THE GOOD SCHOOLS GUIDE

London North

THE GOOD SCHOOLS GUIDE

LUCAS
PUBLICATIONS

www.goodschoolsguide.co.uk

The Good Schools Guide is a registered trademark

Fifth Edition published 2018 by Lucas Publishing Ltd
Good Schools Guide, 10 Greycoat Place, London SW1P 1SB
www.goodschoolsguide.co.uk
ISBN 978-1-909963-17-7 The Good Schools Guide London North fifth edition
A CIP catalogue record for this book is available from the British Library
Copyright © 2018, Lucas Publications Ltd

Printed by Cambrian Printers Ltd

Every care has been taken to ensure that all information was correct at the time of going to press.
The publishers accept no responsibility for any error in detail, inaccuracy or judgement whatsoever.

HOLLAND PARK

since 1958

an Ofsted outstanding and DfE designated teaching school

A place of scholarship; determinedly academic with outstanding A level and GCSE results.

A place of ambition, endeavour, drive and creativity, with outstanding success in placing students in top flight universities.

A place of self-effacing confidence.

A place to find oneself and hear the still small voice.

A place where the potency of academic prowess embraces the human beating heart.

A place which believes that lives and futures can be altered and that chance can be marginalised.

HEAD: Colin Hall
ACADEMY HEAD: David Chappell

AIRLIE GARDENS, LONDON W8 7AF

www.hollandparkschool.co.uk
admissions@hollandparkschool.co.uk

Acknowledgements

Writers

Amanda Lynch
Alison Pope
Beth Noakes
Bernadette John
Carolyn Murphy
Charlotte Phillips
David Hargreaves
Denise Roberts
Emma Jones
Emma Lee-Potter

Emma Vickers
Grace Moody-Stuart
Jackie Lixenberg
Jane Devoy
Judith French
Kate Hilpern
Lisa Freedman
Mary-Ann Smillie
Mary Langford
Mary Pegler

Melanie Bloxham
Melanie Sanderson
Phoebe Bentinck
Ralph Lucas
Sophie Irwin
Susan Bailes
Susan Hamlyn

Design: David Preston

Typesetting: Theresa Hare, Optima Information Design

Editorial review: Beth Noakes and team: Janita Clamp, Melanie Sanderson, Kathryn Berger, Amanda Perkins, Melanie Bloxham

Advertising sales: Charlotte Hollingshead, assisted by Jo Dodds, Publishing Matters

Project management: Katja Lips

Everything held together by: Shari Lord

Junior League of London for excerpts from *Living in London: A Practical Guide*

Photography: Thanks to all the schools who supplied photographs.

Cover photos: St Paul's Cathedral School; Highgate School; Grimsdell Mill Hill Pre-Preparatory School; Belmont Mill Hill Preparatory School; Hawkesdown House

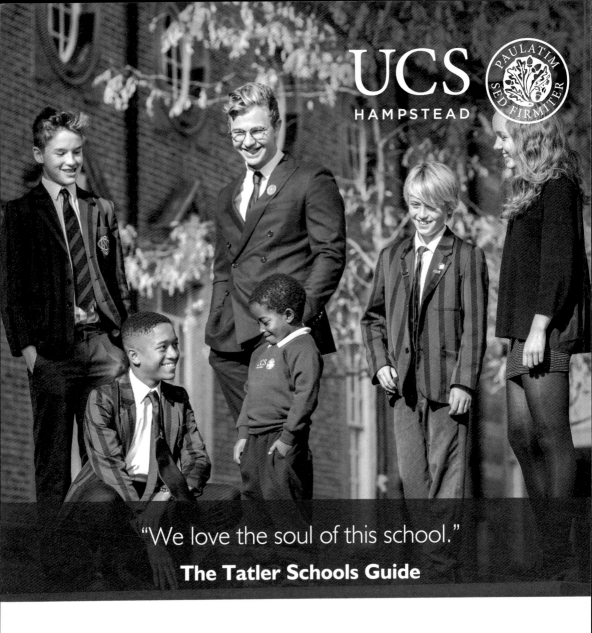

The Good Schools Guide charter

We take our independence very seriously and the separation of commercial and editorial content is absolute. No school can pay to be included in (or choose to be excluded from) The Good Schools Guide, and we do not charge schools for reviews.

In recent years we have helped to defray our costs by selling advertising space and licensing schools to reprint their own reviews for a fee. We make these offers only to schools are that already reviewed by the Guide on merit. Whether or not they choose to advertise has no bearing on their inclusion in the Guide nor on the content of their review. Schools that we have not chosen for inclusion are not allowed to advertise.

Our printed guides and website offer advice on a vast range of education matters. We also have a fee-paying personal consultancy service for parents (Good Schools Guide Educational Consultants). We receive no commission nor any other payment from any school for these services. If you have any questions or concerns about our commercial policy, please contact editor@goodschoolsguide.co.uk.

WITH OUR SUPPORT, SHE WILL THRIVE.

BROMLEY
HIGH SCHOOL

G D S T
GIRLS' DAY SCHOOL TRUST

We are an outstanding GDST and HMC girls' school with an exemplary reputation for academic results, innovation and pastoral care. Our girls from ages 4 - 18 years, develop a love of learning, a spirit of enquiry and an independence of minds.

Visit **www.bromleyhigh.gdst.net**
for information on our Open and Taster Days.

Leading Independent Schools

L E A R N I N G   A N D   A C H I E V E M E N T S   A R E   E X C E P T I O N A L   (I S I   2 0 1 6)

Contents

EXCELLENT
ISI inspection 2018

spirit

Every Heathfield girl has an irrepressible spirit. Uniquely hers, it drives her passion, voice and character. As well as providing an excellent academic education and top-class pastoral care, Heathfield identifies your daughter's distinctive strengths and encourages her to live her ambitions, embrace her spirit and talent so that she develops as the best possible version of herself. **Live life like a Heathfield girl.**

WE HOLD TERMLY OPEN MORNINGS.
PLEASE EMAIL registrar@heathfieldschool.net
TO BOOK A PLACE OR TO ARRANGE A PRIVATE TOUR

Boarding and Day for Girls 11-18
heathfieldschool.net
+44 (0) 1344 898343

HAMPTON SCHOOL

HMC INDEPENDENT SCHOOL FOR BOYS, FOUNDED IN 1557

HAMPTON IS CLOSER
THAN YOU MIGHT THINK

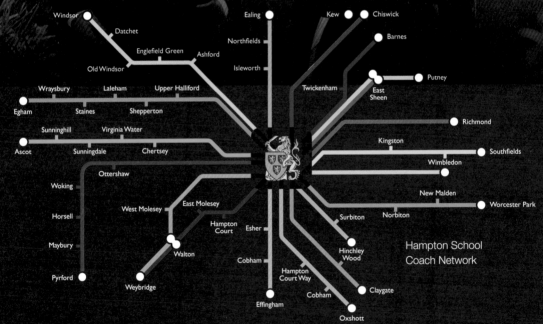

Hampton School
Coach Network

VISITORS' AFTERNOONS
THROUGHOUT THE YEAR

020 8979 9273

www.hamptonschool.org.uk admissions@hamptonschool.org.uk

Entry at 11,13 and 16

Extensive coach network

An outstanding education
in a 27 acre campus

Hampton School, Hanworth Road,Hampton, Middlesex, TW12 3HD
Independent day school for boys aged 11–18 years
Full details available on the website www.hamptonschool.org.uk

Key to symbols

The age range of a school is shown by the colour of the title bar.

Junior School

Senior School

 Girls' school

 Church of England school

 Boys' school

 Jewish school

 Co-ed school

 Roman Catholic school

 Boys' school with co-ed sixth form

 Girls' school with co-ed sixth form

 Co-ed pre-prep, then boys only

 Co-ed pre-prep, then girls only

 Boarding available

1

Peace of mind.

The world can be a noisy place.
That's why children at St James
practise 'stillness' and pause before
and after every lesson. We see them
calm down, refocus and head off
to their next class buzzing with
renewed energy.

For parents, peace of mind comes
from knowing your child will thrive
academically and creatively in a
warm, happy environment. Our
pupils get great results. They just
don't get stressed about it.

Please get in touch today to find out
more about us or to arrange a visit.

ST JAMES
Preparatory School

stjamesprep.org.uk
Earsby Street London W14 8SH
020 7348 1793

London North map

| CENTRAL | 53 |

Camden
City of London
Hackney
Islington
Westminster

| CENTRAL WEST | 257 |

Hammersmith & Fulham
Kensington & Chelsea

| WEST | 409 |

Brent
Ealing
Harrow
Hillingdon
Hounslow
Richmond-upon-Thames

| NORTH | 561 |

Barnet
Enfield
Haringey

| EAST | 651 |

Barking & Dagenham
Havering
Newham
Redbridge
Tower Hamlets
Waltham Forest

| SCHOOLS FOR SPECIAL EDUCATIONAL NEEDS | 713 |

London North SEN schools

St Benedict's School Ealing

a minimis incipe

Outstanding Catholic Independent school for boys & girls aged 3 - 18

"The quality of the pupils' personal development is excellent."

ISI April 2017

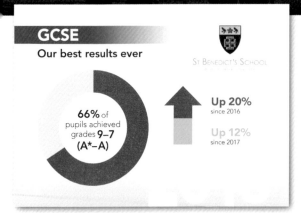

GCSE
Our best results ever

66% of pupils achieved grades 9–7 (A*–A)

Up 20% since 2016

Up 12% since 2017

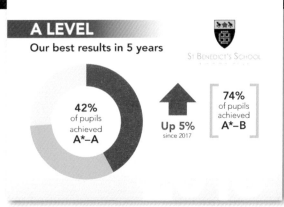

A LEVEL
Our best results in 5 years

42% of pupils achieved A*–A

Up 5% since 2017

74% of pupils achieved A*–B

Book a place on our website or arrange a personal visit with our Registrar, Louise Pepper, on 020 8862 2254

www.stbenedicts.org.uk

✠ EATON HOUSE SCHOOLS

UNFORGETTABLE

Eaton House Schools – where potential is everything

EATON HOUSE BELGRAVIA PRE-PREP, PREP AND NURSERY

- The best Pre-Prep results in 5 years
- In 2018, 40% of 7+ and 8+ pupils received offers to Westminster Under and St Paul's Junior School, amongst many other fine schools

EATON HOUSE THE MANOR BOYS' SCHOOL

- Excellent all round results to the best senior schools
- A cluster of scholarships and a coveted John Colet Scholarship to St Paul's School

EATON HOUSE THE MANOR GIRLS' SCHOOL

- Outstanding results and pastoral care
- 11 Scholarships offered to top London day and boarding schools this year

We are non-selective, register from birth and take children from 3-13. If you want to start a conversation about your child's brilliant future, ring Jennifer McEnhill on **0203 917 5050** to book an Open House Morning.

NURTURING EXCELLENCE
✠ **EATON HOUSE SCHOOLS** ✠

www.eatonhouseschools.com

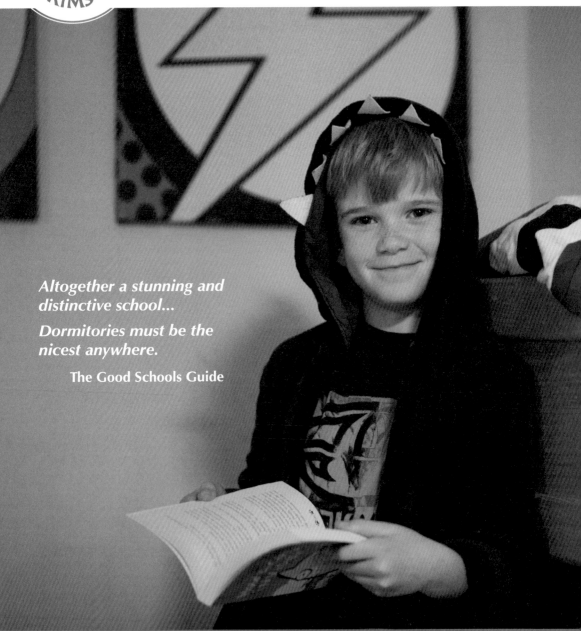

Introduction

Welcome to the fifth edition of the Good Schools Guide to London North. We offer you our knowledge, inside information, experience and opinions on the capital's best schools north of the Thames. Here's our round-up of recent developments on the London educational scene on both sides of the river.

London continues to be a superb place to educate your child, and our London reviewers have once again been inspired by the sheer dynamism, diversity, achievements and aspirations of all the capital's great schools – from local primaries to world famous names. We hope you enjoy reading about them.

London's schools made their regular appearances in the higher echelons of 2018's national A level and GCSE results tables. Looking at the relative performance of London schools, big hitters such as KCS Wimbledon and Westminster are in good company with selective state schools such as Queen Elizabeth School, Barnet, Wilson's Grammar School, Sutton, Tiffin and Tiffin Girls, plus non-selectives such as St Marylebone and Camden School for Girls.

As ever, parents push hard to get into the best and most fashionable schools – so planning well ahead will make your life much easier. This book is here to help, as are the Good Schools Guide Education Consultants (see page 47).

State schools are facing a real-terms funding cut of about 10 per cent over the next few years. Some teachers are reportedly asking for parental contributions to meet basic workplace expenses such equipping science labs; whatever they say, and whatever the social pressures, these are not compulsory. Perish the thought, say the independent schools, as they push fees up ahead of inflation again.

For state schools, look carefully at how each of them is dealing with the funding cuts. According to a survey of some 400 London state school heads by London Councils, nearly half of schools surveyed have increased class sizes, half have narrowed their curriculum and half say they have had to cut teaching staff. Try to scrutinise whether the cuts in the schools that you are looking at are falling in areas that are vital for your child.

Schools also report difficulties in recruiting and retaining staff. High house and rental prices are putting teachers off applying for jobs in London and causing others to move away from the city. Good management – staff feeling really valued – and disciplined, motivated pupils, so that it is a pleasure to teach them, can help to teacher stem defections: make sure that when you visit you get to chat to some teachers well away from their superiors.

The government's ideological support for grammar schools means that there is money around for the (few) London grammars – for as long as this government lasts.

Arts subjects are undoubtedly suffering from the double whammy of exclusion from the EBacc and funding cuts. London textiles teacher Andria Zafirakou of Alperton Community School, 2018 winner of the Varkey Foundation global teacher prize, announced she was planning to spend her million pound prize money on recruiting painters, musicians, dancers, actors, illustrators, film makers and comedians to become artists in residence in London schools to inspire a generation of children.

Languages are another area where it is worth making sure that your child will be offered the opportunities you want for them. Some London secondary schools are showing a decline in take-up and provision, and a high performing sixth form centre in East London doesn't even offer language A levels, saying there is no demand. Pretty disgraceful for such a cosmopolitan city.

With independent school fees now well beyond the reach of most families, around a third of pupils receive some form of financial help. The Independent Schools Council (ISC) annual census for 2018 revealed that although the lion's share was non-means-tested scholarships and discounts, almost £400 million provided means-tested fee assistance for pupils at ISC schools, four per cent more than last year. Some of these means tested bursaries include help for families earning up to £140,000 a year – which shows you how high some fees have got (see page 48 for GSG help on finding out about bursaries).

More than 200,000 children and young people in London have some level of special education need or disability. In the last 10 years there has been a 20 per cent increase in the number with high-level needs and the types of need are increasingly complex. There are concerns that the level of funding given to schools for pupils with high needs is insufficient to provide the quality support they need.

Special schools are inundated with referrals to a point we haven't seen previously – we see heads with application paperwork stacked literally desk high. One head of an autism unit said the number of applications per place made her school now 'harder to get into than Harvard'. Our education consultants include SEN experts (see page 47).

Glimmers of hope? We hear that the Church of England is recognising a chasm in its school provision and is investigating opening special schools. And with council bean counters noticing the huge sums being spent on independent special schools, and we are now hearing of budgets being allocated to open new in-borough provisions.

The English school system

London has an abundance of good schools – state and private. Many families mix and match, and may have a child or two in each system at different stages of their schooling. A choice of school may depend on logistics as much as ideology. But for those not familiar with English schooling the systems can seem baffling.

State schools

Many families head for London hoping for a place in a good local state school. There are huge advantages: at primary level in particular, your child's friends will almost all be local. You will soon feel part of the local community. You won't spend hours in a car trying to navigate London traffic or have to squeeze onto a rush hour tube or bus. In central London especially, many are used to young children arriving without fluent English and have systems in place to help. And of course they are free.

Primary schools

Primary schools start at 3 (if they have a nursery class) or 4 and most run through to 11, though there are some infants' schools (3-7) and junior schools (7-11), often but not always linked with automatic entry from one to the other. Increasing numbers of senior schools are opening linked primary schools, and will eventually become all-through schools.

The cut-off date by age is 31 August in both state and private schools in England (though some private schools may be more flexible). This means that if your child's birthday is on 31 August they will start in the reception class when just 4, whilst a child with a 1 September birthday will actually be just 5 when they start.

Virtually all British state primary schools are co-ed and non-selective academically (the exception is the London

Oratory Junior House, which takes only boys – and tests for academic and musical aptitude), though faith schools mostly select by church attendance.

State primary schools may not have the specialist teachers, small class sizes or facilities enjoyed by private prep schools but the quality of teaching shouldn't be inferior. If you're lucky enough to live close to a good primary school and have a good state comprehensive down the road then your children's education is sorted. However, state primaries don't prepare children for 11+ entrance exams, so if you are aiming at a selective secondary school you will probably have to rope in a tutor in year 5 or so (see Tutors and Tutoring, page 759).

Secondary schools

There is a much greater variety of state secondary schools: single sex and co-ed, selective and non-selective, plus those that select a proportion of students for academic, music or dance prowess

The vast majority of London secondary schools are non-selective, but a few academically selective grammar schools remain, in areas such as Kingston, Sutton and Barnet. The BRIT school in south London for 14-19 year olds is the only state performing arts school in the country with entry by audition. University technical colleges or UTCs, also for 14-19 year olds, specialise in vocational areas such as computing and engineering and have links with local employers. Studio schools are small schools for the same age group that include plenty of work experience alongside academia and vocational courses. Nearly all other secondary schools are for 11-16 or 11-18 year olds.

Some students move on after GCSEs to a sixth form colleges for 16-18 year olds. These tend to offer a wide range

State primaries may not have the small class sizes, but the teaching shouldn't be inferior

of subjects and to have an atmosphere more akin to a college than a school. Some are academically selective, others offer vocational courses to those with a more practical bent.

Academies and free schools

Increasing numbers of state schools – particularly secondary schools – are becoming academies. These are state funded but often run by academy chains, and the current government is encouraging all schools to become academies over the next few years.

Free schools were originally intended to be set up by groups of parents and some of the early ones were, though many were set up by religious groups, and now most have academy chain backers. UTCs and studio schools are both types of free school.

Both of these types of school are outside local authority control, can decide on their own admissions criteria (though they should abide by the national code), do not have to teach the national curriculum and may employ unqualified teachers.

Private schools

Families moving to London may find it logistically easier to apply for private school places because, unlike state schools, they do not require you to have a local address before you make your application.

Prep schools

Many areas of London are well-equipped with prep schools (boys', girls' and co-ed). They are likely to have small classes, specialist teachers and a relatively biddable intake – if not the sports facilities you will find in a country school. Don't assume the teaching will be better than at a state school – both sectors include those who would be better off in a different profession.

ST MARY'S SCHOOL
HAMPSTEAD

An Outstanding and Inspirational Catholic Education

They are likely to start at 3 or 4 and go through to 11 or 13 – historically, girls have moved on at 11 and boys at 13, though increasing numbers of boys' and co-ed senior schools now have a main intake at 11. Some are divided into pre-preps (3-7) and preps (7-13), though usually with a fairly seamless transition between the two; others don't start till 7.

As the name suggests, prep schools prepare your child for entrance exams to secondary schools, and advise on which are likely to be most suitable. A prep school is judged at least partly by its leavers' destinations, so it will do its best to ensure your child moves on to a decent secondary school, even if it has to dampen down your expectations.

Independent senior schools range from the ferociously selective to those that provide a gentle haven

A stand-alone pre-prep, that goes from 3 or so to 7 years, may be a good bet if you are arriving in London at short notice. Some of the children who join at 3 may move on at 4 or 5, so places do come up. The disadvantage is that they are, inevitably, obliged to spend quite a part of the upper years preparing children for 7+ or 8+ entrance exams.

Senior schools

Independent senior schools range from the ferociously selective such as Westminster and St Paul's to those that provide a gentle haven from hothousing or social integration – with admissions policies to match. A glance at the league tables will give a clue as to the degree of selection they operate.

Historically, girls' independent secondaries have started at 11 and boys' at 13, but increasing numbers – especially boys only schools that have turned co-ed – are switching their main intake to 11, with shrinking numbers of 13+ places. Thirteen plus schools with linked junior schools will often offer 11+ places in their junior schools with guaranteed transfer to the senior school, mostly aimed at state school

pupils and those whose prep school finishes at 11.

Some independent schools go all the way through from 3 or 4 to 18, which can provide welcome continuity and freedom from 11+ or 13+ selection tests. However, few guarantee that a child who is struggling academically will be able to stay on with their peers, and teenagers may well decide at 16 (particularly if they have been in the same single-sex school since 4) that the grass looks greener elsewhere.

Independent sixth form colleges

Independent sixth form colleges, sometimes called crammers, were originally set up to prepare students for university entrance, particularly Oxbridge. They still specialise in this field, generally offering a variety of routes that include full two year A levels and shorter courses for those who need to improve on past grades. Classes are small, the focus is on exam practice and extracurricular options are limited. They are useful for those arriving in London at short notice and students who have rethought their options or need to boost their results.

extraordinary days

**Come and see what Stowe has to offer
at one of our Open Mornings**

"Mixes the erudite with the sporty and
studious, with space reserved for the
eclectic and maverick. Ideal for those keen
to learn within and beyond the bounds of
the classroom."
Good Schools Guide

Stowe

e | admissions@stowe.co.uk   t | 01280 818205   w | www.stowe.co.uk

Applying to a state school

It can be nerve-wracking deciding where you would like your child to take their first steps into school, or spend their teenage years.

The primary schools you are considering are likely to be very local. The main admissions criteria for non-faith schools are generally siblings and then distance – which can be less than a few hundred metres for the popular ones.

Secondary schools are far more varied in their character and in their admissions criteria. These may also include academic selection and/or auditions for performing arts aptitude. You may be able to apply under more than one of these.

Timing

Applications are made through your local authority in the autumn of the year before your child starts school or moves on to secondary school. The cut-off date for secondary admissions is 31 October of year 6. For primary schools it is 15 January before the September start date.

If the primary school has a nursery class for 3 year olds you apply direct to the school when your child is 2; however, you will still need to reapply for a reception (4 year old) place via the local authority.

Academically selective grammar schools, and some that partially select by aptitude for eg music, now do their admissions tests/auditions in the summer term of year 5 or the September of year 6, so that they can give out initial results before the October closing date for applications. This will usually involve registering with the school during the year 5 summer term – so check dates carefully.

It can be nerve-wracking deciding where you would like your child to take their first steps into school

How do state schools offer places?

There are some general rules that most schools adhere to.

- Statement of special education need or Education, Health and Care plan naming the school. These children come first in line and must be given a place.
- Looked after/previously looked after children. These generally come next.
- Siblings. These often, but not always, come third. Check before you move house after your first-born has got a place.
- Exceptional medical or social need. This generally involves a letter from a doctor or social worker explaining why St Cake's is the only school that will cope with your child's needs. Very few children get a place by this route.
- Distance. Generally as the crow flies, but sometimes by the shortest walking route. Sometimes faith schools designate parishes, other schools may designate particular areas as their catchment. Some have specific feeder primary schools. Some grammar schools limit the distance applicants may travel to school by eg giving preference to those from specified postcodes. Your local authority should have information on how close you probably have to live to any individual school (except faith schools) to be in with a chance of a place.

However, London has a plethora of different types of school with different – and sometimes multiple – entrance criteria.

Grammar schools

These are academically selective by entrance exam (usually some combination of maths, English and reasoning tests). Increasing numbers give preference to children who live relatively locally; some also prioritise students on pupil premium. You will be told if your child has reached the qualifying standard before the closing date for applications, but not if he will actually be offered a place.

Faith schools

These may demand that you baptised your child before she was 6 months old and have attended a specific church weekly for the past five years. They are no longer allowed to give points for eg brass polishing and flower arranging, felt to advantage middle class applicants.

Free schools and academies

These may set their own entrance criteria, though they should abide by the national admissions code. They, like most faith schools, also decide which applicants to accept (local authorities make that decision for community schools) and thus are vulnerable to accusations of cherry picking easy-to-teach pupils.

Aptitude

Some schools select part of their intake by aptitude for eg music, dance, technology or languages.

Fair banding

An increasing number of non-selective schools use fair banding to divide applicants into ability bands, taking an equal number from each band via other criteria eg distance. This generally involves computer-based reasoning tests and is not pass/fail.

Filling in the form

You can list six choices of schools in London and we recommend using all of your choices. It's vital in include at least one where you are more-or-less sure of getting a place – even if it isn't your first choice. If you don't, you may only be offered an undersubscribed school some distance away. For faith schools, you will probably have to fill in a supplementary application form and get it signed by your religious leader. If a new free school is opening in your area, you will quite likely in its first year be able to apply direct to the school in addition to your six other choices.

NB Put your school choices in order of preference – if you qualify for a place at more than one, you will only be offered the school highest on your list. The schools don't know where else you have applied, and don't know if you have put them first or last – only the local authority knows that.

Moving to London

As long as you have a right of abode in England, you can apply for a state school place here. However, you can't apply till you have an address in the country and are living here (except for Forces/diplomatic families and those applying to state boarding schools).

If you are applying for a school place not at normal admissions times – ie reception or year 7 – admissions will probably be handled by individual schools, though you will have to complete the in-year admissions form. Your local authority should be able to give your information on which schools have spaces, but it's worth contacting schools direct too.

Don't want the school you are offered?

You can appeal for a place at a school you prefer, but do it quickly. In the meantime, accept the school you have been offered (otherwise the local authority is under no obligation to find you a school at all). Ensure you are on the waiting list for any schools you would be happy with. And do visit the school you have been offered: you may find that contrary to local reputation, it is up and coming and will suit your child very well.

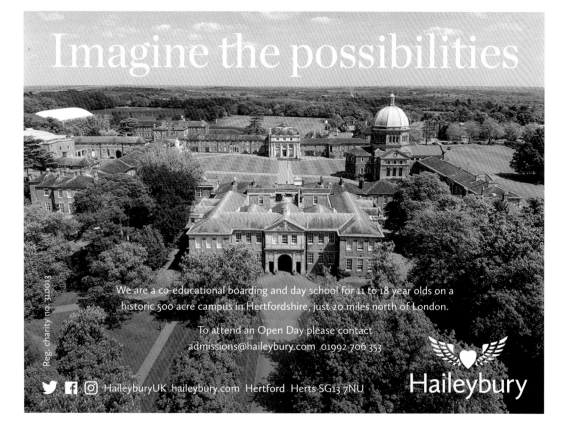

Independent school admissions

Prep schools

London prep schools have never been more popular. Their fearsome reputation for preparing children for entry to London senior schools with a champion's regime of revision, tests and extension work may well suit the bright, robust child but can cause others to flounder.

If a school particularly interests you, request a private visit and make sure it includes time to see the head and watch the school at work. Try to get a balanced view of the school – chat to pupils, staff, other parents and don't allow the marketing manager to dominate your visit. Before (and after), browse the website, prospectus and marketing literature – they'll all be glossy with happy, smiley faces, but do you like the tone and the events they put centre stage? Same old faces, same old names or a good smattering of faces, across the ages? Some preps are very traditional – blazers and boaters are often a clue; others more relaxed – sweatshirts could be a signal. You can probably tell without visiting whether or not your family ethos is likely to be a good fit.

Entry requirements at 3 or 4 vary considerably from 'first-come, first-served' (which may mean name down at birth) to mini-assessment days complete with interview and observations to see just how well Harriet integrates with her peers and playmates. Few will expect children to read and write on entry but such is the pressure for places at favoured schools that, to the dismay of many heads, parents have been known to enlist the help of tutors for their 3-year-olds. In general the play and learning that goes on at home or nursery school should be adequate preparation. At 7 or 8, nearly every prep school operates a formal assessment process, and for many London day schools, the pressure is on.

As their name suggests, the main aim of 'preparatory

They'll all be glossy with happy smiley faces, but do you like the tone and events they put centre stage?

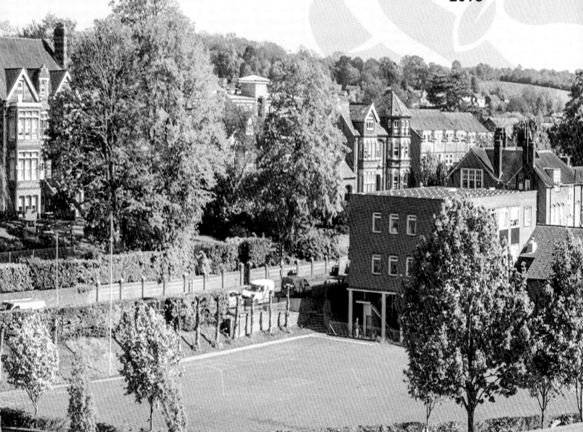

schools', or prep schools, is to prepare children for entry to fee-paying senior schools at 11 or 13. Traditionally, pre-preps take children from 3 or 4 and prepare them for moving on to preps at 7 or 8. There are fewer stand-alone pre-preps than there used to be as their main market, the boarding prep, has declined in numbers. Today, many pre-preps and preps are linked schools, with a more-or-less seamless transition between them and sometimes their senior school too. In London, with fierce competition for 7+ places at top prep schools, quite a few stand-alone pre-preps survive. Their raison d'être is preparing children for these competitive exams, which can mean the pressure starts in year 1 with regular practice papers. Some, whilst having linked prep schools, also send large numbers of children elsewhere.

Preps tend to stand or fall by their senior school destinations. Parents, whether they are aiming to get their 3 or 4 year old into the pre-prep of a chosen all-through school, or their 8 year old into a prep that sends many of its pupils to the top day or boarding schools, are generally looking ahead. Yet all-through selective schools rarely guarantee that children they take in at 3 or 4 or even 7 will have a seamless transfer upwards. If your child is felt to be struggling, you may well be advised to look elsewhere. Equally, a child who fails to gain a place at the pre-prep stage may well have developed sufficiently to sail in there or elsewhere later on. So a school that helps your child to become a happy and confident learner is the best investment.

Senior schools

If your child is already at a prep school then the process of selecting and applying to the 'right' senior school should mainly be taken care of – it's a large part of what you're paying them to do.

It used to be the case that parents rarely challenged a prep's advice about which senior school would best suit their son or daughter, but heads tell us that 'managing parental expectations' is now a significant part of their job. A prep school's reputation stands or falls on the destinations of its pupils at 11 and/or 13; prep school heads spend a large part of their time visiting senior schools and getting to know their pupil profiles. Experienced heads can spot which children should be aiming for which senior schools fairly early on and if this conflicts with parental ambitions then he or she will advise accordingly. No school will 'under sell' an able child, so if you disagree with the advice you have been given you should be able to have a frank discussion about the reasons behind it. The decision about which senior school to apply for should be at least as much about where a child would fit in and be happy as it is about academic ability.

Many prep school heads are concerned that pre-tests don't suit late developers who may not have come into their own academically

State primary to independent senior

Plenty of children from state primary schools do move on to independent secondaries, often with scholarships or bursaries. It is not the state primary school's job to prepare children for independent school entrance exams, so most parents take on a tutor for a year or so to ensure their children are used to, say, writing a story in half an hour, and timing their answers. Neither can you expect a primary school head to advise on likely senior schools, so you will need to make your own judgement on which schools are likely to be suitable for your child.

Applying from abroad

The first step is often an online UKiset test which measures academic English language skills. Most schools will also ask overseas applicants to sit their own entrance test, and are generally happy to send tests abroad, though they may ask applicants to attend interviews in person.

Pre-tests

An increasing number of senior schools offer provisional or definite places based on the results of 'pre-tests' taken in year 6 or 7 (age 10 or 11). Senior schools use these tests as a filter and to give an early indication of demand for places. Many prep school heads are concerned that pre-tests don't suit late developers (often boys) who may not come into their own academically this early.

Pre-tests are age-standardised and include multiple-choice tests in maths, English, verbal and non-verbal reasoning. If your son or daughter is offered a place after completing these tests, he or she will probably still be required to sit the common entrance examinations in year 8.

11+ and 13+ tests

The 11+ test is taken in year 6 for entry in year 7 and comprises papers in English, maths and sometimes reasoning. Many London schools set their own papers, though the London 11+ Consortium of 12 girls' schools sets one common exam – a 75 minute cognitive ability test – and shares results.

The 13+ common entrance – a set of exams common to most independent schools – is taken in year 8. Core subjects

Scholarships available

Where pupils thrive

www.thameschristianschool.org.uk

thames
Christian School

For details of scholarships and
enrolment contact: 020 7228 3933

are English, maths and science and candidates may also sit papers in history, geography, modern foreign languages, Mandarin, ancient Greek and Latin. Tests are taken at the candidate's own school and are marked by the school to which they are applying. Many independent schools set their own tests for candidates (perhaps from abroad) who have not been prepared for common entrance.

Parents feel more responsible for their child's social presentation than their ability to do long division

Most London independent girls' and co-ed day schools accept pupils from age 11, as do increasing numbers of boys' schools. There are still some traditional boys' schools such as Westminster and St Paul's and boarding schools such as Eton and Harrow that start at 13+. Thirteen plus schools with linked junior schools will often offer 11+ places in their junior schools with guaranteed transfer to the senior school, mostly aimed at state school pupils and those whose prep school finishes at 11.

Interviews

While state schools are prohibited from interviewing any but potential sixth form (or boarding) students, the interview is an integral part of nearly every private school admissions process, and tends to send the applicant's parents, rather than the actual applicant, into a spin. Parents feel considerably more responsible for their child's social presentation than for his or her ability to do long division or conjugate French verbs. And, while a school may breezily describe the interview as 'just a chance to get to know the child better', this hardly quells fears about sending young Daniel or Daniella into the lion's den.

Oversubscribed at every point, the selective London independent school tends to concentrate on the academic.

The majority usually only meet the child after a written exam (generally used as a first edit), and the interview itself will probably contain a significant component of maths, comprehension or reasoning. The aim here is to probe intellectual strengths and weaknesses in order to select from the central bulk of candidates or to pick scholarship material. Finding out a little about a child's character is only of secondary importance.

Even the most academic schools, however, are not necessarily just looking for those guaranteed to deliver a stream of A*s. Some use interviews as an opportunity to create as balanced a community as possible:

'I didn't want all extroverts or all eggheads,' said one ex-junior school head. 'Most children who sat our exam scored between 40 and 65 per cent in the written paper, so I was looking for an individual spark. At the age of 7, particularly, the interview is a crucial counterbalance to the exam. Those born between September and December always scored higher marks in the written paper. At interview we would go back to the list and bring in some younger children.'

'I always tell parents if they're paying to coach 3-year-olds they might as well burn £20 notes,' said a school head with the task of selecting 40 4-year-olds

Parents, stand back!

Concerned parents often do their best to control the outcome of the interview, but professional preparation is seen as a waste of time, both by those who interview and by teachers. 'I always tell parents if they're paying to coach 3-year-olds, they might as well burn £20 notes,' said a junior school head who has the daunting task of selecting 40 4-year-olds from 200 applicants in a two-tier interview. 'The only useful preparation is to talk to them, play with them and read them stories.'

Further up the system, the advice is equally non-prescriptive. The head of a west London pre-prep does her best to relax the 7-year-olds she sends to prep school interviews by providing them with as much factual information as she can beforehand. 'I try to prepare them for what they'll find. I usually describe the head — because I'm a smallish woman they might expect all heads to be like me — and I'll tell them what the school looks like. Beyond that I just say, "Look them in the eye, answer carefully and be honest." Children sell themselves.'

Some pre-preps and prep schools provide mock interviews, some will carefully guide children on what books or hobbies that might show to best advantage, but most interviewers say they always know when a child has been coached, and honesty – at least in theory – is the quality they're looking for. 'I tell children,' says one private tutor who prepares children for 11 plus, 'to say what's in their heart, not what their teacher told them to say.'

'I am looking for sparkly eyes and interest. If a child sits there like a pudding, you usually don't take them'

Parents, step forward

Although the school interview is nominally about the child, the school is also interviewing parents and it's they who may need a little preparation while their child can happily be him or herself. A balance between steady, respectful (schools are ever keen to avoid the parent from hell) and interesting (but nor do they like dull ones) is best.

Is it fair?

Personality, of course, will always be the most variable aspect of any interview and all interviewers have a personal bias. They may hate boastful children, or those who say their favourite leisure activity is computer games; they may prefer

Arsenal fans to Tottenham supporters; but some schools do make a strenuous attempt to counteract the sense of one adult sitting in judgement on one child. One senior school sees candidates individually before sending them off to a lesson where they can be observed by another teacher as they work in a group.

The best interviewers can and do overcome the limitations both of the written examination and of the child. 'Children, even very shy ones, like to talk about themselves, their friends, their families and their pets. I get them to describe what they did on Sunday, or I turn my back and ask them to describe something in the room. Sometimes I even get a child to sing or dance. I am looking for sparkly eyes and interest. If a child just sits there like a pudding, you usually don't take them.' Some schools get over the 'what to talk about' dilemma by asking children to bring along a favourite object. If, however, the child pitches up with a copy of Proust or boasts a collection of Roman ceramics, parents shouldn't be surprised if the interviewer is somewhat sceptical.

Although most heads are honest in their report about a child – after all, their reputation depends on it – the interview can also benefit them. 'Occasionally, a prep school head knows perfectly well that a child is not suited to our school, but the parents just won't listen. Coming from us it doesn't sour the relationship with the school.'

How to judge a new school

Start a normal business and you can begin with baby footsteps, holding fire on major investment in resources and employees until you are confident you're on to a winner.

Founders of new schools, however, don't have that luxury. In addition to substantial premises, other chunky overheads include a head, senior management team (possibly compatible, possibly not), a full pack of teachers (ditto), not to mention the pupils.

With such a potent cocktail, the scope for fast track failure even in an apparently well set up new school is almost limitless. So why should prospective parents be prepared to take the risk? And how can they judge whether it will be worth it?

Talented team?

How confidence-inspiring is the head? With a massive extra workload and just one shot at getting things right, 'he'll do' or 'give her a try' just aren't enough. If you doubt the head's ability, give the school a miss. But bear in mind that some of the best heads aren't charismatic orators: their most important attributes are appointing able teaching staff and keeping them happily on board.

Check out the teachers. A good new school will thrive on teamwork. Do they radiate inspiration? And when you talk to them, do you wish you had been taught by them? Teachers in free schools and academies don't have to be qualified. Unqualified ones may be fabulous – or they may just be cheap to employ.

Great governors?

In an established school, all parents need know about the governors is that they are happy with the head – and vice versa. In a new school, however, the governing body's ability to choose a talented senior team, help get over inevitable initial difficulties and, most important of all, replace people fast if they have made the wrong choices, is vital.

You are looking for governors who are good as individuals and even stronger as a team, leading from the front and putting in the time to observe, listen (to you) and learn. Invisibility on open days or other school presentations is a serious warning sign that all is not well.

If your school has an academy sponsor, they will be involved in the governance. Some, like ARK, have stellar reputations. Others are close to disaster areas. Check out not just your school but the others they run. Their Ofsted reports may say more about them as a group than an individual prospectus ever can.

Parent power?

Is drop off time a turn off because of the attitudes and behaviour of other parents or their children? As a group, you are all important in working together to set the school on the right course. It takes extra energy and commitment and you need to know that other parents will chip in. Are they people you could work with? And are their children proud to be there?

Premises

Many new free schools open in uninspiring 'temporary' buildings, with the promise of a move to a fabulous purpose built (but often unspecified) site in a year or two. If the year or two is stretching out indefinitely with no sign of building work finishing (or even starting), beware.

Do your homework

Read the prospectus and study the school website very carefully. The latter should have the most up-to-date information and links to policies on matters such as admissions, discipline, child protection, SEN. How geared up is the school to deal with 'a touch' of dyslexia? Do the less co-ordinated ever get picked for matches? What happens if it becomes successful and oversubscribed and its catchment area shrinks? Will your second child still qualify for a place or will you, and similar other pioneers, be penalised? If you still have questions, ask the school directly or talk to other parents.

Now read on...

For the altruistic, enjoying the inner glow that comes with helping improve education in your local area may be enough. For others, the hope that a brand new school will do your child proud is a more tangible benefit. Whatever your reasons, good luck.

The Good Schools Guide Educational Consultants

The Good Schools Guide has been trusted by generations of parents to provide expert, honest and unbiased information about schools. Our educational consultancy provides the same high standards of expertise, independence and professional integrity to individual families.

Every day our highly-experienced consultants successfully help clients from all over the world find the right schools for their children. However urgent the deadline, however complex the circumstances, call 0203 286 6824 (UK) or +44 203 286 6824 (international) to find out how we can solve your educational dilemmas.

Our consultants

All our consultants have personally visited and reviewed countless schools for our website and publications; many also have professional backgrounds or specialist qualifications in education. Between them they have direct experience of every aspect of both the British and international education systems, not to mention invaluable local knowledge about schools in London and all areas of the UK. Our team includes experts in SEN, school appeals, scholarships and bursaries, grammar schools and relocation to the UK from abroad.

Consultancy built around your needs

Our consultancy packages range from a 30-minute telephone consultation to a fully bespoke service tailored to meet complex, urgent or other specific circumstances. Additional services include accompanied school visits, providing translators and educational assessments and arranging specialist tuition. Our main consultancy services are outlined overleaf; for full details please visit www. goodschoolsguide. co.uk.

London Service

Designed to meet the needs of families new to London who need guidance, not just on schools but on residential areas, commuting, family services, nurseries, playgroups, tutors and much more.

State School Service

This service, run by the GSG expert in state education, is for parents who are interested in state schools only. It can give advice on admissions criteria, catchment areas and grammar schools.

Special Educational Needs

Our team of SEN experts is unique. We have specialists in eg dyslexia, autism, speech and language difficulties and we have extensive knowledge of both mainstream and special schools which cater for children with these difficulties.

Academic assessments

If you are not sure what academic level your child is at, particularly if you are coming from overseas, we can arrange academic assessments.

Scholarships and bursaries

We have amassed information on scholarships and bursaries to create a unique central resource, with information on the fee assistance available at more than 700 independent schools.

Contact us

Phone us on +44 (0)203 286 6824 or send a brief email to: consultants@goodschoolsguide.co.uk outlining what you need. Tell us the age of your child and where you live plus your contact details. We will contact you within 48 hours, discuss how best to help you and ensure we match you with the right consultant. Consultations can be by phone, email or face to face, and we can find a consultant to speak to you within an hour if necessary.

How much?

Ours is one of the most competitively priced tailor-made education consultancy services in the UK. Check our website for current fees.

Our guarantee

The Good Schools Guide has an international reputation for providing unbiased, independent advice on educational matters. We have no commercial links whatsoever with any school. This gives our education consultants the freedom to consider a huge range of schools in order to find the best one for you. You can have complete confidence that if our consultants recommend a school it is because, and only because, they consider it to be suitable for your child. You can also be assured that we maintain the highest possible standards of privacy and all dealings with clients are completely confidential.

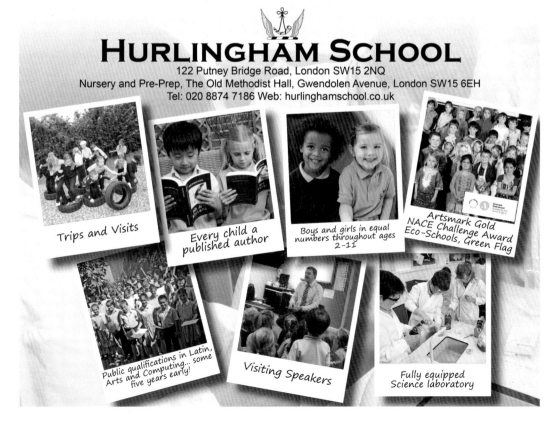

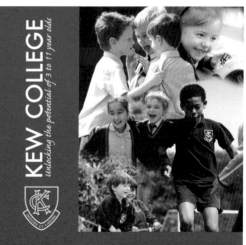

Central

Camden
City of London
Hackney
Islington
Westminster

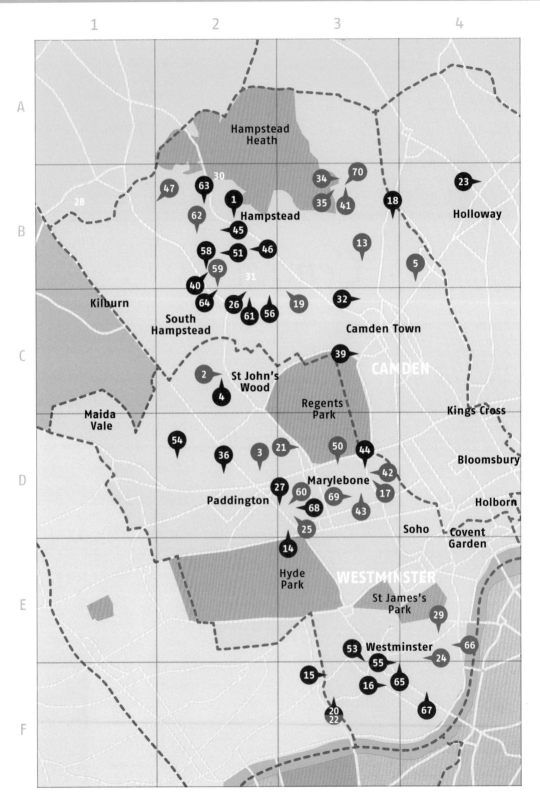

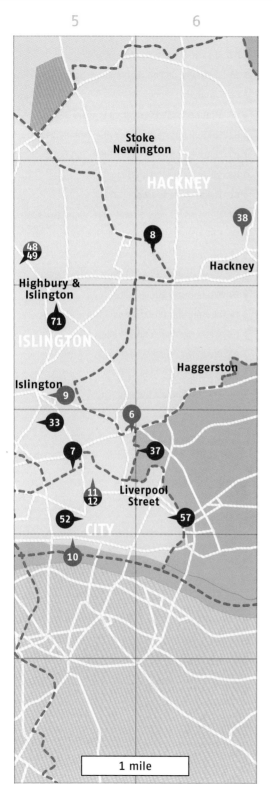

Central London and its state schools

Camden

Camden stretches from the mansion blocks of Holborn and Bloomsbury to Hampstead Heath, with its wooded walks and swimming ponds, and from the council estates of Somerstown to the mansions of Hampstead – which, with its winding, hilly streets, exclusive boutiques and streetside cafés (plus plenty of estate agents) has the ambience of an affluent village.

Camden has long been known to have a good local authority education department – and, most likely in consequence, none of its schools have converted into academies. The only academy in the borough at time of writing is the newish and very popular UCL Academy at Swiss Cottage, which was shocked to receive a tepid judgement from Ofsted in its first report, but is now rated good, has achieved creditable GCSE and A level results and has seven applicants for every place.

The most famous and popular secondary school is Camden School for Girls qv (which takes boys in the sixth form). It uses banding to select pupils of a range of abilities, and such is its popularity that it will only assess those who live within a mile, whilst offers are generally confined to those living within half that distance (apart from a few music aptitude places). Girls are also well served by Parliament Hill School qv and La Sainte Union qv, the latter with a strictly Catholic intake – both with new heads in September 2017. These two are part of a sixth form consortium, LaSwap qv, with William Ellis boys' school qv (on the up after some rocky years) and co-ed Acland Burghley (which received a shock downgrading from Ofsted in 2013 but is on the up with a dynamic head teacher). Hampstead School qv on the western edge of the borough is popular too. WAC Arts College is a newish free school in Belsize Park, offering a creative curriculum to disengaged 14-19 year olds.

A good range of primary schools, though very much weighted on the faith side – Christ Church C of E, Hampstead Parochial, St Paul's C of E, Emmanuel, Holy Trinity and St Silas qv and The Rosary are amongst the most popular, alongside the free school St Luke's in Hampstead. A secular free school, Abacus Belsize primary, opened in 2013 after much lobbying by parents who wanted to redress the balance, and is rated outstanding. Currently at the Jubilee Waterside Centre in Camley Street, it should eventually move into a vacated police station on Rosslyn Hill though there is no timeline as yet. King's Cross Academy opened in 2015 as part of the regeneration of the land behind King's Cross station. Non-church-goers may also want to consider Eleanor Palmer qv (in the news because of some families briefly renting properties close by in order to gain a place), New End, Torriano, Fleet, Brookfield, Kingsgate or Christopher Hatton further south.

City of London
City of London, the original Roman settlement that still makes up the square mile or so of one of the world's financial centres, includes the Barbican, some of the Inns of Temple and many financial institutions. Its relatively few inhabitants live amongst medieval street layouts, Wren churches and 21st century skyscrapers, and it throngs with suited and high heeled City workers hulking in packs outside the packed pubs on Friday afternoons, and no place for coffee or a crust of bread on weekends. It has several independent schools, senior and junior, but no state secondary schools – though the corporation does sponsor city academies in Islington, Hackney and Southwark. Its only state primary school, Sir John Cass qv, is an excellent, multi-ethnic school C of E school, giving priority to regular church-goers.

Hackney

Just north of the City of London and east of Islington, Hackney is an inner city borough that includes trendy Shoreditch and Hoxton as well as the Hackney Marshes and Lea Valley (home of the 2012 Olympic canoeing and kayaking competitions). Once a rural retreat for the capital's wealthy merchants, Clapton has Georgian and Victorian terraces alongside social housing estates. Shoreditch, on the north east edge of the City, has mazes of small streets, thundering arteries, art galleries, clubs and bars packed with City workers and revellers from across the capital.

Hackney's educational landscape is characterised by a high proportion of state and independent schools for the ultra orthodox Jewish community in Stanford Hill. It also has a Muslim free school, the Olive. Its best known – and very sought-after – secondary school is Mossbourne Community Academy qv, whose founding principal was Sir Michael Wilshaw, who went on to be chief inspector of schools. It has complicated admissions criteria involving fair banding and inner and outer zones. The Mossbourne Victoria Park Academy opened in 2014. Clapton Girls' Academy (places allocated by fair banding and distance) is also successful. City Academy Hackney, which opened in 2009, has business and financial specialisms and is rated outstanding; City of London Academy Shoreditch Park opened in 2017. Hackney New School, which opened in 2013 and overlooks a canal basin, has a focus on music and every pupil may learn an instrument free of charge.

Popular primary schools include Lauriston, London Fields, Grazebrook, William Patten, Northwold, Queensbridge, Orchard and Jubilee. Mossbourne has opened its own primary school, Mossbourne Riverside Academy, and Mossbourne Parkside Academy (formerly Brook Primary) is also part of the Mossbourne Federation. At Hackney New Primary, like the senior school, everyone may learn to play an instrument.

Islington

Islington is uncompromisingly urban, with little green space but Georgian squares, trendy converted warehouses, Arsenal football club, canal-side walks and street markets, thick on the ground with City workers escaping for lunch or window shopping the antique shops of Camden Passage.

It used to have the reputation of being a black hole for good state schools, with parents commuting en masse to Hampstead or Haringey, but times are a-changing. Highbury Fields is up-and-coming comprehensive; once popular Highbury Grove sunk in Ofsted's estimation and was converted into City of London Academy Highbury Grove in 2017; St Mary Magdalene qv is a good all-through school with an international flavour. Central Foundation Boys qv is viewed as a 'hidden gem right in the heart of London'. City and Islington Sixth Form College qv has links with some of the top universities and often transforms the prospects of students who arrived with uninspiring GCSE results.

The City of London Academy, a relative newcomer, is sponsored by the City of London Corporation and City University, whilst the newest kid on the block will be the London Screen Academy, a sixth form specialising in film, one of the range of free schools approved by the government and due to open in September 2019.

Primary schools to move house for include William Tyndale qv, Hugh Myddelton qv, Yerbury, Grafton and Gillespie, with St John's Highbury Vale C of E, St Joseph's RC and St Peter and St Paul RC attracting parental bums onto pews.

Westminster

Westminster includes Buckingham Palace and the Houses of Parliament, Mayfair and Belgravia (with its streets of garden squares and creamy white stucco terraced houses, painted in the Cadogen colour code of magnolia). It includes Little

Venice, the area of large stucco houses round the Grand Union Canal; Soho, famous for its sex industry venues but rapidly undergoing gentrification; the massively redeveloped Paddington Waterside area. Also in Westminster are parts of Knightsbridge, with some streets lined with distinctive and imposing six storey red-brick Queen Anne-style townhouses with Dutch and Flemish gables, between high-sided canyons of commercial exuberance. Westminster also includes shabby social housing estates and some very ethnically mixed communities.

It has two of the most popular girls' comprehensives in London, both faith schools with various associated admissions hoops: St Marylebone qv and Grey Coat Hospital qv. St Marylebone has some performing arts places, and Grey Coat Hospital gives some places to girls with a talent for languages; both give a large proportion of places to regular church-goers. Marylebone Boys moved from its second temporary site to its permanent home in Paddington in September 2018. It is linked to St Marylebone and with a similar ethos, but without faith places. All of these schools use 'fair banding' to offer places to children from a full range of abilities. Several academies are doing well: Westminster Academy, King Solomon Academy qv (an all-through school) and Pimlico Academy are all rated as outstanding. A newish sixth form college, Harris Westminster qv, a collaboration between Westminster School and Harris Federation, opened in 2014 at a cost of £45 million, much to the chagrin of other state sixth forms that have suffered massive budget cuts. Students share some lessons with Westminster School sixth formers and it aims to offer a similar level of education.

The church schools tend to be the most sought-after primaries (and the most numerous – more than half are faith schools): Hampden Gurney qv, St Peter's Eaton Square qv, St Saviour's C of E qv, St Joseph's RC and St Vincent de Paul RC qv. Non-church Millbank (beloved of MPs' families), Gateway and Barrow Hill are also well thought of.

The Academy School

3 Pilgrims Place, Rosslyn Hill, London NW3 1NG

020 7435 6621 | office@academyhampstead.com | academyschoolhampstead.com

Independent	Pupils: 95
Ages: 6-13	Fees: £19,470 pa

Principals: Garth Evans BA (late 50s) and Chloe Sandars LRAM Prof Cert FTCL (early 50s) founded the school in 1997. Garth, whose hoary appearance and wry sense of humour bears more than a passing resemblance to Bill Murray, was born and brought up in London. Educated at Westminster and Queen Mary University London, where he read English. Garth's sugar hair, large frame and intent look lend him an aura of wisdom and experience. He enjoys telling the tale of his great grandfather who was part of Scott's expedition to the Arctic. Married to Bee, who is responsible for admissions, teaches geography and is the school nurse. The couple divide their time between London and the south coast near where their (now grown up) children were educated at Sevenoaks.

Garth is charismatic, coming across as a maverick. He sees the big picture and values the important things in life. 'Education is about finding what's your thing, whether that's a maths thing or a guitar thing,' he says. 'The aim is to achieve excellence but dare to have fun while you're doing it.' Although he is the disciplinarian in this establishment, the children remark on his kindness and empathy as well as his intellectual rigour: 'He notices when you aren't happy and makes you feel better,' commented one 10 year old. He started his career teaching English and now teaches maths: 'much better to teach a subject which doesn't come naturally,' he twinkles. He has the older children doing trigonometry and going far beyond what is expected of them – the key thing here is not the grades and 'getting into' a particular school, but instilling a love of learning.

Garth and Chloe met while they were both teaching at Trevor-Roberts, and tutoring too. They decided there was a need for the kind of education The Academy so effectively provides and set up the school in 1997. Chloe, educated at Oxford High School, the Royal Academy of Music and Trinity College of Music, is engaging, thoughtful and thorough. She is passionate about teaching maths, which she does brilliantly, by all accounts, to years 5 and 6. 'It's vital to engage the girls, to make it interesting for them, to show the patterns and make the connections. Many girls switch off maths, and think that they're no good.' Married to Andrew, who left his job in the City to become part of the team, they have two daughters, both educated at St Paul's Girls'. Andrew, educated at Magdalen College School and Cambridge University, deals with the data and the detail (he prefers to describe it as 'the financial, management and regulatory aspects of the school'). He also teaches history. With Andrew's and Bee's support, Garth and Chloe have the time and space to to do the things they love, teaching, inspiring and nurturing the children. Each of the four individuals are key corners of this very stable leadership team.

He has the older children doing trigonometry and going far beyond what is expected of them – key is not 'getting into' a particular school, but instilling a love of learning

Entrance: Entrance into year 2 (though very occasionally they will take someone, a sibling for example, who is in year 1, typically at the beginning of the summer term). This is essentially a school that begins at 6 and they need to be ready for specialist subject teaching from the word go. The school will entertain applications at any time from then on and is refreshingly welcoming and willing to see if they can make it work. Parents and children come in to meet the principals and the children will be assessed while spending some of the day with their peers. Do they fit in, can they keep up? 'We're happy to work with the very strong as well as the weak,' says Chloe; the important thing is to make sure it's the right fit. Maximum of 95 pupils in total (space is at a premium).

Exit: To a range of London day schools, hardly any to board. Deft management of parental expectation.' We are very transparent,' says Chloe.

Parents sent not only the results of practice papers, but the papers themselves as well as the marks (without the names) of the other children in the class so that they can see where their child sits in relation to others. Most get their first choice of school; some go as far afield as Merchant Taylor's, Haberdasher's Aske's, St Paul's and Westminster, others to North London Collegiate, Channing, City of London, UCS, Highgate, Mill Hill, North Bridge House, Francis Holland or South Hampstead. Parents here tend to be sensible and listen to the advice of the experts who really do know where their children will thrive.

Remarks: An intimate, small co-ed Hampstead prep school, tucked into the grounds of a church off the lower end of chic Hampstead High Street, The Academy is not well known but most of those who discover it are delighted. Ofsted, in its recent inspection, was bowled over, awarding it an outstanding in every category, not an easy achievement these days. Chloe, referencing the report, smiles: 'Just because we are relaxed I wouldn't want people to think we are lax'.

Specialist teachers from the start who imbue pupils with a love for their subjects. Parents remarked on how committed the staff are and how skillful at navigating between different abilities, particularly in the early years

Everyone is on first name terms, no 'Sir', or 'Miss' here. Rules are kept to a minimum. The uniform is a low key navy tracksuit, there is no ornate reception area filled with flowers, no grand office where parents can meet the principals in private to discuss their children. The fabric of the building, charming though it is, could definitely do with a lick of paint, yet the informality belies a rigour in the classroom that is less easy to perceive on a brief visit. Expectations here are high, there is an attitude of genuine scholarship, children are taught thoroughly and no one slips through the net. 'We know who the 10 weakest readers are and they will get extra individual reading every day,' says Chloe. The aim is to inspire the children. Specialist teachers from the start who imbue pupils with a love for their subjects. Parents remarked on how committed the staff are and how skillful at navigating between different abilities, particularly in the early years.

'We love curling up next to the radiators in there in the winter,' said one child. 'It's such a warm and comfortable space'

Not a school for a child with serious special needs, however, but they can cope and do an excellent job with pupils with mild dyslexia or dyspraxia. No specialist teaching but rather one-to-one work out of class. One part time SENCo sees only a handful of individuals on a regular basis. Behaviour here is good: 'The discipline is imaginative and creative rather than heavy handed,' commented one parent. 'They look for the positive all the time and treat the child as an individual – a complete person – which is enormously productive.'

Class sizes are small. The child-centred approach extends to making sure that an artificial date such as a birthday doesn't impede or impair progress. As they move up the school the pupils are set for maths and English, but this is done with a great deal of care and tact and there is plenty of movement between the sets. An absence of IT generally, whiteboards and computers particularly, is noticeable. Teaching here is old style, and effectively so.

Parents remark on how nurturing the school is but some expressed surprise at the amount of homework and the focus on academics. 'I thought it was relaxed,' said one mother, 'but actually they have very high expectations and the pace is fast'. This is tempered by a warmth and focused attention that is unusual in most busy London preps. Not only do all the teachers know each child but Sally, a therapist, visits on a regular basis and spends time with individual children who need emotional support for whatever reason, whether for problems at home, difficult friendships at school, or a bereavement. There is a room full of paints and toys where the children can feel completely safe.

The chapel building lies at the heart of the school and is used for anything from whole school theatrical productions and concerts to lessons and even table tennis in break. 'We love curling up next to the radiators in there in the winter,' said one child. 'It's such a warm and comfortable space.' Classrooms occupy the rooms that line the edge of the chapel and when we visited, a class was being taught geography in one corner, while a younger class did classics in another. The central courtyard between the chapel and the main building is reminiscent of an Italian villa – elegant borders, small angular grassy lawns, wrought iron fences, tasteful paving and a few plants sown by the children for good measure. Tucked behind the main building down a narrow path, past the vicar's house, is the hall where they can run around playing team building games like dodgeball or capture the flag. At break time, out come the skipping ropes and hoops. Some heat their packed lunches (brought from home or ordered from the local organic café) in microwave ovens in rooms adjoining the hall and there is a comfortable room with sofas and chairs where children can read and talk.

With the exception of the lavatories, which you might be forgiven for expecting to find in a (grand) house rather than a school, the rooms are small. The library is not much larger than a box room; when we visited, books were scattered untidily on the floor and piled round the edges. However the children love coming in here, curling up on the piles of cuddly toys and choosing the books from the carefully compiled coloured, spotted index. Art takes place in several different rooms at the top of the school; we saw some Picasso influenced self portraits, a collage project based on Matisse and some papier mâché balloons as well as wire sculptures and an impressive array of random clay figures soon to be fired in the kiln.

It would be a mistake to judge the school too much on the premises, however, as they are just part of the picture. The school makes creative use of whole of London, whether it's regular hikes to the Heath for fresh air and exercise, walks to the Royal Free sports hall for team sports, or cultural trips to theatres and museums. Unusually, from the age of 10 the children can go to designated local cafés to buy their own lunch on a Friday.

The informality belies a rigour in the classroom. Expectations here are high, there is an attitude of genuine scholarship, children are taught thoroughly

The big annual event is the musical production. Most recently the whole school was involved in a production of Oliver! performed in the chapel. Every child is involved and 'for several weeks everything revolves about making it splendid, which it is,' observed a parent. Although there are not a lot of concerts, productions and whole school events, when there is one it tends to be exceptional. Music is popular, and of a high standard – Chloe's interest and talent are important influences. One enthusiastic pupil relayed how she loved making up a music poem using different sounds from household objects, whether with a water bottle, a table or a saucepan. The talent contest at the end of the year is another hugely successful whole school event.

Everyone gets to shine, whether by dancing, gymnastics, reciting poetry or singing a song.

There are games – cricket, tennis, badminton, football, handball, table tennis and netball etc – every day, and a double games lesson every Thursday at the Royal Free Sports Hall. They have qualified sports coaches and play matches against other schools, but a parent observed that the number and quality of competitive matches is disappointing, feeling that sport here is more about getting exercise and having fun than anything else. School disagrees and says 'our children.. make very considerable progress in sport'.

When we visited the school had just celebrated its 20th birthday and it's come a long way since the tiny number of pupils it started with. It's still small: the numbers have consistently remained at around 90 for the past five years. This is how they mean to keep it – in a school this size, 'you can properly know every single child,' says Chloe. Shaped like a fish, the school tends to start small (in years 2-4), increases in number in the middle, creating a bulge between years 4 and 6, and then slims down again for the final two years when there tends to be very few girls and about 12 boys.

No organised, structured parents' meetings, PTA, class reps or coffee mornings and very few emails. The school is small enough for things to be conducted more fluidly and informally. If there is a problem the door is open for parents to come and discuss it and 'you can always call Garth on his mobile,' said one mother, 'as can my child if he is having a problem with his maths'. One parent expressed relief that she isn't bombarded by emails here as she has been by other schools, while another observed that it can appear disorganised when they are asked for their consent at the final hour for a rock climbing trip. Parents appreciate the regular updates on progress, together with lists to show where their child ranks in the class.

Parents here are an eclectic mix. Plenty of professionals, doctors, and lawyers as well as academics and scientists, most are local but some originate from all corners of the world, from Scandinavia to China. The one thing they all have in common is they want their children to be happy and to reach their potential. Reams of grateful letters when their children leave, demonstrating again the positive relationships that families form with the quadrumvirate. This all contributes to making The Academy, despite its focus on scholarship, far less of a pressure cooker than many schools of its kind in north London and beyond, though don't underestimate its earnest approach to the work they do.

The American School in London

1 Waverley Place, London NW8 0NP

020 7449 1220 | admissions@asl.org | asl.org

Independent	Pupils: 1,350; sixth form: 240
Ages: 4–18	Fees: £27,050 – £31,200 pa

Head of school: Since 2017, Robin Appleby; has a degree in English from Dartmouth College as well as two masters degrees. She taught in the States (Ohio and then New York) before joining the American School of The Hague and stayed in international education as well as being a trustee on the Council of International Schools, which gave her a chance to learn about how a wide range of international schools work. The two previous heads at ASL had long tenures and she is rather hoping to do the same, though she is from a different mould to the last head and 'may bring a new style to the previous head, though it is early days,' according to parents.

She aspires to a progressive approach to learning and wants ASL to represent 'best practice in US' with the child at the centre of the process. She believes in 'learning by doing,' which very much fits with the long existing ethos and curriculum in the school, with emphasis on understanding concepts, not learning by rote or for exams. She was attracted to the 'sense of tradition at ASL' and started by listening and learning from current staff of this 'highly functioning school'. She is hoping to increase diversity as well as 'make innovative changes that will help prepare pupils for future opportunities'. Robin sees her challenges as including teaching the ways that these first generation technology users can get the best from technology without losing social skills, and developing their emotional quotient alongside their intelligence quotient.

She is accountable to an very active board (around 20 members) who 'are supportive of change but protective of ASL'. They are involved in strategy while she is left to manage the school 'democratically'. She also has an articulate parent body. Staff say that she is 'marvellous' and 'really intelligent' and parents told us 'she is receptive and doesn't hide in her office – we think she is going to get a lot of stuff done!'

Academic matters: Not only the brightest of pupils but also the most motivated come to ASL for an American education. 'Pupils here need to have passion,' according to students, 'and they can't be bystanders'. Indeed, they were articulate and outspoken and aware they 'need to be advocates for themselves with teachers'. Totally American curriculum with an emphasis on critical thinking, collaborative working, questioning and listening. Classes average 20 pupils. Parents told us that 'the instruction is outstanding'.

Lower school has specialist teachers as well as generous sized and well equipped classrooms (though lower school playground needs some enhancing). Space to learn outside, both in plant filled courtyards and the playground and at the learning centre at the school's 21 acre playing fields in Canon's Park. Some phonics in youngest years but emphasis on 'word awareness' and use of 'whole language', with reading schemes, lots of experimenting and learning through play, teaching assistants working with groups and individuals. By grade 1, iPads and technology integrated in learning, with document cameras in all classrooms and pupils being taught coding and touch typing. Spanish taught right from the youngest classes. Maths differentiated in class all the way up. Mixed ability classes allow teachers to team plan.

Each year group has a central hub, promoting camaraderie between classes, with lockers to encourage independence and organisation. Huge lower school library has seating pods like sailors' bunk beds as well as soft floor cushions. Weekly library lessons on how to research and how to find books – particularly useful for their project work. Science room with specialist teachers and parent volunteers allows for experiential learning. Colourful displays of work and motivational messages all around the school rather than neat, copied stories, which gives an indication of priorities – all about what they have understood, with plenty of discussion and expressiveness. 'They teach them to think and be inquisitive,' say parents. No homework is given in the lower school – through pupils are expected to read daily and seem to do projects on subjects that interest them. This 'home learning' has taken a while to be accepted, but parents on the whole appreciate the lack of homework pressure and believe that it helps develop independent learning. 'They take ownership of their own learning.'

Middle school starts in grade 5 (year 6). Grades 5 and 6 share one group of classrooms, and grades 7 and 8 are on another floor – all help develop independence and a sense of moving up the school. Laptops given to pupils in grades 7 and 8 and then in high school it is 'bring your own device'. Language learning expanded in middle school to choice of Spanish, French or Mandarin, but little in terms of maintaining mother tongue languages, though the library has foreign language books in a large number of languages. Science rooms for each year group mean that experiments can be left out and displayed. The Make, Innovate, Learn Lab (MILL) does what it says on the tin – it is used for robotics, designing and making, and plans to 'revolutionise teaching and student learning at ASL by inspiring student to explore, innovate, collaborate, and to change the world'. An indication of the aspirational thinking that fills the school. It is possible to write on all the surfaces in the MILL, so plenty of mind mapping and brainstorming evident. Maths differentiated in class and parents spoke of their pupils being extended and supported. Middle school pupils praised 'supportive teachers' and explained that 'they were slow at marking sometimes, but that is because they have a life too, you know'. They said 'ASL respects what you are comfortable doing and you are not pressured but encouraged'.

Middle school pupils praised 'supportive teachers' and explained that 'they were slow at marking sometimes, but that is because they have a life too, you know'

High school pupils an articulate and motivated lot – with good results to boot, SAT averages of upper 600 in critical reading, maths and writing, and 20 AP programs offered with 92 per cent scoring grade 3 (out of 5) or above in 2018. Indeed, one parent said that 'high school is where things become more challenging and purposeful'. Enormous range of classes on offer each semester, from game design to macroeconomics, from Russian literature to computational circuits, from sport leadership to advanced dance performance. Languages taught as in middle school with the addition of Arabic. Science labs for high school with separate biology, physics and chemistry rooms. English taught round specially designed oval tables with discussion-based learning only (and each lesson is mapped to show how the discussion moved around and who spoke). Journalism encouraged with guest speakers and pupils producing the school magazine. (Impressive recent magazine dedicated to gun crime.) No external exams until AP in upper school, but progress mapped with grade level outcomes for all subjects and report cards based on whether students have met or exceeded these standards (with a section on what they need to be learning). Pupils told us that they have very full timetables as well as a big involvement in sport – they might get three or four hours homework if they are taking a large number of AP classes. 'Teachers stay behind school and are always available to help you – even if they are not your actual teacher.' They suggested that 'math has a good reputation, and social studies and history are good'.

The head believes that 'we have an ethical and moral responsibility to those who need support' and the learning support department tests and teaches pupils both in the classroom and out. Parents we spoke to were highly impressed with the support their children had – 'they gave her study skills she uses all the time' and 'they recognised a need and acted on it to support her'. Special mention by parents on the way the learning support department liaises well with both parents and teachers. Non-English speakers taken in up to grade 3 though EAL support given all through the school.

Games, options, the arts: Drama has the advantage of the theatre, which is well equipped with professional lighting and sound and holds an audience of 450. Plays at all ages fairly full on productions. The theatre also used for concerts – everyone takes music, with youngest pupils learning recorder and then moving on to ukulele with an enthusiastic and experienced specialist music teacher, then in middle school each pupil gets given an instrument and music lessons as well as belonging to a choir. This appears to pay off because even in the high school, where music is a free choice, 120 pupils sing in the high school choir and go on music tours. Two jazz bands, ensembles, quartets, orchestras – plenty of opportunities for music making.

Specialist art rooms, even for the very youngest pupils, with pupils being creative in the widest sense – designing, engineering, building as well as painting, sculpting and drawing. Higher up the school, there is a photography lab and dark room, video classes, ceramics and kilns, textiles, banks of computers for design work, and a light filled art gallery to display work.

'The school is dominated by sport,' according to parents. It's an integral part of school life, running alongside and with at least equal importance to academics. Lower school has its own gym and own specialist PE teachers. Pupils excited by interestingly named 'spy training' (circuit training). Two full sized gyms, a fitness centre and sport rooms for middle and high school, with playing fields out at

Canons Park, a half hour drive away. Wide range of sports during the year – boxing training, fitness suites, gymnastics, athletics, swimming, basketball and of course football. Tournaments against other international schools in London and abroad. 'We like it that our kids get to stay with families when they go on tournaments – my child went to Zurich and learned so much'. New swimming pool means that all the students get swimming lessons and can use the pool for training as well as competitions. Families can use the pool and the gym facilities outside school hours.

Endless clubs – 'we can create a club if we have an idea, we make an application for resources and get given a grant,' pupils told us. A board advertising large numbers of societies included Amnesty, autism awareness, robotics, South Asia, magic, creative writing, computer science, fitness, dance, textiles – the list of clubs worthy of a university freshers' week.

Not a formal atmosphere, but highly respectful (respect is one of the school's core values – along with kindness, responsibility, integrity and the ability to act)

High school pupils expected to be involved in community projects too ('service learning'). Staff members (not just teachers) take groups to local homework clubs, care homes, community centres, gardening projects, community projects, where they help on a regular basis. 'It is the highlight of my week,' said one staff member.

Background and atmosphere: Started in 1951, this is now one of the older international schools and it has been through several dramatic building renovations. Originally designed with open learning areas, it has now adapted these to individual year classes. The theatre was renovated and there's a new art building and fitness suite. Most recent developments continue to make this inner London school a veritable Tardis – there is a large swimming pool under the newly raised and improved playground. The school has a strong sense of identity and stability and pupils said they felt 'safe'. 'The security guard checks if I am getting a taxi and makes sure he knows who I am getting in the car with.' Not least thanks to the extensive security that surrounds a school with some very influential and/or wealthy parents – no access without an ID or appointment, with several guards and a bollarded entrance.

The hub of the school is the meeting area outside the theatre – tables with groups of pupils studying, high school pupils and staff eating, parents making plans and having coffee. The canteen is large, spotlessly clean with a generous selection for all sorts of dietary requirements – pasta every day (including gluten free pasta), hot meals, salads, sandwiches etc. Paid for with ID card so no money carried by pupils. Handy snack bar for eating outside meal times – useful for those staying on for practice or sport or activities. Pupils in grades 5 and 6 don't always like the fact that some days they have assigned seating ('helps avoid cliques and ensures new friendship groups can develop'). Parents considered that 'it is not a tidy or fussy school and it has a warm environment'. Not a formal atmosphere, but highly respectful (one of the school's core values – along with kindness, responsibility, integrity and the ability to act) with obviously motivated staff and pupils making things work. 'Teachers truly care,' say parents. 'They feel they owe it to these children to find out what works for them.' Pupils said, 'there is an awesome social environment, but you have to get involved, you get your social group through common interests'.

School fees are among the highest in London and pupils are privileged to have a raft of highly motivated and professional teachers in a school with seemingly endless resources and excellent facilities. 'Families have good values and no sense of entitlement,' according to one parent – but hard to believe it to be true of all families. 'This is an entitled group of young people, with hired limousines to the prom and branded trainers. I was not comfortable with the fancy cars and the party scene,' another parent said. Pupils told us, 'you need to be persistent and explore what you find interesting'. Teachers are dedicated and motivated, and encouraged with plenty of professional development training to keep their educational practice cutting edge. The teachers tend to stay, which is not always the case in an international school, but if they are prepared to work for demanding pupils and parents, then being in London in such an innovative, dynamic school surely has much to attract.

Pastoral care, well-being and discipline: Emphasis on being emotionally articulate from very early on – 'ways we can show kindness' in kindergarten, and drawings of 'what is in my head' to encourage thinking about feelings. From an early age the pupils are taught conflict resolution. We saw two 7 year olds sitting outside a classroom discussing what had gone wrong in the playground – 'Did you even listen to me?' 'I heard you but I must have misunderstood you.' 'Well, now I am telling you again' – and then later we saw them working together in the PE lesson. Conflict resolved!

Middle year pupils told us, 'this is not a good school if you are rebellious (you go on behaviour report and if you get three of those you might be

The million dollar question – how to get in? 'We are looking for pupils with a passion, who like to learn, will thrive and be independent'

suspended)'. So a clear discipline policy understood by all. They told us 'counsellors are there to give emotional support if you need it'. They were completely unanimous in saying that 'we feel safe at school'. Many of the pupils are very well travelled and streetwise, but quite a mix in terms of life experience.

School counsellors, well-being classes; 'excellent orientation activities really helped me when we first started,' said pupils, and they in turn become student ambassadors. This school is used to helping at transition points. 'There is always a teacher to speak to,' according to pupils, 'or you can speak to your class representative to take it up in council meetings'. 'Everyone is very accepting here – people are all treated the same,' according to middle school pupils, though older pupils told us 'you have to be proactive here'.

Pupils and parents: Articulate beyond their years, these pupils are constantly encouraged to 'speak out', are taught conflict resolution and are expected to be involved at all stages, to give their opinions. They are taught to explain their feelings – 'the social emotional side is encouraged,' according to parents – and 'to advocate for themselves to teachers and to others'. High school pupils run the school magazine; throughout, school council meetings are not only about making suggestions for change, but to organise events – pyjama days, shows, charity events and trips. Pupils here know that they can be heard and instigate change. They have guest speakers who stimulate ideas further. Pupils say, 'you can't be a bystander, you have to speak out for what is right'. 'We think that integrity is important – you have to do the right thing'. Clearly the school's message about core values including respect, integrity and the courage to act (written large throughout the school) has been fully absorbed. Respecting others has led to the provision of unisex toilets.

Parent evenings sometimes involve student-led portfolio conferences – showing the work they have done, which in the younger years can include videos and talking about their work. These are pupils who are used to explaining and discussing their work and themselves. We didn't come across students who were arrogant or self-satisfied – 'you have to be accepting of other people,' students told us.

Parents are involved at every level – making cakes, helping teach science, attending sports matches, hosting visiting international students, volunteering in the library, fundraising and giving money. For many parents from abroad the school becomes their community, and the International Community Committee providing weekly activities to help parents bond and get to know London. All parents we spoke to mentioned the 'welcoming community' that exists at ASL.

Parents largely from the financial sector, though diplomats, journalists, entrepreneurs also represented. Not all American parents, plenty of 'third culture kids' with parents from different countries. The admissions page comes in nine different languages as there are applications from around the world. A few British pupils: 'I wanted a school that had a curriculum that was freer and not focused on one or two subjects,' one local English pupil told us.

Entrance: The million dollar question – how to get in? 'We are looking for pupils with a passion, who like to learn and will thrive and be independent'. 'Parents have offered gifts to get their pupils in but they are not accepted.' Families of younger applicants will all be invited to visit: 'we need to know that we can work with the family, that we have common aspirations'. Higher up the school, applicants need to explain their motivation and interests and school reports will be scrutinised. More families are staying on (only a 10 per cent annual turnover), so not many places come up each year, though even this can be difficult for pupils. 'My kids find the fact that staff and pupils often move quite difficult. Perhaps it is an inevitable downside of a school with an international community.' This is 'an academically challenging school' and pupils need to be able to keep up.

Exit: Most pupils go on to university in the USA. 'We need a UK college counsellor,' according to pupils who felt that there was more support for those applying to universities in the USA. Large numbers to NYU, Northeastern, Middlebury, Georgetown, Cornell, Chicago, Wake Forest, Pennsylvania, Tufts, Yale and Southern California. Far fewer but increasing numbers go to UK universities eg King's College London, Goldsmiths, University College, Imperial; two to Oxbridge in 2018. UCAS translates the students' grades to UCAS points and universities give offers based on AP grades SAT/ACT and subject test results.

Money matters: A big priority is to increase diversity in this exclusive school. Parental giving wherever possible is in the culture (and prominent on the website, where they say 'annual giving is a tradition') and there is now an annual £4m fund for bursaries. School very proud of the fact that 12 per cent of pupils on some amount of financial aid – more than ever before, certainly. The financial stability and strength is evident not only in the buildings and the 'efficient, extremely professional administration' but also in the 'extraordinary resources' which are noted and appreciated by parents.

Remarks: The grande dame of international schools in London, it has plenty to be proud of and yet continues to expand and develop, both in terms of the buildings and facilities and in educational methodology. Teachers and pupils are all striving for better ways of learning and being. The school encourages both inward looking questioning (how to plan and study, how to think through and achieve goals, what is your passion, what motivates you) and outward looking involvement in the world (conflict resolution, what we can offer to others, how to work and plan in a team, world issues). Although this is definitely an American school – 'you cross that threshold and you enter little America' – it has huge resources and extraordinary facilities, and a dynamic learning atmosphere in a central London campus, so you can see why there is huge competition to get in and staff and families stay loyal.

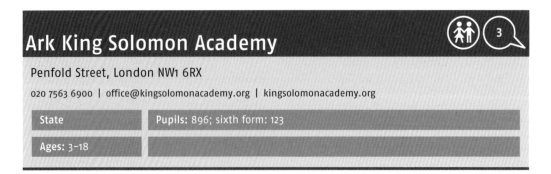

Ark King Solomon Academy

Penfold Street, London NW1 6RX

020 7563 6900 | office@kingsolomonacademy.org | kingsolomonacademy.org

State	Pupils: 896; sixth form: 123
Ages: 3–18	

Principal: Since 2008, Max Haimendorf MA Oxon (30s). One of the first generation of super-bright heads to have chosen teaching as an alternative to banking, Haimendorf graduated from St Hugh's College, Oxford, in biological sciences, and joined the first cohort of Teach First. As part of his on-the-job training, taught science at Uxbridge High School, then worked as the scheme's PR. A period with management consultants Oliver Wyman clarified his career goals: 'Teaching seemed so different from the usual conveyor belt that takes Oxbridge graduates to the City,' he told The Guardian soon after his appointment as the youngest head in England when still in his 20s. At King Solomon, he has taken the core problem ('the endemic issue of educational disadvantage') and addressed it with a Wyman-like mixture of 'creative enterprise and analytical rigour'. Still boyish in looks and enthusiasm, he is much admired by those in the sector ('From the beginning, he was unintimidatable, full of integrity and had a "whatever it takes" approach to the care and outcome of pupils,' said one fan) and beyond. Married to fellow Teach First evangelist Rebecca Cramer (co-founder of Reach Academy Feltham), he recently returned from paternity leave for his first child.

Academic matters: The school's slogan is 'Climbing the Mountain to University' (an image perhaps more suggestive of blood, sweat and tears than joy in learning), and progress from base camp in 2007 has undoubtedly been exceptional. In 2018, 73 per cent of students got 9-4 in both English and maths with 38 per cent of grades A*-A/9-7, making it one of the top-performing state schools in the country. (And KSA doesn't do 'soft', so around half get the EBacc, passing English, maths, science, a modern foreign language and a humanity.) A solid performance, too, at A level, with 65 per cent A*-B grades.

The approach to peak performance here is specific (and inspired by international example, such as the US Charter Schools). KSA keeps a tight control on numbers, never going beyond the 60 that start in reception, making its secondary school, at about 400, exceptionally small. A longer school day (8.20am to 4pm, Tuesday to Friday, with a 2.55pm finish on Mondays) allows for deeper immersion, with English and maths the central plank of learning up to year 11. 'We believe that without mastery of English and mathematics, success in academic study beyond GCSEs is impossible,' says the head. Many pupils start primary with well below average skills, but make outstanding progress in literacy and numeracy in the early years, and the emphasis doesn't let up thereafter. Those in year 7 spend a chunky 12 hours a week studying English lang and lit, plus a further five reading (in and out of school). Pupils are expected to notch up 30 'ambitious'

The approach to peak performance here is specific (and inspired by international example, such as the US Charter Schools)

new words every term and timetabled book clubs encourage 'challenging' discussions about what is read. No dumbing down outside the classroom either, with years 7 and 8 performing, designing and marketing their own unabridged Shakespeare production. Mathematicians, too, stretched both at school and in the public arena (with individuals and teams entering the UK Maths Challenge, Ark Maths Challenge, Times Tables Rock Stars Wrangle and more).

A focus on the 3Rs, however, does not mean other subjects are neglected. In primary, two hours a week are devoted to science, expanded to four at GCSE, when a truly remarkable 75 per cent of students take triple science (a statistic to make many independent schools blush). Here again, a wide range of related extracurricular underpins the main menu (Curie-ous Club, Year 8 Science Fair, Dissection Club, Journal Review Club, Open Labs). French taught for a committed hour-and-a-half each week in primary and nearly all go on to take a GCSE in French or Spanish. Highly structured homework programme from year 7 helps embed it all.

The school has embraced the theory of 'cognitive overload', so the secondary curriculum is kept deliberately narrow, and teaching style is traditional, with teacher-directed lessons and pupils spending a signficant amount of time working in silence. All agree that teaching is outstanding (made so by weekly coaching on professional development). 'We tell our teachers we are going to help them become better teachers,' says the head. 'It means very talented people want to work with us.' Headhunters employed for hard-to-fill slots.

Post-GCSE only 16 subjects on offer, though economics, politics, psychology and business studies are added to the range. The school only teaches A levels (plus one BTec in business studies), believing that 'these are the best preparation for university study'.

About 12 per cent on the SEN register and SEN well supported with three SENCos, on-site speech-and-language therapist, and regular tutorial sessions to help staff with teaching and learning strategies. Aid given both in and outside the classroom, including by Westminster-supplied specialists. Lift for those with mobility difficulties.

Games, options, the arts: Music is heavily embedded in the curriculum, taught for its 'cognitive benefits', 'moral, social and cultural' understanding and 'potential to build effective teamwork' – plus, no doubt, its advantages on the well-honed UCAS form. All supplied with a cello, violin or viola from year 3 and taught to read music, with regular whole-class lessons and small-group instrumental sessions. Compulsory participation in the school orchestra, which is timetabled from year 7 to GCSE. Annual summer orchestra tour abroad for older pupils is much competed over. (No doubt because it offers the opportunity for some 'pure, no-excuses fun!').

Elsewhere, extracurricular heavily entwined with curricular goals. After-school clubs focus on English (with all invited to participate in a year-long creative-writing programme), languages (including Latin), maths, music, and sport, while debating (with entry into national competitions) enhances public-speaking and contributions to the school magazine – The King's Speech – train up potential broadsheet talent. Trips, too, are intended to stretch, so local outings to The Imperial War Museum, British Library, Houses of Parliament and LSE public lectures, and residential adventures include living on a farm, visiting Paris or camping – experiences which are, as the website points out, 'in many schools.. the privilege of those who parents can afford them'.

PE taught for up to 1.5 hour each week, and offered as a BTec; other sports (girls' and boys' football, basketball, cricket, dance, martial arts, badminton, table tennis) available in after-school clubs, played in the spacious, well-maintained playground. School fields football and basketball teams, which compete in Westminster and Ark competitions, and are 'working towards' a netball and a rugby team. Art pursued earnestly (with skills tracked, targets set and 'key words embedded'). If creativity still manages to make it through, enthusiasts can develop 'new techniques' as part of the out-of-class enrichment programme.

Background and atmosphere: KSA is a leading light of the 35-strong chain of academies run by Ark (Absolute Return For Kids), a charitable trust founded by hedge-fund financiers intended to improve the life chances of children by creating high returns on philanthropic investment. The USP of Ark Schools, set up in 2004, is closing the achievement gap between children from disadvantaged and more affluent backgrounds, and the charity aims to apply sound business disciplines to all its programmes, with a strong emphasis on target-setting, monitoring and evaluation.

King Solomon operates very much within the brand, with all energies directed to the end game of making 'a university education something which is accessible, exciting and aspirational'. The curriculum is 'planned backward' with that goal in view, and classes are called after well-known university cities, year groups named by the year in which pupils will complete A levels. Sights are constantly focussed by add-ons such as the Odysseus Project (in partnership with OxFizz), which provides free tutoring courtesy of volunteers from Slaughter and May, McKinsey, The Telegraph, Barclays, Accenture and the Cabinet Office. Societies for medics and Oxbridge offer specialist advice.

An all-through education is, of course, a key part of the strategy ('The disruptive effect of the transition from primary to secondary can often affect confidence, behaviour and academic attainment,' says the head), while the scale is critical. 'We create a community where there are no strangers and no pupil will be left behind.'

The school as family is another leitmotif. But this is not simply an exercise in Victorian paternalism distancing children from undesirable influences beyond the school gates: the modern way is to solidify home-school links and educate the birth family, so the head pays a visit to welcome parent and child into the community and mum and dad are encouraged to participate (including offered handy Positive Parenting workshops).

'We never ask children to do things,"because I said so"', but after that 100 per cent compliance is expected. 'The purpose has been discussed and agreed as a team'

Built as Rutherford School for Boys in the late 1950s as part of London County Council's secondary school building programme, the main building, designed by Leonard Manasseh, is now Grade II* listed. A high point in the development of post-war secondary-school design, its distinctive roofline, Carrara-marbled foyer and varnished concrete and tiled surfaces provide an appropriately imposing backdrop to the endeavour.

Pastoral care, well-being and discipline: The disciplinary style is a further integral strand of the approach. Again, objectives are clear: 'We are responsible for teaching the children in our care how to work hard, and how to be good people.' The school aims, in Manichean fashion, 'to create a light and dark culture'. 'We make it normal, expected and visible that the majority of the group do the right thing.'

Everything is explained ('We never ask children to do things.."because I said so"') but after that 100 per cent compliance is expected. 'The purpose has been discussed and agreed as a team, and everyone

---

Good behaviour rewarded financially (at least, notionally). Elaborate 'payslip' system gives pupils an (imaginary) sum for turning up

understands why it is important.' Morning meetings and time at the end of the day provide moments for reflection on successes and areas of development.

Praise is an important part of the package, with daily 'shout outs' to identify who and what has been done well, as well as class (to celebrate ' the successes of the team') and individual rewards ('to rejoice in personal choices, growth and successes'). Good behaviour is also rewarded financially (at least, notionally). An elaborate 'payslip' system gives pupils an (imaginary) sum for turning up. Those in credit at the end of the week are allowed to take part in Friday enrichment, while big earners win an annual bonus – attendance at a week-long residential course at a leading university.

Those – and, alas, there will always be sinners – who for whatever reason do not make the correct decision are given the chance 'to reflect on the choice they made and what different choice they can make in the future to achieve a better outcome'. To facilitate this, a 'follow-up conversation' with families is also sometimes necessary. Persistent offenders are taught in isolation.

Behaviour in immaculately-ordered classrooms is (perhaps unsurprisingly) impeccable, off-task chatting virtually unknown. Silence – gained by clapping out a quick rhythm – is also expected elsewhere, including in the corridors in years 7-9, with a (slightly) more liberal regime thereafter. (Some have described the silence as 'disturbing', including one visiting head, who was charged for the privilege of witnessing it.)

Parents, however, delighted with the outcome. 'The school has given my daughter a great start in life,' said one. 'Every day she becomes more confident.'

Pupils and parents: Surrounded by streets full of some of the sterner remnants of turn-of-the-century local authority housing, the school sits in one of London's most deprived wards, and its intake reflects its locality, with 58 per cent on free school meals (the government measure of poverty), 75 per cent on pupil premium. Top 20 per cent in the country, too, for ethnic diversity, with over half speaking English as an additional language.

Entrance: Working along the lines of 'give me a child by the age of 7', King Solomon is very much intended to be an all-through school taking pupils from reception to Freshers' Fair. Non-denom and non-selective, after the usual specialist categories (including children of staff, where priority is given to those who teach subjects 'where there is a demonstrable skill shortage'), siblings and distance from the gates are given priority. More than three times oversubscribed at 4, with the furthest successful applicant living less than half a mile away. Don't hold your breath for a place in year 7: all year 6s transfer automatically at this point and the school does not expand (so no new openings at all last year). Sixth form, on the other hand, may have spots available. School also operates its own nursery, with 60 places on offer.

Exit: King's Solomon's raison d'etre is to guide first-generation university goers on the straight and narrow to higher education, a goal now being fully realised with ex-pupils off to study the full range of subject options (from chemical engineering and law to creative writing and psychology). At this point, most don't stray too far from home and London colleges are well represented (Queen Mary, SOAS, Royal Holloway, Goldsmiths, King's, LSE, Imperial), but more adventurous types are off to Warwick, Leeds, Reading, Kent and Sussex. Not huge numbers to Russell group as yet but, no doubt, it's only a matter of time. Offers specialist preparation for Oxbridge and medicine and the first student headed for Oxford in 2018 (history).

Money matters: Being part of the Ark chain of academies brings considerable financial benefits, and after-school clubs (from £5 a term) and trips (including the annual music tour abroad) are heavily subsidised. Ark bursaries also available to underwrite university fees for high achievers.

Remarks: Teaching is inspirational and results significantly better than many schools in affluent suburbs. Some find the approach a bit 'cult-like', but who can argue with the outcome. 'What is being achieved at King Solomon is extraordinary,' remarked an observer. There's no doubt that KSA pupils are safe, happy, secure and – successful.

Arnold House School

1 Loudoun Road, London NW8 0LH

020 7266 4840 | registrar@arnoldhouse.co.uk | arnoldhouse.co.uk

Independent	Pupils: 270
Ages: 5–13	Fees: £19,032 pa

Headmaster: Since 2006, Vivian Thomas (50s). A user-friendly, down-to-earth chap with an easy warmth and an unscholarly taste in garish ties (red flowers and giant yellow fish on the day we visited). Makes a point of being accessible on school gate duty at least twice a week and is generally popular with parents. 'Relaxed, confident, intelligent, and understands how parents feel about their children,' said one. Educated at University College School, Hampstead, followed by St Luke's College, Exeter, where he studied PE and history. Had a trial for QPR aged 17 and dreamt of becoming a professional sportsman but, after failing to make the grade (at football, tennis and rugby), he turned his talents to education. Taught PE and maths at UCS, followed by a spell at an international school in Venezuela. He returned to London to become deputy head at Arnold House, then head of Keble Prep, Winchmore Hill. Married to Rowena, he is a man of varied interests, who 'struggles with golf', enjoys travelling and takes guitar lessons with 'a madman in Dollis Hill who used to play with Ginger Baker of Cream'.

Entrance: Application form (plus the usual fee) due before child's second birthday, followed by an open evening held in April/May approximately two and a half years before the intended entry date. Interested parents (roughly 180 families for 40 places) are then invited to meet the head for a 20 minute chat. As always, it is the parents who are being assessed as much as the child. Don't say, 'I need you to get my son into Westminster'. Do say, 'I'd like my child to be happy and enjoy an all-round education'. Prospective pupils then invited for an informal one-to-one assessment and places offered 15 months before entry date. 'I hate the idea that it'll be down to the little boy, that he might be "not good enough",' says the head. 'What I want to know is, will he be a nice little boy to teach? When you open a book, is he able to be engaged? Or is he climbing the walls, unruly and impolite? I don't want it to be a skills-based test, and I find it astonishing that there are tutoring agencies for 3 and 4 year olds.'

Main entry point is into year 1, with occasional ad-hoc places in other years. Younger siblings and sons of old boys looked on favourably. Partial and full means-tested bursaries are available in years 5, 6 and 7 to prepare boys – most likely from state primaries – for 13+ exams (and bursaries) to independent secondaries.

Exit: Strongly 13-plus focused school. A wide intake means a broad exit, but high fliers get into all the top schools, often with scholarships to boot. Two-thirds go on to London day schools, with the remainder heading off to boarding school. Strong links with City of London Boys, Mill Hill, St Paul's, UCS and Westminster. Boarders go to Eton, Harrow, Marlborough, Radley, Rugby, Tonbridge and Winchester amongst others. Over-ambitious parents are discouraged from entering their son for exams all over the place. 'After many years of headship I know the system inside out. I am very honest with parents. What may look like an opportunity to them is in reality a rejection letter on the mat. Granny's all keyed up, everyone is rooting for him, but I know it's just not going to happen. I'll say, "Your son is moving along quite happily; do you really want him to get that knock back?"'

Roughly 25 out of 30 boys get their first choice school; the remaining five or six take a bit longer. 'When boys are on the waiting list it's my job to turn that into an offer. We have excellent relations with schools, and that's when the prep school head really earns his corn.'

For others the traditional values are its strongest selling point. 'It's just like the perfect country prep school, but in London,' sighed one happy parent

The school offers excellent results with less of the stressful, hothouse hysteria that so often accompanies the 13-plus experience. 'I offer places to parents who understand the Arnold House ethos,' says the head. 'They should want their son to join knitting club, cooking club, play music and sport, and not be getting anxious if he doesn't get three hours homework a night. We are here for bigger things than getting into a top academic senior school.'

Remarks: While some sniff that it is old fashioned, for others the traditional values of Arnold House are its strongest selling point. 'It's just like the

perfect country prep school, but in London,' sighed one happy parent.

Pupils spend time researching Arnold House old boys killed in WW1 before visiting France

In the stressful, results-oriented atmosphere of the London prep school system, Arnold House is an artfully constructed oasis where boys can still be boys. Pupils are even encouraged to have snowball fights and inter-house conker competitions (safely supervised, of course). Admission is non-selective and the school frowns on hothousing, yet year after year leavers gain entry to the holy trinity of Eton, St Paul's and Westminster.

'These boys don't need to be pushed,' claims the head (rather airily). 'It's a question of 'nudging' and bringing a boy nicely, like a fine wine, to the point where he is ready.'

Arnold House was founded in 1905 with nine pupils by a Miss Hanson, who was keen to prove boys could be prepared for public school entrance by a woman. She was successful, and the school has now expanded to fill three adjoining houses in a quiet St John's Wood side street. The buildings lack any particular architectural pizzazz, but inside it feels spacious and well laid out, and is probably one of the cleanest schools we've visited. Even the boys' loos were sparkling, and instead of the usual dank, unloved urinals we found modern boutique-style plumbing with glossy lime green and red cubicles.

Entrance is into year 1, with 40 places split into two classes, though classes are smaller at the top of the school due to natural shrinkage. They are mixed up every couple of years to ensure academic parity and 'social refreshment'. Setting begins in year 3 for maths and English, with subjects taught by specialists from year 5. French from year 1, Latin from year 5, and ancient Greek is an option in year 7. No separate scholarship class, but boys with scholarship potential are identified at the end of year 7 and invited to join specialist lessons.

Lots of examples of creative, value-added education. The Compass Course in years 5 and 6 aims to foster independent thinking, public speaking and IT skills. Pupils work collaboratively to design an EU leaflet, make an animated film, write a play and create a charity PowerPoint presentation. Instead of the bog-standard year 8 battlefields trip, pupils spend time researching Arnold House old boys killed in WW1 before visiting France and finding their graves in the war cemeteries to pay their respects. An inspired way to bring history off the page. There is an embarrassment of before-school, after-school and break-time activities ranging from an 8am Quiz Club to Mad Scientist Club, Bug Club, darts, French Fun and Games plus all the usual sport, music and art activities.

Like many London schools has a shortage of outside space. There is an adequate playground, but boys must travel to the school's seven acre sports ground in Canons Park (35 minutes away) for games. The younger boys travel by coach, years 7 and 8 by public transport. ('You'd expect, with the fees we pay, that the boys wouldn't have to get there by tube', muttered one disgruntled parent.) Here there are classrooms, a theatre, tennis courts and pitches for football, cricket, hockey and rugby. Older boys play team games twice a week, younger boys once a week, and there are additional PE and sports sessions at local leisure centres. A busy fixtures list for A, right down to G teams, means that even the most athletically-challenged pupil has an opportunity to represent the school.

The music department is outstanding and has many scholarships under its belt. Some 85 per cent of pupils learn at least one instrument and many learn two. Twenty different ensembles on offer, from flute group to jazz and African drums, with lots of opportunity to perform in concerts. Years 7 and 8 can use the whizzy i-music suite for production, recording and podcasting.

Art is taught to a high standard and doesn't get quietly sidelined as exams loom for older pupils. No need to feign enthusiasm when pupils arrive home clutching yet another art project. We saw wonderful Cubist self-portraits from year 3 and some very accomplished papier-mâché shells that any parent would be proud to put on display.

SEN support is excellent and, with a year of free one-to-one sessions before charges kick in, is more generous than at many comparable schools. One permanent SEN qualified staff member is supported by three visiting specialists for dyspraxia, speech and language and occupational therapy. Pupils who need extra help are identified in years 1 and 2 and either given classroom support by the six teaching assistants, or allotted one-to-one sessions as necessary. Dyslexia screening for every pupil in year 4 as a 'final trawl' to identify those with SEN needs, which can often mean brighter pupils in which dyslexic tendencies are masked.

So what type of child does Arnold House suit? 'My son has been blissfully happy, but there is a certain rough and tumble that goes with a boys' school, and I think if they are very fragile they might find it easier at a co-ed. They don't have to be uber-sporty though, there's drama, singing, art, something for everybody.'

'We take the boys as they are,' says the head. 'We have boys with IQs below 100 all the way up to 140. Once we take a boy on we're looking to be together as a team for eight years.' He admitted that, occasionally, if a boy looks like he is struggling by year 4

or 5, he will have a meeting with parents to decide 'whether or not this is looking like a good plan'.

Behaviour at the school is generally accepted to be good. 'We expect the boys to rise to a certain level of behaviour. I don't know if you can teach kindness, but you can certainly teach consideration,' says the head. There's the usual system of sanctions and rewards with Good Citizenship badges for 'being a good egg' and Industry badges for trying hard. Senior boys get ties for art, music, games and responsibility. 'I'm always pleased to hear how strict the school is,' said one parent. 'My son is well-behaved, but I occasionally hear of other boys being told off, and they are properly told off.'

School lunches would win a triple gold star from Jamie Oliver. A jolly cook was making roast beef and Yorkshire pud on the day we visited, and the gravy was even made with a dash of wine

Bullying is rare but, as in all schools, it happens. Usually nipped in the bud early by class teachers, but suspension has been used when necessary. 'In 7 years I've had only four situations where I've had to step in,' says the head. 'There isn't a parent I've met who thinks their son could actually be the bully, so it always has to be thoroughly investigated.' The head is very hot on cyberbullying. 'If a boy is being talked about in a derogatory way on Facebook on Sunday night, then it's going to cause problems at school on Monday morning. Even if it happens outside school, I will deal with it.' Only one parent we spoke to was unhappy, feeling that a situation had been dealt with 'too late'.

Parents are a mix of multinational successful professionals, with 50 per cent close enough to walk to school (should they ever choose to leave the 4x4 behind) and others coming from further afield (Notting Hill, Islington, Highgate). Reputed to be a friendly, sociable parent body, though the higher-than-average fees mean there's a lot of wealth sloshing around. 'There are a few amazingly flash cars, but also plenty of beat-up cars like ours. It's an easy, mixed group and I've seen no snobbishness whatsoever.' This is not the place for wags, trophy wives or school gate show-offs. 'It's definitely not a "women who lunch" school,' said one mother. 'All the mothers have, or have had, interesting careers. At my son's nursery I was the only working mum and had nothing in common with anyone, so I find the professional ethos here a relief.'

School lunches would definitely win a triple gold star from Jamie Oliver. A very jolly cook was making roast beef, Yorkshire pud, parsnips and broccoli on the day we visited, and the gravy was even made with a dash of wine.

The Camden School for Girls

Sandall Road, London NW5 2DB

020 7485 3414 | csg@csg.school | camdengirls.camden.sch.uk

State	Pupils: 1,000; sixth form: 450 (including boys)
Ages: 11–19	

Headteacher: Since 2010, Elizabeth Kitcatt BA MA (Institute of Education). Ms Kitcatt has been at the school for many years, joining from Parliament Hill School, where she was head of English. At Camden, under the previous regime, as well as teaching English, she was deputy head, responsible for 'teachers' professional development' and 'school improvement planning'. Looks a bit like Delia Smith and has the same reassuring, measured presence. Clearly strong on detail, but generally considered rather more cautious and less charismatic than her predecessor. 'She's a bit bland,' said one long-term parent. 'She's quite a lot stricter, but otherwise seems to have made little impact.' Determined to maintain the school's high standards and inclusive approach. Enjoys singing in her spare time.

Academic matters: Camden is one of the country's most successful comprehensives. Latest Ofsted rated it 'outstanding' in every respect (except attendance) and commented that 'it rightly deserves the outstanding reputation it has among parents and in the community'. In 2018, 96 per cent got 9-4 in both English and maths, and 49 per cent of grades were 9-7. But the sixth form is the jewel in the crown and A level results are stellar, with 78 per cent A*-B and 49 per cent A*/A grades. 'Top class curriculum,' says Ofsted, and that includes a hard-going compulsory core at GCSE of English, maths, science, philosophy and theology, physical education, French or Spanish and PSHE. Mixed-ability classes of about 28 pre-GCSE, 20 in the sixth form, and work carefully monitored with individual targets set at the beginning of each year. Homework, too, taken seriously, with detentions for slackers.

The sixth form decidedly less mixed-ability than the lower school, as only those who make the grades make the transfer. The curriculum here is traditional and academic with classics, history of art, Latin, ancient Greek (now to AS only due to government funding cuts), economics, psychology and philosophy supplementing the mainstream subjects. Extended Project Qualification (EPQ) also popular. Intellectual stretching taken even further for Oxbridge aspirants with after-school masterclasses covering everything from the Economic Downturn to The Wasteland. Much inspired instruction, particularly in the sixth form. 'It's like an old-fashioned grammar school,' said one parent. 'The teaching is really rigorous.' Lower down, there are those who struggle with more challenging pupils. ('Some teachers just can't control the class,' said one year 9 parent. 'There are subjects where my daughter has completely given up.') Though sciences are well taught with strong results, this is a noticeably arty school – possibly not the ideal place if medicine is your ultimate goal, though several a year do go on to become medics. Special needs well catered for, with sensitive individual support in class or by withdrawal in small groups. After-school homework club for dyslexia and spelling. Middle-class parents, too, tend to pick up the slack when students flag.

Games, options, the arts: 'Art and music are fantastic here,' said one mother with two daughters, one artistic, the other musical. Most parents (many in the media) agree. The school has specialist music status with dedicated music places at both 11 and 16, and this pool of talent forms the core of two orchestras (including a 70-piece symphony orchestra), various chamber music ensembles, three choirs, a wind band, a jazz group, a jazz choir and a recorder group. Both music and music technology offered at A level. Energetic and dedicated head of music. Art, too, is incredibly strong ('Art is really big in this school,' said one student fan) with powerful work on display throughout the halls and a glorious traditional art studio (formerly the gym), with a suitably bohemian skylight, as well as a pottery studio. Textiles equally vibrant. Art is the fourth most popular A level choice (after English, maths and history) with a good number of A*s. The keen also use the EPQ to extend their range (a short film made by a student was recently shown on the South Bank) and about 20 per cent of leavers go on to art-related degrees. Drama too – with the already professional among the sixth form – is strong, with an annual Broadway show and sixth formers mounting their own production; stage management is offered as an enrichment activity.

'Camden girls have a sense of their place within the world that is immediately recognisable,' said one former head girl, and who could dispute her standpoint?

Sport, on the other hand, is probably not the school's forte. An on-site gym, outdoor netball court and attractive dance studio are supplemented by excellent facilities at Cantelowes Park, a few feet from the gates, but play-up, play-up and play the game is not really the ethos here. Plenty of clubs from art, technology and modern languages to specialist make-up and knitting, and sixth formers devote Wednesday afternoons to 'enrichment studies', ranging from creative writing to personal finance and tag rugby. All the more traditional ornaments, too, including a sixth form newspaper and a debating society. Though there's plenty going on, you do have to be self-motivated to make the most of it. 'My son was supposed to do football as an enrichment activity,' said one mother, 'but no one monitors it. He just has Wednesday afternoons off.' School trips (Austrian tour for musicians, ski trip) and work experience abroad organised annually.

Background and atmosphere: Camden, founded in 1871 by Frances Mary Buss, is an iconic school in the history of education. Buss – and her limerickly-linked counterpart, Dorothea Beale, who founded Cheltenham Ladies' College – were responsible for establishing three of the great landmarks in women's education. Buss founded North London Collegiate in 1850, and then, specifically for girls of more modest means, Camden, which opened in 1879 and until 1920 (when it established its own sixth form) regularly sent scholarship girls on to North London for sixth form. The school went comprehensive in 1977.

Relatively restricted site with a motley collection of buildings, from the high-ceilinged, large-windowed Victoriana through 60s concrete to red-brick modern. Good facilities with ongoing development adding new science labs, a well-stocked library, modern computer rooms and classrooms and a building which houses design technology, English and music. Socially, the atmosphere is relaxed but purposeful. 'I was at quite a strict girls' independent school before I came to Camden in year 10,' said one sixth former, 'and I much prefer it here. You're treated like an adult.' Good food – pasta and garlic bread, curry – at reasonable cost.

Pastoral care, well-being and discipline: Deliberately few rules, but Ms Kitcatt is generally noted for having tightened up on the detail, clamping down on latecomers and absentees. Camden Compass spells out the behaviour code, but generally a strong sense of trust and girls are 'let out into the unknown' from year 9. That doesn't mean, however, their activities remain unobserved. 'The one time my daughter was absent without leave, you knew immediately,' said one parent. 'They really have the girls sussed,' said another, with a daughter who'd encountered considerable difficulties. 'I really feel they listened to my worries.'

Highly praised induction programme eases new pupils into the sixth from, where the approach is definitely 'young adult', with signing in rather than register and no requirement to be on site during study periods. 'We see it as transition between school sixth form and college,' says the head. Loose-rein it may be, but a strong team of tutors oversee 18 students each and offer advice on everything from study skills to gap years. Elected prefects organise the leavers' ball and help out younger girls. Parents in general think the outcome is all that could be desired. 'It's a terrific environment and produces really feisty girls, who are encouraged to think for themselves and question.'

Pupils and parents: 'Camden girls have a sense of their place within the world that is immediately recognisable,' said one former head girl, and who could dispute her standpoint? 'Girls are confident beyond belief,' said one parent with a more ambivalent view. Camden is a cool school, an obvious haven for the daughters of the north London, left-leaning media classes. Current and former parents include the sculptor Antony Gormley, Random House chief Gail Rebuck and Tate Modern director Sir Nicholas Serota, and old girls in the same style number Sarah Brown (wife of Gordon), Professor of Networking Julia Hobsbawm and actress Emma Thompson. The mainstream here is street-smart and sociable and frequently blessed by names like Hermione, Indiana and Genevieve. But while all participate in the uniform non-uniform of skinny jeans and stylish footwear, this is not a socially homogeneous institution. The school serves a catchment where the proportion of those eligible for free school meals is well above average, and it educates a plentiful sprinkling of refugees and asylum seekers, from Kosovo to Kurdistan. 'It's multi-dimensional and multi-ethnic,' said one mother. 'It's an urban experience, but excellent.' In the sixth form, there's a significant influx – boys and girls – from the independent sector.

Entrance: At 11, everyone sits an assessment test which places them in one of four bands – 28 admitted from each band. Preference within this to those with an SEN statement/EHC plan naming the school; then looked after children; then siblings; then those with exceptional medical or social need. Eight music places: three offered to those scoring highest in musical aptitude test; next 50 invited back for five minute instrumental performance audition to compete for other five places. Distance the tie-break for the remaining places – generally rather less than half a mile. Camden is definitely one of those London schools which people move house for (and sometimes only pretend to move house – a naughtiness the school clamps down on firmly). If that's your plan, living within a few feet of the gates is your only sensible course of action. In the sixth form, Camden goes co-ed, admitting a further 150-170 new pupils (from about 1,000 applicants), no more than half of whom can be boys. Once again siblings are given precedence (but only if the sibling is still at the school on the date the applicant starts). Other places are dependent on distance from the gates, academic references and GCSE grades, predicted and actual (documentary proof required for all three). Grade 6s essential in

One of those schools which people move house for. If that's your plan, living within a few feet of the gates is your only sensible course of action

at least five subjects, including maths and English language. At this point, a further 15 music places on offer to those who play 'an orchestral instrument to a high standard.'

Exit: Quite a number leave at 16, either because they don't make the grade or because they prefer a sixth form college, apprenticeship or employment. Vast majority of leavers at 18 to further or higher education, including 17 to Oxbridge in 2018, and seven medics. Sussex particularly popular, as are art foundation and music schools.

Money matters: Camden is a voluntary aided school and, as such, has to contribute 10 per cent to its buildings costs. Parents give generously and there is an annual fundraising appeal, with monthly donations from £10. Plenty of further fundraising activities, too, where celebrity watching is the order of the day.

Remarks: One of London's best and coolest schools. Suits the self-motivated, self-assured, creative individualist, particularly those who might find the atmosphere elsewhere pettifogging and unimaginative.

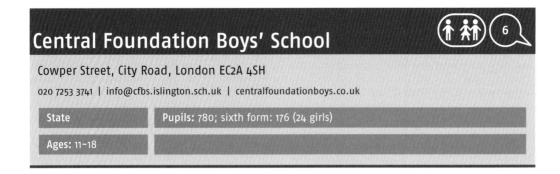

Central Foundation Boys' School

Cowper Street, City Road, London EC2A 4SH

020 7253 3741 | info@cfbs.islington.sch.uk | centralfoundationboys.co.uk

State	Pupils: 780; sixth form: 176 (24 girls)
Ages: 11–18	

Head: Since 2010, Jamie Brownhill LLB (40s). Originally a lawyer, he worked as a construction litigator for city law firm Mayer Brown before deciding to retrain as a teacher at CFB in 2000. 'I wouldn't have gone to just any school,' he says. 'It was very much a sense of vocation and moral purpose that leads one from being a city lawyer to such a challenging environment.' And lucky for the

school that he did make that choice – after just five years at the top he'd completely turned it around, and continues to work tirelessly to keep it on track.

Extremely visionary and not one for small talk, he is prone to sounding as if he's permanently giving a speech, making big, sweeping statements ('One needs to have a vision and follow it through'; 'There's a recognition that a head has an incredible impact' etc), which make him an impressive orator. 'Even in the corridors, he has important words of wisdom,' one pupil told us. Parents talk about being 'blown away' by him. One said, 'Our older sons were educated privately and we looked round 15 schools for our youngest, including private, selective and comprehensives – but this one stood out head and shoulders above the rest, largely because of Brownhill. He sets the tone, the culture and the expectations within the school and we love his inclusiveness, his energy, drive and commitment.' Praise indeed. Another commented, 'We love the fact that he's from the outside world – it gives him a much broader perspective than heads who have spent their entire careers within education.'

Rare is the day that pupils don't have some contact with him – he greets them every morning, runs weekly whole-school assemblies, teaches history to the lower years and he's usually out and about during changeover and break times. His office even overlooks the playground. Staff say he has a finger in every pie (which one admitted can be as frustrating as it is helpful), but ultimately they agree it's enabled him to make the school what it is, with the systems he's brought in for the likes of behaviour and targeting being described as 'nothing short of brilliant.'

Academic matters: GCSE performance has put this school in the top 10 per cent of schools nationally for added value, while the sixth form results mean the school is in the top 15 per cent of KS5 providers in the country – very impressive for an inner city comprehensive with 65 per cent pupil premium (in fact, it was nearer 80 per cent when the head joined). In 2018, 63 per cent got 9-4 in both English and maths; and 34 per cent of grades were 9-7, with the strongest results in maths, English, science and computing.

French or Spanish from year 7, with afterschool provision available in the other. After-school classes also available for Mandarin, Arabic and ancient Greek (all of which can also be done at GCSE), though few continue languages to A level. Setting in English, maths, science, languages, geography and history from year 7, with a reassuring amount of movability. Homework in abundance – building up from an hour in year 7 to two hours in year 11 – and woe betide any student who doesn't hand it in on time.

In 2018, 63 per cent A*-B grades at A level and impressive 44 per cent A*/A. Subject choices are largely traditional – sciences, maths, economics and computing most popular – but the school is part of the Islington Sixth Form Consortium, meaning there's the opportunity to study the likes of photography, psychology, media studies and a whole wealth of languages at one of the other member schools.

Head believes the school's success is largely down to the fact that students are taught in classes with a maximum of 24. There's also a major push on the fundamentals in year 7 and 8, which ensures literacy, maths and learning habits (how you revise; how you organise homework etc) are up to scratch, ready for GCSE learning. Indeed, unlike many schools, where there's an overt focus on years 10 and 11, boys here are developed, with meticulous attention to detail, right from the off. 'It's all part of the culture of learning that is drilled into the boys from the day they start,' said one parent. 'It seems to me that the importance of learning is at the heart of every single piece of communication with the boys,' said another. Perhaps this explains why the boys we spoke to were not only enthused about their studies, but able to directly relate them to their futures. Even some year 7 boys were able to tell us exactly what they wanted to do with their lives and what they'd need to get there.

Head believes school's success is largely due to fact that students are taught in classes with a maximum of 24. There's also a major push on the fundamentals in years 7 and 8

Lessons, which are all taught by subject specialists (most of whom have firsts or 2:1s in their degrees), are well-planned and, according to students, engaging. 'If you don't respond well to a teacher's learning style, they'll adapt it for you,' one told us, whilst several pointed out that teachers are always available by email or after school to go over anything you don't understand.

Teachers (over half of whom are female) say they are helped by the centralised system for dealing with behaviour (same-day detentions even for small transgressions), along with a painstaking focus on tracking and monitoring, which they say means they can get on with the job in hand. We noticed very few teaching assistants – they tend to be used on a temporary basis for getting a child's behaviour sorted. There's a mixed diet of practical, interactive lessons and heads-down learning. Food tech, for example, always involves cooking, whereas in the maths and languages lessons we witnessed, it was very much a case of chalk and talk.

SEN provision – which covers the usual dyslexia, ASD etc – is almost exclusively classroom based (and helped by those small class sizes, as well as setting) and offers exceptional outcomes for students, evidenced by the results. 'I couldn't have asked for better help throughout my son's education,' said one mother, whose son is dyslexic. 'He's

EIFA International School

had the "Why me?" moments when he's had to work much harder, but the school keeps him positive, as well as making sure he has attainable goals and extra support and time where he needs it. Dyslexia has certainly never made him feel he can't achieve as much as anyone else.'

Games, options, the arts: Football and basketball are the top sports, with boys doing CFB proud when it comes to competing against other schools. Cricket is on the up and there's also fencing, boxing, martial arts, table tennis and gym workouts. Whilst the school is good at playing to the boys' strengths (hence winning all those high level competitions), the head is adamant that sport here is for all. Pupils and parents concur. 'There's no stereotypical male bravado around sport at this school. In short, you don't get the jocks,' we were told. On-site facilities include an undercover Astroturf pitch, running track, a couple of gyms and two halls. Off-site, the boys do climbing, swimming and more. 'When a young person leaves here, they really know how to access the community's facilities,' says the head.

Incredibly, every boy who wants to can borrow an instrument for the duration of his time at the school. Not just recorders, but cellos, saxophones and clarinets

Music is integral to school life. Incredibly, every boy who wants to can borrow an instrument for the duration of his time at the school. We're not just talking recorders, but cellos, saxophones and clarinets. No wonder 150 students are heavily involved with the department. From 7.30am every day, there are rehearsals, whether for the three school choirs, orchestra, bands (including house band and concert band), string quartets, woodwind groups etc. The department's equipment is sophisticated and there's a 10-strong staff team, including two full-time music teachers. Expect to see a raised eyebrow if you use the word 'peripatetic' to describe the visiting teachers – this dedicated team say this is the only school in London they work in, where they are considered part of the school community, not just 'teachers who pop in' – the result of which is that they are more than willing to put extra time in for the three main performances per year. Parents describe these performances as 'amazing.' 'We nearly all had tears in our eyes at the last one,' one parent told us. Meanwhile, external opportunities range from singing in the Royal Albert Hall to providing the musical entertainment for local law firm functions. While many of the musical children

are also academic, others aren't – and music gives them a great opportunity to excel.

A delightful, airy and bright art room is home to some serious artistic talent – much of it bold, brave and inspiring. Drama is also seen as important, with weekly lessons for years 7, 8 and 9 in the two-roomed, carpeted drama studio. There are three main performances per year, providing opportunities for both pupils in the lower and upper years. Debating also strong; they were national schools Debate Mate champions recently and were third out 250 schools in a recent competition when we visited.

Day visits to all the usual museums and galleries that this school has on its doorstep, as well as French and Spanish trips (year 9, 10 and 11), an annual ski trip open to all and a rural activity trip for sixth formers. Extracurricular provision focuses on music and sport in the main, with other options ranging from cooking (particularly popular) to arts club and gaming to drama. The school takes full advantage of its location, with excellent links with the City.

Background and atmosphere: There could hardly be a more unlikely location for a school – smack in the middle of the City. Squeezed between, and overlooked by, law buildings and financial institutions, you walk in expecting it to be bursting at the seams. But this place is a Tardis, with a roomy outside courtyard (some of which is covered) and Astroturf pitch, along with ample classrooms of various sizes, break-out rooms, labs, halls, library, dining room, sixth form centre, art block, drama and more. The oldest parts date back 150 years and boast beautifully tiled walls and polished wood floors, albeit with a few areas that look in need of a lick of paint. 'The school even smells of tradition,' said one dad – and he's right.

The school originally opened in 1865 by Rev William Rogers (chaplain to Queen Victoria), who recognised the pressing need for more education in the City. Having initially used temporary buildings in Bath Street, the current purpose built school then opened in Cowper Street in 1869 and the Great Hall came four years later, by which time there were over 900 boys. Post-war, it became a grammar, then in 1975 the school returned to being a comprehensive, with various building works having taken place over the decades – the most significant of which is about to happen. 'The development project, which will cost between £30-£40 million, will involve a science block and a new reception, followed by a new arts centre, then a four court sports hall – along with some more general landscaping and renovation,' explains the head, who points out that the works will be staggered to ensure minimal disruption.

During lesson times, the school is so quiet that you could be forgiven for thinking the place is empty.

It's another story at break times, though, when boys inevitably let off steam – and with everyone changing lessons or having breaks simultaneously, it can be loud. 'It's essential, in my view, to avoid interruptions, so when we learn, we all learn and when we move, we all move,' says the head.

Pastoral care, well-being and discipline: Each year group is organised into eight form groups of 18 students and each of these forms has one tutor who stays with that form as it goes up through the school. Every student is allocated regular tutorials with this tutor. In addition, there are directors of learning (heads of year) who, once a term, do a detailed analysis of each student, looking at issues such as attendance (including at after-school clubs), punctuality, learning and behaviour. Then there's a house system, which generates all the usual leadership opportunities and cross-year friendships.

A high level of engagement with CAMHS means there are no waiting times for students who want to access mental health services within school and there are three student counsellors, focused on supporting students with any work-related issues. 'Students can access both, should they require it,' says the head.

No word gets used more by the head than 'community' and it's this ethos, say students and their parents, that ultimately makes the school such a supportive environment – a place that students want to be. Some older students told us bullying used to be a real issue, but that this head's zero tolerance has helped – measures such as teachers in playgrounds and even bus stops and underground stations, mean there are no longer any hiding places. 'There are instances of bullying,' one boy told us, 'but teachers are good at sorting it out quickly.'

The glass cabinet in the reception area sets the tone for discipline. Displaying beautifully handwritten notes from the headteachers in the 1800s, outlining intricately detailed rules around issues such as not throwing paper and not pulling other boys' hats off, this isn't just a light-hearted look back to harsher times. Indeed, the message remains crystal clear that boys must not misbehave, even slightly. Any that do find themselves receiving a short, sharp shock – notably an hour's detention after school that very afternoon. Talking in class, forgetting your PE kit, lacking focus, failing to hand in your homework – all these things will land you in deep water. No wonder Ofsted marked behaviour here as outstanding and we did not see a single boy failing to pay full attention in class. Teachers who come to visit can hardly believe their eyes. There are more serious misdemeanours, but only occasionally, and these usually relate to violence. 'There is the odd time when a boy flares up and hits out,' explains the head, although it's much less than it

'There's no stereotypical male bravado around sport at this school. In short, you don't get the jocks,' we were told

used to be, reflected by the drop from 190 exclusions per year before he joined to just 10 in the academic year we visited.

Boys are expected to dress immaculately both in and outside school. The messiest you'll see is an undone top button. 'I have a room with every piece of uniform in every size, so if a boy forgets something, they can borrow it,' says the head.

Unusually, sixth formers get a chance to do paid work in school, for example by working in the kitchen and doing lunchtime duties in the year 7 play area. 'It's not that they don't do voluntary work too. It's just that we don't want the students working every hour at Sainsbury's to earn money, which would get in the way of their work. It means everyone wins,' says the head.

There's a strong student voice here – the student council is taken particularly seriously and individual requests are often met too. 'One student in year 7 asked for there to be a skateboarding club and they set it up within a month,' one student told us.

Pupils and parents: There are 35 first languages spoken by students at this truly ethnically diverse school; it's English for 47 per cent of students, then Bengali (16 per cent). Nineteen per cent of students are white British, with other significant numbers being Bangladeshi, Somali, Turkish and Black Caribbean. Because of the banded entry system, some of these students come from neighbouring boroughs, as well as the whole of Islington. The students are a mixed bag socially too – both extremes of wealth and poverty, plus everything in between.

There's no PA, although parents are seen as key to enabling the boys' learning and there's almost 100 per cent attendance at the two annual parents' evenings and other talks and meetings. We found pupils to be articulate and enthusiastic, even in year 7, and there's already a huge sense of pride. Notable former pupils include Anthony Wedgwood Benn (before he became plain old Tony Benn), Kingsley Wood, Jacob Bronowski, Richard Seifert, Ronnie Scott, Martin Kemp, Trevor Nelson and Reggie Yates.

Entrance: More than 600 boys compete for the 180 places. All applicants take CATs (Cognitive Ability Tests), with students split into four ability cohorts. Within each of these cohorts, the boys closest to the school get in. All sixth form entrants must have 6s at GCSE in the subjects they want to study, including English and maths, as well as getting through a detailed interview. 'The way we see it, we have a short period of time to achieve a lot, so we need to know students have the right character and work ethic,' says the head. Attendance in sixth form is 98 per cent (compared to the average of 85-90 per cent for London) and the head intends to keep it that way. Usually, around 10 of the school's own applicants tend to get turned away, while around 25 new students come in (of whom 10-15 are female).

Exit: Around 60 per cent stay on to sixth form, those who don't have generally decided to study A levels elsewhere, including the private sector. Maths, engineering and computer science are among the most popular subjects chosen at university (although there is a huge breadth of subjects overall). Courses include medicine at St George's and business management at Surrey, with one off to Padua.

Remarks: This extremely disciplined, well-ordered and highly academic, urban school runs a tight ship, giving boys who are prepared to toe the line a chance to leave with both excellent exam results and a genuine readiness for the modern world in terms of character, moral compass and work ethic. A hidden gem right in the heart of London, it is a school going from strength to strength and has the feel of a grammar, without the selection. 'It's a hugely well-kept secret, with many parents – including me – thinking, "Why don't all local boys apply?"' summed up one parent.

Charterhouse Square School

40 Charterhouse Square, London EC1M 6EA

020 7600 3805 | life@charterhousesquareschool.co.uk | charterhousesquareschool.co.uk

Independent	Pupils: 200
Ages: 3–11	Fees: £17,040 pa

Head: Since 2009, Caroline Lloyd (40s). BEd in geography from Exeter University (although her parents had wanted her to do a 'proper' degree). Her first job as an NQT was at Charterhouse Square School in 1994, straight after leaving university: 'I was young, determined and desperate to be a teacher.' Indeed Caroline (as she is known to staff and pupils), knew she wanted to teach from the age of 7 and 'used to line up my teddies, pretending they were in class.' However, she had a very specific idea of the kind of school where she wanted to teach and only five schools matched her criteria – Charterhouse Square being one of them.

During her 15 years at the school and prior to becoming head, Caroline experienced teaching in all year groups from nursery through to year 6. After leaving to start a family she returned six months later on a part-time basis as she 'missed teaching so much'. In 2008, the school was purchased by Cognita and the position of head was advertised. Caroline says: 'It was never my intention to become a head, but I was worried that someone new would come in and not see how special the school was' – so she applied for the post. After so many years at the school her application was seen as a natural progression by both parents and children. One parent told us: 'The school was good before with the previous head, but it's great now. The children have just blossomed under Caroline.' Another praised her for being such a consistently visible presence; 'She knows every pupil by name and is naturally great with children. The school just seems to run seamlessly.'

Tall, attractive and immaculately turned out, she could have been separated at birth from the Middleton sisters and would look quite at home sipping Pimm's at a polo match. Her boundless enthusiasm for both her job and life in general is infectious but don't be fooled, this head is no pushover and knows that some people might go so far as to call her a control freak: 'I'm on the school door every morning and most afternoons. I feel that if communication is strong, we can get things sorted before they escalate out of control.'

One can't imagine too many things getting out of control at this genteel school, which has had no permanent exclusions in its 25+ year history; the head concedes that her main challenge is 'managing over-aspiring parents.' She says: 'I've often had to remind parents that I'm actually on the side of the child, especially when they are being pushed too hard to get in to certain secondary schools.'

Entrance: Completely non-selective, entry is by lottery – unless you have a sibling who already attends. Twenty-six 3+ places offered each year and roughly 70 on the waiting list. No point planning the Caesarian or putting names down at birth, you can register up till the end of June the year before entry and a ballot is drawn on 1 July. Head says this comes as a shock for some parents: 'who have been used to pulling out a cheque book to buy their way in' and concedes that 'It can make me pretty unpopular.' Cheque book will, however, come in handy for £4,000 non-returnable deposit payable when accepting a place.

Exit: Most to high calibre selective London secondaries. Fierce competition for places at both (girls and boys) City of London schools and some pupils even pulled out early at age 7 or 10 by parents who think this will increase their chances of getting in. School says this is a shame and 'can be disruptive.' Other leavers to eg Channing, Francis Holland, Forest School, South Hampstead, North Bridge House and Queen's College.

Remarks: Charterhouse Square School is located on the south side of historic Charterhouse Square in Smithfield, central London. The square was built on what was the site of a 14th century Carthusian monastery (an almshouse and chapel remain) and also London's largest Black Death plague pit. The five-storey Victorian building occupied by the school, though smart enough, is easily missed among neighbouring offices and apartment blocks, but any lack of character, not to mention green space, is more than made up for by such a central location. This is a City school and parents know exactly what they're buying into when they make the decision to send their children here. One told us: 'I am able to drop my kids off on the way to work, which is one reason I chose this school. The other reason is that I noticed how happy and well-mannered the pupils were when they were out and about. I know some people think it looks more confined than other schools, but it works for us and my children are very happy here.'

Nursery was having its annual 'animal dress up day' and we were greeted by tigers, bears and monkeys plus unidentifiable but colourful animals

Though it wouldn't suit those who like to plan ahead, most parents seem to welcome the diversity and 'range of abilities' that result from school's non-selective, lottery-based entrance procedure. It's an unusual independent school in other ways: there's no uniform and it's first name terms for all teachers, including the head. One parent told us: 'I love this school for being individual with very individual ideas.' Another said: 'Coming from a convent school background I was initially horrified about the idea of first name terms, but I have to say it works very well and makes the teachers far more approachable to the children, without diluting any respect.'

Head has worked hard to ensure that hers isn't a one size fits all school: 'When I came on board, early years was very formal and a bit of a hothouse. Drama was only every other week and there were no school trips. I think it's about broadening the curriculum so that we can make sure that all pupils can excel at something.' Parents wholeheartedly agree. Teaching described as 'exceptional' and 'instilling a love of learning.' Years 4 and 5 are taught together so that they have the same teacher for two years before the all-important year 6. They work on a two-year curriculum, with the exception of homework, and English and maths textbooks. They are also ability grouped. One parent told us, 'I'm not really sure how it works – but the kids seem to understand it, so that's the main thing.'

Designated SENCo provides one-to-one support and booster groups for children with SEN, which accounts for a handful of the school's intake. The nature of the school building (five flights of stairs) may make it unsuitable for pupils with physical disabilities.

Pastoral care is paramount and school employs a number of highly effective strategies to help pupils feel safe. Older pupils can make use of classroom 'feelings boxes' to share concerns privately with teachers, and the 'buddy' system supports new pupils. Every parent we spoke to raved about this: 'It's a great system as it makes new children feel less intimidated and older children rise to the responsibility of looking after the younger ones.'

Our tour started in the early years foundation stage classes, nursery and reception. Nursery was having its annual 'animal dress up day' and we were greeted by tigers, bears and monkeys plus a couple of unidentifiable but colourful animals. Sweet little add-on area designed for role play was effectively outside, but covered by a canopy and surrounded by a high wall. This, we were told, was to prevent anything landing on the tracks of Barbican station, something that carries a huge fine (on an hourly rate). Thankfully, this has not happened so far.

Small but well stocked library from where children are encouraged to take books home nightly, and a carpeted school hall with beautiful white piano and colourful wall display of ukuleles. Extracurricular activities such as judo and table tennis take place here and all children have the opportunity to learn a musical instrument. 'Informal' Spanish also offered in the early years. One parent said: 'I was amazed when we went on holiday to Spain last year, that my 5 year old daughter was able to communicate with a local in pidgin Spanish.'

> *'Coming from a convent school background I was initially horrified about the idea of first name terms, but I have to say it works very well without diluting any respect'*

Bright, neat, colourful classrooms were full of interested, happy and very polite children and the atmosphere of the school is extremely warm and friendly. Pupils who were leaving told us how they'll miss Charterhouse 'sooo much', especially the teachers. 'What I really like about the teachers is that they are all so friendly. Also, we are often asked to tick a box privately at the end of a lesson about whether we found the classes easy or difficult. If we are really struggling, we can sometimes get an extra private lesson.'

Despite the limitations of a tall and narrow building ('I often had to walk up five flights of stairs when I was pregnant,' the head told us), children don't seem to lack breathing space and fresh air. During the warmer months they spend their lunch break in the private Charterhouse Square gardens; when it's cold and wet they play in the school's 'jungle' downstairs. Organised sports take place nearby at Coram Fields or the Golden Lane Leisure Centre. Pupils do take part in inter-school sporting events, but no regular fixtures because of the issue of 'bussing children around.' One parent did say that this school is perhaps not the right option for the 'extremely sporty child', although another said that her two boys 'are extremely sporty and it meets their needs.' A highlight in the calendar is sports day: 'It's just such a joy, well handled and fun.'

No school meals prepared on site and no dining room because of limited space so until recently all pupils had to bring in a packed lunch. School has now organised for a company to bring in hot food in thermos containers, if the parents require. The head says: 'This system works very well and the advantage is that parents know what their children like and can order accordingly.' We are told the quality and choice is great, with meatballs, pasta, wraps, soups and stews on offer.

Lack of space may deter some, but Charterhouse Square is a wonderful option if you live and work in the City. This is a successful school and a happy environment in which pupils of varying abilities thrive and with comments such as: 'My child loves every day of her school life!' who could ask for more?

The Children's House School

King Henry's Walk, Islington, London N1 4PB

020 7249 6273 | suegarcin@childrenshouseschool.co.uk | childrenshouseschool.co.uk

Independent	Pupils: 113
Ages: 2–8	Fees: £13,920 – £14,730 pa

Head: Since 2016, Kate Orange Cert Ed (Wellington, New Zealand College of Education) – 60s (not that you would know it) with an interesting background in education. After graduating in New Zealand and working for two years as a teacher there, she moved to the UK, cutting her British teeth working for the Thomas's School group in their first school near Sloane Square. However, after two years and with a yearning to work in France, she moved to a village school in Provence, which she says was the most incredible experience: 'I was a New Zealander and this was my first experience of living in a completely foreign environment.' With her schoolgirl French, she even managed to wow officials (from the Mitterrand government at the time), who were sent to the school to inspect this new foreign teacher: 'I became a national cause celebre'. She spent her spare time there acting with a Parisian theatre company, performing at the Avignon Festival. Her love affair with France has persisted.

When she returned to London three years later, she worked in knowledge management for a City law firm for four years. After having children, she taught at an Islington school for two years before moving to The Children's House as a class teacher. She took on the role of deputy head in 2005, taking over as head when the long-standing former head-teacher retired. 'This school just has a lovely feel to it; it's very child centred, which in turn makes it very family centred', says Kate (as she is known to all, even the pupils). Indeed, during our visit, her office door burst open on two occasions with pupils desperately wanting to ask 'Kate' something. As one parent said, 'This school very much operates an open-door policy at all times. You can have a chat to Kate whenever you want, and you often see parents popping by her office in the morning. She's also very quick at responding to emails.' Another parent said: 'I've had both heads and they've both been great, but Kate has a real educational rigour to her and the school has a great academic focus without hammering it home.' Others talk about how dedicated she is and how she knows every-thing about every child in the school.

Married with two grown up children, one in law, one studying architecture, Kate is a classical music enthusiast and belongs to small group of people in southern France who facilitate concerts in Provence, where she tries to spend around three months of the year.

Entrance: Register for nursery as soon as possible after birth; nursery children are now guaranteed to be offered places in reception (£100 registration fee and £2,000 deposit). Places are offered by date of registration and sibling priority. Most places in the pre-prep are filled from the nursery, but 'one or two' spaces might be available in reception, again based on date of registration. Consideration has been given to expansion, but finding suitable premises has been as issue.

Exit: A few leave at the formal entry point to other schools at 4 and 5. Twenty-eight children enter reception at the Upper School in two classes of 14, but numbers naturally reduce to a manageable 20 by year 2, 'although this number does vary from year to year – we don't like to turn anyone away who has come through the nursery.'

The vast majority of 4+ and 7+ leavers go to St Paul's Cathedral School, North Bridge House or The Cavendish with the occasional one to Channing, Highgate, Lyndhurst etc.

Remarks: Founded as a nursery in someone's front room in 1973, when 'there was little in the way of early years provision and nothing in the way of policies and procedures', the nursery is now a fully-formed school in central Islington, housed in a former Hindu Temple, the first of its kind in London: 'Hindu Saints still pilgrimage here, but not during term time', we are told. Situated a brisk 15 min walk from the pre-prep (although there is flex-ibility in pick-up times for parents with children on both sites). Two year olds upwards enjoy a rich

Trips to nearby King Henry's Walk Garden give the children more outdoor space and an opportunity to observe seasonal changes

and dynamic offering (including conversational Spanish, dance, yoga and art) taught by fully quali-fied teachers. 'It's a lovely, friendly place,' said one parent. 'They really care about each child.' At the nursery we were impressed by the large, bright and airy rooms with a plethora of activities to stimulate any child. Although there is no attached outdoor space, children are taken to a nearby garden three times a week and to soft play weekly. Children at the nursery are offered either morning sessions, afternoon sessions or full days.

The pre-prep came into being when a former parent spotted a school to let in the local newspa-per. 'Our nursery parents always felt it was a pity that children had to move on at 4 and 5.' Now they can remain in the fold, housed in a petite and pic-turesque Victorian school building. The classrooms lead off a lovely sheltered playground. 'It's idyllic, like Enid Blyton,' said one parent.

Very much a 'child-led' school, 'We like them to work collaboratively, one child supporting another.' It's not a hothouse, but with the 7+ ever-present at the end of year 2, children are expected to do homework after school on most days (intro-duced gently in reception and year 1) and during the summer holidays before entering year 2. 'A fairly challenging environment', one parent said, but another added: 'Whilst they do take the 7+ very seriously, they do it without panicking parents.' However, as Kate says, 'being a small school, the teachers do get to know the children very well and are quietly assessing their progress on a daily basis. We can then cater for their individual needs and there is a lot of fluidity between ability groups.'

It is a very creative environment in which the arts – music, art and dance – are central to learning. Children might make shoebox interiors as a part of a home topic, create giant tetrahedron mobiles in maths, or paint and embroider textiles in a study of fabric-making. During our visit, the children had just been learning about the Jewish Festival of Succot and had created their very own Succah (a temporary wooden shelter) in the playground.

Specialist teachers extend the core. Spanish is taught from nursery onwards for one lesson a week, and ICT has a dedicated teacher and a full-class supply of laptops throughout. Singing and rhythm are taught by a music teacher, plus a weekly half-hour violin lesson with two professional violinists. 'We could have chosen any instrument, provided the children learned pitch, rhythm and musical notation. Most children play the violin very well by the end of year 2.'

The school prides itself on being very inclusive and an on-site SENCo addresses both minor and significant difficulties. Good support is given to those with English as an additional language, addressing the requirements of an increasing number of bilingual children.

The children are introduced to team games and specialist ball-skills teachers provide additional PE lessons to children in one of the two large adjoining church halls. The well-equipped playground provides further scope for fresh air, exercise and, most importantly, play. 'We have a lot of play resources and use them to extend children's learning with carefully planned activities' – a fabulous wooden pirate ship was a recent addition to the play area. Regular trips to nearby King Henry's Walk Garden provide the children with more outdoor space and the opportunity to observe seasonal changes and grow their own vegetables in the allotments.

Plenty of enrichment. 'The school is fantastic at making lovely things happen for the children,' said one parent. Each class has at least two visits a term, always educational and usually entertaining (storytellers, puppeteers, exotic animals, LSO concerts and an African drummer to name but a few) as well as numerous themed events. During our visit it was Our Wonderful World Week, which is an annual event that has proven very popular; 'Everyone is invited to take part, from grandparents to aunts and uncles, to share something from their country of origin, which could be food, stories, music etc.'

After-school clubs are offered twice weekly, and activities change termly – everything from sewing, fencing, chess, cookery, science, drumming to football skills could be on the agenda. Homework club is also offered 'which helps parents and promotes a sense of independence in the child.' Lunchtime clubs include coding, games and puzzle club.

School uniform is minimal and practical (navy and white with specific school sweatshirts and fleeces). The school encourages healthy eating and children bring in lunch boxes, supplemented by a snack with fruit in the morning (provided by the school).

Traditional values of courtesy and consideration are central to the ethos. Kindness is rewarded here, and if you achieve 10 certificates, you get to choose half an hour's 'golden time' for the whole class: 'Being kind is paramount', said a mother.

Founded by parents, The Children's House remains a parent-driven operation, with active participation from its Parent Committee. All vote for the council of management, which administers the school. Unsurprisingly, families (Islington and Hackney media, lawyers, bankers and artisans) form a tight bond both with each other and the school, regularly arriving to read, organising the summer fair, quiz night, etc. There is a genuine commitment to community links and charity fundraising. 'We couldn't do it without the parents, who are amazing.' The school population is very cosmopolitan, and one of the things parents like most about The Children's House is its home-away-from-home atmosphere, and 'being made to feel so welcome.' One parent told us: 'Literally, my only criticism of the school is that it doesn't go up to 11. It's such a shame to leave such a happy place.'

The school offers three fully-funded bursary places at the nursery and some partially funded bursary places.

City and Islington College

283-309 Goswell Road, London EC1V 7LA

020 7700 9333 | courseinfo@candi.ac.uk | candi.ac.uk

State	Pupils: 1,600
Ages: 16–19	

Director: Since 2015, Peter Murray BA MA PCGE Oxon, late 50s, previously deputy director of sixth form. Read history at Kings College, London, before taking a masters in 19th century social history at Warwick. Drawn to teaching by an inspirational role model at school: 'If you've had a good experience, you think... I might enjoy that....and I did'. Cut his teeth in secondary schools in London and home counties, before moving to tertiary education in Richmond upon Thames College, arriving at Candi (as it is known) in 2000 to co-ordinate humanities, then as deputy for seven years. No stranger to the area, he grew up in Islington, supports the Gunners and saw his younger sister attend the college, operating under a previous name, in the 80s. 'She had a really different and a really good experience,' he muses.

A keen runner and 5-a-side football player, and at 5 o'clock on a Friday evening, showed no signs of slowing down. Although his monochrome office has a touch of the impersonal about it, he expounds vividly on the college achievements, is conversant with the myriad different A level courses and glows with pride at his students' individual successes; 'a lot of our students come from a background where they don't have networking opportunities... where there is not a lot of academic success'. Describes the college as 'schooly, but it's not a school, it's not a university...like university, with safety nets'. Views his appointment as head as 'evolution rather than revolution', aiming to continue the progress of his predecessor in forging contacts with business and industry. 'There's a lot of advantage to be gained from networking and in London we are in a very good position to do that...building students' confidence and knowledge and an understanding of the world of work, building their aspiration'.

Academic matters: A sixth form college for A levels, sheltering under broader academic umbrella of City and Islington College and Westminster Kingsway College, has the advantage of offering a wide range of subjects (over 34 on offer when we visited), delivered by A level specialist teachers, in a tailor-made environment for 16-18s. Class sizes are kept to around 20 (22 max) in the popular subjects, supported by over 140 staff and technical assistants; smaller numbers attend the more unusual options, electronics, dance, graphic communication, Turkish. One parent was impressed by the flexibility in the timetable: 'They've been very open minded about changing course'. Mainstream subjects like physics have seen a surge in popularity, boosted by the college's two female physics teachers, while the college has extensive technical back-up for a range of practical options including textiles, photography and media studies, whose students get to show final pieces at nearby Screen on the Green. Not publishing 2018 A level grades. The head describes the student experience as academically rigorous. Around 60 students take the EPQ, which distinguishes independent learners and researchers. The staff are A level specialists, some with doctorates, some authors of school text books – and unanimously got the thumbs up from parents.

The head gives it straight from the shoulder about the Ofsted inspectors' tour. 'Overwhelmingly they were grade 1 lessons; I didn't have to hide anyone from them, there are no bad teachers here'. The management team he describes as 'fantastic' and 'sparky'; the parents' verdict: 'interconnects

Textiles, photography and visual arts studios look out over the many cranes and offices of the cityscape with film studies further along

well as a team'. The head's mission to create links with industry and academia has a two-fold effect. Describing how aspiring medics get to sit alongside UCL students at the Royal Free Hospital, he commented, 'It is stimulating for the staff, and that comes back into the classroom'.

An inclusion co-ordinator supports a full range of special needs, from mild dyslexia to ASD, with one-to-one support in class or in separate smaller rooms, depending on the level of need. The user-friendly building, complete with lifts, accommodates physical disabilities too.

Games, options, the arts: Wednesday afternoons are for enrichment. Students who aren't lucky enough to be visiting the Supreme Court or meeting a Nobel Prize-winning astrophysicist can enjoy more earthly activities, including football, basketball, netball, boxercise and gym, co-ordinated by a sports youth worker, off site. There's an in-house dance troupe and theatre shows, including an annual talent show and a Christmas production, which take place in the drama studio or at Islington's Almeida Theatre. Students from both music and music tech courses join with others in a combo band, though numbers don't allow for a choir or orchestra. The walls of the corridors display lively posters for a wide choice of clubs: history club, talking religion, talking politics, geo-justice, robot club, as well as political debates about local elections and the London mayor. Teachers make the most of the graphic design students in promoting courses: 'Why learn a language?' asked one eye-catching poster and 'Congratulations on completing your coursework' cheered another message. Trips out include London museums and Tate Modern; residentials for geographers to Derbyshire, while the RS class gets to visit a Buddhist retreat in Scotland.

Background and atmosphere: In an area that Dickens refers to as where 'London began in earnest', the college site at Angel stands at a confluence of the metropolis's business and residential life. To the south and east it touches the City with its commercial and banking quarters, to the north it embraces the mixed residential areas of Highbury, Finsbury and Holloway and the buzzing shops and bars of Upper Street. The college's sparkling glass, steel and chrome structure catches the eye, with its grey themed interior and a city garden. Past the turnstiles and uniformed security checks, the visitor is greeted by a large canteen/hall/chilling area on the ground floor, labelled 'a thriving hub' by one mum. Beyond this is the library, with its purple and grey colour scheme, and shelves of journals. Many of the rooms are convertible to smaller meeting rooms, with soft dividers and screens; an adjacent IT suite houses computers as far as the eye can see.

A tour up the glass stairwell, with Barbara Hepworth-style holes, takes us to the classrooms and workshops above. Textiles, photography, and visual arts studios look out over the many cranes and offices of the cityscape, while film studies are found further along the corridor they call Media Street. Disappointingly little to see of the students' artwork in the designer building, and one mum felt the art and design department could be more inspiring. However, a room full of recording equipment run by dedicated techies provides support for the many and successful media students (alumni include singer, Paloma Faith; actor, David Oyelowo OBE; TV presenter, Reggie Yates; and news reporter, Symeon Brown). Humanities and languages classrooms have a floor to themselves, with seven science labs below; fully equipped with the latest kit and a flock of white coats and goggles; 'It seems to be very well resourced,' commented one parent. A vibrant hub on the first floor, full of upholstered chairs and scarlet beanbags, houses the careers advice centre.

Students not lucky enough to be visiting the Supreme Court or meeting a Nobel Prize winning astrophysicist can enjoy more earthly activities

A lone horse chestnut tree on a patch of green breaks up the austere landscape of the grounds (this is EC1 real estate) while an all-weather court on the roof of the science building next door allows for floodlit matches. Students can take a break between classes at brutalist picnic tables or work up an urban sweat at a game of garden ping pong.

Pastoral care, well-being and discipline: Dress is teen-casual and it's first name terms for teachers; 'that doesn't stop them calling you Sir for two years,' laughs the head. The relationship relies on mutual respect; 'we are trying to turn them into young adults,' he says and students we spoke to were aware of the journey. 'It's preparing me for life after', said one. The young adults recognised the school's high expectations: three warnings for misconduct or poor work, followed by a 'cause for concern' notice. One parent reported that the

tutor had been quick to notice when her daughter's new-found freedom had gone too far, and called a meeting; 'we all three of us got her back on track'. No bullying, except the occasional modern menace of cyber-bullying. A more serious misdemeanour involves discussion with the parents. Serious alcohol or drugs issues are rare and accountable to a disciplinary panel; 'there's less goes on here than in my own sixth form of 90,' owns the head. A mum praised the pastoral tutor system, for 'quite closely monitoring' a particularly shy daughter. The college is conscious that its population is at a fragile stage of adolescence, so employs a full-time counsellor, alongside others including a mental health and well-being worker. 'As a society we are more enlightened,' explains the head. 'In the past people got on with it or sunk'.

Students with issues knew how to contact their tutor, and met with them every week in the normal way to discuss progress. They were in no doubt how to seek out help in applying for university from the full time careers officers; 'They are always telling us who to go to', said one. The higher education department offers advice on UCAS applications, explains personal statements, carries out interview practice using former members of staff and even helps plan gap years. They run a dazzling timetable of tutorials, eg applying for Oxbridge, medicine, teaching, nursing or apprenticeships, along with a range of informative talks ('STEM work experience for Girls' caught our eye) in addition to masterclasses in work-related skills such as online IT courses and young drivers' workshops. 'I talk to universities all the time,' says the head, which explains the respectable number of offers to competitive courses, though it was disappointing to find a capital-centric attitude in the students we met, who appear content to study close to home.

Pupils and parents: Starting afresh in a new sixth form, rather than staying at their secondary school, gives the students a real chance to reinvent themselves, and the ones we spoke to described a variety of reasons for choosing the college: 'it gives you more independence'; 'looking for somewhere you are doing things by yourself'; 'it's more diverse'; 'more subjects'; 'closest to home'. One parent commented about her daughter, 'She hadn't had a good experience, and had a lot of catching up to do with feeling good about learning…it's a place that gives inspiration to the students'. More girls than boys (60:40) and a typical urban cultural diversity: 'The ethnic mix is a real mix; 30 per cent Asian; 30 per cent Afro-Caribbean; 30 per cent white,' says the head, plus a few international students who 'want to have a London experience'. With huge numbers of students, the variety of ambition was also evident: the high achievers gain scholarships with banking or legal companies, others apply for vocational courses, while some are content to munch cookies in the canteen. 'The scale allows the range,' explains the head.

Parents commented on the study body as 'a mixed bag of individuals...from far and wide' and 'it's very diverse'. They meet the teachers at the annual parent evenings, or at individual sessions with the tutor or course leader, if requested. Surprisingly for such a large cohort, the parents all felt involved, and emails and phone calls were answered promptly. The school sends out a termly newsletter, though no-one we spoke to had read it.

Entrance: Five 4s needed at GCSE to study three A levels, higher grades required to take four subjects, and the college sets its own entrance test for maths. Applicants are encouraged to visit the open day in November and apply before the end of January. Oversubscribed, more than four applicants per place, but interviews 2,500 before making offers. A nucleus of students from Islington and Hackney, and has a partnership with three local schools: Elizabeth Garrett Anderson, Holloway and Islington Arts and Media, which have priority, although current cohort attended 200 different secondary schools. A taster day at the start of July is followed by registration at beginning of autumn term and a last opportunity to finalise courses. A handful of international students, who board with local families.

Exit: The head is rightly proud of his statistics: 70-80 per cent to university, one fifth to the Russell

In an area that Dickens refers to as where 'London began in earnest', the college stands at a confluence of business and residential life

Group, a few to Oxbridge. Courses in 2018 included human, social and political sciences at Cambridge, fine arts at UAL, dentistry at King's College London, politics and economics at Exeter, child nursing at Nottingham and medicine at St George's. Several students praised the dynamic careers advice service, which supervises applications.

Money matters: Centrally funded by Education Funding Agency; international students self-fund. Dedicated college advisor supports applications for a host of bursaries, sponsorships and additional expenses, including travel. Parents pay towards school trips.

Remarks: City and Islington College offers students a new beginning with a wealth of courses and great facilities. The students are encouraged to take advantage of their position in the heart of London to forge connections with the world of work and academia. Throw in supportive staff, a savvy head and a blessed central location at Angel and no wonder they are off to a flying start.

City of London School

Queen Victoria Street, London EC4V 3AL

020 3680 6300 | admissions@cityoflondonschool.org.uk | cityoflondonschool.org.uk

Independent	Pupils: 935; sixth form: 260
Ages: 10-18	Fees: £17,901 pa

Head: Since January 2018, Alan Bird, previously deputy head at Brighton College, and responsible for much of the college's day-to-day management. He has also been head of sixth form there. First class degree in economics from Cambridge and a masters from LSE, where he was an Economic and Social Research Council scholar. Has also taught economics at his alma mater, RGS Guildford, and spent eight years as head of politics at Tonbridge. He is a pianist up to diploma standard and a proficient cellist and organist, a good skier, swimmer

and squash player. He is very interested in politics, especially US politics.

Academic matters: Offers A levels – but a move to Pre-U is on the way, initially with biology, history and RS. Others may well follow. All in the sixth can opt to take the Extended Project Qualification in addition to three or four main subjects. School and is on the look-out for a replacement for the ECDL – something with programming built in, a cry we hear everywhere. Links with IT companies being developed to further upgrade the offering. No weak subjects or depts – results at A level and GCSE uniformly impressive. Columns of A*s, As, a few Bs and very little in the lower order columns (90 per cent A*-A/9-7 grades at I/GCSE and 68 per cent A*/As or equivalent at A level/Pre-U in 2018).

Maths much the most popular A level but modern languages hold up and Latin and Greek battle on. Mandarin compulsory in first two years and, seemingly, catching on here rather more than elsewhere. Links being forged with schools and organisations in China. Economics and drama the only concessions to the more 'modern' subjects – no psychology, business or other 'studies'. Lots of academic prizes eg recent successes in Olympiads, the prestigious Erasmus Essay Prize and the international Juvenes Translatores prize. 'My son's teachers have all been wonderful – especially in maths and the arts,' a parent enthused. A second felt, 'My sons are always stretched to be the best they can be but never pushed. They don't let you become so obsessed with work so you can't do other things. The teachers plainly want the best for each boy.' Another was concerned: 'There seems to be a drive to climb the league tables. We don't want that. It's not why we chose the school.' But school assures us there is no shift in the aims in that respect. Around 60 on the school's SEN register – mostly dyslexic or needing help with organisation. Not a prominent feature of the school's mix.

Good library – rather like a top notch public library in design and atmosphere but with 50,000 books, periodicals, CDs and PCs galore plus cases housing the more venerable volumes for show. Unique, in our experience, is the school bookshop – a real one. Super 'science lecture theatre' but memorable lectures seem to be on anything but science.

Games, options, the arts: Sports and arts praised unreservedly by parents despite the trek to the school's main sports centre at Eltham. 'They do fantastic things with them. The music tours are amazing.' More than half learn an instrument; many take LAMDA exams; much-praised joint productions with the girls' school in eg choral concerts with a choir of 200+. Music tech facilities of a high order. Lively drama – productions at all age levels. Smallish, pretty basic, studio theatre but excellent main, flexible 150-seater theatre would do credit to an upmarket fringe venue. Weekly school publication The Citizen produced by students. Four high-ceilinged art studios – all do art and music to year 9 – and much varied and vigorous portraiture on display. We enjoyed the ceramics – especially the satisfying crunch of some material or other underfoot. DT on the bottom floor also lively and fun and more DT and to a higher level (as yet no GCSE) on the cards, to boys' delight.

Football is main winter game and the school is a powerful presence in inter-school tournaments. Basketball, cricket, water polo, swimming and athletics all strong. Current National Water Polo champs and champs in London basketball and football tournaments – no narrow academic focus here. On-site huge sports hall, weights room and pool. Sizeable Astros marked out as pitches. Rest happens 25 minutes' away at sports clubs around the metropolis. Some 200+ on D of E Award programmes; CCF surprisingly lively for a city school but offering mouth-watering, subsidised opportunities – 'I did a powerboat course and got my licence from it,' said one young man.

> 'My sons are always stretched to be the best they can be but never pushed. They don't let you become so obsessed with work you can't do other things'

Excellent range of trips and tours with a focus on educational value and enrichment rather than the extravagance one sees elsewhere. Good use made of London and its riches – a three-weekly trip to somewhere in the capital made by all year 9s. Good range of clubs with a bent towards to the literary and the philosophical – we like The Diaspora Club, The Comedy Society and Modern Language Society, in particular. Many have their own sizeable domains – we passed The Railway Society room – 'thousands of pounds worth of kit in there,' we learned. Debating is popular and lively as is Model United Nations. Lots of outreach and charity work done out of conviction more than duty. Overall impression is of a varied, creative and quirky programme with plenty for everyone from sports stars to unashamed geeks.

Background and atmosphere: A school with a long, complex and obscure history. Its original benefactor, John Carpenter, and his executor intended his legacy to be for 'the finding and bringing up of four poor men's children with meat, drink, apparel, learning at the schools, in the universities, etc, until they be preferred, and then others in their places for ever'. The school as we know it today was finally established four centuries later, in 1837, first just off Cheapside, moving, in 1883, to Blackfriars and finally, in 1986, to a purpose-built, magnificently-sited, establishment between the Thames and St Paul's Cathedral. While it can no longer claim the nobly charitable purpose intended by Carpenter, it retains a liberal, progressive ethos, not least in its determinedly ecumenical attitude to religion and its generous bursary scheme, and much is being done in 'outreach' – eg working with The City of London Corporation's academies, charitable ventures, multiple imaginative and beneficial links.

Wherever you are, great city buildings look in at you through many windows. And the river light is likewise inescapable. The building – which seemed over-warm and airless to us on a mild spring day – is wearing well. It's a little municipal – the signing, wide corridors and atria are reminiscent of an NHS hospital – but the whole is softened by relics from its previous home (we appreciated especially the row of Victorian leaded lights lining the dining room celebrating school luminaries), trophy cabinets, miles of red lockers – and the arts and crafts about the place. Displays stay up for rather too long, we gather, so that people stop looking. Extraordinary things like the fragment of a second century AD limestone Roman head of Mars found as part of an old riverside wall. Large 'concourse' used for events, adorned by plaques and statues to more school luminaries. Also, seemingly, hundreds of PCs everywhere. School houses are named for great figures in the school's history.

Pastoral care, well-being and discipline: Houses are 'important but not that important', we were told, ie sports, chess, intellectual competitions etc run on house lines but 'being in a different house never separates friends'. Sixth formers are grouped by shared subject teacher rather than houses. Every parent stressed how happy their son(s) were at the school. 'The boys in his class are so lovely – friendly, happy and always polite and nice to each other,' one told us, while a second said, 'It's a nurturing environment – they offer help, they set him up with a mentor and try to nip problems in the bud'. A third felt that the boys were 'very respectful of the teachers – it's a liberal ethos and it works'. And a fourth, 'The boys help each other in all kinds of ways'. Few discipline problems, though we heard one class giving a language assistant a bit of a rough time.

Pupils and parents: From all over London and the home counties. Mostly native English speakers, but a great diversity of home languages spoken including Chinese, Hindi, Russian and Tamil. Very few need EAL support. Brains the only common denominator – parents, who like the social mix in the school, are mostly professional, bright, urban and appreciative of broad and liberal educational values. 'They learn to respect everyone,' said one, 'and realise that not everyone can afford parties in limousines.' Formidable list of notable former pupils (known as Old Citizens) includes HH Asquith (PM 1908-16), Arthur Rackham, Ernest (Oh for the Wings of a Dove) Lough, Denis Norden, Julian

Retains a liberal, progressive ethos, not least in its determinedly ecumenical attitude to religion and generous bursary scheme

Barnes, Daniel Radcliffe, Mike Brearley, Anthony Julius, Steven Isserlis, umpteen brainbox academics, legal eagles, cleverclogses of all sorts, among them three winners of the Nobel Prize.

Entrance: Highly selective. By competitive exam in English, maths and verbal reasoning in year 5 for 10+ (40-50 places for which around 160 apply), and year 6 for 11+ (60 places for which around 550 apply) and 13+ (40 places – ISEB pre-test at 10, followed by interviews and conditional offer based on CE – perhaps 350 apply) plus interview and report from current school. At 11+, two distinct competitions, with those after 100 per cent bursaries sifted by taking an online reasoning test in December. Around half of all entrants come from preps, the rest from state primaries. At 16, applicants are tested in their two top subjects – 20 available places for which 75 apply. The school courts the primary/prep sector early – admission in year 6 is unusual and they clearly steal a march on the rest.

Exit: Up to 15 leave after GCSEs, almost all to state sixth forms. All leavers go on to heavyweight subjects at good universities – around 15 per cent to Oxbridge annually (20 in 2018) and the rest to eg UCL, Bristol, Durham, Warwick, Edinburgh etc plus eight medics and five to the US.

Money matters: Around 10 per cent of current pupils on 100 per cent fee remission via 'sponsored awards' available at 11+ and 16+ for bright candidates whose family finances would not stretch to fee-paying school without assistance. All applicants sifted via reasoning tests. Gross parental income to be below £45,000. Around 30 academic scholarships available at all entry points, worth up to 25 per cent of fees. Candidates invited to a 'demanding interview for which no preparation is helpful'. Sports scholarships – good footballers especially welcome. Music scholarships and choral bursaries – these for those who become choristers at The Temple Church and The Chapel Royal.

Remarks: 'A very down-to-earth school,' asserted a parent and we agree. An inspiring yet grounded school with solid values, providing vision, opportunities and a wonderfully civilised start in life for its lucky students. A jewel in London's crown.

City of London School for Girls

St Giles' Terrace, London EC2Y 8BB

020 7847 5500 | admissions@clsg.org.uk | clsg.org.uk

Independent	Pupils: 639; sixth form: 150
Ages: 11–18	Fees: £18,384 pa

Linked school: City of London School for Girls – Prep, 95

Headmistress: Since 2014, Ena (pronounced Enna) Harrop BA MA MA MPhil PGCE (one of the longest list of degrees in The Guide) (40s), a modern linguist, originally from Spain. Her previous incarnations include head of Spanish at Royal Russell and head of modern languages at Royal Grammar, Guildford. She joined City Girls as director of studies in 2010 and – unusually and remarkably – was appointed internally to the headship, clearly to the delight of the entire school. One of the most popular heads we have encountered.

You can, instantly, see why. She is the real deal. Formidably intelligent, chic, softly spoken, charming and beautifully articulate, her credo is the centrality of gender equality and the necessity of the modern world being gender-blind. And, as a head and the mother of three daughters, she lives the dream. Her (teacher) husband took her maternity leave when their last daughter was born. In the words of her pupils: 'She was – before she became head – a kind of figurehead.' 'The message of feminism she promotes in the school is so inspiring.' 'She is likeable, approachable.. collaborative, efficient.' One admitted, 'I was scared when she came on our school trip but she was so relaxed it wasn't daunting at all.' And another, 'When she became head we just thought it'd be great to have more of her.' And every parent we spoke to concurred.

'Independent learning' is a phrase you meet a lot here and, again, the head – with her list of degrees – walks the talk. 'I feel tempted,' she told us, 'to take at least two A levels at this school – economics and art.. and then there's..' A very modern head: a recent assembly was on 'All you need to know about pregnancy and childbirth' and she refers to 'the nappy barrier' to women's achievement. Behind her desk sits a text: 'Feel the fear but still do it.' With Mrs Harrop as role model, a City student will leave as well-equipped to take on and challenge the world – while remaining her essential self – as any young woman could.

Academic matters: Maths rules. As elsewhere with clever students, this has become the most popular – and successful – A level subject, and recent takers outnumbered those who take languages all put together. 'My girls are strategic,' explains Mrs Harrop, 'and they know that if they take a language they are less likely to get an A*/A than if they take maths.' The girls say: 'People really like maths – they see the use of it.' Other popular subjects – in an, admittedly, conservative range as befits the preferences here – are history, chemistry and English. Mandarin, after a very successful course to GCSE, now offered at Pre-U, and should markedly boost the number of language takers which, has, in any case, increased since Mrs Harrop took over. Overall, A level results included a remarkable 82 per cent at A*/A in 2018. GCSE results no less impressive with 95 per cent 9-7. However, although results are obviously a key factor in the school's success, the school itself puts the emphasis elsewhere – on, for example, independent learning and thinking.

Perhaps the most exciting aspect of the extracurricular offering at City is London itself

Lots of computers and library has a bank of borrowable laptops. Librarian seen as 'wonderful', though library itself, possibly, not the most impressive feature – we were bemused by some strange cataloguing and location of books and it felt a bit tired. Although a third of the pupils speak a language other than English at home, almost none need EAL help. Around 12 per cent with a mild SEN of some kind, all supported as needed on an 'as and when' basis but no-one with major learning difficulties here. School not easy for those with mobility difficulties.

Games, options, the arts: Art is, according to all, wonderful. We saw some terrific painting and the results at A level and GCSE are phenomenal. Good hall for display of work and three studios, all richly and messily busy – the colour and variety of the top floor a refreshing relief. DT taken by all years 7-9 in good sized studio with 3D printer and laser cutter plus all else you'd expect. We enjoyed some lively work including inventive year 7 torches. Lots of music – individual, large and small groups, pursued with excellence and enthusiasm. Two good sized teaching rooms at top of the building plus numerous practice rooms. Drama in huge hall and Black Box Theatre at the top of the building. Well-designed literature for shows is evidence of classy production values all through. Draughty outdoor theatre a splendidly imaginative recent innovation – a bit like a Greek theatre, only colder.

A City student will leave as well-equipped to take on and challenge the world – while remaining her essential self – as any young woman could

Games, remarkably, mostly take place on site – planners found flat spaces, inside and out, for two tennis courts, a large Astro pitch, various other big enough spaces for a gym, 25 yard pool, table tennis, newish dance studio (2015). Outside space overlooked by flats – the girls must get used to it. Non-selective approach to some teams gives all enthusiasts opportunities and it works. They do cross-country round the high level walkways. Many representatives in borough games and several notable individual successes on local and grander levels.

But perhaps the most exciting aspect of the extracurricular offering is London itself. 'There are all the galleries and museums – they are so easy to go to from here – you can get there in a double art lesson. It's one of the reasons I came here,' typifies the response. Young Enterprise, likewise, outside speakers, visits, lectures at UCL, the Royal Institution etc, trips and tours – all add to the stimulating mix and the avid seizing of a rich variety of opportunities here.

Background and atmosphere: One of the more surprising school locations in the UK. Navigating the Barbican complex is notoriously tricky, but if you negotiate the grey concrete and glass mini-village to its heart, you will find the school. You get there via brick-paved walkways and the school sits between the ancient church of St Giles, Cripplegate one way, with glass office blocks behind, while the other way are the Guildhall Conservatory, the Barbican arts venue and the city flats with their valiant window boxes – and a large, flagged and lilied, ornamental pond between. Also surprising the eye and breaking up the harshness are the gallant trees and the improbable wodge of ancient London wall which squats defiantly opposite the school's main entrance. The school opened here in 1969 – the first, pretty much, of the reincarnations of venerable educational institutions needing new and purpose-built homes. A bold conception and it wears well. The inside is as stark and workful as Gradgrind could have wished, though lively displays and lots of big windows help relieve the Spartan architecture. Sixth form centre cleverly bolted on. You go in and out a lot as you negotiate the five storeys and we were glad we were not there on a cold wet day. Good-sized dining hall and jolly good menu – Wok Theatre, Italian/Indian Fusion and Big Bowl Salad looked tempting.

The original school began life in 1894. William Ward, who believed in giving girls a broad and liberal education with an emphasis on scholarship, left a third of his fortune – £20,000 – to the City of London Corporation for the foundation of a girls' school. Livery companies, banks and city firms continue to give financial support. The Corporation still administers this and numerous other schools and the board of governors is appointed by the Court of Common Council. The Corporation has an education strategy and its portfolio of schools gives rise to mutually beneficial links between City Girls' and state primaries eg for sixth form community service.

Famously diverse mix of pupils and staff as befits the school's situation in the heart of the city. 'Diversity' is a word you hear a lot here, in numerous contexts. Not least the effect of coalescing people from so huge an area. Likewise, we heard 'exciting' a lot. The girls say, 'It's always busy here – but in a good way, and being in the Barbican is so exciting!' Pupils are bright-faced, smiley, articulate and confident – with no trace of arrogance. They have a sense of their responsibilities to the wider world alongside their own personal ambitions.

Pastoral care, well-being and discipline: Light but 'tightly run' discipline. 'The teachers really care that the girls are happy,' a parent told us, 'and they deal quickly with problems.' 'No-one gets thrown out if they haven't had loads of warnings first,' girls told us. 'They bring in parents. It's mostly just poor behaviour over a long period but it hardly ever happens.' And most pay tribute to the excellence of pastoral care and their 'lovely' teachers.

Pupils and parents: They come from a vast circumference around the city – Chigwell to the north east, Harrow to the north, Shepherd's Bush and Fulham to the west – even as far away as Cambridge. 'It's helped me become a lot more independent and

'There are all the galleries and museums – they are so easy to go to from here – you can get there in a double art lesson'

the school gives us "travel buddies" when we join so that we can get used to the journey with someone experienced.' Parents say: 'The mix of girls is wonderful. They're not a flashy lot and they not tarted-up either.'

Entrance: Numbers of applicants, as at other academically selective London schools, now hitting heights of absurdity and severely straining schools' resources, especially where, as here, physical space needed on assessment days is limited. School is no longer part of the London Consortium so sets own exams in English and maths and what is graphically described as 'an interview with teeth'. Around 900 now applying for the 100 places at 11+ (or 850 for 75 places excl those applying from City's own on-site prep). NB acceptances on a first-come-first-served basis, with offers withdrawn when the 75 places are filled – which generally happens within days. Around 70 applicants for the 10-15 places at sixth form. Sixth form places conditional on school's own exams taken in potential A level subjects and on 9-7s at GCSE in all subjects.

Exit: Around 15-25 leave post-GCSE to board or go co-ed or to sixth form colleges. Early warning given to those who are unlikely to make it into the sixth form. Some parental criticism of the less than gentle manner in which this has taken place in the past but the Harrop regime is softening the approach, though the criterion for staying – eight grade 7s at GCSE – remains in force. Sixth form leavers are starry – 17 to Oxbridge in 2018, with 10 medics and one to Ivy League college; the London University colleges also take a good number. Great range of serious courses – nearly a third STEM and number of linguists now rising. Notable former pupils include Claire Rayner, Hermione Lee, Alison Weir, Elizabeth Emanuel, Romola Garai, Winklemans – Claudia and Sophie – and Daisy Christodoulou. Also Anna Blundy and Dido Armstrong, who both did their sixth forms at Westminster. One wonders whether they still would now.

Money matters: Around 25 per cent on some kind of fee assistance. Bursaries from 25 per cent to 100 per cent. Unusually no academic scholarships, but music, drama and art scholarships of up to £1,500 a year at 11+ and 16+, and an 11+ sports scholarship.

Remarks: By any standards, a top school for girls, with an edge of excitement, modernity and realism. Makes the most of what it is, where it is. Said a parent: 'My daughter is incredibly happy there. She has blossomed. Her friends and the head are amazing. I've only ever heard good things.'

City of London School for Girls – Prep

St Giles' Terrace, Barbican, London EC2Y 8BB

020 7847 5500 | admissions@clsg.org.uk | clsg.org.uk

Independent	Pupils: 93
Ages: 7–11	Fees: £18,384 pa

Linked school: City of London School for Girls, 93

Headmistress: Since September 2017, Rachel Hadfield, previously assistant head for curriculum at Foxfield Primary in Woolwich. Geography degree from Durham; has also been class teacher at Dalmain Primary in Lewisham.

Entrance: Twenty-four hotly contested places at 7+, sitting nationally standardised tests in English, maths and verbal reasoning plus some spelling and writing tests of the prep's own authorship. Register your daughter early to be sure of her being seen: the school assesses a maximum of 150 girls, and is always oversubscribed. Of those 150, the top 50 are called back for a further day's appraisal, during which they're examined in English, maths, science and DT – this last because it allows the girls to be observed in practical activities and working as a team. The 24 places are then offered to those 'with academic ability and the potential to become independent, happy learners.' Girls are seen in the November of the year preceding entry; closing date for accepting or declining offers is mid-February.

Exit: Parents take note: entry to the senior school is not automatic. By Easter of year 5, reserved places (ie places that are guaranteed) are offered only to those girls 'who continue to develop'. Any child who joined the school later than year 3 doesn't get one at all, and must sit for a place along with the external candidates. School insists that 'the vast majority go through'. Some parents' perceptions are different; see below. Destinations of those who do go elsewhere include St Paul's Girls', North London Collegiate, Francis Holland, Channing and Queen's College London. 'We've been hugely successful in placing girls at other schools. Schools like City Prep girls, and they don't get them that often.'

Remarks: Broad curriculum, with specialist teachers from the senior school coming in to teach music, art, DT, PE, Latin (years 5 and 6) and modern languages. The girls learn a different language each year: Spanish in year 3, French in year 4, German in year 5 and Mandarin in year 6. The idea is that the girls acquire an enthusiasm for languages which then helps them to choose the right ones when they go on to senior school, which is certainly commendable. It struck us as odd, however, that they only studied each language for a year before having to drop it and move onto the next one; a year 5 girl we spoke to admitted that she'd now forgotten the Spanish she'd learned in year 3.

'The girls are incredibly competitive, but also very supportive of each other with a strong sense of loyalty'

As well as benefiting from the senior school teaching expertise, the excellent senior school facilities – swimming pool, sports hall, library, Astroturf, tennis courts – are also available, which doubtless explains why there's no difference in fees between the two (though prep fees do include lunch). Sports and gymnastics are strong, and music likewise, with the Y6s doing a Prep Opera every year. Impressive LAMDA results. There are also lots of residential trips which are perennially popular. Wide variety of clubs, and after-school care provides an opportunity for girls to do their homework as well as have fun. ('They have a register to make sure you don't wander off,' said one of our tour guides, earnestly.) Sixth formers from the senior school run clubs for the prep girls, which,

says school, creates 'a big sister culture. They're great role models for the younger girls.'

Other than some worrying reports which we outline below, it took a long while for parental feedback to reach us about this school. Our first invitation was met with complete silence, and even a second appeal didn't yield very much. (This was in contrast to the parents of girls in the senior school, who were quick to tell us how happy they were.) Those who did eventually contact us agreed that the girls are worked hard but achieve highly. A couple remarked on the school's competitive nature: 'The girls are incredibly competitive, but also very supportive of each other, and have a strong sense of loyalty to their school,' said one. Another observed, 'If you're prepared to buy into the idea of City and have a daughter capable of swimming in its often competitive seas, it will be a worthwhile experience for her and for your family.' These parents emphasised that their daughters were enjoying their time at the prep, had made friends and embraced the opportunities on offer there.

However, some of these same parents expressed disquiet about the entry process to the senior school. 'The goalposts seem to have been moved,' said one couple, 'The message about not everyone getting reserved places is stronger now than it was when our daughter got in.' The same worried mother continued, 'Choosing to put a child through an entrance exam when they're 6 is not an easy decision; in our case we hoped to avoid the stress at 11+, which we now find we may not do. I suspect the feeling of rejection and the dent to self-confidence is higher if you don't get a reserved place from the prep and can't stay with your friends, than if you apply and fail as an external candidate.' School told us that an average of four girls leave City Prep's year 6 every year: two out of choice, and two who were 'advised to go elsewhere.' School figures show an average of three girls a year recently have not been given reserved places. This figure seems high to us, given both the stringent nature of the admissions process and the acknowledged high workload put upon the girls during their time here; and we did ask about this. 'Not all girls develop the same,' was the comment. 'Some go upwards and some go downwards; sometimes things happen in families to disturb girls.'

Parents and former parents are divided in their feelings about the school. On one side of the argument, accounts have been passed to us of recent City Prep girls whose confidence, and even health, had been so undermined by the school's approach that their parents voted with their feet and took them out. These parents write with angry eloquence about the school's 'complete lack of nurture and care' and claim that it 'values malleability and obedience over originality and sparky intellect.' They allege that there is poor support for special needs such as dyslexia, and that some of the teaching is sub-standard ('After we moved her, we discovered that she had been so poorly taught that she needed to relearn a year's worth of maths,' said one mother, and another mother reported an identical experience.)

The school insists that it works closely with parents, and that the girls' happiness is paramount. 'We love quirky individuals. We've got lots and lots of those. Girls are allowed to be themselves here.' And indeed, other parents told us that their daughters loved coming to school. One, whose child had excelled there academically, spoke of the school's 'really good pastoral side.' 'The prep is a nurturing and non-threatening environment,' said one

mother whose child was now at CLSG senior, 'and I would have no hesitation in recommending it.'

Picking our way through such contradictory accounts was difficult. We can only conclude by suggesting that since entry to CLSG senior school isn't guaranteed, parents should think closely about whether City Prep is the right choice for their daughter or whether a prep school not linked to any senior school, but with a proven record of getting its leavers into the destination of their choice, might suit their family better. However, we hear encouraging reports of a loosening of tension under the new head.

School has plans to expand by opening a pre-prep – in what is currently a car park beneath the all-weather pitch.

Collège Français Bilingue de Londres

87 Holmes Road, London NW5 3AX

020 7993 7400 | info@cfbl.org.uk | cfbl.org.uk

Independent	Pupils: 700
Ages: 5-16	Fees: £10,230 – £11,205 pa

Headteacher: Since 2011, François-Xavier Gabet (50s). He has degrees from University of Lille – in teaching French and French as a second language. Has taught in French schools in France, Saudi Arabia, USA and Australia and was a French language adviser to the US state of Louisiana. Set up the first bilingual French/English school in Melbourne (while also teaching at Monash University).

He was the ideal founding head for this newish London school and arrived a year before it opened – to plan every facet. Despite his traditional website photo, when we met him he was fashionably turned out in jeans, turtleneck jumper and blazer – looking more like a high-tech dot-com CEO on London's Silicon Roundabout than what one might expect of the head of a prestigious French school.

Steeped in the high standards associated with French educational tradition, he is refreshingly internationally-minded and aims to help his multilingual students recognise the advantages of being part of a global network of schools. While well aware of the rigorous demands of the French system, he asks teachers to be flexible, creative and generous in their approach. He cares about the school's relations with the local Kentish Town community (he does not want CFBL to be a 'French bubble') and works closely with the board (whom

he describes as 'capable, professionally-accomplished and yet humble') to find ways to improve this full-to-capacity school.

Fit, energetic and quite the coolest head this Good Schools Guide editor has met, he is married with a daughter at university in Belgium and a son in secondary school.

Head of primary: is David Gassian, and Cerian Maraviglia is the deputy head of primary.

Academic matters: The French primary model has two divisions – maternelle (reception and year 1) and primaire (years 2 to 6). At the junior section of the CFBL 50 per cent of children have French and English language instruction and 50 per cent follow the French national curriculum. Half the staff are UK qualified and half are French. The teachers are timetabled in such a way that when classes are being taught by French teachers, the English-speaking staff are freed up to support students whose English language skills need bolstering and to ensure that English literacy standards are of a high level.

There are two forms of 25 students each for the youngest classes, 30 per class from the age of 7+. Classes are of mixed ability but the combination of French and English teachers means that they are able to differentiate the curriculum. English and French as a foreign language taught up to four times per week. Other specialists include teachers of PE, music and ICT (interactive whiteboards in all classrooms), while the bilingual French librarian works closely with the teachers in developing the literacy scheme and creating class libraries.

The French secondary model has two divisions – collège (years 7 to 10) and lycée (years 11 to 13). CFBL offers the collège division, following on from the school's primary section. According to the new norms of the French educational system, all students in secondary school are taught English for five hours a week and begin a third language (German or Spanish) in year 11. They are also taught music, sport, IT and art in English.

Students (already working in French and English) have the option to join the international section of the DNB (Diplôme National du Brevet) where 45 per cent of the curriculum is taught in English, preparing them nicely for the new international diploma (DNBI). They are taught history and geography two hours a week in English.

Parents have mixed views – some feel the bilingual programme gives their (French-speaking) children lots of good exposure and immersion in English while others say the level of English is not as challenging as they'd like and that it's essentially French with a few English classes. Bilingual school models are never straightforward, with different perceptions about what exactly they mean. IT is taught weekly – some parents would like to see a bit more, but concede that with the extra time already devoted to languages, this would be challenging.

The pupils work long hours (approximately 30 per week) – the additional English language means more hours than usual – so parents should be clear on this before they enrol their children. This is in addition to the homework load. The French educational system is regarded as one of the best in the world and academic standards are not an issue here. It's deciding if you want to do this with the added challenge of a bilingual or trilingual programme.

No specialist SEN support but class teachers are able to provide some support and there is a part-time educational psychologist too. Parents pay for diagnostic testing. A speech therapist is available.

Games, options, the arts: Though extracurricular activities don't traditionally loom large on the French educational landscape, they do make a great effort at CFBL. More sports on tap here than is the norm for French schools – the football team practises locally and took part in an international tournament. Netball is popular with girls. The school is working on launching a choir and developing interest in instrumental music activities.

He was fashionably turned out in jeans, turtleneck jumper and blazer – looking more like a high-tech dot-com CEO than a head

Sixième students (first year secondary) go on a residential trip with outdoor pursuits activities aimed at integrating new students and team building.

CFBL has an exchange programme with schools in Uruguay, Valence and Berlin for students studying Spanish or German, and strong links with a school in Spain. Mandarin club recently introduced. The head hopes that these experiences will help students and parents value the importance of learning languages and about other cultures.

Background and atmosphere: The Collège Français Bilingue de Londres was born out of a previous French ambassador's call for increased capacity to meet the growing demand for French education in London. With funding from the French government and from French companies (we're guessing banks and perhaps Eurostar, whose London base is conveniently nearby), who formed a charity to acquire the school property, the school's mission is to offer a French curriculum in a bilingual context to 700 students. The school was at one time known as L'Île aux Enfants and located in a nearby building that now houses La Petite École, a feeder primary school.

Housed in a Victorian school building in Kentish Town. The head is aware of the impact that the mass arrival of a French community in the heart of this traditionally working-class area of north London has had and is working to win over the hearts and minds of locals. Most families living in the area were attracted to the Victorian terraced properties and the 'gentrification' of the area is thought to be partly thanks to the school (as well, of course, as the long-standing local Camden School for Girls). Part of the neighbourhood charm offensive was the introduction of French language classes for the local community.

The school backs on to some picturesque residential streets, though it fronts onto a street that is less so, and a bit of planting and tidying of the outside pavements and garden patches would improve the first impression. Step inside, however, and it's another story. The refurbishment is brilliant, taking full advantage of the Victorian features, with high ceilings, large windows drawing in masses of light, brick and glazed tile walls and parquet wooden floors, while incorporating modern touches. The upper school library – with high ceilings and huge windows – is fully equipped with impressive French and English collections, loads of computers and armchairs. Cosy primary library in its own little building on the playground – most of the resources are French, although they are developing the English language collection.

A small portion of the central playground has been forfeited to create a bright and airy cafeteria. Lunches compulsory, with meat and fish served daily and vegetarian options available for those observing kosher or halal diets.

The school has recently acquired an outdoor space a five-minute walk away. This will feature a massive inflatable structure for sports and other activities and will be available to the local community too.

Part of the AEFE (Agency for Teaching of French Education Abroad), CFBL is one of an international network of schools directed by the French ministry of education. The school is managed by a 12-member board – six representing the companies that helped fund the acquisition of the building and six elected by the parents. Its goals are to provide continuity of education to the French expat community in London, but also to prepare students to go to the best French universities. In fact 80 per cent of students who graduate from the Lycée Charles de Gaulle head to British or US universities. The head feels that the internationally-minded, multilingual emphasis of the school serves to provide good preparation for these options later on.

Pastoral care, well-being and discipline: Parents are very pleased with the school, many jumping through hoops to secure places. A parent of a child with SEN described it as particularly caring and attentive to her child. Classes are smaller than most French schools – a maximum of 30 in a class, with a two or three form intake. Discipline is not a worry for parents – one parent speculated that the presence of more UK-trained teachers (there to deliver the bilingual programme) strengthens the pastoral care perspective of the teaching faculty (not always as high on the French teachers' radar). The school runs careers counselling through a jobs forum that parents help to organise. The school employs a full time nurse as well as a part time speech therapist and child psychologist.

Pupils and parents: The community is a blend of expat corporate types on international assignments and more permanent French families who have found themselves in London for other reasons, including entrepreneurs, local business owners and French nationals whose marriages have created bi-cultural families. Parents suggest that the socio-economic atmosphere at CFBL is less 'rarified' than one finds in the more salubrious environs of the Lycée Charles de Gaulle in South Ken. While some end up at CFBL by default (no room at the

Lycée), others prefer this school. The size is another factor – even with its capacity of 700, it is much smaller than the Lycée. French families who find the Eurostar terminal at St Pancras convenient are increasingly moving into neighbourhoods that are handy for the train journey through the tunnel to France and for the school.

More sports on tap here than is the norm for French schools – the football team practises locally and took part in an international tournament

The community is about two-thirds French. Some parents feel the school is less international than they would like, while others who come from France find it very international by comparison. There is obviously an underlying French cultural and educational foundation, but it seems that with a school community consisting of many dual national families, they seek to honour all cultures and traditions. Parents are happy that the children integrate easily, although some say teachers don't make as much of this diversity as they might. A parents' association provides lots of volunteer opportunities for those who want to get involved.

Entrance: Due to the recent opening of new French schools in London, not as oversubscribed as previously. We hear that a maximum of 30 per cent of the places are allocated to children whose parents work for the consortium of French companies that helped to secure the school building. The list of partner companies is available for inspection if required.

Admissions priorities are: siblings (both primary and secondary), children from another official French school (local or abroad), including students following the CNED (the French distance-learning programme), then any miscellany of Francophones fortunate enough to get in. It seems there are some last minute surprises. The nearby La Petite École is a popular feeder, while others opt for local British independent schools while they wait for the coveted place at CFBL.

Exit: Some expat families move abroad and continue their education in the French system. Others, finding the fees an issue (though remarkably good value when compared to most London independent schools), enter local state schools. Students who are less confident about their French language skills may leave after quatrième to do GCSEs in the local British sector, although the English section at the

Lycée Charles de Gaulle is an option for them. Most of the students head to the Lycée International Winston Churchill in Wembley to enter their baccalauréat programme.

Money matters: The fees at CFBL are reasonable by London independent school standards (although CFBL fees are marginally higher than the Lycée Charles de Gaulle). As a charity, school engages in some fundraising activity – such as its annual gala event.

Remarks: An interesting school that embodies all of the academic rigour associated with the French tradition, but with a strong emphasis on languages and English. A sparkling little gem in the heart of Kentish Town, it is a bilingual environment with a truly international mindset.

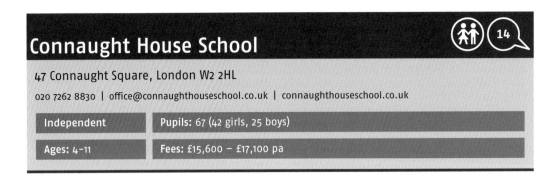

Connaught House School

47 Connaught Square, London W2 2HL

020 7262 8830 | office@connaughthouseschool.co.uk | connaughthouseschool.co.uk

Independent	Pupils: 67 (42 girls, 25 boys)
Ages: 4–11	Fees: £15,600 – £17,100 pa

Principal: Since September 2017, Victoria Hampton (30s), who previously ran the early years part of the school and has taught here for several years. She comes with a wealth of experience of young children, having started and run her own nursery in Oxfordshire, been deputy head of a nursery in Clapham, as well as having a host of qualifications for teaching young children – Montessori diploma, early years foundation degree, Hornsby diploma (dyslexia). She has three young children of her own who will come here and loves being part of the fabric of the school. Gentle, pretty, with a mellifluous voice and perfect diction (which we suspect matches her handwriting), the children clearly love her as do the staff. She knows them all, is actively involved in observing and participating in lessons throughout the school and initiated and implemented changes and improvements in the early years part. One of these was to bring the reception class (known at Junior One) up from the ground floor so that they can have plenty of space, free flowing between two large, high ceilinged rooms.

She is the daughter-in-law of previous joint principals Jacqueline and Frederick Hampton; Jacqueline's mother founded the school in 1952 with just six pupils. It is still an intimate, cosy, family-run school, refreshing in this age of private equity backed independent schools. 'We are a school first that happens to have to run as a business.' Phew – such schools do still exist.

Head: Since September 2017 is Ellie Grunewald MA UEL, BA (Liverpool) PGCE (Kingston), previously academic co-ordinator here.

Entrance: At age 4 into reception (here called Junior One). Sixteen places for girls and boys. 'Very gentle assessments' take place when the child is 3 to ensure that they will get as much out of the school as possible. Children are assessed by two teachers and also have some one-to-one time. Absolutely no preparation is necessary. Priority is given to siblings and second and third generations. After that, proximity to school. 'The local community ethos is something we value very highly and would not like to lose,' says Victoria Hampton. Applications can also be made for entry into the upper end of the school. Academic and music bursaries are available to those applying at 7 or 8. Many come from local nurseries, including Great Beginnings and Paint Pots, and there is some liaison with nurseries after places have been offered.

Exit: All boys have previously left at 7 or 8, mostly to local prep schools such as Westminster Under School, Sussex House or Wetherby, the odd one going north to UCS junior school, but can now stay on till 11. The girls generally opt for London day schools – Francis Holland, Clarence Gate, is currently the most popular, but many also to Godolphin & Latymer, City of London, More House, Latymer Upper, Queen's Gate and South Hampstead High. Those wishing to board generally choose Wycombe Abbey or St Mary's, Ascot. Despite leaving a very small school to go on to these much larger establishments, none of the pupils seems to be fazed – the confidence they acquire at CHS gives them the ability to cope in a broader environment.

This is a rare little boutique in the increasingly branded, competitive world of London day schools and it offers a uniquely personal touch

Remarks: There is no danger of the slightly old-fashioned, wonderfully personal and child-centred ethos of this tiny school changing. The school has not expanded at all since it was first founded. It still occupies the same building, and is very small; you will know quite quickly if you love it or not, but if you don't, be careful not to write it off too soon. This is a rare little boutique in the increasingly branded, competitive world of London day schools and it offers a uniquely personal touch that many similar schools are in danger of losing. Despite its small size, good use is made of the environs. Hyde Park is only a short walk away, and children enjoy lots of outdoor activities there all the year round, including parachute games, obstacle races, rounders and football. Fencing, dance, and martial arts all take place at Little Venice Sports Centre. Tennis, football, hockey, basketball and the annual sports day happen at Paddington Recreation Ground. Swimming is at Queen Mother's Sports Centre in Victoria. There is sport every day of one kind or another. Although we heard some whispering from former parents of boys here – that the boys didn't get to run around enough and there were insufficient sporting opportunities – we could see no evidence of this.

Art and music are the main extracurricular strengths of the school. Plenty of music assemblies and lots of performances. Everyone takes part, and the large, high-ceilinged room in the middle of the building is a comfortable and intimate place to perform. We were treated to a mini concert, which included violin and recorder players as well as piano and singing – impromptu concerts of this kind are not unusual, we were told, and you can see how much confidence is imbued into these tiny performers as a result. The art room is a relatively dark, pokey room in the basement, but the quality of art that is produced defies the facilities. We saw small children beavering away at covering balloons in newspaper to create hot air balloons. We were shown wonderful wooden red buses and fire engines, built by the children, and split-pin dolls clothed in fabulous petite Victorian dresses and hats. Colourful displays adorn the walls – work obviously done by the children rather than touched up by the teachers (what a relief), and bright Chinese lanterns and colourful fish were bobbing from almost every ceiling.

Plenty of drama; each junior form does its own play once a year (these have included the Gruffalo's Christmas and Charlie Cook's Favourite Book), and years 4, 5 and 6 have performed Sleeping Beauty. Drama productions and concerts take place at the Carisbrooke Hall down the road or the Steiner Theatre close to Baker Street. Although this is very much a mixed community school with no particular religious bias, there is an annual carol concert in St John's Church, Hyde Park Crescent, which everyone is expected to attend. 'We would rather it were inclusive.'

Clubs are varied and numerous. They make a huge effort to ensure that everyone from years 2-6 tries everything. There is lots to try, from embroidery, pottery, board games and mini beasts to any kind of dance from country to zumba as well as chess and music. Full advantage is made of the school's cosmopolitan location – recent trips have included to the Globe Theatre, the Courtauld and the Tate Modern, the Celtic Harmony Camp, London Zoo and to the obvious museums – Science, Horniman and Transport.

Plenty of music assemblies and lots of performances. Everyone takes part, and the large, high-ceilinged room in the middle of the building is a comfortable and intimate place to perform. We were treated to a mini concert involving violin players

You need not worry about little Freddie not getting enough attention either. There are only 16 pupils in a class – they try to keep an equal number of girls and boys in the early years (and, in future, higher up). Junior One (reception) has two teachers and a qualified teaching assistant. Forms 1, 2 and 3 have both a form teacher and qualified teaching assistant in each class. All children use personal Fizz books (little laptops, as far as we could tell), there are MacBooks in every classroom and they pride themselves on recruiting excellent teachers with 'diverse interests'. There is a competitive fives player on the staff at the moment. With such a small school, and class sizes, it is relatively easy to pick up any learning difficulties, we were told. They have a few cases of children with glue ear who may need speech and language therapy. Specialist therapists, for, eg, dyslexia are brought in at extra expense for parents but Victoria Hampton herself is a dyslexia therapist, and they prefer to keep as much support in school as possible. We were told that there is usually only one child in each year group who needs any kind of help at all. There are a high number of children with English as a second language, and although they need a reasonably good grasp of English at assessment, because of the high level of teacher support (and a recently introduced EAL club) they usually progress very quickly.

All in all, a very special little school which is loved by parents and pupils alike, where the children feel challenged every day and their parents are constantly amazed by what they know. 'The closest you can get to home schooling,' declared one. If that sounds appealing, take a little trip to Marble Arch now.

Eaton House Belgravia

3–5 Eaton Gate, Eaton Square, London SW1W 9BA

0207 924 6000 | admissions@eatonhouseschools.com | eatonhouseschools.com

Independent **Pupils:** 240

Ages: 4–9 (becoming 4–11) **Fees:** £17,850 – £20,700 pa

Linked schools: For Eaton House the Manor Boys' School, Eaton House the Manor Girls' School, See *The Good Schools Guide London South*

Head: Since September 2017, Huw May (late 40s) MAed, NPQH, Advanced Diploma Royal Welsh College of Music, BMus, previously head of Eaton House the Manor Pre-Prep. Earlier experience in headships include Sydenham Junior School, Roedean Junior School and St Aubyn's pre-prep. A professional singer for several years before taking up teaching, he is a trained ISI inspector.

Mr May lives over the school during the week, returning to his home in Sussex at weekends. Gardening, classic cars (MGs and older Mercedes) and walking his dog Harvey – boy-approved relaxations. He has quickly gained the respect and trust of parents who find him 'approachable' and 'a good listener'. They especially value the fact that he has 'the boys' well-being and interests at heart'. Ambitious for his school, shows vision and is full of enthusiasm for developing each boy's all-round potential, emotionally as well as academically. A parent commented: 'We really value the immersive approach to learning and the school's entrepreneurial spirit; for example, Mr May has set up a partnership with the Science Museum'.

Mr May's arrival, after a brief tenure by respected long term deputy Annabel Abbott, coincided with a change to school organisation plans (see below). He has speedily got a grip, emphasising individual learning plans for each boy, and the school seems as good as ever, with excellent results in his first year.

Entrance: Genuinely non-selective (but this is Belgravia). Main entry is at 4+ into kindergarten

with, on average, 70 places. Places are allocated on a first come first served basis, with priority given to siblings, so it is important to put your name down early. Large deposit payable on accepting a place. There is no financial help on offer. For entry further up the school, the occasional places are subject to an assessment to see if the applicant will fit into the year group. Entry at 8+ is possible, now that the prep is open, but has yet to develop in any volume in its first year. Eaton House Schools Group is happy to let it develop at an organic rate.

Boys come from a wide range of Belgravia nurseries plus Victoria, Pimlico, Fulham and Battersea, with a few from as far away as the City. The majority of pupils have British or part-British nationality (60 per cent) with the remainder mostly European.

Exit: About 40 per cent leave at 7+, and most of the rest of them at 8+, a third of them to Westminster/St Paul's juniors, the rest to a mix of good junior schools (King's College Wimbledon, Dulwich), prep schools (Wetherby's, Sussex House, Westminster Cathedral Choir) and top boarding preps such as Summer Fields, Caldicott, The Dragon and Ludgrove. This would be an impressive record for a selective school, let alone one with EHB's broad intake; Mr May is clear and direct in advising parents on which schools they should aim for.

Eaton House Belgravia now, for the first time, offers options beyond 8+, with several from the pre-prep forming the first, select year 4. Pupils will be able to stay on for three years and then either take the 11+ entrance or spend the final two prep

Majority of pupils live within walking distance, some international families and many parents working in the City

years at Eaton House the Manor south of the river, with others who are aiming for 13+ places at top boarding schools like Eton or Tonbridge (school bus provided for the 10-15 minute journey).

Remarks: Eaton House Belgravia is part of the Eaton House group of schools. The principal Hilary Harper and her husband took over Eaton House Belgravia in 1978 and developed the school into the group it is today. On retirement in the summer of 2016, she sold a majority stake in the group to private equity group Sovereign Capital, though her daughter, chief executive Luchie Cawood, has a significant stake and is thoroughly involved in the schools.

Parents who choose EHB want a traditional pre-prep (and, in future, prep) experience and the school delivers with a 3Rs curriculum, academic rigour and plenty of extras. In particular they value 'the excellent, nurturing male and female teaching staff who ensure they know their boys and care for them'. Classes are small with so far only informal sets for maths and English in years 2 and 3, so that the boys gain a full understanding in all maths and English topics.

EHB offers a very particular brand of boy-friendly teaching. Boys work hard in short bursts in the morning; in the afternoon games are followed by clubs and activities such as football, cookery, coding and Spanish. The extensive list of clubs changes regularly. They are supposed to enjoy the work and to have a riotous time in extras and 'run around after school and relax in supervised activities'. Some parents suggest that 'this would not be the right school for a slow developer, as the boys work at a fast pace and it becomes demanding in year 2 with plenty of homework.' Some teaching talk & chalk (albeit on interactive whiteboards these days), but much based on doing something physical, thinking through what you have done, and then applying it to a problem.

Individual provision ('differentiation') involves weekly consideration of how to support each child: all will at times be taken off into a side room for one-to-one. Not just academic/SEN support: there's Move Fit, run by physiotherapists for anyone who needs to improve coordination, and occupational therapy, for example handwriting and touch typing. In the kindergarten, Lego groups help develop social skills.

Communication between home and school is frequent and well-coordinated. The original plans to grow Eaton House Belgravia Prep organically on its south Kensington site changed in 2018 to expand Eaton House Belgravia pre-prep up to 11 years on its own site. The school is comprised of two immense, linked cream town houses on several levels. The basement houses the kitchen, dining rooms, staff room, some individual music lesson rooms and a well-used science lab where boys enthusiastically carry out experiments and make discoveries. On the ground floor there is a well-stocked, light library and classrooms. The top two floors of the No 3 building, previously administrative offices and living accommodation, have been been converted into classrooms, DT and art rooms for the new prep school.

Boys enjoy their art and we saw some house competition inventive illustrations for selected poems, as well as arresting year 1 wild west T shirts for a forthcoming fashion show. We spotted an attractive watercolour crab on our tour and evidence of interesting artwork in topic lessons throughout the school.

Boys work hard in short bursts in the morning; in the afternoon games are followed by clubs and activities such as football, cookery, coding and Spanish

Mr May is clearly going to add zest to an already excellent musical provision (inter alia he has commissioned an opera for the school). Music takes place in the hall and is timetabled for all. Boys perform in fortnightly music assemblies and termly concerts and take part in competitions and charity events. Parents say that the head of music nurtures and encourages all ages to take up an instrument – drums, piano, singing, trumpet, guitar and violin all taught – with those who are fearful of performing offered strategies to gain self-confidence. The school has a dedicated ICT room, touch typing and coding are encouraged in the curriculum and classrooms have touch interactive boards and now tablets.

There is only one tiny outdoor space, but planning permission has been submitted for a sizeable outdoor learning centre. The fairly small hall/gymnasium is tightly packed when the whole school assembles. By necessity the days are very structured. The school council suggestion of Five a Day interruptions of five minute physical activities by desks is popular and beneficial. Boys are bussed to Hyde or Battersea Park every day to let off steam and play sports. Staff ensure boys are not taken out of sports and bemoan the time spent sitting in traffic. Swimming takes place at the Queen Mother's sports centre. Parents comment approvingly of the sport and 'the diverse clubs on offer including optional weekend activities, so there is lots to do'. A number of football clubs operate outside school hours. The boys enjoy their fixtures, stating that 'If we lose against the Manor, who are bigger than we are, we beat them at chess'.

Boys care about their food, and now this is freshly prepared on the premises, but some parents still believe there is further scope for improvement. The house system underpins all areas of the school and is very effective. It supports a culture of positive reinforcement regarding behaviour and respect, whilst enabling the boys to interact and enjoy the healthy competition on which they thrive. There is real engagement and an understanding of responsibility; 'Boys don't want to let their house down and captains write prayers for assembly'. Good manners are encouraged and one special feature we observed was the practice of one boy in every class shaking our hand, making eye contact and welcoming us to the class. The boys learn to make presentations and recite poetry confidently in public. 'I want them [the boys] to develop

skills for life including adaptability, resilience, and determination and learn to listen and articulate their opinions confidently,' says Mr May.

The majority of pupils live within walking distance, with some international families and many parents working in the City as lawyers or bankers, and most are very ambitious for their sons. 'We don't mind taking a round boy in a square hole' and parents agree that the school happily accommodates boys 'with different personalities and backgrounds, providing a really good real experience'. School advises, 'EHB is probably not the right school for you if you want your son in bubblewrap' and parents agree that the boys 'are not coddled and must be able to cope with academic rigours'. All boys wear uniform shorts and long socks whatever the weather. The pace is fast and there is an expectation that everyone will join in and accept challenges; excellent preparation for the top academic prep schools they are aiming for. 'We are slightly quirky' and the school is not purpose-built or manicured but full of energetic, interesting boys. Boys and staff muck in and this works a treat, as the boys are clearly happy. Staff are always on hand to advise parents about a suitable choice of prep schools where their engaging personalities and good manners will be an asset.

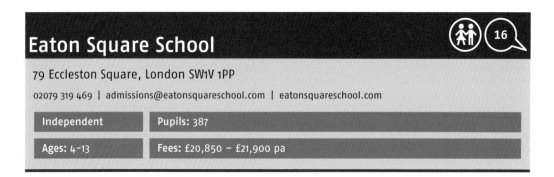

Eaton Square School

79 Eccleston Square, London SW1V 1PP

02079 319 469 | admissions@eatonsquareschool.com | eatonsquareschool.com

Independent	Pupils: 387
Ages: 4-13	Fees: £20,850 – £21,900 pa

Headmaster: Since 2010, Sebastian Hepher BEd (early 50s). Educated at Alleyn's and University of Greenwich. Began teaching career in state sector, at Hurstmere Boys' in Kent, followed by The London Nautical School. Joined Eaton House Pre-Prep in 1990, before being asked to lead Eaton House The Manor in 1993. Under his headship, the school grew from the initial embryonic phase to a thriving prep school. Married, with four children currently at four different schools, with the youngest here. Swims in his local lido every day of the year, come rain or shine. Avid reader of Russian literature. Warm and charismatic, with a good sense of humour. Every parent we spoke to described him in glowing terms. 'He is the reason people gravitate towards the school,' according to one mother.

Teaches reasoning. Also oversees the new upper school in Mayfair.

Entrance: Main intake is at 4+ via assessment. The school runs several nurseries for children from 2 to 4 and these pupils are assessed by head of nurseries and head of pre-prep. They are given priority over other candidates and make up well over half the intake. 'It's not automatic but very rare not to accept a child from one of our nurseries,' explains head. Assessments, in November for external candidates, involve phonic and numerical activities, as well as colouring, cutting and talking to teachers. Between 100 and 150 external children compete for 30 places. Sibling policy, 'as we truly are a family school.'

Occasional vacancies further up the school are quickly filled from the school's waiting list, after the child has successfully completed a series of online tests and spent a day at the school in a classroom setting.

Exit: Most girls leave at 11 and boys at 13. Very few girls stay on for the 13+, usually those heading for co-ed boarding. Pupils progress onto a wide range of senior schools, both boarding and day. Rare to send more than a couple of children to any one school in any given year, though the new Eaton Square Upper School may buck the trend. Recent leavers to Eton, Harrow, Tonbridge, Charterhouse, City of London Boys, St Mary's Ascot, Beneden, Downe House, Roedean, Latymer Upper, Allyen's, Dulwich College, Godolphin & Laymer, Francis Holland x 2, City of London Girls, Queens College, Queensgate.

Head starts dialogue about senior schools in year 5, often encouraging parents look at boarding too even if previously dismissed out of hand by international clientele. Head acknowledges that 'London schools are not the place for the average boy' and that some need to cast their net further. Numbers of boys heading to boarding has increased noticeably and is 'beginning to bubble for the girls.'

Remarks: Situated in three large town houses in the heart of Belgravia. Separate buildings for senior prep, junior prep and pre-prep. One parent likened the children to mountain goats, as they make their way up and down the steep stairs.

Founded in 1981. Recently became part of the Minerva Education Group. Teething problems have left some parents feeling a little raw. One mother we spoke to said, 'The transition to the new ownership has been pretty bumpy, especially as it coincided with an escalation in fees'. Head feels some parental perception has been inaccurate and that school fees have not actually increased more than usual. Indeed, the second year of ownership has actually seen a reduction to the usual increase. On the positive side, Minerva has enabled the school to buy a building on Piccadilly overlooking Green Park for its new senior school, Eaton Square Upper School, which will eventually go up to 16.

Current head is credited with having pulled the school up by its bootstraps academically. It has grown both in size and standing on his watch. One parent commented, 'It used to just be a sweet, local school before Mr Hepher took over. He is much more ambitious and has taken it to another level'. Pupils now follow a more academically rigorous and broader curriculum. Excellent language provision. Spanish being introduced. Extra French classes for fluent speakers. Mandarin offered as a two year course from year 4, though pupils must commit to it for the duration and take a CE exam at the end. Latin for all from year 5.

Head abhors the culture of tutoring and believes 'we need to educate parents.' He has addressed the matter of intense competition for senior places with intelligence and worries that increasing number of schools using pre-tests works against late developers. School prepares pupils well for senior school entry without being a hothouse.

Typically five reception classes and four year 1 classes. Class size fairly small, with a maximum of 16 up to year 5 and a maximum of 18 in final years. Currently only eight pupils in each year 8 class and 11 in year 7, giving plenty of scope for individual attention. Pupils are placed in sets for maths and English at start of year 2 but these are fluid, with 'plenty of room for manoeuvre'.

'When you go into the school, there is a smile on the staff's faces. It's not a school where you drop your child at the door and never get to venture across the threshold'

Parents feel pupils are well prepared for transition to senior school, partly because the curriculum is kept broad throughout. Once 11+ exams are over, girls 'latch onto boys' CE syllabus.' No time wasting allowed here, as can often happen elsewhere post 11+, much to the parents' delight.

From the start, all pupils are encouraged to be articulate and confident citizens. Head believes that good manners are essential. Each class has its own official greeter who comes to the front, shakes hands firmly and welcomes visitors on behalf of the rest of the class. A charming touch.

Thriving pre-prep department. Vibrant, colourful classrooms where emphasis is on practical work, consolidated by written work. 'It's hands on, creative learning here.' Impressive writing on display up the stairs. Everything is beautifully presented, from the work crafted by the children to displays produced by teachers. Charming library area where children can be found earnestly recommending books to each other.

As school is non-selective, there is a huge ability range. Full-time SENCo, supported by highly experienced learning enrichment team. Approximately 30 pupils currently having SEN support (mostly dyslexia, dyspraxia and dyscalculia), either one-to-one or small group sessions. Two children with statements. More able pupils extended through challenging extracurricular activities.

Pastoral care is well structured. Head worries about life being stressful for these children. 'We have a duty of care to shield children from excessive pressure which London and the system place

Fine Arts College Hampstead

on them. Parents who are anxious tend to pass that on to their children. I worry that we're causing a very anxious society. We want to make sure that children are happy when they are here.' Whole school comes together once a week for a reflective and celebratory reflective assembly at St Michael's Church, Chester Square.

Charity is an important part of school life. Huge amounts raised by parents and children. Head is aware of how privileged pupils are here and is hoping to get older pupils involved with visiting elderly residents who live on their own in the Square.

Teachers mostly in late 20s and early 30s; some 10 members of staff have been here a decade. One parent described them as being 'friendly, energetic and good at communicating with the parents. Just what you want'. 'We haven't had a bad teacher yet!' said another, whose children are currently in the middle of the school. Parents demonstrate their gratitude to the staff with a 'parent appreciation breakfast' once a year.

Sensational drama. Huge annual musical performed by year 5 and 6 children at Unicorn theatre in the West End. Professional theatre director hired for the occasion. Years 7 and 8 perform something more challenging such as a Greek play. Younger children perform on stage twice a year. Music also a central part of the school with over 100 pupils learning an instrument. Performances in abundance, from carol services to rock concerts. One parent felt that 'music is certainly more organised than it has been in the past.' Art taught to a high standard. Extra scholarship classes offered to the most artistic; the standard of portfolios is considered exceptional.

Despite its lack of outside space, school takes sport very seriously and coaching is excellent. Mainstream sports all offered as well as ballet, climbing, fencing and kayaking on the Thames. Pupils compete strongly in prep school ski-ing championships, recently bringing back a clutch of gold medals. Legendary swimming squad currently on a four year unbeaten streak. Unusually, pupils swim here from day one. Football also strong, with plenty of practice taking place in Battersea Park. All children make a team of some description. 'The problem is finding enough other schools who can field C and D teams,' laments head.

Extracurricular activity viewed as important. Sensational residential trips. Year 3 heads off to Sussex for a four day adventure. Years 4 and 5 go on a ski-ing and cultural trip to France where pupils practise speaking the language in context and also have daily French lessons. Snowball fights with the teachers apparently one of the highlights. One mother was delighted that the children were made to 'carry their own skis and make their own beds.' A novel experience for some, apparently. Pupils in year 6 go on a classical tour of Rome and Naples. Year 7 spend a week at a château in Normandy. At the end of year 8, pupils go on outdoor pursuits trip to Scotland to celebrate the end of common entrance. Head now setting his sights on a residential trip for year 2. Thirty-four clubs currently offered, at extra cost, including numerous sports, chess, story-telling and cookery.

Pupil composition is predominantly expat, with more than half the pupils from overseas. Americans, Australians, Italians, French, Spanish mostly, with a sprinkling from Germany, Russia and Asia. One mother observed that there had been 'a thick crust of oligarchs' children in the past, but not any more.' Significant proportion does not have English as their first language. School is committed to its international families and has an EAL system in place which supports every child who joins with no, basic or limited English. Currently 14 per cent of pupils require targeted EAL lessons, which are intended to 'help speed up the process of full inclusion in the classroom.' Many of the parents we spoke to felt that its international feel was an advantage. 'It is a British school in terms of manners, etiquette and uniform but feels international in terms of its welcoming and warm approach.' Rare for mothers to work. A sea of nannies at the school gate on the day we visited. Pupils mainly come from local area but radius extends as far as 'Kensington in the north, Fulham in the west, Battersea and Kennington in the south and Marylebone in the east.' School bus service in operation to and from west and south-west London for those who live further afield.

Years 4 and 5 go on a skiing and cultural trip to France. One mother was delighted that the children were made to 'carry their own skis and make their own beds'

Parents are encouraged to become involved, from hearing children read to giving career talks. Strong sense of community here and very active PTA. 'When you go into the school, there is a smile on the staff's faces. It's not the sort of school where you drop your child at the door and never get to venture across the threshold,' explained one mother. Head feels parent body is caring and empathetic, 'partly because of the huge mix of nationalities. Parents who come here are quite open, as they have often changed city and country themselves. You need to be outward looking to do that and this feeds into their children. It creates a lovely atmosphere.' One-upmanship, so prevalent elsewhere in London, is refreshingly lacking here.

Heady mix of traditional British education with an international flavour. Children are happy here as they have the freedom to be themselves. Judging by stampede to get into the building at the start of the day, Eaton Square offers its pupils an joyful start in life.

EIFA International School

36 Portland Place, Marylebone, London W1B 1LS

020 7637 5351 | if@ecole-ifa.com | ecole-ifa.com

Independent	Pupils: 310
Ages: 2–16	Fees: £18,150 – £22,500 pa

Executive Head: Since September 2018, co-founder Isabelle Faulkner, Quebec lawyer and English solicitor, has two children, one at university and one doing the IB.

Head of school: Since September 2018 is Françoise Zurbach, who has been teacher, pedagogical counsellor, and head of school in France and London for more than 20 years. With a French father and English mother, she spent her first 10 years at an English school in Montreal, moving to France and continuing her education in the French system. She spent 20 years teaching in a small French primary school, moving to head Wix primary in London in 2013.

Academic matters: Nursery children in Little EIFA follow the EYFS, taught in French and English; therefore children learn literacy and reading at an earlier age than would be the case in a traditional French setting. Little EIFA offers flexible part-time hours. Primary students follow the French national curriculum using a bilingual French-English model. Each year group (two form entry in most years) has a Francophone (and French-qualified) teacher as well as a native-speaking qualified English teacher, who plan jointly and teach different parts of the programme in both languages, creating a completely bilingual learning environment for every year group.

In the senior school, years 7-9 continue with French curriculum (taught in both languages). In year 10 students may take the diplôme national du brevet as well as follow the IGCSE subjects now that the school has been authorised by Cambridge Exams and Edexcel (68 per cent A*-C in 2018). Senior school staff bring solid international school experience and a good overall understanding of the various curricula – English national curriculum, international curricula and French programmes. School benchmarks student learning via French standardised tests and is inspected by both Ofsted and the IEN (Inspecteur de l'Education Nationale Française).

As the school has 'homologue' status with the French Education Ministry, French (but not English) teachers must be qualified and hold recognised credentials. One parent of a very bright child was effusive about the way he is challenged academically. School engages specialist teachers for children with learning challenges for those who need additional support; there is no cost to the parents for this. Students who are not yet fluent in English or French may also be expected to take lessons with language teachers.

Games, options, the arts: More on offer than in a typical French school. After-school activities are offered by teachers with a special talent or interest, as well as external providers. A range of musical instruments and ensembles including rock bands; activities such as rugby, football, capoira (Brazilian martial arts), ballet, yoga, language clubs, IT coding; a few parents mentioned a creative writing course and one teenage boy refreshingly told us it is his favourite activity; homework club every day. Some parents see it as a way to extend their children's exposure to French or English. Year 2 pupils were very proud to be the winners of a recent European film competition for the animated movie they created.

Early morning drop-off and after-school care till 6pm are available for Little EIFA children; this is convenient for working parents, but also those whose older children may stay after school for club activities. Extracurricular activities incur additional fees but no one we spoke to grumbled about that: they were very happy with the range of activities on offer. There are opportunities to take part in sports competitions and tournaments with other French and international schools in London. Parents told us of a trip to Brussels where the students had a hand in crafting an EU law on the environment.

Background and atmosphere: The co-founders, plus their fellow investors who form the governing board, have had good support from the local Howard de Walden Estate – major landowners in London W1 – who were keen to see EIFA on the menu of international schools available to the local Marylebone gentry. The combination of the strategic planning and foresight of the founders and this collaborative partnership with HdW Estates has enabled this school to secure two impressive buildings for their prep and senior schools. Originally conceived as a prep/primary school in 2013, but parents wanted their children to continue to be educated bilingually, and so a senior school opened and moved into its own premises in 2016.

A huge painting of a London cityscape with silhouettes of children in the foreground, donated by a parent and painted by South American artist Walter Blanco

Little EIFA and the prep school are in a large late Georgian building in Portland Place. Little EIFA is based in a well-organised maze of rooms in the basement level with enclosed outdoor space exclusively for the youngest children. On the ground floor are the reception children and the library, stocked with 5,000 books – half French, half English (on the day we visited full of relaxed but fully engaged children with their noses in books), in bright rooms with original period features such as lofty Wedgwood-blue painted ceilings decorated with crown moulding and fireplaces. Other primary classes perch higher up on top floors with large windows that brighten the rooms year round.

The senior school is a short walk away on quiet side street with a nicely refurbished building that contains bright classrooms fully equipped with all the requisites – science lab, study hub, an amazing large art studio with walls of windows on two sides, and an inviting canteen that serves as a multi-purpose space. This room features a huge painting of a London cityscape with silhouettes of children in the foreground, donated by a parent and painted by South American artist Walter Blanco as part of a school event. Children's work gets equal prominence, and there is also a collage of maps of all

the countries the children come from featured on another wall. There is a clean, uncluttered feel despite the ample careful displays of student work and art. Daily recreation and breaks take place at nearby Regent's Park. Students use the library at the prep school or visit nearby Marylebone Library.

EIFA is an urban school; parents say that some families come expecting more, but what makes it all worthwhile is the positive EIFA school culture – that is the major draw for families we spoke to.

Pastoral care, well-being and discipline: Parents tell us that EIFA has a strong sense of community and this is part of the attraction. The diversity of families helps to create an ambiance where acceptance and respect are the norm. The school is young, and there is a definite 'pioneer spirit' among those families who joined in the early years and who speak with pride about what the school community has created. Communications are good and parents feel well informed and able to approach the school teachers or administration whenever needed. Senior and junior school parents describe the teachers as versatile, devoted, nurturing and impressive. The kids we saw in the classrooms, study hubs and library looked happy and were welcoming and at ease with their visitor. Some parents attribute the good behaviour to the school's small size. No uniforms except for PE and games classes. Active parents' association regarded as refreshing by many who find this parent engagement a welcome change from the norm at other French schools. It's also an important support that can help to integrate parents new to London. Meeting minutes and photos of activities are on the website.

Pupils and parents: The increasing number of French-medium schools on offer in London has enlarged parental choice; those selecting EIFA want what it says on the tin – an international school with a French bilingual programme. Over 40 nationalities; the French, Americans and Canadians are the main groups but there are many bicultural, bilingual families of mixed nationalities; some local residents, others expats. A few French families seeking the dream life in 'France's sixth city – London' (with perhaps one parent commuting to France for work). Though some of these families have returned to France, the school has not yet seen the impact of Brexit and continues to grow. In many respects a 'neighbourhood school' and many children walk or ride their scooters, but some travel longer distances – the school's outsourced school bus service covers to Highgate and Hampstead to the north, Notting Hill to the west, and Fulham to the south west. Parents do not seem to mind having play dates scattered across London.

Entrance: This young school, which has only recently opened a secondary department, does not yet have waiting lists for the senior school. It is currently relatively non-selective, with admission is based on completing a straightforward application form and providing school reports. Does not require fluency in English or French for entry up to year 8.

Exit: Parents say that some families who aspire to the French Bacc opt to move at 11 to the bilingual school in Kentish Town or one of the Lycées, and some, particularly those whose parents are not French speakers, transfer to British independent schools, but an increasing number of families are choosing to stay on for senior school as it introduces IGCSEs.

Money matters: International school prices are to be expected here. The school has needs-assessed financial aid. Low student-teacher ratio (6-1), and since extras such as English or French language support and special needs support are not extra,

the fees are competitive with those of other international schools. Lunch is included in fees and is compulsory unless the child has dietary restrictions. It is prepared by outsourced caterers, and is tasty by all accounts (and our own sampling).

Remarks: This is a niche school with high aspirations that ticks the right boxes for families who appreciate a certain discipline associated with French education (we saw lots of immaculate handwriting), and the opportunity to acquire or maintain French language fluency, but who at the same time like the quirkiness of an international school that draws on global themes and topics to enhance the students' learning and world view. The principal was quick to say, 'EIFA is not a French school, it is a bilingual (French/English) international school.' The rich displays of African masks made in art classes, green Irish shamrocks to celebrate St Patrick's Day, student rehearsals for Wizard of Oz, beautifully written essays on Macbeth and even stir-fry chicken noodles for lunch serve to illustrate her point. Worth a look.

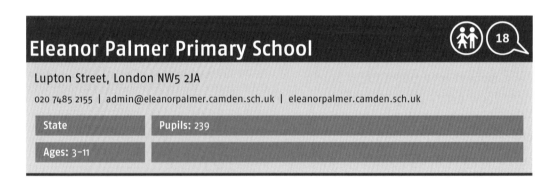

Eleanor Palmer Primary School

Lupton Street, London NW5 2JA

020 7485 2155 | admin@eleanorpalmer.camden.sch.uk | eleanorpalmer.camden.sch.uk

State	Pupils: 239
Ages: 3–11	

Head: Since 2003, Kate Frood MA,OBE (50s). Knew she wanted to be a teacher from the age of 8 and started her career doing just that at nearby Fleet Primary in 1983. Aside from a four-year stint as a maths consultant to Islington Council, has taught in Camden ever since. Trained when child-centred learning (as opposed to testing) was the focus, and this has remained fundamental to her approach. In order 'to keep her hand in and share ideas', continues to teach year 6 maths. 'She really knows what kids can do and – more importantly – what they can't,' said a mother. 'She makes sure every child is well-prepared for secondary.' Liked and respected by parents. 'She's a brilliant head, incredibly good behind the scenes and incredibly forward thinking,' said one. 'Problems are dealt with before they turn into problems.' Awarded the OBE for 'services to education' in 2014. One daughter who attended Camden School for Girls.

Entrance: Hugely oversubscribed, with about eight applicants per place for a single reception class of 30. Proximity is key and there's been much tut-tutting about families renting to squeeze through the gates. (Camden now scrutinises applicants carefully, particularly looking for those who own or let another address locally.) Full-time Camden-funded nursery of 26, but bagging a place here does not guarantee admission into reception (children have been rejected in the past).

Exit: Pupils here tend to go on to local community secondaries, generally the cluster round Dartmouth Park – William Ellis, Acland Burghley and Parliament Hill – plus some to Camden School for Girls. A few, too, to selective state schools, and a further sprinkling to independents. By and large, however, this is a parent body committed to state schooling.

Remarks: Housed in a medley of low-built mid-20th-century buildings on a reasonably spacious, but very urban, site, the school has well-cared for and imaginatively used grounds, including an adventure playground and colourful entrance ornamented with art, fish, running water – and a prominent plaque declaring 'racism is unacceptable'.

Academically, the school falls firmly into the Outstanding category, with high standards in the core and a rich offering well beyond. Heavily committed to topic-based study, with themes such as World War 2 or Victorian childhood taught using imaginative links between history, geography, art and literacy. 'We see learning as an adventure,' says the head, an adventure explored through plenty out-of-school visits and and in-house contributions from storytellers, artists and experts.

The school has both a national reputation for maths teaching and a highly-praised literacy strategy. Children read daily for half an hour and end every afternoon with a class story. Great emphasis, too, placed on the best children's literature, with new titles added regularly and a handy booklet of recommendations. Year 5 studies and performs a Shakespeare play. French for all from year 3, taught by the classroom teacher. Homework (including daily reading and times tables) from the start, and ICT well embedded, with access to a myriad of laptops and iPads.

Eleanor Palmer is a 'teaching school' – one of just 350 in the country – teaching teachers how to teach. This, according to parents, can have both its upside and its down. 'It means,' said one mother, 'the staff are young and hugely energetic, willing to work after school and at weekends, but some are also pretty inexperienced.' Head, however, tends to restrict the rawest recruits to the younger years.

The ethos of the school has been shaped by the work of Carol Dweck – whose perspective is that effort and persistence are what really count. 'This teaches children to see mistakes and failures as positives and makes for a very energetic and inclusive culture,' says the head. So, no star charts, no ability sets; instead, each child is encouraged to achieve their personal best, with marking emphasising steps forward rather than what's gone wrong.

Special needs is led by the head, aided, in school, by support teachers and learning support assistants, and, out of it, by an educational psychologist and occupational therapist. Parents feel the SEN offering has improved in recent years. 'The head is very responsive and things like touch typing are now standard.'

Two hours of PE weekly, with a dedicated sports co-ordinator mentoring both those who struggle and those who excel, as well as arranging participation for all in out-of-school tournaments. Plenty of alternatives, too, to conventional team sports, with dance and skipping workshops, fencing and taekwondo sessions. The school is also 'very committed' to walking. Nearby Parliament Hill used for class activities and sports days.

Specialist music teacher visits twice weekly, overseeing a 'strings programme', which provides all pupils from the age of 8 with (free) group tuition by a specialist in violin or cello. Multiple opportunities to perform in concerts and musicals.

'We see learning as an adventure,' explored through plenty out–of–school visits and and in–house contributions from storytellers, artists and experts

Head very much of the '50 things to do before' philosophy, and her objective is that all leavers should have completed a substantial tick list of activities, from growing their own vegetables to visiting a farm. Trips, trips, trips make the most of the wealth of galleries and museums a bus ride away, as well as of opportunities further afield (everyone gets four residential stays, ranging from camping in Epping Forest to a year 7 week at a Michael Morpurgo's Farm for City Children.)

As the leader of a 'multi-cultural community', the head has taken up the option to skip the daily act of Christian worship. Instead, the red-letter days of all the major religions are covered in assemblies and younger pupils are taught philosophy by trained philosophy teachers. The school is also a level 2 Unicef 'rights respecting' school, which entails listening to children's views and including them in such decisions as the fairness of team selection. Every class draws up a charter based on agreed rights, and then lists how adults and children will respect these. 'Once behaviour is seen in this way there is little need for rules,' says the head. Local councillors, politicians and lawyers, too, are invited in to teach pupils about their rights and responsibilities as citizens. Charity link to school in Sierra Leone.

Kentish Town is more affluent than formerly, particularly after a recent influx of French émigrés, and the popularity of the school means the sharp elbowed have gained ground in recent years, but you'll still find a good cross section of traditional locals and recent refugees alongside the organic set. About 20 per cent receive free school meals, a national average, but well below what might be expected for the location. As the head concedes, this can be a positive, as those from more affluent backgrounds provide 'a critical mass of high-achieving, motivated, liberal, middle class kids – so all my working class or refuge kids get caught up.'

Parents, too, feel the balance works ('I think it still has that community school feeling,' said one) and are full of praise for its warm and nurturing atmosphere. 'Our children have been extremely happy here – and very well educated.'

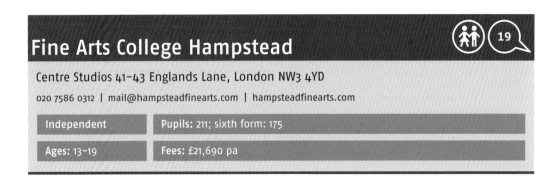

Fine Arts College Hampstead

Centre Studios 41–43 Englands Lane, London NW3 4YD

020 7586 0312 | mail@hampsteadfinearts.com | hampsteadfinearts.com

| Independent | Pupils: 211; sixth form: 175 |
| Ages: 13–19 | Fees: £21,690 pa |

Principal: Candida Cave (50s) set up the college in 1978 with Nicholas Cochrane – who has recently retired as co-principal. They studied at the Ruskin School of Drawing and Fine Art, Oxford, started teaching at a tutorial college and found 'we were quite good at inspiring people'. The decision to set up a college of their own was something that just 'came about', but clearly had a market, and has grown steadily ever since. She remains a practising painter and playwright, while teaching art history. Parents and pupils are great fans of the warm and relaxed approach. 'Candida Cave is what all parents dream of in a teacher, but think they'll never meet,' said one. 'She's imaginative and nurturing, but not a pushover. My daughter just fell in love with her.'

Academic matters: A very broad, almost exclusively arts-based curriculum (no science in the sixth form, though a few mathematicians). The visual arts remain, as one might expect, exceptionally popular. Photography is the number one subject choice but also large numbers for fine art and art history, English literature, textiles, graphic design, film studies and media studies. The fine arts approach provides a strong traditional grounding (from classical busts and life models), which leaves many students with strong enough technical skills to bypass foundation courses. (The college also runs a two-term post A level portfolio course, to ensure preparation for art degrees and art college is tip-top.) An extensive curriculum (29 subjects in all) of liberal arts, social sciences, modern languages (French, Spanish and Italian) and classical studies (Latin, Greek, ancient history and classical civilisation) can be taken in virtually any combination. Strong results overall at A level (20 per cent A*/A, 50 per cent A*-B grades in 2018), with English and fine art particularly stellar. Exceptionally high 'valued added' between GCSE and A level (fourth highest in the country) produced by caring teaching in small groups (classes never exceed nine).

'My daughter had failed spectacularly at two other fee-paying schools,' said one appreciative mother of a daughter now at a Russell Group university. 'She thought she was a dunce until they took her under their wing. They produced an incredible turn around and she went from Cs to As.'

Principal, Candida Cave, 'is what all parents dream of in a teacher, but think they'll never meet'

Also offers GCSEs, with two year groups of about 20 in all. 'We find there's a real need in year 10,' says Candida Cave, 'particularly when schools start saying, you should drop this or that.' GCSE subjects include biology and some physics but probably not the place for nascent medics. In 2018, 76 per cent 9-4 grades. Staff long-serving and enthusiastic (including three ex-students and Candida Cave's daughter), with a fair proportion who also have alternative lives as professional artists, film makers, etc. Teaching style relaxed but enthusiastic; student style, co-operative competition. 'It's very much teaching in discussion, they want to impress each other in a nice way,' says Candida Cave. Good information given to parents and pupils about progress, with fortnightly reports and two parents' evenings. Rated outstanding by Ofsted in latest report.

Games, options, the arts: Plenty of opportunity to display talent, with an annual art exhibition, music and drama recital, and short films shown at the local Everyman Cinema. (One girl was recently runner-up for the Young Film Critic Award at

Bafta.) Loads of outside speakers and cultural outings, with annual study trips to Florence, Paris and Venice. Not at all a hierarchical place, and students organise their own entertainment – 'a certain number tend to take the lead each year' – including charitable fundraising (for Breast Cancer awareness, the Red Cross, a local hospice) and other social events. Certainly not the ideal environment for the sporty (and few here care) but GCSE students have fencing lessons plus PE at a local sports centre and the college's long-standing football team plays against other sixth-form colleges. Popular table tennis, too, on site.

Background and atmosphere: Started in 1978 in the YMCA in Tottenham Court Road, teaching art and art history. 'We started because there wasn't anyone else specialising in the arts,' says Candida Cave. Moved to Belsize Park in 1982, started offering GCSEs in 1994, and then, in 2002, added a converted Victorian dairy, which now forms the hub of the school, providing rambling lateral space around a cobbled courtyard; is gradually taking over more buildings including what used to be the local hardware store. A good mix of classrooms (some more spacious than others) and excellent studio space, for art, drama, photography (with its own darkroom for traditional-style printing) and media studies. The atmosphere is intentionally informal and teachers are called by their first names. 'The college was very much founded as a bridge between school and university. Many students come here because they're looking for something more flexible.' Students congregate in the common room, where free coffee is on offer, but no food supplied on site. Some bring sandwiches, the majority visit the multitude of local eateries. Dress code vaguely artistic and bohemian (the odd fur gilet and extreme make up, the majority in UGGs and tracksuits), but kept well within limits. 'If it offends, we tell them to dress properly. It's just common sense.'

Bought by Dukes Education in 2015.

Pastoral care, well-being and discipline: 'What we liked about the college', said one parent, 'is the industrious informality. They take the job seriously, but don't wear it too formally.' Pupils' work and well-being is immaculately monitored. Everyone has a personal tutor, whom they see for an hour and a half each week. The tutor goes through reports, helps with essay-writing and advises on university applications. All GCSE pupils sign in at 9am and again at 1.30pm. If pupils are not in class an email is sent to parents within half an hour. 'Pupils turn up because they want to,' said one parent. 'But, equally, they know that if they can't be bothered to turn up, the attitude will be, don't bother to come back.' Most have no problems with this. 'I've never been to a school before where all

the other pupils want to learn,' said one boy. Students sign a contract of behaviour, so know exactly what is expected, and misbehaviour, social or academic, is followed by an oral warning, a written warning, and then a parental meeting. 'We've not excluded anyone for eight to nine years, and not even suspended anyone for a long time,' says Candida Cave. 'We're run here on mutual respect and they do seem to rise to that.' Most see the college as a place where they can be confident concerns will be dealt with quickly and in confidence. Definitely a haven for those for whom more boisterous or insensitive environments have just not worked. 'The college made my daughter believe in herself. I feel I owe them,' said one parent.

Staff long-serving and enthusiastic (including three ex-students and Candida Cave's daughter), with a fair proportion who also have alternative lives as professional artists, film makers, etc. Teaching style relaxed

Pupils and parents: A mix of mostly local professional/artistic families, who tend to be profoundly relieved that their children have found such a civilised and creative niche. Some of those who come to do GCSEs have previously been educated abroad. Others have had enough of boarding school, or failed to fit into more conventional schools. Alumni include Orlando Bloom and Helena Bonham-Carter.

Entrance: All applicants are interviewed with their parents and the college makes offers based on two criteria: candidates 'really want to be here' and 'they intend to go on to higher education'. Minimum five GCSEs with 4 or above for A levels, but this liberal benchmark is generally well exceeded, not a few arriving garlanded with a multitude of 9-8s. Most from local independents and leading boarding schools, a few from the state sector and schools further afield.

Exit: Around 30 per cent leave after GCSEs. For the rest, a generous sprinkling into every permutation of arts and media – from film studies and fine art to fashion retailing and creative writing – but also to history, psychology and sociology. Sussex, Falmouth, Nottingham Trent and Leeds currently popular. One to Oxford (modern languages) in 2018.

Money matters: One scholarship of 100 per cent (based on academic merit, a statement of why they deserve a scholarship, and an interview). Two of 25 per cent may be given for outstanding exam performance at GCSE ('We wanted to show we appreciated their intelligence.') A limited number of bursaries awarded to students who have previously been educated in the state system who would not otherwise be able to afford private education.

Remarks: A low-key, calm and friendly place, with strong teaching and results, particularly in the arts. Ideal for the 'arty, urban misfit' who has wilted in a more conventional environment.

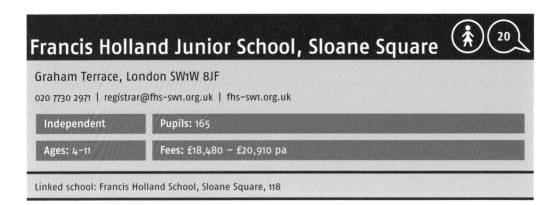

Francis Holland Junior School, Sloane Square

Graham Terrace, London SW1W 8JF

020 7730 2971 | registrar@fhs-sw1.org.uk | fhs-sw1.org.uk

| Independent | Pupils: 165 |
| Ages: 4–11 | Fees: £18,480 – £20,910 pa |

Linked school: Francis Holland School, Sloane Square, 118

Head of juniors: Since 2015, Caroline Spencer-Kruger, previously deputy head.

Entrance: Assessments at 3. Some 150 girls tested in January for 24 places. School assesses 'girls' potential and readiness to learn.' School was horrified when a parent asked about tutoring for their 3 year old and advises, 'Parents need to read to their children, take them to the park and talk to them. That's the best preparation for these tests.' Places occasionally available further up the school and prospective pupils are then assessed in the classroom setting. Barely a spare seat in the house.

Exit: Fairly evenly split: one third to the senior school, one third to other London day schools and another third boarding. One parent remarked that she thought it would be 'a hard jump to go from Francis Holland Junior School to a large co-ed. Girls are protected here and can be quite gentle. I'm not sure they are always ready for the hurly burly of senior school.' Popular day destinations are St Paul's, Godolphin & Latymer, Latymer Upper, JAGS, North London Collegiate and City of London Girls. Current boarding favourites are Wycombe Abbey, Downe House and Cheltenham Ladies'.

Remarks: A small, academic school, tucked away behind Sloane Square. One form per year of 24 maximum. Shares a site with senior school. 'Low pressure in the early years,' says school. Reception children have naps after lunch in first term when sleepy. From year 4 it hots up, with summer exams in maths, English and science from then on. No

setting but plenty of differentiation. The consensus among parents we spoke to was 'You need to be academically robust to cope here. There are so many projects and tests, and parents are expected to be able to support their offspring massively. It feels almost relentless at times.'

More academic than senior school: 'The girls here are clever and motivated,' said one parent. 'Strong foundations are laid but the girls work hard for it,' according to another. The standard of work on display was astonishingly high. The girls themselves feel that they are well prepared for the 11+, but 'we don't feel too much pressure.' Year 6 pupils kept working to proper timetables once 11+ exams are over; no coasting here. Teaching is superb and staff considered by the parents to be high quality. Teachers come over from senior school to teach PE, science, French (from 8) and some art. Well motivated staff. 'We're a strong team'.

Bright classrooms, inventive displays, beanbags and colour everywhere. Wonderful library, shared with senior school, and huge numbers of books at every turn.

Girls have beautiful manners and stand up with military discipline when adults enter the room. Highly articulate and fluent. Very keen to show their projects to us when we visited and tell us what they had learnt. Highly engaged in lessons, from early years upwards. Pretty tartan uniform. One girl in top year thought it would be worth staying at the school just so she could get to wear the new kit.

Plenty of time for fun, with highly-anticipated trips to Cornwall in year 6 and Canterbury in year 5.

Girls have beautiful manners and stand up with military discipline when adults enter the room. Highly articulate and fluent. Very keen to show their projects to us

Sport is a real strength. Ballet taken seriously: compulsory in the first years, fabulous ballet studio. Highly anticipated Princess Margaret ballet competition every summer term – her daughter is an old girl. Lots of music and drama, including impressive end of year 6 musical. Girls take the initiative by providing the costumes, designing the posters and rehearsing on their own at break times. Great emphasis placed on creativity throughout the school. Junior choir from year 3 and a very select chamber choir for the most talented singers. Significant numbers learn instruments from year 1 onwards. 'Girls need time to be bored. They should not have every moment of their lives timetabled.' Wants them to discover what interests them for themselves. Plenty of clubs on offer including chess, speech and drama, pottery, art and French.

A very caring school in which older girls are expected to, and do, look after the younger ones. Year 6 pupils write and illustrate books for year 1 pupils. Lots of raising money for charity. All year 6 girls are prefects, though badges confiscated for poor behaviour.

Families are 'more and more international'. 'A bewildering number of languages spoken in the playground at pick up time,' according to one mother. Children come from nearby Westminster, Chelsea, Knightsbridge and Pimlico.

'A happy school,' is the general consensus amongst parents. Bullying very rare. School feels girls are 'traditional and polite'. One pupil acknowledged, 'It will be the saddest day of my life when I leave Francis Holland to go to my next school.' School described as 'vibrant', and it was certainly buzzing on the day we visited. A real energy about the place. Francis Holland girls have a wonderfully stimulating start to life here, with devoted care and attention from outstanding teachers. No wonder there's a queue to come here.

Francis Holland School, Regent's Park

Clarence Gate, Ivor Place, London NW1 6XR

020 7723 0176 | admin@fhs-nw1.org.uk | fhs-nw1.org.uk

| Independent | Pupils: 500; sixth form: 127 |
| Ages: 11–18 | Fees: £20,040 pa |

Head: Since January 2016, Mr Charles Fillingham (early 40s). Urbane and very approachable, he exudes a calm pleasure in his role and the school. A modern linguist, with degrees from University of Wales, Bristol and King's London. His career has been spent between maintained schools and independent – he had a spell at The Grey Coat Hospital and was deputy at City of London School for boys. He commutes from Surrey each day and spends what free time he can rescue with his wife and two young children, 'though I try still to read French literature'. Like so many other heads, a marathon runner. His three deputies are women: 'They are all in position entirely on merit – but it also really matters for the girls to have outstanding female role models.' Much liked by parents who were particularly wowed by his deftness and approachability in an Q&A session led by pupils very early in his tenure: 'he was easy, natural, and played fair'.

Academic matters: Punching in many ways well above its weight. 2018 saw 55 per cent of A level grades at A*/A, and 72 per cent of GCSEs 9-7s. Given the entrance is not nearly as academically selective as many, they're doing extremely well and across the full range of subjects. This wasn't always the case – a recent big hike in a couple of STEM subjects.

Mr Fillingham, not surprisingly, takes particular pleasure in the immense value-added over which the school presides. Many girls are outperforming their own expectations of themselves, and he's in no doubt why: 'Small classes, immensely hard-working and well-qualified teachers'. This sounds too good to be true, but parents back up the claims: 'totally committed teachers'; 'wonderful care when my daughter needed to work from home' etc. There's no arguing with results. There would be appear to be a slight tilt towards the arts and humanities in terms of subjects being studied, but two girls went off to Imperial recently, six to study medicine and another dentistry. These successes have elicited pride and pleasure from both staff and pupils.

Equally telling, the school seems not to suffer from the level of attrition which has led bright and ambitious girls to move to chic co-ed sixth forms after GCSEs, with some 80 per cent staying on. 'We don't begrudge a girl her deserved success when she wins a place at another school,' says Mr Fillingham equably. 'We will miss her and wish her well'.

The school's strengths in the classroom owe a good deal to unobtrusive but effective early intervention. There are three teachers dealing with pupils' special needs – often related to dyslexia and dyspraxia. 'All the girls who come here are pretty clever,' says the head, 'and so we ought to be able to help them manage these problems'. Although a number of girls don't speak English at home, the school has not had to make special provision for EAL. Modern languages are thriving in the school – everyone takes at least one for GCSE, and Mr Fillingham is now busily fundraising for the school to buy a house in France as a study centre.

Scarcely any mess, even in the sixth form common room. But everywhere buzzed and, while the place felt busy, we divined no sense of tension or crowding

This sensitive integration of pupils from a range of cultural backgrounds is part of the explanation for the school's academic success, which has undoubtedly been assisted by a high degree of staff retention. 'We're losing one member of staff after 42 years this summer,' says head, 'and will be the poorer for it'. He insists that his experience of older colleagues has been only positive and uplifting and that their diligence and enthusiasm has benefited staff as well as students.

Games, options, the arts: Despite being located a stone's throw from Baker Street, the school takes sport seriously – and it shows: the place abounds with buzzy girls who exude the kind of energy which comes from plenty of exercise. It may help that Regent's Park is just across the road, and this allows pupils to make full use of the fact that central London is still full of green spaces.

'The sport is good, but not desperately competitive,' said one parent, 'which has been great for my daughter. She has got into teams which, at certain other schools, wouldn't have happened. And that was great for her.' Tennis and rounders are both flourishing and the netball and hockey teams went on a tour to South Africa last year. Hockey takes place a five minute coach journey away at Paddington Recreation Ground and, for those of an equestrian bent, there are trips to the stables at Hyde Park. There's also a splendid swimming pool in the basement (the head has just extended opening hours) which perhaps explains the fact there is so much competitive swimming and water polo. The school also has a fitness suite and a gymnasium, and gymnastics is big news.

This is an intensely musical school. On our walk round the school we passed a brass ensemble and a string trio, and as well as three orchestras and Jazz group, there are also innumerable chamber groups and five choirs. Recent tours to Russia and the USA testify to music's popularity and another is now planned to China. The head is particularly pleased that the two Frances Holland schools (including the one in Sloane Square) recently shared a platform for a splendid concert, fruit of the work of both schools, to mark the founder's birthday. About two-thirds of the girls have instrumental or singing lessons – hence, the most recent big school production (The Sound of Music) seems to have a particular resonance. Photographs adorn the walls, and the memory is clearly fresh for all those lucky enough to participate or attend. Drama is also lively and very strong, with inter-form competitions for all years, and a dizzying array of short plays.

Masses of clubs ('and they actually meet,' said one parent): touring the school, it was easy to spot how easily and cheerfully engaged pupils seemed in all they were doing. The two art studios conveyed a special joie de vivre – lots of lunchtime and after-school activity goes on here as well – and pupils' work exhibits, in addition to drawing skills, plenty of exposure to different materials and textures.

'We have this mantra about being kind,' says Mr Fillingham, 'and it has to reflect a reality'. All sixth formers do volunteer work – sometimes at local primary schools or in local charity shops – and there is an annual Francis Holland Summer Camp in which pupils spend a residential week with other local children in the Westminster borough. Duke of Edinburgh Award is popular with many girls, and several continue it right through to gold. There's also music and reading with elderly people and with Swiss Cottage School, and a series of links with children's centres in Sri Lanka and Tanzania. A host of activities are also anchored around wider fundraising: the Help Fund raised £17,000 recently. 'There's a big spirit of giving back,'

Masses of clubs ('and they actually meet,' said one parent): touring the school, it was easy to spot cheerfully engaged pupils

a parent said. 'It's made the school a much bigger deal in my eyes.'

Background and atmosphere: The school was founded by Rev Francis Holland in 1878 and endowed with an uplifting motto, taken from Psalm 144, 'That our daughters may be as the polished corner of the temple'. There's a definite patina of that ecclesiastical temper in the building into which it moved in 1915, although nowadays, of course, everything is bright and lively. Still, architecture tells a story and it maintains close links with St Cyprian's Church across the way and still holds many concerts and services there.

The school's pride in confident and ambitious education is palpable, and the most important way this manifests itself is in an atmosphere which is effervescent and unstoppably cheerful. We're not talking about manic high spirits, but something purposeful and upbeat.

The environment supports this – and, in addition to its ascetic advantages, the place looks intelligently cared for. There was no litter or graffiti (God forbid) and scarcely any mess, even in the sixth form common room. But everywhere buzzed and, while the place felt busy, we divined no sense of tension or crowding. Girls up to GCSE have a uniform – it's worn easily and properly, and the effect is reassuring rather than pompous. Sixth form girls dress 'as for their workplace' and seem to accept this without the need for too many stand-offs. Rumours of gripes following a ban on wearing black trainers at school shows among some younger girls, but – in the words of the parent of an indignant daughter – 'that's all good growing-up stuff'.

'I think it's very telling,' another parent said, 'that the staff get along with each other so well. They work late; they turn up to watch plays and concerts; they compete at school quizzes. It's a community which functions.'

Pastoral care, well-being and discipline: There are thoughtful systems in place to harness the abundant goodwill one sees. Every girl has a form tutor who is themselves supported by a deputy, and any concerns are fed through to a head of year and to the pastoral deputy head. There are no houses – formal competition within the school tends to be inter-form. Like most schools which aren't too large, they capitalise on the strength that virtually every pupil is well known to several teachers, and anxieties and inconsistencies are usually quickly picked up. A counsellor also visits on three days a week to provide collateral support. There are a range of opportunities for pupils to shine, starting with a head girl and a small cohort of deputies, as well as a school council. One of the head's recent innovations has been arranging for senior girls to read routine announcements at assembly ('quite empowering, actually,' he reflected).

Parents welcome the clarity of the system and the commitment offered by staff as well. 'London girls can be quite feisty,' one parent reflected, 'and the school offers early and thoughtful engagement when there are problems.' Although there is a system of detentions in place (usually for lateness), the head is emphatic that the girls are sympathetic company and very reasonable. There have been no exclusions, temporary or otherwise, in recent times

Pupils and parents: Lots of communication with parents. There are six sets of reports a year, which sounds like overkill, but the head believes that 'calm, regular, communication serves everyone best', and there is also at least one parents' evening annually per year group. 'Very often, both parents do demanding jobs, so the feedback is essential,' he adds.

Frances Holland attracts what, if poorly managed, could be a challenging constituency of parents, in which the elite professions (lawyers and bankers in profusion) are generously represented. The head insists: 'We enjoy the loyalty of all, and we try to return it in willingly – and even-handedly.' And that loyalty seems to extend to one of the school's most famous alumna, Joan Collins.

Entrance: At year 7, some 600 girls apply for just 75 places. Prospective parents are encouraged to come to an open morning during their daughter's year 5 or at the start of year 6. The school tries hard to make the essentially heartless business of selection as humane as it can. As part of the London 11+ Consortium, the process now consists of a cognitive ability test (rather than maths and English exams) with great emphasis on the interview. At sixth form, candidates are tested in their probable A level subjects as well as interviewed. At this point, there are usually around 20 places and about six successful applicants.

Exit: Girls arrive from a whole range of feeders – 45 schools last year supplied 75 girls. Some two-thirds of the girls come from prep schools, the others from primaries or international schools abroad. Once they're in, Frances Holland sees it as an article of faith to stick by them, come what may, until A levels. In other words, indifferent performance at GCSE debars nobody from the sixth form: 'The gain in trust and goodwill outweighs any hit you may take in the league tables,' opines the head. Three to Cambridge in 2018, and nearly all the others to Russell Group universities plus several off to study art or drama. 'The calibre of advice for those seeking entrance to US colleges is superb,' said one parent (though none off there this year): this is very often a source of grievance in independent schools, so – praise indeed.

Money matters: Fees are mid-range relative to London, and the school tries hard to ensure there are as few extras as possible. Special trips are billed separately, as are music, yoga and speech and drama lessons. A recent change has been to ensure no extra charge is made for books ('a useful

discipline for all of us,' comments the head). Lunch, about which we received glowing opinions, is also part of the package. There are a good range of scholarships at 11+ and 16+ for academic, musical and artistic excellence. There are also a number of bursaries, depending on individual needs and circumstances.

Remarks: A distinguished school which communicates sanity, high standards and sterling example. Teachers and pupils talk easily in classrooms and in corridors – men and women alike – and seem to enjoy one another. Mr Fillingham evidently relishes his work: 'Frankly, I find the people with whom I work – staff, pupils and parents – easy to like and impossible not to admire.'

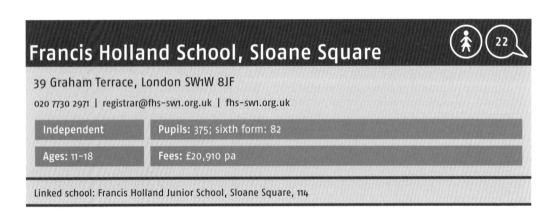

Francis Holland School, Sloane Square

39 Graham Terrace, London SW1W 8JF

020 7730 2971 | registrar@fhs-sw1.org.uk | fhs-sw1.org.uk

Independent	Pupils: 375; sixth form: 82
Ages: 11-18	Fees: £20,910 pa

Linked school: Francis Holland Junior School, Sloane Square, 114

Headmistress: Since 2012, Lucy Elphinstone MA PGCE MEd FRSA (50s). Educated at Barnstaple Grammar School, Devon, and Newnham College, Cambridge (English). Very varied career, including stints in publishing, bookselling, catering, property and ghost-writing. Wide teaching experience from 3 to 18 years, and countless leadership roles including head of a pre-school, head of English at King's Taunton, director of studies in two prep schools, director of drama and resident tutor at Fettes College. Came here from Downe House where she was head of sixth form, senior leader and Oxbridge co-ordinator. Four highly successful adult children. Living in London for the first time since her 20s and loving the culture. Hobbies include ski-ing, watercolour painting, Scottish reeling and Victorian children's literature.

Keen to build up girls' resilience to help them deal with the challenges ahead, including multiple changes of career. Wants pupils to be confident risk-takers. In her assembly on the day we visited, she encouraged girls to take on board Christopher Robin's advice to Winnie the Pooh: 'You are braver than you believe, stronger than you seem, and smarter than you think.' One parent described her

as 'ambitious for the school and highly visionary'. Another claimed, 'She's shaken the school up. It was good before but she has lifted our spirits.' Girls consider her to be 'a great role model.' Dynamic, vivacious and engaging.

Academic matters: In 2018, 41 per cent A*/A at A level; 80 per cent A*-B. Maths and English currently popular, with ever-increasing numbers taking science and economics. Compulsory Extended Project Qualification in sixth form, introduced by head to develop girls' research skills and to prepare them for the next stage. Photography, art and design and computing recently introduced at A level. Eighty-four per cent 9-7 at GCSE. Spanish, chemistry and history results impressive. Setting in English, science and maths by year 9.

Excellent reports about provision now on offer to pupils with special needs: 'no longer just lip service,' said one parent. All pupils screened for dyslexia on arrival. A handful of pupils have EAL requirements and are seen on a one-to-one basis by specialist staff. Extra support continues to sixth form.

Some teaching described as 'fantastic', but one parent we spoke to felt there were 'still some

School has a renowned menagerie of animals, from gerbils and snakes to chinchillas, and younger girls get to take them home at weekends

members of staff who need weeding out. They aren't inspiring the girls and aren't getting the results.' Approximately a third of staff has been there at least 10 years. Recent appointments, particularly of younger members of staff, seen as very positive. Staff feel 'empowered' by head.

Academic success is recognised with flamboyant prize-giving at nearby Cadogan Hall, with performances by talented dancers and musicians. The girls were hugely excited to see staff wearing their graduation gowns and 'felt proud' to be part of Francis Holland. A great success, introduced by head, who is clearly keen to celebrate success in all fields.

Two parallel classes throughout senior school. Classes start at 16 on average and rarely go above 20 in lower years, diminishing to six to eight in sixth form. Would split sixth form classes if they exceeded 10 pupils. From year 11, all girls have an academic mentor, so everyone is fully supported and no one is left floundering. Girls genuinely feel that staff are keeping a close eye on them and that they are guided through university entrance 'incredibly well'.

Games, options, the arts: Sport now taken very seriously, at all levels, and is compulsory for all. Head believes, 'Sport is important as it teaches you that you can't always win, but you can pick yourself up and carry on'. Recently appointed head of sport who everyone is raving about. Well-equipped gym and netball/tennis court on site. Outdoor sports in Battersea Park, including tennis, hockey, athletics and rounders. Top years can try pilates, yoga, squash and boxercise as well as more traditional team sports. Most parents are delighted that fixtures are now arranged on Saturday mornings and the school wins the majority of matches.

Music is flourishing. Nearly 60 per cent learn an instrument. Choirs, orchestras, chamber groups and jazz groups galore. Two choir tours to Europe each year. Head wants creative and enterprising pupils and girls recently set up own theatre company. Highly successful theatrical collaborations with boys from nearby Cardinal Vaughan School, with minimal adult input. Parents consider drama to be a real strength. Speech and drama very popular with many reaching top grades in exams.

Impressive selection of clubs including debating and philosophy, as well as animal club for younger girls. School has a renowned menagerie of animals, from gerbils and snakes to chinchillas, and younger girls get to take home animals for the weekend. Girls encouraged to become proficient in public speaking: debating club from year 6, and mock elections and English Speaking Union events arranged. Broad horizons and an informed awareness of current affairs expected.

Background and atmosphere: Set up by the Rev Francis Holland, Canon of Canterbury, in 1881 as a C of E foundation but all faiths welcome. Sister school to Francis Holland Regent's Park: the schools share a governing body, staff training days and have the same ethos. Same site as junior school, in a Tardis-like building behind Sloane Square. Head aware that being in the same place from 4-18 years has its disadvantages and is keeping her eye out for property nearby. Beautiful interior decorating: stunning new entrance hall lifts morale on arrival and upper sixth common room seriously plush. New Centre for Creative Learning with rooftop garden, performing arts studio and ICT suite should aid school's vision of developing 'creativity, innovation and enterprise'.

She encouraged girls to take on board Christopher Robin's advice to Winnie the Pooh: 'You are braver than you believe, stronger than you seem, and smarter than you think'

School described as 'vibrant', and it was certainly buzzing on the day we visited. A real energy about the place. Francis Holland girls have a wonderfully stimulating start to life here, with devoted care and attention from outstanding teachers. No wonder there's a queue to come here.

Pastoral care, well-being and discipline: Described by parents as being 'nurturing'. Lower sixth and year 8 girls are paired with year 7 girls in Big Sister programme, to make sure they settle on arrival at the school. Head concerned that 'high performing parents have high expectations of their children.' Aware that girls can feel pressurised to perform and a well-being programme, including mindfulness, has been set up to help girls to cope, when it all becomes too much. Head is a trained counsellor and pastoral care is high on the agenda.

Strong ethos of service fostered, whether fundraising for school in Uganda or organising tea parties for elderly in Battersea. Girls are expected to give something back.

Head would expel a girl for drug taking; those caught smoking pay money to a cancer charity, phone their parents from head's office and do community service within the school grounds. Won't tolerate unkindness or rudeness and girls we met were fantastically polite. Sixth formers allowed out for lunch but 'school food is delicious so we prefer to stay at school for lunch and just go out for a coffee,' said one.

Pupils and parents: Happy, confident and charming girls who seem ready to take on the world. Well-heeled and polished with ready smiles. Couldn't wait to tell us how lucky they felt to be here. High octane, international families: mainly French, Spanish, Italian, Russian and American. 'A bewildering number of languages spoken in the playground at pick up time,' according to one mother. Most live within a three mile radius of school. Communication with parents now greatly improved with weekly e-newsletters and reports. 'We are delighted that we finally know what is going on,' said one.

Notable former pupils include Vanessa Mae, Sienna Miller, Cara Delevingne and Rose Tremain.

Entrance: At 11+, a cognitive ability test (rather than maths and English exams) with great emphasis on the interview. Part of the London 11+ Consortium. Some 500 girls sit for 50 places. Bar raised each year. At 13+, exams in English, maths, science and French. For sixth form, by entrance or scholarship exams in proposed A level subjects.

Exit: A trickle leave after GCSE. Most sixth formers to university. Occasionally one or two Oxbridge places. As one girl put it, 'I have applied to Oxford, but it's just one of my choices. It's not made into a big deal here. My other choices are great too.' Art foundation courses also popular. Medicine, economics, history and psychology are favoured courses; Durham, Bristol and Exeter regular destinations. Increasing numbers to American universities, especially for liberal arts degrees, and not only those with a direct American link; others to Spain, France and Canada. Head of careers is a very successful recent appointment; she asks girls at beginning of sixth form, 'What is your dream?', and then helps them to chase it. Higher education fair organised by school. Girls well supported once they leave, throughout university and beyond if needed. Relations with alumnae now actively fostered.

Money matters: At 11, four academic scholarships, as well as music, art and drama scholarships. Bursaries at 11+, 14+ and four in sixth form. Daughters of clergy offered remission on a third of fees.

Remarks: This school is undergoing a transformation and the excitement is palpable. Expectations are high and challenges are being set, but the girls and staff know they have a strong leader and are following her willingly. 'An excellent appointment,' said one parent. 'We feel seriously lucky to have our girls here on Mrs Elphinstone's watch,' said another. Though small, this school is now punching above its weight. An exciting and exhilarating place to be.

Grafton Primary School

Eburne Road, Holloway, London N7 6AR

020 7272 3284 | graftonschool@grafton.islington.sch.uk | graftonschool.co.uk

State	Pupils: 510
Ages: 3–11	

Head: Since 1993, Mrs Nitsa Sergides OBE (awarded in 2012 for services to education), 60s. Qualified as a teacher in 1973, followed by 19 years of teaching at another local school. Became deputy head of Grafton Primary in 1991, and head two years later.

Cypriot born Nitsa (as everyone calls her) is the embodiment of Mediterranean warmth. Her pupils adore her, 'lovely to all of us, talks to us like family.' Her teachers are loyal (incredibly low turnover of staff) and parents marvel at her dedication: 'She's quite amazing, her enthusiasm never wanes and she genuinely wants the best for everybody.' 'She is truly exceptional. Apart from her incredibly nurturing side, she has a gift of being able to get hold of every resource going for the school.'

Nitsa came to the UK at the age of 13 with teaching firmly on her radar; 'I think I was 7 when I realised that's what I wanted to be.' Now in her third decade at Grafton School, she still wants to make a difference. 'I believe that children must be given every chance to succeed regardless of background or ethnicity. We try to create opportunities some pupils may not otherwise have.' This could be a yearly trip to the coast (which for some pupils is their first experience of the sea), or the chance to learn a musical instrument.

One pupil told us, 'I have friends from so many different cultures and we are like a big family.' We heard the word 'family' used frequently and there is a sense of unity

One of Nitsa's proudest achievements is that she hasn't had to exclude a child for 11 years, 'I always believe more in preventative measures rather than reactive measures.' She also believes that, given the correct guidance, inner-city schools can be as good as any: 'My three children are all products of Islington comprehensives. My son is now a neurosurgeon and both my daughters are barristers.' Married for 40 years to an engineer, 'my bouncing board', she loves visiting art galleries and museums and spending time with her grandchildren. Such is her infectious enthusiasm that we left her office grinning.

Entrance: Standard local authority criteria of siblings, proximity to school and children in care etc. Competition for places is fierce – most recently 354 applicants for 60 places. As word spreads about this school there is concern about wealthier parents buying property in now trendy Holloway to get their kids a place, with predictable consequences for Grafton's rich diversity.

Exit: Mixed bag on offer for secondary schools in the Islington area. Most go on to Acland Burghley (if they live close enough), Highbury Fields, Highbury Grove, Mount Carmel school for girls, St Mary Magdalene or others including Islington Arts school, Central Foundation Boys' School, Camden School for Girls, Highgate Wood, Parliament Hill and William Ellis. A few try for grammars like Latymer or Dame Alice Owen or independents such as City of London.

Remarks: A tricky one to find, Grafton Primary sits adjacent to the Holloway Road, off Seven Sisters Road, accessible by car via a tiny slip road. Most pupils walk to school thereby avoiding the perils of Holloway's one-way system.

We were expecting great things and we weren't disappointed. Rated outstanding by Ofsted for the past 10 years and awarded the title of Beacon School, Grafton defies its demographics. A staggering 55-60 per cent of its pupils would qualify for free school meals (although in Islington, these are fully funded for all pupils), 25 per cent of children have SEN, 12 per cent with statements. Grafton is genuinely inclusive – big on equal opps for pupils with disabilities and a vast ethnic mix. One pupil told us, 'I have friends from so many different cultures and we are like a big family.' We heard the word 'family' used frequently and there is definitely a sense of unity and loyalty as well as pride in this school.

Grafton has recently become a teaching school, meaning that it now trains teachers and support staff from other primaries. It is also one of only a few pioneering schools to have been chosen to introduce the CAME maths programme (Cognitive Acceleration through Mathematics Education), which promises to have a significant impact on both pupil and teacher development. Maths is already a very strong subject at Grafton. Up to 20 per cent of year 6 achieve a level 6 in maths Sats.

On entering, one is immediately struck by the spectacularly colourful lobby. Rarely have we seen so much artwork, sculpture, ceiling displays (including a wonderful tree of life installation which ran the length of the lobby and through the school's office). Grafton has partnerships with art professionals, a specialist art and design teacher and an artist in residence, believing that time given to creative subjects helps children achieve in other areas.

The interior of the school is charming, if a little cramped (could be because every inch of space is covered with student displays). The Victorian building is DDA compliant and has a lift for wheelchair users. A £3.5m refurb means all classrooms are now up to spec and there's a new sports hall and reception play area. Library is still a work in progress but promises to be a great space.

Outside is an oasis of calm – amazing, considering proximity to the very urban and not very pretty Seven Sisters Road. Grounds are fairly large for an inner-city school and in addition to the playground there is a quiet formal garden with benches for students to have lunch and read (undergoing a refurb during our visit) and a wildlife garden. This mini eco system with pond and bug hotel feels a million miles from the city. 'Many parents volunteer their time in the garden and elsewhere', we are told. At the end of the wildlife garden is a glass building that we thought was a greenhouse; it's actually the art room, a quirky space crammed with creative materials.

In the assembly hall we were treated to a music assembly in Swahili, just one of the 34 languages spoken here. On site translators assist parents from the three main non-English speaking groups – Somalian, Turkish and Bangladeshi, and the school told us, 'We do what we can to make parents from all sectors of society feel included.'

The pupils we met were a highly articulate bunch – happy, confident and engaging. They loved their school and the opportunities it offers. One told us, 'Julia Donaldson has visited the school and some Paralympians came to talk to us, which was amazing and inspiring.' Another said he loved the cricket and football 'and we've won many tournaments.' A few negative comments about the lunches (free of charge for all pupils) and we thought that some of the food did look pretty unappetising. It seems almost churlish to mention this when for some pupils it may be the only cooked meal they get in a day.

Parents and pupils generally seemed extremely happy with their school. One parent did mention that she would like more sporting activities within the school day as opposed to just afternoon clubs, although she added that the Grafton school day is such a busy one, she's not sure where they would fit it in. Another told us, 'The school is amazing at being proactive, especially with day trips. If they're not hopping on the bus to St Paul's Cathedral, visiting the zoo or going to art galleries and museums, they're doing a walking tour around London. That's the benefit of being so inner city with free bus travel.' The quality of teaching came in for particular praise. One mother told us, 'My older children go to private schools and I know that the teaching my youngest is getting here is better than they received at her age.' She also said that there is a very high ratio of staff to pupils – 1:6 in the first two years – again, as good, as if not better than at some independent schools.

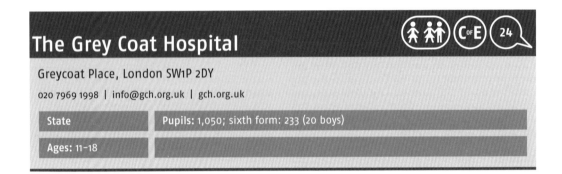

The Grey Coat Hospital

Greycoat Place, London SW1P 2DY

020 7969 1998 | info@gch.org.uk | gch.org.uk

State	Pupils: 1,050; sixth form: 233 (20 boys)
Ages: 11–18	

Headteacher: Since 2011, Siân Maddrell BA (40s). Educated at Surbiton High, followed by a degree in French at Durham. After gaining her PGCE at Oxford, she began her teaching career at Grey Coat in 1992, soon becoming head of modern languages and one of the first advanced skills teachers in the country. Left Grey Coat in 2000 and later became the first vice principal of Pimlico Academy before returning as head.

Friendly, thoughtful, efficient and clearly devoted to her school. Takes great pride in her pupils and their achievements. Not above picking up stray litter in the playground.

'We want to enable girls to take charge of their learning, make decisions based on Christian values, live in the world as independent women and meet the challenges of the 21st century,' she told us. 'We just try to focus on our pupils. It's a very ambitious school and the students will tell you that the expectations and aspirations are really high for everybody. It's about empowering the pupils to do their best. We want girls to be confident enough to be able to seize every opportunity.'

Enjoys sport, theatre and travel – 'I'm very interested in other countries and cultures.' Married with two sons, so 'most of my free time is spent with my family.'

Academic matters: School is regularly rated outstanding by Ofsted. Recently received congratulatory letter from schools minister praising pupils and staff for attainment and progress as one of the top 100 non-selective state schools in the country. Has also won local awards for the success and value-added progress of its disadvantaged pupils.

In 2018, 86 per cent got 9-4 in both English and maths, and nearly 50 per cent of GCSE grades were 9-7. Girls take between nine and 13 GCSEs. At A level, 68 per cent A*-B and 38 per cent A*/A grades. Good range of subjects on offer to GCSE, including Latin, business studies and computing. Pre-U offered in Latin, Greek and art history, all of which are taught at neighbouring Westminster School. 'The pupils love their lessons at Westminster,' the head told us. A level subjects include film studies and sociology as well as more traditional fare. Biology, chemistry, English, history, maths, psychology and religious studies currently very popular. EPQ is becoming increasingly fashionable.

Grey Coat is a specialist language college and has an outward looking, global focus. 'We encourage an international outlook as well as strong grades,' says the head. 'It is important for our students to gain an understanding of other countries and cultures and to have an open and inclusive approach, as well as to develop their linguistic skills.' All students study Spanish and a second modern language (French or German). Many continue with two foreign languages to GCSE. Opportunities to study Mandarin and Japanese out of school hours. Japanese exchange offered to girls in year 10; other exchange trips to Germany and Spain.

International May Fair for younger pupils is an annual highlight. Students are encouraged to represent a country – through fashion, food, dance, ecology and culture. The competition is judged by staff and the prize, awarded to the most impressive tutor group, is a trip to Paris. School is excellent at offering incentives to pupils; girls are encouraged to be competitive. Pupils regularly win local and national science and maths competitions.

Grey Coat prides itself on being an inclusive school. SEN pupils make good progress academically and are fully involved in school life. All year 7 girls are screened for learning difficulties on entry to school. Small support groups for literacy, numeracy and social skills run at lunchtime for younger girls. Five per cent have a statement of special educational needs. Gifted and talented extension programmes in place for more able.

Average class size is 27, with a maximum of 30. No setting in year 7. Year 8 pupils setted for English, maths, science and languages.

Games, options, the arts: Good level of participation in wide variety of sport. 'We are the Westminster sports champions in practically everything and we provide a rich variety of sports,' says the head. Opportunities for fencing, squash, indoor rowing and athletics as well as team sports. Currently Westminster netball champions. 'We've struggled a bit with athletics as we have to bus the pupils over to Battersea Park,' admits bursar. Massive sports hall at Regency Street site. Annual gym and dance display.

Creative subjects taken seriously. Excellent facilities in art and design; these remain very popular subjects and the quality of art displays is very high. 'The standard of art work is mind-blowing,' according to one parent. Music and drama both strong. Instrumental and singing lessons are subsidised by school's foundation. Good range of choirs, bands, string and jazz groups and orchestra. Several concerts every year. Successful gospel choir recently reached semi-finals of BBC's School Choir of the Year competition.

Roughly 15 pupils a year achieve D of E gold award. Good spread of clubs, including maths challenge, debating, football, trampolining and creative writing. External inspirational speakers come in regularly to motivate and encourage the girls. Workshops led by outsiders a regular feature of the education offered here. School takes part in BBC News School Report, enabling pupils to make their own news reports for a live audience. Students develop their journalistic skills and have a ball.

Strikingly beautiful building in Greycoat Place, freshly painted and well polished. Statuettes of Grey Coat boy and girl adorn the front façade of the school

Lots of time for fun here too. Talent show at the end of the Easter term is eagerly anticipated while staff pantomime is apparently 'the best day' of the school year. 'It's absolutely hilarious watching the teachers,' said one pupil. Post-GCSE celebration for year 11s includes a fashion show of their textiles work.

Background and atmosphere: Originally founded for boys – by eight merchants of Westminster on St Andrew's day in 1698. In 1706, Queen Anne granted the Grey Coat Hospital Foundation a royal charter and her portrait hangs in pride of place in the Great Hall. Original wooden boards detailing the names and donations of 18th century benefactors line the stairs. In 1874 Grey Coat Hospital became a girls' school, under church management. Whole school was evacuated during the war and its buildings suffered significant bomb damage.

A C of E school – head says 'Christian values play a key part of Grey Coat.' Church services held each term either in Westminster Abbey or St Margaret's, including a service on Ash Wednesday and a July celebration to which new pupils (and their parents) are invited. 'It's a lovely event – beautifully done,' said a parent. Confirmation services take place at Westminster Abbey and school has its own chaplain.

School occupies two fabulous buildings in the heart of Westminster. Huge quantity of traffic and people encircling it on the streets outside. Strikingly beautiful building in Greycoat Place, freshly painted and well polished. Statuettes of Grey Coat boy and girl adorn the front façade of the school. Wonderful entrance hall, glistening with trophies and artwork. School celebrates the achievements of the girls at every opportunity. In 1998 the school celebrated its 300th anniversary by opening a new upper school building on Regency Street, having sold another site on Sloane Square.

Original building at Greycoat Place is used by the younger pupils (years 7 to 9) but lots of coming and

Heathside Preparatory School

going of pupils from one site to another. Fantastic new arts block includes swish drama studios where recent productions have included The Tempest and The Winter's Tale. 'Drama is a subject that is taken very seriously at Grey Coat and the performances are very professional,' we were told. Facilities hired out to National Youth Theatre in holidays.

Welcoming staff. Healthy female/male ratio and mix of long-servers and newly qualified teachers. 'A positive balance,' says the head. Variable staff turnover.

Symbiotic relationship with Westminster School. Grey Coats go there for lectures, some lessons and Oxbridge preparation, while graduate trainee teachers from Westminster come here to gain experience of teaching in a state school. 'It's wonderful for our students that they have these opportunities,' says the head.

Pastoral care, well-being and discipline: Pastoral care is a major strength of the school. 'Each girl is part of a tutor group family and a year group family, so each feels looked after here,' says the head. Strict code of conduct, but relatively few behavioural issues here. Older girls are given plenty of responsibility, with 40 prefects in final year. Girls can become ambassadors for their year group in years 9 and 11, having successfully explained at interview why they should be chosen. 'There is a strong sense of community here,' says the head. 'We have counsellors, student counsellors, and older students working with younger pupils. It's about creating a sense that we're all in this together.' It certainly seems to be working well. A learning mentor is on hand to help girls organise themselves if needed, as well as a drop-in school nurse.

Girls start off in smaller, lower school – helps them cope better with the progression to upper school. 'It's rare to hear of anyone being miserable here,' a parent told us. 'The school keeps a close eye on its pupils and intervenes quickly if things are going awry.'

Food thought to be 'very good, with lots of choice,' according to one pupil. Vast quantities of pizzas being eaten at break on the day we visited. Oyster card system in place so girls don't need to carry money and the canteen is open from breakfast onwards. School is confident that 'we'd know if a girl wasn't eating.'

Head is justifiably proud of the excellent attendance record of 98 per cent throughout the year – rating it the third highest in the UK. 'All our pupils came in when the recent tube strike was on,' says the head. Pupils with 100 per cent attendance and punctuality for a year get a trip to the theatre.

Pupils and parents: 'A real mix,' the head told us. Twenty-eight per cent of pupils eligible for pupil premium. Two-thirds from minority ethnic groups.

A third whose first language is not English – more than 50 languages spoken at home, including Yoruba, Swahili, Spanish, French and Dutch.

> 'We encourage an international outlook as well as strong grades,' says the head. 'It is important for our students to gain an understanding of other cultures'

Big inner-city blend of families, including daughters of politicians and education professionals. School recently hit the headlines with the news that prominent politicians are sending their daughters here. Old Greys include TV presenter Sarah Greene and Tamsin Dunwoody. Recent leaver is Ebony-Jewel Rainford-Brent, the first female black cricketer to play for the England team (she presented awards at a recent prize-giving). Many old girls remain loyal to the school and return to the annual school celebration service in Westminster Abbey each year.

Entrance: Huge catchment area from the dioceses of London and Southwark. Pupils travel from as far away as Essex and Kent and are rarely local. Total of 151 places offered in year 7. Fifteen language places (following an aptitude test which 450 sit); 88 C of E places; 28 other church places; 20 open places.

Priority given to looked-after children, then siblings, church attendance for church places and a distance tie-breaker. The comprehensive intake is placed into bands following an assessment test – 25 per cent places to band 1, 50 per cent places to band 2 and 25 per cent to band 3.

Open events for year 6 pupils in September and early October each year. Sixth form open events in November. Relatively little movement of pupils. 'We are a very stable population,' says the bursar. Once pupils are here, they tend to stay put, even if it means travelling long distances. In-year admissions are dealt with by the local authority. A few boys in sixth form, all 'charming,' according to one member of staff.

Exit: Around a third leave after GCSEs, usually for schools closer to home or offering subjects not available here. Their places are taken by a fresh intake – the head says 'it's a fresh start for all.' Around 90 per cent go on to higher education. School encourages pupils to aim for top universities and some 40 per cent go to Russell Group universities as well as art colleges. Popular destinations include Oxbridge (five places in 2018), Exeter, St Andrews, Leeds, Durham, Nottingham, Bristol and Manchester, plus one off to a dance conservatoire in Italy in 2018. Popular subjects include medicine, sciences, maths, English, religious studies and classics.

Money matters: Parents' Guild raises money each year for both the school and charity. Recently paid for a beautiful stained glass window by Michael Coles. Parents are asked to contribute a small amount of money on a monthly or annual basis.

Remarks: A sensational mix of high academic standards strongly supported by caring and devoted staff. No wonder they are prepared to travel for hours each day to be part of this buzzing school. The girls we met were charming, articulate, interesting and purposeful. Their pride in the school was striking. Not only are they ambitious and successful but they're also happy. On the day we visited, groups of girls were sitting cross-legged on the tarmac playground at break time, chatting and laughing as though they didn't have a care in the world.

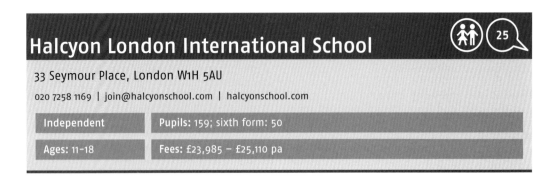

Halcyon London International School

33 Seymour Place, London W1H 5AU

020 7258 1169 | join@halcyonschool.com | halcyonschool.com

Independent	Pupils: 159; sixth form: 50
Ages: 11–18	Fees: £23,985 – £25,110 pa

Director: Since 2015, Barry Mansfield (50s); studied history at Nottingham and did his PGCE at UEA (history and English). His first teaching job was in an international school in Athens, followed by Nairobi, then Dubai, where he became head of English and learned about IB schools. He worked in Sofia Antiopolis in France, then Jeddah, where he set up the diploma programme, before teaching in Bern International School in Switzerland (and setting up the MYP) while simultaneously doing an MA (Open University) in educational leadership.

All that IB experience fits very firmly with his commitment to the ideology of students as active learners. He believes that learning has a social, interactive component with enquiry based, collaborative learning at the heart of Halcyon. He is 'quietly spoken and has a calming, steadying presence' and 'whilst he sets rules and guidelines his is not a dictatorial role, which allows others to have a voice,' according to parents. 'He listens, thinks things through and comes up with a solution'; 'I have never met a head who listens like that'. An egalitarian who doesn't have his own office but shares an open plan space with colleagues. He has one son who went through the IB programme.

Academic matters: Teachers are passionate about their subject, which they discuss with students and other staff. Middle years programme followed for first five years, which involves enquiry-based learning – as much of it student-led as possible. Pupils like the fact that there is plenty of independent

work. Modern, neat, floodlit classrooms – we saw students working on their laptops on beanbags creating, researching and preparing for tests with other students. Subjects – language and literacy, mathematics, sciences, humanities, geography, modern languages and mathematics – all taught within a global context and in a cross-curricular way in order to gain not only knowledge but what parents referred to as 'soft skills like public speaking, discussing and learning to bridge differences and work together'. This leads to the IB Personal Projects which they present to the community at the end of grade 10 (year 11). Huge numbers of oral presentations, videos, multimedia work in addition to essays as opposed to just a handwritten paper. Very few hard copy books as the school provides access to countless online resources. The curriculum content is put online (ITunesU) by teachers and accessible to students and parents, offering all resources and assignment details as well as remedial and extension learning options.

IB diploma continues with three higher level subjects and three standard level subjects across a required range which means they all do, for example, maths and a second language (Spanish, Mandarin or private tutoring of mother tongue languages). To further broaden the school's offerings, students explained that they could take online Pamoja courses and study with the support of the in-school coordinator. So pupils are also able to do IT, psychology, economics, business management and film, for example. Second IB results in 2018 averaged a creditable 35 points, with the first medic and the first Ivy League placement.

Both pupils and parents spoke about the close monitoring and watching possible in small classes: 'Kids get pushed, they don't get lost or coast'

Science in well-equipped labs with students doing some experiments and accessing the internet to explore further. Interactivity means that students can do research and share their results with the class by airplaying to large screens in each classroom. Outdoor learning day an example of the creative teaching with all lessons happening in Hyde Park: students measured respiration for science and exercise; some used iPad apps to paint and others did pencil drawings of trees; others did English Shakespearean play acting or exploring senses for writing poetry; some tested pollutants in the water in the Serpentine (environmental sciences).

All teaching and learning has a clear assessment criteria so pupils feel they can learn from feedback. Emphasis is on what they learn from both their work and the assessment rather than simply giving grades. Both pupils and parents spoke about the close monitoring and watching possible in small classes: 'kids get pushed, they don't get lost or coast; when they need more, they get more because the teachers are very good at differentiating'.

New SENCo because none in place when Ofsted visited (and judged the school outstanding in all categories). Whilst all the use of technology is helpful for the child with dyslexia, and the small classes and self-initiated work allow each pupil to go at their own pace, there is no specific support for SEN and the school will only take children with learning differences if they are sure they can match needs and can accommodate them within the classroom. No pupils with EHC plans.

Games, options, the arts: Art room displays of work from oil pastels to 3D model making, sculpture and papier mâché masks, mosaics, installation art and fabric printing. Two enthusiastic specialist art teachers and a design technology teacher extending the popularity of both art and design technology.

Music is a challenge in a small school but noise limitations overcome by using electronic instruments and headphones, and the music room has a good supply of electronic keyboards for creating and composing music. Some bands – ensemble, contemporary band, small choir. Soloists get to play in assemblies and at graduation. Now expanded to use some traditional instruments.

PE twice weekly compulsory up to grade 10 (year 11) then optional in the sixth form. Table tennis in school and some gymnastics and plenty of dance, otherwise swimming, football, basketball and other sports at local leisure centre or outdoors in Hyde Park. Too small for many team sports but running club and table tennis team, and football (mixed training, separate fixtures). So not the right school if you want competitive sports.

Plenty of drama in school featuring a number of student-driven performances/direction/lighting that seem to be a highlight for many pupils.

A number of extracurricular activities are not teacher-led, but are generated by students themselves – eg Model United Nations conferences which students organise entirely, and they work hard to include students from local state schools as well as other private international schools, plus Global Issues Network, charity fairs, school trips, student driven assemblies, school plays. Emphasis on pupils taking responsibility and leadership roles as often as possible.

Grades 6-11 attend a one week residential team-building trip each September as part of the curriculum to reinforce community early in the year.

Students from all over the world are very supportive of each other – and they laughed when we asked about stealing, which they couldn't imagine in their school

Sharing and celebration of work and achievements in class and assemblies, but also on the school website, which again lets the pupils speak for themselves by showcasing their work and activities.

Background and atmosphere: The school opened in 2013 in buildings that are in part grand and old, as its landlord is the neighbouring synagogue, but due to a full renovation benefit from a number of state-of-the-art classrooms. Meeting room and large assembly hall. The school has a strong commitment to sustainability such as a vegetarian canteen and a virtually paperless operation. There is also a modern extension with super high-tech labs and modern classrooms. They are renting more space as the school grows and this allows for some purpose built facilities including an open plan learning space as well as a larger art room. The location could hardly be more central, and pupils say they 'use London as a classroom'.

Pastoral care, well-being and discipline: Well-being coordinator runs mentoring system which includes each pupil and a member of staff, with some pupils trained so they are 'qualified' in conflict resolution and mediating. The role of well-being, rather than being responsive, is to give pupils agency so they feel that they are 'recognised and have a voice', with not much room for frustration or disenchantment or being ignored. Pupils all spoke of the amount of interaction they have with teachers who 'know you really well and are almost like friends' and 'are interested in what I have to say'. The head says that the pupils are not a blank page on which staff need to impose their systems, but are involved in their own self-directed learning. The staff are there to 'advocate for students all the time'. The school uses 'guiding principles not rules'. Assemblies and discussions about bullying, but students from all over the world are very supportive of each other – and they laughed when we asked about stealing, which they couldn't imagine in their school: 'we respect each other and our possessions'. High security of interest to some parents, thanks to this secular school having a synagogue as landlord. Pupils not mollycoddled, however: they have exit rights at lunchtimes to increasingly wider zones and more frequently as they go up the school.

Pupils and parents: About one third from US, and second largest number are British, with a good mix from other nationalities so a real third culture kids atmosphere. Parents we spoke to said they didn't want to be in an American school but wanted an international environment and liked the fact that kids learned so much from each other's different cultures and backgrounds. Parents also liked the central London position – that is why they had moved to London, they said, to make the most of the city. Small year groups but pupils make friends through multi-aged courses and activities in school, as well as outside clubs and from inter-school connections. Articulate and inquisitive pupils said school is 'welcoming and friendly, you speak to everyone – and students who leave come back to visit and join in'. Active involvement by parents – careers talks, cake baking, trips, twice-termly meetings of class reps with the head.

Entrance: 'Holistic approach to admissions' which involves parent and pupil interviews with admissions team and the head, two years' school reports and two teacher references for younger pupils, three of each for older pupils. They need an academic profile of average or above and good enough English to access the very full-on IB diploma.

Interactivity means that students can do research and share their results with the class by airplaying to large screens

'Families are as important to us as the students': they are looking for those who will engage and are not expecting a focus on scores and data, and who will 'embrace the digital learning style'. Pupils told us it works for pupils who are motivated and curious, and that the admissions team were 'interested in my education and me and not only in talking to and selling the school to my parents'.

Exit: Early days for the school still, but expectation is that up to half may go to university in the US, about a quarter to UK universities, and the rest to other countries (eg Australia, Canada, The Netherlands). Second class of graduates headed off to study eg medicine at Liverpool, international law at UCL, sports admin at Miami, politics and international relations at Manchester and computer science at Delft University of Technology. An experienced universities and careers counsellor on staff.

Money matters: An expensive option and no green fields or grand library buildings to show for it, but this is a charity and all the money is being put back into the school teaching as well as gradual repayment of backers with 'transparency and prudent running of the school'. Teachers are well paid and un-rushed, with the calm that comes from having time to do the job properly. Bottomless resources in terms of technology – laptops, iPads, large screens, video recording, electronic instruments etc. Spotlessly clean. Excellent administration so good communication and clear information sharing.

Remarks: Advanced, not only in terms of digital technology but also in attitude. The school focuses on the pupils and listens to them, making sure they are happy and learning at their own individual speed, with no pupil left behind or slipping. Well-being a priority, proactive and central to learning, which is rare in pressurised London. A friendly school that not only cares and supports but also energises pupils to strive, self-motivate and learn.

The Hall School

23 Crossfield Road, London NW3 4NU

020 7722 1700 | office@hallschool.co.uk | hallschool.co.uk

Independent	Pupils: 460
Ages: 4–13	Fees: £18,795 – £19,365 pa

Headmaster: Since 2013, Christopher Godwin, previously head of Bedford Prep. Read geography at Loughborough, then masters in Middle Eastern studies at Durham. Joined Bedford in 1993 as second master and director of studies before taking over the headship four years later. With no experience of London schools, his post came as a surprise to some parents, although he quickly won hearts and minds with his keenness to maintain the ethos and values of the school, along with his gentle and unassuming nature and fresh pair of eyes. 'There's a track record of people taking this job who are greying and in their early 50s,' he laughs, 'but I hope I've brought a new energy to the school.' Parents and pupils concur, praising his emphasis on 'positive psychology rather than rules, rules and more rules,' as one parent put it. 'There's a strong pastoral element to his thinking,' said another.

Sees the next phase as making the school even more responsive to 'the world we now live in', with a growing focus on preparing boys for what their next schools require and embedding ever more IT into an already technology-heavy curriculum. Known for being open and available to parents and a great team builder among staff. Often seen out and about in school and is not precious about his office, whose conference table is often used by boys themselves. Teaches current affairs to year 5s upwards, geography to year 8s and frequently reads stories in junior school. Heavily involved in the assessment of boys. Keen and active sportsman, particularly rugby – now as coach rather than player.

Entrance: This is the top north London boys' prep school for those looking towards the country's top academic secondary schools, so competition for entrance is hotter than hot, with applications restricted to those registering before their first birthday – and even so, the school is three times over-subscribed. At 3, parents are invited in to discuss whether a child will apply to enter at 4 or 5 (32 places at 4, 22 at 5). 'This can be down to issues such as birth date, speed of development, grasp of English if they come from a bilingual family and, of course, the parents have a say too,' says head,

although he stresses that it all comes down to the individual boy, rather than any set guidelines. All applicants are tested in the same year – 4+ entrants in January for coming September, 5+ entrants in late April/May for the following September – for which parents have been known to tutor their offspring at as young as 3 (although the school says it frowns upon this).

Is not precious about his office, whose conference table is often used by boys themselves

Boys are assessed in groups of six. 'We are looking for a hunch about their potential, measurement of underlying intellect that they'll develop in the long term, as well as how interactive, sociable and curious they are and their ability to concentrate for appropriate lengths of time,' says head. 'It's very detailed, with lots of personal attention, so that we get boys who are right for the school and who we can take right through the school.' Inevitably, there wind up being strugglers and – as the head puts it – 'those who feel adrift from their year group', and these boys have been known to be guided elsewhere, although school insists this is rare and it's clear that increasing effort is made to help every boy keep up. Favours siblings, but no guarantees and many haven't got places in recent years. Occasional places arise higher up the school, with a formal registration process for the waiting list. 'They do a good job of picking the right boys,' said one parent. 'Those that don't get in shouldn't get in and those that do are generally a good fit.'

Exit: Most pupils to St Paul's, Westminster or Mill Hill, others to, for example, UCS. Sizeable minority to other mostly single sex boarding schools, such as Eton, though co-ed boarding schools becoming more popular (and increasingly encouraged by the school), including King's School Canterbury, Sevenoaks and Arundel.

In 2018, five scholarships to Westminster, one to St Paul's, one to Eton, two to UCS and a choral scholarship to King's Canterbury.

Exceptional guidance in secondary school choices. 'We encourage parents of boys in year 4 upwards to start looking widely. We don't leave it with a year to go,' says head. The match is made by a meticulously planned programme of assessments, which include annual verbal and non-verbal reasoning and day-to-day performance, and which are all tracked on a graph for each boy. Scholarship form in year 8 for those completing the demanding exams of Eton and Westminster, but not all scholarships derive from this form.

Remarks: Prep schools don't come more ambitious than this. Catering to the needs of boys who are intellectually curious, academic and highly motivated, this is a school that stretches them in every direction, the result of which is a cohort of fiercely intelligent and extremely articulate boys. Yet there's nothing precocious about them and we found the school environment to be surprisingly relaxed.

Two classes of 16 in reception, reshuffled to three of 18 in year 1. By year 8, four classes of 12 to 14, with a scholarship form and two fast common entrance forms. Staff are a broad age range, including at the senior end, and have notable experience and oodles of enthusiasm. 'They're strict, but you can have a real joke with them too,' said one boy, and we certainly found humour abundant in the classrooms and corridors, with a refreshing ease of communication between pupils and staff. 'The lessons are unbelievably interactive. You never just sit and listen,' said another pupil.

Specialist French, science, music, sport and ICT more or less from the word go. Latin added in year 5, Greek in year 7 for scholarship candidates. Setting in core subjects from year 5 and Latin from year 6. 'But even if you're in set 3, you're still really smart, so there's never a feeling of being bottom of anything,' said one pupil. Three sciences, taught in a more combined way than in the past. ICT provision has long been outstanding, with digital learning embedded into just about every subject and clearly apparent when we visited, with plenty of tablets being used across the board. Advanced coding and programming is praised, as is the collaborative work using shared computer files. Head still not resting on his laurels, though, with £250,000 spent on further ICT, including a new virtual learning environment. Homework starts gently, then builds up and peaks at two preps of 45 minutes for years 7 and 8. No Sats but exams taken very seriously, with all subjects examined twice yearly in the upper forms. 'The teaching is so good that you actually don't need to revise for exams,' said one boy, 'although most of us do

Even the DT room, where boys were making splurge guns ready for their production of Bugsy Malone when we visited, is carpeted

anyway.' Does well in national competitions, such as the Townsend Warner History Prize and national Maths Challenges.

The school itself is divided up, with junior school (reception to year 3), middle (years 4 and 5) and senior school (years 6-8) on separate sites all within a short walk of this upmarket residential area. Junior school is made up of two well-ordered Victorian buildings, with the head living in a flat above. Middle school is a 1970s building that was probably cutting-edge at the time, but could do with a rethink in terms of use of good space now. Senior school is the original red-brick school building, with lots of quirky design features, including split level classrooms, which make for a cosy learning environment.

Classrooms generally on the small side, especially in the middle school, but well-ordered, and many are innovatively designed (especially the history room, with its very own upstairs library and historically decorated walls) and welcoming. Even the DT room, where boys were making splurge guns ready for their production of Bugsy Malone when we visited, is carpeted. Lovely, bright art room, with separate pottery room that boasts two kilns. Wathen Hall, which is the main hall, feels a bit past its use-by date and would benefit from something more airy and with better use of space. Well-stocked, two-story, library with library sessions once a week. Stand-out common room, known as the Pit, with a focal snooker table and split level, contemporary and airy environment.

Like most north London preps, outside space is limited, although the junior school has a colourful and imaginative playground, whilst the older boys use one all-weather pitch, which school admits 'can get crowded' at playtimes. Sport, however, is prioritised, with £2m recently invested in the sports field at East Finchley, which the boys are transported to by coach two afternoons a week, and where they play football, rugby, hockey, cricket and tennis. Gymnastics and fencing in Wathen Hall. Every boy gets a chance to represent the school at some point in a team game (nine football teams) and the school is currently looking to extend its fixture list outside London. Some parents concerned that sport generally favours the best boys, however. 'All boys get to play, but if you're good, you get much better training,' said one. 'If the boys aren't sporty, they're not really bothered with them,' said another. County and national representatives at chess, fencing, skiing and tennis. Annual skiing trips to France and biannual cricket tour of Sri Lanka. 'We competed against teams that got 1,000 runs in 10 games in the last tour. The quality of cricket was amazing,' said one boy.

Over 80 per cent of boys play an instrument, with an army of peripatetic teachers made available, on top of which there are two specialist music lessons a week for all. 'It's not unusual to find boys playing three instruments,' said one boy. Plenty of encouragement to join the large orchestra, string quartets, jazz group and choir, all of which regularly win music awards. 'You get to sing in some amazing places if you're in the choir,' said one boy, listing Southwark Cathedral, St Albans Cathedral and Eton Chapel. 'There are some great music trips too,' said another, citing a year 7 trip to South Africa. The annual bands night is popular and boys rave about the new recording studio. Drama taken seriously, with boys of all ages encouraged to perform in plays, concerts, public speaking and most notably debating. When we visited, an actor in residence (an MA student from the nearby Royal Central School of Speech and Drama) was about to begin his year-long post.

This isn't the kind of school where every boy knows each other (not helped by the lack of single campus) but school does what it can to encourage peer support, with older boys helping out in the junior school and becoming ambassadors for subjects, such as geography. From year 5 upwards, the four houses have so-called 'bungalows', which comprise cross-year groups of eight boys who meet regularly and are led by a year 8 boy to discuss topics such as new ideas for activities or views on the rewards system for good work. In addition, there's a lively school council, that makes a lot of recommendations around meals ('I really don't like the food,' admitted one pupil) and equipment for the playground, as well as decisions about various charity fundraising. Boys say the atmosphere is highly supportive. 'Everyone is really friendly here,' said one.

School accommodates all the usual SENs free of charge, including dyslexia and Asperger's, and is open minded about discussing pretty much any difference, provided the underlying intellect is there. 'My son is dyslexic and the school just took it in their stride, which had a hugely positive effect on his confidence,' said one parent. Learning support department, which is run by a full-time staff member (BEd and certificate in dyslexia), involved in identifying issues, as well as monitoring and supporting them either in the short or long term, bringing in outside expertise where necessary. Only one statemented child when we visited. Huge range of clubs, including cookery, Mandarin, model making, computer maths games etc.

Lots of links with the local community, with teachers offering services at other local schools, whilst boys join forces with other schools to do everything from enrichment maths to drumming workshops. Boys are also encouraged to help out at the community centre 100 yards away. More religious than many nominally Christian schools, but it's a culture that's easily accessible by boys of other faiths or indeed of none, with some assemblies more spiritual or modern or even focusing on current affairs, although expect daily hymns and grace before meals.

The jury remains out on how nurturing the school is. A strong reputation persists that it has a competitive atmosphere, with a focus on academics at the cost of emotional support. But the school itself, along with the parents and pupils we spoke to, made convincing arguments that problems are nipped in the bud, with good pastoral care from teachers, two matrons and the part-time school counsellor, who has links with the Tavistock Clinic. In consultation with parents, the school undertakes a pastoral review every three years, with clear recommendations made. 'Despite its reputation, I've found it to be an incredibly child-centred school, with a caring and supportive environment,' insisted one parent. 'I think people see academic success and believe it must be down to a harsh environment, but actually the environment is genuinely caring and warm,' said another.

'It's not unusual to find boys playing three instruments,' said one boy. Plenty of encouragement to join the large orchestra, string quartets, jazz group and choir, all of which regularly win music awards. 'You get to sing in some amazing places'

School doesn't promote rules as such, but there are clear expectations (many of which are dotted on posters around the school), and sanctions to back them up, most commonly detentions. But boys say punishment can be inconsistent. 'You can wind up with a worse punishment for running to pass a boy a book in the corridor than being really rude,' said one. 'And sometimes you turn up for detention, but the teacher has forgotten all about it.' Parents told us there's far less bullying under the current head, who has made the message loud and clear to both pupils and parents that it won't be tolerated.

Parents mostly high-flyers – bankers, media types, lawyers etc – many of whom have extremely high aspirations for their boys, which can mean the head has his work cut out. Mainly local, but some travel from Notting Hill, Holland Park and Islington. Very active PA and parents socialise regularly, although some years are rather cliquey, with very strong personalities, according to the parents we spoke to.

This is a school that offers boys with high academic potential a dazzling start in life. Most leave not only with great academic results, but excellent general knowledge, huge intellectual curiosity and an appreciation of all things cultural. Myths abound that these are boffins that are hothoused, but in fact we found they are boys with a great sense of fun and who are highly motivated, genuinely enjoying being stretched. For the right boy, this school is hard to fault, but boys who wind up struggling could feel left out in the drive to achieve. As one parent put it, 'The school does all it can to help such boys, but if you don't have a particularly bright son, the bottom line is he's better off somewhere else.'

Hampden Gurney CofE Primary School

13 Nutford Place, London W1H 5HA

020 7641 4195 | admin@hampdengurney.co.uk | hampdengurneyschool.co.uk

State	Pupils: 240
Ages: 3–11	

Headteacher: Since 1997, Mrs Evelyn Chua (50s). Born in a small town in Malaysia, Mrs Chua came to England to do her A levels at boarding school, before proceeding to study piano at the Royal Academy of Music. After a postgraduate degree in music education in the US and a brief stint as a classroom teacher, she took on her first headship at Hampden Gurney, when it had the lowest attendance of any primary in Westminster. The school is now one of the borough's most oversubscribed, and Mrs Chua's super-head status been widely recognised both by parents ('She's like the leader of a ship, you can approach her with any problem') and her professional colleagues (she received a Teaching Awards' Leadership Trust Award for School Leadership). Strongly motivated by her faith, she's focussed, dedicated and slightly formidable. ('The children are not scared of her, but they don't want to go up to her office.') Married with two children, she sees the school as her second home. 'Everything about it has her stamp,' said one mother. 'She could easily rest on her laurels,' said another, 'but she doesn't, year after year after year.'

Entrance: Open mornings held in the autumn term. The school is affiliated to the High Anglican Church of the Annunciation in Bryanston Street near Marble Arch, and gives firm priority to long-term church-goers. (Alternatives venues for worship include St John's Hyde Park, St Mary's, Our Lady of the Rosary.) Hugely oversubscribed with 150+ applying for 30 places.

Exit: Outstanding advice and preparation given for secondary school transfer, with early information meetings in year 4 and one-to-one talks with the head further along the line. About 60 per cent to independents (Westminster, St Paul's, Highgate, UCS, City and Laytmer Upper), many on scholarships and bursaries. Also to top-flight faith schools (St Marylebone C of E, Grey Coat Hospital, the London Oratory and Twyford C of E). About 50 per cent of year 6 apply for scholarships and bursaries, aided by a team of support assistants in the lead up to exams: 'Because of the amount of pressure they're under they need mentoring,' says the head. Parents definitely see the benefit. 'The school is amazing at preparing them,' said one grateful mother. 'It was definitely one of my reasons for going there. You know your kids are going to be given a choice.'

Remarks: By any measure, Hampden Gurney is an 'outstanding' primary school, lauded not only by Ofsted, but by numerous external bodies (Primary School of the Year, Outstanding Progress Achievement, National Association for Able Children in Education Challenge Award). Teaching – it goes without saying – is a strength. 'The head recruits really well,' said one parent. 'She's brilliant at finding enthusiastic young teachers, who bring in new ideas, and the staff are very committed to getting the best out of children.' Early years comes in for particular praise. 'They manage to get everyone reading very quickly, while being very nurturing.'

Broad curriculum includes timetabled Spanish, creative writing and humanities. Two hours a week of science as a separate subject from year 1 (helped by a small roof garden with a pond and greenhouse, and regular outings to science attractions, such as the Science Museum). Computer suite with dedicated hour-long weekly lesson, plus whole class set of laptops. Well-stocked library – one of the best children's libraries in the borough – central to promoting enthusiasm for reading, and pupils test their writing skills in out-of-school challenges, such as the Sunday Times' Goosebumps story-writing competition.

All undergo a thorough-going programme of aspiration raising. 'We inspire the children because we accept that every child has got ability somewhere and can achieve,' says the head. Loads of positive reinforcement plus Building Learning Power programme to instil resilience, perseverance, concentration, and organisation. Infants given extra help through a buddy system which matches them with older pupils. 'It's someone away from class to whom the children can express themselves.' After-school clubs maintain the focus and set sights high. Design club, for example, is intended for 'future engineers, architects and artists,' while journalism club lays the ground for the next generation of Fleet Street's finest. The home-school relationship is critical to the mix, and parents meet teachers at the beginning of the year for a briefing on curriculum, expectations and homework (from year 1). 'There's quite a lot of homework and it's encouraged to be done,' said one mother approvingly.

Special educational needs well supported. Dedicated SENCo and learning mentor work closely with classroom teachers (who are given specialist training) and parents. Outside experts called upon when required. School celebrated, too, for its gifted and talented approach ('Our policy starts with the expectation that there are gifted and talented learners in every year group,' says the head). Early identification then monitored by a full-time specialist, who develops reasoning and creative thinking through after-school clubs, visits, masterclasses and summer schools (at St Paul's, City of London School for Girls and Oxford University). 'It's OK to be a geek,' said one parent. 'It may not be precisely cool to be clever, but you're not penalised by your peer group for wanting to do well.' Head works personally both with those who struggle and those who excel and all acknowledge her talent as a teacher. 'If you're not improving or not where she expects, she will focus on this. She cares deeply about the success of every child and can really inspire children.'

Arts taken seriously. In-class tuition in theory of music and composition (including electronic works), plus the chance to learn either ukulele or recorder. Weekly music club run by professional musicians and links with both the Royal Academy of Music and Royal College of Music for projects and workshops. Individual lessons in piano, saxophone, clarinet and violin at a reasonable cost. Children's choir performs at mass and elsewhere (the Royal Albert Hall, for example, with the BBC singers). Dedicated art teacher. Dance club, taught by qualified dance instructor. Despite its tight urban location, the school manages a good range of games (netball, basketball, tag rugby and football), athletics and gymnastics. Swimming from year 1 at nearby pool. Plenty of sports clubs (some run by year 6) during and after school, on site and in the nearby park. Some inter-school competition, where the school performs with credit ('They often win because the school teaches them not to give up; you can do it, you will succeed'), but, for the very sporty, out-of-school options may be required. Stimulating range of clubs (girls' football, musical theatre, chess, origami, cooking, martial arts) and trips, both local and more wide-ranging (year 6 residential trip to the rolling Surrey hills).

Gifted and talented monitored by a full-time specialist, who develops reasoning and creative thinking through after-school clubs, visits, masterclasses and summer schools (at St Paul's, Oxford Uni)

Established in 1863 in memory of the Reverend John Hampden Gurney, rector of St Mary's Bryanston Square, the school's ethos is still strongly High Anglican, with compulsory attendance at weekly sung eucharist. (Parents, too, invited into school for weekly prayer group.) Termly visit to the church in Bryanston Square and year 6s take positions of responsibility as servers at mass. Order and discipline underpin it all. Firm emphasis on attendance and punctuality. Escalating punishment system (warning, missing play time, time out, Mrs Chua), but these are well-behaved children. 'Everyone comments on it if you go out on a school trip. They sit there and listen and all ask questions,' said a parent. 'It's a joy.' Wide-ranging pastoral strategy. House system – with houses named for local heroes Alexander Fleming, John Wesley, Michael Faraday, Florence Nightingale – develops cross-year bonding, and gentle competition (with certificates for academic prowess and good behaviour). 'The house system encourages everyone to work as a team.' Motivational speakers (Colin Jackson, Cherie Blair) invited in to teach about rejection and reflection. Strong, too, on promoting British values with hands-on experience of democracy, through school council, mock elections, voted-upon school prefects (including head boy and girl) plus visits to parliament and local council. 'They're taught to ask thought-provoking questions about life,' said one father. Smart red-and-blue uniform, with separate PE kit.

'It's a small school and everyone knows everyone. We all see each other at church, in the park'

If Hampden Gurney didn't stand out in so many other ways, it would still be distinguished by its building. Opened in 2002, it was described by the RIBA as 'innovative, bold and dynamic.' Admirers refer to it as 'the beehive', the less well-inclined 'the car park'. Whatever your perspective, it's a clever solution to a tight urban site, offering covered outside play playgrounds on each of its three floors, and identical plans for each age group to proceed from nursery at ground level to top-of-the-school and top of the world in year 6.

Parents, who mainly live close by, are a healthy mix of those who could afford to go private and the just-about-managing. Overall a fairly cosmopolitan lot, often European (Western and Eastern, so German, French, Russian, Polish), almost all practising Christians. ('If you really didn't believe in God it might be a problem,' said one mother.) Strong community feel. 'It's a small school and everyone knows everyone. We all see each other at church, in the park, on weekends.' Energetic PTA, which raises more than £20,000 a year 'for all the softer stuff' such as arts and music provision. Voluntary subsidy of £40 per pupil contributes to school maintenance.

Most parents are delighted with the school ('My children have enjoyed themselves from day 1. The school really makes learning fun'), praising its well-structured discipline and high aspirations ('There's pressure, but within reason; it's certainly not excessive'). That said, some acknowledge the approach might not be ideal for all. 'You have to be a well-disciplined child who likes learning. If you're a wonderfully creative, dreamy child, it might not be the right place for you.'

Hampstead School

(ʘᴥʘ) 28

Westbere Road, London NW2 3RT

020 7794 8133 | enquiries@hampsteadschool.org.uk | hampsteadschool.org.uk

State	Pupils: 1,244; sixth form: 239
Ages: 11–19	

Headteacher: Since 2006, Mr Jacques Szemalikowski MA BSc PGCE NPQH CPhys MinstP FRSA (50s). This head needs no Red Bull! Positively explodes with energy, a dynamo. Five minutes in his company and you are left exhausted. 'I don't know anyone like him – I always think he must be thinking 10 different things as he's speaking,' one parent told us. 'And you know that if any of those 10 things need acting on, he'll do them – probably today!' He joined to make a difference, and in his tenure as headmaster of Hampstead School, he has.

A graduate in astrophysics, and a teacher for 25 years before his first headship at The Warwick School, Redhill; parents also like the fact that he has four children of his own ('It means he really gets it'). Crystal clear on expectations – a misbehaving student can find themselves holed away for the day in the internal exclusion unit, 'our naughty step'. He makes no apologies for his rigorous approach to education, both for his students and staff members alike, and works hard to raise aspirations for every child: 'Our students have played football at Arsenal and spoken in the House of Lords – the message is always "You can do this too".'

Doesn't teach ('It's a luxury I can't afford – I'm too involved in sector improvement'), but is on the gate every morning and afternoon, plus all breaktimes, and does a daily hour-long walk round the school 'so I get to know every child and every teacher'.

Parents praise his selection of staff, who get enviable professional development training, although this can be a double-edged sword, with many staff securing promotional posts in other

For the gifted and talented (known here as 'high potential learners' due to the growth mindset), there's also the Brilliant Club

schools, leading to high staff turnover. That said, the calibre of new teachers is impressive; 'We have an excellent reputation, so we are lucky to get excellent applicants.' As for the school's awards and competition wins, no stone is left unturned when there's an opportunity to fix another framed certificate up on the foyer wall – 'We are proud of what we achieve here, but it's even better to have it externally validated,' head says.

Academic matters: Has not released any 2018 results for GCSEs or A levels. Does well for value added throughout the school and the sixth form is in the top five per cent of sixth forms in the UK for progress. Consider that nearly half the pupils are bilingual (63 different nationalities), five per cent are statemented and nearly 50 per cent are on pupil premium.

So what's their secret? For starters, students are tracked from the moment they arrive (well, the summer before, actually). They have individual charts and are monitored several times a year. As soon as a student starts to slip or is found not to be doing their best, staff put in interventions ranging from one-to-one support to subject clinics. For the gifted and talented (known here as 'high potential learners' due to the growth mindset), there's also the Brilliant Club, involving university students mentoring the school's brightest. Homework levels 'reasonably high' but 'fair' and 'not unmanageable,' report students, and there are opportunities for after-school homework sessions – great for those lacking a quiet study space at home or for the particularly dedicated.

Extra help available for those who arrive with little English – catch-up is rapid. For SEN, support is provided both in and outside the classroom. 'My son, who is statemented, is a completely different child, thanks to this school – when he left junior school, he was introverted and didn't have friends and had the reading age of a 9-year-old,' one parent told us. 'Now, he loves reading, is at the level he should be and has a really nice mix of friends. Between the SENCo, head of year and his form tutor, they've completely nurtured him and given him all the support he needs while never overwhelming him.'

Big emphasis on (and take-up of) science, with the option of triple rather than double science for students who attain at least a level 6 at the end of key stage 3. In the top 20 UK state schools for continuing into science A levels. Maths also strong; school is very involved in maths challenges, with students achieving above national average numbers of gold, silver and bronze certificates. The school offers free Saturday school maths masterclasses for gifted mathematicians from years 5 and 6 of local primary schools. Other popular subjects include English, media, psychology and economics. Virtually no subject is offered at GCSE level which can't be carried through to A level. Choice of 19 A levels and four BTecs, including catering and hospitality – with multiple exit points for flexibility.

French and Spanish from year 7, plus opportunities to learn community languages. Setting from year 7 in maths and science, but it's fluid and reviewed annually – 'for instance, we dropped setting in English altogether this year because we found results were stronger without setting.' PE qualifications taken by every key stage 4 student, and nutrition and food is no add-on either – 'We don't just teach our students how to cook, we teach them how to cater for kings and queens.'

Games, options, the arts: Fizzes with activity. Music is popular and heavy investment in this department has meant that each of the school's 1,300 students is offered the opportunity to learn a musical instrument. Around 100 students have periplectic music lessons and a large number get involved in musical activities, including senior or junior orchestra, guitar orchestra, a very popular jazz band, junior choir and many more.

Buzzing extracurricular activity. The school's debating society and Model United Nations do well (the latter team has beaten Eton three times in the finals)

Drama also strong, with great on-site replica fringe theatre, partnerships with the Hampstead Theatre, Royal Court and Tricycle all help to inspire and, as one student noted, 'we get the opportunity to do things like professional lighting too.' Performances most terms.

Art thriving, with photography particularly loved by students. Masses of outside partnerships to keep things fresh (and competitive) and – true to the school's aspirational ethos – they're not satisfied with their gold award from Arts Council of England and were currently trying for platinum when we visited.

Note these three subjects aren't just exam options and extracurricular – all key stage 3 pupils get one hour of each subject per week.

Sport is going from strength to strength since the addition of a new four-court sports hall, dance hall with sprung floor, fitness suite, multi-use Astrourf and basketball/netball courts, which join the existing on-site indoor pool. Limited playing fields, though, as you'd expect for a London school. Strongest sports are football, basketball, table tennis (there's a ping pong table practically everywhere you look outside), athletics and dance. Winning matters, with a stuffed-full trophy cabinet in the foyer, but the sporting ethos goes wider to ensure every student gets involved in exercise.

Buzzing extracurricular activity. The school's debating society and Model United Nations do well (the latter team has beaten Eton three times in finals). Less academic options include gardening (they have an allotment which grows produce for the catering department – rhubarb and beans when we visited), poetry, rugby, dance and aikido clubs, plus several music ensembles.

Background and atmosphere: Hampstead Schmampstead – this school is no more in Hampstead than Arsenal (FC) is in Arsenal. Situated in between colourful but definitely not posh Cricklewood, Kilburn and semi-posh West Hampstead, you can see the flag before you see the school. Red and emblazoned with the school logo, it waves proudly high above this impressive large red-brick building. The main building, formerly the old Haberdashers' Boys' school, was built in 1908 and promises great things, with banners everywhere: 'Best ever GCSE results', 'Read more, earn more, learn more', 'Leaders of tomorrow' and so on. 'They do it in American schools a lot because it reinforces key aspirations at all times,' explains head.

'We're not a marching in silence in hallways kind of school,' students told us, 'but you know what the school rules are and what happens if you don't follow them'

But though you still wouldn't know it at this point, the rest of the school is unrecognisable from even five years ago. Brand new, all-singing-all-dancing facilities to the tune of £18.5m mean that most of the previous archaic-looking classrooms have been replaced – think bright, light, carpeted modern rooms and particularly large and shiny science labs, with lovely wide squeaky-clean corridors to get from A to B. There's a refurbished and roomy

library – 'there is nothing you can't access in here,' said our guide proudly, although the number of books isn't anything to write home about. Dining and outdoor recreation areas are also new, as is the large assembly hall and aforementioned sports facilities. A well-equipped ICT and catering block is home to industrial spec kitchens, completely with TVs for cooking demos – we half expected Jamie Oliver to jump out to present one of his programmes. And back in the main building, there's a good sixth form centre with huge common room overlooking the central atrium.

Wheelchair access throughout – the school is completely DDA compliant. There is a disability resource which can cater for up to seven students with complex needs, complete with washrooms. These students are fully integrated into mainstream lessons.

Students' pride in their school is evident in the total lack of graffiti, vandalism and litter.

We noticed how they spoke of their school in terms of 'we' and 'us', not 'them', and their sense of ownership in the school means they aren't afraid to speak out. So while in many other schools the best that student councils do is get new fountains brought in, students here recently helped bring about a complete overhaul of the whole detention and reward system and new in-house catering ('the food is all cooked onsite now and it's so good,' one student told us).

Commendable efforts to involve the outside world, with lots of local partnerships and charity work. Enrichment days three times a year – with recent examples including year 9 trip to the coast, year 7 maths puzzles with experts, and business studies students visiting Brent Cross for an Apprentice-style activity. The school culture involves loads of celebration and rewards for achievement and improvement.

Pastoral care, well-being and discipline: 'If punctuality and attendance ain't your bag, this ain't your school,' found our reviewer during our last visit, 'and we've tightened that up even more now,' the head told us this time round, with pupils informing us that turning up even one minute late now lands them in deep water. The senior management team, head included, are at the gates to greet pupils from 8.40am, after which sluggards have to report individually. (Early risers' club offered from 7.30am onwards.) And the head is so intolerant of absence during term time that he's become the go-to headteacher in England to discuss the matter on Radio 4. 'If a teacher prepares a scheme of work using their highly professional skills in a school that's hard to get into and you get an empty chair, that's not only a waste of public money, but it's disruptive,' he says. 'And if you feel you can make the work up, then what's the point in coming to school ever?'

Head is so intolerant of term time absence that he's become the go-to headteacher in England to discuss the matter on Radio 4

The only two exceptions, he says, are illness and two days a year for religious holidays.

Uniform was reintroduced under current headship – 'it puts everyone on a level playing field – essential in such a diverse school,' he says. Different ties denote whether or not a student has been trained in HABZ (Hampstead anti-bullying zone, a model that has since been rolled out across other schools), and any student feeling vulnerable can approach those who have one – extremely popular among students. Non-teaching heads of year are the go-to people pastorally, say students; ditto for parents. Counsellor also available and well-used. 'Mental health is high on our radar – we train staff in mental health first aid and at every level, we're about building relationships with students,' says head. Buddying, mentoring and restorative justice schemes all bolster pupils' sense of security.

'We're not a marching in silence in hallways kind of school,' students told us, 'but you know what the school rules are, why they're there and what happens if you don't follow them' – and the internal exclusion unit, agree all, is a good deterrent. Classes during our visit were well behaved for the most part, with the exception of the odd class joker and one particularly raucous languages class. 'They'll be kept behind for that,' our guide whispered as she shut the door. If a student is found in a corridor during lesson time, they can expect a staff member to stop and question them within seconds (as we saw for ourselves) – woe betide them if they don't have their book signed with permission from their teacher (even to go to the loo). Good level of security – brings to bear the stark reality that you are in an inner-city school.

Only one permanent exclusion in living memory, but around 50 temporary exclusions per year – 'broadly in line with national figures,' points out head, who says they are the result of 'a range of behaviours that contravene our expectations of conduct, plus always for any form of aggression and bullying.' All include a meeting with both child and parent and restorative justice intervention if necessary.

Pupils and parents: From barristers earning £2m a year in moneyed West Hampstead to recent refugees in temporary housing, the demographic is hugely diverse – all the more admirable when you consider how far the school has come. One pupil told us: 'There are no cliques according to how wealthy your family is or their ethnicity – everyone mixes.' Seventeen per cent is white British – the largest group. An appreciation of the diversity of the school is prevalent – Black History Month, Gay/Transgender Month, trips to Auschwitz etc, and we saw posters for a forthcoming Irish night (Cricklewood has many families from Irish descent), to name a few. No shying away from big celebrations around Christmas, Easter and Eid, as at some other diverse urban schools. Around 95 per cent attendance rate at parents' evening, but no PTA. Communications from school praised by parents – 'that goes for general information to conversations about your own child,' said one. We found the students – who come from Kilburn, West Hampstead, Willesden and Cricklewood (and further still if they've moved during their time at the school or enter at sixth form) – polite, chatty, comfortable in themselves and ambitious.

Former pupils include Sadie Frost, Rachel Yankey, ex-MP Julia Drown, Alec Bogdanovic, Jake Lensen, Tobias Hill, Zadie Smith.

Entrance: From up to 71 primary schools (no named feeders; totally non-selective), and covering three boroughs – Camden, Brent and Barnet (admissions managed by Camden) – the school is now oversubscribed in every year. A far cry from before Mr Szemalikowski's time, when the school had a 'terrible reputation,' according to local parents. Around 20-40 external applicants join in year 12 (and some in year 13 who are disillusioned with their current place of learning); entry requirements vary according to the level of course, but applicants should have at least a grade 6 at GCSE in the subject they want to pursue.

Exit: Around 70 per cent stay for sixth form, the remainder go to other sixth forms or colleges or enter employment (increasingly on apprenticeship schemes). Of those that stay, there is some drop out after year 12 (mainly due to the high number of one-year courses available) and around 70 per cent who leave after year 13 go to university, with an overwhelming lean towards maths and science based subjects, although many also into humanities, arts etc. Most to London universities (Kings, Imperial and UCL all popular) 'because they can't afford to move away.' But some go slightly further afield to the likes of Sussex, Herts and Surrey. Over 20 per cent to Russell Group.

Remarks: The head's energy and vision has turned this school around, while new facilities have given it a long-awaited facelift. A melting pot of culture and diversity, with a whole host of activities to keep even the most apathetic child interested, we think this is what all urban comprehensive schools should look like. But although there is room to make mistakes here – the kind that any youngster might make on their journey into adulthood – it's not for the fainthearted. Large and imposing, with high expectations, you have to toe the line.

Harris Westminster Sixth Form

Steel House, 11 Tothill Street, Westminster, London SW1H 9LH

020 3772 4555 | enquiries@harriswestminstersixthform.org.uk | harriswestminstersixthform.org.uk

State

Pupils: 600

Ages: 16–19

Principal: Since 2014, when the school started, Mr James Handscombe MA (Harvard) BA (Oxon) mathematics PGCE NPQH (early 40s). Previously deputy head at Bexley grammar school, Mr Handscombe started his career in what was perhaps his most formative experience, as a maths teacher at Tonypandy comprehensive school in south Wales. Youthful, purposeful, wholly unaffected but intimidatingly intelligent, he is relishing running the innovative and above all scholarly sixth form he is leading here at HWSF. Married with two school age daughters, he met his wife as a student in Oxford. A truly vocational teacher, Mr Handscombe could have done almost anything with his brilliance and brains, but the children he teaches are the lucky beneficiaries of his calling. Educated at a comprehensive in Sheffield, he went on to achieve a top first in maths at Merton College Oxford followed by a masters at Harvard.

His students admire him as a 'well rounded intellectual'. He is 'not boring or plain but has real cross-curricular knowledge,' one told us. He confided to us that he likes to see himself as a polymath. A regular tweeter, his 140 characters tend to be about an array of subjects from U2 lyrics to mathematical juggling. He described to us, as well as to the world at large on the HWSF website, his insecurity and lack of confidence when he arrived as a very young man at two of the best and most prestigious universities in the world. However he concludes that 'it doesn't matter where you come from: the only thing that matters is how interesting you are to talk to.' The three nouns, ambition, perseverance and legacy, emblazoned across the HWSF website and elsewhere lie at the heart of his journey as well as those of his students. It is ambition that propelled him, perseverance that enabled him doggedly to pursue that difficult path, and finally produced the legacy that he is now bequeathing to his students and with which, he hopes, they in turn will imbue generations to come.

Academic matters: This is a highly academic school. It takes the brightest and best students from all over London and the suburbs. Its continuing association with Westminster School is influential in setting the tenor of scholarship and creating high expectations among the students. Its aim, it states, is 'to nurture a community of scholars'. Its A level subjects are the 'facilitating subjects', those most valued by the top universities. Most popular subject by some margin is maths. The department is very strong with high calibre teachers who excel in their field. French, Spanish and German offered as modern languages. Classics, history of art, drama and German are all taught at Westminster School. Music, art, politics and economics are also offered alongside the sciences and the humanities.

HWSF follows the Westminster School timetable as well as the curriculum, right down to Saturday morning lessons. 'A real shock' to many students (and teachers) when they first arrive, observes Mr Handscombe, but they start to enjoy the quieter commute on a Saturday and the opportunity to become immersed in their academic study. As at Westminster, students here have set exeats each term when school is closed on Saturday. 'The core of Westminster School is threaded all the way through HSWF,' says Mr Handscombe. 'There are links at every level.' Teachers share schemes of work, the senior teams meet regularly, they share the same chair of governors, the two heads meet regularly and there is lots of mentoring as well as lesson observations. The same 'loyal dissent' that has characterised intellectual debate and classroom discussion at Westminster for generations is being fostered in its sapling.

Teachers here are young, energetic, and ambitious for their pupils. 'Learning is amazing' is a phrase you hear frequently and it is written all over the place, even on the cushions in Mr Handscombe's study. All pupils take four A levels, some more.

Although there are a few people with mild dyslexia, Asperger's etc, they are all high performers and have to be able to keep up. 'Provision for students with exceptional needs is via the Student Support coordinator and the Harris Federation SENCo,' says Mr Handscombe.

Results are strong. In 2018 – the third set of A level results – 47 per cent of grades were A*/A. Students take the more challenging Pre-U in a number of subjects including English literature, modern languages, Latin, art and design and art history. High percentages of students achieved a distinction in these subjects (in most subjects well over 50 per cent). 'Our students work hard at hard work,' says Mr Handscombe. The results are a by product of this, not the main end game.

Games, options, the arts: An idiosyncratic feature of extracurricular provision at HWSF is the Tuesday afternoon 'Lab' – a time for scholarly work, collaboration, one-to-one sessions with teachers, and an important building block on the path to entering the country's top universities. On the same afternoon 'Lab lectures' take place. Stimulating speakers at the top of their field come to the school to lecture, whether it be on human rights, politics, climate change or science. A select number of students are invited to principal's tea with them afterwards for the opportunity to network and discuss thoughts and ideas in a more intimate setting.

The same 'loyal dissent' that has characterised intellectual debate and classroom discussion at Westminster for generations is being fostered in its sapling

Cultural perspectives – courses not part of their A level study – form part of the timetable. For eight weeks students study three from a wide range of colourful and intellectually stimulating cross-curricular courses. These include beginners' Mandarin, business start ups, The Other in literature, gender trouble from Freud to Beyoncé and introduction to grand opera. Designed to widen cultural horizons, inform the debate and prepare for interview, the programme also helps with the schools' challenge 'to convince them that learning is amazing'.

Students also become members of a weekly subject society. A president is elected to run the society and to chair discussions and debates. In addition there is a wide range of extracurricular societies from the hugely popular Afro-Caribbean Society (ACS, which boasts over 100 members) and the Intersectional Feminist Society (the IFS, in which there are plenty of young men as well as women) to Diplomacy (a highly competitive and mind-bending board game).

All students are encouraged to play sport on Thursday afternoons ('it's part of our ethos to be fit and healthy,' says the website) at venues across London. Football and netball are co-ed, athletics buoyant. HWSF students are the reigning athletics champions in the borough of Westminster. They also do a wide range of minor sports from archery and fencing to trampolining and table tennis. Debating society and bridge club for those who would prefer not to do sport, but they are no less competitive.

Art is offered as a Pre-U and each year a few do go on to do foundation courses, to study fashion or history of art at eg the Courtauld, or to train as architects. The art room is on the seventh floor: bright, busy and creatively chaotic. Music, also on the top floor, is offered as an A level – a few take it each year – and there are individual music rooms and instruments (guitars, electric and acoustic, pianos and drum kit) for recreational purposes. Carols at Christmas, a spring concert at St Margaret's on Parliament Square, as well as a few informal performances each year, either in the classroom or in the hall on the ground floor.

The library, on the ground floor, is like a magnet. Well stocked with books (generously donated by the Wigoder family foundation) as well as with very hardworking and focused students, it is always busy. It opens at 7.30am and closes at 6.30pm, yet at the senate meeting we were fortunate enough to attend, one of the requests from the student body was that the library hours be extended.

Background and atmosphere: Founded in 2014 HWSF, as it is known, forms part of the Harris chain of academies, or MAT (multi-academy trust). The school building is essentially an office block spanning eight floors (good for fitness though you can qualify for a lift pass if you can prove a need for one). Grey, functional, clean lines, minimal decoration; if it weren't for the unmistakable buzz of young bright people you would think there was not much of an atmosphere. However, a stone's throw from St James's Park tube and a short walk from Westminster Abbey and the Houses of Parliament, you can't escape the sense of purpose and excitement of being in a historic part of London where things are made to happen.

Despite its relatively short history, tradition is important here, and we were lucky enough to be present at the leavers' ceremony for the upper sixth. It was held in the splendid Westminster Abbey, and the young students filed in below the flying buttresses, bright eyed and full of optimistic confidence to listen to the various speeches and thanks of their principal and heads of house. Humorous and erudite, the speeches reflected the intelligence and acuity of this cohort. James Handscombe's final words were significant: 'You are the brightest and the best and I hope you will remember that learning is amazing, and that one day some of you will become teachers.. give me a call if you do.' There is a barely veiled intention that some of the students will return one day and take on the mantle, whether by contributing financially or becoming part of the teaching team.

Assemblies are held in Westminster Abbey once a month, and in St Margaret's once a week. As part of the intention to create a sense of history and ethos in the school Mr Handscombe and his team, and the wider Harris MAT, have set out to instil longevity in the institution, a place that will have a dramatic and lasting impact on these young people's lives.

The main aim is that the students are taught to think for themselves and become the kind of students universities are looking for. So far the work is bearing fruit in terms of both the results they get and also how former students are faring at university. The school keeps in touch with its alumni and a key part of their work is to track their progress and development beyond their time here.

A stone's throw from St James's Park tube and a short walk from Westminster Abbey and the Houses of Parliament, you can't escape the sense of purpose and excitement

This is an institution that is not just run by the staff. The senate (student council), its president and two vice presidents (the proud wearers of yellow lanyards, setting them apart from the rest) also play a key role, as well as the house captains. Students and teachers are given equal weight in the voting process. The process is rigorous. Of the 40 who apply for membership, 20 will be interviewed and 10 appointed. The president we met could run for office, at a national level, tomorrow. Seriously impressive.

What is striking about the students here at HWSF is that their passion for learning and for scholarship is nakedly evident. Whereas their cool cousins at Westminster School might be paddling madly underneath but floating serenely on the surface, all the paddling is laid bare here, and proudly so.

Pastoral care, well-being and discipline: These are highly intelligent, high functioning young adults, who are knitted together by a shared thirst for

These are highly intelligent, high functioning young adults, who are knitted together by a shared thirst for scholarship

scholarship and who are generally held in high esteem by their teachers. They respect themselves and the institution. They look smart (dress code is suits but there is some flexibility). Behaviour is generally good. 'The most common transgression is bunking off a lesson to do other work,' says Mr Handscombe. He hopes he will never have to permanently exclude anyone, and hasn't so far; 'it will be a sign that we've failed. The secret of behaviour management is to give them learning, intellectual stimulation. They know that they have to manage themselves, and if I have to step in, we've got a problem…it's a deal, we give them excellent teaching, stimulating assemblies and talks, and they work hard and behave well.'

Pupils and parents: Looking over the sea of 250 pupils in year 12, the immediate impression is the racial mix. No one culture, religion or skin colour dominates. For many, English is their second language and some need support with their English. Some 40 per cent of pupils are on pupil premium. They come from schools all over London and some from as far as Essex and Kingston, Bromley and Barnet. One of our stunningly intelligent and articulate guides said with complete poise, 'A lot of students go out to get their lunch; I always eat in the canteen though as I am pupil premium.'

The largest proportions currently come from Lewisham, Westminster and Croydon. No-one knows anyone else when they arrive, however. There are no large swathes of pupils from a particular school or area. What these pupils have in common is a love of learning and thirst for intellectual rigour. 'It's the scholarly engagement that is key to the melting pot,' says Handscombe, 'and we will fight to preserve that'. One pupil admitted, 'I didn't know what scholar meant before I came here.'

We often found it difficult to distinguish pupils from teachers. Many teachers are young, most pupils mature, confident, assertive but relaxed. Students here are polite, but not overly deferential. They look you in the eye and politely disagree.

Entrance: Students choose to be tested in the two favourite subjects that they want to study for A level. Some 80 per cent take maths exams. There is a mixture of translating and writing for languages, and essays in the humanities and English.

Physics exams consist of standard science questions with a focus on problem solving. The content is relatively basic (year 10 standard) but the questions harder than GCSE standard. Promising candidates can choose the subject they would like to be interviewed in – 'We want to see how clever they are – we're interested in their teachability, enthusiasm, aptitude, speed of learning and ownership of learning,' says Mr Handscombe.

A maximum 650 are interviewed from (in the recent intake) over 1,500 applications for 300 places, with priority to those on pupil premium who reach the required standard.

Exit: To a wide range of universities, including Bristol, Manchester, Royal Holloway and Queen Mary as well as Oxbridge. In the third batch of leavers, 18 students secured places at Oxbridge and one went off to Harvard. They choose a wide range of courses. Popular ones included economics, law, physics and biomedical sciences. Some seepage at the end of year 12, with around 10 per cent likely to trip over the requirement to achieve at least four Ds in end of year 12 exams.

Remarks: A melting pot of the brightest and best pupils from all over London. HWSF is a genuinely stimulating and scholarly environment in which to study. The end game isn't to get into top universities, though that is what most students do, but to instil a love of learning and breadth of knowledge that will serve these students well throughout their lives. Students feel fortunate to be there. The staff feel privileged to teach them. A stunning combination.

Heathside Preparatory School

16 New End, London NW3 1JA

020 7794 5857 | info@heathsideprep.co.uk | heathsideprep.co.uk

| Independent | Pupils: 400; boarders: 15 |
| Ages: 2–15 (boarding from 10) | Fees: £15,600 pa |

Headmistress: Since the school's foundation in 1993, Melissa Remus Elliot MA PG Dip (50s), who is also joint owner. She grew up all over the US, following her father's work, and attended Duke University and The American University, Washington. She worked as a Washington intern and on several Broadway shows before moving to the UK and becoming a teacher. During three years' teaching she formulated an idea of her ideal school and set up Heathside with her business partner and co-head (now retired), Jill White, becoming the youngest head teacher in the country in her 20s. She also got an MA in counselling aspects of education at The Tavistock Clinic.

Married with four children, all at or graduated from Heathside, 'which gives me a good insight into what actually goes on in the classrooms'. Overflowing praise from parents: 'a very open-minded and dynamic person, relentlessly striving to find ways to make the school better'; 'open and honest in a very refreshing way'; 'both pragmatic and inspirational'; 'extraordinary ability to retain a thorough portrait of each child'; 'unbelievably energetic and gung-ho'.

Academic matters: The school is not selective and the broad range of ability is addressed by excellent ('exceptional,' says Ofsted) teaching, with plenty of assistants in the younger years, and small groups, particularly for maths. ('Children learn in different ways,' says the head. 'We have up to nine groups in one year.') The staff, many-long serving and well-qualified (a Cambridge PhD, for example, is a recent recruit), are notably impressive, with an assured command of their subjects, and the ability to impose discipline and engage interest with the minimum of effort. Children settle instantly, seem really enthused, and concentrate well despite visitor distractions.

The curriculum has been lauded by Ofsted as 'exemplary', and mainstream subject teaching (with specialist teaching from year 3) is approached with imaginative vigour – so year 6s are absorbing poetry, history, the classical tradition and the art of storytelling by comparing The Odyssey with John Wyndham's The Day of the Triffids (discovering that the latter provides a rather pacier intro). Maths and science, too, are celebrated and made fun with an action-packed Science Week and activities such as National Pi Day. French taught throughout, Latin added in year 2. Clubs for German, Italian, Mandarin. Pupils are unusually confident, articulate and lively. 'We have a new word in the vocabulary – volatile,' said a teacher. 'Not new at Heathside,' quipped a year 6 wit.

Heathside has always been a school where learning rather than testing is the priority, but, until recently, 11+ has necessarily been a pressure point. The expansion of the school to GCSE is helping to ease the tension. Too much so for some (one year 5 parent complained, 'The only specific 11+ preparation my son is getting is an extracurricular class at 8am in the morning'). Another mentioned the dreaded 't' word.

Year 6s are absorbing poetry, history, the classical tradition and the art of storytelling by comparing The Odyssey with John Wyndham's The Day of the Triffids

Few pupils with a statement of special needs (none at the time of the last Ofsted inspection), but dyslexics and dyspraxics are well supported by a full-time SENCo. Most learn, at no extra charge, in compatible groups ('Everyone has different learning styles; with some kids the penny drops and they're away,' says the head). One-on-one support also available at an additional cost. The school copes imaginatively, too, with those on the foothills of English. (Recent arrivals, for example, were prepared for joining a class studying Romeo and Juliet, by reading the play in their native language the day before.) Those with autism or severe Asperger's would struggle ('There's too much activity,' says Melissa), and Heathside does not admit those with behavioural difficulties: 'They need a bit more space to iron out their problems.'

Games, options, the arts: The dazzling extracurricular offers a rich counterpoint to the main programme. Long-serving head of music directs a packed schedule of choirs, chamber groups (cello, strings), bands (rock and jazz), senior orchestra, and individual instrumental lessons with dynamic efficiency. Drama, too, is approached with US-style energy, and recent productions of Bugsy Malone, West Side Story, Lion King, Guys and Dolls encourage whole school involvement by alternating up to seven casts. Those looking for official recognition of their diction and projection take LAMDA awards. 'We want to provide them with skills for life.'

Not the school if manicured acres of playing fields are a must, but despite its decidedly challenged outdoor space, exercise and sport are creatively and effectively addressed. Neatly serried rows of muddy wellies testify to the fact that Hampstead Heath, a five-minute walk away, is essentially the school playground, with most pupils spending time there most days, overseen by a forest school trained teacher. ('The way they use the Heath is one of the main reasons I sent my daughter here; it's a wonderful resource,' said one father.) More formal instruction is carried out at a variety of nearby leisure facilities (Swiss Cottage and UCS), while specialist coaches for cricket and football ensure teams (many unisex) do well (though perhaps not quite as well as claimed) against schools of a similar size and bigger. Sports day held at nearby Parliament Hill Fields running track. 'I really feel there is enough sport here for even the sportiest child,' said one parent. The senior school offers kung fu and tai chi and intends to become a centre of excellence for tennis.

A wide range of after-school clubs, with chess notably strong (Heathside has been the English Primary School Chess champion for eight years), and regular trips (to Surrey, Dorset, Iceland), as well as outings to West End shows, museums, art galleries, etc.

Boarding: Now plays host to a small number of boarders in the Heathside High building. During its emergency inspection in June 2018, Ofsted found the management 'disorganised and unsafe' (the head of boarding had recently left), though pupils told inspectors they were happy, with 'lots to do'.

Background and atmosphere: Founded in 1993 on the site of a former prep school, the younger years occupy a warren of intertwined buildings in the centre of Hampstead village, with the littlest contained in a converted and extended church hall (used for gym, yoga, music and drama, as well as assemblies). A second building, just around the corner, was only occupied by year 4 when we visited (and, as a result, seemed a remarkable oasis of calm).

The new senior school, Heathside High (you can see the musical already), contains years 5 to 10, and will gradually provide an education up to GCSE (and, perhaps, beyond). Linked by a shuttle bus with the Hampstead site, it sits in a quiet and leafy residential street, a five-minute walk from Golder's Green station. Housed in what was once a turn-of-the-century mansion (and, more recently, a nursing home), it is well equipped and exceptionally light throughout.

Pastoral care, well-being and discipline: Parents uniformly praise the family atmosphere. 'We chose this school because of its reputation for being warm and nurturing,' said one parent, 'and it's been just that.' Children clearly feel completely at home,

North Bridge House Pre-Prep School

'Would you like a cake?' one child kindly offered visiting parents; 'I like your earrings,' another complimented Melissa. The school even has an in-house dog, Ziggy (acquired on the day Bowie died). Like all the best homes, there can occasionally be a slight sense of chaos on the admin side. 'We'll suddenly get a message that there's a school trip the next day,' said one mother, and the website is not always up-to-the-minute, but the promise of a fire pit with hot chocolate can sweeten even these tribulations. 'The confidence and happiness of the children is the most important thing,' says Melissa, and few here would doubt she's got her priorities right.

Pupils and parents: Heathside has its fair share of evidently affluent families (from around the world), but equally attracts more low-key locals from quite a wide tranche of north London, who've often started out elsewhere and turned to Heathside desperately seeking an alternative. (One family got an instantly sympathetic hearing for their 5 year old who 'felt stupid' at his local primary.) 'It's a rat race out there,' says the head, 'and parents say, I don't want any of that for my kid. We want parents who share our philosophy.'

Entrance: At 2 and 3 into the tiny nursery (places, at this point, mainly to siblings and those who sign up from the delivery room). Expands into three classes of 15 in reception. Melissa also does her best to accommodate those who've missed the boat, but are struggling elsewhere, and claims she receives 'a deluge from the state sector in year 7'. Queues, too, in year 3 – the hardest year to get into. Prospective entrants visit for a day to ensure they're a good fit.

Exit: A smattering to selective schools at 7. Prepares everyone for 11+, making sure grammar, punctuation, spelling and maths are more than up to speed. The majority happily proceed to the usual range of local independents (Highgate, UCS, North Bridge etc), often with scholarships, as well as to top-of-the-range Westminster and St Paul's. Now the senior school is up and running (with year 9 and 10s), some parents (and pupils) are heaving a sigh of relief.

Remarks: A Hampstead prep rapidly expanding into an all-through school, with, as one parent described it, 'an adventurous, common-sense and human approach'.

Hereward House School

14 Strathray Gardens, London NW3 4NY

020 7794 4820 | office@herewardhouse.co.uk | herewardhouse.co.uk

Independent	Pupils: 172
Ages: 4–13	Fees: £16,500 – £16,950 pa

Headmaster: Since 2014, Pascal Evans (40s), formerly at Westminster Under and Colet Court. Gentle, reflective, low-key – but do not be deceived: Mr Evans has a very supple mind (with a law degree from Oxford) and is a man of wide-ranging talents and interests – passionately interested in football, and a serious runner who still puts in some 40 miles a week. 'I like the thinking time,' he says. 'Most of the knottier problems can be untangled in the course of a longish run'. Married with a Japanese wife and two teenage daughters – both trilingual.

Entrance: Most boys arrive in the September following their 4th birthday. As one might expect of a relatively small school which lies in the heart of Belsize Park, it's heavily oversubscribed. But Mr Evans and his colleagues are emphatic that they want an entrance process which is humane, conducted according to a criteria that is rational and democratic. Parents need to try to get their sons' names down by 2, but the testing is very gentle and every effort is made to take siblings of existing pupils. The emphasis is to identify families who can share the school's values and ethos and enable them to work for the best interests of the child. 'As the boys grow older it's always reassuring if one spots a child who, say, loves music, or sport,' says the head, 'quite as much as a potential scholar. But we're also looking to see if we can help them to taste or become immersed in new experiences.'

Obviously, there are a lot of Hampstead children here, but the reach goes further than that – lots from Islington as well as others from central London. There's some busy school bussing, but lots of tube and bus rides, as well – inevitably – as journeying on foot and by car.

Exit: Destinations testify to the school's ability to cater handsomely for the upper as well as less lofty academic echelons. 'Unstinting time spent on individual children,' said a parent, 'and an equal commitment to the needs of different children are having a big impact on selection.' When pre-testing was introduced by many top senior schools, a range of good prep schools found some pupils unexpectedly short of offers. There are indications that Hereward House was, briefly, among them – but, if so, it certainly wised up very quickly. Locals UCS and Highgate most popular destinations in 2018, but also Westminster, Haileybury (scholarship), St Albans, Mill Hill and Brighton College (scholarship) – as head says, 'pastoral boarding at its best can be transformative for some boys'. This kind of 'catholicity' used to be typical of London prep schools, but vaulting parental ambition of the last two decades can all too easily leave children and parents feeling second best. It is much to the credit of Mr Evans and his staff that they want no part of that.

Remarks: One of the charms of Hereward House is that it is small enough to be intimate – people know one another. The youngest children are carefully nurtured in basic social skills and helped towards physical literacy. Music and games, play and art and drama are all given due emphasis. Of course, all the time this is going on they are receiving a careful grounding in the rudiments of reading and writing and numeracy, which serves as an excellent springboard for the time when they gradually gravitate away from the form teacher to subject specialists.

Because of the size, systems here can be low-key. There are fewer than 20 staff members, but they tend to be versatile as well as highly capable. Obviously, the need for expertise is understood: there are two permanent special needs teachers and extra assistants brought in as required. But the culture supports turning one's hand to come-what-may: the headmaster teaches a decent number of lessons and views marking prep, setting classes and carrying chairs up and downstairs as a natural and perfectly appropriate task. The supremely capable director of music is also head of classics. In a modest-sized school, everyone pitches into the drama – the majority of senior boys were heavily involved in the recent production of The Sound of Music. 'Staff here,' says the head admiringly, 'just knuckle down. I find their example continually reassuring and admirable.' In the words of one parent: 'The teaching my son is receiving is of the highest calibre – the delivery is sympathetic and often original, and the substance is challenging'.

The potential downside of 'smallness' of course, could be the lack of choice. The 2016 ISI report, while mainly very complimentary, did suggest that the extracurricular curriculum lacked an element of range as well as some ICT provision. The school has since invested heavily in both hardware and systems management, and the results are welcomed by all parties, although the school website feels mundane and clearly needs some love. Philosophy and Mandarin have also been introduced and new clubs have appeared – coding, Greek and LAMDA (arts and drama) all have their own enthusiastic followers. 'He has more after-school clubs from which to choose than he can ever manage,' said a parent, 'and he comes home enthused'.

A serious runner who still puts in some 40 miles a week. 'I like the thinking time,' he says. 'Most of the knottier problems can be untangled in the course of a longish run'

Above all, there is no trade-off in terms of quality. Because the school is on a relatively small site, there may be a patronising assumption on the part of bigger preps that their own standards are higher. Yet the academics and music at Hereward House are outstanding and the drama and the sport are excellent. Given the number of pupils, it doesn't field the endless numbers of teams of the bigger prep schools, but plays excellent football, cricket and cross-country and uses local facilities (whether it's Primrose Hill for the youngest children or Brondesbury Cricket Club for the older ones) to best advantage. Nor has it sacrificed choice – judo, basketball, hockey and tennis are among other sports played to a high standard. Results hold up well and – admittedly it's not yet a premier league sport – the school's five-a-side soccer players can hold up their heads with the very best.

The school's biennial music concert may not be held in a state-of-the-art 21st century acoustically-perfect concert hall in school grounds, but it's a powerful expression of schoolwide dedication and there are ensembles concerts every term which draw in roughly half the school ('and there are many, many other boys doing excellent music in addition to these,' says the head.) 'Outstanding,' said one parent with a very musical child. 'How they bring off this range of talent and dedication in a small school defies all probability'. It's unsurprising, then, that Hereward House pupils have won top musical awards to Eton and Westminster in the past two years. There's also been a surge of popularity in recent times in chess, which is a lesson in forms 2 and 3. 'It's a great activity,' says the head, 'and a powerful education in its own right. I'm glad some of our boys are proving highly successful at it, but what I really value is that it's reaching out to all levels here.'

In the 2016 ISI report, inspectors raised an eyebrow at a system of governance. It isn't hard to see why: the founding head (and still proprietor) is chair of governors. Her grandson is the bursar, and the previous head (who departed at the end of 2014) sits on the governing body. And yet, like all quasi-family schools, the potential downsides are nullified when relationships between the key players are strong, and a former senior school head has recently become a governor. Mr Evans exudes calm and satisfaction, and demonstrably believes he has the latitude to function effectively while benefiting from the support of those who have known the school longest of all.

We saw impressively relaxed and happy staff and children, and this – given the constraints of space – suggests that every aspect of pupils' lives has been thoughtfully and effectively considered. 'In six years as a parent,' said one mother, 'there's never been a day when either of mine haven't wanted to go to school. I don't take that for granted.' There's also lots of good interaction with the local community, enacted through fundraising

> 'In six years as a parent,' said one mother, 'there's never been a day when either of mine haven't wanted to go to school'

initiatives, fun runs, a carol service at the local church and links with the Simon Community for the homeless. Facilities are good (a lab had just been upgraded and the playground relaid when we came round) but there's an eye to what's practical and reasonable, rather than lavish – and therein lies a clue to the underlying ethos of the school. It wants its pupils to give their best in every area of school life and, perhaps above all, to find ways to be themselves while always behaving generously to others. To execute that vision, in the heart of one of the most affluent and challenging parental constituencies in the prep school world, demands clarity of vision and steadfastness of purpose. The head's low-key manner, and his gentle appreciation of his staff, pupils and parents speaks not just well of him and of them, but also suggests the governors who appointed him know their school as well as their man.

Holy Trinity & St Silas

Hartland Road, London NW1 8DE

020 7267 0771 | admin@holytrinitynw1.camden.sch.uk | camden.schooljotter.com/holytrinitynw1

State	Pupils: 210
Ages: 4–11	

Head: Since 2013, Lorraine Dolan (40s) BEd and masters in education, both from the University of North London. Her first job as an NQT in 1996 was at Holy Trinity and St Silas; 'My plan was never to stay at the same school for long but to have an open mind.' However, when Annie Williams took over as head of the school in 2001, Ms Dolan, who respected her greatly, found it difficult to move on. Fourteen years later Ms Dolan started to get 'itchy feet', and when Annie Williams took a sabbatical Ms Dolan became acting deputy head and from there decided to move into leadership. She subsequently left Holy Trinity to take up the post as deputy head at St Paul's Catholic school in Wood Green. Although she says her time there was a 'great experience',

she couldn't achieve what she wanted as a deputy head. When Ms Williams died in 2012, Ms Dolan had begun looking at headship and when the post was advertised, she applied, believing that she had the skills, understanding and experience to drive the school forward.

Tall, with waist-long fair hair, Ms Dolan looks on first impression like someone who might be in the world of media rather than a primary school head teacher. Although softly spoken and friendly, this ex-convent school girl is definitely no pushover and hides a steely determination. It is a prerequisite for this job. Any weaker souls would not survive the legacy of the former head teacher, who changed the fortunes of a not particularly good school to an 'exceptional school' (in the words of Ofsted) and was a woman who had edited the word 'compromise' from her vocabulary. Ms Dolan says, 'Annie was a force to be reckoned with.' Ms Dolan offers a more 'open door policy' than her predecessor and welcomes parent inclusion in the school. One pupil told us, 'she's very approachable and a great role model.'

She has been described by a parent as being 'very old school, in a good way.' She is very intent on bringing traditional values back into the school and has particularly clamped down on the school uniform, which was a bit hit and miss prior to her headship. As she points out, 'You either have a uniform policy or you don't; you can't have a bit of a uniform.' Another parent told us that Ms Dolan 'doesn't rest on the laurels of Ms Williams and wants to make her own mark. She is around most of the time and is often chatting to parents in the playground.'

Ms Dolan has a grown up son, whom she had in her early 20s, and who, she says, 'has been the making of me in many ways.' The product of Irish Catholic parents, Ms Dolan went to a convent school, where she says she was 'often challenging the system'. Her son forced her to be responsible, and although she wasn't thinking of a career in education at that time, was accepted onto a Montessori teaching course, 'which was perfect as I could take my son with me and leave him at the nursery'. Little did she suspect then where that first rung up the ladder would eventually lead. She and her long term partner are both members of a cycling club, and she also enjoys running: 'Keeping fit is a great outlet for stress.'

Entrance: After the customary priority for looked-after children, the primary admissions criterion is church attendance, either at The Most Holy Trinity Church across the road or at St Silas the Martyr in Kentish Town. Approx 60 per cent come via this route; the remaining 40 per cent of admissions are catchment based. When Ms Williams became head, the school was very much bottom of the parental-choice agenda, but the intake has altered and now gets more professional parents – particularly in creative and media related fields. Not too many, school hopes – 'we have a good social mix and want to keep it that way'. At the moment, remains a class and ethnic melting pot, with the largest minority being Bangladeshi.

Exit: Mainly to the local comprehensives – Haverstock, William Ellis, Parliament Hill, St Marylebone and Camden School for Girls – but school has also developed a relationship with The Hall, one of north London's leading prep schools, and some year 6 boys go there with bursaries before proceeding to leading London independent day schools.

Remarks: Housed in a typical Victorian school-house, a meander from tourist-packed Camden Lock; one has to enter two heavy-duty doors to reach the main reception – the first to the playground and the second to the main building: 'We qualified for extra security', the head told us (part of their recent funding programme). However, once inside with its pristine, soothing interior, you'd never guess where you were – fresh flowers, polished parquet and a big red school bell are all from another era.

Teaching at the school is strong; a number of parents have pointed this out and cited a couple of exceptional teachers, one of whom – Kirsty Mccreadie, the current deputy head – held the school together after the previous head's departure and is described by parents as 'simply the most exceptional, passionate teacher – the cornerstone of the school'. Ms Dolan herself has been very successful in turning the maths results around – something she has been working hard to address. When she first came on board, results had been dipping, but her close monitoring seems to have worked – more or less everyone gets at least level 4 Sats, with around two-thirds now reaching level 5+.

We were particularly struck by an astonishing ceiling display of famous London landmarks – the London Eye, St Paul's Cathedral etc – all made from papier mâché

The teaching staff are generally well qualified, with two MAs, one law degree, three teachers who speak fluent French (so French is taught convincingly from reception to year 2), and a couple of graduate teaching assistants who, according to Ms Dolan, arrived with 'passion and drive'. The excellent teaching is partly the legacy of Ms Williams, who had said: 'I'm very snobbish about teachers – they have to have been to a good university and to have travelled. It gives them a cultural understanding', and partly due to the current head who adds: 'All the teachers are clear about my expectations. It's not OK for one child to slip through the net.'

Despite the fact that the majority of pupils arrive at Holy Trinity with well below average attainment, the school is at the pinnacle of the league tables, with results in English in the top one per cent nationally. Literacy is taught for two hours a day, primarily through poetry and prose. This again, we are told, is largely down to another inspirational teacher – Luke Williams, a specialist drama teacher who teaches English and drama from reception to year 6, through the works of

Shakespeare. Every year the school puts on a whole-school Shakespeare play, including every pupil and member of staff, and has now helped found a borough-wide Shakespeare festival with five neighbouring primaries. Hardly surprising then that, according to Ofsted: 'Pupils' empathy with the works of Shakespeare is quite remarkable'.

All the arts are fundamental to the curriculum. Music is central to the school and one parent told us that music largely formed her decision to send her daughter there: 'The school just feels amazing when you walk in. There is the sound of laughter and always someone playing the piano or another instrument.' Pupils can choose to join the jazz band or one of two choirs, or learn an instrument from a long list of specialist music teachers. However, drop-ins on any of the music groups have been abolished in favour of auditioning for them, as the head firmly believes, 'if you make that sort of commitment, you need to stick to it.'

Art is equally important, and despite limited square footage, has its own department; pupils' work is hung boldly throughout the building. Painting even spills out into the large urban playground (underneath the rattling of the Camden overground train), where one inner-city wall has been reborn as a rural, summer scene (with a 3D vegetable plot to extend the experience). We were particularly struck by an astonishing ceiling display in the upper school hall of famous London landmarks – the London Eye, St Paul's Cathedral etc, all made from papier mâché. The idea for this came from a walk around London with year 6 pupils, who were learning about architecture (from a parent architect) inspired by the imminent development works to the school. One parent told us: 'We're so lucky at this school, there is such a pool of talented and creative parents who can come in and share their skills.' Trips are very much part of the education. Visits to the theatre, opera, ballet and museums are planned on a regular basis.

Mealtimes are also a development opportunity: music is played and, on Fridays, tablecloths laid

Though about 40 per cent of pupils are not Anglicans, the Christian message is strong, with a thoroughly involved parish priest (Father Graham), regular church attendance and class mass held half termly. Grace is said before lunch. Lunch itself is entirely healthy, and mealtimes, too, are considered a development opportunity. Music is played and, on Fridays, tablecloths laid. A firm emphasis on good manners. The 'golden rules' dictate: don't talk with your mouth full; learn to use your knife

---

One parent told us: 'We're so lucky, there is such a pool of talented and creative parents who can come in and share their skills'

and fork correctly. Rules elsewhere are equally clear cut. Attentive good behaviour is the norm, but for those who stray, the first offence means displacement to another class; further disruption means an encounter with the head.

Although standards may be firmly upheld, one parent complained that the pastoral care system is not great and there isn't much of a structure in place. However, the head says that whilst historically issues were not dealt with, she 'has worked very hard to get parents to trust that when they raise a concern about their child, whether emotional or academic, it will be dealt with and monitored.' The children are supported by the class teachers. They have weekly circle time sessions and are encouraged to share their concerns as well as develop their understanding about relationships with their peers.

The school takes a proactive approach to its parents, and offers core subject curriculum evenings to support parents with home learning. Parents respond with energetic fundraising – the PTA raises on average £4,000-£5,000 a year which goes towards buying new computers. Ms Williams herself was no ingénue when it came to fundraising and won considerable support from charities – a legacy continued after her death, with the Annie Williams Education Trust, set up by her husband, which has already received many donations.

Plans are currently under way to expand the school building and make it more accessible, the school being one of 10 schools in Camden identified as in need of updating. This will include a three storey extension at the side to house a new office, reception area and staff room and will allow the hall downstairs to be opened up into a large performance space. Classrooms will be increased in size (as they are rather on the snug side) and a lift will be installed, as this old Victorian building is currently unsuitable for anyone with a disability.

'Superb' is Ofsted's summary of the Holy Trinity and St Silas experience, and pupils agree: 'We love it here, we don't want to leave,' said one year 6 pupil. And a parent added: 'I just love the mixed demographic and the fact that everyone talks to everyone. I once saw David Miliband [a former parent], in the playground chatting to a mother in flip flops and pyjama bottoms, about the best pirate parties for boys.'

Hugh Myddelton Primary School

Myddelton Street, London EC1R 1YJ

020 7278 6075 | admin@humydd.islington.sch.uk | hughmyddeltonschool.org.uk

State	Pupils: 482
Ages: 2–11	

Executive Head: Since 2013, Nathalie Parker, BMus (King's College, London), PGCE (Goldsmiths), BSc psychology (Birkbeck). After various posts in south London including deputy head at an all-through academy, glamorous, smoky-eyed Ms Parker (40s) arrived at what, unexpectedly for her, turned out to be a school in difficulties. 'Its Ofsted and data suggested it was a good school, so when it was immediately put on warning notice it came as a shock.' Even so, she took the challenge in her stride, turning around the culture of the school in a matter of months and recently earning from Ofsted the most outstanding of outstanding reports. Charming and persuasive, she is lavished with praise by inspectors and parents. 'Inspirational,' say the former; 'visionary,' chorused a parent. 'She's very good at team building and organising, and is completely non-ideological in the best possible sense. She's prepared to use what works.'

Head of school: is Tim Barber, BA history (King's College, London), PGCE (Manchester). Now that Ms Parker is spreading her expertise across the local authority, Mr Barber is responsible for the school on a daily basis. After work at primaries in the north of England and north London, he started at Hugh Myddelton as a year 2 teacher in 2011, and has since done virtually every job going. 'It been quite fast moving,' he notes with understatement. Down-to-earth, friendly and enthusiastic, he's also immensely hard working and committed. 'The two make an extraordinarily dynamic duo,' commented a parent.

Entrance: After an understandable dip in applications, word of improvement has now spread and queues are starting to form. This is a community primary so, once the usual reserved categories have been addressed, siblings and distance from the gates are next in line.

Exit: Strenuous efforts are made to ensure every pupil finds the right secondary, whether that's at a local comp (City of London Academy, Highbury Fields), selective state (Dame Alice Owen's, Queen Elizabeth Barnet), or independent (Highgate, City of

London boys and girls, Christ's Hospital). Eleven plus preparation given for entrance tests and interviews, and high flying year 5 girls encouraged to attend City of London School for Girls summer school.

Remarks: What's extraordinary about Hugh Myddelton is the rapidity of its progress from floundering to fantastic, moving from 'causing concern' to can't-say-a-word-against-it in just three years. (Nowadays, it sits in the top three per cent of all schools in England for pupils' progress in reading, writing and maths, and most whizz comfortably beyond the national norm.) The formula for its success lies in excellent teaching, exceptional teamwork and a relentless focus on the needs of every child, starting with incoming 2 year olds, who are given a speech-and-language fillip to ensure they're reception ready. Reading taught as early as possible, through phonics, corridor walls decorated with common words, and a 'talk-for-writing' strategy (originally introduced for those on the foothills of English, now working well for all).

Overall approach is 'keep up, not catch up', supported through tailored work and one-to-one tuition where necessary

Teachers consult daily to ensure each child is receiving what they require, and subject-specialist teams work across the age groups. 'In the English team, for example, all the teachers will look at each book, identifying what's being done well, what's needed to improve.' The overall approach is 'keep up, not catch up', supported through tailored work and one-to-one tuition where necessary. Once reading, everyone is given challenging texts, and writing standards are truly impressive. Year 5 and 6 benefit from an additional teacher, bringing class numbers down to 18-20, ensuring everybody gets added focus in these critical final years.

Special needs particularly well supported, with two internal teachers, a speech-and-language specialist and Ms Parker's psychology-informed background. Teaching assistants given specific training, too, and external experts called on as needed. Those who arrive with little English well catered for ('When my daughter started, she was groping for words,' said one parent. 'Now she loves English.') as are the gifted and talented – the school works with The National Association for Able Children (NACE). 'They're completely aware of who the kids are and are very good at getting everyone to learn without making them feel like losers or driving them to distraction,' said one father. 'They stretch them, but never push them too far.' Homework is made fun with six-week topic-based projects, produced with teacher and parent help, and displayed in the dedicated 'homework gallery'.

Virtually every child reaches the government targets in national tests, but tests are certainly not the main objective of the education here and the curriculum is broad and stimulating ('exciting,' say the inspectors). All taught Spanish by a native speaker ('Though we're thinking of moving to Mandarin,' says the head). Expansive new science and technology room allows hands-on experience of everything from cooking to stargazing. Well stocked library is the venue for book club and a welcoming place for older pupils to listen to younger ones read. Technology well supported with a plethora of chrome books and iPads, but personal mobiles locked safely away every morning on arrival.

Much-enjoyed forest school takes place in Abney Park, Stoke Newington, developing appreciation of the natural world, confidence and independence

Ms Parker, a composer by training, came to the school with the brief of improving the arts and sport, and, alongside her multitude of other achievements, these goals have been fully realised. A music specialist now works with classroom teachers, all learn recorder in year 3, keyboard skills in year 5, and singing thrives with junior and senior choirs. Free clarinet and brass tuition put into practice in school band. Music made real, too, with visits to orchestras at the Barbican and Royal Festival Hall. The visual arts also well supported by Islington Arts Factory, and the school has partnered with neighbouring Sadler's Wells Theatre, bringing subsidised tickets and opportunities to perform.

Generous, well kept grounds, Astroturf pitch and well-equipped gym are all put to good use, with a specialist sports coach teaching hockey, tennis and multi-sports. Basketball and football on offer before school, and after-school clubs include karate, gymnastics and street dance. All interests catered for, however, with clubs for Gutsy Girls (to encourage female leadership), archaeology and debate (with pupils excelling in Debate Mate primary-school league.). Much-enjoyed forest school ('Forest school is number one,' said a pupil) takes place in Abney Park in Stoke Newington, developing appreciation of the natural world alongside confidence and independence. High aspirations fostered, too, by 'spotlight days', when pupils visit City University and talk to students about law, computer science, engineering and psychology. Breakfast and after-school club are a boon for working parents.

Named for Hugh Myddelton, royal jeweller to James 1, the school was originally founded in the 1850s, but moved to its current building – a mid-century gem by Julian Sofaer – in the 1960s. A dazzling new extension added in 2009 was opened by former pupil Cat Stevens. The composite provides a luminous and harmonious backdrop to the calm, well organised and purposeful atmosphere within. Classrooms and corridors are spacious and bright, outside space, blessed by an electronic noticeboard and covered picnic tables, an oasis of green in a gritty urban world.

Behaviour, once something of an issue, is now acknowledged by Ofsted to be 'impeccable'. 'Children won't accept poor behaviour,' says the head. 'They're horrified if someone doesn't open a door.' The 'manners curriculum' focuses on topics such as 'meeting and greeting' and 'how to disagree politely', within an overall culture where the dominant motif is praise rather than blame (with parents regularly alerted to the positive through electronic ClassDojo system).

Pupils given plenty of responsibility – on the school council, as head boy and girl, as anti-bullying champions (the school belongs to the Anti-Bullying Alliance and bullying is a rarity). The message: 'Be reflective, responsible and respectful' is also regularly addressed in assemblies, which explore big world issues (gun law, Brexit, equal pay, etc) in 'thought for the week'. 'I'm so impressed by their general knowledge,' said one mother; while another admires the empathy this instils. 'My 6-year-old son came home the other day and said "I'll get you some money from my money box because women don't earn as much men".' Community engagement also firmly emphasised, and pupils recently won a competition with the bright idea of exchanging their own technical expertise with gardening help from the elderly.

Though money, as always, is tight, the head has been clever at tapping in to local resources, such as The Worshipful Company of Water Conservators and Thames Water, who helped fund the science room, and Foyles, who contributed to the library. Nearby City University provides volunteer students for extra tuition.

About 60 per cent of pupils at Hugh Myddelton are in receipt free school meals, but local professionals are increasingly in evidence. What's more, parental attitudes throughout have changed. 'When we started,' says the head, 'there was a sense of apathy, even hostility, a real sense of them and us.' That's definitely a thing of the past. 'Everything about this school is fantastic,' exclaimed one parent. 'My kids complain when it's the holidays,' said another. A year 6 who's gone through the revolution agrees with both: 'It's now an exciting place to come to school.' Wide ethnic mix, with no dominant group, and kids mix well in school and out. 'The kids love each other and spend a lot of time together. There's a real sense of community.'

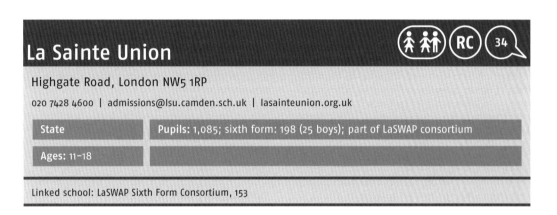

La Sainte Union

Highgate Road, London NW5 1RP

020 7428 4600 | admissions@lsu.camden.sch.uk | lasainteunion.org.uk

State	Pupils: 1,085; sixth form: 198 (25 boys); part of LaSWAP consortium
Ages: 11–18	

Linked school: LaSWAP Sixth Form Consortium, 153

Headteacher: Since September 2017, Sophie Fegan, 40s. Frenchwoman Mrs Fegan (who retains a slight accent) began at the school teaching French in 2008. Since then, she's moved up the ranks from (popular) teacher, to head of year, then deputy head, so no radical changes expected now she's in the top spot. (Though consultations are taking place with girls on ways to improve the school – and tartan trousers could, one day, be an option.) Smartly suited, earnest, evidently devout, she sees the school's mission as promoting 'gospel values so that girls can go on to lead good Christian lives.'

Academic matters: The head is emphatic that this is a 'traditional school offering a traditional curriculum with "no short cuts"': 'We aim to nurture a love of learning, engaging with difficult things and exposing learners to high culture.' (So, year 9 study the work of Bertolt Brecht and Arthur Miller, as well as French poet Lamartine.) Teaching, too, on traditional lines (ie silent, orderly and attentive), with classrooms staffed by the bright-eyed, enthusiastic and energetic. ('Teachers are kind and they help you learn,' said one girl; 'We really trust the teachers,' said another.) Work appropriately challenging and fast paced (a forest of 12-year-old hands, for example, was raised to define the meaning of 'variegated'). GCSE results are strong (81 per cent got 9-4 in both English and maths in 2018; 29 per cent 9-7 grades), particularly in English; RS also noticeably (if, perhaps, unsurprisingly) buoyant.

Inspectors, however, have voiced concerned about the relative weakness of science and maths, and, in 2017, under the new exam system, GCSE maths undoubtedly seemed a bit wavery, with nearly a third missing out on that critical grade 4. 'Maths took a dip,' admitted one teacher, 'but there's an action plan to rectify it.' And indeed in 2018, 82 per cent of pupils did get at least a grade 4. Post-GCSE, membership of LaSWAP sixth form consortium allows a wide choice of courses (over 30 A levels, from further maths to film studies, plus numerous vocational qualifications) either on site or at one of the sister schools, and sixth formers are given very good support.

Pupils, many joining from Catholic primaries, typically start out strong and just get stronger. Testing carried out in year 7 to assess 'needs', then broad banding applied, but no setting. Instead, the school uses carefully considered 'strategies' to address the requirements of its wide ability range. 'We don't say: you're bright, you're not bright. We teach them how to get where they want through hard work and love of learning.' Progress, as the head notes, is 'phenomenal' (significantly above the national average). Those requiring additional assistance are quickly identified, monitored by a senior member of staff, dedicated SENDCo, learning support assistants and SEN governor, and aided by small classes for English and maths, literacy and numeracy catch-up groups, and external help where needed.

Facilities generally good and up to date but, at least in some subjects, a distinctly old-world mood prevails. In DT, for example, the priority is for girls to 'make sure they can make their own clothes', with the advice that the best preparation for starting at the school is knowing how to thread a sewing machine! (First efforts – a small dress – are then sent to an orphanage in Tanzania.)

Games, options, the arts: Impressive extracurricular, with a stimulating range of activities available before and after school and at lunchtime. (Everything from Afro culture to Manga, feminist committee to cheerleading, gardening to first aid.) All the arts flourish ('We want students to have access to cultural capital'), but music a notable strength with instrumental lessons in everything from violin to bassoon, and plenty of opportunity to put skills into practice (school orchestra, soul/jazz group, gospel choir, chapel choir, regular concerts, chapel music tour). Annual art competition, poetry workshops, cross-school drama production (most recently The Crucible) encourage creativity, plus good use made of what London has to offer, with the curriculum abandoned several times a year for outings to the National Gallery, etc. Trips further afield, both nationally (geography to the Lake District) and internationally (Spain). Sport well catered for with own courts and gym providing scope for basketball, netball, handball, athletics, rounders, trampolining and rugby (with one girl recently selected for Middlesex County). Girls compete regularly in Camden competitions (rounders, athletics, basketball), frequently emerging triumphant, particularly in basketball. School council (operating at all levels) gives pupils leadership opportunities, as does Duke of Edinburgh bronze. Mass participation (50 girls) in Jack Petchey 'Speak Out' develops public speaking and political awareness (as do visits from politicians). Outward-looking approach also evidenced by the recent acquisition of the British Council's International School Award.

Background and atmosphere: Founded in 1861 by the sisters of La Sainte Union, a French order of nuns, for much of its history LSU was an independent Catholic boarding school, before becoming an all-girls comprehensive in the 1970s. Boys have been admitted into the sixth form since 1995; LaSWAP consortium includes nearby schools William Ellis, Acland Burghley and Parliament Hill.

Located in the heart of affluent Dartmouth Park directly opposite Hampstead Heath, its convent background has left it with gracious period buildings and spacious grounds, including a beautiful, peaceful garden (plus orchard), hidden behind its elegant 19th-century frontage. This cloistered mood permeates the daily routine, with prayers

'We aim to nurture a love of learning, engaging with difficult things and exposing learners to high culture'

held every morning (inspired by the school's motto, Each for All and All for God, emblazoned on a banner across the assembly hall), compulsory attendance at weekly mass in the school chapel (sixth form non-believers are allowed to sit in silent reflection), and about 10 per cent of lesson time up to GCSE devoted to RE (five per cent thereafter). Charity and social justice both highlighted, and energetic fundraising undertaken for the LSU Tanzania project, North London Citizens' Project, and various local and national causes, with pupils taking a leading role through the house system in deciding when and which charities to support. Regular cake sales and other activities raise significant sums.

Pastoral care, well-being and discipline: A safe and pleasant place to go to school, with attendance and behaviour both exemplary. Girls in tartan pleats and forest-green blazers are generally orderly and well brushed. 'When they enter and leave, they're appropriately dressed. Paying attention to the small details means other things are right as well.' Between 11 and 16, pupils kept on site during the school day, with a keen eye kept out for unhappiness or unkindness, particularly in year 7, when the school runs an effective mentoring scheme with year 10. 'It's the biggest change in their education other than going to university,' says a teacher. 'It's exciting and exhilarating, but it can also be exhausting and a bit daunting.' The home-school bond unusually strong. The online Firefly system documents progress and shares behaviour with parents, who are also aided by workshops on issues such as mental health. Discipline here means instilling good habits: 'We teach children to self-discipline and always know right and wrong. We talk with them and sort them out.' Punishment, when necessary, is quick and clean, with same-day detention, 'so they know they're forgiven and can start the next day afresh.' Plenty of leadership roles for senior students, who act as heads and deputy heads of houses (named for patron saints).

Pupils and parents: Over 90 per cent baptised Catholics, but culturally and socially diverse, united by an atmosphere of respect and cooperation. Pupils – quite often the daughters of old girls – are generally co-operative and industrious. 'There are a lot of studious girls who work hard and get good results,' said one mother. 'If your daughter is that kind of child, she should be able to find like-minded friends.' Parents choose the school for its safe environment and academic focus ('My parents were impressed by its academic success,' said one high achiever) and for the articulate and responsible girls it turns out.

Entrance: Oversubscribed with admissions criteria that don't admit much leeway on the faith front, so realistically only thoroughly practising Catholics need apply. That said, living next to the school gates is not essential, and girls come from north, south, east and west (though a reasonable number worship at Our Lady, Help of Christians, Kentish Town, St Joseph's, Highgate, and St Gabriel of our Lady of Sorrows, Archway). Siblings given priority and 18 places also awarded annually for musical aptitude, with tests held in November of year 6 and Catholics given priority. Faith criteria not applicable to sixth form entrance, when boys and non-believers may apply to LaSWAP, a four-school consortium formed when LSU unites with neighbouring comprehensives Parliament Hill, William Ellis and Acland Burghley.

Exit: Reasonably large exodus post-GCSE, with about half departing for other RC schools (such as Cardinal Vaughan and The London Oratory), or local FE colleges (City and Islington and Westminster Kingsway). At 18, everywhere and anywhere, with top performers proceeding to Russell Group (UCL, Bristol, King's, York) and other leading unis, the vocationally inclined to apprenticeships. One to Cambridge in 2018 to study engineering.

Money matters: Not a rich school by any means either in terms of its students (about a third in receipt of pupil premium) or endowments, but no one seems to suffer the lack. Active Parents and Friends Association raises funds to subsidise school trips, buy computer equipment, and refurbish accommodation (such as the sixth form common room).

Remarks: A safe, calm and orderly place to go to school, with a strong spiritual core, providing a rich all-round education and producing industrious, articulate, responsible girls.

LaSWAP Sixth Form Consortium

William Ellis School, Highgate Road, London NW5 1RN

020 7692 4157 | laswap@williamellis.camden.sch.uk | laswap.camden.sch.uk

State	Pupils: 1,000
Ages: 16–19	

Linked schools: La Sainte Union, 151; Parliament Hill School, 170; William Ellis School, 252

Director: Since 2013, Georgina Atkinson, BA in business and French from Kingston University and L'École Superieure in Montpellier. Did her PGCE at London University, followed by a period of working in schools with sixth forms, teaching business. Subsequently, she worked for 10 years as head of faculty at Saffron Walden County High School in Essex, and then moved on to become assistant principal of Long Road Sixth Form College in Cambridge, where she stayed for the next three years. 'I'm passionate about education, particularly sixth form education and helping students find the right course to match their skills.' Georgina is also an Ofsted inspector.

Working across four schools is complicated; however, Georgina meets weekly with the four school sixth form directors and termly with the heads of the four schools that make up the LaSWAP consortium, to plan strategic overviews. The role of headteacher of LaSWAP rotates termly amongst the four school heads.

Ensuring consistency across four large comprehensive sixth forms is no mean feat, especially when the well-being of roughly 1,000 students is in question – a job made all the trickier by LaSWAP's free flowing arrangement, whereby students could have lessons in any one of the four schools that make up the consortium (La Sainte Union, William Ellis, Acland Burghley and Parliament Hill). To help manage this transient system, Georgina has recently introduced a consortium-wide web based system called e-Tutor, which is available to every tutor in the four schools, and a way of keeping tabs on each student and updating records: 'One of the major benefits of LaSWAP for students is the diversity of such a large place and the fact that students can commute between four different buildings – but because of this, they do need to be monitored.'

Each school already has its own director of sixth form, so Georgina rotates between each school. New LaSWAP office at the front of William Ellis School and Parliament Hill School.

Academic matters: These four comprehensives, geographically within a few hundred metres of each other, created an amalgamated sixth form to provide the widest possible subject variety and range of qualifications. Lucky sixth formers here have a choice of a remarkable 41 A levels, as well as BTecs, NVQs, a choice of six vocational subjects, the new 'flagship' post-16 advanced maths studies, and post-16 GCSEs (for those who need to gain a grade 4/5 in maths or English) About 80 per cent of students follow a purely academic course, the rest take vocational courses, but those who want to can mix and match. Generally around 40 per cent A*-B at A level but cagey about 2018 results. The consortium's strengths lie in the visual arts (with consistently outstanding results) and arts subjects, like RE, film and media studies and English. Languages tend to perform well, but not many students take them up.

'The communication with home is excellent,' said one parent. 'If my son has done something well they email me. Equally, if he's not doing his homework, they'll let me know'

With such a wide and varied intake of sixth form students, we can't help wondering how the recent government move of abolishing most AS levels in favour of linear A levels will impact on future results. Georgina isn't overly concerned – in fact she welcomes the opportunity for students to learn subjects in a bit more depth: 'Students will learn how to learn more deeply and apply this. At the moment, many students acquire the knowledge for the exam, have the exam and then forget it.'

Some criticism for not always taking into account the wide range of ability in this relatively unselective sixth form, but not all would agree – 'In my classes, some people have 10 grade 8s and others mainly 4s, but I haven't found that a problem,' said one boy. A LaSWAP student, we were told, is one who wants to pursue 'more than just academic excellence, with its broad and innovative curriculum.' Teaching (with over 200 'highly experienced' sixth form teachers) is enthusiastic, knowledgeable and well prepared. 'Teachers are good, inspiring

and they listen to you', one student told us, but another one grumbled that 'they enforce too much discipline here.'

All students are allocated a base school, depending on the subjects they choose or where they took GCSEs, but most study on a number of sites. Some subjects are taught on all the sites, the more rarefied – music technology, textiles and dance, for example – on only one. Each student is given target grades on entry based on GCSE results and is carefully tracked thereafter, with good exam preparation and help with study skills, as well as thrice yearly reports. 'The communication with home is excellent,' said one parent. 'If my son has done something well they email me. Equally, if he's not doing his homework, they'll let me know.' The academic side is clearly complex, but well organised. 'I wanted to change one of my subjects early on,' said a student. 'I went to see the head of year and it was sorted by the end of lunch hour.'

Games, options, the arts: The extracurricular here is a significant part of what LaSWAP has to offer, being as varied and extensive as the academic range. The activities, which largely take place on Wednesday and Thursday afternoons, provide 35 options, from ballet and debating to theatrical make-up, DJ-ing and maths masterclasses. Off-site sports include sailing and climbing. The programme is not compulsory, but everyone is encouraged to have a go, regardless of previous knowledge or expertise.

Sport is a biggie here and students with an interest in sports coaching and working with young people can enrol on the sports education and training programme which consists of level 1, 2 and 3 qualifications. If successful, students can progress until they achieve the advanced level 3 diploma in sports development, which leads on to university and/or employment. This takes place at the nearby Talacre Community Sports Centre.

Students also benefit from a wide enrichment programme of visiting speakers and volunteering opportunities that 'stimulate debate and interest in current affairs and the wider community.'

Background and atmosphere: The four schools (La Sainte Union, an all-girls' Catholic school, William Ellis, an all-boys' former grammar school, Acland Burghley, a co-ed comprehensive, and Parliament Hill, an all-girls' comprehensive) decided to unite their sixth form offering nearly 40 years ago. Each school retains its distinctive ethos and students generally enjoy the change of pace. 'I really like the different atmosphere in each school,' said one. Students can enjoy the plush new common room that Acland Burghley has to offer – or the beautiful and serene gardens of La Sainte Union. However, the free-usage of all the various facilities that are not a student's base school has caused a

'Earlier, my daughter's friends were all local. In the sixth form, she suddenly had a whole new set of friends from all over London'

bit of controversy with some students. One told us, 'I thought I'd be able to use the facilities of the other schools, but the reality is I would be asked to leave if I was in the common room of Acland Burghley after school, being a La Sainte Union pupil. It really is for lessons only.' The school says that this is because all students have to be monitored and safeguarded by their head of sixth form, which would be too difficult off site.

And surely even the most disgruntled of students can find somewhere to hang out during lunch times, as the location of these schools would be hard to match. Whilst Acland Burghley is a short walk from bustling Kentish Town with its plethora of restaurants, cafés and quirky shops, both William Ellis and Parliament Hill back onto Hampstead Heath.

Parliament Hill and William Ellis combine to form a joint co-ed sixth form, the other schools retain the pupils they take in at 11, and each has its own director of sixth form and heads of year.

One great plus of the model is the halfway house it offers between school and sixth-form college. 'My daughter originally wanted to leave and go to college,' said one mother, 'but once she'd started at LaSWAP, she found the teachers treated her with more respect and she was given much more responsibility for her assignments.' The advantage for students who opt for continuity is that they remain in familiar surroundings while meeting new people and conquering new horizons. 'In the earlier years, my daughter's friends were all local,' said one parent. 'In the sixth form, she suddenly had a whole new set of friends from all over London.' New students, however, don't feel excluded – 'I felt everybody was in the same position as I was,' said one. 'People had friends from their original school, but they didn't know anyone from the other schools.'

LaSWAP is careful about taking both existing students and recent arrivals to a more independent level of study, with a well-planned induction programme, including a thorough briefing on the outline of each course and relevant dates and department procedures. Students like the friendly, laid-back but organised approach and strong sense of community.

Pastoral care, well-being and discipline: All students register at their base school, where they take most of their lessons. Here they have a head of year and a tutor who monitors their work and well-being, with regular interviews to discuss problems and set appropriate targets. Also a confidential professional counselling service and regular PSHE, with outside speakers, group work and discussions. Georgina is also in the process of setting up a sixth form peer advising system around e-safety and well-being. 'Sadly, as we know, there is more self-harming these days, or at least more people are talking about it. We want to train willing sixth form students to signpost professional support services to their student peers around mental well-being and mindfulness.' Students are also offered the opportunity regularly to access the services of two dedicated higher education advisors.

When a student starts LaSWAP sixth form, they are given a detailed planner (which is a colourful diary-like book), which includes a mine of information. Everything from planning one's workload, to code of conduct and even evacuation points at the four schools. There is also a Who's Who list at each of the base sites including who is the child protection officer etc. (For this fantastic planner alone we thought it was worth enrolling at LaSWAP..)

Dress code is smart casual, and at enrolment the consortium will stress the importance of having at least five outfits which fit this description. However, Georgina says that they don't like to tell students exactly what to wear, but instead she suggests that 'perhaps they look at people who go to work – either from magazines or commuters – and get ideas from that, so as to prepare them for the eventual workplace.'

Pupils and parents: Students from a huge range of ethnic and social backgrounds apply from a vast swathe of north London. Despite the consortium's leafy surroundings on the eastern edge of Hampstead Heath, all four schools are inner-city comprehensives with a socio-economic intake reflective of the term. Generally, pupils are confident and mature and get on well.

Entrance: LaSWAP has some 1,000 pupils. The number has slightly declined over the past few years because of other closer to home schools across London who have opened sixth forms. New entrants make up approximately 40 per cent of year 12. The entrance procedure is intricate, and careful attention must be paid to every step and date. First step is to register interest online. Then, armed with a ticket and a parent, prospective candidates attend the open evening in November. Applications must be submitted by post or by hand in early December – those who miss the deadline are put on the waiting list. All applicants who meet the deadline are offered a meeting at LaSWAP in February or March to discuss subject choice and given offers conditional on GCSE grades. Those with offers are invited to attend the one-day taster sessions held before the start of the summer holidays, when summer assignments are set. Post GCSE results, further enrolment appointments and places are confirmed. Now asks for at least five grade 6s at GCSE (rather than grade 4s, as previously) to study A levels. Pathways other than A levels ensure that individual needs are met.

Exit: Destinations are 'outstanding', and LaSWAP has a significantly above national average success rates to university in general, and Russell Group specifically – the most popular choices are Sussex and London universities, but across a wide range of

degree courses: eg international relations, marketing, philosophy, politics, economics and business. Virtually all of their level 2 vocational learners go on to advanced further education, apprenticeships or employment – a third returning to LaSWAP for advanced applied courses. Three to Oxbridge in 2018.

Remarks: A good compromise between school and a sixth form college, with an extraordinary range of subjects on offer. Tends to suit the motivated and the self starter, but not ideal for those who will be distracted by studying on a number of sites or who require the disciplined parameters of a school sixth form to function at their peak.

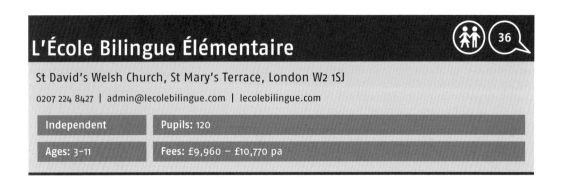

L'École Bilingue Élémentaire

St David's Welsh Church, St Mary's Terrace, London W2 1SJ

0207 224 8427 | admin@lecolebilingue.com | lecolebilingue.com

Independent	Pupils: 120
Ages: 3–11	Fees: £9,960 – £10,770 pa

Headteacher: Since its opening in 2004, Veronique Ferreira, who studied biochemistry at the University of Paris, and after obtaining her teaching licence in 1999 began her career as a primary school teacher in the suburbs of Paris, working with children with behavioural and academic difficulties. This gave her a lot of insights into the different learning styles of children, something that has shaped a lot of the teaching approach she has established at L'École Bilingue. Moving to London, she started in a French nursery school, but as parents continued to speak of their interest in a more bilingual programme, she pondered on how she might introduce a different sort of French primary school model in London. She focused on child development theories, looking at Canadian, UK (including EYFS) and French Breton bilingual educational models. Youthful yet wise beyond her years, her confidence is drawn from her solid foundation in pedagogical studies and the popularity of the school which was her brainchild. Her partner and the father of her daughter, Franck Laurans (head of administration), has provided the business knowledge needed to help her realise her vision for a school that is small, personalised and less rigid that the traditional French models where her students can 'find pleasure in learning'.

Entrance: L'École Bilingue is non-selective, but with only 15 places at the 3-year-old entry class, places are highly sought. Parents like the fact that, unlike other French schools, this is a transparent process. Priority is given to siblings (which can take up three-quarters of spaces), but after that it is first-come, first-served, so sign up early – from birth if you wish. (Nationality/passport are not a factor as in other French homologue schools.) Vacancies for children older than 3 are subject to space; worth a call but most classes are wait-listed, so as soon as someone leaves (and with many expats, children do leave) there is someone to fill the spot. Note that if you miss out on the first round you need to proactively let them know you remain interested.

Exit: The head meets parents individually to discuss the options, and some non-native French speakers may at this point opt for 11+ exams (a very few leave at age 7 or 8) and a move away from the French system. Recent examples include Francis Holland, City of London Girls' School and Holland Park. As the school is part of the AEFE agency for French education abroad, year 6 pupils have automatic access to French secondary schools such as the two Lycées (South Kensington and Wembley) or the Collège Français Bilingue in Kentish Town, which follows the bilingual mode, and the vast majority go on to one of these. While moving from L'École to the ginormous French Lycée is a big change, the Lycée tries to place two L'École students in the same year form group, so that helps a bit. The school has noted that French students repatriating to Paris often seek out bilingual schools there to keep their English language strong.

Remarks: The curriculum is bilingual French and English, and although the French curriculum model is predominant, the head says that she has looked in depth at other curricula, including the national curriculum, the IB primary years and the international primary curriculum, and drawn on elements of all these. Some subjects are taught in French (French, maths, history), some in English (science, English, geography) and some are taught in both languages simultaneously (arts, ICT, drama, music). Children move between English and French medium classrooms so that they are immersed in the relevant language for that part of the day.

Though a small school, the limited space is used to good effect and is immaculately tidy. The compact library is brimming with French and English children's books, a cheerful space where we saw some one-to-one learning taking place; walls lined with colourful boards neatly display creative work by students of all ages; we noticed some tailors' mannequins with student-designed fashions – part of a broader project including all the London French homologue schools in celebration of the centenary of the Lycée Charles de Gaulle. Some special needs support (French and English) available; some children with EHC plans in the school receive individual support either in-class or on a withdrawal basis. Teachers (19 in total, average age early 30s) are a mixture of French and English, all suitably trained and qualified. Staff turnover is higher amongst the French teachers than the English as they may be here as accompanying spouses or may move on to other French medium schools in London or abroad.

Four-course lunches are prepared and served at school by cooks who know each child by name, chivvy those with picky palates to eat their vegetables and report to parents

By all accounts, the pupils are busy and engaged in a wide range of activities. They are especially proud to have been invited – by recommendation of the French education inspector – to participate in the French Parlement des Enfants (a sort of 'junior parliament'). This event has influenced some of the themes and topics that have been studied by pupils in all the year groups. Other academic extras sometimes include a French mathematics competition for French schools in the north of Europe. French assessments are given in year 3 and year 6 to measure attainment against French standards; the school is inspected by Ofsted as well as the IEN French Inspector for the northern European region.

Year 3 goes to Brighton for two nights, year 5 spends three days in East Sussex and year 6 goes to Brittany for a week. The music programme is strong and some children do extra Suzuki violin and piano. Parents sang the praises (no pun intended) of the innovative music teacher who had recently done a 'bilingual Beatles' unit. As with other London French schools, many of the extra-curricular activities are organised by the parents' association, and parents run some of the clubs, which include fencing, dance, art, choir and football. There are no competitive sports on offer; they use the local sports centre – where many students do taekwondo after school; from year 2 they swim at Imperial College pool. There are two major shows – the annual Christmas carol service and an end-of-year show. We saw the former in final rehearsal – joyful voices, silver tinsel halos and red Santa hats.

Though the school is secular, the some of the ecclesiastical architectural features in the former Welsh church nestled in a quiet back street in Maida Vale have been put to effective use, making this a most unusual school building. An enclosed garden behind the school features a vegetable garden for pupils, an eco-pond (with resident creepy crawlies), and an area for messy hands-on learning with sand and water. There is an outdoor play area at the front of the school. A small multi-purpose hall is used for assemblies. Four-course lunches (optional) are prepared and served at school by cooks who know each child by name, chivvy those with picky palates to eat their vegetables and then report to parents on how many ate their carrots. Too much chatter is discouraged during lunches to encourage eating; an adult may read stories aloud instead.

There is a big emphasis on developing the 'soft skills' and the small size means that there is no anonymity in the school. Everyone contributes; everyone has a role to play. The appeal, parents say, is that at L'École they have found a near-perfect balance of strong (French) academic foundations in a very caring environment where everyone knows everyone. The intimacy of the school ensures that behaviour standards are high, and parents subtly suggest that the presence of several English teachers means that discipline is managed differently than in traditional French schools. Parents describe the children as 'kind' and very welcoming of new students. It's also highly inclusive. 'Birthday parties usually involve all of the siblings.'

Parents are big fans of this school, so much so that when they heard of the Good Schools Guide interest in meeting them, they organised a coffee morning (mostly mums, though one dad came) to share frankly their opinions about the school. The small size is an attraction – 'it's digestible for young children'. Another said, 'it's like comparing a mom and pop shop with B&Q'. One recent arrival accustomed to French schools voiced a concern that L'École may lack rigour; others from elsewhere in Europe and the US were delighted with the academic standards. Despite its small size, it appears that communication is patchy; some people seem to be in the know; others (particularly those new to the school) felt they were out of the loop. The school gate is definitely the place to find out what's happening. It seems that parents who are not fluent French speakers can find other parents willing to help and explain things.

Some 40 per cent of families are French (expat and local), 25 per cent are dual French/other nationals, 18 per cent are French/British, and some eight per cent represent other nationalities (including French-speaking north Africans, Canadians and others). Some international families also speak Arabic, Spanish, Italian, etc. Most families live nearby and walk to school, though some are

A vegetable garden, an eco-pond (with resident creepy crawlies), and an area for messy hands-on learning with sand and water

drawn from as far as Fulham, Kentish Town, South Kensington and Hampstead. Because of the school's South Kensington origins, a bus that comes from the Brompton Road area serves families who joined the school in the early days.

The school is owned by founders Franck Laurans and Veronique Ferreira. Parents like the fact that this couple, who 'live above the shop', are firmly at the helm; they feel they provide continuity and sustainable leadership that secures the school's future – at least for the time being. Some subsidies come from the French government for French national students,

Described by one parent as small, friendly 'village' school that draws on the best of French academics and English pastoral education, this bite-size school in the centre of London is worth a visit by parents who want something a bit different.

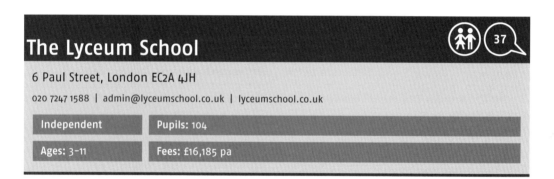

The Lyceum School

6 Paul Street, London EC2A 4JH

020 7247 1588 | admin@lyceumschool.co.uk | lyceumschool.co.uk

Independent	Pupils: 104
Ages: 3–11	Fees: £16,185 pa

Headteacher: Since 2015, Vanessa Bingham (60s). Jolly, unpretentious, enthusiastic, Mrs Bingham radiates both calm and an uncomplicated delight in seeing children at peace with themselves and the world. After teacher training at St Mathias, she began her career as a primary teacher specialising in art, before being catapulted, very young, into an assortment of deputy jobs and, soon after that, into her first headship. Her career had been spent mainly in state education and she's headed an array of primaries in various parts of England as well as being principal of international schools in Hong Kong and China. Married with one grown-up son, she delights in her present role and has exactly the right kind of experience and fond detachment to help the school at a time of critical consolidation.

Entrance: The head's line is that 'everyone who applies and who feels right for us, ought to get a place'. There is no formal testing but the usual practice would be for the head to meet the child and their family to talk through everybody's hopes and ideas.

Exit: A very small year 6 dispersed to Alleyn's, Bromley High, Dame Alice Owen, North Bridge House, The Charter School and UCS in 2018. The school explicitly sets itself to teach to 11+ entry, although they will try to support and guide families who are looking to have their children prepared for 7+ and 10+. There are clear expectations that all pupils, bar the very youngest, will have a little homework, but care is taken to ensure that it leads on from what has being gone that day in school, and is never burdensome.

Remarks: The school began life in 1997. It communicates an unpretentious cheerfulness which is both attractive and impressive, and a strong sensitivity to performing and visual arts. Most of the teaching happens in the basement, which doesn't sound great – and, true, there's not much natural light. But the classrooms tumble over with happy children – a lot of quite concentration was apparent, and the teachers, many of whom have been appointed since the present head arrived, seemed calmly and gently immersed in the children and in what they were doing.

The doors open at 8am each weekday, and parents are welcome to be around until shortly before 9am – coming to assemblies, meeting teachers and so forth. Then it's school time and parents go off (many work in the City, of course, which makes dropping off and collection of children a great deal easier). There is no canteen, but packed lunches are outsourced to a local supplier ('more expense,' said one parent, otherwise a big admirer of the school). Children may provide their own packed lunch. School is finished by 4pm but there are after-school clubs until 5pm, generally managed by the teaching assistants. For some children, whose parents work late, there is a homework clubs until 5.45pm. It's a long day for a young child, but staff pace everything with a view to offering reassurance and, when the moment suggests itself, relaxation.

There's a lively and happy nursery department, with some pupils attending part time and some doing the full five days. 'We did a trial period,' said one parent, 'but very soon there was no doubt in anyone's mind. We'd picked a winner.' There's plenty of learning even here, but evidently gently calibrated to allow the children's days to be full of interest and excitement. By reception, there is more time and focus being given to the rudiments of reading and writing and counting, and the journey obviously picks up pace between years 1 and 6. 'English and maths have to be at the heart of it,' says the head, 'but only ever in ways which underpin confidence and competence.'

One singularity of The Lyceum is the emphasis it places on a topic approach – that is, picking up on a subject or theme which will allow the children to experience it through a host of media and disciplines. 'For me,' said a parent who has had two children go through the school, 'this way of learning has been decisive. It allows the children to get immersed and excited in a way which feels very natural and gives them all a reference point. It really impacts on their experience of school and of each other and spills over into home.' The aim is to stimulate and channel artistic and creative energies, and use these to help reinforce their excellence in traditional subject areas. The library is generously provisioned and clearly a favourite spot for many.

Pupils with special needs are able to draw off a specialist teacher who comes in several days each week. In addition to the qualified teachers, there is also a battery of teaching assistants, and full-time support staff in the nursery and reception years. The most recent two deputies have gone on to their own headships ('The usual mixture of feelings,' says Mrs Bingham of these promotions. 'I'm pleased for them and proud of them, and I'm sorry for us. But it's a good sign').

Theatre and music are at the heart of each pupil's experience. All children learn the recorder and most at least one or two instruments – and, of course, they sing. There is a full-time music teacher and a plethora of instrumental teachers. There's at least one big production each term and a big band, an orchestra and a chamber choir – impressive in a school of around 100 pupils, all of whom leave by the age of 11. They are particularly proud of their summer term concert – the so-called 'summer pudding'. There are endless other concerts and performances besides: a Christmas concert at the Wesley Chapel, a chamber choir concert at St Giles. That's in addition to termly performances for most year groups, often tied in with the particular topics they've been studying during the term. Pictures adorn the walls – very expressive of the wonder of young children. All teachers share in the art, of course, but there is also an art leader to lend an overall coherence.

Communicates an unpretentious cheerfulness which is both attractive and impressive, and a strong sensitivity to performing and visual arts

Both before and after school, clubs flourish: chess, dance of all kinds, French, Spanish, Latin, Chinese – the list goes on and on. There are also visiting speakers and the children seem completely unfazed by visitors and happy to engage with them. Twice a year every pupil from year 3 and year 4 goes away on week-long residentials, with years 5 and 6 going away three times a year. These are designed to extend academic learning (often that which features within pupils' topics), and also offer cultural, social and artistic enrichment. Most are in the UK, but recent year 6 destinations have included Paris, Amsterdam and Rome.

There's no escaping the fact that the school building is less than beautiful and there is no outdoor space. 'I'd worried about that,' admitted one parent, 'but I've come to realise that the children are out of doors and exercising a good deal.' The head and her very diligent staff of 20 or so have expended thought and care on how to turn the space and location to best advantage. One afternoon is spent each week at the Royal Artillery Ground, and they have started to play fixtures with other schools, including netball matches (for boys and girls). Football training is now under way at Finsbury Park, and they swim at the Golden Lane pool on Friday afternoons. One hour each afternoon, weather permitting, is spent on play in Bunhill Park. The school has fashioned an indoor playground for wet weather days. Links have opened up with local community groups – the chamber choir recently went along to sing to a group of local elderly people, and there's much energetic fundraising for good causes, also for elderly people and also for Great Ormond Street Hospital.

Head speaks fondly of children whose behaviour is customarily excellent and also appreciatively of parents. There is an active Parents' Forum with year reps, and head feels the school draws great benefit from their input. The ethos of the school is avowedly traditional, but mainly in the sense of celebrating ageless good manners – being mindful of others and of their feelings. There's no hint of stuffiness and, while it styles itself Christian, it embraces children of all faiths and of none. 'I find the children unusually empathic,' one mother told us. 'They're extraordinarily supportive of each other. Not my experience in other schools!'

Children wear a simple but appealing uniform – navy duffel coats are a nicely archaic touch, as are the girls' hats (felt in winter and a very smart boater in summer). They look confident and upbeat as they go about their days. At no point did we glean anyone taking on airs and graces – a great tribute to the school and its families.

As it is located in the middle of a transport hub, most pupils come to school each day by tube with their parents. Enough use a scooter for the school to create a scooter park in the indoor playground. Parents are made very welcome between 8am and 9am and many of them use that time to ensure they are in close contact with form teachers, who are the first port of call. There are also written reports twice a year and a two week slot at the end of each term during which parents can book to meet teachers for a full half hour. No parent's evenings as such: 'I hate those five or 10 minute slots with everyone else getting cross,' says the head. 'This way nobody feels they've not been taken seriously.'

A cosmopolitan feel – many Europeans and Asians – as befits somewhere in the financial heartland of London. Parents are industrious, unpretentious and seem very grounded. They want their children to have a happy and effective start to their schooling. With just over 100 pupils, the Lyceum has one form per year and, for the moment, seems happy to keep it that way. Fees are mid-range ('but the same as other schools with better facilities,' said one parent), and an effort is made to keep down extras. Nursery vouchers are also accepted.

This is a happy school, calmly and competently working on bringing out the very best in their youngsters, and laudably unprecious. The biggest potential drawback is the building, but it's had the effect of making everyone within the school work harder to ensure children enjoy all the benefits of outdoor space. 'This is real education,' said one parent. 'The children are happy and mindful of one another. It's not greedy, it's not pushy, and people care.' The smooth transition they make to next-stage schooling seems to bear all that out, and is a huge recommendation.

Mossbourne Community Academy

100 Downs Park Road, London E5 8JY

020 8525 5200 | enquiries@mca.mossbourne.org | mca.mossbourne.org/

State	Pupils: 1,322; sixth form: 289
Ages: 11–18	

Principal: Since 2012, Peter Hughes BA (30s), who took over when founding principal Sir Michael Wilshaw left to lead Ofsted. 'They were big shoes to fill,' he admits, and although some parents say he's less inspirational and personable than his predecessor, he hasn't disappointed and is known for being

both exacting and reflective. 'Yes, we've done well, but I always want to know how we can do better,' he says. An Australian, he came to Mossbourne as part of the Future Leaders programme, which identifies, supports and trains potential head teachers. He has taught at Pimlico and Highgate Wood, and was an advanced skills teacher. Gained his BA in education (secondary mathematics) from Charles Sturt University, Australia.

Big on marginal gains, many of the changes he's made are indeed peripheral, including introducing a lottery system to replace the pure distance criteria ('I wanted to stop parents trying to buy their way into the school by moving nearby') and offering an additional 10 per cent of year 9 places to those with the potential to become elite rowers. 'Originally we did this in year 12, but if we're going to complete against private schools, we need to train them at the same age they do,' he explains.

They've created an environment with a 'can do' attitude, where it's cool to learn

About as far from the stereotype of a headteacher as you can imagine, he is young and hip, with a shiny black office that wouldn't look out of place in a trendy media company. Not that he spends much time there. Mostly, he's out and about round the school itself ('I learned from my predecessor that you can't know a school from behind a desk') and he's also often off site altogether. Indeed, as CEO of the Mossbourne Federation, he now oversees not only the Mossbourne Community Academy, but the new Mossbourne Victoria Park Academy (secondary school), Mossbourne Parkside Academy (primary school) and the new Mossbourne Riverside Academy (also primary) in Queen Elizabeth Olympic Park.

Living in Canary Wharf, he is an early riser, often seen out running at 6am with the rowers.

Academic matters: Exceptional results: in 2018, 70 per cent of pupils got 9-5 in both maths and English at GCSE. At A level, 40 per cent of grades were A*/A, 90 per cent A*-C. Not only are these some of the best state school results in the capital, they are also all the more extraordinary when you consider that some of the pupils arrive in year 7 hardly able to read. That said, Hackney is experiencing a rise in the quality of students leaving its primary (and secondary, for that matter) schools, making Mossbourne a less steep learning curve for students than it once was.

School has remained in the top one per cent in the country for value added ever since it opened, a feat the head puts down to several factors. First, they've created an environment with a 'can do' attitude, where it's cool to learn. Second, there are exceptionally strong structures in place, with a strict uniform policy, ferocious discipline and meticulous monitoring with weekly target setting.

The 'personalised learning agenda' is certainly not just government jargon at this school. Third, young and eager teaching staff provide top quality teaching, helped by great facilities. 'Three things are expected of the teaching staff here – giving high quality feedback; providing nurture and care; and being accountable for their results. The rest is up to them,' says the head. You'd have try hard not to do well here, he concludes – and it's true that, walking around, the culture is focused and calm. 'To step outside of that would actually be quite challenging.'

Although some teachers are better than others, they generally do whatever it takes to help kids grasp the subject and are nearly always prepared to go the extra mile, say parents. 'Whatever support you need, they'll give it,' said one.

The banded intake is set on entry in all the main curriculum subjects (English, maths, science, humanities, ICT and modern languages), with significantly smaller class sizes for lower sets and considerable movement between sets. Music, drama, dance, PE, art and design technology are not setted. Three modern languages on offer at GCSE – French, German, Spanish – as part of the core curriculum, and students also have the opportunity to take public exams in Turkish (large take-up), Latin (significant take-up), Bengali, Swedish, Italian. 'We meet the requirements of parents,' says the head, 'so if they speak a certain language at home, but want their son or daughter to learn it in a more formalised way here, we can accommodate that.'

Traditional academic sixth form, offering around 25 A level subjects, the most popular of which are maths (around two-thirds take this), English (around half choose this), history, psychology and the three sciences. Also on offer are Latin and classical civilisation, plus creative options such as music, art and drama.

He is young and hip, with a shiny black office that wouldn't look out of place in a trendy media company. Not that he spends much time there. Mostly, he's out and about

Plenty of computers throughout, many built into the modern white desks – the result of which is that technology is very much embedded into learning. Homework is set in abundance, but head recently introduced a later 4.20pm finish for all, enabling students to spend the last period of the school day either doing homework, preparation for the next lesson or revision. 'It came about because we were asking ourselves if we could improve

South Hampstead High Junior School

students' preparation for A levels,' he says, adding that some students lack a quiet space to work at home and that anything that stops homework becoming a battleground at home has to be a good thing. Crucially, though, students can use this period on some days to take up one of around 30 activities on offer – anything from bicycle maintenance to table tennis and from journalism to debating club – although only if they commit to doing their homework later on those days. 'The overall aim was to provide more structure around homework for year 7s, then slowly remove that structure as students move up the school, so that by the time they reach A level they are independent learners,' says head.

The music scholars programme enables students to perform at the likes of the Jazz Café and Tower of London, and these students are expected to share their learning

Saturday morning school not compulsory, but provides a safe place to do weekend activities such as the City explorers' club, revision lessons, Mandarin and other optional classes (including English for non-native speakers) and, of course, sports.

Outstanding autistic spectrum disorder provision via its own well-resourced teaching centre and well-qualified specialists. 'We take three children per year under this provision, which continues in sixth form and beyond, through the transition into college or work,' says the head. 'Everyone is fully integrated into mainstream school life here.' Parents are impressed. 'The help they've given my son around his dyslexia has changed his life. He went from struggling to write a paragraph in year 7 to writing reams of pages within months, and his growing confidence led to him moving up his sets too,' said one parent.

Games, options, the arts: Sports include football, netball, basketball, cricket and 'best in Hackney' for athletics. Rowing is big and continues growing, with links to the London Youth Rowing and London Regatta Centre, opposite City airport – originally a training centre for the Olympics and still a world-class training facility for the school's rowers, of whom the elite may train 12 times a week. Rowing is part of the PE timetable in years 7-9; recent medals at British championships and European and world indoor event. Impressive sports facilities include a full size sports hall and rowing gym, while all grass sports take place on Hackney Downs. Latest on the building agenda is a performance pavilion, a dedicated space designed by Rogers Stirk Harbour + Partners, where students can train on-site for rowing, as well as providing extra sensory provision for the school's autistic intake and enhancing the school's already notable music provision.

Music is a specialism here, with over 250 pupils having subsidised instrumental lessons. Junior and senior choirs and bands, along with an orchestra, all perform in regular concerts and performances. Meanwhile, the music scholars programme enables selected students to perform in public at the likes of the Jazz Café and Tower of London, and these students are also expected to share their learning back at school to help develop other students. 'My children had never done music before Mossbourne and I now have a leading guitar playing, violin playing child,' one parent told us.

Drama practice mainly takes place in the modern and well-equipped auditorium and lecture theatres, culminating in regular performances and an annual whole-school production, with recent examples including Charlie and the Chocolate Factory, Romeo and Juliet and Little Shop of Horrors.

Plenty of examples of skilled and creative artwork on show during our visit, showcasing strong artistic talent across fine art, clay, screen-printing and more. A dedicated A level art studio means students never have to compromise on space and time to work. 'I always think art is one of the unsung successes of Mossbourne,' one student told us.

Trips to Edinburgh, Belgium, the Isle of Wight, language trips to Spain and Germany; Spanish play, poetry competition, debating, links with London College of Fashion. Lots of careers advice. 'My son talks about his future a lot – way more than I ever did at that age. He has high aspirations,' one parent told us.

Background and atmosphere: Founded on the site of Hackney Downs School, once a successful local grammar school, whose alumnae include Sir Michael Caine and Harold Pinter. By the 1990s, however, it had become notorious as 'the worst in Britain' and was eventually demolished. Mossbourne was rebuilt on the same site, a tricky triangle bounded on two sides by railway lines. Founding principal Sir Michael Wilshaw worked alongside architects, Richard Rogers and Partners, to design a school (costing £32.5 million) which met his requirements. Now one of the largest wooden structures in England (known locally for looking like an IKEA, not least because it's huge and blue on the outside), it was created in a V shape, which holds in its arms a welcoming triangular social area, complete with tables and benches, basketball areas, table tennis tables etc.

Wilshaw believed that pupils need to be kept under constant observation, so the head's office and the classrooms all overlook the grounds. No corridors – hidey-holes for bullying – and no staff-room, since Wilshaw felt teachers need to be involved at break times and after school, when most trouble occurs. Inside (where the IKEA comparison still feels apt, such is the emphasis on modern, innovative and fresh interiors) the triple-height space is light and airy and learning takes place in 'learning areas,' which are split into themes of sport, history, music etc – including one specifically for year 7s, whose transition is a major area of focus. Glittering new sixth form centre.

In each glass-walled classroom – all of which have an open door policy – all students begin lessons by reciting the Mossbourne reflection: 'Throughout this lesson I aspire to maintain an inquiring mind, a calm disposition and an attentive ear, so that in this class and in all classes I can fulfil my true potential'. Sure enough, the students we saw did look attentive and interested.

Active school council and peer mentoring scheme for core subjects. Prefects in year 13. No house system. Pupils we spoke to were articulate, polite and delightful – oozing pride about their school. We were also wowed by the set-up here. It's bright, contemporary and spotless, with superb facilities and seemingly endless examples of attention to detail, including language booths and a huge amount of space for private study.

Pastoral care, well-being and discipline: Woe betide students who don't toe the line here, with staff giving out detentions for things like keeping a watch on during PE, untidy uniform and being more than 10 seconds late when the morning whistle goes at 8.40am. 'We work on the principle that if you sweat the small stuff, the big stuff takes care of itself,' says the head. 'Nothing ever escalates into anything more serious,' agreed one student. 'The most serious offence I've ever seen here is talking in class.'

One of the country's most oversubscribed schools. The head is looking for a balanced intake: 'We want a comprehensive – we don't want a secondary modern'

Among parents, it tends to be the middle-class liberals who struggle, with some thinking teachers can be overzealous. There was also a feeling among some parents we spoke to that new teachers are particularly extreme. 'There's a joke that new teachers

It's bright, contemporary and spotless, with superb facilities and seemingly endless examples of attention to detail

here don't smile until Christmas,' one told us. 'My son got a detention for writing his homework on the wrong page – I mean, come on,' said another. But most approve of the general ethos that if you set the controls, you ultimately give children freedom. 'The heavy-handedness has made my son very driven,' added one parent.

No physical contact between students is allowed ('If a boy has his arm around a girl, how do we know it's not making her uncomfortable, but she's too embarrassed to say, for example?' explains head) and no more than six people in a single group in the playground. Staff always on hand, with stairwells manned between lessons and students monitored after school.

Pre-GCSE pupils wear smart grey and red school blazers and neatly knotted ties, sixth formers graduate to business-like suits and skirts (at or below the knee). No piercings allowed, except for ears, hair must be kept to an acceptable norm. Mobiles banned and students not allowed to enter shops on their way home or loiter outside the gates in groups. Racism a non-issue, and the same can be said for truancy, with a 96 per cent attendance rate.

Pastoral care exceptional. Everything here is about students feeling safe and comfortable so they are ready to learn, with as much access as they need to school counsellors, who come in as and when they're required (the school works with a private company), plus plenty of senior teaching staff (including the deputy head) whose sole responsibility outside teaching is pastoral care. Few personal problems go unnoticed, whether self-harm or being picked on. At the first sign, parents are invited to come and speak to the staff, with two dedicated meeting rooms available. 'We very much believe parents are our partners and are fundamental to the success of the school,' says head. Bullying extremely rare and when discovered, it's dealt with swiftly and seriously. 'My daughter told me about a boy who came out in year 8 and there was no nastiness about it at all, with everyone being really accepting – that would have been unheard of in Hackney in the past,' one parent told us.

Pupils and parents: A large percentage of the intake comes from the adjacent Pembury estate, an urban sprawl which tends to hit the headlines for its shootings and drugs rather than its high educational aspirations. Two-thirds of pupils are from minority ethnic groups (many Turkish Kurds), two-fifths speak English as a second language, 50 per cent are on free school meals. But also a fair number of clued-up, middle-class parents – the kind who used to go private or bus their children out of the borough – who fight from a great distance to get their children the superb education the school offers.

Entrance: Some 1,500 apply for the 216 places, making it one of the country's most oversubscribed schools. The head is looking for a balanced intake: 'We want a comprehensive – we don't want a secondary modern'. Applicants sit cognitive ability tests to divide into four equal ability bands. Fifty per cent of places in each band are given to those who live within the inner zone (up to 1km from the gates); 30 per cent of places go to those in the middle zone (1-2km) and 20 per cent to those in the outer zone (2-3km). Priority is given to looked after children, those with a child protection plan, siblings, those with medical needs and children of staff. Further places by lottery, which head says prevents parents from buying their way into the school by moving into a property nearby, although some parents say the inevitable consequence of the gentrification of Hackney is that this feels less of a community school than in the past. Offers an additional 10 per cent of year 9 places to those with the potential to become elite rowers (zoning does not apply to this group).

The lower sixth form has 200 places. Applicants must meet the demanding criteria of seven 9-4 GCSEs including English and maths, with priority given to pupils already at the school – around 100 of whom generally secure places. All candidates, including those already at the school, must also meet the subject specific entrance criteria in their chosen A level subjects. Whilst successful external candidates used to come mostly from other Hackney comprehensives, they are increasingly applying from further afield, utilising the quick and easy train route from Liverpool Street.

Exit: Those who leave at GSCE leave mainly do so to do vocational qualifications or go straight into work. After sixth form, 90 per cent to universities, nearly half of those to Russell Group universities (a wide mix). Seven to Oxbridge in 2018. Broad array of subjects studied, including music, maths, physics, engineering, law, communications; five medics and dentists in 2018. Remaining 10 per cent mainly into apprenticeships, with around 4-10 students taking a gap year.

Money matters: Money not a problem at this well-resourced school – everything from the buildings to the technology is of the highest standard and whatever the head wants to get done he has the means to achieve.

Remarks: If ever there was a school proving that the right ethos, leadership and sufficient resources can provide not just a good education – but a great one – in the most deprived of areas, this is it. Everything about it is geared around the concept of passive supervision and students feeling safe, nurtured and ultimately ready to learn. This, together with the combination of high quality teaching, excellent facilities and strong discipline and pastoral care, means it's hardly any wonder that results are outstanding and that parents fight hard to get their kids in.

North Bridge House Preparatory School

1 Gloucester Avenue, London NW1 7AB

020 7267 6266 | prep.reception@northbridgehouse.com | northbridgehouse.com/prep

Independent	Pupils: 465
Ages: 7-13	Fees: £18,195 pa

Linked school: North Bridge House Pre-Prep School, 168

Headteacher: From January 2019, James Stenning, currently head of sixth form and deputy head academic at North Bridge House Canonbury. Educated at a prep school in Kenya then Downside school, with an economics degree from Swansea, a PGCE and a masters in education leadership from Buckingham. Began his career teaching economics at St Olave's grammar, thence head of economics and head of extracurricular at Highgate (where economics became one of the most popular A levels, and he was heavily involved in D of E and outdoor education). Joined NBH Canonbury in 2014. Married to Tom, a group account director for an advertising agency. Very keen runner, often taking part in marathons in far flung corners of the globe such as North Korea, Sierra Leone and Nairobi.

Head since 2005, Mr Brodie Bibby BA PGCE MEd (very young 50s). Previously deputy head at Westminster Under school where he taught for four years, Mr Bibby was educated at Truro school and Repton, going on to study archaeology and ancient history at Exeter University and a PGCE at Roehampton, before doing a masters in education at University of Buckingham. He has worked at a range of schools in south London, from Honeywell Primary in Clapham to Finton House in Wandsworth, where he was one of the founding team at the inception of the school, to Hazelwood in Surrey. He also did a spell at the Banda School in Kenya. Married with a daughter and a son, now at London secondary schools, having both been educated here. His wife has a high powered job in the commercial world, he confides proudly.

Big focus on chess, taught by external specialists; pupils compete in school tournaments and have been successful in both local and national competitions

With his chiselled good looks, and snappy dress style, Brodie Bibby is much more rock n' roll than most prep school heads we meet. He met his wife while DJing at a wedding, and his passions as a teacher focus particularly on the dramatic and the sporting. He looks dreamily into the distance while describing a victory at Lord's over Westminster Cathedral School when he started a cricket team at the state primary, Honeywell, and while describing his production of Twelfth Night, which he directed here a few years ago; 'we had three separate casts as we didn't want to turn anyone down.' He also enjoys teaching philosophy to year 3 and history to year 6 and is proud of the mixed ability profile of the school and how closely they track pupils' progress. The ethos here is one of mutual respect, he asserts. Spends a lot of time at their house in Suffolk – playing tennis and golf, enjoying outdoorsy pursuits with his children. Appointed soon after Cognita bought the school, Mr Bibby is Cognita's longest serving head and a sparkling jewel in their crown.

Leaving in December 2018.

Entrance: Entrance into year 3; most move seamlessly from the pre-prep but around 20 places remain for external applicants. Assessments in English, maths and reasoning taken in the January of year 2. Open mornings held throughout the year. Occasional places arise throughout the school so always worth a call.

Exit: Mr Bibby meets with all parents of year 5 pupils in the spring term. He, armed with data, they, with expectation and high hopes. Together they draw up a list of four or five schools and then navigate through the process. One parent commented on how she felt 'held', not overly managed, but supported and directed. Practically all aim for London day schools (the odd one each year may board at eg, Downe House, Sevenoaks or Haileybury), with Channing, South Hampstead, Francis Holland and Immanuel College most popular currently amongst girls, Mill Hill and City of London amongst boys. All girls leave at the end of year 6 (although they no longer have to, they do still leave). Most boys stay until the end of year 8. Some parents of boys who leave at the end of year 6 expressed concern that their sons didn't get the required support – 'school not geared up to boys leaving at 11'. However Mr Bibby avers that the future of CE versus the 11+ is very much decreasing in significance as the 11+ becomes ever more common for boys.

Remarks: Situated on the corner of Gloucester Avenue where Primrose Hill meets Camden Town, North Bridge House Prep School is a big and busy school on a big and busy road. Cramped outside but spacious inside, but there are plans afoot to renovate the playground to make it 'a more green and friendly space'. School compensates by sending the children to Regent's Park, a five minute walk away, where they can kick a ball and let off steam. A feature of all Cognita schools, security is thorough, tight and unforgiving. Everyone is vetted at the door, lanyards flow from reception. The timing of our visit was not long after the terrorist attack on Westminster Bridge, so with year 8 boys going out on daily trips in central London (part of the post common entrance curriculum) security issues were very high on Brodie Bibby's agenda. There are regular security drills and all the staff given guidance on how to talk the children about these issues. Everyone here is conscious of the importance of balancing safety with the need to take risks, but acknowledge that it is not an easy balance to strike in this climate.

The school has moved into its 80th decade, and it's over 30 years that it has been on this site. Mr Bibby arrived here soon after Cognita bought the school. Now under the leadership of corporate dynamo, Chris Jansen, Cognita has had a chequered history. Signs suggest this is soon to change,

A large, bustling, well-oiled machine of a school that – almost always – matches expectations. Children are busy, happy and safe

though change in education is slower than the pace of change Jansen is used to achieving. North Bridge House Prep has always been one of the more successful schools in its stable, but the streamlining, management, sharing of resources and marketing is clear for all to see. Data, tracking the performance of pupils and staff, is an important tool and is used very effectively here. The SIMS system paints a profile of the whole child. The staff are in control and parents feel safe and assured that their child is not lost in the system. Brodie Bibby warmly refers to the 'buzz' and the 'sense of direction' since the arrival of Jansen. There is mutual support and sharing of resources between the heads across the Cognita schools, particularly all four North Bridge House schools.

High praise from parents for the quality of teachers, particularly class teachers. While many said the school feels a bit like a machine – in a good way – they all said that the class teachers brought a very personal feel and that Mr Bibby is available if you need him. SEN support is given primarily in the classroom. However there is flexibility, and occasionally your child may be given one-to-one lessons at the expense of a language if necessary. Range of conditions from ADHD and autism to dyscalculia and dyspraxia. Strong SEN team, says school, and concurred by parents, and it would only turn away a child it felt it couldn't support. There is a 'well-being officer' as well as a school counsellor (available at additional cost).

Children study both French and Spanish as well as Latin from year 6 and some take up ancient Greek. Academics are solid, sometimes inspiring. Ofsted says outstanding. Setted for maths from year 5. Girls and boys are also taught separately from year 6, the intention to prepare them more thoroughly for their respective exams. In years 7 and 8 there is a top, scholarship, stream and three other classes. Technology woven into the curriculum; there are laptops and iPads available on each corridor for use in any lesson. Two imaginatively decorated science labs with planets hanging from the ceiling, and molecule diagrams. Classrooms are high ceilinged, spacious and well equipped. Corridors wide with highly polished floors and well kept carpets.

Lots of co-curricular. Music, drama and sport all thrive here. Plenty of informal concerts in the local church as well as the large summer and Christmas concerts. You don't have to be a maestro to perform. Art room at the top of the school among the roof beams. An inspiring space and we saw cubist self-portraits inspired by Braque. Each child is given an art sketchbook that they use all year. Year 8s were out and about on a street art tour of Brick Lane. Drama productions take place in the 'chapel' (lunch and talks also happen here). Everyone gets involved; recent productions include Matilda and Canterbury Tales. Lots of adventurous trips – PGL and bushcraft, as well as to France, China and Morocco, and post common entrance sailing for year 8 after their intensive trips around London. Football and cricket for the boys, netball and rounders for the girls. Good use is made of Regent's Park and the Astro at Talacre sports centre in Kentish Town. Sports day is a huge event: around 350 parents and spectators attend the event at the Saracens sports ground in Barnet Copthall. There is a lot of focus on chess, taught by external specialists, and the pupils win competitions – national as well as local and within the school. A number of talks from outside speakers – engineers, journalists, army officers and others (parent contacts come in useful here and school recently started an alumni network). Topics range from the building of the channel tunnel to recycling and international affairs. Disappointing library, surprising in a school with such a strong focus on learning.

Discipline is strong. System of house points (four houses, Guinevere, Merlin etc) encourages children to try harder and behave well. From year 6 they can get demerits as well as merits. Lots of positions of responsibility from head boy and girl (though a slight mismatch here as girls are in year 6 and boys in year 8), to heads of houses and sports captains. All traditional prep school stuff that provides the glue and grit that make the system work. Parents a real mixture of busy professionals (in a high proportion of families both parents are working hard), mostly English and based in north London but there are some European nationals, and other overseas parents from further afield – US, Canada, China and Japan. Lots are in the media and the arts, and and there is a smattering of celebrities and a number of first time buyers. With little playground space to congregate in it can take time to find your milieu but most do and speak warmly of their fellow parents.

A large, bustling, well-oiled machine of a school that – almost always – matches expectations. Children here are busy, happy and safe. A good choice for your all rounder who isn't likely to get fazed and is ready to seize the many opportunities on offer.

North Bridge House Pre-Prep School

8 Netherhall Gardens, London NW3 5RR

020 7267 6266 | admissionsenquiries@northbridgehouse.com | northbridgehouse.com/nursery-pre-prep-hampstead/

Independent	Pupils: 190
Ages: 2y 9m–7	Fees: £14,385 – 17,430 pa

Linked school: North Bridge House Preparatory School, 165

Head: Since 2015, Christine McLelland BEd (40s). Previously deputy head at St Nicholas Prep in Kensington (also a Cognita school), and before that worked in the state sector in both secondary and primary schools. She has been a class teacher for all year groups from reception to year 6 and held various senior leadership positions. Married to a teacher, an early years Leader, Mrs McLelland particularly enjoys teaching ICT and maths, the latter because she didn't enjoy it at school and is determined that it should be taught better now. Like many heads we meet she loved school and is proud to report that 98 per cent of her pupils say maths and problem-solving are their favourite subjects. She doesn't teach as much as she would like to now, but can teach anything and does what she can: 'its good for the soul, there are some children who always cheer you up. Spending time with the children is the highlight of my day.'

Started here as interim head in July 2015, following her predecessor's brief tenure and early departure for 'sad personal reasons'. The ship needed steadying. An SIS report in February 2016 identified a number of problems, particularly with the quality of the teaching. Inspectors nonetheless described Mrs McLelland's leadership as 'determined and effective, she is an excellent communicator who takes decisive action.' Parents describe her as 'smart, confident with good communication and marketing skills.' 'She complements Brodie Bibby in the prep very well,' one parent observed. 'Takes a bit of warming up. A bit defensive,' said another, 'but she came in at a tough time on the back of a worrying SIS inspection report and very weak leadership from the previous head.' McLelland describes herself as 'stubborn by nature, I enjoy turning a challenge into a motivation.' We would agree but might add 'with a manner that is a touch brittle'. However, when we met her she seemed to be feeling on the back foot and we were impressed by her fighting spirit. The conclusions of the inspectors 'did not come as a shock,' she asserted and 'a huge amount of work has been done since.'

Full of praise and gratitude for the support and expertise given to her by the Cognita management, Christine McLelland is a woman who isn't afraid to ask for help and seems to work well as part of a larger organisation. We noted that once or twice her vocabulary drifted away from the language of education as she started to refer to 'the product' and 'if you've got a good product the rest of it looks after itself.' Not words that fall naturally from her lips and we detect the influence of private equity backed management. Perhaps not surprisingly there was a high turnover of staff soon after she took over – 'some had a problem with planning lessons,' she says candidly, 'and were just recycling.' Fresh blood has been easy to recruit, however. Many come from the state sector like McLelland herself and she is proud of her high performing team. She loves the children here: 'they are very, very normal,' she says, 'not snobbish or rude but polite, kind and generous.'

Entrance: Children automatically filter through to the pre-prep from the nursery school at the age of 5, so fewer external places at this stage. Applicants are invited in to meet the headteacher – who heads both the nursery and pre-prep schools – prior to admission and places are allocated according to gender and date of birth, with priority given to siblings and children of past pupils.

Exit: Approximately 75 per cent move seamlessly to the prep school into year 3. Brodie Bibby, head of the prep, and Mrs McLelland liaise closely to ensure the transition is as smooth as it could be.

Some still take the 7+ to eg UCS, South Hampstead, Highgate, North London Collegiate, Haberdashers, Belmont, Devonshire House or Westminster Under. The school is focused on journey for your child from 2-18 so while it will respect parents' wishes, you would be naïve to rely on your child getting into a competitive school from here at

7 without external support. Lots of tutoring in years 1 and 2, say parents, an unsurprising consequence but something that is nonetheless bemoaned by both the prep and the pre-prep.

Remarks: The pre-prep (years 1 and 2) is housed in a five-storey red-brick Victorian building in a leafy Hampstead cul de sac. The nursery (nursery, pre-reception and reception) is round the corner in Fitzjohn's Avenue in a similar building with big open spaces for play, exploration and exercise.

This is the base camp of the North Bridge House group of co-ed schools which are scattered around north London. The prep, a 7-13 (years 3-8) school, is in Camden Town, and there are two senior schools, one in Hampstead and the other in Canonbury, Islington. In theory your child could put down roots here and continue seamlessly through the NBH schools to 18, however to find a pupil who has been all the way through from the start continues to be rare.

Some of the infrastructure of the pre-prep in Fitzjohn Avenue seems to be a little tired and worn, from the broken tap in the visitor's lavatory to the uninspiring, sparse and functional head's office. A stark contrast to the classrooms, which were bursting with decoration, displays and colour when we visited. Wide staircases and corridors with high ceilings and large, well-proportioned classrooms create a sense of space and room to grow.

Wonderful outside space includes chicken coop. Pupils eagerly take responsibility for collecting eggs and feeding the chickens – even during the holidays

Fresh air and exercise is important here; pupils play outside at least twice a day. Wonderful space with an Astroturf playground, complete with slides and climbing frame, and chicken coop at the back. Pupils queue up to take responsibility for collecting the eggs and feeding the chickens – even during the holidays. Fresh food is prepared on site and eaten in a wood cabin in the playground which doubles up as a dining and assembly room.

Specialist teachers in music, art, PE and games. Music is a strength and time is made for performances, lessons and groups. The whole school learns percussion, singing and composition, peripatetic teachers also teach guitar, violin and piano, and lessons can continue into the prep. Plenty of opportunities to perform in assemblies as well as in one of the big shows per term (recently Charlie and the Chocolate Factory). LAMDA classes also popular.

Art is particularly impressive, and the lack of designated art room does not appear to have an adverse effect. Each class in the school annually produces a particular themed canvas, in the style of William Morris for example, which parents can then bid for in a private auction. An art exhibition is held at the end of each year and we were lucky enough to see this in the final stages of preparation. A rich collection of work influenced by Monet's water lilies, Kandinsky and sketches of corgi dogs reminiscent of Hockney's sausage dogs, reflect the topic Kings and Queens.

One hour of dedicated IT each week but otherwise use of computers and technology is embedded in the curriculum. These 21st century children are already deft in the art of managing a device and mini iPads and laptops are used across the school.

Safeguarding is an absolute priority in all Cognita schools and the pre-prep is no exception. Rigorous vetting and checking at the door for all visitors, who are issued with a set of rules and banned from using their mobile phones. We were even accompanied to the WC. Strong pastoral care: tabs are kept on the welfare of the children, assisted by a worry box in each in classroom into which the children can place slips and then follow up with the head of pastoral care. An effective system that is used and not just there for show, which is often the case. We saw it in action.

Children split into 10 classes (five in year 2, five in year 1), named after trees (Katsura, Beech, Hazel), one of the many innovations from Mrs McLelland: a move to trees from the birds creates more of an impression of growth, development and strength and can be less easily misinterpreted. Children now mixed into separate house groups too for sport and music competitions etc. Co-ed and inclusive, the school is nonetheless boy heavy. 'There is more competition from other girls' schools in the area,' observed one parent. Many move at the end of nursery to other schools, but on the whole parents are supportive of the school.

Majority of families live in the Hampstead area, within two miles of the school. Some with strong connections to the school – they may be alumni themselves or have other relatives who started their school days here. Eclectic mix of nationalities, with 27 languages spoken. Mix of educated professionals – fair few bankers and lawyers, as well as GPs, PR executives etc. Plenty of working mothers. Fewer big name celebrities than at similar schools.

Provision for EAL support is disappointing, we were told by more than one parent. Surprising for a school which proclaims to be all-inclusive and non-selective and which attracts a number of applicants from non-English speaking families. 'Best to make sure your daughter's level of English is secure before she arrives,' warned one parent. However, school assures us that EAL support for children is provided by learning support assistants across the school and insists that children with little or no English make progress and can catch up with their English speaking peers.

We received similarly confused reports about SEN provision. There are two full time SENCos and Mrs McLelland assured us that they wouldn't turn down a child with specific language difficulty or because of their English; 'we would look at their attention and ability to focus', she says. Yet parents we spoke to warned that school can only really support mild special needs. There were no children with ASD on the school roll when we visited. This is clearly an area that is benefiting from Mrs McLelland's eagle attention, however. A follow up report from SIS in November 2017 observed that pupils identified as having SEN and disabilities, including those with an EHC plan, make good progress because of very good provision and their needs are met 'with great sensitivity and care'. Pupils with EAL make very good progress because they receive 'very effective support.'

Mrs McLelland has been firmly focused on the academic side of things. In 2018 the pupils' attainment in maths put the school in the top five per cent in the country. Mrs McLelland attributes this in large part to excellent teaching from staff who are at the top of their game. CPD and sharing of best practice is high on her agenda. The improvement is acknowledged by the Inspectors. SIS, in November 2017, marked the quality of education as 'good' – a step up from their report in 2016, but probably not good enough for Mrs McLelland, her bosses at Cognita nor the parents. Leadership, management and governance also still fall short of an outstanding grade. We are not usually ones to pay overmuch attention to inspection reports, but Cognita has had a chequered history, is keen to raise standards and, we feel, needs to be called to account.

On the plus side, there has been a gear change in recent months: 'expectations have changed,' says Ms McLelland. Plenty of good, full time teachers with six or seven years behind them, including a relatively high number of male teachers, and we don't often see that for this age group. A native speaker teaches French.

Lots of attention is paid to encouraging the children to achieve academically. A ceremony, full of pomp and mortar boards, is held to celebrate the reception class graduation to year 1. An even grander one for the end of year 2, complete with 'graduation day' prizes, video montage and speeches.

Heartening ethos of 'giving back' – different charities are supported each year. Chosen by the children and the parents, these have included Diabetes UK and Little Village Camden, provides clothing and equipment for disadvantaged women and families.

A school with heart, although it is not always easy to feel the beat of it, on account of its impersonal systems and sometimes mechanical, rather than personal, communication. Schools that are a part of a large commercial organisation can often fall foul of the personal touch, but this suggestion is vehemently denied by the school. They have found just the right person in Chrstine McLelland to marry these contradictions and we are confident that as she continues to find her stride the school can only get stronger.

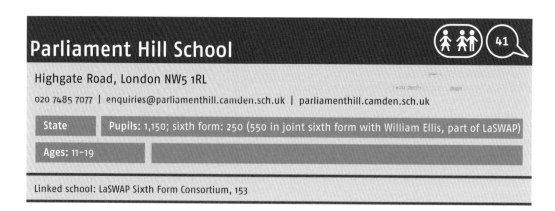

Parliament Hill School

Highgate Road, London NW5 1RL

020 7485 7077 | enquiries@parliamenthill.camden.sch.uk | parliamenthill.camden.sch.uk

State Pupils: 1,150; sixth form: 250 (550 in joint sixth form with William Ellis, part of LaSWAP)

Ages: 11–19

Linked school: LaSWAP Sixth Form Consortium, 153

Headteacher: Since September 2017, Sarah Creasey, previously deputy head and associate head here. She started teaching at a single sex school in Wimbledon, then spent time at Hampstead School before moving to Preston Manor, where she spent 10 years, as head of English and then assistant head. She joined Parliament Hill in 2011.

Academic matters: A huge ability range here, with lots of bright girls and also plenty in need of extra support, whether educational or emotional.

Accordingly, the school offers a range of options. Everyone studies for a core of GCSE subjects which includes maths, English, core science, RE, and short courses in PE and citizenship. They can add on more GCSE subjects, or choose a vocational BTec from a range that includes business, art and design, ICT and health and social care, or go for a young apprenticeship. Most of the latter two options are taught elsewhere in Camden. Everyone is allocated to either French or Spanish classes for the first three years, and can start the other language in year 9; about a third take a modern language GCSE. Other popular options at KS4 include additional AS maths and triple science; ICT AS and photography GCSE are taught after school as twilight classes.

The ability range encompasses those aspiring to read medicine at Cambridge and those working for a BTec in health and social care

In 2018, 80 per cent of girls got 9-4 in both English and maths at GCSE; 36 per cent of grades were 9-7. English has been very strong, maths and science historically rather weaker. However, maths now taught in ability sets from the second term in year 7, and the curriculum has been redesigned substantially. Girls arrive at the school with, on average, much higher verbal than non-verbal aptitude scores – 'but as a technology college we focus on building up their confidence and aptitude in maths and science'. The science department has appointed some very highly qualified teachers over the last few years. Triple science courses very popular, with excellent results. 'They're very good at assessing strengths and weaknesses,' said a parent, 'and throwing lots of energy at weaknesses.'

Downgraded in 2013 from its 'outstanding' status to 'good' by Ofsted, under the new harsher regime, citing the gap in achievement between poorer students and the rest. The school says it was based on 'historical examinations results' and not teaching. Indeed, Inspectors were able to identify many successful features of teaching and learning. Homework and marking – aspects formerly raised by parents as sometimes inconsistent – were areas that Ofsted pointed out as having had 'key improvement'.

Although there has been little fallout since this report from either parents or pupils, school is determined to win back their outstanding status: 'We will continue as a school community to strive for better things...and to be regarded in the wider educational world as a leading school and professional centre of excellence.'

SEN provision has been 'transformed', with an assistant head leading the the way on SEN and inclusion. Few state schools feel that they have sufficient funds to provide all the help every child needs, but 'we feel we've made substantial progress'. The Extra Mile project targets underachieving year 10 girls, who are mostly from white low-income families. The school is also a Potential Plus Partner School which aims to identify 'high learning potential students' by using a programme called Maurice B, which uses cognitive tests to help identify Oxbridge students.

Joint sixth form with next-door William Ellis School, with co-ed tutor groups. It is also part of LaSWAP, which includes La Sainte Union and Acland Burghley schools too, and has over 1,500 students. Each school teaches the core sixth form subjects, but students visit other schools in the group for more minority subjects eg film studies and further maths. The ability range encompasses those aspiring to read medicine at Cambridge and those working for an introductory BTec diploma in health and social care, with appropriate entry requirements. A scheme in conjunction with La Sainte Union targets very able scientists, who study together and take part in organised work experience and masterclasses. English is the most popular A level subject at Parliament Hill, with psychology second. In 2018, 42 per cent A*-B, 19 per cent A*/A.

Games, options, the arts: This is a very physical school and indeed the reason that many pupils choose it above others. Its stunning location almost begs one to be outdoors. Students have the opportunity to experience a wide variety of activities in physical education and the curriculum alone includes dance, swimming, gymnastics, tennis, rounders, cricket, athletics, fitness, invasion games and trampolining. A year 7 student can expect to participate in a minimum of two hours of PE every week as well as learn to swim at nearby Swiss Cottage baths. This doesn't include the extracurricular sporting activities: table tennis, badminton, dodgeball, football, cheerleading and various dance activities.

Dance is the real hot favourite at Parli Hill and one pupil told us that she chose the school because it was one of the few schools in the area that offers dance at GCSE level. Dance at the school comes in many varieties including PHS Dance Elite, contemporary dance and street dance, and there are many opportunities to compete for the coveted Camden Shield by entering any one of the numerous dance competitions, including Rock Challenge and Camden schools' dance festival. (Parliament Hill actually won the National Rock Challenge a few years ago and delighted students were asked to perform at Disneyland Paris.) School also hosts an annual Sweet Summer Dance Show.

Furthermore, year 10 students are offered the opportunity to work towards either a dance leaders level 1 award or a sports leaders level 1 award. Both are designed 'to teach leadership qualities and give students an opportunity to gain experience in leading sports sessions for their feeder primary schools.' Sports teams play successful matches against other Camden schools. School has two tennis/netball courts at the front of the school and a grassy area at the back where the football teams practise, plus a rather ageing hall for gym and badminton with a fitness suite. (New multi-purpose sports centre is part of the school's rebuild programme.)

Everyone takes DT GCSE, with a choice of four options. The single storey DT block was built to an environmentally-friendly design with a green roof, and forms the fourth side of a grassy courtyard, twisting up to meet the original Edwardian building. On another corner of the building is the performing arts block, clad in green glass, which provides music rooms and the dance and drama studios. The top floor corridors are lined with expressive, colourful and imaginative GCSE and A level photography and artwork, and textile designs hang in the stairwells. 'The art department really struck me', one pupil told us when she was looking at secondary schools. (Pretty good photography studio space too.)

This is a very physical school and indeed the reason that many pupils choose it above others. Its stunning location almost begs one to be outdoors. Dance is the hot favourite

Music popular here too and many girls have instrumental lessons and can choose from a variety of musical groups to join including orchestra, rock band, flute group, jazz, string and brass ensembles, or sing in the choir. Those on free school meals get free music lessons. One big annual musical a year (recently Fame) and one main play. Drama also popular and pupils have a large and fairly new drama studio in which to rehearse.

A breakfast club every morning at 8am and plenty more activities ranging from Italian and drama clubs to creative writing and documentary making. They visit museums, theatres and galleries, travel to China and go on physics trips to Switzerland. D of E very popular, as is debating – many students have competed passionately in the Urban Debating League and the Debate Mate Cup.

Background and atmosphere: Opened in 1906, has an idyllic site on the edge of Hampstead Heath.

Plenty of grassy space, including a sculpture park and kick-around area. Buildings range from solid Edwardiana to the 21st century award-winning DT and performing arts blocks. Is at last in receipt of £25 million, paid for by Camden Community Development Programme, which is funding a new maths, English and science block, a multi-purpose sports centre and a dedicated sixth form building – due for completion in 2019. Money is also going towards renovating the existing main Edwardian building (which was very tired in places when we did our tour, especially the loos, which could do with a major spruce up).

Harmonious atmosphere. Despite the huge range of pupils, both ethnically and socially, girls tend to get on well together, with few reports of bullying. Recently one of six in the country to win a Diamond quality mark for cultural diversity. 'Very much a community school', one parent told us – and very 'inclusive.' Bright and engaging students – one who travels from as far as Covent Garden because of the school's reputation: 'I started this school in year 8 as I wasn't very happy at my last school, and heard about Parliament Hill. I was particularly attracted to its location and outdoor space as well as the bright classrooms..I settled in pretty much immediately and everyone was so friendly.' And a parent added: 'The good thing about a school of this size is that almost everyone is going to find another like minded person to hang out with.'

Definitely a sense of personality at the school and of girls who know their minds: 'a lively atmosphere,' as one parent described it. Posters reinforcing 'female power' are dotted around the school – most noticeably near the sports hall. 'Female empowerment is very much part of the ethos at Parliament Hill. Girls here have a real sense of themselves as individuals. These are girls who will make a difference to the lives of other people.'

Pastoral care, well-being and discipline: Many vulnerable pupils here, including refugees and those with learning difficulties, who get 'excellent' support, says Ofsted. Liaises with its feeder primary school to identify girls likely to be in need of extra help with making the transition to senior school: 'Our transition is acknowledged to be excellent and supportive – we work very closely with families.' School also works with outside agencies that provide therapy or counselling to those in need, with a designated key worker in school. It also runs many programmes to motivate disaffected pupils, stretch the aspirations of bright girls and ensure everyone gets a chance to broaden their horizons. One parent told us: 'The school works very hard at narrowing the gap between disadvantaged and non-disadvantaged pupils.'

Assertive classroom management keeps most lessons running without disruptions (although we did pass some slightly rowdier ones on our tour). Big on some areas of discipline like punctuality, attendance and school attire – no uniform, but the rule is 'no gaps, no straps, no shorts' and students will be ticked off if they don't adhere to this. 'It's a problem in the summer,' one student grumbled. Older girls are allowed to go out onto Hampstead Heath at lunchtimes, together with pupils from nearby schools, William Ellis and La Sainte Union, and locals have complained about litter problems. 'We're very concerned. The girls regard the Heath as very special to them, and we're doing work on social responsibility to educate them that it's for everyone in the community'.

Pastoral care is very good, report parents. 'I've always felt they know my daughter very well,' said one. 'They school has contacted me whenever they've had concerns, and they've dealt with any problems quickly and well.' Ofsted remarked how: 'Students speak of the school being an extended family where they feel safe and supported at all times.'

Pupils and parents: 'Amazingly diverse' student population speaks some 50 different languages at home, though few are at early stages of learning English. Over 200 refugees. Nearly half of the girls are on free school meals, but also good support from some local middle-class families. OGs include actress Katrin Cartlidge, BBC journalist Laura Trevelyan, Lola Young, Baroness Young of Hornsey and Emma Hayes, manager of Chelsea Football Club Women.

Entrance: Takes 180 girls into year 7, with admissions organised through the local authority. Priority for particular SENs, siblings, children in care and those with exceptional social needs. Then by distance – generally within a mile and a half. Those joining LaSWAP sixth form to do A levels must have at least eight GCSE passes including three 4 and two 6 grades; various vocational courses available for those with lower grades. Increasingly becoming the school of choice for parents living in the area and not (as was the case historically), second choice to Camden School for Girls.

Exit: Between two-thirds and three-quarters of pupils move on to joint sixth form with William Ellis school, part of LaSWAP sixth form consortium. Some join other sixth forms, eg Camden School for Girls or Woodhouse College, others go to colleges such as City and Islington or Westminster Kingsway to do vocational courses.

Around a quarter to Russell Group universities; 2018 courses ranged from biomedical science at King's College London to Japanese studies at Manchester to international relations and economics at SOAS. Quite a few to art foundation courses.

Remarks: Popular girls' comprehensive in idyllic situation on the borders of Hampstead Heath, with a diverse but harmonious student population. Aesthetically tired, but much needed cash injection in the process of changing that.

Portland Place School

56–58 Portland Place, London W1B 1NJ

020 7307 8700 | admin@portland-place.co.uk | portland-place.co.uk

Independent	Pupils: 290; sixth form: 51
Ages: 7–18 (7–16 from 2020)	Fees: £21,030 pa

Head: Since April 2017, David Bradbury, previously deputy head of South Hampstead High. BSc in physics, MSc and PGCE, all from Keele, plus an MA in education from the Open University. Physics co-ordinator at Bangkok Patana School for a number of years; taught at Chase Terrace High and Newcastle-under-Lyme College; head of physics at Nicholas Chamberlaine School and assistant head at Alleyne's High School. Hobbies and interests include archery, cookery, cryptic crosswords, film, literature and music, as well as hill-walking and board games.

Academic matters: A broader band of ability than in most of the fiercely competitive London day schools – something the school takes pride in and, together with its small class sizes, sees as a 'unique selling point.' Only 12 in a class in years 4-6, an average of 15 in years 7 to 11 (we saw several smaller ones) and smaller still in the sixth form means that attention can be given to each child – you can be sure that there will be both stretching and confidence building. A godsend for the discerning parent who can see through the merry-go-round nature of 11+ and wants to ensure their child is educated rather than exam-processed. Hence the increasing demand for places lower down the school; there is now one class in each of years 4 and 5 as well as two in year 6. Piles on the value added – 'We're always near the top of the value added tables' is the boast.

No Latin or Greek at GCSE ('there isn't the demand from our parents,' we were told). Economics, computing, sport studies and media are offered, along with the traditional subjects. All pupils take at least one of French, Italian or Spanish; not much enthusiasm for taking up a second modern language. If your daughter speaks Italian at home, she is encouraged to do Spanish as her GCSE option. If you want your child to take a GCSE in, for example, Arabic, the school will facilitate it within the timetable, but the onus of paying and finding the teacher is on you.

At GCSE, 26 per cent 9-7 in 2018. The value added shows at A level, where the results are more impressive, most being in the B-D bracket, with a decent sprinkling of As (65 per cent A*-C grades and 10 per cent A*/A in 2018). We saw small tutor groups of as few as five – notably these were in science subjects. Clever ones, with offers from Oxbridge as well other Russell Group universities. Arts subjects tend to be busier (up to 15 in a group). However, sixth form is closing in 2020. Library manned by full-time librarian and a nice place to sit and read. Lots of fiction, used for competitions, book club and quiet study. As an academic resource it is risible (school prefers 'needs developing' and reminds us that the individual heads of departments keep library resources in their offices). Good IT suites and resources for the popular media and film options.

Setting in maths, science and English from year 7. Plenty of movement between sets, we were assured. Sizeable number of mild dyslexics but no additional support in lessons apart from general support from class teacher. Staunch policy of no withdrawals from classes (except once weekly for children who have EAL). School employs four specialist learning support teachers who will arrange to see children outside lesson time in groups of two or three to devise strategies to help them access the mainstream curriculum. No screening on admission. However SENCo oversees general provision and monitoring – 80 to 90 children perceived as having some kind of mild learning disability or difficulty and some have IEPs. Most with more than the mildest difficulties seek support outside school. Inside school, the attitude is healthy – 'I'm not treated as if dyslexia is a crime, unlike at my

Lots of extracurricular stuff – when we visited a stress management workshop was being delivered to all GCSE students

last school,' we were told. Two of the three buildings have lifts but school will be helpful if someone breaks a leg and move lessons to the ground floor.

Games, options, the arts: Well known for sporting prowess despite there being virtually no facilities on site. Pupils are bussed or walk everywhere – mostly to Regent's Park, with pitches and courts of all kinds, Seymour Place for swimming – and the results and achievements, given the conditions, are impressive. Years 7 to 9 have sport timetabled four times a week (one of the advantages of no canteen and shorter lunch breaks: time can be reallocated to sport). Football and netball tours of Barbados, swimming teams win competitions (Westminster champions five years in a row), masses of medals in cross-country and local honours in athletics and team sports. Pervasive pride in school sports, helped, no doubt, by classy Olympians on staff. However most really keen sportsmen and women do their serious sport outside school – girls' football a particular highpoint. Sport now compulsory to year 12 – one afternoon a week minimum of netball or football.

Music and drama similarly 'massive.' Music mostly means pop and jazz (we saw lots of ukulele enthusiasts). There are also a few violinists and woodwinders amongst the jazz pianists, guitarists, drummers and bassists who predominate, but eclectic range of music taken seriously. We were shown round by a budding actor in year 10 who enthused about the opportunities he has been given to develop his talent. Wholehearted, whole school productions annually – West Side Story, Singing in the Rain, The Producers and Annie are recent offerings; not on site as no suitable space but venues include the RADA studios in WC1. Upper school recently performed a resoundingly successful Richard III – which was then a sell-out at the Edinburgh Fringe. Lower school (up to year 9) recently performed Skellig as their annual production. Good-sized on-site drama studio can accommodate smaller productions (we were impressed with the assortment of costumes and props).

Art in the lower school is lively and inventive. We saw ink portraits in the style of Peter Howson, as well as pop art-style Creme Eggs. Fewer than 10 do art A level – facilities limited, though there is a textiles room and school excels in photography.

DT similarly energetic – resistant materials, pewter casting, CAD and CAM, though all in rather small and poky rooms in basement. Lots of extracurricular stuff – when we visited a stress management workshop was being delivered to all GCSE students. Trips galore – we have seldom seen such a full programme. Much use made of London's galleries, museums and exhibitions, plus the nearby wider world and the opportunities it offers for field, sporting and other educational exercises, both here and abroad.

Background and atmosphere: This is a young school, founded only 20 or so years ago by the visionary head of science at St Paul's Girls', Richard Walker. His aim was to create a smaller independent co-ed senior school that wasn't super selective. Part of the Alpha Plus group, it forms one of their 18 UK schools and colleges, bringing the advantages of the economies of scale. Portland Place – the road – is a broad, straight thoroughfare in the heart of Regency London, two minutes from Oxford Circus to the south, two minutes to Regent's Park to the north. It is lined by august embassies (China, Kenya, Poland, Portugal) and the HQs of royal and learned institutions (architects, physicists, radiologists, anaesthetists). The main school building – Portland Place – identifies itself with a modest brass plate and is elegantly splendid. It is rare for us to compliment a school on its decor but a pleasure to do so here. Eye-catching blue carpet up and down the stairs (not just on the ground floor for show as elsewhere), magnificent ceilings, cornices, columns, capitals and fireplaces: nowhere more so than in the old ballroom, rescued from its carapace of false ceiling and fluorescent tubes and very much in use. All in tip-top nick. This building houses the lower years, the hall (used for gym and dance) and the top floors (formerly the servants' quarters) which accommodate music and languages.

A second building in Great Portland Street houses the upper years and has a breathtaking eyeball-to-eyeball view of the BT Tower, seemingly within grabbing distance

A second building in Great Portland Street, five minutes away, houses the upper years and has a breathtaking eyeball-to-eyeball view of the BT Tower, seemingly within grabbing distance. Harford House, also in Great Portland Street and with a facade resembling that of a corporate HQ, is home to art, drama and science. It's a logistical nightmare – five or seven storeys to be up and down all day, three buildings – and it all has to be timetabled, supervised and navigated. We suppose everyone to be very fit – a real bonus for children who need lots of movement and exercise if they are to perform well mentally.

No school kitchen. Pupils bring packed lunches or order in from local cafés (which deliver dozens of paninis etc in little brown carriers). Years 10 and 11 and the sixth hang out in the many cafés in or around Great Portland Street and just love the privilege of this kind of freedom.

Pastoral care, well-being and discipline: Definitely an informal feel to the place. Although pupils are not quite on first name terms with teachers, one can sense an equality in the relationships not seen in more traditional establishments. Good use of sixth form mentors for years 7 and 8 – really fosters inter-age group understanding and friendships, especially helpful in so small a school. Solidly structured pastoral care hierarchy picks up and deals with problems, but there's a pervasive sense of everyone looking out for everyone else. People seem to know each other's little brothers and sisters here. Parents praise the home-school communications and especially the termly parents' evenings. 'The teachers are mostly young and energetic,' enthused a parent, 'and you really get to know them.'

Pupils and parents: More boys than girls (about 60:40 in lower years) – simply because there are so many more girls' and co-ed schools in London. Mixed, as befits its location – trad, moneyed, independent education veterans alongside newbies and newcomers from here, there and everywhere, blended with those who couldn't get into the 'academic' schools and for whom PP has been a jolly lucky find. From the whole urban sprawl – no longer just the north and west but around 30 per cent from east and south too. Mostly UK born and based but also from pretty much the rest of the globe, solar system and beyond, in a great undivided family. Brains? Yes, though common denominator more palpably pleasure, pride and enthusiasm for the place.

Entrance: There are 7+, 8+, 9+ and 10+ intakes – partly to steal a march on the competition and partly to meet the needs of those who dread the 11+ circus and will do anything to avoid it (wise move). 'Informal tests' in English and maths with deputy/head of year. Year 7 has tests in English and maths and a chat with a teacher. For places at 12+, 13+ and 14+, same format plus additional test in science. School keen to dispel image that it's the go-to place for a child on the dys-strata. Child has to be able to cope and pupils who can't will be turned down. Sixth form is closing in 2020 and there are no more year 12 intakes.

Exit: Wide range of post-A level destinations and courses, including sports and exercise science, mechanical engineering and forensic investigations at the newer universities. The odd one to study music and to art college; London, Exeter, Southampton, Liverpool universities popular. About 30 per cent leave after GCSE (mostly to non-fee paying sixth form colleges).

Money matters: No scholarships or bursaries offered at any point.

Remarks: Small, nurturing and refreshingly relaxed. A haven of creativity in the pushy academically competitive world of London day schools. A place for engaged, lively, normal kids – privileged, yes, but Sloanes, no. Becoming ever more popular as more and more people discover it. The challenge will be to maintain its ethos of 'broader academic intake' in the face of increasing demand.

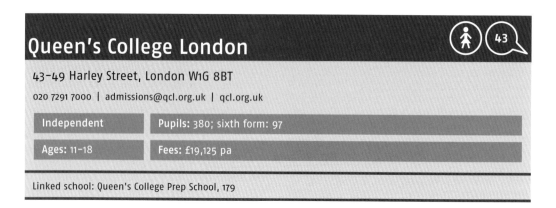

Queen's College London

43–49 Harley Street, London W1G 8BT

020 7291 7000 | admissions@qcl.org.uk | qcl.org.uk

Independent	Pupils: 380; sixth form: 97
Ages: 11–18	Fees: £19,125 pa

Linked school: Queen's College Prep School, 179

Principal: Since September 2017, Richard Tillett, previously senior deputy head at Harrogate Ladies' College. Degree in modern languages and history from Cambridge; taught history and politics at King Edward VI Grammar and was housemaster and history teacher at The Leys before joining Harrogate Ladies' in 2010 as head of sixth form. His wife, Dr Emma Longstaff, is a sociologist who now works in academic publishing, and they have a young daughter. Richard's primary academic interests are Russian history (he is a Russian speaker) and contemporary politics. Away from school life, he is an avid follower of football and cricket, and loves travel, good food and hill walking.

Academic matters: The trend is upwards and results get more impressive year on year. In 2018, 89 per cent A*-B grades at A level, with 57 per cent A*/A grades. Pupils now uniformly take three A levels plus EPQ. GCSE results 71 per cent 9-7 in 2018. The range of subjects is broad, but by far the most popular and successful subject, according to recent results, is English, closely followed by history. Philosophy and ethics is another popular department. Tiny take up of further maths and physics, though several doing biology and chemistry, and top grades uncommon in all these subjects. The number of girls doing a modern language at A level appears to be low too. This is despite the fact that there is a lot of language provision in the

early years – in year 7 they do Mandarin, Spanish, French, Italian and German, and then can choose a second modern language in addition to French in year 8 and 9 before finalising GCSE choices. We swept through a corridor overhearing the songs and languages of different European countries that poured out of each classroom. Results in modern languages are good at GCSE – in French, Italian and Spanish. A shame that this doesn't seem to carry through – yet – to A level. This may change following the appointment of a new head of modern languages from North London Collegiate.

Classics department is lively, we were told, with lots of recital competitions, for example, organised by the London Classical Association, as well as plays, trips and activities. Top Latin set in year 9 is introduced to ancient Greek and a tiny few take A GCSE. The take up of Latin is also low at A level; at GCSE approximately five each year take the subject, some achieving strong A* and A grades.

In some of the EBacc subjects (maths, English, history, geography, and French, but not sciences) the girls take the tougher IGCSE. Results in maths are excellent. No one has got below a B in recent years, with 19 As and eight A*s recently. Parents of girls in years 7 and 8 are excited to report their daughters discovering a love of science and enthusiasm for subjects they had never shown an interest in before. From 2018 girls will take the tougher IGCSE in sciences too.

Reports across the board about the excellent relationships between staff and pupils. Girls here are treated with respect and consideration by their teachers and we were told by a number of parents that the atmosphere was more similar to a university than a school – helped, no doubt, by the 'supervision style' class sizes in the sixth form. Our guides enthused about the teachers 'being there for them' and that they felt they could always trouble them – in or out of lessons – with a question or concern. Small class sizes (15-20) and sometimes tiny in the sixth form – contribute to the particular personal rapport that develops between teacher and student.

Despite its urban centre – Oxford Street and John Lewis only a stone's throw away – Regent's Park is also just up the road and the girls can walk there in 10 minutes

One SENCo only, employed four days a week. Emphasis given to literacy and numeracy in admissions process means candidates with 'spiky profiles' are unlikely to reach the standard. Although the SENCo can meet the needs of pupils with mild dyspraxia, dyslexia, dyscalculia etc, 'we are not a school that specialises in this,' asserts head. School currently supports a handful of girls with ASD, and takes measures such as timetabling a period each day when a student with sensory issues is able to be in a quiet and calm environment, and liaising with another's psychotherapist to manage her anxieties during exams. All staff are trained in managing ASD in the classroom. Girls needing extra support are rarely taken out of lessons but will have 'individual learning plans' which all their teachers will be familiar with so that support can be given all the time during every lesson. Laptops and extra time may form part of the plan. No EFL tuition but will give support for EAL if necessary.

Games, options, the arts: Sport here is surprisingly strong considering this is a central London all girls' day school – and a relatively small one, too. Lots of choice of sports – netball arguably the strongest, but girls can also play lacrosse, football and tag rugby in winter, rounders, cricket and tennis in the summer. Curriculum games now takes place at Paddington Rec – a twenty minute bus journey compared to the former ten minute jaunt to Regent's Park – but with far better facilities: AstroTurfs allowing for whole class teaching of tennis, netball and hockey, an athletics track and gym for senior students. Plenty of fixtures

against other schools – they normally field a first and second team – and games is timetabled heavily in the early years. Twice a week girls will have double games, once a week PE and once a week dance. A gym in the bowels of the school is well equipped and a great space for letting off steam and doing (almost) any kind of sport, dance, ballet or gymnastics and even spinning and zumba. The school's sports uniform – 'a hoody and leggings,' as one parent described it – is very popular with the girls, no doubt a positive influence on the relish for physical activity.

Enthusiasm for sport wanes somewhat in the senior years but they then graduate to yoga, pilates and zumba classes. Swimming takes place at the Marshall Street Leisure Centre. Work has been done and a new house system introduced to create a fuller programme with a wider choice of activities and to encourage the competitive spirit. The appointment of a dynamic head of PE is reaping dividends. 'We are working on two threads,' school told us, 'coaching for excellence and ensuring everyone has a go.'

Drama and music are flourishing, productions here are inclusive, exciting and impressive. A recent show, Belles of the Ball, was devised by the girls with the help of a visiting professional writer and was based on a women's football team formed during World War 1 to raise money for men at the front. In writing and producing the play the girls not only wowed an audience with their final performance but were able to extend and enhance their understanding of a particular period through a very personal and liberating female experience. We spent some time with the head of drama, a former actor, who impressed us with her spontaneity, passion and experience. Lots of lunchtime clubs connected with drama.

School has a full orchestra and a number of ensembles. We heard rave reviews of the singing and tales of girls who had shown no interest in music before starting here, now being entered into choral scholarships for university. Formal recitals and concerts held in the beautiful Waiting Room on the ground floor. Annual jazz concert and a healthy number of girls are starting to choose to take music A level.

The art on the walls and the sculptures on display take your breath away. The art room is creatively inspiring – a barn-like, large, long room with windows in the ceiling and sun beaming in from every corner. However, when we visited the atmosphere was distinctly chilly. The girls were focused but not relaxed. What should have been a buzzy, creative warmth was instead stiff and wary. Perhaps we caught it on a bad day, but we did hear a few reports from parents that suggested we weren't imagining it. Girls who take art have historically done well here; large numbers continue to apply for the handful of art scholarships at the 11 plus. This should be a strength of the school: whether it will continue to be so remains to be seen.

Plenty of opportunity to travel, whether on cultural exchanges with schools in Pennsylvania and France, for example, or on football and cricket trips to, eg, Sri Lanka. Voluntary work or work experience now compulsory part of sixth form curriculum.

Background and atmosphere: Founded in 1848 and given a royal charter in 1853, a pioneer in education for women, this was the first institution in Great Britain to give academic qualifications to girls. Still on its original site in four elegant, well-proportioned Georgian houses, internally it has often been altered through the years in order to provide the best modern education possible. There is a faint whiff of Victorian hospital about it, with some cold stone floors and forbidding doors; however, the William Morris wallpaper decorating the ground floor corridor, tastefully toning in with the pale green school uniform, together with the high ceilings, large windows and frescos, goes a long way to making the school feel tastefully familiar, and comfortable. The school, tucked between expensive doctors' private practices on Harley Street in the heart of central London, with the music blaring out of New Look and Top Shop only yards away in nearby Oxford Street, is deceptively large. The houses extend some distance to the rear and classrooms and corridors are large and airy. An exciting development extending up at the top of the building ('the roof project') has provided a new sixth form centre.

The school is more intimate than many of its kind in London. Older girls frequently smile and greet much younger ones, a sign of refreshing vertical friendships. This is not a school paralysed by hierarchy. Our guides said the thing about their school they were most proud of was the 'community'. 'Everyone knows each other and everyone is involved,' they enthused. A wonderfully atmospheric, wood panelled library with grand fireplaces, dark green wallpaper and serious looking, distinguished people, staring down from paintings on the walls, is where the sixth form currently work. The Waiting Room is an elegant old-fashioned room with an arresting frieze on the ceiling, where once girls waited to be taken to their next lesson. Now PSHE talks are held here, small drama productions and concerts. The 'goldfish bowl', a striking glass-walled computer centre in the heart of the school, is a startling modern contrast to most of the rest of the school, and just outside Daunt Books runs a book stall where parents can place credit and girls can buy books at will. Plenty of computers around the school and a number of classrooms have desks with drawers containing laptops.

Our guides enthused about the teachers 'being there for them' and that they felt they could always trouble them – in or out of lessons

Spacious dining room in the basement, colourful Perspex chairs cheering up the dank basement ambience. Large glass doors open out onto an attractive courtyard area, with surrounding benches, into which girls can spill during the warmer months. Lots of choice, sushi and salad as well as the usual pasta and potatoes. Sixth formers can go out at lunch and sample what Oxford Street has to offer.

Pastoral care, well-being and discipline: Year heads, known as year tutors, help to monitor each individual girl, and there are section heads to oversee, for example, years 7-9 and years 10 and 11. There do not appear to be any serious disciplinary issues. We were surprised to hear no mention of drugs at all among the parents. 'Girls here are respected and treated as adults.' 'They feel listened to, the atmosphere is more like a university than a school' commented a number.

Parents' perception is that there could be more collaboration with boys' schools in the area. School counters this, pointing out participation in the Model United Nations and debating in the London leagues which 'bring the girls into contact with boys', as well as musical events organised with Harrow school.

Pupils and parents: Traditionally regarded as a school that caters for the well brought up, upper middle class girl whose parents regard a good education as of the highest value. The latter persists, and while there remains a faint fragrance of aristocracy, the demographic, as in most central London schools, is highly cosmopolitan. A wide mix of nationalities, Middle Eastern, European and American as well as Scandinavian, Antipodean and Asian; but there is no EFL teaching so they have to speak good English. The culture of the school is very English, however, and the majority of the pupils 'tend to be British,' says school. Girls here are well mannered and polite. They will look you in the eye and can hold their ground. A number of parents said how pleased they were that their daughters had formed such good and healthy friendships. Their view is that the school selects grounded girls who are willing to take advantage of the opportunities on offer. There used to be limos parked outside on Harley Street delivering girls – not any more.

Two of the earliest students, Miss Buss and Miss Beale, went on to found the North London Collegiate School and Camden School for Girls, and St Hilda's College Oxford, respectively. Katherine Mansfield and Jacqueline du Pré also stand amongst the long list of distinguished old girls as well as, more recently, writers Daisy Goodwin and Imogen Lloyd Webber. A distinguished tradition and history in the making.

Entrance: Mainly at 11+ via the London 11+ Consortium (formerly the North London Girls' Schools Consortium). Now a bespoke cognitive ability test (maths, VR and NVR), an 'imaginative interview experience' to explore candidates' skills, aptitudes and intellectual acuity and a common reference form for prep schools to detail wider contextual information on attitudes and character as well as academic performance. Some 500 applicants for 60 places and the numbers seem to rise relentlessly each year. Unusually at Queen's everyone is interviewed, regardless of performance in the exam. Indeed interviews take place between October and December before the exam. 'We like to form a picture of the child without seeing her test results.' They are genuinely selective and are looking for someone who is going to enjoy getting involved and seize the opportunities available.

No automatic entrance from Queen's College Prep but a good percentage come from there. Otherwise over 40 different feeder schools, with about 15 per cent from local state primaries. Another (small) intake at 16+ subject to GCSE results and letters of recommendation from their previous schools. All prospective entrants at this level interviewed by the head of sixth form.

Exit: Some 30 per cent leave after GCSEs, mostly to board or move into the state system. Post A level leavers to top universities eg King's, LSE, Birmingham and Exeter, with two to Oxbridge in 2018 and two off to study medicine.

Money matters: Several means-tested bursaries available at 11+ and 16+, funded by the Old Queen's bursary trust fund. Academic, music and art scholarships, for up to 25 per cent of fees, for both internal and external candidates. Would hope always to be able to find a way of keeping a pupil in need.

Remarks: An elegant school offering a broad education to bright, interesting girls. There is nothing generic about Queen's College. A very individual place where each girl is genuinely treated as an individual Will suit your all-round daughter who will thrive in a structured, nurturing community that takes a personal interest in every child. Stimulating teaching with strength in both breadth and depth. An excellent preparation for life for a young woman in the 21st century.

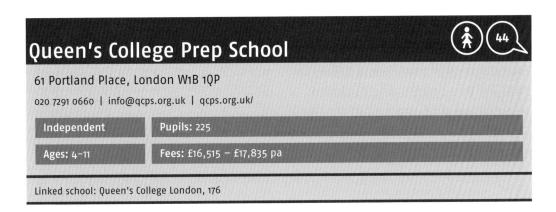

Queen's College Prep School

61 Portland Place, London W1B 1QP

020 7291 0660 | info@qcps.org.uk | qcps.org.uk/

Independent	Pupils: 225
Ages: 4–11	Fees: £16,515 – £17,835 pa

Linked school: Queen's College London, 176

Headmistress: Since 2016, Emma Webb (40s) married to an ex-RAF officer with two children at school in Cheltenham. She read sociology and social policy at Royal Holloway whilst also working for British Airways, so more time at the grindstone than in the pub. After qualifying as a teacher and a spell in the state system and Davenies Prep, she followed her high flying husband to Saudi Arabia, where she spent 10 years, latterly as deputy head of primary at the huge, cutting edge British International School in Riyadh. A great tech fan, she is busy transforming the school systems from paper to screen and incentivising both staff and children. According to parents she has 'ironed out some of the idiosyncrasies' but 'maintained all of the best bits'.

Entrance: More put down at birth now for two classes in reception and although there is no active sibling policy, the head is confident that younger girls naturally follow their elders. The few occasional places higher up the school, almost all due to globe-trotting parents, are in high demand. This is a genuinely international school with parents who come from, literally, all over the world. A large percentage of parents work in the professions. Most of the girls live nearby, or at least north of Oxford Street, but a few come from Kensington or the City.

Exit: The head says that her ethos is to prepare girls for all schools and that she is direct with parents about the right school for their child. 'We advise parents on the school that we feel is best for their daughter rather than our results table.' She is also a fan of boarding and in the past girls have gone to Downe House, St Mary's Ascot and Wycombe Abbey, although none in 2018. In the main, parents either choose the usual London academic (often single sex) senior schools such as City of London, Godolphin & Latymer, South Hampstead or North London Collegiate or opt for the slightly less intense environment of Francis Holland (Regent's Park), Queen's Gate or Queen's College itself. The leavers win a fair number of scholarships, mostly to FHRP or Queen's College.

Remarks: Past the pointy hat of All Soul's Langham Place and the sexy art deco glamour of the BBC, you turn the corner into more sedate Portland Place, framing the distant trees of Regent's Park. Here, QCPS has some unlikely neighbours, including the decidedly odd couple of the People's Republic of China embassy and the openly hedonistic Quintessentially concierge company.

Tour de force is brand new STEM lab, paid for by parents. Any budding scientist would have a field day here and head's enthusiasm suggests she would love to join them

The hall is covered in imaginative artwork and you are immediately aware that you are in a busy school, even if some of the years are out on trips. The layout, spread over two original houses, is slightly confusing to an outsider as they are not joined on every floor but girls, scurrying purposefully, prove that it is no worry to them. The 19th century houses were designed for entertaining so the ceilings are high and the windows are large, at least until you reach the attic, but even there the seductively colourful and popular art room and the classrooms for year 6 are bright and airy. The dining room in the basement does strike chords of the 'downstairs' element of Upstairs, Downstairs

---

A serious comittment to the creative arts is made at QCPS and Miss Rosy's Dance Academy plays a large part (she also runs holiday classes)

but the classroom at the back escapes any gloom by opening onto an interior garden.

The tour de force is the brand spanking new STEM lab, paid for by parents, full of exciting labelled drawers and bins for pipettes and goggles as well as a row of startlingly clean, white lab coats embellished with the green school logo. Any budding scientist would have a field day in here and the head's enthusiasm suggests that she would love to join them, given half a chance.

The school was described by a parent as 'not a sausage factory', but EW is still keen to ensure that the academic standards attained by the girls gives them the widest choice of secondary education. She is particularly keen on maths and the sciences taking an equal place in the curriculum, along with the subjects more traditionally taught to girls: 'I want to encourage them to build bridges in ballet shoes', a comment that was endorsed by 'I waxed lyrical about the maths provision to my husband'. The sciences are condensed into two and a half of the three terms yearly higher up the school, allowing the pupils time to conduct an experimental project (not 100 per cent successful in the case of the irrigation of the vertical gardens on show).

Her enthusiasm for STEM has not allowed EW to neglect other subjects, with English teaching being praised as well as the introduction of Mandarin, Spanish and Italian as extracurricular options alongside French. The fact that none of the teaching staff left at the end of her first year is proof that they are all happy with the new hierarchies that she has established and certainly, on our visit, there was nothing but smiley faces. She has appointed a 'fab head of learning support' and believes that this is 'one of the highest impact hires' that she has made; parents would agree with her. Staff appear to handle the challenge of teaching a child with no English on arrival (provided it is at the lower end of the school) with absolutely no fuss and great success.

A major play for the creative arts is made at QCPS and Miss Rosy's Dance Academy plays a large part, with grateful London parents, casting around to entertain their children, remarking on how brilliant it is that she also runs holiday classes. The music department under the roof is noisy and enthusiastic, led by a teacher whom one parent described as 'magnificent' and, as he is South African, there is even the chance to play his native marimbas. As well as the slightly unconventional percussion-playing opportunities, there are the more usual events such as the Harvest Festival and nativity plays (a camel-based offering last year) in All Souls church, and annual musicals.

One of the head's targets is to increase the sports provision, in particular competitive sports – 'the single best change EW has made'. She has appointed a new head of sport and the offering is going to be widened to include current favourites such as cricket, now that scoring a century at Lords is open to all. Unfortunately, all inner London schools suffer from having little outside space and QCPS is no exception, the girls having to walk to the gardens at the end of the street to let off steam outside on non-sporting days.

At the beginning of the day an Early Birds breakfast club helps out over-stretched parents and after school ends, teachers run a variety of additional activities. External help is also summoned and your daughter can choose from a selection including coding, cooking, gardening, sign language and yoga. The food is alone in being given a low rating, despite a new catering manager and an attempt to move away from 'nursery food'.

EW is very much a new broom, which goes down well with current parents, one of them saying that 'the school has a more modern, professional feel' and that it is aiming to be 'a platinum brand in a competitive market'. This sounds as if the school's charm might be at risk, but we were persuaded that the head is simply trying to make it fit with the aspirations of modern London families.

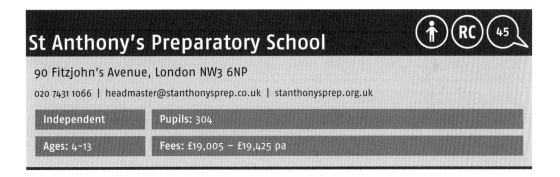

St Anthony's Preparatory School

90 Fitzjohn's Avenue, London NW3 6NP

020 7431 1066 | headmaster@stanthonysprep.co.uk | stanthonysprep.org.uk

Independent	Pupils: 304
Ages: 4–13	Fees: £19,005 – £19,425 pa

Headmaster: Since 2010, Paul Keyte (early 50s). Educated at Bloxham and then read philosophy and theology at Oriel, Oxford, where he got a first. Says he rather fell into teaching but 'loved it, and so stayed': after spells at Dulwich and KCS Wimbledon, he was director of studies at Winchester and deputy head at both Highgate and South Hampstead.

A warm-mannered and, as befits a philosopher, a reflective man. Evidently deeply thoughtful about the nature of the school, its potential strengths and pitfalls, and tries hard to interpret the school's Catholic mission to a multi-ethnic and metropolitan constituency. Although his own teaching background is rooted in senior schools, his pride in the school, and affection for pupils and staff, is palpable.

A pragmatist, when the need arises: 'Schools face ever more outside scrutiny. We have to embrace change and feel easy about accountability – but without losing what's special'. St Anthony's has always been a touch quirky – teachers always known by their first names, and music and drama given strong prominence within the curriculum. But, as Mr Keyte makes clear, parents tend to enjoy school idiosyncrasies only to the extent that they don't get in the way of children's happiness and

well-being, and the ability to get to an appropriate senior school.

Plenty of action to back up his words: major refurbishment of the plant over the past eight years and, although it is split-site, both parts are now brimming over with fresh paint, ever-changing (and enticing) wall-displays of pupils' work, smartscreens in every classroom – and a huge drive forward in the range and quality of sport: 'children need to be fit and resilient,' he says. 'Life throws a lot at them, very early on.' He has even discreetly overseen the introduction of a dress code for staff – done with a light touch. 'Not rocket science, is it? We have to lead by example.'

Entrance: For the past few years, main entry point has been at reception, where there is now a two form entry. Boys come from about 25 different feeder nurseries: Catholic pupils have typically been at either St Mary's down the road or St Christina's in St John's Wood. Although the school is keen to maintain a strong constituency of Catholic pupils, everyone has to go through the assessment procedure. 'Given that most of the children are only 3 or 4,' explains the Head, 'we try to make it feel like a play day as far as possible, and to identify those most likely to respond to our style of teaching and learning'. Occasional spots for boys coming in at other times, but the general rule is to take a tour and then, as early as possible, register.

Exit: Leavers' destinations showcase how adept the school has become at nurturing a whole range of interests and appetites: predictably, a broad sweep of London destinations, especially Westminster, St Paul's, CLSB, Highgate, UCS and Mill Hill. But there's been a surge in popularity for Merchant Taylors' and Habs, and for the Catholic London Oratory and Cardinal Vaughan. Some boarding schools are also becoming popular with St Anthony's families – Eton, Winchester, Harrow, Sevenoaks and Tonbridge have all featured strongly in recent years. For Catholic parents especially, so also have Stonyhurst and Worth.

Like so many London prep schools, St Anthony's has had to adapt to a ruthless and rapidly changing world in which many pupils are under pressure to join junior departments of their senior schools aged 11, rather than hold off until 13. For many pupils, years 5 and 6 leading up to the 11+ is the time of maximum pressure. 'The heyday of common entrance feels quite distant at times,' says the head. 'But for those staying all the way, we make sure these last two years are the most enriched: to release the full academic potential of youngsters, and spice it up with the individuality which St Anthony's has always sought to foster.'

Remarks: Taking children mainly at reception, the aim is to offer at once a broad and balanced curriculum. 'English and maths open up a whole world of learning,' says the head, 'and we want our pupils exploring all of it.' Science and ICT are there right at the start, but from year 1 there is French and Mandarin as well as everything else one would expect – history and geography, art and DT. Religious studies is also taught – but with an eye and an ear for pupils of all faiths and of none.

By the time pupils are 10 and have moved to the senior school, everybody studies Latin and there are after-school opportunities to do ancient Greek and Arabic as well. There's a specially equipped classroom for DT, as well as lashings of art, music and drama. 'We don't want any part in the reductionism in the curriculum one sometimes hears about,' says the head. 'Creativity is at the heart of the school.' There are also a host of out-of-school hobby and discussion groups – philosophy and chess among them alongside the arts. 'My son has been given masses of opportunity in which to find his voice,' said one parent. Another added: 'The staff have a genuine love of learning, and are superb at communicating it.'

Because testing, in all its iterations, has become such a big feature of life for prep school children

from the age of 10 or 11, St Anthony's deploys a range of tests (such as CAT4, PIPS and MiDYis) to acclimatise pupils. 'They are useful visitors,' says the head, 'but life here is dictated, first and last, by what we believe to be enriching in its own right. Dedicated Study Skills department – one full time teacher and one part time, and two of the TAs have special training. There are regular diagnostic assessments to identify anyone needing extra input.

'My son has been given masses of opportunities to find his voice,' said one parent. Another added: 'Staff have such a love of learning, and are superb at communicating it'

All qualified teachers at St Anthony's – from the half dozen or so who have been there for over 20 years to the young Turks. Five TAs have recently studied for their PGCEs while working full time at the school. 'They are astonishingly dedicated,' says the head, 'and many are already academically highly qualified.' One parent, whose son had won a scholarship to a famous school, said what he liked most was that his son had felt 'inspired, rather than under pressure'.

Limited play areas (it is in the middle of Hampstead, after all), although it does have its own rather splendid swimming pool ('Thank God,' says one parent). Normal games see pupils take a 10 minute coach ride to Brondesbury playing fields. 'There's the odd day when traffic is a nightmare,' said a father. 'But they do well at getting them out at break and into the fresh air.' Since we last visited, a quiet revolution has taken place in the profile of sport, perhaps not unconnected with the appointment of outstanding sports teachers. Recent pupils include a boy who went on to captain the first XV at a major rugby-playing senior school, and two members of the Lawn Tennis Association. The main staples are football, rugby and hockey in winter and cricket and athletics in summer, but efforts are made to offer reasonable choice. Cross-country is enjoying a surge of popularity: 15 teachers ran a half marathon recently and another is an elite marathon runner. 'This level of commitment', says the head, 'rather rubs off on the pupils.'

The school is explicit that it wants all pupils physically literate, and there are competitive fixtures with other schools from year 4. 'They have to be fit enough to cope with life's assorted pressures,' says the head. Inevitably, 'some have to learn they are not always the best in the pack, but the idea is that everyone who wants to represent the school

South Hampstead High School

at sport can do so.' There is a clear underlying message here – for parents as much as for children: emotional resilience is all-important, and teamwork and games can, or should be, a significant part of the learning.

As always, masses of drama, music and art, with regular visits to museums, theatres and galleries. One of the head's early moves was to triple the number of music lessons, and the fact that the school also acquired a grand piano and built a new music studio left no doubt that he and the governors were dead set on protecting the school's reputation as a bastion of the creative arts. There's a full orchestra and a jazz orchestra, and the head of music allegedly claimed that every boy who finished his time at St Anthony's could take grade 5 theory in music – quite an achievement, if true.

A high-powered staff room – Oxbridge and doctorates all over the place – but school culture fosters collegiality and old hands willingly share best practice

Plays are performed annually – every pupil takes part in a play for their year group each Christmas and summer, and there are myriad further opportunities for performance – in designated school assemblies and so forth. There's also a major Shakespeare production every year – the most recent ('a triumph,' said one parent) was Macbeth. Art is every bit as strong – a raft of student work has recently been gracing the Saatchi Gallery, and the walls of the school are filled with pupils' latest creative output.

Founded in Victorian times, the school moved from Eastbourne to Hampstead in 1952, and was a family affair until recently – indeed, the present bursar is one of the founding family. It has long enjoyed the reputation for being ever-so-slightly alternative. 'Terms like "wacky" and "bohemian" fall too easily from the lips,' chuckled Mr Keyte. 'Schools always spawn myths, and one myth is that it always used to be wackier than it is now – now being 30 years ago, 10 years ago, or here today.' One parent said, 'The place fosters individuality, but they also foster awareness of others. My sons' friends at the school were all lovely kids.'

In fact, there is strong continuity: it's less academically assertive than some of its competitors, and continues to invest huge time, as well as significant resources, in its arts and mixed curriculum. What is gently shifting is the extent to which it can compete, on all fronts, with the best. The plant is hugely impressive, there is a long waiting list

and the staff are evidently completely committed. Taken over by Alpha Plus in 2009. 'They've offered massive support – moral and material,' says the head, 'and through the links they offer to other schools. In academic, pastoral and administrative terms, we are part of a powerful shared network of understanding and best practice.'

Good local community links and endeavour, and energetic and impassioned fundraising. A particular charity to which the school has attached itself – Mary's Meals – seeks to provide food for the neediest children all over the world, and pupils raised over £58,000 for the key school charities recently. 'Not bad,' says the head, 'and it came from the heart, I assure you.'

The prevailing atmosphere is of calm – children always generate a degree of noise, but the motif is jolly rather than manic, and there was a laudable absence of rush around the classrooms and in the school canteen (the food is widely regarded as excellent). It may be a boys' school, but it is blessedly short of that testy laddishness which serves to exclude rather than embrace. There is also a strong and experienced senior leadership team – of whom the bursar, head of junior school and academic deputy head are all women.

High ceilings and shrewdly-adapted Victorian buildings have managed to foster a sense of space and light. A school for all-comers, all types, and for all seasons. The sense of children at ease around the place is emphasised by the way they wear their uniform – a green and grey affair, which sits comfortably on them. The effect is to suggest an identity, and it's easy to see it's worn with pride – but, mercifully, without swagger. A big emphasis on kindness and tolerance. We heard teachers talking to classes and individual pupils, quite unaware that anyone was around, and the tenor was consistently one of calm benevolence. The payoff is obvious – the children seem remarkably patient and tolerant of one another. Very strong sense that the care of the children is anchored by affection and good sense.

A high-powered staff room – Oxbridge and doctorates all over the place – but school culture fosters collegiality among staff, and old hands willingly share best practice with newbies. Form tutors are the first point of contact for parents, and share concerns with senior teachers as well as with the pastoral deputy head. Stout denials from all parties that parents are anything other than strongly supportive. 'We aim at prevention,' said one long-serving teacher. 'We encourage anyone – child or parent – to tell us if they're worried or doubtful about something. It breeds trust, and it usually means stuff gets sorted out before it gets difficult.' It seems to work too – the headmaster has, in all his years here, invoked the sanction of detention precisely twice.

Reports get sent home twice a year, and there are two annual parents' evenings, as well as a lot of informal meetings. 'We aim to be around,' says the head. 'A lot of goodwill is built up, and a great deal of information exchanged, simply by teachers being around – not least at the school gates.'

Pupil constituency is noticeably more European than many other schools of its kind – hardly surprising given that St Anthony's is the only all-boys Catholic prep school in north London, and hence a favoured destination for the many Spanish, French and Italian who live around here. It also won a string of 'outstanding' commendations in its recent diocesan inspection, which helped to cement its credentials with this particular parent body. On the other hand, it's also a mainstream Hampstead prep school, with lots of parents drawn from the professions, the media and the City. Some remarkable old alumni – David Suchet and Antony Gormley among the older generation; a more recent luminary is Jack Steadman of the indie band, Bombay Bicycle Club.

A very likeable school. Conscious of its individuality, but not in thrall to it. 'A nice balance of informality and old school,' said a parent. Smack in the middle of north London, it is championing values more abiding than merely those of fame and fortune. It achieves considerable success, but not by stepping over the bodies of others. As the head says: 'Working in a school isn't just for the glamour and the good times. The test of vocation comes when it's difficult.' The affection with which St Anthony's is viewed by parents and staff seems to suggest they, like the pupils, are only too glad to have bought into this wisdom.

St Christopher's School

32 Belsize Lane, London NW3 5AE

020 7435 1521 | admissions@stchristophers.london | stchristophers.london

Independent

Pupils: 240

Ages: 4–11

Fees: £14,700 pa

Head: Since January 2018, Emma Crawford-Nash MA BEd (Cantab), mid 40s, previously head of the prep department of Manchester High School for Girls. She got the top exam results in her year at Cambridge and a distinction in her MA. She has been teaching since 1995, specialising in English and the performing arts, and has also worked at Haberdashers' Aske's School for Girls, St Paul's Cathedral School and Nottingham Girls' High School, where she was deputy head of the junior school. Passionate about helping girls to do and be anything they want, she's also interested in theatre, music, dance, running and girls' education in developing countries.

Entrance: St Christopher's is one of London's highest-achieving academic prep schools, with results at 11 the envy of many of its neighbours. This, however, is a school which selects primarily on ability. Part of the selection procedure is standardised tests, so summer birthdays don't lose out. 'It is not an academic assessment. We observe how they play together and how they interact with other children.' The school operates a split entry and although all are assessed at the same time, girls with September to February birthdays will generally join in reception, whilst March to August birthdays join in year 1. Tests dates and results are co-ordinated with other leading selective north London prep schools. Early registration is essential (as near birth as possible) for those already resident in London. Entry lists are closed at about 300 to be assessed for 38 available places. The school, however, is always willing to be flexible for those who've just arrived. Siblings are given an automatic offer, unless it is considered 'they will not flourish'. Not flourishing, however, is fairly loosely interpreted. 'If you have two clever daughters and the third is not as bright, some parents think she'll upset the exit poll, but that's not the way we work.' Parents confirm that year groups cover a (relatively) wide spread of ability. Occasional vacancies after entry. One 100 per cent means-tested scholarship available per annum and other support available as necessary.

Exit: 'We're fortunate in London that there are so many great schools, and we are proud of the achievement of all our girls. There's no scholarship board here. We don't want to make some pupils feel instantly diminished.' That said, this is generally a school of bright sparks and ambitious parents and the majority proceed to the highest performing London day schools. City of London, North London Collegiate and South Hampstead top the list, with St Paul's Girls, Channing and Highgate close behind. Quite a number of scholarships amongst them. A handful to board and an occasional few to Henrietta Barnett.

Remarks: St Christopher's was founded in 1883 by two local literary lesbians, but established in its current form in 1950 by the writer Rosemary Manning. It became a charitable trust in the 1970s. Housed in a large Victorian family house (with modern additions) in fashionable Belsize Park, this is a top-flight prep school for top-flight north London parents and the ethos and atmosphere are reflective of that. The education the pupils receive here is thoughtful and exciting. It concentrates on the fundamentals, but only after the fundamentals have been carefully considered. 'We have to ask the question "what are we educating children for?" It's a world we know nothing about, a world very different from our own.' The school has carefully analysed the impact of technology. 'The girls think technologically and it can be much more difficult to get them to listen to a story and concentrate.' The issue is addressed by concentrated focus on the task of reading and understanding and girls read aloud every day from reception to year 3 and regularly thereafter. 'If you can't read, you can't do maths.' No concessions are made when it comes to literature ('We don't use abridged texts') and Dickens and Lewis Carroll are digested in the original. An excellent library underlines the school's priorities.

'Children today have a very boring existence, chauffeured here and there, and we wanted to create an environment where they were allowed to be imaginative'

Much of the timetable follows the national curriculum ('It would be foolish not to – there are some very interesting things – but we cut away the trivia. We don't reject it, we tweak it') and the approach is based on 'child-initiated learning' with pupils taught to question and take responsibility for what they learn. Work is then tailored to the needs of each pupil, with maths books, for example, customised to the age and stage. (Though those in need of learning support are in the minority – mainly younger siblings – parents consider this tailoring, too, to be strong.) Spanish ('one of the most

widely spoken languages in the world') is taught throughout, Latin from year 5 and French as a club from year 3. Specialist subject teaching from year 4, with drama added to the curricular mix, joined by history of art in year 5. Flexibility of mind is encouraged by the inclusion of chess. ('It's a brilliant thinking exercise.')

Hard-working, well-qualified staff, particularly in the final two years. 'I cannot imagine better teachers than the maths and English teachers in years 5 and 6,' said one parent. 'They are really transformative.'

Despite the school's outstanding scholarship record, there is no scholarship class and no setting, except in maths in the final two years. Nor is this a school that crams for exams; preparation lasts just one term, when practice papers are given weekly. 'They're not missing core subjects from year 5, they still have time for all the extracurricular, they're not pressured and processed.' The approach here is enriching and the school believes there is as much value in creativity as in the core subjects.

Music is generally considered strong and enthusiastic, with two music classes plus a singing class each week. What's learnt here is put into practice with a junior orchestra, a wind group, a string group, piano club, junior and senior choirs and a chamber choir. This is media-land, too, and there is also a thriving film club, where girls learn to make their own. Cultural outings are very much part of the offering, with regular visits to theatres and museums and a young writers' workshop.

Sport is perhaps less important than it might be elsewhere (some parents complain that unless you're in a team, this can be a rather neglected area). Netball court and gym on site and regular matches against other schools in netball and rounders. Short tennis is also taught in the summer term and senior girls play lacrosse. Swimming lessons only in year 3 at nearby Swiss Cottage baths, sports day held at Hampstead Cricket Club. Though the outdoor space here is not unduly extensive, it is used very effectively, with an outdoor classroom, an Alice Garden and a science-themed garden. 'Children today have a very boring existence, chauffeured here and there, and we wanted to create an environment where they were allowed to be imaginative.' Indeed, the thread that runs throughout St Christopher's is that a good education is stimulating, interesting and exciting. The extracurricular is therefore addressed as energetically, with everything from public speaking to self-defence and Indian dance and, while there may be a Florence Nightingale workshop, the message that banking is as worthwhile a career for girls as nursing is instilled with visits to the Bank of England and a mock Dragons' Den. All staff are required to run two clubs a year and the offering is extensive.

Four houses, Brontë, Nightingale, North and Pankhurst, provide the basis for inter-house competition. The school has a strong family feel, sheltered and relaxed. There are no school rules ('We just ask for respect in the classroom and for them to be polite to teachers.') Good behaviour is instilled by discussion. ('Why did you do that? How do you imagine that would look?') Occasionally parents feel that emotional difficulties are not picked up as quickly as they might be. ('If you mention a problem, they take it seriously, but it's not always spotted,' said one.) Assembly every Friday is non-denominational. School meals exclude pork, shellfish, ham and nuts in order to cater for all. The facilities here have been brought thoroughly up to date, too, with a smart extension providing additional classrooms and impressive IT. The uniform of green Aertex shirts and blue trousers is practical and durable.

Over a third of pupils live within walking distance and the rest travel from affluent nearby postcodes like St John's Wood, Maida Vale, Islington and Highgate. Parents are often intellectual, professional, international and Jewish – and occasionally celebrities. 'They are interesting and incredibly well-informed. They are very involved and desperately keen to support their children's education.' ('Sometimes too keenly involved,' remarked one father. 'There are a lot of non-working mothers who once had high-powered careers and are now directing their energies on their children.') Occasionally expectations have to be gently adjusted.

A high-octane education producing confident, well-informed and articulate girls. 'The nice thing about St Christopher's is that it provides an excellent education without trying to breed a master race,' said one happy customer.

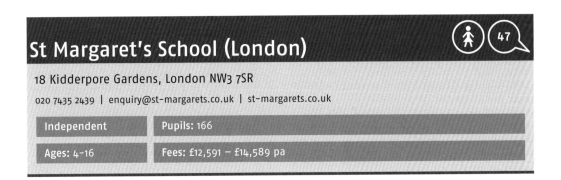

St Margaret's School (London)

18 Kidderpore Gardens, London NW3 7SR

020 7435 2439 | enquiry@st-margarets.co.uk | st-margarets.co.uk

Independent	Pupils: 166
Ages: 4–16	Fees: £12,591 – £14,589 pa

Principal: Since 2008, Mark Webster BSc (early 50s). Educated at Highgate School and University College London (where he read psychology), PGCE at Cambridge. Spent 15 years at the Royal School, Hampstead (first in primary, then IT, psychology and maths, before becoming deputy and acting head). Never planned to become a teacher – 'If you'd asked me early on what job I wanted to do, I'd have said teaching was 999th out of 1000'. A chance encounter changed his mind. 'I was working in publishing, when I met someone who said their job in teaching was fantastic. I'd never met anyone who felt that way about work.' Now equally enthusiastic about his chosen profession, Mr Webster continues to be hands on in his approach and still teaches mathematics.

We were initially struck by Mr Webster's bold shirt of candy coloured stripes, which belies his very calm manner. He is not extrovert by any means (as his shirt may imply), but is calm, thoughtful and extremely warm and friendly. He takes the time to consider our questions, and responds diplomatically and graciously. Parents unanimously agree that he is a 'brilliant head teacher and a real leader.' During our meeting there are a number

of students who pop into the head's office for a variety of reasons ranging from charity fundraising questions to other Christmas related issues. Clearly students feel he is very approachable, and whilst he does operate an open door policy like some other heads, unlike other heads, students actually take him up on this.

He says one of the benefits of working in a small school is that 'I have the privilege of knowing every student.' He enjoys the proximity and seeing the children grow up: 'You feel you can make a significant difference.' Unlike, he says, a much larger school, where perhaps you don't have the hands-on input: 'I can sleep well at night as I know I've done my very best.' Fundamental to his approach is the view that education is about instilling a sense of curiosity – 'Qualifications are a passport to the next stage, but if you remain curious you will never be bored'.

He himself retains a passionate interest in art, history and reading. Also plays football for Highgate Old Boys. A tactful, sympathetic enthusiast, Webster is a good fit for this family-like school. Possibly slightly unusual to have a male head teacher in an all girls school, but that doesn't seem to bother the parents. 'He is wonderful, we are so very lucky.' Married to a teacher; they have two young sons.

Academic matters: St Margaret's recently topped the Sunday Times Small Schools league table. When you consider that in 2018, 68 per cent of GCSEs were graded 9-7, it's not surprising, especially as the school is relatively non-selective and the ability range always includes the very able and those with more modest aspirations. One parent told us: 'I was a bit worried as I do have a very academic daughter and I thought she might not reach her full potential, but the luxury of a school this size is that teachers can cater for each individual in a mixed ability class.'

GCSE options include Spanish, French, art ('which is amazing,' one student told us), psychology and drama alongside the compulsory subjects. All girls are required to take the science trilogy (taught in a compact, but efficient lab) and the vast majority go on to do at least one science A level. A modern language is compulsory.

Setting introduced when necessary but, with limited space, teaching is usually differentiated rather than physically separated. Extremely low turnover of staff (the French teacher has been there for 25 years) – 'I've only had to write one reference in eight years', the head told us. This is largely because most departments are very small 'so teachers can actually make the role their own and achieve what they actually came into the profession to achieve.' This consistency can only be a good thing for the well-being and academic progress of the students.

School does cater for pupils with mild SEN, but 'we don't have the depth of resources for learning support that a larger school would have,' says the head. Two SENCo support plus a couple of teachers trained in dyslexia and dyscalculia, but the main support comes from classroom teachers. All abilities equally well catered for – 'We aren't results-driven and we try to exhaust every avenue'.

Games, options, the arts: The head's view is that education is a 'can-do', 'must try' matter, and is inspired by the celebrated art historian Sir Ernst Gombrich's attitude: 'You don't have to like it, but it's important to understand why other people do. We compel them to try lots of things. They may moan, but we make them give it a go'. Drama is taken seriously. Shakespeare is now a biggie here. 'Our drama teacher has a big pedigree in Shakespeare.' From year 7, pupils have a non-Shakespeare year where they are encouraged to devise their own pieces to perform. The head says: 'We want to encourage them to devise their own roles by exploring situations.' Other productions have included Matilda and Wind in the Willows. Music,

too, is important with a variety of traditional and less traditional extra-lesson options – anyone who wants to can join the ukulele club: 'It's a very egalitarian and upbeat instrument.' A number of choirs, plus a junior school orchestra. At least half of girls have private instrument lessons at the school. Art immensely popular, with excellent results at GCSE: two studios, one reasonably spacious, the other definitely petite. Dance popular too.

'This school allows every girl to flourish. It formed my daughter into the happy, caring girl she is today'

Outside space is relatively restricted, with a largish garden transformed into an Astroturf playground. A local hall is used for gym and the school now has a sports area for netball, tennis and other sports two minutes' walk away. Minibus takes girls to Hampstead Heath for rounders or running, to Hendon Leisure Centre for aerobics, rock climbing and badminton and the Welsh Harp for rowing. Inter-house and inter-school matches from year 4 upwards. In David and Goliath mode, the school is unafraid to compete with much larger north London schools like Channing, despite the fact that 'We often lose'. One parent told us: 'For the super sporty, this school may not be your first choice'

Plenty of extracurricular going on: street dance, choir, theatre, cookery, cheerleading, philosophy, orchestra, chess, tennis and origami. Trips local and international, from walks on Hampstead Heath to Tuscany and Iceland.

An unusual incentive which the head introduced is '125' (a tribute to the school's 125 anniversary), which provides pupils with a list of activities to attempt before they leave the school: 'To complement the academic, performing and sporting curriculum we offer, the girls undertake activities throughout the year as part of the school's Skills Grid. The range includes the practical, the cultural and the altruistic: everything from touch typing, learning a magic trick or "doing something nice for someone who can do nothing in return".'

Background and atmosphere: Founded in 1884 and one of the oldest schools in Hampstead – it moved to its present site in a quiet, suburban Hampstead road in 1943. A large, elegant red-brick house accommodates 155+ girls and the head says, 'The house element has become a pivotal cornerstone of how I think about the school. Everything emanates from it being a house – the relationships, the attitudes etc. We've spent quite a lot of money on knocking down a lot of walls.' We believe he meant that both literally and metaphorically.

Fairly recent building work has completely altered the layout of the ground and lower ground floors to incorporate a new school hall. The idea was also to open up the ground floor as much as possible to give the house a much more open plan feel, thereby creating more light and space. Everything is transparent – even the head's office. The school has also added a pretty roof terrace to encourage reading and quiet study for the upper years.

On entering the building we were treated to the melodic voices of a few girls doing choir practice. We watched for a few minutes entranced. It all added to the warm and cosy atmosphere of the St Margaret's experience (it helped that it was nearly Christmas at the time of our visit). We were struck by how deceptively big the school seems on the inside. Yes, there are areas which are exceedingly tight and narrow, and would definitely not suit any physically impaired student, but the floors upwards seemed endless and the corridors often led into quaint hidden areas. Although classrooms were snug, they were adequate for the number of students in each class (no more than 20). None of the students we met or chatted to seemed particularly fazed about the spatial issue. As one parent said, 'they don't know any better, as some have been here since infants and go all the way through.'

We were charmed by the lovely reading area for the juniors and the loft-style library. It definitely felt as if we had entered a bygone era – not a conventional school by any means (think the Brontës). This, it seems, is what some parents most love about the school. One told us: 'Both the head and the school are very unusual in education and sadly part of a dying breed – not caught up in the madness of it all, but eminently sensible.'

The girls who showed us around were happy, polite and totally unpretentious. We were taken aback by one student who openly admitted she had had 'difficulties' in some areas, but unlike other schools she had been to, everyone at St Margaret's was 'friendly and caring.' (Again, another of the school's many charms is that it didn't select one of its obvious 'stars' to show us around the school and do the whole PR number.)

Senior and junior schools both occupy the same building and have the same head, with different uniforms but little separation between them. Uniforms are smart – red and white in the junior school, black and white in the senior. The uniform was changed a few years back for the seniors as they didn't like it. Girls are listened to here. There are two 'agony aunts' (senior students) available at all times for confidential chats, and a school council. One pupil told us: 'We voted for a tuck shop at the school council and now we have one. We can choose what is sold.' The school has three houses and pupils of all ages work together to raise funds for charities of their own choice and compete at sports.

The small, friendly and homely atmosphere 'allows the girls to achieve whatever they can – but in a safe, non-confrontational environment', said one parent.

Pastoral care, well-being and discipline: Discipline not a significant issue. Though head insists this is not the garden of Eden, disciplinary issues tend to be confined to infringements of uniform – 'We can live with earrings if there's no drink or drugs'. Bullying – 'We get a case every year' – is dealt with promptly. Detentions, it seems, are an alien notion: 'we haven't needed to give one since 2011.' One parent who is a teacher herself working in an inner city school told us: 'I have to laugh sometimes when my daughter comes home and says "OMG! One of the girls threw a pen in class".' Girls generally very well behaved and extremely supportive of one another – 'an extended family', one said.' Another told us: 'My daughter went through a very difficult time one year because of social media. I was alerted to this by her form tutor, who in turn had found out from three of her close friends, who were very concerned. She was closely monitored and supported throughout and got through it.'

Parents, too, tend to be very supportive; they are known to choose the school for its caring environment: 'You get ups and downs with some of the girls, but if you ever get a problem it's dealt with straight away,' said one. Most parents feel one of the school's greatest strengths is its pastoral side, allowing girls to fulfil their potential and know exactly who they are. One parent told us: 'This school allows every girl to flourish. It formed my daughter into the happy, caring girl she is today.' Another told us: 'What struck me about this school when I first looked around, and what still remains true five years later, is that the girls all seem to have that wonderful, quiet confidence. Not that brash sense of entitlement that some wealthy kids can have.'

'Both the head and the school are very unusual in education and sadly part of a dying breed – not caught up in the madness of it all, but eminently sensible'

The school has its own head of pastoral care but also relies on a school counsellor when needed and proactively encourages bonding with a variety of trips. 'The girls mix across the years and are often close to girls in the year above and below,' said a parent.

Pupils and parents: Nice, well-behaved, confident girls from a cosmopolitan range of backgrounds reflecting the school's north London location – a large chunk of second generation French and Italians. A fair number come from within walking distance, then in an arc stretching from Wembley to Islington (school minibus on offer for those who require it). Very much a family school in every sense – 45 per cent of pupils are sisters or relatives of current or ex-pupils. 'A lot of people like the sense of support and nurturing.' The school rarely advertises and most newcomers hear about it by word of mouth and favourable newspaper coverage. The internet has slightly altered the traditional intake, as it is accessible worldwide. One parent told us: 'What I like most about the parents who send their girls to St Margaret's is that they defy the Daily Mail stereotype of bling parents.' Daphne du Maurier was a pupil.

Entrance: 'Loosely selective.' From reception to year 2 assessment involves girls coming in for the morning and working with the class teacher. A handful of places offered from year 3 upwards and potential candidates take a standard set of English and maths assessments. Guaranteed transition from within at 11. 'Once we've made the commitment, unless there are particular special needs we can't support, we stick to it.' Now part of the London 11+ Consortium and external candidates take its cognitive ability test. They do operate a basic sibling policy: 'We're not über selective, but we have rejected siblings if we don't feel the school is right for them.'

Exit: About 75 per cent of junior school girls stay on to the senior school, though a small number move to more selective senior schools such as Henrietta Barnett or South Hampstead High School. There's no intention of opening a sixth form, despite parental requests: 'One of the things about being a small school is that you are aware of the things you can't offer, in terms of space and subjects, which is why we will never have a sixth form.' However by then most parents agree it is time to 'move on.'

Notably successful with applications at 16. Most popular choices at that point are local co-ed sixth forms such as UCS and Highgate, more selective schools such as St Paul's, and similar atmosphere girls' schools such as Channing. A reasonable number goes to the state sector – St Marylebone particularly popular, and a few to Camden, Henrietta Barnett, Woodhouse and the Ark Academy. Good guidance on offer at both 11 and 16 – 'It's really important to make an informed choice. Not every school will suit every girl and they are used to being supported here'. School also works with them on interview practice and personal statements. One parent told us: 'Prior to looking around a few schools, I was advised to by Mr Webster to look out for things which would never have otherwise occurred to me – like to not be swayed by all the high tech stuff.' St Margaret's girls generally get their first-choice sixth form.

Money matters: Not an expensive school by any means, though a number of girls receive bursaries to cover all or part of their school fees: 'A reasonable proportion on some sort of financial help.'

Remarks: A gentle, nurturing school with a strong and secure family atmosphere providing a stimulating, tailor-made education. 'A little gem,' to quote one parent, though possibly not the ideal venue for the child who needs plenty of space to run around or one who requires the challenge of a big stage.

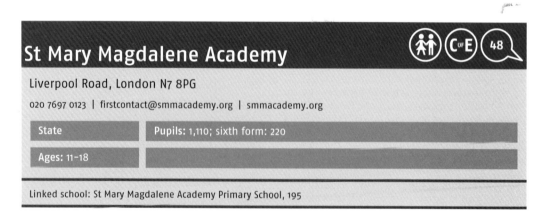

St Mary Magdalene Academy

Liverpool Road, London N7 8PG

020 7697 0123 | firstcontact@smmacademy.org | smmacademy.org

State	Pupils: 1,110; sixth form: 220
Ages: 11–18	

Linked school: St Mary Magdalene Academy Primary School, 195

Head: Since 2012, Vicky Linsley (late 40s): since she joined the school as deputy head in 2008 much credit must go to her for the transformation of this school to a highly oversubscribed 'extremely well run' school with fantastic results, supported pupils, and teachers who stay because they are proud to be at SMMA. Vicky Linsley was a scholarship child who went on to do history at Nottingham and then to Oxford for a masters degree and her teaching qualification. She taught and then worked freelance while her two children were little, consulting in schools that were in special measures – 'an opportunity to learn what works and what doesn't and bringing about change' – and she still inspects schools with Ofsted and works as a consultant with schools looking to improve.

Youthful, energetic and very pragmatic, the pupils call her 'inspiring' and 'really, really nice'. They all see her in assemblies, checking pupil progress, and in classes, and like all staff, she eats with them in the canteen. She also has a weekly current affairs class (The Week) with year 12 pupils. She is generous with her praise of pupils and her pride in the school. An eloquent speaker, which helps her to build partnerships with businesses to the benefit of the school (Deloitte, Virgin Trains, local businesses). She is admired and respected by the teachers who find her 'approachable, she always has five minutes for us, even for small matters'. She has nurtured many and entrusted them with responsibilities, often from Teach First programme or from simple assistant positions, maintaining a surprisingly stable staff body – no staffing vacancies when we visited and, unusually for any school, no shortage of maths or science teachers. And the 'being kind' ethos of the school is led from the head down – examples abound from supporting children in care, who love her, to taking in hot cross buns for every staff member at Easter.

Academic matters: The school has no qualms about saying that it has 'a clear focus on academic achievement' and it works to develop 'globally-minded citizens who are happy and successful'. For financial reasons it has stopped teaching the IB, but the ethos has strongly influenced the curriculum and teaching – encouraging independent and team learning, keeping timetables very full and having the equivalent of creativity, activity and service through the Inspire Programme.

The results have been rising annually and are impressive for a primarily non-selective school – 27 per cent of GCSE results were 9-7 in 2018. Eighty per cent of pupils achieved grade 4 and above in both English and maths. The sciences are especially strong with almost all pupils getting grades 9-6. Also strong emphasis on languages, resulting in 100 per cent top marks in Mandarin (more about China connection later), with Spanish and French also successful. Religious studies (unsurprisingly for this church school) get excellent results too. At A level, 35 per A*/A and 65 per cent A*-B grades in 2018. 'Good results thanks to a really excellent work ethos built up over time in the school' and 'not stressful thanks to three year GCSE programme and the school culture'. Around exam time pupils can be found coming in early for breakfast and morning study time.

'Good results thanks to a really excellent work ethos built up over time in the school' and 'not stressful thanks to three year GCSE programme and the school culture'

Years 7 and 8 include some streaming in lessons (reviewed termly), plenty of extracurricular learning – before and after school and in extension activities. Early establishment of ground rules about behaviour and study skills ('the SMMA way'). 'They have to learn to self regulate – we have 1,300 pupils and they need to learn about manners and being polite'. The pupils who have got into the school on the language aptitude test are expected to take Mandarin enrichment classes as well as the European language (choice of German, Spanish or French) taken by other pupils; those who join the Mandarin Excellence Programme have four hours of Mandarin each week. The school is a Centre of Excellence for Mandarin Teaching and has the Confucius Classroom Award which ensures an extra three full-time Mandarin teachers from China, who teach not only Mandarin but also Chinese culture. Annual subsidised trip to China. Progress tracked and standards high even in those first two years of secondary school by having them all follow ISEB curriculum (same as for those sitting common entrance in private schools).

In year 9 pupils start their GCSE curriculum: 'having three years gives us time to teach more than just the content of the curriculum', and pupils appeared more motivated, having chosen their subjects and knowing they were working towards an exam. Extra time also allows for more outings in year 10, which helps to 'raise aspirations and give a sense of purpose for exams'. 'We aim to give a broad and balanced curriculum so kids really enjoy learning, and they want to learn more because we have more time for content'. Class size drops to 25. Generous selection of subjects, but core subjects the priority – strong maths and science teaching thanks to recruitment and retention of good teachers – we saw several Oxbridge graduates who had chosen to teach here, and people returning to teaching after careers in industry. Pupils said that 'teachers have our interests at heart and know what we like' and 'teachers care about you'. And parents raved about the youthful vitality, energy and enthusiasm of teaching staff.

Library for years 7-11 with full-time librarian used for English lessons and weekly library lessons – all part of study skills lower down the school. Also used for book clubs after school; the school is clearly almost as busy before and after school hours as during. Parents say the school has 'nailed the curriculum and ensures the kids get the results they want'. Certainly, no one dreaming or looking out of windows when we visited.

'Our teachers are organised, knowledgeable and enthusiastic.'
'They relate subjects to real life and raise ethical questions, not just teaching to get grades'

Sixth form of 120 pupils per year completely selective by GCSE results, and once in, they are expected to have a very full timetable of lessons, extracurricular activities, exercise and a real commitment to enrichment, with many collaborative projects – encouraging leadership and entrepreneurship. Pupils appreciated 'plenty of choice at A levels, but if you reconsider your subjects, you can change – the timetable seems to work for you to be able to take any subject combination you want.' Staff teach all the years, including sixth form – keeping them as challenged as their pupils and allowing pupils who stay on to sixth form to know their teachers. 'Our teachers are organised and knowledgeable and enthusiastic.' 'They make it applicable to real life and raise ethical questions, not just teaching to get grades,' according to sixth form students. 'They get us involved; lessons are really interactive'. Maximum of 15 pupils per A level class. Not very much dedicated space for sixth form, though a glass gallery space for 'quiet study', one floor of the library and some corridor break out areas for teamwork. They have their own common room (though pupils found this 'dreary' and lacking in 'sofas and character'), supervised by full time graduates who also supervise study areas, help with essays and 'keep work going generally'. This type of subtle mentoring works to raise expectation and support as these graduates are also available to help with UCAS forms and encourage the idea of going to university. Every student in sixth form taken to visit a university (some now lucky enough to go first class on train with a parent or friend thanks to a new partnership created with Virgin Rail).

Special needs supported by SENCo with ASD specialism and part-time dyslexia specialist; all pupils screened before joining school. Some 13 pupils in school with EHCPs, and 70 accessing support in or outside school. Pupils from neighbouring Courtyard special school (for pupils in years 9-13 with autism) come across with helper to SMMA for lessons sometimes – especially for drama, maths or art. Those who just need an extra bit of help can have tutoring sessions with maths and English graduates in the main hall. Parents say 'they don't give up on anyone' and that thanks to target tracking they are 'on it like a car bonnet if they slip'.

Games, options, the arts: School is open from 7.30am when children can be found in the chess club, martial arts training, extra lessons, or just coming in for £1 breakfast. The day often ends late too, so there is plenty of time for extra activities. Clubs timetable has clubs before, during and after school. Games in huge soundproofed state-of-the-art gym – no whistles or shouting needed to get classes playing team sports (basketball, hockey, dance, trampoline, cricket, badminton) for weekly two hours PE. There is an Astroturf on the roof for football and sport unless it is pouring. They use Finsbury Park for athletics. This is an urban environment and so the playground is not large. A mad keen footballer we met said that he gets to play 'all the time' – and has plenty of matches against other schools too. Girls' teams encouraged and included – no sense that anyone is second class here. They play at the Arsenal Hub, have Arsenal trainers and get reduced price tickets to matches. Recognition for effort or achievement for sportsmen and women given at weekly assembly.

Arts rooms aplenty – sixth formers use theirs like a studio and so are able to leave their work out. Textile, pottery, art and tech GCSEs enhanced by equipment like 3D printers and laser cutters. You don't have to be doing tech GCSE to be involved in Formula E club, building an electric car and then racing it at Goodwood racing track. Proper, spacious cooking facilities for both food-tech and popular after-school clubs and enrichment programme. Music a growing part of school life, partly thanks to MiSST (Music in Secondary School Trust), with every new pupil being lent an orchestral instrument and having small group lessons, as well as individual music lessons ('excellent peripatetic teachers,' according to some parents) for those who continue with their instrument. So 300 music lessons timetabled in somehow as well as orchestra, rock band, string groups and then the annual huge musical productions – an incredibly inclusive, all-singing all-dancing affair, 'a semi-professional experience for the kids with lighting, costumes, musicians.' 'My shy child just came out of herself through the school musical production'. For some 20 pupils the highlight of their year is going to a music residential to Radley School.

Inspire programme includes masterclasses (talks by Jeremy Corbyn and Nick Robinson recently, and the Grayson Perry talk was a sellout), workshops (Deloitte Consulting sent their chef to give classes, the RSC brought in a group to work on Hamlet) and City trips – not only to offices but also to British Film Institute and theatre outings (local Almeida theatres generous with free tickets to SMMA). The programme also encourages pupils to join competitions and get onto programmes such as STEM courses, Oxford Girls' Maths Conference and Women in Leadership conferences, and to go for visits or internships at City firms they have partnerships with – RBS, Cushman Wakefield, Société Générale, UBS.

The school has an immersion programme, allowing overseas pupils to come for periods up to a term. Students every year from China, Indonesia, Korea and even Kazakhstan attend school as part of 'global citizenship', which is a founding principle of the academy. Once the students leave, friendship and global citizenship encouraged as pupils become email penpals. The school also welcomes some 20 headteachers from China for a week each year for the same purpose. A multitude of clubs and possible activities to be involved in; parents and pupils felt that you were encouraged to do anything you were interested in: 'With the job market changing so fast, it will prepare our children to have flexibility, interests, skills and ideas, rather than just careers'.

Background and atmosphere: This is a London Diocese sponsored school aiming to serve the community – the motto 'show by a good life that your works are done by gentleness born of wisdom' sets the tone of the school. A sense of kindness and action and learning emanates. RIBA awards for this purpose built school which one parent called a 'Tardis, a building that flows nicely and does not feel cramped'. Mostly built around a closed atrium with all classes looking inwards to the central library and chapel built on stilts over the canteen. The windows onto the corridors, the open study areas and flow of the building give an atmosphere of transparency and openness. No rooms feel out of bounds and several teachers were working in corridors. Pale wood, excellent acoustic management, curved edges, large windows, glass-topped atrium all help to soften the edges of an otherwise totally urban and closed in school off a fairly main road. Once inside, the building feels spacious, and the tightly managed systems for moving round the school allows students to move smoothly and freely – we didn't see any pushing or shoving and pupils said 'there are no hidden corners or blind spots', 'we are really safe here'. We were struck by the calm and quiet in such a vibrant and active school – there are no bells in between lessons and

playtime is managed well with room for all sorts of activities in the playground without impeding each other (thanks, in part, to the outside amphitheatre which provides seating and space for ball games).

Pastoral care, well-being and discipline: Christian ethos and school motto 'gentleness born of wisdom' emphasised as teachers and pupils can be seen treating each other with respect (and everyone on first name terms). Fabulous, engaged and open-minded students listened to each other and spoke kindly of each other when we met them. Teachers don't interrupt each other or the pupils and they all eat together. Mealtimes are a pleasantly calm and orderly event with pupils and teachers sharing food, space and conversation. The canteen is in the centre of the school, like a kitchen being the heart of the home, busy and used (from breakfast club to after-school snacks via the feeding of the 1,300 at lunchtime) and spotlessly clean. Pupils called food 'healthy and tasty' but of course raved about Friday chips.

The school is mostly non-selective and pupils come from a wide range of ethnic, socioeconomic and cultural backgrounds, reflecting the diversity of the area

Spiritual, moral, social and cultural education embedded in the school through all the curriculum lessons as well as assemblies and activities and in form time. Full-time chaplain for guidance and support. 'Reverend April is my son's favourite person in the school because she is such a kind, generous presence, comes to cheer at basketball matches, and may well be the heart of the school in her eyrie in the centrally placed chapel.' A part-time psychotherapist (appointment by self-referral or suggested by staff). Pupils said there was 'no bullying, but if you see something you can go straight to a teacher or report it anonymously on school website anti-bullying page'. Teachers spoke of restorative justice meetings – how would you feel, how would the other person be feeling. The need to be 'kind' is the leading principle.

'Academy guardians', or tutors, work with Guardian Groups of pupils in the same house but across all year groups. 'It means we know older pupils and they tell us how to do things and we say hello to them round school'. It also means the older ones look out for the younger ones. The family groups meet with their academy guardian, who acts as first port of call for any issues, each day – twice a week they sit together in assembly, but groups are mostly for organisation and keeping pupils on track. The system seems to create a 'close and small community and allows us to get to know them really well and they trust us,' say the guardians. Pupils also said they liked having the same pastoral group throughout school because it 'is like my family away from home'.

The deputy head for expectations and standards, who is in charge of pastoral care, meets heads of year, the SENCo and chaplain every fortnight to ensure pupil well-being. They work on the premise of 'what would a good parent do?' in all dealings with pupils, and he leads assemblies about humanity, compassion and expectations in order to ensure happy, and therefore successful, children.

Discipline by detention set by teacher, heads of year and if necessary involvement of parents. 'Certainty of consequence more important than severity of consequences' – so pupils not intimidated or fearful. Parents appreciate the fact that they get phone calls not only if there is a problem but also if there is something to celebrate when their child has excelled.

Pupils and parents: The school is mostly non-selective and pupils come from a wide range of ethnic, socioeconomic and cultural backgrounds – this is central Islington and the school reflects the diversity of the area well, with families who could afford independent schools choosing SMMA as well as pupils from the neighbouring housing estates. 'We chose it over an independent school because there is no sense of entitlement here, and our child has really polite, kind friendships with kids he would never have met at a north London independent school'. Around half on free school meals and some eight looked after pupils. But parents told us that the school has high expectations and everyone is expected to comply – strict uniform policy evident, tight punctuality enforced, and serious work ethic encouraged. And the curriculum guide given at the beginning of each year includes not only the outline of what will be taught and the exam they are preparing for, but also 'practical ways to reinforce your child's learning', 'how you can help' and 'resources for pupils and parents to support learning'. Learning is clearly expected to be a whole family endeavour. Once a pupil is accepted, all siblings tend to follow – one family has seven children going to the school, and the Mandarin teacher had all four of her boys here. Parents get plenty of letters and email communication as well as phone calls. What they liked was that they felt listened to – suggestions by staff, pupils or parents are heard and responded to positively. Such an open approach.

Entrance: Of the 180 places in year 7 – 210 from 2019 – some 30 come directly from the attached

Christian ethos and school motto, 'gentleness born of wisdom', is put into practice. Teachers and pupils can be seen treating each other with respect (and everyone is on first name terms)

primary school, then preference to children in care and siblings of pupils in the school. Ten per cent selective on language aptitude – no prior language knowledge needed (400 children sat for those 18 places recently). The remaining places are given 30 per cent to Islington Church of England primary school pupils (catchment area around one mile) and 70 per cent on distance from school (currently about a half a mile from the school). A further 18 admitted in year 9 via language aptitude test. At sixth form, top third stay on to form half of the selective sixth form, which has 120 pupils in each of the two years (20 come from a link with Switzerland). Entrance requirements at sixth form are at least seven GCSEs at 4+ including English and maths, with 6+ in proposed A level subjects – 7 for maths and 8 for further maths.

Exit: Some 60 per cent leaves after GCSEs, especially if they came in from the primary school or need a less academic experience. They traditionally go to Woodhouse, Camden Girls or City and Islington College. Many more look at other schools than leave in the end, and one student even said, 'Why would I go somewhere less good than here just to have a change?' Three to study medicine in 2018; some 40 per cent go to Russell Group universities. Increasingly abroad (Science Po in Paris, British Columbia, McGill – French scholarship place). All sixth formers get work experience with one of the partnership firms, help with their personal statements and plenty of exposure to other worlds through the masterclasses and visits, as well as the paid for visit to a university with the school. So pupils given the expectation and real support to get to university.

Money matters: Most parents happy to pay for school trips, though there is support for those who find this a challenge. ParentPay cards also serve as ID cards and enable parents to replenish student accounts for lunch money.

Remarks: A shining example of an excellent school. Parents and pupils are aware that they have picked the golden ticket if they can get an education here – the results are evidence of top quality teaching, and the children's involvement and happiness are enhanced by the wide enrichment programme, whilst the pastoral care provides a tight safety net.

If you want a top notch inclusive comprehensive education, this is the place to go.

St Mary Magdalene Academy Primary School 👫 (C of E) (49)

Liverpool Road, London N7 8PG

020 7697 0123 | firstcontact@smmacademy.org | smmacademy.org

State	Pupils: 210
Ages: 4–11	

Linked school: St Mary Magdalene Academy, 190

Headteacher: Since 2016, Ruth Luzmore (30s), who has brought her enthusiasm, warmth, appreciation and energy to this one-form entry, successful primary school. As the daughter of a primary school teacher she never thought she would follow the same career path, but memories of a very happy primary education, and experiences as a teaching assistant, led her to teaching. She studied in the evenings at Birkbeck College for a degree in politics, philosophy and history whilst earning a living in the daytime. She has continued working days and studying evenings since, gaining a masters in leadership at the Institute of Education whilst working as deputy head in another Islington primary school and now, as head of St Mary Magdalene Academy (SMMA) Primary, she is working towards a PhD in enquiry based professional development. She says, 'it is good to have a life outside the job, which otherwise can be all-consuming'.

Her commitment to working hard and the importance of education for social change can be seen here – involving teachers with an active senior leadership team, engaging parents through the parent-teacher association, good email and newsletter communications. The school also gives a voice to pupils, who not only have a school council but say 'teachers listen to you' and 'you can talk to Ms Luzmore or teachers about any issues'. Since arriving she has appointed a deputy head and several of the teachers, so has staff loyal to her: 'they are open to change and we are evolving policy together'. Many of the TAs have been at SMMA for years, some having taught the parents of current pupils and monitored in the playground – 'that way the care continues from the classroom into the playground and they can be aware of pupils' issues'. 'We keep them because we are a team and all genuinely care for each other.' Staff meetings weekly (if needed, 'I don't waste time on unnecessary meetings') as well as a Friday breakfast meeting to check diaries and plan for the week ahead. 'I like being part of the academy group because it means I run a small, friendly school but can look outwards too, to the senior school.'

Entrance: Strict admissions criteria managed by the academy admissions secretary (advantages to being linked to the academy infrastructure). Priority to children in care, then children who regularly attend one of the three local churches – St Mary Magdalene, St Luke's or St David's, then residents of Islington who attend another church, then siblings (some years as many as half the reception class is made up of siblings), then distance from the school (has been as local as within 0.3 of a mile). Oversubscribed in reception and there is a waiting list for each class.

Exit: Almost all go on to the secondary school of SMMA, though a few to Dame Alice Owen, Highbury Fields, City of London (both boys and girls).

Remarks: Having a previous literacy coordinator as head has ensured that literacy is a real backbone of the school: 'they need to leave not only reading but enjoying reading for pleasure'. Phonics taught formally using Sounds Write system for a short session each day, but then literacy taught in the widest possible way – topic based, class readers, buddy reading, reading road maps to lead pupils through age-appropriate books, as well as staged reading books for the younger pupils. The library maintained by the academy librarian. Writing in evidence on the boards and neatly marked homework in books with the emphasis on self-expression. Spelling homework given weekly.

195

'Enough homework to please parents but not so much kids spend all the weekend working,' according to one parent.

Maths coordinator makes sure that national curriculum covered but also, wherever possible, that maths included in topics ('units of enquiry') and in practical ways (eg visiting fruit snack bar run by sixth formers, raising money for charity – 'generating money is empowering for the children and helps them to realise money needs to be earned'). No setting in maths – 'we don't want to put limits on anyone's ability' – and extra tutoring groups by deputy head in order to extend or support pupils in particular topics. There are booster classes after school which are, apparently, 'really fun and help with your learning,' according to pupils. Pupils said, 'there are different levels of work and you can choose your challenge'.

'Bring a parent to lunch' scheme allows parents to see lunch at school and parents say school is receptive to feedback – not only on the shepherd's pie

Mandarin or Spanish taught from reception. Other subjects do not follow the national curriculum tightly, but skills included within units of enquiry. These allow child-led learning to extend subjects further into areas of the children's interests rather than needing to follow national requirements, with pupils encouraged to have 'intellectual conversations around themes, so that the year 6 conflict module started with Middle Ages and battles and moved right on to Trump and Kim Jong Un'. Parents said that 'kids become obsessed with the theme for six or seven weeks, we prepare it during the holidays, discuss it over meal times – they are always thinking about it. It gives them a chance to really get into a subject in depth'. Year 1s were learning about people's jobs – a lovely set of dressing up clothes and equipment for role play. 'I was disappointed the kids didn't chose me to come to speak in class, but I suppose my job is less interesting to them than other work,' said one parent. Learning done 'in a playful way,' according to parents, and pupils said, 'teachers are not too strict, they give us chances, listen to us and are fair'.

Good results at KS2, above national average in all subjects. However, it is the ability to discuss and articulate ideas that makes this school shine – pupils are used to developing ideas and forming opinions and backing their ideas up. After Sats in year 6, pupils create an 'exhibition where they present a poster with their opinions and collected thoughts which they explain to visiting parents and teachers – a sort of conference (PhD students in the making?). Topics covered included 'How terrorism affects society', 'How do we work for political honesty' and 'The influence of government on health care around the world'. Mentor teachers work to support these mini presentations.

Music taught by inspirational and dedicated teacher – both in class and during Wednesday's 'singing assembly' – the four-part harmony sung 'put goosebumps on my skin, it was so impressive'. Peripatetic music teachers for some 10 different instruments. Pupils enthusiastic about the music, acting and dance. And they, plus parents and teachers, all look forward to the annual Shakespeare production that involves the whole school learning, acting and dancing the play.

One afternoon PE per week with specialist teachers ('really good PE teachers,' according to pupils we spoke to) as are the language teachers and the dance teacher, who comes in for at least a term each year to help prepare for Shakespeare production. Swimming in years 3 and 4. Recent win at the London Schools Football Championship particularly impressive for a one form entry school and a cause of great delight. Girls' football well coached, according to pupils. The fact that there are a good number of male staff helps with regular break-time football practice. Playground spacious – pitch, table tennis, outside learning area, outside toilets etc but money currently being raised to improve the amenities and possibly to include making even more use of green roofs and flat roofs outside classrooms. Reception shares really well-equipped Astroturf playground with neighbouring Islington nursery. School lunches cooked on the premises and eaten from china plates in older years. 'Younger years get to the salad bar so there is less left for us,' bemoaned older pupils, who also said 'you have to eat vegetables, which makes you get used to healthy eating, but we wish older children could get seconds'. 'Bring a parent to lunch' scheme allows parents to see lunch at school and parents say school is receptive to feedback – not only on the shepherd's pie.

Pastoral care a highlight thanks to the full-time school chaplain who works in the academy. American by birth, upbeat, leopard-print wearing and totally involved in the school and the pupils. She leads a prayer meeting for parents and staff, she knows all the pupils by name and comes to support them in sports fixtures. She runs one of the mid-morning assemblies and helps ensure that the Christian knowledge and ethos is embedded in the school. One pupil said, 'We don't just talk about values, we use them too'. They said that 'problems are sorted out straight away and you can talk to teachers about every issue, even things at home'. 'We learn about bullying and are trained as mini-mentors.' There are 'worry boxes' in the class-room for anonymous concerns.

SEN supported by academy SENCo, and several pupils had individual TAs. 'We have helped a few pupils acquire an EHC plan' and there are some 20 on the SEN register for medical or educational needs, though 'if I had a child with additional needs I wouldn't probably send them to SMMA,' said a parent, unsure if there is sufficient extra support. Pupil premium used in part to pay for extra helper in reception: 'We focus on reception because if we invest lower down the pupils have a solid knowledge to carry up the school, so we aren't trying to catch up in year 6'.

The school shares a governing body with the senior school with one of the primary parents voted in. Parents involved as much as possible – invited to help with trips, raising money, running clubs, attending weekly Friday coffee morning, in the autumn term welcome BBQ, and at the inclu-sive and community spirited Christmas fair. 'We are raising money for the school but we want eve-rything to be as affordable as possible for everyone'.

Our opinion: everyone knows everyone in this small, friendly school with different year groups playing together and parents who are involved. A really solid, well-planned education with plenty of extracurricular clubs and activities, creating artic-ulate, thinking pupils who have been listened to and encouraged to engage in, and have meaningful conversations about, all their learning.

The St Marylebone C of E School

64 Marylebone High Street, London W1U 5BA

020 7935 4704 | info@stmaryleboneschool.com | stmarylebone.school

State	Pupils: 1,116; sixth form: 330 (around 80 boys)
Ages: 11–18	

Headteacher: Since 2014, Kathryn Pugh MA (Cantab) PGCE NPQH (mid 30s). A Cambridge graduate with first class honours in English, she joined St Marylebone in 2005 as an English teacher and learning co-ordinator, and was promoted to assistant head in 2008, before succeeding the long-serving and legendary Elizabeth Phillips OBE. This is only the second school she has worked at. She arrived here after cutting her teeth (as she puts it) at Riddlesdown Collegiate, a large co-ed compre-hensive in Surrey, where she taught English and drama. Straight after leaving Cambridge she spent four years working in business and media, and then in theatre and communication for 18 months in Malawi, as well as for the Teacher Support Network, an educational charity.

Tall and willowy, Ms Pugh looks more like a Chanel model than headmistress. She cycles to work each day and is described by her pupils as 'inspirational', 'accessible', and 'empathetic'. We were regaled with tales of her contorting herself into yogic positions during English lessons as well as her passionate encouragement of 'complete ran-domness in lessons'. Said to be a fruitarian, she is described as looking strikingly beautiful in her red cape, while standing in the midst of girls in green cartwheeling and cavorting. She 'mucks in – not afraid to get her hands dirty during the fairs'; and 'She's so dynamic,' enthused one parent, 'everyone wants to do their best for her, both her pupils and her staff...the school is lucky that it has so many years of someone so ambitious and committed.'

We spoke to her surrounded by her senior man-agement team. This is a woman who clearly prefers to see herself as prima inter pares. Her predecessor was a great delegator, and responsibility continues to be very much shared. She wants to talk about the school and its achievements and defer to her colleagues. She is deeply uncomfortable when the questions focus on her. Appreciative of a strong and supportive team, Ms Pugh is doing sterling work channelling the goodwill of both her staff and a diverse parent body.

Academic matters: Results are excellent. At A level, 71 per cent A*-B with 37 per cent A*/A in 2018. School keen to point out that girls who take further maths and chemistry perform brilliantly. While English, maths, art and politics are the most popular sub-jects, school does have 10 STEM ambassadors, and offers two sixth form maths/ICT scholarships to students likely to go on to study STEM subjects at university. Psychology, sociology and economics among the options – the first much the favourite, with a spread of results. German now phased out in favour of Spanish. High take-up; French and Spanish students achieved excellent results with a high percentage of top grades – a great improvement since our last visit. Supervised study periods during year 12 help the less-disciplined with their homework. Relatively good teacher:pupil ratio, with setting from the start, and school invests in retaining good staff. Our student guides were keen to tell us how many of their teachers had doctorates and were specialists in their fields.

Offers a good choice of subject options – 'an amazing variety,' enthused one parent. A future skills award and child development have replaced health and social care; dance, Latin and business studies canter alongside the front runners at GCSE and all are in the ribbons. In 2018, 72 per cent got 9-4 in both maths and English with some outstanding performances (45 per cent 9-7 grades). RS results are knock-out and the curriculum is praised for its earnest inclusiveness. The Englishes are good, so are the single sciences. One full class takes triple science each year, though most take the double award. Maths more than respectable. School does, after all, have a maths and computing specialism as well as performing arts. All students study both French and Spanish in key stage 3 and over 75 per cent take at least one language at GCSE. Art, geography and history strong and popular. School has policy of taking some subjects – ICT, RS – early to excellent effect.

Our student guides were keen to tell us how many of their teachers had doctorates and were specialists

Gifted and talented programme now called Aspiration and Challenge, with the idea of achieving excellence for everyone. High Achievers' programme for those with high academic ability; Scholarship programmes those talented at dance, music or drama. Two SENCOs, a full-time SEN teacher, learning support assistants and specialist centres for students with learning difficulties. It is a centre of excellence for severe emotional and behavioural difficulties. Can provide for moderate physical difficulties too. EAL is an important area also (about half of the cohort speaks a language other than English at home) and this department plays a vibrant part in celebrating cultural diversity.

Games, options, the arts: It has a performing arts specialism – with 14 places awarded to those talented in dance, drama or music. It is perhaps not surprising, then, that sport has a lower profile. That is not to say that there are not opportunities

available, and there are a surprising number of athletically ambitious girls. Our guide was a pentathlete, excelling at high jump, long jump, shot put, 800 metres and hurdles, participating in clubs both in and out of school. Cross-country is also popular. Grey Coat Hospital School is the big rival at netball; they also play Portland Place and Holland Park. Plenty of inter-house sports competitions too (five houses across the year groups – Hardwick, Dickens, Barrett, Nightingale and Wesley). Annual sports day at Willesden Green. Other sports on offer include football, trampolining, rugby and tennis as well as the D of E awards scheme. They have managed to fit an underground sports hall into this already over-filled space and have a seven metre climbing wall. Sport very much available even if not always enthusiastically taken up.

Dance, drama and music are outstanding and production values are high. 'The girls take huge pride in their performances,' we were told, 'even if not everyone can take part. It is inspirational.' The inspiration is further fuelled by the innovative and outstanding three storey building that incorporates the visual and performing arts space, with dance studio and gym in the basement. This makes a huge difference – not least to the amount of space it frees for other curricular activities. In all respects the arts reign here. You can make everything from jewellery to ceramics and print your own photos. Up-to-date laser cutters in the well-equipped DT workshops. Graphics also well regarded. Debating, dance and musical performance of all kinds thrive. Scholars' concert happens in the Wigmore Hall; some musicals, eg sixth form production of Chicago, performed at the Rudolf Steiner Theatre; whole school production of Grease in the old-fashioned, polished-wood-smelling school hall.

Some disagreement among parents as to whether there is an opportunity for everyone to get involved in these productions and performances. Grumblings in some quarters that only the best are given roles – and here, there are a lot of girls considered to be glittering. So your aspiring Milly who doesn't quite make the grade may well end up sitting on the sidelines for much of her school years. School quick to point out that over 150 pupils across the school took part in whole school production at Christmas. We, like Ofsted, were impressed with range of other co-curricular activities which don't necessarily require high-confidence performance skills: book clubs, green committee, Young Entrepreneurs, Fair Trade group etc. However, opportunities like GCSE photography work in the highly professional Metro Studios only available to the three or four girls whose applications to take the course are considered sufficiently impressive. This is the reality of a state-funded school, but it must be trying for the also-rans and would-bes.

Background and atmosphere: Tucked between Princess Grace Hospital and Marylebone High Street and close to the teeming runway that is the Marylebone Road, the school is a leafy, contained oasis of calm and purpose. St Marylebone Parish Church is a focus point and contributes to the peacefulness. This is where assemblies and concerts happen as well as religious services. A closely-knit jungle of buildings from red-brick Victorian, complete with heavily green gloss painted corridors, to modern glass and concrete are packed onto this one compact site. Further down the High Street on Blandford Street is the sixth form building, which is modern, purpose-built, and feels more like a tiny university campus than a school.

Five forms per year, and with only 750 in the main school with up to 330 in the sixth form, St Marylebone is a relatively small inner London comprehensive – and this shows. As intimate as it can be, spread over two sites, it is an unintimidating place, with plenty of smiles and polite greetings between staff and pupils as well as between the pupils themselves. No space for lockers, so girls have to learn to be adept at carting their lives around with them and being organised about what they need for each lesson. Lunch is eaten in form rooms, though year 10 examinees and upwards are mercifully allowed out to settle in the numerous cafés round about at lunchtime. Sixth formers have their own canteen in Blandford Street.

Pastoral care, well-being and discipline: Pastoral care is very strong, affirm several parents. As well as there being systems of support in place among the staff and pupils, there is a strong mentoring facility between the older and younger pupils. This is an intense time of life for any teenager, but one senses that in this school the experience can perhaps become more intense than elsewhere. School says that the intensity is 'offset by a very caring community feeling which identifies and helps deal with problems' – and denies that this is a school of 'precious princesses'. Maybe it is part of the performing arts culture.

Girls, on the whole, very supportive of each other, though there is a lot of competition and this has to be managed. Behaviour is good. Cases of bullying rare, we were told. A smell of smoke doesn't linger in lavatories here, and a zero tolerance approach means that your child may well end up with detention just from talking in class. The bar is high, girls feel lucky to be here and want to behave well. Parents commend the fluid communication lines whenever a problem arrives. Lots of positive feedback when a struggling girl starts to perform well, as well as the more obvious commending of high performance. Much appreciated are the proper, old-fashioned termly reports which don't just parrot at you what the class has done

but actually talk about your own daughter. Good, realistic and collaborative target-setting also works.

Pupils and parents: Broad social mix, made up of the heady variety of backgrounds and cultures that you would expect in an inner London comprehensive. Much more middle class than many of its kind, however, because this is the golden apple if you are after an excellent education for your creative daughter who also likes to perform. A higher proportion than usual of parents are actors, barristers, artists and, yes, even bankers, than you would find at just any ordinary central London comprehensive, many of whom have been privately educated themselves.

Tucked between Princess Grace Hospital and Marylebone High Street, the school is a leafy, contained oasis of calm and purpose. St Marylebone parish church is a focus point and contributes to the peacefulness

The gritty detail is there are approximately 65 per cent from ethnic minority backgrounds and from 90 different countries. Over 50 per cent of pupils are bilingual. More than 60 languages spoken at home. Sixty per cent C of E members; the largest second religious group is Muslim. School clearly tries hard to integrate the social mix – has an annual World Culture Day among many other initiatives – and attracts fierce loyalty. Girls travel some distances to get here – from as far as Hackney in the east to Ealing and Shepherds Bush in the west, Kilburn, Kentish Town and Islington in the north as well as Wandsworth and Southwark in the south.

Entrance: As maddeningly oversubscribed as you would expect – something like 1,000 applicants for 168 places. Looked after children and those with statements have priority. Sixty per cent C of E places, 40 per cent 'open', with distance the only criterion. Fourteen places annually given to those with outstanding aptitude in an aspect of performing arts (music, choral, dance or drama). Applicants divided into four ability bands with equal numbers accepted from each band. Tie breaker of how near to the school you live. In the sixth, 330 places – priority to existing students, though they have to fulfil requirements (minimum of five 9-6 GCSEs, with at least grade 5 in maths and English). Boys are taken into the sixth and, again, more apply than there are places for. Performing arts and maths/ICT scholarships for sixth formers. School receives five applications a week for occasional places.

Exit: Up to 40 per cent leaves after GCSE and goes to further education colleges, the independents, eg Latymer Upper, or other state schools, eg Camden, largely for a greater range of A level subjects or more vocational courses. Most stay, though entrance to the school's own sixth form is not a given, even for their own. Sixth form leavers to good universities and a range of courses; seven to Oxford and Cambridge in 2018. A few each year to read music. Students go on to study a decent mix of arts and science subjects, from biomedicine at Edinburgh to Spanish and Hispanic studies at Bristol to criminology at Manchester. A few each year to read music,

usually several to art foundation, dance foundation and drama school – immediately or after a gap year.

Money matters: National funding programmes largely cut so bidding for extra money from various sources takes up a lot of time. The result, however, is a school that is well-staffed and well-equipped, if not to lavish private school standards.

Remarks: If your daughter is outgoing, confident and creative this is an excellent choice. St Marylebone is an exceptional school. It has the benefits of the moral ethos of a Church of England school but is ethnically diverse and serves many different communities. With a bright young head at the helm, its future looks as rosy as its history.

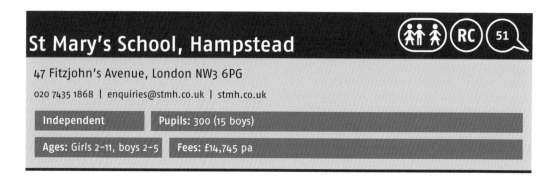

St Mary's School, Hampstead

47 Fitzjohn's Avenue, London NW3 6PG

020 7435 1868 | enquiries@stmh.co.uk | stmh.co.uk

| Independent | Pupils: 300 (15 boys) |
| Ages: Girls 2–11, boys 2–5 | Fees: £14,745 pa |

Headmistress: Since 2016, Harriet Connor-Earl BA (RE – from Brighton). In her late 30s, she is young for a head teacher – but definitely not green. She has been in the teaching profession for many years, starting off her career at a state secondary school in Haywards Heath before a stint in New York teaching at St Columbia Elementary School: 'I taught grade 8, but a lot of the expectation was teaching to test, so you couldn't be creative.' She still enjoyed it and benefited from the experience. When she came back to the UK, she worked for two years at Chapter School for Girls in Kent, followed by four years at Warden Park School. Subsequently she became director of studies and boarding housemistress at Ardingly College Prep School, Sussex, before being offered the post of head at St Mary's: 'The minute I walked in the chapel, I fell in love with it and the school..and the girls were the kindest and happiest I'd ever met.'

Children, she says 'are wonderful and curious and the best bit about humans.' She simply loves working with them and her career in teaching was preordained, from when she used to line up her teddies in her pretend classroom to having a mum and two aunts who are all teachers. We liked this head almost instantly (the aroma of the warm pain au

chocolates and coffee we were offered did nothing to change our mind). With her wonderfully posh name, Mrs Connor-Earl is all the things you would hope the head of a cosy independent girls' school to be – understated and elegant, straight up but with a twinkle or two. Her girls would probably like to be her one day, and the parents would secretly like to be her mate.

She didn't have an easy task, following in the footsteps of her much respected predecessor. One parent told us: 'I loved Ms Rawlinson so much I was determined not to like Ms Connor-Earl, but actually that changed pretty quickly.' Most parents agree that Ms Connor-Earl is a lovely, approachable and welcoming head with bags of energy and a tough job of putting her mark on a school where some parents don't like change. One parent said: 'She has injected fresh ideas into a slightly tired school, which although well regarded for its pastoral side, was less so for its academic achievements. She now runs a much tighter ship and her enthusiasm and experience have brought about positive changes.'

A committed Catholic, she is married and has one son. Enjoys family skiing holidays, cooking and renovating her house in Brittany. She has successfully completed the 110km London to Brighton cycle challenge and raised over £3,000 for charity.

Entrance: All year groups are oversubscribed and prospective parents are encouraged to register as early as possible. Non-selective academically. Places go first to siblings, then to Catholics. Family-orientated ethos means that other faiths and cultures are also warmly welcomed. Nursery arrangements are particularly parent friendly. Children are admitted from 2 years 9 months and can stay to lunch or all afternoon with minimum notice. Boys make up a third of nursery entrants. A few further places for girls often become available in year 3. Some full bursaries available.

Exit: Plenty of offers from leading academic secondary schools, with several scholarships. Large numbers to South Hampstead and Channing, followed by Francis Holland NW1 and Highgate. Others to eg City of London, Queen's College, North London Collegiate and St Paul's Girls, or to state grammar schools (St Michael's, Henrietta Barnett) or boarding (Queenswood, St Mary's Ascot). Secondary school advice is a strength, starting with individual parent meetings in year 5. 'Parents trust us and listen to what we recommend', says the school. Boys leave by the age of 6, many to neighbouring Catholic prep, St Anthony's, others to Devonshire House, UCS, Hereward House, Habs, Highgate or The Hall.

Remarks: Founded in 1871 by the Congregation of Jesus, the school moved in 1926 to its present site, a spacious turn-of-the century building with polished mosaic floors and vast country-like gardens. Against this gracious period backdrop, facilities are thoroughly up to date, with a super new science lab, a large, bright assembly hall and a well-stocked library. Significant recent investment in IT: new iPads and laptops in every classroom and MacBooks in the music department to help pupils create digital music.

In 1992, when there were too few teaching nuns to manage the school, a charitable trust was formed to continue the good work under lay management.

A non-selective school, it still manages to pull off high-flying results at 11. Teaching (as described in their most recent ISI report) is 'excellent' – sharp, lively and very pupil focused: 'The teacher worked out my daughter in three minutes', said one parent, and 'communication with the staff is excellent', said another. Results are achieved by encouragement and risk taking, rather than a hothousing ethos. The head says: 'I don't believe that children should be assessed at 3 and 4 years old, and I also won't choose one girl from a family and not her

sibling. Yes, it means I won't have 32 girls going to St Paul's, but I will have 32 girls going to the right school for them.'

The head has introduced an assessment programme, with pupils monitored from year 1 so they get used to the process and gain the experience: 'By the time they get to year 6, they are used to exams and we can pretty much safely say what they will achieve academically.' She has also introduced the four Rs into the school's ethos (Risk taking, Resilience, Respect, Reflection). One parent told us: 'Mrs Connor-Earl encourages girls to take risks and leave their comfort zone. They are rewarded for challenging themselves and making mistakes, to help them achieve more academic progress and build their self confidence.'

'Mrs Connor-Earl encourages girls to take risks and leave their comfort zone. They are rewarded for challenging themselves and making mistakes, to help them achieve'

The brightest are stretched through a curriculum enriched with plenty of arts-related activities and sport. 'We wanted to make teaching more relevant and incorporate risk taking and thinking independently.' Interesting extra work for those who need stretching (lunch-time puzzle club, for example, is a big hit). Fluid ability grouping throughout, then setting in maths and English in year 6 in the run up to 11 plus.

Excellent support is available, with one full-time SENCo and various special needs teachers – depending on cohort – providing help in class and out of it (in lovely, bright teaching spaces). 'We would never turn anyone away. We try and cater as much as we can for all children – we assess them on a case by case basis.' One parent told us: 'You really feel they care about every single girl.'

Strong sport (new Astroturf) with a double court for netball and a well-equipped gym. All the usual team games: rounders, netball, hockey, football, plus swimming at Swiss Cottage baths (for years 3 to 6) and athletics in Regent's Park. Gymnastics particularly popular, with pupils competing at regional and national level. High achievement too in music and excellent dance and drama (including an all-encompassing production in year 6).

Heaps of extracurricular going on with everything from spy club, illustration, knitting, origami, gardening, cooking, yoga, various music clubs and chess etc to a wealth of languages including Mandarin, Latin and Spanish. We particularly loved the idea of year 5 book club with the head herself in her lovely, tranquil office accompanied by freshly baked cookies (it sounds so wonderfully Enid Blyton; we hope it's accompanied by lashings of ginger beer).

An after-school club until 6pm every day supports working families, with emergency places bookable on the same day. It includes a quiet area where children can complete their homework or read with a teacher.

Plenty of trips too. For year 4s it's their first residential trip with a night away, for year 5s an activity week in Devon and for year 6s there is a trip to the Alps post-exams and a trip to France to meet penpals and make croissants. Little ones go to a safari park or the seaside. Ex-pupils are also invited back once a year to enjoy a pizza and DVD night with the year 6s. Cake concerts are popular, with gluten-free brownies on offer. One year 6 pupil told us, 'There's a lot to like here and I'll be completely upset to leave.'

> ## 'We would never turn anyone away. We try and cater as much as we can for all children'

Boys are well integrated and given appropriate scope in the Big Boys' Club, where they play football and let off steam on imaginary motorbikes. 'It lets them be boys in this all-girls environment,' said one mother.

Very much a Catholic school, with about 70 per cent Catholic families. 'I think one of the most wonderful things about it is that the Catholic ethos permeates every aspect of the children's life', said one parent. Those who wish can be prepared for first holy communion by much-loved Father Chris on his twice-weekly visits to the school chapel. Pupils take part in mass and study Catholic Christianity. 'Many of our parents have had a Catholic education themselves and want that for their children' – but even those who haven't feel included. 'As a non-Catholic', said one parent, 'I was quite concerned at the outset, but Father Chris is so lovely and gives such interesting talks. They really teach the children how to be good and loving members of the community.'

Pupils are smiley and notably well behaved. They have a certain girlish innocence which is often so sadly lacking in today's techno age. Our two lovely guides giggled conspiratorially when we asked if they ever had the need to confess anything to Father Chris, to which one replied: 'Well, I did once borrow my brother's toy without asking and so did confess.' Everything here is geared towards doing things 'the St Mary's way'; those who slip up are gently reminded of 'expectations'. 'We want pupils to do their best.' Most pupils adore the school ('my daughter can't wait to get back after the holidays') and parents are equally appreciative: 'I can't say a bad word about this place. I have had three daughters come through this school, and I almost want another one just so she can come here.'

Mostly professional families from Hampstead and the surrounding areas, with a wide range of backgrounds (Europe, the US, Asia and the Far East). About half speak at least one other language at home (with good in-school support for newcomers on the foothills of English). Very welcoming parents, we are told, 'which can be unusual, especially in the London private school bubble. But here they are grounded and down to earth.' Despite its Hampstead location, this is a fairly understated place and, unusually for a prep school, offers a number of full bursaries.

St Paul's Cathedral School

2 New Change, London EC4M 9AD

020 7248 5156 | admissions@spcs.london.sch.uk | spcslondon.com

Independent	Pupils: 246; boarders: 28 (boy choristers)
Ages: 4–13	Fees: £14,031– £15,105 pa; Boarding choristers £8,736 pa

Headmaster: Since 2016, Simon Larter-Evans, previously head of boarding, housemaster and head of English at the Yehudi Menuhin School. He studied ballet at the Rambert Academy, then spent four years as principal dancer, performing in the UK and abroad. After 15 years working in commercial management, publishing and IT industries, he gained a first class degree as a mature student in English literature, drama, theatre and performance from the University of Surrey, and a PGCE from the Institute of Education. He has been a teacher of English and head of year 9 at St Edward's School, Oxford, and a teacher of English and drama at Pangbourne College. He is married to Dawn, a director at Accenture, and they live 'over the shop' in a house within the school.

Friendly and approachable, he has quickly won over the SPCS community. 'He has a great manner with both parents, teachers and staff,' wrote one parent. 'Really lovely!' enthused another. 'Open to new ideas,' was another comment. A general feeling that the school, already good, can only get better with him at the helm. Interests include photography, gardening, cooking, cycling and writing. His study is lined with an erudite collection of books, and he is currently doing a PhD on psychological development in young musicians and dancers.

Entrance: Register early – school is massively oversubscribed. Single form entry of 20 in reception. First list is closed at 70, then reserve list of 40. After that, the school keeps names and addresses but doesn't charge a registration fee. Informal style assessment – number games, drawing pictures, telling stories, etc. Staff look for children who are able and who will get on well within the school. Preference is given to siblings as long as they're able to access the curriculum.

Year 3 entry of a further 12 pupils. School doesn't follow any kind of formal 7+ assessment programme, but children are tested in English and maths 'just to see where they are.' A few join at year 7, as others leave and places become available.

Choristers (boys only) can join at any time, including mid-year, but are unlikely to be accepted after year 5. The school takes around six per year. Auditions are held by Andrew Carwood, director of music at St Paul's Cathedral, who looks for a desire for music, an innate openness of the voice, and the ability to hold a tune.

New buildings planned which will enable two form entry to reception from 2020.

Exit: Diverse destinations, reflecting the intake: St Paul's, Westminster, Forest, City of London Boys' and Girls', Alleyn's, North Bridge House, Portland Place, Queen's College, Channing, Highgate.

Majority of girls leave after year 6 for London day schools. The few who stay on go to mixed schools with a 13+ entry eg City of London Freemen's. Excellent track record of scholarships, both academic and specialist. Choristers do very well, often winning music awards to top senior schools eg Eton, Winchester, King's Canterbury, Uppingham.

Remarks: The Choir School dates from around 1123, when eight boys in need of alms were provided with a home and education in return for singing the Cathedral Office. It wasn't a particularly child-friendly place, however, and by the early 19th century the stipend paid for the boys' upkeep was so inadequate that they were usually dismissed to roam the streets once service was over. Victorian philanthropist Maria Hackett, shocked by their predicament, campaigned tirelessly for 60 years to get them something better, and the present school was eventually founded in 1874 in Carter Lane. Threatened with demolition in the 1960s, it moved to its present brutalist modernist site in New Change. Originally for choristers only, it became a day school in the 1980s, and co-ed in the 1990s. The swimming pool that once occupied the basement is now the English department; needs must.

Year 7 English students had come up with their own scholarly questions about Shakespeare that they wanted to research

It is, to modern sensibilities, a very ugly building, but it's a truly lovely place to go to school, sheltering under the lofty and awe-inspiring splendour of St Paul's Cathedral, and flanked by St Paul's Cross, with its inscription that recalls 'such scenes of good and evil as make up human affairs'. The original roll of eight pupils has grown to 250, spanning reception to year 8.

Not a school for those seeking flashy facilities. Major building works are planned during the summer break in 2019 which will improve and expand both residential and teaching spaces, plus enable important outreach work. For now, however, the building remains a homely rabbit-warren of rooms, many of them low-ceilinged and endearingly scuffed. Pupils allude happily to the 'garden', the school's outdoor space, but it isn't very green, and the school's biggest space isn't that big. On the other hand, weekly assembly is held in the Quire of the cathedral itself, affectionately referred to as 'the school chapel', and how many schools can say that? Tell Out Your Soul was sung full-throatedly by children clustered four to a hymn book – not enough to go round, rather charmingly, in this most august of settings. Worship was friendly and child-centred but still assembly as we used to love it: a good sing, a bit of pi-jaw, a few notices, then off to the strains of the organ. Except that it's the St Paul's Grand Organ, and visiting tourists were agape.

They teach the International Primary Curriculum here; both head and staff like its theme-based approach. They're certainly doing something right. Everywhere we looked, we saw children who were confident, articulate, comfortable with wider learning. In a year 7 English lesson students had come up with their own scholarly questions about Shakespeare that they wanted to research: 'Did he copy work from Christopher Marlowe?' 'What was the political landscape when he was writing?' 'Who did Shakespeare take inspiration from?' and, bluntly, 'Are any of his plays not considered to be any good?' Year 5 maths lesson invited similarly independent thinking: children worked in pairs to 'mark' each other's (anonymous) mistakes on a recent exam paper, and embraced the task with relish, although the gleeful written comments may not have been quite what the teacher had in mind – 'What do you think you're doing?' 'You haven't put the units in, you idiot!' and, more generously, 'Don't forget to wright [sic] the answer.' The only modern language taught is French, but the children also do Latin, and Greek is offered for those who stay on to year 7. Pleasant and well-stocked library is used enthusiatically by the whole school. After a morning on the go teachers are still cordial and full of vim, and the standard of work on display is extremely high – we loved the year 3 postcards from Ariadne to Theseus, complaining about being dumped on a desert island. Science taught in dedicated science lab.

Full time qualified SENCo delivers integrated learning support in lessons, aided by team of assistants. School is able to cater for mild dyslexia, dyspraxia, etc. and doesn't see it as a barrier. At the other end of the spectrum, however, several parents contacted us to express concern about the teaching lacking stretch and challenge for the most able pupils, particularly in the middle years. 'They do differentiate in most lessons but they don't really challenge the most able with extension activities,' wrote one who seemed to speak for several. 'There are several gifted children in both maths and English for whom this is the case, and those parents are quite frustrated.' School strongly contests this. 'Extension materials are available in classrooms, and children are directed to them, or can elect to do them. The puzzle wall outside the maths room contains sums which are fiendishly difficult. But it it's true that we are not a hothouse, and we work hard not to make school a misery.'

Sport described as 'very inclusive and energetic' by parents, and boys and girls are equally encouraged to play all sports. Team games are played in nearby Coram Fields and Victoria Park, and the school has its own training playground on site. Swimming down the road in the pool at City of London boys.

Drama is 'inspirational, exciting and contemporary,' according to one parent, and recent shows have included Dr Jekyll and Mr Hyde performed by the year 8s and A Midsummer Night's Dream by

Sport described as 'very inclusive and energetic' by parents, and boys and girls are equally encouraged to play all sports

the year 5s. Lots of clubs after school, and trips to all sorts of museums and galleries, both in London and further afield – the year 3 camping trip in Essex was 'the most fun ever,' according to pupils.

However, the stand-out activity, as you'd expect, is music, described by a mother as 'Superb! Very uplifting and of a fantastic standard.' Twenty visiting teachers deliver 450 individual music lessons weekly. Senior and junior orchestra, three choirs and an abundance of ensembles including early music group. Outstanding ABRSM exam results, with merits and distinctions at grade 8 common – all the more remarkable given that no child here is older than 13. Music-making here is inclusive – 'It is the norm to sing in a choir or play instruments,' confirmed one mother – but raised above the ordinary by the choristers, whose musicality pervades the entire school community.

Choristers' cathedral life happens before and after school, but their day school life is the same as the other children's. 'The school does a fabulous job of keeping the choristers integrated into the wider school,' wrote a grateful mother, 'but also manages to build a close sense of community and support amongst the boys.' For those who can cut it (for senior choristers, autumn term finishes at 4pm on Christmas Day), the musical training is unrivalled. 'I think the whole chorister experience is rather magical and has probably fundamentally changed my son's life and attitude to life for the better,' marvelled a parent. 'It has given him a love of music, a real sense of confidence, calm and an ability to slow down and relax.' 'It's busy, but in the best way, and it's become such a big part of my life,' confirmed a year 7 treble, before delivering a stunning rendition of Take O Take Those Lips Away that left us open-mouthed with admiration.

There are usually around 30 choristers and they all have to board. (They can also be of any faith – the school has no issue with this.) Boarding house is a little sparse, but welcoming: L-shaped common room offers books, board games, DVDs, sofas, a Wii, and the ever-popular Lego and K-Nex. Bedrooms were, we thought, rather cramped by modern standards, with up to eight boys to a room, but new accommodation is planned for 2020. Run by a mix of male and female staff. 'The boarding team are responsive and have endless patience for worried or slightly disorganised parents. The communication is very good and open,' wrote one

Westminster School

mother. Parents can visit them in the evenings to help with homework, etc. There's time off on Saturday afternoons and boys can also go home on Sunday night, 'which really helps, because obviously we miss him!' according to a parent.

Behaviour is lively but generally impeccable throughout the school. House points system not unlike Hogwarts, with points won and lost for your house through good or bad behaviour. 'The sanction of removing house points is extraordinarily potent here,' remarked the head, and detentions are rare. Achievement and good behaviour rewarded through commendations, gold certificates, etc.

SPCS families are professionals from all walks of life – 'comfortable, but not super-rich,' according to school, which aims to keep its fees as low as possible. A few bursaries, funded directly out of fee income and limited to children in year 3 and above. The only scholarships available are for choristers, whose education is paid for by the cathedral. Strong international contingent – at least a dozen languages spoken here. A SPCS mother wrote, 'The school tends to attract interesting families from a wide mix of backgrounds.' Alumni include England cricket captain Alastair Cooke, Walter de la Mare, Charles Groves and Simon Russell Beale.

This is a kind, nurturing, but exciting place to learn and to grow up. 'Overall, it is a fantastic school. Caring, and academic without being too pushy,' was one parent's verdict. 'I'm delighted my children have been educated there. It's been a special time in their lives and they've all benefited from it in different ways.'

St Peter's Eaton Square

Lower Belgrave Street, London SW1W 0NL

020 7641 4230 | office@stpeaton.org.uk | stpeaton.org.uk

State	Pupils: 308
Ages: 3–11	

Head: Since 2016, Miles Ridley BA PGCE (late 50s). A degree in English and drama from Essex launched him into a career on the boards as an actor. Ten years on, married and with a family, he took a teaching certificate at Goldsmiths College and began teaching in a primary school in Lewisham, moving quickly from class teacher to senior leader and SENCo. After 10 years at this school, which his own children attended, he thought a change would be good. Applying for the SENCo post in a secondary school more for the experience of the application than anything, he found himself heading a department of 25 teachers and assistants within the very large SEN dept. Further training as a teacher of hearing impaired children led to jobs in both primary and secondary schools as SENCo and senior teacher, followed by a position as SEN consultant for Westminster. He joined St Peter's as assistant head and took on the headship when the previous incumbent was headhunted elsewhere.

A quietly urbane man with owlish glasses greeted us, fresh from an editorial meeting with the pupil magazine sub-editors. Married to a lawyer, with two grown up children, committed to the school's Christian values and not above making the tea himself, from a handy kitchenette in the corner of his otherwise minimalist office. 'I'm a bit old school and like the idea of nurturing well-rounded young citizens..I want to know their moral education has been well supported.' He has made a start already by condensing the behaviour policy into four principles: everything you do must contribute to yours and everyone's learning, be polite, kind and safe; 'It fits into everything we do, more than I dreamt of,' he says. Popular with parents, who greet him each morning in the playground, and approachable to children, he has made a name for himself in introducing the school magazine and transforming the school's SEN support. 'He has been really supportive; any problem, we go straight to him,' said a mum. A child's verdict, 'He's kind of laid back but doesn't let us chat very much. He has rules'.

Entrance: Admission by Westminster LA criteria: priority given to looked after children, those baptised at St Peter's Eaton Square church, those who attend the affiliated church and then congregations of other C of E churches. Most of the 10 children from their own nursery gain a place, but have to apply. Oversubscribed three to one, until top years, when some filter off to local prep schools. Catchment area is mostly Westminster,

A quietly urbane man with owlish glasses greeted us, fresh from an editorial meeting with the pupil magazine sub-editors

but some other boroughs, including Lambeth and Wandsworth.

Exit: About 50 per cent go to state secondaries including state boarding schools. Top of the list most recently are: Holyport College, Chestnut Grove, Lady Margaret School, Marylebone Boys' School and Notre Dame Roman Catholic Girls' School. Some successes with independent day schools too, including Latymer Upper, Queen's College and City of London School, with one or two applying to board at eg Pilgrims ('not without tutoring,' one parent murmured). Exit at age 7 or 8 discouraged.

Remarks: Academically up with the front-runners, with well above national average results in Sats. Parents praised the maths teaching, which adopts the Shanghai Approach, not press-ganging, but a method learned from visiting Chinese teachers. 'It's very systematic; they do it in groups,' said one mum. Literacy was also mentioned: 'My son started off uninterested in reading and is now one of the best in the class'. We saw formal grammar being taught as early as year 2, while junior cruciverbalists were compiling a famous character word-search. Latin is taught from year 3. Class sizes are kept at 25 with two classes per year group, except at the top of the school, due to (mostly) boys leaving early.

The class teacher is often supported by a TA and year 6s volunteer to read to younger children. A typical London turnover of staff (or, as one child put it, 'Teachers leave very often'). We heard about Science Day, when students rotate as science detectives, carrying out experiments with each new teacher; 'We made slime with borax and PVA glue and food colouring'. There's a no homework policy, 'because they were sending sheets home and only a certain number of kids did it', explained one mum. We heard replacing traditional homework with school supported Home Learning had upset some parents. Lower numbers of children with SEN than average but school supports some with learning difficulties, Down's, ASD and complex needs; 'we would never say, "no",' remarks the head. One mum reeled off a list of extra equipment that had been provided for her daughter with cerebral palsy, as well as a general readiness among staff to manage her medical needs and frequent out-patient appointments. 'They treat her like a normal child. They administer medication at lunchtime and have never complained'.

Music is abundant across all years and from year 4 in the form of group violin lessons. 'There's lots of research about how learning a musical instrument gives you extra brainpower,' says the head, justifying his choice of instrument. 'It's portable but it's a step up from the recorder'. One mum criticised the lack of variety of instrument teaching: 'They made things so hard for the peripatetic teachers that they all quit...it was interfering with core subjects'. All children participate in singing and drama, with house singing competitions and a choir which performs at church and local concerts, including in Victoria Station and Trafalgar Square at Christmas. Nativity plays for infants, and year 6 leavers raise the roof in a full production, the likes of Pirates of the Currybean; 'they are spectacular,' commented a teacher. Proximity to the West End shows enables actors to perform at the school, as well as easy access to museums and theatres on school trips.

No sports fields. Youngest children do yoga, while others start the day with Shake and Wake dance moves

Artwork was prolific in the classrooms; we particularly liked year 2's pop art self-portraits and the models of revolving stages in year 5, inspired by a visit to Cirque de Soleil. A termly school magazine, SPARK, sponsored by an international publisher/local well-wisher, showcases the children's activities in glossy magazine form, as well as providing a platform for aspiring writers and helpful advice from the young agony aunts, eg 'When someone makes you feel angry, drink some water to calm yourself'. The school has no sports fields, only a tiny green soft surface playground and basement hall, used by a specialist PE coach. The youngest children take yoga, while others start the day with Shake and Wake dance moves. Sports day takes place in Battersea Park and year 6s walk to nearby Hyde Park for outdoor pursuits, after their Sats. Swimming at the nearby Queen Mother sports centre, from year 2. Parents run an after-school football club in Battersea Park, and help to ferry children there, to cut down costs. One mum lamented the lack of space for sports: 'shame there isn't more space to run and get energy out of themselves'. Year 6 enjoys a residential at Sayers Croft, which introduces caving, pond dipping and orienteering – all without phone or iPod help; 'it was really easy', said one boy.

A Christian school, in name and ethos, with regular visits to the high C of E Romanesque church in

Eaton Square. Christian values are evident round the school, from the motto 'Together, we will realise the potential God has given us', to the daily hymns at assembly. The Saint Peter's Way code of conduct, with its four simple principles, is familiar to each child and used as a way of managing behaviour. 'It works', says the head; 'I have had emails from the public praising the children's behaviour'. As for bullying, 'we teach the child to understand the difference between teasing and bullying'. The school promotes positive behaviour but also operates a red and yellow card staged sanctions system to encourage children to reflect on their actions. Staff aim to be consistent: 'Children want someone to be in charge; if you are not in charge, one of them will be'. We saw charts of traffic light warning steps in each class and incentives in the form of house points. A celebration assembly rewards good conduct with 'star of the week' and the four houses (named after the gospels) compete for house points. One mum commented it was 'very Hogwartish' and reported that the thrill of winning the house competition was so great there was no need to supply a prize. If the resident agony aunt's advice doesn't satisfy all mental health needs, the school offers mindfulness classes for anxious students.

Christian values are evident round the school, from the motto 'Together, we will realise the potential God has given us', to the daily hymns at assembly

Founded in 1815 by the parish of St Peter's at the east end of Eaton Square, the school started in Eccleston Place and moved later to its present site in Lower Belgrave Street, 'practically in Victoria Station,' laughed one mum. A Victorian red-brick frontage, with imposing square tower and large round windows, squeezed between office buildings and mansion flats, with original front-yard style playground (now hidden from prying eyes with hoardings), all within earshot of the London-Brighton line. Teaching space is chiselled out of every available corner, from the upper attic storey, where high ceilings give a gothic feel to the building, down to the basement nursery. Red painted doors outside and spidery fire escapes lead to blue doors and creamy new paintwork inside, with some lovely original artwork by Axel Scheffler on the walls. Fortunately, our guides knew where they were going, as we were quickly disorientated by the internal layout, recently redesigned, with plenty of small tuition areas.

The older years occupy the top floor, with banners of spelling words draped across the ceiling and an international map woven into the rug. Two-person desks facing the front in year 6, while further down the school we saw four to six children to a work table and in the youngest classes the bright picture carpets were used for group times with comfy cushions for reading. Most rooms have a touchscreen board ('like a massive iPad', suggested the children) with books stored on shelves to the side. A separate computing suite with desktops and a roving iPad chariot provide enough computers for a whole class. If you stare closely in the reception class you will glimpse the pet snails. The kitchens on the ground floor serve up lunch on long tables in the adjacent hall; jolly, illustrated menus announce a diet of school favourites, as well as Meat Free Monday. Lasagne and chocolate cake were voted tops.

As one parent put it, 'the playground is the thing you notice more than anything' due to the restricted size, lack of climbing equipment, and, when crammed with whooping children, the intense noise. Another parent mitigated, 'it's so not a reason not to send your child there'. Smartly framed boards on the outer walls inform parents of class news and neatly stacked balls wait temptingly for use in PE. 'The site is absolutely minute,' says the head. 'We hope that Westminster chooses to close off the road, and we can use it as a playground.' The children, however, don't appear fazed by the lack of outside space. Our guides personified the St Peter's Way dictum, in being kind, polite, and articulate. 'The children always show you round,' said one mum. 'What better advert can you have?' We agreed. They led the way in trim blue and yellow uniform, complete with stripy ties. 'I would rather wear my own clothes, but I can understand why there is a school uniform', said one. Another informed us the clothes were available to buy at 'John Lewis slash Peter Jones'.

Parents, we heard, were 'driven, aspirational with a disproportionate number of barristers, lawyers etc, to whom standards are important...a real cross-section of that part of London'. The head adds, 'Parents are quite vocal and I am happy for any and all to come to me with their concerns'. A school council ensures the children have their say too. Many families live in Westminster or Lambeth and walk or use the bus or tube to school; the head is on a mission to reduce idlers in four by fours at the school gate.

The new PTA was described as 'really involved' with a talent for fundraising; recent initiatives include a quiz night, Christmas fair, and Burns night supper. There are clubs before, during and after school, including breakfast, debating, drawing, yoga and French. Parents are satisfied with communication, via the 'very nice reception staff', who filter emails 'to stop the teachers from being harassed'. Enquiries are answered promptly, and parents and children appeared to understand the meaning of 'open door policy'. 'I've never had an issue in almost 10 years with teacher access,' said one mum. One small boy said, 'Mr Ridley is happy if children go to him, unless his sign is up'.

A top scoring school which provides an all-round education with a Christian soul. Ethical values underpin the direction and modern teaching methods provide a firm grounding for the school's metropolitan population. As one parent put it, 'it offers what a private school might be without the price tag'. Good things come in small parcels.

St Saviour's CofE Primary School

👫 CⁿE 54

Shirland Road, Maida Vale, London W9 2JD

020 7641 6414 | office@stsavioursprimary.co.uk | stsavioursprimary.co.uk/

State	Pupils: 240
Ages: 3-11	

Headteacher: Since 1994, Lindsey Woodford, BA in education from London University. A warm, humorous, approachable woman with none of the lofty airs that waft around some heads. 'She's fun and she's ballsy, but she's strict. It's a winning combination.' Happy to muck in, she even joined a team of parents in a sponsored swim to raise £12k to Astroturf the playground. 'I don't know many other headteachers who'd don a wetsuit and swim 3.5km in the Thames. She's pretty game.' Her office, far from being a scary place, is crammed with 100-200 soft toys which have colonised every available surface. She is ably assisted by Ripley, her border terrier, who is adored by the children. Pupils who have done well (or are perhaps just feeling a bit glum) are occasionally awarded Ripley Time, which means being allowed to sit in her office for a supervised stroking session.

In her spare time Ms Woodford enjoys embroidery, crime novels, antiques and baking. We can vouch for her excellent homemade biscuits (gooey peanut butter flavour the day we visited). Very much hands on – small children approach her for a hug as we walk through the playground (and you can't fake that). Previously deputy head at St Michael's in Highgate, following stints at schools in Bucks, Brent, Haringey and Ealing, so oodles of experience. A local girl, she was born at nearby St Mary's Hospital and attended Parliament Hill School in north London. She is married to the contractor who created the nursery in 2000. The ultimate accolade comes from a grateful mother. 'I'm proud of how my daughters have turned out and I feel they have been formed by Ms Woodford as much as they have by me. I owe her a lot.'

Entrance: Heavily oversubscribed one form entry school. Over 90 applicants for nursery and 140 for 30 reception places. Nursery is mornings only, though afternoons are available for a fee. No catchment area; pupils come from as far afield as Camden, Kentish Town, Kensal Rise and Harlesden. After the customary preference given to looked-after children, admission boils down to enthusiastic worship at one of two affiliated churches, St Saviour's and St Mary on Paddington Green. This means 'at least three Sundays every month for at least a year before application'. Prospective parents might want to reconsider that sneaky lie-in every fourth Sunday, as admission is uncompromisingly awarded to the 'most frequent worshippers'. And don't even think of slacking off once you've got your foot in the door as progress from nursery to reception depends on continued regular worship – a rule that is enforced. 'We hate to lose children but it does happen,' admits the head.

> '*I don't know many other heads who'd don a wetsuit and swim 3.5km in the Thames*'

Admission for siblings languishes way down at no 8 on the list of criteria, though occasional places in later years are well worth applying for as later places are awarded 'on need'.

Exit: Pupils progress to a wide variety of schools. Favourite state schools include Greycoats, St Marylebone and Twyford High School, plus

Paddington Academy, Holland Park and St George's. The head is also very open to the independent sector ('We love a good badge') with pupils winning places at Highgate, St Paul's Girls', Latymer Upper, City of London, UCS, Merchant Taylors', Channing plus boarding schools like Christ's Hospital and Wycombe Abbey. It's enough to turn an expensive prep school head green with envy.

'For the last two years we've got a child into St Paul's Juniors at 11 plus. We're very proud of that.'

Secondary transfer meeting in September where both state and independent school admissions are explained and various bursaries and scholarship options discussed. 'It's never too early to come and talk to me.' Parents who are considering the independent sector are given advice from year 2 onwards, plus suggestions for specific tutors. Ms Woodford is brutally honest about a child's chances of success. 'I don't mind where children go on to as long as it's the right school for that child'.

Remarks: Nestling in a quiet side street amongst the tall wedding cake mansions of Maida Vale, this Ofsted outstanding state primary has won more awards than you can shake a stick at. But, despite the wealthy area, this is no middle class ghetto school.

'It's truly comprehensive,' said one parent. 'You've got people who live in million pound houses and families who live in local authority housing by the canal. Everybody just gets on with it and befriends each other.'

It's now an annual day when lessons are suspended and every corner of the school is given over to different creative activities such 3D printing, learning the ukulele, an apothecary's garden, dance

Broad international mix with 35 languages spoken (the largest groups being white British, followed by Eritrean and other African). A tranche of bankers, diplomats and media types alongside a large number of low income families just above the free meals threshold. Twenty-four children on free school meals (approx 10 per cent) when we visited, though the number waxes and wanes. Winner of Mayor's Gold Club Award for succeeding against the odds in improving pupils' achievements. 'It doesn't matter to us that we get a badge for it, what matters is our free school meal pupils do at least as well, if not better, than other pupils. We buck the trend,' says the head.

The socially and culturally diverse mix makes the school's outstanding results all the more impressive. Over 60 per cent of pupils regularly achieve level 5 in Sats, and they are top of the Westminster league table for pupils achieving level 6 (expected level for 14 year olds). 'They really encourage each child to discover something they can excel in, whether it's art, English, maths or anything else,' said one happy parent. 'It's not just about sitting exams, it's about becoming a well rounded, caring, bright little person who wants to learn.'

Our immediate first impressions were that St Saviour's is an exceptionally smiley school. We got eye contact and a friendly grin from pupils and adults alike as we waited in reception, and the smiles kept on coming throughout our tour. In an age when so many children look down and mumble when addressed by an adult, the confidence of these pupils shines out. Clearly, the social graces are given the same importance at this state primary as they are in the private sector.

Bog-standard Victorian school building, but preferable to the cramped conditions so often seen in converted premises used by some London independents. Here the classrooms are large and light-drenched with walls of vast windows. Trad architecture could feel forbidding in dark stairwells, but they've done their best to create a bright, cosy and well cared-for learning space. Walls covered in excellent artwork. Comfortable sofas, toys and a multi-sensory room in the early years section. Pupil loos are clean and colourful (no smells) and only one wet tissue apologetically stuck to the ceiling.

Separate junior and senior playgrounds. Outside space is limited, typical of most inner city primaries, but they've made the most of what could have been a rather dank concrete area. Good range of outdoor toys including space hoppers, a climbing wall and some rather grand-looking trees in pots. Small side garden growing potatoes, rhubarb and herbs and we even spotted the head's mum who had popped in to tend the plants. Truly a family-oriented school.

Setting starts in reception, with four groups per class. Some groups might have just two pupils, while others are much larger, depending on the needs of each individual year group. Teaching assistants work with higher ability as well as lower ability pupils. 'We focus on what each child needs.' Weekly Spanish lessons from reception onwards with a linguist Star of the Week award.

Regular pupil progress meetings to identify and keep track of underperforming pupils. Each child on the SEN register has a target sheet so progress can be tracked in lessons and support groups, and to ensure no child slips through the net. A qualified SEN specialist working part time is ably supported by battalions of TAs trained in many different types of strategies and interventions. Success

We got eye contact and a friendly grin from pupils and adults alike as we waited in reception, and the smiles kept on coming

of the school's support safety net self-evident in outstanding results for all pupils, regardless of background. 'I have a dyslexic daughter and they are very clever with their thinking,' said one mother. 'If you can't learn your times tables they'll come up with another way to teach them to you. They teach each individual child, rather than sticking to a formula.'

Provision in sports and the arts is a huge strength at St Saviour's. Thriving PTA holds monthly fundraisers to generate over £65k a year, most of which is used to fund three specialist teachers for art, music and sport. This means, in addition to the standard PE hour with class teachers, all pupils have a weekly session with a professional sports coach. There are also dance lessons with a West End choreographer, covering fun stuff like Bollywood, musicals and Strictly Come Dancing. Then there's swimming in year 4, cycle training in year 5 and the year 6 pupils do a course of horse riding lessons in Hyde Park. Opportunities to try tennis, golf, cricket and tag-rugby and to compete in teams against other schools.

Art is taken seriously here and is of a high standard. The PTA-funded artist in residence works with each year group on a project relating to subjects they are studying in class, for example year 3 pupils made a giant sarcophagus when they were studying the Egyptians. We saw excellent William Morris designs done by year 5 while studying the Victorians, screen prints of the Tudors by year 4, and some awesome studies of real fish done by gifted and talented pupils. Pupils identified as G&T in art are given additional opportunities to work on projects with visiting artists (such as designing the 3D climbing wall), plus there are regular drama and music workshops run by outside experts.

For working parents there's an (oversubscribed) wrap-around care scheme running up to 6pm and a two week summer holiday camp. All staff members (including the headteacher) are responsible for an extracurricular club running from 3.30-4.30pm. Pupils can choose from horticulture, ICT, arts and crafts, media, football, website, cooking, construction, choir and many other options. More innovatively, there's a coding club, and coding is also taught as part of the curriculum in years 3 and 4. 'Coding is a big buzz in education at the moment and we're right at the forefront of that,' says Ms Woodford.

What sets St Saviour's apart is the head's boundless enthusiasm and creativity. 'What we do here is we don't say no. We consider all ideas and are willing to try new things'. STEAMco was a concept some parents had seen at a festival. It's now an annual day when lessons are suspended and every corner of the school is given over to different creative activities such 3D printing, learning the ukulele, an apothecary's garden, dance, sculpture, making furniture out of newspaper, launching home-made rockets, cooking and much more. Pupils are free to browse at will – some try everything, others stick with one experience all day. Year 6 pupils built an electric goblin eco-car designed to spark an interest in engineering, which they subsequently raced at Goodwood. Then there's Maths Week. Every class pitches a business idea to Ms Woodford and she decides whether to 'lend' them £20. The class must turn a profit and pay her back, plus one per cent interest, by the end of the week. Business pitches mostly involve making and selling various sweets and cakes but pupils have fun and grasp the idea of profit, loss and interest.

Coding is taught as part of the curriculum in years 3 and 4. 'Coding is a big buzz in education at the moment and we're right at the forefront of that,' says Ms Woodford

Pastoral provision is outstanding. Each child selects two staff 'listening partners' that they can talk to about any fears or worries. Some staff members are chosen by 20 children, others just a handful, but even the catering staff and site manager have their listenees. Then there is a Buddy System in which each year 6 pupil is paired up with a reception 'buddy'. The buddies read and play together, go on trips and can be invited to tea by the respective parents. There is a daytime 'sleepover' where pupils bring a pillow, toy and sleeping bag and lie in the art room reading stories to each other.

Few behavioural problems. A general policy of positive behavioural reinforcement, high expectations and aspiration seems to work well. Much ado is made of the Star of The Week system, with postcards sent home, a mention in the newsletter and announcements at school. Four houses (named after planets) and team points awarded for a variety of endeavours. 'The school is strict and that's what I love about it. They will not tolerate any bullying and they don't like cliques either. Pupils are encouraged to be friends with everyone, so nobody is left out,' said a satisfied parent.

St Vincent de Paul RC Primary School

Morpeth Terrace, London SW1P 1EP

020 7641 5990 | office@svpschool.co.uk | svpcatholicprimary.org.

State	Pupils: 250
Ages: 3–11	

Head: Since 2015, Nathaniel Scott-Cree BA (early 40s). Teaching degree from Roehampton Institute of Higher Education, followed by a masters in Catholic school leadership from St Mary's Twickenham. Originally from the Surrey/Sussex borders, his first job was at St Osmund's School in Barnes, followed by a complete contrast in locality – Brixton – where he taught for six years at Corpus Christi School. He says: 'It was a very well run school. Parents moved to put children in there.' He left to become deputy head at St Vincent's Primary School in Marylebone, where he stayed for the next six years before being offered this headship. He has always taught in Catholic schools, which he says is his 'personal preference', and is 'very committed to them.'

Mr Scott-Cree is young in terms of head teachers: 'not the youngest,' he says, but he clearly has a wise head on his youthful shoulders plus bucketloads of dry wit. His straightforward, honest and no spin approach instantly endears him to us. It was his dad who initially suggested teaching to him as being a 'good option' and he also felt committed to doing a job which makes a difference: 'I wanted to help improve children's chances in life and I believe that to be through education.'

His commitment to the job is evident in the changes he's brought to the school: the new house system; tighter security (more about those later); changes to the syllabus; better communication between the school and parents – and he's even teaching himself Latin in order to teach it to his students. He says: 'When I started here I decided to continue with Latin and run with it. I now teach two lessons a week in Latin for years 4 and 5.' He is liked and respected by both pupils and parents, who tell us 'he's really blended in well with the school.'

Married to a deputy headteacher at another school, Mr Scott-Cree has three children of his own, and although he wouldn't dissuade any of them from a path of education ('if they believe it to be their true vocation etc etc'), he would point out the difficulty of teaching nowadays and all the bureaucracy around it: 'I probably wouldn't cut the mustard if I was entering the profession now,' he says drily. We beg to differ. Any spare time he has

he mostly enjoys 'doing nothing', he says jokingly, but other than that he enjoys reading, listening to music and watching a good film.

Entrance: Always oversubscribed. Nursery children are not guaranteed entry into the main school at 4+. Priority given to practising Roman Catholics, with distance from the school used as a tiebreaker. First priority goes to looked after Catholic children, then baptised, practising siblings, then baptised Catholics. A waiting list is kept for occasional places.

Exit: Most pupils get their first choice secondary school. For most girls it is Greycoats (if it's good enough for the former Prime Minister's daughter..); other popular choices for boys and girls include Sacred Heart, London Oratory, Cardinal Vaughan and St Thomas More as well as independents including Westminster Cathedral Choir School.

Remarks: School was founded in 1859 by the Sisters of Charity of St Vincent de Paul to enable them to work with the poor of Westminster. Moved to current premises in the shadows of Westminster Cathedral, conveniently next door to St Paul's bookshop, in 1974. For a young and impressionable soul eager to soak up all London has to offer, fewer locations could beat this school in the heart of London.

It is hardly surprising that pupils come from a wide variety of countries and backgrounds. Around three-quarters speak English as an additional language. Indeed most of the parents we spoke to, although fluent in English, spoke it as a second language. Many parents choose the school for its diversity, but mainly for its strong Catholic ethos. One parent told us: 'As Roman Catholics ourselves, this school has a great reputation locally for its strong ethos of upholding values, discipline and academia, but also being a loving and caring environment.'

This is a Catholic school foremost and whilst pupils are taught to understand other faiths and cultures (Judaism and Islam weeks etc) there is a strong Christian ethos to adhere to. The head says:

'The behaviour at SVP is outstanding, but it is naive to say that incidents don't happen from time to time. However we do instil in pupils to love one another as I love you.' Chaplain Father Brian leads assembly ever Wednesday, and there is a collective worship every morning. One parent told us: 'I have sat in assembly for one hour and nobody moves. They are so engrossed and well behaved.' Good behaviour, thinking of others and cooperation goes without saying.

He clearly has a wise head on his youthful shoulders plus bucketloads of dry wit. His straightforward, honest and no spin approach instantly endears him to us

Pupils are monitored regularly to assess their progress and there are plenty of parents' evenings, giving everyone the opportunity to discuss their children. Parents comment on how approachable the head is and that you can pop by his office without an appointment. Mr Scott-Cree has also introduced a small letterbox outside his office, where pupils can write down any concerns they may have either anonymously or as something they wish to share (and confessionals with Father Brian are also offered).

When we entered the school at the start of our tour, we were immediately stuck by the double-door entry and security systems put in place. Sadly quite pertinent in light of the recent Westminster attack, which happened a week after our visit and only a few minutes away. The head says: 'At the end of the day, I'm responsible for these pupils if something goes wrong. Where we are located there are a few unsavoury characters around, and whilst I don't want the school to be a prison, I want it to be as safe as possible.' And one parent added: 'Before Mr Scott-Cree was head, you could just walk in, which is incredible really if you think about it. I feel so much happier now that it's more secure and I feel my child is safer.'

Fairly compact site – outdoor space has been redeveloped to create three separate play areas for nursery children, infants and juniors. Cleverly designed, with lots of greenery and modern play equipment. Plus who could tire of seeing the majestic gothic structure of the neighbouring Westminster Cathedral, which almost borders the playground? Pupils also use the playgrounds and local facilities for team sports and have a dedicated sports coach for all PE lessons. Inside, school is light, modern and well designed but has the very nostalgic feel of a primary school from yesteryear.

Peaceful chapel is very much at the heart of this friendly and well-disciplined school.

Large, multi-purpose hall where children practise for termly concerts and plays and musical performances. School is part of the Westminster Cathedral Choir School outreach programme and the choir performs at Westminster Cathedral as well as singing regularly at family masses. Well-stocked music room with an impressive selection of instruments – from glockenspiels to bongo drums. All have singing and music lessons, provided by a dedicated music teacher. Pupils talk excitedly about how they are encouraged to create their own music. Small charge is made for individual lessons on a wide range of instruments. (No formal library, but that is up for discussion: 'it's a space issue.')

Alongside the national curriculum, pupils benefit from being taught Spanish from the age of 7 (a good chunk of Spanish speakers already at the school). Latin is introduced in year 4. Academic results are exceptional. Staff have high expectations and have created a good learning ethos. The SENCo coordinates additional needs and runs a Units of Sound online literacy development programme for dyslexics.

Polite, engaging and kind pupils were what we witnessed during our time at the school (lots of opening doors for us). It struck us how unspoilt many of these children were: 'I went to Wagamama for the first time,' said one excited 9 year old (as part of a food workshop which included a trip to the restaurant). Other trips have included London Zoo, Legoland and various museum outings. Years 5 and 6 do trips to forest schools and Sayers Croft outdoor centre.

Who could tire of seeing the majestic gothic structure of the neighbouring Westminster Cathedral, which almost borders the playground?

Sports quite big on the agenda and the school has fared admirably (given its size and on-site facilities) at football, swimming and athletics, 'and we have even been to the Olympic Copper Box Arena', one proud pupil told us. Sports now all the more competitive since Mr Scott-Cree introduced the new house system named after saints: St Theresa, St Joseph, St Francis and St Bernadette. One parent said: 'The introduction of the house system has added a healthy competitiveness to the school. My daughter is now desperate to earn house points.'

Yearly nativity plays are performed actually in Westminster Cathedral, with full costumes and music. (We'd be hard pushed to imagine anything more spiritual.) There are two other occasions in the year when they join the parish of Westminster Cathedral for mass. We are told that some parents choose this school for this reason. Sixth formers from neighbouring Westminster School work as volunteers, acting as classroom assistants and helping to run school clubs. ICT room doubles up as a cinema for film club.

Not a place for those who wish to sit on their laurels. Energetic PTA meets regularly to discuss the organisation of numerous fundraising events for the school. Each family is asked to make a small annual contribution towards the maintenance and building fund – for the benefit of the present community and to ensure continuation for future generations. Pupils are active fundraisers and

run regular charity events. The school also works with Mission Together, a charity that encourages children to care about mission through prayer, learning and fundraising.

School was downgraded by Ofsted in 2015 to 'requires improvement', but was upgraded again in 2016 to 'good'. The head says, 'The issues that had affected the school have been addressed and lots of support has been put in place to get it back on track.' However, he adds that the report was limited in its judgment to one particular area, which can have a big impact. However, parents praise the school to the rafters and pupils say they look forward to going to school. One parent added that 'SVP starts with the assumption that there's something great about you and let's work on that.'

Sarum Hall School

15 Eton Avenue, London NW3 3EL

020 7794 2261 | admissions@sarumhallschool.co.uk | sarumhallschool.co.uk

| Independent | Pupils: 184 |
| Ages: 3–11 | Fees: £14,025 – £15,180 pa |

Headmistress: Since 2008, Christine Smith BA Cert Ed RSH (SpLD) (50s). Previously at Lochinver Prep in Potter's Bar, where she is now governor. Originally taught home economics and textiles at Edmonton County School, which she left to bring up her two daughters. Subsequently returned to teach deaf children, later becoming director of studies at Lochinver and setting up their learning support unit. When her children left home, she wanted a new challenge and 'fell in love' with Sarum Hall the moment she visited. Believes she's known for being kind, fair, calm, trustworthy, experienced and well connected in the educational world and, on the whole, parents agree, adding that she's 'lovely', 'nice', 'always smiling' and a 'great listener.' 'Whether it's staff, food or sports day, if you have something to suggest, she'll seriously consider it,' said one parent. Mostly office bound, although she does greet the girls, teaches SRE, and dines with them, daily, along with all the usual lesson observations, assemblies etc. Not a captain that socialises with her crew, we feel, although the head points out that she has an open door policy and provides a long list of ways she supports her staff including organising end of term meals out. Married to an actuary, with interests including tai chi, cooking,

theatre and martial arts (she spent time in Beijing learning about swords).

Entrance: Main intake in September after 3rd birthday. Parents are advised to register their child as soon after birth as possible (non-refundable fee of £100), visit the school on a working day two years before said child is due to start and then confirm their continued interest in writing. Non-selective, although priority given to siblings and children and grandchildren of former pupils (of whom there are many). The rest of the 23-24 nursery places are based on the head's decision. 'I meet with all parents and am looking for those who understand that the arts, and indeed play, are as important as academic learning for children's development,' she says, although presumably that's all of them, unless they failed to research the school before applying. It's all a bit vague for our liking; we feel that fitting in probably plays a vital part.

Exit: Almost all to their first choice of school at 11: Channing, City Girls, Francis Holland, Godolphin & Latymer, Highgate, Immanuel, North London Collegiate, South Hampstead, St Helen's and St Paul's. Unusually for a north London prep, a fair number go on to board too, at the likes of Cheltenham, Queenswood and Wycombe Abbey. Recommendations as to the next school very much the head's own, for which she uses her 'first-hand knowledge of the girls, together with the teachers' recommendations, results, tracking data, and my knowledge of the families, which the teachers are not always privy to.'

Remarks: Nestling among the opulent period homes of this leafy north London street is a contemporary, RIBA-lauded, purpose-built building, with no fewer than three secured doors to get inside the learning environment ('Safeguarding means a lot to our girls' parents,' explains the head). Inside the building, which was completed in 1995 (although the school itself dates back to 1928), the combination of high design standards, light oak floors, high ceilings, masses of natural light and (recently) air conditioning makes for a welcoming, airy space in which to work, move about and play. White walls are tastefully decorated with displays of the girls' work from across the curriculum and there's no shortage of colour, ranging from the odd single fuchsia wall here and there to groups of pastel colour chairs. If anything, there's over-use of pink, but this very much sets the mood of the school, which parents repeatedly refer to as turning out 'very well-mannered young ladies.' These are girls that will hold the door for you even if you're still half way down the hall and who, from year 2, leap to their feet when the head enters and chorus 'Good morning, Mrs Smith.'

If anything, there's over-use of pink, but this very much sets the mood of the school, which parents repeatedly refer to as turning out 'very well-mannered young ladies'

Not that there's any compromise on academic learning. The head's unwavering vision of the school focuses on being both academic (with an expectation that girls go onto further education and huge praise from parents about girls being superbly prepared for 11+), as well as having a strong emphasis on the arts.

New national curriculum forms the cornerstone of learning, but without the dreaded Sats and with embellishment of other subjects, including French from reception, Mandarin in years 4 and 5 and Spanish for one term in year 6. Specialist subject teaching in music, IT and French from nursery, science from year 3, English, maths and humanities in years 5 and 6. Some setting in maths. Big emphasis on cross-curricular teaching, with girls preparing for a performance of Frozen when we visited, having made the characters (art), in preparation to perform the play (drama) in French (languages). Great attention to tailored learning, with plenty of classroom assistance and additional work, for instance, for those sitting boarding school entrance exams.

Music, art and drama all thriving. Music facilities include a spacious ground-floor room, with no shortage of instruments, while the rooftop extension provides three practice rooms and the so-called Rainbow room, which is used for rehearsals, workshops, fencing, the well-being programme (relaxation, yoga etc) and a resting place for girls in nursery after lunch. Majority of girls study one or more instruments after year 2, with plenty of opportunity to perform in assemblies, recital evenings and frequent concerts. Junior and senior choirs, open to everyone. 'My daughter does 8 music-related things a week including choir, music theory, music lessons and two instruments,' lauds one parent.

Drama taught in the Rainbow room, school hall and upstairs in the new playhouse, with performances generally including double year groups, and including recent examples of A Midsummer Night's Dream and Olivia the Musical. Also sit the English Speaking Board exams (and LAMDA if requested) to build up communication skills. Fabulous high-ceilinged studio art room, with girls studying sculpture, textiles, woodwork and more. Facilities include a printing press and kiln. New food studio where all pupils will learn to cook healthy meals. Plenty of outings to exhibitions, including the Royal Academy, with which the school has close links.

IT suite has 16 computers organised on round tables, with half the class using it at any one time. Chrome books and iPads also used in the classroom, although not to any great extent. Well-equipped science lab, with a teacher having introduced sustainability in a big way to the school. Sunlit, well-stocked library, with soft beige carpet and big wooden table in the middle, with 12 colourful chairs and plenty of visits from authors, such as Helen Peters and James Mayhew.

Nursery and reception areas nurturing, with a good mix of tables and chairs and dedicated play areas, including an (again pink) indoor wigwam and freeflow outdoor space on the balcony, with two stylish 'SH' embossed canopies to keep the sun off young skin. Plenty of mingling with older girls, thanks to buddying and monitor opportunities, along with a shared play time once every half term.

Outdoor space had been recently refurbished when we visited and although by no means vast, it's exceptionally well-planned and welcoming, with a new two-storey playhouse in the middle of the play area to provide more surface area of play (and welcome shade on hot days). Girls are free to use the lower level during breaks, whilst the upper level is used for drama, small group workshops and exhibitions. Girls particularly love the five colourful beach-huts. 'With the middle three, each of the houses chooses what goes in them,' explained one girl. 'Our one has sporty things, and the other two are for crafts or being creative.' Surrounding this and the adjacent sports court are wormeries, raised beds and an environmental pond, allowing children grow vegetables and herbs and do gardening club, all of which have helped the school achieve Green Flag status. 'In terms of being green, they've achieved a lot, even by Camden standards,' said one parent.

Daily sport (netball, hockey, rounders, soccer, cricket and tennis) takes place on the court or in the assembly hall, which doubles as a gym for both dance and gymnastics, and triples as a theatre. Swimming once more part of the curriculum, at nearby Swiss Cottage Baths one afternoon a week for one term for year 4. Cross-country at Primrose Hill. Annual sports day becoming more competitive and challenging, after parents complained it was too gentle.

Girls particularly love the five colourful beach-huts. 'With the middle three, each of the houses chooses what goes in them,' explained one girl

Pupil voice much improved in recent years, with eco team and school council having made changes to snacks, lunch menus, uniforms and are regularly involved in décor decisions.

Breakfast club from 7.30am, and homework club until 4.30pm, included at no extra cost. Over 40 after-school clubs (photography, chess and draughts, yoga, board games among them), also included in the fees, unless outside staff need to be brought in. Plenty of outings, particularly to London museums and galleries. Residential trips to Norfolk for year 5 and a château in France for year 6. Homework introduced gently in year 2, rising to around an hour a night in year 6.

The girls themselves 'aren't the most savvy and streetwise,' as one parent put it. 'But all the parents I know like it that way,' she added. 'It can make the transition to senior school a bigger deal, but having nice, polite girls is a good trade-off,' said another. Behavioural problems minimal and nipped in the bud, with strict use of policies and procedures. 'Positive rewards for good behaviour and our constant emphasis on Golden Rules help,' adds the head. 'These are different to school rules because they're about how we should behave, rather than what we mustn't do. We are gentle, kind and helpful. We listen and are honest and work hard. We look after property. We don't hurt anybody's feelings' etc. If a girl doesn't work hard, or indeed underperforms for any other reason, her case gets taken to the weekly curriculum meeting and a plan put in place, with full parental involvement.

Great food (all clean plates when we visited and we cleared our own too) prepared daily on site, with vegetarian option and great excitement about puddings such as Arctic roll and sponge and custard. Served in dining room, with pastel spotty tablecloths to brighten up the four rows of long tables with benches, where staff eat with girls after grace has been said.

Christian background, but head quick to point out that they support other faiths. 'We say the Lord's Prayer daily, go to church three times a year and the vicar comes in for some assemblies. But I recently invited a rabbi too.' Big on charitable fundraising, with each house choosing a children's charity each term, then arranging activities to raise money for it.

Parents and pupils reasonably multicultural, but mainly affluent, white, middle-class. Plenty of bankers, lawyers and barristers. Many girls have brothers at The Hall or Arnold House (and head tries to coordinate term dates). Bursary fund, which is means-tested. One girl on it when we visited, with another about to join. Many of the governors have a connection to the school and have been there for many years, with (unusually) no set system of election or removal.

Learning support unit has one dedicated member of staff (trained to RSA level 7) who comes in four days a week. Copes with mild dyslexia, dyspraxia (five children in total when we visited) and the 'gifted and talented' at no extra cost. Support is mainly in the large dedicated room, but some classroom assistance too. Two deaf children when we visited ('The school has been incredible with meeting her additional needs and going the extra mile,' said the parent of one) and one child with a visual impairment had just been offered a place. But whilst school is well laid out for wheelchair access, no child who uses one has ever attended. Won't take children with serious behavioural difficulties, although never had to turn anyone away or asked a child to leave. Outside help brought in for speech and language when required. School nurse recently brought in, who doubles up as school counsellor. 'Both my kids were flagged as needing extra help,' said one parent. 'The school kept me informed, we had meetings and they made innovative suggestions, all of which has meant the children are now on the right path. I can't fault it.'

This is a small, intimate, highly structured and extremely traditional girls' prep in a stunning modern setting that gets children of a broad range of ability to reach their full potential, without too much pressure. 'I've got three girls at the school – one very academic, one shy and musical and the other in between, and they all shine,' said one parent. 'The school has a knack of fostering natural talent,' said another. Its emphasis on the arts and play, alongside academic learning, means it's not for the tiger parent and and its preciousness, emphasis on authority and very high expectations around manners means it's probably not for the non-conformist child either. 'But if you toe the line, this is a lovely, fun school that you see girls skipping into.'

Sir John Cass's Foundation Primary School 👫 (CₒfE) 57

St James's Passage, 27 Duke's Place, London EC3A 5DE

020 7283 1147 | office@sirjohncassprimary.org | sirjohncassprimary.org

State	Pupils: 247
Ages: 3m–11	

Headteacher: Since September 2018, Alex Allan, previously deputy head, head of the school's Children's Centre and SENCo.

Entrance: The only state school in the Square Mile, Sir John Cass is one form entry. Historically, about 100 apply for the 30 places on offer, with priority given to those who worship regularly at St Botolph's, Aldgate. Desk space decided thereafter by a mixture of church attendance and distance from the gates. The school also runs The Cass Child and Family Centre, an attached children's centre with full provision from 3 months.

Exit: To a wide range of secondary schools, north, south, east and west, notably to City of London's sponsored academies (where City-dwellers gain some preference), selective state schools, and leading faith schools across London. One or two annually to the independent sector. (Has recently started working with City of London School for Girls to help prepare pupils for 11+ testing, and supports children to apply for scholarship and bursary entry at City and other fee-paying schools).

Remarks: Sir John Cass traces its roots back to the school established by the alderman of that name in the churchyard of St Botolph's by Aldgate in 1710. The current gracious grade II* listed building – described by Pevsner as 'neo-Baroque-neo-Hampton Court' – dates from 1908. It formerly housed a secondary school, with all the benefits that implies, including broad corridors, large classrooms and a generous assembly hall. Its listing also relates to its 'boardroom', a glorious panelled reconstruction of a merchant's home dating from 1669, with a plaster ceiling and 17th century hand-painted panels, where lucky members of the student council enjoy regular meetings. 'It's quite a big building,' said a parent, 'but it still has a very intimate, personal quality. It really feels like a family, not corporate in any way.' As well as recent and on-going refurbishment, there are plans for a £5m extension and modernisation, and local building works will ultimately give the school access to a leafy square.

Outstanding choir, under legendary choirmaster, has also made plenty of public appearances

Academically, Sir John Cass has long been recognized as one of the country's best primary schools. Despite the fact that many of its pupils come in with well below average attainment, virtually every child here reaches the expected government benchmark and an exceptionally high proportion soar well beyond it. Success for all is guaranteed through excellent, experienced teaching and, often, by high levels of staffing, which enables children to be taught in small groups when small groups are most needed. (Two teachers, for example, work with reception and year 6.) 'The teachers are incredible,' said one parent. 'They give lots of extra support for whatever kids require.'

Huge emphasis is put on reading from the outset. ('We're less about children catching up than getting it right from the start.') Each classroom has a designated quiet space for private study, and pupils get plenty of extra support, both from City volunteers, who come in to hear children read, and parents, who are encouraged to make nightly reading as customary as tooth brushing. Good, well-stocked library, with full-time library coordinator, and year 6s are furnished with take-home Kindles to embed the literary habit. Regular – but not crippling – amounts of homework. Years 4,5 and 6 use laptops in class, but this is not a place which believes that technology is always the answer. 'Four year olds need to interact with each other and the natural environment'; no whiteboards in the nursery classroom.

A fully qualified native speaker teaches French. (The class we visited seemed encouragingly well beyond bonjour and merci.) Art, too, now has a refurbished studio and expert teaching three days a week, with several nascent Picassos reaching the finals of a recent Diocese of London art competition.

Music a celebrated strength, with a long-established Strings Programme giving all children in years 4-6 a weekly music class and a smaller group session to concentrate on technique. Performance developed further at Christmas and summer concerts, and star performers (who often achieve grades 4/5) invited to study at specialist music colleges and play at the Guildhall. Outstanding choir, under legendary choirmaster, has also made plenty of public appearances (including on the Queen's Christmas speech). African drumming and dancing recently introduced in year 2. Performing arts group meets twice weekly to study drumming, dance, drama and vocal techniques, all taught by specialists. 'Performance makes pupils more confident and articulate,' says school.

Pupils get plenty of extra support, both from City volunteers and from parents, who are encouraged to make nightly reading as customary as tooth brushing

Sport goes well beyond the statutory minimum, with a recently recruited sports coach developing skills in rugby, hockey and multi-sport in the expansive school gym as well as swimming at several local pools. Unsurprisingly, Sir John Cass generally represents the City of London in interborough competitions for tag rugby, cross-country and swimming.

A significant proportion of children here receive the pupil premium and/or come from families whose native language is not English, and additional needs are taken seriously. The attached

---

Project with Leiths cookery school ensures everyone leaves with a repertoire of 12 dishes in their personal recipe book

nursery is very much seen as the foothills of primary, with children encouraged to get muddy and explore materials. Special needs lead is aided by number of teaching assistants specialising in English as an additional language. A Tavistock-trained counsellor also attends weekly.

Lavish menu of trips, both in London (Buckingham Palace, Natural History Museum, Regent's Park) and beyond, which 'help pin down history and geography'. Out-of-London jaunts include a week-long stay at the Hampshire and Cass Centre in the beautiful Brecon Beacons, and a country-town mouse exchange to Caunton Dean Hole in Nottinghamshire, where urbanites can get up close to cows, fresh air and pond dipping. Lunch-hour and after-school clubs include chess and Lego, football and art, as well as inexpensive breakfast and after-school care.

Behaviour throughout is exemplary, with classrooms quiet, orderly and attentive (misdemeanours generally confined to coats not hung up properly on pegs). 'All the children get along. There are no dominant groups, no cliques.' One tiny child came up and gave the head a big hug, another waved as we entered the classroom.

As a voluntary aided Christian foundation, the school has a strong, traditional Christian focus, with a bible corner in each classroom, Christian assemblies and regular church attendance. Whatever their views, parents welcome the faith structure. 'My family are not religious, but I really value the fact that my kids learn about religion with children of all backgrounds,' said one mother.

School lunch eaten by virtually all with appetising food cooked daily on site and crudités laid out (and consumed) on all tables. City Gardeners work with pupils on a well-tended roof garden, so children can eat what they have grown, and a project with Leiths cookery school ensures everyone leaves with a repertoire of 12 dishes in their personal recipe book.

About 30 per cent of families are City residents, the rest are from adjoining boroughs. Though number on free school meals has diminished as more professional families move into the City, the school remains unusually diverse. The school has worked hard on developing the PTA, bringing everyone together. 'The school really represents London,' said one mother. 'It's very open-minded, very inclusive. For me, it's like a dream.'

South Hampstead High Junior School

5 Netherhall Gardens, London NW3 5RN

020 7794 7198 | junior@shhs.gdst.net | shhs.gdst.net/junior-school

Independent	Pupils: 265
Ages: 4–11	Fees: £15,327 pa

Linked school: South Hampstead High School, 221

Headmistress of junior school: Since 2013, Gabrielle Solti BA PGCE (40s), previously head of Notting Hill and Ealing Junior School for 10 years. A local: she attended SHHS junior school herself, taught at Trevor-Roberts and was deputy head of Primrose Hill Primary before taking the Notting Hill and Ealing job. Born into a musical family (her late father, Sir Georg Solti, was once described by the Telegraph as 'the most distinguished conductor alive'), she studied history at Oxford, interned at the European Commission (where she met her husband), then worked at Nestlés in France and the UK before taking a teacher training course at the Institute of Education. Says she is 'passionate about pedagogy – that's what we're here for. We're evolving how we tailor education for girls and get them involved in learning.' A hit with parents, who see their daughters blossoming under her liberal regime. Two children, one at SHHS.

Entrance: Application forms available to download during a two week period in the September two years before entry into reception; school assesses all those who apply within this period. Some 250 apply for the 24 reception places and around 130 apply for 24 more places in year 3 (applications close in the November of the year before entry).

Reception assessment is play-based, in the November prior to entry, in similar age groups of 12-13 girls with four or five staff observing and interacting. Mrs Solti sees all applicants herself. 'We're looking for signs that they will benefit from the academic education we have to offer – for their ability to notice, examine, explain.' A hundred of the 250 return in January in smaller groups when the school 'looks for a range of personality types' and aims at a balanced year group. No barrier against those with summer birthdays – 'we expect a little less of them'.

Year 3 applicants are tested in maths, English and non-verbal reasoning, with high performers invited back for interview and small group activities. At this point 'we are looking at what they can

do', but hoping to see past tutoring to potential, and 'the small group assessments are the most useful in making final judgements.'

Inevitably the assessments are not an exact science, and though nearly all of those accepted do, indeed, thrive, the school is aware that there are plenty more suitable candidates than they have room for in both age groups.

Exit: Virtually all to the senior school, round the corner. Diminishing numbers don't make the move up. 'My job is to assess them properly and help them achieve what they need,' says the head. 'If a child works hard we can usually get them to the right standard.' Occasional leavers to eg Henrietta Barnett.

Remarks: Happily, staff do not have to cram their charges through the 11+ and thus can oversee an education outside of the box. The head introduced the concept of the Growth Mindset ('I can do it...' proclaim posters in each classroom), to encourage girls to take risks, challenge themselves and learn from mistakes. 'Self-assessment – what did I do well and what do I need to improve? – can counteract girls' tendency to be "people pleasers".'

Our extremely self-assured and chatty guides were keen to tell us about Open Homework. 'You're given a word and you can do anything with it, from art to baking'

She is at one with the senior school head in believing that resilience is one of the most important qualities schools can inculcate in girls. Pupils are encouraged to speak up – they have 'talk partners' with whom to share ideas in class, they perform in assembly from the youngest years, talk about their work, debate, recite poetry, perform in plays. By year 6 even the most naturally reticent are confident enough to show parents around the school.

Our extremely self-assured and chatty guides showed us how topic work encompasses a range of subjects. Reception children were painting pictures of jungles to decorate their role play area. We saw pictures of the year 2 (Raging Rivers) trip to the River and Rowing Museum; we viewed year 5's Chinese pottery vases, dropped in on their Mandarin class and heard about their impromptu trip to Liverpool to see the Terracotta Army exhibition – 'you have to grab these opportunities,' says the head. Year 4s sculpt Viking chessmen and have a residential trip to York ('really, really fun'). Year 6s were enthused by their visit to France (which took in a chocolate factory and a goat farm).

Our guides were keen to tell us about Open Homework. 'You're given a word and you can do anything with it, from art to baking'….'I made a board game'….'I made 100 paper aeroplanes'…'I painted a picture.' We liked the display board showing a reasoned discussion on whether girls would prefer to live in London or in a village in Africa.

Sport rapidly improving. They now play football alongside netball and are jettisoning rounders for cricket. Even the youngest ran a mile for Sports Relief recently

Parents approve of the SHHS emphasis on inspirational and powerful women, which begins in the junior school. Year 5s learn about the Suffragettes (a then staff member spent time in Holloway prison), about Rebel Girls and significant Women Through Time. 'It makes the curriculum meaningful to them.'

No setting or grades in the junior school. 'We focus on what they did well and how they can improve.' A few have dyslexia, dyspraxia or are on the autism spectrum, but 'all are academically able. They may need support at different stages and in different ways, and we want to get in quickly with help. We have a wonderful SENCo.'

Sport rapidly improving, and girls use the senior school sports hall and playing fields as well as their own games area. They now play football alongside netball – hurray – and are jettisoning rounders for cricket. Year 5 were off to Sydenham High when we visited to be coached by an England cricketer. Even the youngest ran a mile for Sports Relief recently. Cross-country, yoga, fencing and dance all popular. Year 5s and 6s compete against

other schools, with A-D teams, and PE clubs are open to all. 'We want them to love sport and enjoy being physical.'

Plenty of inter-GDST school competitions. Displayed in the entrance hall we saw awards for cross-country and quiz competitions, and for young choir of the year. The relatively recent house system – with houses named after Bronte, Curie, Parks and Pavlova – provides more gentle opportunities to compete.

There's a good musical grounding with all year 1s learning the violin or cello and all year 2s playing the recorder, and orchestras, ensembles and choirs for those who would like to progress further. Drama performances start early and year 4s were away at the senior school rehearsing for their production of Pirates of the Currybean when we visited. We heard about workshops on architecture and dance, robots and forensic science.

A big party celebrated the 60th anniversary of the junior school's move from Waterlow House on the senior school site to its own red-brick building round the corner in Netherhall Gardens in 1957. Pupils also dressed up in 50s clothes and listened to guests talk about their junior school days in that era – 'we heard about the great smog and how hard it was to get to school'.

This building now houses reception to year 4, plus the science lab (home to skeletons Bob and Bob Junior, where 'we do lots of experiments, so we can see what happens, not just hear about it') plus the art room full of clay sculptures. There's a bright and comfortable library where classes spend half an hour a week ('Really nice. You get to sit and read!') and there are 'star reads' suggested for each year group by previous years. A second building across the road, purchased in 1993 to cope with increasing numbers, houses classrooms for years 5 and 6 plus the music room, another library and the DT room.

Outside space is limited at both sites but reception has its own outdoor classroom with Wendy house, and a row of scooters indicated how many local girls get to school. They also manage to fit in a mini sports pitch and playgrounds with climbing frames. 'At the co-ed school where I used to teach the playground was full of boys kicking a football in the middle whilst girls played little games round the edges,' says the head. 'Here at least half of our girls can be seen running up and noisily at play time. There's space to run, jump, climb and throw balls.'

A creative and liberal start to education where girls are encouraged to speak out and challenge themselves inside and outside the classroom.

South Hampstead High School

3 Maresfield Gardens, London NW3 5SS

020 7435 2899 | admissions@shhs.gdst.net | shhs.gdst.net

Independent	Pupils: 673; sixth form: 163
Ages: 11–18	Fees: £18,654 pa

Linked school: South Hampstead High Junior School,219

Headmistress: Since January 2017, Vicky Bingham (40), previously deputy head at Guildford High. Educated at the European School in Brussels – her father worked for the EU; classics MA from Oxford; PGCE in classics from Cambridge. Started her career teaching classics at Guildford High; off to St Catherine's Bramley as head of classics, before returning to Guildford as deputy head in 2010. 'I didn't always want to teach, but during my final year at Oxford I realised that by the time I retired I wanted to have filled my head with something worthwhile and I felt that teaching classics is important to humanity.' She 'fell into' working at girls' schools and has found them 'unpretentious, unstuffy, moving with the times.'

With an international upbringing, she feels at home amidst the cosmopolitan buzz of SHHS. 'In many families at least one parent comes from overseas.'

We found her energetic, enthusiastic, full of ideas. Sees developing resilience as a vital part of girls' education, via a well-rounded, holistic curriculum. 'The more activities there are outside the classroom, the more chances they have to shine in something.' Very keen on debating and public speaking: 'I won an international public speaking event that gave me confidence and I want the girls to have that chance.' Also passionate about improving school's sporting offering, of which more later.

A big thumbs up from parents and pupils, who have experienced a rapid turnover of heads over the past few years, and fervently hope she is here for the long term. 'She's very focussed on the girls,' said a father. 'I'm a big fan,' said another. 'The girls respect her, she's on their wavelength, she's a big hit at the school.'

A keen walker (with her dog, Max), she took up running at 34 and was first lady in her first race. 'Sport wasn't valued at my own school and I felt it was a waste of my 20s that I hadn't realised I was good at this.' She has gone public with her views on the British values curriculum ('somewhat jingoistic') and tutoring ('it robs children of the critical ability to surmount problems themselves'). The day we visited she hit headlines for her criticism of women who insist on micro-managing the domestic sphere as well as holding down demanding jobs. 'What kind of blueprint are some of us providing for our daughters by infantilising men?'

Her daughter is at the junior school here.

Academic matters: Results at GCSE hard to beat; in 2018, 89 per cent at A*-A/9-7. A levels 67 per cent A*/A, 88 per cent A*-B in 2018. Good showing in languages – everyone studies one MFL in year 7 plus Latin (a choice of French, Spanish, German and Mandarin) and two in year 8, taking at least one to GCSE – and a fair few continue to A level. Maths taken by about two-thirds of sixth formers with impressive results; psychology, history and economics all popular; generally good numbers taking science A level, though physics less popular (the department, we were told, has 'now stabilised').

New 'This is Me' project encourages girls to talk proudly about themselves and their achievements

Everyone studies four subjects in year 12, many dropping to three in year 13: some parents voiced a feeling that taking three subjects throughout would lead to less stress and more time for enrichment. The first term in year 12 sees a Friday afternoon Great Ideas course which is a springboard to an EPQ (increasing take up with strong results), and students are encouraged to enter for national essay writing competitions, Olympiads, engineering scholarships etc with some great successes. The Futures Programme, preparing for life beyond school, taps into the GDST Alumnae Network of over 75,000 members. Journalists, vets, psychiatrists, charity executives come back to talk about their work. In the younger years, the new

Westminster Under School

'This is Me' project encourages girls to talk proudly about themselves and their achievements in an interview-style situation.

'I want us to do more than chase exam results and prizes,' says head, who believes that they get results 'without an insane amount of pressure.' 'I thought it might be hothousy and too pushy, but it really hasn't been,' said a parent. General agreement that any hothouse atmosphere is created by ambitious families rather than by the school.

Universal praise for staff. 'They're well supported by very able teachers.' 'When my daughter struggled with maths, the teacher went to endless trouble to help her understand it. And they're all like that.'

The SEN department here is not rushed off its feet, but there's always a proportion of pupils with specific needs such as dyslexia or dyspraxia, some of which don't come to light until the sixth form. 'Because they're so bright they tend to be able to work with strategies we give them.' Support given unstintingly: one-to-one when needed, but most within lessons. 'A good lesson for a dyslexic child is a good lesson for everyone.' Laptops provided to all those that need them.

Games, options, the arts: Historically, South Hampstead 'has never been a sporty school,' say students, and indeed many parents we talked to cited sport as the weakest link. However, head – who 'sees sport as a cornerstone of pastoral life', said a colleague – is overseeing a transformation. 'Playing as part of a team gives you a sense of pride,' she says, and there are now A-E netball teams in year 7, with increased competition feeding gradually up the school. Lots more competitive matches against other schools and over 20 sports now available thanks to recently expanded PE dept from athletics and badminton to yoga and zumba. Two netball teams recently reached the Middlesex finals, football is increasingly popular, with external coaching, and they have dropped rounders in favour of cricket as a key summer sport with coaching from ex-England players. Years 7-9 now get a full afternoon a week at the four acre sports ground, a 10 minute walk away, as well as PE lessons in the new sports hall deep in the bowels of the reconstructed school building. Sixth formers talked enthusiastically of the 'very competitive' staff v students netball match.

Music a strong point with numerous opportunities at all levels ('My daughter is a fairly average player but has plenty of chances to perform'), ambitious concerts and recitals large and small. And amongst the lunchtime and teatime recitals, choral and orchestral concerts, a ukulele ensemble, the Big Band and jazz groups provide a jaunty air, with the summer Jazz Night a showcase for saxophonists and their ilk.

Art as popular as at most highly academic schools where many parents push their daughters towards more 'academic' subjects. Small but perfectly formed A level groups produce some impressive work in 'relaxing and enjoyable' top floor sixth form art and sculpture rooms. Visits to local galleries and far-flung exhibitions: Vienna, Kyoto, New York. DT product design available to A level but take-up tends to be bijou at this level.

Recent production of Made in Dagenham – based on the 1968 sewing machinists' strike for equal pay at the Ford factory in Dagenham – 'very impressive' and there are plenty of musicals and classical plays, recently Euripides' Trojan Women. However, drama's not generally amongst the high flying subjects at GCSE, few take theatre studies at A level and we heard about some thespians moving to sixth forms elsewhere for this reason. Plenty of opportunities to speak up, though, with debating increasingly popular and compulsory public speaking competitions from years 7-10.

Music a strong point with numerous opportunities at all levels ('My daughter is a fairly average player but has had plenty of chances to perform'), ambitious concerts and recitals, large and small

Huge range of speakers drop in, from Dame Stella Rimmington, Olympic hockey players and Angela Saini (Inferior: How Science got Women Wrong) to Michael Gove (who apparently provoked intense questioning on Brexit). Those invited by year 13s have included Laura Bates (founder of the Everyday Sexism Project).

Clubs for cheerleaders and comedians, Shakespeare and Dr Who devotees, fashionistas and philosophers. FemSoc discusses problems with the patriarchy; Womanities Soc examines the less-than-well-behaved women who have shaped history, created art or literature; the popular LGBTQ+ discussion group is now known as PRIDE. D of E hugely popular: 'nearly all my daughter's group seem to be doing it'.

Background and atmosphere: Opened in 1876 as St John's Wood High School at Swiss Cottage with 27 pupils, changing its name to South Hampstead High in 1887 and moving to a purpose built site in Maresfield Gardens with 300 pupils. And there it stayed, in the same red-brick building with the odd acquisition or two: Waterlow House, bought in 1921, originally home to the junior school, and rebuilt in 1988; and Oakwood, bought in 1991 as the new sixth form centre.

In 2014, after a major £35m reconstruction, the 600 pupils moved back from temporary premises on the Lymington Road sports ground to the multi-storey glass and red-brick home, full of light and air, that rises from an underground sports hall to a rooftop garden, with panoramic views of north London from its upper floors.

The walls are alive with murals and artwork, including the abstract Hampstead Mural panels by the late Gillian Ayres, commissioned in 1957 for the school's then dining room, now joined by five new paintings donated by the artist to celebrate the new building, and which form the school's modern art collection.

Waterlow Hall, lined with honours boards, is the site for assemblies and performances. Currently it is underwhelming from an acoustic point of view and fundraising is underway to transform it into a worthy setting for concerts, plays and speakers.

Oakwood House, the sixth form's own, is more reminiscent of wood panelled grammar school of yore. Sixth formers love the rooftop garden and ground floor grassy area with picnic tables and Mira Cinnamon statue. They have an agreeably informal common room with slouchy sofas and table football and, with staffs' rooms nearby, the head of sixth form is 'very available'.

The previous head, perhaps with the aim of giving the school a more pronounced individual identity, commissioned a variety of blue and yellow penguins with water bottles on their backs, carrying the message of water conservation, which dot the school. The girls, somewhat bemused, have taken the name Penguin for their own magazine, 'the voice of satire and quirkiness'. The current head is 'keen to tap into new traditions' and has turned end of year assemblies into a celebration of the life of the school. 'I cry every time we sing the school song,' said a sixth former unapologetically.

A tradition of celebrating girls' education and empowerment, with a suffrage week of events to mark the centenary of women gaining the vote. 'You learn early on about the value of women,' said a sixth former. 'Virtually all the girls here would say they're a feminist.' 'A good place for a girl to learn – not too precious,' added a parent.

Pastoral care, well-being and discipline: The usual pastoral scaffolding, including one-to-one chats with a tutor on a regular basis, also features a life coach and a counsellor. The counsellor, a child psychotherapist, 'makes herself approachable by coming into assemblies,' and even girls without specific problems go along for a chat and a biscuit, said a parent. 'She's brilliant. They've nailed it.' The life coach is there to help on a practical level – 'perhaps with specific things a girl would like to change

'We do have the usual teenage issues, but the girls are very supportive of each other – they will tell us if they feel someone needs help'

about her behaviour. Some have recurring themes and we encourage them to think about what would work better.' 'My daughter finds her very useful,' said a parent. 'If you are struggling academically, she reorganises your life,' said a sixth former (which sounds fabulous; can we all have one?). 'There will always be a teacher you can speak to,' she added, mentioning how much care she had seen a teacher take with a pupil who became upset in her class.

As a highly selective all girls' school, South Hampstead might seem a likely candidate for widespread anorexia and the like, but no-one we spoke to – parents, girls or staff – felt it was a pressing issue. 'They keep a good watch on the girls,' said a parent. A deputy head confirmed: 'We keep a close eye if we think anything is emerging that suggests an eating disorder. We do have the usual gamut of teenage issues, but the girls are very supportive of each other – they will come and tell us if they feel someone needs help.' Staff are well aware of the dangers of modern communication modes. 'We're constantly talking about screen time, the pitfalls of Instagram reality, of trying to have a thick skin in relation to social media.'

'My daughter struggled socially when she first joined,' said a parent, 'and they were really onto it, very supportive.' Girls agree: 'There's a very warm atmosphere here. Very nurturing.'

This is liberal Hampstead, where being right on and tolerant is more or less a given. So how would the school cope with transgender issues? 'Fundamentally, we are proud to be a girls' school,' says the head. 'But if one of our pupils transitioned we would make kind, considerate, sensitive adjustments to make it possible for them to stay. We're ready for it. Our uniform includes trousers and could easily be unisex.'

Pupils and parents: Characterised by members of the north London liberal intelligentsia, with a good ethnic mix. The bulk of the intake from Camden and the surrounding boroughs, including many international families, with increasing applicants from further west. South Hampstead girls are 'diligent but flexible and creative about their thinking,' says head. They are 'great social campaigners – they like things with edge.' Parents are 'really supportive, like to have an open dialogue, like to give advice; they like us to be honest and transparent'.

Entrance: Nearly all junior school girls (around 46) move up to the senior school without taking the entrance exam. They are joined by some 55 girls from approaching 600 applicants from outside, about 20 per cent from state primary schools.

The 11+ assessment for entry from 2019 onwards will consist a 75 minute cognitive ability test (rather than maths and English exams) with great emphasis on the interview. The intention is to make the tests as tutor-proof as possible and to cut down on the prep school culture of 'endless practice papers'. An aim of the interview will be to find 'children who can think for themselves when they encounter academic obstacles'. 'No silver bullet but we are doing something address the problems' of the advantages given to the tutored and prepped under the current system. Forty per cent increase in applicants recently.

At 16+ by exams in three A level subjects plus general paper, interview and predicted GCSE grades.

Exit: Between 15-20 per cent leave after GCSEs. A few to state sixth forms such as Camden School for Girls and Marylebone, and a few more to join their brothers at UCS up the road or to Westminster, one or two off to board. Sixth form leavers off to study eg classics at Durham, economics and management at Edinburgh, French and Spanish at Leeds, yacht and powercraft design at Southampton Solent. A good handful now to US universities (four in 2018) and to Oxbridge (six in 2018). Several medics (three in 2018). Notable old girls include Helena Bonham-Carter (who opened the new school building), Lynne Featherstone MP, Suzy Klein, Angela Lansbury, Joanna McGregor, Rabbi Julia Neuberger, the late Lynsey de Paul, Fay Weldon, Olivia Williams, Naomi Alderman.

Money matters: Academic and music scholarships of up to 50 per cent of fees, plus means-tested bursaries of up to 100 per cent, available at 11+ and 16+.

Remarks: A busy, buzzy school regaining its pre-eminence in north west London under an energetic head who is determined to empower her pupils. Said a satisfied parent: 'They really do care about the girls and giving them a broad education.'

Sylvia Young Theatre School

1 Nutford Place, London W1H 5YZ

020 7258 2330 | info@sylviayoungtheatreschool.co.uk | syts.co.uk

Independent	Pupils: 240 (25 boarders with host families)
Ages: 10–16	Fees: £14,160 – £14,460 pa

Principal: Since 1981, Sylvia Young OBE (70s), founding principal and true trailblazer. An East End girl, she trained part-time as an actress at Mountview but realised that a performing career wasn't for her. Married, and working as a part-time librarian, when her daughters' primary school asked her to teach some holiday drama classes, and a star was born. In 1972 she started an evening school, enlisting friends from Mountview to help with the teaching and charging pupils 10p a class to cover the hire of the church hall. She started the full-time school in 1981, because all the part-time students kept asking for one.

Decades later, the school is one of the most highly-regarded names in arts education for under-18s, testament to its founder's revolutionary drive (rumour has it she can trace her ancestry back to Leon Trotsky), vision and simple humanity. 'I find it difficult to accept how well known the school's become,' she confided. Parents are more forthright in their praise. 'Sylvia is incredibly inspirational for the children, she is amazing with them,' wrote one. 'We have found Sylvia to be exceptionally supportive. Her culture runs right through the school and we have found it to be a strong and positive one,' said another. Given an OBE in 2005 for her services to the arts.

She and husband Norman still live in their flat on the top floor of the school building. Their two daughters, Alison, a theatrical agent who now works alongside her mother at the school, and Tony award-winning actress Frances Ruffelle, are both grown up and mothers themselves – pop singer Eliza Doolittle is one of the grandchildren.

Since 2005 MS Frances Chave BSc PGCE (50s) has been the academic and pastoral head. Ms Chave read maths at Exeter University, did her teacher training at Southampton, then taught at two large comprehensives (Cranford Community College and Feltham Community College), before helping to set up a third, Overton Grange School in Sutton, where she was deputy head. Came to SYTS because she wanted a change and the school wanted her hand on the academic tiller. Both provision and results have risen under her care, and she loves it here: 'It's a fabulous place!' she told us. 'Being in a school where every single student wants to be there is very special.' Valued by parents and students alike – 'Very welcoming and approachable; she encourages the parents to contact her … always around the school and not locked away in her office,' was a typical comment. Not a performer herself, but loves theatre. Likes walking and cycling in her spare time.

Academic matters: At GCSE in 2018, a creditable 39 per cent of grades at A*-A/9-7. Not stellar, but very respectable given the school's totally non-academically selective intake. One parent expressed disquiet about the academic provision, claiming it was uneven, but the overwhelming majority were extremely positive. 'The standard of the education and the teachers' dedication to the children is second to none.' 'We have been impressed with the academic provision. The teachers mostly seem dedicated and fair.' 'Our experience has been that the academics are strong – they have an excellent set of teachers on the whole and they care, teach well and motivate the children.'

The buzz in all these classes is palpable, and the students achieve great things, coached by top-notch industry professionals for whom they clearly have the utmost respect

SYTS still adheres to the weekly curriculum model it first adopted out of necessity: three days of academic education followed by two days' vocational training. Housed in wonderfully spacious surroundings since 2010, there's no longer a need to push the desks back on Wednesday night and convert classrooms into studios, but, says Ms Chave, 'it really works. From Monday to Wednesday there's a complete focus on academics – it's quite a different atmosphere from the vocational days, and they're not always running off to get changed.' Students love it: 'It's good that they have the academics first, because then you're really ready to get going on the vocational side.' 'It's a really effective use of time, and you don't have to carry around so much.' 'The vocational days are the carrot they hold out to us, and it makes you work really hard on Monday, Tuesday and Wednesday.' A parent commented, 'An

initial concern was that the three day/two day split could mean that the academic side could suffer, but this does not seem to be the case.'

Parents also praised the school's insistence that professional work shouldn't compromise the children's academic attainment. Every week the staff post online what needs to be completed and see that it's done, and when a child is absent longer-term eg on tour, SYTS staff liaise with the child's appointed tutors. One mother commented, 'My son has worked consistently over the past two years and has always had help keeping up with his academics, as the school takes this very seriously.' Another wrote proudly, 'My daughter is a working child and the school fully supports working children, but they do expect them to maintain their grades and work very hard.'

Pushed into three days, the curriculum is necessarily compact. For key stage 3 the core subjects English, maths and science are taught alongside the humanities, art, ICT and Spanish (the only language offered here). Music study is taught as part of the vocational curriculum. At key stage 4, students take eight or nine GCSEs: everyone does drama, English lang & lit, maths and double or triple science, plus two options from music, art, media studies, history and Spanish. As one student remarked, 'There are subjects we can't do. But the ones we do are really well taught.' The lessons we observed were professional and lively, delivered by cheerful, upbeat teachers with excellent communication skills. Students are vocal, attentive, diligent, very keen to get things right.

SENCo is in school on the academic days, aided by a SEN support teacher. The main needs here are mild to moderate dyslexia and some dyscalculia, and children are helped in class or with weekly individual sessions.

Games, options, the arts: Performing arts are, of course, the school's raison d'etre. Thursdays and Fridays are devoted to vocational training in acting, singing and dancing and everyone has to do all three. This was a huge plus for the young folks we spoke to: a boy who had previously attended another performing arts school switched to SYTS because 'at my last school you had to choose a pathway, either dance or drama, whereas I wanted to specialise in everything!' Lots of nodding at this.

Students are taught ballet, jazz, contemporary and tap; speech, characterisation, improvisation, stagecraft and audition technique; singing, aural awareness and technological awareness. The buzz in all these classes is palpable, and the students achieve great things, coached by top-notch industry professionals for whom they clearly have the utmost respect. 'The vocational training is amazing, second to none!' was a very typical comment. We saw the head of music – brusque, scary and

Sylvia Young began her famous agency in the spare room of her house in 1972 armed with a scrapbook of school portrait photos

taking no prisoners – coax an amazing performance of The Impossible Dream out of the year 10s. 'That should give me a tingle, I haven't had a tingle yet!' he admonished towards the end of verse 3, but we certainly got that tingle ourselves. 'Oh, he brings it out of you, I don't know how!' exclaimed a young alumnus who was also watching. 'He's so professional! I didn't have confidence in singing when I came here, and now I'm a singer. This school sets you up for a career in this industry.' Parents have regular opportunities to watch their child perform, and every December the children sing at the Actors' Church in Covent Garden. LAMDA exams taken by virtually everyone, and very high standards achieved. The Lab, an experimental drama club, meets after school and prepares plays for workshop performance.

Sylvia Young began her famous agency in the spare room of her house in 1972 armed with a scrap book of primary school portrait photos, with the aim of creating some extra performance opportunities for her young charges. A young advertising chap called Saatchi liked her style, and it went on from there. Today the agency is located on the ground floor of the school and manned by up to seven staff. All full time SYTS pupils are automatically members. At any point in the day children might be told they have an audition, whereat the school will chaperone them there and back. If successful, the agency deals with all the paperwork and licences. Some of the children become very successful indeed, playing principal roles in West End shows and on tour – one of our tour guides had just extended his contract as young Harry in Harry Potter and The Cursed Child – and you might expect there to be an overly competitive atmosphere as a result, but there really doesn't seem to be. 'It's friendly competition!' insisted the students. 'When we come here we know it's going to be competitive; it's what we signed up for.' Students also learn a mature and resilient approach to the inevitable rejections. 'If they don't get a part, it's not them or their talent that's being rejected, it's that they're not what the director sees for that role,' insisted the principal. 'We teach them that NO stands for Next Opportunity.'

The year 6 pupils go swimming once a week, but otherwise there are no sports; the timetable doesn't allow for it, and the children keep super-fit with all that dance. Would the students like sports, we asked? 'No!' was the unanimous answer. Acrobatics

offered as an extracurricular, but not much else: the children work hard both on and off the premises and it's not unknown for them to commute daily from eg Birmingham – so they're not looking to stay after school for the Philately Club.

Background and atmosphere: 'I was determined to call it a theatre school,' explained Sylvia Young, 'because I was from a drama background. At the time, the others were all called stage schools, and to me that meant little chorus girls with their hair in bunches.'

Initially housed in the Gainsford Club for amateur boxers in Drury Lane – now long gone, a casualty of the Covent Garden gentrification. The lease expired in 1983 and the school had to find new premises in a hurry, alighting on a derelict school in Rossmore Road, Marylebone. 'The building was full of dead pigeons,' Sylvia reminisced, 'so the staff and I went down to Church Street market to buy mops and buckets.' It was a happy move, however, and the school stayed there for 27 years, with each leaver inscribing their name on a brick in the attic walls – a lovely photo-montage in the school's current site shows all the bricks and reads like a Who's Who of British popular entertainment. In 2008, with the school's success continuing to grow, Sylvia put in an offer on a disused Church of Christ Scientist in Marble Arch – Ginger Rogers used to worship there – and here the school is now, housed in air-conditioned space and splendour following a two-year programme of gutting and total refurbishment. The school boasts 10 purpose-built studios, two computer rooms, two science labs, two art rooms, various academic classrooms, a library, and a large and airy canteen. There are even two small outdoor courtyards where students can let off a small amount of steam. School is proud of these central London rarities, but one rueful parent did comment, 'If I have a criticism, it is the lack of outside space in which to run around, especially on academic days,' adding, 'however, I do think that is a small price to pay for the extra benefits of SYTS.'

The school began all those years ago as a community initiative, and its priorities remain the nurturing of children and the family atmosphere, something which everyone we spoke to agreed was one of its best aspects. Students work hard, develop professionalism, make friends and are overjoyed to be here. 'I only have praise for SYTS and feel it was the best decision to send my son there,' wrote a parent. 'He can't wait to get there each day, and is the happiest he's ever been in a school.' 'The kids are immensely supportive of each other and very close,' commented another, 'and there is lots of fun and laughter.'

Pastoral care, well-being and discipline: School is 'very strict' about the everyday things – no chewing gum, neat appearance, punctuality, attendance.

'They HAVE to be respectful to each other and to teachers,' said Sylvia, forcefully. A parent wrote, 'One headmaster from a major public school told us that he always prefers to take ex-Sylvia pupils as they are so much better behaved than from any other school.'

Pupils are very presentable, smartly turned out in traditional red and black uniform on academic days, black movement clothes on vocational days. Refreshing emphasis on common sense, eg 'We got rid of the pink ballet shoes because it was so much kerfuffle changing.' Girls now wear black ballet shoes and can move from class to class in them. Hair is neatly tied back, even on academic days.

Children work to achieve a place here, and discipline problems of the mainstream kind are rare. Reprimands and detentions are usually all that's necessary, and there's a strong culture of rewarding academic achievement. The students we spoke to couldn't think of any recent episodes of bullying – in fact, they were clear that bullying was something they'd left behind at their previous schools – but insisted that staff were approachable and that they had confidence to speak out if anything arose. However, there was a consensus that a school counsellor would be welcome – 'I know that counsellors can't talk to other teachers, whereas here you're worried that what you've said might not be private,' was a comment that had everyone murmuring agreement.

The lessons we observed were professional and lively, delivered by cheerful, upbeat teachers with excellent communication skills. Students are vocal, attentive, diligent, very keen to get things right

Because children come from such a wide radius, some board with host families found by the school. SYTS is inspected as a boarding school and adheres to the national standards. 'We live overseas, and my daughter boards; she has been with the same family throughout her time at the school,' wrote the mother of a year 10 pupil. 'She is happy and well cared for there.' Some other students lodge with their own relatives or friends. For those living at home, journeys of at least an hour each way are common.

Pupils and parents: Children come from 'absolutely everywhere', some from affluent families, others from poorer backgrounds where the extended family is working to put them through the school.

Girls outnumber the boys two to one, but the boys are unfazed – 'We've been doing the performing arts before coming here, and we're used to it.' 'And the boys here are really lovely!' cried a year 8 girl. Some pupils from showbiz backgrounds, but by no means all.

Everyone is united by a common love of performing. 'Our son has a wide and varied friendship group. They're all there for the same purpose, so there is a stronger bond between them,' said a father.

Alumni include Billie Piper, Keeley Hawes, Nicholas Hoult, Matt Di Angelo, Denise van Outen, Matt Willis, Rita Ora and Amy Winehouse.

Entrance: Around 350 apply each year – school takes between 30 and 40. One-form entry into year 6, two-form into year 7. Capacity for up to 26 in each class, but in practice the forms are rarely this big – 'We don't take children just to fill up places – they have to be good.' Thereafter students can join at any point other than year 11, although rarely at year 10 because GCSE preparation begins towards the end of year 9. Auditions are held throughout the year, and children can start mid-year if need be.

At all ages, applicants have to audition before a panel: they perform two acting pieces supplied by the school, plus a song and dance of the child's choice. 'We're looking for potential in at least one of the vocational areas,' said Sylvia, 'a student we feel we could train.' They also have to sit tests in maths and English, but these are diagnostic, and to check that a child can cope with doing in three days the academic study that other schools would do in five.

The school assesses progress regularly, but doesn't make a practice of assessing out. 'We wouldn't ask a student to leave if they're working to their best ability. We find that children develop at different times, and we know that all our students will leave us with a good level of attainment.'

Exit: No sixth form. At 16, around 50 per cent to dance schools – Bird's, Laine's, Urdang. Others to performing arts schools such as Tring Park, Arts Ed, ELAM, The Brit School, BIMM, LIPA. Some to independent sixth form colleges eg Hurtwood House, Ashbourne, often on full scholarships.

Not an obvious Russell Group route, but one student off to do A levels at Westminster School recently and another to Wimbledon High. 'I'm always thrilled when I hear of our students who've gone into law, medicine, forensic science...' remarked Sylvia with pardonable pride.

Money matters: Fees are extremely reasonable for an independent school in central London, remarkably so given all the top-quality specialist tuition students receive. Lots of children here on some form of financial assistance – equivalent of some £350k a year in bursaries. Children's agency earnings can be put towards the fees.

Remarks: Not a school simply for children who like to have fun on stage. Standards are extremely high, the discipline is exacting, the work hard and the hours long. Children need to have genuine talent, passion, and focus. 'If they don't have all this, then re-think!' advised several parents. But if they do, this is a fantastic school, combining sound academics with first-rate vocational training, and producing confident, happy, polished and likeable young people.

Trevor-Roberts School

55–57 Eton Avenue, London NW3 3ET

020 7586 1444 | trsenior@trevor-robertsschool.co.uk | trevor-robertsschool.co.uk

Independent	Pupils: 180
Ages: 5–13	Fees: £15,300 – 16,800 pa

Headmaster: Since 1999, Simon Trevor-Roberts BA (50s). Son of the founder, Trevor-Roberts studied at Westminster School before reading English at Aberystwyth. In 1983, he joined his father Christopher in the family firm, where he learnt his trade by example. (He has since been joined by his sister Amanda, who heads up the junior school). Mild mannered and reflective, he has a very clear sense of what the school is about: 'We try to get children to enjoy the process of learning.' Continues to teach maths to the 13 plus candidates, because he's found he, too, now has the knack of putting things across clearly. 'I shadowed my father for a long time and learnt how to do it by osmosis.' Parents find him immensely approachable and engaged. 'You always have complete access to the head and he knows all the kids incredibly well.' Married with two grown children, both of whom attended the school.

Entrance: Register as soon after birth as possible. About 80 sets of parents are contacted when their child is 1 and offered a tour. Those who wish to proceed confirm this in writing, and the school assesses the first 50 children on their list in the September prior to the calendar year in which they turn 5. 'We're not expecting any preparation, but we want to make sure it will be a happy transition,' says the registrar. 'We're looking for inquisitive children who want to learn. Getting that is more a dark art than a science.' The school generally tries to give priority to siblings, 'but only if it's the right school'. Often takes in one or two more in year 4, when the year group divides into two classes.

Exit: Girls mostly – though not exclusively – at 11, generally to Francis Holland, South Hampstead and other north London favourites. Most boys (and some girls) at 13, to a wide range of day and boarding schools, including regular placements at City of London, Eton, Harrow, Highgate, Latymer Upper, Merchant Taylors', UCS and Westminster. 'The head is very good at managing parental expectations,' said one former parent.

Remarks: This is a family-run school with a very distinctive ethos, deriving in large part from its origins. Founded by the current heads' father in the 1950s with just 14 boys, it was originally seen as a refuge for the 'unteachable'. 'My father had a reputation for taking those whom other schools had given up on and getting them through entrance exams to leading public schools,' says Simon Trevor-Roberts.

Today, the school can take its pick of north London's brightest, but continues to select a mixed-ability (now co-educational) intake and provide a tailor-made education for all. 'They want every child to work to his or her potential and really do treat every child as an individual,' said one parent.

Children start in year 1 in a class grouped according to the calendar year of their birth. In year 4, this is rearranged to allow everyone to be in place for secondary school entrance. One class of 16-18 in the early years, two classes in years 4 to 6, then a single form again for the final two years. 'We like to move children around so they're not in the same group for eight years,' says the head. 'It gives us the flexibility to allow those who require it a bit more time and accelerate those who need it.' Parents confirm this is skilfully managed. 'They're constantly readjusting their approach for different levels of learning, but not in a way that disturbs the children.'

Specialist subject teaching from the word go, with a classroom teacher for the core subjects, but music, history, geography, science and art all taught in their own space. 'It keeps the week fresh.'

Plenty of imaginative teaching by intelligent (including many Oxbridge), though not always qualified, staff. French from year 1, Latin from year 5, some Greek in year 8, Mandarin taught as a club. Special needs addressed by weekly sessions with the learning support coordinator and outside specialists.

Everyone staying for the final two years sits common entrance. 'We take it very seriously,' says the head. 'Eleven plus is about flexible problem solving; by 13, it's more structure on the page.' Senior schools praise the 'structure on the page' received.

Very good at ensuring the basics are in place. 'Sometimes you have to be a bit tough,' says the head. 'We insist that children use a pen rather than touch type. If you have to write an essay under exam conditions, you have to be able to discipline your thoughts.' No truck with overly formalised exam training. 'Non-verbal reasoning is not a subject,' he says crisply.

Poetry and drama matter and prove great confidence builders. 'My son almost died of nerves the first time he had to read out a poem, but now he loves drama and performing'

Formal homework from year 3, starting out with 20 minutes in English or maths ('It shows them how to work by themselves and for themselves'), up to two hours a night for the top forms. 'They do work very hard, but the atmosphere still manages to be reasonably relaxed,' said one mother.

Good relationships with staff are fundamental ('The teacher is not someone they're trying to hoodwink,' says the head), as is the view that effort should be lauded over achievement. 'Children are perfectly aware there's competition elsewhere, they don't need it reinforced. We want them to be in competition with themselves.' Good work is rewarded with a 'digniora', with recipients queuing in the lunch hour to have their accolade verified and registered. Three merits win a token (designed to reflect the season) to be spent at independent local shops.

Breadth well beyond the exam curriculum is given enormous emphasis. Outstanding music

---

'Children love sport, but I don't want a First Eleven ethos, with the captain of games strutting around,' says the head

– 'We love music' – with a dynamic head. Taught in the classroom from years 1 to 6, with the addition of numerous ensembles (brass, jazz, string, woodwind, chamber choir, rock band) and much external participation (at the Royal Festival Hall, St John's Smith Square, etc.) Twice weekly art lessons (one in year 7) in a bright art department at the top of school, with its own kiln. Extra art and DT on offer for enthusiasts on Wednesday afternoons.

Cultural values that have largely been submerged elsewhere – 'Everyone is encouraged to have a novel on the go' – with half an hour of silent reading daily after lunch. Poetry and drama matter and prove great confidence builders. 'My son almost died of nerves the first time he had to read out a poem,' said one mother, 'but now he loves drama and performing.' 'The plays are unbelievable,' said another.

Plenty of fresh air and exercise, with a good-sized, well-equipped playground, including popular table tennis, miniature railway and chicken coop ('the chickens are a great comfort to quieter, shyer children.'). Primrose Hill, a few hundred yards from the door, enables twice weekly games. Definitely not a school, however, where 'go-fight-win' is on the agenda. 'Children love sport, but I don't want a First Eleven ethos, with the captain of games strutting around,' says the head. 'We do play matches against other schools, but everyone has a go.'

The senior school building, a fine example of the arts and crafts, was the founder's own home and still offers delightful domestic interiors with William Morris wallpaper in the front hall and mid-century classic tables used instead of desks in the top forms. The juniors are housed in their own building with a separate dining room and science lab.

The atmosphere is civilised but structured ('It's a nice mix of the very strict and the nurturing and kind – teachers are always willing to talk things through.'). Pupils sit down to eat their biscuits at break before rushing off to the playground. Everyone has a hot lunch, served through an open hatch, 'so they can see where it is made.' Staff share the dining hall with pupils. 'Eating is socialising.' Food is freshly prepared on site using local produce.

Manners and uniform are both reasonably relaxed (no backs against the wall here). Light blue polo shirt for younger children, dark blue for older ones. Trousers and skirts, 'something reasonable'. 'Jeans are fine, jeans hanging off the hips are not.'

Often the school of choice for the liberal, media intelligentsia (including some famous names), the type of parent who genuinely believes in the well-rounded education, not the rush to the top of the league tables. (Competition here, though it undoubtedly exists, tends to be on the level of how many operas your child has seen rather than where the family went skiing.) Mainly local, some from Notting Hill, Queen's Park, Islington. The head feels 'there's no typical child, but I've heard people say our children are very kind.'

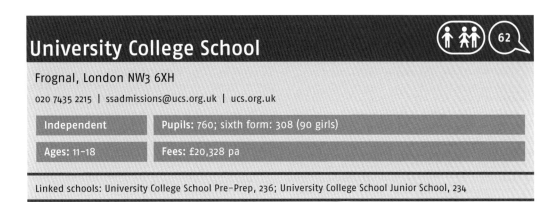

University College School

Frognal, London NW3 6XH

020 7435 2215 | ssadmissions@ucs.org.uk | ucs.org.uk

| Independent | Pupils: 760; sixth form: 308 (90 girls) |
| Ages: 11–18 | Fees: £20,328 pa |

Linked schools: University College School Pre-Prep, 236; University College School Junior School, 234

Headmaster: Since 2013, Mark Beard BSc MEd (early 40s), a chemist. Mr Beard came from Brighton College where he'd been deputy head with a period as acting head between the redoubtable Seldon and the remarkable Cairns – a good place to cut headmagisterial teeth. He is credited with this school's greatly increased number of Oxbridge entrants. He began his career at King Edward's School, Birmingham, where he is remembered as 'a jolly good chap', thence to St Paul's School, as head of chemistry. Mr Beard is married with two young children and enjoys squash, reading and ancient history.

He is energetic, open, likeable, relaxed and clear-sighted. He followed a loved and warmly respected head, Ken Durham, and big shoes can be hard to fill. However, 'I came in to be myself,' he asserted when we met. 'I set out my stall openly and clearly from the start' and whilst Mr Beard's appointment to this major school as a first headship was a considerable vote of confidence, he has more than filled his predecessor's shoes. He flustered some in the school community when, in his first term, he cracked down on aspects of this traditionally 'liberal' school – notably its somewhat relaxed attitude to uniform. 'I have been keen to explain..that liberal scholarship is not the same as liberal attitudes.. There is a school uniform and it is to be worn properly at formal occasions; you should be punctual to lessons, mind your manners and if you have homework, you do your homework.' Many parents applauded. 'Things needed tightening up,' one told us. 'I think he'll make it stricter, smarter and tidier – but within the ethos of the school,'

thought another. He has broadened the curriculum throughout the school and has placed a stronger emphasis on community links with an expansive volunteering and outreach programme now in place. Parents and students recognise the changes they have witnessed. 'He's less overtly charismatic than Ken – more cautious and considered. He will be a very good influence.' Sixth formers concur: 'He'll do interesting things over time.' One thing that remains constant throughout is the 'soul' of the school. There is a buzz across the site. Students love to learn here and teachers love to teach here.

Academic matters: Mr Beard's charges have not let him down. Recent results have been some of the best in the school's history with 70 per cent of A levels graded A*/A, 88 per cent A*-B in 2018. At GCSE, 88 per cent A*-A/9-7 grades. Impressive by any standards.

Far freer choice of GCSE and A level subjects than elsewhere including no blinkered – in our view – insistence on the holy trinity of sciences. Twenty plus A level options, with psychology recently added. Much teaching material tailor-made by school's own staff – that's proper teaching. Universal praise for the English dept. 'It's phenomenal,' drooled a parent. Very good languages dept and exchange system. Mandarin is growing seriously now and Italian is now an option in year 9 and beyond. School has switched to the Pre-U for languages, DT, philosophy and English. We approve. But teaching praised across the board. A sense of academic work being serious but also offering infinite opportunities for thought, exploration and discovery.

Parental approval of Mr Beard's instant moving of A level mocks from March to January. Much appreciation of staff dedication. 'They're always there if you need help. There's a young bunch of teachers and many run extra classes for those who need them,' we were told. There are also support mechanisms such as regular tracking and reporting back to parents, to help boys who need pushing.

All are screened in general literacy, numeracy and reasoning on entry. Mild SEN seen as no problem here. Two full-time and one part-time learning support specialists. Individual support either by withdrawal or classes before and after school – also for those with mild EAL needs.

Games, options, the arts: The school has traditionally focused on inclusivity over winning – an excellent principle but one which can elicit grumbles from motivated and competitive boys and parents. However, this is clearly changing now. Regular Saturday fixtures for up to 18 teams including C and D teams and many extracurricular clubs/practices in eight key sports taking place before school, after school and lunchtimes. Under Beard, there is greater emphasis on performance. There is now an 'elite sportspersons' programme', additional soccer and cricket coaches, increased games options and other initiatives to allow pupils to reach their potential. Top sportsmen are given the opportunity to flourish: the 1st Rugby XV won the Middlesex Cup recently and play flagship matches at Allianz Park – home of Saracens. Recent results in several sports including some individual triumphs suggest that, indeed, a sport fuse is alive and kicking here. They have county/academy rugby players, hockey players and cricketers, England (ISFA) footballers, tennis players very high in the national rankings, international swimmers as well as individual rowers, sailors and fencers. £10,000,000 investment has improved the nearby 27 acre playing field site in West Hampstead, including building a brand new double pavilion.

Perhaps best summed up by a veteran parent: 'It's a wonderful, liberal, free-thinking school. They are accommodating and accepting and they celebrate difference'

'The music and drama are simply brilliant,' a parent enthused. Music has long been exceptional here and we noted the number and quality of ensembles eg the symphony orchestra, chamber orchestra, several chamber groups, umpteen bands of all kinds including jazz and swing and excellent

---

DT and art are outstanding. Evident creativity, freedom and experimental ethos and the dept has more the air of an art college than a school

choirs. Well-provided for. Many pupils take LAMDA exams to high levels. Students write and direct their own plays and performance values are high. DT and art are outstanding. Evident creativity, freedom and experimental ethos and the dept has more the air of an art college than a school. Many media, some wonderfully bizarre and arresting work and all good stimulating stuff.

Far more interesting sounding clubs and extracurricular activities than we meet in most schools. Friday afternoons are given over to sixth form enrichment and staff follow their own enthusiasms in running classes such as Latin American film culture, wine tasting, life drawing, rock climbing, Literary London. Pupils set up clubs to pursue their own interests so we found a medical ethics society, a law and justice society, an eco-friendly club and beekeeping among many others. We wanted to sign up to them all.

Far from being a crammer in atmosphere, independence in all things is key. 'If your kids are self-starters, motivated and organised there is so much on offer, but they have to make the effort to get it. They don't come after you,' an appreciative parent explained. 'There is so much on offer even for the less academic child,' said another.

Exceptional outreach activities include collaboration at all levels with several state schools and pupil volunteering.

Background and atmosphere: The main buildings, dating back to 1907, are solid and imposing but rest comfortably on the southern slopes of the Hampstead hill. An unusual history. Founded by the University of London and various interested liberal intellectuals in 1830, it was designed to give an education to boys from dissenting (ie not conformist C of E) families and, initially, had no form of communal worship – unique at the time. Also no corporal punishment and no boarding. Its earliest incarnation was in Gower Street, hence the designation of Old Gower for an alumnus. So, from the off, it was regarded as 'liberal', and the tradition has been proudly maintained. What does it mean? 'It means, "no rules just for rules' sake",' ventured one parent, and that's at least part of it. Another parent quoted a prep school head: 'It's a school for mavericks.' While we like this observation, we feel it's a bit off the mark and UCS suggests that, while the great majority of pupils are far from being mavericks, the school is inclusive and can certainly accommodate them. Perhaps best summed up by a veteran parent: 'It's a wonderful, liberal, free-thinking school – you can look however you want to look, whether whacky or entirely traditional. They are accommodating and accepting and they celebrate difference.' It also still means no RE or religious assembly and a spirit of tolerance and inclusiveness.

A terrible fire in 1978 destroyed the huge Great Hall but the rebuilt version is almost overwhelming in its size and gravitas – wood panelling, stucco ceiling, huge organ and brass chandeliers. All eat in the handsome panelled refectory – all refectory tables and forms – with a strangely monastic feel. Droolly enthusiasm for the school food. 'No-one complains here,' we were told, and the menu was about the most varied, tempting and creative we can remember.

Later buildings include the 2006 sports centre with excellent pool – also used by the local community; the sixth form centre with large and well-appointed common room, study areas – with and without PCs – and an excellent all-day café; the Lund theatre – a large and flexible space in which most productions happen and which is constantly in use; transformation of library in AKO library, 'a new hub for innovative and creative teaching and learning'. Site now feeling a touch full (head prefers 'compact') although space still for super vegetable garden and beehives, three Astro pitches/courts and little green nooks for sitting and relaxing. Some smartening up going on hither and yon – a little paint and patching doing wonders as part of the rolling refurbishment programme, with the opening of the Kenneth Durham Social Sciences Centre and the construction of a Centre for Innovative Learning and Teaching. The emphasis here is not on every kind of here-today-obsolete-tomorrow IT gizmo but on rock solid teaching.

Girls arrived in the sixth form in 2008 to both trepidation and excitement from staff and boys. But it has worked, and not too much to the detriment of relationships between the school and its all-girl neighbours. 'The boys love the girls coming in the sixth form – it works very well,' one veteran parent assured us. 'They take very confident girls – the multi-tasking, vibrant, feisty ones – and they settle well.' The girls we spoke to bore this out, but they also paid tribute to the efforts made to integrate them before term and to help them quickly make friends once the year began.

Pastoral care, well-being and discipline: Houses are called 'demes' here and matter, but not too much. Praise for the Beard tightened-up regime. 'Some of the younger boys were getting lippy and needed reining in.' But equally, parents, pupils and OGs keen that the school's treasured 'liberalism' is maintained. 'It isn't a school for those who need a highly regulated, organised system,' explained a devotee. Another parent concurred, 'It's very friendly and informal. It's warm and family-like.' Much praise for the home-school communications. 'I have mobile numbers for all my son's teachers and they reply to emails almost before you've sent them.' Even warmer praise for the deme wardens: 'They are phenomenally good on the pastoral side.' Mr Beard has a light touch but a firm view. 'We want them to be the problem solvers of the future, not the problem causers. That's partly what a liberal education should be about.' Few discipline problems. Leavers reflect thoughtfully on their schooling: 'You learn to manage your time. They cultivate you into someone who can deal with a high level of intensity in your work. They build it up so that you don't really feel how much more deeply you are thinking. You become very independent and self-reliant in this school.'

Pupils and parents: From all over north and central London. Pupils are as diverse as the capital itself. They are articulate, thoughtful, independent. Parents are achievers, ambitious, cultured, moneyed – for the most part – and involved. 'Increasing numbers of middle class parents have to work hard to find the fees,' acknowledges Mr Beard.

Entrance: About two-thirds of 11-year-olds come from the junior school in Holly Hill. They move up without needing to take an entrance exam. At 11+, 350+ boys, mostly from local primaries, try for 30 places. Exams in maths, English and reasoning in January. Around 40 per cent of applicants thereafter invited for interview.

Far from being a crammer in atmosphere, independence in all things is key. 'If your kids are self-starters, motivated and organised there is so much on offer'

At 13+, 300 boys apply for some 30 places – mainly from local preps, eg Arnold House, Devonshire House, The Hall, Hereward House, North Bridge House, St Anthony's and Trevor-Roberts, but also Notting Hill and Westminster Cathedral Choir School. Pre-test in year 6 in maths, English and reasoning. About 150 return for an activity morning and interview in the October of year 7. Offers conditional on performance at CE.

At 16+, some 200 apply for around 50 places. Most entrants at this stage are girls, but no actual quota – entry on merit. Girls come from eg City of London, Francis Holland, North London Collegiate, Channing, South Hampstead. Some from Highgate School. Also from St Marylebone School, Hampstead School and

William Ellis. Selection via November assessment and about 50 per cent of applicants interviewed. Assessment is an objective test of thinking, reasoning and problem-solving. All offers conditional on GCSEs.

Exit: Everyone goes off to a good university to read a proper subject. London University is a favourite; many also to Durham, Manchester, Leeds, Bristol, Nottingham. Impressive numbers annually to Oxbridge (19 in 2018, with seven to the US and five medics). The vast range of subjects they pursue is testament to the individuality fostered here.

Notable Old Gowers include: Tristram Hunt, actors Hugh Dennis, David McCallum and Bertie Carvel, journalists Ian Katz, Jonathan Freedland and Paul Dacre, Thomas Adès, members of Bombay Bicycle Club, Will Self, Justin Stebbing, Chris Bonington, Roger Bannister, John Barrett.

Money matters: Around £1m a year disbursed to pupils who would not otherwise be able to afford UCS. At the time of our visit, 52 pupils were on 100 per cent bursaries – one of the most generous provisions in the UK. Most of this funded by the letting of school facilities to the community, charitable work and donations. No academic scholarships but music schols worth up to 25 per cent.

Remarks: A very good school and set to rise even higher under energetic and confident head.

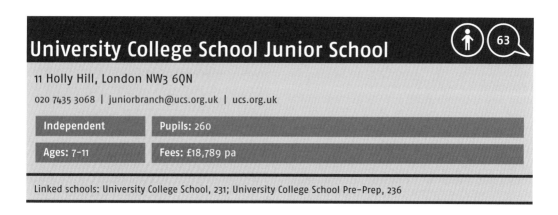

University College School Junior School

11 Holly Hill, London NW3 6QN

020 7435 3068 | juniorbranch@ucs.org.uk | ucs.org.uk

Independent	Pupils: 260
Ages: 7–11	Fees: £18,789 pa

Linked schools: University College School, 231; University College School Pre-Prep, 236

Headmaster of Junior: Since 2014, Lewis Hayward MA Oxon MA ed management (OU) PCGE, a classicist (late 40s). An interesting former life – he began his teaching life in EFL in i) Nairobi and ii) Saudi. Thence to the relative quiet of Holmewood House and Highfield preps' classics depts until he left for Highgate School in 2009, where he became deputy principal. Efficient, professional and articulate, Mr Hayward is a modern head. He is voluble about the mega plans for refurb and new build which will bring up to date this charming school on its compact site, but he is also a man who greets every child by name and who knows not only the bricks and mortar but the concerns and qualities of his charges. 'Stretching without cramming' is his academic credo, and the parents we spoke to recognised this approach. 'He's slotted in very well,' said one parent who's known the place for years. 'He doesn't just say the right things but he works hard and is very approachable.' Another agreed, 'He wants to meet everyone's expectations.' A third told us, 'He had big boots to fill but all his changes seem good.' A sportsman, he runs nine miles daily as part of his commute from south London. He's in school by 6.30am to avoid the crowds and have quiet time. Energetic, focussed, clever – a good appointment for this special prep.

Entrance: Sixty boys are selected at 7+ from the 210-odd applicants. Two part assessment – i) a series of concentration and listening exercises and ii) a formal exam including comprehension, maths and NVR. Newbies join those who come up from the school's own pre-prep (from which entry is not automatic – they sit the same exam) or other local preps eg Hampstead Hill, Golders Hill, Mulberry House. NB sibling policy dictates that 'Having a sibling (current or former pupil) at the school does not confer automatic admission into the school. Siblings must go through the same process as all other applicants at their chosen point of entry. Siblings will not be admitted if we believe that they are unlikely to cope and thrive within the academic UCS environment or if we think that their admission in preference to another candidate would be unfair.'

Exit: Virtually all to the UCS senior school. Any who, by year 4, are not cutting it are supported with one-to-one, and those very few who clearly wouldn't thrive in the senior school are helped by the head to get in to gentler, more appropriate, schools elsewhere. Notable leavers include Sir Roger Bannister, Julian Lloyd Webber, Hugh Dennis, Ian Katz.

Boys in a drama class were wide-eyed and thoroughly engaged in an instant reaction game – no hanging back or bashfulness here

Remarks: In the heart of gorgeous Hampstead village, though you could live there for years and never know it was there. Purpose-built in 1928, the main house is functional rather than beautiful but still works well. Supplemented by a small science block and smaller arts block, the school covers pretty much all indoor needs on site plus a new outdoor terrace, and the sizeable rebuild and refurb – which clearly Mr Hayward is itching to start – will upgrade and modernise as needed.

Academic excellence is a given, and the children here are sponges who mop up everything intellectual, cultural, esoteric, thrown at them. Several long-serving and much loved staff give character, stability and stimulation. Recently, a UCS junior team reached the final of the Prep Schools' Science Quiz and they regularly star in the Primary Schools' Maths Challenge. Average class size 21. A few need EAL help and are supported by SENCo as are those with mild learning difficulties – all closely monitored.

Parents enthuse, but mostly about the quite extraordinary range of extracurricular activities on offer – we've not met anything quite like it at a cramped London prep before, and wonder how on earth they do it. Before-school activities include G&T clubs – open to all – in maths, English, coding, German, Mandarin etc. More at lunchtime and even more after school. 'More than I could have imagined,' beamed one mum, 'almost too many. My son wants to do all that's on offer but he simply can't.'

We watched several lessons and were struck by the diverse teaching methods employed by the much-praised staff. The French names for the parts of the body were being learned by groups of boys, sprawled on the floor, drawing jambes, poitrines, gorges etc. Boys in a drama class were wide-eyed and thoroughly engaged in an instant reaction game – no hanging back or bashfulness here. Self-discipline rather than rules, rule here – most classes were lively but controlled and we also saw several in which boys were silently reading, clearly lost in their own imaginary worlds.

Arts thrive – stunning theatre work on proper plays – The Dream and Private Peaceful most recently. Everyone in top three years gets involved. Serious music – an orchestra, two choirs – each 50+ strong, big band and numerous smaller instrumental ensembles – and everyone takes part in the big annual concert. Virtually everyone scrapes or blows something – 'We get 'em playing,' asserted impressive head of music. Very good art displays in corridors, though some few classrooms sporting boringly blank walls. Art block houses studio and DT room – classes split between the two. We loved the Japanese ceramic pots which boys had made and were decorating in authentic style as we watched. Laser cutter, 3D printer etc and we were impressed by the torches being designed via CAD and then made in the subterranean DT workshop. Best was the super cookery kitchen. Year 6 boys cook a three course meal for staff and parents and it all smelled gorgeous. Good-sized labs in science block, inhabited by enthusiastic boys plus a corn snake, tarantula, bearded dragon and some startling tropical fish. Good-sized library, well-used and sensible tracked reading scheme, punctuated by quizzes to monitor progress. Parents help with reading.

Although on site outside space is limited to little more than a rubberised playground (a small adventure trail is also planned), sports thrive. Outside table tennis and table football. School uses nearby fields plus sports facilities at the big brother school down the hill. Earlier complaints about few opportunities for those not in A or B teams seem to be being addressed now. Lots of trips – field studies to Norfolk; west country rugby tour; ski trip to Italy; football trip to Spain; art trip to Nice, Amsterdam or Barcelona and a year 4 field studies trip to Normandy.

Parents enthuse, but mostly about the quite extraordinary range of extracurricular activities on offer – we've not met anything quite like it at a cramped London prep before. 'More than I could have imagined,' beamed one mother

Strong social network across this very diverse community. 'My son sees a lot of the other boys outside school.' Inside school, too, communication thrives – 'Every class has a council rep who can express grievances and they really do listen to them. The kids feel understood.' 'Older boys mentor the newbies so it's a bit like having an older brother in the school.' 'They just don't tolerate bad behaviour.' Parents stress the friendliness of the place: 'They were wonderfully supportive of me when we had difficulties and I was very emotional.' Consensus: 'It's a lovely, embracing and supportive school for boys from varying backgrounds, interests and personalities. My boys are all quite different but it was the right school for all of them.'

University College School Pre-Prep

36 College Crescent, London NW3 5LF

020 7722 4433 | pre-prep@ucs.org.uk | ucs.org.uk

Independent	Pupils: 100
Ages: 4–7	Fees: £15,720 pa

Linked schools: University College School, 231; University College School Junior School, 234

Headmistress: Since 2015, Zoe Dunn BEd PhD NPHQ (late 30s), an Eng lit specialist with an impressive pedigree and all in this neck of the woods. After four years at The Hall, down the road, Dr Dunn went to The Royal School – up the hill, and now taken over by North Bridge House Senior – first as deputy head and latterly as head of its junior school. After a sabbatical term on a Winston Churchill Travelling Fellowship, she founded and then led a local faith free school – The Rimon Jewish Free Primary School – down the far side of the hill for four terms. A brief maternity leave over, she took up the post here. She sparkles and charms. Clearly super-bright, she is also simply super and you want to find her children to benefit from her enthusiasm and energy. Herself a mother of a toddler (when we visited), she lives locally and engages her charges in lots of local affairs eg charities and arts activities. Keen on outdoor learning and forest school – 'so good for team-building' – she has also revived the house system. Parents are happy: 'She's very strong. All her changes are positive.. She understands the parent body.. She couldn't be more supportive when there are problems..She's pretty powerful but she's so approachable she somehow takes people with her.' One of three good recent appointments for this family of schools.

Entrance: Register (boys only for 4+ entry) up to a year before starting reception. Siblings get no preference – 'We have to maintain the academic standard of the school'. Occasional 5+ and 6+ places.

Exit: Though entry not automatic, most boys go on to the UCS Junior Branch, as the name-change to UCS Pre-Prep suggests. Some to eg St Paul's Juniors, Westminster Under. Girls to South Hampstead, City Girls, Channing. Both kinds to Belmont, The ASL, The Academy, Highgate, Heathside.

Remarks: Tucked away down College Crescent, you wouldn't know it was there, but the anonymous entrance conceals a surprisingly roomy little pre-prep and a bit of a gem. Now overlooked by the imposing brick and glass grandeur that is the newly reinvented and rebuilt South Hampstead High School, UCS Pre-Prep comes as a surprise. But, if you are keen on a 4-18 trajectory through one of London's best schools, this is where you can start. Once a co-ed pre-prep including nursery (whose previous domain is now an arts and science block), it has phased out 3 year olds and is phasing out girls. Class names all follow the bird theme (school was previously called the Phoenix) and are named Hummingbird, Barn Owl, Puffin etc.

Good use of a whole range of teaching and learning media throughout, including interactive whiteboards – often as 'input' at the start of a class to set in motion whatever learning activity is planned. Also iPads and netbooks, but Dr Dunn stresses the importance of traditional skills too. Learning support given in small groups or one-to-one for EAL (25 per cent of the children speak a language other than English at home, though only 10 per cent need support), SEND and as a booster for those showing gifted/talented tendencies.

Outside space limited but school has allotments, use of nearby fields and a surprisingly large gym at the top of the building

Some 35 per cent of these tinies play an instrument (having lessons in school from 4 years old), and all children participate in the twice annual performances, such as Aladdin, which take place in the large theatre auditorium at UCS senior branch – very exciting for all. Specialist art teacher produces wonderfully imaginative work in these creative buds. And art room has a wall that can be endlessly painted and repainted – such a good idea. Selection of so few from so many clearly works.

Outside space is very limited but enthusiastically used, with playhouse and tunnel slide over safe surface flooring. School also has allotments and use of nearby fields and a surprisingly large gym at the top of the building. Also makes use of facilities – sporting and others – at big brother schools.

Families live in the NWs, some Ns and the odd W postcode. Sixteen home languages spoken at the time of our visit and all cultures celebrated when appropriate. School is linked to one in the high Himalayas and a teacher goes out each year carrying artwork from UCS Pre-Prep and brings back similar from a very different place. Parents seem universally happy despite hiccups like The Great Hot Lunch Controversy – resolved democratically, we gather (children bring their own lunches). Unstinting praise for the teachers: 'we're so lucky. phenomenal..amazing..' Summed up by one parent: 'There was never a day when my children didn't want to go to school.'

Westminster Cathedral Choir School

Ambrosden Avenue, London SW1P 1QH

020 7798 9081 | office@choirschool.com | choirschool.com

| Independent | Pupils: 230; boarders: 24 full (choristers) |

| Ages: 4–13 (boarding from 8) | Fees: Day £16,350 – £18,582; Boarding choristers £9,747 pa |

Headmaster: Since 2007, Mr Neil McLaughlan (40s). Married with a young son and daughter, and a man who radiates humour, decency and charm in equal measure. Read philosophy and politics at Durham and spent a few years with Andersen Consulting in London before embarking on a teaching career in 1997. After spells at Stonyhurst and Worth, he took up a post as head of English and director of development at Downside School, before joining WCCS as headmaster. He hopes to be there 'for the duration.' Parents hope so too. 'Lovely guy!' said one. 'So easy to approach!' said another. 'An extremely dedicated head and a great promoter of the school,' said a third. Typically modest, he hopes to do 'lots and lots of small things right.' We think he's doing lots of big things right too. Under his visionary yet kindly leadership, this has become an inspiring school that is going from strength to strength.

Entrance: New pre-prep takes boys at 4+. Entry by assessment, but the school is looking for potential rather than attainment. Most are expected to continue on to the prep school after English and maths tests. Thirty places available; priority to siblings. Other main entry points are at 7+, where 16 places are available, and 8+ (a further 10 places for day boys and six places for choristers). Applicants sit tests in English, maths and non-verbal reasoning in January of the year before entry. Occasional places in other year groups, notably at 11+. The school is always oversubscribed and, once boys have met the required academic standard, will give preference where possible to practising Roman Catholics and to boys with a brother at the school.

Choristers, who must be Catholic and boarders, join at 8+. Would-be probationers have to pass informal and formal tests with the cathedral's master of music, as well as succeeding at the academic assessment; and if they manage all that, they spend two nights at the school to see whether chorister life will suit them. Only then will they be offered one of the six available places. As the school's popularity grows, so inevitably does the competition; there are now half a dozen serious candidates for each choristership, and for the first time in over a decade, the school has not had to go recruiting for them.

Up to full fees assistance for choristers; none for day pupils, whose families just have to fork out. As a result, there is more cultural than social diversity here. Boys come from a wide range of nationalities, among them France, Spain, Italy, Russia, Ghana and Korea, making this a truly international school. With some 80 per cent of the boys now from Catholic families, the school is less religiously diverse than it was, but remains open to day boys of all faiths provided their families are happy to support the school's Catholic ethos.

Exit: The head has worked tirelessly to raise the school's profile, and WCCS's exit record is superb. Boys regularly leave for boarding schools like Eton, Harrow, Winchester, Radley, Downside, Charterhouse and King's Canterbury, and for a raft of top London schools, including Westminster,

St Paul's, UCS, City of London, KCS Wimbledon, Latymer Upper, Dulwich College and Wetherby senior school, often with music scholarships. Others to Cardinal Vaughan and the London Oratory. 'The school is much more linked into the senior schools than it was a few years ago,' reported one satisfied parent. 'Oh yes, the head's always going on about schools,' confirmed one of the boys, equably. In 2018, there were six music scholarships, one music exhibition and one sport scholarship.

Remarks: The school was endearingly shabby once, but not any more. A five-year programme of refurbishment has just finished, and everything is now bang up to date. Visitors are welcomed in the beautiful glass-fronted foyer, where handwritten Music for Mass schedules from 1905 are hung beside huge photos of current pupils radiating health and cheeriness. Throughout the building, ceilings, floors and lighting are all new, and all the classrooms are gleaming and well-resourced, with interactive whiteboards in each one. Large and much-loved playground, covered with Astroturf, where boys play 'crazy games' on the climbing apparatus. 'That was a real selling point for me,' said one parent. 'The boys have a chance to be boys.' 'The way to the heart of little boys is good food and football at playtime, and WCCS excels in both,' confirmed another. We didn't try the football, but we can confirm that the food is splendid, a delicious combination of tasty and healthy.

'The way to the heart of little boys is good food and football at playtime, and WCCS excels in both'

Boarding facilities have also been upgraded. We can't comment on the refurbished boarders' common room, because a curmudgeonly old trumpet teacher therein told us we were interrupting his lesson and to get out, but we did manage to see the sleeping accommodation, which was cheerful, light and airy. The rigours of chorister life notwithstanding, feedback on the boarding experience from both parents and boys was uniformly positive. 'The key thing,' says head, 'is to have good, kind people around the boys, good accommodation and excellent food. An army marches on its stomach.'

Years ago, parents had disquiets about aspects of WCCS. Nowadays, they cannot find enough superlatives with which to express their delight. 'We have been thrilled by both the teaching and pastoral care provided by the school.' 'The staff generate a wonderfully positive energy.' 'It's an amazing school, the teachers are so kind!' 'You couldn't choose a better school, I recommend it

---

'The one ingredient a Catholic school should have is joy,' said the head, simply and without any side, when we asked him

to everyone.' 'A wonderful warmth and care is present everywhere.'

A father of a new chorister told us, 'My son absolutely loves it. He's thrilled to pieces. The first weekend they were eligible to go home, he didn't want to come.' (Poor mum!) And a mother of two day pupils wrote, 'Happiness is guaranteed at this school; it is such a nurturing, caring and stimulating environment. I can honestly say that the only problem I have ever had is to find a way to drag my boys out of the playground and back home at the end of the day.' What's behind this remarkable success? 'The one ingredient a Catholic school should have is joy,' said the head, simply and without any side, when we asked him.

There is joy in the teaching here, that's for sure. A quiet revolution is taking place in the WCCS curriculum that made this reviewer go all excited and wobbly at the knees. Schemes of work have been painstakingly redesigned, with scholarship and a genuine love of learning at their heart. 'The idea is to present knowledge as a unified whole,' explained the head, 'so for instance, whilst they're studying Adam and Eve in RS, they'll be doing CS Lewis's The Magician's Nephew in English. Likewise, we use geometry and graph-plotting in maths to support map skills in geography, and they'll draw antique maps in art at the same time. If the boys are doing the human body in science, they'll look at what the Greeks and Romans discovered about it in history.' The boys we spoke to praised the lessons as 'really good fun,' adding, 'The work's challenging, but in a good way'.

Much emphasis on poetry, with poems studied every week, as well as learnt by heart and declaimed. 'We want them to know the great poets of the English language,' said the deputy head, and to further this, the school has produced its own wonderful anthologies, where the selection is 'unashamedly classic.' In addition to regular English lessons, boys receive two lessons a week on formal grammar and punctuation, and Latin is compulsory from the off – 'Latin is crucial for grammar, it's not an academic luxury,' insisted the deputy head. 'As an international school, the story of the world's great civilisations interests us. But children of this age also need connections, and they need the basics.' All those who have wrung their hands at the disjointed, shallow content of so many modern lessons, lift up your hearts and hope.

This is clearly a scholarly yet joyful environment, and the quality of student work we saw reflected that. We read, misty-eyed, a set of poems by the year 7s about Westminster Bridge (inspired by Wordsworth's sonnet) that were outstandingly creative and well-written; likewise, a history essay on Thomas Becket was not only mature and insightful, but skilful and lucid in its use of language. But mightn't this approach favour only the brightest? WCCS's SENCo emphatically denied it, asserting that boys at the school with SEN benefited from understanding how language works. We were impressed with the support the school gives to those with dyslexia and dyspraxia, as well as to ESL students, such as the two grave and courteous Russian boys we saw having extra English tutorials. And all the staff we met were purposeful, well-bred (curmudgeon excepted), cultivated, devoted to what they do and, according to parents, 'incredibly dedicated.'

As you'd expect, the standard of music here is outstanding. The choristers are completely immersed in music-making at the highest level (listen to the downloads on the website, and marvel), and the day boys, swimming in the same element, also achieve great things. We saw year 8 boys composing their entries for the school's Christmas carol competition, and heard much excellent instrumental playing as we went round the school. 'The music programme is amazing,' enthused one parent. 'My son's piano playing has come on by leaps and bounds in just a few weeks.' Many pupils achieve grades 7 or 8 in their chosen instrument(s) by the time they leave.

Football, rugby and cricket are the main sports here, played at local pitches, and swimming and PE are held at the nearby Queen Mother Sports Centre. Lots of extracurricular activities, including debating, philosophy, chess, scrabble, code-breaking, the Airfix model club, current affairs, and cross-country running. 'But where do you run?' we asked, glancing with some surprise at the surrounding streets. 'Oh!' said our tour guide, 'Green Park, Hyde Park, St James's..'

Lucky lads, you might think. And they are, of course. But what struck us most about this lovely little school was how considerate, well-mannered and sanguine about life its pupils seemed to be. They are achieving great things, while remaining likeable and happy boys. As one mother wrote, 'My son is neither Catholic nor musical, but has been recognised for other things he has to contribute to the school. They're grounded children with good values. It's a perfect place for my son to grow into a confident young man.' We agree with her. For boys fortunate enough to come here, this is as near perfect as it gets.

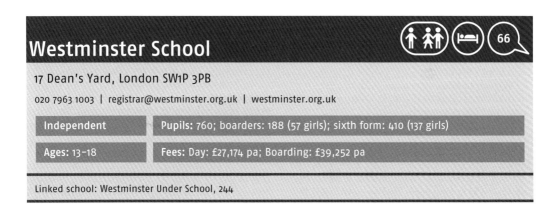

Westminster School

17 Dean's Yard, London SW1P 3PB

020 7963 1003 | registrar@westminster.org.uk | westminster.org.uk

Independent	Pupils: 760; boarders: 188 (57 girls); sixth form: 410 (137 girls)
Ages: 13–18	Fees: Day: £27,174 pa; Boarding: £39,252 pa

Linked school: Westminster Under School, 244

Head Master: Since 2014, Patrick Derham MA (50s), previously head of Rugby School. At 12, he was sent to live and study on the naval training ship Arethusa, run by the children's charity Shaftesbury Homes to prepare young men for the navy. Two years later the ship was abruptly sold due to financial difficulties and, with a day's notice and little idea what a public school was, he arrived at Pangbourne College on a bursary. He eventually became head of school and read history at Cambridge (first class degree), and feels 'my life was transformed by education.'

Taught at Cheam School and then Radley, where he was head of history and a housemaster for '12 very happy years' before being advised by the warden there to go straight for a headship. Five years as head of Solihull were followed by 13 at Rugby, before landing the headship of 'the home of liberal education – the perfect culmination of my career.'

His background ('my mum still lives in a council house in Scotland') has clearly been a powerful motivating force in his commitment to widening access to a good education – as he points out, 'all the great schools were founded with that intention.' At Rugby, he set up the Arnold Foundation to provide bursaries for children who need the stability of a boarding education ('we didn't just cream off the brightest middle class kids'). He is a trustee of the Royal National Children's SpringBoard Foundation, a national charity modelled on the same lines, and vice chair of IntoUniversity, which gives disadvantaged children academic support and mentoring to raise their aspirations.

'It's a breath of fresh air,' said a parent. 'Intellectual risk taking is encouraged. They're never not challenged.' 'It's incredibly inspiring,' said another

'He did an amazing job here and will be brilliant at Westminster,' said a Rugby insider. Very down to earth, personable, fantastic speaker, say Westminster parents. 'You feel like you can trust him'... 'He really cares about getting to know everyone'... 'I like it that he already knows who I am and who my children are'... 'Very responsive to comments'... 'My daughter thinks he's great'.

Clearly no ivory tower head, he loves interaction with pupils and teaches A level history. Parents watching their sons compete in the recent National Schools Rowing Regatta were delighted to see Derham there cheering on the teams (they won the championship eights' title for the first time in the school's history).

Married to Alison, a teacher, with two grown up children. Westminster seems to be in very steady, to say nothing of inspiring, hands.

Academic matters: With these very bright pupils, 'you can teach for the love of the subject and focus on the exam when need be,' says the head. 'It's a breath of fresh air,' said a parent. 'Intellectual risk taking is encouraged. They're never not challenged.' 'It's incredibly inspiring,' said another. Many of the teachers are experts in their fields, encouraged to follow their interests. 'I cannot believe there is a more stimulating place to teach in the country,' said a teacher. 'It is so much more liberal than at my previous school,' said a sixth form student. 'It's not constrained by the syllabus – it's learning for the sake of learning. It really allows you to get a proper understanding outside the exam baselines.' Pupils tend to internalise that love of learning. 'They read and they question and they challenge,' says the head. 'In my first lesson one asked me, "Where is the evidence?" I'd never been asked that before.'

Everyone encouraged to include a practical subject, eg art, electronics, drama, music, at GCSE. Huge range of languages includes Dutch, Arabic and Portuguese. Several parents commented that inspirational teachers had sparked their sons' interest in subjects they had previously hated. 'He'd always been a bit of a maths boy but now he is flying at English and languages too. They've understood how to teach in a way that suits him and developed all these new interests.'

Top exam results are, nonetheless, part of the package, with 97 per cent A*-A/9-7 at GCSE in 2018. At A level/Pre-U, the results were 88 per cent A*/A grades and 95 per cent A*/B. New thinking skills course – designed as a more challenging alternative to critical thinking A level – introduces sixth formers to the elements of informal logic, and helps prepare for university entrance skills tests such as the Oxbridge Thinking Skills Assessment.

High academic ability is obviously a prerequisite, but study skills coordinator works with all those who need support for eg mild dyslexia, dyspraxia or Asperger's, or just lack of organisation, helping them with the skills needed to cope with learning at different levels as they move up the school.

Links with local state schools Grey Coat Hospital and Harris Westminster Sixth Form – the latter sponsored by Westminster School – see sixth formers from these schools joining in German, Latin, art history and drama lessons with Westminster students. 'They've done a really good job at integrating us,' said a Westminster sixth former. 'I'm as good friends with students from outside as anyone else in the class.' Joint senior management meetings with Harris Westminster staff: 'We are going to learn from each other.'

Games, options, the arts: An almost overwhelming range of extracurricular opportunities. Societies often stem from the particular passions of both staff and students, ranging from feminist to secular to geography. English society may see Simon Russell Beale answering questions on playing King Lear at the National, whilst Piyush Goyal, national treasurer of the Indian Bharatiya Janata Party (BJP) party, tells the political society about Indian public affairs. 'I set up a society and had an ambassador from Panama come to talk,' said one student. 'Staff are really supportive when you want to set up new things.' Huge range of journalists and politicians, scientists and thinkers drop in to give talks; poet in residence inspires creativity. Trips everywhere: climbing in Cataluña, Beijing exchange, art history in Venice. Years 9-11 go off for a week's climbing, sailing, hill walking or camping at home or abroad.

'Phenomenal' music, with professional standard orchestral concerts at St John's Smith Square and the Barbican, carol service in Westminster Abbey, masterclasses, eminent musicians from

Nicola Benedetti to Ian Bostridge giving evening concerts. One parent felt that 'unless you are excellent you won't get a look in,' whilst staff point out there are house concerts and ensembles for the less stratospherically talented. 'We like to think there is room for everyone.' Drama equally high performing – Guys and Dolls a recent sell-out but much cerebral fare too, plus house drama and GCSE/A level pieces – and again huge talent required to bag a role in the large scale school productions.

Art, too, 'wonderful', with much emphasis on traditional drawing and painting skills, life classes, film making facilities and a darkroom. Plus, of course, easy access to all of London's galleries and museums. 'My son had no artistic ambition when he arrived, but is now doing art A level. They have totally inspired him,' said one parent, whilst another commented: 'They let these academic boys be so creative – they feel free to explore.'

Sports – known as 'Station' – take place on Tuesday and Thursday afternoons, mostly on the enviably large playing fields in nearby St Vincent Square plus adjacent sports centre (in a previous life one of the Royal Horticultural Halls). In Westminster liberal fashion, no particular sport is compulsory, with a huge range of choices from sailing to judo to golf to girls' football. 'You wouldn't send a very sporty boy to Westminster,' thought a parent, who was grateful that her keen but not-particularly-athletic son had been in teams which he would have been unlikely to make at a more overtly sporty school. However, particularly successful at rowing (and was basking in the glow of recent success at National Schools' Regatta when we visited), fields nine football teams with 'at least respectable' results, and 'we do very well at niche sports such as rock climbing [third in the Independent Schools' Championships] and fencing [bronze medal in U15 Foil]'. Often dominates the London School Cross-Country Championships and the Westminster Secondary Schools Swimming Gala, with pupils representing Westminster in the London Youth Games, and is successful at fives and real tennis. 'You are encouraged to try lots of things and find something you are passionate about,' said a student.

Volunteering taking on increasing importance with head's passion for outreach, with nearly all Westminsters teaching music or setting up debating societies in local primary schools, working on Hampstead Heath or learning sign language to communicate with deaf children. 'People are really involved and really making a difference,' said a student. 'Staff have the time, passion and faith in us to let us get on with things.' Phab week – where year 12 Westminster students host young people with physical and/or mental challenges, taking part in creative activities and seeing London together – is a 'life changing experience'. 'With privilege

comes enormous responsibility to give back,' says the head.

Boarding: The last Anglican monastery in London now houses Purcell's, a girls' boarding and boys' day house with attached chapel. Five other boarding houses, all in or near Little Dean's Yard and all of which include some day pupils. Many rooms surprisingly spacious; younger boys in College, scholars' house, in dorms of up to eight, whilst upper years have their own rooms and those in between may share with one other. 'Because these are all old buildings, the room arrangements can be random, and sometimes we have to improvise.' All boarders are cared for in relaxed fashion by housemaster (male or female), some with own family; resident tutor and matron also on site. Breakfast and supper in College Hall, the medieval dining room of Westminster Abbey, which day pupils may also join.

> 'Lots of people said I wouldn't like Westminster,' reports the head. 'They told me the pupils were arrogant, staff unmanageable, parents difficult. None of this is true.' Westminster families undoubtedly tend to be wealthy and intellectual

The only full boarders are sixth formers, and Saturday evenings tend to be quiet, though school is increasing organised weekend activities, particularly for the 10 per cent or so of overseas sixth form boarders.

Boarders have supervised prep sessions, and there are evening activities in the sports and music centres after prep, but those after a full-on boarding experience jammed full of organised activities may want to look elsewhere. 'He likes it for the independence and to be with his mates,' said a boarder parent, whilst another said, 'It feels like a convenient b&b. Much better than having to pick him up at late after a rehearsal or lecture.' However, a sixth form boarder commented on the 'serious sense of community you can only get from living with others. The people in your own house become quite special to you.'

Background and atmosphere: Whilst some other great public schools overshadow their environs, Westminster is an integral but discreet part of central London, largely located in the walled precincts of the former medieval monastery of Westminster Abbey. Its main buildings surround the square of

University College School

Little Dean's Yard, known as Yard, where pupils spill out after lessons to chat or kick a football or practise basketball. The Abbey, next door and with its own private entrance, serves as the school chapel, used for twice weekly services plus carol and other concerts.

'It is an incredibly tolerant and civilised atmosphere,' said a parent. 'Unlike other schools, they don't try to mould pupils into a particular product. They are quite laissez-faire'

Westminster had become a school by 1179, with pupils taught by monks of the Abbey at Westminster. It survived Henry VIII's dissolution of the monasteries in 1540 and has been in continuous existence since the 14th century, with Elizabeth I celebrated as the school's official founder.

'It is an incredibly tolerant and civilised atmosphere,' said a parent. 'Unlike other schools, they don't try to mould pupils into a particular product. They are quite laissez-faire.' Parents of quirky students are relieved to find a school that is very kind and accepting of eccentricities. 'If he was at any other school he'd be toast,' said one. 'Some schools can be so unforgiving: Westminster is the complete opposite.' Another reported that it has 'catered brilliantly' for each of her very different children. 'It's so wonderful to see these kids spark off each other.'

Has signed an agreement with Hong Kong education company HKMETG to set up a six bilingual 3-18 schools in China by 2028, with 10 per cent of places free to less affluent families, and consultancy fees contributing to the Westminster bursary fund.

Pastoral care, well-being and discipline: Tutors attached to each house oversee the academic side, whilst housemasters look after all else. One parent felt that both have too many charges to know her son well. 'I feel his well-being is my responsibility, not the school's. I don't think anyone there knows him well in the round.' Others, however, described the pastoral care as 'exceptional', and a student said, 'I have always found the school really responsive. Your housemaster is always there and will take care of everything from not feeling well to having too much work.'

Pupils expected to be proactive, motivated and organised, with very full timetables but no compulsion to take part in organised activities. 'But anything you want to try, there's some way of doing it,' said a student.

Pupils and parents: 'Lots of people said I wouldn't like Westminster,' reports the head. 'They told me the pupils were arrogant, staff unmanageable, parents difficult. None of this is true.' Westminster families undoubtedly tend to be wealthy, intellectual, metropolitan, cosmopolitan and no doubt demanding, but most parents are extremely supportive of the school. 'It is very hard to withstand this full on praise and delight.' 'I am a real believer.' 'Fantastic on every front.' And from an initial sceptic: 'I am increasingly fond of it.'

Girls entering the sixth form report a much easier ride than they might have expected. 'I had heard rumours about the boys being awful and arrogant – but they weren't,' said one. 'Some would show off in lessons to begin with, but they calmed down pretty quickly.' 'I suspect they look for a certain confidence,' said another. 'If you were insecure you might find it intimidating.' 'It was quite a shock to the system at first,' said a third, 'but we can hold our own.'

'Westminster imbues in you a sense that it is fine to talk to anyone on equal terms,' said an ex-student. 'You have a real feeling of being special.'

Parents – nearly all are Londoners, with even boarders mostly coming from within the M25 – offered a cornucopia of outings to Dulwich Picture Gallery, tours of Westminster Abbey and the Houses of Parliament, plus quiz nights, drinks parties, concerts in the Abbey, and the opportunity to attend expert lectures with their children. 'Parents very friendly and there's a good sense of community and involvement,' said one.

Old Westminsters span the centuries and the professions: the massive list ranges from Ben Jonson, John Dryden, Robert Hooke, Lord Lucan, Kim Philby, AA Milne, John Gielgud, Tony Benn, Corin Redgrave, Helena Bonham-Carter and Imogen Stubbs to Dido and Mika.

Entrance: Register by the end of year 5 for 13+ entry (boys at state primary and other schools that finish at 11 may apply to Westminster Under School). Computer pre-tests in English, maths and reasoning in year 6; high performers who also have a good report from current school called for interview, which includes short maths and English tests. Entry from 2021 onwards will not depend on passing the CE but on 'continued good conduct and academic progress at their prep school'.

For 16+ places, register between summer and October of the year before entry. Applicants – boys and girls – take exams in their four most likely A level subjects, and are interviewed.

Exit: Excellent and detailed preparation not only for Oxbridge but for American university entrance, with school trips to visit east coast universities. 'The school has been very supportive from an early age,' said a student, 'keeping us up to date with when to take subject tests and when to visit colleges.' Good preparation too for medicine, which is amongst the most popular degree subjects alongside liberal arts.

Up to half of sixth formers do, indeed, go to Oxbridge (61 in 2018, with 13 medics and others off to the US including Yale, Harvard, Stanford and Princeton), most of the rest to London universities, Edinburgh, Durham or Bristol.

Money matters: A number of means-tested bursaries of up to 100 per cent of fees available at 13+ and 16+; applicants must live in London. Bursaries also available at 11+; boys spend two years at the Under School before moving on automatically to the Great

School. Eight Queen's Scholarships awarded at 13+; recipients must board, and the scholarship covers half the boarding fee. This can be topped up by a bursary in case of need. Five exhibitions at this level. Up to eight music scholarships at 13+ worth 10 per cent of day fee and four 16+ music scholarships, plus free instrumental tuition. Four 16+ Queen's Scholarships now available for girls.

Remarks: One ex-student commented that Old Westminsters of her acquaintance have gone into a far wider range of careers than those from other schools. 'They seem to be following their passion. Westminster instils a belief that you can do whatever you want to do.'

Westminster Under School

Adrian House, 27 Vincent Square, London SW1P 2NN

020 7821 5788 | alycia.lee@westminster.org.uk | westminsterunder.org.uk

| Independent | Pupils: 280 |
| Ages: 7–13 | Fees: £19,344 pa |

Linked school: Westminster School, 239

Master: Since 2016, Mark O'Donnell, previously the head of St Martin's Ampleforth and also head of Alleyn's Junior School in south London. Educated at Stonyhurst and St Ignatius College, New South Wales, he has a masters in education from Harvard and a postgraduate diploma in education from Oxford. He is a Fellow of the Royal College of Arts, a Duke of Edinburgh assessor and an alpine ski leader. He is married with three sons.

Entrance: Academically selective (very) at 7, 8 and 11. Some successful applicants are merely 'well above the national average', about a third 'far above'. All candidates need to read fluently well beyond their chronological age and approach the unexpected logically and imaginatively. No obvious feeders, though all the usual central London pre-preps represented. At 11+, a reasonable chunk from state primaries, most of the rest from schools which end at year 6. (The school encourages entrants from 'those leaving at a natural point.') Twenty-two places at 7 (175 applying), a further 22 at 8 (175 applying), then 28 places at 11 (250 applying). At 11+, now uses computerised pre-tests in December before written exams for call-back candidates. About 40 invited at each stage for interview

and further testing. 'We want to understand each child and decide if this is the right school for them.' What makes the fit? 'The school is about passion, enthusiasm, determination and a hunger for achievement. We're looking for boys who are independent, intellectual and individual. Everybody here loves learning.'

Exit: About 90 per cent go on to the senior school (including all those who come in at 11), with a good number of scholarships, but the school is equally happy to prepare for entrance and scholarships elsewhere. About 8-10 each year to Eton (often those with family connections), some with major scholarships. Generally a couple to Winchester, and sometimes a sprinkling to City, Dulwich, Alleyn's, etc.

Remarks: Academically top of the tree. Well-qualified staff (a number with PhDs) provides teaching that is mostly strong, lively and challenging. 'We're looking for boys who will think and problem solve. We want them to work things out, not be spoon-fed.' Most boys seem to relish the offering. 'I really like all my lessons,' said one. 'The teachers are very enthusiastic and if you have a problem they just want to help,' said another.

However, the pressure to be high in the rankings comes as a shock to some.

Specialist teaching in all subjects from year 5. In English, boys are encouraged to 'develop their own voice'. Books are seminal, with even the smallest scouring the library shelves in their lunch hour. Reading lists updated termly and topped up with an in-house bookshop and regular swapshop. Weekly maths competitions hone skills both for lessons and the Intermediate and Senior Maths Challenge, where plenty achieve gold and beyond. Maths and science extension club. Programming from year 3. French throughout, taught by native speakers. Classical studies combined with Latin from year 5, stand-alone Latin from year 6, Greek in year 8. Annual Latin play competition. 'There's a real sense of intellectual endeavour,' said one parent.

Thorough monitoring, with internal exams November and June, plus mocks in the Lent term of year 8, as well as regular subject testing. Lots of rewards for achievement with cups and shields for virtually everything. 'They really ram home competition,' said one parent. Homework load significant at all levels. An hour a night in years 3-5, an hour and a half in years 7 and 8. Some parents have voiced the view that supportive homes are essential. The school says this shouldn't be necessary: 'We don't require parental support and you absolutely don't need a tutor. If you need a tutor, you shouldn't be at Westminster.' However, one parent commented that tutoring is 'rife'.

For a central London prep, notably well-endowed with playing fields, and the expansive garden square opposite the front gates provides an ample supply of pitches

New arrivals at 11 – two forms of 12-14 boys – are given Saturday morning lessons from the moment they're accepted, then segregated for lessons (but not other activities) in year 7. 'We give them lots of attention, before dividing up the whole year group into scholarship and CE forms in year 8.' Those from state primaries can find the transition taxing. 'Catching up to common entrance in two years was difficult,' said one parent. 'There was an enormous amount of work and my son found it stressful.'

Few struggle in the conventional sense, but an experienced SENCo provides support with study skills, exam technique and organisation, arranging clinics where help from peer mentors is particularly productive. Plenty of 'enhancement', too, through debating, history of art etc.

Music of an exceptionally high standard (many boys with grade 8 and beyond and plenty of music scholarships to senior schools). Head of music (also musical director of National Youth Music Theatre) oversees over 500 lessons a week, an outstanding choir and biannual music trips.

'They don't just have a Scrabble club or a chess club, they have a Scrabble competition or a chess competition'

Not everyone's idea of a sporty school, but the athletic ante has been raised recently with the addition of a number of well-qualified coaches. ('One boy attends the Chelsea football academy one day a week, but still manages his academic work.') For a central London prep, notably well-endowed with playing fields, and the expansive garden square opposite the front gates provides an ample supply of pitches and courts as well as an adventure playground. Games twice a week, with regular inter-house and inter-school tournaments in football, hockey, cricket, tennis and basketball. Recently-acquired sports hall just down the road (also able to accommodate mass gatherings of parents) offers further scope for indoor games, including judo, fencing, karate, wall climbing and nets.

Exciting theatrical tradition maintained by an 'inspirational' head of drama, with three productions annually (recent highlights include Lord of the Flies, School for Scandal) and a new performing arts centre. Art now housed in its own light and lovely double studio, with a self-contained art history library. Clubs every night (history, Mandarin, debating, etc). Chess (taught by a Grand Master) particularly popular, with 90 members and England players. Competitions galore, including hotly contested Scrabble tournament. (Some find the atmosphere slightly too competitive. 'They don't just have a Scrabble club or a chess club, they have a Scrabble competition or a chess competition.')

Plenty of external speakers and trips in London and further afield. (Recent adventures include classics to Sorrento, cricket to South Africa, geography to the Grand Canyon.) Philanthropy a core value. 'They learn to enjoy giving and love raising money for disadvantaged children.' (Parents and boys raised £45,000 last year, £18,000 in the popular Readathon.)

Founded in 1943 as a class of 17 boys located in the senior school, then decanted to Ecclestone Square, the school took up residence in its current spacious premises in Adrian House – a red-brick Victorian former hospital – in 1981. The Under

School continues to share both governors and outlook with the senior school, allowing the same careful planning over future development. A large new building, directly opposite the existing school, opened in 2013, providing a lofty dining hall and indulgent stretches of well-equipped teaching space.

Discipline not an issue. 'You don't have to shout at Westminster; we encourage good behaviour through positive behaviour management and high expectations.' Certainly, one boy unbidden held open a door, all answered questions readily and politely. Immaculate uniform, perhaps, not a priority. In PSHE, 'they learn about emotional intelligence and empathy for others. We talk about life. We want them to be able to talk with us about anything and it will be OK.'

At 7 and 8, parents primarily prime-central-London (often City) high achievers. At 11+, more diverse, with pupils coming from as far afield as Dagenham and Guildford. Plenty of bilingual, multicultural homes. Parents tend to be proud (and occasionally pushy). Boys are extremely articulate (one 8 year old, asked how he'd cope with a broken arm, responded, 'I would just have to become ambidextrous') and can undoubtedly be boffiny ('Thus, you can see,' explained one 11 year old).

No scholarships, but a few means-tested bursaries of up to 100 per cent at 11 (which take the recipient through the senior school). 'Our philosophy is that the children who can come here should not be prevented from doing so for financial reasons.'

An exciting, demanding education for the intellectual, industrious child.

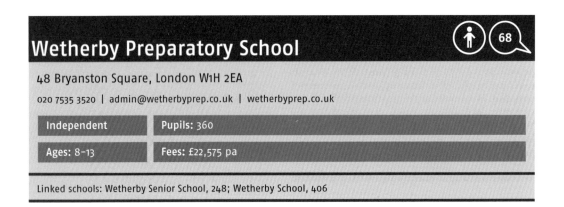

Wetherby Preparatory School

68

48 Bryanston Square, London W1H 2EA

020 7535 3520 | admin@wetherbyprep.co.uk | wetherbyprep.co.uk

Independent	Pupils: 360
Ages: 8–13	Fees: £22,575 pa

Linked schools: Wetherby Senior School, 248; Wetherby School, 406

Head: Since 2008, Nick Baker BA PGCE (early 40s). A grammar school boy, he hails from Bucks, and was educated at Dr Challoner's and University College London, where he read geography, before qualifying as a teacher at Newcastle University. He has taught geography in a range of schools, including Holloway Boys comprehensive, head of year at Borehamwood, a former state middle school, and head of geography at Chesham Prep School (where he went as a boy, is now chair of governors, and which his two sons currently attend). He has taught at Wetherby Prep since it first started in 2004, initially as a senior master before becoming deputy head, and his brief continues to expand as he has also headed the new Wetherby Senior School since it opened in September 2015.

Tall, broad-shouldered and youthful, with a reassuring laugh that echoes from his belly, Nick Baker is hugely popular, with parents, pupils and staff as well as colleagues in the wider prep school world. A keen supporter of Watford Football Club, he celebrates their victories at whole prize-giving events as well as in his blog and emails, and even

the many Chelsea supporters among the families here share in his delight and enthusiasm. Open and affable, his weekly newsletters in Wetherbuzz frequently include anecdotes about his two boys and what his family is getting up to. Hot on values and manners, one of the many 'challenges' he initiated is the Politeness Challenge. 'Much the best news is hearing that Wetherby boys are good house guests,' he says. Parents like the fact that he is so present, both around the school and at the many social events organised for teachers and parents, the Headmaster's Ball, or 'pub nights with dads', for example, as well as the Come Dine with Me event where teachers cook and wait on the parents. The adjectives that we heard most often were 'very professional', 'excellent communicator' and 'very driven and opinionated', but what is most apparent and consistent is that they trust him.

Entrance: At 8 into year 4 (when 200 sit for 40 places). Boys from the pre-prep have automatic entry. Everyone else (including from other Alpha Plus schools like Chepstow House, but apart from

Wetherby delivers what its parents demand: high quality teaching, extensive choice of activities and exceptional communication

siblings who also enter automatically) sits papers in English and maths during an assessment day at the school and also takes part in group activities.

Exit: An impressive number to top academic schools, especially considering the range of ability in each year. In 2018, four to Eton, six to St Paul's, six to to Harrow, four to Westminster. Others to eg Winchester, City of London, Charterhouse and Wellington. Around a quarter to Wetherby Senior School (nine in 2018).

Remarks: Wetherby Prep, and its brother, pre-prep Wetherby School, are currently riding high and widely regarded by parents across London as the jewel in the Alpha Plus crown. Slick as a well-oiled machine, Wetherby delivers precisely what its parents demand: high quality teaching, a broad and extensive choice of activities and sports and exceptional communication. Many of the parents are bankers and Wetherby is the prep school equivalent of a well-resourced City institution. Boys here are polite (everyone stands up when you enter a room – 'our parents like that,' says Mr Baker) but sparkling and not squashed. One occasion which captures the spirit of the school is the prize-giving assembly which takes place every Friday in the Church of Annunciation behind Marble Arch. Parents and children cram into every corner and, after singing a hymn, prizes are distributed. These can be anything from the history prize to the prize for the best joke – let alone for sporting achievements (like running the marathon). Mr Baker conducts the whole occasion with warmth and humour. He clearly knows every child well and there is a lot of boyish banter. A cauldron of competitiveness, when house points are read out there are huge whoops and cheers. These boys really care if their house is ahead – especially if it's about the amount of food waste they are managing to avoid. We also witnessed a charming joy in their peers' achievements. The best kind of competitive spirit. We were most impressed when boys not only moved aside to let us sit down but also folded and cleared our chairs for us amid the chaos of cricket bats, violins, hockey sticks and trumpets at the close of proceedings.

Situated behind Marble Arch in leafy Bryanston Square, the Georgian building is grand and spacious. The signature red painted front door welcomes you into a smart, light, high ceilinged entrance hall, complete with wood panelled, gold leaf scholarship boards and lists of head boys, prefects and house captains of the school. Boys pile past heaving musical instruments and sports equipment, looking smart but tousled in cricket gear, grey and red blazers and caps. A sweeping staircase takes traffic up the several flights, a small back staircase channels them down. All the classrooms are large, light and airy, well-equipped and organised. The basement not only houses a couple of very well-equipped science labs, a fitness suite with rowing and running machines, and the dining room, but also a pet snake which boys can stand and stare at to while away any spare minutes in their busy day. Every boy has his own red locker – no need to lug every book and file around with him the whole time. School laptops seem to be littered at strategic points around the school and are available for anyone to use. There are also 20 desktop PCs in the library, which doubles up as an ICT suite where the boys learn coding, touch-typing and animation. School has recently expanded into a new building a short distance away in Manchester Street.

Tall, broad-shouldered and youthful, with a reassuring laugh that echoes from his belly, Nick Baker is hugely popular, with parents, pupils and staff as well as colleagues in the wider prep school world. A keen supporter of Watford Football Club

From year 4, boys are setted in maths and English and have specialist subject teachers; most other subjects are setted in year 6, when they also start Latin. Three classes per year, with about 20 in each class. With automatic entry for siblings and boys from Wetherby School, alongside selective entry for others, the school is mixed ability but, Mr Baker observes, 'the academic demographic gets stronger year by year. The average CAT score used to be 112 and is now 120.' Full-time SENCo, assisted by one other person, gives support to children with mild learning difficulties, including dyslexia, dyspraxia and mild autism. Support provided ranges from touch-typing to reading groups as well as one-to-one session in maths and literacy outside the classroom. Approximately 16 in the school are getting support at any one time. Lots of prizes and rewards including a meeting with the head – the Headmaster's Good Show – to commend outstanding work. One young 9 year old told us proudly that he was 'very good friends with Mr Baker' as a result of his regular chats with him.

Sport is strong and getting better and better each year, both in terms of what is offered, the facilities and the teams' performances against other schools. The Park Club, in Acton, is now their home ground, and although some parents complain of traffic and the length of time it gets to bus them there, most were very enthusiastic about the excellent facilities, the space and the fact that they no longer need to box and cox in various places around central London. Boys play rugby and football in the winter, athletics, tennis and cricket in the summer. Their annual sports day is a major fixture in the calendar. There are plenty of other sports on offer too – hockey (including roller hockey), horse riding, fencing, rowing, rock climbing and badminton. One gets the impression that when Mr Baker goes to his Alpha Plus governors to ask that the tap be turned on (to make provision for another club, for example), it will be done. Lots of popular 'fathers and staff' fixtures too, in cricket and football.

Parents enthuse about the 'excellent' music. 'Despite the fact that my son is sporty, his favourite club is choir,' observed one father. Dynamic head of music has a modern and innovative approach. Plenty of public performances, impromptu as well as more formal. Breakfast concerts happen twice a term, there is a junior and senior school recital and a band as well as an orchestra and a chamber choir.

Art is well organised and cross-curricular. We saw lots of lino cuttings and Mac books in the art room as well as impressive pieces of work around the school. In DT they were building clocks, and there is a dark room for photography, but the 'backbone of the department is printing,' we were told. Drama could be better, Mr Baker acknowledges; some parents, more brutally, described it as 'almost non-existent.' They use the Rudolf Steiner theatre up the road for productions, 'but it's so difficult to get good drama teachers/directors,' explains the head.

Parents here are slightly more diverse than those at the pre-prep. The numerous school buses run like clockwork and depart and arrive when they are meant to, enabling many parents to entrust their boys to the school transport, so they come from as far as Islington in the north east to Hammersmith in the west. Lots of well-heeled bankers and lawyers, and a smattering of celebrities – what would you expect in this part of London? – but a refreshing mixture of cultures and backgrounds. Nick Baker's openness and inclusivity – both in the weekly Wetherbuzz newsletters as well as in his public addresses – help to contribute to a real family and community feel. An outstanding school, polished and professional, and an excellent foundation for your all-rounder son.

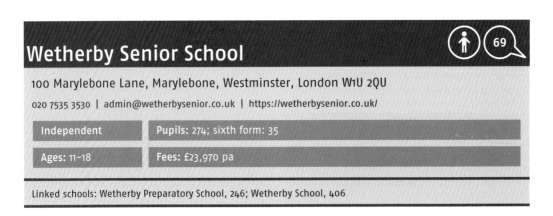

Wetherby Senior School

🧍 69

100 Marylebone Lane, Marylebone, Westminster, London W1U 2QU

020 7535 3530 | admin@wetherbysenior.co.uk | https://wetherbysenior.co.uk/

| Independent | Pupils: 274; sixth form: 35 |
| Ages: 11–18 | Fees: £23,970 pa |

Linked schools: Wetherby Preparatory School, 246; Wetherby School, 406

Head: Since September 2017, Seth Bolderow MSt BA, early 40s. Succeeded the much-loved Nick Baker who helped set up the school and ran it alongside the prep school for two years, but it was time to hand over the tiller to refocus on the prep school. Bolderow was regarded by some parents, who felt that they had bought into the 'Nick Baker ticket', with some suspicion initially. Formerly deputy head of Harrow International School in Hong Kong, Bolderow, whose name isn't the only thing that seems to have stepped out of a Thomas Hardy novel, hails from farming stock in Norfolk and was educated at Norwich school, and Exeter University where he studied classics. He was awarded a distinction for his Mst in Greek and Latin languages and literature at St Anne's College Oxford, and was sorely tempted by a life of academia. However, drawn to the camaraderie of the classroom and sports pitches, he commenced his teaching career at Blundell's, then Uppingham and King Edward's School Bath, before taking on head of sixth form at The John Lyon School and then making the move to the Far East with his girlfriend, soon to become wife. They have two young children. His proudest moment, he says, was delivering his son, less than a year old now, as there was a dearth of midwives at the time.

Quietly modest, head is authentic, a good listener and a man with a clear and defined purpose

Full of appreciation for the wider network of support and expertise afforded by the Alpha Plus group (a common theme among heads of school groups, we find). The director of schools, Jenny Stephen and the recently appointed CEO Mark Hanley-Brown get a special mention, described as having 'education pedigree'. Bolderow's functional office is warmed by evidence of his passion. Piles of Classical Loebs and ancient Greek and Latin texts line the shelves. Quietly modest and understated, he is not one to play table tennis with the boys, as his predecessor was, and he keeps a respectable distance from the parents. While one wouldn't ascribe to him an urbane charm, he is authentic, a good listener and a man with a clear and defined purpose, and has won the admiration and respect of parents and boys alike.

Academic matters: First GCSE results 71 per cent A*-A/9-7; but internal data suggests pupils make very good progress, and systems in place to track progress constantly. 'For GCSE boys', says school, 'projected grades given to boys and parents after year 10 and 11 mocks are tracked against independent baseline data (MidYIS). Using Attainment 8 as an overall measure for each boy, we are adding 0.22 of a grade on average, with 29 per cent of cohort adding more than one grade.' Almost every parent we spoke to praised the quality of the teachers and how impressive both their subject knowledge is and their understanding of the ethos of the school and commitment to it. A blend of experienced and relatively newly qualified, an equal split of men and women, they are recruited from both sectors, state and independent, and while naturally differ in style manage to combine being unpretentious with a traditional approach. 'All of our teachers are really lively,' averred the boys we spoke to.

A traditional academic curriculum includes Latin with German, French and Spanish the choice of modern languages. Native speakers and those who show a particular aptitude will be invited to take the GCSE as early as year 8. Graphic design, no DT. Practical skills are taught, the use of laser cutters etc. An esoteric part of the curriculum is that every pupil to age 16 is taught philosophy and learning skills. The head of philosophy is keen to throw everything at them, from Plato and Aristotle to Kant and Hobbes. The aim, to create independent learners who can think for themselves – qualities top universities are crying out for. Boys setted for maths from year 7 and in English and science from year 9. There are five sets for science. Beginners' sets for German and Spanish in year 9. Class sizes are small, currently 16. Judicious and sensible use of sets and there is movement up as well as down. A healthy broad range of ability when we visited, but as the school fills up, and word spreads, we suspect intake likely to become more and more academic.

A specialist SENCo but no one-to-one support in the classroom. Needs of anyone with learning difficulties are met in the classroom through differentiation. A tiny few need EAL support (about 5/225). Lucid Exact Software used to screen boys once they're here to spot any difficulties, like dyslexia. School works closely with an dducational psychologist who is brought in when there's a problem. They avoid labelling as much as possible, but Mr Bolderow said that around 25 per cent of current pupils are on the SEND register. Whatever their needs, he says, they can all manage in class without individual support.

First sixth form intake in September 2018, most moving up from year 11, with a few places for external applicants. The sixth form will grow organically – from an initial 35 – as the larger year groups move up the school.

Games, options, the arts: Traditional sports, rugby, football, cricket, tennis and athletics, with lots of competitive fixtures. Two afternoons a week are timetabled for games and they play matches against leading London secondary day schools including Latymer Upper, Westminster and Kingston Grammar as well as the top two years of the prep schools. The downside, say a number of parents, is the one hour plus round coach trip to the sports ground, which is Trailfinders in Ealing. Some wonder how much time they actually get to play when so much time is taken up travelling. Nonetheless, the U15 football team had an impressive season, reaching the quarter final of the ESFA small schools cup. They are starting to punch above their weight.

Lots of trips: 'they are always off somewhere,' remarked one parent. Nor do they waste the opportunity to take advantage of the museums and theatres on their doorstep

The director of sport, an ex-Saracens rugby player and elite RFU referee, is highly praised by colleagues and parents. A 'fantastic sportsman, he is increasingly attracting sporty boys,' say some parents we spoke to. One parent was particularly impressed by his attitude to sport and exercise. It is not just about competition and fixtures, but laying down the foundations for a healthy lifestyle and contributing to a mental health. Year 10 boys are linked to gyms and can opt for boxing, spinning etc, and there are a range of minor sports offered from fencing to basketball. Even unenthusiastic sportsman have to do one afternoon of physical activity in the sixth form – other afternoons they can do work in the community or work experience.

Drama is vibrant and everyone gets a chance to be involved. Last year they did a 'promenade' production to great acclaim, as the actors moved round parts of the school performing. This year we witnessed the dress rehearsal for an edgy play set in a prison written by the head of drama. She fizzes with excitement as every head of drama should, and the boys respond positively. Some prefer to do backstage work, whether it be costumes and make-up or lighting and set design. Productions, small and large, throughout the school year, including a Christmas Cabaret. LAMDA very popular in years 7, 8 and 9 and the teacher is in school most days

'The head of music is an inspiration,' say the boys. A French horn player, he has a fleet of colourful plastic brass instruments and with his combination of music technology and practical playing gets all the boys involved. There are already a number of groups including a wind ensemble, brass group and rock school plus DJ Buster teaches them to DJ. While the school is still relatively youthful it is hard to get the strength in depth for a whole school orchestra, although there is a chamber orchestra which will expand to full orchestra as the school grows.

Boys just about manage to play football in a tiny courtyard at the back of the Marylebone Lane building. Two common rooms with table football, and a Nintendo Wii

Art technician specialises in sculpture and this was evident in the displays. Much use is made of the kiln. We saw a variety of silkscreens, and while there is a separate art and graphic design teacher, there is much crossover in the work produced. Boys' artwork is prominently displayed in the headmaster's office and throughout the school, but there is also a lot of artwork that has not been done by the boys – perhaps to fill the space? A number of exhibitions during the school year; the younger boys exhibited their art and graphic design work at the Saatchi gallery.

Lots of trips: 'they are always off somewhere,' remarked one parent, to Croatia (geography),

Barcelona (combined Spanish and football tour), Pompeii (classics) and closer to home. Located in the heart of London, they don't waste the opportunity to take advantage of the museums and theatres on their doorstep.

Activities take place at the end of each day and are built into the timetable. As well as 'academic catch up' clubs in every subject, they can choose from a range of activities, from bridge, to cinema, scientific illustration (an example of their innovative use of cross-curricular expertise) to boxercise.

Mr Bolderow is a governor at Queen's College and already the two schools are forming alliances, whether it be social, musical, Duke of Edinburgh awards or lectures. A relationship is also developing with Francis Holland Regent's Park, so there will be lots of opportunity to experience working alongside girls.

Background and atmosphere: The last link in the chain of the formidable Wetherby schools, owned and managed by the private equity backed Alpha Plus group, Wetherby Senior School caters for the oldest boys in the group but, founded in September 2015, is the youngest school. Alpha Plus have cleverly given all their Wetherby schools the signature colours – the red and grey, evident from moment you arrive at the brightly painted red front door, to the furnishings throughout the school, and the boys in their smart uniforms – and also through each school runs an ethos of traditional boys' education blended with a modern and global outlook.

The school opened in 2015 with 67 boys in years 7 and 9. There are now over 200 and the maximum number will be 600. 'The size is an essential part of our ethos,' explains Bolderow. 'We are big enough to be able to compete, have an orchestra, field a number of different team sports, but not so big as to lose the intimacy that we value so highly.' Expectations are high, but boys can be themselves and there is no particular 'Wetherby mould' that they feel they should fit into.

Set in the heart of central London, the main site is in a surprisingly quiet corner of Marylebone Lane, tucked behind the famous haberdashery shop with its colourful array of ribbons. A Victorian mansion block, it has the benefit of being a traditional building with soul, but high ceilings, large classrooms and a sense of space. A second, newly purchased, similar five storey building, Hannah House in Manchester Street, is largely the base for the junior years, and the centre for the new sixth formers in Marylebone Lane also has space for a gym in the basement. A flow of boys make the five minute walk between buildings, as the division of use is largely by department, but timetables are designed to minimise movement for the youngest boys. The new building has a large cafeteria, signature red benches and grey tables and staff eat with the students. Sixth formers can also have lunch and snacks throughout the day in their café in the sixth form centre in Marylebone Lane.

Pastoral care, well-being and discipline: One message we received very clearly from parents is that the care taken by all the staff and their sensitive approach to the boys' welfare is remarkable. Whether a response to a particular crisis, or the general awareness of the difficulties of being a teenager in the 21st century, the school takes it seriously and responds professionally but with compassion. They will not hesitate to bring in professional counsellors for support and one mother remarked how pleased she was that her son came home buzzing from a series of talks from 'the good lad initiative'. A group of cool young men promoting 'positive masculinity'.

Boys are split into horizontal groups within their year group, known as Tributaries or 'Tribs', and assigned a tutor, who not only sees them every morning for registration but also meets with them for an hour each week. The tutor, overseen by a head of section, is responsible for the welfare of the boys in their care as well as keeping an eye on their academic progress and behaviour. The system works well, was the unanimous verdict of the parents we spoke to, and the communication between tutor and parent is invaluable.

Mr Bolderow sees a different tutor group each Friday to talk about the school. They have about 20 minutes to ask questions and make suggestions. 'This is usually about the food,' admits Bolderow. The chef here (god forbid that you should refer to her as cook) used to work at Soho House and while the food is delicious, there was a plea from the boys to tone down the sophistication of the recipes, since when baked potatoes have been back on the menu. There is a busy school council which consists of representatives from each Trib, and which reports to school in assembly.

A tiny courtyard at the back of the Marylebone Lane building makes it possible for boys to play football, and they do; there are two common rooms here complete with table football, and a Nintendo Wii. A range of lunchtime activities at Hannah House, indoor and out, as well as time in the park. Most of the boys we saw in break were staring at their 'phones, disappointing but a reflection of the age. A number of parents we spoke to would welcome a more robust approach from the school on the use of mobile phones.

Only sixth formers allowed out to lunch. We happened to see a number of younger boys filing into a local tea shop at the end of the day and were impressed by their deportment in the bustling streets of Marylebone.

Pupils and parents: Wetherby Senior couldn't be more of a reflection of its central London location. Thoroughly multicultural, one parent might be Swiss, the other Swedish. Whilst the majority of the boys are long term residents of the UK, the school is a truly global environment with boys from all over Europe as well as Russia, the Middle East and the USA. Most come from London prep schools.

The chef here used to work at Soho House and while the food is delicious, there was a plea from the boys to tone down the sophistication of the recipes

Boys we met and spoke to were refreshingly individual and polite. They look you in the eye, are confident but not arrogant. This is far from a macho culture. Boys here can be any kind of peg, and will still fit the hole.

Entrance: Academically selective at 11, 13 and 16. Tests in English and maths at 11, but school will also give equal weight to the reference from his current school and his performance at interview. For 13+ entrance all boys will sit the Common ISEB pre-test in year 6 together with an interview. Always worth checking for the occasional place. They are looking for boys who will contribute to school life and benefit from the rounded education.

Places available at 16 and an offer is made based on GCSE results.

Exit: At the time of going to press, no cohort has left the school, but all boys are prepared for university, and the expectation is that the most academic will go to the top US and UK universities. 'Staff are experienced in supporting applications to UK universities and the school will be working with US university specialists to support boys who are aiming to study further afield.'

Remarks: Wetherby Senior could not have arrived at a better time. Parents of boys will be flocking to its red door in this overheated senior school market, in which it is particularly hard to find good schools for boys. If the school continues along the trajectory it has set for itself it will only become ever more popular. A marvellous education for the modern teenage boy.

William Ellis School

Highgate Road, London NW5 1RN

020 7267 9346 | info@williamellis.camden.sch.uk | williamellis.camden.sch.uk

| State | Pupils: 850; sixth form: 207; joint sixth form with Parliament Hill School, part of LaSWAP |
| Ages: 11–18 | |

Linked school: LaSWAP Sixth Form Consortium, 153

Head: Since 2011, Sam White, chemistry graduate and previously deputy head of the London Oratory. Good news, say parents: 'He has an exceptionally good manner with boys and parents.' 'The boys like and respect him.' 'Whenever I go in I see him chatting with a boy, and he seems to be genuinely interested in them.' A pupil concurred. 'He has been really keen to get to know us all. He is a good influence on us.'

He was appointed after the school had suffered a budget deficit, got through two heads in quick succession and been slated by Ofsted. A year into his tenure, Ofsted returned and pronounced the school 'good', quoting a teacher's remark that 'The headteacher is leading and pulling everyone here along.'

He felt that he was taking on 'a challenge, but manageable... it was a school that desperately wanted to improve'. His first job was tackling behaviour – 'we needed to re-establish clear boundaries' – and his first two years saw a high rate of temporary exclusions, which has now dropped significantly. He has also continued the work on improving the quality of teaching and, despite some initial staff turnover, maintained teacher morale and encouraged staff to work collaboratively to produce good schemes of work.

Camden is one of the few areas of the country where no schools have converted to academies, and the local secondary schools (which collaborate as a joint sixth form, LaSWAP) work closely together.

Academic matters: Huge ability range, with year 7 reading ages ranging from 8 to 17. In 2018, 63 per cent of pupils got 9-4 in both English and maths at GCSE, with 15 per cent 9-7 grades. Parents report that English, once a weak point, has been turned round by the 'very impressive' HoD; the school now teaches the IGCSE English language.

The school has a language specialism, and everyone starts French in year 7, with around half studying it to GCSE. School has links with the nearby Collège Français Bilingue de Londres. Most take up either Spanish or German in year 8

(offered in alternate years), but this is no longer compulsory, and some spend extra time on English fluency instead. Latin and Mandarin are taught in clubs, and fundraising enabled a recent sixth form Mandarin and geography trip to China.

Around a quarter of boys take single sciences to GCSE. Those with a more vocational bent can take OCR science, and choose from various other courses with a large coursework element such as business studies, travel and tourism, and ICT. Some spend a day a week in years 10 and 11 at Westminster Kingsway College studying eg catering, construction or motor mechanics. New food tech facilities open on site in 2019.

'The extracurricular activities have improved markedly over the past few years,' said a parent, citing her son's sessions at the Royal College of Music, theatre and concert trips

Fluid grouping rather than setting across the curriculum from year 8 (school hopes to group maths and science from year 7 in future) at the discretion of each faculty head. 'If a set of boys has a particular weakness in a subject we may put them together for a term, but there's plenty of movement.' Some parents would prefer more rigorous setting, but praise the willingness of staff to go the extra mile for boys at all levels. 'They will take time and a lot of patience with those who are bright but not pulling their finger out. I don't feel they are just settling for the easiest way of getting them through exams.'

Parents are mostly optimistic, though one complained about a lack of homework. 'We've found the teaching really good so far,' said another. 'My son is very happy here and seems to be doing well.' 'My son, who is very academic, is being well supported,' said another. 'I had severe reservations about some of the teaching during my son's early years here,' said a long-standing parent, 'but I don't now. I've never felt I had to get a tutor in.'

> 'Whenever I've emailed to ask questions, I've had an immediate and pleased reply. They are extremely responsive to an interested/meddling parent'

Teaching assistants are increasingly being trained to help with particular subjects, or with behavioural or language difficulties, rather than being velcroed to a particular child. The school uses some of its pupil premium funding (alongside sponsorship) on its City Year team of volunteers, who act as mentors, support teachers in class, run breakfast and homework clubs and supervise in the playground. The funding also helps with small group and one-to-one teaching, particularly in English, as well as counselling and interventions to improve attendance.

Joint sixth form with Parliament Hill School, which is part of the LaSWAP consortium that also includes La Sainte Union and Acland Burghley. This enables a wide range of courses including a choice of 41 A levels, as well as BTecs, NVQs, vocationally applied subjects and post-16 GCSEs. Students stay in their base school (which for William Ellis boys will be their own school or Parliament Hill) for the majority of lessons, but may go elsewhere for minority subjects. In 2018, 15 per cent A*/A and 42 per cent A*-B grades.

As well as working with Camden to provide one-to-one careers advice, school uses Future First, set up by old Elysians, to help it keep in touch with alumni and get them involved in giving careers advice, work experience and mentoring. It organises career sessions here and brings back old boys to talk about their work.

Games, options, the arts: A large trophy on the head's table when we visited is the house cup. Houses (named after local historic buildings: Lauderdale, Burgh, Willow, Keats and Fenton) are run by 'young, enthusiastic staff'. Pupils gain house points by competing at sports and taking part in talent shows, spelling bees, chess, model building, cake sales et al.

Year 7 and year 9 have a week camping at the school's field centre, The Mill, in Surrey. Boys also go on ski trips, language exchanges and field trips. 'The extracurricular activities have improved markedly over the past few years,' said a parent, citing her son's sessions at the Royal College of Music, playwriting with professionals, theatre and concert trips, Model UN.

Football and basketball are the most popular team sports, but rugby is up and coming – the RFU provides coaching and talented players are encouraged to join local clubs. The eight table tennis tables get enthusiastic use. Takes part in the annual Camden Shield boys' competition, which sees teams from six Camden secondary schools compete in football, table tennis, basketball, badminton, athletics and cricket. Pupils report that team sports peter out in the higher years: 'The teachers do try, but we tend to get a bit lazy in years 10 and 11.' The school has a newish sports hall, with facilities for PE and basketball and a multi-gym, and the playground doubles up as five-a-side football pitches. Sadly, the school cannot afford to hire the field next door, groomed for cricket when we visited, but it does play games on other parts of Parliament Hill Fields and uses the athletics track there. Clubs include cricket, running and trampoline.

Light top floor art rooms display impressive work; a sixth former was recently a finalist in the Camden Art Competition, and students have exhibited their work at the local Lauderdale House. Some parents find the music provision underwhelming, but there are choirs, ensembles and a range of concerts for all, from beginners to advanced musicians, often in conjunction with Parliament Hill School and La Sainte Union, which form a joint orchestra with WE. There are also workshops and masterclasses run by professional musicians. The head of music 'has been very supportive of my son writing and performing his own music,' said a parent, and a school group recently reached the finals of the Roundhouse Band Slam competition. School subsidises instrumental lessons for boys on free school meals.

> Boys are confident, not arrogant. 'My son has had a very happy time,' said a parent. 'He has a sense of belonging and pride in his school'

Not a school that goes in for full-scale musicals, but has recently opened a new drama studio and there are many smaller drama performances, such as the recent drama club interpretations of the Ancient Mariner and Christmas Eve in the Trenches at the Winter Concert. Pupils work with outside organisations such as the Donmar Warehouse, and take part in the Shakespeare Schools Festival. 'They do it thoroughly and well,' said a parent.

Background and atmosphere: William Ellis was a public-spirited businessman who founded several schools in the mid-19th century, believing children should be taught 'useful' subjects such as science and to develop their reasoning faculties, rather than rote-learning religious tracts and ancient languages. William Ellis School, the only one of his schools that still exists, was founded in Gospel Oak in 1862 and recognised as a boy's secondary school in 1889. It moved to its present site, on the edge of Parliament Hill Fields, in 1937. Originally a grammar school, it turned comprehensive in 1978; the red-brick vine-clad buildings still have a grammar school feel. Brand new sixth form study centre.

'My son has had a very happy time here,' said a parent. 'He has a sense of belonging and pride in his school. It fosters a nice attitude and spirit in the boys – confident but not arrogant.'

Pastoral care, well-being and discipline: The head's tightening up on discipline and appointment of an effective head of pastoral care have helped to cut down on the low level disruption that once marred many lessons, and has made boys feel safer inside and out. 'They are much stricter on uniform than they used to be, and you no longer have to hack your way through a posse of boys smoking round the gate,' said a parent. Year 7 has its own quad, with table tennis and picnic tables. The year 7 head has links with most of the feeder primary schools, and boys are invited to summer school before they start.

William Ellis was a public–spirited businessman who founded several schools in the mid–19th century, believing children should be taught 'useful' subjects such as science and to develop their reasoning faculties, rather than rote–learning religious tracts and ancient languages

One parent commented: 'The pastoral care is very good. A few years ago I went through a difficult divorce and they were brilliant at supporting my son.' Another said, 'Whenever I've emailed to ask questions, I've had an immediate and pleased reply. They are extremely responsive to an interested/meddling parent.'

Increasing emphasis on carrots rather than sticks, with boys earning house praise points for good work and good attitudes, from persistence to creativity. 'Relationships can be much more relaxed once ground rules are established,' says the head. Deep Learning Days, part of the PHSE curriculum, see timetables dropped for a day in favour of discussions on relationships, including peer pressure and bullying, careers and the world of work, with plenty of outside speakers. 'We try to make it circular – get the boys to present back to their peers what they have learned. Recently 25 year 9 boys did a play for the rest of the school.' One parent commented on her despondency at a lack of creativity in the PHSE teaching, but another said, 'They are very good at raising the boys' social and political awareness. They don't shy away from issues that can be sensitive, such as homophobia and religion.'

Pupils and parents: Huge ethnic mix, with fewer than a third of pupils from white British background, and others ranging from Irish to Turkish to Somalian. Huge social mix too, from the large social housing estates of Gospel Oak to the multi-million pound houses of Dartmouth Park. 'There were cliques lower down the school, but in years 10 and 11 everyone hangs out together and we all get on,' said a pupil. 'The fact that the boys come from a huge range of backgrounds doesn't seem to matter one bit, which is a very impressive trick for a school to pull off,' said a parent. Old Elysians include Toby Young, Robert Elms, Sean French, Andrew Sachs and Len Deighton.

Entrance: Usual admissions criteria for 130 year 7 places: looked after children, medical and social need, siblings, up to 12 musical aptitude places, then by distance (usually up to about two miles). Generally around 300 outside places for LaSWAP sixth form consortium, with an intricate admissions system and a range of entry requirements for different levels of courses.

Exit: Most (65 per cent) to LaSWAP sixth form. Some go off to eg Camden School for Girls, Woodhouse College, St Marylebone, Fortismere or FE colleges. Around 20 per cent of LaSWAP leavers to Russell Group universities. Destinations in 2018 ranged from economics and Spanish at Reading to banking and finance at Middlesex to film practice at South Bank.

Money matters: Voluntary aided by the William Ellis and Birkbeck Schools Trust, but otherwise is as hard up as most other state schools.

Remarks: Small boys' comprehensive in idyllic situation on the borders of Hampstead Heath, now emerging rapidly from the doldrums under strong, popular and enthusiastic head. 'It can only get better and better,' said a satisfied parent.

William Tyndale Primary School

Upper Street, London, Middlesex N1 2GG

020 7226 6803 | admin@williamtyndale.islington.sch.uk | williamtyndale–islington.co.uk

State	Pupils: 450
Ages: 3–11	

Head: Since 2005, Tanya Watson BMus NPQH (50s). She was raised in America (there's still a suspicion of an accent), then trained as a concert pianist at the Royal Academy of Music. While developing her performance career, she started taking pupils, and was so taken with teaching she decided to commit full time. Undoubtedly a good decision for William Tyndale, since, over the past decade or so, she's carefully nurtured this always popular primary into one of the borough's star attractions. Articulate, organised and capable, she's at the gates every day and is widely admired. 'She's a very strong leader and provides a real sense of order and reassurance,' said one parent. 'She's both very approachable and a little bit formidable,' said another. What parents particularly respect about her, however, is her commitment to extending beyond the expected. 'She's filled my children with confidence and given them opportunities I couldn't have anticipated.'

Entrance: Parent tours held twice a year by appointment through the school office. sixty reception places allocated via Islington Council. After the usual priority categories (including siblings and the children of long-serving staff), entrance is based on distance from the gates (adjudicated by a computerised mapping system). Needless to say, you have to live very, very close (within less than 0.2 miles). The school then operates a waiting list.

Exit: To well over 20 different schools. Popular local choices include Highbury Grove, Highbury Fields, City of London Academy and Stoke Newington, but a sprinkling across the northern reaches of the capital, including to Camden School for Girls and Mossbourne Community Academy. Last year, 14 (three with scholarships) to independents, including Highgate, City of London (boys and girls), and Forest.

Remarks: From the outside William Tyndale, which recently celebrated its centenary, seems a bit of a fortress, commanding the playground and lording it over the children below. Recent additions and a carefully modernised interior have softened the tone, with an inviting streamlined entrance, spic-and-span classrooms and up-to-date facilities (including plans for improved science space).

This is a school where the phrase 'every child matters' is definitely not empty rhetoric. Teachers take time to make detailed analysis of progress and, while standards are immutable, the approach to obtaining them is often tailor made. Results – for everyone – speak for themselves, with children, whatever their background, performing well above expected (and national) standards.

Lewis class delivered fascinating facts about the author of the Narnia books, wrote its own wintry poems, did a snowflake dance

Literacy (undoubtedly a strength) is reinforced (and reinforced again) throughout the timetable. Classes named after famous children's authors (Morpurgo, Rosen, Dahl, etc) and class assemblies give plenty of opportunity to explore their namesakes. Lewis class, for example, not only delivered fascinating facts about the author of the Narnia books, but wrote its own wintry poems, did a snowflake dance, and used castles to discuss structures. Lots of learning poetry by heart, and older pupils take part in a school-wide poetry recital. Maths, too, made fun, with activities, such as the (prize-gaining) Multiplication Bee. Sky-high expectations for all, so timetabled Latin (with proper vocab tests, etc) from year 3 because the head believes 'it improves writing across the curriculum, helps pupils understand the nuts and bolts of English and provides a strong cultural base for their understanding of history.'

Other non-standard enrichment includes regular chess. 'The national curriculum can be a bit thin,' said one mother, 'but William Tyndale provides all the extra flourishes.' Dedicated librarian develops library skills. IT facilitated by iPads throughout. Recently relaunched homework strategy now targets individual needs. ('After consulting parents, the school stopped sending home those projects we all used to do. Now we get homework we know is right for our kids.') Outdoor classroom where all pupils work with the school's 'environmental educator', maintaining both a 'wildlife' and 'growing' garden (with fruit and veg contributed to school dinners).

SEND well supported – at both ends of the spectrum. Three specialists help with reading recovery ('Fantastic,' said a beneficiary) and other challenges. Extra tuition provided before school and during breaks so 'everyone has fair access'. One of the top performing schools in the country, too, for boosting the performance of disadvantaged pupils.

William Tyndale is a school where curricular and extracurricular do not operate in separate spheres. Art is 'exceptional', 'inspirational', 'really wonderful, chorused parents. The school has its own art block and artist in residence, and juniors study art for two hours a week and work with external arts organisations (Stamped Arts, Cubitt Artists) on large-scale projects, such as the chronological history of the school which lines the stairs. Pupils can also gain an Arts Award Explore qualification, by participating in arts activities (for example, the school's Film Club), attending arts events and keeping a portfolio. Understandably, the school has gained an Arts Council Artsmark Gold award.

Music, too, exceptionally strong, with weekly, specialist-taught music lessons in the dedicated music studio. Free recorder lessons for all in year 3, and Hackney Music Hub provides tutors in African dance and drumming in year 4 and samba in year 5. Instrumental lessons (recorder, flute, cello, brass, clarinet) also available. School orchestra plus two choirs (infant and juniors), with regular opportunities to perform in school (musical assemblies, shows, concerts) and outside (Pure Voice, Hackney Music Festival). School won a Sing Up gold award in 2016, and head undoubtedly brings her own expertise to bear. 'After a concert, she will pick out and discuss various themes,' said a parent.

Sport dynamic. Dance, gymnastics, cricket and rounders all on offer, with expert coaches imported for lessons and clubs. ('My daughter was taught by coaches from Arsenal, which she absolutely loved.') Swimming lessons at Highbury Pool. A rare primary school with a third-generation floodlit football pitch (available for hire to aid school's coffers), in constant use for lunch-hour sporting activities and inter-school competitions (mini Olympics, netball and football tournaments). Keen competitors in the Islington Primary School Football League (with both girls' and boys' teams highly successful), and in local hockey matches (with co-ed team), tag rugby and athletics tournaments.

Comprehensive programme of London visits (Geffrye Museum, Museum of London, Central Mosque etc), and extensive range of clubs (sports, music, creative writing, book club etc) with debating club notably strong. (Pupils recently won the London Primary Debate Mate Cup, confronting such knotty questions as: 'This house believes that people should break the law to save the environment', and 'This house believes that children should be paid for good exam results'.)

The school has its own art block and artist in residence, and juniors study art for two hours a week and work with external arts organisations on large-scale projects

School is relaxed and informal, but not slack. No uniform and reasonably scruffy end-of-day look, but no question of come-as-you-please, so no jewellery, nail varnish or hair dye (to prevent jealousy). Masses of positive reinforcement for pupils (with awards for attendance and punctuality) and praise for parents (for making sure kids stay off playground equipment after school). Parents encouraged, too, to talk to teachers about concerns as they arise rather than bottle it all up until parents' evening. Draconian measures, however, for late pick up from (privately run) after-school club. (£20 fine, which increases by £1 a minute per child.) Atmosphere widely praised by all. 'It's a lovely community, very friendly, very disciplined,' said one father. 'It's very uncompetitive, and children are encouraged to help each other. I just don't worry about the children once they've gone in. I feel they're in very good hands.'

Parents a broad mix, so the expected chattering-class professionals (overheard in the playground: 'I forgot your smoothie, have you got a banana?'), but also 35 per cent on pupil premium, and wide ethnic range. Dads unusually well represented at after-school collection.

Parents here are well organised and generous. The William Tyndale Charitable Trust was set up to raise funds for school improvement, and has helped finance significant capital projects, including the new performance stage and sports pitch (£5,000), playground equipment (£10,000) and stairwell art project (£6,000). Regular money-raising events include the quiz night, summer fair and weekly cake sales.

Parents overwhelmingly delighted with William Tyndale. 'I feel so lucky. It's completely brilliant. I can't praise it highly enough.'

Central West

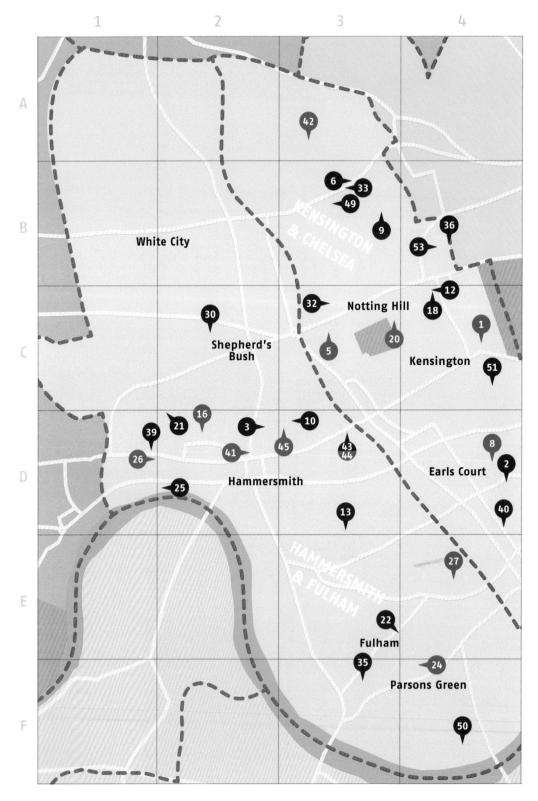

1

2

3

4

A

42

6
33
49

9

36
53

B

White City

12
32
Notting Hill
18

30

1

Shepherd's
Bush

5
20

Kensington

51

16
21
10

C

39

3

43
44

8

26

41
45

2

25

Hammersmith

Earls Court

40

D

13

27

HAMMERSMITH
& FULHAM

E

22

Fulham

35

24

Parsons Green

50

F

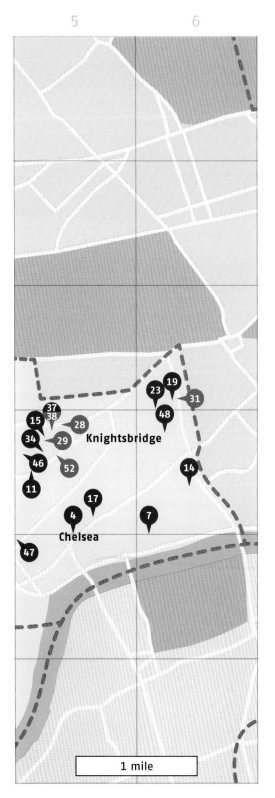

5   6

1 **C4** Ashbourne Independent School   267

2 **D4** Bousfield Primary School   269

3 **D2** Bute House Preparatory School for Girls   271

4 **D5** Cameron House School   274

5 **C3** The Cardinal Vaughan Memorial School   275

6 **B3** Chepstow House School   279

7 **D6** Christ Church Primary School Chelsea   281

8 **D4** Collingham College   284

9 **B3** Colville Primary School   289

10 **D3** École Française Jacques Prévert   292

11 **D5** Falkner House   294

12 **C4** Fox Primary School   296

13 **D3** Fulham Prep School   299

14 **D6** Garden House School   302

15 **D5** Glendower Prep School   304

16 **D2** Godolphin & Latymer   306

17 **D5** The Hampshire School, Chelsea   308

18 **C4** Hawkesdown House   310

19 **C6** Hill House International School   314

20 **C3** Holland Park School   316

21 **D2** John Betts Primary School   321

22 **E3** Kensington Prep School   323

23 **C6** Knightsbridge School   325

24 **F4** Lady Margaret School   327

25 **D2** Latymer Prep School   331

26 **D1** Latymer Upper School   333

27 **E4** The London Oratory School   336

28 **D5** Lycée Français Charles de Gaulle   340

29 **D5** Mander Portman Woodward (MPW)   345

30 **C2** Miles Coverdale Primary School   348

31 **C6** More House School (London)   350

32 **C3** Norland Place School   354

33 **B3** Notting Hill Preparatory School   357

34 **D5** Our Lady of Victories RC Primary School   359

35 **F3** Parsons Green Prep School   360

36 **B4** Pembridge Hall School   362

Central West London and its state schools

Hammersmith and Fulham

A long borough that travels from north to south, albeit with numerous bus routes linking the two ends. Just west of Chelsea, this is a hard borough to pin down, with Fulham's pockets of large mansion flats near the river and Victorian terraced houses within sound of gentle thwonk of tennis balls at the Queens Club – cheek by jowl with council housing and some fairly mean streets. But some of the harder areas are on an upward trend, particularly near the recently gentrified Fulham Broadway and in Hammersmith with bustling King Street, ever improving pubs and new development spreading out from the huge Westfield shopping centre.

A high percentage of children used to attend secondary schools outside the borough, but the arrival in 2011 of two very different schools, and in 2014 a third, has changed the face of secondary school provision here. The Hammersmith Academy had a wobbly start in the face of the sudden and fierce competition from the much publicised and surprisingly popular West London Free School. The latter with its public-school-like stipulation that Latin be learnt by all and that boys play hockey and rugby, not football, was a London middle class magnet. The WLFS's GCSE results have so far not fallen short of expectation. The Hammersmith Academy is modelled on the highly successful Thomas Telford Academy in the Midlands. It has three hour lessons conducted in its splendid circular premises between the Goldhawk and Uxbridge Roads, and the Mercers (the Guild that is behind St Paul's boys and girls, among others) as sponsors.

At the other end of the borough, Fulham Boys has made an impressive start since it opened in 2014. Still waiting to move into permanent premises near Fulham Broadway (now scheduled for 2019/2020), its dynamic Welsh headmaster with his passion for a single sex boys' education (as well as Welsh rugby) has impressed both the boys and their parents.

An emphasis on excellence in everything from academics to sport combine with a strong pastoral approach. However its zero tolerance attitude to discipline ignites mutterings about pettiness, and patchy progress among pupils, particularly those in the lower sets, is causing unhappiness among some. A C of E school, it operates 'fair banding' and has 50 per cent faith places.

Burlington Danes Academy, towards North Kensington, is one of the Ark academies, with the associated financial and expert support that comes with that. With a focus on maths and the performing arts, the school has become a serious contender – results are good and becoming better, and Ofsted judges it to be outstanding across the board. Phoenix Canberra, in Shepherds Bush, benefitted enormously from the tight control and charismatic headship of Sir William Atkinson. While he has gone now academic performance remains reasonably steady with some improvement. A good choice of vocational subjects as well as academic but probably not the place to sit A levels.

Sacred Heart High qv in Hammersmith is a reason for parents of girls to convert to Catholicism and choose a local Catholic primary school (siblings are quite low on the priority list).

In the south of the borough, Fulham Cross Boys' School (once called Henry Compton) and Fulham College Girls' School (both 11-16 years) are now in federation with the new Fulham Enterprise Studio. This is a vocational studio school for 14-19 year olds, specialising in construction and performing arts (production).

Lady Margaret qv in Parsons Green, an all-girls, Church of England school with over 50 per cent church-goer places, feels more like Wycombe Abbey than a London comprehensive. This end of the borough is also home to the highly prestigious London Oratory qv – the holy grail for Catholic parents with sons. Boys are accepted from across London, the admission requirements stringent, but the lucky parents who have succeeded in jumping through those precarious hoops (including Blairs and Cleggs) are satisfied customers.

Popular primary schools include John Betts qv, traditional and small, lots of parents opining that it reminds them of their own primary school, Brackenbury, Greenside and the West London Free School primary school, with automatic entry to the senior school a definite pull for parents. Burlington Danes Primary, part of the Ark MAT, and a feeder for the secondary school, opened in 2015 and all the signs are that it will perform as impressively as its sister school, The Ark Conway Primary School, in the far north of the borough. The latter is in a relatively deprived area on the borders of East Acton, but in a splendidly characterful building (the old library).

There is a plethora of good church schools, most notably the outstanding St Stephen's on the Uxbridge Road which sends large numbers to Twyford C of E qv high school in Acton as well as the West London Free School (its founder's children go there) and the eternally popular St Peter's in the leafy Hammersmith square of that name off King Street. For the Catholics, Larmenier & Sacred Heart in Brook Green and The Good Shepherd off Askew Road feed boys to Cardinal Vaughan and the London Oratory, girls to the ever outstanding Sacred Heart.

Kensington and Chelsea

The Royal Borough of Kensington and Chelsea is one of London's smallest boroughs geographically and yet one of the most densely populated areas in Europe. It includes Holland Park, the area named for the eponymous park, which features leafy streets and some of the largest detached and semi-detached houses in London. Notting Hill of Hugh Grant fame is home to the Portobello Market and hosts the largest annual street party and carnival in Europe, held over the August bank holiday weekend.

The borough houses some of London's wealthiest as well as its poorest. Half the residents educate their children privately, half of the state school pupils receive free school meals, and half of the borough's children go to secondary school in another borough. It is also, on DfE statistics, the best performing area in England for GCSE results.

Of the six mainstream secondaries only Holland Park qv and the relatively young Kensington Aldridge Academy (started in 2014 near Ladbroke Grove), are community schools. Holland Park is rated outstanding and is hideously oversubscribed, but gives up to 10 per cent of places to students who show an 'aptitude in art and design'. Kensington Aldridge, also judged outstanding by Ofsted, operates its sixth form jointly with Charterhouse and Godolphin & Latymer.

The rest have a religious requirement as part of the admissions process. Three are Catholic: St Thomas More (co-ed) in SW3, Sion-Manning (girls) in North Kensington and Cardinal Vaughan qv (boys) in Holland Park. Co-ed Chelsea Academy (Fulham) is C of E (50 per cent faith and 50 per cent open places with some preference for children from K&C primary schools).

Cardinal Vaughan is responsible for weighting some of these figures. A school with consistently high results, a rigorous attention to the more challenging subjects and tight discipline, it is the number one choice of school for the children of a number of prominent political figures.

Fox qv, with its tiny catchment tightly focused primarily on and around Kensington Church Street, is a very vibrant and a reliable primary school choice. Half of the 27 primary schools are either Catholic or C of E. St Barnabas and St Philips and St Mary Abbots – the latter attracting leading lights in parliament – are perhaps the most coveted. Further south towards Chelsea, the Oratory is a popular choice for Catholics and Christ Church qv for the Anglicans. If you're not religious and live close to a salubrious area that incorporates, inter alia, The Boltons, then Bousfield qv is likely to be your primary school of choice. Other less well known schools that have a good reputation in the (slightly) darker corners of the borough include Barlby and Thomas Jones qv. Kensington Primary Academy, an offshoot of the West London Free School in Hammersmith, opened its new premises on Warwick Road W14 in 2016.

Hill House International School

Ashbourne Independent School

17 Old Court Place, London W8 4PL

020 7937 3858 | admin@ashbournecollege.co.uk | ashbournecollege.co.uk

Independent	Pupils: 275; sixth form: 253
Ages: 14–19	Fees: £24,750 – £26,250 pa

Principal: Since 1981, Michael (Mike) Kirby BApSc MSC (60s), who founded the college. Mr Kirby read aerospace engineering in Toronto (he retains a soft Canadian burr) and Birkbeck where he did a masters in statistics. Very tall, laconic and seemingly inscrutable, but a warmth and a smile escape him occasionally and the man is momentarily revealed. After 32 years, unsurprisingly, he and his school mirror each other. Focused and clear-sighted, he has made a place where little distracts from work but where the work ethic is underpinned by the sense of support felt by the students. His involvement with the students is integral to the day-to-day running but the touch is light. 'I know a lot of them personally – they can be a bit wide-eyed and innocent but they're just nice kids and they're great fun.' He still teaches maths revision classes – as ever, we applaud – and, unlike many in his position, sees the students very much in their own home context. 'We positively encourage parents to get involved.'

Prominent member of CIFE (the Conference for Independent Further Education) and the British Council Education Counselling Service, he is the owner and proprietor of Ashbourne. This and the length of his tenure make him unique. He is keen that Ashbourne be recognised as a 'bona fide part of the independent school system', hence his resolve not to be the first resort for resit students – though they do come in penny numbers. He launched and continues to steer a pretty effective school.

Academic matters: Most students come for the two-year A level course, although one year and 18 month A level programmes also on offer – these popular with, mostly, overseas students. In 2018 A level results were 49 per cent A*/A, 75 per cent A*-B. Separate classes for students who want to improve their grades – a growing trend. However, students who significantly underperform – having been warned that they are in danger of doing so – are shown the door. No embarrassment at this – 'We filter,' says Mr Kirby. 'That's how we get the results'.

Small middle school offers two year (years 10 and 11) and one year (year 11) GCSE programmes

but up to date exam results not readily available, so do ask searching questions.

At A level, 37 subjects on offer and all taught in small classes – seven is average, 10 is max and even ones and twos for some subjects. Maths much the most popular subject and with the most impressive results – tend to be mostly A*-B. Similarly with further maths. The sciences also taken by many – again with, generally, a decent crop of results. We witnessed one Eng lit class – all girls. Languages holding up well and business here, as everywhere, gaining a more mixed bunch of results. Unsurprisingly, no Latin, no Greek. All language teachers are native speakers. Lunchtime critical theory seminar much-praised and very popular: 'It's way beyond the A level syllabus so you learn about Marx and Freud and feminism and then apply the theories to film and literature. I learned so much from doing it that way,' an A2 student enthused. All lessons are two hours long. Teachers much praised for their enthusiasm and care. Many are long-serving.

Very tall, laconic and seemingly inscrutable, but a warmth and a smile escape him occasionally

Few SEN students with anything other than mild dyslexia/dycalculia/ADHD and neither building any good for those with mobility difficulties. No SENCo though SEN overseen by affable head of middle school. Mr Kirby says: 'The school is happy to accept those with SEN but makes no special provision beyond arrangements for exams.' A few here have extra exam time, a laptop in exams or a scribe.

Games, options, the arts: Some variance between the college, which claims to offer 'a very wide extracurricular programme', and the students, some of whom seem to know little about it – mostly, apparently, the Brits who don't live locally. However, much enthusiasm from those who do partake and especially from those who have gone on overseas subject-related trips with the college. We are told that the college has now appointed an officer who is specifically responsible for student activities and for ensuring that everyone knows about them.

Art is legendary here and the art room – where we were glad to see some mess – was full of concentrating artists and makers of textiles when we visited. Lots of colour and art seemingly derived from diverse influences. College runs a choir but no orchestra/ensembles. Lots of societies – held in lunchtime and after college; good college newspaper written by students. No sport to speak of and some join gyms etc (there's one next door) but, as everyone agreed, it's the price you pay. Very popular Christmas Revue in which virtually all take part – local fringe theatres are hired for these and other performance events.

Background and atmosphere: Principally in two buildings, separated by Ken High Street. Old Building (in Old Court Place) is tucked down a side road – helpfully guarded by two policemen holding rifles (actually outside the Israeli Consulate) – and so discreet, it's very easily missed. Most sixth form classes take place here. Young Street Building in – you couldn't make it up – Young Street opposite houses the middle school and the rest of the sixth form classes including a huge art room – by far the biggest of the school's rooms. Internally, both buildings are pristine – white walls relieved by stylish and undistracting prints and some larger artwork made on site. Plain carpet, bare wood stairs. Sofas only in one common room and the two staff rooms which are as severely workful as the rest of the establishment. There's nowhere to doss, nowhere to hide. You come here, you work. If you want to mess about, you go out. And they do. Ken High Street, the park, cafés and shops – it's all on the doorstep and, if the inside of the school is cramped, up close London is huge, spacious and full of things to do. Students would welcome kitchen space – somewhere to warm up lunch brought from home (daily eating out is expensive) – but every inch counts here and the common rooms are small. Lockers only for GCSE, art and photography students.

School has recently bought the upper floor of a period building at 47 Kensington Court, which provides, alongside extra classrooms, a new dedicated drama space with elegant top-lighting.

Can accommodate up to 250 students. Teaching rooms are definitely small. Interactive whiteboards in use everywhere and computers everywhere too. The library is all Macs and the shelves have text books and uni guides. Good music room – again, all tech, as far as we could see though there is, apparently, a piano and a guitar. Good film/media room and photography studio has dark room. A

> There's nowhere to doss, nowhere to hide. You come here, you work. If you want to mess about, you go out. And they do. Ken High Street, the park, cafés and shops – it's all on the doorstep. London is huge, spacious and full of things to do

pervasive air of relaxed purposefulness. And a fantastic location.

Pastoral care, well-being and discipline: The parents we spoke to paid tribute to the excellence of home-school communications and this is true equally of local or UK-based families and the overseas ones. Few such colleges offer the community feel and nurturing to be found here – strengthened by everyone being on first name terms and easy exchanges of emails between parents and staff. Staff room doors are glazed and usually open – little sense of 'them and us'. Everyone has a personal tutor – the same throughout their time – 20 tutees to a tutor. This is not the place if all you want is processing to achieve results. The staff gain much praise for being on top of their game educationally but also for 'really caring' and being very approachable. Drug use would lead to immediate expulsion but this sanction very rarely used. Probably not your first shot if you've been ejected elsewhere.

Pupils and parents: Students come from state and independent schools in the UK, as well as from private schools abroad. Around half the students from around 40 different countries – the rest from the UK. Fewer Chinese than hitherto – more now from Vietnam and Malaysia but college recruits from Russia, Botswana, Ukraine and Kazakhstan and elsewhere. All students have to speak good English and must speak English during the school day – even when with compatriots. About 40 per cent of the students have dedicated English-language classes (no extra cost) – up to six per week – however, best not to choose Ashbourne if you need substantial EAL reinforcement. Of the UK students, around third to a half from the state sector. No boarding though college has halls shared with other educational bodies close by and in Hampstead. Some international students' families find their own more local accommodation. Slightly more girls than boys overall and girls vastly outnumber boys in the humanities. Students here don't look like rebels, dropouts or rejects but wholesome and focused – much as at any academic, independent school's sixth form. All relish the social mix and the internationalism. Students on bursaries complement the loaded with no discernible difference. 'It's a bit cliquey,' we were told, 'especially if you're not into smoking and drinking,' but that's what they do at this age – it's part of being a teenager and drugs seem not to feature here, unlike elsewhere. The principal notes that Ashbourne appeals particularly to 'pupils from good local girls' independents who want something different at A level'.

Entrance: January and September intakes makes for flexibility and a great help to those who need time to regroup after, perhaps, mind-numbing GCSE results. Entry via interview – telephone or face-to-face with either principal or director of studies plus a subject-related entrance test. Auditions for drama/music applicants and portfolio for those who wish to pursue fine art – in which the college has a distinguished tradition. Also, most recent school report/grades/predictions and a personal statement. At least 6s at GCSE expected for entry to A level courses – though some flexibility. International students must have minimum 5.5 IELTS or equivalent.

Exit: To a diverse list of colleges and universities – London universities figure prominently, along with eg Edinburgh University. Three to Oxbridge and one medic in 2018. Courses taken mostly point to solid professions and vocations. Many ultimately into law and finance but this is no mere spawning ground for the suited professions. Creatives include artist and photographer Marion Sosa, fashion designer Chau Nguyen, actors Calum Witney and Vicky Pasion, and the writer Dane Weatherman (founder of the literary periodical Black and Blue).

Money matters: Some bursarial help for students of exceptional ability, especially in drama, art and music, which offer a very few full scholarships. Candidates assessed on the basis of academic and (where relevant) performance or artistic ability. Also a rigorous, wide-ranging interview.

Remarks: Solid, reliable and effective place to study. Not for socialites, smack-heads or slackers.

Bousfield Primary School

South Bolton Gardens, Old Brompton Road, London SW5 0DJ

020 7373 6544 | info@bousfield.rbkc.sch.uk | bousfieldprimaryschool.co.uk

State	Pupils: 430
Ages: 3–11	

Headteacher: Since 2014, Helen Swain BEd MA, deputy head for last eight years. Has been in teaching for 26 years and joined Bousfield as a year 6 teacher some 20 years ago.

Entrance: Due to cuts in funding there are now 60 part-time places in the nursery on offer, rather than the previous 30 full-time places. Two parallel classes from reception to year 6, each with 30 pupils. Applications for the nursery are done through the school; applications to the main school are done via Royal Borough of Kensington and Chelsea.

No automatic transfer from the nursery to the main school – parents must reapply. Children who are in care or have an SEN statement/EHC plan are considered first, followed by siblings and then proximity to school (currently approximately 0.5 of a mile and shrinking). Distance measured as the crow flies. Places do become available further up the school, due to high mobility rates of pupils, so worth persevering. Hugely oversubscribed. As one current parent put it: 'If you get offered a place here, you'd be mad to turn it down.'

Exit: Most popular secondary schools are: Holland Park, Chelsea Academy, Lady Margaret's, Fulham Boys' School, St Thomas More Language College, Ursuline High School and Cardinal Vaughan Memorial School. Over a third go on to independent senior schools, including Latymer, City of London, The Harrodian, Putney High and Francis Holland. No special preparation given for those doing 11+ exams. School knows a large amount of tutoring probably goes on, but says pupils get plenty of exam practice anyway. Much parental advice and support given when it comes to choosing next school.

Remarks: Strikingly international, with 41 different first languages currently spoken at home. Sixty per cent have English as an additional language. After English, the most prominent languages are French and Arabic. School sees this cosmopolitan element as a real strength and the high level of harmony being something to celebrate. A significant number arrive with very limited English. It is 'sink or swim, but usually swim.' Much language teaching on offer, including Italian classes laid on by the Italian Consulate and French to all KS2 pupils. Bilingual pupils tend to outperform monolingual ones. Much coming and going due to large expat intake. Lots of French families have departed recently due to job losses in the City. Only about half the class in year 6 have been there from reception.

Superb academic results, particularly given the huge EAL contingent, though school always looking to 'up the ante.' English, maths and science Sats results well above national average. There are plans afoot to introduce some setting for maths and reading in year 6, though lack of space means separating children into groups is a challenge. Pupils' progress is tracked carefully.

When we visited, children were beautifully behaved and all engaged. A sense of calm pervaded the school. Manners and presentation clearly high on the agenda. No uniform. Packed lunch or school lunch. Fruit given to the younger years, funded by government school fruit and vegetable scheme.

When we visited, children were beautifully behaved and all engaged. A sense of calm pervaded the school. Manners and presentation high on the agenda

One full-time teacher and one teaching assistant in each class, as well as extra support staff for pupils with statements and EAL pupils in the early stages of learning English. A great team of dedicated staff, who 'put the hours in.' Many loyal, long-serving teachers (20 members of staff have been there more than 10 years), as well as newer ones. A strong team – 'no prima donnas.'

Bright, vivid displays throughout the school. Some classrooms smallish; every iota of space used. School is a 1950s listed building, with courtyards and coloured panels, which makes expansion and development problematic. Beatrix Potter was born and brought up in a house on the site.

Arts are very strong in the school, though not at the expense of academics. Lots of music, dance and drama going on. School believes performance helps to build children's self-esteem. Pupils are offered a rich curriculum, full of workshops, plays and concerts. More than 90 learn a musical instrument. Guitar and strings ensembles, two choirs but no orchestra. Parents attend practice workshops so they know what a good music practice at home should involve.

Artist Quentin Blake pops in regularly. All leavers receive a prize at the final assembly and Blake says his spirits are raised as each leaver is celebrated

Plenty of sport – gym and games as well as after-school clubs offering tennis, football, cricket and even cheerleading. Swimming for years 3 and 4. Pupils take part in borough events (including athletics) in the summer term.

Quantity of homework has been reduced – parents were completing too much of the pupils' project work ('you can always spot the hand of a parent,' we were told) and copious amounts were being downloaded unthinkingly from the internet. Homework now more focused on the basics, with reading, spelling and maths given from early on.

Some children with SEN EHC plans. More on the SEN register, receiving support of some kind. No specially trained teachers but school feels they have strategies and experience to help those in need. Has experience of pupils with Asperger's syndrome, autism, ADHD, emotional/behavioural difficulties and moderate/severe learning difficulties, as well as dyslexia, dyspraxia and hearing and visual impairment. School is not a centre of excellence for all of these – very occasionally pupils move to special schools, either when Bousfield can no longer adequately support them or when they move to secondary school. Staff say Bousfield is 'an inclusive school' that does its best to accommodate those with difficulties.

Strong parental involvement, with school questionnaires showing overwhelming parental support and high levels of satisfaction. Numerous opportunities for parents to attend curriculum workshops and 'book looks' (when they visit to look at children's books). Parents welcomed in at the beginning of the day.

Some wrap-around care available, albeit not all on-site. Breakfast club on offer and pupils can be escorted to a neighbouring school (with more provision) at the end of the day if required.

Bousfield has close connections with artist Quentin Blake, who attends prize-givings and pops in regularly. All leavers receive a prize at the final assembly and Blake says his spirits are raised as each leaver is celebrated. 'After the ceremony, I go away feeling that at this point in their lives perhaps they really have all won,' he adds.

A great sense of purpose permeates this thriving school, with pupils bright-eyed and focused, offered a lively, dynamic and interesting education. As one satisfied parent lamented: 'I just wish it could go on into secondary school.'

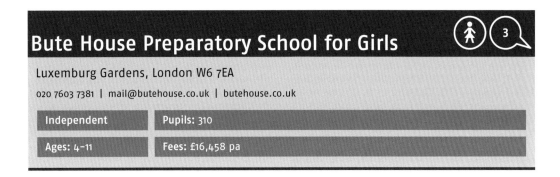

Bute House Preparatory School for Girls

Luxemburg Gardens, London W6 7EA

020 7603 7381 | mail@butehouse.co.uk | butehouse.co.uk

Independent	Pupils: 310
Ages: 4–11	Fees: £16,458 pa

Head: Since 2012, Helen Lowe (50s), BA Oxford Brookes, LGSM Guildhall School of Music and Drama. Married to Phil, whom she met at drama school. They have two grown up children. Having 'got acting out of my system' she started her teaching career in big Essex comprehensives, where she taught drama. She is verging on the evangelical about the profoundly positive benefits a background in drama can have – 'everyone should go to drama school because it's all about people and understanding other people's point of view'. She then went on to teach at primary schools in Richmond and became the literacy consultant for the whole of the borough. Her experience in the independent sector includes being a drama teacher at St Paul's Girls' in the 1990s, curriculum coordinator at Lady Eleanor Holles junior department and head of juniors at King's House in Richmond, where she taught for three years. Bute House is her first 'stand alone' headship, ending the 20 year tenure of the formidable Sallie Salvidant.

Bright and bubbly, Mrs Lowe likes to make an impact. Never one to be seen without her pink lipstick, snazzy glasses and white blonde hair well coiffed. Her confident manner ('I'm very bossy,' she admits with a twinkle) could be overbearing were it not delivered with such warmth and humour. Parents remark on her enthusiasm and ability to make changes without a fuss. Good changes, that few had even noticed were needed – a whole school Christmas celebration at a local church for example. 'I am a great communicator,' she says. Parents agree. She holds open house individual appointment sessions where parents can discuss any of their concerns about the school. She not only puts her point across impressively but listens too. What's more, the parents listen to her, even when it might be news they don't enjoy hearing – that

their daughter won't suit a school they have set their hearts on, for example.

She knows the girls properly, and by the time the 11+ process kicks in, she is well-equipped to write their reports for senior schools and advise the parents on the best school for each one, having taught all girls in their second half of year 5 and first half of year 6. 'I have the best interests of the child at heart,' she avers. This may not always coincide with pleasing the parents but it doesn't faze her. When it comes to decisions about boarding school, however, she is sensitive to the fact that this is a decision that affects the whole family, not just the girl. A refreshingly modern and human touch from a prep school that sends a fair few to the top girls' boarding schools.

Entrance: There are two entrance points: reception – a one form entry where 22 places are allotted by ballot (after taking into account siblings, which could mean that the number is easily halved), and year 3, when girls are selected after sitting the 7+ exam (in the January of year 2). About 400 girls are entered into the ballot, two years before entrance, which is then scrupulously and rigorously drawn – by the chair of governors, with the head, the bursar, the school secretary and a lawyer in attendance. No question of rigging, and absolutely no point in ensuring that little Emily can recite her 10 times table.

For year 3, about 200 register for 38 places. Assessments in English, maths and non-verbal reasoning are carried out in a relaxed way along with various activities which focus on team work and social interaction. The girls are carefully observed by a number of teachers and Mrs Lowe said, 'hand on heart', they weren't just looking for the most academically able and – don't choke on your skinny flat white – they have turned down girls despite

271

their marks being among the highest. They are looking for girls who respond well to learning, with a positive and enthusiastic attitude. This is a school determined to maintain its mixed ability, academically non-competitive ethos (this and the ballot were the two non-negotiables in her interview, Mrs Lowe tells us).

No sibling preference at 7+ assessment, but school 'looks very carefully at sisters'. Occasional places thereafter are competed for by test, and the school has a waiting list for each year. Girls come from the local boroughs and as far as Barnes, Ealing, Kew, Putney, Wimbledon and north London. Vast diversity of backgrounds; the US and Asian contingent is fairly significant and a number are bilingual in combinations of French/Mandarin/Italian/German, to name but a few.

She not only puts her point across impressively but listens too. What's more, the parents listen to her, even when it might be news they don't enjoy hearing

Exit: Majority go to St Paul's, then Godolphin & Latymer and Francis Holland SW. Even if they don't go there, these are the schools to which most parents aspire. The rest either usually board (though none in 2018) – Wycombe Abbey, Downe House, St Swithun's favourites – or go to other all girls' day schools eg Putney High, Lady Eleanor Holles. Recently greater interest among parents in co-ed – Latymer Upper is becoming increasingly popular. Interestingly, around the same proportion of those who enter at 4+ as those who come at 7+ go on to the most academic schools. Bute girls trail scholarships: 36 in 2018. Nine in music.

Remarks: One can be forgiven for thinking that this is the prep school for St Paul's Girls' School; it used to be years ago, but hasn't been since the 1950s, and it's a dangerous mistake to make. Although Bute is lucky enough to share the St Paul's swimming pool and some games pitches, and is only a stone's throw away, it is an entirely separate and distinct institution. You may have won the jackpot to get your daughter in here, in that she will have a fabulous education during her early years, but you haven't been granted a stepping stone into the hallowed halls of St Paul's Girls. There are no friendly ears to be bent. Iris will have as great a chance of getting in there from any of the good London preps as she does from Bute House.

An outstanding prep school, Bute House manages to combine solid substance with flair and panache. There is lots going on: the academics are excellent despite – or probably because of – its non-competitive ethos, but this is one of the most passionately competitive about sports of any of the girls' day schools we have seen. In the classroom, however, there is no setting, streaming or ranking, and marking is all done by comment: 'That's what contributes to the girls being so good and kind to each other – and makes it such an amazingly warm, happy and friendly place,' comments Mrs Lowe.

Learning support is known as 'learning enrichment' here – SEN and G&T girls occasionally removed from their lesson in order that their learning be 'enriched'. The head of the learning enrichment department is a SEN specialist, as are the other members of staff who both support those girls needing extra help and extend the more able girls. Teachers from the LED work in class alongside class teachers as well as sometimes taking groups of girls out of the classroom. The teaching is clearly, for the most part, inspired, and this is true of the learning enrichment programme too. Fifty-two girls are on the LE register, many needing only minimal support. This support is free. Those who don't speak English at home have one weekly support session. Some see the SENCo on a one-to-one basis and some in small groups. Ninety on the G&T register. School says that any difficulties are diagnosed early and dealt with as soon as possible.

We detected some sensitivity around the issue of special needs. The school says that it 'makes it clear in its parents' contract that girls with specific learning difficulties who need a great deal of additional support may be encouraged to look for another school that can meet their needs better'. School is keen to point out, however, that a dynamic SEN teacher coupled with a change in priority and ethos from the top means that everyone here gets the attention they need. However, there does appear to be some tension between the non-competitive academic ethos and the fact that ultimately this is an academic school with parents who have academic aspirations. Mrs Lowe asserts that early identification of any issues should enable all the girls to achieve highly, and she is especially keen to ensure that every girl achieves to the best of her ability. She says she also looks carefully at the transition from year 2 to 3, since this can cause anxiety for parents who perceive that the new intake may well be more academically able, and the flood of new girls will result in their daughter becoming 'lost'. The strong non-competitive academic ethos comes as a shock to a lot of parents who are attracted to the idea of Bute House as a top prep school with a history of a relationship with St Paul's – often in competitive professions themselves, they find themselves feeling frustrated not knowing whether Molly is top of the class or not.

This is perhaps the most colourful school we know – everywhere are displays, pictures and models, all bursting with vitality, wit and fun

Any competitive instincts can find an outlet in the sports programme, however. Bute girls are known in the prep school world to be formidable netball players and there is a D team as well as an A so everyone should get a chance to play. Some mutterings among mothers that this is not the case – but we suspect that the kudos of playing in the A team is such that both daughter and parents aspire to that. Gymnastics is also very popular and of a high standard. Although gym squad, run by external coaches, is only for the most talented, school says that those not in the squad have plenty of opportunity to be involved in gymnastics. Excellent sports facilities, especially considering its inner urban site, with use of St Paul's pool next door, and swimming is strong – plenty of squads and galas so that everyone gets a chance. Mrs Lowe attributes the excellent team spirit among the girls to the lack of competition in the classroom.

An innovative head of drama has been injecting some exploratory imaginative work into the drama curriculum; the class we saw were all lying on the floor with their feet in their air waving their arms. Head of music also young and energetic – a benign 'Jack Black school of rock' type, he arranges lots of different groups, bands and orchestras ('smiley strings', 'string fever', 'jammy jazzers' to name a few). Girls have class music twice a week from reception through to year 6 and most learn at least one instrument, from the double bass through to the bassoon.

Rich curriculum – everyone does French from reception, Spanish from year 5 but no Latin at all. Specialist teaching from reception in drama, music, sport and art (and DT) as well as French. Specialist science teaching from year 4 and proper DT facilities – saws, work benches, as well as a well-equipped art room – first class and unusual in a London prep school. Huge superbly-equipped science lab and lots of outside space – netball courts as well as playgrounds, comfortable sitting areas and plenty of greenery. Every floor has stairwell storage for laptops, which are available for the girls to use when needed. Excellent library, well-stocked, well-organised (there are two librarians) and most importantly well-used. Lots of music rooms for lessons and practice. All the girls do one drama performance once a year. The show at the end of year 6 is a highlight, with a recent production being Annie.

The Bute building itself is a surprise – a somewhat futuristic 1950s neo-greenhouse farrago with add-ons in pine, pink render, louvred glass and warm-toned brickwork in a quiet Victorian terraced street just off fashionable Brook Green, five minutes from the Hammersmith jungle. It has a splendid atrium with the reception and offices and big screens with the news of the day, timetable changes etc; even the day's birthdays – rather nice. One eye catching and charming tradition is the corridor outside the hall, the walls of which are covered by little ceramic tiles, each one made by a Bute pupil as a record of their time at the school. The school, thereafter, in the head's words, 'is a bit of a Tardis' and one is not prepared by the hotch-potch exterior for the spaciousness – of each classroom, the immense hall and outside space as well as of the airiness and uncluttered feel of the whole.

Bute girls are known in the prep school world to be formidable netball players and there is a D team as well as an A so everyone should get a chance to play

The classrooms are a feast. Reception is big and there is plenty of space for everyone at the little tables and around the many activities. Everything is beautifully laid out – pencils in pots, a discovery table with 'new life in spring' exhibits – most remarkable – a canopied and cushioned book corner and lots of lovely dressing-up stuff including some pretty cool shoes. All the children use the garden, complete with lots of climbing things and a real – not a bouncy – castle and sandpit. Reception children have their own times when they also use large wheely toys. This is perhaps the most colourful school we know – everywhere are displays, pictures and models – all bursting with vitality, wit and fun. Many rooms, including the hall, are flexible, and divisible into two. All classrooms have smartboards and, oh joy! – all are air-conditioned. The girls eat in one half of the hall and drool over the food. 'It's just the best'..'it's cooked to perfection!' Free cucumber and carrot wedges are served at break and there are water-fountains inside and outside school.

If your daughter is lucky enough to get a place here she will have stimulating and exciting time, making good friends and building excellent foundations for her future. Your aspirations and ambitions need to be tempered, however; the school she ends up going to next will be right for her, but it may not necessarily be the one you had in mind when you set out on this odyssey.

Cameron House School

4 The Vale, London SW3 6AH

020 7352 4040 | info@cameronhouseschool.org | cameronhouseschool.org

Independent	Pupils: 119
Ages: 4–11	Fees: £18,465 pa

Headmistress: Since April 2018, Dina Mallett, previously head of Cumnor House School for Girls for two years. She spent eight years as deputy head of City of London Girls' Prep and nine years at Dulwich Prep London.

Entrance: All children are assessed at 3, so no need to rush to get your baby onto a list; register up till a year before entry. A popular school – over 200 applicants for 20 places and school acknowledges how difficult it is to choose – 'It's heartbreaking to reject anyone.' Ultimately they look to create a class with a balance of the confident and the shy and some happily in between. They work closely with nurseries and rely on their reports (children come from a wide range including Pippa Poppins, Paint Pots, and Miss Daisy's). Putting school down as a genuine first choice always helps.

Exit: A few boys at 7+ or 8+ to, eg, boarding or Catholic schools (Ludgrove, St Philip's), but school actively discourages year 3 leavers so fewer and fewer now. School has fine tuned the 'stepping stones' options for boys who want to do 13+ common entrance and sends them for two years at 11 to, eg, Newton Prep, Fulham Prep, Sussex House, Wetherby or the Hampshire School Chelsea. Lots of advice given to parents from year 5 onwards.

At 11 girls and boys go to a broad range of schools each year – current favourites include St Paul's, Godolphin & Latymer, Westminster Under, Wycombe Abbey, Francis Holland, City of London and Alleyn's. They nearly always get their first choice school, we're told (due in large part to school's determination that parents choose the school that suits their child, whatever they themselves might prefer). 'And they interview beautifully because they're so confident.'

Remarks: A tiny (one class per year of about 20), cosy, pretty school, but don't be misled into thinking it's just chocolate boxy – Cameron House is a serious player in getting children into sought-after London schools. Wide range of ability, but what all

children have in common is that they are confident and very, very smiley.

They are given a lot of preparation in the final year. In year 6, class sizes shrink so everyone gets more attention, compulsory homework club gives all children an extra hour at school and removes the pressure from the parents. 'We shoulder the worry, and the last thing we want is to see 10 year olds being counselled for stress.' A lot of staff channelled into year 6, when they do group work, prepare for scholarships, have mock interviews and confidence-building workshops. The formula clearly works – they get results, but no-one could describe this as a hothouse.

Approximately 15 children are helped with mild to moderate SEN – dyspraxia, dyscalculia, dysgraphia etc. The school takes a holistic approach. Learning support is timetabled and structured with clear IEPs drawn up – parents pay extra. Programme for the gifted and talented run within the class. In addition a select few are invited to join the Discovery Club and Explorers Club. Cautious approach to the gifted and talented programme. Children are identified towards the end of year 1 – 'We wouldn't want to have to say, "You weren't gifted after all!"'

Children have fun here, whether it's enjoying music, drama or sport, watching caterpillars transmorph into butterflies or playing giant magnetic chess in the playground

A town house with not a great deal of space, but the soft plush tartan carpet throughout the stairwell, lavatories with pretty wallpaper, water filters, attractive blue furnishings and every teacher referred to by their first names – without even a Miss or Mister attached – give the school a homely, uninstitutional feel.

Children have fun here, whether it's enjoying music, drama or sport, watching caterpillars transmorph into butterflies or playing giant magnetic chess in the playground (a good excuse to see the lovely Dina, to get the chess pieces). Even maths can be made to be an excuse to dress up and laugh – Bubbles the maths clown visited, the hall was filled with balloons and children came to school dressed as shapes. In Book Week everyone dresses up.

Nearly everyone plays an instrument or has singing lessons – the lessons happen in a little Wendy house type hut in the playground. Major dramatic productions – The Lion King, A Midsummer Night's Dream among them – take place in a closely guarded secret venue – 'Let's just say a theatre off Kensington High Street,' is as far as school will be drawn. 'We aim high' – list of impressive artistic accomplishments for such a small school includes getting to the final for young choir of the year at the Royal Festival Hall. They have an orchestra, string quartet and three choirs.

One of school's challenges has been to stop the boys leaving at 7+ or 8+ – signs of success. Although previous year 6 classes have had few boys, some none at all, when we visited there were an equal number of both sexes. 'Parents are starting to realise that they can get their boys into Westminster Under, St Paul's Juniors or Latymer at 11, and there are plenty of stepping stone options between 11 and 13.' Children are kept a lot more active here than at many similar schools. Games takes place three times a week – children can do cricket, football, hockey and netball as well as martial arts in the huge loft space at the Boudokwai centre. Lots of matches (most of which they lose, commented one parent) but the advantage of being a small school is everyone gets to have a go – it's not just the sporty types who do everything.

A lot of expat families, mainly from the US, Canada and Australia, reflecting the cosmopolitan area. We saw masses of glamorous long-haired mothers off to the gym after drop off. Lots of City types, but also more than the usual number of creatives – artists and actors, as well as doctors and art dealers. All parents are very involved and enjoy the open door policy of the school.

A charming school that will discover your child's strengths, nurture and support them.

The Cardinal Vaughan Memorial School 👤👫 (RC) (5)

89 Addison Road, London W14 8BZ

020 7603 8478 | mail@cvms.co.uk | cvms.co.uk

State	Pupils: 964; sixth form: 357 (152 girls)
Ages: 11–18	

Headmaster: Since 2011, Paul Stubbings MA. Educated at Worcester Grammar school and Durham University, where he read classics. His conversation is littered with his experiences of 'damascene' moments – his love of Latin and Greek, his vocational calling to become a teacher. One wonders (though he didn't say it) whether it was a similar enlightened moment that drove him to fight for the headship and steer the school away from the dangerous rocks of conflict between the Westminster diocese and a section of the governing board. He certainly stepped into the breach when horns were locked over a tussle between whether the school should be a 'pan London Catholic school' or whether priority should be given to local residents of the borough. He was promoted from deputy head, pastoral – aka the enforcer, and feared by many in the role. He refers to himself in that incarnation as 'the chief chastiser – good at scaring kids, but not nastily'. One former parent described him at this time as a sergeant major, famous for issuing multiple detentions as snowballs flew on one of those rare fun-filled winter days. A smooth negotiator is certainly not the role one would immediately assume for him, but since he has taken the reins the school has been running without much jolting, and both parents and staff are delighted. He is completely 'home grown', and has taught here in various roles since his teaching practice placement in 1988. He officially started as a classics teacher in 1989 and still teaches Latin to year 7.

Since morphing into the top man, he sees himself as more of an avuncular figure to the students and confesses that he misses the ongoing day-to-day bustle. However, he embraces having to articulate the direction of the school and describes his vision as the replication of qualities of Cardinal Vaughan himself – namely his energy and foresightedness, firmly rooted in a Catholic foundation. He regards the school as embodying the best of tradition and 'the old', whether is be the traditional hierarchy or the gowns the teachers still wear. 'The only times hierarchies don't work,' he says, 'is when they cease to be benevolent'. However, he acknowledges that change cannot be avoided: 'I have to row this school forward in order for it to stay the same'.

As we left his large modern study, he with a flourish of his gown, two boys were waiting outside whom he confided he was about to exclude. The lines here are straight and inflexible, and if you cross them you can be in no doubt of the consequences.

Academic matters: Consistently impressive results and school makes no bones about aiming for academic excellence in its comprehensive intake. Sunday Times continues to rate it as the highest attaining comprehensive school in the country. School has specialist status in mathematics and IT and computing is BIG here – computer science is now part of the curriculum – an innovation that puts paid to the any suspicion that the school might be stuck in the past. A level results 78 per cent A*-B grades, 51 per cent A*/A in 2018. Range of subjects offered not immense but includes economics, music tech, Latin, philosophy and sociology. It has to be said that the 'newer' subjects do not attract vast numbers. School also offers applied A level in business – Bs for most. Most popular – and successful – A level subjects are maths and Eng lit, both astonishingly good. GCSEs: again not a huge range of options – French and Spanish now the only modern langs, though Latin thrives and Greek is available at GCSE. Most popular subjects are engineering – a double qualification – French and ICT. Everyone takes RS. In 2018, 55 per cent 9-7 grades overall. And remember, this is a comprehensive school.

This degree of success is not achieved by having independent school sized classes. In the lower school class sizes are 28-30, though music, DT, art and IT groups have 20 pupils. At KS4, class sizes vary but core subjects are taught in groups of 25-30. Most sixth form classes are under 20. Girls and boys seem to achieve similarly though there are some mutterings about sixth formers being 'encouraged' to drop subjects rather than continuing to A level if it is felt they are unlikely to do well. Accolades abound – the Vaughan is in the top 20 of just about every league table, often near the top. It is regularly named 'top Catholic comp in the country' by those who have such plaudits to give away. Parents and pupils, for the most part, add to the encomia. No-one could eulogise the school's shiny new facilities – apart from all the IT stuff – or accommodation. The level of achievement here is down to

Consistently impressive results and school makes no bones about aiming for academic excellence in its comprehensive intake

the quality of the teaching and the staff and pupils' pride in the place. We heard of 'lovely teachers', the good monitoring of progress and much high praise, especially of the music dept. Bright pupils speak warmly of their 'inspiring' teachers – 'they are amazing – best in the business' – and they mean it.

All applicants are tested – to ensure that school takes across the ability range and to better enable banding once they arrive. School takes 'more than our fair share of children with an EHC plan' and it is a beacon of hope for those parents of children with significant difficulties, seeming, as it does, to offer real education in a compassionate community. Majority with SEN, though, are mild dyslexics and dyspraxics. Who goes where is decided, of course, by the LA but school is concerned about the sheer additional physical space taken by extra LSAs who accompany some of the children with more severe SEN. And this is understandable. Many rooms are small and rather poky and corridors are not spacious. Busy SENCo and others give in-class support but parents give mixed reports. One parent felt that her dyspraxic son's problems were picked up very late and that the support he was subsequently offered was barely adequate. Similar reports from others. School, however, tells us that such comments are 'vastly outweighed by parents delighted with our SEN arrangements'. School unashamed of its high octane essence. 'Here we have traditional, hothouse academic teaching. It can be a bit of a shock for those who come in from outside.' G&T pupils offered Greek – where else in the state system is this a growth area?

Games, options, the arts: Despite having to travel for 30 minutes on a bus (to Twickenham) for rugby and football, these sports are not only popular but also strong. Vaughan teams are not to be messed with and are widely respected by their competitors in West London. The first XI recently won the cup in the QPR league, the second XI, no slouches either, won the shield. Athletics and cricket in the summer. Fixtures on Saturday mornings, though if you get a detention you are in danger of being dropped from the team – no leeway there. There is also a gymnasium on site in the 1990s extension known as the Pellegrini building, painted in bright blues and turquoises; the well-known 'boys at games' fragrance welcomed us as we observed a volleyball game. Rock climbing, basketball, table tennis also on offer. Girls in the sixth form can play netball, and some do rock climbing.

Several parents referred to a divide in the school between the 'sporty' and the 'musical' side. Music is certainly as keenly practised, respected and given an equal, if not even greater status as sport, and we were very impressed both with the sumptuous musical facilities and the array of opportunities for performance. When we visited there was great excitement as the head of music rushed in to show Mr Stubbings an article in the Financial Times about a carol composed by one of their 15 year olds and performed on Radio 3. Large practice rooms and smart rooms for performance. There are several grand pianos for simple practice, you understand, and a plethora of choirs from the elite Schola Cantorum – replete with claret-coloured cassocks and leather-bound hymn sheets, providing music for the school's liturgies – to the sixth form choir and the school choir. As well as a full orchestra, chamber orchestra and various trios, there is the hugely busy Big Band that performs in concerts and events all over London.

Various venues are used for concerts including the Albert Hall, Cadogan Hall, St John Smith Square and Westminster Cathedral. The Schola goes on regular tours outside the UK, including Italy – all the grandest places in Rome – plus Spain, Greece, Holland, Germany, the USA and France. The Schola now has its own Songschool – just like in a regular cathedral choir school – in which the choir rehearses; a real boon. Those with a talent for singing also get the opportunity to sing in operas at the Royal Opera House as well as the ENO; recent productions have included La Bohème, Die Zauberflöte and Carmen. More light hearted musical productions take place in the summer – Guys and Dolls, Sweeney Todd, The Pyjama Game, to name a few. Other than the annual musical there is little drama to speak of – never a strength here and not an academic subject. School's original main building began life as a theatre and we wondered why so little use is made of it in this way – the stage and gallery are intact, if a little dog-eared. Good art: we liked what we saw of the ceramics, sculpture, mobiles, printing et al – lively creative stuff – and equally good DT: wood, metal and plastic work. Three workshops and lots of benches means there is plenty of room to work and create. Engineering and graphics popular at GCSE – this is where lots of that work takes place. Plenty of imaginative and rewarding extracurricular trips and visits – especially for the musicians; parents glow.

Background and atmosphere: The Vaughan is located in posh Holland Park – wide, quiet streets lined by well-appointed Victorian villas and mansion blocks. Shepherd's Bush, on the other side of the monster roundabout round the corner, is a

world away, whereas Kensington High Street – about 15 minutes walk the other way – seems a natural neighbour. Founded in 1914, the school is a memorial to the third Archbishop of Westminster, Herbert, Cardinal Vaughan. It began life as an independent school with 29 pupils but became a grammar school in 1944 and a comprehensive in 1977. Girls were first admitted to the sixth form in 1980 and their presence is firmly established. They are not just a token presence, either – the ratio is 60 boys to 40 girls, which is significantly higher than their cousin school in the neighbouring borough. No chance of going co-ed throughout – simply no room. The original building – Addison Hall, which Mr Stubbings affectionately refers to as Hogwarts – was a musical theatre, but its exterior – possibly what attracted its purchasers – is more reminiscent of a Rinascimento palazzo in pink stone. It now boasts an entrance with highly-wrought grillwork in which the school's motto, Amare et Servire, and crest are displayed. The Old Building, as it is known, houses years 11-13. The New Building was built in the 1960s and much added to since then. It has an attractive exterior with a pretty little garden and an impressive reception area, which abuts the main hall – full of pupils on supervised private study when we visited – no 'free' periods here. DT and IT are housed in the Pellegrini Building, named after a former head. Some roomy places inside but the overall impression is of a rather cramped school with little space – especially outside – and many rather bleak areas.

The original building was a musical theatre, but its exterior – possibly what attracted its purchasers – is more reminiscent of a Rinascimento palazzo in pinkstone

Situated in these leafy, pricey avenues, you'd expect an upmarket local school population. But it isn't so. School takes from all over, some travel from as far as the northern reaches of Barnet, Harrow and Hillingdon, others from the furthest reaches of Southwark, Merton and Kingston. The only common denominator is a commitment to the Roman Catholic faith. Previous head was wearily, but pugnaciously, defensive of the charge of being socially or academically elitist. He wrote, 'people ask why our pupils' performance goes so far beyond national averages. After all, our top results at A level and at GCSE, over the last five years, have improved six times more than national results. Is it because, as some would like to believe, we "cherry pick" pupils from privileged backgrounds? I don't think so.' Mr Stubbings, too, is often accused of running an elitist school, with only some eight per cent of pupils on free school meals (against 21 per cent in the local authority as a whole). His retort? Selection is random.

We saw lots of Vaughan pupils out and about and they definitely do not frighten the horses. 'Old-fashioned good manners' expected and, in general, displayed

The life of the school is imbued with its Roman Catholic inspiration. Everywhere are photographs of pontiffs, cathedrals and the school's own choir singing in various glorious cathedrals. Year groups go on retreats at Tyburn Convent and at Farm Street and the school day and week are punctuated by regular mass, confession, Benedictus, Angelus and so on – all lessons begin and end with the Sign of the Cross and some teachers have prayers in each of their lessons – to a degree rare even in RC schools. But there is also a spirit of enquiry. Vaughan pupils address seriously 'the Dawkins delusion', 'the problem of free will' and 'the just war theory'. Philosophy pupils attend Heythrop College for talks on philosophy of religion, epistemology and ethics, and theology pupils explore the history of Israel. The ethos is embraced and warmly defended by pupils when appropriate. They are aware of the privilege of being here and of the secular – and other – pressures that might have it otherwise. While most parents express great satisfaction with the school in general, we heard a few murmurs from those who are less than ecstatic. 'It's fine as long as all goes well'.. 'they're not brilliant at dealing with problems'.. 'they're not great at getting back to you' (school says, 'we pride ourselves on excellent communications with parents and prompt responses to their queries') and 'it's best for the really bright'. School warmly disputes this too. And most are truly grateful for what they receive.

Pastoral care, well-being and discipline: Discipline couldn't be much tighter. The boundaries are clear and few transgress. Immediate expulsion for 'supply' of drugs – sharing them with a friend; fixed term exclusion for possession. 'We don't have a drug problem in this school because they know the score,' asserts Mr Stubbings. The senior sixth former who was our guide was so concerned with punctuality that he didn't allow us to admire the work in the art room. The atmosphere is orderly and you could hear a pin drop walking through the corridors during lesson time, despite the open doors into the class rooms. Occasional bullying is 'firmly and speedily dealt with'. The occasional idiot caught smoking in the streets – sixth form pupils are allowed out of school in breaks – is punished. 'If they're in my uniform it'll be exclusion,' says Mr Stubbings. We saw lots of Vaughan pupils out and about and they definitely do not frighten the horses. 'Old-fashioned good manners' expected and, in general, displayed. Catholic ethos underpins everything and is palpable. Sex ed taught 'by the RS dept for the moral side and the science dept for the biological details'. Four houses – Campion, Fisher, Mayne and More.

Pupils and parents: Pupils come from a wide area covering most of London, some from as far away as Hertfordshire and Surrey. Around half are from ethnic minority groups. Some 30 per cent speak English as an additional language. Here the offspring of a few of the well-heeled 'old' RC families from Kensington learn alongside those of their Filipino, Portuguese or Spanish live-in domestic staff and the children of Irish immigrants from Wembley, in a context hard to find elsewhere. Parents very appreciative of parents' evenings when teachers come to find them rather than the usual ghastly queuing for a two minute slot with a glazed-eyed teacher. Notable former pupils include actors Richard Greene – Robin Hood in earlier days – and Roger Delgado, footballers Bernard Joy of Arsenal and Fulham and the last amateur to represent the England national football team, Paul Parker, Kevin Gallen of QPR and Eddie Newton, novelist Helen Oyeyemi and comedian Dominic Holland. Also WWII flying aces Donald Garland VC and Paddy Finucane DSO and recent Olympic rowing gold medallists Martin Cross and Gary Herbert. Many seem, however, to have careers in the City.

Entrance: Pupils come from over 50 schools. Around 830 apply for the 120 places at 11+. At sixth form, around four apply for every place. Most of the sixth form entrants will be girls – lots from Sacred Heart – and the entrance requirements at that stage are primarily academic, although they do have to have been baptised and a priest has to attest to mass attendance – 9-6s at GCSE in the subjects they will study in the sixth. School has long been (in)famous for the rigour of its admissions' criteria and stories abound of devoted little church-goers being rejected on account of imperfect catechism or knowledge of parables. 'Nonsense!' bellows school. Early baptism (within six months of birth), weekly attendance at mass, holy communion – all are taken for granted in applicants; no mention now of the 'family involvement' that was so contentious. Applicants split into three ability bands, 12 music places. School uses 'random allocator' for the 70 or so places that remain after priority places have been taken (Catholic children in care, siblings etc).

Exit: A regular mighty handful to Oxbridge (14 in 2018), all doing solid subjects at real colleges. Most of the rest to heavyweight universities to do heavyweight subjects – law at King's, maths at Imperial etc plus medics and vets – and a sensible fistful to eg sports psychology at Bournemouth. A notable number to architecture and engineering. Some 10 per cent leave after GCSEs – most to join other schools, a few to employment, another few to other RC colleges.

Money matters: School asks for a voluntary contribution for the Governors' Fund and the vast majority stumps up – some more, some less, but no-one comes after you if you don't. A few instrumental bursaries for sixth form entrants who must have reached at least grade 6 on an orchestral instrument.

Remarks: Some see the Vaughan as a 'quasi grammar school' and its cousin in Fulham as a 'quasi public school'. Whatever label you attach to it, our view is that it is the kind of school many parents in London are crying out out for but few, very few, ever find. A unique opportunity if you are lucky enough to qualify, however it won't suit all boys. Be sure your son is someone who responds to rigorous discipline and doesn't flake (or rebel) under stern authority.

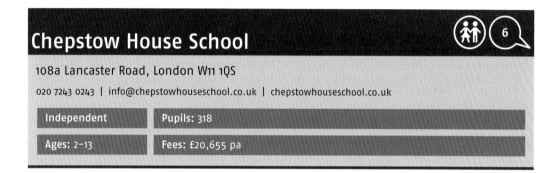

Chepstow House School

108a Lancaster Road, London W11 1QS

020 7243 0243 | info@chepstowhouseschool.co.uk | chepstowhouseschool.co.uk

Independent	Pupils: 318
Ages: 2–13	Fees: £20,655 pa

Headteacher: Since 2010, Angela Barr BA Ed (50s). Has been head since school started. Previously head of the lower school at Pembridge Hall, another Alpha Plus school. Studied geography and education at Christchurch College, Kent University and then taught in a state school in Essex before taking off and travelling around Africa for a year, with her husband Simon. 'I loved school and always wanted to be a teacher,' she says with passion.

Marked her 50th birthday celebration with another trip to Africa (Namibia) with her husband – this youthful, warm and attractive head is a spirited and independent character who lives for the moment and is all about the 'doing now.' Indeed, it's not often we come across a head who has zip-wired across the Thames to raise money for charity. One parent told us: 'She really is up for anything.' Another said: 'It was truly amazing and helped raise some much needed money towards the Evelina Trust at St Thomas's. It shows the sort of head she is.'

Teaching, she says, is her hobby – 'I love it so much it doesn't feel like a job' – and she is by all accounts a very hands on head who personally supports youngest pupils with their reading. 'I am a big believer in getting children reading,' she says. Also works hard to make sure her staff are teaching with all the different learning styles in mind – 'essential in a co-educational school.' Parents have told us she is on the front gate to greet pupils every single morning, and knows every child by name and even their siblings: 'It gives a really personal element to the school and helps the younger ones settle in.' 'Firm but fair' we are told, and whilst she is open to new ideas and welcomes feedback from parents, 'she also won't be led by them, however influential and high powered they are.'

Still ambitious for the school as 'it's still growing' and, more importantly, 2018 saw the first set of (very creditable) 11+ results.

Entrance: Non-selective, so it's a case of registration at or as soon as possible after birth (embryonic stages even better). Current cost £150 – non-refundable if you don't get a place. School allots five definite places a month, and tries to stagger them among children born at the beginning, middle and end of the month, so no advantage in booking your Caesarean for the first of September. Attempts are made to keep an even number of boys and girls and those who drop out are replaced like with like, as far as possible, from the waiting list. That way they don't get a surfeit of, say, boys born in August. Priority given to siblings. The school now includes

Little Chepstow Nursery which can accommodate 40 children, all of whom will be guaranteed a place at the school if they have spent the full two years there. Chepstow House is expanding gradually to year 8 by 2019, with entry points at 7, 8 and 11.

Exit: Pupils can now stay on until 13, with first year 6 leavers off to eg Francis Holland NW1, South Hampstead, St James Girls, St Paul's, City Boys, KCS Wimbledon. As a result most pupils now continue through, although there is a handful whose parents still opt for the 7+ to gain entrance to schools such as Wetherby, where competition is possibly less rife than at 11+. One parent told us: 'It's a shame Chepstow House doesn't go on until 18.' (We couldn't help feeling that there is no pleasing some.) Those staying on to 13 have applied for schools ranging from Eton to Canford to Wetherby Senior to Westminster.

Remarks: Born into the now well-established stable of Alpha Plus Group schools, this nearly fully matured school has much to live up to – no doubt in part due to the huge demand there is for good schools around the sophisticated area of Notting Hill. However, so far the school has risen to meet that demand with style. It moved to its stunning new home on Lancaster Road in 2014 (bang opposite its rival Notting Hill Prep), into a building formerly known as the Isaac Newton Centre. Tucked away from the hubbub of the Westway, the impressive black wrought gates are the only giveaway that there may be a school around. On entering what looks more like a portcullis than a gated entrance to a school, followed by a short walk through a tunnel, one arrives at the bright, glass-fronted reception.

Chepstow House is built all on one level..but what a level. The corridors are endless. With red carpet throughout, it feels more like a large, glamorous chalet, than any school we've been to. A very shiny and exquisitely maintained school, where even the teachers – blonde, long limbed, healthy – look as though they have stepped out of their own teachers' version of Tatler (we felt decidedly old and washed out). Children, too, look enchanting in their quaint red berets and jackets, girls in tartan pinafores, boys in red tank tops and grey shorts (some parents worry about their sons getting cold knees in the winter – although they can graduate to corduroy trousers from year 4 upwards).

It does feel very moneyed, but not pretentiously so, quite understated but with a few eye-catching facilities. We particularly liked the main hall (which also doubles up as the dining area and performance space) – and is designed with a semi-circular upper level, which parents can stand on and look down to watch their children perform. 'A bit Shakespearean', one parent said. Colourful

A spirited character who lives for the moment and has zip-wired across the Thames to raise money for charity

mosaics of various animals adorn the walls, 'which most of the children have helped to make.' We were also struck by the imagination of many of the teachers, particularly in the gloriously colourful art room, with an assortment of interesting objects dangling from the ceiling or on the walls. The art teacher was enthusiastically describing her latest art project, which involved recyclables, at the time.

Another thing that caught our eye (and the first time we'd seen this in any school we've been to) was a very realistic looking fully clothed 'dead body' in the science lab, with an exact replica of a cordoned off area as a murder scene (even down to the windows with No Entry tape strips across). The science teacher – who clearly has a great sense of humour – told us that it was the pupils' job to find out how he died, by carrying out a series of forensic investigations. Genius and imaginative, we thought. The drama room, too, was an interesting space with the ceiling swathed in colourful Moroccan-style chiffon material. Much thought had gone into the aesthetics of the school, evidently.

Classes named after birds (get to year 6, and you make Eagle status). With a teacher and teaching assistant in each class the children get lots of support and attention. French and music start from reception. Three sets for maths in year 2 and lots of differentiation in the lower years. Maths Whizz, used from year 3, is a programme which individualises each child's maths programme 'to stop anyone falling through the net.'

Each child has the use of an iPad – technology skills are learned on the job as well as in a separate lesson devoted to IT. We saw children as young as 4 year using iPads in the nursery. Any learning difficulties are identified quickly, says head. School sets high standards for reading and writing, and tracks development and progress in-house with a reading test as well as SEN assessment. One parent told us that her child is severely dyslexic, and needs a lot of extra support: 'Chepstow House picked up on this really quickly and were really on top of it.' This was echoed by other parents in similar situations.

The sense of purpose is palpable. During our visit, children were focused and interested in their lessons. We were amazed by the quality of writing from children as young as year 1. Gone was the giant, looping, large-spaced scrawl we often see from 5 and 6 year olds, instead replaced by neat, legible writing kept between the lines. 'We spend a lot of time working on both their gross motor skills and fine motor skills. We even do magic spells with them, where they learn to pick up things with small tweezers.'

Music is vibrant and the pupils are introduced to a number of different genres. A number of pupils have violin, guitar or piano lessons taught by peripatetic teachers. Sport has also been taken up a notch since the school has grown and Chepstow competes successfully with other local independent schools. It's also very inclusive: there is an A and a B team for most fixtures, and everyone has the chance to compete. Sport is on site from reception to year 2 – from year 3 upwards they go off site for sports such as football, cricket and hockey as well as regular swimming and access to a climbing wall. 'I love the sport here; boys get to do netball and girls get to do football,' said one happy pupil. Lots of extracurricular, too, from fencing, dance and martial arts to Spanish, coding club and even skateboarding.

Ofsted was glowing in its report and the only minor thing criticism was the need for some sort of external covered area for pupils to play in all weathers. This has been addressed, and indeed the outside play areas are some of the nicest we've seen in a city school in terms of space and facilities. Lots to play with and play on, colourful and interesting and all beautifully maintained by the onsite manager and a couple of ex-parents who oversee the 'grow your own' area.

Parents from all over the globe – plenty of Americans, Australians and Canadians, a fair few from Scandinavia, Eastern Europe and Russia, as well as French and Italians. Attracts the less traditional English who prefer co-ed at this stage. Parents are in media, finance, law as well as in the arts. Head makes good use of the parents' experience. One parent arranged for someone from Sky News to give a talk in assembly while another organised expeditions to private art galleries hosted by another parent.

Parents are generally very supportive and enthusiastic. 'It's a tight ship – with high energy,' we were told. A very active parent committee, which managed to raise a gobsmacking £390,000 last year – through galas, fairs and produce selling (together with the head's zip-wire challenge). The school also ran a separate charity appeal for the partner school in Ethiopia, which raised enough money to build an children's home in the grounds: 'It was quite a year last year; I think it'll be a quieter one this year.'

With red carpets throughout, it feels more like a large, glamorous chalet than any school we've been to. A very shiny and exquisitely maintained school

Lots of smiling faces, both parents and children, when they arrive first thing. Kiss and Drop, as it is enchantingly called, is a system for parents who don't want to come into school and hang around until the official start time of 8.30am. Head welcomes everyone and is proud of school's open door policy. 'We are not hiding anything,' she says. Nor does she have to. These children are very lucky indeed to have such a focused and privileged start to their education.

Definitely one to watch if you live in or near this very oversubscribed area of London.

Christ Church Primary School Chelsea

1 Robinson Street, London SW3 4AA

020 7352 5708 | info@chchchelsea.rbkc.sch.uk | chchchelsea.rbkc.sch.uk

State		Pupils: 210	
Ages: 4–11			

Head: Since 2009, Avis Hawkins, BSc NPQH (40s). Read psychology at Royal Holloway with a view to becoming an educational psychologist, but got the teaching bug while training at the Institute of Education. Started her career in a state primary in Lewisham, then opted for a school in special measures (now 'inadequate' rating) for the challenge; 'That made me the teacher I am'. Appointed deputy at Christ Church in 2000 and was the natural choice to step into the role when previous head retired.

Attractive, energetic and disarmingly open, she has both children and parents on her side; 'So personable and friendly,' said one. Another added, 'Not the kind of head who just sits in their office', though with the white and grey Danish-look furniture, complete with functional teaching table – no leather sofas here – she might be tempted. 'Open door' policy taken literally; pupils appeared in her study and opened up cupboards and drawers in her desk during our chat. Her wide smile only wanes when lamenting the tight budget. In response, she has recently created an enrichment assistant, who

---

Makes the most of local contacts. Recent visitors include a fashion designer, artists from the nearby Saatchi Gallery and volunteers from the Chelsea Physic Garden

makes the most of useful local contacts, whom she invites to talk to hand-picked groups of children. Recent visitors include a fashion designer, artists from the nearby Saatchi Gallery, and volunteers from the Chelsea Physic Garden. 'I am taking experience-based learning and applying it to the curriculum', she explains. Married with three children, two at the school, her hobbies range from food to DJ-ing. There is no doubt she leads by example. DJ Hawkins is one to watch on the education scene.

Entrance: Vastly oversubscribed C of E voluntary aided school, with perennial waiting list. Priority given to siblings and families attending St Luke's or Christ Church, Chelsea; remaining places for other C of E families and locals. Takes from RBKC and Wandsworth, with a few from as far afield as Hammersmith and Lambeth. Single class intake at reception, with occasional places further up the school. One parent told how 'wealthy families used to take them out at 7', but it appears the wealthy have now got wise too, and none leave unless forced by relocation.

Exit: Increasing numbers, 30-50 per cent, to independents, including Godolphin & Latymer, Alleyn's, Dulwich, Westminster; lots bag bursaries and scholarships. Many to top London state schools: Lady Margaret, The Grey Coat Hospital and Chelsea Academy, plus newly established Fulham Boys School. One parent felt, given increasing numbers opting for independent secondary schools, more help could be given to parents with bursary and scholarship applications.

Remarks: Located in the hushed affluence of a terraced square, in an area of celebrated artists, writers and politicians, this charming Victorian school has an exterior that harks back to a bygone age, when Chelsea was no more than a collection of small parishes, and church, schoolroom and public house all clustered together on one corner. 'A village school in the heart of London' was how one parent described it and the charm lingers on, with lollipop cherry trees and a butcher's boy bike poised to deliver lunches to a nearby nursery. However, step inside and you have a Narnia experience: the interior has been redesigned to a spacious and functional plan, with chic grey walls, birch wood trimming and rows of navy pillars. Purpose-built in 2005, the main building on the north of Christchurch Street opens out to accommodate an internal playground for reception, with multi-coloured apparatus, as well as an open central stairwell and roomy classrooms for years 1-3. Behind doors we found a cookery room, art studio and ICT suite, as well as cosy beanbags in the reading room (emphatically 'not a library') and a multi-use hall with gym and dining tables. As one parent put it, 'Every nook and cranny has to be made useful'. Outside and across a wide pavement (or The Piazza) the older years occupy what was the infant school, opened in 1850 by the patron, Earl Cadogan, we are reminded on a stone plaque. Three classrooms housing the older years have a more studious feel, with individual desks facing whiteboards, but each has its own corner with plump cushions for bookworm breaks. Opposite stands Christ Church, a Victorian gothic parent building, visited on feast days and Fridays by the school, while at the fourth corner of this tiny crossroads is the playground, discreetly hidden behind a tall wall of ivy, masking the children's shouts from the genteel residents. The large play area has been landscaped to accommodate a sports pitch, gardening plots, a pergola and free play areas. 'I would like a bit more playtime,' sighed one child, and we were not surprised. Several parents commented how well maintained the buildings were, and one ventured, 'environment helps behaviour'. The charming neighbourhood is reminiscent of a scene from Mary Poppins; all it lacks is a dancing chimney sweep.

This is a school that claims to take a holistic approach to education, nonetheless, it manages to hit the spot academically. Class sizes are 30, with a 22:1 student to staff ratio, but with lots of small groups or half-class sessions at specialist subjects. The head assures us, 'if you're looking for a school at the top of the league tables, we're not the school for you', but it is hard not to be impressed by these children's achievements on paper. When we asked the children what the school could do better, they suggested more time in the library. Numeracy and literacy is managed by the leadership team as a through-school experience, not split into key stages. Verbal reasoning and non-verbal reasoning are taken in year 6; 'We pay lip service to the 11+ exams,' says the head. 'Aspiration is important'. The national curriculum is supplemented by half-termly 'curriculum weeks' when the whole school shares a topic. Recent themes include healthy living; fashion; local studies. We witnessed a Friday afternoon English class hard at metaphor and metre – no slouches here. Inclusion is a watchword too, with several SEN children supported within each year group. A range of difficulties, from dyslexia to ASD, are managed by a dedicated department and visiting OT, SLT, nutritionist and school nurse. The head welcomes the differences: 'it makes everyone aware of social behaviours'.

'A village school in the heart of London' was how one parent described it and the charm lingers on, with lollipop cherry trees and a butcher's boy bike poised to deliver lunches to a nearby nursery. Inside you have a Narnia experience

Not surprisingly, the staff profile is 'very static'; several boast 10+ years of loyal service, so the head continually makes waves with professional training programmes. The school forms an alliance with four other local primaries, mutually inspecting and monitoring each other and offering suggestions. The head also has a knack of finding restless retirees and enlisting them into some extracurricular activity: a retired headmaster takes gardening, as a curriculum topic, directing the wheelbarrows, tending the chickens and watering the kale beds. Another ex-teacher runs cricket sessions in morning break, and several volunteers have become student teachers, and later join the staff. As one mum put it: 'They are very good at growing their own'.

There's a daring zing to the curriculum, or, as the head puts it, 'I am trying to make the curriculum wide enough and rich enough so children can find their talents beyond the three Rs'. This is evident in music, where a specialist teacher with his own band inspires over 50 per cent of the school to take up an instrument. Youngsters can pick up a ukulele, trumpet or drums, as well as the more usual options, funded for a term by the school. Any child showing musical promise can go on to one-to-one lessons, at their own expense. As an Artsmark school, there's an artist in residence in each year group, who encourages messy creativity in an upstairs studio. Year 1 recently completed a metal-bashing project, while the corridor was arrayed with giant paper planets – another group's work. A recent leaver went on to star in the West End production of Matilda, a talent no doubt fostered in the ambitious Christmas and Easter shows; productions have included King Lear and Richard III (abridged). A specialist sports teacher co-ordinates trips over the bridge for team games in Battersea Park or to the beautiful Royal Hospital pitches nearby. There's room for football and netball on the hard court in the playground, dance for boys and girls in the hall, and swimming from year 2 at nearby Chelsea Sports Centre. Lately, they introduced teams to borough tournaments, and the girls' netball team ran off with the cup. A mass of after-school clubs include Mandarin, chess, judo, and knitting as well as a kayaking experience up river to Putney. One parent had to pinch herself when faced with the list of clubs, for fear she had confused it with the exclusive school up the road.

Christian values appear modestly within the school, as a poster on the doorway or mosaics of Biblical scenes on the walls. There is daily assembly, led by the head, or a celebratory one each Friday, known by the visiting vicars as 'The Oscars'. Here the children applaud each other's achievements and two Students of the Week are named from each year. Other incentives to good behaviour include an afternoon's golden time, sparingly reduced for poor behaviour. Anything more serious involves meeting the behaviour specialist, but we had difficulty finding anyone who had ever witnessed this: one parent said, 'They are all incredibly well behaved and respectful', and 'the last thing they would do is exclude a pupil'. The youngest children have a designated 'shepherd' from year 6 to sit with them at lunch. The system looks after the lambs but also instils a sense of responsibility in the older pupils. One mum worried that responsibility was not always shared evenly between the children: 'They could mix up responsible roles, like reading in church'.

Unlike many London prep schools, the pick up was not dominated by hooting 4x4s; instead, parents chatted outside in groups. The school's community spirit was evident; 'phenomenal at bringing everyone together. Very welcoming', thrilled one mum. Many meet up crossing the bridges from Battersea. One dad stressed the 'connectivity between teaching staff and parents'. There are parent workshops in maths and English, with crèche, to coach parents in helping with homework. Day to day queries are dealt with by phone or teacher meeting. More than one mum reported how they got an overnight response from the head and an invitation to meet the next day. Children are a more mixed bunch than at some local schools, or as the head put it, 'a mix of privilege and none', though all looked equally smart when dressed in the navy and cherry uniforms and stripy ties. Perhaps on World Book Day when the children walk up the King's Road to Waterstones in their PJs, they appear more individual. Their eyes lit up in anticipation of the trip, and again when discussing the lunches. Parents and offspring raved about the improved catering. The kitchen is literally a home-grown affair, using eggs and produce from the school's garden, cooked up into healthy meals by two mums, who have a background in catering, with a sprinkling of advice from the community nutritionist. One of the cooks even delivers carry-outs by bike to a nearby nursery. The result is an education in healthy eating and sustainability. According to the kids, it tastes good too, especially the pizza and apple crumble.

We agreed with the mum who said: 'I knew it was good, but I was surprised how good it was'. A diminutive state primary school, which rivals the local independents in the brainy stuff but which displays ingenuity and imagination in its broad curriculum. The resourceful head syncs her band of dedicated staff and parents to strike up a winning tune and lively, inquisitive children take up the chorus. Well, Chelsea is famous for its smart set.

Collingham College

23 Collingham Gardens, London SW5 0HL

020 7244 7414 | london@collingham.co.uk | collingham.co.uk

| Independent | Pupils: 200; sixth form: 170 |
| Ages: 14–20 | Fees: £8,040 – £20,850 pa |

Principal: Since 2012, Dr Sally Powell, BA PGCE MPhil DPhil (Oxon). Degree in English literature from Royal Holloway, London. Masters and doctorate in Victorian literature. Teaches English literature A level for four hours a week and tends to take the fast track group. Still passionate about teaching. 'It would be a deal breaker for me if I had to come out of the classroom,' she states. Enjoys gothic revival novels and is a huge Brontë fan. 'If I can teach Wuthering Heights then I normally do.' Has been here for 15 years, previously as vice principal and deputy principal. Over 20 other members of staff have also been here more than a decade. 'I'm the new girl!' she jokes. Loves theatre and art and often accompanies school trips to plays and exhibitions. One teenage daughter who is destined to come here for her A levels. 'She would come here now if I would let her!' she says. Warm, enthusiastic and welcoming.

Parents like the fact that head knows every pupil by name as well as their background. They describe her as 'easy to talk to,' 'kind' and 'wonderful – she champions the children.' Nobody we spoke to had anything but praise for her.

James Allder BA is the deputy and also teaches geography. Very knowledgeable about the school. They make a good team.

Academic matters: In 2018, 22 per cent of A level grades were A*/A and 58 per cent were A*/B; 22 per cent of I/GCSE grades were A*-A/9-7. A good mix of academic and vocational courses offered at A level with maths, business studies and economics currently popular. A staggering 25 subjects possible at GCSE, including Arabic, classical Greek and photography as well as the predictable mainstream subjects. Pupils generally take eight or nine GCSEs. Rare for pupils to come here to retake GCSEs – pupils tend to take them all here over the full two years, starting in year 10.

Pupils can either take A levels over two years or opt for the more intensive one-year course. For fluent French speakers, a dedicated A level class is laid on so they can complete the course at speed. No restrictions in terms of subject combinations, however unconventional. 'It is entirely bespoke.' Head feels that strongest departments currently are English, economics and chemistry but also singled out art as being extraordinary.

Revision A level and GCSE classes also offered at Easter (three weeks) and Christmas (three days), with intense practice of exam-style questions. Open to in-house pupils as well as those at other schools. Small groups guaranteed. Just the ticket if your offspring needs structured handholding in the exam run up. Head says it is a great way to recruit future pupils. Once they see what is on offer, many are keen to jump ship. Some 11+ and CE tuition also offered in the holidays and after school.

International students, though a tiny minority, have mandatory English classes for eight hours per week. All these students are prepared for IELTS test, a requirement for study at British universities. Where necessary, extra support is available either in groups or one-to-one. Many non-native speakers are timetabled to take classes in art, photography or PE in which they can work alongside fluent students and improve their language skills.

'We have students who are top end ballet dancers, tennis players, skiers or violinists and the school fits in around their lives and schedules. It is a different type of schooling'

One of the college's main selling points is the small classes, with a maximum of nine pupils at GCSE and eight at A level. 'A luxurious way to learn and a luxurious way to teach,' says head. School bends over backwards to put on whatever class is requested, even if only one pupil is taking the subject, eg Japanese. Masses of individual attention. Mixed ability classes: some are highly academic, others distinctly less so.

About 20 per cent currently has some form of SEN – overwhelmingly mild dyslexia, dyspraxia or slow processing. College has taken high functioning autistic students in the past but you have to be pretty independent to thrive here, so not the place for someone at the severe end of the spectrum. SENDCo offers learning support on individual basis. Weekly study skills workshops put on for all pupils with topics ranging from how to organise one's files to how to take notes and how to memorise material. Pupils also offered one-to-one support from teachers, at an extra cost, either for a short boost on tricky topics or longer term help. For example, if you are dead keen to do economics but your maths is not quite up to scratch, you can have individual tuition with the economics teacher in school to get you up to speed. Parents welcome this in-house support rather than having to find an external tutor.

Many teachers here are academics, often with doctorates, and love the intellectual life. 'That is what makes our A level teaching so very strong.' College shares some teachers with Imperial, a stone's throw away. Deputy explains that 'the flexibility of our timetable means some teachers are part time and many of them do something else as well as teaching here. Both art teachers, for example, are professional artists. That gives a real depth and breadth to their knowledge. Lots of the maths department are musicians too.' One parent we

spoke to commented that the majority of teachers are inspirational, though possibly not all.

Head is excited about the 'electus programme' which aims to stretch the most able. The bright sparks selected take additional classes, go on visits and write a dissertation over the summer holidays, similar to the EPQ. It is intended to be an opportunity to explore cross-curricular themes and provide something to talk about in their personal statement. Head is convinced there are more opportunities for able students here than at larger schools.

Games, options, the arts: Extracurricular provision limited. Pupils who are talented musicians or on the sports field tend to pursue these passions externally. 'By the time you are 16 or 17, you know what you are interested in. They are in London, so they can find a place where they can do whatever they want. We have students who are top end ballet dancers, tennis players, skiers or violinists and the school fits in around their lives and schedules. It is a different type of schooling,' explains head. One mother we spoke to felt many of the pupils here are not the sort who care much about making a sports team or school orchestra anyway. 'Collingham does not attract many of those types,' she said.

If you are dead keen to do economics but your maths is not quite up to scratch, you can have individual tuition

Two hours of sport per week for GCSE pupils, mostly football in Kensington Gardens, plus tennis and rounders. In the sixth form, students can choose between football and yoga. 'We play in a small inter-college football league but we are not particularly good,' confesses deputy. 'Definitely not a sporty school. Quite the opposite,' said one parent. Annual music concert is run by the students and includes varied performances from rap and computer generated music to drama and poetry recitals. 'We've seen it all. It's an open stage', and is apparently great fun. Everyone is encouraged to take part and money raised goes to charity.

High standard of art displayed on the walls around the school, despite the small size of the studio. Photography is popular and school has its own dark room. Pupils have had work exhibited at Royal College of Art competitions. Parents feel able artists thrive here. No drama performances at all. 'Not the school for you if you are looking to take part in musicals like Seven Brides for Seven

Garden House School

Brothers or Oklahoma!' jokes head. LAMDA exams can be taken by those with a dramatic bent.

Plenty of trips and outings arranged including to Houses of Parliament, law courts and recording studios. Teachers are encouraged to get the pupils out and about as much as possible to support the curriculum, whether to attend lectures, visit exhibitions or see plays. Residential trips to Paris, Amsterdam and Florence as well as ski-ing in the Alps and walking trips to Snowdonia for the more energetic. A level pupils and GCSE pupils come together for these, which helps to foster a feeling of community which could otherwise be lacking. Activities week includes a charity walk, art and drama workshops and work experience. Everyone must get involved in some capacity, even if they are reluctant to travel too far afield.

Background and atmosphere: Founded in 1975 as Collingham Tutors. Based on two sites, half a mile apart, one for GCSE students and the other for A levels. GCSE pupils come over to use the two labs, the art studio and to study Spanish in particular. The building in Collingham Gardens was previously Gibbs' Prep School where Prince Edward was educated, and before that was a magnificent terraced home, with servants' quarters up at the top. Though the vast drawing room on the first floor has been transformed into a study room/exam hall, it has retained it grandeur. The whole building still feels like a home, with its thick carpets and ornate mirrors.

Pupils tend to get on well as a group. One parent we spoke to felt the distinct 'lack of nastiness and cliques' was refreshing. 'They are quite a sophisticated bunch, though.' A level pupils are free to come and go during the day, as long as they are back for their lessons. Supervised study periods between classes for first year of sixth form, so there is a little more structure and less to-ing and fro-ing than one might expect. GCSE students need to be in school all day other than lunchtime, when they can go off site, as there is no outdoor space. Most are thrilled to be able to enjoy the delights of the Gloucester Road in the middle of the day. Many lunch at cafés in the 'French quarter' in South Ken, though it has been known for pupils to head to McDonald's. 'They are generally far too cool to bring in a packed lunch!' laughed one mother.

School is good at celebrating achievement. A board of 'high fliers' is in pride of place in the entrance hall with their photos, grades and university places for all to see. Acts as a spur to the current students to try to get themselves onto the board in due course.

Pastoral care, well-being and discipline: Excellent. Lots of individual care offered. Everyone has a personal tutor who regularly meets with them on a one-to-one basis to discuss both performance and well-being. Half-termly target setting and termly parent meetings. Given the size of the school, anyone who is struggling is picked up at lightning speed.

All meals freshly cooked, made to order. Those with eating disorders can be monitored in a subtle way by the lovely cook. 'We are quick to pick up on what is going on'

Zero tolerance of drugs, alcohol or bullying. On the day we visited, there was a group of pupils standing across the street, cigarettes in hands. Though not ideal, head would rather that staff can see what is going on and who is out there than have them skulking down back streets. College will not accept any behaviour that will disrupt classes, though this is rare. 'There are very few opportunities for disruption, but young people are young people and they can make wrong choices from time to time..' concedes head. Pupils wear their own clothes and the dress code is 'informal but respectful.' Pupils are sent home for inappropriate attire. No hats or hoodies inside. 'There is a university-like feel to the place and most students rise to that challenge.' School occasionally needs to have a conversation with a pupil about garish hair but tends not to over-react if it is subtle. 'The worst thing for a student is for me to like it!' jokes the head. 'Essentially, it is an elegant building and we expect people to behave in an elegant fashion.'

Some pupils who come here have had a fractured school history, possibly because parents have moved around or because they have experienced bullying. Some have just fallen under the radar in bigger, more conventional schools and crave a fresh start. There is certainly a band of more fragile students. One mother commented, 'It is wonderful there is a school like Collingham to scoop up these children who have lost their way elsewhere. Once they get here, they can finally breathe again.' Another said the school had been wonderful with their child's depression and never judged her. 'Everything at the school was fitted in around her recovery.' In-house counsellor on hand to help with issues such as self-harming and depression.

Small, manned café in basement, open from early morning to evening serving main meals and snacks. You could eat all your meals down there. 'Sometimes I do!' quips deputy. All freshly cooked, made to order. Those with eating disorders can be monitored in a subtle way by the lovely cook. 'As a community, we are quick to pick up on what is going on'. Everyone seems to be looking out for everyone here.

Very rare to be expelled. 'If a child is getting the tone wrong then we are there to support them. We help them to develop those social skills.' Deputy explains, 'We will give them a second chance but not necessarily a third, fourth of fifth chance..'

Small classes help with low self-esteem. One mother commented that her two children have been transformed by coming here. 'Within six weeks they have become totally different children. I cannot praise the school enough for this.'

Pupils and parents: Over 95 per cent are UK students though the college is strikingly cosmopolitan with a diverse range of parental backgrounds. Ninety per cent of pupils speak English at home and five per cent speak French. Over half of pupils come from London and home counties day schools with another 20 per cent from British boarding schools. Steady flow of pupils from neighbouring Lycée, keen to have a more intimate school with a less didactic style of teaching. Others from eg Dulwich College, Eton, Westminster, St Paul's Girls' and boys' and neighbouring Queen's Gate as well as boarding schools such as Bryanston and King's Canterbury.

'It is wonderful there is a school like Collingham to scoop up these children who have lost their way elsewhere. Once they get here, they can finally breathe again'

Mostly affluent, dual-income professional families. Many from creative backgrounds, particularly the media. One mother commented that some pupils are very spoilt, though there are others from more modest backgrounds.

Good communication between the school and parents. 'Much more than you would find in other schools,' states head. Parents feel they are kept fully informed and that anxieties and concerns are acted upon. Head believes parents discuss matters freely with the school partly because 'there is no long gravel drive to navigate. We are much more open house. They come in off the pavement, straight into the hall and my office is just there.' Certainly not an intimidating school. Head says parents tend to be 'warm and lovely'.

Notable former pupils include actress Minnie Driver, author Paula Hawkins and assorted members of the Jagger clan.

Entrance: No open days. The vast majority comes through word of mouth. Prospective A level and GCSE pupils are interviewed individually by principal or director of studies, and must also provide a satisfactory school reference. Every student is considered on a case by case basis. 'We spend well over an hour interviewing a pupil with their family. We really try to get to know the family dynamics. We want to know how supportive they are going to be – that is important to us'. School would never take a pupil who had been expelled from their previous school for drugs because 'the parents who are sending their children to Collingham are sending them here in good faith that we are policing and monitoring, as best we can, our students' behaviour. We are not in the business of taking other people's problems'. Head admits it can be heartbreaking because they may have just made a silly mistake. 'They may be a delightful student from a delightful family but regrettably that is our policy'. She has a box of tissues at the ready in her office for inevitable tears which are shed when pupils are turned down or when parents and children talk about difficulties they have encountered at their previous schools.

Normally, 10 new students join year 10 and 20 join year 11. Entry is also possible throughout the academic year. Around 60 per cent of the GCSE pupils continue into the sixth form provided they have a minimum of five GCSEs at grade 4 or above. Those wishing to take maths or a science need a minimum of grade 6 in that subject at GCSE. Normally around 60 students enter the school for the first year of sixth form, with year 13 entry taking on an additional 10 A level pupils and 20 one-year pupils.

Exit: Those who leave post-GCSE tend to go to state sixth forms. Some return within weeks, as they realise it can be better to be a big fish in a small pond.

Most sixth formers head to university, many inevitably to London. Bristol, Leeds and Oxford Brookes also currently popular. Pupils select a range of courses including engineering, history and English. The more artistic tend to opt for art foundation courses at eg Central St Martins.

Some parents think it is 'Oxbridge or nothing' and Collingham feels it is key to manage parents' expectations. Oxbridge preparation includes extension classes and help with entrance exams. Mock interviews set up with experienced retired teachers so pupils have practice in being grilled by a stranger. One to Oxford in 2018; some off overseas to University of British Columbia (English), Isart Digital Montreal (game programming) and Peking University (pre-university programme).

Money matters: Fees depend upon numbers of subjects being taken, length of course and whether full or part time. 'We try to keep fees as manageable as possible and we offer multi payments.' High performing students from state sector are sometimes awarded a means-tested bursary, to a maximum 30 per cent reduction in fees.

Remarks: Head explains, 'We are the last, or one of the last, domestic-orientated sixth form colleges in London. The others are very international. We have carved out a niche for ourselves that we are jealously guarding.' Parents and pupils rave about the friendly, supportive environment here and feel cherished in this intimate environment.

Colville Primary School

Lonsdale Road, Portobello Road, London W11 2DF

020 7229 6540 | info@colville.rbkc.sch.uk | colville.rbkc.sch.uk

State	Pupils: 430
Ages: 3–11	

Head: Since 2011, Jagdeep Birdi BA QTS (40s). Studied history, English and education at Lancaster, then headed for the Big Smoke, where he has since taught across five different London boroughs. For the 11 years before he joined Colville, he was deputy head at Ronald Ross, Wimbledon, then at Sir John Lillie, Fulham.

Despite the school leaping from its place in the bottom 200 schools in the country to one of the top 200 since he joined, he's not one to wax lyrical about vision, strategy and grand plans. Not for him the stereotypical headteacher mini-speech packed with well-practised bullet points of what makes the school, and him, great. In fact, this modest, mild-mannered man even struggled to answer our questions about what it is that makes the school stand out, although you don't have to talk to him for long before his passion and dedication for both education and this school reveal themselves. It is this heartfelt, unaffected and laid-back attitude – in which aspiring for the best is seen as the most natural thing in the world – that staff say sums up his leadership style. This style, they told us, makes him approachable, collaborative and empowering and is ultimately responsible for him having made such a difference here, turning the school into one that attracts and retains excellent teaching staff and causes kids to treat the school's core values of respect, aspiration and perseverance as instinctive. It can be no coincidence that the amount of private donations have shot up under his headship – reaching over £100,000 in the last four years alone – which have led to huge improvements in three key areas: the physical environment of the school, the number of teaching staff and the high number of extracurricular clubs (42) at the last count.

Kids – of whom there are above 400 (set to rise to 500 as the current 'bulge years' are officially replaced by double intake years) – feel they can chat informally to him too and do exactly that at lunch, which he joins them daily to eat, while he greets both children and parents at the gate every morning and afternoon. 'I know every parent and I know every child,' he says, again in a tone that suggests this is completely normal. 'His natural manner is to make us feel as if we're an important part of the school – that our views about the school matter as much as the teachers,' said one parent. Another told us, 'If you raise something with him as being in need of change, he will go ahead and make the change or give you a very good reason why he can't. I don't think you could find a more accommodating head.'

Kids feel they can chat informally to him and do exactly that at lunch, where he joins them daily

His first-floor office – a Big Brother set-up, with floor-to-ceiling glass overlooking the key stage one area of the school – seems an unlikely choice for such an unassuming leader. Until, that is, staff explain that actually, it means they can see when he's free to talk to and, perhaps more crucially, it places him firmly at the heart of the school rather than being hidden away in some corner office.

Entrance: After the customary priority for looked-after children and those with special needs, siblings are next on the list. Then it's down to distance, which currently stretches to 0.45 miles, although this is rapidly shrinking as news of the school's continuing improvements spreads. Indeed, there are now over 200 applications for the 60 reception places. Even if families move to another part of London, they tend to stay, with some children coming from as far as Hackney and the far side of Barking. Cohort is truly ethnically diverse, with a whopping 46 languages spoken and no dominant group among them (even the most common language spoken apart from English only has 18 speakers). Refreshingly, the fact that 62 per cent of pupils come in speaking English as a second language is considered a bonus, not a drawback. 'These children know how to acquire a language – that's a good thing,' says the head, adding that diversity is seen to enrich the school. Seventy per cent of pupils at the older end of the school are on free school meals, whilst that figure drops to just 10 per cent at the bottom end, telling you all you need to know about the change in reputation of the school.

Exit: The largest share – half the pupils – go to the local comprehensive of Holland Park, whilst around a quarter go to Kensington Aldridge Academy. The rest go to a wide range of comprehensives right across London, with a handful per year group now moving into the independent sector.

Remarks: 'Let's not beat around the bush – this school used to be appalling when my child, who is now in year 6, joined,' said one parent. 'Colville was the school that nobody really wanted for their child and the one that poor low-income families got lumbered with,' reported another from the same year group. But in the last five years, standards of attainment achieved by the school have shot up, with Colville having received two ministerial congratulations in the last two years alone – and the parents, particularly those of the older kids, can't believe their luck.

'Teaching was poor,' acknowledges the head. 'The school wasn't in a good place.' So what happened to all those substandard teaching staff? "A number of teachers chose to leave during my first few months,' smiles the head. 'Now we get top-notch teaching staff coming in and the teaching is rigorous, particularly in maths and English,' he says, adding that the school has specialist teachers for computing, games, art, music and French, all of whom teach from reception upwards. But it's not just the quality of the teaching staff – who we found to be successfully engaging children in every classroom we entered – that's noticeable here. It's the sheer number of them, with some classrooms we visited having four teaching staff for 24 children. Refreshingly, many are male and most of the teaching assistants are graduates. Even when these

Children running around loudly and happily and making full use of the new plush, large, wooden climbing structures

classes reach the 30 mark, it will be an impressive adult-to-child ratio and it clearly makes a difference. Indeed, we watched staff working their way round the classroom, making sure that every child understood exactly what was being taught and helping them with the nuances of their learning so that nobody is left behind.

The extra adult bods in classrooms also means there's more room for learning-through-doing. In fact, we didn't see one instance of chalk-and-talk during our visit, but instead clusters of desks in which small groups of children, helped by adults, worked together interactively to put the teacher's words into practice, often in fun and innovative ways. And before you wonder if all that makes for a chaotic and noisy learning environment, it doesn't. There is a noticeable sense of calm and purpose throughout this school.

Except, that is, at break time, which takes place in the reasonably sized tarmacked playground that takes up around half of the school's neat, rectangular plot that's tucked behind the fashionable Portobello Road and which is overlooked by high-rise flats and town houses. Playtime here does what it says on the tin, with raucous children running around loudly and happily and making full use of the new plush, large wooden climbing structures. There's also a school garden and separate edible garden (which, by the way, has links with Wholefoods in Notting Hill). Everyone seemed to be part of a group and we failed to spot one face that wasn't smiling. 'You don't get left out here because we have a playground buddy system,' one pupil told us. 'We once had an issue with another child upsetting ours, but the school put a stop to it immediately,' reported one parent, with others agreeing that any unkindness or friendship problems are generally nipped in the bud. A school survey, completed just prior to our visit, found that 99 per cent of children felt the school is a respectful environment, where pupils are respected whatever their background.

Originally, the school opened in 1879 as Buckingham Terrace Primary, when six teachers – poor things – were charged with 550 pupils. During the WWII these pupils were evacuated and when they returned after the war in 1945, the school reopened as Colville Primary. The old laundry building (girls were taught laundry back in the day) has now been converted into a modern, welcoming space for reception, whilst another outdoor building, complete with glass roof both inside and out, is home to the nursery. The rest of the school is taught in the three-storey main building, where the (mainly) large classrooms boast high ceilings and such large windows that even with the blinds almost completely pulled down, the rooms ooze light. There are three school halls, one of which doubles up as the dining room – known as Le Bistro – where removable round tables are covered in red and white table cloths and even vases of flowers. 'We wanted to make it homely and the children love it,' a member of staff told us, although one pupil told us the one thing she'd change about the school is the food. That said, only 20 or so kids choose to bring in packed lunches.

The well-stocked library is a welcoming environment, complete with areas to spread out on cushions and read, whilst the art studio/come food tech room is huge and, again, boasting plenty of natural light. 'I never thought my son would like art, but he loves it now,' said one parent, who praised the specialist art teacher's links with local galleries, including the Saatchi gallery. Music is also taken seriously, with the specialist teacher working in a large, well-equipped dedicated space. All children are given the opportunity to play instruments here, with a steady stream of six peripatetic teachers teaching in small groups and individually. There's a school choir (which has performed at the likes of the Royal Albert Hall) and orchestra. Other facilities of note include the break-out rooms for specialist support and the large ICT suite. Truth be told, much of the school could do with a lick of paint, and it's never going to look state-of-the-art due to the age of the building, but if you focus on the available space and how it's used, we think most people would be hard pushed not to be impressed, particularly for an inner city primary. And the £4.5 million refreshment has now made some exciting changes.

Sport is reported by parents and pupils alike to be fun and inclusive, with all the usual options, some of which are taught on site, whilst others, including swimming, involve a short walk to the local leisure centre. There are links with major local football clubs and Lord's cricket ground and dedicated coaches regularly visit to teach and enthuse the children. 'Sport is brilliant in comparison to other inner city schools,' one parent told us.

The school's motto, 'Inspiring success', is clearly not an empty phrase here, but something that they really aspire to for every child. Part of this involves setting – in phonics and reading from October half-term in reception, and in maths from year 2 – whilst another area of focus for the school is SEN. With seven statemented children when we visited, and plenty with extra needs ranging from those on the dys spectrum to those who may not

have quiet areas to study at home, the school has made sure it is a learning environment where individual support is prioritised and provided both inside and outside the classroom. Without really planning to, the school has also gained something of a reputation for specialising in hearing loss, with three children in this situation attending at the time we visited. There's a big push on reading at home, with parents expected to regularly sign off reading records and there's a fair amount of homework, usually at weekends. 'Fridays aren't my favourite after school day,' admitted one parent. 'But I agree the homework is necessary as the children will be in for a shock when they reach secondary school otherwise.'

The summer and Christmas fairs are a very big deal here. 'One of our parents went to RADA and it meant last year's Santa's Grotto was better than Harrods',' says the head

Behaviour is generally good, with pupils we met having a clear understanding of the school's behaviour code and, by and large, respecting it. A traffic light system in every class helps keep them on the straight and narrow too – nobody likes the shame of being moved onto red or, God forbid, purple (the extra colour that pupils tell us is saved for the likes of 'disrupting the class or being rude'). Youngsters who really overstep the mark find themselves in the head's office, although he says, 'the only time any child has had to be sent to me in the last six months was for setting off the fire alarm.' It also helps that good behaviour and work is rewarded with privilege points, which can be redeemed for toys out of the special cupboard when they reach increments of 10. 'Ten points will buy you a nice little toy, but if you save up 30 or 40, you can get something like a Bop-it,' one pupil told us, visibly excited by the prospect. Children who do particularly good work are invited to share it with key stage leaders and/or the head, as well as getting a special mention in class assemblies. The school says it's strict on uniform, but in reality, that just means that unlike in the past, when kids could wear any old red jumper, there's now a school version, along with the usual grey bottoms and black leather shoes.

Signs of life can be spotted early in the day here, with before and after-school provision, as well as a breakfast café where parents can come with their children. In addition, the 42 before and after-school clubs range from breakdancing to violin and ballet to gardening club. There are regular school day trips to the capital's museums, Kew Gardens and Holland Park (the latter for forest school), whilst year 4s upwards get to go on residential trips. Community links are a strength, with children involved with everything from Jamie Oliver's (for cooking sessions) to Salvation Army (where the choir performs to the elderly).

Parents are increasingly involved in school life. It wasn't always the case, pointed out one parent, who suggested the idea of having student reps to the head, which he promptly took up. 'The PA is increasingly active too,' she said, although some parents told us they'd like to see more events put on for parents to help bring the school community closer still, whilst another said a common complaint is that the school often only tells parents about school trips last minute – a shame as many

like helping out on them, but don't generally get enough notice to get time off work. The summer and Christmas fairs are a very big deal here. 'One of our parents went to RADA and it meant last year's Santa's Grotto was better than Harrods,' says the head.

We found this school to be refreshing, unpretentious, aspirational and spirited. It is also testament to the fact that, with the right leadership, a poor performing school can become a school of choice within a short space of time – not just for parents, but children too. 'Every single day, my children look forward to going to school,' one parent told us. 'Everyone loves it here,' agreed one of the pupils we spoke to.

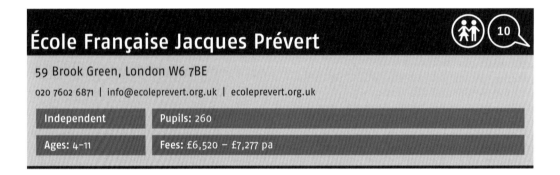

École Française Jacques Prévert

59 Brook Green, London W6 7BE

020 7602 6871 | info@ecoleprevert.org.uk | ecoleprevert.org.uk

Independent	Pupils: 260
Ages: 4–11	Fees: £6,520 – £7,277 pa

Director: Since 2016, Delphine Gentil, who was a head for 10 years in a country school in France before applying to the French authorities to be moved to Jacques Prevert. She is in London with her two children, who attend the Lycée Charles de Gaulle, and her husband commutes regularly from France. She is sporty and cycles and swims regularly. Cheerful, enthusiastic and clearly hardworking, she is thrilled to be in London and hopes to extend the minimum three year contract (maximum allowed by the French state is five years).

She is enamoured by the greater freedom she has in England regarding the curriculum, the budget choices and the collaborative work between London's French schools. More pastoral care, more awareness of the need to support pupils with SEN (her special area of interest) and improved English curriculum have been her particular input to the school in her short tenure. Excellent Ofsted report reflects her efforts. Parents say she is 'excellent' and 'respected by staff, parents and teachers', although some parents also bemoaned the turnover of heads imposed by the French department of education. Parents praised 'the great lengths she goes to, to make sure pupils acquire diverse experiences rather than just learning about things "the French way", including supporting teachers' projects such

as going to the opera in Holland Park, going to the Hindu temple in London, getting out to see art and theatre, bringing in experts from other cultures'.

Entrance: Admission at all times of the year, not academically selective, priority given to children from French schools (either in France or abroad). French aptitude test if pupils are not from a French school and are over 6 years old, to ensure they will be able to access the curriculum, though children can join the infant section without knowing any French. Some 80 per cent French pupils and a few British, Turkish, Canadian etc. British families choose it if they live locally and want a reasonably priced small independent school (all the scooters parked up showed evidence of locally living pupils and a sustainable travel plan). Means-tested bursaries available to French citizens.

Exit: Pupils mostly expect to move on to the nearby French Lycée (which remains the parents' main choice with a number of pupils joining the International Section if their English is good enough – all applicants for IS got places recently). It used to be a feeder school to the Lycée, but a secondary school place there is no longer guaranteed. If not, then they might choose the newer Winston

Churchill school in Wembley or other French schools. A couple each year to English schools – Francis Holland, for example – though parents aware that they will get little, if any, advice on transfers to to non-French schools.

Remarks: The school follows the French curriculum entirely; half staff brought in from the French authorities, so they are French 'fonctionnaires', and half the staff are locally employed. The head has managed to bring about some changes thanks to good resources – interactive whiteboards and updated classrooms to make the most of the small, awkwardly shaped rooms in the 'charming and historic' red-brick house facing Brook Green in Hammersmith. Parents appreciate the setting, 'leafy and facing the green and in a lovely part of London'. Two sets of stairs (one for going up and one for coming down), a tiny playground, canteen in the basement with good quality (mostly organic) food made from scratch on the premises. Lunch menu published weekly, though kids bring in packed lunch on Wednesday when they all have half day.

The school has been updating its IT provision – 70 new iPads to back up the small suite of computers in the well-stocked basement library. Enthusiastic French librarian brings in guest authors and teaches library skills. Pupils are encouraged to borrow from both the French and the English libraries. Emphasis on rote learning and neatness, with a strict French national curriculum to follow and emphasis on reading and writing only after year 2. Before then, plenty of work on fine and gross motor skills, language acquisition and memory. Specialist teachers for English and music.

Four hours a week of English work with English teachers, who follow an adapted curriculum with differentiated content and teaching according to pupils' level of English. If a pupil comes in with no French (one of the 20 per cent non French pupils, for example), they are given extra support in French. One parent told us that 'at the end of year show you can't hear their English accent or know whose mother tongue is English'. However, parents pointed out that this is French school, not a bilingual school, so all English teaching is a bonus. Pupils seem to reach a surprisingly high level of English thanks to some inspirational English teaching – quite a few pupils named English as their favourite subject (though science and lunch time followed closely on our straw poll). French parents said that English tends to be the main language in the playground (helped by playground assistants speaking English). That, together with PE and science often taught in English, helps their children acquire really fluent English and become truly bilingual; all of the pupils we spoke to slipped easily from one language to another. Parents and the head are aware of the 'challenge of a good level of English instruction in a French school'. The very much improved English teaching and newly developed English curriculum was raised by most of parents as being a real asset now, achieved by no longer requiring these English teachers to be bilingual and therefore having a greater choice of teachers. Parents said 'the quality of instruction is superb', giving as an example the fact that this small school had several pupils who came in the top one per cent of 30,000 French students in an international maths competition.

Lunch playtime either in the small playground or opposite in Brook Green, sports at local centre include swimming as well as rock climbing, ice skating and rugby, alternating between years and terms. Littlest ones have gym in school hall. Dedicated music room and teacher who helps pull together end of year show and Christmas choral performance. Some art by class teachers enriched by visiting artists who help on projects and for inspiration. Thanks to increased interest in supporting diversity by the current head, there are pupils on a register with different levels of educational support – some with in school and in class differentiation and awareness, some with outside support, families frequently using French speech and language and other therapists. The odd pupil with a teaching assistant (paid for by parents). Building totally unsuitable for anyone who can't manage the many stairs.

Parents said 'the quality of instruction is superb': this small school had several pupils who came in the top one per cent in an international maths competition

The head is very keen to work on pupils' well-being, since she 'can see how pressurised both they and their parents are, living and working in London'. She has introduced workshops looking at mental health and self-esteem, and 'who they are as a group and how to behave in a group', with lectures and training by a psychotherapist who works with pupils, parents and teachers. Pupils are an enthusiastic bunch, wanting to share their love of the school – 'I love everything' repeated by several pupils we spoke to. If they had come from schools in France, they appreciated the art and music and sport, which don't happen much in France. If they had come from English schools, they liked the clear rules and purpose. Working parents also appreciate pre- and post-school care in morning club from 8am onwards ('my child just loves morning club,' said more than one parent) and after school in clubs and then daycare until 5pm.

In many families both parents work, but they are very involved in this close-knit school – either on the management committee or in the PTA, or as class representatives, meeting three times a year to discuss class issues. They help to run the many subsidised extracurricular clubs, taking pupils to outside school clubs, organising rotas and finding leaders to teach, for example, coding, football, karate, chess, zumba, art, cooking. The school management board appoints the local staff who are not appointed by the French government. Parents can

see the head informally, as she is at the school gates each morning and evening, or by email or appointment. Head regularly meets with 13 other French curriculum schools in London and they share good practice and joint training.

Parents all mentioned the 'outstanding value for money' aspect of the school – 'much more reasonably priced than other London private schools, and one of the cheapest French schools in London too'. But they also all raised the fact that pupils 'feel looked after and loved, in an environment where they are safe and taken care of'.

Falkner House

19 Brechin Place, London SW7 4QB

020 7373 4501 | office@falknerhouse.co.uk | falknerhouse.co.uk

Independent	Pupils: 200
Ages: 3–11	Fees: £9,780 – £19,080 pa

Headteacher: Since 2017, Flavia Rogers BA PGCE (30s). Educated at Falkner House followed by St Paul's Girls' School, then studied history at Exeter University. Taught in New York at the Nightingale Bamford School before coming back to London, where she taught history at Kingston Grammar School. She has been at Falkner House since 2008.

Falkner House is truly a family business in every sense; Mrs Rogers' grandmother, Flavia Nunes, was Falkner House's founding head, and she works alongside her mother, Anita Griggs (school principal) and sister Eleanor Dixon (head of Falkner House Boys). They have the central London education system embedded in their DNA. Mrs Rogers has three children, all of whom are at Falkner House, so she feels she has an unusual perspective of being both consumer and producer. 'Seeing things from the angle of a current parent is incredibly useful and means I have insight into what life is really like for children and families at the school. For example, do we really do what we say when we say we have very little homework in the lower school? How does this translate at home?' She has known her husband Sam since they met at St Paul's and she lives across the road from Falkner House. In her off-duty hours she is an 'obsessive reader' and her favourite place in the world is the family house on the south coast.

Mrs Griggs and Mrs Rogers are an exceptionally tight team. They spend a huge amount of time together (every weekend as well) and clearly love what they do and love working together.

Entrance: Register as soon as possible after birth. Some enter at nursery (including boys), but a nursery spot does not guarantee passage to the main school. In the January before entry, about 160 girls compete for 24 reception places in an assessment that looks for 'focus, working memory and enthusiasm,' as well as more elusive qualities such as 'grit' and good manners.

Retains the echo of a post-war family home, with the head's office elegantly kitted out with antiques

'A child cannot be prepared and we don't assess whether or not they can read.' Many will inevitably be disappointed, but parents are let down as gently as possible. 'No selection system is perfect. We don't get false positives, but we sometimes get false negatives.' Occasional places (an average of one a year) are again filled by assessment. 'I'd rather leave a space than have the wrong fit,' adds the head.

Exit: The 'next step' is considered thoughtfully, with parents invited in for a planning meeting in year 5. 'We take endless care to ensure girls not only get into the best schools but the schools that are best for them.' The majority, now as always, to London's academic girls' schools (St Paul's, Latymer Upper, Godolphin & Latymer, City, Francis Holland SW1, Queen's Gate, Putney High). A small number of girls go on to board, with Wycombe Abbey, Cheltenham Ladies and St Mary's Ascot featuring strongly. Girls frequently leave garnered with academic, music and sporting scholarships.

Remarks: Flavia Nunes set up Falkner House in 1954 with the intention of providing girls with the same standard of academic excellence enjoyed by their brothers – by no means a given in those days – and the school continues to provide a broad and challenging education taught by a dedicated, energetic and innovative staff. 'They're the real stars,' says the head.

Reading is central to the offering. All younger girls are expected to read nightly at home and a love of words and books is encouraged by regular attendance at two libraries, essential reading lists and a weekly library lesson from year 3. Poetry is learned by heart and recited in class and competitions; recently launched own poetry anthology of verses 'every Falkner House child should know'. Girls become articulate and confident, both on the page and in conversation.

Beyond the three Rs, a rainbow of opportunity. French throughout, classics from year 3, Latin from year 5. The arts, too, are taken seriously. Music is exceptionally strong and varied with plenty in the way of performance (wind band, string group, choir, chamber music ensembles). Art room buzzing and history of art taught from reception, with regular outings to museums and galleries. Dance and drama included in the core curriculum, with regular outstanding class productions, and a popular after-school ballet club allows those who wish to take external exams.

Technology here is not just for display on the timetable, but blazing a trail – a hardworking teacher has reinvented the year 5 and 6 curriculum to be delivered on iPads. Recently Apple named Falkner House one of six groundbreaking schools worldwide for its innovative approach.

Light approach to both homework and exams. The latter are introduced in year 4 as 'It's important for girls to learn to take both the test and the results in their stride; to learn their best is good enough and what we value is their effort over the result.' says the head.

This is a highly selective school and few have serious special educational needs. Mild difficulties, however, are addressed successfully by experienced staff and high flyers given regular extension work.

Despite a handkerchief playground, sport played competitively to a high level. Coaches ferry girls to Battersea, Kensington Gardens, Latchmere Leisure Centre and Chelsea and from year 3 the school fields A, B, and often C squads in netball, athletics, swimming, rounders and cross-country. 'It's a culture of "play the game within the spirit of the game",' says the head. 'We do not kill to win.' Win they do, however, producing recent champions at the London Schools Swimming Association and the British Schools Team Fencing Championship. Numerous extracurricular activities include clubs, trips (abroad and in the UK) and treats (on Founder's Day school stops for the day and each year sees a themed carousel of events for the girls to enjoy.

'A child cannot be prepared and we don't assess whether or not they can read,' says the head. Many will inevitably be disappointed, but parents are let down as gently as possible. 'No system is perfect'

Fresh food cooked daily – and described as 'amazing' by our guides, with staff monitoring manners and a balanced diet. 'We've taken out all mention of healthy eating,' says the head. 'All children here eat healthy food, so why create more anxiety?'

The school is still located in the two spacious, multi-storeyed Victorian houses where it was founded and retains the echo of a post-war family home, with carpeted corridors and the head's office elegantly kitted out with antiques. Tradition, too, maintained with daily 'prayers' (Christian hymns and the Lord's Prayer) held in the delightful, parqueted assembly hall. All faiths welcome. Remembrance Day, carol service and the Queen's Jubilee accorded due dignity. 'The girls should understand the culture.'

Other traditional strands include both a house and prefect system. Head girl, deputy and prefects appointed for half term stints, so all get a go, while other routes to glory include sports person or artist of the week, eco monitor and badge girl (responsible for helping the teacher).

Head's mission is to endow pupils with self confidence, independence of mind, kindness and good manners, and girls clearly enjoy the process. 'It's fun,' said one. Though the inevitable friendship groups form, all seem to get on. 'No-one is not friends,' said another. Top year girls are paired with those coming into reception, and this union of 'big and little sisters' means new arrivals are never left stranded. 'We play with them and introduce our 'little sisters' to each other.' Precocity definitely discouraged (no nail varnish, no jewellery and only 'sensible' shoes).

The girls are strongly encouraged to be self-sufficient. 'I'd prefer parents not to come in and hang up the children's coats – children come to school to learn independence,' says the head, who is also firmly anti-PTA (school says it prefers to get to know each and every parent individually). Nevertheless, the home-school link is strong and parental involvement expected with homework and music practice. Parents regularly invited to attend events, from mini concerts to Father's Day breakfasts. The school website, updated weekly, keeps all in the loop, while the flexible early birds and late birds system allows drop off and pick up from early morning till late afternoon. 'If you're stuck in traffic you can just telephone,' said one parent. 'It's fantastic for working mothers.'

Families mainly within walking distance, then spreading out to Hammersmith, Chiswick, Fulham and the City. Highly qualified, often working in financial services and a mix of nationalities. Unsurprisingly, some can be a tad competitive, something the head keeps firmly in check. 'If someone rings up to demand why their daughter's not in the netball team, you just have to say, "I'm sorry you're cross, but let's try and be reasonable. There are other people better at netball".'

Given the location, families tend to be affluent. The website includes requests for housekeepers and year 6 parents are politely asked to plan family holidays 'to avoid jet lag before the 11+'. No formal bursaries or scholarships, the school always helps out existing pupils in financial difficulties.

Opened a boys' prep for 4-11 year olds in Earls Court in 2017, plus a co-ed nursery.

Fox Primary School

Kensington Place, London W8 7PP

020 7727 7637 | info@fox.rbkc.sch.uk | fox.rbkc.sch.uk

State	Pupils: 359
Ages: 4-11	

Executive head: Since 2006, Paul Cotter BA PGCE (40s), who is executive head of the federation of Fox Primary and Ashburnham Community School, Chelsea. Previously deputy head at Avondale Park Primary, North Kensington. As successful head of Fox, became acting head of Ashburnham, and oversaw the transformation of the smaller school at World's End. Sees the formal union of the two schools, both with multicultural populations but from different social spheres, as a positive; 'Fox has benefited from the whole experience. We've had to reflect upon our own practices'. Described as 'approachable' by the parents, and visible at the school door every day. Not content to sit back on laurels and watch the RBKC high-steppers bid for a place by renting a house on the doorstep, he is currently implementing the local authority's new entry system, with more equitable lottery-style admissions; not to mention managing a huge building project on the side.

Head of school since 2013, Ms Emma Madden BA (Cantab) MA (IoE); mid 30s. Like Paul Cotter, joined Fox from Avondale Park Primary in 2007, swiftly rose through the ranks of assistant, deputy, then associate head. Married with two children,

husband works as an environmental campaigner. To call Ms Madden purposeful is an understatement. Barely through the door, we were treated to a lightning lecture on the school's educational approach, whilst she fielded calls for advice from staff. Parents are rightly respectful of her leadership qualities. A young dynamo in the school, she takes great pride in the school's training record, and quickly dismissed our suggestion she might have time for extra-mural leisure pursuits. She is at the door every afternoon, keen, committed and capable; but don't expect a relaxing chat over coffee.

Entrance: LA managed, prioritising looked after children, SEN and siblings. Current catchment area extends from Westbourne Grove in the north to Cromwell Road in the south, includes more billionaires' basements than you can shake a stick at, and a small local authority housing estate. After priority groups, places allocated to those within the catchment area by random allocation. Unsurprisingly, given the international demographic, some occasional places, but loyalty is encouraged; 'We only want people to come if they intend to stay,' says the head of school, with a nod at the 'stay till 8' brigade.

Exit: Roughly half of all leavers go to Holland Park School, where results have soared, a few to Chelsea Academy. Others (with helping hand from a tutor) successful at top London day schools, including St Paul's Juniors, City of London Boys and Girls, Latymer Upper, Godolphin & Latymer. Parents say Mr Cotter makes no judgement about where the child goes, as long as it's the best fit.

Remarks: Perfection comes in small packages, and the teaching at Fox Primary is no exception. The small classes (two of 24 per year) and the impressive KS2 Sats results (the majority exceed level 5) have consistently put the school high in the league tables. The head pointed out they were recently the highest performing school in the country for two years running. The key to its success is spotting and training good staff, of which they are justifiably proud; 'It has huge respect for teaching as a profession,' a parent remarked. The Mayor of London must agree, to have awarded the school the Gold School award. Emma Madden is unashamedly serious about the school's role as a training centre, providing professional development for two London boroughs as well as courses for newly qualified teachers and TAs. She even runs literacy and numeracy training sessions for parents. In addition the school is a maths hub for central and west London, sharing methods among teachers as far as Shanghai.

Two hives produce Fox honey, which is sold. These city children are not just playing farms, they grow their own lunch and supply produce for a local restaurant

We were surprised to hear that, though energetic and youthful-looking, some staff had more than 10 years experience, and a few up to 20. The best of the newly qualifieds in training at the school are persuaded to join. 'There's a lot of support for young teachers', said a parent. 'I guess you want that fresh voice, but you want it to be quality'. The school has children with statements supported by the two special needs teachers, one a science specialist, but overall number of SEN children is lower than average. EAL proportions are high. One parent remarked how quickly the class teacher had noticed and dealt with her daughter's reading and maths difficulties. Support came in the form of small group work and individual attention; 'she's flying now,' commented the delighted mum.

The 1930s municipal school building sunk between chic terraces and mansion flats off Kensington Place is no great shakes. Classrooms are high ceilinged, utilitarian design, with steel framed windows, many brightened up by pots of geraniums. The younger years enjoy the ground floor rooms, where round tables in primary colours, a carpeted reading corner and bunting brighten the space. They make the most of their direct access to the rear playground, where netball posts share the tarmac with raised vegetable beds sprouting sunflowers and courgettes. Mounting a brick-built staircase to the half tiled upper corridors we met a class of older children, in quiet discussion at a large group table. Another group was colouring the Brazilian flag in a geography lesson, strains of gentle music in the background. We heard from one articulate boy that a parent had visited earlier to teach them some Portuguese in addition to the Spanish, taken in class. On the top floor a music activity had children, grouped in front of the whiteboard, following acoustic patterns by clapping out rhythms. A display of the SS Windrush emblazoned the white walls of the oldest children's room in celebration of black history month, as had a visit from Lenny Henry. The children we met were unpretentious yet confident, happily engrossed in their work. PE in the hall, involved youngsters shooting hoops in sensible royal blue T shirts and track suits. No uniform otherwise, though Hackett rugby shirts were all the rage.

Parents, though devoted to the teaching methods, were once unanimous in wishing for a larger site. Sure enough, there has been a recent new extension with classrooms, a hall and teaching suite, to accommodate the extra 100+ children.

Fox values displayed around the school: collaboration, loving learning, independence, creativity mean there is a healthy balance of academic and creative subjects. All children learn recorder in year 3, with individual instrument lessons offered further up the school. A school orchestra practises before lessons. Shows are big at Fox, with end of year productions carrying an ethical message (Charlie doesn't just find sweets in his chocolate factory but Fox's moral values too). Previous productions have included Matilda, Grease and Mary Poppins, with class teachers scripting a part for every child. Parents are happy to watch three Mary Poppinses singing in chorus. 'They are really nice events,' said a parent, 'with a lot of real warmth towards the child who stands there'. Other children join the inter-schools' debating team. A makeshift studio in a classroom at the top of the school allows the specialist art technician space to do her thing. We saw satisfying slab pots and displays of accomplished paper cutting. Some talented children's work had been exhibited at Leighton House Museum and The Tabernacle, Portobello Road.

An experienced PE teacher, 'adored by the children' ensures every child in year 6 represents the school in an activity: football, tag-rugby, hockey and netball run alongside judo and athletics in local leagues. Table tennis is a big success, with an all-weather table in the playground, and involves ex-Fox students in national tournaments. With many working parents, clubs after school in subjects such as martial arts, chess or 'thrifty accessories' are popular, one parent told us; 'The day people sign up, parents are queuing into the street'. There is a breakfast club for early bird children, and if they are still motoring after school, play care runs till 6pm, with tea too.

Founded in 1842 by a doughty female philanthropist, Caroline Fox (curiously under-celebrated at the school, we thought), when modish Notting Hill was no more than muddy fields. Originally a charity school for the local labouring classes, Fox Primary moved to its present site behind the antique shops of Kensington Church Street in 1935. Since then, the utilitarian architecture has withstood a sea change of bohemian chic in the neighbourhood, retaining a sturdy presence at the end of a quiet cul de sac. Within the high walls surrounding the school, some of the noble intentions of the founder re-emerge in a save the planet philosophy. A children's eco committee rakes out compost, feeds the wormery and monitors rubbish, and has achieved the Green Flag award. Solar panels operate on the roof, while a water butt supplies the gardening teacher with rainwater to cultivate some tasty extras for lunch. The chickens have now given way to beekeeping and two hives produce Fox honey, which is sold for school funds. These city children are not just playing farms, they grow their own lunch and even supply produce for a local restaurant.

Founded in 1842 by a doughty female philanthropist, Caroline Fox (curiously under-celebrated, we thought), when modish Notting Hill was no more than muddy fields

This is a foodies school. Lunches are cooked on site, with meat delivered by Lidgates butchers on three days; the rest of the time it's a meat-free menu. Some choose to bring packed lunches. 'Food's excellent,' said a parent. Favourite dishes included chicken and rice and yogurt fruit compote. Fox publishes its own cookbook, with toothsome photographs by one of the parents. Not a turkey twizzler in sight, instead delicacies such as pigeon breast in fennel, top secret pancakes and a recipe from the high table: Mr Cotter's vegetable loaf. A Food Explorers week is an opportunity for children to try

unfamiliar tastes. One mum welcomed the experience: 'I feel that if the other children are eating it, she will'. Trips out have included the Holland Park edible garden, London Wetland Centre, as well as the walkable South Kensington museums site. Older children have been to Whitstable on a geography field trip and paddle-boarding at the British Sailing HQ.

'We celebrate success a lot,' remarks Emma Madden, both among the four houses (named after species of fox: arctic, desert, silver, red) and at afternoon assembly, timetabled at 3pm, to keep the mornings free for the most concentrated tasks. Children are motivated in class by the chance of becoming 'Star/Speaker/Reader of the week' or by competitions, eg 'Who can invent the healthiest snack?' with a trip to a local café as a reward. Homework is regular but not excessive, numeracy once a week, reading and spelling daily. Discipline is not an issue with such an oversubscribed school. 'Behaviour is very, very good', remarks Emma Madden; 'children need to have clear expectations'. Parents' concerns are managed by face-to-face meetings with teachers in the playground each morning, or by email. 'They are learning to control that,' said a parent, conscious that high-achieving parents are experts at monopolising a teacher's attention. The school's Twitter account, no doubt managed by one of the school's two network managers, is full of up-to-date bulletins of the children's day. Despite this, one mum felt notice of school decisions did not always get through. 'I know the information is there, but it's just letting the parents know…it's been a full time job keeping up with it all'. Parents' evenings twice a year bring opportunities to chat to the class teacher, as does the annual International evening, a festival of the multi-national flavour of the school.

The parents are a committed lot; 'Fox is fortunate as it is in an affluent area,' said one mum (very low numbers on free school meals). Despite the area being known for its cosmopolitan beau monde, the school's parents include a few past pupils as well as professionals from business, legal and arts spheres. Fundraising by the parents, via the usual coffee mornings and cake sales, has succeeded in equipping the IT class with a set of iPads. The PTA has charitable status and organises summer and winter fairs with the aim of creating benefits for children from all backgrounds – Caroline Fox would be proud.

For the fortunate who break through the over-subscribed entry lists, can breach the formidable railings outside and are not bewildered by the airport-style security checks inside, it is a rare find: a quality education with a broad curriculum, led by a staff with vision and commitment. As one mum said, 'It's a brilliant school and we are very, very lucky'.

Fulham Prep School

200 Greyhound Road, London W14 9SD

020 7386 2444 | prepadmin@fulhamprep.co.uk | fulhamprep.co.uk

Independent	Pupils: 708
Ages: 4–14	Fees: £16,869 – £18,729 pa

Executive head: Since September 2018, Will le Fleming has been in overall charge of the senior, prep and pre-prep schools. He was previously deputy head and director of the senior school at St Paul's Girls' School. Educated at Eton and Cambridge, he is a teacher and writer whose work in education began with Historic Royal Palaces, managing a substantial programme of teaching for all ages from primary to A level. In 2009 he moved to St Paul's School where he was rapidly promoted to undermaster, a post including close involvement in admissions and liaison with prep schools.

Head of prep: Since September 2018 is Neil Lunnon, previously deputy head pastoral at Wellington College, where he has spent 24 years. He also spent three years at Eagle House Prep as deputy head.

Head of the pre-prep: Ms Di Steven Bed (late 40s). Educated at Glasgow University with PGCE from Dundee and an NPQH. Thoroughly professional and immaculately turned out, Ms Steven is imbued with the skills of guiding and bringing up young children for over 25 years. She has been at the school for over 13 years and took over from Jane Emmett at the pre-prep when Jane started the prep. With her lilting Scottish accent, spoken in soft, undulating tones, her clear boundaries and high expectations, she is a safe pair of hands and well equipped to oversee the 250 pupils in her care.

Entrance: The pre-prep is non-selective in reception, with 90 places offered on a first come first served basis (from date of registration). Priority and discount offered to siblings (there are normally between 25 and 50 siblings each year), and school will carefully consider both the balance between boys and girls and when their birthdays fall in the year. Five open mornings a year give everyone a chance to visit; parents who have registered are invited for an official tour with Ms Steven. After reception, occasional places can arise, but your child will be informally assessed, spending a morning at the school. Automatic transfer to the prep. Outside entry into the prep is by assessment and interview at 7+, 8+ and 11+, or occasional places in other year groups. Entry into year 9 in the new senior school consists of the ISEB pre-test in year 6 for external candidates – their purpose to make sure the candidate will be able to manage GCSEs. Some limited scholarships available for year 9 (academic, sport, art, music and drama).

Exit: Most of the pre-prep move on to the prep; children won't be prepared for the 7+ or 8+ and Ms Steven will tell you candidly but pleasantly if your child is not suited for say, St Paul's Juniors or Putney High junior. Despite this, between two and five children out of 90 do sit the exams each year. Some leave at the end of years 2 or 3 when often families move to 'the country'. Several boys a year move to boarding preps at 8, but most girls and more and more boys now leave at 11+ to a huge range of London day schools as well as a few girls' boarding schools. At 13+, it's mostly boys who have stayed on and are going to boarding schools, though the odd one is destined, (post pre-test in year 6), for eg Westminster, Hampton, St Paul's or KCS. School has a reputation for matching the right school to the child, rather than being swayed too much by fixation on brand or location. This may explain the breadth of destinations in terms of ethos, type of school and location and the fact that there are no large groups going to any one school. In the past pupils have gone to eg Hampton, Dulwich, Godolphin & Latymer, City of London, Putney High, Emanuel School, Francis Holland etc, or to board at Benenden, St Mary's Ascot, Harrow, Charterhouse Marlborough, Eton or Winchester. They can move up automatically to the new senior school. A clutch of scholarships each year, including academic ones to top academic schools.

Remarks: This is a very large prep school, and it's getting bigger as it expands into an all through school to 18. From small beginnings in 1996, with a few tinies in a scouts' hut near Putney Bridge, it's become a bustling hub of a school, now on three separate sites (the pre-prep is still located near Putney Bridge, senior school on its new site at Castle Court in Broomhouse Lane) with minibuses weaving their way between, and also ferrying children from all over west London, Wimbledon, Ealing, Kensington and Kensal Rise. A proper prep school that doesn't just cram for the notoriously narrow 11+, but teaches a broad curriculum, covers common entrance (and beyond) and prepares each child for life at senior school, it has been a remarkable success. So much so that the next phase in its development is to carry on through GCSE to A level. The plan is that it will grow incrementally but always remain small, relative to other senior schools, at fewer than 300 pupils in total between years 9 and 13. Sibling discount; some bursaries for families in difficulties. Scholarships available for years 7 and 8.

Situated in a cosmopolitan corner of London, the demographic of the school reflects its local area. There are currently 29 different nationalities in the school, including an increasing number of Turks and large numbers of Europeans including Scandinavians, as well as Americans and Canadians. There is also a core group of British families here and the parental body is 'remarkably down to earth,' observes one teacher. 'You're unlikely to spot celebrities in the playground here, and most of our parents are allergic to anything flashy.' They generally adopt a 'sensible attitude,' and there are 'surprisingly few helicopter parents'. The number of scooters at the pre-prep, parked neatly in rows and (almost) in colour codes, is testament to how many make their way to school without harming the environment.

We witnessed 10 year olds designing clay pots using Aztec art and saw some flamboyant portraits of kings and queens, decorated with fabrics and beads

The main building for the prep school (years 3-8) is a large Victorian building, complete with large paned windows, wide corridors and staircases, polished parquet floors and heavy iron radiators. Situated just behind Queen's Club in Barons Court, it is lucky enough to have plenty of outside space which is used for sport as well as play. A climbing wall, Astroturf pitches for football and cricket (played by both boys and girls) and even a red, old style telephone box tucked into a corner. In London a primary school with this much space is more likely to be state than independent and FPS (as it's known) certainly has the edge over its competitors in this respect, many of which are housed in cramped premises over several floors in town houses with barely any outside space at all.

School has a reputation for matching the right school to the child, rather than being swayed too much by brand or location

The quality of the teaching is good, though not necessarily uniform in style. Parents particularly praise the quality of teachers in years 1 and 2 and one mother of a boy enthused about the muscular male teaching in the top years of the prep, something that she felt was important for her son. A healthy mix of long term teachers as well as fresh blood. Year 3, the first year of the prep school, continues with class teacher based teaching, 'helping them to make the transition,' but specialist subject teaching is introduced in year 4. Children are divided into five sets for maths from year 4, Latin is introduced in year 5, and those further up the school have the option to do ancient Greek. Classrooms are spacious and numbers vary between 16 and 20 in each class. Between years 4 and 6 there are four to five classes in each year. Years 7 and 8 have three classes, mainly boys staying to take common entrance, but usually including one or two girls.

Parents appreciate being told exactly where their child stands in relation to the rest of the class, as well as receiving a report every term. 'It gives me a much more realistic sense of how my child is doing than I received at his previous school,' remarked one parent. The transparency extends to the advice given about senior schools; a comparison of pupils' scores in tests with the pass mark of a particular school helps to keep expectations realistic. As with many prep schools that continue to year 8 (and now beyond), the school attracts genuine specialists in their field and the rapport between staff and pupils is positive, we're told.

The music 'is totally amazing,' said one mother; 'sometimes they can field two school orchestras who put on stunning, ambitious performances.' There are also plenty of choirs, a wind group, jazz group and brass group. Busy parents come in especially to support the orchestra. One mother was delighted that her son, who had shown no previous interest in music, was loving it here. Children excel at their individual instruments and the music room, where class lessons take place, is overflowing with bongo drums, xylophones and keyboards. Plenty of large drama productions: years 3 and 4 recently performed Robin Hood and Alice in Wonderland, year 6 Annie. The pupils also enthused about the teachers' annual Christmas production as well as the Christmas talent show that included a Trashion Show complete with clothes made out of rubbish and recycling.

Lots of sport, with an emphasis on team sports, and focus on the traditional – football, rugby, cricket, netball and rounders, with tennis, hockey, swimming and basketball too. Sports take place at the old WASPs ground in Acton, swimming at Fulham Pools. The size of the school, in the middle years at least, gives strength and depth and they hold their own in competitive matches against other schools (although one parent with children in the top two prep years commented how disappointed they were that matches had been thin on the ground). There are sports tours (a recent netball tour to Cardiff where they trained with the Celtic dragons), lots of medals and awards and a tangible sense of pride among both staff and pupils at their sporting achievements.

Art and DT are given generous time in the curriculum (each class doing a term of each and then rotating). The departments are bustling but, like so much here, efficiently organised and calm. We witnessed 10 year olds designing clay pots using Aztec art and saw some flamboyant portraits of kings and queens displayed in the corridor, painted and then decorated with fabrics and beads. In DT their construction skills 'were being challenged'. Years 6-8 get to use glue guns. 'We keep everything very organised so that the children can find things and become independent; they learn not to rely on the staff,' explained the head of DT. Plethora of after-school and lunch time clubs (chargeable), from magic club and newspaper club to fencing and gardening. Good use is made of the city, with regular trips to the Royal College of Music, the Natural History Museum and theatres as well as residential PGL trips for the older children. Our guides enthusiastically recounted stories of getting stuck on the mud slide on their recent trip to Wales.

Well-stocked library, books ordered neatly, with interesting displays, beanbags at one end, large oval tables at the other. The tidy spaciousness nurtures focus and concentration. The grand entrance hall, with smart chairs, mood lamps and magazines, is more reminiscent of a Harley Street waiting room than a busy prep school, as is head's super plush grand office, in the style of a chic boutique hotel suite.

The simplicity of the ethos, governed as it is by the 'three Cs – courtesy, commitment and consideration', helps to keep children focused on what's important, without fuss and a weighty rule book list of dos and don'ts. Although there are more boys than girls, particularly in years 7 and 8, the school refreshingly appointed a head girl this year rather than a head boy. Senior schools, we were told, remark on the confidence of the FPS pupils – they don't have an air 'of being beaten down by life' – and this is something the school feels passionate about, preserving their childhood and sense of freedom for as long as possible. The broad church quality of FPS, and its

inclusive approach, go some way to diminishing the 11+ pressure, as does the new senior school. However, school is also very conscious that within this the academic needs of each child have to be met. Has introduced a scholarship set at the top of the prep to stretch the brightest (when we visited they were celebrating academic scholarships to St Paul's, Hampton and Sherborne). Particularly proud of the Trivium, a general studies course that pulls in knowledge from different areas of the curriculum and involves, for example, pupils presenting to an audience on the French elections, big game hunting or African drumming. This is something that the whole prep school participates in, not just the brightest.

Trivium, a general studies course, involves pupils presenting to an audience on the French elections, big game hunting or African drumming

Currently 20 per cent of pupils need extra support – whether because they have been formally diagnosed with SEN (only mild dyslexia, dyspraxia catered for; no one here has an EHCP, although there are pupils here with ASD and ADHD), or 'just need a leg up – a helping hand with study skills etc' and don't necessarily need the help of the SENCo. One parent wondered whether she should be pushing more for support for her dyslexic so: 'They don't seem to be very on it,' she remarked. Full time SENCo has four staff in her team dealing with every need including EAL (the numbers of which are high here at around 40 per cent).

On the whole, the school receives resounding parental support. The positives include the swiftness and sensitivity of the school's response when things go 'wobbly', the pride their children take in their school, the breadth of the education, and the fact that the focus is on each child's individual needs and capability, rather than unrealistic expectations of the cohort as a whole. A large school, without doubt, but one which doesn't lose sight of the small detail. The four houses successfully nurture loyalty and cohesion, and teachers on the gate each morning greet everyone by name. However, dissenters question whether they can raise the academic game enough to ensure that sufficient pupils are meeting the ever-higher targets of London day schools. Although the senior school may go some way to reducing the pressure this, together with a determination to allow the children to enjoy their childhood for as long as possible, sheltered in the vibrant broad church that is FPS, is likely to be one of the new prep head's greatest challenges.

Garden House School

Turks Row, London SW3 4TW

020 7730 1652 | info@gardenhouseschool.co.uk | gardenhouseschool.co.uk

Independent	Pupils: 475
Ages: 3–11	Fees: £17,700 – £22,800 pa

Principal: Since 1973, Jill Oddy BA. She also runs three pre-prep schools in New York. As a long-serving member of the administrative department – who appreciated the school's move in recent years to Turks Row just behind Sloane Square – proudly remarks: 'She has tremendous vision.'

Head of girls' school: Since September 2017 is Annie Lee, previously head of All Hallows in Somerset. Music degree from Exeter, masters from St Mary's Twickenham and PGCE from Homerton College Cambridge. Has taught music at various schools including KCS Wimbledon and Wimbledon High; has also been head of Highfield Prep.

Head of boys' school: Since 2006, Christian Warland, with BA from Exeter, (40s), left his work in the City as a lawyer and seems here to stay. He has found the change very satisfying: 'We spent considerable time analysing what went wrong in the City whereas here we are constantly forward-looking and this is very positive.' An old Garden House boy himself (and son of the principal), his three sons have been, or are being, educated at Garden House.

All three heads value taking time to get to know the children, from shaking hands with them and making eye contact first thing in the morning to teaching. Head of boys teaches ICT to year 2 and current affairs to the rest.

Entrance: As part of the school's desire to involve parents from the start, the family is seen as a unit. Usually girls are interviewed by head of lower school in January for the following September and boys by headmaster in October/November. Regular tours are organised for prospective parents, Tuesdays for the boys' school and Wednesdays for the girls', and there is no entrance examination, thankfully, so it really is important to secure a place on the lengthy waiting list with £120 as soon as possible. The school states that GH children live in Kensington, Chelsea, Fulham, Battersea and Westminster and that English is spoken at home by at least one parent, so very much a day school serving its local, smart area. Once a place is offered,

a registration fee of £2,000 is payable. There is a 10 per cent discount for all siblings at the school together. Around 50 boys and 45 girls join reception. Entrants at 8+ (by exam and interview) are nearly all boys, to replace the 30-40 who leave at this stage; scholarships and generous bursaries available at this stage. There is a small amount of coming and going as families relocate so it is definitely worth checking.

Exit: Boys leave at 8+ (30-40) and 11+ (12-15) for top London day schools, including St Paul's Juniors, Sussex House, Westminster Under, Northcote Lodge, Wetherby Prep; one or two to boarding prep schools such as Summer Fields, Ludgrove and Cothill House. Nearly all girls leave at 11; just under half go on to boarding schools including St Mary's Ascot, Downe House, Wycombe Abbey. Francis Holland by far the most popular day school destination, followed by Queen's Gate, Godolphin & Latymer, St Paul's Girls' etc. Some go on with academic, art or sporting scholarships and awards.

Remarks: The exterior of the school, originally a British army barracks, is well maintained, but what awaits inside is quite magical. We were struck by the attention to detail and aesthetics; the entrance hall is beautifully arranged with rocking-horse, pupils' models and high quality art works by professionals, including an appealing watercolour of the school by a parent, Martin Millard, whose wife helps in the library. Classical music plays and flower arrangements and lighting produce a calming, civilising effect after the noise and bustle outside. Every corridor and every room shows a care for the surroundings, whether it be the recital room, art room, well-equipped ICT suite or classrooms with vibrant displays, and this contributes to the attention paid to individual pupils. As a current parent remarked: 'This is above all a nurturing school, where boys and girls receive a wonderful education. It is so nurturing both for parents and children.'

Heads are proud of broad curriculum and use of cross-curriculum planning. Every class has

Boys were enthusiastically producing leaves in IT and art for FebFest, and the older girls spoke of performing at Cadogan Hall

a teacher and classroom assistant, with specialist teachers for music, drama, games, French, IT, ballet, Latin, fencing, art from year 2 upwards and RE in the upper school. Boys and girls are taught separately after kindergarten but come together for playtime and musical and drama performances, as well as some trips. Average class size is 15 for girls and 14 for boys, with mixed ability teaching for all and some streaming only in mathematics. There is a learning zone on the website and plenty of interactive boards and laptops for research. There is a well-qualified learning support team with a range of expertise, including speech therapy, so pupils can be assessed in-house; some classroom assistants are trained in dyslexia. Alongside the learning support, there is also a gifted and talented coordinator, and year 6 get help with creative writing and mathematics ready for 11+ exams. The boys and girls share the same broad curriculum, but many boys sit 8+ exams, so there is a different emphasis at this stage even for those staying till 11. Practice papers and internal assessments throughout the year help pupils to cope with different styles of questioning. Plenty of advice and guidance available to parents but tutoring is discouraged as unnecessary pressure.

The attractively-equipped kindergarten accommodates tiny tots in a separate building attached to Holy Trinity Church. There are morning sessions for 24 children and afternoon sessions for 12, and they share a play area with the C of E primary school over the road.

The behaviour policy, using traffic lights, is well thought out. A parent commented on how seriously the children take it and said that the red light is very rarely used – 'it is brilliant, a clear not emotional system.' The head was also reassuringly definite that she would have no hesitation in using the red light and contacting a parent if the need arose: if, for example, a child were bullied.

All three heads are keen for school to be fun and stimulating, as the enormous array of activities and events demonstrate. During our visit boys were producing leaves in IT and art enthusiastically for FebFest, and the older girls spoke of the delights of preparing music and performing at Cadogan Hall in the spring term to a packed audience. The FebFest programme, involving the whole school from year 2 upwards, is linked to a fictional character travelling the world and hearing music from many cultures and heritages. The school is handy for galleries, exhibitions, museums and concerts. Music is popular with pupils as the teacher makes 'music enjoyable using actions' and 'is not too serious but friendly.' We heard the boys singing with gusto, and the percussion teacher clearly had year 1 boys enthralled. Every year the chamber choir goes on tour to Normandy and sings in the chapel of Emmanuel College, Cambridge. The musical calendar is packed. Four productions a year at the Royal Court and the Christmas concert is held in the Holy Trinity Church. Numerous events and competitions include Varsity Challenge, House Shout and Garden House has Talent.

Sport is taken seriously with football, rugby, cricket, rounders, hockey, lacrosse, tennis, netball at nearby Burton Court and Ranelagh Gardens as well as swimming at the Queen Mother's Pool. As a parent remarked, 'It all happens seamlessly despite the school not having its own extensive grounds, as so much is in easy walking distance.' Pupils were keen to explain how inclusive the school is, with team places and encouragement even for the less talented.

Active and supportive PTA with a predominantly Anglo-American parent body. The pupils feel they are respected by the teachers; as one parent remarked, 'There is always a seasoned staff member who has expertise and experience alongside another with energy, who comes across as positive and not world-weary. The school is amazing'.

The entrance hall is beautifully arranged with rocking-horse, pupils' models and high quality artworks by professionals; classical music plays and flower arrangements and lighting produce a calming, civilising effect

Fridays are half days, though older children can do supervised homework until 2.30pm. Popular with parents who feel younger children are ready for the shorter day by Friday, and with those who want to leave early for the country.

Not a cheap school, although the Harrods uniform is also available secondhand and there is a complimentary bus service at 4.00pm to Fulham.

Sparky teachers, male and female, give a sense of energy in a school community in which the ethos is care, respect and kindness for all.

Glendower Prep School

87 Queen's Gate, London SW7 5JX

020 7370 1927 | office@glendower.kensington.sch.uk | glendowerprep.org

Independent	Pupils: 238
Ages: 4–11	Fees: £19,200 pa

Headmistress: Since 2012, Sarah Knollys (rhymes with tolls) BA PGCE (40s), educated at Wycombe Abbey and St Paul's Girls', Exeter (a degree in French and Italian) and Roehampton Universities. Started teaching career as SEN assistant at Finton House School, London; rose from form teacher to maths co-ordinator, SCITT mentor, key stage 2 manager, senior management team and school governor at Allfarthing School, London, a busy state school in Wandsworth (1993-2000); founding head, Maple Walk School, London (2005-2012). Married to Christopher; they have two teenage sons.

Bright and bubbly, Mrs Knollys exudes warmth and is highly accessible. She is the kind of person who rolls up her sleeves and gets on with it, whether it be teaching netball, transforming school lunches or wearing her slippersocks round the school on Red Nose day and dressing up in something crazy on Fun Friday. She is a woman who gets things done – as can be seen from her previous job at Maple Walk, the pioneer New Model school which started 'out of a trunk' as she puts it, with two pupils, and increased exponentially to 150 pupils by the time she left.

This is her first experience of a single sex school. 'I thought I'd miss the boys,' she remarks, 'but I don't miss the scraps in the playground – and our girls are very feisty.' She loves the girls, she says, because of their enthusiasm for everything, their lack of shame about excelling in science and maths and the more stable class dynamic – which can often be distorted by a predominance of one gender, she explains. She makes herself available to the parents, emails are responded to promptly, and she is there every morning to greet families. She is particularly on top of the 11 plus process, which starts with private meetings with her as early as year 4.

She is a good listener and we were told by one girl that 'she took on board our suggestions so we have much better lunches now, we no longer have to serve the younger children their lunch, and the loos and sinks are much nicer.' Her visible presence around the school includes teaching year 6 Latin, supporting maths in year 5 and English comprehension in year 4. That way she can properly understand each child and write detailed reports for the senior schools as well as giving fully informed advice to parents. She has one-to-one meetings with everyone from the kitchen staff through to the teaching staff and the parents. No one gets special treatment but everyone gets proper attention. This is a woman who throws herself into every aspect of the job and has been seen wiping her tears away during a music assembly. 'These are my girls,' she says unapologetically.

They are fiendish at netball and compete at national level as well as against other local schools

Entrance: Selective at 4 years. Far too many applicants for the 36 places. The girls are assessed on an informal basis – essentially to see if they interact well and can do the basics competently. Any parent who thinks coaching at this age is a good idea – forget it now. Sensible sibling policy means that often there are a fewer than 36 places open to newcomers. The tinies are assessed for 40 minutes in small groups. Older children applying for an occasional place will be assessed for longer – a morning or perhaps a full day, careful note being taken on whether they can cope and how they interact with their peers. No particular feeder nurseries. Occasional places occur but school unlikely to fill them after year 5 – the cohesion of the year being seen as paramount. It's worth a call, though. Some bursaries available for needy local girls or those already in the school who fall on hard times. Unsuccessful applicants for 4+ entry and later applicants to the school will be placed on a waiting list for consideration should an occasional place arise.

Exit: Recently, quite a number to top boarding schools – Cheltenham Ladies, Wycombe Abbey, Benenden, Heathfield, St Mary's Ascot. A wide range of offers from London day schools – including the odd co-ed one; girls tend to go to St Paul's, Godolphin & Latymer, Latymer Upper and Francis

She is the kind of person who rolls up her sleeves and gets on with it, whether it be teaching netball or transforming school lunches

Holland SW1, though some further afield to eg South Hampstead, North London Collegiate and Putney High. A range of awards – 15 in 2018, mainly academic, but also for art and sport.

Remarks: Think purple. Think elegant. Think Glendower. Natty purple berets, charming purple checked and striped uniform, purple website, purple chairs and folders in the class rooms, purple benches and tables in the playground as well as the purple scooters that the girls arrive on. Plush carpets and sweeping staircase in a building that feels much more like a comfortable home than a school. The 1830s white building – Thomas Cundy III? – on Queen's Gate occupies a large corner plot facing Stanhope Gardens. Part of the adjacent building integrated with the school through a major development and refurbishment programme. The resulting six storey building is remarkably spacious. An airy, panelled and white-painted entrance hall, complete with wonderful large Quentin Blake originals, greets the visitor and is also used, with the doors opened to the adjacent library, as an assembly space. Library attractive and well-stocked. Excellent displays of work everywhere, lots of up-to-the-minute equipment in all rooms, which are remarkably orderly with inviting and interesting-looking work and resources.

From the moment you enter Mrs Knollys' study with its oak panelled walls, large Victorian partners' desks and oil portraits on the walls, you know this is a school with history. Founded by two spinsters in 1895, one of whose eyes (Edith Lloyd's) follow you around the room from above the fireplace, Glendower is a charitable trust, and has always been run as a not-for-profit organisation. A nostalgic relief as spanking new profit-making companies pop up throughout the city, establishing expensive schools to meet demand.

Girls get lots of attention here. One teacher/assistant to 11 girls, class sizes of between 16 and 18. Not a school for those with serious SENs but school will pick up and support those with mild difficulties and make individual learning plans for those who need them. Between five and 10 per cent of girls are on the SEN register, more are being monitored. No stigma, just lots of support. There's a handwriting club during lunch break, some who have been diagnosed dyscalculic get support from outside – Emerson House for example; a learning support assistant will go into the classroom to give support with organisational/processing skills etc. No extra charge for this. Some five per cent come needing a little extra help with English and EFL is given in small groups or one-to-one as needed. Parents a real mix, US, Chinese, European – lots of bilingual, trilingual, English as a fourth language – but they are here for the duration – not much to-ing and fro-ing. Specialist teaching right from the start – French, music, drama and PE, and by year 4 almost all teaching is specialist. The academic programme includes DT and ICT, and Mrs Knollys is no Luddite – plans afoot to introduce tablets in the classrooms. Science is well-equipped and busy. The girls enthused about identifying cells under a microscope using iodine.

The post 11 plus programme is excellent and includes touch typing, Latin and lots of public speaking – balloon debating competitions against other schools is a popular one. Poetry competitions all through the school, poems recited by heart, girls vote for the winners and finals judged by eg famous actresses and poets. Lots of music – and the twice weekly music assemblies can feature anything from Bollywood dancing to a harp recital. Most girls play at least one instrument and many take musical theatre exams. 'Music is as natural as breathing here,' glows Mrs Knollys. 'No-one is concerned about performing and there are no divas.' This

Think purple. Think elegant. Think Glendower. Natty purple berets, charming purple checked and striped uniform, purple website, purple chairs and folders in the classrooms, purple benches and tables in the playground

school is no slouch when it comes to sport either, despite having no grounds to speak of. They are fiendish at netball and compete at national level as well as against other local schools and among themselves in inter-house matches. We saw several girls snatch some precious moments during break to practise their shooting skills. Theatrical productions and swimming take place at Imperial College, athletics in Chiswick. The girls also play tennis and rounders. Lunch: 'we are no longer vegetarian!' – another change introduced by the attentive Mrs Knollys. Fish on Fridays. Only vegetarian options on Mondays but the rest of the week meat galore. Food cooked fresh on the premises and they eat in their own dining room – no packed lunches here – hurrah!

Godolphin & Latymer

Iffley Road, London W6 0PG

020 8741 1936 | registrar@godolphinandlatymer.com | godolphinandlatymer.com

Independent	Pupils: 820; sixth form: 215
Ages: 11–18	Fees: £20,943 pa

Head mistress: Since September 2017, Dr Frances Ramsey MA PGCE DPhil (Oxon) (40s), previously principal of Queen's College London. Educated at co-educational boarding schools, the Dragon, then Oakham, she read history at Oxford and her doctorate is in medieval history. Prior to becoming principal at Queen's College, she was director of studies at Westminster School and master (sic) of the Queen's Scholars for 17 years. Parents at Queen's spoke of her 'vision' and her presence – 'she is always there', said one, 'and available,' said another. Married to Christopher, who is a professor of archaeological science at Oxford, and has two teenage children. She is a keen horsewoman and rides on most weekends, enjoys alpine skiing and likes to visit historical sites.

Academic matters: Generally extremely impressive. In 2018, 97 per cent A*-A/9-7 at GCSE, and an improved 72 per cent A*/A at A level; and a stellar points average of 40 for the IB, with six students getting 43+ points. Even more impressively, this is achieved without (too much) pressure. All the parents we contacted were adamant that the school successfully balanced high academic standard with a rounded and friendly environment. 'Our daughter achieved straight A*s at GCSE whilst playing netball for the school, performing in school productions, and having a great time with her friends,' wrote one father. The school doesn't have a prize-giving because, they say, it isn't part of the G&L culture to single girls out for academic achievement: 'It's celebrated and praised, but we want the girls to take responsibility for their own successes.' The girls agree. 'We're worked hard here, but in a good way,' reported one. A parent confirmed, 'There is a competitive atmosphere in the school, and the expectations of the girls themselves are very high, but I think much of this is driven by the girls themselves, and I have not seen any undue pressure from the staff.' 'The amount of homework set is very manageable and appears to be less than other comparable schools,' added one mother.

Humanities continue popular, with a high take-up of subjects like English, history and philosophy. Interesting language curriculum: compulsory Mandarin in year 7, plus Latin, plus optional French, German or Spanish. The following year girls can drop the Mandarin, but only if they take up another language. From year 10 they can study Russian, Italian and Greek. Maths and science are strong and at least a third of the sixth form chooses to continue with them. 'The beauty of a girls' school is that the girls want to do everything,' says school, adamant that it would never consider bringing boys in at this stage.

Around 30 per cent of sixth formers opt to do the IB. 'We think it's a great programme, a philosophy of education rather than individual syllabuses tacked together.'

The walk from bustling Hammersmith is short, but the streets become abruptly quieter and leafier, and stepping into the school grounds is like entering a time-warp

School says that it's 'very happy to receive applications from students with individual learning needs' – the term SEN isn't used here – and there are two members of staff employed to support them. That said, we have to add that not a single current parent of the many we contacted mentioned any such issues, suggesting that few girls here need this kind of help; and given the school's very selective intake, this many not be the place for pupils with more than mild difficulties. Parents of a recent leaver, however, were extremely positive that their daughter – who went on to one of the top universities – had received 'marvellous' support for her dyslexia from G&L staff, and were the more grateful that no charge for this help had ever been made.

All girls here treated as gifted and talented, and the emphasis is firmly on stretching and challenging everyone as far as they can go. It evidently works. As one parent wrote, 'The staff are dedicated to ensuring everyone achieves their potential and willingly give up their time to offer in-school clinics, extra lessons and other help when needed.' Another wrote, 'The amazing results speak for themselves.'

Games, options, the arts: Sport at Godolphin used to have a bit of an exclusivity tag, with parents complaining that their daughters got sidelined if they weren't good enough for the A team. Not any more: the school has worked hard to extend the provision, and the word that both parents and pupils now use to describe it is 'inclusive'. In fact, every parent who contacted us praised the sporting provision and described the sports teachers as 'incredibly dedicated.' Hockey, netball, basketball, tennis, rounders, cricket, gymnastics and athletics are all flourishing, and the number of teams has dramatically increased to around 12 per year group. The school already boasts a full size Astroturf hockey pitch, three netball courts and 12 tennis courts, but there's more to come. A new £6m sports centre offers badminton courts, volleyball, trampolining, a climbing wall, fitness room and a dance studio. Lots of extracurricular options on offer too, such as rowing, pilates, squash, fencing, karate, kickboxing and yoga, plus dance options including zumba, hip-hop and street. No pool in the new centre – to include one would have put completion back by another five years – but the girls we spoke said they were fine with it. 'If I want to swim, I go swimming!' was the prevailing view, and there's certainly enough else to do.

Music and drama have always been strong at Godolphin, and continue to be so, although oddly enough none of the parents we spoke to said much about them, choosing to concentrate on the sport instead. The Rudland Music School, with its contemporary glass frontage, is home to state-of-the-art facilities. Lots of choirs, bands and ensembles for girls to join, and opportunities to learn all the usual range of instruments. Several drama productions a year, some of them student-led, and everyone has a chance to get involved. These are staged in the Bishop Centre (named after a former headmistress), formerly St John's Church and now a marvellous multi-purpose performance space, with flexible staging and seating expertly deployed by the school's own dedicated theatre technicians. Speech and drama exams are a popular extracurricular choice.

Art, housed in a pleasingly scruffy corridor with paint-splattered walls, is clearly flourishing, with some wonderful work on display, and lots of girls choosing to take the subject for GCSE and A level. Loads of clubs on offer, covering everything serious and non-serious – we thought the Inaccurate Classical Film Society looked great fun – and the school arranges a remarkable 150 trips a year to every conceivable destination. Plenty of opportunities for community work, and all year 11s get involved with Model United Nations. School is non-denominational, but has a strong Christian society.

Background and atmosphere: Built as a boarding school for boys in 1861 and called simply the Godolphin School, it became an independent day school for girls in 1905, hooked up with the Latymer Foundation and was renamed Godolphin & Latymer. A few decades of state-aided existence followed, until it was threatened with going comprehensive in 1977, and, rather than lose its academically selective ethos, it reverted to being fully independent again.

All girls here treated as gifted and talented, and the emphasis is firmly on stretching and challenging everyone as far as they can go. It evidently works

The walk from bustling Hammersmith is short, but the streets become abruptly quieter and leafier, and stepping into the school grounds is like entering a time-warp: red-brick Victorian tranquility was our first impression, quickly succeeded by admiration at the school's ultra-modern thumbing-in system. These contrasts abound throughout the site and create much of Godolphin's undeniable charm. The school hall – far too small for whole school assemblies these days – is delightfully old-fashioned, and adorned with traditional honours boards celebrating scholastic achievement; the library is a miracle of modern planning in a limited space, offering different rooms for silent, quiet or collaborative study. Sixth form common room and study areas on the top floor are light, airy, well-equipped, and obviously used by the girls with relish and affection. Facilities everywhere have been tastefully incorporated alongside the original buildings, and the effect is an enticing blend of monastic calm and youthful buzz. A lovely garden, complete with pond, is used by the girls for quiet reading.

An average of 23 pupils per class, slightly high for an independent school, but no sense of pupils being packed in. Everyone praised the friendly, supportive and lively atmosphere. Dolphins, as they're known here, are an eager and zesty bunch, joining in and seizing the opportunities here with both hands. One mother summed it up: 'A lively group of competitive girls, all with different talents, but sharing a great enthusiasm for life.'

307

Pastoral care, well-being and discipline: Previously not rated that highly by parents, but as with the sports, the school has worked hard to raise its game in this area. There are two tutors per form group and the emphasis is on celebrating every kind of achievement. The result? 'Fair to outstanding, depending on the staff involved,' was one parent's verdict, but they all said how happy their daughters were and how much they loved their school. 'My daughter feels empowered and respected by the school. She feels the school belongs to her, not that she is a minion that belongs to it'; 'Pastoral care is diagnostic, not just a knee jerk reaction,' were typical comments. Communication with parents, once a source of complaints, is now almost universally rated as excellent.

Behaviour is relaxed, 'but there's no mucking about,' according to the students. No uniform for sixth formers, who are able to wear jeans provided they look 'appropriate'. For the rest of the school the uniform is modern, smart and smartly worn.

The variety and quality of the food came in for particular praise, with all parents and students seeing this as a vital part of caring properly for busy girls, and we can confirm that the smoked salmon and cream cheese bagels were wonderful.

Pupils and parents: As you would expect in this part of London, parents are hardworking, professional, mostly affluent, and ambitious for their daughters. Considerable cultural diversity, with numbers of students speaking more than one language, but inevitably less social mix than there used to be before the abolition of assisted places. Girls are confident, articulate, cheerful, and full of self-belief without being arrogant.

Entrance: Competitive, and becoming more so each year. At 11+, 820 applicants for 110 places,

but school aims to keep the admissions process as fair as possible. School is part of the London Consortium, which now sets a common 75 minute cognitive ability test (verbal and non-verbal reasoning plus maths) with great emphasis on the interview. School looks for 'curiosity and a willingness to think for yourself: girls who are going to enjoy the learning experience here.' Emphasis also placed on primary school report. No guarantee of sibling places – girls have to be able to cope with the pace of lessons here – but 'will always look very carefully at siblings, and for occasional places siblings are given priority.' About 25 per cent of girls come from the state sector.

At 16+ around 12-15 places available, all of them keenly competed for.

Exit: A small number – around 10 per cent – leave after GCSE to board, or to co-ed sixth forms at schools such as Westminster. At 18, almost everyone to university: 15 to Oxbridge in 2018, 15 to the USA/Canada, and pretty much all the rest to Russell Group institutions, apart from two off to study in France and one to Italy.

Money matters: Music scholarships available at 11+ and 16+, art scholarships at 16+ only, worth anything up to 50 per cent of the fees. Around 10 per cent of girls on means-tested bursaries – available to families with incomes up to £140,000 pa. Owing to its history as a state grammar, the school has no endowment, and the bursary fund exists solely through fundraising.

Remarks: To have your daughter offered a place here is a real gift. As one parent expressed it, 'I am a huge fan of Godolphin & Latymer. I have two daughters there, both very different girls, and both have really thrived.'

The Hampshire School, Chelsea

15 Manresa Road, London SW3 6NB

020 7352 7077 | info@thehampshireschoolchelsea.co.uk | thehampshireschoolchelsea.co.uk/

Independent	Pupils: 300
Ages: 3-13	Fees: £17,100 – £ 18,855 pa

Headmistress: Since September 2018, Dr Pamela Edmonds BEd MEd EdD, previously head of St Cedd's School in Chelmsford. Over two decades in senior leadership roles in prep and all-through

schools, in the UK, Singapore, Thailand, Japan and Spain, including teaching the IB in south east Asia. An ISI inspector, she has climbed Mount Fuji, enjoys sailing, squash, theatre and ballet.

Entrance: Entry points at age 3 into the nursery, age 4 into reception, age 5 into year 1 and age 8 into year 4 – informal interview and assessment, designed to put children and their families at ease. Small entry point into year 7, 'but we're quite selective at that age, because of needing to guide them to the right schools.' Occasional places in other year groups do sometimes come up – always worth enquiring.

Exit: To a wide range of destinations, mostly London day schools. Girls move on to places such as Francis Holland, More House, Queen's Gate, Emanuel, Latymer Upper, with occasional St Paul's Girls' and CLSG successes. Most leave at 11, but no pressure to do so, and some opt to stay on until 13 because they like it here. (The school has forged sporting links to other schools with 'small clusters of girls' at this age, which we thought eminently sensible.) Boys leave mostly at 13, to the likes of Latymer Upper, City of London, Emanuel, Dulwich, Wetherby sometimes St Paul's, King's Wimbledon and Westminster. School is proud of its track record: 'No child here leaves without the school that's right for them.'

Remarks: Founded in Surrey as a dance school in 1928 by June Hampshire, mother of actress Susan. On moving to London in the 1930s the school became mainstream and for many years was seen as a very traditional prep. Since becoming part of the GEMS group in 2007, however, it has modernised considerably and now has a reputation for delivering sound up-to-date academics in an atmosphere of kindness and friendliness. Years 1 to 8 are accommodated in the main premises on Manresa Road, a wonderfully spacious grade II listed building; it used to be the Chelsea library and still has the same air of calm tranquility.

None of this has come at the expense of tradition, however, and bookworms would adore the fabulous school library: cavernous, marble–columned, galleried

Sheltering beneath the architectural grandeur is some pretty impressive modern technology: a splendid science laboratory, one of the best we've seen in a central London prep; height-adjustable interactive whiteboards; individual computer desks in the classrooms; and an excellent ICT suite where we saw children hard at work designing a restaurant. None of this has come at the expense of tradition, however, and bookworms would adore the fabulous school library: cavernous, marble-columned, galleried, and home to thousands of

books. We thought it looked a tad underused, but the forthcoming appointment of a librarian is set to change that, whereat this will surely become one of the great strengths of the school's provision.

Kindness really does seem to be the way here, and everyone we spoke to agreed. 'The teachers never, ever shout; they're really sensitive to the needs of the children'

The school hall is a great space for PE, concerts, plays, assemblies and dance – the Chelsea Ballet School visits every week. Lovely spacious classrooms, and a well-sized and equipped garden for the children to let off steam. Team games such as rugby are played off-site in Battersea Park, and the children go swimming at Chelsea and Fulham swimming baths. Lifts throughout the building mean that children with physical disabilities can be accommodated.

Broad extracurricular provision includes judo, table tennis, fencing, archery, football, rugby, cooking, chess, cards, computing, debating, art, drumming, ukulele – 'We're constantly seeking to add to our clubs,' affirmed head, adding that they hope to lay on activities at weekends in future. Music provision is good and there are plans to get it better. Children can learn piano, cello, violin, etc, and take part in choir, and there are regular concerts plus the annual Summer Arts Festival. No orchestra yet, and drama is currently confined to class rather than whole school productions, although the imminent arrival of a second drama teacher will bring more opportunities in this area. Lots of trips, including annual week-long jolly for the older children to places at home and abroad. Parent body is dedicated and 'very proactive, very influential in supporting the family feeling of the school,' according to staff. Recent events organised by the PA include a Fathers' Day breakfast and a United Nations day where parents drew on their own variety of backgrounds to run stalls showcasing food from countries around the world.

We liked the pupil work that we saw on display, particularly the French, and this struck us as a school where children are free to flourish at their own pace. Teacher pupil ratio is 1:9, ensuring all students get the attention they need, and there's particularly strong SEN provision, both for those with diagnosed difficulties such as dyslexia and those assessed as gifted and talented. Full time SENCo is called head of enrichment, and is integral to the school. Speech and language therapist comes to the school to help on site. EAL is well catered for in-house: much demand for this, since this is a school with an international intake, reflecting the locality. Both parents and children very contented with their choice: 'The school gives an excellent balance between holding the kids accountable for high academic standards and a well rounded extracurricular activity programme,' was one parent's verdict, and a pupil told us, 'I like everything I do here!'

Early years are housed a few streets away in Wetherby Place, in premises which felt rather small when contrasted with the main school. However, there's been a lot of refurbishment, and it's clearly becoming known as a smart choice for local parents: there is a waiting list for reception places, and the school recently opened a third class to accommodate the increasing numbers. Teaching rooms are bright and airy, and classes are small: 13 max for nursery, 14 max for reception. We saw child-friendly, child-centred learning and positive reinforcement everywhere, and the standard of work on the walls was high. The little ones go over to the main school for lessons such as art and PE

and to use the library and play areas, thus ensuring that they remain part of the wider school, and a shuttle bus means that parents can drop their children off to either site.

In both locations, we were impressed by the peaceful, happy atmosphere. The bottle green and grey uniform is smartly worn, and children move about with a sense of calm purpose. Kindness really does seem to be the way here, and everyone we spoke to agreed. 'The teachers never, ever shout,' was one comment, 'they're really sensitive to the needs of the children.' As a charming and articulate young leaver put it, 'I've loved this school. I would have stayed here until I was 18 if I could.' 'My daughter's been made really welcome here, and we couldn't be happier,' confirmed a father.

Perhaps not the go-to choice for those seeking non-stop high-octane buzz from dawn till dusk, but a successful and busy school for all that, offering a supportive and relaxed environment in which children can be themselves and achieve their potential without having to compromise their nicer nature.

Hawkesdown House

27 Edge Street, London W8 7PN

020 7727 9090 | admin@hawkesdown.co.uk | hawkesdown.co.uk

Independent		Pupils: 130
Ages: 3–8 (gradually becoming 3–11)		Fees: £16,350 – £19,170 pa

Head: Since April 2017, Jenny Mackay, BEd from Westminster College, Oxford. Previously deputy head of juniors at both Lady Eleanor Holles and Streatham and Clapham High. Has also taught at Dulwich College, Eaton Square and in Dubai. Still teaches year 3 comprehension and drama.

The day after running the London Marathon, Mrs Mackay took up her role as head. She recalls mentally rehearsing her speech to teachers as she pounded along the Thames. 'I had to take it fairly slowly on the stairs on my first day!' she jokes. Keen theatre-goer and bookworm. Has travelled extensively. Proactive head who enjoys networking and spreading the word about Hawkesdown. As one parent put it, 'By cold calling the heads of local preps, and inviting them in, she literally rebuilt the relationship between Hawkesdown and these schools.' Stands cheerily at the entrance every morning welcoming pupils and parents, aware that minor problems can often be nipped in the bud through a timely word at the door. Married.

Entrance: Names down as soon as possible after birth. Pupils can join at 3 in the nursery or 4 in reception. Occasional places thereafter. Parents invited into the school two years before starting, to meet head individually. Confirmed or waiting list places offered 12-18 months ahead of start date.

Nursery is capped at 16, but room for 20 in reception. 'We appreciate that many families may want their children to complete their own local nursery, and so we are happy to take them in reception too. We have good relationships with many local nurseries and want to maintain this in the years to come!' head tells us. Sibling priority at every stage.

Gradually becoming co-ed and expanding up to 11: its first girls joined the nursery in 2018 and it will take girls into reception in 2019, with the first year 4 class in 2022.

Exit: Informal chats begin with parents at the end of year 1 to identify possible prep schools. Most boys currently leave at the end of year 3 though sizeable proportion leave after 7+. They head for a mix of boarding and day preps, with most favouring London. Westminster Cathedral Choir, Chepstow House, St Paul's Juniors, Thomas' Kensington, Westminster Under, Caldicott, Summer Fields, The Dragon and Papplewick all perennially popular.

Some boys sit for one or two schools at 7+ or four or five schools at 8+. 'When one leaves depends upon where one is heading. If parents have a clear future school in mind, this will dictate which year they want to sit exams'.

From 2022, boys and girls will be able to stay on to 11.

Remarks: Founded in 2001 as part of a group of schools that includes Devonshire House and Lyndhurst House. Named by its owner founders, Mrs F Loveridge and Mr M Loveridge, after Hawkesdown in Devon where there is an ancient fortress. This was to reflect the team spirit, hard work and sense of community of those who built it. School motto is 'Endeavour, Courage and Truth.'

Not a dreary worksheet in sight. Pupils were busy being explorers on a magic carpet in one class and pouring out gunk into measuring cylinders in another

A free-standing pre-prep. The big change on Mrs Mackay's watch is the beginning of the expansion of the school to year 6 and the introduction of girls, starting in nursery and filtering up to the top over time. Head believes, 'I do not think it matters at this stage whether a school is co-ed or single sex. We don't teach to gender.' School is responding to parents' desires to have their sons and daughters in the same school and to have the option to stay to 11. Exciting times ahead. Mrs Mackay's calm professionalism will surely mean Hawkesdown takes it all in its stride. Parents are delighted she is at the helm for this regeneration. No major building modifications needed to house additional pupils. School will become one-form entry, with an occasional bulge year.

School went through a difficult patch when there was an interregnum with deputy head becoming acting head. Shrinkage in numbers enabled school to plan forward. One mother stated, 'It is definitely back on track'. Another commented that 'the school now has a sharpened sense of direction.'

Huge emphasis on literacy and numeracy from the off and many pupils read well by the age

of 5. On several occasions, head stressed, 'we are not a hothouse, but we do get the best out of the children.' No setting as small classes allow differentiation and no child is under the radar. One father praised the 'customised' teaching.

Inspired teaching much in evidence on the day we visited and not a dreary worksheet in sight. Pupils were busy being explorers on a magic carpet in one class and pouring out gunk into measuring cylinders in another. Without exception, the boys were captivated. 'I want the children to have a very creative experience, so they look back on these years with happy memories,' states head. 'The children have all this fun but still get into great schools'. When school expands to year 6, it intends to keep its foot on the academic pedal from the get-go. French from nursery.

Homework is equally imaginative, taking the form of a Take Away Menu, with starters, main courses and desserts that allow for various creative activities linked to the term's topic. Pupils complete a meal over the course of the term. The menu of tasks might include learning how to sign language one's name, paint blind or create a Florence Nightingale lantern. 'They really enjoy it and it gives them a chance to choose and be more independent in their learning,' explains head.

Head is not in favour of after-school tutoring. She wants her pupils to 'have a life. They need to work hard in school but then have down time, so they are refreshed for the next day. We need to think carefully about what we expose children to.' One parent admitted there is a smattering of tutoring but 'not that much. The parents put in the work, though!'

Experienced SENDCo, on-site four days a week. All pupils screened for dyslexia in year 2. School does what it can to help with physical disabilities but there is no lift and it is not the easiest school to navigate. Approximately seven boys currently receiving speech and language therapy and one boy is having weekly one-to-one additional sessions. EAL support offered.

Non-denom but with a Christian ethos. Hawkesdown aims to be 'a place of fun and success to remember with warmth. A place where a boy can start his school life happily and make his early friends with confidence'. All newcomers are given a stylish teddy bear, named Jack. Jack is an acronym for school values: joy of learning, all in, confidence and independence, kindness and respect. Children are rewarded with stickers when they demonstrate JACK values. Gold stickers also given for tying ties or shoe laces independently and for demonstrating community spirit.

Pastoral care is a priority. School very aware of mental health issues and accepts that taking prep school entrance exams at the age of 7 or 8 can be hard. Masterclasses and workshops for parents to help alleviate pressure on their offspring. Head has noticed a reduction in families being hellbent on supremely academic schools for their sons at all costs. Mrs Mackay knows that 'if you put pressure on children they crumble, especially if they are getting it from home too.'

Took up her role as head the day after running the London Marathon, rehearsing her speech to teachers as she pounded along the Thames. 'I had to take it fairly slowly on the stairs on my first day'

A highly nurturing place that values each pupil's unique qualities. No such thing as a typical Hawkesdown pupil: 'We have the loud, quiet, quirky, those who struggle to tuck in their shirts, those who want to save the world ... we are very much about the individual.' Though many schools pay lip-service to this, Hawkesdown delivers.

Children have a say in running the school and boys recently requested to serve themselves at meals. Bedlam on days when rice and corn are served, but generally works well and children feel empowered. Not all child-led initiatives are approved and drinking hot tea at meals was firmly rejected. Orange squash on Fridays currently being trialled at boys' request.

Hawkesdown pupils do not go hungry. Food three times a day, including a sandwich mid-afternoon. Sophisticated vegetarian options include polenta cakes and asparagus tart; rice cakes for snacks. Everything freshly cooked on site.

Located on a pretty road off Kensington Church Street, next door to Fox Primary, so the street is awash with children first thing in the morning. Purpose built as a school. Fairly cramped premises with tiny outdoor courtyard but Kensington Gardens is used for daily 'huff and puff'. Not bad as a back garden. PE takes place in school hall, as well as nearby Holland Park. Football, cricket and tag rugby offered, as well as judo and fencing. Tournaments and matches galore, both locally and further afield. Everyone gets the chance to play in a team if they want to. Possibly not the right school for the uber-athletic. Chess taken seriously and is a compulsory lesson from year 2 upwards.

About 30 per cent currently learn either the piano or violin. Choir meets regularly and performs at the carol service, Notting Hill Christmas market, harvest festival and summer concert. Annual event singing to elderly at a local residential care home. Parents feel that 'art has taken off recently' and

walls are adorned with vibrant displays. Collages aplenty, and different years groups collaborating to make dragons and jungle scenes. Art exhibition in the summer term, where every child has something on show.

After-school clubs are mostly run by staff, but with some outside agencies too. Internal clubs include art, drama, storytelling, cooking, brain benders, board games, football and cricket. External clubs include chess, Chinese Dragons (Mandarin with some art thrown in) and Relax Kids (mindfulness and yoga). Sport, anything IT related, art and drama are always a hit, but all have respectable numbers attending. Many are free. Year 3 spends three days and two nights on a PGL adventure at Marchant's Hill in Surrey. Day trips to HMS Belfast, Wetlands Centre, Hampton Court, London Zoo and Royal Observatory.

Mostly dual-income professional families. Majority British but with sizeable contingents from America, Europe and Russia. About 40 per cent of pupils are fluent in more than one language. Most live within walking distance, and tend to walk, scoot or cycle to school. 'Parents need to be fully committed to the school and want to be part of it. They need to value our ethos,' states head. Most are very involved, but school is not afraid to tell parents to be more visible if they have not been glimpsed for a while. They are encouraged to attend assemblies, concerts and matches, as well as annual prize giving, sports day and carol service, and attendance is very high. Parents and grandparents read to the children twice a term to share a love of reading. Parents recently watched delightedly as their children sashayed down the catwalk in eco-friendly outfits, complete with compere. Parents report that school events are invariably jolly and entertaining.

Parents watched delightedly as their children sashayed down the catwalk in eco-friendly outfits

---

No bursaries but head explains that 'if someone was struggling while already at the school, we would have a discussion and see what we could do. We are a family and people do go through hard times.' No sibling discounts.

Changes are afoot. The introduction of girls and the extension to year 6 mean that this school is positively buzzing. Hawkesdown nurtures its pupils, encourages fun but also achieves academic success. Happy memories guaranteed.

Hawkesdown House

Hill House International School

17 Hans Place, London SW1X 0EP

020 7584 1331 | info@hillhouseschool.co.uk | hillhouseschool.co.uk

| Independent | Pupils: 656 |
| Ages: 4–13 | Fees: £13,200 – £16,200 pa |

Principal: Since 2002, Richard Townend (early 70s) – organist, scholar, and son of the founder. The present head is calm, shrewd, gently impassioned by the vision of the school which he runs – and a wonderful foil for an egotistical and anxious world. The running of Hill House, while ultimately in his hands, is shared among his wife and two sons. His beliefs are refreshing simple: 'bring children up with plenty of love and affection, and an example which allows them to understand the boundaries by which we must all live'. To that, and an inspiring academic education, add lots of fresh air, games, skiing and mountaineering, swimming and music. The morning of our visit, he was taking a vast choir practice of over 90 children, preparatory to a school assembly held at St Columba's Church. That isn't how most heads operate today – more's the pity.

After some stinging criticisms from Ofsted in 2014, the school found itself forced to address a range of health and safety issues, and to oversee some structural shifts designed to safeguard academic progress. It is a mark of the head's quality that he believes much good resulted from the whole episode. It was also very telling that the Ofsted debacle was chiefly notable for provoking an outpouring of parental, pupil and old pupil love and faith.

Entrance: Prospective parents have to go on a tour of the place – there's no booking: you just show up at one of the advertised times (these happen four days a week). 'Hardly sounds very onerous,' says the head, 'but just occasionally you'll get someone who tries to avoid it. No tour, no place. Simple as that.' If you like the place, then you fill in an application form. There is a waiting list, but – given the fast-changing plans of young parents and the fact that many go abroad – vacancies often crop up. The school tries to sidestep entrance tests, especially for the youngest children. Mrs Townend, wife of the headmaster, is in charge of admissions. She and her team make it their job to be friendly and accessible. Now offers 8+ music and art scholarships.

Exit: Wide range of schools including boarding schools. Most pupils go on to London day schools: girls' destinations include Frances Holland SW1, Queen's Gate, JAGS, St Paul's, Putney High, More House. Boys to Dulwich College, Wetherby Senior, KCS, St Paul's, Dulwich, Westminster, inter alia. Boarding destinations include Stowe, Gordonstoun, Harrow, Abingdon, Benenden and Charterhouse.

Remarks: The youngest, aged 4 and 5, go to Small School to learn their rudiments – physical development, communication and language and social development. With lots of free play as well as structured lessons, the aim is to build up confidence and competence. They move from Flood Street to Pont Street when they are 5 or 6, and start to focus on English, handwriting, maths and reading, supplemented by supporting subjects as well as lots of music, drama and games. Then it's on to Cadogan Gardens and gradually learning to adapt to specialist subject teachers as well as the all-important form teacher. Aged 10 and 11, the girls and boys have separate classes, as they set about preparation for senior schools. Most girls leave at 11, while the great majority of boys stay to 13.

There is more art, music and drama than one can imagine. The head is a fine organist

'The genius of Hill House,' said a parent, who is also an old pupil, 'is that they apply intelligence and thought to getting a child happy. Being happy means feeling reassured, not indulged. When they are surrounded by teachers who focus upon them with a fond and shrewd eye, they feel reassured. They can start to learn.'

There are three special needs teachers to support those with particular needs. The ethos of the school is to attend carefully to anything which may stand between a child and their ability to meet their potential, but also to guard against anxiety. 'Early intervention and calm management seems to level most things out very satisfactorily,' the head observes.

'When they are surrounded by teachers who focus upon them with a fond and shrewd eye, they feel reassured. They can start to learn'

Staff reflect the school's commitment to diversity and cosmopolitanism – a spread of ages and backgrounds, but with a healthy quota of bright and fit young ones heralding from all over the word, as well as those from within London and the M25. This is a family school and, as presently constituted, nobody who isn't a Townend would appear able to climb to the very top of the tree. While this might work to demotivate a lesser teacher, the staff here palpably relish the wonderfully idiosyncratic extended family to which they, and everyone connected to the school, belong. The proof of that can be seen in the extraordinarily high rates of staff retention. The head's deep knowledge of his staff, and fond regard for them, is an eloquent advertisement for the school.

'Almost too much sport,' one parent said, 'except that it seems to embrace all pupils, and so the effect is everyone of them feels involved and wanted'. All pupils play sport at least once every day. Given that the school buildings are housed in the heart of Knightsbridge and Chelsea, this poses some logistical demands, but the sight of boys and girls in rust-coloured breeches is well-known to residents of SW3 and typically presages a visit to or from various indoor and outdoor grounds (Duke of York's, Battersea, Queen's Club – the list goes on for ever). Longer journeys are also made possible by a fleet of six minibuses, operated (as with everything else here) by in-house drivers. As well as all the usual rugby and netball, football, hockey and so forth, there are limitless opportunities for individual sports and a full complement of inter-school fixtures. A particular emphasis is placed on swimming – to which the late Colonel Townend, the school's founder, attached a passionate importance.

There is more art, music and drama than one can imagine. The head is a fine organist and, back in 1972, a fine two manual organ with mechanical action containing 456 pipes was especially commissioned for the school and installed in the music room in Hans Place. There is also a stock of over 300 orchestral instruments, which are loaned to boys and girls for the duration of their time at Hill House, and everyone gets a slice of the action. 'I've just watched my son play at Peter Jones,' said one parent, 'and my daughter at St Columba's Church. They're not prodigies, but they're thrilled to be involved. And so am I.' Among many other offerings, there is an annual Christmas musical

as well as a regular dance and drama club. The school has three art galleries and children's work is displayed everywhere – all of it is framed. In a typical Hill House touch, the frames are bought at the local Habitat and knocked together expertly by the school's works department. The impression is terrific.

Hill House famously has an overseas annexe in Switzerland. Since 1960 this has been located at Glion, a mountain village over 700 metres above sea level looking out over Lake Geneva. The children are given an experience of a boarding school environment in the setting of a mountain village: there are geography CE project courses – and, of course, skiing.

The founder, Colonel Townend, opened the school in 1951 and was still in post in his 90s. His somewhat autocratic manner, the Knightsbridge address and the fact that the young Prince Charles arrived as a 7 year old newbie in 1956 have led many to assume that this is a school for toffs. That is quite unfair. Its vision has always been both forward-looking and international. It was among the very first of the so-called prep schools to welcome girls, its fees are a good deal lower than many local competitors, and its pupil constituency much broader socially than its elite addresses suggest. True, the place is superbly equipped, but it is also quite crowded, teeming with life. The children and staff are both industrious and relaxed. Both genders and all ethnic groups are fully represented at every level.

The staff here palpably relish the wonderfully idiosyncratic extended family to which they, and everyone connected to the school, belong

There is a series of handsome London houses – Hans Place is the site of the original school and this is where the headmaster and school offices are located, but there are other houses in Flood Street, Pont Street and Cadogan Gardens. Two idiosyncrasies seen in each are revealing: a discreet investment by the school in the latest chemical technology to ensure the loos are odour-free (an issue in some schools) and the fact that all the catering is done in-house by support staff who have mainly worked here for years and years. No agencies, no fuss and consistently terrific reports of school lunches. The day of our visit we passed chefs chopping mounds of fresh carrots alongside mountains of fresh fruit. That isn't typical fare in school kitchens, more's the pity.

The school has a huge local reputation – arguably one of the few fixed points in that restless, rootless world of Knightsbridge. It embraces the local community in the fullest sense, inviting local societies and residents' associations to concerts and plays and festivals, loaning its facilities at knock-down rates (or, where appropriate, free) and also doing a mass of fundraising for local children's charities.

The ethos of the school revolves around being tolerant, well-exercised, stimulated and kind, and contexts for nurturing each of these are embedded within every aspect of the school curriculum. There is a well worked-out chain of communication embracing form tutors, year and section heads, senior tutors and housemasters, all ultimately reporting to the pastoral deputy head (the only very senior figure in the school who is not a Townend) and finally the headmaster himself. 'What matters,' says the head, 'is that every child knows there is someone to whom they can confidently turn.' Anecdotal evidence suggests this is overwhelmingly true. 'The key to it all,' said a parent, 'is an atmosphere of great friendliness and patience, accompanied by an underlying structure and sensitive discipline.'

The school draws in families from south, west and east London – lots of children commute by bus and tube – as well as those who walk to school from various smart Knightsbridge or Chelsea squares. We detected none of those snobbish hierarchies which, in some schools, can make relationships toxic. Parents are welcomed as part of the school community from the first minute, and many are first-generation users of independent schools. All form tutors – the first port of call between parents and school – set aside 30 minutes before and after school when parents can go and see them. There are reports at the end of every term (a particularly full one every summer) and an annual parents' evening to discuss children's progress with individual subject teachers.

The uniform is conspicuous but no more costly than others, and a big effort is made to keep extras to a minimum. Individual music lessons and Friday clubs are charged as (inevitably) are the trips to Switzerland. Some bursary help is available 'in exceptional circumstances' – the school works especially hard to try to look after families which have encountered bereavement.

'Almost too much sport,' one parent said, 'except that it seems to embrace all pupils, and so the effect is every one of them feels involved and wanted'

Hill House challenges many of the complacent assumptions of our age. The fact that it's in Knightsbridge and that the uniform is so conspicuous could mislead one easily into inferring the opposite of the truth. The reality is a superbly effective and brilliantly resourced school – one which operates in a glorious time-warp in its preference for doing everything within the family and among the extended family: no school in the country can enjoy such deep loyalty from its support staff, which says a lot. Children of any race or social background will be gathered up here and utterly integrated.

Just like any family business, there are inherent vulnerabilities – and we suspect it may have been that which nettled the inspectors. But the commitment of the Townends to the constituency they serve is massive and wholehearted, and the palpable love and loyalty of all its constituencies (including old pupils), let alone their various successes, says everything.

Holland Park School

👫 20

Airlie Gardens, Campden Hill Road, London W8 7AF

020 7908 1000 | admissions@hollandparkschool.co.uk | hollandparkschool.co.uk

State	Pupils: 1,300; sixth form: 240
Ages: 11–18	

Head: Since 2001, Colin Hall BA PGCE (mid 50s). Born and brought up in Durham, he was educated at Durham Wearside grammar school. He graduated with a history degree from Sheffield and went on to to do a PCGE at Cambridge. His career has been meteoric. Each employer recognised his hunger and determination, as well as fierce loyalty (a number of references are reproduced in the staff planner for the benefit of his aspiring teachers). He arrived here from Longford Community School in Hounslow, his first headship; prior to that he had senior positions at Cheney School in Oxford and King Edward VI Morpeth in Northumberland. He still manages to find the time to teach English, which is the subject he has chosen to teach since his first job at Thurston Community School (now College) in Suffolk (his greatest joy, he says, is reading, and he read Sons and Lovers when he was 10). There is a more than a touch of Napoleon about him. A dynamo of man, we have rarely met someone who combines a seemingly unlimited supply of tenacity, fastidious attention to detail, boundless energy, aspiration for both pupils and staff alike and a total and passionate commitment to his vocation.

We were invited (unusually) to attend a staff meeting in the morning. Teachers here are (mostly) younger than 35 and Mr Hall invests as much nurturing and guidance in them as he does the pupils. Marking is assiduously scrutinised, lessons observed, goals and targets set. A canny head, he is also excellent at working the money and the room. The great and the good make up the body known as 'the friends of Holland Park'. Prizes such as the 'pupil premium award' are swept up, Alan Bennett attends whole school events, HRH the Duchess of Kent (known here as Katharine Kent) has her own set of keys to the building.

Deeply aspirational; 'no child is outside of our grasp,' he insists, 'no child is without ambition'. It does not surprise us at all that Michael Gove, the former education secretary, asked to come and 'observe Colin Hall' (although Mr Hall, with a disarming humility, says it did surprise him). Nor does it surprise us that when you Google him, Colin Hall appears among an elite band of 'super heads'. What is more surprising is that despite his Napoleonic appearance, parents describe him as having a big heart, a sensitive and empathetic approach. He also has a reliance on and affection for his trusted loyal advisers, the senior leadership team, but most notably his right hand man, David Chappell, associate head ('everyone is some sort of head,' remarked one parent. There are five deputy heads and five assistant head teachers as well as an associate head).

Academic matters: This is, unquestionably, a good fit for a bright, motivated pupil who has a particular flair for the humanities and English. A rigorous banding is applied across all subjects from the start. Band 1 pupils are considered by staff at pupils to be the crème de la crème. These are the ones taken on day trips to universities, for example and are the participants at the glamorous Perfect Tense event in the summer term when star pupils, selected by staff for 'outstanding achievement', are celebrated at a black tie awards ceremony in Holland Park – attended by the 'friends' of the school as well as by

parents and staff. One pupil we spoke to remarked that 'even those in the top of band 2 rarely get to go to Perfect Tense.' While this isn't necessarily true, school admits to the disparity in numbers – approximately 65 per cent of band 1 pupils compared with five per cent of band 4 pupils are likely to be celebrated at Perfect Tense. Pupils (and parents) are keen to move up a band if they can swing it.

All this contributes to personal drive and aspiration and the results speak for themselves. In 2018, 74 per cent of pupils got grades 9-4 in both English and maths at GCSE. At A level in 2018, 50 per cent of grades were A*/A. Not a wide range of A levels offered, but all 'proper subjects'. English and biology currently most popular at A levels. Fewer than 10 take Spanish and/or French. A tiny few do design or music.

'They lit a spark in my son,' remarked one parent, 'with a combination of inspirational teaching and incentivising notes of encouragement from the head'

Teachers here are thoroughly committed. They have to be or they wouldn't last. Parents talk of a high turnover of staff, particularly in the maths department, but Mr Hall holds on fast when he strikes gold with a talented teacher. Lots of opportunity for career development and promotion. English, humanities and art are all strong here and the staff, in those subjects, long serving. Class rooms could be mistaken for museums – ordered, uncluttered, tastefully decorated and minimal. Mr Hall's attention to detail spares no corner. Lesson plans are scrutinised, progress reports monitored and the delivery of lessons constantly observed and remarked upon. We were given copies of the lesson plans of every lesson we saw, as well as examples of marking. All extremely thorough and impressive. The lower bands have the advantage of the some of the best teaching. No-one is allowed to coast here. Parents particularly enthusiastic about geography, history and English teaching. 'They lit a spark in my son,' remarked one parent, 'with a combination of inspirational teaching and incentivising notes of encouragement from the head'. However, another parent deplored a 'boot camp approach' – evidenced by an inflexibility and greater concern for the results and statistics than what might be best for the individual.

A measure of staff commitment is the practice of opening the school on Saturday mornings as well as for one week during the holidays – for what are called 'interventions'. About 200 children will come in on a Saturday to benefit from extra support and teaching. There may well be sports fixtures and practices on Saturdays too. As many as 600 students have lessons over the the Easter holidays. Teachers aren't paid extra for this; their professionalism demands it of them. Parents are impressed by the thoroughness with which progress is tracked. 'If my son gets a lower result than expected, the teacher will ring me to discuss why this might have happened.'

Many pupils take GCSEs early (a practice that is unlikely to be able to continue under the present regime). By year 10 some have already taken four or five subjects including French, Latin, English literature, history and RS. A few parents regret this suggesting, that their children weren't allowed enough time to enjoy the subject and study in depth, cramming in a short time instead. Others feel disappointed that their child might have been able to achieve an 8/9 in a subject if they had taken it at the normal time. Pupils we spoke to bemoaned 'the exam culture', the constant pressure and the stress this can cause.

We were impressed when we saw a number of double basses and guitars in a music practice room, owned by the school but available for pupils' use

Not the school for a child with special educational needs, whether mild or severe, and by Mr Hall's own admission 'you have to be very sure you can meet them.' The school does have lifts, so can accommodate physical disabilities, and perhaps even a case of mild autism. There are a number of students here with 'emotional and behavioural difficulties', we were told. Full time SENCo but one parent remarked on the high turnover of people in this role. In class support provided wherever possible; occasionally a student may be withdrawn from class to be given extra support.

Games, options, the arts: Excellent sporting facilities – lots of outside space, Astro and tarmac for netball, tennis, football and cricket on the doorstep, as well as a spanking, shiny, well-equipped gym with basketball courts etc in the basement, not to mention the 25m competition swimming pool. One of our year 11 guides enthused about netball. Girls in the team are keen and committed and will turn up for practice at 6.30am on a freezing winter's morning. There are house matches every term and a house sports week. As well as rugby, football, cricket and netball, plenty of minor sports

also offered, including lacrosse, badminton, table tennis, athletics and rowing, and there are netball and football tours as well as a ski trip.

However, parents agree that the uptake and quality of boys' sport is patchy. Football is popular and the school competes impressively against the local competition which includes Cardinal Vaughan, Burlington Danes, Chelsea Academy and Latymer Upper. Matches and practice sessions are timetabled on Saturdays. Rugby and cricket, on the other hand, have some way to go. Although two hours a week is allocated, most do little above and beyond this; 'My son is getting overweight and has no way of letting off steam,' complained one parent. Perhaps the work pressure is such that students are afraid of committing too much time to doing anything outside the classroom? Either that or, as one parent put it, 'the boys aren't being enticed to do more sport'. However, the school will support pupils' enterprising initiatives – setting up an American football club, for example. A cricket tour to Ampleforth College in Yorkshire caused a great flurry of excitement, but 'the standard is low and enthusiasm quick to wane,' observed one parent.

The major drama production of the year is performed not by pupils, but by staff. The leadership team puts on an annual Shakespeare play each Lent term, well attended by the whole school community; it is clearly a strong bonding experience. Photographs of performances adorn the walls, and particularly amusing characters (who can't act for bacon, confesses one of the leadership team wryly) are discussed for months afterwards. With the exception of an annual 'drama evening' in March where a wide range of age groups perform a selection of pieces – perhaps from the A level or GCSE syllabus – it would seem that there is little drama for the students, apart from what takes place in the classroom during a drama lesson, or when studying a play during English. Apart from the school hall, used primarily for assembly, there is nowhere to put on productions on site, and no mention of any attempt to borrow or lease any local theatres.

A small but impressive choir is growing in quality and stature, and is led by one of the talented deputy heads. We were impressed when we saw a number of double basses and guitars in a music practice room, owned by the school but available for pupils' use. Some pupils receive financial support from the school to play their chosen instrument. Lots of prizes for music. There is clearly very positive encouragement coming from the top (and it helps that Katharine Kent is a strong supporter of the arts, especially music). An orchestra gets cobbled together from pupils who play an instrument outside school, but there is little continuity. When we asked one pupil why there are not more musical groups, she replied tartly, 'probably because

The leadership team members are ever present and enforce good behaviour – from attire to skullduggery

they can't make us do an exam in it.' School is part of the tri-borough music service (which includes Westminster, Kensington and Hammersmith); however, one parent talked of the music as taking place 'in fits and starts'. Peripatetic music teachers are not accommodated as there is huge resistance to any pupil missing an academic lesson to fit in an instrumental lesson.

One of the assistant head teachers runs the dance department, which is burgeoning. Two dance studios in the school, and several teachers; dance is a popular mainstream subject as well as after-school activity. We saw boys and girls, gawky and graceful, making shapes and loving it. When asked about drama productions, most parents we spoke to talked of dance performances.

The art department is exceptional – and pupils heavily rewarded with prizes and praise for creativity. Mr Chappell, the exceptional associate head, is currently steering a very talented group of students from year 10 through to the sixth form through A level art in the bohemian environment of Thorpe Lodge. A run-down and enchanting building, once inhabited by the governor of the Bank of England and with its own magical gardens, Thorpe Lodge is situated within the school gates and a stone's throw from the main building. Here, the art students are given free rein to express themselves, and so they do. Huge self-portraits in oil, spectacular installations and a plethora of other work was currently in progress when we visited. DT is well equipped with several laser printers as well as 3D printer. With the art scholarship students and a passionate teaching team, the school well deserves its reputation as an excellent choice for those with a creative bent.

Background and atmosphere: What you see now when you enter the shimmering glass building, replete with tasteful furniture, aesthetically pleasing fixtures and fittings, not to mention the delicate fragrance of Jo Malone candles, bears almost no resemblance to the 60s monolith that was Holland Park Comprehensive several years ago. Mr Hall and his leadership team (referred to by one parent, wryly, as the 'men in black': though there are two women on the team, the preponderance of young white men – who when we visited were wearing black gowns – give some weight to the analogy) have wrought a remarkable change. It neither looks

nor, more importantly, smells like a school. Fresh flowers, designer furniture (Ercol tables and chairs even in the classrooms as well as the front hall and communal areas), no mess, no clutter, and above all no damage. Everything is immaculate. The staff room is tastefully adorned with simple two seater pale blue sofas and blue Smeg fridges, banks of daffodils decorated the assembly hall on our visit, thoughtfully framed posters, paintings, poems and catechisms adorn the freshly painted walls.

The building itself is all glass and (sun) shine. Every one of the 1,400 pupils is housed here. With the exception of A level art in Thorpe Lodge, all lessons and activities take place in this one building. Everything is open plan, from the library to the unisex WCs. It's not possible either to smoke in the lavatories, or curl up in a discreet corner with a book – the building is easy to police and its corridors regularly patrolled. There is nowhere to hide. We were standing on the 'bridge' during break and it was like observing an installation – a river of smartly dressed, well-behaved young men and women moving seamlessly and smoothly up and down stairs and along the wide spacious passageways.

Pastoral care, well-being and discipline: Hall and his henchman is a phrase that slips easily off the tongue – even if it is said with some irony. There is little scope for miscreants. The leadership team members are ever present and enforce good behaviour – from attire to skullduggery. The open design of the building ensures that no misdemeanour goes unnoticed. If you're sent out of the classroom for poor behaviour – it's like being sent into a goldfish bowl. Uniform, attendance and behaviour all strictly observed. How else would the delicate Ercol chairs and tables that adorn all the classrooms contain not one scratch or speck of flicked ink or graffiti? These young adults are taught to take care of their surroundings, of themselves and of others.

Art students are given free rein in the bohemian environment of Thorpe Lodge, a run–down and enchanting building with its own magical gardens

In conversation, Mr Hall defies this appearance of zero tolerance. 'The development of individual relationships is so much more important than casting things in black and white,' he insists. He proudly states that no-one has been permanently excluded for five years, while accepting that sometimes the last resort is the only option. Parents are involved as soon as their child is excluded from lessons. Punishments include doing serious work over a period of two to three days – no break or lunch with friends. Restorative justice is a firmly held belief here – and constructive discipline.

Students are rigorously monitored. If they are disorganised, late or disruptive, are they getting enough support from home? Tutor system is key in pastoral care structure. If there is a lack of motivation in the class room, are individual teachers doing enough to support and guide – are workbooks being marked quickly enough, for example?

Pupils and parents: The school has had a glamorous history since its founding in 1958. It was the school of choice for the liberal left in the 60s (Tony Benn and Roy Jenkins both chose to move their sons from Westminster and Winchester respectively to Holland Park), and with Angelica Huston among the alumni, the school had a decidedly cool reputation. Colin Hall has restored much of this glamour during his 15 (plus) years. Although one parent referred to a 'champagne socialist' element among the parent body, it's no longer the choice of just the trendy left. A number of high profile members of right wing political parties are attracted to the school's rigour and aspirational ethos, but the creative, media element is still strong.

Parents who once might have saved and scrimped to go private are celebrating that their children can be educated to such a high standard, funded by their taxes alone

Located in one of the most fashionable and expensive corners of London, its demographic is very different from many schools of its kind across the capital. But only because standards are high. Parents who once might have saved and scrimped to go private are celebrating the fact that their children can be educated to such a high standard, funded by their taxes alone. You will still find here the odd Etonian or Wykehamist who has chosen to return to London in the sixth form. The catchment is narrow (currently a half mile radius) but it's not impossible to get a place if you live further afield if you can get in on the art scholarship ticket. Pupils here are smart, focused and polite. Ofsted rated behaviour outstanding and we agree. They know how much devotion comes from the top down into their education and they respond to it.

Entrance: The catchment area is getting smaller by the year. Now you have to live within about half a mile of the school to have a chance of getting in.

About 1,600 applicants for 240 places. Can be as many as 50 appeals, with only a tiny few successful ones. Banding tests take place in the autumn of year 6. Siblings get priority; 24 places (10 per cent) are reserved for the specialist 'art aptitude test', with distance no object – 'you could live in Glasgow and get a place'. Normally about 380 apply for these 24 places. Applicants aren't interviewed, nor do they need to provide a portfolio, just two drawings under exam conditions. There's an art aptitude waiting list as well as a main waiting list – possible to sit on both. Large numbers from local primaries but particularly Fox up the road. Growing numbers from the independent junior schools.

Entrance into the sixth form is tough. 'This is a very academic sixth form,' we were told – the high standard of the sixth form regarded as a role model to fuel the aspirations of students lower down the school. At least seven GCSEs graded 9-6 including English and maths. Minimum of 7s in the subjects you want to study. Priority will be given to pupils from Holland Park, otherwise proximity to school will be the decider between two equally competing candidates.

Exit: After GCSE very few NEETs – almost all who leave join colleges, apprenticeships or other sixth forms. One or two to the independent sector but mostly to Holland Park sixth form (about 50 per cent) or to other state sixth forms. After A levels, 87 per cent to university. Around two-thirds to Russell Group universities, including six to Oxbridge in 2018. Quite a high number take a gap year. Most popular are the London University colleges – particularly UCL and King's. Students choose to read a variety of courses from veterinary medicine, medicine, engineering and law, to English, classics, architecture and theology. A few to art college.

Money matters: Now an academy, but retaining its very close links with the Royal Borough of Kensington and Chelsea, it remains the area's flagship comprehensive school. Always well funded by the Royal Borough, this is now matched by funding from the Education Funding Agency. It has all the appearance of an exceptionally well-funded school, so we suspect Mr Hall is very clever at tapping any available and potential resources.

Remarks: Ofsted rates the school outstanding under every category – indeed 'beyond outstanding' in several, and the inspectors are superlative in their praise for the school. It would take a harsh critic to disagree. This is a sparkling environment and your child will emerge polished and bright if s/he is academically ambitious, prepared to toe the line and thrives under pressure. Comprehensive it may be, but it won't suit every child.

John Betts Primary School

Paddenswick Road, London W6 0UA

020 8748 2465 | admin@johnbetts.lbhf.sch.uk | johnbetts.lbhf.sch.uk

State		Pupils: 240
Ages: 4–11		

Headteacher: Since 2015, Jessica Mair BA QTS NPQH (late 30s). After a degree in drama and education at Roehampton University, earned her teaching colours at London primaries from World's End to the East End, before spending two years in Argentina, as deputy head of St Andrew's Scots School: 'It was a very good experience, to be immersed in a different culture and way of thinking'. More recently, deputy head at Queens' Manor Primary, where, as head of inclusion, she was responsible for its special needs unit. She describes herself as 'a change agent', which gave her the courage to take up the reins at John Betts after a popular predecessor's 26 year tenure.

Visibly competent and professional in manner, she reveals the secret of her success: 'If you find out what a child is good at and make sure they are happy and settled, they will fly and make progress', a philosophy she acknowledges that has been handed down from her own headteacher at Queenswood. She and her 'very strong leadership team' have introduced careful changes in the traditional workings of the school, swapping individual desks for work tables, updating the curriculum to reflect a contemporary urban population and starting up an orchestra. Parents appreciated the changes: 'she's modernised us a bit...new staff, new ways to attract the children'. 'Very impressive, very together,' said one mum; also impressively quick up and down the many school staircases. 'I think it's important that children run to school', she laughs, leading by example.

Entrance: Vastly oversubscribed. Places are allocated by London Borough of Hammersmith and Fulham criteria: priority to looked after children, SEN needs, siblings, then according to catchment area, which in some years is no further than one tenth of a mile. Occasional places are snapped up, when families move abroad or out of town.

Exit: Fewer children leave at KS2 than in the old days, as shrewd parents have become more appreciative of the 'bargain' of a John Betts education. At 11, half go to independent schools: Latymer Upper, St Paul's (girls and boys), Godolphin and Latymer, Frances Holland, Harrodian; half to state secondaries: West London Free School, Hammersmith Academy, Holland Park, Twyford C of E High School. Occasional child to an independent boarding school.

Remarks: Eight classes of 30 (one per school year with a 'bulge' year for a double class intake), with a teaching assistant to support each class teacher, as well as learning support staff, for SEN children. The national curriculum is taught in a topic-based approach over two years, so both years 3 and 4 may be studying the same topic, but with differentiated work, to challenge them at the appropriate time. 'Our children are very good at asking significant questions,' comments the head. There is a 'London school turnover' of staff, including a new deputy and leadership team, who work alongside others, some of nearly 40 years standing.

One mum described how her son left school with the sports prize, and credited his confidence to the school's ethos: 'I feel he can deal with anything'

The curriculum includes French from year 2, Italian from year 3 and students from nearby independent schools visit in the lunch-hour with an introduction to Latin. A feast of extracurricular clubs compliment the children's day: chess, coding (IT, to you and me); as well as yoga, netball, and skittleball. Years 3 and 4 swim at nearby Latymer Upper School and a football team, coached by parents, plays in a local league. One mum described how her son left school with the sports prize, and credited his confidence to the school's ethos: 'I feel he can deal with anything'. There is a tuneful school choir and, since the recent introduction of individual instrument lessons, a nascent orchestra.

Performances for the parents have included Wind in the Willows, Fantastic Mr Fox and scenes from Harry Potter. Drama club, we heard, is 'incredibly well attended'.

John Betts, a Victorian physician and philanthropist, established the school in 1859 under a trust and it continues to operate as one of only two voluntary aided non-denominational schools in London. The founder's desk fills the head's office and his portrait on the wall oversees that his original vision continues, as a non-denominational school with Christian values. 'The values that are handed down at John Betts are still here,' a former parent told us. 'My son has been taught to be kind, and tolerant and independent'. Sitting on the north east edge of Ravenscourt Park, the building is sometimes mistaken for a church, with its stately gabled frontage and marble portico. The local area embraces both community housing and smart stucco villas of Ravenscourt Park, so there is a vibrant cross-section of locals, 'a good reflection of London,' commented the welcoming receptionist. A short bus ride down the road are the business hubs of Hammersmith and Shepherds Bush, but inside the school's sleek new lobby, you are greeted by an oasis of calm and orderliness. We were slightly bewildered by the labyrinthine layout of the school, the three buildings of contrasting age and style interconnecting with stairwells and walkways.

The local area embraces both community housing and smart stucco villas of Ravenscourt Park, so there is a vibrant cross-section of locals, 'a good reflection of London'

Downstairs the younger children enjoy a low level suite of modern rooms, and an ICT studio, with smoky picture windows, which open directly into the playground. A glass canopy shelters the children walking to and from the adjacent 1980s extension, which houses a year 5 class. As we peek in, groups of six children round work tables are chatting constructively about maths. The individual tip-lid desks are stacked outside waiting to be auctioned at the Christmas fête. 'They made it very static,' explains the head. 'Tables allow the children to have experience of moving round the room'. An old school hand-bell marks the boundary with the original Victorian school house with its raftered ceilings and gothic windows, where we find a multipurpose room for music, art and breakfast club as well as an interconnecting classroom for the two bulge classes. The lively displays of work hung from washing lines include rock cycles and

Dr John Betts must look with pride from his gilt-edged portrait in the old study to see how the school's original principles are flourishing

ancient Greece, as well as a useful board of speech bubbles, encouraging the children to pipe up confidently with their own ideas: 'I noticed that...' and 'I disagree because...'. The head explains, 'We encourage chat'.

Behind the school, the playground has been given a make-over, thanks to the generous PTA, with an all-sports pitch, climbing equipment, a huge Four-in-a-Row and painted chess boards. Summer sports day is held in the open spaces of Ravenscourt Park.

There is just one hall at present, which converts to the dining room, with congenial round tables. Lunch is cooked on site, by a private catering company, and staff eat with children. Hot lunch is compulsory, to ensure the kitchen is viable, but judging by the aroma of the day's special, Moroccan chicken with apricots, with homemade bread and carrot cake as sides (vegetarian option too), there would be no difficulty persuading children to eat here. Whole school assemblies use the hall every Friday, and British values (as recommended by DfE's Spiritual, Moral, Social and Cultural development programme) are promoted, in the form of kindness, tolerance, resilience etc. 'We're not just responsible for preparing them for the next step, but preparing them for the rest of their lives', explains the head.

Good behaviour is encouraged with gold awards at assembly, and house points for the three houses, Eagle, Falcon, Hawk (the school council's ice-cream sundae names for houses were vetoed). Mindfulness and yoga encourage well-being among the students, and if these are too soporific, there's always Wakey Shakey in the playground. There were no reports of bullying – the school council explores both 'bullying' and 'victim' behaviour patterns, and the police visit to teach 'bystander awareness'. One mum reported, 'My daughter takes part in a little nurture group that is all about exploring emotions in a private space for children to talk'.

Teaching tailored to the individual is conspicuous round the school. One mum explained, 'They craft the lessons to engage everybody'. We visited a year 2 maths class, where the majority of the children were involved in a carpet time activity with the class teacher. Nearby a child with special needs was enjoying independent calculations at the computer, while a cluster of faster learners gathered around a table for extension work with the TA. The sense of industry and enthusiasm was contagious and we were pleased to see 'hands up' was still in favour here. 'They work really hard to differentiate and that takes a lot of work behind the scenes,' explained one parent. NHS therapists and SEN support workers visit the children with additional needs. 'Learning support might be for a more able child', explained the head. Despite this, one parent confided, 'tutoring does happen at the school'.

The staff got the popular vote from the children – 'my son just falls in love with each class teacher,' said one mum – and the 'family feel' of the school is upheld by having several ex-parents as employees; others run school clubs. Head takes advantage of the wealth of experience in the cosmopolitan community; we spoke to one mum whose sporting background was used to advise on specialist PE provision. 'I would not have put a hockey stick in a 5 year old's hands,' she said, but applauded the responsible way the specialist PE trainer had supervised the class, 'then the class teacher gets skilled up from watching,' she explained.

We heard about the 'very dynamic PTA' whose reps 'do a good job of keeping everyone up to date'. In addition, the head writes a newsletter each week, and there's a policy that all enquiries receive a response in 24 hours. Parents were aware they could have a quick chat to the class teacher after school, or make an appointment for a longer discussion. The head encourages face-to-face or telephone calls and has a firm view on emails: 'written word can be easily misinterpreted, clear communication is key'. Parents all stressed the 'very close community' feel of the school, and meet frequently at the many events, Christmas and Easter concerts, international day and the summer show, for which the whole school makes costumes, paints sets and sings (year 6s get the speaking parts). Parents help on school trips, popularly to the Kensington museums, Imperial War Museum and even The Royal Opera House, and years 3 and 6 get to go on residentials. 'It's a compliment to the school,' commented one mum, 'that I felt I wanted to put myself up for election for parent/governor....the PTA had quite a few candidates'.

Children looked smart in navy, white and grey uniforms with touches of green and yellow on their stripy ties. The school uniform list on the website speaks volumes: suitable shoes, hair ribbons and no zip up tracksuits. However, the website did come in for criticism from parents: 'desperately needs doing,' said one, who commented that the children on the school council would have a hand in designing a new one. 'The school council is not just a name, they are given autonomy,' she reported. A head girl and head boy are elected, along with prefects, giving the older children an opportunity to write a job application and undertake an interview, the head explained. 'It gives them exposure to talking to adults and public speaking experience'.

Possibly the best bargain in education west of Notting Hill; local authority funded. Extras for school trips made up by parents; PTA funds those who can't pay: 'We don't want any children to be priced out of the school,' said one parent.

Dr John Betts must look on with pride from his gilt-edged portrait in the old study to see how the school's original principles of curiosity and compassion are flourishing. Traditional and modern practices enrich the teaching, add to this mix a dynamic head, a lively modern curriculum and energetic parents, and – local fee-paying institutions beware – this school is a rattling success.

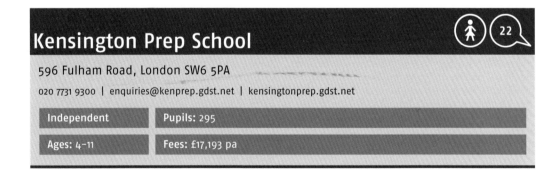

Kensington Prep School

596 Fulham Road, London SW6 5PA

020 7731 9300 | enquiries@kenprep.gdst.net | kensingtonprep.gdst.net

Independent	Pupils: 295
Ages: 4–11	Fees: £17,193 pa

Head: Since September 2018, Caroline Hulme-McKibbin BEd (Homerton College, Cambridge), previously principal since 2009 of The King's School Macclesfield Infants and Juniors. Degree from Homerton College, Cambridge. Taught in state primaries in Trafford then at King's Junior when co-education introduced; became academic head. After a career break to have family returned in 2003 as vice principal; 2005 head of Alderley Edge School for Girls' junior section. Husband a business consultant, two daughters. Interests include netball umpiring, theatre, reading. The previous head, Prudence Lynch, retired after 15 years.

Entrance: Girls come from 40 local nurseries and most live locally, many within walking distance. There are over 200 applicants for 44 places at 4+. Register any time up to September prior to entry the following September, with assessments in January. Girls are seen in groups of five or six and observed during play with every aspect graded. 'I couldn't care if they can recite the three times table. I want to know if they understand the three-ness of things in another context.' An understanding of English is important: 'It's no good if they have no basic understanding of what is going on and what adults say to them'. At 7 + there are a very few places but it is always worth trying as occasional places do crop up. Siblings accepted provided they can cope, but this is not automatic.

Exit: School aware that most parents choose KP for its excellent results. 'Fewer are considering boarding schools and the majority want selective, academic girls' day schools.'

A record number of scholarships in 2018: 32 (17 academic, 14 music, one art). Favourite destination is Godolphin & Latymer followed by Putney High and Francis Holland SW1. St Swithun's and Wycombe Abbey are the most popular boarding destinations.

The girls we saw were fully engaged in a breadth of activities without realising they were being assessed. 'The girls hear about fairies or the Big Bad Wolf visiting'

Parents we spoke to who had experienced the ruthless competitive examination process commented on how they have complete confidence in the school system, and how well prepared the girls are so that they feel very secure. One recalled that the girls did knitting on a Friday afternoon to keep them calm. The process is carefully managed with plenty of meetings in years 5 and 6 alongside an open door for advice from the head.

Remarks: Founded in 1873 in Kensington, it was the first school to be established by the Girls' Day School Trust and today the only stand-alone prep school in the group. In 1997 it moved to its present site, previously a secondary Marist convent in just over an acre of grounds. Clearly values belonging to the GDST, which provides expertise and financial support alongside independence. The trust cares

---

We saw the multimedia recording studio, and the eco greenhouse which complements the outside garden and pond

about the ongoing professional development of its leaders and staff. 2016 saw the completion of a £2.7 million building project appropriately titled Creative Spaces for Growing Minds. We saw the multimedia recording studio, and the eco greenhouse which complements the outside garden and pond. We were delighted to see the girls thoroughly enjoying their spacious classrooms with breakout areas and retractable doors, as well as the improved specialist drama, art, science and IT suites and two new lifts making the school thoroughly accessible throughout.

We witnessed a year 2 geography project work on the hi tech 'explore floor'. A carousel of 10 minute activities meant groups of six learnt about the United Kingdom in a stimulating, exciting way. Some learnt to use directions accurately and programmed small robots, others learnt to recognise London landmarks, whilst others learnt the difference between physical and human features. The girls we spoke to 'love the freedom to do what you like in learning. The teachers make maths and science fun.' Perhaps that explains why they do so well, winning the GDST Maths Competition twice recently, and four year 6 girls qualified for the UK MT Maths Challenge designed for years 7 and 8.

The dining room looks inviting with its bright colour scheme, modern lighting and freshly cooked food on the premises, which we sampled and enjoyed. There are a few classrooms with traditional desks but all have plenty of light and space. Accomplished artwork decorates walls, many of which are crammed with questions and ongoing thinking by pupils, not often seen on a school tour. Self-directed, independent and collaborative ways to learn abound, and in such an academic environment, girls need to be robust and willing to participate if they are to thrive.

With two courts on site as well as nearby Fulham pools and King's House Sports Grounds for sports day, girls are given plenty of opportunities to play in fixtures. In truth the games department is eclipsed by the starry music department. Girls perform at Cadogan Hall and there are three choirs, four orchestras, chamber ensembles and a main orchestra with over 100 players. A biannual overseas music tour takes place to Europe, for example to Holland and Venice, with a planned visit to Budapest. An artist in residence works alongside the art teacher as well as providing clubs. There is no pottery but we saw accomplished models. There is an extensive club programme which includes football and trips galore.

The early years section is superbly resourced inside and outside with free flow. The girls we saw were fully engaged in a breadth of activities without realising they were being assessed by experienced staff. One parent shared how 'the girls hear about fairies or the Big Bad Wolf visiting, and in year 2 a fairy lives in the classroom and girls can write to her if they have a concern and receive a reply.' Parents love the fact their daughters are happy and have fun at school. A director of individualised learning and assistant learning support coordinator ensure pupils are given extra support at different levels where necessary. This may be small group support by a teaching assistant or teacher within or outside the classroom.

A school counsellor is in school three days a week. The online communication system supports homework with iPads and a learning platform showing how mathematics has been taught in the lesson.

Parents we spoke to remarked, 'The school has a lovely community feeling and right from the start girls know how important it is to be kind and good.' This is a caring, not a cosy school where girls need to be willing to be challenged. Inspectors awarded the school the highest possible grades across the board in the latest report. They rated the quality of pupils' learning and achievements exceptional. This is not a school for the fainthearted, staff or pupils, but it is one where all share the excitement and creativity of learning. KP is the ideal school for a high flyer. The pace is fast and the girls are happy, have fun and are zippy.

Knightsbridge School

67 Pont Street, London SW1X 0BD

020 7590 9000 | registrar@knightsbridgeschool.com | knightsbridgeschool.com

Independent	Pupils: 401
Ages: 3–13	Fees: £19,500 – £20,700 pa

Principal: and founder, since the school opened in 2006, Magoo Giles (50ish), known universally and affectionately as Magoo. Married with two children, one in the school. Via Summer Fields, Eton, the Coldstream Guards and two years as personal equerry to the Queen, he spent six years as head of nearby Garden House Boys' School. If he wasn't a teacher from the off, he should have been – he exudes ebullience, dedication and high educational values. With the backing of 50 friends and family members, he got hold of the building on the corner of Lennox Gardens and Pont Street – formerly home of The Hellenic College – and began to create a dream come true. Magoo is energy, enthusiasm, loquacity and huge fun in pinstripes. He is not out to process children for any particular school but to ensure his school maintains the values, atmosphere and friendliness that make a sound learning environment for all. Parents praise his pastoral care for their children. His school was celebrating its 10th anniversary when we visited. Hard to believe it's not been a fixture for far longer.

Headteacher: Since 2015, Shona Colaço MA PGCE MSB CBiol (50s), previously head of science, director of studies and, finally, deputy head at Hampton Court House School; a biologist by training. Married and with two children, she has upped the profile of science in the school and has also developed leadership courses for her staff – which can, of course, lead to their leaving to lead elsewhere. 'I am as ambitious for my colleagues as for our pupils.' Parents approve: 'The school needed someone more academic'. If listening to Magoo is like being showered by freshly uncorked champagne, chatting with Shona is a reassuring glass of fine wine. She is calm, efficient, warm and experienced – and just as much fun as Magoo, only quieter. Their rooms adjoin, an open door between them, and you can't avoid thinking 'dream team' when you see – and hear – them working together. A wise and mature appointment for a fast-maturing school.

Entrance: Nursery is just for siblings and most entrants join at reception into which they take four classes with a maximum of 18 children in each. They close the lists at 200 applicants and Magoo sees all candidate parents and children – the child does activities with the head of early years while the grown-ups chat. Occasional places thereafter

– younger candidates spend a day with their own age group and older ones sit tests and are interviewed. All is designed to ensure that children will fit in and involve themselves and that school and child will suit each other. Most from local nurseries eg Miss Daisy's, Tadpoles, Chelsea Pre-prep and Pippa Poppins.

Exit: Most girls leave at 11 and boys at 13; Queen's Gate currently the most popular at 11, then Francis Holland SW1 and Harrodian; Wetherby most popular 13+ destination, with the odd one or two to Prior's Field, Uppingham and St Paul's. Wise approach to children going to the best schools for them. This is not the school for you if you want your sprog spoon-fed for a school with a name you can brag about.

Remarks: On the corner of Pont Street and Lennox Gardens in a tall, six storey, once private, house complete with grand, limed oak staircase, back stairs, ballroom, erstwhile kitchens, spacious halls, interesting and large triangular corner rooms and lots of little rooms and passages. Few vestiges of the late lamented Hellenic College and its Grecian legacy can still be found about the place. An upmarket prep was the natural successor to its prior tenant and Knightsbridge School has quickly established itself as the natural school for its local constituency of sophisticated, moneyed and cosmopolitan residents. Despite its location, the road is extraordinarily quiet much of the day. The school encourages its families to walk to school, in the interests both of health and out of consideration for neighbours.

Much of the ethos is encapsulated in the little KS book given to pupils. It is quite wonderful, whisks us back to our grandparents' childhood and we will carry it everywhere

Quiet learning in every room. Every class has a teacher and an assistant. We have seldom seen such engaged children, at all levels. Bright, young (mostly female and blonde) staff – all smiles and energy. Curriculum trad and sensible, complemented by brand-new Macs and iPads and laptops with in-class charger units and all used with proper educational values rather than for their own sakes. We even spotted some books! Those on school's SEN register are supported in-class, in small groups and individually. Speech and language and occupational therapists come in as needed. Full time SENCo of whom warm reports. Tribute from one

particularly grateful young dyslexic learner: 'Learning support changed everything for me. I don't go to ICT classes, I have one-to-one instead. I'd never have got to Harrow without her help.'

Much enthusiasm for many teachers eg 'he is brilliant!' Parents praise the care and attention given to their children. Rare and only gentle grouse from both parents and children is about a high turnover of staff – especially among the younger ones. To some extent this reflects the school's success in creating new leaders but, as one harder-nosed, parent observed, 'They all want Knightsbridge on their cv'. Also some wise and older staff, so youth and energy are balanced by experience and thoughtfulness. But the hope that a house tutor would stay with a child throughout its KS career seems unlikely to be fulfilled very often. Parental praise for academic support given to those who stay into year 8. Somewhat quieter praise for support given to those who take 11+ entrance tests. 'We need more help with English and maths and less other stuff when the exams are coming.' But this may express perennial parental anxiety more than anything else.

Art room on top floor with pitched ceilings and skylight. Art activities limited by space and resources but what we saw was imaginative and pleasing. Projects on eg 'fish' and 'looking out of the window'. No real DT though some textile work; 3D printer in Mac room. Though the (very well-cared-for) building has its airy spaces, on-site activity space is limited. 'We do miss having a playground.' One good gym in the basement is supplemented by the excellent and capacious facilities at St Columba's church opposite with its huge hall – used by the school for everything that needs real space. Otherwise, buses take children to local parks etc and no-one complains of a lack of exercise – despite the lack of space. Hot days make much of the place airless and stuffy, despite fans and windows.

Much of the ethos is encapsulated in and by the little KS book given to pupils. Its 96 pages include everything from The KS Code and Song ('You're on the winning team all the way at KS/You get the most from every day'); selective capital cities (no Brazil, Nigeria or Israel but Monaco?); rules of various games including poker; wives of Henry VIII; 12 famous women (one is Coco Chanel); famous speeches; 'thank you' in 24 languages; the periodic table; signs of the zodiac; instructions on how to tie a tie and some predictable hymns. It is quite wonderful, whisks us cheerily back to our grandparents' childhood and we will carry it everywhere.

Parents and children enthuse about the range and variety of activities and clubs on offer – impressive for a prep, especially a day prep. Lots of rewards (Supers) and some demerits (Subs) and a well-understood system for both. Trophies, cups

If he wasn't a teacher from the off, he should have been – he exudes ebullience, dedication and high educational values

and shields galore. House system which works vertically and horizontally and important for competition in sports, quizzes, arts etc. Effective tutor system clearly trusted by the pupils and especially in moments of anxiety or distress. Also Place2Be – recently won award – a counselling resource with its own room and handled with tact. Parental praise for the home-school communications which are frequent and close. Teachers in the junior school are Miss, Mrs or Mr plus First Name. On Magoo's door is, simply, Magoo. Food looked jolly good to us – especially scrumptious fruit bowls – but a few junior gourmets grumbled about lack of choice.

Most families live in Kensington, Chelsea, Belgravia. A few from such outbacks as Fulham and Battersea. Lots of Americans. But, at time of our visit, around 20 home languages spoken so an interestingly diverse constituency reflecting the neighbourhood. Smallish percentage of pupils need and get EAL help but the staff can muster several languages between them and induction of ESOL pupils is carefully handled. International families love the fact that so many are from overseas, 'so my children don't feel alien like they would in other preps – it's a real melting pot,' said one. Very lively and popular Parents' Association particularly valued by the recently arrived international families who make friends and quickly involve themselves. Five PA committees and a Knowledge Society which invites guest speakers for parental enlightenment, education and entertainment. Every parent we spoke to stressed how 'super-happy' their offspring were. Lots of involvement in local charities and eco initiatives – a palpable concern not to upset the neighbours – many of whom are current parents – clearly a priority.

KS Foundation – largely supported by parents – offers two 100 per cent bursaries annually for children in years 7-9. NB this is an important opportunity, especially for state primary leavers who want to go to senior schools which start at 13+. The commitment can extend to helping bursary-holders into senior schools which will offer continuing significant financial support. Otherwise, no fee assistance lower down the school unless in cases of dire, short-term need.

A lovable school with a warm and community feel that surprises in such a location. If you have no other reason, it's worth moving to Knightsbridge for.

Lady Margaret School

Parsons Green, London SW6 4UN

020 7736 7138 | admissions@ladymargaret.lbhf.sch.uk | ladymargaret.lbhf.sch.uk

State		Pupils: 736; sixth form: 162
Ages: 11–18		

Headteacher: Since 2015, Elisabeth Stevenson MA PGCE, previously deputy head at Grey Coat Hospital. Degree in medieval history plus later, part time, degree in early modern European history at Birkbeck. Taught history at Rickmansworth School before moving to Grey Coat in 2000 as head of history, then assistant, then deputy head. An excellent training ground for Lady Margaret, with which it has much in common. Although only a year into her tenure when we visited, her leadership, innovations and smiley presence were palpable. Parents and girls seem enchanted by her – 'so involved and visible about the school'; 'she speaks so well'; 'look – her door is open, it always is – that speaks volumes' – and in fact, both doors into her room – to the atrium and to the garden – were wide open: she could hardly be more accessible. Entirely visible around the school, Ms Stevenson is completely invisible on the school website, even if you put her name in Search, which seems a shame.

A practising Anglican, she celebrates the 'Christian values' and the 'centrality of worship' to her school's ethos. 'It frames and shapes the day,' she told us. 'Every assembly begins with lighting a candle and ends with a prayer. And we say grace at the end of each school day.' But she will not rush

Kensington Prep School

to embrace the option of admitting 100 per cent of pupils on the basis of a shared faith: 'I think as a Church of England school we should serve everyone in our local community, not just the church community.' She has ideas and principles but is not dogmatic. 'I don't think education is something that happens to you. It's about engaging. Schooling should be characterised by kindness and engagement.' Girls concur: 'She runs a tight ship and is very organised but is so approachable!'

Academic matters: They are doing something right here. Despite a scrupulously banded intake, the results they produce defy any reasonable expectation. It must be all about aspiration and ambition. Psychology, Eng lit, maths and history the most popular A level options in a range that includes history of art and IT. Forty-three per cent of grades were A*/A and 69 per cent were A*-B in 2018. Fine art – see below – and history the most successful but few subjects saw many grades below C. Everyone takes core GCSEs which here include RS. Equal numbers for French and Spanish – no other languages timetabled. Around three-quarters take all three sciences. Fifty-seven per cent of all GCSE grades were 9-7 in 2018 (88 per cent got 9-4 in both English and maths). RS, perhaps unsurprisingly, the stand-out success. We were interested in the approach here: 'Not all the RS teachers are from the Anglican tradition. They are very open to all religions and always willing to debate and discuss.' We toured the school and witnessed class after class of girls, head down or in earnest collaboration – evidence of the head's claims that 'girls don't have to be ashamed of working hard here.. they are ambitious and want to do well – even the naughty ones!'

She has ideas and principles but is not dogmatic. 'I don't think education is something that happens to you. It's about engaging. Schooling should be characterised by kindness'

Overwhelmingly positive approach. The school uses the WWW (What Went Well) remark and an EBI (Even Better If) comment on every piece of work. We think this a sound way of keeping teachers up to the mark quite as much as pupils. We enjoyed many features of work and evidence of thinking here eg the What Is Your Favourite Book display board and were intrigued by the choices: – lots of Roald Dahl (predictable), one Pride and Prejudice (estimable), one Ulysses (impressive, if implausible) and one 50 Shades of Grey (lamentable).

At the time of our visit, 10 girls had statements or EHC plans and a further 60 received some kind of SEN support. Level of support varies according to need eg differentiated work and resources, LSAs in lessons, withdrawal, small groups and in-class support where needed. SEN department runs homework club, reduced timetables and curriculum support sessions. Also external agencies provide eg additional therapies such as speech and language and drama. School would welcome anyone including those with mild ASD but the site prohibits entry to anyone with complex physical problems. Those who need EAL support also helped by the SEN dept and on a similar basis.

Games, options, the arts: Art is exceptional. It inhabits six separate studios and rooms including a designated oil painting room. We were delighted by some of the most interesting, careful and creative work in painting and drawing we've seen anywhere; large numbers of fine art A levels are awarded A*s. Lively textiles, food tech lab and a sizeable DT workshop testify to the emphasis placed on head and hand collaboration here. Annual fashion show and competition display girls' own handmade work. Music, likewise, is celebrated here – both in theory (fabulous ICT suite for music) and in practice – lots of lessons, practice rooms, four choirs, ensembles and enthusiasm. Dramatic productions staged with verve and hard work and with impressive results. Until now, drama has not been a 'subject'. However, girls who chafe at the lack of timetabled drama will chafe – and leave for other schools in pursuit of it – no longer. It's now possible to take a GCSE in drama – Ms Stevenson very clear about its usefulness on the timetable in terms of character development, team work and expressiveness.

Energetic sports include rowing at Fulham Reach, games at Eel Brook, five minutes' walk away, or at Barn Elms, by public transport. Tennis in Bishop Park. Lacrosse, badminton, cricket – no shortage of sporting opportunities whatever your thing. And successes, both individual and in teams, across the board. 'Very well-run' D of E programme. 'Fantastic' dance opportunities – street to ballet on offer and parents rave about the choreography and production standards – 'they rehearse so hard!' A sense of trying everything and having a go.

Background and atmosphere: Parsons Green is a purlieu on the eastern edge of Fulham, in this hip part of London. A three-bed house will set you back more than £1.5m. Facing the triangle of grass shaded by ancient plane and ash trees which is the actual Parsons Green, the school is housed in a row of attractive buildings from several eras. Parsons Green tube station is a convenient two minutes' walk away. The school has an interesting role in the history of women's education. Founded in 1841, Whitelands College was a teacher training college 'to produce a superior class of parochial schoolmistresses'. Whitelands College School followed a year later. In 1917, when the school was threatened with closure, the remarkable second mistress, Enid Moberly Bell, rescued it and reopened it as Lady Margaret later that year. (She also moonlighted as the vice-chair of the Lyceum Club for female artists and writers.) Her life-partner, Anne Lupton, financed the purchase of the school's second building, Elm House, and named the school after Margaret Beaufort, of whom Erasmus, no less, wrote on her tomb: 'Margaret, Countess of Richmond, mother of Henry VII, grandmother of Henry VIII, who donated funds for three monks of this abbey, a grammar school in Wimborne, a preacher in the whole of England, two lecturers in Scripture, one at Oxford, the other at Cambridge, where she also founded two colleges, one dedicated to Christ, and the other to St John, the Evangelist.' The school's transmogrifications since founding reflect the changing times and mores – from a grammar, to a voluntary aided and now an academy.

Art is exceptional. We were delighted by some of the most interesting, careful and creative work in painting and drawing we've seen anywhere

The Christian backbone of the school is proudly proclaimed by the 12 foot wooden cross with the Tudor rose ingrained on it which leans against the wall of the most modern of the buildings – a plate glass and marble statement – at one end of the extensive frontage. The two main buildings are handsome Georgian townhouses which retain some elegant features of their former selves and a mass of small rooms, passages and staircases. The school – when you are in it – is far larger than you'd guess from the outside, having accrued buildings, outside space and assorted additions. Most of it is well-maintained and treated with respect. We saw no litter. The girls, too, are well-turned out in their black with red stripe uniform. We witnessed the head turning down the odd collar and a girl or two pulling down a shorter than average skirt on her approach. 'She has smartened us up,' we were told. Sixth formers wear home clothes and treat this privilege with respect.

Excellent – and one of the best-stocked we've seen – library, a little cramped but full of girls actually working, something we do not often encounter. Good study areas elsewhere including one 'informal' and one silent one in the sixth form centre. Excellent Busby Auditorium – a real lecture theatre seating 140 – used for talks, rehearsals, presentations etc. Good and tidy displays about the place. One large tarmac playground. School food not seen as irresistible. About half bring lunch from home, most sixth formers go out to get it. But with pasta and salad bars, hot choices and fruit pots, it looked OK to us.

Pastoral care, well-being and discipline: Well understood pastoral care system. Problems first to form tutor, then head of year. School counsellor around two days a week for support. But girls attest to 'happier' atmosphere under new regime and a new emphasis on self-esteem. 'The head wants us to develop into confident young women.' When girls get into trouble – and in rare cases of exclusion – it is because of persistent behavioural lapses rather than anything else. Social media abuse a persistent hazard here as everywhere. 'We have a very strong community feeling but we do have girls who behave badly on occasions. We deal with it very quickly,' explained the head – this view supported by both parents and girls. Pastoral care described as 'amazing' by parents and school is assiduous in home-school comms. 'We have the numbers of absolutely anyone we might need,' said a parent. Parents also feel involved – 'they do listen to concerns'.

Pupils and parents: About as diverse as it gets. Some from local, affluent families who also apply for the local independents. Many from far less privileged homes. Great mix of backgrounds. Some 18 per cent speak a language other than English at home – a relatively small proportion given the school's location. Very active PTA – lots of drinks dos and other events. A few parents feel a bit pressured to involve themselves and cough up for school appeals but they stress these are, of course, voluntary and some keep away though everyone we spoke to praised the school's sense of community.

Entrance: Banding via non-verbal reasoning test which tests maths and a piece of independent creative writing. Sixty-seven foundation places reserved for girls who regularly attend C of E services. Fifty-three open places reserved for girls of any other, or no, religion. Applications divided into three ability bands making six categories. For each category, distance measurements are then applied. No priority for those with SEN unless statement or EHC plan submitted naming Lady Margaret. First priority to looked after, or previously looked after, girls, then (up to a third of places to) siblings. In effect, in the year we visited, this meant: 17 girls admitted from each of foundation bands 1 and 3, and 33 from foundation band 2. In the open bands, 13 were admitted from bands 1 and 3 and 27 from band 2. There was no point in living more than 0.3 of a mile away if you applied for an open place, but some foundation entrants lived up to five miles away. Church-going essential for the latter – at least twice a month for previous three years. Hundreds apply for the 40-50 sixth form places – applicants, like existing pupils, need six 6s at GCSE and between 9-6 for individual A levels.

Exit: About three-quarters stay on after GCSEs. One of the most impressive leavers' lists we have seen from an academy. Two to Oxford in 2018 and, while Oxbridge isn't the measure of all things, it suggests the school has an ambition for its alumnae lacking elsewhere. Otherwise, a good spread of universities from the newbies to the redbricks and, again, a diverse mix of courses chosen – from IT through midwifery to anthropology Two medics and 11 off to study art in 2018. Rather extraordinarily, everyone seems to leave for either university or an art college. An interestingly diverse list of leavers over recent decades includes Diana Garnham, ex-chief executive of the Science Council, Nigella and Horatia Lawson, Lady Zoe Barclay, actresses Kelly Hunter, Joanne Adams and Jessie Burton, film director Mahalia Belo, upcoming soprano Louise Alder, Martha Fiennes – oh, and Janet Street-Porter.

Money matters: Parental contribution asked for and willingly donated in most cases.

Remarks: Outstanding school for an ambitious, motivated, outward-looking girl. The anxious faces of the parents handing in their applications for next year's places said it all.

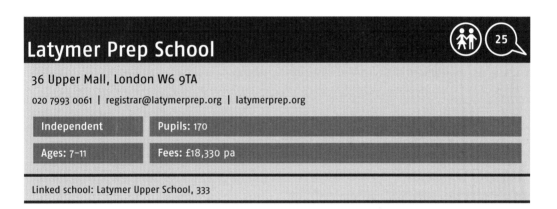

Latymer Prep School

36 Upper Mall, London W6 9TA

020 7993 0061 | registrar@latymerprep.org | latymerprep.org

Independent	Pupils: 170
Ages: 7–11	Fees: £18,330 pa

Linked school: Latymer Upper School, 333

Head: Since September 2017, Andrea Rutterford, previously deputy head at Devonshire House prep in Hampstead. She has also headed year 3 and year 5 at Highgate Junior School.

Entrance: Highly selective, with around 220 competing at 7+ for the 38-40 places. They take an exam, with half invited back for some science-related activities and team-building exercises and observation. The gender split is nearly 50/50, with each year in two classes of 20 (occasionally 21). Families are mainly local, within 30 minutes' travel time, although the reach of the school has expanded in recent years to stretch as far as Kensington and Notting Hill.

Exit: Majority to the senior school, although transfer is not automatic, with all pupils required to sit the entrance exam, but does not prepare for other senior schools.

Remarks: Rivercourt House, an attractive 1800s villa overlooking the Thames, is the main building. Full of light, with an elegant staircase and plenty of original features and creaky floorboards, it has the feel of a well-to-do, kindly aunt's home and is an enviable environment for youngsters to learn in. Next door, Latymer House accommodates more classrooms, food tech, cookery, IT and art – all very well equipped, with plenty of space. Both utilise walls and corridors to the max to display children's work. Even a window had lovely artwork draped across when we visited.

Opposite the rather limited outside space is an odd 1930s building, whose outside spiral staircase leads to the Seahorse Drama Studio, with a truly professional feel. In addition, pupils also regularly parade down the underpass under the A4 to Latymer Upper to make use of facilities such as the dining hall, sports and music facilities and drama hall (with recent productions including My Fair Lady, Toad of Toad Hall and Peter Pan). Other links with the upper school include shared teacher training on inset days and teachers doing regular observations of year 7 teaching to get a feel for standards. All this, agree parents and pupils, makes the transfer into the upper school pretty seamless. 'They don't get scared because they're already familiar with it,' explained one parent.

Expect specialist teaching from day one, so whilst each class has its own form room, pupils go to subject-dedicated rooms to learn. Of particular note is the large, fantastically well-equipped art room at the top of the school, where pupils were busy painting clay pots they'd made, and a delightful, well-stocked library. Delicious baking aromas drifted out of the food tech room when we visited, whilst in the science lab, pupils could hardly have looked more animated.

The curriculum is future-orientated, with all pupils learning Mandarin and Spanish, and technology is genuinely embedded throughout all subjects, with regular use of iPads in class, including art. This is not at the expense of more traditional learning, however. 'We want them to read and write before they can swipe,' says school.

Music is strong, with every child playing a musical instrument and half of them playing two, for which one-to-one tuition is timetabled into the curriculum. Big on brass, with lots of children learning the French horn or trombone, whilst the cello also remains popular. Two main choirs – enthusiast singers (no audition necessary) and the chamber choir – accommodate 90 children in total. Music tech also a focal point. 'I was certain my kids had no talent with music and I've been truly shocked what they've brought out in them,' said one parent.

Full of light, with an elegant staircase and plenty of original features and creaky floorboards, it has the feel of a well-to-do, kindly aunt's home

The focus on sport that the upper school is noted for is seen as equally important here, with specialist sports coaches teaching both girls and boys rugby, football, netball, cricket, dance, rounders and – the particular strength of the school – swimming. New £14m new sports facility behind the 1930s building has revolutionised facilities. Sport is inclusive. 'Our aim is that every pupil leaves with one sport they like doing. That might not sound very ambitious, but actually girls often fall away from sport because they're not given the opportunity to find something they love. Not here.'

Over 20 school clubs, including zumba, film studies, The Latymerian (school magazine), chess, bridge, drama, coding, Warhammer and karate. Most are free, although a few bought-in ones, such

---

'You're encouraged to ask questions. In fact, if we are really interested in a particular area, that can drive the class in a new direction'

as zumba, do charge. No after-school care, but the prep room remains open until 4.30pm. Plenty of day trips to places including V&A and Kensington Gardens, whilst residential trips include Norfolk (year 5) and Italy (year 6).

This isn't a school that believes in lots of rules. 'There's just a general expectation of respect and being nice,' said one pupil. And with the exception of some year 6s who have passed their 11+ swanking around a bit, it's all pretty low-key, with a genuine feeling of innocence. About the worst behaviour you'll see, say teachers, is children running to the next class, when they should walk.

As for bullying, it's hard to imagine here. 'Of course children sometimes fall out, and there are situations in which children lack empathy or fail to see the implications of what they've done. But there's very little deliberate unkindness. We think that's down to modelling by the staff and the fact that, for the children, the absolute worst thing for them is feeling they've disappointed us. They can't bear it.'

'You learn through trying,' is an unofficial mantra of the school, with the staff encouraging intellectual risk-taking. 'We are constantly reminding the children that the point when you're not quite sure is the point when you learn. Getting to the top therefore isn't the be-all-and-end-all and we encourage them to see that and value the moment when they're not quite sure.'

There are pupils with SEN, including dyslexia and Asperger's, and they've also had students who are registered blind or deaf. 'We delight in being open'; anyone with any kind of learning challenge is encouraged to make full use of the upper school's learning support department (now known as the 'academic mentoring department' to remove stigma), which is run by three specialist and extremely well-liked women. 'They offer unbelievable support,' said one parent.

There's a lively PA, which does all the usual fundraising and organising of school fêtes and social events, along with each class having a 'rep' and 'dep,' whom the school closely communicates with. 'If there's ever an issue or misunderstanding, the rep and dep won't encourage parents to write saying, "We all think this or that". It's much more a case of them coming in informally and early to nip it in the bud.' Parents agree this works, and several praise the way they are encouraged to come into the school in the morning and afternoon, never hurried on as in some schools. They can also come in to help with reading.

We saw relaxed, engaged, happy and confident (but not precocious) children, who are clearly at home and keen to learn. 'You're encouraged to ask questions,' one pupil told us. 'In fact, if we are really interested in a particular area, that can drive the class in a new direction.' 'Teachers always tell us, it's our enthusiasm they want to build on,' explained another. For this reason, comment a couple of parents, it's probably not the best school for shrinking violets. 'I think a really quiet and withdrawn child might feel a bit lost here,' said one.

Unlike in the upper school, there is a house system, all named after birds. 'It gives a sense of healthy competition and gets them out of their year groups,' said one parent. There's also a school council, although it's not particularly active.

This is a charming prep that children genuinely adore. 'My child is often up at 7am fully dressed and asking when it's time to go,' said one parent, whilst another said, 'The children might not come out looking as neat as they went in, but you know they've had a really lovely time.' Despite the expectation on high academic achievement (which some parents say can be tiring), there's a big emphasis on a rounded education, and above all it's lots of fun, with warm relationships between staff and pupils. This throws some children who come from more formal pre-preps or primaries, with parents also sometimes starting off feeling slightly hesitant about how relaxed and open the atmosphere is. But they soon feel liberated and by half term in year 3, children seem to have fully subscribed to the ethos of the school. As one pupil summed up, 'this school is like one, big warm hug.'

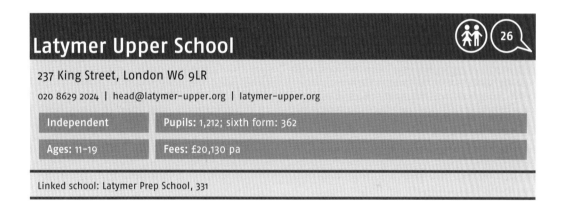

Latymer Upper School

237 King Street, London W6 9LR

020 8629 2024 | head@latymer-upper.org | latymer-upper.org

Independent	Pupils: 1,212; sixth form: 362
Ages: 11–19	Fees: £20,130 pa

Linked school: Latymer Prep School, 331

Head: Since 2012, David Goodhew (MA Oxon), originally a local boy who has now moved 'back home', living 10 minutes down the road with his French wife, Céline, and two young sons. Read classics at Oxford and previously deputy head of Durham School. Spends at least one hour every day walking round the school – visits lessons for a few minutes, which both pupils and parents say sums up his 'hands-on approach' and 'openness to ideas for change'. Not stereotypical headmasterly, parents and pupils describe him as 'very approachable.'

Clearly, though, capable of stern decisiveness when needful. We were sad to hear of the departure in February 2018 of seven year 9 pupils found to have been smoking cannabis in a local park. The school – in sacrificing, we understand, high-achieving pupils and this number of fees – clearly intends to send an unmistakeable message to anyone tempted to offend in like manner.

Academic matters: Grades have been steadily improving over recent years and although research

from the University of Durham found pupils are achieving either in line with – or better than – their abilities, results remain a notch short of stunning. A levels in 2018 saw 70 per cent A*/A grades, with 91 per cent at A*-B. GCSEs were over 90 per cent A*-A/9-7.

Key aspects of the innovative curriculum include the Global Goals course in year 9 that critically examines the 17 sustainability targets set by the UN. This leads nicely into the UCAS-accredited World Perspectives, which has replaced the 11th GCSE in the middle school. Exploring global political issues, pupils love it and parents delight in their children 'watching more news' and 'talking about bigger issues at the dinner table.'

All year 7s learn Mandarin (carried on from the prep school, if they went) Spanish and all pupils expected to do a modern language at GCSE. IT has been ditched in favour or computing and coding and technology is genuinely embedded into all learning, with all pupils from year 10 upwards given an iPad. 'I do all my essays on it, plus I can do things like surveys,' said one pupil, while one upper sixth pupil has even designed a rowing app that is now used by the GB rowing team.

Majority of teachers hugely admired, with several references to them going the extra mile and being 'very imaginative in their teaching methods'. 'Staff really care, not just academically but in a pastoral way,' summed up one parent. 'I could frankly hug all of them,' said another. 'The teachers try and inspire you – there's no fobbing off of pupils' questions, ever,' remarked a pupil.

Careers and university advice is outstanding, thanks to a knowledgeable and dedicated team, including a careers specialist and international university admissions specialist. The latter post was brought in due to the recent surge in applications to American universities. 'Because of our rounded approach to education, it means our students are often drawn to the American university model of taking seriously areas like sport, music and drama, and the fact that you can delay specialisation,' explains the head.

Parents and pupils rave about the learning support department, which is now known as the 'academic mentoring department' (to remove stigma). Run by three specialist women who nobody seems to be able to praise more if they tried, pupils can visit for one-to-one sessions any time, whether they have severe dyslexia or just a piece of challenging homework, at no extra cost. The department's peer mentoring scheme is popular, whereby older pupils help younger ones, with benefits to both sides. 'If anything, the department could be bigger, though, as it's always full,' said one pupil, who added that on results day, this is where you'll find students running to give staff a hug. School reckons on around 10 per cent needing some kind of support, with just two statemented.

Games, options, the arts: Famed throughout the western (London) world for rowing (Henley, National Schools Regatta) and swimming (ESSA, Bath Cup, Otter Medley); these remain some of the school's strengths and are pursued with much enthusiasm and success. In the past a number of parents have complained that girls' sport has been taken less seriously than boys', but there's also notable accomplishment in for both in football, hockey and cricket (girl footballers coached by QPR trainers), plus netball and rugby, all of which are taught by professional coaches. Sport is also known for being inclusive, plenty of C, D and E teams, with enjoyment of sport valued as much as sporting prowess. One parent also points out how 'my son has been encouraged to try out sports he wouldn't normally opt for, which has been great for him.'

The impressive £14m sports centre (2016) – including swimming pool, sports hall and bouldering wall – enables a full programme of sports

> **'Staff really care, not just academically but in a pastoral way,' summed up one parent. 'I could frankly hug all of them'**

and fitness activities, including netball and cricket training before school and at lunchtimes whatever the weather, and there are now greater opportunities for teaching more sports simultaneously, as well as enabling classes in fencing, climbing, yoga and pilates. Sports grounds at Wood Lane used by the England rugby team for training.

All pupils take DT, art, music and drama to the end of year 9 and then choose, although we wonder how they decide. Art is outstanding, with talented and impressively free and imaginative artwork in just about every media, displayed everywhere from the head's office to the four good-sized studios. Similarly, DT is fantastically equipped, with an emphasis on creativity. One excited pupil passionately talked us through some of the machines: 'I once asked to build a stomp rocket powered table tennis ball dispenser for a project. I was allowed and it worked!' he added.

Performing arts also taken seriously, with a commendable theatre (plus other studios) and plenty of year group plays, plus an annual all-school one. Meanwhile, each week 800 individual instrumental lessons are taught by 40 visiting music teachers in air-conditioned, sound-proofed, purpose-built rooms. Group music lessons focus on getting children enthused with practical work, not simply focusing on theory. Singing takes place across several choirs through to grungy bands, and everything in between. Students even have their own record label, 32 Bit Recordings, with profits from releases going into the school bursary fund. 'The arts aren't considered an alternative to academia here,' said one pupil. 'There's room for people to excel in both.'

Astounding range of extracurriculars on offer, with over 100 clubs, as well as a good range of outside speaker. Trips, it seems, are organised to pretty much every corner of the earth, with the Horizon fund ensuring that no pupil is excluded for financial reasons. The annual 'activities week' causes much excitement, where students do anything from cycling coast-to-coast to building a shelter for teenage mums in Uganda. 'It all comes back to our rounded view of education,' says the head. 'Skills learned in leadership, resilience and teamwork matter every bit as much as academia.'

Background and atmosphere: Located on the banks of the Thames in west London, the grounds occupy a rectangular plot between the main entrance in King Street and the busy A4 into London, under which runs a cunning underpass, through which children parade to the prep school, sports centre, pool and Latymer boat house.

But if you didn't know better, you could be forgiven for thinking the school is a church, since your eye is immediately drawn to the huge stained glass windows of the gothic, red-brick main hall, which is nestled behind a long, low gothic arched wall. Dating from 1890, the hall now has several smart newer buildings surrounding it, most recently the striking glass-fronted library and science block, while the old car park has been transformed into a charming 'piazza', complete with giant outdoor chess set, which students describe as the hub of the school during nice weather and exam time.

Back in the main hall, expect portraits of old heads and war memorial tablets, along with brown glazed tiles on the walls and blue carpets on the floor, which very much set the mood throughout the old building, with its seemingly endless supply of nooks and crannies, hidden staircases and innovative linkages between buildings. 'Pupils can be here five years and still discover new areas,' said one pupil. Wooden lockers, which are dotted around the school, had just been replaced with metal ones when we visited ('so much nicer,' said a pupil), while the mezzanine areas of many classrooms give a nice warmth to many of the teaching areas.

One excited pupil talked us through some of the machines: 'I asked to build a stomp rocket powered table tennis ball dispenser for a project. I was allowed and it worked!'

In contrast, lots of light wood and huge windows feature in the newer buildings, the most exceptional of which is the science and library block. The ground-floor library is exemplary and one that many towns would be proud of – well-stocked, not just with books and DVDs but computers, with genuinely studious looking pupils. Meanwhile, the corridors of the three floors of science boast interactive periodical table, television with live newsflashes and even live lizards and fish (not together) behind glass, among other innovative features. 'We're just about to do a class on how much vitamin C exists in fruit drinks,' said one excitable teacher as we walked past one of the well-equipped labs. On top is a roof garden, weather station and observatory.

Other areas of note through the school include the huge dining room (now extended) and the

well-used sixth form common room, with plentiful and colourful booths and sofas. Outside, expect inevitable queuing and log jams at changeover times, as a result of 1,400 students in limited space, but nobody seems to really mind.

Originally a boys' school, girls started coming in sixth form in the late 1990s, after which it became fully co-ed in 2004. Now 50/50 across every year group, with the head genuinely astounded that anyone could think single sex is preferable. Certainly, nobody could argue that uptake for maths and science among girls isn't strong here. Active school council, which recently put together an initiative for more recycling bins and voted against bringing in a house system.

Pastoral care, well-being and discipline: There was a perception in the 1980s (and, some argue, rather later) that the school was 'a bit rough,' admits the head. 'Not now. The behaviour is excellent.' Parents and pupils concur, putting it down to warm, mutually respectful rapport with staff, as well as pupils knowing exactly what's expected of them.

Head acknowledges that any school would be foolish to believe bullying is non-existent. What matters, he says, is what you do about it on the rare occasions it occurs. 'There's a big focus on encouraging pupils or parents to report it immediately, after which it's dealt with quickly and sensibly,' concurred one parent. Despite some sixth form drink and drugs related expulsions some years back, the head says the zero tolerance to drink, smoking and drugs means it's not a problem now (and wasn't a big one then), which parents and pupils agree with.

Teachers genuinely interested in pupils' well-being, and although there's not huge interaction between the different year groups, pupils seem at ease with different ages.

Pupils and parents: Around 90 per cent from within a three-mile radius, who arrive by tube, bike or on foot. Diverse population for an independent school, which the school is clearly proud of. 'We attract a real mix from city investors, media types and academics living in leafy streets through to families on the White City estate, which is surely better than just those from a privileged bubble mixing with each other. What life lessons that does that teach you?' explains the head. Parents agree, describing the school as 'grounded'. 'Privileged, yes, but posh, no,' said one. Communication with parents – both via the school and the Parents' Guild – is considered good.

Incredible list of alumni, including Hugh Grant, Alan Rickman, Christopher Guard, Imogen Poots, Mel Smith, Gus Prew. Also Walter Legge and Raphael Wallfisch, and Pete Townsend's dad, who was expelled. Then there's Kulveer Ranger, Keith

Vaz, George Walden, Joshua Rozenberg, Andrew Slaughter, Heston Blumenthal, Dr Hilary Jones and Lily Cole. 'If you're lucky, you get to meet one of them at a prize giving,' said one pupil.

Entrance: Of the 170 places available at 11+, 40 come from the school's own on-site prep. Of the remaining 130, 50 per cent come from local state primaries, with the other half coming from other preps. Some 1,200 candidates altogether. The entrance assessment consists of its own English and maths papers (no longer reasoning, with the aim of creating a more level playing field for the untutored), with successful candidates invited for interview. There's no 13+ entry.

At 16+, over 200 candidates for 30 places. Although attracting a high calibre at this age, entry for sixth form doesn't set a ridiculously high bar, with the school expecting minimum eight or nine GCSEs including maths and English, with 9-7 grades in the subjects they wish to study (or related subjects).

Exit: Careers and university advice considered second to none. Oxbridge (23 places in 2018), Bristol, Leeds, UCL Edinburgh, Durham, Warwick, the US (13 places, plus five to Canada). Seven medics, one musician to Berlin, others off to Milan and Leiden.

Money matters: Founder Edward Latymer, a wealthy puritan, pledged funds on his deathbed in 1624 to educate and feed 'eight poore boies'. So when the previous head came into post in 2002 and there were just seven free places (even less than Latymer's pledge) he took action.

The school has since raised over £13m specifically for the bursary programme, with around 175 pupils now on means-tested bursaries; the majority 75-100 per cent of fees. The school has just launched its most ambitious fundraising campaign in its history and the aim is for one in four students to receive bursarial support by 2024.

At 11+, academic scholarships (usually a one-off £1,000) and music scholarships (one of 40 per cent, others up to 20 per cent). Sixth form drama (40 per cent), music, art and sports scholarships (nominal amounts).

Remarks: Oodles of pupil pride about pretty much every aspect of the school, with only minor niggles from pupils and parents. 'If you're not academic, you'll struggle. But it's not just about the academia as there's this constant focus on being well-rounded,' said one pupil. If you're after a school that encourages academic curiosity and a real passion for life, this is it.

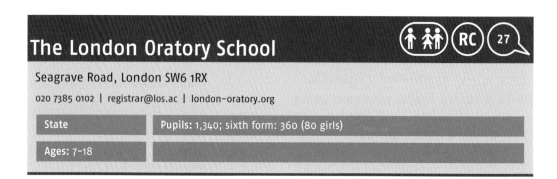

The London Oratory School

Seagrave Road, London SW6 1RX

020 7385 0102 | registrar@los.ac | london-oratory.org

| State | Pupils: 1,340; sixth form: 360 (80 girls) |
| Ages: 7-18 | |

Head: Since January 2018, Daniel Wright MA, previously deputy head of St George's College Weybridge. History degree from Cambridge; began his teaching career at Gordon's School, moving to Godalming College in 2004 as head of history then director of faculty. Took up his post at St George's in 2015.

Junior housemaster, who runs the Junior House on a day to day basis, is Pheona Mackay. She is ex-RAF and feared by the parents, though loved by the boys. 'She obviously adores the boys,' said one parent, 'but I am a bit worried about approaching her.' Her attitude appears to be that the job of educating the boys is the school's, the less interference from parents the better.

Academic matters: Junior House boys are tested at the end of each term and reports are sent to parents, which detail their results, progress and targets. Otherwise, you get to meet your son's teachers only once a year. Some complain about poor communication lines between school and home, but say that on the whole they put up with this because they trust the school. 'You might not get to hear about a concert until two nights before,' remarked one parent. The school is totally integrated into the senior school – junior house boys even have lunch, as the senior boys do, in classrooms that become 'house rooms' at lunch time. However, there is little interaction with senior boys. Playtimes are organised so as not to coincide with the traffic of burly teenagers, and the whole of junior house has lunch at a different time from the senior boys.

Consistently impressive results at both GCSE and A level. School fiercely competitive with its notable rival – particularly regarding academic results. When considering A level scores school would like it be noted that they have a broader range of ability in their sixth form as their entry requirements are lower. What we like particularly is the range of subjects boys are choosing to take at both GCSE and at A level. Large numbers do maths and sciences – and a healthy helping of A*/9-8s in these subjects – but the humanities and languages are not neglected. History particularly popular, and double figures do art and DT each year. Heartening in an (almost entirely) boys' school to see this range, and we were particularly encouraged by a thriving German department. A level results in 2018 were 78 per cent A*-B and 45 per cent A*/A grades. At GCSE, 85 per cent of pupils got 9-4 in both maths and English; 47 per cent 9-7 grades. School will endeavour to facilitate any language if there is a demand, however low the numbers – Russian, Arabic, Chinese, Portuguese and Polish all offered and a good solid classics department encourages a number of people to take Latin and Greek GCSE. A few go on to A level.

Good results can partly be attributed to good and committed teaching, but must largely stem from an excellent work ethic that is drilled in from the start. Homework is rigorously monitored and it's a detention for repeated failure to produce it. Setting from year 9 and a number of GCSEs are taken in year 10. Sixth formers have to work together in a large room during study periods. No lounging around on comfy sofas here. A member of staff is ever present to monitor behaviour and we were conscious of our noisy footfall when we peeked in.

The less academically able are offered a sixth form course in advanced business – a hybrid of two A levels and an AS, leading to qualifications in business and computing, a practical alternative to a sixth form college course for those who can't bear to leave. Now offers the Extended Project Qualification. Classes felt by some to be too big – can be as many as 30 at GCSE; sixth form numbers are higher than elsewhere too. However, with 10 or so a year gaining places at Oxbridge, the Sutton Trust continues to rank it among the highest performing state schools in the country. Standards here are high and pupils strive to maintain those standards.

SENs catered for – attracts standard numbers of the usual spread of needs. Currently school estimates there are approximately 40 with EHC plans – a range of those on the autistic spectrum as well as some with emotional issues, social and/or communication issues. School can accommodate pupils with cerebral palsy. By all accounts the SENCo is 'magnificent' and there is an army of teaching assistants as well as learning support staff. In-class help along with withdrawal where appropriate. Murmurings of discontent in certain quarters – particularly parents who have sons with no identifiable special need, but may simply be dreamy or disorganised. 'Faulty communication lines and support is not swiftly forthcoming' are the central complaints. Wheelchair-friendly and SENs seen, in general, as just part of life.

Games, options, the arts: Junior House boys are committed and robust. The day starts early with an hour's choir practice from 8am, if you are in the Schola. All boys play two instruments – one orchestral, normally supported by the piano. For potential applicants, who must be of at least average academic ability, musical promise is the only criterion which counts here, once you have demonstrated your Catholic credentials – all the boys have musical potential. Not all boys are in the Schola – some just follow an instrumental course. The Schola sings every Saturday evening in the Brompton Oratory. Junior house boys play every instrument you can name, under the care of innumerable peripatetic teachers of high quality, and use all the senior school facilities. They tour, record and give stunning concerts They work hard and play hard.

One parent remembers how much her son enjoyed knitting and crocheting while in the Junior House. Boys here will throw themselves into anything

Not just music, sport too. Tag rugby is organised against other junior schools. They swim once a week in the school pool, and water polo is a popular after-school club. Plenty of other after-school clubs too – including Lego, programming and chess, but many boys are just too tired at the end of the school day. Art is vibrant and boys get to use the facilities of the senior school. They learn about eg Da Vinci in lessons then put their learning into practical effect in the art room. Not a lot of drama, but plenty of musical productions – again, use of the senior school facilities greatly enhances the experience. This is true, too, of science. Science is taught in the senior school labs, and they get the benefit of having specialist teachers from an early age – not just the form teacher.

This is a big rugby school. If your son is a keen football player he will struggle to find much here apart from the house soccer competition. Rugby fixtures against a huge number of schools including the top public schools, many on a Saturday. Six teams in the first form alone, and more than 20 in total, so plenty of opportunities for everyone to have a go. Boys are bussed to Barn Elms in Barnes for training – a round trip of not much less than an hour.

Water polo also popular, with fixtures against other schools; hockey and cricket other main activities at present – all weather 4G playing field installed 2016; also a good, well-used, on-site 17m pool and gym. Also popular is D of E. CCF perhaps the biggest in any state school, both army and RAF – tours, camps and expeditions of all kinds. Lots of sixth involved in community work – helping at local schools and care homes, soup kitchens on Saturdays, the offices of a local charity etc.

A delightfully refreshing and modern attitude to educating boys: 'Arts are very important in a boys' school'; plans for a dance studio, which is in the pipeline. 'The boys will respond really well to dance classes.' That's right, says one parent, who remembers how much her son enjoyed knitting and crocheting while in the Junior House. Boys here will throw themselves into anything. The key thing is to make it fun.

Senior school music is also excellent, fuelled by those who come up from the Junior House, all of whom have exceptional aptitude. Some 600+ pupils learn at least one instrument. Bands, including the popular jazz group, choirs and orchestras thrive and are well-housed in the arts centre. The chamber choir recently went on a tour to Prague, and recorded their first CD with music sung on the tour. The Schola Cantorum is a choir of professional standard and considerable significance in the world of RC – and secular – music: three visits to Rome in as many months, including representing the Vatican in Al Gore's Live Earth initiative. They record for films and TV, were one of the main choirs at the mass for the beatification of Cardinal Newman on the Papal visit to Britain and are regarded with deserved respect. They sing at the weekly vigil mass at the Brompton Oratory. A recent performance of St John Passion was by all accounts breathtaking – but this is the norm here. Concerts take place at St John's Smith Square as well as the school theatre, and there are plenty of other choirs – these boys (and girls) want to sing. A recent highlight was the girls' choir performance at the Vigil Mass in Westminster Cathedral.

School's on-site arts centre is an impressive asset and includes stunning 300-seat galleried theatre in which full scale shows are mounted –a minimum of four performances each year, including one musical. When we visited, Sophocles' Antigone was in rehearsal – the sixth form play. Recent productions include Guys and Dolls, The Government Inspector and Henry V, as well as

Good results can partly be attributed to good and committed teaching, but must largely stem from an excellent work ethic

Joseph and his Technicolour Dreamcoat – performed by the junior boys. Good display spaces – a stimulating photo show by member of staff was good to see, along with a vast Paolozzi brutalist sculpture. Pupils go on to study art/art history and architecture at prestigious institutions. No photography or textiles on offer, though both are available in extracurricular clubs.

Lots of overseas trips in the holidays – foreign exchanges, cultural and historical visits. Rugby tours to far-flung places and singers and instrumental players performing far and wide.

Background and atmosphere: Founded in 1863 by the Oratorian Fathers, the school moved to its present site and buildings – in the lee of Chelsea FC's massive stadium – in the 1970s and has worn surprisingly well. Splendid extension and refurbishment of main teaching area recently completed – nominated for architectural award. A bright glass central atrium with pods of different sizes round the edge – for smaller groups and lessons away from the main central area, which is the school library. This is where sixth formers come during their free periods. There is calm peacefulness, no doubt enhanced by the Seven Virtues of Man, which are encapsulated in images and text in panels that climb to the glass roof at the top. Around the outer edges the Beatitudes are depicted. On ground level in the centre is a stunning modern statue of Mary with an adolescent Jesus, complete with apron and the tools of his carpentry trade. A welcome change from the Madonna and child, and so fitting in a school where mothers and sons are working out this next phase in their relationship.

This stunning new development is a modern and dynamic contrast to the old-fashioned class rooms for years 7 and 8, complete with the old style wooden desks, storage inside and inkwell on top. Everyone eats by house in their 'house rooms' (aka classrooms outside feeding times) with six separate serveries. An unusual system, but it seems to work. Some rooms and corridors, notably in the sixth form areas, are scruffy and lacking in soul, but with plans for landscape gardening afoot for the sixth form garden, as well as the creation of a quiet room for reflection and contemplation, it is apparent that there is always attention on improvement and change. We liked the brick courtyard, Chapel Courtyard, with its lead flashing. No football in break and at lunch time here. Health and safety has stopped that. The infrastructure has undergone a profound makeover since we last visited and the boys and staff reinforce an air of engagement and pride, a sense of collaborative energy and achievement.

The chapel, opened in 1992 by Basil Hume and dedicated to St Philip Neri and St Edward the Confessor, is simple in design and has a warm and gentle feel. Services here are intimate and spiritual – only room for one of the houses each day and for the young boys in Junior House; part of the Schola sings, eg, Faure Requiem. Beautiful. Major ceremonies held in the famous, huge, Italianate Oratory Church in South Kensington. The Catholic ethos underlies all aspects of the school but not obtrusively or obsessively – it is simply a given and central also to the plans to develop the community involvement of the school. Long-standing commitment to local primary schools and charities – such as SURF and the SVP soup kitchen – with sixth formers carrying out voluntary work and the music department involved in outreach programmes.

There is calm peacefulness, no doubt enhanced by the Seven Virtues of Man, encapsulated in images and text in panels that climb to the glass roof at the top

The Junior House really is tiny, with only 80 boys in all (20 in each of years 3-6) and can't really be regarded in a school in its own right. Parents talk of the shock arriving here after a state primary – 'This is not like a primary school. You entrust your children to the teachers here. You're not sure what goes on from the time you drop them at the gate,' said one parent. It is in a separate wing – situated, rather appropriately, in the heart of the music school – with four classrooms, a choir room and several practice rooms (as music is everything here), all recently refurbished. Old-fashioned classrooms, old-fashioned desks that lift up to contain a motley jumble of books and stationary. The music practice rooms adjoin and creakings of strings or blasting of brass form the background noise. It operates rather like a choir school, or an old fashioned prep school – only without the boarding. It is one of very few state choir schools.

Pastoral care, well-being and discipline: Discipline is acknowledged to be tight – rules are strict and enforced strictly. Any mobile phones spotted on the premises will be confiscated and have to be collected by parents. The approach is 'compassionate', but zero tolerance for physical violence – automatic suspension for anyone who tries to sort a problem by 'raising a hand against someone else'.

House system – there are six houses with 200 pupils in each house – encourages friendships between the year groups and boys in the sixth can mentor those younger who need support over a subject or a problem. Parents mostly praise the staff for their pastoral care – especially the deputy heads – of whom one has been in the school for 20+ years since the start of her career and the other who is a past pupil of the school. However – as with the academics – a complaint we keep hearing is about communication channels and the prompt resolution of problems. There is a culture of deference among parents here, however, so it still takes some boldness to take a proactive step. The sixth form girls talk of close relationships across the two year groups – a benefit of having only 80 girls in total.

Shift in emphasis is taking time to seep through decades of rigorous and sometimes steely discipline. Aim is to see less 'reaction' and more proactivity, and that through charitable service programmes, and the self-reflection programme that goes with that, the young adults at the school will acquire a taste for 'goodness' and doing and being good. Part of this vision has been the establishment of the charitable foundation that is linked with the school.

Pupils and parents: From a vast geographical area, most London boroughs, inner and outer – some leave home before dawn breaks to come here. Over 50 languages spoken at home; serious Roman Catholicism the only – but unifying – common denominator. A higher number of professional families than in most inner London comprehensives, and the school still has a traditional public school air about it. Parents are warming to drive to involve them in all ways – social, educational and practical. Parents' groups for sports, music and food.

A lot of boys in Junior House have brothers in the senior school, and 'being such a small school, the parents tend to bond quite closely and stick together,' said one parent. The pace is fast and it's 'hard core,' said another. 'While there is a sense of exclusivity – the bar is so high to get in and you feel so lucky – these are very normal boys, not precious and geeky'. A wonderful start in life for your musical, resilient, self-motivated, Catholic little boy.

Reports in the main school are now termly and home-school contact far more a normal thing, though complaints persist of parents not being kept in touch. Children appreciate the knock-ons of greater parental involvement and find it supportive and helpful. The boys themselves are relaxed, friendly, ambitious and hard-working. Classes are head down and concentrating. We heard no raised voices, saw few inattentive faces. Pupils have a sense of pride in themselves and in the school which one would wish to see replicated everywhere. The only boy who wouldn't like it here, we were told, was someone who didn't want to involve himself.

Sixth form girls are no mere modern import designed to boost results. They date back to a link with a girls' school in the 19th century and were incorporated into the sixth in the 1950s after a merger. Their numbers are small but, says head, 'they add so much to the school'. It was good to see girls and boys out and about in the lunch hour clearly in relaxed friendship and at ease – no cattle market or points system here. Popular among politicians – Tony Blair and Nick Clegg both sent their sons here. Notable former pupils include Simon Callow, rugby union star Michael Swift and Hayley Atwell.

Entrance: Admits up to 20 boys at 7 into year 3, up to 10 of whom are choristers. All applicants tested for general academic ability and for music aptitude; potential choristers also tested for choral aptitude and suitability. Priority to practising Catholics who attend mass frequently, baptism before 6 months, siblings. All get automatic entry to the senior school.

Entrance to main school simpler than hitherto, but heart-sinking for anyone other than an assiduously practising Roman Catholic family. In fact, don't bother to apply unless you are a pillar of your local church and known to your priest, who will have to vouch for your bona fides – both pupil's and family's; early baptism essential. After long-running legal battle no longer includes 'Catholic service' – eg church flower arranging – as part of points system. Admission process involves completing the school's Supplementary Information Form and a local authority Common Application Form. Nine hundred plus apply for the 160 places.

Junior House boys transfer automatically and parents praise the seamless transition. The current oversubscription criteria are based upon mass attendance, early baptism, siblings and attendance at the Oratory Primary School in Chelsea, with a ballot system as tie-break.

Sixth form also oversubscribed. Requirement is grade 6s in six GCSEs and at least a 4 in maths and English. This is the stated requirement, but parents we spoke to said the standard was in fact much higher. Beware the postman if your son looks like he won't make the standard expected at A level. A letter is likely to arrive during year 11 to warn that you need to find a place elsewhere. Forty places attract 200 applicants and, again, the RC credentials are what counts, plus 'expected performance at GCSE and suitability for an A level course which will be sought from each pupil's current school'. Girls join from Sacred Heart, Gumley, the Ursuline Convent and a few from Lady Margaret's.

Exit: All Junior House boys move up to the main school. Most (about 70 per cent) stay on after GCSEs; almost 400 in sixth form. Regularly win Oxbridge places (10 in 2018), covering the range of disciplines. Around half to Russell Group; four medics in 2018. Fairly equal spread of arts, sciences and practical subjects. Otherwise to good universities everywhere to read everything. Refreshingly few silly subjects pursued – these pupils have been properly taught and sensibly advised.

Remarks: Much that is excellent and not just the obvious – the music, the academics, but also the attention given to spiritual and emotional development. An ideal choice for a son (or sixth form daughter) who toes the line. Approach with caution if you have a scatty child who balks at authority.

Lycée Français Charles de Gaulle

35 Cromwell Road, London SW7 2DG

020 7584 6322 | inscription@lyceefrancais.org.uk | lyceefrancais.org.uk

Independent	Pupils: 3,660; sixth form: 583
Ages: 3–19	Fees: £5,726 – £11,980 pa

Proviseur: Since September 2018 Didier Devilard, previously proviseur of the Lycée Victor Hugo in Toulouse.

Academic matters: Lycée Charles de Gaulle is the premier French school in Britain and one of the largest in the world. The raison d'être is to provide French education leading to the French baccalaureate, regarded by many as one of the most robust school-leaving qualifications there is. With many dual national French-English families enrolled, the Lycée also offers GCSE and A levels.

The French model has the following divisions: maternelle (reception and year 1), primaire (years 2-6), college (years 7-10) and lycée (years 11-13). In primaire and college, the school offers the French curriculum in French. From the final year of college (year 10) students either move over to the British section to do GCSEs and IGCSEs followed by A levels or continue through to the French baccalaureate. Parent perspectives on the Lycée vary significantly depending on their own cultural expectations of what constitutes a school education, but most parents seem to feel that overall the kids are well taught, learning lots, enjoying the challenge and loving the school's international community.

Primary class teachers do everything (including art and PE) while specialists support IT and music. The quality of the art is down to the creativity of the teacher but we've heard of some great stuff with cross-curricular projects and older classes partnering with younger ones. Parents say there's 'frequent assessment and evaluation' so a struggling child is quickly identified. A primary parent with British school experience describes the French system as 'less flexible, but of high standard.' Class sizes are about 28, with an assistant in each class. Classroom arrangements are fairly traditional, with desks in rows, though we saw some more varied arrangements.

College is another story. Some students entering college come from schools where the entire enrolment is less than the year group they are joining. Students move around for different lessons in what one parent described as an 'anonymous teacher environment.' Students have advisers whom they see for maybe 30 minutes per week and there's no expectation of pastoral care on the adviser's part. They monitor pupils' progress through frequent assessment and parents are kept informed. The problem is that it's public knowledge, so if you are bottom of the heap everyone knows, which can take its toll on the self-esteem of less confident adolescents. The survivors – and there are plenty who thrive on the mounting pressure – develop strong independent skills and learn to manage their time and work successfully, attributes French parents expect to see.

The French curriculum is followed in the French section for the oldest students (confusingly called the 'lycée'). In year 12 there are three French baccalaureate pathways: economics and social science, literature and science, where the subjects studied vary as do the number of hours devoted to each. The word is that there is pressure from both school and parents to go down the prestigious science route. Because so many students are fluent in English, many do a GSCE in English within the French bacc stream.

The international version of the French baccalaureate (which follows the French bacc curriculum but has more courses in English and leads to the same official French bacc exams) has recently been introduced, so it's too soon to evaluate. (Not to be confused with the IB diploma.) Students join this programme in year 10; transfer from this programme into the British section is only available in year 12 and depends on availability of space. No 'bacc-light' – this programme reputedly demands an even heavier time commitment than the regular bacc.

It's hard work, rigid and requires lots of memorisation. 'The French system crams knowledge into your brain and we know the brain is a muscle that can be stretched'

The British section offers the GCSE/A level pathway. Students must be fluent enough in English to manage. Discipline is also an issue – nobody with a rap sheet gets in. Occasionally this route is apparently recommended for students who may not succeed with the French bacc.

Year 10 pupils do a wide range of about 10 courses, including French of course, but also a third language (pupils are spoilt for choice – Italian, Spanish, German, Arabic, Russian, Greek and Latin on offer). French IGCSE exams are compulsory, which pleases parents, though there seem to be some questions about timing with kids sitting exams too early.

In year 11 students generally drop one or two subjects as they get into their A level subjects. Parents rave about the maths, chemistry and physics, but suggest that those interested in the arts tend to look elsewhere (French education is not noted for intellectual autonomy or commitment to creativity, which are fairly fundamental for art). French and PE are compulsory throughout.

Deciding which route to choose – French bacc or British A levels – can be daunting. Those opting for the British tend to be dual nationals, non-French who joined the Lycée because their kids were in a French system and Anglophile French families setting down permanent roots in the UK.

The appeal of the French bacc is its strong global reputation, with its slavish commitment to developing intellectual rigour. But it's hard work, rigid, requires lots of memorisation and absorbing of new information. 'The French system crams knowledge into your brain – and we know the brain is a muscle that can be stretched,' said one French parent.

But some French students aiming for a UK university question the need to do the full-blown bacc when they can focus on more specialised A levels. Plus it's no secret that class sizes in the British section are smaller (about 12 compared to 28 to 30 for the French section) and the teaching style is more conducive to project work, class discussions and debates.

The French bacc classes, 'no wishy-washy child-centred approach,' are more traditional, 'cruelly elite' in a 'sink or swim' learning environment. 'Teachers instruct with minimal empathy. You listen and absorb the learning, which can be a challenge for students with strong personalities inclined to engage in debate and, God forbid, challenge the teacher.' Then there is the matter of 'loyalty to French heritage.' If they move to the British section some families lament the move away from the French educational tradition, even though it may be the right decision educationally. British section kids have more time for extracurricular activities. Places in the British section are competitive; with the Lycée full to capacity, expansion of this programme seems unlikely. But more French students are considering the advantages of the A level university pathway, so there are more applicants than spaces.

Ongoing discussion amongst parents about A level results. The small size of the A level cohort means there are limited courses offered and timetabling clashes can prevent kids from taking the courses they want, leading some frustrated families to change schools after GCSEs. It has also been suggested that some French parents whose children are in the British section have a hard time overcoming the 'pedagogical cultural divide' between the French and British systems; they simply don't understand the flexibility that British teachers have in delivering the curriculum.

Some French parents with children in the British section have a hard time overcoming the 'pedagogical cultural divide' between the French and British systems

The governance and management structure of the Lycée is naturally focused on the French curriculum. For a British deputy head, finding a way to sit within that institutional culture is undoubtedly a challenge. Although the policy of rotating the head makes sense for Lycées worldwide, it probably has an impact on attention to GCSEs, A levels etc in the British section. Each new head has to get up to speed with the whole (and for them, anomalous)

British programme, along with all the other challenges of running such a large institution. It's a steep learning curve for even a top educationalist.

French bacc results are excellent, above the French national average. In 2018, 76 per cent of students got 'mention bien' or 'mention très bien' grades.

A levels are by comparison less impressive, particularly French, given the context, although the school points out that students only have three hours a week for French and take the exam a year earlier than other schools. Parents think this differential in results between the French bacc and A level has been taken on board by the school.

Although French nationality, language and heritage is the common denominator here, some kids are not completely fluent in French. It's full immersion, so if a child isn't capable of fully functioning in French by the age of 5, parents say they'll struggle when reading and writing begins. Others move their children out as they get older because parents lack sufficient French language to fully support them – unless they have a French-speaking nanny at home to sustain the French speaking day and supervise homework. English as a second language is taught from primary, with some setting for levels in consideration of the native speakers. In college, students are streamed for English. Other languages are available but no mother tongue instruction other than French and English.

For students with special needs, the educational psychologist and speech and language adviser recommends what sort of specialist might help manage the student's learning (dyslexia is not uncommon) but the school itself does not provide much support in-house. School has disabled access in all but one building but the logistics of the daily timetables and student movements mean that students with mobility challenges would struggle here.

Many teachers (average age early 40s) are civil servants, with professionalism and benefits for which French teachers are renowned. Forty-five per cent have been at the Lycée for more than 10 years.

Games, options, the arts: On Wednesdays, primary classes end early but extra activities like cooking, crafts, IT, sports and games are offered. Human Rights Club, Justice in the Heart and House of Students are student-led activities the British and French section students do together, but French section students have less time to devote to these.

Curriculum-related residential trips abroad include India, Berlin (history), Paris (Comédie Française), Greece (classics), Venice (Italian), New York (art), Moscow (Russian). Compulsory work experience programmes in years 10 or 11 are organised by parents.

A few hundred students do sports, many on Saturdays at the sports facility in Raynes Park,

If you're approaching the area during pick-up you'll think you've alighted at the wrong end of the Eurostar

competing against London schools and schools abroad. There's a school sports day but parents warn: 'Don't expect to get a ribbon unless you place first, second, or third.' Music is popular, with ensembles, orchestra or choir to choose from.

Background and atmosphere: School was founded to serve London's French population, but also to further France's 'mission civilisatrice' – making French culture and education available to the Brits. During the Second World War it became the home of the Free French and the head sits in the office once occupied by General de Gaulle, so the school's name has meaning. British section was created 60 years ago to offer the French programme in English, but the differences in the French bacc and A levels meant that a marriage was not practical, so the British section sits within the organisation as a 'stand alone'. Over the years the Lycée has spread and now occupies a city block across from the Natural History Museum. If approaching the area during pick-up you'll think you've alighted at the wrong end of the Eurostar.

Part of the AEFE (Agency for Teaching of French Education Abroad), the Lycée is one of more than 100 overseas schools directed by the Ministry of Education and is governed by a committee including the French ambassador and other diplomats. Heads are rotated, with posts lasting up to five years. British section is managed by Simon McNaught.

Facilities have been renovated to absorb increasing student numbers – a combination of interconnected new build and Victoriana and using lots of cheerful colours. Buildings open out at the back to play area shared by all ages. Parents say 'it looks confusing, but the kids figure it out in a day or two.' Primary is in a building shared by upper classes on the top floor. There's a large hall for dramatic and musical performances, music and art rooms; PE is outside in the central yard, at local sports facilities or own grounds in Raynes Park. The yard has large canopies with seating areas to provide all-weather cover; no indoor play area.

A large library mushrooms over several floors, separated into college and lycée sections. Classrooms have desks in traditional rows. Computers in the libraries, study rooms and computer lab, but not much evidence of technology inside the classrooms.

Lunch is served in a bright, clean cafeteria. Youngest have their own lunch room; lunch is compulsory unless there are extraordinary dietary needs. Varied three course menu looks just short of Cordon Bleu by usual school standards. Considering that the chef turns out more than 2,500 meals a day, the food looked and smelled very appealing; fish always on offer for those with kosher or halal preferences.

School also boasts an impressive medical centre, staffed with sympathetic nurses and a full-time doctor. Parents are happy with home-school communication, and it's easy to have a quick chat with the primary teacher at dismissal. The formal communication cycle is 'front loaded' with year-group parent events at the beginning of the year; after that it's up to parents to seek out the teachers – but they'll be in touch if there's a problem.

Pastoral care, well-being and discipline: With such an enormous student body, parents' reports are mixed. Some parents insist the kids 'don't get lost, are well looked after,' while others say that once in college 'students are a number and their teachers hardly know them.' The school tries to put students joining the college in classes with three designated friends to ease the culture shock of coping with the sheer scale of the Lycée. This is less a concern for rising Lycée primary students already familiar with the environment.

Playground attendants are a prominent French feature – supervisors keeping an eye on everyone. College students may leave campus provided they have parents' permission (most don't); in the top years most go out for lunch. A nifty school diary is issued to track home-school communication; the back cover has every student's photo, identification and timetable so anyone trying to slip out can be identified and sent back to class.

The children are cheerful and polite; primary teachers remind them about the importance of greeting people respectfully. No lockers – backpacks are stored here and there. No reports of any significant behaviour issues; everyone knows what is expected. If students fall short, they may be given more homework or required to attend school on Saturday. School psychologist offers counselling for students. Secondary school year group leaders have offices in their own sections of the school, with a secretary to manage the 300 or so kids in each level.

Parents warn that drop off and pick up can be stressful. By staggering start and finish times the school manages the flow of traffic pretty well under the circumstances. But parents need to be prepared for the possibly overwhelming feeling of chaos and confusion at the start.

Pupils and parents: The French connection is the common denominator. Vast majority are French nationals with at least one French parent, some dual nationals (eg British/French), a few British. Other nationalities include Canadian, American, Italian, Spanish, Lebanese, Moroccan and Russian. Many parents are in London on short-term assignments – diplomatic, financial services, media, industry. The generously subsidised fees (not available in the British section) widen the socio-economic net, attracting families who may not normally aspire to private education. Parents prefer this more realistic reflection of society to the rarefied atmosphere of economic privilege that they associate with many London independent schools.

Students come from all over – some with long commutes on public transport – but they feel it's worth it. In some cases the main wage-earner commutes to France or travels internationally but the family has chosen to stay in London in order to keep the kids at the Lycée.

The generously subsidised fees widen the socio–economic net, attracting families who may not normally aspire to private education. Parents prefer this

The APL (parents' association) organises after-school activities, raises funds, supports the athletics programme and serves as a sounding board for issues of community interest. Some non-French speakers say it's difficult to become involved. Eclectic list of 'vieux garçons et filles' includes Jacqueline Bisset, the late Natasha Richardson, Gyles Brandreth, Lady Olga Maitland, Roland Joffé.

Entrance: Registration process begins around April of the entry year, with decisions sent in early May. Highly oversubscribed, entry is described as 'a nightmare, haphazard and chaotic.' Families normally apply to other schools as well; some start off elsewhere to await an offer. There's a priority list of criteria: children of French diplomats, siblings (in primary only), children from another official French school (locally or abroad), including students following the CNED (the French distance learning programme), then any miscellany of Francophones fortunate enough to get in.

Siblings trump everything else in primary so families bank on getting one tiny first foot in the door, knowing the others are pretty much a shoe-in. One French national tells us she put her children on the waiting list from the earliest time allowed. Her eldest was unsuccessful but a few days after the term began the younger one was offered a place, posing a dilemma for managing two-school runs

simultaneously. When she explained this to the school, they somehow magicked up a space for the second child.

Best tip for locals is to transfer from one of the official AEFE Ecole Homologuée nursery schools such as École le Hérisson, L'École des Petits (Fulham) or La Petite École. Feeders for primaire entry include the annexe schools – Wix (Clapham), South Kensington, Ealing and Fulham. Year 7 feeders include École Jacques Prévert, L'École Bilingue, L'École des Petits and L'École de Battersea. For year 10 (British section) and year 11 (French section) it's the College Bilingue in Kentish Town (CFBL). Beware, though – not all schools with emphasis on French language are official AEFE schools, so check the Lycée's website if you're banking on this as your golden ticket. Families do move on so vacancies arise mid-year, but school always refers to the waiting list. According to one successful mother, 'this is the only hope for a local family wanting their child to go to the Lycée' and requires strategic planning of Napoleonic proportions.

No admissions testing and once a child is in, parents have no worries about future entrance exams such as 11+ or CE.

Exit: The Lycée prides itself on its careers department, with advisers specialising in UK, US and French universities. Careers counselling begins in year 11; a major careers forum involves experts and university reps from three continents. Some parents feel more coordination is required to rationalise the Lycée exams and Oxbridge and Russell Group entrance criteria, and more focus needed on writing UCAS personal statements.

Roughly one quarter go to French universities, with 10 per cent of bacc graduates gaining entry into the Grandes Écoles. British destinations include Oxbridge, UCL, Exeter, Bristol, Warwick, Imperial, LSE, Bath, Kings, Queen Mary, Durham, Reading, Edinburgh; French destinations include Sciences Po and the Sorbonne; others to eg McGill in Canada, Morocco, Norway, Belgium, US and Switzerland.

Money matters: A 50 per cent AEFE subsidy (except for those in the British section) makes for bargain tuition by London standards. Some welfare grants and bursaries – and APL has been known to rally when a family falls on hard times.

Remarks: This is a huge institution yet parents say children are happy, well taught and love the cultural diversity. The waiting lists are testimony to the school's overall success. With the French and Francophile population growing daily, it seems that the entente cordial is alive and well in this petit coin of London.

Mander Portman Woodward (MPW)

90–92 Queen's Gate, London SW7 5AB

020 7835 1355 | london@mpw.ac.uk | mpw.ac.uk

| Independent | Pupils: 651; sixth form: 598 |
| Ages: 14–19 | Fees: £28,578 – £30,678 pa |

Principal: Since 2016, John Southworth, previously a vice principal. Engineering degree from Leicester and MSc in defence technology from the Cranfield Institute of Technology. Has been a major in the army, director of co-curriculum at The Perse, principal of Lansdowne College and vice principal of MPW since 2014. Parents at Lansdowne College commented that his army background showed through in his bluff manner: 'He's very much his own person. He said exactly what he thought, and it turned out to be right.'

Academic matters: Once primarily a 'crammer' helping students with short-term goals, such as exam retakes or Oxbridge entrance, today MPW is a thriving sixth form college, with over 70 per cent taking two-year A level courses. What marks it out is the range and flexibility of options on offer, with 44 subjects provided in any combination. A long day (9am-6pm) and 36 classrooms allow a timetable that suits almost all ('It doesn't always look pretty, but that's the price you pay for flexibility'). The college also provides a stand-alone one-year A level programme, handy for aspiring medics moving from arts to science or those with weak results wanting to try their hand at something new. Results overall are strong (34 per cent A*-A, 66 A*-B in 2018), particularly in light of the wide-ranging intake, and a hefty dollop of star performers deliver top grades.

Without doubt, an exam-oriented place, with a persistent spotlight on the syllabus and exam technique honed by regular timed tests and ample supplies of homework, but students confirm it's far more than an exam factory. 'The teachers' knowledge is so broad, they make subjects more interesting because you're able to explore in more depth.' All pupils get plenty of close attention in classes never larger than nine – which means there's no place to hide. 'At my old school,' said one pupil. 'I used to sit at the back and not pay attention. You can't do that here.' Well-qualified staff, many of whom are public examiners or have published text books, receive extravagant praise ('brilliant', 'second-to none', 'amazing') not only for their expert subject knowledge but for their

willingness to go above and beyond. ('Even when I was away from college in the middle of exams I would email them and they would reply within 15 minutes,' said one former pupil.) Teaching style is egalitarian and conversational with technology firmly embedded in the delivery. 'Virtual learning is an efficient and engaging way of getting information across. There's now such a wealth of information available on line that students need to develop the skills to pare it down.'

About 50 a year take GCSEs (or IGCSEs) either as a two-year course for those joining in year 10, or as one year from year 11 (excellent for those recovering from ill health or recently arrived in the UK). Results good, with 52 per cent A*-A/7-9 grades in 2018.

Without doubt an exam-oriented place, with a persistent spotlight on the syllabus and exam technique honed by regular timed tests

About a fifth of students here have some form of special educational need, and the school copes well with mild difficulties, with an SEN specialist, general learning and study skills and individual education plans. ('We're clear what we can do, and if we can't do something we will tell parents there are places much better equipped to help.') MPW continues to provide its traditional refuge for those taking resits, with a remarkably flexible range of options to allow for gap year plans. Recently introduced University of London International Foundation Programme, developed and assessed by LSE for overseas applicants looking to UK universities without the requisite qualifications. Also offers Association of Accounting Technicians (AAT) level 3 diploma in accounting – successful graduates achieve professional status as AAT bookkeepers.

Games, options, the arts: Art is a particular strength, with dedicated studios for ceramics, textiles, graphic design and photography. Music taught as an A level, but no school orchestras or groups, so 'not a big school for music.' Extracurricular, once very much an also ran, has become mainstream as MPW has developed its identity as a sixth form college. Today, you'll find the usual add-ons – student council, Duke of Edinburgh (bronze taken by all year 10s) and Bank of England Interest Rate Challenge. Sport has 'improved massively' (though, as one parent commented, 'It's still nothing like at school'). Compulsory once a week for GCSE students, optional thereafter. Big menu of activities on Wednesday afternoons, with a fleet of coaches delivering to a host of venues. Well-qualified coaching staff in rugby, football and tennis, supplemented by experts in activities like golf. Rugby popular and successful, with matches against leading independents like Dulwich College and Epsom. Football, too, has an enthusiastic following. Those allergic to team sports can enjoy tennis, dance and yoga, and all students have free access to a local gym. Plenty going on outside the classroom: debating, poetry competition (recent theme, Remember, advertised on whiteboards through the college), college magazine, widely attended lecture series. Students also make full use of local museums and theatres with regular trips. Diminutive basement canteen provides healthy-eating options, but local eateries a big draw.

Background and atmosphere: Founded in 1973 by three Cambridge graduates who hoped to apply the best bits of the Cambridge tutorial system to a school, providing more choice and less tradition. Now part of the MPW group, with branches in Cambridge and Birmingham, the London HQ is housed in a series of high-ceilinged, stucco-fronted Victorian buildings in South Kensington. Indoors, all very 21st century, with computers everywhere (including folding into desks). Excellent facilities, too, for the myriad of subjects on offer, including fully-equipped media suites, computing and film rooms, separate art studios for photography and ceramics, new drama studio, and five specially-designed science laboratories. Co-ed throughout (slightly more boys than girls), the atmosphere is grown up, academically disciplined, but socially relaxed. Pupils have a strong sense of community. 'We had an absolute blast, while getting the A level grades we needed to get on the courses we wanted,' said a recent leaver. The size undoubtedly helps. 'My year group feels like a family and I can approach anyone to talk to.'

Pastoral care, well-being and discipline: Pastoral care is central to the MPW approach. Each student is assigned a director of studies, who acts as the pivot of their personal and academic life (as well as the main point of contact for parents). 'It's very personalised learning. We feel if they're nurtured, they'll prosper.' Directors of studies gain a detailed overview of the student's strengths and weaknesses, help manage the workload and deal with other aspects of daily life. 'As well as reading 10 drafts of my personal statement,' said one overseas student, 'my director of studies advised me on practical matters like getting a GP and organising the paperwork needed for a school trip to Italy.'

'As well as reading 10 drafts of my personal statement,' said one overseas student, 'my director of studies advised me on practical matters like getting a GP'

A level students only required to be in college when they have lessons. GCSE pupils kept under close supervision between classes and given timetabled library sessions to complete homework. Parents are kept in the loop, with plenty of feedback, positive as well as negative. 'They shouldn't feel that every time they receive a call from the college it will be bad news.' Classrooms and libraries orderly and focused, corridors silent. 'The amount of time spent on behavioural management here is miniscule.' This serenity, however, is achieved by clearly defined boundaries. 'We're very consistent on enforcing the rules. You have to attend, have to behave and have to be on time.' Two or three generally expelled annually. 'The most common reason is a lack of work ethic, which is a corrosive influence on others.' Immediate expulsion for drugs, too, whether on the premises or off, and random drug testing. Fresher's week type activities help integrate newcomers. 'Over 50 per cent of the college is new in any one academic year, but these are well-rounded young people and make friends quickly.'

Pupils and parents: Significant number of refugees from leading independent schools, day and boarding, plus the usual international clientele (about 25 per cent). At A level, incomers are those looking for greater freedom and informality, or for A level combinations or subjects not offered at their current school. Pupils tend to be articulate, friendly and mature.

Entrance: More or less non-selective academically, but the average applicant will have good middling GCSE grades (three 7s, three 6s, a couple of 4-5s). 'We have a strong top end, but we'll take someone with six 4s.' What they won't take is someone who doesn't fit the mould. All students are interviewed

Latymer Prep School

by the head or senior member of staff to establish whether they have a strong work ethic and understand that 'the price of freedom is behaving like an adult'. 'We're looking for the curious and motivated.' School references assiduously pursued. 'We want to be sure they're not involved in bullying or other misdemeanours.' International students given admissions tests and interviews. Majority of GCSE students stay on for A level, even if they arrive with other plans. 'Once they've seen it, they find they like the atmosphere.' Some join in the second year of A levels after a hiccup elsewhere.

Exit: Around a third leave after GCSEs. Normally 70 per cent or so to leading universities (particularly in London – Imperial, UCL, and LSE all popular). Four to Oxbridge, plus four medics and a vet in 2018. About 30 per cent annually to professional degrees (medicine, dentistry, veterinary medicine, science and law) and high numbers, too, to leading art colleges. Specialist preparation for Oxbridge, medics, lawyers, etc.

Money matters: Tutorial colleges will never be the cheapest A level or GCSE option, but most consider MPW good value for money. For the 'talented', there is a limited range of scholarships and bursaries and, for those planning 'worthwhile' travel in a gap years or holiday, there are also travel scholarships worth up to a £1,000.

Remarks: A positive, professional place, with strong teaching and outstanding pastoral care.

Miles Coverdale Primary School

Coverdale Road, Shepherds Bush, London W12 8JJ

020 8743 5847 | admin@milescoverdale.lbhf.sch.uk | milescoverdaleprimary.co.uk

State	Pupils: 241
Ages: 3–11	

Headteacher: Since 2008, Mrs Taranum Baig BEd with French, NPQH. Has studied at the Sorbonne. Previously acting head and deputy head of Dairy Meadow Primary, Ealing and acting deputy head at Stanhope Primary, Greenford. About to become an Ofsted inspector. Born in India and moved to London as a child. Conscientious and hard-working, though encourages staff not to stay too late at school, so they can get a healthy work/life balance. Gentle sense of humour. Likes travelling and heads abroad as often as possible. Enjoys tennis in her spare time. Married. No children. Head says her vision for the school is best summed up by a quotation of Martin Luther King, 'Intelligence plus character – that is the goal of true education.' Head adds, 'irrespective of background.'

Entrance: At 3 into the nursery. Admissions to the nursery are managed by the school office, but from reception to year 6 they are handled by LA, Hammersmith and Fulham. A place at nursery does not guarantee a place in reception. Heavily oversubscribed. Roughly 130 applicants apply for 25 places in nursery; 130 applicants for 30 places in reception. Intake drawn according to local authority's admissions procedure. One form entry.

Exit: Pupils go on to Fulham Cross, Phoenix High School, Hammersmith Academy and Ark Burlington Danes Academy. Some move to schools out of the borough.

Remarks: School is named after Miles Coverdale, who in the 16th century produced the first complete printed translation of the bible into English. Today, the school accepts all faiths. About to celebrate its centenary. School has gone from strength to strength on current head's watch. She puts this down to high expectations of pupils and staff 'knowing the data' (school keeps a close eye on anyone falling behind), quality of teaching and an excellent team of governors. 'A combination of delivery and accountability,' explains head.

Housed in a vast red-brick, Victorian building in the busy heart of Shepherd's Bush. A mixed, multi-cultural area which is reflected in the ethnic diversity of the pupils. Sixteen ethnic groups currently. Largest contingent are West African, followed by white British/other. Sixty-six per cent do not have English as a first language. Languages spoken at home include Somali, Arabic and a variety of Eastern European tongues. Thirty-one per cent of pupils eligible for free school meals.

Head acknowledges that a number of pupils come from unsettled backgrounds, so 'we can give them the stability they sometimes lack at home.' A very inclusive school.

Rated outstanding by Ofsted and placed in the top 100 schools nationally over last three years. Academically, each year group performs well above national average. Head confident that pupils can begin with low attainment levels but will have excellent results under their belts by the time they leave. 'We maximise potential.' Children fully engaged in their lessons and teachers full of energy on the day we visited. School works hard to narrow the gap between higher and lower attainers. Booster classes given to year 6 before Sats to make sure everyone performs well. A handful achieves a remarkable level 6 in maths and in grammar, spelling and punctuation before leaving. School has been awarded a gold club award by Boris Johnson for 'succeeding against the odds in improving pupils' aspirations and achievements.' Head is delighted that she has been made a National Leader of Education and the school has been designated a National Support School, in recognition of the continued school improvement work with other schools at local, national and international levels. A real feather in her cap.

Currently nearly 30 children with statements of special educational need. Early targeted support is the order of the day here, with maths and reading intervention groups for those falling behind. Specialist unit offers speech and language classes for children with language impairment (the only one of its kind in the borough). Pupils here are seen as being very much part of the mainstream school. These classes provide support for 20 pupils, between the ages of 3 and 7, in two classes of 10. Wide variety of difficulties catered for, from those who are unable to produce speech sounds to others who find it challenging to recall words. Most pupils then transfer to their local mainstream school at 7 or, if still in need of on-going help, stay at Miles Coverdale where they receive additional support. Full-time speech and language therapist. Children must have a statement before being accepted. A counsellor visits twice weekly to help with children with social and behavioural problems.

Strikingly attractive, bright and colourful school. Most classrooms are huge, often two rooms knocked into one. Food technology room where all pupils are given the opportunity to cook; large ICT suite; welcoming library, complete with dinosaur statue made by a member of staff. New library is wonderful: comfy sofas, bright murals of book characters and inventive furniture, all of which underline the emphasis on reading within the school. Even the most reluctant readers must be enchanted. Lots of small rooms dotted around the place for one-to-one support or small group sessions. Two playgrounds, one for each key stage, with plenty of equipment and a quiet area 'which doesn't get used very often!' Separate outside play area for reception pupils, complete with sandpits and water tables.

Staff consists of a mix of long servers of more than 20 years and more newly qualified. Low teacher turnover. Head keen on constant training of staff. 'We see ourselves as a learning community. We all need to keep learning. Every member of staff needs to keep developing to have an impact.' High pupil/teacher ratio, with two or more assistants per class of 30. High morale among the dedicated staff. One parent felt 'the teachers are close to the parents. They're welcoming and friendly. If you have an issue, they are happy to discuss it. They don't tell you to arrange a meeting and come back another time. They are very willing to talk to parents.' A teacher we spoke to happily gives up his free time to take pupils to events at weekends, such as chess tournaments.

Her vision is best summed up by a quotation of Martin Luther King, 'Intelligence plus character – that is the goal of true education.' Head adds, 'irrespective of background'

Music is a strength of the school. Music co-ordinator encourages the children to join musical events going on out of school. 'I keep my eyes open for those with that something extra, then I push them on. I even go to the auditions with the parents'. Dynamic department which uses IT to great effect. Choirs put on performances for elderly in local nursing homes. Drama is also strong. Plays include an annual Black History performance as well as Christmas and year 6 productions. Poetry recitals, debates and presentations also encouraged. According to one mother, the performances are highly anticipated and 'parents always love the plays they put on.' Numerous outings and trips for all age groups including to Royal Opera House, Lyric Theatre as well as frequent workshops including with English National Ballet and maths magicians. Children are exposed to a variety of enriching experiences from Shakespeare to street dance. Head says, 'The reason for us arranging these activities is that the core of the children here doesn't have access to this sort of experience otherwise. I want them to be introduced to the multi-cultural aspects of British-ness, to British values.' Residential activity trip for year 6 leavers. A hugely busy extracurricular timetable on offer here.

The school participates in inter-school sport tournaments and events but a lack of silverware reflects the dearth of recent victories. Coaches come in from nearby QPR football club. Fencing and football popular and cricket also offered in the summer.

> *'The teachers are close to the parents. They're welcoming and friendly. If you have an issue, they are happy to discuss it. They don't tell you to come back another time'*

Extended school day available to help working parents with a breakfast club and a nearby after-school play centre, meaning children can do a 10 hour day. Pupils able to attend up to three clubs a week and all are free; current clubs include karate, basketball and dance. Homework club for pupils who need help. A popular five-week summer school is led by teachers and support staff and includes maths and literacy lessons as well as plenty of fun 'for those children who don't get away on holiday all summer.' Head very aware that many families struggle to cope and the school does all it can to give the pupils a chance to enjoy life as well as excel academically.

High parental satisfaction. Those we spoke to were very supportive of the school and felt there were plenty of chances to get involved. A number of the parents work here as support staff. One mother said she was happy to 'let the school get on with it' as she felt 'it takes good care of the boys and girls.' School reaches out to parents and adult classes are held within the school buildings during the day, including English, computer-literacy, sewing and bike-riding. Workshops also on offer which show parents how they can best support their children with maths. Coffee mornings held regularly at the school for parents. A feeling among the parents that they are very lucky to have found this high-achieving school. One mother we spoke to had experienced seven other schools before coming here and she believed that this one was head and shoulders above the rest.

Outward looking school which is very involved in local community. Teachers work with numerous outside agencies and school provides placements for work experience, teacher training and volunteering. Now has much higher profile within the community and is seen in a positive light by neighbours. Christmas and summer fêtes sponsored by local businesses. School takes fundraising seriously and raises a substantial amount for charity each year.

Head says, 'We are what we are. We're successful. The results speak for themselves'. Year 1's mission statement sums up the ethos of the school: to 'respect each other, sing out loud, smile often and work hard.' Head has certainly transformed this school from one which had 'a poor attitude and negative feel' to one that is firing on all cylinders. Seriously impressive on every level.

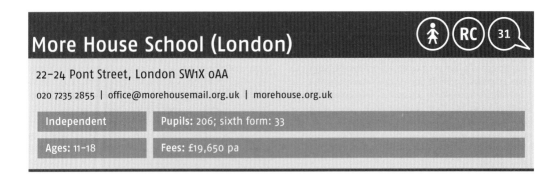

More House School (London)

22–24 Pont Street, London SW1X 0AA

020 7235 2855 | office@morehousemail.org.uk | morehouse.org.uk

Independent	Pupils: 206; sixth form: 33
Ages: 11–18	Fees: £19,650 pa

Co-heads: Since 2014, Amanda Leach, previously deputy head here for eight years. BSc in sports science from Liverpool and PGCE from Exeter. Has taught at Cranbrook School, Kent, and Uffculme School in Devon. Spent a year teaching EFL in Rome. Joined More House in 1998 as a science teacher, and has also taught ICT and PE here. 'Why would I want to leave here? I love it so much,' she enthuses. Married with two daughters; husband is director of sport at Bedales. 'I love being outdoors with my family. My kids are into gymnastics. We are not allowed to sit still for very long at home!' Described by one parent as being 'approachable and down to earth, though we don't see much of her.' Another said, 'I love Mrs Leach. She is breathing new life into the place. She has lots of energy and is a total delight.' Enthusiastic, effervescent and warm. Can be seen cycling to school from Putney every morning and girls wave to her along the Kings Road as she races past. A breath of fresh air.

Since 2017, Michael Keeley BMus. After studying music at Goldsmith's College he completed his teacher training at Birmingham University. In 1990, he became assistant director of music at the Godolphin School in Salisbury, then on to More House as director of music in 1993, promoted to deputy head in 2014 and then co-head. He continues to sing at St Paul's Cathedral as much as his teaching commitments will allow.

Academic matters: Wide range of academic ability. As one parent put it, 'There are less intellectually confident girls here who are nurtured, but there are also some very clever girls, whose parents have chosen the school because it is Catholic.' Core subjects taken in year 7 alongside Latin, history of art, dance, music and drama. All girls take two modern foreign languages and those that are bilingual can take that GCSE early. Maths, science and modern languages taught in ability sets. Religious studies compulsory for GCSE and many choose to continue with it at A level. Heads favour the philosophy and ethics course as it 'encourages girls to question their spirituality.' Pupils take eight to 11 GCSEs. Twenty-nine per cent 9-7 in 2018.

French currently popular at A level, though subjects wax and wane, depending upon the cohort. School happy to have only one or two pupils taking a subject at A level and class sizes seldom above four. Polish, Russian and Arabic all fell into this category recently, with no take up for physics or chemistry. Timetable built around what girls want to do and school tries to be flexible in terms of what it offers. Twenty-six different subjects currently taught at A level. In 2018, 33 per cent A*/B and 18 per cent A*/A grades. Extended Project Qualification taken by lower sixth. No plans for Pre-U or IB due to school's size.

Ms Leach has tightened up on academic rigour, making some significant changes since her appointment. Templates now printed in exercise books to ensure that feedback from teachers is detailed and effective and that there is constant dialogue between staff and pupils. School is also getting better at monitoring girls, with assessment points five times a year to ensure those not making enough progress are quickly identified. Colour-coded boards in staff room help teachers to see when a pupil is falling behind in subjects other than their own and gives a more holistic view of each girl's overall progress. Staff appraisals take place more regularly and twilight sessions help ensure staff members are on board with changes being implemented.

Excellent provision for girls with specific learning difficulties. The department comprises a full-time SENCo, speech and language therapist and a part-time ESOL teacher. EAL girls have extra English support until it is up to scratch. School can support girls with dyslexia, dyscalculia and dyspraxia; currently one or two per year group have quite severe difficulties. Currently two girls with Asperger's. About 25-30 girls currently receiving one-to-one support, with others having help with maths and English in small booster groups. Some girls stop support lessons around year 9 and then come back to having support nearer to GCSEs. 'It is flexible. Girls can dip in and out, depending upon their need.' All subjects offer weekly intervention classes for year 11 and above, from October through to start of exams. One parent feels that 'girls have to flag up their need for support themselves, but once the school is aware of it, provision is made pretty quickly'.

Enthusiastic, effervescent and warm. Can be seen cycling to school from Putney every morning and girls wave to her along the Kings Road as she races past

Gifted and talented programme for the brightest pupils. 'The top end is identified within three or four weeks of being here. A learning mentor then sits down with them and asks them whether they are being challenged in each subject. We listen to them'. Extension work might include Italian classes for able linguists. School explains, 'It's not just a case of giving them an extra worksheet. It's more undercover than that, but we know who has a special talent or ability. We take notice, but they don't feel pressurised.' Scholars and gifted pupils are invited to join More's Household, which offers lunchtime talks, given by internal and external speakers. Girls here regularly enter and win external prizes, such as national poetry and storytelling competitions. One girl recently made the finals of The Big Bang UK Young Scientists Fair.

Games, options, the arts: Creative and performing arts at the heart of the school. Deserves its artistic reputation and currently boasts a textiles specialist, a painter and a mixed-media artist. Heads believe that the art department is good at seeing where a girl's artistic talents lie and then giving her the opportunity to develop her interests whether in clay, textiles or fine art. Weekly, after-school life-drawing classes put on for sixth formers. Numerous visits arranged to London galleries.

Three-quarters of girls have individual music lessons. All year 7 girls play an instrument (brass, string or woodwind), bought through PTA fundraising. Strong choral tradition. All year 7 and 8 girls are in a choir. Optional thereafter. In the last choral concert, 130 girls sang alongside staff, parents and alumnae. Annual international music tour. On a recent choir tour of Rome, girls performed with papal choir in St Peter's in front of Pope and 75,000 spectators. All musical tastes and talents catered for, from chamber choirs to karaoke and geek club, which involves hand-bell ringing for the Christmas concert. 'The music is exceptional. All-inclusive. You don't have to be talented in order to be allowed to perform,' according to one parent.

Drama is another strength of the school. Sold-out drama productions of As You Like It and Grimm's Fairy Tales. Biannual play and musical which run on a carousel system. Musical is staged in a professional theatre. If a smaller production is put on one year then a junior production is also staged so that as many girls as possible can perform. 'Everyone is given a chance,' and certainly no shortage of opportunities for those who want to be in the spotlight.

'The top end is identified within three or four weeks of being here. A learning mentor then sits down with them and asks them whether they are being challenged'

'PE is being taken much more seriously than in the past,' according to one delighted parent, and sports department is well led. New PE kit has made a world of difference and hoodies without pockets mean that girls are more likely to catch the rounders ball. Practice takes place all over London, including the climbing wall at Imperial College, athletics in Battersea Park, swimming at St Mary's, Paddington and tennis in Cadogan Gardens. For the first three years, all girls participate in netball, rounders, hockey, athletics and dance as well as a healthy active lifestyle programme. Years 10-11 may also do circuit training, fitness classes, spinning and climbing and sixth form takes part in boot camp. Two girls recently selected to represent borough in London Youth Games netball team. Annual sportswomen's dinner in summer term celebrates athletic achievement. Teachers run the London marathon and raise significant amounts for charity in the process. 'The great thing about sport at More House is that everyone participates,' commented one parent. As heads explain, 'We are competing against bigger schools. Sometimes we win, sometimes we lose, but all girls get the chance to play in a team.'

Plenty of early morning and lunch time clubs, such as a thriving debating club, as well as play-dough modelling and knitting for those who prefer something more sedate. 'We want the girls to keep their childhood as long as possible. We also offer flower pressing. We don't want girls to bypass that lovely age.' Touch-typing compulsory for all in year 7. Confirmation preparation also offered. Most clubs are run by sixth formers and year 11 girls; some are run by professionals. Enviable overseas trips to Europe as well as ski-ing in America. Year 8 trip to France is a particular highlight, involving canoeing and camping overnight. Those that cannot afford the trips are subsidised, and alternative trips are also organised in London. 'Always lots going on here. That's why I am such a fan of the school,' said one satisfied parent.

Background and atmosphere: Founded in 1953 by canonesses of St Augustine at the request of a group of parents who wanted to send their daughters to a Catholic London day school. Since 1971, the school has been under lay management. Named after Sir Thomas More, the Tudor theologian.

In the heart of Knightsbridge, though not as glamorous as its location might suggest. Described by one parent as being 'essentially two houses in Pont Street with minimal outside space. Pretty scruffy and quite dark.' Much of the school was looking distinctly tired when we visited, but all has been transformed: classrooms ripped out, new furniture installed and redecorating throughout. One delighted mother told us, they have 'been busy tidying up the place, decorating where it was needed and making it more aesthetically pleasing.'

Heads determined that the school should 'not be a pressure cooker. We're not waiting for that top to blow off.' This is a very nurturing environment in which girls are constantly encouraged. One mother commented, 'At parents' evening, the teachers always highlight the girls' strengths and are keen to build on these, rather than just dwelling on what they can't do. It boosts the girls' confidence.' Very small classes which do not change from year 7 to GCSEs. 'That's my one gripe about the school. It would be good for everybody if the classes were mixed up regularly,' said one mother. Almost all classes have no more than 16 girls up till GCSE. Sixth form classes range from one pupil to 10 (but mostly much fewer). Family feel to school and all age groups mix well together, partly due to flourishing house system.

Pastoral care, well-being and discipline: Catholic heritage and ethos strong, with many crucifixes on display around the school. Currently 40 per cent Catholic, though there are girls of all faiths and none. School has its own chapel and the chaplain takes mass once a week. 'Catholicism is quite a big deal here,' said one parent. 'We get the balance right between Catholic and non-Catholic,' believes Ms Leach. 'It's part of our foundation, to respect each other and to be kind. I'm not a Catholic, though I went to a convent school and then on to a missionary school, so faith is very much part of me.' Spiritual growth fostered here. Girls also raise decent sums for charity and this is seen an important part of their education.

Heads keen that girls should develop a sense of perspective, and they are frequently reminded that 'It's not failure you should worry about. It's how you pick yourselves up'

Parents cite the pastoral care as being a main strength of the school, and those we spoke to felt that issues were dealt with efficiently and effectively. Heads keen that girls should develop a sense of perspective, and they are frequently reminded that 'It's not failure you should worry about. It's how you pick yourselves up. I don't paint a perfect image of myself. We all have ups and downs. It's my duty to help the girls through their difficulties.' Ms Leach stands at the door each morning as the girls file past. She can usually spot when something is amiss with a pupil. Girls know they can, and do, knock on her door any time. Layers of support in place, including tutors, and all 'minis' (year 7s) have a 'big sister' in sixth form. Because it is such a small school, eating disorders and emotional difficulties are spotted quickly. Hard for pupils to hide under the radar here.

Excellent relationships between staff and pupils. Girls see their teachers as approachable. As one parent put it, 'The teachers know the girls so well, that's the beauty of a small school.' Occasional short-term suspensions for rudeness to a member of staff but school is not overly quick to punish girls. 'If a girl has messed up, she's going to get an earful from her parents. I tend to ask them what they'd do differently next time.' Saturday detentions recently introduced for persistent offenders.

Pupils and parents: Roughly 70 per cent British. International contingent from all over, including Spain, France, China, Russia, America and Middle East. 'A mixed bag. Some with lots of money, who are driven in and out by chauffeurs, and others who are struggling. Quite diverse, with a good percentage of different cultures,' according to one mother. Girls travel from all over London.

Parents mostly professional. 'I don't think I have the most demanding parents in London. That's a reflection of the girls who are here. These parents want the best for their daughters. They are not idealistic in terms of what their daughters

are capable of. They are realistic and know we're going to do the best job we can for them.' Parents feel the communication is good: 'We are kept fully informed, both with the good and bad. We are kept in the loop.'

Entrance: One open day only but private tours throughout year. Part of London 11+ Consortium. Prospective pupils spend a half day at More House in the autumn of year 6, which involves an interview with head and sample lessons. The process now consists of a cognitive ability test (rather than maths and English exams) with great emphasis on the interview. This is pivotal in many ways. Head always tells girls that they will be able to answer all the questions as they are about themselves, so no need to be nervous. Increasing numbers of applicants every year but lists are closed once 150 have registered. Normally 32 places available (two forms of 16) though some bulge years of 48 (three forms). Girls are either offered a definite place or put on the wait-list. Very few turned down completely and when they are it is 'because they are not More House material as they are off the scale at either end. I can't support the very lowest ability or very highest ability, given the cohort I've got. I don't want one girl on her own at the top. If a girl can't be challenged intellectually by peers here, she's better off elsewhere. It would be great for my results to take them on, but I won't do it,' explains Ms Leach. Occasional vacancies further up the school are filled quickly. Three or four join in sixth form. School is looking for potential as much as performance at each stage. 'I want to find the golden nugget that's hidden somewhere in a girl. I want to watch them blossom.'

Exit: About 60 per cent stay on for sixth form. 'The ones who leave are those who are too cool for school. I'd rather have the ones who want to be here.' Some depart for co-ed establishments or go to local sixth form colleges. Post A level, many go to art college. Others head to universities all over: Queen Mary's, Exeter, Reading, Nottingham and Kent popular in 2018. One parent felt the school 'isn't striving to get everyone into university. That's not what they are about. They try to support the girl in finding out what is best for them.' Even if a girl is deemed to be Oxbridge material, there is no pressure on her to apply if it's not the right course for her. Usually one girl to Oxbridge every couple of years though none recently. School is now focusing on more careers advice for girls and is aware that it should tap into the expertise of its alumnae more.

Money matters: School offers a number of academic scholarships and exhibitions as well as creative and performing arts scholarships to year 7 and lower sixth. Entry bursaries for those starting the school in year 7, as well as special governors' bursaries offered in response to a particular set of circumstances, and come with provisions attached. Normally only awarded to girls who are already at the school and in examination years. Five per cent off school fees for eldest daughter when there are three or more sisters attending school at same time.

Remarks: If your daughter needs a large, competitive school with plenty of space, this is probably not the place for her. But, as one satisfied customer put it, 'If you're after an all girls Catholic school in central London, this is a great choice. It's not for everyone, but if your daughter wants a small, happy and supportive school, this couldn't be better. If I had my time over, I'd send my daughter here again like a shot'. School is aware that many parents do not know about More House yet, but that 'word is getting out as we're getting better and better.' The way things are moving, this school is not going to remain a secret for much longer.

Norland Place School

162–166 Holland Park Avenue, London W11 4UH

020 7603 9103 | office@norlandplace.com | norlandplace.com

Independent	Pupils: 235
Ages: Girls 4-11, boys 4-8	Fees: £16,104 – £18,072 pa

Headmaster: Since 2002, Patrick Mattar LRAM MA (early 50s). Degrees in music and education management and administration. Educated in Solihull. Came here in 1989, as head of music, straight from the Royal Academy of Music. This was followed by six years at Wetherby, first as director of music then deputy head. Returned here as headmaster in 2002. Married with two teenage sons and laughs that 'parenting does not get any easier!' Wife is director of lower school at Sussex House.

Music is his passion. Performs piano recitals at charity concerts, auctioned off by school. Parents rave about his talent. He admits that practising 'takes up a lot of time but I enjoy it.' Also admits to being a keen cyclist.

Softly spoken, with an infectious laugh. Parents find him approachable, compassionate and hard working. 'A superb head who has given great stability to the school,' enthused one mother. Another commented that 'the school is jolly lucky to have him'.

Entrance: Non-selective at 4 (48 places at this stage, half boys, half girls). Names down as soon as possible after birth; ideally the form will be dropped off at the school on the way home from the maternity ward. Places fill up sharpish. Each month, four definite places are allocated to two boys and two girls, on a first-come, first-served basis, so it helps it your child is born in the first half of the month. Other children placed on waiting list. Head jokes, 'Have your child in December or January when everyone else is too busy thinking about Christmas to register!' Siblings still have to register but get wait list priority and school has 'not yet failed to get a sibling in.' Head sees all parents (but none of the children) who have places in reception to explain the ethos of school. He considers it important that parents share his philosophy. Those with 'definite' places visit in the summer term just over a year before entry, those on the waiting list may be invited in the following autumn or spring term. Short, informal tests in English and maths for occasional places thereafter, as they materialise further up the school (though does not take in another class of girls at 8+ to replace the leaving boys). Head explains, 'We are non-selective but we are very much part of the London academic environment, so parents need to be aware that their child must be able keep up with the pace'. Nursery heads are seen as an invaluable source of advice about whether a child would suit the school and vice versa.

Exit: At 8, boys disperse to a range of schools including Wetherby, Sussex House, St Paul's Juniors, Westminster Under and Fulham Prep. A few head to country boarding preps, such as Caldicott. Girls' destinations, at 11, include Francis Holland (NW1 and SW1), Godolphin & Latymer, Queen's College, City of London Girls, Notting Hill and Ealing with a sprinkling to boarding (eg Wycombe Abbey, Downe House). A couple of academic and music scholarships every year.

Inspired science teaching with emphasis on experiments. Recently, year 4 girls have been busy imagining they were water particles

Head is aware that he is 'operating within a tighter academic belt' and that increased competition for London day places is a reality. School still gets similar numbers into same schools as it always has, 'though perhaps they need to work a little harder across the board to get there,' he smiles. Some parents complain about too much homework in the final years. Tutoring goes on here as elsewhere. Head finds it helpful when parents ask whether coaching is a good idea and encourages open dialogue, rather than secrecy, on this matter. He is conscious of the 11+ pressure but also notes that 'it's incredible how motivated, rather than battle weary, the children are by year 6. Many of the girls are switched on by the whole process and enjoy it.'

Head believes that 'if a child is struggling here, you have to be very careful about where you send them next. Sometimes boarding can accommodate a richer variety of pupils than London day schools.' Gives as much advice as parents want on the next stage but states 'it's always up to the parents at the end of the day.'

Remarks: Founded in 1876. Situated in the heart of noisy Holland Park Avenue in three large town houses, connected by steep stairs and narrow corridors. Bit of a rabbit warren. Not the most spacious of schools but good use is made of the two smallish playgrounds decorated with murals and climbing wall, so children have the chance to let off steam regularly. Staggered break times for practical reasons.

Mainly local families from Notting Hill, Holland Park and Shepherd's Bush. Most walk or come by scooter. Mainly professional families, many of whom are second and third generation Norlanders. Predominantly British, though with significant numbers of bilingual Europeans (Spanish, French and German). Fifty-five currently have EAL requirements, catered for through classroom differentiation and a year one EAL club. Alumnae include George Osborne, Rosalind Franklin and Arthur Bliss.

The school is structured around the fact that the boys scatter at 8 and the girls at 11. For the first three years, pupils are taught in two parallel (but age differentiated) co-ed classes. In year 3, the girls and boys are separated so boys can focus on 8+ exams while girls head down the 11+ route. Effectively, school becomes single sex from start of year 3, though spelling remains co-ed and some mixed classes are re-introduced once the boys' exams are over. Up to 24 per class, down to fewer than 20 in the one remaining class in the final years. 'We purposely allow numbers to fall off a bit in the last three years.' One parent we spoke to wished the school also offered 7+ preparation, but no imminent plans for this.

Parents favour the broad curriculum throughout. Lessons are exciting. Inspired science teaching with emphasis on experiments. Recently, year 4 girls have been busy imagining they were water particles. Specialist teachers for PE, art, music and French (which is introduced from the word go). Latin taught by head, post-exams in year 6. He also teaches reasoning to years 3-6 – 'A great way for me to get to know the children.'

Wide range of academic ability. 'As we're non-selective, we don't have a certain type of child. We love the variety we get.' Setting is fluid and discrete. School favours plenty of differentiation from the start (parents consider the most able to be well stretched and the weaker ones are effectively supported). From year 2, maths and English are divided by ability into separate classes and split lessons continue up to year 6. 'In effect, we are streaming pupils, though not for all lessons. What we are aiming for is very small group teaching.' It works well. Head says, 'I don't want rivalry amongst the children and we don't seem to get that.' Children do not fall by the wayside here, as they can do in larger establishments. Every child is kept on the radar.

Though most children make a team at some point, head thinks it is important that children learn to cope with the harsh reality of team selection. 'It teaches them to persevere and prepares them for disappointment at senior school'

All children are screened for dyslexia at the start of year 2, through a computerised test. Twelve currently have mild specific learning difficulties. School does its best to support those who are struggling but concedes the building lay-out is not ideal for those with physical disabilities. Visiting speech and language therapist. Some have one-to-one (at extra cost) or small group support. In lower years, pupils can attend early morning groups for consolidation sessions. Mr Mattar himself has undergone medical training to support a current pupil who requires extra physical help, reflecting the school's consistently caring approach.

No laptops or other devices brought in from home. Small ICT room where computer skills are taught in half classes. Other than researching, homework is not done on the computer. 'Parents support this – they are quite a traditional parent body.' Head is mindful of the fact that senior schools are old-fashioned in terms of entrance exam requirements (cursive handwriting, decent spelling, accurate punctuation and grammar). 'If that changes, we'll change what we do in school too,' he states categorically.

From year 2 upwards, the whole of Thursday afternoon is dedicated to games. Twice weekly PE lessons also taught in the playground or hall, with an emphasis on acquisition of skills. Football and cricket for boys; netball and rounders for girls; swimming for years 2 and 3; tennis, touch rugby and rock climbing. Years 3-6 participate in matches and tournaments with neighbouring schools. Though most children make a team at some point, head thinks it is important that children learn to cope with the harsh reality of team selection. 'It teaches them to persevere and prepares them for disappointment at senior school. We are encouraging, though, and get them to keep trying.' Some parents complain about insufficient sport, especially at the top end of the school, though most believe this has been partly addressed through the wide variety of clubs offered, including 'netball shoot off' and 'catch it' club. Number of clubs per child is restricted to avoid pupils becoming wiped out and to allow adequate downtime at home. Most clubs are run internally, others by external providers (chess, ballet and football).

Abundant opportunities for pupils to take to the stage. Children here learn to conquer any fear of public speaking early on. A flamboyant musical in year 3 marks the boys' last year in style, as does the departing year 6 girls' performance

Plentiful opportunities for pupils to play music together, from string and woodwind ensembles to recorder and guitar groups. Sixty-five per cent of pupils learn one or more instruments. Superb ABRSM results, from grades 1-6. Recently, over a quarter gained distinction. Large music room, chock-full of instruments including a set of drums, ready for samba playing on sports day. The whole of year 5 is currently trying to master the ukulele. Copious choirs. The chance of selection is high

– 'that's the strength of a small school. Some are disappointed but that's life,' states head.

Art plays a strong part in the school. Large, airy art room. On the day we visited, there were stacks of clay on every surface and an assortment of mini creatures ready for the kiln. Children can try their hands at a rich variety of art, from weaving to screen-printing T-shirts. DT is combined with art in final years.

Abundant opportunities for pupils to take to the stage. Children here learn to conquer any fear of public speaking early on and giving each child confidence is an aim of the school. Younger years perform termly assemblies as well as a nativity play in the local church. A flamboyant musical in year 3 marks the boys' last year in style, as does the large scale performance put on by departing year 6 girls. Plenty of drama lessons and clubs to supplement the extravaganzas.

Parents feel that issues such as bullying are stamped out quickly and effectively. All pupils play together in the playground; 'very inclusive,' according to one parent. Everyone (including head, teachers and pupils), looks after everyone else. A very nurturing place. Without exception, the teachers we met were bubbly and enthusiastic. None has been here more than 10 years, though head believes he has a good number of 'seasoned ones' as well as a more youthful contingent.

Refreshingly, Norland is not afraid to celebrate individual achievements at weekly assemblies and termly prize-giving. Each Friday there is a 'sports person', 'musician' and 'art duck' of the week. Three head girls selected, one per term, in the final year. Ample opportunities for leadership.

Residential trips from year 3 onwards, becoming increasingly far flung as the pupils become more adventurous. All pupils go – no stragglers left behind, as can happen in other schools.

Parents are welcomed into the school and volunteers run library sessions. Head comments, 'The community of the school is a huge thing'. Lots of like-minded families who become close and go off on holiday together. Seemingly, a cohesive group of relatively unpushy parents. Emphasis on fundraising and children are expected to do their bit for charity, including getting their hands dirty. Head feels it is important for them to experience giving back, not just to be aware of it.

Very traditional school (from the berets and boaters to the emphasis on good manners and fair play) but combined with a forward-looking approach. On the day we visited, the school was awash with happy, sparky children who appeared to be thriving in this caring environment. According to one parent, 'the great thing about Norland is that it doesn't dim the flame of learning' through excessive exam focus. No wonder there is a stampede from the maternity ward.

Notting Hill Preparatory School

95 Lancaster Road, London W11 1QQ

020 7221 0727 | admin@nottinghillprep.com | nottinghillprep.com

Independent	Pupils: 370
Ages: 4–13	Fees: £19,800 pa

Headmistress: Since 2003, Jane Cameron BEd (50s), three grown-up children. She was persuaded by the parents at Acorn Nursery not to retire or abandon her 'babies' to the vagaries of other schools but start her own prep so that their children could continue to benefit from her huge enthusiasm for education. Here is a woman who would love to stop the clock, not because she isn't entirely happy in her own skin (she clearly is) but because she loves every aspect of her job – children, staff and parents. One new boy in reception, in a case of mistaken identity, proudly announced to his mother 'we had assemberlee with David Cameron and she was very nice'; however, Jane Cameron (as she is universally called) would certainly have a poll rating way above that of any politician in this corner of north Kensington. Retiring in 2019.

Entrance: Luck or an elder sibling has to be on your side to get into NHP as approximately seven names go into the scrupulously fair ballot for every one that finds a place. One parent, whose offspring squeaked in, said it was a great relief as it is 'definitely the right place for us'. Siblings are always accepted and although it is not automatic for children from the Acorn Nursery (still attached to the school) to get in, it is certainly no disadvantage. Recently moved to three form entry but demand still far exceeds supply.

Exit: Almost all move on to independent secondary schools, although the occasional leaver goes to Holland Park or Cardinal Vaughan. The usual suspects at 11+ are day schools such as Latymer Upper, Godolphin & Latymer, City of London, Francis Holland and at 13+ St Paul's, Westminster, City of London, UCS, Harrodian. Several to co-ed and boys' boarding schools, including Eton, Wellington, Rugby and recently Bradfield, with a few girls plumping for boarding at Benenden and Downe House. If any of the 'secure, cushion or stretch schools' turns down one of her pupils she banishes any sense of failure by telling them that it's just the same as a restaurant saying 'we'd love to fit you in but we just don't have enough tables'.

Remarks: Turn left at the bottom of Portobello (still an unlikely mix of market stalls, genuine and fake French bakeries, shops selling incense and Poundland), and you find yourself in the less exotic Lancaster Road. A typical Victorian schoolhouse, overshadowed by the rather solemn Serbian Church next door, houses the lower school with years 3 to 6 filling a purpose-built (2011) building on the other side of the road. Yards away, round the colourful corner of Ladbroke Grove, they have squeezed a brand new block for years 7 and 8, also including massive spaces for music and art. The architectural styles are something of a hotch-potch and the outside space is not exactly state of the art although, to their credit, they have managed to squeeze in the unlikely duo of hens and an adventure playground. The only drawback: it takes smart timetabling to avoid children having to be endlessly escorted from A to B.

She banishes any sense of failure amongst pupils by telling them that it's the same as a restaurant saying 'we'd love to fit you in but we just don't have enough tables'

JC's determination to maintain her original ethos is immediately apparent on meeting everyone, from the very small people sitting on the floor, right up to the confident, friendly, amusing, only just children like the head boy and girl. This is a Thinking School and the evidence is everywhere, with hands shooting up when asked which habit was being studied this week. 'Managing impulsivity' naturally means different things at different ages, but the Edward de Bono six hats concept (the basis on which Thinking Schools operate) has definitely sunk in all the way up the school, even if the interpretation varies. We sat in on a fascinating year 6 philosophy for children (P4C) class and wanted to vote ourselves when it came to choosing the question for discussion, in fact we would have paid big money to stay and listen to the intelligent arguments raised.

Seven academic and one art scholarship awarded to the 2018 leavers show that the system works and there is no need for parents to worry that philosophy is going to stop their children learning the basic building blocks. The ethos of the school is easily absorbed, particularly that learning how to learn is, at this stage, more important than anything else. Not a school that believes in offering a huge language choice (no Mandarin here): French all the way up, together with Latin from year 5 and Greek (optional) in years 7 and 8. Apart from the four founding teachers, there are another 15 who have been here for more than 10 years, but the average age is only 35 and the head says they lose very few, unless they are Antipodean, with quite a high percentage returning to the fold later in life.

The lower school head of SEN (who has been here since the school opened) is an articulate enthusiast for early intervention, and the children being given extra help responded happily to questions. One parent told us that when her son was diagnosed with ADHD 'they were really wonderful at supporting him', and we were convinced that a large SEN department was well on top of any problems.

***

The architectural styles are something of a hotch-potch and they have managed to squeeze in the unlikely duo of hens and an adventure playground

Music is huge at NHP; JC is so fond of music, in particular singing, 'I'm tone deaf but I love joining in,' that the new 'music person' will have enormous support in filling the large boots left behind by much-loved predecessor. There are several choirs including a chamber choir, which you have to audition for, as well as ones for the less sonorous, in fact being unable to sing is not considered an option here and you are encouraged to play an instrument even if 'you can't play for toffee'.

The vast new art room (plenty of room for the next Anish Kapoor) will give the subject much more visibility. Reception and year 1 take to the stage at Christmas with a sometimes slightly unorthodox nativity play which, last year, was written jointly by the head and director of music. It featured an angel who had difficulty managing her impulsivity, when joined on her way to Bethlehem by sundry others including cowboys/girls and footballers. Stealing an idea from the Old Vic, year 8 are given the task

***

Being unable to sing is not considered an option and you are encouraged to play an instrument even if you 'can't play for toffee'

of writing and staging their own play in 24 hours, only at NHP it is spread over a week, whilst year 3 and 6 produce plays in spring and summer terms.

Differing opinions on the amount of sport available, from both parents and pupils, some claiming that it was a bit light on the ground – 'they could definitely do more' – and others saying that 'they were brilliant getting him into sport'. At the moment the girls are confined to hockey as a team game, but apparently there is a move afoot to petition the authorities for the right to choose to play rugby with the boys. Not surprisingly for a Thinking School they have been told to go ahead and ask, provided they can get enough mates to sign up. All in all, we felt that the consensus from the pupils we talked to was that they weren't missing out and there were plenty of after-school opportunities if you wanted to do more, including martial arts in year 1 and Boxclever higher up. 'There really is something to interest every type of child,' said one parent about non-sporting alternatives, including chess and coding.

Outwardly, NHP may appear a laid back school but discipline is key albeit, hopefully, self-imposed. Messing around lands you with an orange card and 'culpas' are handed out for more serious or repeated offences. These can land you with a spell of community service or a detention at breaktime, luckily a rare occurrence. The modern terror of online bullying plus the perils of the internet are areas that the head is extremely aware of, running talks for parents as well as strict monitoring throughout the school.

On asking Jane Cameron – who is definitely the guiding light behind this school – what she was proudest of, she answered, 'This may sound fluffy, but it is having created a community where everyone is happy'. Not a bit fluffy in our view (unbiased, despite meeting an equally keen Tintin fan), this judgement backed by a pupil telling us, with a huge smile, that coming here was 'the best decision she'd ever made'. Loud applause from parents, which carries weight, as this a collection of sophisticated, worldly individuals used to having their voices heard.

Our Lady of Victories RC Primary School

Clareville Street, London SW7 5AQ

020 7373 4491 | info@olov.rbkc.sch.uk | olov.rbkc.sch.uk/

State	Pupils: 236
Ages: 3-11	

Headteacher: Since 2016, Chris McPhilemy, previously acting head teacher (and before that deputy head) at St Mary's Catholic School in Wimbledon.

Entrance: Pupils come from the parishes of Our Lady of Victories, Our Lady of Mount Carmel and St Simon Stock. Priority goes to baptised, practising Catholics; all applications must be supported by letter from the parish priest. Siblings of families living within the parish boundaries get priority. Random allocation is used to offer places to other applicants. Children attending the nursery are not automatically guaranteed a place in the reception class, which is always oversubscribed. Contact the school for occasional places in older age groups.

Exit: To state schools and independents in many different directions. Co-eds St Thomas More, Holland Park, Emanuel, St Benedict's, Latymer Upper. Boys, London Oratory, Cardinal Vaughan, independents Westminster, St Paul's, Dulwich College and City of London Boys. Girls, Sacred Heart, Hammersmith, Gumley House, independents More House, Queen's Gate, Francis Holland, Godolphin & Latymer. A few to Catholic boarding schools eg St Mary's Ascot, Worth and Ampleforth.

Remarks: Very high standards across the curriculum continue to make this a successful and sought-after primary. All teaching is graded outstanding. Lots of attention to detail, personal successes, the pupils are encouraged to take pride in everything they do. Continuous assessment and monitoring ensure everybody reaches their potential, and those who need additional support are identified. Parents tell us enthusiastic staff always want to make sure the children really enjoy themselves and develop socially as well as academically. School aims to pick up SEN early; pupils are supported by differentiated teaching, specialist teachers and therapists in small groups or one-to-one. International clientele so lots of EAL tuition for those who need it.

Tall Victorian buildings with lots of stairs, however, good-sized classrooms, beautifully decorated; the school has gold Artsmark. Displays show that even the tiny children have beautiful handwriting. Nursery and reception classes have been redesigned so 3 to 5-year-olds are taught in a large, open plan space with its own playground. French starts at key stage 2, other languages via clubs, year 6 have French penfriends and make an annual trip to Cannes. Sadly, Latin has disappeared from the curriculum. After-school verbal reasoning club in the run-up to 11+ exams. Inner city location means outdoor spaces are tight, but they are well-maintained and decorated with mosaics made by the children. Younger horticulturalists grow many colourful flowers and shrubs through the gardening club which they organise themselves.

Encouraged to be involved in the school community, parents run cookery classes, listen to readers

The school has a Sportsmark; multi-purpose hall is large enough for short tennis, gymnastics and ballet lessons. Outdoor sports take place at Battersea Park; professional coaches, including ex-Middlesex cricketer, teach good range of team games. Specialist teachers for both art and music, pupils can have individual instrumental tuition on a range of five different instruments, and often join the young musicians' performances at the Albert Hall. Enticing range of extracurricular activities, clubs, trips and special visitors; year 5s can complete their cycling proficiency certificates at school.

Parents say pastoral care is very good and inclusive, the weekly newsletter keeps everybody up-to-date with events and pupils are given a voice through the school council which meets regularly with the deputy head. Food is often on the agenda, as the school has Food for Life Award, everything is cooked on site and where possible locally sourced. Encouraged to be involved in the school community, parents run cookery classes, listen to readers and raise large amounts of money which go towards paying for improvements and equipment for the school as well as for outside charities. Catholic beliefs remain at the heart of the warm, family atmosphere of the school. First rate and first choice school for Catholic families in Kensington.

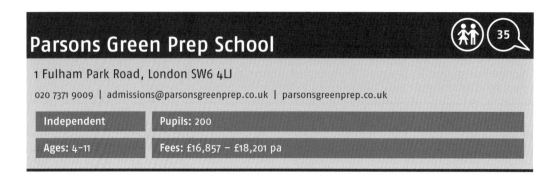

Parsons Green Prep School

1 Fulham Park Road, London SW6 4LJ

020 7371 9009 | admissions@parsonsgreenprep.co.uk | parsonsgreenprep.co.uk

Independent	Pupils: 200
Ages: 4-11	Fees: £16,857 – £18,201 pa

Headmaster: Since January 2018, Tim Cannell (50s), formerly head at The Prebendal School in Chichester, who joined PGP in September 2017 to cover Helen Stavert's maternity leave and has been appointed permanent head. Educated at Chigwell School and Davies College, followed by University of Winchester (formerly known as King Alfred's College). Read theology and has a masters degree in education management. Taught maths and RS in several prep schools – Bialla International School, Papua New Guinea, and Eagle House and Moor Park in the UK – where he was variously day master, housemaster and director of studies. A keen cricketer, he also enjoys playing squash and listening to music. Member of IAPS and CSA; has two grown-up children, both Cambridge graduates.

Tim's hobbies and interests include walking and being outdoors, gardening, watching and taking part in sport, exploring new restaurants and renovating an old barn.

Mrs Lucinda Waring (40s) is the founding principal (since 2001) and majority shareholder. Originally trained at St Nicholas' Montessori College in Knightsbridge, she founded her first nurseries at the age of 26. Naturally inspiring some envy amongst her high-flying parent body, she aims to remain firmly 'back office' but has stepped up recently to aid the transition of the new head. The school is very much her vision – to create a school where children could thrive without undue pressure; she is on top of every detail and the children know and greet her throughout the school. She is married with one child.

Entrance: Parents can register from birth (£150 registration fee). Once on the waiting list, entrance into reception via pre-entry checks, including a full academic report from current educational setting. Entry into year 1 upwards by school report and morning activity session. Easy-going families preferred. Sibling policy: 10 per cent off for siblings.

The maximum number entering reception is 44, with almost twice this number on the current waiting list. Pupils enter from Fulham nurseries in the main. Occasional places in year 1 upwards (with references and assessment). A deposit of £2,000 per family to secure the place.

Exit: Preparations for exit at 11 plus are thorough and commence from year 4. Perhaps there is little the school can do to alleviate the inevitable pressure parents and children feel, but one parent said, 'Children need to be confident enough to be able to think: yes, I can do it! That's what this school gives them'. Staff insist they will speak up in the face of ambitious parents to try and ensure that children will move on to schools where they will above all be happy. Recent destinations range from St Paul's Girls' School, Godolphin & Latymer, City of London Boys', Dulwich College and King's College Wimbledon to More House, Portland Place, Arts Educational, Kew House, Francis Holland (Sloane Square), Harrodian, Queensgate, Benenden and Lady Margaret.

Remarks: The school has undergone a name change, becoming Parsons Green Prep (previously Eridge House). Despite the marketing-friendly name change, and ambitious air of the principal, there are no plans to expand the school: 200 pupils would be the absolute maximum.

The school was founded in 2001 in a formerly derelict Victorian villa in an enviable location and with that rare thing, some outside space behind a high garden wall, offering privacy and enough room to run around. The original building was restored and modern additions blended, offering new classrooms and the large assembly hall used for everything from staging productions to PE. The end result is a smart blend of light, modern-seeming classrooms large and small, wide enough corridors with spick and span displays and lots of stairs. Come August and with class sizes finalised, the staff may be busily swapping rooms so that each class is accommodated in the best possible space.

The playground is Astroturfed throughout, with just enough room for football, tennis and netball, and a good in and out space for the early years, with wooden play equipment and smaller quiet area with outdoor chess tables. Very physical older children may need more space, not that it will be easy to find in central London. The stockpile of micro-scooters racked on the playground walls points to pupils mostly living nearby.

Founded in 2001 in a formerly derelict Victorian villa in an enviable location and with that rare thing, some outside space behind a high garden wall

The school sets out to provide a creative curriculum, but is well ahead of the curve at primary level in putting STEM subjects at the heart of the maths curriculum, following three years of careful training and planning. Every class has a STEM lesson once a week and there's a new engineering after-school club.

Parents say: 'Reading in the early years is extremely well taught'. Maths and English are taught in small ability groups. One of the numeracy tools has been effectively adopted from Montessori methods. The Mac suite has been upgraded and there is improved wireless technology around the school. Years 5 and 6 have their own individual android tablets with keyboards.

We were impressed by the individual targets on each child's work in every lesson. Teaching aims to take pupils from their learning comfort zone, where they might be engaged but not excited, to their learning challenge zone where they are encouraged to take risks. The school is currently increasing its expertise in stretching the able, gifted and talented. We found children eager to talk to us in every classroom we visited, either explaining clearly what they were working on, or coming unprompted to share their work.

Parents praise cross-curricular topic work, saying 'subjects are really brought to life', such as the year 6 challenge to design a theme park, using mathematical knowledge to design the rides and calculate their profits, whilst utilising art and creative writing to design the posters. Humanities teaching seems fun, too: we observed Horrible Histories style hygiene tips for the Tudors, whilst philosophy for children inspires pupils to interrogate the world around them. Science day saw staff joined by a team from the Science Museum – children made gigantic bubbles, launched rockets and made goop.

French is taught weekly throughout the school with a specialist French programme, which continues after school, for those children who are already fluent French speakers. The occasional pupil exits to the Lycée.

Two assemblies per week. Christmas concert not a carol service. When we visited in October, they were looking forward to going crazy on Christmas decorations.

A third of the 36 staff has been at the school for more than 10 years. We have rarely heard so much praise for teaching assistants: in the main extremely youthful, so they have sufficient energy to keep up with their charges. 'Right people in the right places,' says principal and 'no staff who get stale'. Parents say: 'often young and enthusiastic about teaching'; 'lovely teachers allow children to be children'; 'willing to try a multitude of different ways to captivate children'. Teachers feel looked after by the school and are part of a very thorough programme of ongoing training. They describe themselves as 'creative, motivated and committed.'

Teachers are addressed (by everyone – parents, other staff) as Miss or Mr plus first name, so eg Miss Lucinda, which we found a bit Beatrix Potter-ish, but the principal says, correctly, 'it's friendlier for the children'.

Most parents are content with 'sensible homework', none during school holidays until key stage 2, and there is a dedicated homework session at school. Children are deliberately not over-loaded. Trips could be to the local community supermarket or fire station, but also make the most of London from Fulham football club on the doorstep to Pudding Lane. From year 3 residential trips begin with camping and a French day trip.

Seven per cent of pupils have EAL needs. The school seems to have fewer than average number of children with learning differences, but a SENCo in place to ensure their needs are met.

Parents universally describe children who love going to school and 'can't wait to get in at the gate'. We can report beaming smiles and diligent application in every class we visited, and parents agree, describing the school as 'a happy place to learn'; 'intimate, caring, quietly competitive' and 'children do not feel any pressure at all and yet are making good progress'.

Some gripes about sport persist: 'No way near enough sport,' said one parent and another added, 'Not enough boys in year 3 to field a football team'. However, sport is evolving: now offers tennis throughout the year with new tennis coaches, and a coach from Chelsea FC runs three after-school clubs each week. Year 2 upwards play football, tag rugby, cricket, netball, rounders and have weekly swimming lessons. The school has recently joined the Independent Schools Association, which means more sporting competitions. The usual summer sports day and swimming gala. The upper school makes use of Hurlingham Park. Keen sports players had better be early risers as squad practice takes place before school most days.

Children are taught guitar, piano, violin and now drum lessons – singing and guitar most popular. There's an orchestra and a choir.

'The summer performance is always excellent,' said a parent. Most recently A Midsummer Night's Dream and The Wind in the Willows. 'Would like more drama opportunities,' said another. A few entries for the LAMDA drama exams with several distinctions.

Chess is huge here, deliberately encouraged to develop logical thinking. Greatly improved clubs, say parents. Those now on offer pre- and post-school or at lunchtime encompass the fun and fashionable, including photography, fencing, orchestra, Mandarin, soccer, chess, baking, sewing, ukulele, running and study skills. Hot lunches and after-school clubs cost extra.

The school is very clear about the standards expected of the children, and parents see pastoral care as a real strength of the school: 'My child had been unhappy at a different school, but has thrived here'; 'I really like the atmosphere: it is very caring

but with high standards of behaviour'; 'bullying isn't tolerated and the staff has been quick to act' and 'not much gets by the staff'. The new buddy benches in the playground have been a big hit, too.

Frequent mentions by parents of this school being well suited to a child who might be quite shy initially: 'a sensitive soul ' or 'young in year or late developers'. But parents with more than one child here, the majority, report it suiting all sorts of temperaments and abilities: 'outgoing children can shine'. A teacher believes it works well for 'bright children who are not afraid to take risks and who want to learn'.

Parents are without doubt a smart, city crowd: 'Friendly, international and professional with lots of dual-working parents,' said one. Many agree on a friendly welcome from other parents. Every other parent describes the school community as 'international' but the principal says this is more perception than actuality. Parent volunteers do everything and anything from weekend hospitality for the science lab chicks, to designing the logos for the houses, to being part of the eco committee growing and harvesting crops in the school garden.

Any parents with low-flying or tiger-ish tendencies, this may well not be the school for you. Those who are searching for somewhere to nurture and inspire happy, confident children – look no further.

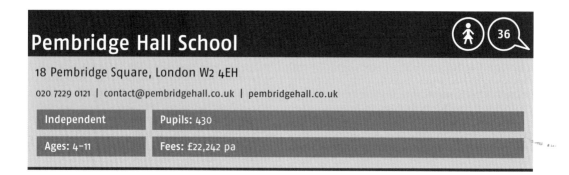

Pembridge Hall School

18 Pembridge Square, London W2 4EH

020 7229 0121 | contact@pembridgehall.co.uk | pembridgehall.co.uk

Independent	Pupils: 430
Ages: 4–11	Fees: £22,242 pa

Headmaster: Since 2012, Henry Keighley-Elstub BA PGCE (40s), previously deputy head at Wetherby Prep. Educated at Eton and Leeds University, where he read classical civilization. He has taught history at Ludgrove, Cothill and Chesham Prep, where he was head of department and also senior master. As well as this being his first headship, it is also his first experience of an all girls' school, and one that finishes at 11 years rather than 13. 'I was worried about that at first,' he admits, 'but now I barely notice, and communicating with an 11-year-old girl is equivalent to talking to a 13-year-old boy.' Married to Sarah who works at IBM ('I have no idea what she does', he confides. 'Perhaps she's a spy.') They have a young daughter.

Mr Keighley-Elstub, slight of build, has an immediately warm, engaging and enthusiastic personality that makes even the stiffest person unfurl. His conversation is littered with verbs and adjectives like 'skip along' and 'groovy'. His upbeat, chipper approach is directed at everyone. As well as the girls, the parents and the teachers it embraces the peripatetic music staff, games staff and the odd visitor. Despite being an Old Etonian with an unusually complicated name both to spell and pronounce (think 'Keithly'), Mr Keighley-Elstub is remarkably down to earth. He attributes this to his Northern pedigree (his father was a Yorkshireman but practised as a GP in Wimbledon where Mr Keighley-Elstub grew up). His family used to turn up at Eton in a clapped out old VW, but 'that wasn't remotely embarrassing,' he avers. 'Eton's not smart at all. The greatest compliment anyone could pay me,' he continues, 'is to turn up to meet me in jeans.' If he weren't so refreshingly open you wouldn't guess it – he looks immaculate in his well-cut suit and playfully shrieks when he discovers the odd crisp on the floor in a classroom.

We joined a river of red blazered and straw boatered girls as they walked immaculately to the church

He loves music – his wife is a violinist and he has recently formed a staff choir. He is also an enthusiastic sportsman (running is his thing) and he is determined that the girls here start winning some matches for a change. He champions all departments – art, music, sport and drama – equally and works to get them all to enjoy working together rather than being at loggerheads, as happens so often. He is relishing the challenges of his first headship and is not unaware of the benefits of running a school that is part of the Alpha Plus group. He talks of the wealth of resources available to him, from legal to financial as well as the supportive but 'hands off' nature of the governing body. Although ambitious with lots of energy, he is clearly here to stay for some time – 'I couldn't leave while there is still so much to do,' he says. 'I want to transform a good school into an outstanding one'.

Entrance: Names down at birth – 'but realistically that means within two weeks of birth,' says head. He is keen to dispel the myth that you need to plan a Caesarean and father needs to put the form through the letter box as the baby arrives. It absolutely makes no difference at all on what day of the month your child is born. They divide the months into thirds and take an equal number from each third. Non-refundable registration fee (currently £150) does not guarantee you a tour of the school. Personal tours with the head offered as soon as you are off the waiting list and offered a place (something Mr Keighley-Elstub has recently introduced – prior to his arrival tours with a member of staff offered at deposit decision time – close to starting). The competitive market (for children more than the schools) and wealthy catchment of West London means that parents don't blink at paying these sort of sums without even being given the chance to see the school before making a decision. The alternative to long waiting lists is a selection process at 3, and that would mean 'we may miss the wild wacky ones that add colour to the place,' says Mr Keighley-Elstub. Nevertheless, close liaison with feeder nurseries (he mentioned

The Acorn, Rolfe's, Strawberry Fields, Minors and Ladbroke Square) to make sure girls will manage.

Exit: Plenty of scholarships, academic, sporting as well as musical and artistic, each year (14 academic, music and art scholarships and exhibitions in 2018, the majority to Francis Holland NW1) and fine boards in the upper school hall to commemorate them.

Most popular day destinations in 2018 were Francis Holland NW1, Godolphin & Latymer and St Paul's Girls. Most popular boarding destinations were Downe House, St Mary's Ascot and Wycombe Abbey. Plus a large contingent going to Bute House at 7+ in 2018.

Remarks: Situated in a particularly leafy, white stucco square in Notting Hill Gate, the lower school is in a tall building a minute's walk from an identical building containing the upper school. In between is Wetherby pre-prep – the boys' equivalent – and also owned by the Alpha Plus group. In the basement of number 10 (the upper school) is Minors Nursery – another Alpha Plus establishment: no wonder such direct communication about the character and ability of the girls can be made.

Girls here are well spoken, eager to please and confident. Lots of awards and prizes and opportunities to speak publicly and take responsibility

Round the corner in St Petersburg Place is the splendid St Matthew's Church where whole school assemblies take place each week. We joined a river of red blazered and straw boatered girls as they walked immaculately to the church. An overwhelmingly white collection of girls for such a multicultural part of London; they are international – American, Russian, European as well – but only about 10 out of 400 girls receive EAL help. Mr Keighley-Elstub described the ethos as 'lightly Anglican' but a very English education, which seemed to be requirement of even the most foreign of families.

Girls here are well spoken, eager to please and confident. Lots of awards and prizes and opportunities to speak publicly and take responsibility to build that confidence. We were particularly impressed with an astonishing game designed by a 10-year-old girl out of a cardboard box, which intricately displayed the planets and included chance and question cards which she had devised herself. She then explained through a microphone how to play the game to an audience of about 450 people in the church, including parents as well as teachers and children.

Classrooms spacious, bright and airy with wonderful high ceilings and tall windows. Lovely wide corridors and staircases that seem to go up and up for ever. Lush red carpet (to match the uniform?) in the lower school, upper school mirrors the lower school but in blue. We saw some very impressive still life work in the very studio-like space at the top of the school, which had brilliant ceiling windows, creating an excellent space to be creative. Well-equipped science labs in the basement with a good old-fashioned full-sized skeleton in the corner. Super space in the basement for drama and productions with a wealth of colourful and imaginative costumes and hats. All years get a chance to perform: year 5s do a Shakespearean medley, year 6s do their annual play in the local Tabernacle Theatre. Both buildings have large halls which double as dining rooms at lunch time. Wide choice of healthy cooked lunches and imaginative fruit (watermelon and pineapple – not just your regular apples and bananas). How refreshing not to see children eating packed lunches at their desks.

Healthy number of male teachers and the arrival of Mr Keighley-Elstub has seen barely any staff turnover at all. He feels proud of having injected renewed energy and purpose into the place and acknowledges that when he arrived there was a lot of reassurance to be done. Parents were rattled and there was a lack of direction. Those we spoke to referred to a terrible lack of communication. Many considered moving their daughters but remarkably few did, explaining that the pastoral care remained excellent throughout and they didn't want to uproot a happy child. Emphasis is now on communication – particularly with parents; improvement and consolidation of the academics; and improvement of sport.

Girls are starting to win netball matches now – and we were proudly told of how they beat Glendower recently. Netball and hockey played in nearby Avondale Park and Holland Park, athletics at the Linford Christie stadium in Wood Lane and swimming at the Porchester Baths. Plenty of inter-house matches so that everyone can have a go. Tennis as a club rather than a school sport, and rounders possibly on its way out. 'I don't see the point of it,' says Mr Keighley Elstub. 'It's rather a poor man's cricket'. He is very open to the idea of introducing football and cricket for the girls but so far there doesn't seem to be the demand. Several outside spaces in both buildings for fresh air between lessons and 'unless there's the threat of a tornado out they go,' says head, who can't understand why the girls had been treated with such velvet gloves in the past, with the mere threat of rain resulting in their reading inside.

Three classes of 20 in each year. Setting only in maths from year 3. Serious preparation for the 11 plus starts in year 5 but the groundwork is now being laid much earlier. Mr Keighley–Elstub teaches years 5 and 6 so he can give well informed advice about senior schools. He is not afraid to tell a parent if they are being overly ambitious academically but will look at the whole child and advise which is the most appropriate school on that basis. Vast majority of parents here are in finance – though the odd one is glamorously famous, you wouldn't describe this as a trendy school. Mr Keighley-Elstub famously put a stop to the cashmere scarves as part of the school uniform and supplied by a parent: this isn't the image he wants to nurture.

Large, busy, and traditional with a dynamic head, Pembridge Hall can only get better and better and could be an excellent choice for your enthusiastic daughter.

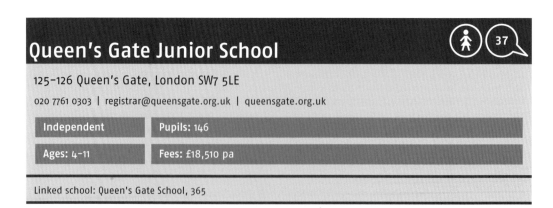

Queen's Gate Junior School

125–126 Queen's Gate, London SW7 5LE

020 7761 0303 | registrar@queensgate.org.uk | queensgate.org.uk

Independent	Pupils: 146
Ages: 4–11	Fees: £18,510 pa

Linked school: Queen's Gate School, 365

Director of the junior school: Since September 2017, James Denchfield, previously head of lower school at Queen's Gate Senior. English and history degree from Goldsmiths College and PGCE from the Institute of Education. Taught English at schools in London and Norfolk before joining Queen's

Gate Senior in 2009. The following year he became head of English, and has since progressed to head of remove then head of lower school. Has also worked with the North London Girls' Schools' Consortium (now the London 11+ Consortium), including helping to set the English paper.

His daughter was a pupil here; he also has a young son. He lives in south-west Hertfordshire, where he enjoys walking and bird watching.

Entrance: Around 100 applicants for each of the 23 places at reception. One 7+ competitive academic scholarship worth a third of the annual fees. Assessment morning with groups of 8-10 children given tasks and observed by the headmistress and other staff.

Exit: Around 90 per cent to the senior school. Rest to a range of good London schools and a few to boarding.

Remarks: A few doors down from the senior school and an equally discreet entrance belies the warmth, fun and productive activity that goes on here. Up to 23 tots in the first two years – each in a good sized room with teacher and two teaching assistants. Happy, absorbed children are relaxed and busy in rooms that are stimulating without being frantic. Some older classes quite noisy with a buzz of activity but everywhere, even the art room, is orderly and purposeful. Quiet, sustained work for the oldest girls, who would change nothing about the school save its lack of outdoors, and really like their friends. Rooms light and recently refurbished – and at a sensible temperature. Good sized hall – like the senior school, the old salon in grand architectural style. Good-sized library, well-used with a real, 'very hard-working' librarian shared with big sister school. Lots of multi-purpose spaces and facilities. Good IT suite.

Some older classes quite noisy with a buzz of activity but everywhere, even the art room, is orderly and purposeful

Lots of music – choirs and an orchestra. Very lively art; we encountered Dragolina, an immense dragon being constructed for the coming Chinese New Year – and were glad to see good old-fashioned crayon work. Tastes of French, Spanish, German, Italian and Latin as the girls progress through the school. Fun, but some parents query the purpose: 'they really don't know any French at all when they go into the senior school'. Teaching of eg science done by senior school staff. By bus to sports facilities all over the place – ensures plenty of indoor and outdoor sports. Lots of lovely after-school clubs three days of the week – 'So hard to choose, Mummy!'

Parents happy. 'It's traditional, though things are livening up. It really suits my daughter.' Staff now mostly young and pretty international. We warmed to the sight of children spontaneously hugging their teachers (probably illegal!) A safe, cosy and well-structured start for your precious daughter. And once she's there, you could really forget about her education for the next 14 years and trust them to give her all she needs.

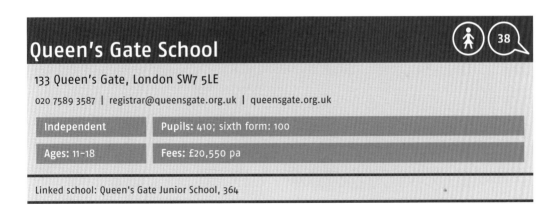

Queen's Gate School

133 Queen's Gate, London SW7 5LE

020 7589 3587 | registrar@queensgate.org.uk | queensgate.org.uk

| Independent | Pupils: 410; sixth form: 100 |
| Ages: 11–18 | Fees: £20,550 pa |

Linked school: Queen's Gate Junior School, 364

Principal: Since 2006, Rosalynd Kamaryc BA MSc PGCE (50s). Petite, chic and with a lovely soft Irish voice, Mrs Kamaryc immediately comes across as the warm, calm and practical person to whom you'd want to entrust your precious daughter. A mathematician who still teaches – in her case, the bottom GCSE set. 'I just love teaching,' she says, and 'counts it a privilege to walk the school' once a day.

St James Senior Girls' School

Mrs Kamaryc has an impressive pedigree, this being her second headship. She began teaching in Scotland and spent 10 years as head of Wykeham House School, Fareham – via Forest School and Woodbridge School. Parents enthuse: 'She gives terrific support to the girls,' we were told. 'She's extremely capable, a very safe pair of hands with a very clear vision for the school.' 'Very approachable though can seem a little shy.' Her catwalk walk at a school fashion show wowed everyone. 'She commands respect but she can kick up her heels too. She's fun.'

Academic matters: 'It punches above its weight academically,' one parent told us and the results bear this out. French, English, maths, art and geography shine brightly. Tiny sets at A level – often ones and twos – a rare privilege and at half the cost of the top tutorial companies. They will run an A level course with one pupil and don't ditch the subject – or its teacher – if it has no takers in a given year. Art and maths have biggest numbers. If a subject has more than seven takers they split the group. Some depts seen as better than others. 'English and history are very strong; art is amazing,' we heard repeatedly and 'though the teachers are all lovely, their actual teaching isn't always great – a little dull and uncreative sometimes.' But A level results are remarkable these days, 55 per cent A*/A, 79 per cent A*-B in 2018.

'We do some gruesome stuff,' chortled the dynamic head of art as we gaped at the 'urban zombies' and various startling depictions of blood and vomit

Good range of GCSE subjects for so small a school. Ancient history and classical civilisation, Latin and Greek, computing recently introduced and lots of modern languages, including Mandarin, available – and not just for native speakers. Good results in English, geography, French, drama, art – but no weaklings here (80 per cent A*-A/9-7 in 2018). 'We chose it,' said a parent, echoed by more, 'because it is not obsessed by exam results.' 'It's not a hoop-jumping school.'

School has 1.5 staff on learning support team – much praised. 'Incredible support for my daughter's mild dyslexia. Possibly not for much else,' thought a parent, and this is borne out by the head.

Games, options, the arts: Parents glow and when you make it to the loftily-situated art dept you understand why. The main studio entrance is festooned with trompe l'oeil blue velvet curtains and abutted by a display of white paper insects; inside is a huge range of work, all demonstrating boldness, creativity and imagination. 'We do some gruesome stuff,' chortled the dynamic and experimental head of art as we gaped at the 'urban zombies', the girl under a blanket of fresh minced steak and various startling depictions of blood and vomit. It was reassuring to turn to the multi-coloured shoes on every step of the staircase, the cardboard relief masks, the fun, wit, skill of it all. DT even more surprising; facilities include a laser cutter, 3D printer and vacuum former. Products we saw included acrylic pencil and iPad holders and electronic dice. We warmed to a girl (flatteringly, given our age) mistaking us for a potential parent, who insisted on telling us: 'If someone wanted to do product design, they really mustn't go anywhere else.' Art and DT results from here are outstanding.

'Our drama teacher is so dedicated and lovely.' We interrupted a rehearsal of Darkwood Manor – a bit of Gothic horror written by the girls, gory in their white and cicatriced faces, blood and masks. No theatre, though a small semi-studio – 'we don't need a 100 seater theatre,' claimed a proud parent. Good music room with lovely Broadwood grand and reassuring number of real instruments plus modern keyboards with headphones. Many learn instruments and school music is lively and popular.

Sports regarded as much improved during Mrs Kamaryc's tenure, though almost all involves bussing hither and yon. 'We don't mind, it's not an issue,' parents feel, though some pupils we spoke to yearned for playing fields and pitches. It probably isn't ideal for your jumping bean, though on offer now are rowing, squash, fencing among others and girls love it all. 'We have 95 clubs,' we were told and a buzz of jolly fun activities and try-outs pervades the place. Some little sorrow that not everyone joins in with all this opportunity as fully they might.

Background and atmosphere: Queen's Gate is a smart, elegant road in anyone's book. You walk past this school and back again without knowing it's there, so discreet is its little brass nameplate. 'It's a fantastic location,' gush Kensington mummies, 'just like a house.' And so it is – three houses, in fact, knocked together and inside – apart from the fabulous cornices, ceiling roses etc, it's yer actual rabbit warren. 'Yes,' nods a wise mummy, 'but good teaching can take place in a tent.' We lost count of the number of floors and semi-floors above the basement (ICT, lab, lockers and gym and still somehow redolent of the butler's clipped footfalls and scurrying maids). Some upper floor corridors are so narrow that we fear future generations of Tubby Tillies may get stuck. Not that we saw any such here, of course.

Main entrance hall embellished with wall-mounted bell, a set of gongs, a digital clock, fire extinguisher, staff pigeonholes, a vintage radiator, a vitrine bulging with silver trophies and a venerable wooden post box we couldn't open. All this somehow seemed to sum up the whole. Wonderful main hall confected from the two adjoining salons from the houses' glory days – newish wooden floor and matching brass chandeliers. No playground, just a couple of tiny roof gardens for the younger years. Otherwise, breaks are taken in classrooms – and these, on, admittedly, a dark January day, were some of the most overheated we have encountered. Pupils and staff were busily fanning themselves as the rude bell shattered the silence and doors opened. 'It does get very hot,' a youngster confided, 'and sometimes it gets very cold.' Black (for pupils and staff) and white (for pupils) dining rooms, wonderfully elegant and decidedly different. Food reckoned to be good – around half bring in their own. Some come for breakfasts which sounded more than worth sliding out of bed and down the road for.

'We celebrate all faiths and cultures.' Evidence was the great excitement – and splendid dragon – we witnessed in preparation for the Chinese New Year

Main library is a beautiful room with splendid polished oak tables and equally venerable stock in many cases (nothing wrong with that) and a lovely place to work. Sixth form has surprisingly spacious common rooms with sofas. Also a kitchen and a work room, but work decidedly not happening when we peeked in.

No uniform, most dressed perfectly sensibly though this feature of the school clearly stresses a few. 'Some girls bring in ridiculous designer bags,' one mum kvetched, but no-one looked especially coutured to us – though perhaps we are not the best judges. Certainly a divisive issue for some – though not exactly on an 'in/out of the EU?' scale.

Pastoral care, well-being and discipline: Everyone praises the pastoral care. 'They are very good at sorting out individuals,' one father told us. 'My daughter is very happy there.' Another praised the good relations between the girls, fostered by the staff and the care taken to build inter-year relationships. A third described the amount of extra time and effort put in by the teaching staff. A fourth said: 'My daughter feels there is always a teacher to chat to if she has a problem' – and so on. Each term

'It's a fantastic location,' gush Kensington mummies, 'just like a house.' And so it is – three houses, in fact, knocked together

has a 'pastoral day' and a trip to France in year 7 is 'brilliant for bonding us'. Very little sense of serious disciplinary problems being on anyone's radar.

Pupils and parents: Head stresses: 'We're a very English school with an international community. Many of our parents came here from overseas as students – and stayed. We are a Christian foundation but we celebrate all faiths and cultures.' Evidence was the great excitement – and splendid dragon – we witnessed in preparation for the Chinese new year. Largest number of overseas nationals probably Italian, followed by French, Spanish, US, Aussies, Qataris and a few Russians. Much-loved by its old girls, many of whom are current parents; good supportive parents' group. Only, but repeated, gripe is that 'communications are not great' – a surprise to the school but something they are addressing.

Notable OGs include HRH the Duchess of Cornwall, various Redgraves, Sieffs, Guinnesses, Amanda de Souza, Jane Martineau, Nigella Lawson, Lucinda Lambton, Tracey Boyd, Aurelia Cecil, Trinny Woodall and Imogen Poots. Former head of MI5 Eliza Manningham Buller used to be on the staff.

Entrance: Around six applicants per place at 11+. Part of the London 11+ Consortium. Assessment process now consists of a 75 minute cognitive ability test (rather than maths and English exams) with great emphasis on the interview. Waiting list for all years, but occasional places occur (maths and English tests plus interview) so worth a phone call. A few in at year 12 but 'we are very selective' and six 9-7s at GCSE are a requirement. Head meets all prospective parents before anyone is tested on anything.

Exit: Almost all stay to A level. Of the 10 per cent or so who try pastures co-ed, boarding or state, some scuttle back tout de suite. Head says that she encourages them to 'be brave and look elsewhere' at this stage. You'd be brave – or rash – to move from so small and nurturing a community to a place where no-one knows a thing about you. Year 13 leavers go to a wonderfully eclectic bunch of good universities around the globe, with several off to the US (two places in 2018). Oxbridge is not uncommon (one place in 2018), solid Russell Group for most but around a quarter much further afield.

Art, art history and classics more common than science, though two medics in 2018.

Money matters: All 11+ entrants are automatic scholarship candidates and 25 per cent fee remission offered to high flyers. Art, drama, music and sports scholarships also available – apply on registering. Similar 25 per cent remission available to sixth applicants. Means-tested bursaries too, but no point in applying until a place is offered.

Remarks: A lovely school for lovely girls in a classy and sophisticated milieu. Tiny classes, delightful teachers, charming friends with a faint St Trinian's spicy edge. Not for you if you want gritty urban reality – except, perhaps, in the art room.

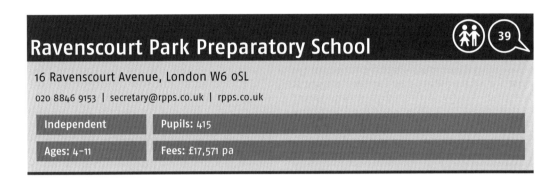

Ravenscourt Park Preparatory School

16 Ravenscourt Avenue, London W6 0SL

020 8846 9153 | secretary@rpps.co.uk | rpps.co.uk

Independent	Pupils: 415
Ages: 4–11	Fees: £17,571 pa

Head: Since 2015, Carl Howes MA (Cantab) natural sciences, PGCE from St Luke's Exeter, previously deputy head at St Paul's Juniors, following head of maths and second master at King's House School, Richmond. His wife is a Twickenham primary school teacher; son, 20s, and teenage daughter. First RPPS head to come from outside, Mr Howes is committed to the school's ethos: 'I very much appreciated the thriving, happy community I inherited.' Seen most days in the playground, smartly attired, welcoming all; parents we spoke to describe him as 'highly approachable', 'a good listener, quiet but straight talking'. Mr Howes comments, 'I enjoy the connection with the children and as a head you have to make an effort': he clearly does, as prior to our visit, he was away on year 5's Devon residential trip. He takes assemblies, debating club, teaches year 4 and 5 mathematics sets, some sport to younger pupils. He has introduced Headmaster's Awards which acknowledge pupils' effort and attitude. Pupils we spoke to found him 'kind, generous with his time, turning up at weekend tournaments'. 'He's a perfect adult: he understands children and what they find interesting and funny'. We found him charming, measured in approach, with a fascination for educational matters, coupled with intelligent discernment to ensure RPPS equips pupils for, as he puts it, 'the challenges of an unknown world'.

Two terms into his tenure, school inspectors judged RPPS 'excellent in all areas,' of which he is justifiably proud. He appreciates staff are 'forward-looking' and 'responsive' adding, 'I am not a micro manager'. Parents we spoke to recognise he has 'a light touch' which 'empowers the teachers', whilst upholding high expectations and 'sifting out what really matters'. To relax, Mr Howes cycles to work, runs five kilometres on Saturdays and plays the saxophone. When asked about his future ambitions, he has no wish to lead an empire, enjoying the holistic education and size of RPPS.

Entrance: Register on child's first birthday, not before, for one of 60 non-selective reception places allotted by ballot with siblings given priority. Later applicants join waiting list with a few occasional places arising each year when families relocate. The expectation is that all will stay until the end of year 6 in gender balanced classes of 20. The majority of pupils come from local day nurseries.

Exit: Most parents seek day school places; very popular destinations include Latymer Upper and Kew House. Also popular were Notting Hill and Ealing High School and Godolphin & Latymer. Mr Howes has good relationships with senior schools and can advise accordingly. The school caters for a range of ability with impressive results, including 12 to 15 scholarships every year. 'If I could, I would like to abolish 11+,' summed up one parent, disenchanted with the process but pleased with how RPPS strives to address the stresses and strains, whilst others agreed how extremely well the teachers and headmaster know each child's ability and personality.

Remarks: Maria and Ted Gardener, former teachers, founded the school in 1991. With the addition of the Gardener Building in 2011, the school consists of four separate buildings on one site, close to Ravenscourt Park where most PE and games lessons take place. Some parents are nostalgic about when the school was smaller, believing the parent body was more cohesive, but acknowledge more families have benefited and are pleased 'it has kept its heart'. Part of the Gardener School Group Ltd with Kew House and Kew Green Prep, RPPS benefits from shared resources, expertise and fixtures. Some parents we spoke to talked about it being a business, especially the fact 'the fees go up every year at the higher end'. Others bemoan the lack of bursary places which they believe 'makes the school less diverse, to its detriment'.

The homely Old Vicarage building houses the early years and year 1 in well-equipped classrooms with dedicated outside play area for supervised groups. A spacious science lab ensures pupils can carry out experiments. They are encouraged to solve problems and create models; we saw a sophisticated Galileo-inspired pendulum. Some parents criticised half termly homework projects as too demanding and questioned whether models were produced by other competitive parents. Homework and costume provision for theme days can cause difficulties for working parents but the 8.00am–6.00pm school day and after-school clubs are much appreciated. Children appear relaxed and enthusiastic. They stood up as one, politely greeting us with 'good morning' in every class, and readily explained what they were doing. They were clearly absorbed in the task at hand, from year 5s in an English class reflecting on the plight of refugees, to year 1s explaining how to access and record work on their PCs in the IT suite. All classrooms have interactive whiteboards and iPads are used throughout. Pupils enjoy fun ways of learning to do computer coding, creating animations, games and stories collaboratively, and all are made aware of e-safety.

Fantastic facilities include a light, spacious art room with its own kiln. We saw high quality art work in different media displayed throughout the school, including a stunning recreation of a Van Gogh-inspired painting made by classes using coloured curled card. Parents value the creativity on offer but some wish 'more of the artwork could come home'. Overlooking the playground, conveniently situated on the ground floor, is the excellent library. Librarians ensure it is accessible in break times and we saw pupils thoroughly enjoying the wide range of materials on offer. There is an attractive dining room where tasty, fresh food is prepared, monitored by a food committee including some parents.

All buildings contain cheerful rooms where learning support or small group work is undertaken. The SEND register is reviewed after standardised assessments each term during pupil progress meetings and 25 were on the register when we visited. The department is well regarded. Parents find the SENCo and her team 'really

responsive' and praise the school as being 'inclusive'. 'They cope very well with pupils with pre-identified minor learning difficulties.' There are withdrawal lessons and/or provision made in the classroom to cater for individual learning difficulties. Teachers are available to talk to, with no extra charge for learning support.

Spacious science lab for experiments. Pupils encouraged to solve problems and create models; we saw a sophisticated Galileo-inspired pendulum

Staff are energetic and dedicated. As one parent explained, 'They tick all the boxes', and best of all, 'they really know their pupils'. Pupils we spoke to described RPPS as 'a friendly community' where 'everyone is made to feel the same, equally valued' and their teachers as 'encouraging', 'very fair' and 'kind'. We saw Mr Howes in a new guise at the dance assembly, when he joined some colleagues in street dancing. This was part of the school's commitment to growth mindsets, an educational strategy which Mr Howes and his senior team have introduced to encourage all pupils to make mistakes and develop resilience, so they will try something new and persevere. Year 2s had no problem explaining this approach to us with a helpful visual chart in their classroom. Mr Howes explained the two year rotating cycle of values being shared in assemblies including intellectual humility, respect and tolerance, part of the school's holistic ethos.

Parents were unanimous in their appreciation of the staff's open door policy, which ensures prompt responses to their concerns whether small or great, and agreed they are never made 'to feel a nuisance'. Communication is considered 'excellent', ranging from the website with parent portal and Parkside newsletter to the weekly 'onthefridgedoor' which encapsulates the week's events and pupil achievements, including a paragraph from the head. Parents commented on 'the solid system' for pastoral care with clear guidelines. Pupils we spoke to happily explained 'reminder notes' alongside the RPPS Code of Conduct. 'There is always someone to share your concerns with,' they agreed, 'and plenty of opportunities for responsibility with school council representatives and librarians, to name a few'.

At KS1, the boys and girls have games lessons together; at KS2, the boys do football, rugby and cricket and the girls do netball, hockey and rounders. There are regular fixtures and 18 sports related clubs each week on offer. Relatively recently, the girls' netball team qualified (again) for the IAPS finals and year 5 had its first football and netball tour to Jersey. 'Music is fantastic,' parents agree and approximately 230 individual instrumental lessons take place in school weekly with 15 peripatetic teachers. All praised the wide variety on offer: three choirs, two orchestras, music theory club, chamber music ensembles, rock bands, an a cappella singing group and recorder, guitar and brass ensembles. Children can take graded examinations in school and many are involved outside in the National Children's Orchestra, Junior Academy, the Tri-Borough Orchestra and National Youth Harp Orchestra. A recent year 6 pupil achieved grade 8 with distinction in the violin. The specialist facilities include a 160 seat performance hall with sound and lighting, music suite and teaching rooms.

RPPS follows a full primary curriculum beginning with EYFS and working towards 11+, making use of specialist subject teachers and classroom assistants. Parents believe the pace is 'spot on' with increased homework and more emphasis on English and mathematics from the summer term in year 5. Parents praise the life skills RPPS develops, and how staff encourage pupils' independence, dealing with homework and 'organisational skills like packing for a residential trip, which sets them up for senior school so well'. Once the examinations are over, children enjoy themed topics and a diverse range of activities, home and away. Year 6s we chatted to were very excited about their forthcoming production and there is an annual ski trip to Austria after the exams as well as a biennial music tour, the last one to Tuscany. Throughout the school the curriculum is enhanced by theme weeks and staff take advantage of nearby galleries, theatres and exhibitions as well as parents sharing their interesting careers. French is taught throughout with Spanish as part of the many extracurricular clubs, which also include pottery, cookery, chess, dance, science, debating and even cheerleading.

This popular school caters for families with children of different needs and abilities. Many walk to school, with the majority within a two mile radius and a few from Holland Park, Kensington, Olympia. The pupil body is reflective of the area with the majority being of white British origin and a quarter from European backgrounds, often bilingual. Parents in variety of professions, including some in marketing alongside the ubiquitous lawyers and bankers. 'You can get involved as much or as little as you like,' they told us and many do participate, regularly attending concerts, listening to readers or engaged in the Parents' Association of Friends.

Parents agree the school 'is nurturing, inclusive, welcoming and truly caters for all-rounders', unlike schools 'with greater emphasis on the academics where pupils need to be more robust and confident'. Not the right school for parents obsessed with their children obtaining top grades in everything or those seeking a traditional, highly competitive environment. Even teams are colour coded rather than A, B, C, D, emphasising participation and lack of labelling. With mixed ability there is a balanced atmosphere which does not stop the very able from flying, but does mean all are respected and encouraged. As one parent remarked, 'RPPS is a really fun, positive and nurturing environment for the kids, who become so confident and happy about their place in life'. Others said, 'This dynamic school caters for all sorts, any character; that is one of its strengths'. The 11+ preparation is a 'well-oiled machine' with 'loads of opportunities for different characters to learn and flourish' as recent results demonstrate.

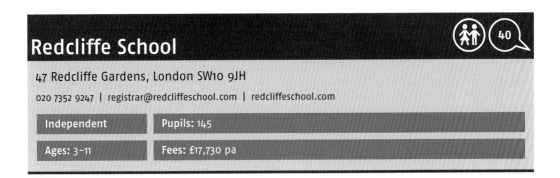

Redcliffe School

47 Redcliffe Gardens, London SW10 9JH

020 7352 9247 | registrar@redcliffeschool.com | redcliffeschool.com

| Independent | Pupils: 145 |
| Ages: 3–11 | Fees: £17,730 pa |

Headmistress: Since September 2017, Sarah Lemmon (40s). SL is so happy in her work that she leaves her husband and son (an ex-Redcliffe pupil) outside Bath and commutes to London every week. Raised in Co Wicklow until she was 17, she has spent all her post-school life in London, not because it is the dull filling in a green sandwich but because she genuinely loves the city. Once graduated from Froebel College, she tested her natural instinct to become a teacher by doing a stint in the outside world but is clearly delighted that she made the choice to switch to education. She started teaching here 12 years ago and has climbed the ladder to the top, via the headship of the pre-prep, a cv that makes parents comfortable that she knows the school from the bottom up and, judging by their comments, certain that she is doing a great job.

Entrance: Approximately three children are put down for each nursery place but there is a lot of natural attrition due to some London parents' habit of applying piecemeal and keeping their options open until the last minute. It's a first come, first served, non-selective school with a front of the queue policy for siblings and the registrar says that she 'can't think of a time when there has been a problem with this'. All children are assessed for entry to the main school via a gently selective process and for the occasional places available further up. The vast majority of children in the nursery move into the reception class, although a few go abroad or to the local Ofsted outstanding primary, Bousfield, and there is the occasional movement in both directions.

Exit: Redcliffe is becoming co-ed throughout but boys have tended to transfer at 7+ or 8+ to conventional preps such as Sussex House, Wetherby Prep or St Philip's, with the occasional parent choosing the country boarding option. The trend for senior London schools to take boys at 11+ is increasing but, just in case, the head is already sounding out schools like Thomas's Battersea and Eaton House, who will be prepared to take in any of her leavers aiming at 13+ senior schools. She also runs an annual event for parents, bringing in heads from six senior schools. Girls at 11+ mainly join the old favourite London day schools but the excellent results allow them to aim at the schools for high achievers such as Godolphin & Latymer, JAGS, City of London Girls and Putney High. An impressive proportion of academic scholarships, considering the size of the school, with the odd one for sport or music.

Remarks: As one walks past an uninspiring example of ecclesiastical architecture, almost the only clue to the existence of the nursery and pre-prep is the sound of piping voices. In what was once an undercroft is now a surprisingly light and airy space, with a multi-purpose hall on one side and a cheerful passage leading to the nursery and classrooms for reception and year 1. The nursery is much praised by parents, one knowledgeable mother commenting that not only had they managed to persuade her son to sit on the carpet quietly for 'a decent length of time' but also that he came home burbling about the fun projects and activities that had filled his day. Meals, quite often a

Pupils can join clubs for budding artists or chefs, practise for a parliamentary career in debating or pave the way for a life on the boards

trying time at this stage for both small and large people, are no problem here as apparently the food is 'brilliant', and a parent told us that her candidate for the 'world's fussiest eater' wolfed it all down.

The pre-prep is not just about play, judging from some of the extremely neat writing and maths displayed on the walls, but there is an obvious emphasis on building confidence as well as academic skills. The most quoted example is how they successfully encourage every child (from reception onwards) to take turns at presenting work in assembly. We were told by parents that in some cases 'this was a minor miracle', persuading an acutely shy child to happily stand up in front of 150 people and start talking. SL, who believes in making sure that you never ask children to do what you would not do yourself, makes sure that the teachers lead the way by all taking assembly themselves.

Facing the busy road that runs on down past the pre-prep is the modest facade of the late Victorian building which houses the main school. This was originally the home of the school's founder, Lady Daphne Edwards, about whom little is known except that she left her house plus enough cash to a charitable trust, enabling the school to flourish and arrive at its 70th birthday. The trust funds have been well looked after and SL says that they have the wherewithal for expanding their space to match their co-ed ambitions, which aim to grow the school gradually from one to two forms in a year when there are sufficient pupils.

The common hustle and bustle of most junior schools feels muted as there are only around 100 children in the building and the housekeeping, despite the challenge of a cageful of fluffy chicks, is well on top of the dust bunnies. The sense of calm is apparent all the way up from the semi-basement, with its hall, tiny Maurice Sendak kitchen squeezed into the corner and classroom at the back, to the attic with its new, purpose-built music rooms and cosy staff room under the eaves. Children move about with purposeful expressions and an obvious certainty about their next destination, so this is definitely a well-orchestrated operation, although rather charmingly relaxed on the surface.

Despite this cool rather than hothouse atmosphere, Redcliffe children leave with the full academic package: they may not have been offered the exotic curriculum options available in the larger local preps but they have no trouble in passing the 7+, 8+ and 11+ and succeeding in the ferocious competition for places at demanding senior schools. Naturally, there is some concern that the different requirements for boys (online pre-tests) will mean some additions to the current curriculum, but as English, maths, verbal and non-verbal reasoning are already on the timetable, SL believes that she is on top of this. They will certainly all be good at maths as the teacher of years 5 and 6 is apparently 'amazing'.

Unable to take children with anything beyond mild dyslexia; there used to be murmurings that the SEN provision was possibly a little stretched and problems were not picked up fast enough, but the evidence is that this has changed. SL and her new SENCo are much more aware of where help may be needed, and the genuine family atmosphere of the school is a huge advantage.

Knowing that she is going to have older boys in her charge, one of SL's new initiatives is to increase the opportunity for the children to enjoy sport, always logistically a problem in inner London. Friday afternoons are for games in the form of optional clubs, rather than lessons, and an extended school day on Friday (until 3 o'clock) will allow them to ramp up the sporting provision. The new sports facility is only a few hops, skips and jumps away and there are beaming faces at the mention of the summer sports day. Redcliffe might not be the perfect spot for a football fiend looking for the rough and tumble of team games but, having said this, they have a potential international swimmer in their ranks, so an awareness of sporting potential is certainly there.

London parents are looking beyond academics, even when the school is tiny, and pupils can join clubs for budding artists or chefs, practise for a parliamentary career in debating or pave the way for a life on the boards by aiming at LAMDA exams. Trying to ensure that her charges do not lead too cloistered a life, the head casts a termly fly into the parental talent pool and lands a willing soul to talk to them about the world outside as well as posting a weekly blog herself.

Enthusiastic comments on the standard of pastoral care from parents – 'it's like leaving your child with a relation rather than a babysitter' – and from older girls, who appreciate the thought that has gone into the new flowery summer frocks – 'I might even wear it after I've left' – show that the new head is sensitive about making changes. She is well aware that finding the correct balance between remaining a small traditional London prep school and being a forward thinking modern co-educational establishment is no easy task. We left feeling confident that she would crack it.

Sacred Heart High School (Hammersmith) 🚶 Ⓡ🄲 ⁴¹

212 Hammersmith Road, London W6 7DG

020 8748 7600 | info@sacredh.lbhf.sch.uk | sacredhearthigh.org.uk

State	Pupils: 1,021; sixth form: 300
Ages: 11–18	

Headteacher: Since 2014, Marian Doyle MA NPQH (50s). Previously deputy head since 1997. Before that, she taught English and RE at Haggerston School, Hackney, Phoenix High School, Hammersmith and latterly Holland Park School, Notting Hill Gate. A world away from the previous head (a deeply traditional woman who reigned for 23 years with what girls describe as a combination of awe and fear), Doyle is softer around the edges and fresher in her outlook. Not only does she look more modern (she wore fabulous killer heels when we met her), but the school itself feels more alive, with walls now adorned with colourful canvases of the girls at work and many inspirational quotes. School systems (from admin through to bullying policies) have also had an overhaul, thanks to the head's key vision of the school being run seamlessly. A parent herself, she is big on boundaries and 'tough love', but is also approachable and smiley, and is regularly seen around the school, popping into lessons and talking to the girls at break times. 'She is very keen to make sure that we like it here,' said one girl.

Academic matters: Impressive results, by anyone's standards. In 2018, 51 per cent 9-7 grades at GCSE; 54 per cent got 5+ 9-5s including both English and maths. Sixth form opened in 2013. In 2018 A level results 32 per cent A*/A and 58 per cent A*-B.

Maths the strongest subject, followed by English. RE, history and geography also stand out. In terms of languages, Spanish and French are on offer, and a group of around 15 girls are put forward for Latin GCSE, which they study at St Paul's. Science highly promoted, with 60 per cent doing science and maths post-16.

Each year group has five form groups, with setting across all subjects from year 7 into five or six groups, depending on the subject, with plenty of flexibility to move about as necessary. Class sizes vary, with many as large as 35.

Expectation for all pupils to do at least two after-school clubs (which they call enrichment), which has been accommodated by changes to the school day (which now comprises five 60 minute lessons and finishes at 3.05pm) and an expectation that staff stay longer to run these clubs on Tuesdays and Wednesdays. Outside facilitators brought in too. Subjects include all the usual suspects such as choir, sport, maths challenge, science clubs, drama etc as well as more unusual offerings including yoga and gardening.

One full-time staff member (qualified teacher, as well as a dyslexic specialist; has the national SENCo leadership award) is responsible for SEN, although no special unit. She puts in place three tiered levels of support – firstly, qualified teachers' support in mainstream, with the aim that specialist subject teachers can support in their areas of expertise; second (if necessary) additional support before and after school; finally (again if necessary) involvement of school counsellor or outside services, such as speech and language and occupational therapy. Difficulties catered for include dyslexia and other needs that are physical, such as hearing loss or severe long-term conditions, communication and language difficulties, ADD, ADHD. School also claims there are some serious mental health concerns. School reckoned there were 65 in total with SEN when we visited, five of whom are statemented/with EHC plan. Very rarely, if a child's needs cannot be fully met, the school works closely with parents and the local authority to find alternatives. Help for gifted and talented through a range of enrichment and additional opportunities.

'The help my daughter has received for her dyslexia has been second to none, including trying out a range of different techniques, and the communication with us has been excellent too,' said one parent. 'Her self-confidence has rocketed and she's doing really well in exams.'

School is designated as a national teaching school, leading the West London Teaching School Alliance, which means working closely with 28 other primary and secondary schools in west London to improve standards of teaching and share best practice on issues including initial teacher training, professional development, research and

The school itself feels more alive, with walls now adorned with colourful canvases of the girls at work and many inspirational quotes

development, succession planning and mentoring. Head says it's her vision for the school to become known for its drive for excellence. 'I put the same level of effort into training and development for the staff as I do teaching the girls, because I believe the two are inextricably linked,' she says.

Although the teaching staff we saw were a pretty glum-looking lot (particularly unwelcoming when we went near their classrooms), girls are clearly impressed with their level of commitment. 'Lessons are really engaging,' said one. 'They make sure nobody gets missed,' added another. Indeed, girls are regularly reminded of a quote from one of the founders: 'For the sake of one child, I would have founded the society,' after which they're told, 'You are the one child.'

Games, options, the arts: For a small inner-city site, they certainly pack in the sports facilities, all of which are utilised to the max, with the girls doing at least two hours of PE per week and with the option of PE as both a GCSE and A level subject. In addition to the two tennis/netball courts (which double up as rounders pitches), there's a gym and activity studio for the likes of dance, pilates and yoga. The new £8m sports and science block is home to a massive sports hall that can facilitate three teaching groups simultaneously. 'It's four times the size of our gym,' enthused one girl. Also new is a running track and outdoor gym of the ilk you see in parks, all of which means the long-standing link with Hammersmith and Fulham Health and Fitness Centre will start to diminish. Rowing, softball, basketball and volleyball on offer, along with all the usual suspects, and after-school clubs include street dance, yoga, cheerleading, fencing, trampolining and football, among others. Plenty of inter-house sports competitions, the highlight of which is the annual sports day held at St Paul's fields (originally owned by Sacred Heart but sadly they sold it off years ago), and the school has increasing success in the borough in hockey, rounders, netball and athletics.

No shortage of peripatetic teachers for musical instruments including piano, flute, trombone, drums etc. There are junior and senior choirs, various ensembles, and the girls talk highly of the general music classes, as well as about the annual Battle of the Bands. 'Music is really good fun here,' one girl told us. We particularly like the random pianos in the corridors, all of which girls say get played regularly for practice, making for a lovely ambience when walking through the corridors.

Links to various theatres, including the Donmar, and the drama school LAMDA, give a flavour of how seriously drama is taken here, with annual all-school productions such as Hairspray and Annie. Art and DT studios are spacious, with state-of-the-art equipment and some extremely talented artwork produced by the girls. No cookery on offer when we visited, but this is being reexamined.

Background and atmosphere: The school, or 'convent of the Sacred Heart,' is built on a site steeped in Catholic history dating back to the early 17th century. During its 330 year history, four different orders of nuns have taught here. Today's Tudor-style, red-brick buildings were built in the late 19th century and there's no shortage of religious reminders inside, notably the huge, austere-looking religious murals all the way along the wide, spacious corridors of the cloisters, as well as the chapel, which doubles up as the main school hall. 'We have daily morning prayers,' said one girl, 'but apart from that, the presence of Catholicism in our everyday life is through the school's ethos and values.' 'The school provides a good moral compass, but there's no hard-line religion,' agreed a parent, who added that there's a sensible and modern approach to sex education too, within the context of the Catholic Church teaching.

'I put the same level of effort into training and development for the staff as I do teaching the girls, because I believe the two are inextricably linked,' she says

In 1948 the convent school was reorganised as a secondary grammar school, continuing as a grammar school until 1976, when it received its first comprehensive intake. The school then took on academy status in 2012.

Most pupils use the entrance on Bute Gardens, whilst sixth form and visitors use the main entrance on Hammersmith Road, where you'll be greeted by a single receptionist behind an oak veneer desk and a couple of rows of cream leather chairs. The hum of traffic is loud, but it doesn't take many more steps into the school to feel as if you're in an oasis of calm – not at all what you'd expect from an inner-city comp. Even during class switch-over times, when the extra-wide corridors are packed with animated girls, it somehow manages to avoid the feeling of chaos that many other

schools have (probably helped by the very strictly policed one-way walking system).

A steep stone staircase leads down to the converted basement, which forms the buzzy social space and café for sixth formers. The rest of the girls eat in the dining room which, head admits, 'could be more funky' and where the 'food is 'ok.' Those who have packed lunch eat at temporary tables that are laid out daily in the wide corridors.

Asked what they'd improve, girls told us they could do with more quiet study space, especially in sixth form. 'We are allowed to use the library,' said one, 'but it's not ideal.' Indeed, when we visited, the library was being used by an entire class and was by no means quiet, although in fairness it is two-story, with doors shutting out such sound on the top level. Well-stocked and imaginatively designed, it is also very light and inviting. Classrooms are bog-standard, with stand-out facilities for drama and music. Great excitement about the new science block, which should transform this current provision beyond recognition.

Girls encouraged to be proactive, rather than spoon fed, with lots of emphasis on them doing things, rather than talking about things. When we visited, a group of girls had gone to Mexico to rebuild houses for those in poverty. A further group of six girls went to Lourdes with the Handicapped Children Pilgrimage Trust. Impressive amounts of charitable work overall, including £10,500 raised for a sister school in Kenya for disabled children via activities including sponging teachers, making teachers eat chilli, sponsored walks and rowing the distance of the Channel in the gym. School is also part of a worldwide network of schools in 45 countries which creates opportunities such as a head girls' meet up to discuss leadership ideas and pupil exchanges across different countries.

Plenty of school trips to universities, BBC, Houses of Parliament, businesses including JP Morgan and all the usual museums and art galleries. Residential trips largely music-related, including to places such as Austria and Paris, whilst whole school European ski trips take place each year.

Strong student voice, with elected student members having requested that the science garden become more appealing, as well as having offered responses to the school's Equality Plan.

Pastoral care, well-being and discipline: Although current head is considered 'less scary and strict' than her predecessor, she is equally dedicated to high standards, pointing out that your daughter will be in detention if she arrives even five seconds after the bell goes. 'The point is that in professional life, if you had a meeting at 10am, you wouldn't arrive just after 10am,' she explains. 'We also want a calm start to the day.' It clearly works – there are few detentions in reality, with the girls we talked to never having been late in their entire six years. Other zero-tolerance aspects of school life include school uniform (especially length of skirts) and good behaviour, although pastoral care is highly praised here, with all the parents we talked to calling it 'very nurturing and caring.' Pupils are frequently reminded they can talk to form teachers, non-teaching pastoral support managers, the chaplain or two full-time school counsellors. In addition, there are strong links with Child and Adolescent Mental Health Services (CAMHS) and the charity Mind. 'One of my daughters went off the rails and had some counselling, which promptly nipped it in the bud,' said one parent. Head is by no means resting on her laurels, though. 'Like most schools,' she says, 'we have seen an increase in mental health issues and are very aware we need to talk about it in a more real and open way.' Peer mentoring scheme between year 7s and year 11s encourages cross-year relationships and older girls to take a leadership role.

Pupils and parents: This is top of the state school list for many families, not only in west London, but as far as Islington (with Tony Blair's daughter being the obvious example). Although it's non-selective and fully comprehensive, the majority of families are middle-class and with English as a first language. That said, there is genuine poverty among some of the girls, with head reporting that this is increasingly the case. 'We have 14 per cent identified as having free school meals and many others with an income only just above the threshold where parents struggle to make ends meet,' she says.

Strong PA and links between parents generally. 'It's unusually sociable among parents for an inner-city comprehensive, with lots of mums' nights out, quiz nights and family-focused activities,' said one parent. Good communications between school and parents, although some parents think the annual parents' evening, which falls in the summer term, is far too late in the academic year.

Entrance: Parents keep an extremely beady eye on the admissions policy of this heavily oversubscribed school, and many are unswerving in their commitment to find some way for their daughter to become one of the approximately 198 pupils to enter year 7. But you'll need to start early, as all girls need to have been baptised before they were 6 months old (although we did to talk to one parent who did it slightly later due to illness in the family) and to have attended one of 11 feeder schools, all named on the website. If you meet all the criteria, you won't need to sweat so much about how close you are to the school. Be warned that siblings don't automatically gain entry and are sometimes turned away. Separate admissions procedures for girls with an SEN statement/EHC plan. Parents praise the transition from primary school. Up to places for 40 external applicants to sixth form, for which you'll need eight 9-4s at GCSE, including subject-specific requirements.

Exit: Clear expectation to remain at the school to do A levels, and the majority do so. Others commonly go onto Cardinal Vaughan or The London Oratory, with a handful going into the independent sector, including UCS, St Benedict's and Latymer Upper. 2018 leavers off to do courses including aeronautical engineering at Imperial, anthropology at Exeter, English and drama at Bristol and fashion communication at Condé Nast College.

Remarks: An exceptional and relatively small inner-city state school that provides girls who are prepared to behave impeccably with a traditional education and sense of community that will set them up for life.

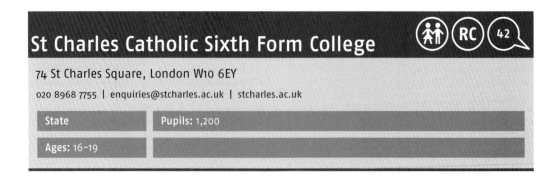

St Charles Catholic Sixth Form College

74 St Charles Square, London W10 6EY

020 8968 7755 | enquiries@stcharles.ac.uk | stcharles.ac.uk

State	Pupils: 1,200
Ages: 16–19	

Principal: Since 2015, Elaine Taylor BA MA PGCE. BA in history and sociology from Queen Mary's and MA from Institute of Education. Joined the college in 2009 as vice principal. Previously at St Francis Xavier College in Clapham, where she was assistant principal. Has also held positions of head of sociology, psychology and politics. No longer teaches but is very hands on with EPQs. 'Teaching was the only job I ever wanted to do, though I never thought I would be a principal!' she confesses. Married with two grown-up sons. Strong Irish roots and nips back to Ireland at the drop of a hat. Tries to switch off at weekend by walking and gentle exercise, as aspects of the job are stressful, particularly in current financial climate. Family is her priority at weekends and during holidays. An approachable, friendly and welcoming head. Well-respected by parents.

Academic matters: College offers a variety of courses at levels 1, 2 and 3. Pupils can take A levels or vocational qualifications or a combination of both at level 3. Hasn't released 2018 A level results, but usually around a quarter at A*-B. School offers three levels of study – advanced (A levels and vocational level 3), intermediate (GCSEs and BTec level 2) and foundation (BTec level 1 and functional skills in English and maths). Two per cent of pupils make up level 1. Ms Taylor explains, 'Level 1 students are those who have done very badly in their GCSEs at their old school, or students who have not been in the country very long and need to develop their numeracy and literacy skills.' Level 2 pupil numbers have grown to 150. 'They are usually students who have not done very well in their GCSEs either, but not atrociously, gaining mostly 4 and 3s'. Most of these pupils progress on to level 3 at the college. Limited numbers of GCSEs offered and level 2 pupils tend to take maths and English GCSEs, alongside level 2 BTec programme. In recent years, the proportion of A level students has been declining in favour of those choosing the BTec route. Nearly 30 different A levels offered, including ICT, Italian and photography; newly introduced BTecs include media and music. 'We might cultivate the combined pathway a little more,' explains head, 'as it gives pupils greater flexibility'. Possible to start at level 1 and move on up to level 2 then 3. 'Some stay with us for four years and end up at university. We support them along the way.'

Around 40 level 3 pupils take the EPQ. Ms Taylor is very enthusiastic about this qualification: 'We are trying to develop it, as nearly all our students take three rather than four A levels now, and the EPQ will be a good differentiating tool when applying to universities. They all start off enthusiastically but a 6,000-word dissertation can be quite hard work!' Subjects range from whether the African elephant can survive, to debates on the influence of gender on crime, to the railway industry.

Well-resourced learning support centre, providing support for 10 per cent of pupils. College currently has 4.5 learning support teachers and three learning assistants who support the small number of pupils with EHC plans. One parent raved about the support her SEN son received: 'They really understood him and worked with his strengths.' Her son was given an individual tour of the school before arrival, so he would not have to deal with the hurly-burly of the regular show-round. Roughly 130 pupils qualify as having some sort of SEN, ranging from those who just need a bit of extra help with structuring essays to those who require a full-time assistant in every lesson. A fair number with dyslexia, Asperger's and autism. Around 50 qualify for extra time in exams. Support offered ranges from one-to-one to pairs or small groups, from one hour a week upwards. Help given to those who have English as an additional language but pupils need to be able to fully access the curriculum. Fully wheelchair accessible.

Basketball team has recently won the national finals. 'We are like the Leicester football team: we came from nothing and won the trophy,' beams head

Over 30 teachers have been here for more than a decade, and a sizeable number were pupils here themselves. Average age of staff now late 40s – early 50s 'because people don't want to leave us!' Ms Taylor feels that pressure on staff has become worse than ever and she is saddened that tighter budgets have led to staff cuts. Every member of staff is now up to their full complement of teaching and staff development has been curtailed. 'The impact on the staff, the teaching and learning is significant.' Principal laments that teaching is not the attractive profession it used to be and the college now finding it very hard to recruit in areas such as economics, business, maths and science.

Games, options, the arts: 'We don't force students to do enrichment but we really try to encourage them to do so,' states Ms Taylor. Sport offered includes football, basketball, rugby, boxercise, futsal, netball, trampolining, table tennis, dance and zumba. Basketball team has recently won the national finals. 'We are like the Leicester football team: we came from nothing and won the trophy,' beams head. Successful at football too. Fully equipped fitness gym is well-used, including female-only afternoon. Indoor and outdoor multi-function sports area means some sport takes place on site but footballers trek to Westway to practise.

College has own dance and theatre studio. Drama is offered at A level and performing arts at BTec. Annual musical, open to all. Wicked, Mamma Mia and an American showcase have all featured in recent years. Considered to be a highlight of the year. No students play instruments at school, no orchestra and no choirs. Not the place for your child if they are desperate to be part of a music ensembles. Art is very popular, with notably strong department. Pupils choose between fine art, photography (school boasts own dark room) or art BTec. Textiles has been discontinued, but plenty of opportunities to experiment with a variety of media.

College is outward-looking. Other enrichment opportunities include pupils teaching computer skills to local senior citizens one afternoon a week – so popular, there is a waiting list. Others work for charities or Young Enterprise, and help with regeneration of local area. Regular outside speakers range from chief executives from Mastercard to religious leaders of all faiths. Lots of work experience.

Trips tend to be subject-related, including a cultural trip to New York every year for psychology and sociology students; a geography trip to Sicily where pupils visit Mount Etna; travel and tourism trips to Lanzarote. Getting harder to subsidise pupils who cannot afford it. 'We'd like to do more but it's quite a commitment for teachers to take a trip away too. They need their weekends!' comments Ms Taylor. Lots of visits closer to home, including to theatres and art galleries.

Background and atmosphere: Just off Ladbroke Grove. Tucked between a Catholic church, a Catholic girls' secondary, the Catholic Children's Society and a convent. Named after St Charles Borromeo, 16th century Italian archbishop who believed in the redeeming power of education. Founded by Cardinal Basil Hume in 1990.

Accepts all faiths and none but Catholic ethos pervades, though in terms of numbers only about 35 per cent Catholic, 30 per cent other Christians and 22 per cent currently Muslim. Compulsory RE programme, comprising one hour lesson a week. Ms Taylor explains, 'It is important to have a general religion programme. It is an opportunity for students to mix with students of other religions, to discuss a range of issues and to hear what others believe. It's good preparation for the world outside.'

Very inclusive, defined by Catholic values, with Christ at its centre. An explicitly Christian set of values from the Gospels, with a focus on inclusivity and service to others. A banner above the entrance proclaims, 'Show mercy to others as God shows mercy to you.' Voluntary mass every Friday and a daily morning prayer. Christmas and Easter services. On-site chapel. Annual trip to Lourdes to help the sick, organised by the full-time chaplain who also acts as an unofficial counsellor. Pupils find him approachable and he can often be spotted deep in a game of chess with one or other of them. One parent assured us that religion was 'not overwhelming'.

Pastoral care, well-being and discipline: Everyone is in a tutor group which meets daily, under one of the pastoral managers. 'This daily contact just

> '*Some students have challenging lives outside and it is part of the mission to encourage them to take the right path*'

keeps them on track,' explains head. External counsellors visit the school weekly. Even though this is a sixth form college, many school-like structures are in place. Ex-pupils say how much they miss the pastoral care once they go to university.

Zero tolerance of any form of physical violence or drug related incidents, both within the college grounds or in the vicinity. Immediate expulsion for these offences with suspension for lesser transgressions. 'Discipline is a headache,' according to one mother, though probably no more so than in some other London schools. Giving your ID card to another student results in suspension for three days. Security guards at the gate are strict about checking for ID and no-one allowed in without it. Pupils initially surprised how strict the college is, but head believes that 'the safety of the students is the most important thing. Some students have challenging lives outside and it is part of the mission to encourage them to take the right path'. Attendance and punctuality are strictly monitored. Knife tunnels erected sporadically, in liaison with police, so pupils 'know that we are monitoring them.' If pupils are late to lessons then they are not allowed in. Pupils can be late to school in the morning three times a term, as college recognises that public transport is not always reliable, but after that no leniency shown. One mother divulged that her son was worried he would be bullied as 'it's a rough place, but the college handled his needs well.' Principal disagrees that the college is rough, telling us 'this is simply not the case.'

Head believes the issues that pupils face are becoming more complex. She explains, 'We have many students who have mental health issues. More and more young people are coming to us who are already in the CAHMS [Child and Adolescent Mental Health services] system. There are many who have very difficult home lives and some are already living independently.' There have been incidents with suicidal pupils in the past. 'This often occurs on a Friday, with the thought of the weekend ahead.' Others have suffered historical abuse. Social media often the source of arguments. 'The exam competition is worse now – everything has to be an A. We put so much pressure on the young,' worries head. College is often a haven for those with complicated domestic lives and Ms Taylor believes it is her job to provide stability for those who are troubled.

Pupils and parents: Diverse, international set of pupils who come from 165 different schools. Pupils trek in from far and wide. Wide ethnic mix, with African students making up the majority. Over 40 per cent are on free school meals; most from low-income backgrounds. Lots of siblings and cousins. 'People hear about us very much through word of mouth.'

Parents are kept in the loop regarding their child's attendance, punctuality and behaviour via the parent portal and communication with tutors and pastoral managers. Two parents' evenings a year, so most feel as though they know what is going on.

Entrance: College is non-selective and places are offered based on a successful interview and reference from previous school. School interviews over 2,000 students a year. Pupils need to write a statement outlining why they want to study in a Catholic college. Priority given to disabled and looked after children, followed by pupils from Catholic partner secondary schools, then Catholic students from other secondary schools and finally non-Catholics. In reality, not many are turned down, but acceptance is dependent upon reference and interview. Ms Taylor states: 'We want to recruit as many students as possible, though there has to be some integrity about who we take.' Some start but do not last long – about 100 students are lost during the year. Prepared to take some from pupil referral units, in line with its inclusive policy, 'though we won't take them all.' If a pupil's reference is poor in terms of attendance and punctuality then unlikely they would be accepted.

For A level route, minimum six GCSEs at 9-4, including English language. Minimum five GCSEs at 4 or above for level 3 BTec vocational study. For intermediate route, four grade 3s or above at GCSE.

Foundation level is suitable for pupils with GCSEs below grade 3.

Exit: Of the level 3 pupils, about 85 per cent go on to university. Large numbers to Russell Group, with London a firm favourite as students can save money by living at home. Increasing numbers are deferring as they are not sure that they can afford it and others not even applying as they are put off by student debt. Popular subjects include business, sociology, psychology, Arabic studies and international relations. Just a trickle chooses history or English.

Many opt for art foundation courses and college has good links with Central St Martins. Others head for London College of Fashion. One artistic past pupil is currently using his considerable creative skills in a tattoo parlour.

Some proceed straight to the world of work, particularly into retail, with increasing numbers opting for apprenticeships in business, IT or administration.

Money matters: Bursary payments made to nearly 40 per cent of pupils – grants for those in financial hardship studying full time. All charged a one-off resources fee when they start, to cover costs such as photocopying. College hires out its facilities to bring in much needed cash.

Remarks: Principal states, 'We want every student, no matter what their starting point to do the best they can. Everyone these days is measured by their exam results but education is so much more. We are trying to do something a little bit different to others. We take on students that sometimes need a second chance, because sometimes life does not go according to plan'. For those prepared to play by the rules, this college can and does turn lives around.

St James Junior School

Earsby Street, London W14 8SH

020 7348 1793 | admissions@stjamesjunior.org | stjamesjuniors.co.uk

Independent	Pupils: 246
Ages: 4-11	Fees: £16,425 – £17,910 pa

Linked school: St James Senior Girls' School, 382

Headmistress: Since 2009, Catherine Thomlinson, BA in English and history from Roehampton (40s). A St James' disciple to her fingers' ends, having

spent almost all of her teaching career here after being educated at sister school, St Vedast (brief spell in South Africa before coming back to the fold). Two children, a son and a daughter, both of whom attended St James from age 4 right through senior school. A thoroughly lovely lady who radiates kindness, humanity and good humour, and this despite having a shocking cold when we met. The study oft proclaims the head, we've found, and Mrs Thomlinson's was sparely but beautifully furnished, bright and calm. Amidst some exquisite pictures of quiet seas, a joyous tract reads, 'Let your light shine!' – and hers most assuredly does.

Despite her lifelong loyalty to the St James traditions, Mrs Thomlinson has not been afraid to modernise. She has pushed through substantial curriculum development, including DT, French and dance; and both boys and girls now do cookery, woodwork and sewing. Introduced interactive whiteboards for upper junior classrooms ('a fantastic tool'), and is looking to bring these in throughout the school. Major development of EYFS provision, following criticism in recent inspection report. Parents report improved communication. Continues to uphold strong emphasis on speech, drama and music, 'because they really touch the emotional intelligence'.

Entrance: 'We don't take children on an academic basis,' says head, and accordingly there's no entrance exam at age 4; instead, the school holds informal assessments that involve meeting both child and parents, plus a report from child's nursery where applicable. Children of alumni and siblings have priority, as do those whose parents registered them early for a place. School looks for 'a certain confidence, and for children and families who value what we value'. Places higher up the school occasionally become available, and children who apply aged 7+ take assessments in reading, writing and mathematics to establish whether they're able to manage within the standard of the established class.

Exit: Girls and boys now both stay on till year 6, with the majority (80-95 per cent) going on to St James Senior Girls or St James Senior Boys. The latter is out at Ashford (comprehensive coach service provided by St James Schools). School says that 'all children are given thorough preparation and guidance for the 11+,' and that 'we are happy to support all our pupils in whichever path they take'. Other school destinations include Merchant Taylors', Latymer Upper, Ibstock Place, Emanuel, St Mary's Ascot, Queen's Gate, Aldenham and Hampton.

Remarks: A frieze of the goddess Athene gazes down benevolently from one of the foyer walls, and this may explain the air of gentle wisdom that really does pervade this unusual and admirable little school. It nestles quietly within residential streets, the outside resembling a monastery, with its high walls and expanse of sheer red brick, but the tableau through the security gate wasn't in the least forbidding. Children played cheerfully in a pretty, cloistered courtyard under the eye of a watchful but serene-looking teacher, and the whole was framed by light and airy corridors – a preponderance of new glass giving a modern, clean balance to the Victorian charm of the original building. The atmosphere, as far as we could judge, was one of kindness and peaceful activity. Parents all confirmed this: 'It's a very happy place.' 'It's an extremely happy school.' 'A warm and nurturing environment.' 'My child has loved being there from the very beginning.'

Children played cheerfully in a pretty, cloistered courtyard under the eye of a watchful but serene-looking teacher, and the whole was framed by light and airy corridors

The school's ethos places an unusually high emphasis on generosity, mutual respect and 'being the best human beings we can be,' and achieves this through a number of distinctive practices. Every lesson begins and ends with a 'moment of stillness'. Such moments 'give you that sense of ease and reflection,' says head. These pauses, as they're known, are popular with parents and children: 'It gives you a chance to be still,' said a year 6 child, whose demeanour was courteous and mature beyond his years. Parents agree. 'One of the main benefits of St James is the peacefulness,' was one comment, and 'One of the reasons we send our children to the school is to learn early on to take a pause, allow the noise to stop,' was another.

All the children, even the little ones, learn Sanskrit, in accordance with the school's belief that the Eastern philosophies have much to teach us; and both children and parents insisted to us that this was one of the things they 'really loved' about the school. St James describes itself as 'multi-religious', and philosophy itself is a very important part of the curriculum. The school teaches a Socratic method of dialogue and questioning, and the children are taught to develop open-ended questions and to debate as a class ('No putting-down of others' opinions is allowed,' says head firmly). The school motto – 'Speak the truth, be generous and kind, be your best' – seems to mean more here than such saws do in other schools. St James's policy of teaching boys and girls separately, then bringing them together for social activities (break-times, lunch, productions, trips, etc) may also be a key factor in establishing such good relationships between the children. 'You can see the boys, but you don't always have to be with them,' said a grateful year 5 girl, with which one of the boys countered, 'The girls think they're best, and we just get on with being even better.' We suspect this is amiable posturing: a number of parents confirmed to us that their child's closest schoolfriends included those of the opposite gender.

Academic performance is strong, with the standard of written work exceptionally high, both in content and accuracy – all the more impressive, given that the school's intake is not academically selective. 'I'm a great advocate for academic rigour,' confirms the head, adding, 'but I'm just as passionate about children finding out what they love.' All classes have weekly sessions in the well-stocked library, run by a dedicated librarian, and there are regular visits by children's authors. ('My son very quickly developed a love of reading,' reported a satisfied parent.) SEN provision is good, with about 30 EAL children cared for within the classroom set-up. We applaud the emphasis on using Shakespeare as a teaching resource at all levels, more so than in any other school we've visited. We saw verses from The Winter's Tale charmingly illustrated by the reception children, and read some excellent commentaries on Polonius's advice to his son ('To thine own self be true') by the year 3 boys. 'We love Shakespeare,' the head acknowledged. 'We did A Midsummer Night's Dream and The Tempest last year. And Mozart's The Magic Flute. We have a great cultural reservoir to draw on – why not give them the best material?' Why not indeed.

And in fact the drama on offer is very impressive, with all the children involved in at least one performance every year. 'We like big productions!' beamed a member of staff, before hurrying off to oversee preparations for Fiddler On The Roof, for which the school hired the Britten Theatre at the Royal College of Music because 'we like to be ambitious'. Previous big productions include My Fair Lady, The Railway Children and The Sound of Music. For in-house performances, the school's hall has been recently refurbished and hosts frequent verse-speaking, plus dance for both girls and boys as well as drama productions. Music is strong, with 70 children taking instrumental lessons at school on 'pretty much anything they want', and regular concerts, often featuring the school's orchestra. The children sing every day in assembly – repertoire by Mozart, Purcell and Vivaldi is popular – and have music lessons every week. Artwork of an astonishingly high standard adorns the walls, produced in the attractive art room under the gaze of the stuffed menagerie up on the shelf: a goose, a grouse, a heron and a weasel.

All children have a period of games or sport every day, be it gym, dance, swimming or ball skills, and the upper juniors (years 3-6) go off-site once a week to Barn Elms to hone their skills at netball, rugby, cricket, athletics, cross-country and the like. There are lots of inter-school competitions, and the children told us proudly about recent triumphs over Wetherby and Fulham Prep. Swimming is held in nearby Fulham Pools, and ISA golds and silvers have been a feature of recent years. St James Junior is a member of Forest Schools UK, with two of its staff trained as forest leaders, and there are many trips to Minstead Study Centre in the New Forest. 'I've been seven times!' enthused one upper junior boy, 'and I enjoyed it SO MUCH!' A varied programme of outings closer to home has encompassed museums, art galleries, theatres, and the usual London fare. Excellent range of lunchtime and after-school clubs includes guitar, yoga, cookery, gymnastics, model-making, archery, fencing, lacrosse and the perennially popular Mad Science Club. The head actively encourages all her staff to take up hobbies themselves, and the staff music band, we're told, is going from strength to strength. Use of ICT across the school has increased, although actual ICT lessons are still for year 6 only. Children are 'encouraged to use ICT at home,' which may or may not be enough preparation for the increasingly ICT-based curriculum they'll face at senior school. But the junior school's stated priority is to develop clear cursive handwriting in its pupils, and from what we saw, they definitely succeed.

We saw verses from The Winter's Tale charmingly illustrated by the reception children, and read some excellent commentaries on Polonius's advice to his son

Food here is vegetarian, so that all the children can eat together, and is included in the fees. We were impressed by what we saw: a delicious-smelling vegetable curry, fresh bread being baked, home-made leek and potato soup, and lots of genuinely appetizing fresh fruit. The number of clean plates testified to its popularity with the young clientele, and one solemn little girl was particularly enthusiastic about it to us as she lowered her elbow into her coleslaw. No problem, though – the lower juniors (years R-2) wear smocks down to lunch, which we thought eminently sensible.

All aspects of the pastoral care were rated excellent in the latest inspection report, which commented on the 'family atmosphere of mutual respect,' adding that 'the pupils thrive in the positive, caring environment' and are 'very well cared for.' The pupils concur. 'It's fun here,' 'The teachers are very kind,' 'Everyone is really nice,' 'You don't feel you have to be afraid of anything,' 'You can be yourself,' 'You can be proud of yourself,' 'The teachers are proud of us and they trust us,' were some of the many tributes we heard. This is all the more inspiring, given that the School of Economic Science, which founded the St James schools, attracted some very different comments from its embittered pupils a few decades back.

But all that is history. St James Junior impressed us as such a kind and enlightened medium in which to culture young minds, that we occasionally had to remind ourselves that this was a school we'd stepped into and not a Botticelli painting. It was almost a relief to see one small boy aim a punch at another, to hear an indignant cry of 'I was first!' and to meet a teacher who was unmistakably knackered after her morning's work. But these tiny wrinkles only served to throw into greater focus the sweetness and calm of this remarkable community. Not a school for budding Piers Morgans, we suspect. But who cares?

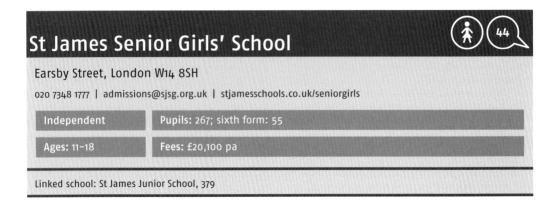

St James Senior Girls' School

Earsby Street, London W14 8SH

020 7348 1777 | admissions@sjsg.org.uk | stjamesschools.co.uk/seniorgirls

| Independent | Pupils: 267; sixth form: 55 |
| Ages: 11–18 | Fees: £20,100 pa |

Linked school: St James Junior School, 379

Headmistress: Since 2014, Mrs Sarah Labram BA (40s), formerly deputy head (academic) here. A classicist with a degree from King's College London, she is totally imbued with the St James ethos: a former pupil and head girl, whose two daughters were both educated at the junior and senior schools. She joined St James in 1996 as a classics teacher and has risen through the ranks to become head of department and then deputy head.

A hands-on head with a winning combo of directness, warmth and enviable serenity, she is often out and about around the school and clearly knows her pupils well, chatting easily with them in the corridors. Has an open-door policy, with pupils popping in to say anything from 'It's my birthday, would you like a piece of cake?' to 'Can I tell you about my sports achievement?' Refreshingly, pupils also have no qualms about poking their heads into her office to ask things like, 'Can you sign our permission slip to stay in at lunchtime to practice dance?' if nobody else is around. 'She's definitely not a head that you only see for bad or serious stuff,' one pupil explained, and although they welcome her lack of preciousness and her cordiality, they are quick to add that underneath it all, she commands respect. 'I was late for assembly the other day, and I won't be doing it again,' one pupil said. Parents feel they're in safe hands and praise her responsiveness, kindness and efforts to involve them eg to give talks (a dad had come into talk about climbing Everest when we visited), try out the school food, hear updates about the school and present their own views etc. That said, her introduction of the three new roles of head of lower, middle and upper school means any parental concerns are usually dealt with lower down the food chain.

Teaches Greek to year 9s. 'Teaching is what I love and classics is my passion – I'm not giving that up!' she laughs, adding that it ensures that she understands what's expected of other teachers. 'I soon see if something works or it doesn't,' she explains. 'And the inevitable informal chats in the classroom give me an insider's view of pupil needs too,' she adds. Lives in south east London and hobbies include theatre, classical music and walking.

Academic matters: Girls take the IGCSE in the three sciences, for greater rigour. At GCSE, 69 per cent A*-A/9-7 grades in 2018. Stunning success in art, biology, classics and physics, and at least respectable everywhere else. At A level the subject options include drama and theatre, Spanish, psychology and history of art. In 2018, 81 per cent of A level entries were graded A*-B (55 per cent A*/A). Results creditable in most subjects – few grades below B – and art, economics, French, and physics particularly impressive. School also offers EPQ to give students the opportunity to get deeply involved in a subject that interests them, to pull together learning from other subjects and to develop extended research and writing skills – all good preparation for university.

As with the boys' school, philosophy and spirituality are a major part of school life. Yes, girls are expected to work hard (we saw heads down in every classroom we visited) but every lesson is underpinned by the kind of big questions and ideas that form the cornerstone of all western and eastern wisdom traditions – but without being tied to the dogma of one. The result? Girls are encouraged to get the magic, awe and wonder of each subject – the wow-factor in addition to good, solid teaching. Plus, we found the girls could link pretty much everything – be it Latin, English or those knotty teenage issues like body image and social media – to guiding philosophical principles. 'It's not just about philosophical and spiritual concepts, but how they might be important when, say, you're trying to understand the relevance of maths in your life or how integrity might be important if, perhaps, you fall out with your friends,' explains the head. There's also a big push on mindfulness, meditation and quiet time (five minutes at the start of the day and after lunch). 'I love the way they create space for inner reflection and how the school is so confident and unapologetic that this is their offering,' said one parent. 'If you don't buy into meditation or mindfulness, it probably isn't the school for you,' said another.

Has an open–door policy, with pupils popping in to say anything from, 'It's my birthday, would you like a piece of cake?' to 'Can I tell you about my sports achievement?'

Sanskrit is continued for those who join from the junior school (introductory course offered to those joining in year 7) and available as an option at GCSE and A level. At least one a year chooses to study it at university. 'It's great for grammar,' says the head, 'as well as for the philosophy and culture that surrounds it. Plus, it marks you out as interesting and it's well respected.' In addition to Sanskrit, French and Latin from year 7; and Spanish (for those who don't carry on Sanskrit) and classical Greek (for the most able linguists) from year 8. Setting in English and maths from year 7; Latin and French from year 8; and science from year 9. Homework taken seriously – an hour and 10 minutes for year 7s, building up to a couple of hours a night in year 10 and 11. All the usual monitoring and targeting, with girls all initially tested in year 7, from which they are ranked (although they're not told where they sit).

SEN mainly consists of mild to moderate dyslexia, dyspraxia, dysgraphia and dyscalculia, with some mild autism and ADHD. Support mainly classroom based, with some one-to-ones and small group work taking place outside the classroom. 'Dyslexic girls often find Latin particularly hard, so we'll do small group work on study skills instead for year 8s, for example,' says head. 'The scaffolding they've put around my daughter has been amazing – it feels like they really care about getting her the best outcome,' said one parent. Strong gifted and talented provision. ICT not embedded as much as in some schools, though there's a decent ICT suite.

Heavy on careers advice, with girls given opportunities for 'tastes of reality' all the way through – much of which is embedded into lessons – with advice at every stage, which become increasingly intensive from year 9 up.

Games, options, the arts: This is a compact inner city school, so anything involving running takes place at the Chiswick playing grounds or Barn Elms multi-sports facility, both a coach ride away. On site, they cram in netball, aerobics, gymnastics, health-related fitness and dance etc and off site lacrosse, netball, athletics, rounders and tennis are the main sports. Does well in regionals and nationals for lacrosse (two Wales and one Scotland under-19 for lacrosse when we visited), along with some successes in cross country and netball. 'There's a drive to improve variety,' says the head, pointing to the recent introduction of football, table tennis, karate, cross country running and gymnastics – although this is mostly after school, to the disappointment of some pupils we spoke to. 'I wish there were more sports and more space,' more than one told us, and it was disappointing to find that some had reached sixth form having not been enthused by any sport. 'Sport is the one downside here,' some parents agreed, with one elaborating: 'It would be nice to see more of the less naturally sporty girls helped to find one sport they can love for life and to appreciate the value of teamwork that comes with that.' They have their own adventure club – the St James Challengers – and D of E. No swimming.

Artwork here is exceptional – and is, not surprisingly, on display throughout the school, much of it professionally framed. Two good art rooms in which, largely, the traditional skills are taught by much-admired staff. Visiting instructors add to the core curriculum. Now offers 3D design technology.

Singing is huge – every Wednesday and Thursday, the pupils get together to sing and we lost count of how many times the summer concert was mentioned. Orchestras, choirs, ensembles galore – for which practice is before school or at lunchtime – and 75 were taking individual music lessons from peripatetic teachers when we visited.

Drama popular and lively, with a new drama studio providing a great dedicated space that can be fully blackened out. School takes part in the Shakespeare Schools Festival. Years 7-9 and 10-13 alternate in doing a play or musical every year (the older ones teaming up with the boys' school – with other joint events including the summer concert, leadership days and dinner and dances for the sixth-formers.)

Small, but much used, cookery room, with year 7s taught not just how to cook, but a wider perspective of the role of food in societies and a way to use it as a form of sharing and nurturing relationships (eg they cook lunch for elderly folk from local old people's homes).

'I've been blown away not only by the quality of people these girls get – and it's they who organise the speakers – but by the quality of the questioning from the girls'

All the usual day trips you'd expect in the heart of London – theatre, ballet, museums, London Zoo, Bletchley Park etc – plus plenty of residentials, to the likes of Isle of Wight, Devon and further afield to the battlefields and Greece. Community service trips to places like Calcutta and South Africa, where the girls get involved in housing street children. Occasional overseas trips for choirs and sports teams etc.

Extracurricular clubs impressively varied – everything from politics club to computer science and Italian to arts – which take place before school, at lunchtimes and after school. Minerva Society particularly popular – after-school talks, including the likes of politician Natalie Bennett. 'I've been blown away not only by the quality of people these girls get – and it's they who organise the speakers – but by the quality of the questioning from the girls,' said one parent. 'They are more insightful, sharp and ethically on point than my colleagues that I attend talks with.'

Background and atmosphere: Founded, along with its sibling junior school and senior boys' school, in 1975 by the School of Economic Science (SES) (see our online review of the senior boys' school for background and history), at which time the school was based in Queen's Gate, later moving to Notting Hill Gate and then, in 2001, to its current location in a leafy residential West London street.

Located down a quiet road, within sight of Olympia, the main gate leads into an attractive courtyard, which forms the centre of the whole school, in which the junior and senior schools co-exist happily. Indeed, there's nothing remotely unusual about seeing young boys and girls making their way along the polished wooden-floored corridors here – which is really rather nice and makes for a smooth transition from juniors up to seniors.

It would be unfair to say this three-storey school is bursting at the seams, but there isn't a great deal of elbow room, with compact (but very light and airy) classrooms – which probably look smaller than they are due to the clunky, traditional wooden desks, all facing forward for chalk-and-talk type teaching during our visit, although we were assured there's plenty of interactive teaching too. Recent improvements include a new sixth form centre, library and a fourth science lab. Good-sized and well-equipped music room. Big and airy school hall, plus gym and a refectory, all sitting on top of one another. Overall, the buildings are well cared for – lots of white-painted corridors, blue carpets, good wall displays and useful noticeboards. Outside space is limited, though care has been taken to provide little trellised alcoves for quiet chat around the tarmac playground, complete with climbing wall, and there's also the courtyard.

The food is vegetarian and the tables are laid invitingly – hot home-cooked food plus fresh fruit, salad, bread and cheese. Girls love it or hate it (older ones are more enthused). We loved it.

Girls seem down-to-earth, happy and supportive of one another, many draping their arms around each other as they walk from classroom to classroom. 'I can't think of a girl here that you wouldn't describe as nice,' one pupil told us. Plenty of room for difference, with no feeling that there's a St James 'type' and plenty of room for growth if your daughter arrives as a shrinking violet. 'My daughter was terribly shy, but now speaks publicly, is head of house and organises outside speakers for the school. I'd never have thought it possible. She has blossomed as an individual, thanks to this school,' one parent told us. Girls aren't overly sophisticated, but not too sheltered either. Academically, hard-working, conscientious and reflective. The sixth form have privileges – no uniform, going out at lunchtimes etc.

Pastoral care, well-being and discipline: Highly praised, with the form teacher – who moves up the school with the class where possible – at the heart of pastoral care. And if you can't talk to your teacher (which all girls told us they could), then there are plenty of buddies and mentors. All the spiritual and philosophical emphasis mentioned earlier undoubtedly helps guard against the usual teenage problems. And although there's no school counsellor, there's a trained well-being coach. Bullying rare. 'Girls are sometimes unkind, but it's usually down to thoughtlessness and we deal with

'My daughter was terribly shy, but now speaks publicly, is head of house and organises outside speakers for the school. I'd never have thought it possible. She has blossomed as an individual'

that quickly when we need to,' says the head. Pupils concur. Plenty of assemblies on everything from LGBT to mental health. House system taken seriously – with girls all wearing their house T shirts on Fridays and alternating in eating in the staff dining room.

Misbehaviour, when it happens, is low-level – chatting in lessons, failing to hand in homework on time, untidy uniform etc is about as bad as it gets, for which you get 'a slip'. Three slips in one half term lead to a detention and three of those leads to an extended detention, which basically means community service and reflection. 'At that point, you'd want to be looking at the root cause,' explains the head. We met several sixth formers who'd never had a single detention. Only one temporary exclusion, and no permanent ones, under current headship. No school council when we visited (suggestions box instead), but it was about to be implemented.

Who wouldn't fit in? Girls who don't appreciate quiet time. 'There's lots of wriggling and squiggling at first – that's normal, but then they get so used to it that it becomes completely normal, then by year 12 and 13 they are such advocates,' says the head. We found she was spot on. 'I'm so passionate about the value of meditation,' said one sixth former. Also not a school for the highly competitive. 'You don't measure yourself against other people here,' one pupil told us. A parent added, 'Whilst this is an airy and bright school, despite its metropolis location, young people who need to be very physical would find the St James offering challenging, I think.'

Pupils and parents: Mixed as befits its west London location. Around half white British; a fifth from Asian backgrounds (many of whom are attracted by the influence of the eastern philosophies); and the rest a huge mix including Chinese, black Caribbean and Eastern European. English as a second language a non-issue as even they speak English well. A tiny minority of the staff are members of SES, some are ex-pupils, but the vast majority of pupils are now from families who have no direct connection whatsoever. When we mentioned SES to the pupils we met, they shrugged their shoulders. 'We know it was relevant to the founding of the school, but it's just not part of our school life now,' said one.

Some pupils travel significant distances, mainly from the west, with some taking at least an hour on public transport, though most pupils are more local. A growing contingent from the north west pocket of London eg Willesden and Hampstead. Parents range from the relatively wealthy to those who save every penny to send their daughter here. Lots of dual income families. Quite a few old girls' children come here. Lively PA, called The Friends, with all the usual quiz nights and stalls at sports day etc. One parent was disappointed by the lack of class reps. Former pupils include actors Emily Watson and Sasha Behar and novelist Laura Wilson.

Entrance: St James Junior girls move seamlessly through – NB now at year 7 rather than year 6. The rest come from preps and state primaries – around half from each. Main prep feeders are Pembridge Hall, Orchard House, Chiswick and Bedford Park, Glendower, Ravenscourt Park Prep, St Nicholas Prep, The Falcons School, Bute House, Garden House, Kew Green Prep, Thomas' Battersea and Thomas' Kensington. Some also from St Mary Abbots, Barnes, Belmont and Fox primary schools. Around 200 apply for around 25 places (the other 25 taken by juniors). School is part of the London 11+ Consortium which sets a cognitive ability test (maths, verbal and non-verbal reasoning) and has a common reference form. 'An imaginative interview experience, which explores skills, aptitutes and intellectual acuity of the candidates.'

There's the odd space available in most higher years. Entry criteria for sixth formers is at least five GCSEs at 9-5 including at least a 7 in the subjects chosen.

Exit: Up to 40 per cent leave after GCSEs – all for good, healthy reasons: some to co-eds, some to schools that offer alternative A levels or courses, often to state schools, occasionally to board or to nearer home. Some gap years. Around 70 per cent to Russell Group universities, with popular destinations including Bristol, Exeter, Durham, York, King's, UCL and SOAS – and increasingly, East Anglia. One to Cambridge in 2018. Science or medicine related courses popular, the rest choose across a vast range – art through to zoology and everything in between. Many pursue careers in which they contribute to the community, notably teachers, medics, nurses and working for charities.

Money matters: The school operates a means-tested bursary scheme. All current and future parents may apply. Future parents need to be registered with the school. This is not a rich school so don't look for masses of help.

Remarks: This small school is 'like a family', according to the pupils we met, and we got that impression too. Girls are supportive of one another and this, coupled with the emphasis on spirituality and philosophy, makes it a school that provides so much more than the academic rigour, which is a given. They take the view that it's no good being a straight A* student academically, if morally you are a C student. No wonder the school turns out such generous-spirited, honourable, sharp young women who know not only how to reach their full potential, but who have grown up understanding how to use that potential to the advantage of wider society. A gem for ethically minded families.

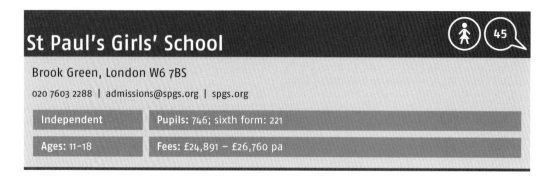

St Paul's Girls' School

Brook Green, London W6 7BS

020 7603 2288 | admissions@spgs.org | spgs.org

Independent	Pupils: 746; sixth form: 221
Ages: 11–18	Fees: £24,891 – £26,760 pa

High mistress: Since September 2017, Sarah Fletcher MA PGCE NPQH, an Oxford historian (early 50s), and previously head of City of London School. Before that she was head of Kingston Grammar School, where her regime was creative, modernising and human. And before that, a deputy head and director of studies at Rugby; she has taught at, among others, Wycombe Abbey, St George's Montreux, Habs Girls' (head of history) and Lawrence Sheriff Boys' Grammar in Rugby – a diverse and venturesome academic career. And an excellent preparation for one of the top jobs in the independent day school sector. Helped to develop and launch both the Pre-U and the EPQ. Her passions outside education are the clarinet, art, theatre and fresh air.

Academic matters: Pretty close to unbeatable. School can afford a lofty disdain for league tables as it is always at or near number one (60 per cent A*s and 90 per cent A*/A grades at A level/Pre-U in 2018; 99 per cent A*-A/9-7 at I/GCSE). The common claim to prioritise a broad education is undoubtedly justified here: many parents chose the school amidst a plethora of offers from other London powerhouses for this very reason. 'It really does feed a broader intellectual curiosity,' said one. Another commented: 'The teaching is second to none – exciting and stimulating. The teachers really get the children and make the most of them.'

Those few with special educational needs often have coping strategies in place before they arrive, but the school is well set up to help. 'They've been astonishingly good at responding to my daughter's needs, and put in plenty of support for her,' said a parent, 'so it hasn't been too much of an issue. But they have made it clear that she is expected to meet the standards of the school.'

There is a tight group of almost entirely academic subjects at GCSE and A level, which includes Italian, Chinese and Russian in the wide range of languages, though with relatively few takers at A level, and the recently added government and politics and theatre studies A level. Maths is by far the most popular A level subject, as one would expect, with a fairly even spread between the runners up biology, chemistry, English and history. Most A levels (19 out of 23) and the Pre-Us are linear, with all exams at the end of year 13.

The school considered offering the IB but decided against it. 'We decided that A level and Pre-U are more flexible instruments – you have time to do things outside the curriculum that are not measured, and you can be a specialist or a generalist. It also gives more time for the bespoke Paulina unique co-curricular opportunities.' These include the Senior Scholarship project, which sees girls between years 12 and 13 carrying out projects with titles ranging from Is There Beauty in Chaos? to Visualising Polytopes in 4 Dimensions; and the Friday lectures from luminaries such as Shami Chakrabarti from Liberty and documentary maker Michael Cockerell on his latest work, The Life of Boris Johnston.

Games, options, the arts: With a legacy of Gustav Holst as first director of music and in-house composer, music has always been exceptional. Indeed, the recently renovated music department and singing hall – 'where Holst and Miss Gray [the then high mistress] listened to girls singing' – are an important nerve centre of the school. There are orchestras, music ensembles and choirs open to all, but the symphony orchestra and senior choirs are by audition only and perform at astonishingly high levels.

Art, too, is high profile. When we visited, the impressive coursework for the school-directed art GCSE course was on display in the hall. 'Art here is very special,' commented a student. The top floor art rooms include a terrace with a panorama of the London skyline where girls learn about architecture. There are spaces for digital art, animation, ceramics, sculpture and print-making as well as painting and drawing. DT is a GCSE option only as part the art and design course but an example of the talent was an impressive pupil-designed bus shelter that adorned the entrance drive when we visited.

Drama has perhaps been a poorer relation in the past, but there is now a separate drama department. It is a successful GCSE and A level option (though a mother commented that she was unusual in encouraging her daughter to take two arts subjects at GCSE: 'Lots of parents only want their daughters to do academic subjects'.) The purpose-built Celia Johnson Theatre hosts several annual school plays, with smaller scale productions in the drama studio. Students devise and direct their own plays, including the year 12 Colet Play, which has been performed at the Edinburgh Fringe on several occasions. Girls also join in St Paul's Boys' School productions.

'The girls get caught up in the energy of the place,' says school, and a parent commented, 'My daughter always comes home having done amazing things'

Lacrosse is the main sport, with 7.30am practices for team players ('they all love it, so it's fine', commented a less devoted pupil), international tours and players often making county and area squads. The school also competes successfully at sports including netball, basketball, rowing, cross county, fencing and swimming. However, there are opportunities for the less talented too, with teams down to D and E in the lower years. 'My younger daughter is in a team even though she's rubbish,' said a parent honestly.

One parent commented: 'It's very inclusive. There's choirs and orchestras anyone can be in, and the same for drama and sport.' Amidst so many very talented girls, however, some of the younger ones in particular can take time to gain confidence and find their niche. 'My daughter plays an instrument but hasn't been asked to take part in anything so far. She and her friends like singing, but they found the choir too highbrow. And they were very disheartened when none of them got through to the second round of auditions for the school musical.'

Another parent said, 'There are huge opportunities, but it's up to them to make the most of it.'

Huge numbers of clubs, seminars and trips: writing courses, physics and maths competitions, conferences in Paris, museum visits in St Petersburg, dance shows and debating competitions. 'The girls get caught up in the energy of the place,' says school, and a parent commented, 'My daughter always comes home having done amazing things.'

Background and atmosphere: Some 400 years after John Colet founded St Paul's School 'for the children [not girls, naturally] of all nations and countries', the Mercers' livery company, guardians of his estate, decided girls were also worthy of an education and set up St Paul's Girls' School. Its red-brick main house, designed by Gerald Horsley, with marble-floored corridors, and panelled and galleried great hall, has a gracious, traditional and peaceful feel. 'But if you go in at break time it's very buzzy,' said a parent. 'They're all running round the hall, there's music blaring out.' Lack of uniform gives an informal air, with most girls dressed in ubiquitous jeans or shorts and tee shirts.

The school has an undeserved reputation for being 'very formal, starchy, cold, highly competitive, ruthless and unforgiving'. But once families join, say staff, 'they find it's much friendlier than expected, and more informal. We like to do things in a friendly, collegiate way.' Parents agree: 'It's a much more normal place than you'd think from its image. It's much nicer from the inside than from the outside.' 'They really care about the individual.'

Impressive admin: 'It's really well run, which means a lot to us,' said a mother. 'Induction week in particular is brilliantly organised. They told the girls what would happen, and it did. They're very accommodating and very professional.' Another said, 'Unlike at my son's school, I don't feel I have to stress about homework and deadlines. I leave it to them.'

Pressure to achieve tends to come from highly-ambitious girls and their families rather than from the school. However, some feel that the school could do more to mitigate anxieties. 'Success is taken so seriously that it sends out a message of pressure,' said a parent. 'Lots of girls really worry about how they are going to do in school exams. You can feel very unsuccessful if you aren't brilliant.' Some parents of younger girls feel the homework can be overwhelming. 'It tends to take much longer than intended because they're perfectionists,' said a year 7 parent. 'She and her friends take all evening doing homework.' 'I don't know how they cope if they miss anything, because lessons move at such a fast pace,' said another.

'We had the preconception that you had to be pretty, funny and clever to fit in here,' said a mother. 'But my retiring daughter has come home beaming from day one.' Another said that her daughter has found it tough: 'It took her a while to make friends. Coming from a state primary was particularly hard from a social point of view. But she's already gaining in confidence. They make the girls feel really proud of being there.'

Girls are encouraged to take the initiative. 'If you come up with an idea, the school will back you up and support you all the way,' said a sixth former, citing the in-house second-hand clothes shop, housed in a restored Victorian coal cellar that previously acted as a junk room, set up and run by students to raise money for local charities.

Pastoral care, well-being and discipline: 'We like to think it is a kinder school than it was,' say staff, with an increased emphasis on the pastoral side. 'We have clear boundaries but lots of room for independent expression. We treat the girls like adults as soon as possible.' 'There's a marked lack of rules,' agreed a parent. 'There's a respect and a feeling of equality between teachers and girls.'

Some of these highly-ambitious girls do succumb to eating disorders or other expressions of teenage angst, but the school is very conscious of the problem and encourages a relaxed approach to eating. The food, said a pupil, is 'amazing. I feel as if I am eating in a restaurant every day. Food is important to Paulinas.'

Small tutor groups of 12 girls keep the same tutor for two years in the lower school and three in the middle school. The sixth form has a vertical system to enable those in different forms to share experiences. The sister scheme sees girls from the middle and upper schools help new girls settle in, and two year 13 girls are attached to each lower year group, available for mentoring and encouragement. 'The sixth form isn't hived off in its own area but is very much part of the school. The girls are role models and figures to look up to for the younger ones.' Two 'very approachable' school nurses, a school doctor and three counsellors make up the non-teaching pastoral team.

Pupils and parents: Intellectual, ambitious, often multi-national families. 'I sometimes feel that my daughter's in a minority having two English parents. Lots of girls speak a second language fluently.' From a range of backgrounds – journalists and artists, academics and scientists, with a large proportion of bankers and lawyers ('You can spot those with bursaries,' said a parent wryly, 'because their dads aren't bankers.') Largest single cohort from Bute House, which regularly sends up to 20 or so girls here; the rest from a wide range of preps and primaries across London and beyond.

'There is a view that you must be super-confident to succeed here, but girls vary here as much

'We have clear boundaries but lots of room for independent expression. We treat the girls like adults as soon as possible'

as anywhere. We do have a place for sensitive, quieter girls, and we enjoy the challenge of bringing them out. However, some parents still don't feel that their daughter is tough enough.' Parents agree that eccentricities are well tolerated. 'Of course the top dogs are the cool girls,' said one, 'but you can be a total geek and it's not a problem.'

Old Paulinas include (amongst many) Harriet Harman, Shirley Williams, Carol Thatcher, Stephanie Flanders, Rosalind Franklin, Rachel Weisz, Imogen Stubbs, Marghanita Lanski, Dodie Smith and Rachel Johnson.

Entrance: A computer-based test in November, aimed to be tutor proof and to identify 'girls with intellectual potential', deselects around 20 per cent of applicants. 'There's a vast industry preparing girls for St Paul's, and we don't want to miss bright sparks who haven't been tutored.' The rest take maths, English and comprehension exams in January, with those shortlisted invited back for interviews. 'Our admissions process is a very careful, solemn business. We try to make it humane as well as thoughtful, and we discuss every candidate in detail.' The school optimistically asks parents to state if their daughter has been tutored, 'though we know they will answer what they think we want to hear'. They are trying to increase the proportion of successful state school applicants (currently around 15-25 per cent), and run a series of enrichment days for gifted and talented year 4 and 5 children from local state primaries. Parents are given information about bursaries and encouraged to attend an open evening. 'We don't positively discriminate, but we do try to see through disadvantage.' The school is clear that it is looking for a particular type of girl. 'Our girls devour intellectual material very quickly. Those who want to work at a slower pace will be happier elsewhere.'

Exit: No-one is asked to leave because of poor academic performance (though they might reconsider someone who showed a lack of interest in learning). 'We make an undertaking to see them through, and every year we take through one or two girls whose GCSE performance is less than starry.' Minimal numbers leave after GCSE (a few are tempted off to co-ed sixth forms, particularly Westminster).

Vast majority stays the course and moves on to do mostly solidly academic subjects at a very

Wetherby School

narrow range of top universities. Around half get Oxbridge places (47 in 2018); 13 off to Yale, Harvard and other Ivy League universities; virtually all the rest to Durham, Edinburgh, Bristol, London with a few to other Russell Group universities.

Money matters: Various music scholarships at 11+ which are currently the value of tuition in two instruments. The same music opportunities are available at 16+ along with art and drama scholarships, each worth £250 a year. The school aims to fund 20 per cent of girls through its means-tested

bursary programme – 'we would like to feel that any girl from any setting could plot her way here' – and staff visit likely families at home to ensure they are not running a fleet of Ferraris from a multi-million pound mansion. Those on 100 per cent bursaries also receive a grant towards music or PE lessons, school trips, textbooks and travel.

Remarks: Unmatched environment for girls who thrive on hard work and have an appetite for intellectual experiences. 'What is on offer is exceptional. They have so many wonderful opportunities.'

St Philip's School

6 Wetherby Place, London SW7 4NE

020 7373 3944 | office@stpschool.co.uk | stphilipschool.co.uk

Independent	Pupils: 105
Ages: 7-13	Fees: £16,200 pa

Headmaster: Since 2016, Alexander Wulffen-Thomas BA PGCE (30s). The suit, tie and polished shoes are neat, tidy and conservative but the first impression is that he might be happier outside (runs up the stairs at speed). Born in the wilds of West Yorkshire, one away from the tail end of a large family, brought up in Cheshire and schooled at St Ambrose Prep, St Ambrose College and then Stonyhurst. Read Russian – 'it's a country with a soul' – at Durham, then used his languages to find a job in the City. Left in his late 20s as it involved too much time in front of a computer screen dealing with dreary problems such as money laundering regulations and went to work at Westminster Cathedral Choir School, initially in an Evelyn Waugh-type role as a teaching all-rounder of history and games. Obviously more successful than the original as he landed the post of deputy head and then applied for the job at St Philip's, seeing it as a natural progression for someone with Catholic values and a leaning towards traditional teaching.

Married to Olivia; one dog – attends the school; no children as yet.

Entrance: The main intakes are at 7 (approximately 10 boys) and at 8 (another 10 boys). Usually three to four applicants for each place and mainly from local pre-prep and state schools as most of the boys live nearby. They are oversubscribed but make their choices based on teacher's impressions as well as academic potential; this is definitely not a hothouse

school and they take in boys with minor learning difficulties as long as they can cope with the mainstream curriculum and routines. St Philip's does not hide the importance of its religious roots and the majority of boys are from Catholic families, often children or relations of previous pupils. However, the school is also catholic with a small c and about 10 per cent of the boys follow different faiths. When we asked some Catholic pupils whether this was ever awkward they responded convincingly in the negative, although possibly with a hint that the others might be missing out.

Exit: A minnow compared to some of its competitors in London, St Philip's rightly holds its head up high in the academic stakes, although its new leader is emphatic that this is not a 'show-off school and the pupils' work does the talking'. Parents are helped to make the choice of 'where next' by an excellent app produced by the head, and most boys move on to their first-choice school. Most popular destinations currently Wetherby Senior, Ampleforth, Dulwich College and Portland Place.

Remarks: Housed in a tall red-brick building in South Kensington, the only advertisement is a charming plaque depicting a very blue St Philip Neri, and you could easily miss the word underneath announcing that it is a school. The spiritual aspect remains very important and assembly in the morning tends to be RE with sporting analysis sandwiched between the opening prayer and the collect for the day (presumably when their horse was in training it also included prayers for the creature's chances in the 2.30 at Kempton).

One parent said that her 'totally talentless' child kept returning with 'frankly miraculous' objects

It is a logistical triumph that they fit 100+ boys into this space, but it may help the pupils to organise themselves as there is literally no room for discarded items of clothing or belongings. On a hot day, the blazers hung neatly on the back of chairs and the old-fashioned desks were bare, lids firmly down. We did look inside a few, with the head's permission, but nevertheless feeling rather guilty due to the Keep Out notice in one, and found the usual variety of orderliness but absolutely no sign of any illicit items. Outside, there is a communal garden, which ticks the fresh air box but results in sighs from all concerned as it comes with major drawbacks, such as a noise cap, which is not ideal for small boys wanting to let off steam.

An individual school from day one; not many of its rivals can boast having owned a racehorse or having had a headmaster who doubled up teaching the boys with acting as chauffeur at the beginning and end of the day. Mr Tibbits – the name in itself a joy – started the school as the result of a complaint by a priest at the Brompton Oratory about the sad lack of education for Catholics in the neighbourhood. He was an exceptional teacher but may have been helped by fortifying himself for the task with a glass of sherry before lunch and a glass of red wine with the cheese whilst the boys unhappily chewed their way through Spam and mash, followed by blancmange. Nowadays, this miserable experience – no-one was allowed to leave until the last plate was clean – has been superseded by packed lunches, but the very mildly eccentric atmosphere remains. Only two more headmasters bridged the gap between his death in 1967 and Alexander Wulffen-Thomas's arrival in 2016, and maybe for this reason the 21st century is slightly less in evidence than at some of its rivals.

A high proportion of the teachers have been here for a long time but there is young blood, the head intends to move from one to two 'gappies' next year and there's a new multi-talented deputy head. Parents and children speak very highly of the teachers, not only about their competence but also about their kindness, one small boy taking a great deal of trouble to explain – vocally and by mime – how one teacher gave you a minus mark but was 'really kind' whilst she was doing it. They believe

in ensuring that the basic building blocks are carefully laid and regularly checked, with daily spelling and twice weekly maths tests in lower forms, and also encourage learning by heart through poetry competitions. Higher in the school all the teaching is praised but maths and Latin are exceptionally strong, and science may well benefit further when they are able to provide the intended new lab. There are 'no mountains of homework', but parents are relaxed and confident that their boys will do well.

Art is hugely popular, taught in a surprisingly bright and airy basement with one parent saying that her 'totally talentless' child kept returning with 'frankly miraculous' objects. Not afraid of the big time, pupils are entered in Royal College of Art competitions and 12 students had their work displayed in recently. Music is an intrinsic part of life, from playing the piano at assembly to singing in the Schola, and all pupils are encouraged to play an instrument or sing, with up to half of them performing at the school concert.

Sport is important; possibly to compensate for the lack of space back at base, they have invested in acres of well-manicured games fields in Barnes where the whole school decamps on two afternoons a week, leading to boys having 'smiling faces when you pick them up after a games day'. Despite their tiny numbers they field teams that are not frightened of taking on larger boys from much larger schools and quite often succeed in beating them. Swimming is a weekly lesson and the boys have recently organised squash teams who play in tournaments at Queen's club. Most importantly, neither the boys or their parents seem worried that they will be at a disadvantage on the games pitch when they move on. On a daily basis, table tennis is played in the garden with a staggering number of boys whizzing round the table at any one time, and logically they are bound to turn out a champion at some point.

Mr Tibbits – the name in itself a joy – started the school as the result of a complaint by a priest about the sad lack of education for Catholics in the neighbourhood

Homework clubs take place every day with some of the choices being languages, judo, art and fencing, but Airfix was definitely the favoured option of both one very enthusiastic boy and the head. There is no impression that this is a 'strict' school but the boys jump to their feet when the head walks into a class with a crisp 'Morning, Sir' and shake your hand, looking you straight in the eye. One parent, on being asked how they dealt with the inevitable small boy playing up, said that whilst discipline was not obvious, there were 'no hiding places; it's a tiny school in a tiny place'. When asked, the head told us that this was an advantage as every member of staff knew every child, which meant you could spot trouble and deal with it even before the boy was aware of it himself.

Lots of expeditions and a school skiing trip every year. On asking one boy whether he had learnt the history of Canterbury Cathedral at school before the impending visit, he replied 'Well, it would be silly if we hadn't,' then 'St Thomas a Becket' accompanied by an excellent 'being stabbed' routine.

The SENCo is a form teacher who co-ordinates any help needed and specialists are called in from outside when parents and teachers have planned a course of action, one parent confirming that they 'get it' when you have a child who might have social problems.

The fees are low by London prep school standards, partly because of the no frills approach – boys bring their own packed lunches – and partly because they have not invested in a shiny new look. Current parents seem very laid back about this, feeling that the whole nature of the school might change if it presented a more polished exterior, a sentiment echoed by the head's wish to keep this as a 'discreet school that speaks for itself'. A bursary fund can accommodate discounts up to 100 per cent of the fees, with an independent financial auditor assessing all applications.

At somewhere both as small and individual as this it could be easy to overestimate the importance of the teaching staff, but St Philip would be proud of this lot and the boys they turn out – shiny haloes all round.

Servite RC Primary School

252 Fulham Road, London SW10 9NA

020 7352 2588 | info@servite.rbkc.sch.uk | serviteprimaryschool.co.uk

State	Pupils: 240
Ages: 3-11	

Executive head teacher: Since 2002, Kathleen Williams BEd NPQH (40s). Has spent all her teaching career in borough of Kensington and Chelsea. Previously deputy head of St Mary's Primary, Ladbroke Grove. Married with a young child, who (she hopes) will soon be a pupil here. 'I couldn't think of my son going anywhere else. I want him to have the grounded education which Servite provides,' she says. Loves theatre, opera and all things musical. Friendly, capable and calm; an experienced pair of hands. Servite works in partnership with less serene local schools, in order to help raise standards and strengthen leadership. Head is ably supported by associate head teacher, Claude Gauci, who takes over the reins when she is out nurturing other schools. They make a robust team. Head admits that teaching is a demanding profession, but 'we're lucky. It's a privilege to be part of this happy school.'

Entrance: At 3 to nursery but a separate application is required for entry into reception. If they don't meet the strict criteria, then nursery children don't make it through to reception. Oversubscribed: approximately 60-80 apply for 30 places in nursery and 170-200 vie for 30 places in reception. Ever-decreasing catchment area (currently about half a mile). Pupils come predominantly from World's End estate and Earls Court. Priority given to baptised, practising Catholics who worship next door at Our Lady of Dolours. Occasional places further up school, though pretty rare due to low pupil mobility. V few non-Catholics. School currently at full capacity with 30 pupils per class.

Exit: Not a feeder for one particular school. Vast majority go to local Catholic state schools, including Cardinal Vaughan, Sacred Heart, St Thomas More and London Oratory, as well as a handful each year to Chelsea Academy. One or two go down the independent path, usually to Queen's Gate on bursaries. No special preparation given for 11+ and school seems to have escaped fanatical tutoring which goes on elsewhere in final years. A breath of fresh air.

Remarks: This successful school is tucked away behind an unprepossessing façade on the Fulham

Road, opposite Chelsea and Westminster Hospital. Surprisingly spacious once inside with large, light classrooms and three playgrounds for different year groups (the one for the smallest children particularly colourful and welcoming). Impressively large hall which transforms into a dining room, gym and theatre and boasts sophisticated lighting and sound equipment.

'We have an open door policy,' says head, 'but within a structure. Not mayhem! Boundaries are set in a respectful way and issues are dealt with quickly'

Head believes Servite offers a broad education, which encourages self-confidence and independence. Children are well prepared for life at secondary school by the time they leave. 'Servite gave my daughter the firm foundations on which to build,' said one grateful parent. Parents value the close association with the church which backs onto the playground. Pupils visit on holy days and every week one class celebrates mass there. Only three school rules – follow instructions; use kind and helpful words; keep hands, feet and objects to yourself. Pupils seemed to be adhering to these when we visited, though last rule appeared hardest to uphold.

Significant proportion of male teachers now. Staff consists of dedicated long-servers whose average age is 40. Appear devoted to the school and appreciate its family feel. 'They go the extra mile,' says head, 'and attend events at weekends such as school family mass with parents. No matter where the teachers live, they come to these events and the parents really appreciate it.' New teachers aren't taken on if they won't make a strong commitment to the school, beyond the classroom basics. Palpably strong relationships between teachers, parents and pupils. 'We have an open door policy,' says head, 'but within a structure. Not mayhem! Boundaries are set in a respectful way and issues are dealt with quickly.' One parent said, 'The school is professional but understanding'. Problems tend not to fester for too long.

Academic standard has been raised and school now boasts impressive results. Able children are extended through creative writing groups and extra maths support. Some bright sparks achieve high levels in maths. Links fostered with Imperial College and Royal Institution to extend knowledge and develop understanding of science. Spanish, music, dance and art taught by specialist teachers. Homework every night from the beginning. Project work given to older children to encourage effective time management and independent learning. School has pupils with a range of special needs, including autism, cerebral palsy and moderate specific learning difficulties. Behaviour support, learning support and pupil referral units offer considerable help to those in need. Currently five children with EHC plans.

School reflects the international, mixed community in which it finds itself. Head comments that many pupils come from 'poor, working families, where parents are often in domestic service.' Many families struggling but tend not to be on benefits. One in five pupils is entitled to free school meals. Roughly 60 per cent has English as a second language. Many pupils hail from Philippines, South America, East Africa and Western Europe. Main languages spoken at home are Spanish and Tagalog. Extra language support catered for through small targeted group work and some one-to-one support on offer. Parents happy with speedy progress made by those with limited English on arrival. 'Now you wouldn't know which ones were behind with English when they started,' commented one.

Fantastic, flexible wrap-around care on offer but school admits it's hard to sustain at a competitive price. Includes breakfast at start of day as well as tea, activities and opportunities to do homework at the end of the day. Children can be looked after from 8am-6pm. Parents aware they are lucky and are the envy of other schools nearby which don't have extended care on-site.

Impressive range of sport on offer and given as taster sessions. Netball, football, athletics and swimming taught either on site, in Battersea Park or Chelsea baths. Dance and gym compulsory. A wide assortment of clubs including taekwondo, yoga, zumba and street dance. Football, drama and cooking currently very popular. Parents pay for these. Good use made of the local community and has strong links with neighbouring Chelsea Football Club. School participates in Educate through Sport initiative and an English reading programme offered by the club. Paul Canoville, first black player for Chelsea, regularly visits the school as part of its programme to promote positive attitudes towards racial diversity.

Excellent use made of its central London location. 'You name it, we've been there!' says associate head. From designing apparatus for Cirque du Soleil acrobats to jump over in the Albert Hall to PGL visits to Weymouth, the pupils have fun here. Parents pay for school trips, but school helps those who are genuinely struggling to meet the cost. School payment plan in operation and parents encouraged to save for trips on a weekly basis.

Impressive art, drama and music. Annual art show to which parents are invited. Fantastic, carved Viking longboats on display and amusing portraits done by pupils of the staff line the stairs. Christmas nativity put on by youngest children and year 5 performs The Passion at Easter. Two nights in July are devoted to a musical production, generally led by year 6 leavers, and about which parents rave. Years 1-6 learn a class instrument, including ocarina, violin and ukulele. Currently 75 taking one-to-one lessons in piano, violin or guitar.

Effective communication between school and parents via weekly newsletter. Parent council is parent-led and discusses initiatives such as school meals and uniform. Money raised by PTA tends to be spent on travel expenses for school trips, restocking library and equipment for playground.

School lives by its motto: 'Learning to love and loving to learn.' Family feel to the place. Children skip in each morning and enjoy their time here. On the day we visited, ambulance sirens blared incessantly on the road outside while the children danced around merrily in the playground, totally oblivious to the noise and fumes that engulfed them.

Above all, a welcoming school. No wonder head won't be considering anywhere else for her son.

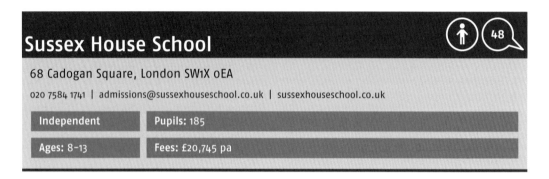

Sussex House School

68 Cadogan Square, London SW1X 0EA

020 7584 1741 | admissions@sussexhouseschool.co.uk | sussexhouseschool.co.uk

Independent	Pupils: 185
Ages: 8-13	Fees: £20,745 pa

Headmaster: Since 1994, the engaging, cultured Nicholas Kaye MA ACP, Cambridge English graduate followed by music research (60s). Whilst deputy head here, following a brief spell at Asra Hawariat School in Addis Ababa, of which he is a trustee and fundraiser, the opportunity arose to acquire the school from the Vernon Trust, which he seized with typical energy, creating an independent charitable trust. Sussex House has never looked back, going from strength to strength, achieving the recent accolade of Best Prep School award. Parents admire this 'erudite man' and the boys sum him up as 'diverse, really talented, passionate about music, poetry, architecture, and a playwright'. His study/Victorian parlour is crammed with book shelves containing leather-bound volumes and novels by past Old Cadogans, an ornamental pianoforte ('The best pianoforte is the concert Steinway in the ballroom,' remarks the head) along with a cornucopia of porcelain, potted plants, objets d'art, furniture, rugs and oriental carpets illuminated by wooden lamp stands with large lampshades.

As one might expect in this very traditional institution, there are school photographs, house shields and embroidered banners made for the Jubilee and carried in procession on special occasions such as the annual All Souls' Day Requiem at St Mary Magdalene, Little Venice, which we attended. Conducted by Mr Kaye, this was an uplifting service in which the Sussex House choristers sang exquisitely. Mr Kaye enthusiastically teaches 10 periods to the top years with a focus on creative writing and literature. All the parents we spoke to agreed 'he has an excellent rapport with the boys'. One parent remarked, 'The headmaster has a key role in setting the tone of the school. Even more amazing is the fact that he sees the best in every child and gets the best out of every child.' Another commented, 'He teaches the VIth [year 8] English in his study and they appreciate their elevated status. The sessions are challenging, quite adult, like an Oxford tutorial'. He is very ably supported by his PA/registrar who firmly declares, when questioned on the future, 'We are certainly not ready to hang up our boots yet!' And fortunately they show no signs of it.

Entrance: At 8+ and only later if there happens to be a place available. Thirty-six pupils are selected on the basis of a rigorous, competitive entrance examination in English, maths, reasoning and interview. Strong English is a key requirement and there are no boys in the school with EAL requirements; however, it does cater for up to 23 boys on the SEN register who are given support without additional charge. Parents suggest, 'Not a school of mixed ability, although mild learning difficulties such as dyspraxia are dealt with'. Prospective parents are all given a personal tour by the registrar, meet the headmaster and are invited to a special evening led by members of the VIth form. The majority of boys live within a few miles of Cadogan Square. Regular

'The headmaster has a key role in setting the tone of the school. Even more amazing is the fact that he sees the best in every child'

feeders are Garden House, Eaton House, and other central London pre-preps. There are no sibling discounts on offer but bursaries and scholarships are available according to need and are up to the full remission of fees in cases of genuine need.

Exit: Majority to Eton, then St Paul's, Westminster, Winchester and City of London.

Remarks: Mr Kaye chose the aspirational school motto 'Lead me to the rock that is higher than I', and, as he explains, 'This implies a journey which, unlike climbing Everest, is never complete'. Unusually for a day school, there is an Anglican school chaplain who leads important services in the local church which acts as the school chapel.

This is a distinctive, remarkable school which is unashamedly academic. After being greeted by gowned school marshal, Sergeant Khim Sherchan, formerly of the Gurkhas, you are ushered into a grand Norman Shaw arts and crafts town house with William Morris wallpaper, stunning fresh flower arrangements, a realisation of Morris' tenet 'Have nothing in your house that you do not know to be useful or believe to be beautiful'. Parents who would prefer something more modern and spacious, where boys can let off steam at break times kicking a ball, should look elsewhere. Up the wide, ornate mahogany staircase is the ballroom, which provides a venue for daily assemblies, lessons around polished tables and tea time concerts. These concerts are an example of how every effort is made to encourage budding musicians at all levels. The music is stunning and every year concerts with a professional orchestra take place at the Cadogan Hall along with an annual musical at the Fortune Theatre. We heard a talented 9 year old play the violin with incredible skill and learnt he is also a valued member of the football team. One parent we spoke to remarked, 'The school is small enough so that each boy finds a niche.' Creativity abounds and is an intrinsic part of life at Sussex House along with its nurturing approach, and why many parents choose it over other top prep schools. As a parent commented, 'The wonderful drama is performed in the West End, giving unparalleled opportunities for this age'.

During our visit we saw some excellent architectural models in the making, in readiness for the annual exhibition with the theme of Iconic Chelsea.

The clubs and art lessons include opportunities to do pottery and oil painting as well as making use of laptops for presentations about artists. The subject specialist staff are long-serving and popular with their pupils. All the boys we met commented on how the staff are prepared to give up their own time to help individuals. The boys themselves are a superb advertisement for the school: intelligent, polite, lively, responsive and articulate. 'They are confident without being arrogant,' commented a parent, adding candidly, 'That is not to say that they are not sometimes boisterous, and need careful handling in this confined space by their form teacher and/or the deputy head.' They are given Stars for rewards and Stripes for punishments. The year 8s are prefects and wear gowns unless they fall from grace and are no longer allowed to wear a gown: a great incentive. They have opportunities to exercise at Battersea Park at least twice a week, and A, B, C and D teams regularly play fixtures against other schools. The school day includes regular walks to Nicholls Hall for gym, fencing and music. Fencing is excellent here and the school magazine, The Cadogan, records many sporting achievements and activities, as well as superb poetry. The classrooms for younger boys still house old-fashioned lacquered desks, which are confining, and it is important to be aware that break times are spent inside the school, which would not suit all boys.

As one might expect in this very traditional institution, there are school photographs, house shields and embroidered banners made for the Jubilee

Average size of classes 18, with 12 in the top year when a scholarship group is formed. The curriculum is carefully tailored to suit the needs of individuals who will sit various school examinations. Mr Kaye would love to have a six day week, 'but that is not possible', so much is packed in: orchestra practice and Greek before school, for example. As there is no dining room or kitchen, boys must bring packed lunches; 'not ideal,' state parents, but lunch time is a social occasion with the form teacher followed by numerous, popular clubs including architecture and discussion group. One ex-parent remarked on how 'well-rounded SH boys are', and that out of 250 boys at Eton in her son's year, three of the 12 chosen for the Eton debating competition were SH boys. The boys we chatted to would love to play rugby, but revel in football alongside options such as fencing, tennis, cricket, golf and swimming. They appreciate the spacious new science laboratory and find the art they do inspiring.

For those parents seeking a Summer Fields in central London, Sussex House fits the bill. Parents agree, 'It really does prepare boys for boarding at 13+ and gives them a wonderful, well-rounded platform'. It is not surprising that so many Old Cadogans hold the school with great affection. They include novelists Edward St Aubyn, Jason Goodwin and Richard Mason, along with actors Daniel Radcliffe, Jasper Britton, and Christopher and Jay Villiers, composer Michael Csanyi Wills, and many more recorded in the annual, very impressive magazine.

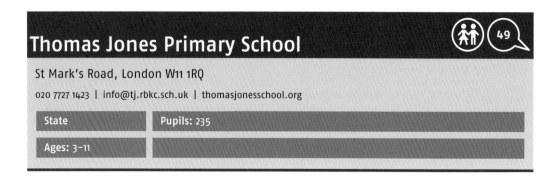

Thomas Jones Primary School

St Mark's Road, London W11 1RQ

020 7727 1423 | info@tj.rbkc.sch.uk | thomasjonesschool.org

State	Pupils: 235
Ages: 3–11	

Head: Since 2001, Mr David Sellens OBE (for services to education), BA English, Goldsmiths (40s). Cut his teeth in teaching at New End Primary School in Hampstead, where he worked for five years as the youngest member of staff; 'I had a lot of energy, and the head at the time afforded me the luxury of opportunity.' His energy and enthusiasm swiftly saw him on the leadership team, at a time when the national curriculum was being implemented. However, feeling slightly constrained and wanting to do things his way, he started looking for a post where, he says, 'I could make a difference.' The role of deputy head came up at Ashburnham school and the young, enterprising Sellens, bursting with ideas, hotfooted it straight from artistic and aspirational Hampstead to a school south of the river in dire straits; 'I was suddenly thrust into an environment where results and aspirations were very low.' He and the new head, working closely together for sometimes up to 80 hour weeks, turned the school around over the next four years into Ofsted outstanding and awarded beacon status. Shortly afterwards, he was alerted to the fact that nearby Thomas Jones Primary School was on the verge of closure and, keen to become a head teacher, he applied for the post and promptly set about changing the fortunes of the school. Fourteen years on, he has exceeded the expectations of even the most optimistic.

In his second decade of tenure, Mr Sellens still appears like an enthusiastic and irrepressible newbie to the post. He is a hard man to pin down and his boundless energy sees him flit from one room to another, starting with the 8.45am meet and greet of all pupils and parents at the school gates; 'You'll like this,' he assures us; 'apologies if it gets a bit loud with the bell.' He describes his approach as radical rather than traditional. He teaches year 6 pupils English and says he doesn't pay 'too much attention' to the national curriculum. When asked if he sees himself as a bit of a maverick (after all, this is a head who walks into assembly eating a bowl of porridge and banana extolling the virtues of having a healthy breakfast, a head who ditches the traditional end of year musical, opting instead for Under Milk Wood), he says that although this comment has been levelled at him many times, he sees himself more as an individual who occasionally likes to 'buck the trend.'

He always carried with him a strong sense of social justice which is what motivates him daily

Mr Sellens admits that he is 'incredibly fussy' about a lot of things. 'I'm fussy about [the state of] buildings, pupils' attire, their demeanour.' He also insists that pupils make eye contact with people and greet visitors with a handshake: 'He has meticulous attention to detail', one parent told us. This head is also big on homework – year 6 pupils can do up to two hours a night. Even with this 'bossy' approach, he says that he doesn't face much protest from pupils or parents, as there is a sense that 'it is being done for all the right reasons and the outcome is extremely strong.' One pupil said he was 'controlling – but in a good way.'

Brought up on the south coast, Mr Sellens says he was the typical story of an 'industrious' child from a humble background who won a place at grammar school and worked hard to better his situation. He always carried with him a strong sense of social justice which is what motivates him daily; 'I want to give every pupil the opportunity to shine, to look back and think they don't have regrets and it doesn't matter what they do, as long as they enjoy doing it.' When asked if he has any children of his own, he replies 'no', then pauses, has a think and says 'yes, 235 of them!'

Entrance: The catchment is so small for this one form primary school that you virtually have to live in the grounds to get in (we kid you not – one pupil who lives two doors away last year didn't qualify. Such was the outcry, she eventually managed to secure a place). The head says he is sometimes overwhelmed by the number of prospective parents, 'some with children who have yet to be born.' Distance from the school is now measured from the centre of the school outwards. (Mostly therefore to those in the nearby housing estate and their siblings).

Exit: Mainly to the local comprehensives – Holland Park or new Kensington Aldridge Academy; some try to gain bursaries or scholarships to independent schools. Last year, three children secured bursaries and scholarships to nearby Notting Hill Prep and further afield Christ's Hospital, West Sussex and King Edward's, Surrey.

Remarks: There are primary schools, and then there's Thomas Jones Primary school. Former secretary of state for education Michael Gove has waxed lyrical about this school on many occasions, claiming in one speech that it offers a better education than nearby £20,000+ pa prep school which taught the heirs to the throne. He said: 'There are state primary schools every bit as ambitious, as supportive, as exciting, as the smartest of private prep schools – like for example, Thomas Jones Primary in West London.'

Named after Thomas Jones of North Carolina – a passionate crusader against the evils of slavery in the early part of the 19th century – this state primary in the borough of Kensington and Chelsea (a short walk from bustling Ladbroke Grove) is as true to its ideological namesake as it is to his inspirational work. By any stretch of the imagination it is a major achievement for a primary school serving a deprived inner city area to secure a rolling five year average of over 99 per cent of children achieving level 4 and above in maths and English – about three-quarters achieving grade 5+ and a few achieving level 6 in maths (often top in the borough for both subjects). What makes Thomas Jones's achievement even more remarkable is that barely any pupils who sit the tests come from an indigenous English-speaking background, with one in three speaking Arabic as their first language. Moreover, 30 per cent of last year's cohort were on the SEN register.

Nowhere is London's diversity of culture or chasm of social inequality better highlighted than at this school. One side of the school (Lancaster Road) is flanked by grand period properties where a three bedroom maisonette can set you back a mere £2m. The other side (St Mark's Road entrance) is a stone's throw away from a large, austere housing estate, 'not fit for purpose' we are told, which accounts for roughly 70 per cent of the school's intake. More than half of the pupils live in difficult circumstances and are entitled to free school meals; some of them, we are told, 'don't own a desk and do their homework on an upturned tray or in the local library.' One parent we spoke to told us that the strength of the school is its diversity, 'and that it caters for all.'

We wondered whether this was part school and part holistic retreat. Large (glass-encased) scented candles, wafting scents of vanilla or lavender, flickered on teachers' desks in almost all classrooms

There is nothing ordinary about this school – certainly not if one compares it to other inner city state primaries. The interior is so immaculate and shiny we could see our own reflection in the wooden parquet flooring and the walls looked as if they had been freshly painted; 'we keep them white so it's easy to match and cover any dirt marks.' When asked how they manage to keep a primary school of 230 children so unbelievably pristine, Mr Sellens tells us that the pupils demonstrate real pride in the school and often ask to be on the 'cleaning rota.' For a bog standard (architecturally speaking) 1970s prefab, as this school is from the outside, the inside came as quite a revelation. Light and bright 'to create an illusion of space', the open plan and organic design is quite remarkable both in terms of its functionality and aesthetics.

The artwork which adorned the walls had been carefully selected and beautifully displayed, and we were particularly struck by some stunningly creative models of castles made from toilet rolls and other household objects, displayed outside the year 3 classroom. We also liked a large, colourful mosaic of Elmer the elephant with a large caption reading 'It's good to be different.'

And then there are the candles! This most certainly was a first for us and we wondered whether this was part school and part holistic retreat. Large (glass-encased) scented candles, wafting scents of vanilla or lavender, flickered on teachers' desks in all classrooms bar the ones with the youngest pupils. The result was a calm, almost hypnotic ambience, 'the antithesis of what some students get at home,' the head told us. We even heard classical music (from Schindler's List) emanate from the year 6 classroom as they were in deep discussion about their current literature book. As Ofsted remarked, 'Immersion in the plays of Shakespeare and high quality literature, such as Lord of the Flies, has instilled in pupils a love of literature and has enabled them to reflect with confidence.'

No doubt the school's recruitment policy has played some part in its outstanding achievement. Many teachers are recruited straight from university and stay for a few years before moving on, possibly to jobs outside London where they can more easily afford a home. 'Some of them are very talented, they are enthusiastic and idealistic..they want to teach in this type of environment – even if sometimes they don't stop for very long.' It is now a teaching school and can train its own. Sellens attributes the quality of what is afforded to pupils to his skilled and deft team and especially the deputy Lindsay Johnson, who exudes gravitas and energy. She has worked at the school for 20 years and is, in Sellens' words, 'the lynchpin of the school's success.'

The head told us it is important to him that all students look exactly the same and 'exquisite in their uniform, so there is no way of telling their background'

We were taken on a tour of the school by six well-mannered, extremely articulate and very lovely pupils of varying ages, who each in turn solemnly shook our hands, looked us directly in the eye and said 'welcome to Thomas Jones primary school.' This editor couldn't have felt more revered if she were the Duchess of Cambridge. Pupils were as pristinely turned out as the school they inhabited. Hairclips and bobbles matched their uniform and we were hard pushed to find a strand of anything out of place. The head told us it is extremely important to him that all students look exactly the same and 'exquisite in their uniform, so there is no way of telling their background.' Those from deprived backgrounds can get help with the cost of the uniform.

Future plans for the school include a beehive, which the school says is its modest way of

This is a head who walks into assembly eating a bowl of porridge and banana extolling the virtues of a healthy breakfast, who ditches the traditional end of year musical, opting instead for Under Milk Wood

contributing to the eco-system and 'teaching the pupils to care for something.' This will add to the existing mini outdoor nature reserve set amongst pretty, manicured gardens and (slightly sparse) play areas. Indeed, dare we say it, our one criticism of the school would be the lack of outdoor facilities (although we appreciate this is an inner city school) or much time given over to sports, which seems to be a criticism echoed by a couple of parents we spoke to. One told us: 'There's not much in the way of drama or sports at this school which is probably indicative of most state schools nowadays. Sadly, when schools are monitored so closely, something has to give.' However, netball, football and athletics teams, training after school, sometimes with professional coaches, have enjoyed significant successes in borough leagues in recent years.

Ofsted – which regularly rates the school as outstanding – has praised it for high aspirations: 'Year 6 pupils don white coats for science lessons and eagerly respond to the school's expectation that they are preparing for university.' We also noticed that pupils called their smart navy blue school bags their 'briefcases' and year 6 pupils are expected to pick up a daily newspaper, because as one former student told us, 'pupils need to experience language they don't normally use.' It is not unusual, according to Mr Sellens, to hear the children talking about going to university or becoming barristers or doctors when they leave school.

Everything about this school is aspirational. You won't find a 'home corner' filled with dolls, cookers or microwaves in the gorgeous and colourful nursery. Instead there is a medical corner filled with realistic medical apparatus and costumes. Similarly, we loved the weekly interchangeable corner in reception which encouraged playing various professional roles such as doctor or teacher. It has a gold healthy schools award and year 4 children were recently treated to a trip to a Jamie Oliver restaurant and have been learning how to make sushi wraps using healthy ingredients – and fish fingers and baked beans are banned from the school menu because 'we want to afford them food they wouldn't get at home.'

Thomas's Fulham

Hugon Road, London SW6 3ES

020 7751 8200 | fulham@thomas-s.co.uk | thomas-s.co.uk

Independent	Pupils: 429
Ages: 4-11	Fees: £13,770 – £20,016 pa

Linked schools: Thomas's Kensington, 401; For Thomas's Battersea and Thomas's Clapham, see *The Good Schools Guide London South*

Headmistress: Annette Dobson, 40s, opened the school in 2005. A slightly low key dresser with a laugh that reaches her eyes, one only has to look at her feet to see that snappy shoes and clear-headed dedication are not the sole preserve of Theresa May. Wanting to be a teacher from the get-go (maybe influenced by her mother's voice teaching in an adjacent classroom), she swam into the professional A stream by graduating from Homerton College, Cambridge. After a spell at North Bridge House, she crossed London to Thomas's Clapham, heading up the lower school, collecting a postgraduate degree and completing a study in phonics.

Thoroughly aware of the need to keep abreast of the numerous practical and technological changes in her world, she still keeps her feet firmly in the playground by maintaining a close, personal involvement with each child. On Monday mornings she stands by the door and shakes them all by the hand and, far more amazingly, remembers their names, a nice touch that illustrates the emphasis she puts on manners as well as her commitment to approaching her charges as individuals. Genuinely passionate about improving her school, she even spent her sabbatical visiting educational establishments around the world, although luckily she shows her human side by admitting to having eaten pretty well along the way.

Entrance: At 4, a non-academic assessment takes place in January for September entry. Eleven years of experience makes the head fairly certain about the kind of child that would or would not relish the opportunity of beginning their education here. She is tactful but clear that it is potential team players as well as bright individuals she is looking out for. There is a strong sibling policy (on average about half the slots go to siblings), which usually leaves a minimum of two children applying for each remaining place. Parents can feel very pressurised; one observer said that a 'parent was completely manic to get child in', but the process is fair with advance information for parents, and one

child came out saying, 'I like this big school'. Places do become available further up the school, mainly due to the constant whirling merry-go-round that lands London parents anywhere from Manhattan to Moscow at the drop of a city chapeau. At this stage, children spend half a day at the school to make sure they will fit in and also need a letter from their previous school.

Exit: As you would expect from such a professional outfit, detailed practical information and knowledgeable help on the which, when and how of senior schools is handed out to help parents navigate this educational minefield. In 2018, roughly half the pupils moved to Thomas's Clapham or Battersea to prepare for the 13+. Others to a variety of schools, including King's College School, Putney High, Wycombe Abbey, Emanuel, Queen's Gate, St Mary's Calne, Whitgift.

> *One commented that her child, coming into the school with zero skills, did 'really well in her first year'*

Scholarships are won but head confirms that there are not many available at this stage, and this is not an academic hothouse, a point echoed by one parent who felt that a very clever child might not get as far here as in a more competitive environment. Parents seem pleased with the advice given on senior schools and the head's statement that they 'aim to work in tandem with parents to find the best fit for a pupil' is backed up by the results.

Remarks: This youngest outpost of Thomas's private empire has settled in a handsome Victorian school building, gazing out over the top of a smart new asphalt athletics field, at the green park beyond. Nineteenth century it may be, but with sparkling two-tone brick, huge windows and a tidy colour-coded interior, this is definitely not a modern version of Dotheboys Hall and there is absolutely no air of laissez-aller neglect: in fact the energy and enthusiasm of the school is almost instantly apparent.

With walls covered in pictures from an exceptionally imaginative art department housed in a large beamed outbuilding and neat, well-conceived timetables for music and games on the stairs, the atmosphere is vibrant. Happy, eager children look you straight in the eye and teachers appear to be enjoying themselves as much as their pupils. Judging by the cheerful munching of buns at break and excellent reports from the head girl, the food served on primary coloured plates (matching the house colours) keeps the energy levels up through a satisfyingly full school day.

All children, including those whose idea of art is to splash a lot of paint about (actively encouraged last year by a gigantic Jackson Pollock themed bonanza) can learn the fun to be had out of being creative

Particular praise is handed out by parents of reception teachers, one commenting that her child coming into the school with zero skills did 'really well in her first year' and others saying that almost all the class are pretty independent, at least at the laces tying end of the scale, by the end of the year. All the way up reading is heavily encouraged, with pupils taking home a daily diary including a book page that parents have to sign off. A library complete with cheerful librarian is nestled under the roof. Maths is taught imaginatively, not just as learning numbers but as a link to other subjects, and science appears to be popular, apparently due to explosion experiments, luckily under control in two purpose-built labs. French is introduced in reception and croissants and conversation feature in a biennial French day in Fulham and a week's trip to France for year 6. History and geography are both taught with the emphasis on connections to the outside world, and with classics added in years 5 and 6, round out the rest of the curriculum. Like most schools with an ecumenical viewpoint, RE is taught from a moral guideline and historical angle.

The arts – particularly music and drama – form a central part of life, over half the children learn an instrument and nearly three-quarters sing in a choir. Very popular plays are put on in the school's own theatre by all year groups, and after-school or lunch time clubs encourage would-be gymnasts, thespians, musicians and ballet dancers to go further and take external exams, such as LAMDA and the Royal Ballet School. All children, including those whose idea of art is to splash a lot of paint about (actively encouraged last year by a gigantic Jackson Pollock themed bonanza) are able to learn the fun that can be had out of being creative.

Despite the practical problems of operating on a small campus set in bricked over West London, the head (a fresh air fiend) runs the full mile to bring the outdoors into the pupil's daily routine. Little ones do PE and ballet, in the lower school they have general games and later on they can pick from a wide offering of conventional single sex sports. Some take place in the park opposite, which is regularly filled with small people jauntily dressed in the school's red and blue uniform complete with stripey socks. Otherwise they walk or are bussed to nearby facilities, a necessary evil for London schools and which makes the head look longingly at the space available to her peers in the country. Despite the logistical problems, there is enthusiasm all round about games, both competitive and recreational, and particular pleasure when a team beats other schools in the group. Sporty children can choose further exposure by joining popular extracurricular clubs for gym or judo, golf or tennis, while swimming, sailing and kayaking are available if they want to get wet. Classroom themes regularly incorporate outside expeditions, both in London and further afield, often with the help of the Exploration Society to give them a more adventurous time away from the tarmac. Recently launched 'Thomas's Outdoors Programme', includes week-long visits in Lent term for year 5 and 6 children from all the schools to Thomas's Daheim, school's new 'mountain outpost' in Upper Austria.

Takes an early warning approach, starting in reception, to spotting any learning problems, which are jumped on quickly by full-time staff, backed up by specialist help from the outside. The head, who used to teach in this field, reckons that it is part of her job – 'we love off-piste children here, they are so often better at problem solving' – to help find the solution to each child's difficulties. Equally, she feels that tutors should only be employed to mend a particular gap in the wall rather than act as structural engineers, a policy which can be hard to get across in a city full of aspirational parents. Rules clearly exist but are wisely enough applied to make for few confrontations and the vice-head is on standby to have words with the inevitable, occasional small child trying it on. All the last year are encouraged to take a responsible role and show particular pride in overseeing the playground, although they sensibly admitted that they grabbed a teacher pretty quickly if anyone looked in need of first aid.

Twenty-first century technology connects parents, described as cosmopolitan, via a Twitter feed, and a newly updated portal allows them to follow their child's every move. Most of the content is popular (particularly the photographs), but one parent remarked that she preferred talking to the teacher rather than looking at her boy's exploits on an iPad. The head, however, convincingly counters this by saying that she will never allow face-to-face contact between teachers and parents to be lost. In another minor quibble a mother said that she was probably old fashioned but found receiving online reports irritating, as she likes to keep the real thing. An unsurprisingly lively PTA backs up the school and

works its socks off to raise money for charity with the Bake Sale streaking home in the popularity stakes. Thomas's ethos to 'give not take' seems to have sunk in well as children often donate a book to the library to mark their birthdays and sometimes turn up with money for charity that they have raised off their own bat.

Promoting the Thomas's motto Be Kind quite so prominently might have backfired, but the evidence of the success of the strategy is everywhere. From the top ('fabulous, fantastic head') to the bottom (smiley children leaving the assessment clutching balloons), this is a school that really does succeed in doing what it says on the shiny tin.

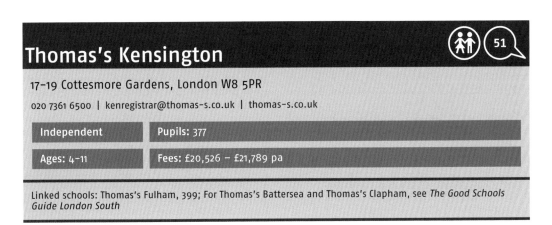

Thomas's Kensington

17-19 Cottesmore Gardens, London W8 5PR

020 7361 6500 | kenregistrar@thomas-s.co.uk | thomas-s.co.uk

Independent	Pupils: 377
Ages: 4-11	Fees: £20,526 – £21,789 pa

Linked schools: Thomas's Fulham, 399; For Thomas's Battersea and Thomas's Clapham, see *The Good Schools Guide London South*

Headmistress: Since 2012, Jo Ebner BEd MA PG Dip Couns Cert FT NPQH (late 40s), previously head of the Royal School, Hampstead (now absorbed by North Bridge House and owned by Cognita); 'I got the school to a place where it was worth buying,' she says. Educated at North London Collegiate (where both her mother and her daughters were at school too) and Homerton, Cambridge, she also trained at the Tavistock Clinic as a school counsellor and completed her MA at the Institute of Education, London. Tall and statuesque, Miss Ebner has long brown, lustrous hair, is highly emotionally intelligent, with a self-deprecating sense of humour. She has three children – now in or approaching their 20s – and shares her comfortable office with her adoring golden retriever, Maddie.

Her first teaching job was at Primrose Hill primary school ('from the age of 7, I was determined to be a teacher,' she avers). She set up the first counselling service when she was at South Hampstead High School. She also taught at a primary school in Willesden and at the North West London Jewish Day school as well as a successful stint as deputy head of The Hall junior school in Hampstead. A deeply committed educationalist, she is heavily involved with the GSA (Girls' Schools Association),

serves as a governor of several schools, including St Mary's Ascot, and has written several articles on parenting.

One of the first things Miss Ebner did here was to remove the position of lower school head. She is very much in charge of the whole school. While she operates an open door policy and parents praise her direct approach when dealing one to one, her reputation at the moment is that she can be distant, 'certainly not cuddly,' observed one, but 'very cheerful, involved and approachable,' said another. She teaches religious studies to year 2, and set up a mindfulness course for parents, staff and pupils – 'it is really helpful in the run up to exams,' she confides. She regards communication as being vital, 'the bottom line, as with any relationship, is that it's about trust.' A transparent approach will nip things in the bud so she makes herself available – parents can drop in to discuss any issues with her. However, she doesn't cosy up to them – avoiding the dinner party circuit so that she can remain objective about what is in the best interests of their children.

Passionate about investing in her staff and striving for the highest quality of teaching, whether through further professional development or promotion, she is regarded by parents as having made shrewd recruitments as well as keeping good teachers and teaching assistants who mature and develop under her leadership. Her teachers value her big picture approach to their futures and the encouragement she gives for them to seize opportunities. She set up a bespoke masters programme for all Thomas's staff, in conjunction with Roehampton University. At the time of our visit a few teachers doing this masters programme were enthusing about their research on, eg, the pros and cons of setting.

Entrance: Three classes of 20 (split 50:50 boys and girls), so in theory, 60 places at reception. However siblings take priority (though will only take siblings they think will thrive) so you should expect only about half that number of places. Over 100 tinies are interviewed the year before entrance. They are not looking for children who have been tutored and prepped but who are adaptable, willing to get stuck in and have plenty of initiative. The pace is fast here and your child is likely to have a number of different teachers during a typical day. Register at birth to be sure that you get on a list for assessment. Once the list reaches 180 it will close and your only chance will be a waiting list place, currently limited to 50 names. Occasional places rarely arise but there are formal assessments at 7+ and 8+, where school will consider applications from up to 10 children for each of years 3 and 4. School only ever offers a couple of places at this stage.

Children here are fizzing with energy that a highly dedicated team of teachers channels very successfully. Thomas's kids are exuberant, confident and very busy

Exit: There is an option to continue to Thomas's Battersea from 11 to 13 and about a third choose to do this, mostly boys, and girls who are going down the boarding route – automatic transfer, subject to the head's recommendation. Some of these have been successful at the pre-test during year 6 and are armed with offers from top 13+ schools from King's Wimbledon and St Paul's to Eton and Winchester. Lots of help and preparation to ensure the transition is smooth, as despite being part of the Thomas's group, they are different schools with a different make up and transition isn't necessarily seamless. Battersea teachers come to the school to meet the children who are moving, and a number of events are organised to help with integration, from games in the park to cupcake decorating, as well as coffee mornings and drinks parties for the parents.

To one child's (and his father's) enormous delight, one week the mystery reader was his grandfather reading via Skype from the USA

Otherwise a range of schools as one would expect as there is a broad range of ability here. Latymer Upper and Godolphin & Latymer currently very popular, followed by The American School, Francis Holland SW1, Queen's Gate and St Paul's boys and girls. A cluster of academic scholarships as well as the odd music and drama scholarship each year.

Miss Ebner makes it clear that the school does not prepare pupils for 7/8+. If you want your son to apply to St Paul's Juniors, Westminster Under etc, you're on your own – the school will not do any extra preparation. Boys do still occasionally leave at 7 or 8 to go to these schools – it's not impossible – but it is not something the school will actively encourage.

Remarks: A stimulating, creative but also nurturing school in a very fashionable corner of London, Thomas's Kensington has a cosmopolitan flavour to it without being flashy or ostentatious. Children here are privileged but not spoilt, and fizzing with energy that a highly dedicated team of teachers channels very successfully. Thomas's kids are exuberant, confident and very, very busy. Lots of drama perhaps contributes to their looking you in the eye and explaining things with an articulate awareness that belies their young age.

Situated on three sites in a leafy, salubrious triangle of elegant properties at the south west corner of Hyde Park, Thomas's Kensington was the first school in the Thomas's quadrumvirate (the others are Clapham, Battersea and Fulham). Founded by Joanna and David Thomas in the early '70s and the family members are still the proprietors. Their two sons, Ben and Tobyn, are heavily involved as joint principals. Joanna and David, who have a flat above the junior section of the school in Victoria Road, are still very present around the school. The involvement of such a charismatic family and their wholehearted dedication to the place gives it a distinctive, family feel. Joanna and David Thomas are highly respected among the parents who generously donate to the CAIRN trust, a charity they set up to educate children in Nepal.

All three buildings are elegant, spacious and well looked after. Reception children enter the junior section on Victoria Road thorough a little passageway and wooden gate into a secluded garden and play area. Lots of scooters and bikes parked inside the black wrought iron gates of the pale blue painted Georgian mansion. Most kids live close enough to walk and scoot so there is a refreshing lack of Chelsea tractors at drop off. Lots of fresh air for all; the little ones are split into small groups from each class at playtime and spill out into the little Astroturf courtyard between the reception classrooms. This is just one example of how the classes are mixed up here so that friendships can be refreshingly fluid betwixt classes. From year 1 they walk 10 minutes to Kensington Gardens for fresh air and exercise.

School is mixed ability – assessments for entry are not primarily focused on any kind of academic prowess. This, and the tendency to take siblings, makes for a broad range. Lots of focus on reading. Children are listened to four times a week and a 'mystery reader' regularly turns up at school. To one child's (and his father's) enormous delight one week the mystery reader was his grandfather reading via Skype from the USA. Any difficulties are picked up quickly by class teachers and any special educational need is coordinated by the SENCo and her team. Parents praise the school's responsiveness when support is required, and an occupational therapist as well as a speech and language therapist come regularly into school. A number of children go to the Kensington Dyslexia Teaching Centre (just around the corner). Controversially, school made the decision to teach mixed ability maths and English groups all through the school until year 5. The decision was made partly as a result of the masters research that one of the teachers is doing at Roehampton. The evidence apparently suggests that setting is not beneficial to either the less or the more able students. A number of parents of able mathematicians are not supportive, parents of children who are not at the top of the game are more open to the idea. School says the research is still ongoing. French is setted – some strong French speakers in the school. Spanish and German offered as after-school clubs (parents recently requested Italian, so this is to be introduced). Latin taster in year 4 and then taught as part of the curriculum in years 5 and 6.

The creative and performing arts and sport are all given a lot of emphasis here and the school positively hums with activity beyond the classroom. Thomas's children stand out as being sparky and articulate, and the extensive drama and dance provision must play some part in this. All children, girls and boys, do ballet during their lower school years. Chelsea Ballet comes to the school to teach pupils once a week. Each year group puts on a large-scale production in the theatre. We watched year 4's fabulous production of Aladdin – worthy of any professional production, complete with tiered seating and first class lighting as well as stunning costumes. Watched by parents, staff and pupils, but what was particularly noticeable was the warm support of fellow pupils, one year 6 boy spontaneously rising to his feet to make a congratulatory speech at the end of the show. Year 6 was due to perform Arabian Nights at Imperial College. Music also flourishes – everyone given a violin to learn in years 1 and 2. A number of groups and choirs to participate in, including a full orchestra and a chapel choir. Concerts are performed at the Cadogan Hall as well as on site. Lots of sporting fixtures – primarily against the other Thomas's schools, but others too, eg Fulham Prep. Main sports – netball, hockey and rounders for the girls, football and cricket for the boys, plus tennis for both in the summer term. Parents praise the inclusive approach – children are encouraged in music and athletics, for example, even though they might not be showing a particular talent.

We watched year 4's fabulous production of Aladdin – worthy of any professional production, complete with tiered seating and first class lighting

Even more impressive than the wealth of opportunity within the school is how much energy is put into a community spirit and to giving something back. From the CAIRN charity – Joanna and David Thomas's baby – supporting children in schools in Nepal, to various outreach programmes in local state schools, children here are busy raising money or sharing resources and thereby instilling and being instilled with a sense of public responsibility, generosity and kindness. Independent-state school partnerships have been established eg providing and teaching Latin in local state schools, collaboration between orchestras and choirs, and whole school community days when children from each year group carry out various projects in the community from reading to local nurseries to art, drama and music productions. The TSF (Thomas's Schools Foundation) is focused on working with local state schools, to widen educational opportunity and to provide bursaries. Joanna and David, together with Ben and Tobyn, are all actively involved in leading the whole school community to support the Foundation.

A remarkably cohesive and vibrant school. Bubbly children that are nevertheless polite and well behaved; 'It can be noisy,' acknowledged one parent, 'but with laughter not screaming.' Privileged, yes, but spoilt, absolutely not. These children are developing a strong sense of social responsibility and couldn't be better prepared for the complex global environment they are growing up into.

Westminster Tutors

86 Old Brompton Road, London SW7 3LQ

020 7584 1288 | info@westminstertutors.co.uk | westminstertutors.co.uk

Independent	Pupils: 45; sixth form: 40
Ages: 14-99	Fees: £5,500 – £25,500 pa

Head: Since 2007, Virginia Maguire BA MA MLitt (40s). Moved on from her previous role as director of studies at David Game College (proprietors of Westminster Tutors) to running this tiny jewel in the crown of his group of tutorial colleges. She spent five years lecturing at a Thai university, 'learning that there are completely different ways of perceiving the world around us', which may account for her ease with the varied nationalities of the pupils in her charge. Her presence is notable in this educational microcosm, not just because of the proximity of her office but also because of the reaction of her charges. She may feel particularly at home because her mother was a pupil, but whatever the reason, she is obviously capable and respected. When not at her desk, she is a keen open water swimmer but 'definitely not of the Channel kind'.

Academic matters: There is a maximum capacity of 45 students of which, in any given year, there are likely to be about five doing GCSEs (including retakes), about 20 taking A levels and 15-20 doing A level retakes or Pre-U studies. Occasionally, they enrol people in their 20s who need to take different or extra qualifications for career or further study.

Occasionally the students are taught in a group (three maximum) if their target levels are the same, but almost all the teaching is one-to-one. They offer a wide range of subjects from classical Greek to physics and psychology and the head prides herself on being able to cater for obscure requests. For the more obvious subjects she has a pool of tutors and personally makes the match between pupil and teacher. One parent asked if the tutor could be changed if the relationship didn't work and believed it when she was told that it wouldn't be a problem, although luckily the situation never arose.

The school may be diminutive in terms of pupil numbers but in the quality of its staff it rates as a Titan. The teachers tend to be stars in their fields with a level of letters after their names that would make most of their profession blush. Head recruits mainly by word of mouth and from direct applications, mixing very high-powered people close to retirement or only wanting to work part-time with younger artists, musicians, writers and PhD candidates. The only rule is that they must have a 2:1 or first in their first degree; however this year, 40 per cent have Oxbridge degrees, 70 per cent masters and 35 per cent already have PhDs. The average period that they work here is three or four years but they often come back at different points in their careers.

Each student has an individual timetable and the system is immensely flexible, making it a logistics nightmare for the smiley, hugely competent college secretary, who has been struggling with spreadsheets for over 10 years. The students all praised the teaching and describe the tutors as being 'really on top of it' and one parent described it as 'brilliant across the board, all A*s'. Parents liked the 'old-fashioned, comprehensive reports that offer an accurate assessment with no false promises' and felt 'confident that we know where we are'. A pupil agreed that the report was fair and highlighted the areas where she needed to progress. One girl described a teacher as 'she knows what she's doing' (presumably a relief to her parents..) and other students talked about great personal attention such as being emailed in the holidays if they voiced a worry.

> *Each student has an individual timetable and the system is immensely flexible*

They efficiently combat the lure of Xbox and Netflix by constant communication with parents so that even potentially wayward students switch from sci-fi movies to science homework. GCSE pupils have homework diaries and if necessary A level students have study slots built into their timetables. The net result of this highly individual (in every sense) and carefully monitored approach is results – 36 per cent A*/As and 78 per cent A*-B grades at A level in 2018 – that exceed those of their competitors in the tutorial field and are impressive by any measure. Recently rated outstanding in all categories by Ofsted.

Games, options, the arts: Bearing in mind that the school is above a row of shops in central London with no outside space and that the 40 odd students are not all here on a daily basis, it will not come as a surprise that sports do not feature as a significant part of the curriculum. There is a circuit training session once a week but almost all other outdoor activities are organised by the parents or the children themselves, with a staff versus students bowling outing as the only competitive event that we found. When it comes to options and the arts, the school is much better placed as all art, music, English and humanities students have tutorial guides who often include lessons in the real world of art galleries, concerts and stage performances.

Background and atmosphere: Although it has the legal status of a school and has to abide by the same rules as its much larger competitors, the head is happy that there is not a 'schooly atmosphere'. This is hardly surprising given the nature and appearance of its founder. Miss Freeston inhabited a smoke-filled den in Victoria, giving the distinct impression that there might be a bed hidden under either the piles of books launching an attack on the ceiling or the ancient, smelly dogs on the hairy sofa. You might have thought she was just a parody of a mid-20th century female academic, particularly as she always wore a mid-calf, much sat in tweed skirt and layers of doubtful moth-eaten cardigans. However, you would have been foolish to underestimate her ability to understand people as well as texts. The exterior may have presented the unmistakable combination of erudition and dottiness, but under the holey woollens was a sensitive, thoughtful woman with a formidable understanding of bright, if lost, teenage girls. It was for this reason as much as her belief in the value of education that she started Westminster Tutors in 1934.

The school has kept the same ethos and atmosphere despite its move to South Kensington and the current building is still more of a rabbit warren than a conventional educational space. It might not impress parents or students looking for a polished, modern environment and it is not for teenagers needing wide open spaces. It is quite clear that the money goes on the staff and not on the classrooms: for instance, chemistry experiments take place in a galley kitchen. This slightly unusual classroom surprisingly passed an inspection from the A level boards with flying colours and without any culinary or chemical disasters. Orchids, a guitar and a chess set might not be what you expect in a tiny maths classroom but you probably would not expect a teacher who is also finishing a doctorate, either.

Pastoral care, well-being and discipline: The head appears to have Miss Freeston's understanding of the young but she is a thoroughly modern woman and the pastoral care is described by Ofsted as excellent in 'spiritual, moral, social and cultural' areas. A parent talked of the head as being 'good at keeping an eye' and several parents remarked on the quick response they received if they contacted the school. The only hard and fast rules are attendance and safety, both of which are seldom a problem. The head reserves the right not to enter students for exams but says that the threat has always been sufficient so far. The only odd rule that she is enforcing at the moment is banning them from sitting on the strange red sofa outside the café opposite, presumably due to the smokey nature of its usual occupants.

The teachers tend to be stars in their fields with letters after their names that would make most of their profession blush. Head recruits mainly by word of mouth

There is an elected head boy and head girl but they admit that their duties are mainly social, including that 'we have enough milk for tea'.

Pupils and parents: Over 50 per cent of the enrolments are by word of mouth, including a large number of alumni who want their children to have the same experience. A parent told us that they had chosen the school over similar options because the alternatives felt like 'crammers and were run on military lines'. He also said that he was 'happy coming into a place covered in modern art, and it just felt right'.

The intake tends to come from a mixture of top public schools and London state schools with a fair sprinkling from abroad as the transition can be handled more easily in an operation where teaching provision is adaptable. One student told us that it suited her better than her previous school because 'you can't just hide at the back'.

There is no obvious archetypal parent although most tend to be successful in their fields or professions. It can be an option for parents of fairly modest means as some pupils only need to attend for a year to get back on track or be helped into a top university.

Entrance: This is a totally non-selective school but the majority of the intake are above average academically. They may have found it difficult to succeed in the competitive world of a large, hothouse London day school or have come from another educational system. The head interviews parents and potential students and considers whether they would be suited to this very individual environment as well as their previous academic performance. They do not take students who have been expelled for serious breaches but are sympathetic to anyone who might have struggled to stay afloat in a larger pond.

Exit: The head tries to give very personalised university and career advice and is proud that she publishes the destinations in full rather than just choosing the highlights. In 2018 71 per cent went to Russell Group or Ivy League universities, including one to Oxford. The majority of people choose the school because they want to make a successful transition from A levels to a top university but this is not always the case, and recently one student left to do a BTec in mechanical engineering and one to

a retail apprenticeship because it was agreed that this was a better route for them. Parents agree that they are 'on the money' about university choices and come up with good suggestions to add to their children's ideas.

Money matters: Inevitably not a cheap option but compared to alternatives with larger classes it offers value for money.

Remarks: Students are shoehorned into tiny classrooms, reminiscent of the dormouse being stuffed into the teapot at the Mad Hatter's Tea Party and there is definitely an element of the unusual in the workings of this place but there is also an academic wizard at play here. The head may hanker after a swimming pool but the students lack for nothing in the level of teaching or encouragement in learning how to learn.

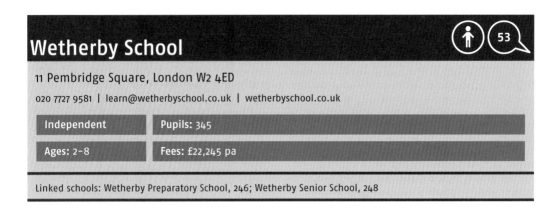

Wetherby School

53

11 Pembridge Square, London W2 4ED

020 7727 9581 | learn@wetherbyschool.co.uk | wetherbyschool.co.uk

Independent	Pupils: 345
Ages: 2–8	Fees: £22,245 pa

Linked schools: Wetherby Preparatory School, 246; Wetherby Senior School, 248

Head: Since 2009, Mark Snell BA PGCE (mid 40s). Educated at Eastbourne College, University of Westminster (a degree in business studies) and Brighton University, where he gained his teaching qualification. His first job was at Eaton House the Manor. Utterly down to earth, direct, no nonsense and unpretentious (although one parent observed that his 'oikishness verges on the pretentious given his background'). With his buzz cut hair style and his gruff manner, Mr Snell is so robust and hearty he could pass for the manager of a medium sized football club. He is also deeply committed and completely devoted to the boys and their needs. 'I enjoy life and don't give a stuff what anyone thinks of me,' he says. Most parents love him ('he still makes time to for me to discuss my son even though he's no longer at the school') though a few dissenters bemoan his encouragement of the alpha in these already uber alpha boys.

Deputy for two years before taking over as head, he is completely au fait with the ethos of the place and is hugely respected by his fellow Alpha

Plus heads. ('Nick Baker is a great bloke,' he says. Nick Baker – head of Wetherby Prep – thinks the same of Mark Snell, though he put it slightly differently.) Previously head of maths at King's College Wimbledon, and prior to that he taught at Westminster Under where, he says, he really cut his teeth and learnt a lot of what he knows now ('though I'm thick as two short planks,' he repeatedly assured us). Despite his 'street' manner, he was born into prep school aristocracy and teaching is very much in the blood. He was brought up in a south coast prep school with his three siblings. His father inherited and ran Mowden School near Brighton (now a prep school to Lancing College), and the wider family are involved with Ludgrove Prep School (in Berkshire). His wife also teaches ('though she is much cleverer than me'). They have a son and a daughter, both school age.

His subject is maths, and though he kept telling us how dim he is, he had us stumped on more than one occasion as so many of his explanations were put in arithmetic form and he relishes statistics.

He really knows each individual and can give informed advice on where next. 'If parents choose not to listen, that's fine,' he says; 'that's their prerogative, but I know the schools, understand the assessment data'

Teaches maths to years 3 and 2, and loves it, he says. An added advantage is that he really knows each individual and can give informed advice on where next. 'If parents choose not to listen, that's fine,' he says; 'that's their prerogative, but I know the schools, understand the assessment data, and I know the boys.' Very accessible – to the boys especially, but to parents too. Many spoke of their complete confidence in him, his judgment, and his recruitment of teachers ('you feel confident that he will never employ a duff,' enthused one parent). A loyal Seagulls fan, his faux wood panelled study (a present from parents, along with most of the colourful decorations) has several Brighton and Hove flags and memorabilia and is brimming with evidence of his personality and the affection families past and present have for him.

Entrance: Non-selective. Register the month your baby is born, and ideally the day he is born. If you try to register any later than when your baby is 3 months old, you're too late. School gets approximately 35 applications a month – or about 360 a year for 88 places (four classes in each year group). Staggered entry by the month to avoid a preponderance of December (say) babies. You only get to see round the school if you are going to be offered a definite place. If you are on the waiting list there is still hope, but not a lot. Parents feel they have a golden ticket if their son gets a place here and are unlikely to turn it down for anything other than 'act of God'. Lots of international families and a number of children speak more than one language at home, but not much EAL support needed, as most arrive here fluent in English. No longer as local as it once was, parents prepared to travel far for the first class education they feel their son will get here.

Exit: High numbers to the most academic prep schools. In recent years as many as 40 per cent to Westminster Under, Sussex House and St Paul's Juniors. Increasing numbers, currently 45 per cent, to Wetherby Prep, where entrance is automatic and the standards are rising, so why go through the stress of exams? The other 15 per cent elsewhere – eg locally to King's College Junior School

and Latymer Prep or to board at Summer Fields, Caldicott or The Dragon.

Remarks: The Wetherby brand is currently putting even Balenciaga in the shade. It is hard to find anyone, past, present or potential parent, who doesn't positively glow about the school. They single out the quality of the teaching – not only does Mr Snell recruit excellent teachers but he motivates them and makes them go the extra mile. Homework is 'innovative and thorough'. Communication with parents is 'exceptional', plus the 'school really understand boys and how to educate them.'

Lots of competitions and games inside the classroom as well as out. Learning here is fun, whether it's a project on the Romans or a fabulous end of year party, which incorporates an ice cream van and a bouncy castle. School is lucky enough to be able use the square opposite and the boys get lots of fresh air and exercise during breaks throughout the day. Reception and nursery children have their own outside playground, complete with springy tarmac and climbing wall, which is in constant use. On top of this they have several gym and swimming lessons (at Kensington Leisure Centre), as well as sport (in Hyde Park and Westway) in the afternoons. Lots of football and tag rugby in the winter, cricket in the summer. Plenty of fixtures against other schools, in swimming as well as field sports, and an annual sports day at the Wetherby sports grounds – at the Park Club in Acton. Dads' and boys' Saturday morning football is hugely popular, as are chess club, martial arts club, arts and crafts and drama. The choice of clubs is huge, from chess and cookery to Lego and French.

Learning here is fun, whether it's a project on the Romans or a fabulous end of year party, which incorporates an ice cream van and a bouncy castle

Plenty of music too – a choir in each of years 1, 2 and 3 as well as the wonderful Wetherby singers, created for those who couldn't make it into the choir but still love to sing. 'They make a terrible noise,' growled Mr Snell, 'but parents love it.' More than half the school learns an instrument – peripatetic teachers for guitar, violin and piano. There are instrumental concerts at the end of each term in St Matthew's church up the road as well as impromptu recitals in the hall. Drama part of the timetable as well as offered as a club. There is a performance at the end of each term, and the year 3s perform a major production (in recent years Peter Pan and The Jungle Book) at the Tabernacle Theatre.

Despite being non-selective the pace is fast here. Boys are expected to work hard right from the word go. We saw boys as young as 3 and 4 reading and writing (beautifully). Standards are high and everyone is aspirational – teachers, head and parents alike. Children who need support are usually identified early – good systems in place for spotting and diagnosing any difficulties. What is done about it next depends on the level of support required. At the more severe end – boys with moderate learning difficulties – many parents choose to take them to Emerson House in Shepherd's Bush to get that support. Others are taken out in groups for extra support – it could be the top, middle or bottom group in maths or English; others may have one-to-one support lessons. School employs one full-time and one other teacher who has half her timetable, dedicated to learning support.

There are 22 boys in each class, and they get lots of attention. Ratio of pupils to teacher (or teaching assistant) is high – more than one teaching assistant in every class room as well a lot of floating teachers. Lots of differentiation – and boys taught according to academic capability not according to syllabus. 'We teach them when they're ready to learn'. Only in the final year, year 3, are they grouped according to ability, in maths, English and reasoning. Relatively high number of male teachers (14) unusual for this age group. 'We can attract a different kind of teacher – Alpha Plus pays very well, especially at this level, and we rarely lose anyone to another school,' says Snell. Although they couldn't fault the education in the classroom, some parents boldly suggested that more attention could be paid to the importance of moral values. The idea of being 'nice' to each other, so focused on in girls' schools, is missing here, they said. These are alpha boys with alpha parents and, parents observe, there is a limited public spiritedness where writing cheques replaces baking cakes.

School is currently expanding up to 360 pupils. The new building in Pembridge Villas, once the site of Chepstow House, is already being used for reception and Little Wetherby (the nursery). New kid on the block is another pre-prep, Wetherby Kensington. Despite an increase in the number of places, we doubt there will be less pressure on them. A busy, successful, well-run, well-resourced school, full of happy, spirited boys. For as long as this formula remains the same Wetherby is likely to remain the brand parents want.

West

Brent
Ealing
Harrow
Hillingdon
Hounslow
Richmond-upon-Thames

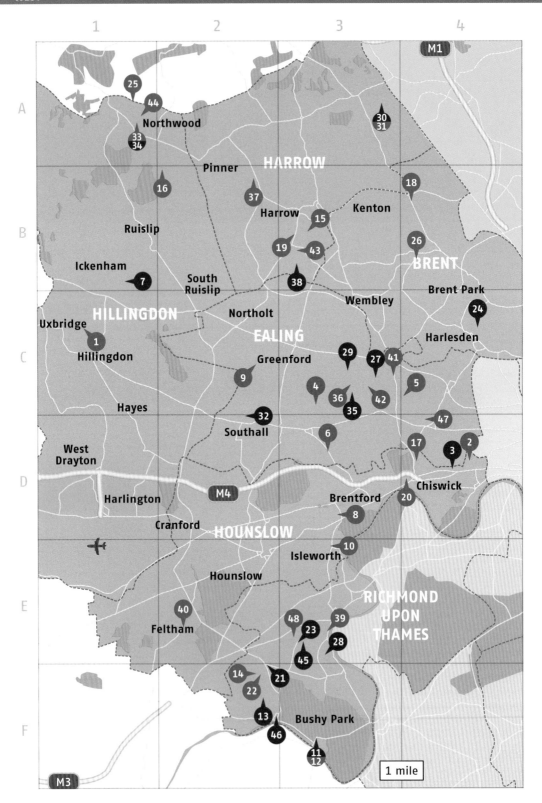

M1

25

44

Northwood

33
34

Pinner

HARROW

30
31

16

37

Harrow

15

Kenton

18

B

Ruislip

19

43

26

BRENT

Ickenham

South
Ruislip

38

Wembley

Brent Park

7

HILLINGDON

Northolt

24

Uxbridge

EALING

Harlesden

1

Greenford

29

27

41

C

Hillingdon

9

4

5

Hayes

36

42

32

35

Southall

6

47

West
Drayton

17

2

3

D

Harlington

M4

Brentford

20

Chiswick

8

Cranford

HOUNSLOW

10

Isleworth

Hounslow

RICHMOND
UPON
THAMES

40

48

39

E

Feltham

23

28

45

14

21

22

13

Bushy Park

46

11
12

F

1 mile

M3

WEST

West London and its state schools

Brent

Gritty Brent with its huge ethnic mix is largely famous for Wembley Stadium, whose Norman Foster designed arch can be seen from many viewpoints. Next door is Wembley Arena, the art deco building originally built to house the swimming pool for the 1934 British Empire Games, which now hosts acts from Bruce Springsteen to Beyoncé. Plenty of redevelopment is going on around, with 5,000 homes promised over the next 10 years. Wembley is classic MetroLand — the term coined by poet Sir John Betjeman for the expansion of London in the 30s along the Metropolitan line. It has lots of detached, semi-detached and terrace houses from the period.

Southern areas such as Kensal Rise and Queen's Park are rapidly acquiring a cachet amongst young arty professionals and City workers. Chamberlayne Road, with its mix of cool bars, cafés and boutiques, was even dubbed the hippest street in Europe by Vogue magazine.

The leafier northern part of the borough hosts JFS qv, the extremely popular secondary school (despite a few recent hiccups) that is the largest Jewish school in Europe. It moved from Camden to a purpose built site in Kingsbury in 2002. Islamia Girls School, in Brondesbury, is rated as outstanding. Kingsbury High and Queen's Park Community schools are good local non-faith schools. Ark Academy in Wembley is a newish all-through school. The new Lycée International de Londres, which opened in 2015, is no doubt affecting the demographics of the area, though rated by Ofsted as requires improvement. Probably the most controversial is the Michaela Community School qv, set up in 2014 by head Katharine Birbalsingh (who it is fair to say is not publicity shy) and renowned for its boot-camp discipline.

One of the best-rated primary schools is North West London Jewish Day School. St Joseph's and Our Lady of Grace are popular Catholic primary schools, whilst Malorees is an outstanding non-faith school, as is Oakington Manor School in Wembley, which has its own centre for children with speech and language difficulties.

Ealing

Ealing, a sprawling West London borough, comprises Acton and Ealing to the East, Greenford, Northolt and Perivale to the North and Hanwell and Southall to the West. It is the fourth most ethnically diverse borough with 55 per cent of residents coming from an ethnic minority. This is reflected in the make up of the schools.

An influx of residents (there are large Polish communities particularly in the north in Greenford, Perivale and Northolt, as well as Somali residents in Acton and Hanwell, and Indian communities in Southall) has resulted in most of the primary schools expanding from two form entry to three and in some cases four. The question many are asking is how the secondary schools are going to meet the greater demand for places.

One of the most popular secondary schools at the moment is Drayton Manor qv. Residents describe it as structured and old fashioned with good results but perhaps lacking a creative edge. The more arty child may be better suited to Brentside High, a modern site with shiny new facilities. Elthorne Park qv remains top of many parents' list, on a spectacular site with extensive playing fields. Results here are impressive too. Cardinal Wiseman (Greenford), Greenford High (Southall) qv and Twyford C of E High School (Acton) qv come out top on the results table but Elthorne is hot on their tails. A stone's throne from Elthorne Park, also backing onto the extensive green fields close to the River Brent, is the Ealing Fields non-denominational, co educational free school (opened in 2016). It promises an all round education with a focus on character, resilience and life skills as well as academics. With Professor Guy Claxton as its patron, and the simple motto 'brave hearts, bold minds', it is has found a niche in the local provision. The more established and traditional Ellen Wilkinson qv in West Acton is a good choice for girls keen on science and maths.

Twyford's reputation is phenonomenal. Parents are prepared to move mountains (by which we mean dedicate themselves and their week ends to the local church) in order to get their children in here. We agree, it is good, and probably worth the sweat, particularly shining in music and languages. William Perkin C of E, part of the Twyford Church of England Academies Trust (along with Twyford), has got off to a very impressive start since 2013. It's popular with parents and judged to be outstanding by Ofsted in all categories. Situated in a relatively deprived area of the borough, the main admissions criterion is proximity to school (rather than, like Twyford, years of churchgoing). Alice Hudson is unstoppable, and plans continue to create a third school in the Twyford C of E Academies Trust, to be known as North Twyford C of E High School. With her track record, despite some setbacks in finding premises, the hopes of residents in the borough are high.

Practically all primary schools are good, some outstanding. Popular primary schools include Derwentwater, Berrymede and the new Ark Priory and Ark Byron in Acton (Ark Byron has finally moved from the premises it shared with Ark Priory into brand new premises on the edge of Acton Park), Fielding (which as its name suggests is lucky enough to have a green field rather than just usual tarmac playground), North Ealing qv (known for good results) and Montpelier qv in Ealing, plus Hobbayne, Mayfield and Brentside in Hanwell. Southall alone has 18 primaries, including one Sikh faith school. North Primary qv and Havelock are considered to be outstanding and the rest, with one or two exceptions, good. In contrast, Perivale has only three primaries, one of which, St John Fisher, is Catholic and outstanding. In Northolt and

Greenford (19 schools between them) ones to consider are Vicar's Green and Gifford.

Harrow

The little village of Harrow-on-the-Hill was where wealthy 16th century farmer John Lyon obtained a charter from Queen Elizabeth 1 to found a Free Grammar School. Harrow School qv is no longer free nor a grammar, but one of the country's leading public schools.

Harrow, with Hertfordshire to its northern border, is undoubtedly one of the leafier of the London boroughs, dotted with small detached and semi-detached houses and a good proportion of garden-for-money, though the affluent areas of Harrow-on-the-Hill (with its pretty, winding high street and rows of cottages), Pinner (with its clutch of timber-framed buildings) and Stanmore contrast with more deprived areas such as Wealdstone. The Metropolitan tube line has shaped the area, with large areas of commuter suburbs being developed in the 20s and 30s. It is extremely diverse ethnically and religiously, with a large Indian population.

Nower Hill High qv and Whitmore High are the top rated secondaries along with the girls' Sacred Heart Language College. St Dominic's Catholic Sixth Form College qv has an excellent record.

Around half of its students are Catholic, nearly all the rest Hindu or Muslim. New state comprehensive Pinner High School opened in 2016 in buildings vacated by the former private Heathfield School for Girls.

Harrow has several high-performing Catholic primary schools eg St Anselm's, St Bernadette's and St John Fisher. The Moriah Jewish Day School does well too. Popular non-faith schools include Newton Farm, Grimsdyke, Pinner Park, West Lodge and Whitchurch Junior.

Hillingdon

Hillingdon sits right on the western edge of London, a mix of green belt land and residential suburbia, with the Metropolitan and Piccadilly lines providing a quick link to the centre. The M4 and the M40 run through on their way west; Heathrow airport is in the borough, as is part of the Colne Valley Park, the first real countryside to the west of London.

Uxbridge, with its fine tube station, grew up at the point where the ancient London to Oxford road crosses the River Colne. The western edge of the town has a peaceful network of rivers that once powered watermills — flour milling was its major industry for many years. The town grew in prosperity after the arrival of the Grand Union Canal in 1793, and then again after the arrival of the Tube.

Haydon School qv in Northwood is one of the most popular secondaries (specialises in languages and applied learning, with lots of BTec options), alongside Bishop Ramsay C of E in Ruislip, Douay Martyrs Catholic school and Vyners, both in Ickenham, and Queensmead in Ruislip.

Amongst the primary schools, Catholic St Swithun Wells, Sacred Heart and St Mary's all perform well. Other popular primaries are Whiteheath Junior, Hillingdon primary, Oak Farm Junior and Breakspear. Guru Nanak Sikh Primary Academy, half of whose pupils enter the school knowing little or no English, is vastly oversubscribed.

Hounslow

Hounslow, which abuts the Thames at Brentford, is a gateway to all roads west. The M4 runs more-or-less along its northern boundary. Heathrow airport, just over the border in Hillingdon, is a major employer, and the population is very diverse, with large numbers of families speaking English as an additional language.

Chiswick House, designed by Lord Burlington, is a

grade 1 listed Palladian mansion with a garden of historic importance. The Griffin brewery, which has stood by the Hogarth roundabout for hundreds of years, has been churning out millions of pints of London Pride since the 1950s. Bedford Park, near Turnham Green tube, was the first garden suburb, planned in the 1880s by Arts and Crafts architect Richard Norman Shaw. Strand-on-the-Green was once a riverside fishing village, and still feels like it.

When the court sat at Kew, the rich and famous built big, ostentatious houses in Osterley and Isleworth. Though most have gone, Syon House on the Thames has been a home of the Duke of Northumberland for over 400 years. It, like fine, Tudor Osterley House, was remodelled by Robert Adam, while Capability Brown laid out their parkland. Old Isleworth is still a picturesque enclave of period houses.

Isleworth's Gumley House School qv is in a Queen Anne house surrounded by lovely grounds The Green School qv (girls, C of E, Isleworth) and St Mark's Catholic School (co-ed, Hounslow) are other popular faith-based schools. Heathland School and Lampton School in Hounslow are high performing non-faith, co-ed schools. Cranford Community College takes large numbers of disadvantaged children, the vast majority from ethnic minorities, and is rated outstanding.

Belmont primary qv caters for an affluent area of Chiswick and gets some seven applicants for each place. Spring Grove, Grove Park, Blue C of E and Chatsworth are other popular primary schools, as are St Mary's RC schools in Chiswick and Isleworth.

Richmond-upon-Thames

Straddling both sides of the Thames, Richmond's borough limits can confuse even locals (just as well they don't go in for drumming strangers out of town: they'd probably never leave).

But whether cosying up to Kingston (south bank) or Hounslow (north), schools suffer from similar overcrowding. The LA has been tackling the problem, tacking on classrooms and building new schools from scratch. Meanwhile, living as close as you can to the desired school (dustbin in playground ideal if has own postcode) has never been a better idea.

Richmond comprehensives were, until recently, no better than they should be and, in many parents' eyes, rather worse, given the excellence of the local primaries. Waldegrave (girls only to year 11; boys in sixth form) remains the star performer, among the top non-selective schools in the UK for every measure. Also doing well are Grey Court School and Orleans Park.

Senior leaders of successful schools have been giving a leg up to two of the borough's outliers, Twickenham Academy and Hampton High, to overcome some pretty underwhelming results and go on to better things in the future. Parent feedback is increasingly positive.

Of the borough's three newest secondaries, St Richard Reynolds, a Catholic school in Twickenham (with linked primary), is the beneficiary of a recent glowing inspection report and is, it says, 'passionate about improving the life skills and chances for children created in God's image.' (Doesn't say anything about chances for those who aren't.)

Turing House, a free school for 11-18-year-olds sponsored by the Russell Education Trust (RET) missed out on the same site and is currently making do in temporary premises, an underwhelming office building in Teddington, with a move to a permanent home still to be finalised.

Also in temporary accommodation is The Richmond upon Thames School. Newest of the lot, its first intake – 150 year 7 pupils – joined in 2017. Though it goes only to 16 – now an anomaly in a borough that has been busily bolting on sixth forms elsewhere (to mixed reviews) – the plan is for pupils to transition seamlessly to Richmond upon Thames College, on the same campus, for their post-GCSE education.

Currently, however, top sixth form destination for many Richmond families remains out-of-borough Esher College, known for consistently good A level results (nearly 60 per cent A*-B grades in 2018) and wide subject choice (not matched by the diversity of the intake, say locals).

Popular primaries north and west of the Thames are Orleans, St Mary's Church of England and Archdeacon Cambridge's C of E and Hampton Junior, together with Collis, one of first to be surgically enhanced, now boasting indoor facilities so good that at least one envious visiting teacher had to be coaxed to leave for own less impressive establishment. Downsides headed by danger of low-flying helicopter parents (as well as flight path noise).

Borough-wide praise for staff, whose own enthusiasms translate into impressive extracurricular activity. St John the Baptist's joint head is a Shakespeare nut, busily abridging the plays, one highlight a performance of Macbeth in nearby Hampton Court Palace. Hampton Hill, in contrast, excels at music. It holds a Sing Up platinum award, and boasts numerous ensembles and choirs including – wonder of wonders – a boys only vocal group, as well as an audition-entry chamber choir. Chase Bridge, meanwhile, also equipped with lovely new buildings, makes the most of links both with army music centre Kneller Hall and Twickenham stadium (both nearby).

At primary level, both Richmond's budding free schools have finally bloomed. Deer Park School moves to permanent premises in East Twickenham in 2019, above a Lidl (loyal Waitrose customers may require some re-education to come to terms with the concept). Twickenham Primary Academy, meanwhile, sponsored by not for profit GEMS Learning Trust (a branch of the for-profit international group GEMS Education), is up and running in refurbished offices close to

Twickenham Green, offering an abundance of 'laughter and delight' (measurement criteria will be interesting), as well as a longer school day (let's hope the two are compatible).

ACS Hillingdon International School

Hillingdon Court, 108 Vine Lane, Hillingdon UB10 0BE

01895 259771 | hillingdonadmissions@acs-schools.com | acs-schools.com

Independent	Pupils: 580; sixth form: 100
Ages: 4-18	Fees: £10,640 – £24,400 pa

Head of school: Since 2017, Martin Hall (50s), who hails from Aberdeen, moving to Glasgow to study economics and philosophy then further south to Worcester College of Education where he did his PGCE (secondary economics), working first at St Olave's Grammar school and then off to Tanzania for two years' voluntary service. 'It was very formative, it made me content with small things and realise that a good teacher can achieve wonderful things regardless of a school's facilities'. One gets the impression that this tall, affable man still has an outdoor spirit and a desire to do good. He came back to the UK for more teaching jobs but then returned to Tanzania as a teacher and there he met his wife. That was his first experience of IB teaching, to which he is now committed: 'more room for experiential learning'. After a further stint (six years) at the Inter-Community School of Zurich, where he was secondary school principal, he moved back to Tanganyika International School as the director – 'like being the CEO' – overseeing two campuses and gaining a good head for business.

He was drawn to ACS Hillingdon because it allowed him to get back to the the UK, to be closer to teaching again, and he immediately liked the warmth of the school and the 'ambition and pluckiness' he felt that this small school has. Pupils are excited about him teaching economics – they 'are lucky to have him so involved, even though they like their other economics teacher'. He is aware of the challenges – a transient population, a lack of tradition, a need to provide a huge range of curricula for the pupils with so many different academic trajectories. However, his wide experience and open nature make him feel he may have solutions – building up a coherent curriculum and creating identity, encouraging experiential learning as much as possible: 'learning is not just about communicating knowledge, it must be transformational'. After several changes of head and an acting head here, everyone very much hopes he does indeed have a vision and will stay to carry it through.

He has all three of his children at ACS and his wife teaches at a local primary school. Parents say they don't see him often – most contact is with the principals of high, middle or lower school. New high school principal September 2018, middle school principal in post since 2014, lower school principal in post for more than 20 years.

Academic matters: Non-selective and taking pupils at all times of the year from all different academic traditions means this school needs to be flexible and adaptable and have a good range of curricula to offer. The IB middle years programme has been dropped and the school now offers its own special blend of IB, British and American courses, with average IB points of 33 in 2018, though some high flyers who do very well.

Reception and year 1 have their own spacious bungalows and playground, and the linked indoor outdoor learning, teaching assistants and generous facilities make it a dreamy place for kids to be. 'Parents choose this over the local state schools in order to allow their children to learn through play – it matches a more international style of school where pupils don't start formal learning until after they are 6 years old'. Teachers and teaching assistants supported by specialist art, music and PE teachers.

We have rarely seen so much opportunity for building and making – Lego, straws and cardboard

Lower school continues the comfortable atmosphere, with a sofa in each classroom, groups of tables, teamwork, collaborative projects and thematic learning. Maths and English every day (EAL support extensive in these early years if needed, and highly differentiated reading schemes), with technology, humanities, Spanish and science interspersed. iPads used regularly, with technology lessons ensuring they know how to upload video and recordings and photos of their work onto the intranet site to be shared with parents and saved at the end of the year in a digital file. Lower school pupils can then use their technological skills for creating, building and innovation and STEAM (science, technology, engineering, art and mathematics) integrated in all their learning. We have rarely seen so much opportunity for building and making – enough Lego, straws and cardboard to make anyone's fingers itch to design. Native language enrichment ensures pupils keep up and develop their mother tongue, and they learn Spanish in lower school as well as having a language of the month so they can learn to appreciate each other's cultures and are exposed to different languages to match the different nationalities. Parents called the lower school 'phenomenal', with good structure and purposeful development.

Middle school pupils have homerooms where they meet and where they have their lockers, but they move to specialist teaching rooms, gaining independence and study skills. Spanish and French for all in middle years, plus combined sciences, humanities, music and PE. Choice of drama, dance or visual arts each term. And again, generous lashings of designing and using technology, including building robots, in all their learning – presentations, videoing, displaying, investigations and finding solutions. 'I wish my child could have more lessons with the technology teacher – she is fantastic and they learn so much'. The school has a Genius Bar that is available to resolve problems with devices – don't we all wish we had access to that!

We met pupils who were following the IB diploma fully, some who were taking the odd IB course as part of acquiring the High School Diploma – plenty of choice

Teachers expect pupils to question and learn from mistakes: no rote learning happening here. 'We teach them to be ready for things we don't even know will be in their futures'. Pupils were expected 'to ask yourselves what would you have done in that situation'. Pupils going on a school visit to Apple asked designers 'what was the worst mistake you ever made?' as they realised that it is from mistakes that we make the most exciting developments. Parents are concerned that since abandoning the middle years programme, neither pupils nor teachers are clear of the curriculum. 'The middle years seems to have lost its way – my child doesn't have a clear idea of where they are or where they are going'. 'It is all very laid back and chilled, but that is not what I am wanting from a school'. Though in annual parent surveys, most say their children

are challenged by the curriculum and some parents appreciated the flexibility of not having the MYP.

A new suite of science rooms sits on top of the new part of the school building, large light rooms dedicated to physics, chemistry and biology, with a technicians' prep room and space for experimenting and exploring. One side houses science rooms for middle school and one side for upper school. The success of the new science labs can be seen in the students' extended project choices, with conference level posters of research: 'How does temperature affect the concentration of iron in fresh and frozen spinach?'; 'How do the different lengths of hydrocarbons affect the rate of combustion?'

Upper school involves more independent learning. Students have weekly sessions with university guidance counsellors in the first term to ensure they are on target with deadlines and that they have chosen pathways that will suit their further education goals. 'My daughter enjoys the breadth the IB offers over the science A levels she would have taken in her old school'. Pupils have a choice of IB courses, American AP courses or High School Diploma courses, but they all have to be involved in CAS (creativity, activity and service). We met pupils who were following the IB diploma fully, some who were taking the odd IB course as part of acquiring the High School Diploma – plenty of choice and options to be busy and extended. Pupils seemed motivated and engaged: 'The IB course is really hard, and even though I have an unconditional place at university and don't need the grades, I owe it to myself to do as well as I can in the exams'.

Upper school students have a wood-panelled library worthy of an Oxford college, whilst the middle school library provided a generous study space and chill out zone, and the lower school library had sofas and hidden corners to lose yourself in a book. Three full-time librarians make sure that despite the modern acceptance of iPads, technology and screens, all the pupils read and love books. Pupils leave with healthy above-average grades, though the head says 'there is room to improve on the IB results'.

Most of the learning support is based around EAL and language acquisition together with supporting pupils' mother tongue languages. There is some dedicated learning support – both outside the classroom and inside, based in the spacious learning support rooms in the Pavillions. The use of technology through the school does help to support different learning styles. Parents also liked the way that particular strengths were noted and pupils extended and challenged with extension work or put into advanced classes – especially in maths.

Games, options, the arts: Exceptional artworks in a huge range of media cover the walls, including photography displays, with a large number of pupils choosing the art option at IB and achieving well above average on a regular basis (last year 25 per cent of pupils achieved a grade 7 out of 7 in IB art). Four dedicated art teachers clearly going above and beyond as we saw printing, graphics, modelling, painting, mosaics, collage, displays, oil, portraiture and in depth analysis. A pottery kiln is an added bonus – pupils were making plaster casts of their hands and using these to make sculptures based on Anthony Gormley's work – serious stuff, particularly for the lower school.

Film studies a relatively new IB course – very popular, with excellent sound, filming and editing suites as well as trips to nearby Pinewood Studios.

A large space dedicated to STEAM activities – science, technology, engineering, art and mathematics. Basically problem-solving in practical ways, learning to work in teams, design and build experientially and practically. The technology room includes a student built 3D printer, alarms, pupil built robots, drones and innumerable devices worthy of the most advanced of homes.

Regular PE lessons take place within the school timetable (twice weekly) but it is the after-school sport that is extensive – sports fields 10 minutes away host a range of sports according to the season, with teams for all levels and both sexes, and competitions against other international schools both locally and abroad. 'There is an emphasis on participating, thanks to the encouragement and the general ethos of the school,' according to one dad. Swimming at a local pool. Specialist PE teachers ensure that the cabinet of trophies is well stocked with wins by the Hawks.

One parent said 'the sport culture is excellent, there is a balance between academic development and strong sport involvement. Sport is used as a positive balance to develop a rounded person'. 'We see sport as an integral part of our child's school life': even though it takes place after school, 'they come home less stressed and fitter than if they had not done the sport between school and homework'. Parents commented, however, on the few galas and matches with other schools. And one pupil complained about mixed sex football teams as numbers were too few for separate teams.

Music taught by specialist music teachers twice weekly from reception onwards, with middle and upper schools having use of a dedicated building, Harmony House, with individual practice rooms (plenty of peripatetic music teachers for individual lessons), music lesson rooms and generous suites of computers for composition work. 'I like it that they are able to extend their musical interest – my child is now part of a rock band'. A choir used by pupils also allows pupils to help complete their CAS requirement.

After-school activities included theatre, fencing, golf, cooking, eco club, street dance, kickboxing, zumba, track and field, chess and language enrichment. Older pupils involved in Duke of Edinburgh, National Honour Society and International Schools Theatre Association.

Background and atmosphere: Set amidst a leafy, residential suburb is what was the 1855 grand country home of the Mills family with their 13 children. It became a convent in 1920 and was bought by the school in 1978. Its listed building status means that the fine stucco work, high ceilings and elegant windows are lovingly maintained – and now used and enjoyed by pupils and staff. A glorious red room used for recitals overlooking immaculate lawns and manicured planting. Modern buildings have been added on – slightly incongruous, but very spacious and practical gyms, classrooms, canteen, with a brand new science floor on top. High school uses the older buildings, lower and middle school the more modern section and the youngest classes have their own bungalow and playground space next to the learning support Pavilions. Clean, spacious rooms with a feeling of grandeur and history in some, and practical efficiency in others. Really well equipped with excellent, very up to date facilities.

A change towards more 'local international families' – those that came for a short time on placements but have stayed and are now very much local families

The grounds have room for tennis courts, a multisport all-weather sports field, vegetable patch looked after by the eco club, and efficient parking for the 37 school buses at drop off and collection times. School playing fields a short bus ride away. Overall a great feeling of space – staff room enormous, wide corridors for pupils to move around, huge science labs, extra rooms for team working and studying, generous numbers of art rooms, meeting rooms, music rooms. Such a luxury to have space for learning and playing and yet so close to London. Perhaps that is why such a large number of pupils are bussed out of central London?

Parents felt that they had good access to teachers on the whole, though were not sure about the current reduced reports that don't give grades and are rather too general. Parent-teacher meetings in October, and pupils show their work to parents in February, which means that by the time the spring term report comes in parents can have a surprise – 'and no report should be a shock to a parent'. The school is therefore changing to three reports with narrative each year.

School lunches a flexible arrangement as pupils can decide each day whether they are eating school lunch or packed lunch (a fingerprint system avoids money being brought in). Large salad bar (special low salad bar for the tinies), good range of hot food, sandwiches and soups, and interesting menu from a different country each day. No pushing or shoving, things run smoothly and calmly and mealtimes chatty but not noisy.

Pastoral care, well-being and discipline: Pupils from too many countries to be anything other than accommodating of each other – parents hugely grateful of the fact 'that we are family to each other' and that 'kids are kind'. Many parents mentioned the small size of the school as a positive: 'everyone knows each other' and 'teachers are really available for students and they know them well'. Parents and pupils appreciated the fact that there is a 'positive peer group' and 'international mix of kids adds a real richness and creates a nice social network'.

'I haven't had to expel anyone – a short discussion with pupil and parents quite enough to right any wayward behaviour. And that is limited to some roughness in the playground or leaving premises without permission – never anything worse than that,' says the head. This is not a traditional or rigid school – kids set their own standards in the main and stick to them. There is a sense that pupils are reasoned with rather than told. And parents confirmed that they are emailed or phoned if there are any issues to avoid them escalating, though some noticed increasing amounts of 'mouthiness' going on in middle school years.

Pupils and parents: Some 70 per cent of pupils come to school on one for the 37 buses that either collect from homes or from collection points. Buses do not travel further than one hour – large collections of families around Gerrards Cross ('we have Gerrards Cross coffee meet ups whilst the kids play on the green – a village community for us'), Richmond/Chiswick and St John's Wood (also known as little America). Though the map of where families live is quite an impressive spread. A growing number of local British families. Hard to define which country many pupils are from – 'most of us have several passports and may not even have lived in the country our passport is from' – but considered to be 35 per cent American, 17 per cent British, plus small numbers from some other 40 or so countries.

Parents work in a range of areas – banking, oil, film, increasingly military and diplomatic. The school sees a change towards more 'local international families' – those that came for a short time on international placements but have stayed and are now very much local families. There is less transience of pupils than previously, though this may change since military and diplomatic families get moved more often.

Entrance: Admission at all times of the year after visits, references, school reports and questionnaires from pupils. Non-selective, but pupils must have enough English to be able to access the curriculum at middle school and upper school level, though children accepted without English in lower school. Would not accept children needing one-to-one support, though there is a learning support department for mild learning differences. Some mobility difficulties can be accommodated but the old, listed building not suitable for wheelchairs.

Exit: Students liked the amount of career input – 'I have an internship this summer thanks to the school' – and appreciated the school counsellors helping with university choices. References and university applications to UK based on MAP (Measurement of Academic Progress) data obtained on all students, and internal tests and marks from teachers. If they stay all the way through school – and increasing numbers are: 'we extended our stay in the UK so that our child can finish at ACS' – then they usually leave for universities in the UK eg Bournemouth, Imperial, King's, SOAS, Birmingham, Warwick; or in the USA – Boston, Emerson, Florida State, Northeastern, Parsons, Syracuse. A peppering to other countries including Canada, Australia and the Netherlands.

Money matters: School fees do not include bussing service nor lunch nor learning support, but huge range of facilities and equipment an indication that the school is not cutting corners. Privately owned by a not-for-profit corporation with two sister schools in the UK and one in Doha. In the process of becoming a charity, which will enables them to offer more financial assistance (scholarships previously only for two final years, but now financial awards from 20-100 per cent available at 11, 13 and 16). Being part of a group of four schools helps ensure financial stability as well as shared experience, administration and management.

Remarks: This school gives a well rounded education, humane and with priorities about looking after the student's well-being rather than school's image. Not wildly competitive in any area, with the drive coming from the students rather than imposed from outside. Music, sport and art balance the enquiry-led academic life of students in spacious and generous grounds with very good facilities. 'We chose this school because it felt very relaxed and there was a happy buzz in the school with children laughing and talking,' say parents.

The Arts Educational School (London)

Cone Ripman House, 14 Bath Road, London W4 1LY

020 8987 6600 | pupils@artsed.co.uk | artsed.co.uk

Independent	Pupils: 235: 180 girls, 55 boys; sixth form: 108: 81 girls, 27 boys
Ages: 11–18	Fees: £15,390 – £16,990 pa

Headmaster: Since 2012, Adrian Blake (40s) BEd MAPgDip NPQH. Trained as an actor and worked professionally before finding he liked education, and retraining. Started his career as lecturer in performing arts at North East Surrey College of Technology, followed by a spell as director of thinking and learning and advanced skills teacher at Greenshaw High School. Moved to Lambeth Academy to become assistant principal, then came to ArtsEd in 2009, initially as director of teaching and learning. This background may help explain his consummate ease with modern education and its jargon – unusual in a performing arts school head. A fast-talking enthusiast, who seems genuinely to know the names of every single ArtsEd pupil past and present. Still teaches 15 periods a week (extracurricular martial arts included), and greatly liked by parents and pupils alike. 'He is truly inspirational, and the children really respect him'; 'Very present in the lives of the students, and my son especially enjoys his lessons'; 'A very dynamic character whom the pupils love and want to impress,' parents told us. Married to a deputy head at a nearby state school.

Academic matters: Several of the pupils we spoke to said that they'd come to ArtsEd because they weren't excelling academically – 'I really just like acting, I'm just not into this academic stuff,' was a comment echoed by most. If so, they appear to have found the right school to help them find their academic feet. 'I'm enormously passionate about learning, and when you put creativity into leaning, everything is richer,' asserts head, and the figures support the claim. In 2018, 30 per cent 9-7 at GCSE, with 68 per cent of A level passes at A*-B and 39 per cent A*/A. Creditable results for an academically non-selective school.

Maximum class size of 24, and students are taught a core of subjects that covers all the basics, including French and the humanities. At GCSE students take double science; it's rare for anyone to take triple science, although not unknown. One mother attested to the subject's overall popularity: 'My son loves the lunchtime science club, which is

really igniting his passion for the subject.' Homework is, according to everyone, kept to reasonable levels, and the children are given at least two days to complete any assignment – an important piece of commonsense in a school where pupils have so many other claims on their time. 'Although there isn't as much homework as at other private schools, I'm confident that the teachers are gauging the pupils' needs well, and I feel my child is in safe hands,' wrote one parent. Others were equally positive about the academic provision overall. 'The staff are very inspiring. Since being at ArtsEd my daughter has become very keen to succeed in her academic studies – I've never seen her so determined to do well,' commented a grateful mother.

'It's such a professional environment,' a sixth former told us, 'and the work ethic you're taught is fantastic'

In the sixth form students choose A levels, or a mixture of BTec and A levels, and at this stage the options are almost entirely arts-based: dance, drama, art, music, film studies, etc. English, history, and French are there for the more academically minded, plus maths, which is, according to head, very popular. No science A levels offered: the sixth form is built according to demand. Sixth formers we spoke to praised the teaching and the high level of individual attention given. 'The teachers are one of the reasons I love it here – they give you so much time,' was a typical comment.

Full-time SENCo offers support to the 25 per cent of students with dyslexia and other SEN, and this provision was particularly highly praised by parents. A mother, whose son moved to ArtsEd for the sixth form after receiving inadequate support elsewhere, wrote, 'With the help of the excellent SENCo team, my son has thrived and achieved really good academic results in all his subjects. He is more confident in his academic ability now and feels understood and supported with his dyslexia.' New dedicated sixth form SENCo as well.

Games, options, the arts: Students in years 7 to 11 choose to specialise in either dance or drama (see Entrance), but everyone receives classes in both disciplines. The vocational and academic teaching is interspersed throughout the day, and the amount of time students are required to spend in school increases as they move up: younger students stay until 5.30pm doing vocational work two or three days a week, in the sixth form it's every day. This is no hardship to the students or their families – it's what they all joined for. Lively and busy programme of shows and presentations including two major productions a year, all of them resourced and rehearsed to an extremely high standard. 'It's such a professional environment,' a sixth former told us, 'and the work ethic you're taught to have is fantastic.' 'You come in each day and there's such a buzz that you just want to stay!' said another.

Extremely good facilities, some of them shared with 'the degrees', as the ArtsEd undergraduate students are known here. The amazing Andrew Lloyd Webber Foundation Theatre that hosts the school's major dance shows and concerts is at the heart of the school, along with several smaller studio performance spaces. The school can boast many successes in national initiatives such as the National Theatre's Connections and the Independent Schools Association Drama Festival. Students are encouraged to get involved with all aspects of production, and film is also increasingly popular, with regular access to the purpose-built film and TV studio.

Music is taught at all levels and lots of instrumental lessons available. One recent leaver went on to the Royal College of Music to study the oboe. When we visited, the school resonated to the rhythms of an African drumming class, complete with enthusiastic whoops and wails.

'Sporty kids wouldn't like it here,' was the unanimous opinion of the students we spoke to. The school has no outside facilities of its own but the students go off site for sports each week, and there are regular kickabouts at lunchtime. But no-one is here for the sport, of course, and with so much dancing going on, the children keep superfit. Visual arts are also strong and creative, as the variety of work on the walls confirms.

ArtsEd isn't a stage school or an agency; the emphasis is firmly on academic success and vocational training, and it does not go out and seek professional performing work for its pupils. That said, professional directors and producers regularly come to the school looking for the right child for a particular role, and the head will always consider what he calls 'enhancing opportunities'. An ArtsEd year 8 pupil was appearing in Harry Potter and the

'Since being at ArtsEd my daughter has become very keen to succeed in her academic studies – I've never seen her so determined to do well'

Cursed Child when we visited and we met a young lad who'd enjoyed six months in Bugsy Malone. The industry likes ArtsEd youngsters, it seems. 'I know a high-level producer who won't consider stage school children any more, because they're prepared in a certain way – but he comes here!' remarked the head, with pardonable pride.

Background and atmosphere: ArtsEd grew out of the Cone Ripman School, founded in 1939 and itself the result of a merger between two previous dance schools. Originally located just off Oxford Street in Stratford Place, the outbreak of war forced a move to Tring in Hertfordshire where the school shared premises with the Rothschild Bank at Tring Park Mansion House. In 1941, the school was able to move back to Stratford Place, but kept its Tring premises as a second, boarding school. In 1947 both places were renamed The ArtsEducational School, to reflect Grace Cone's and Olive Ripman's commitment to a proper academic education for their young performers. Gradually the two schools diverged, and are now good friends but completely independent of one another (in 2009, to avoid confusion with its former partner, Tring changed its name to Tring Park School for the Performing Arts). ArtsEd moved to its present premises in a leafy part of Chiswick in 1989, renaming the building Cone Ripman House in honour of its founders. Cone Ripman House does nothing much for the eye on the outside, it has to be said, but has been extensively modernised and refurbished within and looks airy and streamlined.

The original Cone Ripman School was for girls only, and even today ArtsEd is still girl-heavy. This is almost always the case with performing arts schools, but seemed particularly so here, where only a quarter of students are boys. A sixth former admitted that she 'wished there were more boys', but the boys themselves were philosophical about it. 'It's a bit of a problem, but you make friends across the years,' observed a year 10 lad, equably.

Parents and students alike described this as a happy school. 'Everyone knows everyone, and everyone's so kind to each other'; 'It's a really nice atmosphere, it allows you to progress.' Parents concur: 'Our daughter has been at ArtsEd for two years and they have been the happiest school years of her life. ArtsEd is like a big family,' wrote one. Everyone praised the 'positive competitiveness' the school fosters, and insisted that no matter who got which part, 'we're in it together, we work as a team.' Chances to shine abound. 'If you audition for a part and you don't get it, you know there'll always be another opportunity,' a level-headed teenager told us. 'We offer developmental opportunities throughout the year,' confirmed the head, 'and parents will see their children do any number of things.' 'Watching your children in demonstrations of work is amazing; you can see them and their cohort growing in confidence,' agreed a parent. The young people we met were quiet, polite, respectful and proud of their school.

Has been awarded an Independent Schools Association Excellence Award in recognition of 'excellent academic standards, alongside specialist performing arts provision and record numbers of pupils achieving places at universities and conservatoires'.

Pastoral care, well-being and discipline: Students work hard to win their place here, and still harder once they arrive, so behaviour problems are rare. Occasionally there are the friendship group issues that you'll find at any school. However, everyone here knows the importance of getting on with each other, and staff work actively to promote harmony and healthiness, both physical and emotional. 'In my old school there was a lot of bullying, but everyone here gets along, and the teachers always talk to us if there's an incident,' said a year 7 girl. Parents agreed: 'Staff are kind and approachable and my child has great respect for them.' The head was adamant that there were no eating disorders in the school, and the canteen certainly seemed well-used and well-liked, selling a commendable variety of healthy and appetising dishes. A few sixth formers live too far away from the school to travel there daily from home, and instead lodge in nearby digs (this isn't allowed for younger students). The school isn't affiliated to any boarding provider, but helps students find host families, and has set up an 'away from home' group that meets every fortnight.

All students are assigned a staff mentor in year 10, and in year 11 the head personally meets all year 11 students to talk about future plans. The school prides itself on developing 'emotional resilience and bounce-back-ability' in its pupils. 'We really grow the understanding, and we enable them to do their best at auditions,' said the head. Parents valued this aspect of the school very highly. 'The school emphasises professionalism in preparing them for a demanding and sometimes brutal industry,' was one comment. 'ArtsEd students leave school very well prepared for the big wide world,' was another. 'You make connections here,' a sixth former reflected, 'and you're well-connected when you leave.'

Pupils and parents: Inevitably, many of the children come from families of film-makers, actors, writers and dancers, but not exclusively so, and the students we spoke to were adamant that 'you don't have to have a showbiz background to do well here'. Not much ethnic diversity when we looked round, perhaps reflecting perhaps the differing aspirations of London's various communities. Most of the children we spoke to were local, but the school recruits from a wide radius – one year 7 student travels up from Brighton each day, and we met a sixth former who'd relocated from Ireland.

ArtsEd alumni include, to name just a handful, Julie Andrews, Darcey Bussell, Martin Clunes, Nigel Havers, Bonnie Langford, Tuppence Middleton, Finn Jones – the list is impressively long.

Entrance: Twenty-four places at Y7, but school won't take full number if there aren't 24 good enough to take. Places do come up in other years: always worth checking. Entrance is by audition: students can try out for either the dance or drama pathway – or they can try for both, in which case the school will offer a place on the one they feel is best suited to the student. Written assessment in maths and English is simply to gauge academic progress: the school is academically non-selective. A number of additional places available at year 12. Similar entrance procedure, albeit more detailed and tougher: audition, workshops, interview.

Everyone praised the 'positive competitiveness' the school fosters, and insisted that no matter who got which part, 'we're in it together, we work as a team'

School looks for 'potential... that real passion', but not for would-be stars. As head observed, 'I don't do divas. Everyone's talented here. Staff are talented. We're all here because we're passionate about the arts, about education, about training.'

Exit: Typically with this kind of school, a few leave after GCSEs, having decided to pursue other life choices, in particular to study science at A level, since it isn't offered in the sixth form here. ArtsEd students have successfully applied at this stage to schools such as Latymer Upper and Tiffin. At 18, around 80 per cent to an impressive array of prestigious conservatoires: RADA, LAMDA, Royal Central School of Speech and Drama, English National Ballet School, London School of Contemporary Dance, Trinity Laban, etc. A number move upstairs to the highly regarded ArtsEducational degree schools in acting and musical theatre. Some pursue a career in film at places such as Bournemouth &

Poole or the National Film & TV School. Others go abroad to institutions such as the Juilliard or the New York Film Academy. A few go into the industry immediately: a recently sixth form leaver went straight into playing the lead role in The Curious Incident of the Dog in the Night Time. A small number to university, mostly to read arts subjects.

Money matters: ArtsEd fees are remarkably reasonable given the high level of specialist tuition the students receive, and lower than those charged at many other independent schools in this part of London. For those who need help, the school offers means-tested bursaries of up to a third of the fees

for students in years 7 to 11. In addition, eight full-fees scholarships are available in the sixth form. The school does not receive any government or local authority funding.

Remarks: A dynamic, purposeful, well-oiled institution where creative youngsters learn to work hard and achieve highly. 'With the school's expert guidance and support the transformation in my child has been remarkable,' said one mother, and another reported her daughter as saying, 'Mum, I don't think there's another school in the world that is as good and as fun as ArtsEd.'

Belmont Primary School

Belmont Road, London W4 5UL

020 8994 7677 | office@belmont.hounslow.sch.uk | belmontprimaryschool.org.uk

State	Pupils: 470
Ages: 3–11	

Head: Since September 2018, Elaine Lacey, previously deputy head at the Blue School in Isleworth.

Entrance: Preference given to siblings. Next in the pecking order are those who live within the Primary Admissions Area – 'catchment' to you and me. In recent years, even living in the catchment has not guaranteed a place at the school. Children in public care and those with medical/social needs come high up in the pecking order. After that – don't even try. Parents are known to rent property within the area just to qualify, and then..? More hope from year 2, however, as a steady trickle leaves to go to prep school/move out of London. Places are snapped up, though, and school tends to be full all the way through to year 6.

Exit: About half to Chiswick School, although the numbers are decreasing with the advent of competition in the area. A clutch to West London Free School and Hammersmith Academy as well as the usual numbers to Twyford, Lady Margaret, Gunnersbury and the Green School. The rest (about 20 per cent) to local independents, including Godolphin & Latymer, Notting Hill and Ealing High, Latymer Upper, Hampton, Ibstock Place. The occasional one to St Paul's Juniors at 8 as well as at 11. Lots of outside coaching during years 5 and 6 to prepare for independent school entrance exams.

School asks for a financial contribution for the school reports required for entry into such schools.

Remarks: The reluctance of the previous head and staff to welcome us to look round this super, oversubscribed, well-funded state primary (or indeed respond to our messages) bemused us – especially considering that Belmont is one of the most successful and popular state primaries in West London, with seven applications for each place.

Pupils bubbled with enthusiasm and love for their school as they showed us round. An abundance of facilities – from musical instruments, playground equipment, books and materials to the brand new stage for dramatic performances. Results are excellent, showing much higher than expected progress between key stages 1 and 2 and a quarter of pupils in their final year gaining well above expected levels in reading and maths.

The school caters for an affluent corner of Chiswick and the catchment area is becoming ever tighter. Families from sumptuous houses in the Bedford Park area can no longer expect to get a place. Were it not for the council accommodation on the school's doorstep, you might not get the social mix one would expect in an inner London state primary school at all. Our first impression was that there was an unusually high proportion of white middle class kids; the head was keen to give precise statistics and told us that 52 per cent of Belmont's pupils are from minority ethnic groups (in this case Eastern Europe and a few affluent UK residents from say, Canada or Sweden). This ain't your typical London primary.

School is housed in a large, three-storey brick building that benefits from the high ceilings, large windows, well-proportioned rooms and wide corridors typical of Victorian buildings of its kind. A generous refurbishment programme has resulted in shiny polished floors and child-friendly primaries and pastels (plenty of aqua and primrose) painted on the walls – helping the building to fall firmly on the side of happy, modern school rather than gloomy Victorian institution.

Belmont is beautifully mapped out, with two classes at either end of each spacious floor, each one charmingly named after fruit – apples, pears, cherries. The main hall in the middle space between classrooms is used for play (reception and year 1 – lots of dressing up and imaginary play goes on here), assemblies (years 2 and 3 on the middle floor) and drama and gym (years 5 and 6 on the top floor). Yet more rooms house musical instruments galore (drum kits, pianos, flutes, various percussion), two well-stocked libraries, two ICT suites (the juniors have the luxury of one computer each, one between two for the infants) and dedicated SEN provision. Teaching up to the end of year 2 is mixed ability; setting in maths and English from year 3. Two sets – the higher being slightly the larger and having, therefore, up to 32 children to the lower set's 28-ish. The upper set has just one teacher, no classroom assistant being needed with these children because, of course, they are motivated and keen to learn. We couldn't see much problem with the lower sets either.

About 20 per cent of children identified as having special educational needs but a very small proportion of these have EHC plans. School has coped in the past with more severe special needs, but children must be able to climb stairs.

About a quarter of pupils don't have English as a first language (about 43 different first languages other than English recorded) but no marked difference in the performance of these children – credit to the school. Dedicated part time EAL teacher as well as SEN coordinator with a team of teaching assistants give support in the classroom. Sats results in all subjects are at least 10 per cent above local and national averages and are far higher by year 6. Those with EAL needs are seen individually or in small groups for as long as necessary, until they are up to the general standard. Teaching assistants support individuals, pairs or groups under the supervision of the SENCo. A reading recovery teacher sees individuals who, by year 1, are falling behind – with 'fantastic' results. When we visited, there had been a relatively high turnover of staff

(we were assured that this is a result of career progression, maternity – no reflection on the school). Five male teachers – always a bonus. Years 3 to 6 have 40 minutes of French weekly. Everyone has two hours of physical activity a week.

All classes have class music lessons and learn singing with a specialist teacher. In addition to class music, many learn individually – often more than one instrument. Recorder is offered to the whole of year 3 and there is a choir. Swanky staging facilitates an annual production from year 6. Other year groups, sometimes working together, also put on shows each year. Photographs on display suggest a high level of dramatic productions, much supported by parents, many of whom are 'in the arts'.

Good sports provision. A school sports partnership linked to Chiswick School and an outsourced sports programme (football, netball and athletics) in addition to members of staff teaching sport. On Friday afternoons here there is 'enrichment time', when for 30 minutes children can choose from a wide variety of activities, from Glee Club to comic making. Strong after-school club provision. These include, as well as the sport and music, Big Bang Science and Doughlightful – a clay modelling activity.

Pupils bubbled with enthusiasm and love for their school. An abundance of facilities – from musical instruments, playground equipment to the brand new stage

The Belmont Home School Association – PTA to you and me – raises between £20,000 and £30,000 each year. This has helped make the playground ever more luxuriant, with designated spaces for quiet reflection, a wilderness garden, covered areas for performances with costume boxes, lots of bike sheds, a super climbing wall painted by parents and plenty of gardening boxes replete with flowers, herbs and plants.

The early years spill out beautifully into carefully designed outdoor play areas, secure from the rest of the large playground. The nursery is particularly roomy and attractive – 52 places with sessions of a maximum of 39 children, an à la carte choice of mornings or afternoons or a combination of whole days and half time sessions. Three large rooms, own toilet facilities and a large kitchen area ('mummy sometimes comes in to help us cook', said an excited 3 year old) as well as access to the hall and library. Few chic little independent nurseries provide as much as this. Everyone eats in the school canteen and the number of pupils having cooked lunches delivered by the borough increases all the time. The rest bring their own.

Ofsted hasn't done a full report since 2007, when school was judged 'outstanding' (confirmed by an interim assessment in 2011). Staff are greatly aided by a posse of 'liberal middle class' parents only too eager to help in all areas of school life, including arranging fundraising events to enable disadvantaged pupils who might not otherwise be able to afford to take part in trips etc. They are aided, too, by an excellent governing body, as well as by a good relationship with her local authority. A very small number of exclusions in previous years, but none for some time. A proper

and well-understood system of sanctions. Also an established homework system with extension work on the school website for those who want to push their offspring further.

Many parents commented that they were sometimes frustrated by the blank wall that meets their follow-up questions on their child's progress and results. 'Teachers can be cagey', remarked one parent, 'which makes me nervous. I might be surprised'. If you can cope with this and a certain complacency ('we don't need publicity', we were told at one point), then this is a no-brainer – an excellent state school with most of the advantages of an independent school but without the fees.

Drayton Manor High School

Drayton Bridge Road, London W7 1EU

020 8357 1900 | adminoffice@draytonmanorhighschool.co.uk | draytonmanorhighschool.co.uk

| State | Pupils: 1,502; sixth form: 333 |
| Ages: 11–19 | |

Head: Since 1994, Sir Pritpal Singh BSc MA FRSA. Educated at Highgate School, where he was a boarder; he has maintained close links with his alma mater. Read chemistry at London University. Deputy head at Cranford Community School, as well as head of science, head of chemistry and head of year group at several other comprehensive schools. Knighted for services to education in 2005 and has received the accolade of head teacher of the year.

A true visionary who has turned the school into the success it is today. No mere figurehead. Very visible around the school – he still greets pupils daily after 23 years in the job. Dedicated to his pupils and justifiably proud of his school. Parents and pupils see him as an excellent role model. Treats everyone with respect and dignity: 'We show that everyone is valuable. Subtle things, we need to live it out. You have to give of yourself, consistently'.

No longer at the chalkface. 'Some heads feel that teaching is crucial to their stature. I loved teaching and was at ease in the classroom, but feel that I have nothing to prove. It's better for me to walk around the school and drop into lessons, see lots of students in the lunch queue or at the bus stop. That way I get a better spread of contact.'

Calm, assured and with a warm sense of humour. 'He is very composed and that is reflected throughout the school. There is a sense of peace

about the place, no matter when you visit and that comes from the top,' commented one parent.

Married with two grown-up sons, one of whom is an engineer, the other works in IT. Family is important to him. Loves sport and coached rugby for 14 years. Also enjoys listening to music, with a particular weakness for the Rolling Stones. A well-travelled man, who holidays all over the world, from the Caribbean to South Africa and Australia.

Relishes his job and considers himself fortunate. 'I could have been a pauper in India. I just happen to have been born into a family that valued education'.

Academic matters: In 2018, 23 per cent of grades were A*/A at A level, 53 per cent A*-B. At GCSE, 74 per cent got 9-4 in both English and maths; 19 per cent of grades 9-7. Has awards for exceptional GCSE results and letter of congratulation on EBacc results received from minister of state for school standards.

Thirty subjects offered at A level, including media studies, sociology and psychology. Popular A levels currently maths, biology, chemistry and history. Government and politics, as well as history, recognised nationally as superb departments. BTec qualification also offered in creative media and applied general qualifications in business. Wide choice of GCSE subjects including computing and economics.

Pupils can take between five and 12 GCSEs. Modern languages offered including Spanish, French and German, though no Mandarin nor Russian. One parent we spoke to wished her daughter could have taken two modern languages at GCSE but this is not possible. On average, 35 pupils learn Latin in first year with around 20 pupils taking it for GCSE in year 10. 'The students love it; the parents love it and it adds something to the character of the school. It attracts good, interesting staff and it adds an extra dimension to the school,' says head.

Average class size is 23; maximum 31. Five one-hour lessons a day. School recognises the benefits of setting by ability – English and maths from year 7 and science, French and Spanish from year 8. Head states, 'Differentiation is a strength – all our pupils are pushed, whether very able academically or not.' Awarded 'outstanding' in last Ofsted inspection.

EPQ is embraced here, with a broad range of subjects chosen by pupils ranging from bovine TB to Jane Austen. Not compulsory and about one third of the year end up taking it. Head encourages the pupils to take it on if manageable without over-extending them. 'It's a conversation we have with the student and family.' Pupils were highly focused in the lessons we observed, whether being tested on GCSE biology modules or role-playing gritty scenarios in drama group. Head delights in the fact that 'they enjoy being challenged. They can listen for long periods of time. They can express their opinions with confidence'.

Over 300 pupils are on the SEND register, well above the national average. School offers excellent provision for those with milder end of learning difficulties such as dyslexia, dyscalculia and autism and those with social, emotional and mental health difficulties. Staff are trained to deal with attachment and anxiety disorders as well as school phobias. Baseline assessment on arrival. Beautifully designed new inclusion centre. 'Probably the best facilities in the school for the students who need the most support,' explains head. 'They all arrive early as they love coming to this area.' Great improvement on the huts that they have replaced. Pupils respond well to the consistent experience they get here. Alternative curriculum offered to those that need specialist support in the first few years in phonics, literacy and numeracy. EAL pupils also withdrawn from class for extra help if needed.

School stretches the very brightest sparks too. Gifted and talented pupils might be given extra lessons or be sent off on a trip. One mother we spoke to commented that her clever son 'was very well supported and extended throughout.'

Homework club in library for those who find it hard to concentrate at home. The pupils we spoke to did not find amount of homework too onerous, with one even shyly confessing that she enjoys the homework. Booster revision sessions laid on for A level and GCSE pupils after school, in holidays and at weekends, so no-one is left to flounder in exam season.

Teachers are ambitious for their pupils and are rated highly by the parents. 'You really feel at parents' evenings that the teachers know your child inside out.' Pupils feel most teachers are 'easy to talk to.' Over 20 members of staff have been at school for more than a decade but there is a healthy balance with plenty of youthful faces too. Head admits that recruitment of excellent staff 'can be challenging with teacher shortages' and it can be hard when a head of a faculty leaves but 'we are like a gyroscope. It takes a lot to knock us off our stride'.

Games, options, the arts: Wide array of sport offered from rugby and cricket to gymnastics and dance. Some pupils perform at national level, including at handball, acrobatic gymnastics and swimming, as well as county level. School is regular winner of cups and tournaments across borough and new display cabinets are being built to house the abundant silverware. Netball particularly impressive – 100 per cent victorious in borough league fixtures. Girls' and boys' football teams currently strong, as is rugby. Excellent facilities including a floodlit all-weather pitch and sprawling school playing fields on nearby Greenford Avenue. Everyone is encouraged to participate at some level, whether house dodgeball or more giddy heights.

'He is very composed and that is reflected throughout the school. There is a sense of peace about the place, no matter when you visit, and that comes from the top'

The arts faculty is made up of art and design, drama, music and media subjects. Numerous choirs, bands including ska, rock and funk, ensemble groups, junior and senior orchestras and chamber groups, many of which rehearse at lunchtimes. Concerts galore, both formal and informal. Numerous opportunities to take part in musical events, from participating in national orchestra days to hearing musicians at Albert Hall. Currently 150 students learn an instrument. Head is ambitious to improve the music department. 'We want to be world class, with the best facilities,' he states. Excellent new art, design and technology studios too. Though some impressive work on show, including sensational portfolios, art is not a popular A level. Top notch drama centre. School takes part in Shakespeare Schools Festival and pupils regularly attend productions at Lyric Hammersmith and the West End. Annual summer showcase is highlight of school year. 'The shows are sensational,' according to one parent.

Sixth form enrichment options include chess, debating and trampoline sessions. Pupils participate in National Citizen Service and fundraisers for children's charities. School promotes learning outside the classroom and pupils go on exciting visits both at home and further afield, including ski and snowboard trips to Maine, homestay visits in France and residential stays in Devon.

Background and atmosphere: Opened as a grammar school in 1930, before becoming a comprehensive in 1973 and an academy in 2011. Still feels like a grammar school, with its stained-glass coats of arms in the library and its Latin motto Nec Aspera Terrent, meaning 'hardships do not deter us'. Sums up ethos of school.

Current head is only the fifth head in school's history and many of the buildings are named after his well-loved predecessors. Yellowing old school photos line the corridor, reflecting the changes in its history from genteel 1930s arrangements to hippy groupings from the 1970s.

An £8 million building programme, including a new humanities faculty, outstanding new library and refurbished science labs, has transformed the school. Beautiful central piazza, complete with immaculate topiary and a total absence of grime or litter make for stunning premises. Vivienne Westwood's striking Union Jack on a main corridor adds a dramatic punch to what could otherwise feel like a National Trust property.

Pupil successes are celebrated, whether at congratulatory breakfasts, coffees, lunches or a year 13 boat trip to Craven Cottage. Prizes awarded in all year groups for effort and progress, as well as for humour and good character, and for courage.

Pastoral care, well-being and discipline: Each year comprises 240 pupils, organised into nine tutor groups. Each pupil sees their tutor every day. 'I love my tutor,' smiled one boy. Each member of the senior team is attached to a year group so gets to hear swiftly if there are issues that need to be dealt with. 'When I meet with heads of year, I expect to be told the key things that are going on in each year group. Very quickly I know what I need to know. I've got my finger on the pulse, as have my deputies,' states head.

Discipline is important. Schools keeps rules to a minimum but expects them to be obeyed. Only sixth formers are allowed mobile phones and punishments for others in possession of them are no-nonsense. Third time caught with a mobile phone counts as defiance and can be met with an exclusion. 'Even for sixth formers, if they are caught doing anything iffy then the sanctions kick in. They respect that,' explains head. Strong policies in place regarding social media. 'Our values are clear

School is regular winner of cups and tournaments across borough and new display cabinets are being built to house the abundant silverware

on social media – it all comes down to good manners.' At risk of permanent exclusion for possession of drugs and offensive weapons. Four or five permanent exclusions annually. One mother summed it up: 'The kids respond to the discipline. There is not much wriggle room!' Another parent said, 'The children know where they stand. They know the consequences for bad behaviour and the school carries through with these. No idle threats at Drayton.' One mother commented that some boys mess around in class but that generally there is zero tolerance of larking about. Head thinks it can be a relief for the pupils to have to comply with strict rules: 'They can blame me. It allows them to perform at a high level.' Over 95 per cent attendance rate.

Head believes a caring ethos is at the heart of the school. 'We insist on high standards, starting with good manners. Being courteous and considerate comes before academic prowess. How we treat other people is the number one priority. That is our bedrock. It's the Drayton Manor way.' This sense of decency is expected not only in the classroom but between lessons, at break time and even at the bus stop. 'The whole continuum from home to school is important for us. It does not end at 3.30pm. They need to learn that this is their life now.'

Head recognises that it can be hard being a teenager. 'It's important they know there is more to life than just being popular. The children feel safe here and can develop their own personalities. They can express themselves without being made fun of.' The pupils in turn say they can trust the staff and feel that if they tell the teachers about any problems, they will make it better. 'Pastoral care is not just about having the structures in place but trying to work out what it feels like to be one of the students. We think a lot about it,' says head. One girl we spoke to said the school had supported her incredibly well when she suffered a bereavement and another mother expressed her gratitude for the way it had built up her daughter's shaky confidence. Very few suffer with depression, anorexia or self-harming.

Ninety-five per cent of food is home-made, including breakfast for early birds from 8am. Chef worked in a Michelin-star restaurant and certainly wowed us with delectable pastries. Lots of options, including halal, gluten-free, vegan and vegetarian, though one pupil told us 'it would be easy to get away with just eating a cookie every day for lunch as no-one checks'.

Pupils and parents: Socially mixed intake, from affluent professional families to the very deprived. Pupils head in from north and west Ealing and Hanwell. One third white British with many different ethnic minority groups. Sixty-five per cent EAL and over 50 different languages spoken at home. Parenting support classes offered. Above average number of pupils on free school meals.

Excellent home-school communication. 'We all have our part to play for the greater good. Students, staff as well as parents.' Head genuinely likes meeting people and enjoys being around at events such as parents' evenings. PTA raises funds though car boot sales. Money raised recently has been spent on a digital piano, art supplies and lighting kit.

Old Draytonians include footballer Peter Crouch, BBC business editor Kamal Ahmed and Lord Justice of Appeal Sir Michael Fox. Many old boys and girls come back to talk to current cohort about their experiences.

Entrance: Non-selective. Priority given to looked after children, then siblings, followed by those who live closest to school. Successful court case means that children gain a place at Drayton Manor if it is the nearest school to their home. If you live a mile from the school but it remains the nearest school to home, then you will have priority over children who live half a mile away but have other schools from which to choose. Massively oversubscribed, with roughly six applicants per place. Waiting list for all years. Generally, a grade 6 is needed at GCSE in order to pursue the subject in the sixth form, whether existing pupil or from outside. Fifty or more pupils join in year 12, to replace those who leave after GCSEs (they usually head for vocational courses elsewhere or employment). Head explains, 'People realise that if you live miles away, there is no point in applying for a place; roughly speaking unless you live 0.8 miles away or less, you won't get a place.' Siblings make up around half the school.

Exit: Up to 50 per cent leave after GCSEs. Popular choices include Leeds, UCL, King's, Sussex and Brunel. Subjects range from international politics to mechanical engineering. Eighteen off to study medicine in 2018.

Interview practice for those applying to Oxbridge or for medicine, as well as shared careers workshops, at Highgate School. Oxbridge society prepares pupils for applications, including test practice. Two or three head off to Oxbridge most years (two places in 2018). Head says pupils don't always know what they are capable of so encourages those who would never have considered university to believe that they can achieve it. He explains, 'This is a seven-year programme. You can't just turn it on in year 12. Students need to learn how to crack the code. Those from other countries have to learn how England works. They need to learn not to be intimidated by institutions.'

Money matters: Sixth form bursary. School uses its pupil premium to fund learning support, masterclasses, mentoring, Easter revision and some subsidising of school trips. Voluntary contribution of £10 per family per year.

Remarks: Head said, 'I think you can see why I have stayed so long. It is remarkable how the students have responded to my approach.' Certainly, the pupils we spoke to were thoroughly impressive: modest, polite, caring and articulate but with a developed sense of fun. They could not wait to tell us how much they liked Drayton. An inspiring and exciting school that provides a truly outstanding education.

The Ellen Wilkinson School for Girls

Queen's Drive, London W3 0HW

020 8752 1525 | office@ellenwilkinson.ealing.sch.uk | ellenwilkinson.ealing.sch.uk

State	Pupils: 1,350; sixth form: 270
Ages: 11–18	

Headteacher: Since 2014, Rachel Kruger B Mus Ed, B Mus Hons, BSc (pure maths), MBA (late 40s). She arrived here in 2012 as deputy head, and taught maths and music. In 2013 she became acting head and took over as permanent head in March 2014.

Originally from Stellenbosch in South Africa, Ms Kruger studied Bloemhof Girls' High School in Stellenbosch. She has spent the last 15 years in schools in Ealing. Prior to starting at Ellen Wilkinson, she taught maths for 11 years at co-ed comprehensive Dormers Wells High School, and music at Uxbridge High School for two years before that. She now feels she has come full circle, relishing the atmosphere of this all girls' school. She is clear about the benefits of single sex education for girls. 'I love seeing the girls in year 7 playing hide and seek,' she says. 'I doubt you would find that in a mixed school.' The women in the senior leadership team all went to girls' schools.

Modelling behaviour and expectation for her pupils is key for Ms Kruger. You can immediately see why she is hugely popular with parents, staff and girls. Wreathed in smiles and generous with her warm greetings to everyone she passes, she exudes positive energy. 'Everyone respects her,' said our guide. 'The girls benefit from her warmth,' commented a dad. She combines a tough, focussed approach with the soft femininity of the floral print dress she was wearing when we met. Just being in her company makes one feel that anything is possible and nothing is too much of a problem. Open and relaxed in conversation, she is easy to talk to and parents warmly appreciate her approachability and her ability to listen and deal with things quickly and effectively. They describe her as 'a good leader' and 'effective manager'.

You can immediately see why she is hugely popular with parents, staff and girls. Wreathed in smiles and generous with her warm greetings to everyone she passes

She clearly loves her job and puts her heart into it, is active in the head teachers' group among Ealing schools, and receives lots of support through mentoring from other female leaders, as well as giving support in return. She knows the girls, and unusually for a head of a busy secondary school, still finds the time to teach maths. A love of learning is one of her defining qualities. A trained opera singer, she is currently studying for a law degree. No plans to change career, however. 'I just want to keep learning,' she twinkles, 'and it has the added bonus of setting an example to the girls: they can see my disappointment if I don't do as well as I would like and they witness me striving to do better.' Parents remarked on her gutsiness in singing a solo at a winter concert – 'if the girls are expected to do this, so should I be.'

Academic matters: In 2018, 71 per cent got 9-4 in maths and English GCSE, 30 per cent 9-7s. English, sciences, languages (including Arabic and Latin) all strong. RE is a noticeably popular subject at which girls do well here. A specialist maths and science college since 2002, a healthy proportion of the girls take maths, biology and chemistry A level. Further maths, psychology and philosophy are recent additions to the A level choices. In 2018, 47 per cent A*-B and 23 per cent A*/A grades at A level. Several vocational options at level 2 and 3, including business studies, and health and social care. Suggestion in some quarters that sixth form is less stimulating and a few start to look elsewhere after GCSE. Lots of setting – maths and English from year 7, science and languages from year 8. Mandarin now offered as part of the curriculum from year 8. School runs maths and science taster sessions and master classes for feeder primary schools, with excited pupils trying out practical experiments in real science labs.

Food tech, product design as well as textiles offered at GCSE. The latter particularly popular. We saw examples of a project on headpieces in Alice in Wonderland. One year 11 pupil won an award with the London College of Fashion and went onto work with print designers in East London. Lots of extracurricular academic clubs, including Latin.

Busy careers library, particularly well used by years 9 and 11; 'we're giving support with careers a lot, but apprenticeships too,' says the careers officer.

A number of students need learning support and are taken out of class for one-to-one sessions. Those on EHC plans tend to be girls with a physical disability who need practical help. Lots of careful differentiation takes place in the classroom, we are assured, and careful monitoring as to who needs more support. 'We are gradually moving this support away from the just the SEND department and giving the support in the class room,' says Ms Kruger. One full time SENCo, one deputy and one EAL teacher. Higher level teaching assistants and several other teaching assistants in both SEND and EAL departments. Some 70 per cent of students speak English as a second language, supported by a strong EAL team and school, deservedly proud that the results of the EAL students are well above national averages. Value added scores strong, among the best in the borough.

Games, options, the arts: Frequent drama productions as well as concerts, jazz band and string quartet. All girls do drama in years 7 and 8 and a fair number continue to GCSE. The shiny polished Victorian main hall is used for annual theatrical productions as well as concerts and there is a good sized drama studio. A number of successful musicals are preformed each year, including Oliver!, Little Shop of Horrors and Les Misérables and they performed the Rocky Horror Picture Show at a local theatre. 'The standard is professional,' observed more than one parent. Music is a passion of Ms Kruger's, and she encourages lots of concerts

Three large and spacious art studios, bursting with industry and colour, are an inspiring place to explore different styles

throughout the year, the winter concert being a particular highlight, with other different kinds of opportunities for the girls to perform and develop a musical interest.

PE facilities have been transformed by the recent addition of a new sports hall. Successful basketball and netball teams; girls here also play football, run cross-country and our guide plays handball for Ealing. School enters teams for a number of competitions, tournaments and fixtures against other schools. Minor sports clubs too, including trampoline, badminton, and ultimate frisbee. They recently received funding from London Youth Rowing and were awarded Middlesex Education Provider of the Year for tennis. Lots of outdoor space, with grass and all weather hockey pitches as well as tennis and netball courts enabling the school to host a number of competitions across the borough. Ellen Wilkinson prides itself on being a 'sports leadership academy', one of very few schools in London to have this status and based on the fact that the school offers the Sports Leadership Award at both level 1 and 2. Perhaps more importantly, our guide confirmed that it's 'cool to be sporty'.

Three large and spacious art studios, bursting with industry and colour and situated around a green grassy area, are an inspiring place to explore different styles for budding creatives. Art GCSE results are good, and A level results, though less consistent, are solid.

Extracurricular clubs range from sporting and music to academic and learning support. However at lunch time girls can also choose to do a variety of activities from tapestry to debating and dominoes to eco learning. It's up to the girls how much they get involved.

Background and atmosphere: Named for the Mancunian Labour MP, Ellen Wilkinson, who led the Jarrow March in 1936 and became the first female Minister for Education in 1945, the school was founded in 1974 and is still the only all girls comprehensive school in Ealing. With nearly 1,400 pupils it is a large school.

First impressions as you arrive in the new foyer are of a thoroughly modern, state of the art school, with clean lines, minimal decoration, and monochrome appearance punctuated with bursts of colour – a fresh bowl of flowers strategically positioned, for example. The new building,

which houses senior staff offices, administration and conference rooms, as well as the entrance hall, is replete with white stone floors, glass walls and Perspex chairs. The smell of fresh paint blends in with the scent of freshly cut flowers. The library – also recently finished – is designed in the same style, and on a clear winter's day, when the trees are bare, there is a clear line of vision from one building to the other.

In between, however, there is a hotch-potch of different styles: Victorian, polished wood floors and high ceilings, lined with gold leaf embossed honours boards, and a tranquil Japanese garden surrounded by 60s two storey blocks, where the girls can enjoy lunch in the warmer months.

The grounds feel extensive with a number of netball courts as well as 'the field' – a wonderful large green space, only spoilt, when we visited, by an unsightly amount of litter. School already onto this with plans to fence the field off. This is where the girls do athletics and can sit outside and eat lunch.

New girls in year 7 are given a map when they arrive and then packed off on a treasure hunt to acquaint themselves with the territory.

There is a distinct professionalism about everything here. A tightness. Things are done well. Crisp. Effective. Even the uniform has smartened up with crisp white shirts beneath their maroon v necks.

Pastoral care, well-being and discipline: An area that has vastly improved under Rachel Kruger's compassionate but firm leadership, confirmed by all the parents we spoke to. There was a lot of low level disruption that needed tackling. Part of this was to revamp the pastoral team, another to ask the students to write their own code of conduct. 'A strict but comfortable school, everyone is kept in order but we don't feel pressurised, we understand the rules are for our benefit', confided our guides. One parent commented on how swiftly a problem between a teacher and her daughter was resolved by the head of year. There are systems in place and they seem to work. Staff work hard with parents, and communication is improving, we were told. Fathers attend workshops on sex education, all parents now want to get involved.

'We help everyone to find their own way through acceptance; kindness is a big word here, ultimately it's their choice whether to do the right thing,' says Rachel Kruger. Politeness and good manners are essential requirements here. Swearing at a member of staff will result in exclusion. 'We will do everything we can, use as many resources as possible before permanently excluding,' assures Ms Kruger. Pastoral systems include peer mentoring – both internal and external – and the five star canteen with a focus on hygiene and health is part of the campaign against any kind of food disorders. Ms Kruger acknowledges the challenge of gender identity. 'They are legally women until they are 18,' she says firmly, 'and therefore can remain in EWS, but they get fantastic support' from Gendered Intelligence – a community based project that delivers educational programmes as well as offering advice and counselling. Ms Kruger puts safeguarding before everything, something that was reflected in the recent safeguarding audit, which was outstanding.

Pupils and parents: Most parents and daughters here made a conscious decision to choose Ellen Wilkinson above any other school. The odd pupil has chosen it because someone in her wider family has been here, many because it is a real community school with a local feel. Some teachers are former pupils. One parent said her daughter chose it 'because of the extracurricular clubs, diverse cultures and because it's sporty.' Most like the all girls atmosphere, but this is definitely not a religious school. One Muslim parent said her two priorities were that her daughter be 'happy and safe'; Ellen Wilkinson fits the bill.

A genuinely relatively balanced mix of cultures and religious groups with about 20 per cent white British, 30 per cent Asian, 20 per cent black and 20 per cent Arabic, others include Japanese (some choose this over the local Japanese school), Chinese, Polish and other European. Sixty-six different languages are spoken in the school. Although in some families the mother might speak very limited English (though the father's English is fluent), 'all groups integrate', affirmed everyone we spoke to; there are no cliques based on race.

They all share a common interest in developing the confidence and aspirations of all the girls. 'They will be the leaders of tomorrow', affirms Ms Kruger. Tolerant, broadminded, self aware and thoroughly 21st century, our guides looked slightly baffled at our questions about diversity. Girls here are proud of their school and have a strong sense of giving something back and contributing to society.

Entrance: Always oversubscribed, with over 500 applicants for 216 places. Priority given to looked-after children, siblings, children of teachers at the school and those with specific medical or social needs. Then distance to the school is the deciding factor – currently around 1.5 miles.

About 40 girls from other schools join the sixth form each year, with a baseline of 5+ 9-4 GCSE grades for A level courses, including 6s in their A level subjects. Those who don't make the grade can take two or three BTec courses.

Exit: The majority go on to university. One to Cambridge and two medics in 2018; large numbers to the London colleges (UCL, Kings, Queen Mary's, SOAS and Goldsmith all popular destinations) to read a range of courses from biomedical science and chemical engineering to photography and Japanese. The STEM specialism here is clearly effective, as most go on to study maths and science related degrees.

Around 40 per cent depart after GCSEs to sixth form colleges elsewhere (eg Harris Westminster, William Morris, St Dominic's in Harrow and Hammersmith Academy), a few to further education colleges.

Remarks: A school with history, substance and a wealth of experience that is more than keeping up with the times and has a refreshingly modern and progressive outlook. Under its current leadership, a warm wind blows through its wide corridors which, together with high expectations and standards, makes for a thoroughly healthy and successful institution.

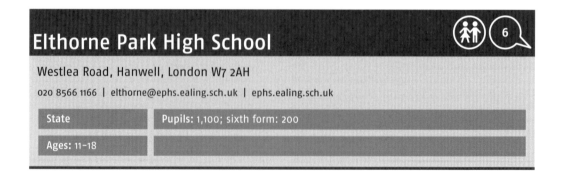

Elthorne Park High School

Westlea Road, Hanwell, London W7 2AH

020 8566 1166 | elthorne@ephs.ealing.sch.uk | ephs.ealing.sch.uk

State	Pupils: 1,100; sixth form: 200
Ages: 11–18	

Headteacher: Since 2012, Eliot Wong BSc PGCE Dip Ed NPQH (40s). Married with a school-age daughter, Mr Wong is a west Londoner through and through. Educated at St Peter's Primary school in Hammersmith and then Burlington Danes, he graduated with a first class degree in mathematics from

King's College London before following his vocation in teaching (maths). He still finds the time to teach further maths to a class of about five who choose to do it ('it's the most enjoyable thing I do') as well as running revision classes for GCSE. Sixteen years of his career have been spent in schools in Ealing. Previously deputy head at Brentside High School, and before that assistant head at Cheam High School. He has also worked at Cardinal Wiseman (head of maths) and in Woking.

Thoughtful, determined and with a razor sharp logical mind, Mr Wong has achieved much improvement. Graphs depicting GCSE data are moving in a healthy northerly direction and the latest Ofsted inspection in 2015 graded the school as good (from a requires improvement in 2013) with the proviso that it only missed an outstanding because there were only two years of available results data. Far from being disheartened by missing out on an outstanding, Mr Wong sees this as an opportunity to innovate and change continually: 'once you achieve an outstanding, there is a risk of complacency,' Mr Wong smiles. An advocate of Jim Collins' hedgehog concept, Wong believes if you focus on doing one thing really well everything else will fall into place. In his view it's the teaching that you need to concentrate on. 'If you teach really well, behaviour improves and parents are happy.' He measures the quality of teaching in a number of different ways, including regularly observing lessons and checking exercise books.

A simple but effective change he has made is to the school's mission statement: from 'achieving in a learning community' to 'achieving excellence in a learning community.' He has introduced rigour, challenge and aspiration and observes that 'most staff have responded very positively'. A regular tweeter, he celebrates his students' achievements in the public sphere as well as making sure his school remains prominent not only on social media but also in the mind of the local authority, from which he has been effective in extracting funding (for the new £14m expansion, for example). He is proud of the liberal atmosphere that is immediately noticeable, but asserts that 'we are old fashioned in some senses – in that we work hard and show a positive and respectful attitude.' However, this is achieved not by 'imposing draconian measures' but through 'trust (and verification) and expectation'. That is the Elthorne way, he says, and applies as much to the staff as to the pupils.

Excellent teachers and motivated pupils are only two legs of the three-legged stool; another focus of his is parental involvement. He has introduced the 'text challenge', challenging parents to support their children with weekly texts about particular issues, in current affairs, for example. Mr Wong is deeply conscious of having to find ways to add value not only to aspirational families but also disadvantaged families. 'If you want to get the best out children you can't drag them, but you need to stimulate them with interesting, engaging lessons and the support of their parents.' This is the ACE formula – Achievement, Challenge, Excellence. It seems to be working.

> 'If you want to get the best out children you need to stimulate them with interesting, engaging lessons and get the support of their parents'

Mr Wong is well respected by the pupils (they panic if they are on their phones when he appears in the playground), but parents speak of their frustration with his failure to respond to emails, and to complete references on time, and complain how difficult it is to get hold of him. An industrious, and thoughtful head, however (his office is decorated with hundreds of yellow post-it notes), he is highly committed and canny.

Academic matters: Huge improvement in results. In 2018, 78 per cent got 9-4 in both English and maths GCSE and 60 per cent got 9-5; at A level nearly a quarter A*/As and almost three-quarters A*-B. ALPS value added rates the sixth form as 'outstanding' for teaching and learning and results. Each year five or six pupils take further maths A level.

Elthorne Park is currently the top performing school in South Ealing and Hanwell (and has held this position for the third year running), and is in the top quintile of schools nationally in terms of GCSE attainment (including English, maths and two sciences). Out of over 5,000 non-selective, co-ed schools in the country Elthorne recently ranked 91st in performance tables, putting the school in the top two per cent.

Ofsted identified particularly imaginative teaching in modern languages with high standards of marking. Over half the year takes at least one language and French, Spanish and German all get a good smattering of 9-6 grades, Polish too. A foreign exchange is organised for each language and about 50 pupils go on a language exchange each year. Elthorne's modern language results are in the top five per cent of the country. Mr Wong says he will support anyone who wants to learn Latin (and ancient Greek) but a visiting teacher will have to come in specially or the pupil will have to go elsewhere.

The quality of teaching is closely observed and monitored. 'Book looks' at least half termly to check that marking is up to standard and each teacher is observed three times a year. Each year to GCSE has six classes with about 26 pupils in each. Setting in maths from year 7, English and science also broadly set as well as modern languages. Excellent DT department, offering separate exams in food technology, textiles, resistant materials and graphic products. Music, drama and theatre studies are strong, as well as all three sciences, particularly chemistry. All departments run 'intervention sessions' to support pupils who are falling behind.

Some 75 per cent of students have been taking Ebacc subjects for some time but 'I will no way force every student to do subjects that aren't suited them,' avers Mr Wong. BTec courses in media, business and health and social care also available as well as level 1 courses in eg motor vehicle maintenance and salon services. The ASDAN Award Scheme provides a course in basic skills, life skills and general knowledge for those students who wish to limit the number of GCSE courses they study.

Innovative style of teaching includes 'flip learning'. Students in the sixth form (and some classes lower down the school), given an iPad and required to research a subject before a lesson. The lesson can then be conducted in a more discursive way – students therefore learn to think, as well as to carry out independent research.

He still finds the time to teach further maths to a class of about five ('it's the most enjoyable thing I do') as well as running revision classes for GCSE

Enrichment lessons form part of the curriculum for years 7 to 9 – an effort to broaden the academic experience so that pupils are not confined to Ebacc subjects. They might study, eg, Japanese or film. Gifted and talented pupils can used it as a springboard to enhance their skills.

One parent observed reluctantly that there remains a culture of low expectation at Elthorne, however, citing as an example the practice of basing target grades at GCSE on earlier Sats results. Parents also commented on a lack of support with regard to A level choices and the university process. There is a lack of clear communication and flexibility about options, they say. This results in a few going elsewhere for sixth form when their inclination would have been to stay. School's response to this is that the senior leadership team now interviews every year 11 student and discusses the extracurricular guarantees made to every student, which range from travel abroad to gym membership and personalised help with Oxbridge applications. Communication when a child is not

reaching targets, on the other hand, is very good, observed another parent. A subject teacher will send a text, and similarly if a child gets detention, the parents are sent a text.

The number of students with SEN is not high – less than 20 per cent – but a relatively high number of students (between two and three per cent) with EHC plans. 'They are attracted to us as we are a nurturing school, and they are well supported,' says Mr Wong. The SENCo has a team of 10. Children are supported in class as much as possible with teaching assistants attached to subjects. EAL tuition takes place outside the classroom. One parent observed how little support you get if you are a middle class kid with dyslexia – we have heard that before. A £14m expansion project, the Additionally Resourced Provision for Special Needs, opened in 2017. This is a hub of activity working to support children with speech, language and communication problems and those with specific learning needs (SLCN – speech, language and communication needs). The new development also houses facilities for all the students, including a new hall and drama studio, a life skills room and two extra ICT suites.

Games, options, the arts: 'Expressive arts are at the heart of our community,' says Mr Wong. We were impressed with just how much goes on in here – in creative arts, drama, music and sport. Elthorne teams have excelled in the borough in various sports including cross-country, netball, basketball, rugby, football and cricket. Girls' sports are especially strong. The current year 11 girls' netball team has been unbeaten for the past four years and the U13 girls' football team is national champion. There are regular competitions and matches – inter-form and inter-school as well as regional. An annual sports day, which includes track and field athletics as well as softball, takes place at Perivale sports ground.

For budding thespians there is the opportunity to perform extracts from Shakespeare plays at the annual Shakespeare Festival. In addition there is an annual major whole school production, often a musical (recently they performed Grease). Students get involved with all aspects of the production – costumes, choreography, music, set and props. Decent drama studio where lessons and rehearsals take place. Performances happen in the hall.

Gifted musicians are identified and giving lots of opportunity to compete and perform. Numerous concerts and recitals plus a classical music competition and annual rock concert. Plenty of ensembles – brass and guitar as well as a chamber and whole school orchestra. Macs in music rooms where students are taught music composition. The popular summer festival and barbecue brings together performances and displays – art and DT as well as drama and music.

Lots of trips and activities including annual ski trip and Spanish, French and German exchanges (with a twin school), as well as geography field trips and visits to eg Oxford University and the theatre. Plenty of extracurricular opportunities such as public speaking competitions, D of E, bushcraft and PGL trips, the STEM challenge (EPHS were recently regional winners) and UK maths challenge. A plethora of clubs take place after school, from debating to film and volunteering in the community.

Background and atmosphere: Elthorne may be in Hanwell but it stands out from other schools of its kind because it's situated on the edge of the seven and a half acres of green space that is Elthorne Park. Children can spill into this area during lunch break (supervised), and the football pitches and sports areas are a tremendous additional resource. The main buildings are positioned around a central courtyard – a mixture of low, single storey, temporary, and two storey buildings as well as the shiny, modern sixth form centre. Eight modern, spacious and well-equipped science labs, a suite of specialist music rooms, a purpose built drama studio, four art studios with a dark room, graphics and kiln facilities. Specialist DT including food technology, textiles and resistant materials. Plenty of Macs available for use in graphics as well as in music. Large sports hall as well as separate school hall where lunch, assemblies and drama happens. Purpose built sixth form centre. A feeling of space – no cramped corridors and a comfortable well-resourced library.

Maroon uniform creates a somewhat dour impression and can be worn scruffily: 'they are not super strict about ties and tucking in shirts here,' said our guide with warm appreciation. This school is far from dour, however, but vibrant and buzzy. While Mr Wong clearly has a firm grip, the school has a relaxed feel; children are not deferential but their behaviour seems to fall on the right side of the line.

Pastoral care, well-being and discipline: Mr Wong describes the school as a healthy mix of old-fashioned and more relaxed values. While there is a finely tuned system of 'levelled' detentions (ranging between a 15 minute personal detention with a teacher to a head teacher detention on a Monday night) as well as a three strikes policy and a system of internal isolations, the key element is trust. This can't be imposed, says Wong, through draconian measures, but through example and respect. He talks about 'the Elthorne Way,' an expectation of high achievement and excellence through a healthy symbiotic relationship between staff and pupils. Students appear relaxed, but that doesn't mean they aren't polite and well behaved. Mr Wong works hard and expects those around him to work hard, both staff and pupils. 'I believe in hard work and striving for excellence,' he says, 'I don't believe in excuses.' Trust is key – but trust with verification. We will trust them, he says, but we will check on them. The students have a voice – the student council have regular breakfasts and lunches with staff and there is an annual student survey. They, too, are listened to and treated with respect. When it comes to drugs and weapons, however, the line is clear and inflexible.

Mr Wong works hard and expects those around him to work hard, both staff and pupils. 'I believe in striving for excellence,' he says, 'I don't believe in excuses'

Parents warmly supportive – and appreciative – of the school's approach to incidents that happen outside school hours, often with the local community. They step in quickly and with tact and understanding. Behaviour – according to most parents – is 'on the whole good'.

Pupils and parents: Just under 50 per cent of families here are white British. The rest split fairly equally between black, Asian and Eastern European. Some support for EAL but most have learnt good English at primary school. Local Ealing families who, on the whole, are keen their children do well and will work hard with the school to achieve this. Relatively low number of pupils are on free school meals (25 per cent compared with a national average of 28 per cent). Stable student population.

Entrance: About 1,000 apply each year for 240 places in year 7. The four main feeder primaries are Fielding, Oaklands, Little Ealing and St Mark's – perception among parents is that Fielding dominates. As the primaries expand, so there is greater pressure on places. Proximity to the school the main criterion (after the usual criteria have been taken into account – children in public care, exceptional medical or social circumstances etc). Catchment has shrunk from a 1.5 mile radius to a one mile radius. Parents want their children to come here and consider it to be outstanding – regardless of what Ofsted says. Siblings given priority. To get into the sixth form you need a minimum of five 9-4s including English and maths at GCSE with at least a 6 in chosen A level subjects.

Exit: Of the upper sixth approximately 75 per cent go on to university, with about a quarter of these to Russell Group. Brighter pupils attracted elsewhere for sixth form, observed one parent. 'No NEETs for the past three years!', says head proudly. Some 93 per cent stay in education post-GCSEs, around 50 per cent stay at Elthorne to study advanced courses in the sixth form – over 70 per cent of these study A levels, but all sixth formers study advanced (level 3) courses which may include BTecs. About 20 per cent each year go on to art school and one or two each year go to the BRIT school.

Money matters: A local authority funded, well-resourced school – reserves, we were told, are greater than five per cent. Lower than borough average spent on supply staff, large proportion of budget spent on teachers and education support staff. Almost double spent on learning resources and ICT compared with local and national averages.

Remarks: Value added – an often overlooked measure – is strong here: mid and high achievers will make significant progress, especially compared with their peers nationally. If you have a motivated child, keen to do well, this school won't hold him/her back but will inspire and work to meet that potential. A school with a genuine liberal arts and creative ethos. A precious gem in this age of emphasis on Ebacc subjects. Let's hope it will preserve its arty tradition as it consolidates the academics in the face of pressure from on high.

Glebe Primary School

Sussex Road, Ickenham, Uxbridge UB10 8PH

01895 462385 | office@glebeprimary.org | glebe.hillingdon.sch.uk

State	Pupils: 600
Ages: 3–11	

Headteacher: Since 2017, Melanie Penney, previously assistant head and deputy head.

Entrance: For nursery places apply direct to the nursery and for the school apply through the local authority. Usual criteria apply.

Exit: One or two go to the independent sector and a few to local grammars, but the majority head to Vyners School in Ickenham (over half) or Douay Martyrs.

Remarks: Set in the deepest London suburbs (Ickenham tube is near the end of the Piccadilly and Metropolitan lines) and built in the 1970s, the school caters for a mixed intake. Ten per cent of pupils come from military families stationed at the local RAF base and often only stay for a short time. Most pupils are drawn from the local area but the catchment area has shrunk in recent years as the school has grown more popular, with some pupils even transferring from schools that previously had a better reputation.

Sats results are above the national average but a recent Ofsted report found that 'more able pupils have not always done as well as expected.' However the school told us that this point has been addressed 'through setting and focus groups for more able children over the last few years' and as a result, level 5 Sats results have risen to well above the national average. There is a joint project for gifted and talented pupils with a neighbouring school and Glebe recently won the Hillingdon Maths Challenge. School also has links with nearby Brunel University – for science and PE lessons.

'It feels like a little village school and it has a very caring environment'

The school's go-getting motto is 'We can and we will!' and first impressions reminded us more of a private school than a state primary. Photos on the wall of the head boy, head girl and house captains show the ambitious nature of the place and the school is keen 'to replicate some of the best aspects of independent schools, such as widening opportunities in sports, music and introducing a house system and prefects.'

Much of the games teaching is delivered by a specialist sports coach. Sports include football, netball, cross-country, athletics, cricket and tag rugby (supported by an enthusiastic year 6 teacher). The school takes part in inter-school competitions and recently won the Uxbridge football competition.

All children get the chance to study a musical instrument. This starts in year 2 with recorders and free tuition on the keyboard from year 4. Parents can pay for tuition in violin, cello, clarinet or flute if they want their children to take music exams. Two guitar clubs after school and when we visited we saw a group of year 4 children strumming away confidently. School choir performs regularly in different concerts, including one at the 02 Arena. 'The music provision is wonderful,' said an appreciative parent. Former pupils include TV presenter Sue Cook and London 2012 athlete Julia Bleasdale.

The school is a regional centre for those with impaired hearing. The SRP – specialist resourced provision for hearing-impaired children – has two teaching areas and a speech therapy room. Each classroom has a Soundfield system, amplifying the sound of the teacher's voice. There are places for nine hearing impaired children and the school employs two specialist teachers of the deaf. All the children are on the roll of their mainstream class and school aims for them to be taught in class alongside their hearing peers, with support if necessary.

School has recently moved into a new two-storey building, to great parental relief, and can at last serve hot lunches.

Parents are very supportive and reckon the school has a strong nurturing ethos. 'It feels like a little village school and it has a very caring environment,' said one. 'All the children are aware of each other and support each other.' Another told us: 'I wouldn't hesitate to recommend it to anyone. I feel that I struck gold when I found Glebe.'

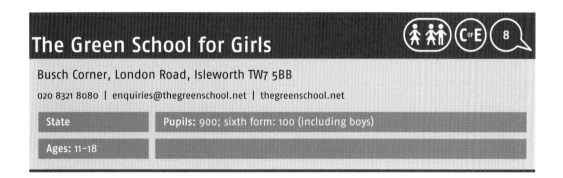

The Green School for Girls

Busch Corner, London Road, Isleworth TW7 5BB

020 8321 8080 | enquiries@thegreenschool.net | thegreenschool.net

State	Pupils: 900; sixth form: 100 (including boys)
Ages: 11–18	

Executive Head: Since 2015, Sally Yarrow (late 40s) BMus PGCE, educated at Aylesbury High grammar School and Hull University before completing her PGCE at Goldsmiths. Started her career as a music teacher and music remains her passion in education. Previously deputy head at St Marylebone school, a consistently high performing all girls C of E secondary, she fits like a glove here but has nonetheless stepped out of her comfort zone, having been at St Marylebone for almost her entire career. 'I could have stayed there for the rest of my working life, I loved it and was very happy, but I was ready for a new challenge,' she confides. With two school age boys of her own, Mrs Yarrow is approachable, youthfully girlish and enthusiastic, and deeply principled. Very popular with parents and pupils who regard her as having made a real impact. One parent described her as shrewd with a definite presence. Many of the girls see her as stern and strict, 'which is no bad thing,' affirmed another parent. On a very local level, she introduced whole school assemblies in the capacious sports hall, a hugely popular fixture with the girls which gives the school a sense of unity and purpose. She is definite about her vision and expresses it without any

fudge or waffle. Her expectations are high but her approach is entirely child centred. 'It is all about what's best for the pupils', she says. 'We are a fully comprehensive, inclusive and diverse school and I am very proud of that.'

Her title is now executive head of the Green School Trust and she oversees both the girls' school and the new Green School for Boys. Parents confident that Stephen Burns, previously deputy head, will be an effective head of school responsible for the day to day running of the Green School for Girls

Academic matters: Consistently impressive GCSE results. Sixty-nine per cent of pupils got 9-4 in both maths and English and 30 per cent of grades were 9-7 in 2018. History, maths English and religious studies perform particularly well with high numbers of 9-7s. Science is also getting stronger. A level subjects include art and design, film studies, sociology and psychology as well as BTec level 3 in health and social care. High numbers choose biology, psychology and religious studies at A level. Value added scores are good (Progress 8 is a positive 0.5, placing the school in the top three per cent of schools nationally) – pupils make good progress, a valuable indicator of good teaching and a well run school. Parents comment about their daughters in the lower sets being stretched just as hard as if they were in the top sets. High expectation runs through all the layers of the school. Number of pupils with English as an additional language is very high – there is the option to take a GCSE in a native language, or indeed any language in which a pupil excels, in year 9.

A level results do not match the impressive GCSE scores – 'yet,' Mrs Yarrow intervenes. 'We lose a few of the high achievers after GCSE, and the girls for whom English is not their first language find the challenges are greater at A level – but this is something we are very much working on at the moment,' she explains, adding 'there is a huge amount of support for sixth form provision.' In 2018, 46 per cent A*-B and 22 per cent A*/A grades. The school is part of a Hounslow sixth form consortium (others include Gunnersbury, Brentford, Gumley and Chiswick), so girls in the sixth form here can travel to other schools for certain lessons, which may include boys. Extended Project Qualification (EPQ) is popular and highly successful. It taps into all the skills and qualities that Mrs Yarrow is so determined to develop here, self-reliance, resilience, being able to think and stand on one's own two feet. An enrichment programme in the sixth form, 'broadening horizons', incorporates academic literacy, discussion and discourse. It is aimed at developing academic minds; their form tutors are known as 'coaches' and they coach them with their studies. Opportunities for stretching as sports leaders, in Young Enterprise and LAMDA. Sixth form mentors, or co-tutors, work with particular forms as part of their leadership development, and they assume positions of responsibility whether as prefect, head girl, or one of four deputy head girls or assistants (a mirroring of the schools' staff senior leadership team).

Additional support given to those who need in it in years 7, 8 and 9 in maths and English (known as the Bridge Group). There can be as many as 15 pupils taught in a lesson of their own by the very experienced SENCo as well as a teacher and learning support assistant. Girls are taken out of language lessons to attend these classes. Less than one per cent of students have a statement/EHCP.

Setting for maths from year 7, and from year 8 in English and science: 'This may change; there is a fairly broad range within the sets,' avers Mrs Yarrow, who is mindful to ensure that teaching in the lower sets doesn't create a false cap of attainment. Teaching methods, language used by staff and senior leaders' attitude all encourage the building of a growth mindset and resilience. 'This is one of our school priorities,' says Mrs Yarrow, 'along with the application of performance skills to all the subjects and to life.'

Games, options, the arts: Wide choice of sporting activities include rowing, netball and badminton. School participates in various borough competitions including the National Youth Rowing Competition. Plenty of facilities on or adjacent to the site – netball courts as well as rugby and football pitches. Tag rugby one of the main sports here. A large, modern and squeaky clean sports hall can accommodate volleyball, dodge ball, trampolining and self-defence as well as netball, basketball and badminton.

DT GCSE options are textiles and food technology, but no electronics or resistant materials. Eighteen sewing machines as well as three embroidery machines and two overlocker machines, but only one textiles teacher. If your daughter wants to do A level textiles she will currently have lessons at one of the other schools in the Hounslow consortium. Everyone does food technology in years 7 and 8. Art is a popular A level. We saw some impressive ceramics, a very tangible pineapple in particular.

Very popular with parents and pupils who regard her as having made a real impact. One parent described her as shrewd with a definite presence

Old hall used for fashion shows (a fundraiser) and drama productions. There is also a drama studio – where we witnessed a very noisy game known as 'the splat game' designed to warm up the acting genes. Lots of productions by all year groups. Annual school productions have recently included Archie Dobson's War, Much Ado About Nothing ('slightly adapted,' we're told) and The Ash Girl. The sixth form theatre company recently produced, performed and directed The Great Gatsby.

Since the arrival of Mrs Yarrow, a huge and healthy increase in numbers wanting to join choirs and bands. Music has had a heavy injection of hers. Girls describe it, with infectious enthusiasm, as 'a really fun subject'. Music technology popular; lots of fancy equipment – Apple Macs and keyboards, and we saw a year 10 class writing a rap song. Lots of practice rooms for the large numbers who play an instrument – many play more than one, and music permeated several mainstream lessons we saw.

Debating club also very popular – open to any year group and recently, we were told, they examined issues from gay marriage to stem cell research and thrashed out the question of whether Black History Month should be abolished.

Plenty of residential trips – especially in year 9 – to Spain and France as well as ski trips to Austria.

Hampton Court House (Senior School)

Duke of Edinburgh awards, bronze (year 10), silver and gold.

Careers advice and support strong. School awarded level 3 Investors in Careers.

Background and atmosphere: Although this is a Church of England school with a Christian ethos, it is overwhelmingly multi-faith. About a third of pupils are from Muslim families. One parent explained that girls' schools are popular 'because girls won't lose the attention of their teachers to the boys, the discipline is good and they can choose science subjects without feeling overshadowed by the boys'.

A five form entry school, the Green School is on the large side but not vast. Swathes of green tartan stream into the welcoming café Sorrento opposite the school. Not shouty girls, but considerate and polite, and all different cultures and backgrounds seem to integrate well as they pile into their waffles before the start of school. They file in an orderly fashion into the vast sports hall for assembly, in time to the soothing classical music that bounces off the sporty walls, and the hall becomes a sea of green uniform.

A school steeped in history (it was originally founded in 1796), the main building is a handsome 1906 Edwardian brick and timber building situated on the busy junction at Busch Corner in Isleworth. This now houses the library and a performance hall (where the clock has always been wrong) as well as some classrooms. Linking them are long, wide corridors which smell of freshly polished wooden parquet floors. Gold leaf plated wooden merit boards from the 1950s line the walls, and cupboards stuffed with silver cups nestle in corners. A satisfyingly traditional smell of learning, scholarship and achievement. The library, despite its traditional feel, is buzzing with activity. This is where girls come to do their homework – both during and after school hours. Books here are well thumbed and there are plenty of computers.

The modern buildings are bright, filled with sunlight, with lots of space. Our guides particularly enjoyed lingering in the sociology classroom, a favourite subject here. The sixth form centre is civilised with attractive space to eat and talk as well as have meetings, perform plays and listen to talks. An area to chat and use mobiles is screened off from an area to work and use computers (we presume for work). The school canteen is comfortable, streaming with sunlight through the large windows when we visited. All the girls we met said the food was good. Many get in early to eat breakfast here at 7.30am.

The school is divided into five houses – named here after trees (Willow, Oaks, Beeches etc) for the purpose of competitions, whether sporting, academic, or other – there is an inter-house Christmas carol competition, for example.

Pastoral care, well-being and discipline: The pastoral care here is universally acclaimed. A number of parents described how much their daughters have grown in confidence here – whether as a result of performing in plays and assemblies, playing sport or being encouraged to question and challenge their teachers during lessons. While there is respect for the staff among the pupils, it works both ways, enabling the timid types, prone to being overly deferential, to emerge from their shells and speak up for themselves. The school motto, Let your light shine, seems to have genuine resonance.

Recently, we were told, they examined issues from gay marriage to stem cell research and thrashed out the question of whether Black History Month should be abolished

The very congenial school chaplain is in school three times a week and she takes part in assemblies and services. By all accounts she plays a key pastoral role for students and staff alike.

There is a clear disciplinary procedure which appears to be appreciated by pupils, parents and staff. Final step after three warnings. If a girl needs to be removed from a lesson for being disruptive, she is sent to the Improvement Area. Curriculum parking is when a student is removed from a lesson and 'sent to an appropriate parking lot' to work. Detentions here are known as 'learning meetings'. 'You don't sit around doing nothing but discuss a solution.'

Naughty behaviour seems to boil down to disrupting lessons and occasional bullying behaviour. The girls we spoke to looked wide eyed when we asked about drugs. This is a school of predominately good girls. Any incidents of bullying are dealt with quickly through the year leader and heads of year. Response is speedy and effective. Girls seem quite confident that they would go to the teachers if they needed to.

Social media – as in all secondary schools at the moment – is causing the most sleepless nights for heads. Here mobile phones have to be stored in lockers during the school day and if they are found on a girl during a lesson they are confiscated. The strict policy is bearing fruit – fewer social media related incidents this year than in previous years. A more relaxed policy is adopted with sixth formers, however.

One girl, who said she never used to like school, now enjoys coming to school and said she 'feels safe'. Parents, too, are confident that any issues of bullying, social media abuse or self harming will be dealt with swiftly and effectively. One mother described how 'in tune' the school is with its community: there is a genuine understanding of and empathy with the issues that face teenage girls at this time.

Pupils and parents: An immensely diverse, multicultural C of E school. Many Muslim pupils, some Hindu, as well as devout Christians and some of no faith. Many parents are practising Christians but plenty are not. Pupils come from Brentford and Chiswick as well as Staines and Isleworth and a wide range of local and far flung primaries. Over 30 per cent of pupils are on pupil premium. One parent talked of it being a 'balanced community', families from all walks of life, earning a living in so many different ways, but what virtually all parents have in common is a shared belief in high standards. They are committed to supporting their daughters to reach their full potential.

Entrance: As this is a Church of England school, parents are expected to be committed to the Christian ethos and give full support to the school. Girls are expected to attend Christian acts of worship and take part in the religious curriculum. A hundred of the 155 places are reserved for practising Christians, 30 places allocated to 'other world faiths' and 25 are community places. Priority to siblings (including brothers at the Green School for Boys) and those who live closest.

Sixth form admissions (boys as well as girls) according to predicted GCSE grades and proximity.

Don't be shy about making an in year application for an occasional place. As with all areas of London there is movement and there are often new arrivals in years other than years 7 and 12.

Exit: A challenge for Mrs Yarrow is to keep as many of high performers as she can for the sixth form and encourage them to appreciate its strengths. In 2018, 60 per cent left after GCSEs. After A level students go to a wide range of destinations to read an equally wide range of subjects. One off to Oxbridge in 2018 and one to study medicine; others to destinations ranging from LSE, Imperial and UCL to the University of the Arts (film and TV studies). A small number to art foundation and five per cent take gap years, including apprenticeships or internships with eg the BBC.

Remarks: We agree that this is a genuinely outstanding state secondary. The high standard of pastoral care and the attention that's paid to each individual and their needs makes this a good fit for almost any girl, but especially those who are aspirational, hard working and committed to doing their best. A tolerant, diverse school with strong Christian values – of the very best kind. Those with sons too keep an eye out – the new Green School for Boys is one to watch.

Greenford High School

Lady Margaret Road, Southall, Middlesex UB1 2GU

020 8578 9152 | office@greenford.ealing.sch.uk | greenford.ealing.sch.uk

State	Pupils: 1,755; sixth form: 539
Ages: 11–19	

Headteacher: Since 2009, Mathew Cramer MA PGCE NPHQ (mid 50s), a north Londoner by birth and son of a commercial artist. Mr Cramer was educated at Highgate Wood Comprehensive and went onto read philosophy and literature at Sussex University followed by a masters at Warwick and a PGCE at King's College London. His career started with a brief spell in Hong Kong editing textbooks, since then he has spent his entire career teaching in west London. He came to Greenford to teach English in 1995; prior to that he was at St Mark's Catholic school in Hounslow, where his wife is now head of

media. Warm, understated with a beguiling, dry sense of humour, Mr Cramer is an experienced and extremely effective head. His office is reassuringly cluttered, with an eclectic mix of pictures on the walls, from ancient maps and Greek temples (his mother is Greek Cypriot) to Hokusai's 'Great wave off Kanagawa' juxtaposed with boldly colourful paintings by his students.

Modest about the achievements in his 10 years at the helm here, Mr Cramer says the school was always successful, 'a very warm school built on positive relationships between staff and pupils.

I've tried to establish a culture that is happy but aspirational,' he says. 'I try to give lifeless buildings an identity, find ways to demonstrate that learning is exciting and give school a sense of vibrancy.' Passionate about literacy, he focuses heavily on reading skills when they arrive. At this point only a third can read above the standard of their reading age, and a third are well below the standard. 'It's essential they can access text,' says Mr Cramer.

Thoughtful and sensitive, Mr Cramer is very much a people person. Parents describe him as 'gentle but firm. He enjoys a good debate.' He puts staff recruitment amongst his highest priorities – 'it's all about the staff,' he says; 'the results of employing the right person for a particular role are tangible and visible.'

The school is flying high and has been for some time, receiving a number of awards, including the Gold Award from Boris Johnson, awarded for the highest progress figures. Mr Cramer notes this with a healthy mixture of scepticism and pride, and is more concerned to tell us about his bugbears: 'litter drives me mad,' he says.

Academic matters: A fully comprehensive, non-selective school, Greenford High has to cater for two extremes, without overlooking the middle tranche. It does an impressively good job. Japanese, GCSEs and A levels at one end of the spectrum, and a BTec in business and enterprise at the other. DT product design, fine art and photography as well as business and economics are all offered; science labs are well equipped, science teaching effective. The high expectations for academic students do not just include a university exit, Russell Group, perhaps or even Oxford and Cambridge, but Harvard and Princeton too. At the other end of the scale, some apprenticeships are harder to achieve than a university place. Some 500 students were competing for one apprenticeship with Honda; it was a Greenford boy who won it.

His office is reassuringly cluttered, with an eclectic mix of pictures on the walls, from ancient maps and Greek temples to Hokusai's 'Great wave off Kanagawa'

Years 7 and 8 now have nearly all lessons their own 'middle school' building, and pupils graduate formally from year 8 into year 9 – they get a 'degree' to show they are ready for the GCSE course that starts from year 9. The only test is their attitude to learning. Those that are not ready continue for longer in middle school. 'This solves a number of problems,' says Mr Cramer, 'not least it stops year 8 from being a fallow year.' Setting from year 7 in maths and English (about nine sets in total), science is setted later (moderate setting in yr 7; more refined at KS4). Every pupil takes RE GCSE at end of the year 9, 'a gateway GCSE', 80 per cent pass, a third achieve A*/A, and 'even if they don't do as well as they would have done had they waited until year 11, it will have motivated and challenged them,' says Mr Cramer. At the end of year 10 they all take a language GCSE (which they have started in year 7 and could include Spanish, French, German or Japanese), some take two languages, some take a community language – facilitated, but not taught, by the school. A study club after school for years 10 and 11 supports their organisation, revision and individual learning. Some classes have a mixed year group – eg years 9 and 10 are mixed as are years 10 and 11 – usually for options at GCSE.

GCSE results in 2018 impressive, 35 per cent 9-7, and 77 per cent got 9-4 in both English and maths – some of their best results ever, which placed the school in the top 200 nationally. At A level in 2018, 44 per cent A*-B grades (22 per cent A*/A). Key Stage 4 ALPs grade (measuring student progress against the national picture) was a level 2 – Outstanding. At A level, ALPs grade was a level 3 – Excellent; these scores have been consistently this high for the last 10 years.

Particularly strong GCSE results in business and economics (business handily appeals to both ends of the academic spectrum and Southall has one of the highest number of small businesses), all three sciences, computing, Japanese (though small numbers take it), German and history. Most popular subject at A level, by some margin, is maths, with pleasing results. Excellent results at A level too in media, film and TV studies (best results in the country), DT product design, physics and fine art.

Greenford used to be a language college and 60-70 per cent of students continue to take a modern language at GCSE. Japanese has always been strong – 'it's always about the personalities,' says Mr Cramer. 'We were lucky to have an outstanding Japanese teacher and we continue to attract excellent teachers'. They are proactive – whether it be inviting the wife of the Japanese prime minister to the school or beating Eton and other high achieving independent schools at the Nihongo Cup run by the Japanese embassy. The experience spills into pupils' later lives: one ex-pupil is now working for big business in Tokyo. With difficult decisions impending on funding, however, the fate of Japanese here lies in the balance.

School is consistently in the top five per cent of the country for progress, and while the SEN progress is still above average at +0.15, SEND pupils make lower progress compared with other pupils

'I try to give lifeless buildings an identity, find ways to demonstrate that learning is exciting and give school a sense of vibrancy'

in the school. A fair number of pupils have support with their learning, but only a handful on EHC plans. Mr Cramer is visibly pained that these pupils make less progress than their mainstream peers despite the fact that they are still making more progress than the national average, and confirms that this is one of their targets.

The university style campus is not necessarily conducive to people with EHC plans – but the new block, in development, will have an ARP area to work with students who have different needs, and a capacity for 20 students.

Greenford High has pulling power, attracting high quality teachers. One of the physics teachers we met is possibly the only Somali female physics teacher in the country. The school has a partnership with Teach First, as well as with the Institute of Education, and trains 30 teachers a year – many stay on. Healthy mix of the long established, stable and experienced, some of whom form part of the senior leadership team, and the young and dynamic, bringing fresh ideas and fuelling the tangible vibrancy in the classroom.

Games, options, the arts: Sport is strong – as in other departments at Greenford, standards are high. An Olympic judge runs the gymnastics, an ex-England player coaches the basketball. Excellent facilities in relatively new building (funded by PFI). Well-equipped and well-used gym. Lots of space on site, including fleet of MUGAs as well as grass pitches (though notorious Ealing soil means they're waterlogged for much of the winter months, we were told with wry raise of the eyebrow). Football and netball strong (though there was an observation from one quarter that if you are not particularly keen you can end up not playing much sport at all). Both genders shine in gymnastics and trampolining. Boys and girls taught separately for PE.

Despite corrosive cuts, school manfully continues to offer excellent art, DT, textiles, cooking and photography (three art teachers have had to go as department has shrunk from five to two). Impressive display of design products – toys and automated hoovers. School is proud owner of a laser cutter as well as a 3D printer. All pupils do art in years 7 and 8, between 15 and 20 do GCSE, a few do fine art A level and about about 4-6 a year go on to art colleges. 'It is important that we don't forget those students,' says Mr Cramer.

School very supportive of Cadets, Scouts and Duke of Edinburgh Award. Some 150 trips a year, including to Lille, Berlin and Tokyo, to Cambridge, Oxford and Reading. Mixed year groups help to spread the cost – school helps as much as it can with funding. 'There is not a culture of the haves and have nots here, much to parents' relief,' pointed out one father. 'School is open to any initiative and will run with it, but the students need to be proactive,' commented a mother.

Music – very few take it to GCSE or A level (music tech only). However there have been successful barber shop quartets. Drumkit and guitars available for anyone who wants to have a go. 'As with so much of the approach at Greenford,' observed a parent, 'if the pupils show enthusiasm and drive, the school will support them and nurture any talent or interest.'

Drama is taken by everyone in years 7 and 8, and 20 or so continue to GCSE, though it is not available at A level. Small theatre where students put on comedy shows.

Background and atmosphere: Founded in 1939, Greenford started life as a typical suburban grammar school, surrounded by farmland. The original 1930s buildings still stand and now form part of a new block. The school has gone through a number of different personalities since then and is now a large comprehensive with 1,800 pupils, increasing to 2,100 with the new middle school building, which houses years 7 and 8 and provides a 'small school' within the school.

One of the teachers we met is possibly the only Somali female physics teacher in the country

The school buzzes with an atmosphere of endeavour, echoing its motto 'learning to succeed'. Mr Cramer likens the modern university campus style of the site to Sussex and Warwick Universities. The new buildings, opened by David Miliband in 2008, are constructed out of various materials, painted in bright array of colours and named alphabetically after key people (A for Aristotle, B for Brunel, F for Fitzgerald – Ella, not Scott). Each building has vibrant murals painted up the stairs, along the corridors, in the entrance halls – penguin book covers, famous theatrical production posters and a Scrabble board, a surrealist portrait of 'the Greenford giraffe' outside Downing Street, a double Helix climbing the stairs, a large map of England with university sites pinned to it. 'We wanted to make the place feel vibrant, that learning is stimulating and fun,' says Mr Cramer, 'and the students appreciate it, they respect their environment, we have very little vandalism.' The campus is surrounded by irregular grassy mounds, referred to as 'Teletubby hills', contributing to the overall sense that this place is an oasis of opportunity in the middle of its suburban setting.

The main reception, as you enter the school, resembles a busy airport – lots of people coming and going, a sense of industry and purpose. High tech gates and lanyard creations, but amidst all that security the atmosphere is human, friendly and flexible.

The canteen is café style, with a mix of round and long tables and a little tuck shop. Post-16 accommodation includes a common room with table football and a large quiet area filled with computer stations to work and prepare for the next stage.

Pastoral care, well-being and discipline: Strong emphasis on an ethos of helping others – not reacting out of self-interest but for the good of the community and the good of others. Initiatives like hosting a dinner for senior citizens in the school hall – organised and run by post-16 pupils – helps to reaffirm these values. Assembly – taken in year groups, so each year gets together once a week – reflects on a range of issues from moral choices to healthy eating and child exploitation. Each assembly ends with an act of worship – relevant to all faiths.

They are proactive – whether it be inviting the wife of the Japanese prime minister to the school or beating Eton at the Nihongo Cup run by the Japanese embassy

Cyber issues addressed head on. System of cyber mentors contributes to an awareness and support system for any abuse of social media. School receives £50,000 each year from the John Lyons Foundation towards this. E-safety talks regularly attended by all students – 'as a result, social media bullying and related issues are not a major concern here,' assures head.

'This is not a detention bound school,' commented one parent, 'but there are rules and there are standards, and they are high ones. If you want to get the best out of the school you are expected to work with them.. You have to look smart, hand homework in on time, but these things are done by cooperation rather than the coercion.'

Behaviour, on the whole, is good. Teachers here earn respect and get it. There is genuine concern and care for the pupils, so that although good results are expected, it is the result that would be good for each individual. On the more contentious issues, we were assured that incidents of knives in school are rare and the school takes a sensitive approach to the government initiative Prevent. Issues relating to religious extremism are tackled by the head in assemblies and through outside speakers who come to give talks. Homophobia more of a prescient issue than gender fluidity.

Pupils and parents: A diverse mix of different cultures and nationalities, about 40 per cent Muslim. Despite the diversity, the community is well integrated. When Pakistan play India in the test match, we were told, the school comes alive with excitement and the fault lines are more visible. Only five per cent white British. Other white communities from Eastern Europe, predominately Polish. Others come from all over, from Eritrea to Afghanistan, a fair few from Somalia. Many are very aspirational. Turnout for parents' evenings is always high, observed one parent. Lots are keen for their children to excel at the sciences. The demographic has shifted slightly in the last 10 years – mainly with the decrease in numbers from the Sikh community – and the school has now started to attract families with very able children – families who in the past might have chosen to send them to grammar schools or choose independent schools.

One parent commented, 'kids here are not very privileged but become privileged from being at Greenford'. Pupils are politically aware, will hold mock elections during an election even if it coincides with exams, are flexible and ready to think on their feet.

Entrance: Most oversubscribed school in Ealing. Receives more applications than any other school. There were 1,667 applications for 300 yr 7 places for September 2018; 435 first choices, 426 second choices. Siblings given priority. 'This is a family school,' says Mr Cramer; 'a family could live in Slough and get a place at the school' (many do – as many Sikhs moved to Langley and Slough). 'We don't have a catchment.' However the next criterion is proximity to the school and most live within half a mile, though 10 per cent of pupils live further away.

Exit: One to Oxford and one to Cambridge in 2018, plus six medics. Mr Cramer makes lots of trips to Oxbridge colleges to make himself, his school and his students known. Approximately 230 go on to university each year but there is also a lot of investment in apprenticeships. 'You have to be realistic,' affirms Mr Cramer, 'university is not for everyone but it does offer the chance to lead a different life'. The occasional place is won at top US universities, too. One former student is now studying at Harvard, another at Princeton.

Remarks: If you want a strong head with a big heart, a diverse community which shares a desire for a high standards and has high expectations, whether it be for results, or attention to well-being, and if you are lucky enough to fall within the criteria for getting into this hugely oversubscribed school, you need look no further. But this is a school that gives to those who give: the more you put in the more you get out. Slouchers beware.

Gumley House School FCJ

St John's Road, Isleworth TW7 6XF

020 8568 8692 | general@gumley.hounslow.sch.uk | gumley.hounslow.sch.uk

State	Pupils: 1,072; sixth form: 170 (15 boys)
Ages: 11–18	

Headteacher: Since 2016, Caroline Braggs BA PGCE MA NPQH (50s), previously deputy head. Read theology at Heythrop College, London University, gaining her PGCE at the Institute of Education and MA at University of Surrey. Has taught at three other Catholic schools before but is delighted to be the head here as 'Gumley is the place I want to be.'

When Idi Amin expelled all Asians from Uganda in 1972, Ms Braggs and her family packed their worldly possessions into two suitcases and ended up as refugees in Birmingham. She was just six at the time. Ms Braggs comes from a family of strong and practical women and her can-do attitude makes her a powerful role model. She believes that what this school does best is 'Educating the whole person. Gumley empowers the students to take their place in society. It teaches them to pick themselves up and be resilient when faced with challenges in the outside world. We prepare them for the future, for a global and a changing world.' As a refugee, she knows first-hand that versatility and adaptability are vital when facing life's challenges.

Ms Braggs attends all school events with gusto, regularly staying late into the evening. Pupils appreciate her dependability and her friendliness. One girl commented, 'Everybody finds Ms Braggs very easy to talk to. She listens to what we say.'

Any smidgeon of spare time is spent at the theatre, travelling (she is a frequent visitor to Madeira) and relaxing with extended family. 'My nieces and godchildren are my life,' she beams.

Academic matters: Generally very decent results, but hasn't publicised any GCSE or A level results for 2018. Around 26 subjects offered at A level. Currently, English, maths, sociology and chemistry are popular sixth form choices. Part of a consortium with Gunnersbury and St Mark's, so those favouring less conventional subjects such as classical civilisation can study them at their sister schools. Conversely, their pupils venture over here for media studies and economics. Compulsory RE at GCSE. Parents feel that teaching is 'generally very good throughout', though one mother we spoke to felt homework 'could be more structured and meaningful.' The school disagrees with her view, telling us that 'our research and knowledge does not highlight homework as a general problem.'

Gumley has a language specialism. French, Italian, Spanish and Mandarin offered, as well as Latin for the most able. Annual language festival celebrates the diverse languages spoken by pupils. School also has partnerships with schools in Africa, China and India, reflecting its international make-up.

SEND provision considered to be excellent. Three fully qualified teachers and nine learning support assistants. Gumley can support the milder end of physical and learning difficulties, including ASD, dyslexia and speech and language needs. Everyone is screened for literacy levels at the start of year 7. Those requiring help are offered extra tuition, in-class support and reading clubs. Wheelchair access throughout.

Head feels pressure on staff is worse than ever, and that recruitment and retention of teachers is a problem here, as it is nationally. Pupils rate their teachers highly as 'they listen to us and care for us. They want us to do well.' One girl we spoke to praised her teachers' speedy responses to emails, often well into the evening. Many teachers go well beyond what is expected.

Chasing league tables is not Gumley's style. Head explains that 'academic excellence is of paramount importance, but in tandem with the development of a young person's mental and emotional well-being.' She elaborates, 'We do not lose sight of the person while aiming high academically. Education is not just about maths, science and so on. It's about making someone fully human and able to take their place in society.'

Games, options, the arts: Sporty pupils are not short of opportunities here. Athletics, cricket, football, badminton, netball, rounders, gym and dance all offered. Excellent outdoor and indoor sports facilities, including eight tennis courts, five netball courts, a gym and dance/drama studios. Well-used Astro pitch. Athletics at park across the road. Gumley has secured numerous titles within the borough and at the London Youth Games.

Music is an integral part of Gumley life. Keen singers and instrumentalists are spoilt for choice, with a gospel choir, chamber choir, orchestra, string ensemble and woodwind ensemble. Christmas and summer concerts are described by parents as 'exciting' and 'impressive'. Recent choir tour to Brussels Cathedral. Music department encourages pupils to try out different genres of music, one day experimenting with edgy rhythms on the drum kit, the next day performing traditional choral music. Enthusiastic staff choir.

When Idi Amin expelled all Asians from Uganda in 1972, Ms Braggs and her family packed their worldly possessions into two suitcases and arrived as refugees in Birmingham

Energetic drama productions ranging from Shakespeare to West End-style musicals. Pupils become fully immersed in the productions, including watching professional adaptations as preparation. 'It's the whole caboodle with drama,' states head. High profile drama festival to which parents and carers are invited, as well as local primary school children. Annual poetry festival involves pupils writing their own poems. Gumley boasts its own poet laureate. Local and national poets and artists are invited in to inspire pupils.

Annual art exhibition. One talented pupil won the Young Brit at Arts Award, beating off competition from over 2000 competitors. 'Our art is outstanding,' explains the head, and the masterpieces adorning the walls support this. 'We are a school that allows exploration of all types of art,' she explains.

Impressive range of after-school clubs, all free of charge, including maths, STEM, eco, Latin, as well as 11 sports clubs, and music clubs including Gumley Glee. Trips abroad include annual language exchanges with schools in Spain, Italy, France and China; geographers head to Iceland; history and politics pupils to New York and Washington. Head joins the pilgrimage to Lourdes. For those looking to challenge themselves physically, there is ski-ing in Austria and a water sports week in France. Something to tempt all tastes.

School is good at encouraging the girls to think about careers from year 7 on, to look beyond the school gates and to be adventurous in their choices. Gumley also has a business and enterprise specialism and has developed close links with a range of businesses. Lots of industry workshops and work experience organised by school, including with British Airways, GSK and Merrill Lynch. Alumni, including bankers, engineers, scientists and film directors, give career talks to the pupils. They give their time for free, hoping to egg on the next generation. The phrase goes 'once a Gumley girl, always a Gumley girl.'

Background and atmosphere: Founded in 1841 by Marie Madeleine D'Houet, an aristocrat in post-revolutionary France. Inspired by the spirit of Ignatius of Loyola, she established her own religious order – the Faithful Companions of Jesus (FCJ). In setting up Gumley, she hoped to empower local women. Part of a group of four schools in England under the trusteeship of the FCJ; the others are in the Wirral, Liverpool and London. School motto is Vive Ut Vivas ('Live that you may have life'). Head sees foundress as an inspirational figure as 'she did not put a ceiling on herself. I want the pupils to realise that the power to determine their path in life is in their hands.' The school still follows the guidelines laid down by Marie Madeleine, as the head explains. 'She always said to the sisters that they should never tell a child off publicly. Take them aside and do it quietly. Never speak to a child as though their feelings do not matter'. Head stresses that being gentle is not about being weak; her mantra is the same as the foundress': 'strong in action and gentle in manner'.

A Catholic school (now an academy) for girls with a handful of sixth form boys, who choose Gumley for specific subjects such as economics, government and politics, and media. Boys are fully integrated, including a deputy head boy. Some non-Catholics attend who join in fully with spiritual element of school. Head is certain that 'they enrich the community. Though they don't have to participate, they often want to.' Respect for different backgrounds and faiths is fundamental to the school. Head firmly believes that the two most important commandments are to love God and to

Pupils try out different genres, one day experimenting with edgy rhythms on the drum kit, the next performing traditional choral music

love your neighbour, and that these should be seen in action around the school.

Education is based on gospel and FCJ values with a focus on excellence, companionship, dignity, gentleness, justice and hope. The pupils themselves feel Gumley 'teaches us to be virtuous and hopeful.' Bethany, the chapel in the grounds, can be used for quiet reflection throughout the day, and is particularly well-frequented in exam season, given its location bang next to the exam hall. Also used for a weekly mass (school has its own chaplain). Retreats implemented across all year groups, so pupils have time for quiet reflection away from the hustle and bustle of school life.

Gumley pupils are keen on fundraising. Substantial sums raised for variety of charities, both high-profile and local, especially those supporting children, the elderly, homelessness and Catholics. Pupils venture out into the community, visiting hospitals and offering story-telling sessions to local primaries. 'We teach them to put faith into action, through the understanding of linking charity work with the curriculum,' explains head.

Spacious campus. The central Queen Anne house is set in 10 acres of pretty grounds. Lawns are punctuated with numerous picnic tables, which are well-populated in the summer term. A large canopy covering an outside eating area lends an attractive Mediterranean touch to this corner of Isleworth.

Pastoral care, well-being and discipline: Pupils, parents and teachers all rave about the outstanding pastoral care. 'We strive for pastoral excellence,' explains head. Team is made up of two pastoral managers, two on-site counsellors and a teacher responsible for inclusion. One person oversees the smooth transition from year 6 to 7, and parents are impressed by this 'great induction and inclusion programme'. All pupils are in a tutor group. School will not economise on pastoral care and pays for staff supervision 'so they do not take difficult issues home with them'. The well-being of the whole community is central here.

Pupils are taught how to protect themselves, particularly online, and to think of the implications of present action on their prospects. Gumley emphasises the importance of learning to communicate with people from every walk of life. The head believes that 'if you can communicate with all sorts of people, you will fly'.

Discipline taken seriously. Low truancy rates. Rare to expel a pupil, generally only for extreme behaviour. School does all it can to support those who are pushing the boundaries but sometimes a parting of the ways is inevitable. Forgiveness and reconciliation are part of the Gumley ethos. 'Girls and boys are not known by their failings,' says head. Success is celebrated, including through awards for achievement, progress, perseverance and contribution to school life. Gumley favours the carrot over the stick.

Food considered to be fine and there is a choice on offer, though sizeable minority prefers to bring in packed lunch from home. One parent we spoke to felt 'there could be healthier food options at the canteen'. Breakfast for early birds from 8am onwards.

Pupils and parents: School composition is predominantly Catholic. Wide mix of nationalities with over 65 languages spoken at home, notably Portuguese and Polish. Three or four pupils arrive per year with minimal English, and support is offered to those whose English is not up to scratch. Broad ethnic and social mix.

'Our art is outstanding,' explains the head, and the masterpieces adorning the walls support this

Parents feel communication from school is generally good. However, one mother commented that the school would benefit from 'a report system that better informs parents of students' grades and progress.' School says it is 'stumped' by this parental comment as monitoring reports are sent home every eight weeks.

Entrance: Open mornings and evenings in the autumn term for prospective pupils. Non-selective academically in year 7, when 210 are admitted. Governing body in charge of admissions. Catholics taken before other faiths; all families are expected to support the Catholic aims and ethos of the school. Majority from Hounslow, Ealing, Hammersmith and Fulham deaneries. Priority given to siblings, children whose parents work at the school and those living closest.

Pupils entering the school in the sixth form need English and maths level 5 and three different subjects at a minimum of level 5, with at least 6 in A level subjects. No faith requirement for those arriving for the final two years.

Exit: Some depart after GCSEs, either to sample co-ed, or because they want to take vocational courses, or for geographical reasons. Of those who stay the overwhelming majority opts for university. Recent university courses range from engineering at Loughborough to Chinese studies at Sheffield to film and TV at Southampton Solent to politics and French at Manchester. Usually one or two to Oxbridge. Some choose art foundation courses, such as Central St Martins. Others prefer apprenticeships, including in the civil service and in engineering, which often translate into real jobs on completion.

Money matters: Gumley asks for voluntary contributions to the school development fund. Recently it has been used to help cover the upgrade of the security system, keep text books up to date, build a new roof, replace windows and make improvements to the music suite.

Remarks: Head wants pupils to be the best they can be. 'It's not the career, it's not the job, it's who you are that matters.' Gumley pupils are well-equipped to face the challenges of the 21st century.

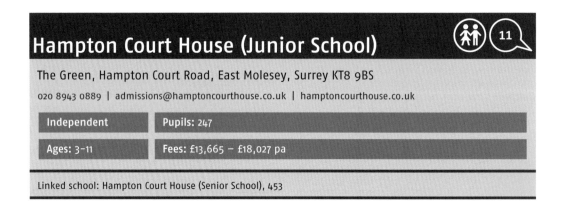

Hampton Court House (Junior School)

The Green, Hampton Court Road, East Molesey, Surrey KT8 9BS

020 8943 0889 | admissions@hamptoncourthouse.co.uk | hamptoncourthouse.co.uk

Independent	Pupils: 247
Ages: 3–11	Fees: £13,665 – £18,027 pa

Linked school: Hampton Court House (Senior School), 453

Headmaster: Since 2001, Guy Holloway MA (Cantab), NPQH, known as 'Guy' to all, who is also head of the senior school.

Entrance: Into the nursery at 3, or year 1 at 5+, following an informal interview with child and parents. During visit child will be observed by the teaching staff for both academic and social behaviour, and will meet with the head of lower and early years. If applicable, a confidential report from the child's current school will be requested. Head wishes to ensure that parents are committed to the school's ethos and approach to learning. At 10, children are tested in English and maths. More selective in recent years, but potential is still considered carefully. With approximately 35 languages represented at the school, the majority of students have at least one British parent. School runs buses from Chelsea, Kingston and Richmond and pupils come from central and west London and surrounding parts of Surrey.

Exit: Despite being an all-through school, pupils are all prepared for 11 + and 13+ examinations and scholarships. Most – some 70 per cent – stay on, but some move to a very wide variety of destinations: Lady Eleanor Holles and Ibstock Place currently most popular. Not surprisingly there are also

families returning abroad as work commitments dictate. Increasingly parents are choosing to keep their children at HCH senior school.

Remarks: Very special indeed is the opportunity for all children from early years to year 4 to receive a bilingual education in English and French with fluent French speakers, so all can become at least competent and develop good accents. From age 6, pupils can also follow the French curriculum for the Centre National d'Enseignment à Distance, which we saw in practice as a year 5 group successfully completed assigned writing tasks to time. Grammar is taken seriously, along with teaching accurate use of punctuation, as seen in pupils' books. All learn Latin from year 5 and Spanish is lively and enthusiastic. Language options include Mandarin. HCH is one of the leading prep schools for this in the UK. French is taught through other subjects (such as mathematics and humanities) and we saw year 1 pupils completing maths addition work happily asking questions in French and slipping back into English with ease. It all seemed perfectly natural and there was support from classmates as well as teachers.

Many nationalities are represented amongst staff and pupils and the curriculum reflects this, so children learn to appreciate and respect other

There are trees to climb, grounds to explore including a sizeable pond, and the stunning house itself in beautiful countryside

cultures. We saw a year 5 English class tackling creative writing and were impressed by the articulate, confident responses to our questioning, whilst attentive year 6 pupils were appreciating Beowulf. Parents value the imaginative cross-curricular opportunities teachers take to make topics more meaningful eg Queen Victoria in history alongside Great Expectations in English. We saw year 2s, basing their designs on South American wildlife, making imaginative moulds in art, which would later be used to produce Fair Trade chocolates

As well as a concentration on the 3Rs, art, drama and music are seen as central to education here – hooray! Talented musicians are given every opportunity to perform and share in music-making, and more than 50 children have music lessons in school. IT is well provided for with a designated room full of Macs with big screens. All sports are taken by qualified sports teachers and everyone up to year 4 has weekly swimming sessions at Imber Court Pool, a short ride away. In addition, after-school tennis lessons are on offer with tennis specialists. Early years children have their own garden, and all can freely enjoy the wonderful space for outdoor play. There are trees to climb, grounds to explore including a sizeable pond, and the stunning house itself in beautiful countryside. One parent remarked, 'HCH is not an imposing,

austere place: instead, very warm and welcoming. My child has had an amazing childhood at HCH. They read books and then play outside enacting them, letting their imaginations run freely'.

A French parent we spoke to was very impressed with communication and the fact that teachers are approachable, know pupils by name and show interest in the families attending. 'The school is small enough to defuse situations so difficulties can be resolved at an early stage.' School is flexible about keeping children down a year or bumping them up one in consultation with parents. This can work exceptionally well, especially in a case of mild bullying, exceptional aptitude or slowness, but it can pose a problem if the child is destined elsewhere.

SEN provision is considered 'outstanding' as far as Ofsted is concerned (praise for the IEPs), with a few requiring direct support for dyslexic traits and social and communication skills. There is specialist one-to-one EAL support.

The food is amazing. The chef also oversees all food at a Fulham free school and is a key player in the government's School Food Plan programme. We saw healthy, appetising food choices with plenty of seasonal options.

Freedom to run about in home clothes and be encouraged to gain a love of learning without the usual constraints can, in many cases, lead to happy, self-disciplined, motivated children. Nevertheless, some parents flee after a while and are not assured that the ethos works in practice or that all claims are realised. This is not the right school for those conservative parents who prefer a more conventional, pedagogical approach and obvious rigid hierarchical structures.

Hampton Court House (Senior School)

The Green, Hampton Court Road, East Molesey, Surrey KT8 9BS

020 8614 0857 | admissions@hchnet.co.uk | hamptoncourthouse.co.uk

Independent	Pupils: 109; sixth form: 20
Ages: 11–18	Fees: £18,027 – £19,506 pa

Linked school: Hampton Court House (Junior School), 452

Headmaster: Since 2001, Guy Holloway MA (Cantab) NPQH, known as 'Guy' to all. With his own Russian/German background, he is passionate about the importance of languages, both ancient and

modern. He studied at King's College School, Wimbledon, before reading English at Peterhouse, Cambridge. He spent many years in Paris, first at the international PR firm, Burson-Marsteller, and then at the École Active Bilingue, where he was head of English in the section Britannique. For several years he was a volunteer with Save the Children UK, working with disadvantaged children. He is now patron of the children's charity Their Future Today, which supports abandoned and institutionalised children in Sri Lanka.

Part of the 1993 founding team which opened the Harrodian School, where he was director of studies, he is a co-founder of HCH. A committed educationalist, he lectures at the Institute of Education's London Centre for Leadership in Learning. He believes in giving pupils a global perspective so they have an appreciation of cultures and informed tolerance, partly borne out by the international flavour of his staff appointments, including a Spanish head of pastoral care and a German head of mathematics. He runs a weekly seminar – a comprehensive history of music course for all children in years 1 to 8 – and teaches cultural studies to years 10 and 11. He believes staff have a responsibility as role models, sharing the love of their subjects with their pupils. He acts on his beliefs, eg, he encourages all in the acquisition of vocabulary and shared his personal discovery, lustrum, in assembly on the day we visited.

'Don't expect one of the local hothouses without uniform. You won't find the mechanistic, predictable approach, but instead a joy in the educational experience'

Guy sees his future as 'married to HCH'. He champions creativity and is justifiably proud of the school's culture, which 'enables pupils to fulfil their passions' and nurtures individuals so that they develop quality relationships as a life skill. He is approachable and totally committed to the school's ethos: 'We believe in questioning our beliefs' and 'The primacy of the idea over the person'.

Alongside his fascination for psychology and learning, Guy has a diverse range of cultural and linguistic interests alongside languages, including foreign travel, literature, chess and concert-going, and he is an active member of the Rose Theatre Players. He enjoys directing films as well as plays (over 30) at HCH and recalled many ambitious productions to us with pride.

Academic matters: The study and celebration of languages and the arts are integral to HCH, which is a UNESCO associate school and the only school in the UK to be granted Institut Francais status by the

One parent said how proud she had been of the way her daughter and friends had been protective and inclusive of a pupil with ADHD, and another commented on the positive approach staff showed

French government for its commitment to French language and culture. In a liberal, civilised, relaxed, atmosphere where staff are addressed by first names, individuals are encouraged to pursue their passions to the full, whilst learning how to appreciate art, music and drama. The staffing reflects this, with native speakers and professional performers as role models; so important. Undoubtedly languages are a strength at HCH with high numbers of 9/8s at GCSE. Everyone takes at least one language to GCSE, with nearly a quarter studying French/Spanish in the first year of the sixth form.

In 2018, 85 per cent of all GCSEs at 9-7. HCH has gained the Good School Guide award for best performance in English independent schools by boys in both psychology and Spanish. This is not a result-driven academic school; instead, the head describes it as a 'shared intellectual environment'. Pupils are prepared for 13+ as well as GCSEs and now A levels. As one long-standing parent put it, 'Don't expect one of the local hothouses without uniform. You won't find the mechanistic, predictable, step by step approach for all at HCH, but instead a joy in the educational experience where pupils gain a rounded introduction to life, and where it's not just about passing exams'. Unavoidably, not all parents are convinced, and some question the fact that, despite degrees, teaching staff do not necessarily have teaching qualifications, whilst others praise their 'inspirational enthusiasm' and the attention and support given to each individual.Ofsted has judged that 'the mostly good or outstanding lessons enable pupils to make rapid progress' and recognised HCH as 'good and increasingly outstanding'.

The school is a lead school in the Network of Excellence in Computer Science, with an emphasis on programming. 'If a child needs to be extended and takes a subject a step further, this is acknowledged and encouraged'. Pupils do need to be motivated and exert self-discipline as this will not be imposed from above.

In 2015 HCH opened its gates to a newly-established sixth form led by experienced, traditionalist headmaster Tristram Jones-Parry MA (Oxon), previously head of Westminster and Emanuel, and teacher of mathematics. Guy explained that the decision was made initially to offer 'heavy duty A levels as well as psychology'. We caught the end of a physics lesson with a small, predominantly male group of the first cohort of sixth formers in one of three new specialist science laboratories. The sixth form has been in the spotlight with its novel late start. Lessons run from 1.30pm to 7.00pm and the school is linked with Oxford University research, promoting a later start for under 20s which aims to maximise the benefit of improved sleeping patterns. Sixth formers can stay on to enjoy a diverse range of speakers, as part of the Form Seven adult education programme involving topics such as Napoleon and the Battle of Borodino, women and enlightenment science, and 18th century French art history. Second A level results in 2018 saw 76 per cent A*-B, 51 per cent A*/A grades.

School is very accepting and inclusive of SENs. SEN department comprises a SENCo, who comes into school twice a week, plus three others: one maths specialist, one specialising in early intervention, and the other very experienced in dyslexia and dyspraxia. They work in small groups or one-to-one, as best suits the child. Seventeen per cent of pupils are on the SEN register – mostly mild to moderate dyslexia or dyscalculia, but school will support ADHD and dyspraxia. One parent commented how proud she had been of the way her daughter and friends had been deliberately protective and inclusive of a pupil with ADHD, and another commented on the positive approach staff showed, allowing the pupil to let off steam by running up and down the corridors when necessary.

Games, options, the arts: The arts and music are superb, with imaginative use made of music composition linked with filming and animations, and pupils winning prizes for artwork and photographs. Small classes mean staff all really know the pupils. Talents are recognised and promoted and the school is sufficiently small to be flexible, a great plus if your child carries out arduous sports or music practice or has to attend rehearsals outside school. Many do, including a current ballet pupil dancing at the Royal Opera House; others attend West End show rehearsals and music performances, and there is a genuine respect for the work ethic involved. As Guy comments, 'Our current national gymnasts complete hours of training a week, and that requires real commitment and dedication'. In the lunch break we heard a young Cambridge choral scholar master successfully putting the choir through its paces, practising a Rutter anthem in the Great Hall. More than 60 students have one-to-one music lessons in school.

There is a varied sports curriculum, with fixtures against local schools in football, netball, cricket and athletics with coaching in rugby VIIs and hockey too. Sixth formers can use a gym across the road if they wish. Each year group has one full sports afternoon a week and there are daily lunch-time clubs as well as after-school clubs in judo, archery, table tennis, football and athletics. The school grounds are extensive and include a netball and tennis court, football pitch and a smaller 5-a-side football pitch. Pupils enjoy running in Bushy Park and Hampton Court Green. One parent did suggest: 'There are lots of clubs but it would be good if they had some physical activity every day of the week, building exercise into their daily lives', although acknowledging that 'healthy eating is considered and the food is amazing'.

Background and atmosphere: Completed in 1757 by the Earl of Halifax, Hampton Court House was intended as an extravagant gift for his mistress Anna-Maria Donaldson and was designed by architect and astronomer Thomas Wright. He was responsible for special period features including a heart-shaped pond and enchanting shell-lined grotto with its painted blue ceiling with gilded wooden stars, and an octagonal ice-house now used for drumming practice. Set within nine acres, the beautiful Georgian mansion has a stunning entrance hall with columns, gallery, ceiling, fireplace, conservatory, winter garden with palms and dining room, all tastefully decorated and looking out at the vista of Bushy Park. After Mrs Donaldson's death the house passed through a succession of tenants and was sold to Marmaduke Blake Sampson in 1871. He was city correspondent to The Times and Argentine consul in London, and was responsible for adding the picture gallery. Much later it passed to the tea-planting Twinings, until in the 1980s, quite extraordinarily, it was a Save the Children home for refugee Vietnamese children.

As one parent summarised, 'we appreciate an all-through school where time is found to explore ideas and there is a conventional output but not process'

Following considerable restoration and refurbishment of the house, the school started its life with a pre-prep and prep in 2001, expanding upwards until it opened its sixth form in 2015. The irregularity of the classrooms, along with the abundance of comfortable sofas and country house items of furniture, may seem quirky to those parents used to pristine, purpose-built establishments. Nevertheless, much thought has been given to light, and the ambiance is spacious; pupils are not as crammed in as they might be in some central London schools.

This school has a palpable atmosphere and culture of kindness. As one parent explained, 'HCH is a microcosm of society based on respect and developing useful, responsible citizens ready to take their place in the world.' Parents rightly value the warm welcome and friendships made at HCH with fellow pupils and staff. We noticed the relaxed way in which ages and genders mixed happily and naturally at lunch, moving about with ease, whilst parents are delighted at the way pupils support one another, enjoying activities such as camping, chess, or performing in concerts and plays.

Pastoral care, well-being and discipline: At HCH the belief in developing quality relationships is key, whilst reflecting and learning from one's mistakes in a community based on mutual respect. Guy explains, 'I may hold a door open for a pupil but expect a pupil to hold a door open for me'. First names are used throughout, but despite the non-uniform, each pupil has an almanack in which there is a clear code of conduct and dress. When we visited we were impressed by the pupils' smart appearance. Undoubtedly some individuals would not thrive in such a liberal, non-hierarchical setting, and Guy admits that it is important to match the individual to the right school and that some have left because of this. Parents often visit several times for reassurance, but tend to agree that 'The teachers know all the pupils, and because of the small nature of the school, they are often able to intervene and defuse situations'.

The irregularity of the classrooms, along with the abundance of comfortable sofas and country house items of furniture, may seem quirky to parents used to pristine, purpose-built establishments

School actively promotes mindfulness, and nutritional advice and time management skills are included in a comprehensive well-being programme. In the past the head has expelled a boy over drugs, and is very aware of safety and security. He regularly chats with the gatekeeper, who can spot if a child is looking miserable or has a concern.

Pupils and parents: Pupils come from a 30 mile radius, with many from Kingston, Surbiton or Hampton, and there is a school minibus which collects from Chelsea, Richmond and Kingston. Not surprisingly, there are a number of international families including some French, who want their children to maintain levels of French 'whilst immersing themselves in English and English culture'. HCH attracts the unconventional, the liberal, the arty. As one parent summarised, 'we appreciate an all-through school where time is found to explore ideas and there is a conventional output but not process'.

Sufficiently small to be flexible, a great plus if your child carries out arduous sports or music practice

Former pupils include environmental campaigner and filmmaker Ayrton Cable, winner of Diana Award and nominated for the International Children's Peace Prize for his work in Malawi; two international ice skaters; many young actors and actresses eg Rupert Sadler, Harriet Turnbull, Nell Tiger Free and Isabella Blake Thomas; not forgetting a heavy metal singer, Austin Dickinson.

Entrance: Main entry points at 11+ and 13+. Interview for candidate and parents plus maths and English tests. Parents are welcome to visit more than once as it is essential pupil and family believe in school's distinctive ethos and approach to education. New sixth form applicants need at least six grade 6s with 7s in subjects to be studied at A level.

Exit: Will prepare for 13+ exams and, unsurprisingly, incredibly diverse range of destinations, including lycées abroad, state schools, Eton, Wellington, Westminster, Bryanston, Kingston Grammar, Wimbledon High, Surbiton High, with some scholarships, although in recent years more are staying on. There is some turnover of children because families move abroad, but those remaining develop a widening circle of friends. Some 60 per cent leave after GCSEs.

Money matters: Up to three scholarships – academic, music, arts – each year, worth 10 per cent of fees maximum. All 11+ candidates are automatically entered.

Remarks: Ideal setting for individuals who can be trusted to be responsible and will thrive on civilised, relaxed values and learn from enthusiastic, approachable teachers who share their passions for their subjects. Several parents acknowledged, 'We visited three times before making up our minds because the school offers something different'. In recent years the school has become more selective, but the head, quite rightly, remains interested in individuals and what they have to offer. As one parent remarked, 'This is a place where it is ok to be different and ask questions, and not be considered a nuisance'.

Hampton Pre-Prep and Prep School

Gloucester Road, Hampton TW12 2UQ

020 8979 1844 | admissions@hamptonprep.org.uk | hamptonprep.org.uk

Independent

Pupils: 232 (6 girls)

Ages: Boys 3–11, girls 3–7

Fees: £12,060 – £13,935 pa

Linked school: Hampton School, 459

Head: Since 2015, Tim Smith, BA, MBA (40s). Previously deputy head academic, The Hall School Hampstead, for five years, originally joining in 1994 as games and French teacher, becoming head of learning support and then head of middle school. Also deputy chair of governors in Camden state primary.

Full of the joys of spring. Actually, make that all seasons. 'I love coming into this wonderful place every day,' he exults on the website.

A linguist, he's arty (a regular at the Barbican; partner is head of exhibitions at the Royal Academy) but has only ever wanted to teach. 'Always wanted to play schools,' he says of childhood in New Zealand. Years of wrestling with nervy North Londoners haven't dimmed enthusiasm for career he describes as 'exciting, rewarding, engaging, motivating, joyful and hilarious.'

A shrewd operator, choice of SW London school with less toxic parental vibe – at least for now – compared with NW London is deliberate. Ditto prep finishing at 11 rather than traditional 13, as many senior schools up year 7 intake at the expense of common entrance places. Keen to avoid ivory tower complacency, an occupational hazard for preps, he thinks (state schools often do it better) and keep the innovations coming to improve quality of teaching – 'the light at the heart of school'.

His emphatic approach has come as a bit of a shock to parents though (largely) in a good way. 'Quirky,' was a description we heard more than once. 'Eloquent,' ditto. Felt to have made real effort to get to know pupils. 'Had the measure of our son quite quickly,' said mother. Excitement of the job? Like other heads, says no two days are the same (we're dying to find the first school where they are). Unlike them, explains how. Easy to forget you're dealing with children, he says, who 'do lots of extraordinary and enlightening and motivating things no matter how hard you try or how much you want them to ... go in a certain direction.'

Doesn't pull his punches, particularly when it comes to nervy parents who tell him they only 'want the best' for their child. Do they imagine teachers 'munching on breakfast of baby seals and endangered penguins [and thinking] "I can't wait to come into school and be mean to children?"' he wonders.

Short shrift also given to their fears that strengthened links with Hampton mean school door, as one expressed it, 'no longer open for all boys'. Stresses that nothing is set in stone, academic standards largely going to be determined by intake and any change will be gradual – with no wholesale notices to quit. 'Won't be gathering children up by their ankles, and flinging them into park because they're not clever enough.' A relief all round, then.

Entrance: In a crowded part of the world where limitless parental aspiration meets finite school places, school's willingness to go extra mile a real help for parents – one family wrestling with decision was given mobile number to call during hols for extra reassurance.

Pirates covered by coordinates in maths and top marauding destinations in geography

Main intake at age 3 into co-ed nursery (20-22 places) and into boys only prep in year 3, when between 14-17 places on offer depending on how many boys leave at end of year 2 (some lured away by well-regarded state primaries). Screen for learning needs in kindergarten, then it's assessments for reception, and years 1 and 2, plus reports. Entry to prep currently automatic-ish for existing pre-prep pupils. Others have tests plus interview with head and report from previous school.

Exit: Girls at end of year 2 to local all-through schools such as Surbiton, LEH, preps (Newland House, Twickenham Prep) and state sector.

In year 6, healthy numbers to St James Senior Boys' School, Claremont Fan Court, Halliford and St George's College Weybridge. Hampton School, however, biggest destination of the lot with just under half moving there. Assured places scheme available from year 2 to year 5 based on combination of assessments, teacher reports, exam results and in-depth discussions by admissions committee unsurprisingly a huge parental incentive. Other boys welcome to sit 11+ on equal footing with external candidates. Eight scholarships in 2018 (four for Hampton senior school).

Remarks: Relationship with big brother Hampton School wasn't exactly a secret even before change of name (from Denmead) in early 2016. Part of Hampton School Trust since 1999, founded in 1924 by one of English masters in own dining room after own son's left-handedness made him an educational pariah.

Pre-prep, just a hop, skip and jump away across pretty public park, is where it all starts. 'The jewel in the crown,' thought one parent. Housed in original school buildings with grassed front garden and miniature lych gate entrance, home-like feel and nurturing ethos makes it a popular standalone option for daughters as well as sons.

Long-serving pre-prep head, Mrs Murphy, gets star ratings from all for ability to get the best from pupils, effortlessly wrapping up fun and learning together with cross-curricular approach felt to be particularly successful (pirates covered by coordinates in maths, on board rules in English and top marauding destinations in geography). Lots of experienced teachers who make connections but ensure pupils 'make the vital links for themselves.'

Attractive two-storey building houses eight airy classrooms, brace of IT suites, art and music rooms and efficient-looking library, all under nature and neighbour friendly living roof, angled to blend in with residential surroundings.

Plenty of greenery courtesy of allotment with raised beds and that horticultural essential, a potting shed, part of revamped outside space that also includes playing fields (shaping up nicely on day of visit) and all-weather area. Back gate on to Carlisle Park provides extra overspill games space, senior school's 27 acres and theatre also coming in handy for large scale events.

Other changes are less root and branch than nip and tuck and made only where demonstrably better than what's gone before (we liked the lesson bell, lifted from French educational system and featuring mellifluous four-note leitmotif).

'What we do is based on substantiated, evidence-based, peer reviewed, professional practice,' says Mr Smith. 'We're not pulling mad ideas out of a hat.' (Harvard University, no less, called in to help with review of pastoral care). Far more emphasis on tracking – no doubting where your child is and what they're capable of achieving, while assessments are regular without being excessive and can't be prepared for (and don't get Mr Smith started on tutors – 'A racket'). Formal exams limited to maths and English, with verbal reasoning added to English and NVR to maths from year 4.

Team of 20 academic staff in the prep (around equal numbers of men and women), 12 in the pre-prep (all female) and just under 30 non-teaching staff, including three gap year students.

> *'Won't be gathering children up by their ankles and flinging them into the park because they're not clever enough.' A relief all round, then*

Two sets for maths and English from year 4, three in years 5 and 6. Will often double up on teachers to support and challenge (school's headline staff to pupil ratio of 1:18 doesn't reflect this) while three-strong learning support team (same again for pre-prep) help small numbers (around seven) with ADD, ADHD and mild SpLD. Their highlight is the 'ladder of success' – top rung winners who successfully complete daily tasks acknowledged in assembly with 'huge, noisy fuss...' and edible prize. Individual support for EAL pupils (around 35 across whole school) in pre-prep and in class in prep.

Curriculum 'shouldn't be a mile wide but only inch deep,' says Mr Smith, who also comes up with own three Rs – 'richness, relevance and rigour'. Thus subject list doesn't bulge with the outré or unusual – French is only language taught, for example – but concentrates on core range done well, and given more time. Mr Smith is also bumping up recruitment of subject specialists – like parents, feels currently too many generalists, particularly in top years.

With staff training and appraisals also being revamped, teachers 'go the extra mile,' says parent, encouraged to go exploring if lesson takes a different tack. Universal praise for English, boys learning to 'critique their own work and improve it,' says approving parent. Love of books reinforced all the way through –school will set reading as only holiday homework, for example.

Maths felt to be improving, online resources used increasingly to advantage. Results in all-through confidence – year 3 boys eager to explain division by four ('divide by two and by two again'), others in year 6 yomping through hinterlands of mean and mode. 'Teachers aren't going to blow you out of the window if you get it wrong,' reported one. 'Make teaching fun.'

Exam pressure – which pupils agreed could be tough – similarly well handled, focus on preparation without panic. Boys able to rattle off practical techniques that help. 'Make the point, use a quote and explain,' said one.

Ad hoc prizes (including sweets and – from one teacher – even more popular tennis balls) are popular incentives, though discipline felt by parents to be excellent – 'Only takes a look for boys to be quiet.' Masses of reinforcement, from weekly award of courtesy cup in prep to flowers, cloth and special pud for best behaved pre-prep lunchtime table. Easily understood golden rules for younger pupils, though slightly tortuous house point system for year 4 upwards (fine detail runs to several pages) is being revamped. 'Too complex,' agrees head.

Trips range from creative writing workshops to suitably bloodthirsty Saxons vs. Viking experience – firmly linked to curriculum, while clubs span debating to cooking, changing by season. Otherwise, sport's the big thing, with three sessions a week and easily the highlight for majority of pupils. Biggest stars can, thought one parent, get the 'c-leb' treatment (the eternal problem) though another praised numbers of teams (A to D for rugby and football) and regular swapsies so Bs get at least second dibs on training and attention. Means that while truly uninterested might struggle, anyone who's keen but with a modicum of talent is felt on the whole to have a good time. Results justify the effort with frequent successes, school handicapped only by size (some larger Richmond-based opponents can choose from bigger pool of talent).

Swimming has been major casualty of timetable rejigging, axed in the prep (though still offered for years 1 and 2). Not everyone's happy about this – 'focus is on football and rugby to the detriment of any other sport,' said parent, but Mr Smith isn't budging. 'We're not going to use valuable curriculum time to teach them to splash around in some grubby pool when parents can do that themselves on a Saturday.'

Art, however, has had a reprieve. Initially pared back and rotated in 10-week blocks with drama and DT, has regained weekly slot on the timetable after fears that talented weren't getting enough time to hone work to scholarship standard.

With around 60 prep and pre-prep pupils learning instruments (beginners to grade 5), a choir, orchestra and wind band and several scholarships in recent years, performing arts are good, think parents, though anticipate better things to come. 'Don't have enough children, scratching, blowing, tweeting and trumpeting,' agrees Mr Smith. Added space for more of everything – instruments, informal as well as class-based concerts plus whole school annual production all on the way, activity across the octave and decibel range should increase.

Parents very sociable, newcomers quickly brought into the fold. While the many working parents can inevitably end up missing out on coffee mornings, 'Always someone who'll scoop up your child.' Helped by before and after-school care – 7.45am start (8.00am in the pre-prep), 5.30pm finish – more activities after school would make life even easier, felt one parent.

Mr Smith stresses (and will probably have to keep on stressing) that ethos of school won't change 'simply because ... we apply tenets of the admissions policy ever more carefully as time goes by.' Some current parents have yet to be convinced. Prospective parents eye up growing numbers gaining places at Hampton and make up their own minds.

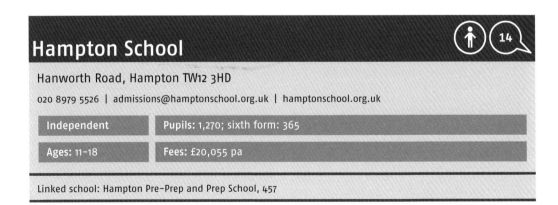

Hampton School

Hanworth Road, Hampton TW12 3HD

020 8979 5526 | admissions@hamptonschool.org.uk | hamptonschool.org.uk

| Independent | Pupils: 1,270; sixth form: 365 |
| Ages: 11–18 | Fees: £20,055 pa |

Linked school: Hampton Pre-Prep and Prep School, 457

Headmaster: Since 2013, Kevin Knibbs MA (early 40s). Joined Hampton as deputy head in 2007. Previously history master, head of lower school and senior master at Bolton School Boys' Division. Educated at King Edward VI Grammar School, Chelmsford and read modern history at Oxford (gaining two football blues in the process). A career schoolmaster who still teaches history to youngest boys. 'I happen to run a big business, but that's not why I chose teaching in the first place,' he tells us. Not one to hog the limelight. At his happiest when talking about the boys, of whom he is fiercely proud.

Very visible head who can often be spotted at weekends on the touchline and towpath, supporting Hampton boys and chatting to parents. Friendly, approachable and generous spirited. 'I am lucky to lead a school that is on this trajectory and I want to keep it going. It's a privilege to be in this job. I love it. I hope that comes through.' It does.

His wife is one of the chemistry teachers. He has a weakness for off-piste ski-ing in Colorado.

Academic matters: Results going from strength to strength with record grades. At GCSE, 93 per cent A*-A/9-7 in 2018. Boys performed outstandingly well in the free-standing maths qualification with over 90 per cent scoring the top grade. Hamptonians also impress regularly in national competitions, including as winners of the UK Maths Trust challenge for two years running, and in winning essay and poetry prizes. In lower years, all boys study chemistry, biology and physics as separate subjects, computer programming and coding, at least one language out of French, German, Spanish, Russian or Mandarin, and Latin, which is compulsory in years 7 and 8. Setting in maths and modern languages from third year.

Head acknowledges that 'we are a springboard school and people want our staff. Any of my senior team could run their own school but I am clinging onto them'

At A level, 68 per cent A*/A grades in 2018. Currently physics, chemistry, history, philosophy, German and Mandarin (short course) offered at Pre-U. At A level, maths remains perennially popular with regularly 30 per cent taking further maths. As one teacher explained, 'maths is like a magnet for these boys.' High uptake of chemistry, physics and economics too. In sixth form, all boys follow an enrichment programme which includes six week courses on topics including university life and finance, mindfulness and current affairs. School offers its own extended project qualification, with recent essays focusing on quantum gravity and the feasibility of time travel.

School is no slouch on the computer front, with eight different ICT suites and a new coding room. Boys bring in their own iPads and use them in every subject. School council currently hotly debating whether to replace text books with ebooks.

Around 185 pupils have some kind of SEN. Support offered tends to be small group intervention (currently around 40 such groups) with lunchtime drop in sessions popular, especially as exams start to loom. 'Some of our highest achieving boys are on our learning support register and that's how it should be,' states head. Forty pupils are classified as EAL, though none require additional support.

Over a third of staff has been at school for more than a decade. Each year roughly 10 per cent leaves, so constant flow of fresh blood, including some sparky graduates who are grabbed straight out of university and are trained on the job. Head acknowledges that 'we are a springboard school and people want our staff. Any of my senior team could run their own school but I am clinging on to them.' Approximately 40 per cent of teachers are female. 'That's changed a lot. When the boys leave here they know exactly who is in charge,' smiles the head. Pupils feel their teachers are friendly. One of the younger boys explained, 'Homework got the better of me at the beginning. But if you email a teacher to say you are struggling with the work, they are more than happy to go through it the next day. You just need to give them the heads up.' All the lessons we observed were lively and led by dynamic teachers, many of whom have grammar school backgrounds themselves and like the down-to-earth ethos of the school.

Games, options, the arts: School is well-known for its excellent sports provision, with at least 17 different sports offered. Over 27 acres of playing fields so all facilities (bar the Millennium boathouse) are on site and head has been known to joke that he would move the Thames if he could so that it could flow closer to the school. All-weather 3G sports ground very well used, including at break time when swarms of boys congregate there and kick balls about with great gusto. 'It's good for morale and improves concentration in the classroom,' states head. One boy told us that 'my mum loves the 3G grass as I never come home muddy!' Another told us that he fell in love with Hampton the moment he saw the huge number of pitches stretching into the distance.

Sports practice mostly takes place at lunchtime to enable those travelling home by coach to participate. Football and rugby in the winter; athletics, cricket and tennis in the summer; rowing throughout the year. Minor sports include fencing, sailing and windsurfing. Boys can choose which sports they want to play and the school excels at most. As always, Hampton is competing at the highest levels in national schools' competitions and churning out some exceptional sportsmen, especially in football, rugby, rowing, athletics and cricket. Deserves its reputation for being one of the top football, rugby and rowing schools in the country. No hockey offered which one parent found 'disappointing, as many boys would be keen to play it.' School stresses importance of participation for all, and multiple teams are fielded in all age groups. One mother we spoke to was not so sure, saying that 'in reality, there may be some who struggle to make a team.' Starry old boys include Olympic gold medallists Greg and Jonny Searle as well as Surrey and England all-rounder Zafar Ansari.

Very visible head who can often be spotted at weekends on the touchline and towpath, supporting Hampton boys and chatting to parents. Friendly and approachable

Head insists that school is not just for those who can perform brilliantly on the games pitches. 'There are many quiet, effective learners who find their own niche. We want to make sure that all boys get opportunities'. Boys agree that 'there is no hierarchy of worth. Being in the first XV is not seen as being any better than being in the Voices of Lions.' School has worked hard to encourage this view and head is adamant that that academic, musical and dramatic successes are now celebrated just as much as sporting triumphs.

With over 50 clubs on offer, including model aviators, debating, and photography, there does seem to be something for every taste. Over 200 boys take part in D of E scheme each year. Adventure Society, open to all years, offers a heady mix of kayaking, power-boating, orienteering and sea-cliff climbing. For the more sedentary, chess is thriving: five teams regularly represent the school. One pupil is currently national chess champion. Beekeeping society is the latest club on the list.

Performing arts have taken off in the last decade and serious resources have been funnelled towards both drama and music. The Hammond theatre seats 380 and boasts a hydraulic orchestral pit, hi-tech lighting and sound systems and, one pupil told us, watching plays here 'feels like being at the West End.' Numerous plays performed every year, from junior plays to large-scale musicals such as Chicago and Les Misérables. Lower school play is normally a performance of an original work by a visiting community playwright. Well-equipped art/DT department, and some stunning artwork lines the corridors, though surprisingly few take these subjects at A level. School produces a steady stream of Arkwright engineering scholars.

Around 400 boys have music lessons, many on more than one instrument. Significant numbers attain grade 8. Two current pupils with diplomas. Plenty of performances from rock, jazz, keyboard to strings and boys have 23 music ensembles to choose from. Celebrated male voice choir, Voices of Lions, enjoys a high profile and performs at Edinburgh Fringe. The lively rendition of Drunken Sailor in school assembly was apparently 'legendary'. Nine Hampton musicians have received organ scholarships from Oxbridge in recent years.

Background and atmosphere: The school was set up over 450 years ago thanks to a bequest of property and land by local brewer and businessman, Robert Hammond. Formerly a grammar school (went independent in 1975). Situated in suburban West London, on a greenfield site. Not the most beautiful of schools, though the warmth and friendliness of both staff and pupils makes up for the lack of architectural splendour.

School is outward looking and has developed links in the local community and abroad. Boys help in local primary schools and put on a Christmas party for elderly locals. School provides a Latin class for GCSE pupils from local state schools. Also has an association with a safe haven in Malawi. Hampton is proud of being a 'beacon school' for Holocaust education and raises awareness of more recent genocides. Certainly not a school that just looks after its own.

Close ties with neighbouring girls' school The Lady Eleanor Holles School. Since the appointment of the current head there, there is 'an enhanced desire to work collaboratively, especially at sixth form level'. Schools already share much, including drama productions, language exchanges and Oxbridge interview preparation. School firmly believes it gives the boys the best of both worlds, and it is hard to disagree.

Pastoral care, well-being and discipline: School takes great care to integrate boys who arrive at 13 with the well-established 11+ cohort. Pupils are supported by a pastoral team, including their form tutor and head of year, as well as sixth form mentors, though one parent we spoke to said 'the lack of a house system and small tutor groups may mean that some boys may slip through the net, no matter what the school tells you.' Some reports of bullying in the early years, though parents felt this was generally stamped out quickly. Head runs a weekly pre-school drop-in for boys to approach him on any matter they wish and he meets with head boy and his deputies once a fortnight and jokes that 'they tell me how to run the school'. This head has his ear to the ground.

Head has helped establish Hampton as a national leader in mindfulness. 'We're one of the

Lady Eleanor Holles School

early pioneers of it,' he says proudly. Believes it is a useful tool for helping these boys deal with 'the ups and downs of teenage life in this high achieving setting.' Mindfulness, life issues and well-being/resilience taught for nine weeks as part of the curriculum in fourth year, followed by a top-up session before GCSE study leave begins. Numerous teachers, including the head, have also done the course. One pupil we spoke to admitted that 'it can be a struggle to balance everything as there is so much going on here, but mindfulness helps.' Boys can frequently be seen practising mindfulness techniques before exams and performances. Head believes that it is no coincidence that since it has become a mainstream part of the school, 'the academic results have improved and the school has become a kinder, gentler and calmer place'. Head adds, with a smile, 'If it's good enough for Jonny Wilkinson ...'

Pupils and parents: Diverse mix of boys. Many parents have state school backgrounds and choose it for its unpretentiousness. Increasing numbers of European parents whose sons are bi/trilingual. Languages spoken at home include Gujarati, Urdu and Korean. Many boys walk or cycle to school and older boys can drive, as long as they park at a distance. Extensive coach network (run jointly with LEH) attracts families from all over west and south west London and Surrey. Coach journeys with girls apparently awash with 'witty banter.'

Celebrated male voice choir, Voices of Lions, enjoys a high profile. The lively rendition of Drunken Sailor in school assembly was apparently 'legendary'

Parents are very involved with the school, often helping with careers advice and fundraising. Head admits the parents can be demanding, but 'we're better off than some schools in that respect. We seem to attract families which do not tip over the fine line between aspirational and obsessional.'

Entrance: Highly selective. A 40 per cent increase in registration since 2011. Now more than six applicants per place. No sibling policy. Pupils generally enter the school at 11, 13 or 16. The 11+ route is normally for 125 boys; current batch from 75 different feeder schools (54 per cent of them joined from state primary schools, the remainder from preps which finish at end of year 6). At 13+ a further 65 boys enter the school, from about 25 different independent prep schools. Around 10-12 boys join in sixth form though few places up for grabs at this stage.

At 11+, entry is via school's own entrance exam (maths, English and reasoning) plus interview and reference. For 13+ entry, boys must sit the pre-test at 11; from 2020 offers will not depend on common entrance scores. Entrance at sixth form is via personal statement, head teacher's report, written and online assessment and interview. Boys must also get a good clutch of GCSEs, with a minimum six 9-7 grades including English and maths. The staggered entry at 11 and 13 works well and one teacher made it clear that 'we're standing firm with the 13+.'

Head devotes hours to speaking to prospective parents and says he tries 'to be clear about our ethos to parents. The families we choose need to be on board. It has to be the right fit for their son.' Warns parents not to 'force the pace' but to aim to put their son in an environment where he will be happy. Looking for boys who are academically able, inquisitive and hard-working, but they also need heaps of stamina to keep up here. A willingness to join in and try new things is crucial. 'Along with appointing staff, it is the most important thing I do,' says head. He manages to make the selection process as personal as possible and sends out good luck cards to all 1,200 applicants before entrance exams. A characteristically thoughtful gesture.

Exit: School is keen to point out that 'we do not cull anyone post-GCSEs' and there is no minimum number of GCSEs that internal boys must gain in order to be allowed to stay into the sixth form. 'We do talk to parents and pupils openly, however, if a boy is struggling. They might choose to put in place a contingency plan.' Those boys who leave at 16 tend to do so because school does not offer the subjects they wish to study, such as photography.

Up to 20 boys head for Oxbridge each year (14 in 2018) in a wide range of subjects. Head explains, 'We don't get obsessed about it. It is certainly not a case of Oxbridge or die. Some boys actually turn down Oxbridge places if there is a better course for them personally elsewhere'. Vast majority tends to head for Russell Group universities. Occasionally, boys venture to the Continent while others choose medical schools (six medics in 2018), drama schools or conservatoires. Favoured universities at the moment include Warwick, Durham and Nottingham. Boys opt for a wide range of degrees from astrophysics to zoology. A handful disappears off to Ivy League colleges in the US, often on sporting scholarships. Twenty or so take gap years. As head of careers explains, 'We try to set out the options for the boys and support whichever path they want to take.' Boys regularly return for career advice long after they leave.

Money matters: Fifty-six boys are on full bursaries and another 127 are on substantial bursaries. Plans afoot to provide more such places and this is a matter close to the head's heart. 'In terms of the school's future, to maintain our grounded feel, and with fees going up, we need to make sure that more bursaries are available. We do not have a big endowment so have to do it through fundraising.' Academic, all-rounder, art, choral and music scholarships carry a remission of up to 25 per cent of fees. 'If there are financial issues, we do try to help,' says head.

Remarks: Hampton is riding high. Though head is conscious that 'we can sometimes hide our light under a bushel here,' they would be justified in shouting their achievements from the rooftops. There is currently a real energy about the school and boys appeared to be genuinely happy.

One of the aims of the school is for Hamptonians to strive 'for personal success while supporting those around them.' If the boys who showed us around are anything to go by, they are accomplishing their goal admirably. Hampton is producing young men of integrity. No wonder the head is so proud of them.

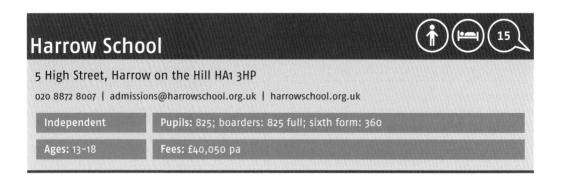

Harrow School

5 High Street, Harrow on the Hill HA1 3HP

020 8872 8007 | admissions@harrowschool.org.uk | harrowschool.org.uk

Independent	Pupils: 825; boarders: 825 full; sixth form: 360
Ages: 13–18	Fees: £40,050 pa

Head master: From April 2019, Alastair Land MA (Cantab), (40s), currently head of Repton after three years as deputy head here. Educated at Manchester Grammar School and Trinity College, Cambridge (first class hons in natural sciences). He comes from a lineage of skilled horticulturalists who nurtured his early interest in science. A man with a vocation to serve, he seriously considered a career in the armed forces (and hasn't closed the door on one in the church), but above all he 'always knew he wanted to teach.' His first job gave him the opportunity to combine the two and he spent nine years at Eton as biology teacher and commanding officer of CCF. Thence to Winchester College where he was master in college and senior housemaster. Father of two young sons.

Interim head during the autumn 2018 and spring 2019 terms is Mel Mrowiec, founding head of Harrow International School in Bangkok and a long-serving teacher and deputy head at Harrow.

Academic matters: Teachers, parents and the boys themselves describe Harrow as an 'academic' school. Harrow's results don't appear in league tables – head says he's fed up with the 'one-dimensional snapshot' they deliver – but results are impressive. At A level in 2018, 64 per cent A*/A grades, 88 per cent per cent A*/B and 84 per cent A*/A at IGCSE. IGCSEs taken in English, French, German, Spanish, history, geography, maths, as well as biology, chemistry and physics. Drama and PE introduced at GCSE recently.

Thirty-one subjects on offer at A level – all the usual, plus business studies, government and politics, history of art, music technology, photography and theatre studies, with a range of languages. Maths is the most popular subject at A level, with nearly two-thirds taking it. Half the boys do four subjects at A level rather than the usual three (one boy recently did nine). Sixth form electives are a recent innovation for sixth form pupils – a chance for boys to experience university-style teaching in specialist areas and have increased from five to eight periods a fortnight, with boys taking three one-term courses – the last relating to their chosen university course. Cerebral subjects on offer include programming, the history of western art, the greats of European philosophy, psychoanalysis and its impact on European culture, conflict and creativity in creation, post-genocide Rwanda and financial mathematics. Now offers EPQ.

Dazzling array of languages on offer – French, German, Spanish, Italian, Russian, Turkish, Polish, Japanese, Arabic and Chinese. All three sciences are compulsory at IGCSE. School has its own observatory with three telescopes and astronomy offered as a GCSE. Timetabled reading periods and new seminar programme for years 10 and 11. At GCSE classes range between 14 and 20 pupils while at A level the average is eight and none are greater than 12.

Embracing technology: all new joiners asked to purchase a (subsidised) laptop to be used in all lessons.

Even though it's played in the depths of winter and is a very muddy affair, the boys love it and only wish more schools played it

School caters for mild dyspraxia and dyslexia. One-to-one help given off-timetable, at no additional cost. Dedicated band of teachers (or 'beaks' as they are known at Harrow) includes many writers of scholarly books. Women make up 19 per cent of staff.

Games, options, the arts: There's no doubt about it, Harrow is a very sporty school, with hordes of teams regularly trouncing their opponents. Sport played five afternoons a week, 32 sports on offer and director of sport encourages even the less enthusiastic to 'have a go' at something. Main sports are rugby, soccer, cricket and Harrow football. The latter is played with a pork-pie shaped ball which absorbs the wet and can be propelled by any part of the body. Even though it's played in the depths of winter and is a very muddy affair the boys love it and only wish more schools played it (Harrow is the only one). When we visited pupils were counting the days till their Harrow football match against an OH team. Last year lots of their fathers had played and there was even one grandfather in the side – 'but we were very careful with him.'

Vast expanse of playing fields, sports centre with indoor climbing wall, weights room, 25m pool and sports hall, courts for tennis, rackets and squash, nine-hole golf course and Olympic-sized running track. School boasts national champions in rackets, fencing, fives and judo, two boys playing rugby for England and number of cricketers playing at national and county level. The mother of a gifted sportsman was full of admiration for the way the school nurtured her son's sporting talent whilst keeping him focused on his academic studies and helping him achieve stellar grades. 'The school sees each boy as an individual and were very supportive and flexible,' she told us.

Head of music admits that when he arrived there was a perception among rival directors of music that Harrow was 'an old-fashioned school where little value was placed on music and the arts.' To his delight he found the reverse was true and there's a 'wealth of musical talent.' Half the boys learn musical instruments and 50 per cent of these achieve grade 8 or better by the time they leave. Practice sessions timetabled for younger boys. Loads of orchestras, choirs and strong tradition of singing. More than 100 concerts a year, with recent performances at the Royal Albert Hall and Royal Festival Hall. Steady stream of boys to top universities and conservatoires to read music too.

Excellent Ryan Theatre seats 400 and is used for school and professional productions but annual Shakespeare productions take place in the beautiful arts and crafts Speech Room. A huge, wood-panelled half-moon, it boasts authentic Globe-style staging and seats the entire school. Wonderful art and, befittingly for a school where photography pioneer William Fox Talbot was a pupil, photography. DT, sculpture, art and photography now in a new state-of-the-art facility that also includes a new digital design suite. There's no lounging around with nothing to do at weekends either – scores of extra-curricular activities to choose from, everything from the Alexander Society for boys interested in military history to the Turf Club for horse racing fans.

Boarding: All pupils board at Harrow. We visited two very different houses – Druries, which dates back to the 1790s and is a maze of charming nooks and crannies, and the ultra-modern Lyon's, or the Holiday Inn, as a few wags have nicknamed it. 'It's the best piece of real estate around here,' joked one boy, hugely appreciative of its light, airy, five-star rooms. 'There's room for us to move around and not cause too much havoc.'

He comes from a lineage of skilled horticulturalists who nurtured his early interest in science. A man with a vocation to serve, he considered a career in the armed forces

Each house has common rooms, games rooms (kitted out with plasma TV, pool and table tennis tables), garden and 'yarder,' an area where boys can run off steam and kick a ball about. Two boys sharing is the norm in the first year but by year 11 (or even earlier) they get their own room, complete with desk, shelving, computer and, occasionally, en-suite shower. All pupils' names etched on wooden house boards, with head of house's name picked out in gold. Boys can make toast and heat up soup in their houses – 'and the more ambitious make Pot Noodles,' said one boy. We trust he was joking. Meals are eaten centrally and food gets a firm thumbs-up – from us too, if the lunch we had with sixth formers was anything to go by. Boys are allowed to go out for a meal with their parents on Sundays but there's no weekly or flexi-boarding. Two weekend exeats in the autumn and spring terms and one in the summer.

Background and atmosphere: Harrow is one of only four all-boys, full-boarding schools left in the UK (along with Eton, Winchester and Radley). Boys have been educated here since the 13th century, but the school was founded in 1572 under a royal charter granted to local farmer John Lyon by Elizabeth I (Lyon's, the newest boarding house, is named after him). The aim was for the school to provide free education for 30 local scholars, a number later increased to 40 by the governors. School sits in picturesque Harrow on the Hill, surrounded by 400 acres and with panoramic views across London – of it, yet remote from it, as we said last time. On a clear day you can see Canary Wharf from the head's study and it's just 25 minutes by tube to Green Park. Visitors to the undulating school site take note – flat shoes are a must.

School is steeped in tradition and history. The 17th century Old Schools contain the beautiful Fourth Form room, with names carved into every inch of panelling, from Byron to Robert Peel. It's also where Professor Flitwick's charm classes were shot in the first Harry Potter film (lots of tourists gazing admiringly when we visited). The stunning Vaughan Library, designed by architect Gilbert Scott (he also created London's St Pancras Station) has chess sets on tables and stays open late during exam periods. War Memorial Building commemorates the 633 OHs who died in the First World War. You can't help but be profoundly moved by the Alex Fitch Room, an Elizabethan wood panelled room with stained glass windows and a Cromwellian table, given by a grieving mother in honour of her 19-year-old son after he died in the First World War. She asked that it should be used for the purpose of boys meeting their mothers and that a light should always be left on over her son's portrait. Plaques and memorials commemorating quirky events are everywhere. Charles I rested here while preparing to surrender and little inclines have memorable names like Obadiah Slope, wittily named after Trollope's unctuous Barchester Towers character.

> *Charles I rested here while preparing to surrender and little inclines have memorable names like Obadiah Slope, wittily named after Trollope's unctuous character*

Harrow Songs are legendary. No Harrovian, either past or present, fails to mention the strength of feeling they engender and the lump in the throat they provoke. Songs have been an important part of the school since 1864, when the head of music wrote the first song, and they are considered to be

> *It's the sort of place where a Yorkshire farmer's son will be sharing a room with the offspring of a City banker*

'a unifying force.' In November each year the whole school assembles in Speech Room in honour of its most famous alumni, Sir Winston Churchill, for the Churchill Songs. Like rival Eton, school has its own jargon. 'Skew' is a punishment, 'tosh' is a shower, 'tolley up' is permission to work late and so on.

Pastoral care, well-being and discipline: Pastoral care is meticulous, with highly structured system of resident housemasters, assistant housemasters and matrons. Harrow's 12 houses are integral to the school and boys are fiercely loyal to their own house. Some houses are regarded as stricter than others and parents we spoke to said it's important 'to pick and choose carefully.' One of the houses – West Acre – was recently the subject of an ITN documentary series, following the life of the school for a whole year. Housemasters in post for 12 years and as well as doing most of the admissions assessments each gives their house its character and reputation. They also work round the clock – 'at the beginning of every term I say to my wife "see you at the end of term",' one housemaster told us with a grin.

Harrow takes a pragmatic approach to technology and social media but the boys are so busy there isn't much time to sit around and play computer games. Pupils understand that bullying is 'completely unacceptable' and head says that it has plummeted, 'not down to zero, but pretty close.' School does a bullying survey every winter and housemasters, year group tutors, matrons, two school chaplains, health education tutors and school psychologist pick up on most things. Discipline is clear and firm but the place feels pretty relaxed, with boys knowing exactly where they stand. 'You are given freedom but if you abuse the freedom you would be punished,' one boy told us. Zero tolerance on drugs and use or supply in term-time or holidays means expulsion. Anyone found with spirits suspended and warned while smoking is handled through 'escalating sequence of sanctions imposed by housemasters.'

Smart uniform of dark blue jackets (bluers), grey flannels (greyers), white shirts and ties, plus, of course, Harrow's infamous boaters. Boys wear them or carry them and either love them or loathe them. They're allowed to write their names and draw pictures on the inner rim and spray them with varnish to protect them. Members of Philathletic

Club (school's top sportsmen) get to wear bow ties. Sunday wear is black tailcoat and the whole kit and caboodle.

Pupils and parents: Pupils come from all over and school is proud of its 'broad and varied intake.' We said last time that it's the sort of place where a Yorkshire farmer's son will be sharing a room with the offspring of a City banker – and it still holds true. Between 10 and 15 per cent are progeny of OHs, while 20 per cent are from overseas (some expat, others from vast range of countries – 40 at last count). Twenty-five with EAL requirements. Most boys are C of E but there's a 'significant' RC community. Small numbers of all other main faiths or none.

The boys we met were engaging, appreciative of the fine education they get and very proud of their school. 'It doesn't give you a sense of entitlement, just a great responsibility to give something back,' one boy told us, while a sixth former who'd joined from a state school at 16 said that he'd been 'pushed and challenged' and that there was 'a lot more opportunity for debate' than at his previous school.

Parents reckon the school suits all-rounders who work hard and like sport. 'It's very disciplined and the boys are busy all the time so they have to be organised,' one mother said. 'There isn't any time to get up to any mischief and the boys are really tired by the end of term. There's a real camaraderie about the place and the boys make life-long friends. I can't fault it.' Another reckoned that even though it's 'strict,' any boy would thrive at Harrow, as long as they can cope with being in a large school where they won't necessarily be 'king pin.'

The mother of a gifted sportsman was full of admiration for the way the school nurtured her son's sporting talent whilst keeping him focused on his academic studies

Long and distinguished list of former pupils – seven former prime ministers (including Sir Robert Peel, Lord Palmerston, Stanley Baldwin and Sir Winston Churchill), 19th century philanthropist Lord Shaftesbury ('a towering figure – we refer to him a lot,' says the head), Jawaharlal Nehru, King Hussein of Jordon, Lord Cardigan (who led the Charge of the Light Brigade), General Sir Peter de la Billière, plus countless other men of military renown (20 holders of the Victoria Cross and one George Cross holder). The arts and sciences are equally well represented, with a dazzling list of luminaries including Lord Byron, Richard Brinsley Sheridan, Anthony Trollope, Terence Rattigan, John Galsworthy, Cecil Beaton, Edward and William Fox, Richard Curtis, Benedict Cumberbatch and James Blunt, plus Crispin Odey (one of the UK's most successful hedge fund managers), Julian Metcalfe (founder of Pret à Manger), cricketer Nick Compton and Tim Bentinck (better known as David Archer).

Entrance: Very competitive. Around 600 apply for the 160 places on offer at 13. Prospective pupils supply school reference and sit pre-test in year 6; most are expected to be invited for assessment at the start of year 7, through tests and interviews. Offers are made – subject to CE or scholarship exams 18 months later. Sixty-five per cent expected at CE. 'Some weight' given to sons of OHs and boys' siblings – 'but brothers don't automatically get in,' said a parent. Boys arrive from more than 100 regular feeder schools. All-boys' boarding preps like Caldicott and Cothill top the pack but others from a myriad of co-ed and day schools.

Total of 24 new pupils a year into the 340-strong sixth form. Candidates need at least seven or eight 9-7s at GCSE but many will have straight 9/8s. Candidates write a CV, plus letter to the head explaining why they want to come to Harrow, and take tests in their proposed A level subjects. The best attend a day of interviews and assessments.

Exit: Very few leave after GCSEs and nearly all sixth formers off to university, with 19 boys off to Oxbridge in 2018. Other top destinations include Exeter, Bristol, Edinburgh and UCL; several heading for the US eg Brown, NYU, Stanford, Chicago and Yale.

Money matters: School has given franchises to Harrow Beijing, Harrow Bangkok and Harrow Hong Kong, with a fourth likely to follow in the next few years. These are all successful enterprises carefully monitored by Harrow and also fund generous bursary schemes at home.

Wide range of scholarships and bursaries at 13 or 16. School offers means-tested bursaries of up to 100 per cent of fees to pupils who win a scholarship of any sort. Up to 30 scholarships a year for academic excellence, music, art or talent in a particular area (normally worth five per cent of fees). There are also Peter Beckwith scholarships for gifted and talented boys whose parents can't afford to send them to Harrow. Two awarded each year to boys aged between 10 and 13 – these can cover fees at a private school from the age of 11 and Harrow fees from 13.

Remarks: Parents looking for a top notch, blue chip, full boarding, all boys' school will be hard-pressed to beat Harrow. This is a school on top of its game.

Haydon School

Wiltshire Lane, Eastcote, Pinner HA5 2LX

020 8429 0005 | info@haydonschool.org.uk | haydonschool.com

State	Pupils: 1,864; sixth form: 436
Ages: 11–18	

Headteacher: Since 2006, Robert Jones (40s). Read economics at LSE and taught in Hong Kong for four years before returning to the UK. Moved to Haydon in 1999 and quickly moved up the ranks to become assistant head, then head. Married to drama teacher. Two sons – one grown up, one at primary school. Originally from Manchester, he's a huge Man United fan and looks rather like an ex-professional footballer himself. Still plays football and coaches Ascot United under 7s (his son plays for the team) and keeps fit by running a number of half marathons each year.

Academic matters: Specialist language and applied learning college offering more than 30 GCSE and BTec options. 'We want to offer as broad a curriculum as possible,' explains the head. Language provision is excellent, with students starting off with French and Italian or Spanish and German; older pupils can take on further languages such as Mandarin. 'Around 100 opted for Mandarin this year,' says the head proudly. In 2018, 74 per cent got 9-4 in both maths and English (28 per cent 9-7 grades); at A level 45 per cent A*/B, 68 per cent A*-C. Parents praise the quality of teaching and particularly the revision lessons offered around exam time.

Students need six GCSEs at 9-4 (including maths and English) to study four A levels. Those who do not have a good pass in English or maths are able to retake these along with three A levels. One SENCo and a team of learning support assistants support around 20 or so statemented pupils. There is also a special centre where students can be taught in small groups.

Parents like the fact that class sizes are around 25, but some would prefer more streaming. 'At present in year 7 there is streaming just for maths,' said one parent. 'I would like to see this extended to other key subjects such as English and science as is the practice in other local schools'.

Games, options, the arts: School has scored successes in a host of sports – at both local and county level. Particular strengths are rugby, rounders and indoor athletics and there is even an ultimate frisbee team in the sixth form. New sports hall added to extensive sports facilities.

Originally from Manchester, he's a huge Man United fan and looks rather like an ex-professional footballer himself

Haydon has benefited from new facilities in recent years, including £5 million art and design building and £2 million music and performing arts centre (three music rooms, drama studio and music mixing room, plus one-to-one teaching rooms). School has two orchestras, jazz band, samba band and wide variety of other music groups. Four big concerts a year as well as annual musical or play. Thriving art department achieves excellent exam results. Students can study art, textiles and photography at A level. Lots of school trips too – to France, Germany, Italy, Peru and Swaziland.

Background and atmosphere: School is situated on the edge of the Northwood Hills in Pinner, with spacious playing fields. Rather nondescript 1950s buildings – originally two grammar schools that merged in 1977. Food in the sixth form café is so good that the staff choose to eat there. Food in the canteen for the rest of the school received less favourable reports but new caterers now in situ. 'The boys' changing rooms are a real state,' one student told us, but we weren't shown these on our tour; lots of building work was going on when we visited. We were very taken with the pool table and primary colours in the rather groovy sixth form common room though.

Pastoral care, well-being and discipline: A new positive reward system has recently been introduced. 'The reward system is a great motivator,' one parent told us. 'My child strives to get good news notes, commendations and other rewards.' Meanwhile a year 8 student said: 'I really look forward to the awards assembly. It's a way of showing how hard we are working.' One of the top awards means pupils get a special lunch with the head (mums sadly aren't eligible to compete for this award).

Students excluded for threatening behaviour or repeated disruption in lessons (four permanent exclusions last year). Parents are happy with school's approach to behaviour. 'I have always found that a high level of discipline is maintained from the minute the children arrive at the school,' said one. When we visited, students seemed well behaved and friendly.

Pupils and parents: 'Haydon has a really good reputation round here,' a student told us, 'and all my friends at other schools wish they were here.' The school offers both pupils and parents a chance to voice their opinions – parent voice group meets four times per year.

Entrance: Most students live locally (within a mile or so of the school). Admissions criteria are: children in public care, then siblings, then children living nearest to the school, then employees' children. An additional 60 students join in the sixth form.

Exit: Around 40 per cent of pupils leave after GCSEs – for college, other schools, apprenticeships or employment – and up to 10 per cent after year 12. Some 80 per cent of sixth formers to university, and about a third of these to top universities eg Southampton and Nottingham (the largest percentage of any state school in the borough). One to Cambridge in 2018 (veterinary medicine) and one to study medicine at Oxford.

Remarks: A friendly comprehensive that really does cater for all, with strong vocational courses as well as the more traditional A levels – all taught to a high standard. 'I would have no hesitation recommending Haydon,' said one parent. 'I feel my children are lucky to attend the school.'

International School of London

139 Gunnersbury Avenue, London W3 8LG

020 8992 5823 | mail@ISLLondon.org | isllondon.org

| Independent | Pupils: 400; sixth form: 75 |
| Ages: 3–18 | Fees: £19,000 – £26,300 pa |

Principal: Since September 2018, Richard Parker, who has been principal of ISL Surrey primary school since 2015, and was also co-principal of the London campus. Started working in a law firm in the City, which may have been the inevitable job choice for a Cambridge graduate in history, but he left law and went to the Institute of Education, London, trained as a secondary school teacher and taught at several state London schools before he and his wife moved to teach in international schools in Spain, Argentina, Hong Kong, Portugal and Brunei. Two children.

Academic matters: Early childhood classes start full time from 3 years old and parents said it was a blessing to have all children at the same school with the same school hours. Long days for little ones, but the option to have a rest in the afternoon helps. Not that there was much sleeping when we visited – children were busy eating and cleaning up

and playing. Lots of equipment and adults meant children were cheerful and well occupied. A very well-designed play area just for the early years with plants, wooden toys and climbing benches and even a mini amphitheatre, where story telling and plays take place. Small classes and high teacher:pupil ratio. Parents confirmed that much of the learning takes place through play.

Primary class size varies from but is never more than 22 pupils, which together with the fact that we saw a classroom assistant or extra teacher in many of the classrooms means that the high teacher:pupil ratio continues up the school, and confirms what the pupils explained to us as 'lots of support and help whenever you need it'. Parents said that the longstanding head of primary knows every child by name and is very present and responsive. The school follows the Primary Years Programme, an international curriculum leading to the International Baccalaureate. Learning is done in six week Units of Enquiry and the aim is for each topic to cover all subjects. Much of the learning is student interest based and interactive, with peer to peer teaching and debate. The aim is for pupils not only to acquire knowledge but to have conceptual understanding, gain skills and develop beliefs and attitudes which they can demonstrate through responsible action. This interdisciplinary learning seems to be appreciated by pupils, who told us that school was fun and they looked forward to coming to school, and parents, who appreciate that pupils 'learn how to learn' and that the school has a 'liberal' approach to education'. Several spoke about the advantages of 'a fully integrated curriculum'.

'You are graded on how you work things out, not on the result only, and teachers mark on your critical thinking'. Clearly the message on reflective learning has got through

The end of the Primary Years Programme is celebrated at a grade 5 exhibition. Parents we spoke to felt that since the curriculum is fairly child led, the level is well matched and work is differentiated by ability – possible with such small classes. However, some suggested that native English speakers may not be overly stretched. The language programme is a distinguishing feature of the school. Regular teaching in their mother tongue as well as intensive English lessons ensure that that pupils maintain their own language while acquiring a second or third language. Parents said that every child showed real fluency within two years. This basic tenet of ISL maintains that children will learn a second language better if they maintain and develop their first language – any language learning enhances language development as well as being good for personal and educational development. We saw pupils in tiny groups or individually learning Swahili, Finnish, Arabic, Spanish or French, and the library has an impressive selection books in 18 different languages.

The Middle Years Programme does not feel very different from the primary years. Pupils, however, felt that there was more work and more independence required. The language programme continues alongside the MYP with its emphasis on global contexts and key concepts. The aim is to acquire skills to help with learning and life. There are self-initiated personal projects, work on laptops (given by the school or supported with bring your own device initiative) and an emphasis on independent reflective learning. One student said, 'It teaches you how to work and gives you explanations', and another

said, 'You are graded on how you work things out, not on the result only, and teachers mark on your critical thinking'. Clearly the message on reflective teaching and learning has got through. Facilities are not extensive, but the school is well equipped. Two science labs, plenty of laptops, a large well-stocked current library which includes newspapers and magazines, interactive whiteboards, and endless language learning rooms. The mother tongue language programme and intensive EAL continue where needed in middle years.

The IB diploma programme is housed in a building some 10 minutes' walk from the rest of the school, and so it feels like a sixth form college with fingerprint entry registration and a spacious, bright common room overlooking the small courtyard garden. The library is at the top of the building in a quiet study zone with many students wearing headphones. Smaller classrooms cover the various IB subjects on offer – economics is very popular, as are maths and the sciences (biology perhaps even more than physics and chemistry). A huge, light art room. Languages, unsurprisingly, often taken at higher level IB as most students are multilingual. In 2018, 33 average points, two getting 43, and 84 per cent bilingual diplomas.

A grade 10 foundation class (15/16 year olds) particular to the school gives intensive English lessons and preparation for the IB curriculum. Students follow a range of subjects (English, maths, science, humanities, PE, mother tongue) and the course focuses on developing their academic English so that they can move successfully into post-16 education. Most stay on to take IB diploma at ISL.

Games, options, the arts: Extracurricular subjects and the arts have taken on new energy recently – one parent said it was unrecognisable now with the number of clubs and non-academic subjects being taught. A new music teacher who is proving very popular and dynamic has increased the music uptake and output – all grade 3 pupils take violin now, and grand primary and middle years musical theatre productions clearly a matter of great excitement and preparation. Similarly, a new middle years drama teacher seems to be a good influence, using the large bright space at the top of the main school.

For art, classes are divided into three and students do a rota of visual art and design technology with both hard and soft materials. Laser cutters and 3D printers, sewing machines and collage, mask making and woodwork. A lively hive of activity and creativity with much emphasis on the planning and design elements.

A real highlight of the school for the pupils is the 'makers' space' where student-led technological creations can take place – either as part of a lesson or in breaks and after-school clubs. Video recording and editing, creation of a 3D printer,

Not much evidence of chauffeur driven pupils or security guards for little princes and princesses, despite fairly chunky fees

video game design, innovations and machines of every sort. Dyson would be thrilled, as are the students, with the possibilities to make and create. Students said to us that the school makes you want to learn more but without making it feel like work. We certainly got a sense of learning through creating in that classroom.

Sports led by three person PE team – dance, hockey, basketball, volleyball, football. Swimming every year in junior school with kids bussed to Brentford Sports Centre. The school has a gym and playground but uses a nearby playing field for wider sports activities. A recently signed contract will see the school having access to newly built sports centre at nearby Gunnersbury Park. Sports rarely involves many inter-school competitions but some fixtures arranged with other international schools. Lots of time and clubs for tennis, yoga, basketball and football. Parents felt that kids get an excellent sports education despite paucity of on site sports facilities, partly because they are taught general skills – such as kicking or throwing – rather than a specific sport. More competitive children use local sports clubs.

Other after-school clubs clearly well used – Glee Club was one child's favourite for musical theatre; there's also eg journalism, badminton, chess, Lego robotics, global issues debating. Many clubs led by students from the diploma programme, presumably in order to gain points towards the IB and to fulfil the community or action side of the programme. DJ-ing taught by one student who proudly told us this had resulted in his club members getting their own equipment and setting up as part time DJs.

Background and atmosphere: An older red-brick building with modern additions on two sides forms a U-shaped school round the playground/school bus parking area. All pupils now come in through the main reception area (fingerprint entry system as well as more usual registration in class) and there is a flow to the school despite its many additions. It was bought in the 70s and was one of the first schools to offer all three IB programmes (PYP, MYP and DP). It is one of three schools owned by a Lebanese family who are still very involved, although there is an active board of governors too. Some links and support from the conglomerate of the schools, but this school is the largest

and most established, with the heads reporting directly to the board and the proprietors. It is liberal in outlook, catering for an almost exclusively international student body. This makes it wonderfully international in outlook and values including a great openness to other cultures. It also makes it painful for pupils who stay longer and live through friends leaving regularly. This turnover is part of the reality of ISL though an effort is being made to appeal to more local families, and not a moment too soon, according to parents. There is an active alumni body and one of its aims is to ensure links between ex-students of all ages are maintained. The transitions programme supports families and students when friends leave as well as supporting families who are new to the school – with a good family mentoring system.

Door-to-door bus service is available but with growing London traffic problems school strongly recommends that families choose to live in neighbourhoods like Kew, Chiswick or Ealing.

Pastoral care, well-being and discipline: Part of being an international school means that all the students have something in common, and pupils told us that was why they all got on so well and there was never any bullying, stealing or behavioural problems – they said, 'we are all different and that makes us the same'. They mentioned talks about drugs, mental health, guidance, sexting use of the internet and alcohol, and parents felt that kids had a good education in ethics and values – words like empathy used from early years. No-one could remember incidences of discipline so we couldn't get examples of this – though a discipline policy available in writing.

Student council in evidence and clearly plenty of input from pupils and parents. Some parents felt that the school listened to parents too much – the school is very anxious to please, rather than having the confidence to state its position. But perhaps the active and eloquent parent teachers association is hard to ignore.

Learning support department consists of SENCo for both lower and upper schools who sees pupils regularly as well as coordinating speech and language therapy and outside professionals. Pupils frequently self refer to full-time counsellor, who also supports teachers and sometimes meets parents. Counsellor also gives talks on relationships and general health (though sex education left to the biology teachers).

Parents spoke of the a 'warm atmosphere' and in particular the 'smooth transition', with school praised for its warm welcome to the many new faces each year. Good relationships between different year groups enhanced by vertical integration – clubs, mentoring, joint drama and fundraising activities etc.

School lunches delicious and prepared in house, with limited choice. A continental school feel with everyone eating the same food together.

Pupils and parents: Large numbers of Italians, Japanese, Americans, Dutch, French and British represented in the pupil body – which is why some families choose it. Also popular is its location – mentioned by every parent we spoke to – near Kew, Chiswick and Ealing. All family friendly areas and good for parents working in town. Not much evidence of chauffeur driven pupils or security guards for little princes and princesses, despite fairly chunky fees. Some of the classes are small lower down the school so less choice of friends for some, but 'more of a community than a school' and 'like family'.

Regular transition workshops to support parents. 'Strong' parents' association organises cookery clubs, outings, welcoming and pairing up of established families with incoming families as well as having regular meetings with school to both support and offer suggestions – and parents say school 'listens to us and is open to implementing parental suggestions'

Entrance: A rolling admissions policy to match the needs of relocating families. Initial contact through admissions team who work hard to ensure that visits and questions and contact generally runs smoothly and easily, since 'parents are already stressed enough'. Interviews by Skype if needed and sight of current school reports. They don't expect kids to have fluent English, but do expect behaviour they can manage and learning needs they can support. Learning support for up to two hours if needed included in fees, and extra (for example individual classroom assistance) paid for

by parents. Sensible experienced admissions staff keen to maintain non-selective mix at the school, including those with learning needs. Registered as Tier 4 sponsors for visas.

Exit: Over three-quarters stay in the UK to universities including SOAS, Exeter, Cardiff, King's and Westminster, with several to art colleges like City and Guilds. A smaller proportion of students move to universities outside the UK including ESSEC Business School, Paris, Vrije Universiteit Amsterdam and Sciences Po, Paris.

Money matters: Privately owned by the Lebanese family who started with this International School of London and now also run the International School of London in Surrey and one in Doha, Qatar. The Makarem family are still on the board, have weekly updates and visit regularly.

Fees are substantial and often paid by employers. No extra charges for the mother tongue language programme (as long as there are at least five students), learning support, day outings, most clubs, but extras include transport, lunches, intensive English, and 'capital development fee'. No bursaries.

Remarks: A perfect school for a child to get intensive English language learning whilst actively maintaining their mother tongue and ideal for families who want to remain near central London. This school seems to be changing and flourishing with new and better facilities and management, whilst having a solid background of experience in international teaching. We liked the international culture of the school and the calm, purposeful atmosphere.

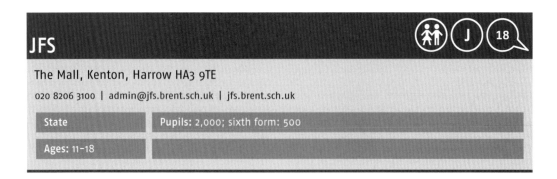

JFS

The Mall, Kenton, Harrow HA3 9TE

020 8206 3100 | admin@jfs.brent.sch.uk | jfs.brent.sch.uk

State	Pupils: 2,000; sixth form: 500
Ages: 11-18	

Headteacher: Since June 2018, Rachel Fink, previously head of Hasmonean Girls School. A chemistry graduate from UCL, she has an MA in Jewish studies from King's College London and a teaching degree from Michlalah, Jerusalem College for Women, and is a former JFS head girl. She spent

10 years teaching science in high schools in Israel, is a graduate of Cambridge University's Co-Exist interfaith programme and has been a member of a Partnerships for Jewish Schools' working party on mental health. Her husband, Stuart, is also a teacher.

Academic matters: Consistently in the top one per cent nationally of non-selective schools, JFS continues to achieve pretty stunning results. In 2018, 49 per cent of A levels A*/A, 76 per cent A*-B. At GCSE, 51 per cent 9-7, although interestingly the percentage of entries at grades 9-4 was 91, suggesting perhaps that the school's intake is top-heavy at the high achieving end.

Teaching here universally praised. 'The school is incredible academically'; 'The teaching is amazing'; 'I feel I'm being really stretched, especially in maths'; 'The teachers praise you so much, they really notice your achievements,' said students, while parents added, 'The teachers for the most part are either good or wonderful'; 'Most of my son's teachers have been spectacular'; 'They really push pupils to achieve their potential'; 'The academic standards are excellent.' Strong uptake of the EPQ, and an ongoing and wholehearted commitment to A levels; only one BTec offered and there are no plans to introduce the IB.

Year 7 pupils set for English maths, Jewish studies, Hebrew and PE, but in mixed ability groups for other subjects. Excellent support for both high and low ability students, and a large and well-equipped SEN department supporting the latter. 'The support to my child has been fantastic – staff have bent over backwards to help him,' an appreciative parent told us. Ofsted commented in its most recent report that more need to be done to support those towards the bottom of the middle, some of whom don't make such rapid progress as their peers. Parents, however, told us that the school catered well for difference. 'My children are different in every way and the school's been brilliant with both of them.' 'The school has found a way to reward each of my children for what they do well.'

School is very well-equipped, with interactive boards in every classroom, and no fewer than 14 science labs. Indeed, science was praised as a particular strength of the school. 'The resources here are really good. The teachers are some of the best in the school, and they always get outstanding results,' said one young physicist, proudly. Annual science festival, and the department creates plenty of science leadership opportunities. One-year GCSE astronomy course available to sixth formers as an optional extra, and Science Support Club for years 7 to 11. We dropped in on the year 7 Math-a-Thon, a highly impressive but good-humoured event where you could have heard a pin drop as the competitors stepped up to the platform and got to work in an atmosphere of palpable excitement.

French offered to all year 7s and Spanish to all year 8s, along with Ivrit (modern Hebrew). However, modern languages came in for something of a battering from both pupils and parents – 'They aren't great, but this is no secret,' wrote one mother gloomily, and pupils we asked tended to concur, dismissing Ivrit in particular as 'the subject everyone intends to drop in year 10'. Whilst admitting that they'd had some trying staff shortages in recent times, school insists: 'We're fully staffed, and we've got some really cracking teachers in that department.' And at least one student agreed: 'I think the languages teachers have really helped me.'

Science was praised as a particular strength. 'The resources here are really good. The teachers are some of the best in the school, and they always get outstanding results'

History and politics are extremely popular here, and classical civilisation is a recent and successful innovation – 'a really good course,' according to students. Jewish studies widely regarded as excellent, and won universal praise for its intellectual breadth and inclusivity. 'It's been taught in a way that's allowed my son to challenge the material, rather than trying to indoctrinate him,' said one parent, and another confirmed, 'My children have felt comfortable to question the teachers, who have always responded well.'

Games, options, the arts: Impressive array of trophies on display reflects the opportunities and facilities for sport on offer: netball, football, badminton, basketball, trampolining, fitness, athletics, rounders – etc. When we visited, the school had just won the Middlesex Regional Cup for Football in year 12, and everyone we spoke to clearly enjoyed this part of the school's provision. Magnificent climbing wall very popular and much-used.

Superb artwork everywhere we looked, including some really huge canvasses – 'They're not short of ambition,' commented the head of art. Drama also flourishes on a big scale, staging musicals like Little Shop of Horrors, Guys and Dolls and Fiddler on the Roof alongside Shakespearean offerings such as Twelfth Night and Much Ado About Nothing. Music is high-quality, lively and wide-ranging – 'The music department is really friendly.' 'They adopt you as one of their children if you go to rehearsals,' according to pupils. Students can learn 'any and every instrument', and there are regular concerts as well as an annual music festival and the ever-popular staff recital.

Sixth form newspaper held in high regard, and student journalism is strong throughout the school. 'Someone who likes to write and have their voice heard can always do so here,' said an aspiring reporter. 'Loads' of student-run societies, including the sixth form medical society, which lays on talks by prestigious visiting speakers – professors Jane Dacre and Alan McGregor recently headed the bill.

Lots of excursions, and many parents praised the year 9 trip to Israel – 'Incredible' and 'the highlight of my child's year.' High take-up of gap years in Israel arranged by the school.

Background and atmosphere: Founded in 1732, moved to Bell Lane in London's East End in 1832, where at one time it had 4,000 children on its roll and was the biggest school in Europe. The site was bombed during the war, and in 1958 relocated to Camden. Expanding numbers, plus the need to upgrade school facilities, led to the move in 2002 to its present purpose-built home in Kenton. The new school building was designed to be light and airy, to have learning at its heart, and to have the synagogue placed where it would be the first thing visitors would see. The latter is certainly the jewel in the school's crown, with beautiful stained glass windows and a library and study area in the gallery. It's in constant use, both for services and Lunch and Learn sessions. Elsewhere the building is curvy and lightsome, with wide corridors and a progressive feel, although here and there carpets and paintwork were showing their age. Sixth form area is particularly inviting, with spacious and attractive study areas.

Sixth form newspaper held in high regard, and student journalism is strong throughout. 'Someone who likes to write and have their voice heard can always do so here'

The school is divided into four houses named after leading lights in the Anglo-Jewish community (Angel, Brodetsky, Weizmann and Zangwill), and is orthodox in the sense that its denominational authority is the Chief Rabbi. However, it admits children from a wide variety of Jewish backgrounds, both practising and secular, including around 10 per cent from overseas. 'The school prepares you to mix with any background,' said a very likeable sixth former. 'It's great for getting you out of the Jewish bubble, and it's a great place to be secular as well as observant.' All faiths are represented on the staff, 60 per cent of whom are not Jewish.

We liked the liveliness and warmth of this school community. 'JFS is really good, really welcoming, and I settled in quickly,' said one student. 'You can have so many friends in all the different year groups, because there are so many activities,' said another. To us, as we moved round the school, the students seemed cordial, purposeful, orderly

and well-turned-out, wearing their blue uniform with care (mostly); carrying themselves with confidence, and, we thought, joie de vivre.

Pastoral care, well-being and discipline: In 2014 parental complaints about some students' behaviour led to an unannounced visit by Ofsted and the lowering of JFS's status from outstanding to requires improvement. Something of a shock, one imagines, but the school rallied, and following a monitoring visit from Ofsted six months later, was judged to be 'taking effective action to tackle the areas requiring improvement' and acting 'professionally and resolutely'. Measures have included restructuring the senior leadership team, new appointments on the governing body, improved information gathering about attendance, introducing a clearer sanctions policy, and working with an independent school improvement adviser contracted by the school's local authority.

Has it worked? Well, the school is, if anything, more oversubscribed than it was before, and responses from parents and children were overwhelmingly favourable. 'We have always been struck by the excellent behaviour we've witnessed in the JFS students we met,' wrote one mother. 'In my opinion, the recent downgrading only demonstrated what a ridiculous body Ofsted is,' said another. In December 2016 the school was regraded as good in all areas except the 16-19 study programmes where it was graded outstanding.

'Everyone feels safe here,' was a typical student comment, and school says, 'We have a strong message to the students: bullying is not tolerated,' adding that recent surveys of parents indicated that 90 per cent of parents felt that bullying was dealt with effectively. That said, JFS is a big school, and a few people expressed concern to us that behaviours such as blanking and name-calling sometimes slipped under the radar. As one mother put it, 'The school deals with bullying very well once they're made aware that there's a problem.'

Pastoral care was very highly rated. 'There's so much support,' said a grateful year 7 child who admitted having taken a while to find her feet, and students throughout the school concurred. 'Any issues have been taken up when I raised them,' said one. 'The mentoring system is second to none', said another. Parents added, 'The staff are always easy to contact – I've only had trouble once in the past nine years getting a teacher to get back to me,' 'One of my children had some anxiety over exams and self-esteem issues. The school has been exceptional and extremely supportive over this.'

Everyone agreed that, despite the school's size, their child had felt noticed and encouraged. 'When choosing schools, we didn't want JFS because we felt it was too big,' wrote one parent, 'however, from the first day we could not have been more impressed. The transfer process from primary to secondary school was flawless, and both our children made friends quickly.'

Pupils and parents: A broad social mix of families, with about eight per cent on free school meals. Students are confident, articulate, 'sometimes audacious.'

Entrance: Heavily oversubscribed, with around 800 applications for 300 places at year 7. Check school's website for ladder of admissions criteria. Following the famous court of appeal ruling in 2009, students no longer have to have a Jewish mother, but families need to complete a certificate of religious practice. Around 35 external applicants are accepted to join the sixth form each year, on the basis of GCSE results and religious practice.

Exit: Around 10 per cent leave after GCSE to try something else. Of those who stay almost all go on to higher education, either directly or after a gap year. Some 70 per cent to Russell group universities in 2018, with eight to Oxbridge, plus two off to medical school and one vet. Usually a few each year to music conservatoires or drama schools. Gap year option arranged by the school to study in Israel is always popular, with some even doing a second gap year.

Remarks: Still the school of choice for Jewish families wanting the best education – both Jewish and otherwise – for their children. As one parent wrote, 'When my son received his place at JFS, my husband and I felt we'd won the golden ticket, and our feelings haven't changed.' As another put it, 'I can't imagine sending my children anywhere else.'

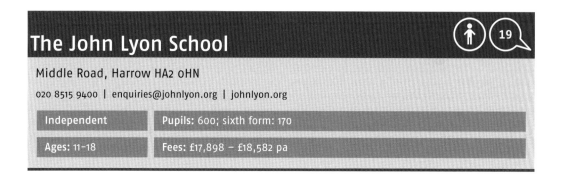

The John Lyon School

Middle Road, Harrow HA2 0HN

020 8515 9400 | enquiries@johnlyon.org | johnlyon.org

| Independent | Pupils: 600; sixth form: 170 |
| Ages: 11–18 | Fees: £17,898 – £18,582 pa |

Head: Since 2009, Katherine Haynes, BA MEd NPQH (40s). Attended Oxford High School for Girls ('No doubt, that's the reason I'm driven in the way I am'), before reading maths at Warwick, followed by an MEd. Then taught in the Midlands, becoming head of maths at Edgbaston High School, followed by Warwick School, where she first started out as a school inspector and took the professional training scheme for headship. Her appointment at John Lyon made her the first woman ever to head an HMC boys' day school, but she had no hesitation in taking up the challenge. 'I felt I could provide a different perspective and saw what was possible. I wanted to make it more academic and put it on the map.' Has acted decisively on this brief, expanding the academic and extracurricular offering and polishing the pastoral care. Parents undoubtedly appreciate her approach. 'She's vibrant and dynamic, with no airs and graces, no nonsense,' said one fan. In term time she 'lives and breathes' the school, and all praise her involvement with pupils ('She really has time for the boys') and their families ('We were so impressed she invited parents of new boys to dinner at her house'). Continues to work as a school inspector, and, in her limited free time, enjoys gardening and travelling.

Academic matters: Small class sizes (20-23 in years 7-9, 18-24 at GCSE, 10-16 at A level) mean that pupils are well known by staff. ('A good relationship with teachers helps with their work,' says the head.) Currently reducing GCSE numbers from 10 to nine, 'to give more scope to go beyond the curriculum'. IGCSEs in maths, English and all sciences ('The exams are harder, but they make the transition to A levels smoother'). Carousel of languages, with Mandarin taster in year 8 (including a successful exchange programme with Harrow's sister school in the Far East), Latin from year 8, classical Greek from year 10. Post-GCSE, the school remains happy with A levels, adding classical civilisation, psychology, government and politics, music technology, computer science and, soon DT, to the subject range. Also major emphasis on the EPQ, with an impressive 100 per cent achieving A*/A most years. Results overall very solid (63 per cent A*-A/9-7 at GCSE; 31 per A*/A at A level in 2018), a reflection of the effort to instil self-discipline, hard work and high expectations. Parents believe the school gets the balance just right. 'The grades are good, but you're not made to feel awful if you're not at the top of the league tables.'

About seven per cent of pupils receive some sort of learning support (typically for dyslexia), which is provided by two specialist teachers in the learning support department. Those with English as their second language – the school does its best to accommodate families relocating mid year – also aided by a qualified EAL teacher. Gifted-and-talented programme, too, for those in need of 'enrichment'.

Games, options, the arts: Though the school overlooks some of the playing fields of Harrow, its own expansive 25 green acres are a five minute minibus-ride away. These have recently been updated with a state-of-the art MUGA (multi-use games areas) pitch, providing excellent floodlit facilities for hockey and tennis alongside football and cricket (and archery). Pupils also have access to Harrow's nine-hole golf course, squash and tennis courts (clearly made good use of, since one boy recently gained a tennis scholarship to the US). On site, there's a gym, 25m pool and fitness suite, with sporting options including basketball, judo, and badminton.

Drama a popular choice at GCSE and A level, with aspiring thespians busily practising their lines outside the two well-used drama studios on our visit. Boys also mount productions at Harrow School's Ryan Theatre and have the opportunity to work with professional companies, including the Donmar Warehouse, the Lyric Hammersmith and the Royal Shakespeare Company. Music – praised by parents as 'phenomenal' – benefits from a purpose built recording studio.

Parents undoubtedly appreciate her approach. 'She's vibrant and dynamic, with no airs and graces, no nonsense.' In term time she 'lives and breathes' the school

A 'rounded' education given a firm emphasis, with a timetabled programme of 'skills-based' activities including everything from cooking to changing a tyre. Out-of-lessons options also extensive, with a particularly high take up of Duke of Edinburgh (an impressive 30 pupils successfully completed gold recently). CCF also on offer, as part of the Harrow School cadet force. Plenty of trips (football to Iceland, cricket to South Africa, joint ski trip with Harrow, Wellington and Dulwich) and societies, from computing to chess. 'It's a very broad ranging education,' commented one contented father.

Background and atmosphere: John Lyon School – established in 1876 to 'educate local boys' – forms part (along with Harrow School) of the John Lyon's Foundation, and sits a street away from Churchill's alma mater in leafy Harrow on the Hill. The two schools have a happy, but not smothering, relationship, with heads of departments meeting for lunch, boys enjoying use of each other's more covetable facilities.

One of the head's greatest achievements has been a 10-year plan to modernise the outdated buildings. First on the list was the introduction of a dining hall. 'I wanted somewhere the whole school could sit and chat.' Moving the library to a new location has provided an attractive central space, where staff and students can socialise over a hot or cold meal (though the food itself is perhaps not a highlight – 'It's OK,' said one boy politely). Other, much-appreciated, improvements include a sixth form centre, occupying the entire Victorian school house, which provides both learning and leisure space for older boys. Next on the agenda is a flagship STEAM (the sciences plus art) building where DT, computer science and maths will unite with art.

A rebrand is also in the pipeline, which, it is hoped, will put the school more prominently in the spotlight. 'People describe us as one of the best kept secrets in London,' says the head, who clearly now intends to let the secret to leak out. 'We want to bring across the vision of what we represent: heritage and innovation, creativity and resilience.' Other widely acknowledged USPs include 'the family atmosphere,' the 'friendliness' and the attractively small scale. 'It's not too big,' said one father. 'Everyone knows my son's name, from the registrar to the guy who sits on the front desk.' Some feel the rebrand is long overdue. 'The school doesn't beat its own drum enough; it's sometimes seen as an also ran, which it definitely shouldn't be.'

Pastoral care, well-being and discipline: Great praise for the care and attention boys receive, with parents united in the view that the school does its utmost to develop every inch of potential. 'My son is a bright child, but not A*, nor is he massively sporty, but John Lyon is a lovely, nurturing, comfy school, which gets the absolute best out of him.' Confidence building in the public arena very much part of the package. 'My son has really flourished here and is turning into a nice young man who is able to talk to anyone.'

Boys generally motivated and ambitious with little evidence of teenage rebellion. 'We promote a code of conduct rather than having endless rules, so it's usually possible to pull back before declaring "time's up",' says the head. Even so, if that code is broken, lines are firmly drawn.

Girl-free zone compensated for by good links with neighbouring schools, so debating with North London Collegiate and Northwood College, drama with Royal Masonic.

Pupils and parents: Primarily local, very cosmopolitan, with over 50 per cent from Asian families, whose children will often be the first in the family to go to university. 'They're aspirational and hard-working and want to do the best for their children,' says the head. Boys are positive, focussed and keen.

Alumni include Michael Bogdanov, theatre director, Timothy West, actor, Stephen Pollard, journalist and Alastair Fraser, cricketer.

Entrance: At 11, 75 per cent come from local primaries (about 200 apply for 80 places, with increasing numbers making John Lyon their first choice); English and maths exams plus group activity. At 13 (when three or four forms expand to five), all from local preps, with main feeders Durston House, St Martin's, Orley Farm; English, maths, French and science exams (no pre-tests). The school is academically selective, but here the term 'potential' is not just rhetoric. All applicants are interviewed by senior staff (at 13, all by the head), with the intention of snuffling out 'those happy to be busy, active and willing to push themselves'.

Small intake into the sixth form, plus occasional mid-year admissions.

Exit: Around 30 per cent leaves post-GCSE for local sixth form colleges. Of the remainder, 70-80 per cent to their first choice of university, with significant numbers to leading London colleges (LSE and King's), then Russell Group (two Oxbridge in 2018) countrywide. University advice up-to-date and thoughtfully tailored to individual needs (including STEP classes for mathematicians). 'We're ambitious for boys and see what's possible,' says the dynamic head of university applications. High proportion to professional degrees in science (one medic in 2018), law, economics, architecture and finance.

Money matters: Good value. The John Lyon's Charity continues to help with means-tested bursaries.

Remarks: A small, thriving school, with historic links to Harrow School, which provides a well-rounded, well-grounded education in a welcoming atmosphere.

Kew House School

6 Capital Interchange Way, London TW8 oEX

020 8742 2038 | admissions@kewhouseschool.com | kewhouseschool.com

Independent	Pupils: 525; sixth form: 160
Ages: 11–18	Fees: £21,387 pa

Headmaster: Since 2013, Mark Hudson MEd (50s). Previously senior deputy head and director of technology at top performing Thomas Telford School – joined in 1996 as director of technology, becoming deputy head two years later and senior deputy head in 2006. Before this, head of design and technology at Bishop Fox's Community School in Taunton for 11 years, preceded by post as a DT teacher at St James's High School in Exeter, after a year in the same role at Kingsfield School in Bristol.

An 11+ 'failure' (made grammar school for sixth form), he's an articulate advocate for children at risk of being written off too early. Wants to offer 'the very best of contemporary educational practice' and overcome inertia that, he says, governs too much of what schools do. 'I'd rather children experienced education than having it inflicted on them.' Goal is to bring disenfranchised pupils in out of the cold. 'There are far too many out there,' he says.

He's co-written textbooks, been involved in A level curriculum design, enjoyed a spell as a teacher fellow at the Royal College of Arts and had a hand in the building of four new academies sponsored by Mercers' Livery Company which wowed school's owners, the Gardener Schools Group, prompting the job offer here. Clincher was the chance to build his own senior school from scratch.

It's a long way from childhood dream of being a dentist. 'I was quite enchanted by it. It's such a nice environment to work in, to meet people and make them feel better.' (Either had exceptional dentist or exceptional teeth.) Academic requirements put this out of reach, however, and instead he had an interim period studying town and country planning. So 'stultifyingly boring' that quit in third year, switched to a design-based degree and never looked back.

These days, doesn't teach regularly but likes to drop into DT lessons ('can't help myself') and wow pupils with technical skills (no coincidence that design department is next to his office).

Out of hours, he's a self-confessed petrolhead and drives 'a very nice' Jaguar. No doubt curbs temptation to talk shop at home (wife head of lower school at feeder prep; they have two grown up sons also in design and engineering-related careers). Also walks, swims and plays golf.

Felt to be down to earth. 'He was moving the mouse mats back into place in the IT room,' said approving parent on an open day visit. He also fitted some of the table top plug sockets in the sixth form centre, and very nice they look, too. (DIY, unsurprisingly, is another interest.)

Commands healthy levels of respect from parents. Personable deputies fulfil the good cop role, thought one. ('We swap,' says Mr Hudson, deadpan.) Felt by pupils to be more approachable than he looks. 'Can give off aura of being stern but that's necessary, it's in the job description,' says one. 'But he's very nice.'

With applications for year 7 at gratifyingly healthy levels and waiting lists in most pre-GCSE years in operation, he's concentrating on growing the sixth form. School currently operates full service of A levels, despite the financial pain of tiny classes (we saw two pupils rattling round in vast art room, same number again in food technology lesson, some other subjects in single numbers). However, expects numbers to increase over the next two years. In the meantime, 'I'm happy to offer personalised tuition,' he says.

Should be kept in check as long as his down-to-earth mother is around. 'Normally they wait till you've died, don't they?' she asked, when he broke the news

Directors are so delighted with what he's achieved so far that they've named the new sixth form block after him. Though grateful, he fears it might create the wrong impression about his ego. Should be kept in check as long as his down-to-earth mother is around. 'Normally they wait till you've died, don't they?' she asked, when he broke the news...

Academic matters: School, until recently the back up choice at 11+, offers an alternative in competitive west London. Instead of super selectivity, takes students from across the ability range. 'Far more professionally satisfying to see a student come in with moderate or even limited academic prowess and see them grow into someone who can do really

well.' Thus prize-giving only happens in the sixth form. 'Immensely divisive if go by results alone,' says head.

He's also less than keen on termly/annual reports and 'speed dating' parent-teacher events – don't flag problems quickly enough, he reckons. Instead reports – shown to pupils first – are sent out every half term and parents are invited (and expected) to comment and get in touch. Works for proactive parents – welcome to drop in at any point and have own café. 'If there's an issue, you go in,' said one. Others – 'have to train them up,' says Mr Hudson – felt you could end up slightly disconnected from what's going on.

Average class size 22, far smaller in sixth form (maximum class size of 12) with pupil to staff ratio of around nine to one. Good choice of subjects at GCSE – options include computing, PE, food tech and four languages (including Latin). Start GCSE curriculum in year 9 – time to change option subjects if have made wrong choice.

More generous still with A levels – currently 25 including computer science and music technology, Latin, statistics, product design and business studies. Most take three subjects (plus EPQ) and occasionally four (one pupil also racing through art in a year). Most popular subjects maths, sciences, politics, economics.

Unwilling to release results of first set of A levels in 2018 'due to the stats not working in our favour because of so few candidates, even though the results were very good'. GCSE results in 2018 45 per cent 9-7 grades. Inspectors approve so far – no recommendations for improvement in ISI compliance report (early 2018).

Admissions policy stresses (as do we) that parents must support the school's educational approach particularly as applied to length of lessons. Most are 90 minutes, while art, design and food tech, CAD, games and science lessons are all three hours long, joined by some GCSE option subjects higher up the school. No question of going out on an educational limb, says Mr Hudson. Tried and tested elsewhere, including at Thomas Telford. Adds up to a day's extra teaching time each week (and means less homework).

Benefits are manifest, says school, from easier trip planning (no complex negotiations with other subject teachers over missed lessons) to reduced time in corridors. 'Keeps the school calm,' says Mr Hudson. 'In my experience, 90 per cent of all pastoral issues take place when children are moving around.' Classroom time is also more productive – normal 40-minute lesson can be substantially truncated by late arrivals and packing up time. Head not keen on shattering siren of school bells so there isn't one. No clocks in classrooms, either.

The teachers we talked to were enthusiasts. 'Love them,' said art teacher. 'Can get things done.'

With no staff room, teachers are easily found either in classrooms or the café and willingly, say pupils, give up time at breaks or after school

Food tech teacher, pointing to fab-looking deconstructed Pavlova, agreed – even enough time to make the tiny meringues on top.

Undoubtedly requires sustained razor-sharp teaching and planning to ensure that interest levels (staff as well as pupils) don't flag. Some parents query if this happens all the time. Others are full of praise. Supplementary tutoring takes place as elsewhere. If gives a short-term boost or catch up, Mr Hudson accepts the need – and invites tutors to work with the school – but shouldn't be a permanent prop.

Some pupils we talked to felt that longer lesson time took a while to get used to. 'When you first start, feels a bit weird,' said one pupil, but worth persevering as boosts concentration and can build better independent learning skills – particularly useful in the sixth form.

Pupils rate help from teachers – 'focused on the individual,' said one. With no staff room, teachers are easily found either in classrooms or the café and willingly – say pupils – give up time at breaks or after school, plus holiday revision days (compulsory) in all subjects, with after-school homework club staffed by different teacher each night. No sanctions for unfinished homework. Instead, teacher and pupil will sit down and work it through. 'They're here if you struggle,' said a pupil.

Approach felt to be particularly helpful for pupils with specific learning difficulties (generally mild to moderate) as ensures time and space for extensive differentiation. 'Would definitely think of sending dyslexic son here,' said prospective parents. Four-strong SEN team, some smaller group lessons but focus is on effective staff training and integrated support in lessons.

'Great thing about the SEN is that it's embedded in everything they teach,' said parent. School's excellent reputation for SEN puts off some prospective parents (watch the shutters come down during open days). It shouldn't, says school, which stresses relatively small numbers involved. While 130 or so have an ed psych report, only 55 currently receive extra support in their lessons. Around 10 per cent of pupils have previously been educated overseas but vast majority of these bilingual – just one currently supported as EAL pupil.

All requires and largely gets strong and generally young teaching team, most reckoned by parents to be in for the long haul. Staff turnover 'modest', says school. In total, nine staff departures since launch, with six out of the seven founding team still there. In rare cases where teachers don't fit in will move on fairly quickly, think parents.

School's proud boast is that never use supply teachers – pay own staff for cover instead, better for pupils. Curricula are all written by school's teachers, nothing shop bought. Not all homework is online but aim is to get more of it that way, making lost assignments a thing of the low tech past and ensuring that anyone who's missed school finds it easy to catch up.

Games, options, the arts: 'We don't have the rolling acres,' says Mr Hudson – a distinct understatement with just a couple of courts on site (though nicely screened with vegetation) used for informal footie sessions at break.

Not the place for athletics, think parents but highly aspirational, with just about every other sporting activity catered for and no more than a 10-minute walk or bus ride away. Swimming and indoor sport is even closer, held at local leisure centre just the other side of the road. Rowing – growing fast – at picturesque Strand-on-the-Green riverside. Cricket, rugby and football all on local pitches with good complement of girls' teams. Some individual successes (year 9 Surrey netball development squad) and team wins (recent national table tennis champions in ISA competition).

Activities list also impressive – 90 or so in total, changed termly. D of E, with speedy sign up, now takes the most enthusiastic through to gold ('fastest accredited school,' reckons head).

Reports – shown to pupils first – are sent out every half term and parents are invited (and expected) to comment and get in touch. Works for proactive parents – welcome to drop in at any point and have own café. 'If there's an issue, you go in'

Lots of outside speakers, some parents (politicians, engineers, actors) and trips, some curriculum-linked, many local (Kew Gardens, Wetlands in Barnes) others residential, ranging from survival skills in Cornwall to art appreciation in Rome (could work vice versa, too). Older pupils may travel much further afield – one sixth former off to Great Barrier Reef – extended project topic. Good works happen locally (supports autism unit in Chiswick primary) and further afield (building eco-bungalow in resource-poor village in Laos).

Art is exciting as well as impressive – highlights on view included stunning A level project, inspired by 1970s slogans and street protests with raw, powerful words and images reproduced on clothes pegged on a washing line. Year 9's workbooks instead featured technically adept delicate plant images. Currently in single (well-lit) room, a second home to the most dedicated, with handy balcony for spray painting. Additional room for A level work on department head's wish list.

Lively drama with plenty of productions (High Society the latest in list that includes Joseph, Little Shop of Horrors and Pygmalion) though sixth form currently feel they're less involved that years 7-11 (down to small numbers, not neglect). Now offered as A level and can study for LAMDA exams and pupils regularly (and successfully) enter local competitions and festivals.

Music coming along nicely – lots of Steinways round the place and plenty of ensembles, selective and otherwise and including parent and staff choir and joint concerts with Gardener prep schools. The very enthusiastic may be home late – head doesn't care for disrupting curriculum time so all individual music lessons (around 100, beginners to diploma standard, learn in school, 50 outside) happen between 4pm and 6pm three days a week

Background and atmosphere: School's owners – the Gardener Schools Group – run two successful preps in the area, Ravenscourt Park and Kew Green, both relatively recent additions to the local educational scene. Opened in 2013, this is first (and so far only) senior school in the group. Maria Gardener cited by parents as reason for looking at KHS in the first place. 'She's a special needs teacher herself and gets it when so many other heads and owners don't,' said one. Some events (eg quiz night, occasional concert) bring prep and senior school parents together – creates nice atmosphere.

Art is exciting as well as impressive – highlights on view included stunning A level project, inspired by 1970s slogans and street protests with raw, powerful words and images

Setting does take a bit of getting used to. From the road, it's a quintessential red-brick office block, surrounded by heavy traffic and redevelopment (views from one window in sixth form block are big on bare earth and builders' rubble). Inside, however, head has had a free hand (and what appears to be considerable budget) to design it as he sees fit – and results are excellent.

Space is effectively, imaginatively and even beautifully planned, as well as being conspicuously neat and tidy. It's super quiet, too (making crash of a couple of doors in need of soft close fittings particularly noticeable).

Areas, subjects and staircases zing through the entire colour spectrum (pupils must travel to end of the rainbow and back several times a day). Even the displays coordinate with the paintwork, striking aboriginal inspired designs in terracotta and burned yellows a perfect match with the paintwork while the dinky but well-equipped labs are primary coloured, ditto canteen which features one of the few clocks (Swiss railway).

Lighting is just as eye-catching. Most stunning is newer, second block housing sixth form independent learning centre on the ground floor, notable for massive lampshades in contrast with smaller clusters twinkling away in corners, all helping to concentrate light where it's needed. 'Like Soho House,' say parents. Other practicalities also well catered for – densely packed row of power sockets at counter top height makes laptop charging a doddle. Younger years, who use upper floors for maths and languages, can only admire from a distance.

Uniform, in contrast, surprisingly preppy – blue blazers, jumpers and shirts plus brown skirts or trousers – some girls pushing to wear either. Parents seemed generally happy. 'I like it, the kids don't,' said one. Freshman-style hoodie popular with all. Parents have no problem with absence of official kitbag but one wish list would include same colour shoes for all (currently black or navy for girls, brown deck shoes for boys), particularly at concerts when 'you really notice it.'

Other sensible touches include absence of lead weight backpacks. Only sixth formers have lockers. For other years, daily textbooks (normally no more than four) come in and go home in strong plastic folder (previous iteration, in cardboard, proved too flimsy for the job). Saves back pain, time and trouble. 'They don't get lost because they go in and out all day,' said parent.

Pastoral care, well-being and discipline: Vertical tutor groups mean siblings can be together (if want to). Same personal tutor ensures continuity and in-depth knowledge of pupils. Fine as long as teachers don't leave and pupils like them, and generally felt to work well. It's possible for pupil to request change of personal tutor if the chemistry isn't there. Very rare, say pupils, who felt would 'need a very good reason.' Could make request a bit Beadle and Oliver-ish – off-putting for all but the most robust souls.

Worth enlisting support of head boy and head girl, current duo (nominated by staff, final choice through pupil vote) busy working through lengthy wish list.

Notting Hill and Ealing High School

Sixth formers want to be allowed off the premises during 45-minute lunch break (can't be done in the time, says school). School food is a work in progress though vegetarian options have improved, thought one pupil, and sixth formers can now order appetising-looking sandwiches. Not cheap ('most expensive croissants in west London,' thought a parent). School doesn't feel 75p is particularly unreasonable.

Sanctions are unambiguous – instant exit for drugs and alcohol, only possible leeway is student who owns up to having a problem, but no guarantees. Break school's strict phone policy (allowed in school only if switched off) and it will be left in reception for parents to collect (only happens once). Forget school tie and you have to borrow one of senior teacher's cast-offs (one girl unfazed by shiny, multi-pleated number).

Some nice touches – like name tags, worn by all pupils (school reminds them to turn over when on public transport) that mean that year 7s know each other and are known to all. 'Unusual but inclusive,' said parent.

CCTV throughout the building also helps, say pupils, who felt that people are 'generally nice to one another.' Parents agree. Smartphones as ever a big out-of-school issue.

Mr Hudson urges parents to opt for Nokia retro phones – with limited success, even with the nostalgic joy of playing Snake. Cyber-bullying, as elsewhere, remains a problem. School has upweighted resources here – onsite counsellor recently recruited – and parents feel school is getting to grips with a difficult area. Rare that pupils asked to leave for bullying but would happen if behaviour consistently 'detrimental to others – important that parents realise you stand by your principles,' says Mr Hudson.

Pupils and parents: Families thought to be less anxious and more down to earth than at other schools – some very affluent, many dual income. 'Very normal, very relaxed,' thought one. 'Perhaps more comfortable because they're more experimental, so quite chilled.'

Pupils generally make own way to school. Drop offs possible but infra dig beyond initial newbie phase. Mostly families relatively local – Kew, Chiswick, Barnes, Putney, anywhere within reach of Kew Bridge station (overground) or Gunnersbury (District line – a 10 minute walk). Currently need to do bit of dogleg to dodge busy motorway feeder road – a worry to parents – though working with developers to make this safer. Some pupils bike to school (plenty of cycle paths) and helmets must be worn. 'When forgot, teacher was on my case immediately.' The canny (or 'lazy toads,' says Mr H) catch bus a single stop from Kew Bridge, dodging busy roads and saving their tired legs.

Families thought to be less anxious and more down to earth than at other schools – some very affluent, many dual income. 'Very normal, very relaxed,' thought one. 'Perhaps more comfortable because they're more experimental, so quite chilled'

Entrance: Now over 450 registrations for 88 year 7 places (four classes of 22) from almost 90 prep and primary schools, including Avenue House, Heathfield House, John Betts, Kew Green Prep, Orchard House, Prospect House and Ravenscourt Park School. Very occasional places in other year groups (school currently completely full – except for sixth form).

Aim is for balanced cohort of 'inquisitive, intelligent students displaying a confident sense of identity and an original approach to learning, problem-solving and creativity'.

So while entrance exams (maths, literacy, but no reasoning) count, there's 'greater weighting' for reports, achievements and interests, and presentation on subject of choice. 'Currently lots on single use plastic – the Sir David Attenborough factor,' says head. 'And cakes. We like cakes.' Staff may also visit current school. Process ensures that bright and articulate who may struggle to express themselves on paper get a fair hearing.

Exit: Have tended to lose half a dozen or so after GCSEs, many to state sector, but it's being balanced by new intake. First leavers in 2018 off far and wide, with a couple to Loughborough, others to Oxford Brookes, Bath, Nottingham Trent, Liverpool, Chester, Reading, Birkbeck and St Mary's Twickenham.

Money matters: No scholarships, bursaries or even sibling discounts though most SEN support included in the fees. Everyone expected to eat at school. 'School does not provide facilities for packed lunches.' On the bright side, sixth form coffee machine which charges £1 for everything, even, according to pupils, hot water for own teabag, is to be supplemented with Quooker or similar in the near future. 'Was charged for short period but now [a] dispenser is in place,' says school.

Remarks: Inclusive, different and surprisingly beautiful. Essential to understand and commit to approach – especially those extra long lessons. Emphatically not the place for clockwatchers.

Lady Eleanor Holles Junior School

Burlington House, 177 Uxbridge Road, Hampton Hill TW12 1BD

020 8979 2173 | registrar@lehs.org.uk | lehs.org.uk

Independent	Pupils: 196
Ages: 7–11	Fees: £16,731 pa

Linked school: Lady Eleanor Holles School, 486

Head of Juniors: Since 2016, Paula Mortimer BEd (40s), previously head of St Christina's school in St John's Wood. A science specialist with a degree from Oxford, she has taught in preps and all-through schools, latterly as deputy and acting head of Channing Junior School. Also has experience as SEN coordinator. Still loves teaching. 'I have no plans whatsoever to stop spending time working with children in the classroom,' she says. A hands-on head, she is known for fostering honest, open relationships not only with staff, but with pupils and parents. Very committed to pastoral care. 'For me, a role as head is all about ensuring children are secure and happy first and foremost, as that's what makes them successful learners. They're two sides of the same coin.' Particularly keen to see children take risks in the classroom. 'That's how they learn.'

Head of whole school is Mrs Heather Hanbury (see senior school entry).

Entrance: School's own entrance tests in English and maths at 7+, and top performers invited back for an activity session. About 48 places, split across two forms. Only two girls trying for every place, but don't be fooled – the older they get, the faster the ride, so best for those who seem exceptionally bright and eager to learn. That said, they do take some borderline performers. 'Some show high potential, but have not had the fire in their belly if, for example, they've been at a pre-prep that just drills facts into them. We are looking for what girls are capable of, not what they've already achieved – along with a can-do attitude.' Pupils come from a combination of primaries and many from pre-preps like Athelstan House, Denmead and Jack and Jill.

Exit: Some 75-85 move up to the senior department – low for an all-through school, but the school insists that in any one year, usually only three or four girls do not progress due to not being academically able. Thankfully, no exam separating those who get in vs those that don't – instead, girls are assessed on the basis of their classroom work and

school exams and offered a guaranteed place in year 5. The few who don't make the cut get lots of support and extra help to prepare for tests to other schools and they may still sit the LEH entrance exam if they wish. Those who want to try for a scholarship also sit the entrance exams, along with the outside applicants. Those who do get a place, but decide to go elsewhere, opt for Tiffin Girls, St Paul's Girls or Nonsuch, with others going to Kingston Grammar, Sir Williams Perkins, St James' Girls and St Catherine's.

Remarks: A warmer welcome to a school you will not find, thanks to the lovely receptionists – and this really sets the tone for this surprisingly informal school where girls thrive academically, and then some. Four or five thick, bound photo albums take up the entire coffee table in the reception area, packed with pictures of the girls at carol services, on school trips, doing drama productions etc – also giving a flavour of school life here, where enrichment and extracurricular is seen as important as the demanding class-room based learning. Not in a 'You will do five after-school clubs a week!' kind of way, but in a 'let's provide the girls with both self-drive and exciting opportunities that they'll choose to take up' kind of way. 'My daughter recently told me she's taken up chess – I knew nothing about it. Absolutely brilliant!' said one parent. When we visited, two whole classes were absent for enrichment purposes – one practising for a big drama production in the senior school and one on a visit to the BFI, all dressed in Roald Dahl-themed costumes, complete with face-paint.

The school building started life as an attractive old house, although build-ons over the years mean that outside it is now a rather dull looking three-storey block with a one-storey extension in unattractive brick and PVC windows. However, unlike preps elsewhere, it has fabulous outside space – real space. A super garden area with excellent climbing frames and other apparatus, courts and pitches, much of it, of course, shared with the senior school. Particularly valued by girls are the 'hedge homes' – little dens in the hedges abutting the brook separating the school from the grounds. The girls use pebbles for money and run these little domestic havens just as they would their brick and drainpipe equivalents.

Inside, everywhere is carpeted, which makes for quiet corridors and a civilised feel. Classrooms are airy and light, where teachers pack in the learning, although by no means all with chalk and talk – we saw plenty of interactive examples. A sense of purpose and attentiveness pervades, but it feels as if the girls are having real fun too – and their work is displayed in every corridor in witty, appealing and imaginative ways. Great cross-curricular approach to much of the teaching – something that the girls talk excitedly about, giving us example upon example. If they learn about the ancient Greeks, they make Greek vases. If they learn about circuits, they design and make a working toy car. Arts and crafts and DT throughout are unusual and clever – girls showed us examples of 3D mazes they'd made, along with personally designed carry-bags, clever photography, moving toys and home-made slippers. Even the plastic plates they use at lunch (where food has mixed views from pupils, but mainly good) are each designed by a girl in the school. Particularly great excitement about the animated films the girls make, using their own clay and cut-out models, in year 5.

> *To get in at all, she'll have probably have been top dog in her pre-prep or primary school – here, she'll enter a melting pot, where everyone is academically superior*

The wow-factor science lab is designed for interactive learning, with five hexagonal shaped high tables with Bunsen burners and plug sockets in the middle with six stools round each, plus state-of-the-art flatscreen Apple TV on the wall. 'We recently hatched chicks in an incubator,' girls told us. The library, though inviting and well-stocked, is small and barely adequate for this number of girls – which staff acknowledge, although they point out that they haven't given up trying to work out a solution and they claim that the lack of brilliant library is somewhat compensated for by revolutionising the use of iPads in learning. Good traditional hall for productions, assemblies and younger girls' gym, and they use the fabulous senior school theatre. Decent ICT suite.

Weekly music lessons in a good-sized dedicated room, whilst around three-quarters have private music lessons in the senior school, and a further 20 per cent learn a musical instrument outside school. Junior choir (for years 5 and 6 – you have to audition), chorus (open to anyone), orchestra and string group (which has performed in Hampton Court). 'My daughter adores her trombone classes – they really enthuse her,' said one parent.

> *A sense of purpose and attentiveness pervades, but it feels as if the girls are having real fun too*

Drama is also big here and the girls love it, as we saw for ourselves during a practice session in the senior school theatre. Big singing and acting voices for girls so small – a treat to watch. The school takes part in everything from poetry recitals to debating competitions to Shakespeare festivals. Superb sports (great preparation for the legendary sporting culture of the senior school) and girls are lucky to use many of the older girls' facilities. In winter, the focus is on swimming, netball and gymnastics and in summer, on swimming, rounders, athletics and some tennis.

Back in the classroom, there's very little setting, although girls are sometimes taught in smaller, mixed-ability groups if it's felt it will aid their learning. French and extracurricular Mandarin are offered as languages, although the languages model is being reviewed. Specialist teaching in science, music, PE and computing from year 3, with everything else taught by the form teacher – then specialist teaching for everything from year 5.

Academically, this school holds a reputation of being a hothouse, which clearly infuriates staff and parents alike. 'Come and see the school for yourself,' urges the head, who believes the label 'hothouse' becomes lazy shorthand for selective schools that do well. 'They are just little girls who have a growth mindset.' The 'growth mindset' is a phrase you hear a lot here – with the school avoiding words like 'bright' and 'intelligent' like the plague. 'Those are fixed labels that are high risk because once you are told you're bright, you might not take risks in the classroom for fear of failing – and taking risks is how you learn.' Homework seems fair – 20 minutes a night up to year 5, then 40 minutes. 'The school understands that if you're a working parent, you might not have time to do hours of homework – I applaud that,' said one parent.

Teachers (who, disappointingly, when we visited, were all female) have lots of autonomy, teaching how they want to, not how they're prescribed to. They are, however, encouraged to constantly try new techniques (of their choosing) to keep things fresh. We found imaginative and lively examples throughout.

Mild SEN – although note it's not called that here, with them favouring LDD (learning difficulties and disabilities). Help just as likely to be for a spelling group that need short-term strategies as for anyone with dyslexia or dyscalculia, which means no stigma. Short-term bursts of intervention is the name of the game here, with a major focus on arming the girls with tools and techniques to keep up with the fast academic pace.

Pastoral care strong, with deputy head at the helm. They take a proactive approach, with lots of staff meetings to discuss, 'Did you think what X did was out of character?' 'Did you think X has been a bit distracted lately?' etc. and they discuss it with girls if appropriate – and indeed parents, who they aren't afraid of calling to ask if everything is all right. Likewise, parents feel welcome to call the school. Girls praise the strong system of buddies, including coach buddy, house buddies and peer mentors, who help people out in the playground if they're sad. 'They even designed their own hats,' the girls told us, explaining that the buddy brings the woeful girl back over the little bridge into the junior school area to a special bench, where they can talk. 'It gives the peer mentor great skills of mediation,' one parent pointed out. Lots of leadership roles (science leaders, head girl, house captains etc) and there's a term of mindfulness teaching for year 5s. Plenty of opportunities for personal attention time – not just in the natural flow of the day, but via specific appointments, in which pupils are encouraged to share news about something amazing they did at the weekend as much as to discuss something that's worrying them.

> **'Come and see the school for yourself,' urges the head, who believes the label 'hothouse' becomes lazy shorthand for selective schools that do well**

Bullying minimal, due to zero tolerance attitude, anti-bullying assemblies, golden school rules, talks about making the right choices and – perhaps most innovatively – a contract that each girl signs every year. If they break the contract, the head shows them the document and their signature and they get a firm questioning session – girls consider this deeply shameful. 'Girls put a huge emphasis on best friends, so we do a lot of work around that, explaining that boys don't do this and they don't have to feel disloyal having more than one really good friend.'

Misbehaviour negligible, with little need for discipline – forgetting homework and calling someone a bad name is the worst of it, for which you get a 'sanction,' three of which in a half term mean you have to stay in during a breaktime. But it's very infrequent. 'You lose perspective of behavioural issues in a lovely school like this,' said previous head, recounting a story of someone who recently took the pebbles (remember the currency in the hedges) back to their desk in a plastic bag so they didn't have to share it. 'The result was huge gasp, shock and outrage – because that's as bad as it gets here.' Parents and pupils concur.

> **We saw for ourselves the reassuring skips down the corridors and beaming smiles in the classrooms**

Trips to interesting places – including the National Archives at Kew to look at Victorian prison records (after which they 'used metaphors to write poems as if we'd been in prison') and the Globe theatre, plus residentials to Surrey (year 5) and France (year 6).

Parents tend to be much like the pupils here – academically brilliant, with a go-getting attitude. Not all super-rich, with many parents holding down a couple of jobs to pay the fees, something that the school values as enriching the school community. Lively PA, called The Friends, is open to both senior and junior school parents. Most families live within a half-hour radius and arrive either on foot, by car or via the super-efficient coach system that is shared with both the senior school and neighbouring Hampton School for boys. Juniors get a coach buddy to make the whole thing less daunting.

Word of advice if your daughter gets in: try to prepare her psychologically for the transition period. To get in at all, she'll have probably have been top dog in her pre-prep or primary school – here, she'll enter a melting pot, where everyone is academically superior. But whilst this can be difficult, girls find it humbling too – probably explaining why we found girls to be so pleasingly modest. No know-it-alls in sight. Overall, we found the girls to be conscientious and bubbly (the ones who showed us round didn't stop talking, such was their enthusiasm for seemingly every detail of the school) and very happy learners. 'My child loves going to school,' is a phrase we heard time and time again – and we saw for ourselves the reassuring skips down the corridors and beaming smiles in the classrooms. 'Anything you'd change about the school?' is one of our common questions to parents, to which we twice got the answer, 'Only that I didn't get to go there myself.'

Lady Eleanor Holles School

Hanworth Road, Hampton TW12 3HF

020 8979 1601 | registrar@lehs.org.uk | lehs.org.uk

| Independent | Pupils: 700; sixth form: 200 |
| Ages: 11–18 | Fees: £20,196 pa |

Linked school: Lady Eleanor Holles Junior School, 483

Headmistress: Since 2014, Heather Hanbury, previously head of Wimbledon High. MA Edinburgh, MSc Cambridge in geography then land economy. Prior to teaching, she spent nine years working in various management consultancy roles in the City, then as a corporate fundraiser – 'real world' experience that both pupils and parents value. Moved into teaching because she was so frequently told she 'should' – 'but I initially resisted it because I don't like to do the expected,' she laughs. Eventually had a change of heart and took a PGCE with the express ambition of becoming a head. 'I always wanted to run things. I like making organisations efficient, effective and happy' – something that everyone agrees she's achieved, with bells on.

Began her teaching career at Blackheath High School in 1996, quickly rising through the ranks to head of sixth form, before moving on to Haberdashers' Aske's School for Girls, thence deputy head of Latymer Upper School. Teaches all year 7s for half a term each ('I get to know them, but more importantly, they get to know me – far better than helicoptering my way into sixth form teaching,' she insists). And although she does herself down when it comes to her teaching abilities ('I do the least damage,' she laughs), girls say she's actually very good. The only school where we've heard pupils describe their headteacher as 'very sweet,' they gush over her assemblies ('She recently did a fantastic one on friendship and talked all about the movie Mean Girls,' enthused one) and say she is 'involved,' 'interested' and 'approachable' – attending every event imaginable, even wearing sports kits to matches.

In school, she adorns glamorous suits (no staff member we met would have looked out of place at a wedding), hums with energy, has just the right amount of modesty (as is the LEH way), is quick to smile and laugh and is intent on injecting some fun into school life. Her office is among the nicest, largest and swankiest we've seen – in fact, if you replaced her desk with a bed, it could pass as a luxury boutique hotel room.

Lives with her husband in Hammersmith. Interests include bridge ('I'm not very good,' – there's that modesty again), cooking and theatre.

Academic matters: Few teach academia better and it's done via thrilling, not drilling. 'What's the point in boring them into submission?' says head – although she admits it's not always easy, particularly around GCSE learning, 'which can be very routine especially for bright, lively minds.' 'I really admire the school's ability to go sideways in any subject, bringing in current affairs or going cross-curricular, for instance,' said one parent. Results outstanding – 92 per cent A*-A/9-7 at GCSE in 2018. It helps that staff clearly delight in what they do and all teach their own degree subject. Pupils told us teachers are always available, with the staff room practically empty at lunchtimes, as teachers run clinics or answer pupil queries from their departments. Sixth formers increasingly help the younger ones ('It's easy for them to remember the bits people find tricky in years 8 and 9,' explains the head. 'And it's good for them too – there's nothing like teaching to help you learn yourself.') Traditional subjects taken at GCSE, with computer science being offered since 2017.

'I always wanted to run things. I like making organisations efficient, effective and happy'

Committed to A levels, rather than the IB or Pre-U, with the academic offering upped via EPQ, plus an enrichment programme across every subject. 2018 saw 75 per cent A*-A grades (95 per cent A*/B). Good range of subjects, including classical civilization, psychology and economics, although maths and sciences remain the most popular. Sixth form feels quite a separate entity here – these older girls are revered and there are lots of sixth form only areas, including their smaller classrooms which cater for more tutorial style learning, in which there are no more than 12 girls in any one class.

Setting in maths during year 7, with groups reviewed annually. Languages include Latin, German and French from year 7, with the option of Spanish and ancient Greek added at GCSE (although French remains the most popular language at GCSE). The school has one of the biggest German A level cohorts in the country, and Spanish is growing. ICT embedded into learning, with increasing use of iPads in lessons. A culture of enquiry and exploration fostered throughout.

They also collect lots of silverware. 'It's great because if you don't like running around after a ball, you can sit in a boat instead – although many do both,' says the head

Meticulous record keeping for monitoring and targeting, although they don't make a big show of it to pupils or parents. We found girls have quite a competitive attitude to learning, although they are also quick to support and praise others' achievements, with lots of patting on backs and high fives. Some criticism from pupils around the timetable, which includes nine 35-minute lessons. 'By the time you've settled into a lesson, that only leaves half-an-hour – and you've got four of those before break,' said one.

Few with more than mild learning difficulties here, for whom SEN support is embedded into classes, with some one-to-ones where required – and it must work as they get the same results as everyone else. Seriously good school to consider if you have mobility problems or are wheelchair-bound – flattish site, lifts and wide corridors, plus can-do approach – although we were surprised no girls in this situation when we visited.

Games, options, the arts: Legendary for sports and the facilities in this 23 acre plot are outstanding for a girls' day school, including three spectacular and very green lacrosse pitches (which many of the classrooms overlook – lovely, especially in summer); six outdoor courts; a massive modern sports hall; and indoor swimming pool (recently refurbished). At the front of the school are grass tennis courts and croquet lawn ('embarrassing, really, but rather fun!' laughs the head). Some parents choose the school on the strength of the sports alone. Lacrosse, not surprisingly, is the main winter game and played to win – which they do. Rowing also a speciality – a welcome rarity in a girls' school, for which

boathouse facilities are shared with neighbouring Hampton School, and they also collect lots of silverware. 'It's great because if you don't like running around after a ball, you can sit in a boat instead – although many do both,' says the head.

Other sports include gymnastics, netball, swimming, basketball, fencing, rounders, athletics, tennis and badminton. Don't like sport? Head told us there's plenty of girls in this situation and that's fine too, although one girl we spoke to felt sport can be a bit elitist. 'You start out with A-E teams in year 7, but now we've got an A team and half a B team – if you're not in those, you don't get anywhere near as much attention,' one of the older girls complained, although others disagreed with her, which led to an interesting debate. Sports tours to eg Barbados and America.

Artistic talent was being exhibited in the fabulous new art rooms and corridors in all its splendour when we visited – much of it so good that you'd hang them in your own home. Beautiful ceramics displayed in a glass cabinet. Lively textiles and photography.

Music exceptional – the Holles Singers reach the finals of the BBC Youth Choir annually. We lost count of how many other choirs there were – some for which girls audition, others open to all. Orchestras and ensembles galore, with bands ranging from rock and pop to jazz. 'Unbelievably, we even have a symphony orchestra!' smiles the head, wide-eyed. Sixty per cent of girls learn an instrument with a peripatetic teacher. Brass particularly popular, with many budding saxophonists. Plenty of space for all this in the shiny purpose-built arts block (where the arts studios are also based).

Purpose-built theatre (again, in the same block) has the wow factor even when empty, but what a treat to hear a girl practising a solo song for the annual musical when we visited – she was amazing. Drama here is outstanding, with each year group performing something annually. The two big set pieces are joint musicals with Hampton School (years 11 up) and the summer musical (for years 7 and 8). 'They are something else – so professional,' said one girl.

Extracurricular life here is thriving. Particularly lively debating society, model UN and lots of charity and community work, including going into local schools. D of E and CCF take-up good. Masses of day trips to museums, theatres etc, plus residential trips from year 7 upwards – language exchanges, ski trips and battlefields, among them. Other recent examples include Greece and Italy (classics), Berlin (history) and Iceland (geography).

Background and atmosphere: The school was established in 1710 under the will of Lady Eleanor Holles, daughter of John Holles, 2nd Earl of Clare. This makes it one of the oldest girls' schools in the country. It began life in the Cripplegate Ward of the City of London, then moved to other premises in the City till 1878, thence to Mare Street in Hackney (that building now houses the London College of Fashion). The current school, purpose-built and designed in the shape of an E, opened in 1937. Such a long history is scarcely uncommon in many of our great public schools but rare in girls' schools. A palpable pride underpins the place. The staffroom has seen many distinguished names. They include Pauline Cox, former head of Tiffin Girls', Margaret Hustler, former head of Harrogate Ladies' College, Cynthia Hall, former head of Wycombe Abbey, and Frances King, former head of Roedean, who all taught here.

Very long, horizontal, featureless and functional, the two-storey main building doesn't delight the eye but then again, it doesn't offend it either. Inside, the corridors are wide, the rooms are light and everywhere is well-kept. Some areas are somewhat hospital-like, with lengthy corridors and polished wood floors. The pupils insist, though, that 'the thing that brings it alive is the girls.' Latest add-on – the arts, music and drama block – was finished in 2013 and provides the stand-out facilities mentioned earlier, as well as a jazzy new refectory. Big main library is well-stocked. Fabulous DT room, with much pride around the 3D printer ('I can't believe one exists, let alone being in our school!' said one girl). Lots of innovation in the cookery room – the girls were making their own versions of Bakewell tart when we visited. Excellent sixth form centre features small teaching rooms – ideal for a history seminar or session on poetic form. The sixth form library is notable – light and overlooking the pitches – as well as being well-stocked (including more mature books and careers and university materials), with neat tables for study and rows of PCs. Nice sixth-form café and common room too.

Girls have quite a competitive attitude to learning, although they are also quick to support and praise others' achievements, with lots of patting on backs and high fives

Focused and purposeful atmosphere. Girls are well turned out in grey uniforms and the sixth formers look fresh and neat in casual dress. A sense of order pervades throughout. It's cool to be clever and cool to be good at sport. And because they expect a lot from the girls from an early stage, there's a big push on them taking responsibility for themselves from the off. 'If you don't turn up for a practice, you don't stay on the team.' Strong

It's more carrot than stick here, with rewards of sweets if you don't get any pink slips and a pizza lunch if your class does particularly well

links with Hampton School – just across the playing fields – not just in drama, music, rowing and coach trips as we've mentioned, but also in careers and university preparation and increasingly for the younger years too eg extracurricular clubs. 'It almost feels co-ed without having the distraction of boys in the actual classroom – what could be better?' delighted one parent.

Pastoral care, well-being and discipline: House system is a big deal here – there are even inter-house jigsaw competitions. 'It's about so much more than an annual sports day,' says the head, and girls love the leadership responsibilities and opportunity to make new friends that come with it. Much praise for the pastoral care system – a clear structure and everyone knows who to go to. Teachers described as 'supportive mentors'. One parent told us her daughter needed to take significant time off and that the ongoing support from afar was 'incredible.' Good system of buddying, and a feeling that no transgressors would get away with it for long. No noteworthy sins of the drink/drugs/ fags kind and minor bullying problems are dealt with swiftly. A culture of openness means that it's all right to tell someone if you're not happy. We were particularly impressed with the cyber mentor system, which involves sixth formers being trained to go into classes without teachers to discuss any online problems. 'The training means they know when a line is crossed and they report it to us to intervene,' says the head. In fact, e-safety overall is taken very seriously here, with a dedicated e-safety officer. School counsellor available three days a week. School wants to increase its offering around specific mental health issues. 'I think we're at the point we were with bullying 10 years ago – in that it's time to bring it out of the closet and admit it's ok to have issues and deal with them. It's about de-stigmatising,' says the head.

Despite the school's reputation of being highly pressurised and hothousing the pupils, it's the girls who seem to be the ones putting pressure on themselves, rather than it being imposed from above. 'It's just the culture of the school,' one girl told us. All are therefore grateful for the talks on how to cope, especially at exam time, and pupils told us they know where to go if they feel it gets too much. 'And we support each other too,' they say. One parent told us, 'I get especially fed up of hearing about the hothouse reputation as it's my experience that the school actually works very hard to take pressure off the girls, persuading them to rest in the holidays and to balance their work with fun stuff in term-time too.'

Low-level misbehaviour, such as forgetting homework, leads to a 'pink slip.' Three of those in a half-term and you get a strongly worded letter. But it's more carrot than stick here, with rewards of sweets if you don't get any pink slips and a class pizza lunch if your class does particularly well in something eg charity work.

Girls praise the mixing of year groups, which they say leads to friendships they might not otherwise have had – 'due to houses, extracurricular clubs and the buddy system' – but it didn't stop some girls complaining to us that there are cliques that can be hard to penetrate. Food much better than it used to be, girls told us. 'There's loads of choice too – you can grab a sandwich or have a full-on hot meal.'

Strong links with Hampton School. 'It almost feels co-ed without having the distraction of boys in the actual classroom – what could be better?' delighted one parent

Who wouldn't this school suit? Girls who aren't prepared to work hard, try new things (no matter if you're no good at it – it's the trying it in the first place that matters here) or who are set in a certain mindset, said the girls we met. 'You find yourself becoming someone completely different than when you started – it's really quite incredible,' said one girl.

Pupils and parents: Parents tend to be much like the pupils here – academically brilliant, with a go-getting attitude. Not all super-rich, with many parents holding down a couple of jobs to pay the fees, something that the school values as enriching the school community. 'There aren't as many very wealthy families as I thought there'd be when I joined,' says head. Lively PA, called The Friends, is open to both senior and junior school parents. Mainly white British, although younger years are more ethnically mixed, with the second biggest ethnic group being Asian. From a wide area – Ealing, Windsor, Woking, Wimbledon and Chiswick, and all points in between. Public transport links aren't great, but an impressive coach map shows the multitude of routes they cater for (joint with Hampton boys' school) at the beginning and end of the school day (some later to cater for girls who do clubs) and which 50 per cent of the

girls utilise. The rest walk, cycle or dropped off. Lots of parents have boys at Hampton.

Entrance: Around a third of entrants come up from junior department. Of the remainder, about two-thirds come from the private and a third from the state sector – around 40 different schools in total. Private ones include Newland House, Twickenham Prep, The Study, Bute House, Holy Cross Prep, Kew College. Four to five applicants for each place. Tests in maths, English, non-verbal and verbal reasoning and a problem solving paper. Expect the unexpected in the interview. 'We can tell a mile off if we are hearing not the girl themselves, but their parent or tutor. I'm absolutely allergic to that,' says the head, wincing. 'I don't even care if they do something silly in the interview – at least it shows they're being themselves.'

School sets its own exams for sixth form applicants, who need a 7 in subjects they want to study – and, in fact, 9-7s in pretty much everything. 'The odd 6 here and there is ok, but we want girls who can leap in with the rest and move fast,' says head. Reports from current schools also count, along with an interview.

Exit: The school loses around 10 per cent of girls at sixth form – most to other high-level, but (crucially) co-ed sixth forms. A few leave for financial reasons. Around 80 per cent to Russell Group universities. Destinations include Oxbridge (11 in 2018), Durham, Bristol, London, Exeter, Edinburgh, St Andrews and a few to Europe and USA (four in 2018). Mainly traditional degree subjects, with lots studying medicine (16 in 2018), English, history, sciences. Notable old girls include Lynn Barber, Charlotte Attenborough, Carola Hicks, Annie Nightingale, Saskia Reeves, Jay Hunt and Gail (University Challenge) Trimble.

Money matters: Drive under way to increase the number and value of bursaries. Means-tested and reviewed annually. Academic scholarships worth up to 10 per cent of fees at 11+ and sixth form level. Music scholarships up to 10 per cent. At A level, academic, music, art, drama and sport scholarships available – each worth up to 10 per cent of fees. Music exhibitions worth up to 7.5 per cent – and that's at 11+ and A level.

Remarks: This is a school that bangs the drum very loudly about empowerment, constantly reminding girls they can do anything if they put their minds to it – and they excel in giving them the tools to achieve that. Not for the faint-hearted, the girls work hard – and we mean hard – but they play hard too. If your daughter has the potential to be a determined, committed learner with a can-do attitude, this could be her ticket to a highly successful future.

The Mall School

185 Hampton Road, Twickenham TW2 5NQ

020 8977 2523 | admissions@themallschool.org.uk | themallschool.org.uk

Independent   **Pupils:** 280

Ages: 4–13 (4–11 from 2020)   **Fees:** £12,240 – £13,767 pa

Headmaster: Since 2011, David Price BSc MA PGCE (50s), married with two children in their late teens. Brought up and educated in the Black Country, his first introduction to the western edge of London was Kingston University for his MA. After a spell as head of English at Latymer Prep he went down under to teach at Melbourne Grammar School. He says he felt a bit homesick there, so he returned to his 'pom' roots, moving on to be head of juniors and director of studies at The Mall, before becoming top dog.

Calm and understated, no fireworks, 'a mediator and negotiator', he inspires confidence that he knows exactly what the school is about and his role in its performance. Equally, the parents trust him to run a tight but friendly ship which will land their sons safely in their chosen academic port. Known to be behind his desk if needed, he also gets about a lot, often at the school gates talking to parents, invoking the comment that he uses these opportunities as 'a sounding board for new ideas'.

Entrance: The largest feeder for the first come, first served pre-prep is Jack and Jill Nursery, usefully sited on the green next door, but children also arrive from a variety of other nurseries or straight from the home version. Two forms move from pre-prep up to the main school but will now increase to three from year 3 onwards creating additional places at the existing entry point of 7+ and an occasional place at 8+. At these stages, potential pupils come to an assessment in maths and English during a day in the school where both sides have the chance to eye each other up.

Boys from a wide variety of backgrounds, often with two working parents, come here from all over west London, although one parent counted its proximity to their house as a huge plus. Despite tending to move on to similar schools, they can end up in very different lives, for instance Zac Goldsmith with his mayoral ambitions or the actor, Alex Pettyfer, who reverted to his schooldays by playing Tom Brown in a TV adaptation.

Exit: Until 2020, boys will be leaving at 11+ and 13+ so, during this period, a small percentage will still move on to leading boarding schools such as Eton or Harrow but the vast majority (increasingly more at 11+) head to local independent day schools, top of the list being Hampton followed by King's College Wimbledon, Reed's, St George's Weybridge and Radnor House. Several boys to St Paul's each year and the occasional one to Westminster.

Remarks: The pre-prep, five minutes down the road from the prep school, has an exceptional, brand-new playground complete with a huge pirate ship and interactive games on the walls, imagination and energy equally well catered for. We badly wanted to play and boys have been known to cry on having to leave. It's small, and not so small, boy heaven. Incredibly tidy; even the smart red scooters have their own designated parking spaces inside neat white lines and a nice man was sweeping up the leaves that had dared to deface it.

Equally, parents trust him to run a tight but friendly ship that will land their sons safely in their chosen academic port

Inside, the newly refurbished classrooms are equally colourful with interactive whiteboards, matching, bright plastic chairs and lots of lesson related photographs and images on the walls. We particularly liked the washing line strung with pages of handwriting on a pirate theme. 'He had a brown hat …. and no legs' was our favourite description of Captain Hook.

Juliet Tovey oversees it with a practised eye, having been involved in education all her career, teaching in a variety of state and private schools as well as working as a local authority maths consultant. Not much chance that she'll get caught on the hop as she runs 20 kms a week.

The two classes in reception and year 1 (maximum 18 per class) are each taught by a teacher and an assistant, the mornings being mainly for maths and English, the former prominently using the domino look-alike Numicon bricks. A reward system in each class allows all boys a daily start on the rainbow, with progress either to sunny uplands or downwards to a very unthreatening cloud. Apparently, they rarely stay in the rainy zone for long and can redeem themselves right up to the final bell.

One mother informed us that she had been told off by her son for arriving early. KiddyCook aims at future masterchefs whilst tennis and chess clubs are full to bursting

Everyone has a hot lunch in the newly decorated basement where once a week there is a 'top table' for the four boys who have managed to avoid spag bol down their fronts and the temptation to talk with their mouths full. This innovation has worked extremely well and JT says it really does encourage good behaviour. Once the boys are fed, the afternoon is taken up with music and PE lessons and learning to swim in the pool at the main school.

One parent told us that JT had been 'fantastic over the transition from pre-prep to the big school' and the boys feel at home straight away because they are used to the feel of it, from coming swimming, on visits in year 1 and to Friday assemblies where they bravely march up to receive their commendations in front of the whole school, a sure sign of a confident small person.

The main school is nearing its 150th anniversary but has been on this slightly squeezed site since 1922, the only major interruption a fire in 1960 that wiped out all the buildings except the stable block. Possibly not a disaster, because they were able to rebuild and now have managed to cram in a 130 seater theatre, music rooms, an art studio, a DT workshop and science labs. Outside space is strictly limited but there are playgrounds, an outdoor classroom with ponds and a veggie patch, which had so impressed one leaver that he announced in the school magazine that he 'would like to become a naturalist'. There is also an indoor swimming pool, excellent for little ones as it only has a fraction of the normal chlorine levels and the temperature is more like a warm bath than an arctic lake.

The high academic standards are definitely a prime reason why parents enrol their children here: 'we wouldn't have put our boys in the school if we didn't think they could keep up with the pace'. Classes are an average of 17 (no more than 20) and will continue at this size after the top two years have been phased out. Form teachers and tutors (from year 4), about a third of whom have taught here for more than 10 years, closely monitor progress. Enthusiastic praise for the teaching – 'the academics are extraordinary' – is handed out all round, but French taught in French by Frenchwomen, 'part of the DNA of the school,' says DP, probably scores highest, swiftly followed by every other subject on the curriculum. A new science teacher has raised standards in her subject to the level that year 5 and 6 gained third place in the National Inter-School Science Quiz championship. IT which, admitted DP, had been 'a little on the back foot', has been sharpened up with speedier Wifi, more computers and an IT whizz permanently on hand to crack any problems.

The concentration in the classrooms is palpable, whether it be year 8s pouring over history textbooks or year 3s filing the edges off acrylic heart keyrings. That 'students step up to the challenge', as one parent stated, is clear when you look at the number of scholarships, including 21 to Hampton and nine to St Paul's over the last six years.

Tackled on the subject of SEND provision, JT talks about the benefit of enrolling boys at reception because they can start evaluation from day one and identify any potential problems before they move up. Once in the main school, there is regular appraisal and a supported English class in years 4 to 6, taught by the SENCo; at the moment about 12 per cent of all pupils need additional support including a tiny number of EAL boys.

The new head of sport has hit the spot with both students and parents as he has brought in 'a certain level of organisation' which both felt was somewhat lacking, in particular when it came to uniforms and matches. Swimming is the big thing here, they are borough champs and amongst the top five junior schools in the country. Field sports, rugby, football and cricket are played in Bushy Park, luckily only a stone's throw away, and although this is not known as a sporty school there is a concerted effort to find an opportunity for every boy to represent the school in some form of team.

Parents talk happily – 'big, big plus' – of the extracurricular activities that take place after school and allow them to do a late pick-up (until 6pm), with one mother informing us that she had been told off by her son for arriving early. Kiddy Cook aims at catching future masterchefs whilst tennis and chess clubs are full to bursting right up the school. Although the judo master is a 'tough guy', he obviously holds no fear for the boys as his judo clubs are hugely popular.

Arty boys are successfully encouraged with three year 8 boys winning scholarships to senior schools recently. Almost three-quarters of the boys play a musical instrument and they hold a Summer Prom and inter-house music competitions as well as training junior and senior choirs. Budding thespians are well catered for in the new theatre and it was smiley faces all round when we asked boys about their acting experiences at school.

Pastorally, the overall consensus is that the 'children are happy, due to the teachers and staff, who are patient and untiring' and have a motherly approach to new boys, who are given an older buddy to run to, which goes down well with parents. The proof of the pudding came from three separate parents remarking that one of the main reasons that they had chosen the school was because they wanted their sons to turn out like the boys who had shown them round. Most parents felt the rewards system employed (points on a credit card) was an incentive to behave as well as succeed but there was a comment that the criteria on awards were not explained clearly enough. We tackled DP over this and, encouragingly, he said

that he would address the subject at the coffee mornings he holds with parents.

The resolution that DP and the governors have made to close the top two years will bring about a sea change and we listened carefully to parental reaction. The dust has settled and the general consensus appears to be that the move will prove to have been an intelligent, forward thinking response to the increase in entries at 11+ by local senior schools. However, the way that it was handled led someone to say that 'it was a shock we could have done without'. In our opinion, this considered decision to alter the shape of the school will not affect either its ethos or its efficiency.

Apart from the all singing and dancing pre-prep playground this is an unflashy, sensible, feet on the ground school. They concentrate on what they do best, giving boys a superior academic grounding in a safe environment and preparing them to succeed in senior schools.

Maple Walk School

62a Crownhill Road, London NW10 4EB

020 8963 3890 | admissions@newmodelschool.co.uk | maplewalkschool.co.uk

Independent	Pupils: 195
Ages: 4–11	Fees: £10,047 pa

Headmistress: Since 2012, Sarah Gillam, BEd from Homerton College, Cambridge. Originally Dorset born, but started her career at Lyndhurst House Prep school in Hampstead. She left education for a while to 'gain some experience in the professional world' but came back to education as she missed teaching and the children. Her 30 year career includes two middle school headships and one head of junior science. Prior to her role as head of Maple Walk, Ms Gillam worked for six years at the now defunct White House Prep school in Wokingham (although during her tenure, it was an outstanding prep school, she says). She was attracted to the post of head at Maple Walk 'because of its wonderful history and story' and because she felt it was a school with great potential.

Warm and likeable (she was very concerned that we should have nice biscuits with our coffee), slightly distracted but perhaps it was nerves, so keen was she to impress. However, the parents we spoke to praised her ambition for turning 'a small villagey school' into a 'proper prep school'. One

parent told us: 'Ms Gillam takes very seriously the reality of living in London and has worked hard to make sure the pupils are well placed and prepared to take exams for secondary school. She has done this with a more rigorous curriculum.'

Ms Gillam herself says that she has been very keen to work on the process of transforming this school – already an amazing galleon – into a tighter ship with more rigorous applications and monitoring of crew. She has worked at strengthening the senior leadership team and now has an excellent range of advisors. Also an ISI team inspector, Ms Gillam says this can be a great resource for the school as she gets so many ideas from other schools as well as being able to confer with specialists 'who are at the top of their game.' She still teaches RE from year 3 upwards for one lesson a week.

Described as a very visible head who is always wandering around the school, is very approachable, open to ideas and someone who 'patently cares about her job.' She has an open door policy and as one parent said, 'is probably quite frustrated that more people don't walk through it more often.' Ms Gillam has three grown up daughters, one of whom is also training to be a teacher: 'If you have this as a vocation, it is something I would always encourage.' Any free time she has, she enjoys cooking, travelling and spending time with her family.

Entrance: Some 200 applicants for 20 places per form. Siblings get preference, then in order of registration – waiting lists for several years ahead. The advice given is 'get them on the list as soon as possible.' For spaces higher up the school, the head meets the parents and the child has a trial day in the relevant class, 'to check that they will fit in socially and academically'.

Exit: To a wide variety of schools, including Aldenham, City of London, Emanuel, Queen's College, John Lyon, North Bridge House, Wetherby Prep and St James Senior Girls in the private sector, and St Marylebone, Hampstead School and Twyford CofE School in the state sector. A fair percentage generally awarded art scholarships at Holland Park School.

Remarks: The New Model School Company (NMS) was set up by Civitas (but is now an independent entity) when research identified a gap in the market for a low-cost chain of not-for-profit independent primary schools. Maple Walk was the first NMS school, starting in a rented room in a sports centre off Ladbroke Grove in 2004 with one teacher, two pupils and school materials stored in a trunk. A year later the fledgling school of a dozen pupils moved to the upper floor of a church hall off Kensal Road. In 2009 the school – by now with classes up to year 4 – moved to its own purpose-built premises in Harlesden, which have impeccable ecological credentials: a sedum roof, solar panels, a ground source heat pump, plus a no-car travel plan.

'There's a nice, cosy, community feel,' said one. 'I liked the fact that it is small, pioneering and affordable,' said another. 'It's a really vibrant, eclectic community'

Although the school has had a reputation for being a no frills, low-fee-paying school and a decent alternative for the independent sector, parents we spoke to felt that it was now time to redress this reputation because, as one parent told us, 'it punches above its weight.' Another parent said: 'They do far more than you would expect from a school of this size and have really upped their game.' The general consensus seems to be that it delivers a great education and is a school which pushes each individual to strive. Indeed it made a recent Telegraph's top Ten Value Prep Schools: 'Excellent value for money', one parent said.

The education is traditional, with reading taught by phonics, French taught from reception, history taught chronologically and Latin taught in year 6. Maths is set from as early as year 1, but there is movement between sets. The school says: 'We recognise that within each class there are pupils of widely differing mathematical aptitudes and we aim to provide suitable learning opportunities for each of them.' The school follows the increasingly popular Singapore maths scheme, although this is 'often supplemented by other resources.' English is not set, but there is differentiation within the classroom for the more able and also for those who need more assistance. One parent told us: 'One of the perks of a school of this size is the small classes and that each class has a teacher and teaching assistant, so you know your child will get a lot of individual attention.'

The teaching was praised by parents and pupils alike: 'They have really nice teachers who know the children well.' 'Teachers are absolutely on it.' The head's after-school secondary transfer club introduces exam techniques to older children, and the year 6 class teacher 'is very experienced at secondary transfers'. 'They do their absolute best to make sure they are well prepared,' said a parent. Certainly parents are happy. 'They seem to be getting a very good grounding,' said one.

The school can cope with mild SEN – 'we don't assess children coming into reception, but we do ask parents to be honest and transparent and we may talk to their nursery if we have any concerns'. One-to-one literacy and numeracy assistance at extra cost; some children get speech and language support outside school.

Sport has very much been an area of focus for the school, with a 'competitive but inclusive policy.' Whilst onsite sport facilities are pretty basic, the school has the use of nearby Roundwood Park for tag rugby, hockey, football and netball etc. For the particularly keen, an early morning (7.30am) cross-country run is offered to both pupils and their parents. We were told of an inspirational PE teacher who encourages even the most uninterested of children to give competitive sports a try, even at the cost of sacrificing a win for the school. One parent said: 'My son is not great at cricket, but this teacher put together a team of all the least talented cricket players in the school to encourage them to have a go at a competitive game against another school. They loved it.'

An emphasis on children becoming confident public performers: the annual Craigmyle poetry competition (named for the charitable trust that paid for the new site and building works) involves everyone from reception upwards reciting a poem by heart, and there are public speaking competitions, music concerts and drama performances. 'The children are very confident,' said a parent. 'They have nice manners, they can talk to adults, they look you in the eye.'

This is a busy, busy school. Lots going on to excite and motivate – indeed their most recent Independent Schools Inspectorate report praises the range of extracurricular activities. This includes photography, art portfolio club, Spanish, chess, dance, puzzle club, drama and football.

The curriculum is further enriched by a wide range of educational visits for all year groups, whether it's mud-larking on the Thames or visiting the Imperial War Museum. There is the year 5 residential trip, which has included a bushcraft trip where students are taught basic survival skills, and the annual year 6 week-long residential camp – which could be staying at a château in France or a PGL adventure course on the Isle of Wight. One pupil told us: 'I really like the variety of things on offer here. There's lots of great stuff to do, but it's also quite academic.'

The school copes well with its limited premises. 'Of course that would be the one thing I'd change about the school if I could, but without physically moving the school, there's not much you can do', said one parent. But the outdoor space still manages to squeeze in playgrounds for infants and for juniors – with a climbing frame, football/netball court with climbing wall (also funded by the PTA, Friends of Maple Walk). There are interesting-looking outdoor 'pods' for music classes with peripatetic teachers. The gardening club grows vegetables in tiered beds and a butterfly/bee-friendly area is in concept. The children learn to swim at a local pool and try out a different sport each half term.

The active PTA has raised funds from auctions, casino nights and summer fairs to name but a few, for part-time specialist dance and sports teachers, and parents have donated computers, including a suite of Netbooks that travel round different classrooms. The school has a broadly Christian ethos, with some religious assemblies and nativity plays, but all faiths are welcome and Jewish and Muslim parents come in to talk about their religions.

Despite the low fees, it is still very much a white, middle class demographic – albeit mostly journalists, artists and musicians rather than bankers and lawyers. A much larger percentage of families now live locally (previously the majority from Queens Park and Willesden Green) and the fact that it is so predominantly white and middle class probably represents how the area has changed. But as the school says, 'it doesn't stop us hoping and trying to attract a more diverse demographic.'

Parents cite the 'village school' atmosphere as one of their main reasons for choosing Maple Walk. 'There's a nice, cosy, community feel,' said one. 'I liked the fact that it is small, pioneering and affordable,' said another. 'It's a really vibrant, eclectic community.' Parents emphasise how happy their children are – 'mine will look back and feel they've been part of something really special and exciting'.

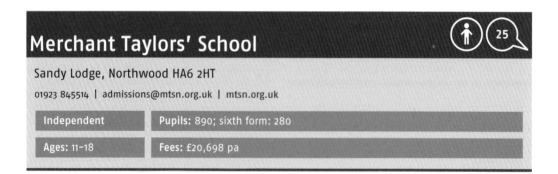

Merchant Taylors' School

Sandy Lodge, Northwood HA6 2HT

01923 845514 | admissions@mtsn.org.uk | mtsn.org.uk

| Independent | Pupils: 890; sixth form: 280 |
| Ages: 11–18 | Fees: £20,698 pa |

Head master: Since 2013, Simon Everson MA PGCE, born in Hertfordshire then educated at Solihull School and Cambridge (English) before completing a masters in philosophy at Nottingham. Has taught both in state maintained and independent schools as well as in Japan and was latterly head at Skinners' School in Tunbridge Wells, where he also took over a local failing school, guiding its transformation to academy status. Was adamant that very few schools would tempt him away but couldn't resist the lure back to Herts and MTS, where he took over 'a school with wonderful tradition, but one that's vibrant and relevant now.' Still 'loves the classroom' and 'borrows classes' when time allows. Moved immediately upon appointment to reintroduce significant financial benefits to scholars, with scholarships for the brightest and most able across the board now worth at least 10 per cent of fees:

'We are determined to seek out excellence and reward it.' Enjoys walking, bird watching and Scotland and is a recently qualified apiarist (bee-keeper). An electric guitar sits tucked in the corner of his office – 'I wanted to put myself in the boys' shoes and remember how it feels to struggle to learn something new,' he says. Businesslike and sincere. Married to Ginny, a psychotherapist.

Academic matters: A school populated by an intellectually curious and highly motivated cohort. Academic rigour – and ultimately success – is par for the course here but head is clear that they do not want to create a monoculture: 'We reject the philosophy of moulding children into specific types.' Boys inspired by staff who, in head's words, are 'fiercely intelligent – no school is better than the quality of its staff', and are striking to visitors either for their youth, energy and enthusiasm or wit, wisdom and worldliness. Humour and empathy pervade the classrooms, evident as much in the way staff speak to the boys as the quirky touches around the buildings – we've never seen fairy lights or a Ferrari flag in a biology lab in any other school. Dead Poets Society springs to mind more than once on our tour.

We've never seen fairy lights or a Ferrari flag in a biology lab in any other school

Traditional curriculum, not known for any single specialism – boys as likely to read medicine at university as English – and, although one parent said that academically 'it's not for the faint hearted,' school adamant that it's 'not merely a conveyor belt to top results'. 'Exam results are a given,' says school; 'it's about what else they leave with.' Boys take IGCSEs in majority of subjects with consistently outstanding results: 86 per cent A*/A in 2018, with 71 per cent of A levels graded A*/A and 93 per cent A*-B. Flexible setting in maths and science from year 7 (set together), with some 'banding' in English literature from year 9. 'We tend to separate out the boys who read; the ones who can handle Chaucer and Shakespeare with no problem'. Top half takes maths IGCSE in year 10, with one third also taking French a year early. It's French and Latin in the languages department in years 7 and 8 with the addition of German, Spanish or Greek in year 9, all available at A level. Around 60 per cent take the EPQ. Maths, economics and the sciences top choices at A level with around half the number opting for humanities and English but with no less stellar results. Small numbers for languages – although school still timetables minority subjects such as Greek even for lone students.

Excellent standard of art and DT, which has 'outstanding' teaching, according to parents – MTS has a produced higher number of Arkwright Scholars than any other school since the scheme began in the 1990s. This strength likely to snowball since the 2015 opening of school's cutting edge new DT building. Atmosphere surprisingly relaxed and no sign of the macho testosterone culture that's endemic in so many boys' schools. 'We achieve results by inspiring boys,' says head. Enrichment programme for most able scholars 'turns seamlessly' into Oxbridge preparation.

Huge sense of collective pride in outstanding work with Phab, funds raised throughout the year and an annual residential care week

Learning support (mild dyslexia, dyscalculia some ASD) viewed in the same way as educating the most able children: 'they just need a slightly different educational experience to everyone else,' although school also quick to point out that even those with individual needs 'must be able to keep up with the pace here.' New SENCo 'with a wealth of experience' recently appointed to monitor and work with specific learning difficulties – but strictly no withdrawal from class. ESL students must be instantly able to access curriculum as are fully immersed from day one. Can accommodate pupils with mobility problems, including wheelchairs.

School really shows its mettle in university application process and careers advice, an area which head says has reached 'Rolls Royce quality.' Parents describe the UCAS application process as 'incredibly well organised', with each sixth former assigned to the head of department of their chosen subject who acts as advisor and referee. Personal references from tutors are the cherry on top of the holistic application process. Boys encouraged to begin thinking about future careers early with a World of Work day in year 11, plus a joint careers conference with the girls of nearby St Helen's School. OMTs highly visible as mentors to current pupils, who are encouraged to use active database of over 600 old boys willing to offer work experience, and allowed time out of school to pursue such opportunities. A unique 'entrepreneur in residence' runs a start-up business from the DT building to give boys an insight into a world beyond the corporate giants who will doubtless be clamouring for their affections come milk round time.

Games, options, the arts: Sport seen as a hugely important part of the universal education at the heart of the MTS ethos, with sportsmanship and camaraderie as high on the agenda as winning. Part of the strong community feel comes from the whole school, including 80 per cent of the teaching staff, heading out to the (spectacular) sports fields together twice a week. Rugby, hockey and cricket are major sports and although there are varying degrees of success in the former (there was almost a hint of pride in the boy who self-effacingly told us he was in the 'least successful rugby A team on school record'), hockey and cricket are flying increasingly high with victories aplenty, and the fixture list growing annually to encompass more top schools. School boasts over 60 county and five national sportsmen and the U17 cricket team were recently crowned national champions. This in no small part due to dedicated directors for each major sport (hockey coach is ex-England international), as well as regular visiting coaches; recently the Australian cricket team, who requested that their pre-Ashes tour training take place at MTS. Sport for all – every boy competes for the school as often as is feasible with as much celebration when the 'Super E' rugby team (unbeaten) brings home a victory as the more elite squads.

A unique 'entrepreneur in residence' runs a start-up business from the DT building to give boys an insight into a world beyond the corporate giants

With over 20 minor sports from riding to kayaking, sailing and golf boys have no excuse not to find something they love. One of our guides was not overly keen on main team sports but was on the first team for fives. Two others were keener on playing electric guitar in their band – but that was seen as valuable too. One or two grumbles about lack of footie until sixth form, but that doesn't stop boys having a good kick around the quad at break times, and school provides goalposts for the purpose. World class facilities include all the usual suspects plus all weather hockey pitches ('better than the Olympic ones,' one keen player assured us), heated indoor pool, athletics track, lakes for sailing and kayaking, squash and fives courts, an assault course and fencing salle.

Endless opportunities to get stuck in outside of the classroom and sports field at lunch times and after school. Every sport imaginable, from sub aqua to cycling, has a society and there's chess, bridge and stamp club for those more inclined towards brain sports. Boys can flex their journalistic muscles by contributing to one of six school magazines or try their hand at societies ranging from the possibly unique dissection society to debating, most of these included in fees. Music and drama 'amazingly active,' says head, with ensembles and choirs galore, including Dixieland, Merchants of Groove and swing band in addition to a host of more traditional offerings. Two major theatrical productions take place each year in the Great Hall, in addition to smaller endeavours and a fiercely fought house drama competition. Parents rave about quality of productions, with recent extravaganzas including Grease. Active CCF (one of the largest in the UK) in conjunction with St Helen's, and D of E schemes offer super opportunities to follow outdoor pursuits and take part in trips to eg Morocco, Canada or Nepal. Huge sense of collective pride in relation to outstanding work with Phab, with funds raised throughout the year and an annual residential care week staffed by senior pupils, who consider it a great honour to be selected to take part.

Copious amount of trips. Rugby and hockey tours to South Africa and Australia and cricket to Barbados. Years 7 and 8 classics trip to Naples, geography to Iceland and history to Istanbul. Eleven language trips each year and six language exchange programmes across year groups.

Background and atmosphere: Founded in the City of London in 1561 by the Worshipful Company of Merchants, then the largest school in the country. Relocated in 1933 to its current location – a 250 acre site comprising a core of listed art deco buildings plus a host of sympathetically incorporated modern additions set before endless playing fields leading down to a lake that homes countless wildlife species. Visitors greeted by exquisite formal gardens and a handsome fascia. School lacks dreaming spires and turrets but gives an immediate sense of purposefulness and solid endeavour. Some areas (entrance hall, library, politics and economics centre, sixth form common room, new history building) more pristine than others but a sense of calm and mutual respect prevails.

'Civilised' a word that comes up again and again, along with a sense of a truly cohesive community spirit. Older boys mentor the younger, the whole school eats together (no exceptions, no packed lunches) and assembles together – 'invaluable', says head. 'We are a corporate body not a disparate group'. There's also a great sense of the traditional juxtaposed with gleaming new facilities – a feeling that a boy who has walked the corridors of MTS would not be remotely overwhelmed walking into an Oxford or Cambridge college for the first time.

Merged with ex-Northwood Prep, which has changed its name to Merchant Taylors' Prep.

Pastoral care, well-being and discipline: Discipline 'almost always low profile due to our hugely positive culture,' says school. Boys are not 'spiky' or 'entitled', transgressions rare and bullying almost non-existent ('I couldn't believe how much friendlier it was than my prep school', said one happy boy). Vertical tutor system praised almost unanimously by parents and boys with only a few grumbles relating to tutors moving on to pastures new mentally checking out in advance. For the most part, parents described them as 'almost part of the family', and many keep in contact with former tutees way beyond the A level years. Thriving house system facilitates yet more cross-fertilisation for friendships and opportunities for boys to shine in competitions, with pupils praising weekly house assemblies covering topics from 'the art of small talk' and 'how to tie a bow tie' to rocket building in teams. Plenty of chances for responsibility at the top of the school. Head boy voted in by 50 per cent student vote, supported by 10 elected monitors and a JCR of a further 30 boys. School run on Christian ethos, with services held in chapel and all faiths welcome, but there's also a Muslim prayer room and societies for all main faiths.

Pupils and parents: 'What makes a Merchant Taylors' boy?' we asked. 'Well, we don't really do posh,' came the smiling reply. Our opinion: smart, charming, self-effacing and diverse. Not a hooray Henry in sight or any trace of plums in mouths, but a group of boys wearing their school tie with humility and an awareness of privilege rather than entitlement. Fun to sit with (yes, even year 10s) in the dining room and totally at ease with adult company. Minds of staff and pupils alike on higher things than the tedious minutiae of shiny shoes and tidy haircuts obsessed over at so many schools. Head says school is 'always hanging on the coat tails of the pupils' enthusiasm', and keenly supports pupil-led initiatives, most recently a drone club, instigated by one young scientist. Perhaps because around a quarter of boys receive some level of financial assistance, social awareness is a key factor in their all-round pleasantness – 'It just wouldn't be the done thing to crow about wealth or status,' said one parent. 'Many families make huge sacrifices to send their sons here.' School concurs: 'Those from affluent backgrounds wear their wealth lightly'.

A school where three worlds don't so much collide as mesh. A hybrid London/country school with appeal to local, north and west London and Herts/Bucks families. The London crowd loves the spacious campus, laid back feel and multitude of sporting options on offer, especially in comparison to nearby competitors, and those from the shires enjoy the slightly edgier, more worldly feel than they find in schools closer to home. Reflective of local area, around 40 per cent British-Asian, a large Jewish contingent and all other main faiths represented. Wonderfully inclusive – 'there's zero tolerance of racism or homophobia,' boys told us – and although firm friendships are formed on the tube trains and coaches that transport boys in from eg Highgate, St John's Wood and Ealing, plus suburbs from St Albans and Harpenden to Beaconsfield and Gerrards Cross, all reported that new friends are constantly made through tutor groups, form groups which are mixed up each year, subject choices (from year 12 forms are grouped according to A level choices) and activities.

> *The London crowd loves the spacious campus, laid back feel and multitude of sporting options on offer, and those from the shires enjoy the slightly edgier feel*

Unlike many secondaries, parents maintain close contact with school, attending events and committees in droves. Head reported around 200 attendees at one of his recent termly parent forums. In turn, school has unique relationship with many OMTs well beyond the A level years, with tutors speaking with deep fondness of past tutees' achievements. Actor and alumnus Riz Ahmed chose MT as the backdrop for one his first movies and Grammy Award winning OMT band Nero (the lead singer read philosophy at Oxford, incidentally) recently returned as the surprise act at leavers' ball. Other famous alumni include Nobel prize-winning medic Sir John Sulston, Lord Coggan (former Archbishop of Canterbury), Sir Alan Duncan and Boris Karloff, as well as a host of others from the worlds of politics, business, sport, the military and the arts.

Entrance: Selective with two main intakes at 11+ and 13+. At 11+ around 380 boys (roughly two-thirds from state primaries) apply for 60 places. At this point, applicants tested in maths, English and a general paper with those delivering the goods on paper invited back for a one-to-one interview ('not as intimidating as it sounds – they always leave with a smile on their face,' says school). Worth remembering that many will be applying for several schools, so not as competitive as it first appears.

A further 100 places available at 13+ with fewer applicants (about two to one, though many places taken by boys from Merchant Taylors' Prep) for each place but larger hurdles to clear: boys hoping for entry in 2021 or before are interviewed first in May/June of year 7 (registration by end of February) on strength of prep head's report with high fliers offered 'unconditional' places at that point in the expectation that the exam will present no problems. Those offered a 'conditional' place after interview will need to pass every paper in the CE-style exam in January (English, maths, science, humanities, MFL and optional Latin).

Potential entrants from 2022 onwards (born after 31 August 2008) will face an entirely new process aimed to fall in line with other public schools. Applications will need to be made by June of year 5, followed by an interview in the autumn of year 6. Conditional offers are made shortly after, subject to performance in examinations in January of year 6 (English, maths and a general paper). Parents asked to pay deposit in year 7 confirming that MTS is their first choice school. Those who accept a place will then take 'setting examinations' in almost all subjects in January of year 8. Candidates will no longer be able to try again at 13+ if not successful at 11+.

School clear that parents tutoring boys heavily for the exam 'are not doing them any favours – we're looking for intellectual curiosity, a passion for something, reasoning skills and ways in which boys can make a wider contribution to the school.'

At 16+ exams in four A level subjects; offer confirmations depend on GCSE results.

Up to 40 or 50 feeders at 11+, with preps including Radlett Prep, Manor Lodge, Buckingham College, Reddiford and Gayhurst. At 13+ large numbers from Merchant Taylors' Prep, St John's, Durston House and St Martin's, plus a few each from The Beacon, Davenies, Orley Farm, York House and St Anthony's, amongst others.

Exit: Very little fall out after GCSE. Eighteen to Oxbridge in 2018 with vast majority of remainder to top universities. London colleges feature highly (particularly Imperial, LSE and UCL) as do Birmingham, Bristol, Durham, Nottingham and Warwick. Very strong numbers to read medicine (five in 2018), economics and engineering but diversity across the board from sports science to English, humanities, law and the occasional one choosing film or drama school over university offers, or heading to university overseas (one to Toronto in 2018).

Money matters: The old school tie doesn't come into the selection process and school prides itself on staying true to the ethos on which it was founded – to offer an excellent all-round education to boys from all walks of life and offer financial aid to those who would most benefit – these days, around 200 boys at any one time. Academic scholarships awarded to boys who perform particularly well in the entrance papers, with scholars benefiting from an enrichment programme. Up to five major academic scholarships at both 11+ and 13+ worth at least 10 per cent of fees. Also sport, art, drama, DT, music and all-rounder scholarships.

Remarks: A rare breed – a London school with a country feel, offering the best of both worlds to boys from the city and the shires. Sitting coolly around the top of the league tables, seemingly without trying too hard, a testament to teachers who inspire without applying undue pressure. Wonderful breadth of sporting opportunities for both the elite and the enthusiastic. Not the most obvious choice for macho rugby types, or for the parent hoping for their son to leave school with a public school swagger, but for those looking for an environment that actively encourages boys to 'lean in to difficult questions', get involved in enriching activities outside of the classroom, and that values the quirky and erudite, look no further.

Michaela Community School

North End Road, Wembley, London HA9 0UU

020 8795 3183 | info@mcsbrent.co.uk | mcsbrent.co.uk

State

Pupils: 600

Ages: 11–19

Headmistress: Founder and head since the school started in 2014, the vibrant and dramatic Katharine Birbalsingh MA Oxon NPQH (early 40s). A graduate of New College Oxford (French and philosophy), she did her teacher training at the Institute of Education. Previously deputy head of a South London state secondary, she spent all her years since university teaching in inner London state secondary schools, working her way through the usual channels. She has come a long way since her ground-breaking speech to the Tory party conference in 2010. Condemning the state of an education system that 'kept poor children poor' to roaring applause, Ms Birbalsingh, in her 30s at the time, looked startled at how well her speech was being received. Naïve politically, and not even a Tory, the accolade took her by surprise but she found herself without a job immediately afterwards.

She is clearly loving being in charge of this ground-breaking school ('I always planned on being a head,' she confides), and being able to fashion it according to her principles and beliefs. 'It's like being the conductor of an orchestra, but it's very important that it still works without me,' she insists. That is the beauty of systems and attention to detail. Passionate about social mobility and empowerment through knowledge, she and her team have created, in Michaela, a finely tuned collection of instruments that play beautifully in time and in sync. 'The systems here are tight and will only get tighter the more the school fills up and the older children influence and educate the younger ones.'

The tools are teaching from the front, silence in the classroom (until called upon to speak), repeated memorisation of facts leading to deep retention of knowledge

'When they arrive in year 7 quite a lot is about damage control,' she says. 'Some don't know their times tables, their reading is limited..we need to start teaching them the right habits for learning... we also have to help some of the parents to step up... However we don't do anything that's a waste of time – I don't believe in targets, they waste time... Every decision we make is whether it's right for the kids, not whether it's right for Ofsted.' Parents warm to her straightforward approach. She sticks to her boundaries and is uncompromising about what she believes to be right. They also notice her respect for her staff and others around her, and how much she herself is respected.

Confident, articulate, determined, driven and very brave, Ms Birbalsingh is an inspirational role model for both the boys and girls at her school and they feel very fortunate to have her.

Academic matters: Despite there being no GCSE or A level results yet (first year 11 in September 2018, sixth form opens in 2019) to give testimony to the academic success of pupils here, it is already clear that the progress they are making and the standards they achieve are remarkable. The tools are teaching from the front, silence in the classroom (until called upon to speak), repeated memorisation of facts leading to deep retention of knowledge,

regular self-quizzing, testing and open competition, as well as a challenging curriculum. Everyone does all the same subjects – English, maths, French, humanities, science, music and art. A pupil who is struggling may be allowed to take a reduced number of GCSEs; most will take eight though the bright ones will do nine, having done RS early in year 10. Pupils have two group music lessons and two art lessons a week. The library is stacked to the gunwhales (just under 4,000 books) in the grey, functional office-style bookcases, with classical literature, contemporary literature, predominately fiction and plenty of poetry and plays. There are class readers, Friday readers and Group readers. By year 9 all pupils will have read seven Shakespeare plays (including Macbeth, Julius Caesar and Othello) – the full versions, in the original. They will have memorised huge chunks of them and studied characterisation, plot device, pathos and humour. Reading is given great emphasis: the 'academically gifted' read over 100 classics from Homer to Orwell from the quality-controlled library. In English and maths as a whole the school's tests show pupils making double the expected level of progress.

Not all teachers at Michaela have a teaching qualification, something the school is proud of as it feels they are not all moulded from the same clay, but all are graduates from top universities including Oxbridge and Russell Group. They are motivated and enthusiastic. Ms Birbalsingh understands the pressure points on the profession only too well, so in her (or 'their' school, she prefers – 'this is very much a collaborative effort') there is no detailed marking, and box ticking exercises are limited to a minimum. Teachers are needed to supervise on staircases during 'transition', when the pupils march quickly in silence between lessons: if they were marking each essay in minute detail they wouldn't have time for this. Staff read all essays and make comments, but give detailed feedback to a class as a whole so everyone can share understanding of where the strengths and weaknesses lie. No pupil is spared. They are told exactly where they rank among their peers, and are praised for their performance in detail about what they did right, just as they are chastised about where they have fallen short – not enough focus in class, overlooking the opportunity to catch up in support lessons after school, not being diligent enough while self-quizzing. Teachers relish the opportunity actually to teach, impart knowledge, wisdom and learning. The job here is not about classroom control. These classrooms and corridors and dining rooms are strictly controlled at all times. Teachers are respected as being the ones whose age, wisdom and experience give them a natural authority. 'This', says Ms Birbalsingh, 'allows the children to be children, and they feel safe knowing where the boundaries are and understanding the consequences if they cross those boundaries.'

Orley Farm School

The plan for A level is that the most rigorous academic subjects will be prioritised – maths, further maths, physics, chemistry, biology, English literature, French, art, music, theology and philosophy, but Ms Birbalsingh is busily visiting outstanding sixth forms to learn about what works best – she and her team will fashion the sixth form just as they created years 7-11, with meticulous attention to detail and a fundamental belief in the acquisition of knowledge imparted from specialist teachers who love their subject.

They are told exactly where they rank among their peers, and are praised in detail about what they did right, just as they are chastised about where they have fallen short

Expectations are unashamedly high. Oxbridge and other top Russell Group universities are all within reach for many and the year 9 students are being taught to appreciate that already. One year 9 girl said that she 'isn't focusing on Oxbridge' as she wants to go the LSE. Pupils are streamed in four sets but there is fluidity between the sets and they are not referred to in front of the pupils. Oxbridge hopefuls can be found even in the lower half of the year group. One girl who arrived from the Sudan started in the bottom half of the year group; now, two years later, she is in the top.. 'but we never say "bright" or "able", only "are you working hard?" We celebrate the pupils who spend the most time on their homework – here there is no "bottom set mentality",' avers Ms Birbalsingh. Ms Birbalsingh has been busy networking at Oxford and Cambridge colleges, preparing a strategy, paving a path.

SEN is not a comfortable acronym at Michaela. Labels are seen as damaging. They would prefer to focus on the effort involved. 'Weakest pupils need more rigour, more focus and more practice,' asserts Katie Ashford, one of the deputy heads and an English teacher. Ms Birbalsingh accepts that some students need extra support – they have put on an extra lesson for those who 'are so far behind' in maths for example, but the focus is on each child.

Several parents remarked on their sons' appetite for homework. One year 9 boy works for two-and-a-half hours each evening. The incentives are there – they love to earn their merits, and as they start to see the fruits of their labour in their improved scores, a virtuous cycle is set in motion.

The teachers are wholeheartedly supportive of the regime at Michaela. You only have to read their book Battle Hymn of the Tiger Teachers – the Michaela Way to get a sense of their dedication, and total commitment to the ethos and practice here. Ms Birbalsingh almost purrs when questioned about the quality of her teachers: 'We have the best,' she affirms, citing their quality of life as part of her pulling power. Parents and pupils we spoke to agree.

Games, options, the arts: The art room here is disciplined, with as clear lines and boundaries as you find everywhere else in the school. Lots of charcoal and pencil drawings adorn the walls ('it's so difficult to find an art teacher who knows how to draw these days,' observes Ms Birbalsingh.) Tasteful artwork – and carefully displayed, detailed portraits on the walls of each floor of eg Mandela, Boris Johnson and David Cameron. Clear simple lines – minimalist. Not fussy. Not messy.

Sport takes place one afternoon a week in a sports centre round the corner. Just football and dodgeball – not a lot of choice – but they get exercise and the opportunity to play matches against other schools as well as the chance to shine if sport is their thing. There are table tennis tables in the yard as well as basketball hoops – a chance to let off steam and be competitive between lessons. Apart from performing excerpts in class from the Shakespeare plays they are studying – eg Julius Caesar – not a lot of drama. 'We don't have the facilities – this is not what we are about,' is the explanation.

There is a focus, however, on a co-curricular programme that stretches the academic and cerebral. Visitors' programme includes talks, starting from year 7, from speakers ranging from hedge fund managers to barristers and politicians: recent examples include Boris Johnson, Nick Gibb, David Lammy MP and journalist turned teacher Lucy Kellaway. A rhetoric programme from year 9 paves the path towards Oxbridge applications. A scholars' programme will be run with the Brilliant Club from year 10 to challenge pupils with independent research projects and essays.

Every pupil will go on two trips a year, to the Natural History Museum, the British Museum, the National Gallery, the Globe Theatre and Cambridge University. Extracurricular clubs include films (pupils watch six classic films a year including Frankenstein, Romeo and Juliet and The Imitation Game), Future Leaders (pupil prefects are selected to lead conversations at family lunch), Lizard Point (stretching online quizzes of locations and regions) and competitions (Times Table Rockstars, Poetry Declamation, Dates and Capitals). For the more athletic child there is football, table tennis and basketball and those with an interest in music can do chamber choir and flute choir.

Background and atmosphere: Founded by Katharine Birbalsingh in September 2014 as a free school 'with a private school ethos', the school makes an initially forbidding impression. An office block in the heart of a very industrial part of Wembley (the tube trains roll regularly past the dining room windows). Huge iron gates and a security system more fitting of a high security prison need to be negotiated before you enter the reception area.

Once inside the austere grey walls, the remarkable thing is that there is complete silence. Even in the reception and waiting area, the silence is broken only by the occasional whirr of a photocopier and the whispered exchanges behind the desk. On arrival all guests are presented with a list of rules – including 'Do not talk in normal voices in the corridors – only a whisper please!' 'Do not demonstrate disbelief to pupils when they say they like their school', and 'Do talk to the pupils at lunch and at break.'

As you tread carefully through the corridors you observe children at their desks in rows, arms folded on the desk except when they are eagerly throwing up their hands or writing carefully in their books. In the class room there is plenty of interaction. Teachers lead from the front but lessons are delivered not like a lecture but as a series of questions and answers. Feedback from the front (no marking policy – marking can waste too much teaching and supervising time).

'Family lunch' is another unique feature of the school, and key to the school motto 'Work hard and be kind'. It begins with the whole school chanting a poem in time

'Transition' – when the children move between classrooms at the end of a lesson – is astonishing to witness. Like clockwork the system slips into place. Teachers station themselves at key points of the staircases and the end of the corridors. Children move at a rapid pace without running or talking. There are smiles and nods of hello – this isn't a prison, after all – but the focus is on supreme efficiency. Every moment of learning time counts and movement between classes can be a drain on these precious minutes. Here at Michaela there is a determination among staff, shared by pupils (remarkably), not to waste this valuable learning time. Once in the classroom, every pupil knows their role, and books, piled at the correct place on the window sill, are retrieved and distributed quickly and quietly down the line. By the time the teacher commands 'Go!' – dot on time – they are ready to begin the lesson. Merits and demerits are distributed as an acknowledgement of this performance.

'Family lunch' is another unique feature of the school, and key to the school motto 'Work hard and be kind.' It begins with the whole school chanting a poem in time. We heard Coleridge's Kubla Khan. Everyone eats the same food, vegetarian menus carefully chosen to suit all faiths and eating requirements. Hot, freshly cooked food but no canteen. Food is served by the children on individual tables of six. Each child is given a role and they all know exactly what they are doing, whether it's pouring the water, dishing out the food or clearing up. During the course of lunch each table will discuss a topic that has already been chosen by the teacher in charge – 'Does what you're taught at Michaela affect your behaviour outside school?', for example. Once the food is eaten it is time to record 'appreciations'. Individual pupils stand up and declare their thanks to the 150 pupils, guests and teachers present, for anything they like, from the care their history teacher took to giving feedback on an essay, to the help his mother gave him in getting him to school that day. The audience applauds, with two sharp claps, merits are awarded for effective articulate speaking, a demerit for any suggestion of ridicule or lack of respect.

At break, lunch, mid-morning and afternoon, children spill out into 'the yard', or as one pupil, remarked, 'it's essentially a disused car park', but it serves its purpose – fresh(ish) air, table tennis tables, football, basketball, a chance to let off steam and above all a chance to talk. This is where friendships are formed and ideas – other than classroom ideas – can be exchanged. Pupils clearly value it a lot, as part of the system of punishment includes being 'banned from the yard'. Apart from during lunch – which is formally structured with general group conversations rather than private individual conversations – this is the chance they have to talk to each other properly.

Pastoral care, well-being and discipline: Everyone in year 7 attends behaviour bootcamp a week before the start of the new school year in September. This is when the system – of detention, merits/demerits, how to manage 'transition', how to walk fast but in silence through the corridors, how family lunch works, which way to walk past your chair when leaving the classroom, how to address a teacher or any other adult, and what attitude to bring with you to Michaela – is carefully, systematically taught, reinforced and embedded. It is an invaluable week for teachers too, new ones especially. By the time term starts everyone understands the systems and can row together. One of our guides ('a girl who struggles academically,' we were later told) was articulate and polite to the nth degree, and proudly told us there was no bullying in the school. There are barely any moments to bully. The reasons pupils don't run in the corridor is that there would be an opportunity to knock into someone, for a fight to brew; for the same reason they walk in a particular direction around their chairs, and cross their arms on top of the table, to avoid surreptitious shoving, a sneaky peak at a mobile phone or anything else that may lead to demerit or detention, but ultimately being someone you don't really want to be.

Unashamedly strict, this is a 'no excuses' school. The discipline is centred on a system of merits and demerits – six detentions and you are in isolation, three demerits have you removed from a lesson. Detention is used regularly but intentionally. The time is not wasted. Each pupil is fully occupied with self-quizzing while they are in detention, and some even start to appreciate the progress they can make while being punished.

Kindness is as much a part of the ethos as achievement. Children are taught to understand that the strict regime is for their own benefit. Family lunch and appreciations, as well as everyone working to serve and clear the food, all contribute to an ethos of gratitude, kindness and empathy.

Parents need to support this approach, and it's often they who find it more of a challenge than their children. Faced with the prospect that a mobile phone would not be returned until the end of the half term, after a child had been caught using it in school, the parents have the choice of accepting it or finding another school.

Pupils and parents: Extremely diverse, pupils here come from a number of different cultures and are of different faiths, but no one dominates. Some walk to school, most take buses from all over London, but mainly from the north west, a few take the tube to Wembley Park and walk across the road to the school. One thing they do have in common, however, is that these are not pupils from highly privileged backgrounds. Half the pupils are eligible for pupil premium. Parents are told that they need to be prepared – 'Michaela', they are told at open evenings, 'will be like the personal trainer in fitness regime and that is what you are signing up to.' The occasional child leaves – not because they can't take the strain, but more often because their parents can't. However the majority of parents, pleased that their children are being taught to such high standards and that behaviour is excellent, are fully supportive of the firm line taken by the school.

Entrance: There are 120 places in year 7. Priority given to siblings, but otherwise the main criterion is a lottery system for people living within a five mile radius of the school. As word spreads, and the school becomes increasingly oversubscribed, proximity to the school will become ever more essential.

Application is through Brent Council, and for an occasional place, ring the council to get placed on the waiting list.

Exit: If Ms Birbalsingh's vision is realised, expect a number of pupils to go to top UK universities, including Oxbridge. The first set of results for year 11 will be in 2019 (though some took RS in 2018), for the upper sixth in 2021.

Remarks: A challenging and rigorous academic education with high expectations for every pupil. For the right child this is a truly extraordinary and superlative school. Not for the faint hearted, the cynical or the fragile. Strict, but with a warm heart beating below the surface, Michaela creates a safe, but stimulating environment, and the chance to fly.

Montpelier Primary School

Montpelier Road, Ealing, London W5 2QT

020 8997 5855 | admin@montpelier.ealing.sch.uk | montpelierschool.net

State	Pupils: 682
Ages: 4–11	

Headteacher: Since 2003, Mr Am Rai (40s). BA in sociology, Birmingham Poly, MA in educational management and administration at University of London, Institute of Education. Married, two children. Very experienced head who had already worked in seven London state primaries prior to his arrival at Montpelier. He had been twice seconded to rescue failing schools. And you can see why. He is a man of very clear vision and sound, liberal educational principles. He is highly articulate, straightforward and frank in conversation. In two hours' conversation, we were wearied by no jargon, no pseudo-academic parroting, no political posturing – so refreshing. There is no disguising Mr Rai's confidence and his ambition – both personal and, more overtly, for his pupils. The results are there for all to see. Montpelier's most recent Ofsted – with only two days' notice – achieved a full house of grade 1s, and school is now a National Support School, helping others to improve. The results top the borough's and top most other boroughs too. The children are stimulated, creative, challenged, smiley and rewarded. A very good head.

Entrance: Oversubscribed at all levels but high turn-over among local international community means that occasional places at all stages are not uncommon. All managed by Ealing LA and, if you have no special circumstances, you need to live up close and purposeful if you are to get in. And families increasingly swap their large homes in less well provided for bits of the borough for flats round the corner from this school.

Exit: Some leave for local preps at end of year 4. Of the remainder, around 30 per cent go to the local hotshot comprehensive – Drayton Manor HS. Around 15 per cent to Ellen Wilkinson HS – the local girls' comprehensive. The rest either to local RC or CE high schools or to the local independents – Notting Hill and Ealing, St Benedict's, St Augustine's. Increasingly, some to the Tiffins, to Bucks, Berks or Middlesex grammars, to St Paul's Boys' or Girls', Latymer Upper or John Lyon, and some parents even move house after their bright buttons gain places there or at eg Henrietta Barnett. No disaster schools in the area – another good reason for coming here.

Remarks: Sited on a corner of two quiet, tree-lined roads and adjoining a pretty park. The surrounding streets are similarly well-appointed, orderly and solidly middle class – this is suburban bliss, though the North Circular grinds along only a couple of hundred yards away. The nearest schools are all independent and, not surprisingly, they are the chosen destinations for a sizeable minority of Montpelier leavers.

Three connected school buildings, and only one – due for renovation – makes the heart sink. The latest is a clever extension housing reception and admin. Infants and reception on ground floor – makes sense. Four playgrounds with good play equipment though not over-provided with soft flooring. Reception classes have integral loos, so no tots trailing down corridors. No overheated classrooms here – though we visited on a dull January morning – and no class feels over full, despite 30 in each and staff. Windows have replaced doors wherever possible – school has a light and open feel. Reception in large classroom with a teacher, a nursery nurse, a student teacher and a teaching assistant. Corner with fresh fruit and drinks available all day for whoever feels inclined. Some 40 per cent bring food from home but the school lunch menu – outside caterers – looked varied and appetising.

You can see why. He is a man of very clear vision and sound, liberal educational principles. He is highly articulate, straightforward and frank in conversation

Infants' classes full of quiet, concentrated activity – seven or eight things going on in each room: water, measuring, building, weighing, word work, writing etc. Every class has a whiteboard and IT used imaginatively round the school – connecting people and activities and joining things up. Learning legacy boards provide testimony to what has been learned during the term. Monitoring and appraisal embedded into everything – each child has her own targets for the core skills and a list of 'I Can' statements to keep parents abreast of what has been mastered and what still needs to be done. This complemented by the clever use of iPads by teachers who photograph work and load it onto a parents' portal so that latest work can be admired at home. Now a National Teaching School, with the head and several teachers giving support to other schools on teaching and leadership.

Lots of imaginative cross-curricular learning: displays everywhere are evidence of lively thinking and teaching. Year 2 work on portraits looked at what portraits can teach us rather than being merely an excuse to draw ourselves. Super project on Medusa – each child had made a Wanted poster with clever text – and another class displayed illustrations of The Lady of Shalott with sensitive use of quotes. Oxford Reading Tree used throughout with built-in encouragement for parental participation and each child has weekly guided reading session to build comprehension skills rather than just skimming speed. A good hall/gym, a nice little library – properly used for lending and reading – two IT suites, art room, and every class has an art week in which they can drop everything else and experience sustained and concentrated work on a project of their own. Unusually strong music – 150+ learn an instrument in or after school – and school provides child care for siblings until 5.00pm to facilitate music activities. Everyone has an afternoon of sport weekly. Not much but better than many.

Remarkable amount of support given to those who need extra help with eg language, writing task or maths. We saw one-to-one sessions and numerous small groups in all available spaces. Also, for those with an SEN to whom – until recent changes in government SEN provision, at least – school has given exemplary support. And organised time made to equip those who arrive with no English with key words and skills. As socially diverse as any school in the capital. Around 55 per cent speak a language other than English at home – huge range of languages and cultures – among which highest proportions from the Middle East and Japan, then India and various bits of Europe. Families include a lot of 'corporate nomads' ie those with three or five year contracts who may be relocated anywhere on the globe. After-school language (French, Spanish, Arabic, Mandarin) and many other clubs.

The first thing that strikes you on an ordinary school day is how quiet it is and how class after class of 30 diverse children work absorbedly and happily together. In this large, highly organised school – and it is a large primary by any standards – children look relaxed and secure and, even amongst the smallest, there is a sense that school is about learning. Few behavioural problems – jumped on smartly when they occur. Head 'will exclude if a child is spoiling the lives of other children', but no-one excluded for bullying in eight years prior to our visit.

Parental talk of 'the warm community feeling', express gratitude that 'the children are looked after well and are happy,' and pay tribute to the truly multicultural ethos – 'all faiths and beliefs are celebrated'. Very active PTA and lots of community activities eg annual international food fair and remarkably effective fundraising summer fête.

Most staff – many are young – highly praised. Head is seen as dynamic and approachable by some and by others as remote and over-protective of his staff. No-one, however, wishes they had sent their children elsewhere, and none would dispute that he has made a stunning success of a school which, before, had been content to be good enough. 'We judge things by the happiness of our children,' asserts head wisely.

Newland House School

32–34 Waldegrave Park, Twickenham TW1 4TQ

020 8865 1305 | admissions@newlandhouse.net | newlandhouse.net

| Independent | Pupils: 425 |
| Ages: 3-13 | Fees: £11,544 – £12,918 pa |

Headmaster: Since 2010, David Alexander BMus Dip NCOS (50s). Previously head of Norland Place School and Haddon Dene School. Warm, welcoming and with a good sense of humour. Very kind and doesn't have a bad word to say about anybody. Justifiably proud of his charges. 'Our 13-year-old boys are a delight, as are our 11-year-old girls. I'm very proud to know any of them. I like what the school has done for them.' Parents say, 'What you see is what you get. Pupils and parents respect him but he knows how to laugh too.' Believes one of his main jobs is to steer parents towards the right school for their child: he wants his pupils to be at the top of their game at their senior schools. The children adore him because he's such fun: he is currently keen for the school to buy a boat which can act as a floating classroom on the Thames. Holds a commercial flying licence and commands a reserve RAF squadron at weekends. Mr Alexander selects the head boy and head girl by deciding which pupils he would most like to have lunch with.

Moving on in July 2019.

Entrance: All change, with new term time only nursery in own building (was former pre-prep), and 7+ entry being phased out (last intake September 2018). Now has 50 per cent more spaces in reception following recent pre-prep expansion into brand new premises on main school site. Nursery places offered on first come first served basis – but only to families who have been offered a reception place. Often oversubscribed – best register your child as soon as possible after birth. At 4+ entry is on a first-come, first-served basis, with siblings given priority. Sixty places available at this stage and a waiting list in operation.

Academic and music bursaries available – up to 50 per cent of fees, negotiated on a yearly basis.

Ten per cent discount for third sibling when all are in school together.

Exit: Predominantly to private day schools, occasional boarding, with Surbiton High, Sir William Perkins's, Reed's School and St James School heading recent destination lists. Hampton, King's College School and Kingston Grammar regularly feature. Girls leave at 11 and boys at 13. Girls can stay on to 13, but don't. 'It would be a leap of faith,' says head. Consistently high number of academic, sports, music and all-rounder scholarships. Head puts this down to outstanding teaching and the fact that the children are in a happy environment and so want to learn.

Remarks: Pre-prep is run by the approachable and calm Tracey Chong. All-female staff ('by coincidence') give it a homely air. Its brand building, right next door to the main school unites the two parts of the school and means additional places in reception. 'The teachers at the pre-prep are lovely and smiley and it rubs off on the children,' said one parent.

The pupils call the head 'Sir' and scramble to their feet when an adult enters the room

Classes at the prep are mixed ability, maximum 20 children. Lessons are lively and fast-paced with specialist teachers for PE, art, music and ICT from the start. Separate sciences taught from year 4. Children set for English, French and maths from year 5. Days are long, especially for those who start with the full cooked breakfast on offer at 7.30am.

Once the girls leave at the end of year 6, the boys are placed in two mixed ability classes and one small scholarship set; vacancies left by girls are not filled. Greek on offer to potential scholars. Parents love the fact that children get so much individual attention at the top of the school. 'A real strength,' said one. Children are well prepared for 11+, 13+ and scholarships. As the head puts it: 'We are a preparatory school. It's our job to prepare them for the exams for entry to their next schools.' Parents report that a massive amount of coaching goes on in the final years, of which the head is critical. 'It's not necessary. We are all fighting a coaching culture but people get sucked into it.' Head gives out CE results to boys as they sit around a camp fire on the year 8 trip to Wales. 'A lovely touch, and the boys never forget it. It's a gesture typical of the school,' said one parent.

Classrooms are spacious and light, with traditional wooden desks arranged in neat rows.

Head gives out CE results to boys as they sit around a camp fire on the year 8 trip to Wales. 'A lovely touch, and the boys never forget it'

Impressive ICT suite, tablets about to be introduced but head keen this shouldn't be a gimmick. The school enters a huge number of national and international competitions with frequent success. Recently won three World Maths Day trophies, out of a total of five awarded to UK schools. DT department is the envy of other schools and recently assembled a car for the Shell Eco-Marathon that achieved a mileage of 1,000 miles per gallon. Currently a group of senior boys is investigating the effect of tyre pressure on the environment and presentations have been made to MPs.

Plenty of choirs for each year group, new pop choir for year 7/8 boys is thriving. Several hundred individual instrumental and singing lessons take place every week. Lots of bands, ensembles and orchestras. Children have taken part in performances at the Kingston Music Festival and concerts at the Barbican with the London Symphony Orchestra.

Art clubs include weekend activities where parents can become involved. Local artists exhibit and sell their work in the reception area and include a couple of inexpensive pieces so that children can buy a picture if it catches their eye.

Sport is a real strength of the school. Boys play rugby, football and cricket; girls play netball, rounders and hockey. Swimming, cross-country and athletics also on offer and even more sport possible through numerous after-school clubs, including golf at neighbouring club. Main playing fields are five minutes away by minibus; two multi-purpose, all-weather courts and four cricket nets on site. Lots of tournaments and matches mean everyone gets the chance to compete.

Full-time head of SEN. Head believes 'a good learning support culture enhances what you do'. Provision for mild dyslexia, dyspraxia and dyscalculia, though not the place to send a child with severe difficulties.

Many long-serving staff. Head did away with 'teaching' and 'non-teaching' labels when he arrived. 'We're all teaching the children in different ways,' he says. One satisfied parent commented that staff were 'prepared to go the extra mile for the children.' Two gap year students help with sport and a French assistant teaches conversational French.

Parents are typically hard-working professionals. 'The school reflects the local community and lots of the children arrive at school on foot or by scooter,' says head of pre-prep. Active PTA raises substantial funds, half money raised goes to charity, the other half to the school – recently paid for a climbing wall. Activity-based wraparound club from 7.30am to 6pm.

A competitive, purposeful and demanding school which has retained old fashioned values (the pupils call the head 'Sir' and scramble to their feet when an adult enters the room). Pupils are challenged on all fronts and, as one parent put it, 'By the time the children reach year 5, they are under pressure to perform. It's not a soft school but, for the right child, there simply isn't anywhere better in the area.' One mother felt that 'it's not for the retiring child. I think they'd get trampled underfoot.' The head disagrees and feels the school caters for all personalities and abilities as there is so much on offer and so many chances to shine.

North Ealing Primary School

Pitshanger Lane, Ealing, London W5 1RP

020 8997 2653 | admin@northealing.ealing.sch.uk | northealingprimary.co.uk

State	Pupils: 714
Ages: 3–11	

Head: Since 2014, Sally Flowers, previously deputy head. She joined the school as assistant head in 2011.

Entrance: Larger intake now due to three form entry but pupils still need to live within a mile of the school to get a place (no official catchment, admissions by distance as the crow flies).

Exit: Majority go to Brentside High, a few others to Drayton Manor, Ellen Wilkinson, Twyford and Cardinal Wiseman. A handful each year to grammar schools. One third go private – St Augustine's, Latymer, St Benedict's, Notting Hill and Ealing and John Lyon.

Remarks: Hidden away behind the main road, the sunflowers and flower tubs welcomed us in as we walked across the playground to the school entrance. The school is divided into three main areas. Reception and nursery classes are housed in a bright and airy modern building at the back of the site where outdoor classrooms are covered for use in all weathers, allowing free flow back and forth. 'The children are so lucky to have a new building and they love being able to explore inside and outside,' enthused one parent.

Years 1 and 2 are in equally bright classrooms and at the end of their corridor is a dedicated music room. There is also a hall where we observed new reception children doing a movement class. 'Bend knees!'

Children are also separated at play time: nursery, reception and year 1 all have their own separate playgrounds. Years 2, 3 and 4 have the back playground and years 5 and 6 are at the front. The school even has its own garden which backs on to Pitshanger park.

Years 5 and 6 are housed in the old part of the school (100 year old Victorian building). Classes here a bit cramped but bright wall displays, eg a display about the local Brentham estate in Victorian times, make them feel welcoming and warm.

Healthy eating policy – no sweets allowed in lunch boxes. 'We don't check the staffroom, though'

Key stage 2 children are set for maths and we observed an able maths group being taught in the library, preparing for the Primary Maths Challenge. Around a third of year 6 students achieve level 6 in their maths Sats and results in reading and writing are among the best in the borough. 'We saw a great improvement in our reading levels after we introduced guided reading,' explained the deputy head.

Music and drama are particularly strong, with the school choir taking part in local music festivals. Children can learn the recorder in key stage 2 and there is also the opportunity to study the violin, cello or guitar. Each year the head directs the year 6 production; last year it was Bugsy Malone. 'The standard of the drama is really high, thanks to the head's passion for theatre,' explained one parent.

Sports are also very high profile, with a glass cabinet bulging with cups in the school reception. Netball, football and all the usual sports teams win prizes each year. There are numerous sports clubs before and after school most days.

Very active PTA organises regular quiz nights etc. 'As well as raising money, these events are a great way to meet other parents.'

Hot dinners are cooked on the premises – half the children have school dinners and half bring packed lunches. The school has a healthy eating policy – no sweets or chocolates are allowed in children's lunch boxes. 'We don't check the staff room, though,' quipped the deputy head. Senior staff are on duty at lunch time and there's a staggered system so that no one has to wait too long. There is also a tidy classroom competition each week where the school cleaners choose the tidiest class and their prize is to go first at lunch.

All the usual EAL, SEN and inclusion provision. Anti-bullying guidelines are adhered to and there is a buddy system where older pupils support younger pupils. Former pupils include Peter Crouch and Honor Blackman.

A very friendly and welcoming local school that achieves excellent results.

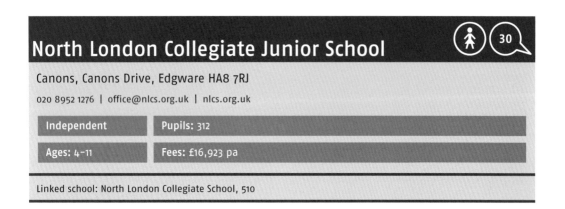

North London Collegiate Junior School

Canons, Canons Drive, Edgware HA8 7RJ

020 8952 1276 | office@nlcs.org.uk | nlcs.org.uk

Independent	Pupils: 312
Ages: 4–11	Fees: £16,923 pa

Linked school: North London Collegiate School, 510

Head of junior school: Since 2003, Jo Newman BEd (50s). An old girl of North London, Mrs Newman read geography and education at Homerton College, Cambridge. After leaving, she dabbled briefly with the idea of retail – 'I love people and I think I would have been equally happy in a number of jobs' – before starting her teaching career at Haberdashers' Aske's Boys' Prep. Deputy head of the NLCS First School, then moved briefly to Spain for her husband's work. On her return, spent three years as head of Channing Junior School. Warm, can-do sort of person, excellent at team building (her last three directors of studies have moved on to headships elsewhere) and involving others. Cares passionately about education (part of a recent sabbatical was spent visiting schools in New York) and those in her charge. 'She knows every girl well,' said one mother, 'and really fights for their happiness.' Married to an accountant, with two adult daughters (both of whom attended the school), she spends off-duty moments cooking, visiting the theatre and walking.

Entrance: Some 250 try for 40 places at 4. A first edit establishes whether children have good basic 'pre-school' skills (such as holding a pencil and being able to use it) and takes numbers down to 90. A second evaluates 'learning, listening and following'. 'They look at pictures, play games, engage in conversation.' Reading and writing definitely not required. 'They will not be asked,' says the head firmly. Children assessed carefully in relation to those of the same age. ('There's rarely a month's difference in their assessment groups.') Much time spent, too, working with nurseries to encourage applications. An early refusal does not mean don't ask again. 'We try to get across to parents that, if a child is not ready at 4, please bring them back at 7.' At that point, a further 8-10 places, with about 127 applicants, again assessed in two rounds. 'We want to know what they can do, not what they can't; we'd rather they spelt "enormous" wrong than "big" right.' Also assessments for occasional places for those already registered.

Exit: Virtually all to the senior school (90 to 95 per cent). 'We're aiming to provide an all-through education and the expectation is that girls will move up to the senior school.' All sit the entrance test, however: 'Our research shows that it gives them confidence they're as good as those coming from outside.' For one or two this might not be the right route, and parents are advised well in advance. 'The art is to make the right decision for each girl.' Some girls leave to board, a trickle to leading state schools, such as Henrietta Barnett and

Watford Grammar School for Girls, but no cramming for entrance tests. 'We prepare them for secondary education not for 11+,' says the head. 'Our aim is to instil a love of learning and a breadth of opportunity.'

Remarks: North London is, as it always has been, an unashamedly academic school, whose aim is 'to enable girls to recognise academic excellence and realise that it's attainable'. This is achieved through outstanding teaching and a holistic approach to learning, not by hot competition. Here the goal is always 'personal best' rather than 'beat your neighbour'.

National curriculum followed throughout, but work often goes well beyond and around it. (In years 2 and 3, for example, girls learn to play chess.) Classes throughout primarily taught by a form teacher, with specialist subject teaching introduced early on. Senior school staff ease final year girls into their prospective home, though the junior school also has its own subject specialists. A medley of foreign languages on offer (Spanish in year 3, German in year 4, Mandarin in year 5, French in year 6) as an introduction to the senior school range.

'Learning habits' (flexibility of mind, empathy, collaboration, resilience, reflectiveness, good judgement, self-assurance, curiosity, focus, risk-taking, persistence, initiative, originality) introduced early and made explicit. Year 6 guides on our trip were fully genned up on the terminology, pointing out their 6-year-old peers in full creative flow ('We're making pop-up sea creatures,' said one year 1. 'It's very creative and very fun,' glossed an older girl).

Golden Book Oscars awarded for best author, etc, with teachers striding the literary red carpet dressed as Voldemort and other fictional stars

Homework from the off, with reading and spelling in reception and year 1. Older girls get about 40 minutes. 'It's not all work, work, work,' said one. 'You don't feel scared or embarrassed if you can't finish.'

Two school libraries, clearly much-loved habitats. Golden Book Oscars awarded for best author, etc, with teachers striding the literary red carpet dressed as Voldemort and other fictional stars. Prominently displayed list of 50 Books to Read Before You Leave Junior School ('I've read 47,' confided one year 6), with 'more mature' literature for the eldest.

Special needs carefully monitored. 'We look out for obvious signs in assessment,' says the head. 'We're very attuned to early identification.' Strong in-school support, led by a SENCo, for those with dyspraxia, etc. 'Every case has a conference.' The site itself works well for those facing physical challenges, and the school has, when required, incorporated additional aids, such as a hearing loop.

'She knows every girl well,' said one mother, 'and really fights for their happiness'

Extracurricular – 'the hidden curriculum' – very much the bedrock of a North London education, whatever your age or stage, and girls here are active and energetic participants, whether in the latest theatrical production or music competition. A multitude of after-school clubs (with late transport on offer) ranges from cookery to bridge, and many take a range of three or four activities each week.

Drama important, with an annual play for each year group and a major year 6 extravaganza. 'It feels like a professional play,' said one, 'with costumes and make up.' Over 90 per cent learn one or more musical instruments, with plenty of performance opportunities. (Two all-comers' choirs, plus an auditioned year 5/6/7 choir competing on the international stage.) Games three time a week, plus swimming lessons, plus after-school sports club, plus school teams. 'Squads are very exciting,' said one girl (and perform well against other schools).

Like its senior counterpart, the junior school was founded by the formidable Frances Mary Buss, one of the Victorian era's most dynamic crusaders for women's education. The school originated in Camden Town, but, in 1929, purchased Canons, the former home of the Duke of Chandos. The First School (reception to year 2) opened in 1993. Today, the junior school is housed in its own building, in two separate parts, one for the First School (with its own hall, library, adventure playground and playhouse); the other for years 3-6 (with a science lab, ICT suite and art studio). Girls also make use of the large, leafy grounds, senior school's excellent sports facilities (including pool) and dining hall.

Older girls poised, purposeful and articulate. An encounter with representatives of the junior school council demonstrated school democracy in action. Their aim: 'to improve the school'; their achievements: the introduction of an adventure playground, a bird feeder, a poetry competition (with a cup) and a raffle (with the prize of shadowing the head for a day). Sadly, a motion to supply sushi at lunch fell by the wayside.

Classroom teachers take responsibility for pastoral care, with a not-many-rules policy that stems from the founder. Discipline not really a significant issue. 'No one gets in trouble,' said one girl. 'If we do something wrong, we apologise.' Occasionally, there might be 'a warning' (for 'saying a rude word'), even more rarely parents are notified and the miscreant misses break.

More problematic issues dealt with sensitively, aided by a school counsellor and good communication with parents. 'We don't want little problems to become big problems,' says the head. She herself is very involved, with an 'open-door' policy. Parents kept well informed, with a regular curriculum newsletter, home-school diary ('Today x lost a tooth,' read one, the tooth itself carefully enclosed) and plenty of information evenings. 'Parents can be anxious, and we want to make them feel comfortable.' Parents themselves very proactive: 'All you have to do is mention an exhibition and they trot off to the museum.'

The school runs an extensive coach service importing girls from a large swathe of north and west London and Hertfordshire. Families – from all over the world – often have both parents working (so supervised breakfast and after-school care a godsend.)

A stimulating education, provided in an idyllic setting, producing articulate, confident, enthusiastic girls.

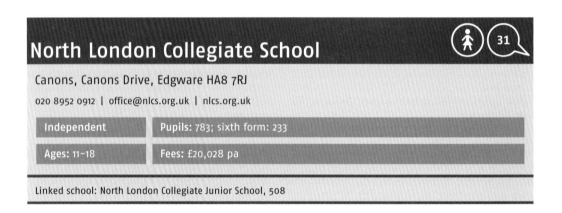

North London Collegiate School

Canons, Canons Drive, Edgware HA8 7RJ

020 8952 0912 | office@nlcs.org.uk | nlcs.org.uk

Independent	Pupils: 783; sixth form: 233
Ages: 11–18	Fees: £20,028 pa

Linked school: North London Collegiate Junior School, 508

Headmistress: Since January 2018, Sarah Clark MA (40s), previously head of The Queen's School, Chester. Read history and classics at Newnham College, Cambridge. Has also been deputy head at Wellingborough School in Northamptonshire. Married to a history lecturer, with two teenage children. Avid supporter of Chelsea FC and loves to cycle, paint and write fiction. Active and breezy, she speaks exuberantly about working in single sex education. 'Girls can really be who they want to be. They don't hold back because they don't feel they need to be cool in the same way they would if there were boys around.' We hear she has been extremely hands on and immersed in school life from day one.

Academic matters: North London provides an unashamedly ambitious, academic education, consistently sitting in the top five schools nationally in terms of its exams results. In the sixth form, it is one of the rare London schools to offer both the IB and a mixture of A levels and Pre-Us. Virtually all pupils do outstandingly well in all exams. (In 2018, 85 per cent of A levels were graded A* or A; average IB a disappointing 37, from just seven students. Superhuman outcome at I/GCSE, with 97 per cent A*-A/9-7.) The school puts this down primarily to the quality of the teaching: 'We don't teach to the test, we work well beyond it.' Parents agree teaching is 'inspirational'. 'The staff remain stable but are never allowed to get stale.' Girls are expected to (and do) work very hard, with plenty of homework from the off. 'You work as hard as you need to or want to,' said one recent arrival. Research skills are carefully nurtured and girls learn how to address their workload in a disciplined and organised manner.

Post-GCSE, English, history, physics and maths are notably popular. ('No gender bias! Hurrah!' commented one parent.) Modern languages (six on offer including Mandarin, Russian and Italian) and classics are unusually strong, with Latin for all in years 7-9. Traditionally, many took five AS levels, with many keeping a balance of arts and science, but the new A level regime has reduced this to four, with any slack addressed by 'an independent research essay'. Parents praise the school's flexibility in meeting individual interests, particularly in the sixth form. 'There's no pick-one-from-column-A procedure,' said one father. 'They don't mind if only one girl opts for a subject. They're willing to give one-to-one teaching

> *You could never be bored here, though you might end up exhausted. Every possible interest is catered for, from philosophy to animal welfare*

if necessary.' Girls are free to choose what really interests them. 'They'll only query something if they feel a girl is being pushed by her parents or considering a subject which would put her out of contention for certain degrees.' Equally, however, they won't micro-manage any downside once choices have been made. 'No one told us our daughter wasn't very good at history and much better at English, which she was doing as a fifth AS level. We had to fight for her to be allowed to change.'

About 40 pupils have some kind of learning support. All receive an 'individual education plan', with students seen by a SENCo without losing lesson time. Despite its extensive and complex site, the school is also happy to cope with physical disabilities – 'as long as the pupil can communicate and access the curriculum' – working with parents to ensure the right support is in place.

Games, options, the arts: You could never be bored here, though you might end up exhausted. Every possible interest is catered for, from philosophy to animal welfare. Last year, pupils had a choice of 40 clubs and societies, 30 overseas trips and 30 concerts and productions. Actors to the Edinburgh Fringe, musical groups to Tuscany, and eager proto-journalists produced enough journals and publications (50 this year) to stock a newsagent, on topics as diverse as economics to Ebola – not to forget the cutting edge Wintour, named after celebrated old girl Anna Wintour, editor of American Vogue. 'We feel it's the extracurricular involvement which helps produce the academic success. There's something for everyone, something to capture the imagination.' Activities for senior girls take place after school, those for younger ones in the lunch hour. Finding time can still prove a problem. 'Sometimes it's hard to fit it all in,' said a year 8 girl. 'You have to decide.' No doubt, all part of the learning process.

Lacrosse is the dominant sport, though plenty of choice, too, for those not unduly captivated by fresh air and outdoor competition, with a fitness suite, trampolining and dance in a smart new dance 'space'. Well-used and buzzing art department, packed with enthusiasts and a range of high-quality work.

Extensive range of enrichment activities (Duke of Edinburgh, Model United Nations, debating, Young Enterprise) help develop public-speaking skills and an appreciation of the world elsewhere. The school has a strong international perspective and offers exchange programmes with schools in the USA, Australia and Germany. In 2011, North London opened an overseas campus in South Korea, NLCS Jeju, and students have the opportunity to visit the campus and do internships here, with NLCS Dubai new in 2017. Charity also firmly emphasised, including raising money for and teaching at a school in Zambia and visiting a local school for severely disabled children.

Background and atmosphere: Founded in Camden Town in1850 by the formidable Frances Mary Buss, a highly effective crusader in the cause of education for women. (She also established Camden School for Girls, with whom North London continues to share a Founder's Day.) The school bought its current spacious, 30-acre semi-rural site in 1929 to use as a sports ground, and relocated here fully in 1940. The estate formerly belonged to the 1st Duke of Chandos and, during his time, Handel was composer in residence. The central core of the building is a country house of 1760, now joined by a multitude of varied later additions. Pupils appreciate their attractive surroundings. 'It's so beautiful,' said one. 'When I first came here, I was blown away by the grounds.'

> *Active and breezy, she speaks exuberantly about working in single sex education. 'Girls can really be who they want to be. They don't hold back because they need to be cool'*

The atmosphere is calm, orderly, and purposeful, and most find it an enjoyable place to be. A recent arrival from the junior school, when asked if she'd thought about alternatives, said, 'I stayed here, because I couldn't see a fault with the school.' Some parents, however, find it quite protective (a good thing or bad, depending on your perspective).

Though the school is academic and fast-paced, it's not pushy. There are no academic rankings or prizes below the sixth form, for example. That said, a girl who doesn't tick along at the same speed could be less content. 'The academic stuff is just baseline,' said one parent. 'They're expected to get involved in clubs, societies, music, sport and community service.' Some also feel that a girl who needs plenty of validation or isn't super confident may occasionally feel swamped. 'I do know people who have pulled their daughter out, though it's usually more about the parents wanting their girls to be top in everything, which is just not going to happen at NLCS.'

Long list of illustrious old girls includes: Judith Weir, Stella Gibbons, Susie Orbach, Marie Stopes, Stevie Smith, Myfanwy Piper, Dame Helen Gardner, Gillian Tett.

Pastoral care, well-being and discipline: Girls here are generally industrious and motivated and heavyweight disciplinary issues are rare. The general approach can be summarized as: 'give girls plenty of freedom, make them engaged and feel valued'; purpose and focus will then follow. It undoubtedly seems to work, and even the youngest here appear remarkably poised and mature.

This is very much an education preparing girls for life as well as exams. The school feels that single-sex education gives them the freedom and security to experiment and develop confidence. Career aspirations are set high and reinforced with photographs of high-flying former pupils ornamenting the corridor walls. 'Our old girls often work in environments of domineering boys from public schools and hold their own. The school helps give them the courage to do that.' An active alumnae office furthers access to a valuable network. Student voice here is important and heard, with a school council and elected prefects – 'the Big 6' – who play a significant role.

'Our old girls often work in environments of domineering boys from public schools and hold their own. The school helps give them the courage to do that'

Brown and blue uniform for younger girls, sixth formers can do their own things (big shawls this year's 'look'). Most appear stylish and smart, with few fashion extremes.

Pupils and parents: Mainly cosmopolitan, ambitious, middle-class professionals, many of whom run their own business or work in financial services. Girls come from every conceivable ethnic background (over 50 languages spoken at home), but an increasing number of Europeans (French, Dutch, Russian) and Americans, as well as the traditional high percentage of Asian and Jewish families. An extensive coach service, with long arms stretching out north, south, east and west, makes this a far from 'local' school. 'The girls reflect the demographic of London,' said one mother.

Entrance: At 11, 65 places for external applicants (joining 40 or so coming up from the junior school). Apply between June and November of the year before entry, with exams in English and maths in January of the year of entry. About 600 apply, with about 200 interviewed. 'We're looking for teachability and girls who will thrive and flourish with the pace of life here. We want flair and interests, a decent vocabulary and logical ability.' Excellent at establishing whether these qualities exist. 'The interview process is very good,' said one parent. 'It's rare for someone to slip in who isn't suited.' About 20 extra places available at sixth form. Apply between July and November of the year before entry, with tests in four subjects. Occasional places awarded throughout to fill any vacancies, when those already registered will sit appropriate exams.

Though the school is academic and fast-paced, it's not pushy. There are no academic rankings or prizes below the sixth form

Exit: Once girls are in, the expectation is that 'we see them all the way through'. A handful move on after GCSE to co-ed or state schools (but a few find the grass greener elsewhere). No-one asked to leave on the basis of exam results. 'They do not cull,' said one mother. 'Even if a girl is struggling, they'll do everything they can to keep her if she is happy.' Almost all get into their first-choice university, with 25 to Oxbridge in 2018, 13 medics, two dentists and a vet and most to top universities including in the US (seven in 2018, one with a scholarship).

Money matters: North London has always prided itself on being affordable and accessible and offers plenty in the way of scholarships and bursaries. Academic scholarships (of up to 50 per cent of the fees) are awarded on the basis of performance in the entrance exams at 11 and 16. Music scholarships at 11 (girls must pass the entrance exam as well as the audition in which grade 5 is generally the expected minimum). Means-tested bursaries (reviewed annually) range from 10-100 per cent of fees and can be awarded in conjunction with scholarships. Bursary funding is partially underwritten by the South Korean franchise, and the school is looking for other projects to further extend these opportunities.

Remarks: An outstanding school for the girl who is quick and hard working and enjoys being busy and involved. Probably not the ideal place for those who might feel the pressure to be 'top' in an environment where everyone is.

North Primary School

Meadow Road, Southall UB1 2JE

020 8571 7749 | admin@north.ealing.sch.uk | northprimary.co.uk

State		Pupils: 420	
Ages: 4–11			

Headteacher: Since 2015, Nicola Forster BA NPQH PGDip (mid 40s). With a personal pedigree from the best Ealing schools, Ms Forster took a degree in geography and education at Roehampton, before beginning work in the first (of eight) London primary schools. She was promoted from acting head at Hathaway Primary to head at Ryefield Primary, Uxbridge, before joining North Primary, following its troubled spell making headlines over the solar eclipse. Inspired to teach by her mother's example, 'I learnt from an early age how you could influence children's lives through teaching,' she is at ease in her trainers and sportswear ('I'll put on a dress for the town hall!') despite having just run four times round the neighbouring sports fields with the children for Sports Relief.

Parents showed guarded respect; 'It's early days; we all look at results,' said one, who had had experience of four successive heads at the school, but they applauded her candour: 'Her door is open, which parents do like'. Children approached her with ease in the corridor, addressing her formally as 'Mrs Forster' but responding familiarly, 'Yeah, cool!' Divorced with two teenage girls at the local secondary school, she is a keen runner. She has already introduced a new assessment system for the children and plans a shift of emphasis in the curriculum; 'We have very high attainment in literacy and numeracy; I'd like to increase the range'. She has refurbished some of the buildings, including a stylish makeover in a Victorian classroom to create a colourful office for herself and her deputy, and is planning to install a multi-use games area to rival the local boys' independent school. She applauds her school's participation in the national evaluation scheme, Challenge Partners: 'it's really helpful to hear other people's points of view, to help us tighten our systems'. We forecast that, barring rare astronomical incidents, she is on course for a successful run

Entrance: London borough of Ealing admissions criteria. Many come via the outstanding children's centre next door, Grove House. Catchment area includes the residential area west of Hanwell and north of Uxbridge Road. Oversubscribed.

Exit: Most to local secondaries: Villiers, Dormers Wells and Greenford High school are popular choices. Some go to selective state schools: Tiffin, Upton Court.

Remarks: Astoundingly high Sats results have earned this school its reputation. The head attributes much of it to the expertise of the staff and good resourcing; the parents put it down to commitment of the families and community environment. Two form entry with 30 children to a class, supervised by one teacher and a teaching assistant. Despite 98 per cent EAL – 22 different tongues, mainly Indian languages, but some Somali and eastern European – the teaching is in English, and the school is proud of its EAL lead status. There is some EAL support for the 30 per cent who arrive without any English, and bilingual staff throughout the school and offices. The corridors sport a handful of translated signs, but if interpreters are needed, it tends to be informally, by word of mouth, between community groups. Lower than average numbers of SEN, nurtured in individual sessions or small groups in a corner of the hall. One mum was dissatisfied with the SEN support: 'My child has had one-to-one; it has sometimes been a bit tricky'.

'I learnt from an early age how you could influence children's lives through teaching'

The classes are named after flowers (Cornflower, Poppy etc) after the school's address in Meadow Road. No rural signs now; the school is in one of London's more economically deprived suburbs, with twice the national average on free school meals. Drawing from an area between Hanwell and Heathrow airport, and home to a large Asian community, Southall is famed for its productive and hard-working ethos. 'There are very high expectations from parents and teachers,' says the head. A dad acknowledged the pressure this puts on the staff: 'We've had an up and down period in the last few years...recently some teachers left', but he reassured us, 'teachers do get along with the pupils; the pupils are encouraged to achieve'. The head describes the staff as a real blend of ages and genders, some home grown, some from overseas.

A single storey brick and slate schoolroom, with ornamental weather vane, is what remains of North Primary's village school origins. Adjoining is a Victorian arts and crafts extension, in keeping with the scale of the residential street, while additional low-level classrooms from the 1970s spread out into the playground at the rear. 'The premises need a revamp,' said one parent, as the defunct climbing equipment in the rear vouched, but the high ceilings and echoey brick corridors, lined with pegs, lend an air of trusty tradition to the building. The reception and year 1 classes on the ground floor enjoy direct access to the playground, where there is an outdoor classroom, as well as a giant number square and Snakes and Ladders, painted onto the tarmac. Indoors the classes are peppered with scarlet tables and chairs, with carpet-time nooks. Upstairs year 2 was studying the Great Fire, with 3D help from a flame-ridden dolls' house in Pudding Lane. We saw some budding authors, composing alternative endings to traditional fairy tales.

Year 2 was studying the Great Fire, with 3D help from a flame-ridden dolls' house in Pudding Lane. Budding authors were composing alternative endings

The first floor hall houses a gym frame and ropes for PE and accommodates assemblies, including the popular singing assembly, as well as whole school gatherings once a week. Old and new buildings are connected by a modern dining hall, serving a halal menu twice a week, fish and chips with Eve's pudding on the day we visited. Beyond is a corridor resplendent with children's work (design your own Greek urn was our favourite), with a full library at one end. We peeked into a discrete sensory room, for SEN time, and an ICT room, hiding 30 computers inside tip-up desks. The upper floor classrooms are a delightful mix of modern and traditional: whiteboards displaying familiar columns of spellings and fractions, while high-ceilinged rooms are ventilated by the original telescopic winder poles. Lively year 6 classes were in session when we visited, discussing the construction of pyramids, while in a side room, a pair of young boffins were enjoying higher-level learning tasks, cracking a secret code.

Visitors are greeted at the door by a colourful montage of art on the walls, reflecting the diversity of the school, with a collage of religious symbols served up on paper plates, and an appliqué wall-hanging of local landmarks, from the famous Southall water tower to shops selling Asian sweets. In the reception class exotic instruments lay ready to play at one of the many school celebrations: Eid, Easter, Diwali, Holi, Chinese new year; 'It's one big party,' laughs the head. Some take the form of shows for the parents, such as The Elves and the Shoemaker or the traditional nativity play, with contributions from their own Bollywood dance troupe. There's a diverse choice of sports, too, football, cricket, netball and golf, as well as an American football club after school. Sports day is held at the local Spikes Bridge Park. Plentiful after-schools clubs include the three Rs: reading, rugby and recorder, as well as a hip Digismart computer club; some charged extra, some free.

Mindfulness, from year 4, prevents the myriad amusements causing sensory overload. The deputy head keeps a model brain on his desk to teach the children the mechanics of destressing; 'It helps them deal with test situations,' says the head, and 'The stressed child would have a specific adult to link to'. Parents were satisfied there were no serious issues with bullying: 'In the main...it's a misunderstanding more than anything serious,' said one dad, and 'The kids are all respectful to the adults'. Communication with parents was felt to be good; 'there is a system', which includes face-to-face chats with the head or class teacher; 'Morning and night, someone is on the gate,' reassured the head. Emails to the office produce a quick response; 'School is good at getting back to you,' said one mum. The school has a Twitter account and a weekly newsletter, as well as a (disappointingly plain) website. There is a strong parent council – 'Which helps the standards...where some parents have issues, but don't know how to voice them,' said a governor – as well as a student council, which has been known to travel to the town hall for meetings with the mayor. Other school trips include the Kensington museums, the RAF museum and a residential to Surrey for the older ones, while the youngest children's outings include learning to make and post a mother's day card at the post office.

Dressed in their scarlet jumpers and white polo shirts, the children we saw were both relaxed and purposeful as they prepared for a trip to the local sports field. As one dad said, 'The kids feel safe and respected and enjoy going to school'. A strong PTA funds extras, such as new playground equipment, via quiz nights, a ladies' night and the lavish Mela, or summer fête, a cornucopia of sweets. The head was astonished at the generosity of the participants. One parent commented, 'It's a very good community environment, everyone is fairly local, the community helps with volunteering'. Another said, 'Parents are quite involved and do a lot to make sure their children do well... A lot of parents bounce ideas off each other; it's an Asian thing'. Some parents are former pupils. The head is quick to recognise the parental input: 'Children are very focused, families are very supportive; families are ambitious...the parents are like private school parents'.

A fusion of traditional and progressive values makes this school special, from code-breaking science lessons to Bollywood spectaculars, from Gulab Jamun to fish and chips. The community support is palpable and the academic success skilfully orchestrated by the head and watchful governing body, who make the most of the rich diversity among the children, in language, culture and learning. North Primary is clearly a rising star in Ealing's firmament.

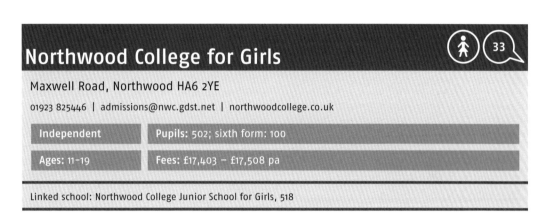

Northwood College for Girls

Maxwell Road, Northwood HA6 2YE

01923 825446 | admissions@nwc.gdst.net | northwoodcollege.co.uk

Independent	Pupils: 502; sixth form: 100
Ages: 11–19	Fees: £17,403 – £17,508 pa

Linked school: Northwood College Junior School for Girls, 518

Head mistress: Since September 2018, Zara Hubble (very youthful looking 40s), previously head of Northwood College junior school. Educated at Westonbirt School and City of London Girls, after which she took a Montessori nursery teaching course then a BEd specialising in KS2 at Southbank University. Cut teeth at St Hilda's in Bushey before joining Heathfield, where she taught year 6 and ultimately became head of year 7. Moved to Northwood as part of merger with Heathfield in 2014, becoming head in 2015. Likeable, calm and poised, with two daughters at university. Keen skier and book lover.

Academic matters: In the ferociously academic context of this corner of North London, school is by no means at the top of the pile when it comes to results – but neither does it either pretend or want to be. Value added is the name of the game and head is delighted to be in top four per cent nationally in relation to this, if not topping academic league tables. Broad-ish church intake, coupled with ethos encouraging every girl to outperform her potential, means that academic superstars can coexist happily alongside their more pedestrian peers, with neither group feeling undue pressure. School more interested in 'building a portfolio of skills relevant to each girl' than cracking the Oxbridge whip – 'girls need a raft of skills beyond the academic. Soft skills can mean the difference between success and failure.' Listen up, neighbouring hothouses.

It's compulsory Spanish in years 7 to 9 in the languages department (not popular with everyone), with French or German as an option. Mandarin on offer from year 9. Classrooms we visited were formal in format – old school even: girls in rows facing the front and lecture style lessons. That said, lessons were interactive (think periodic table bingo) and when questioned in class, the girls we saw were incredibly articulate, confident and considered in their answers. Parents cite RS and English teaching as 'really impressive' and results bear this out, with the former producing 'ridiculously high' grades at GCSE and A level.

Girls take nine or 10 GCSEs from a traditional curriculum with compulsory language and three sciences, plus options including art, classical civilisation, drama, Latin and Greek, home economics, RE and textiles. IGCSEs now taken in some subjects, at the discretion of each departmental head. In 2018, 70 per cent of GCSEs scored A*-A/9-7. Similarly broad choice of A level options, although disappointingly low uptake of the more 'artsy' options – including English, history and languages – reflecting parent demographic aspiring to careers in the sciences for their daughters. 'Our families value STEM subjects,' says school. 'It can be a challenge to persuade them otherwise...but it's one we're happy to grapple with.' After sciences, psychology and RE most popular A level choices. Very respectable A level results in 2018, with 77 per cent A*/B grades and 50 per cent A*/A.

Because large number of girls move through from junior school, any SEN usually identified years before arrival in senior school, with seamless transition a major benefit for girls requiring support. Most mild SENs managed in lessons, with only occasional withdrawals. School supportive of girls pursuing interests or sports to a high level outside of school and will adjust timetable to accommodate if possible. Bespoke programmes occasionally put in place, for example to help girls be more outgoing.

Independent thinking is school's raison d'etre – even, according to the girls we spoke to, above and beyond sport, music or drama. Girls formally taught thinking skills from nursery upwards with a full-time cognitive development director to ensure consistency of message and integration across all parts of the curriculum. Even the youngest in the school evangelise the benefits of eg looking at problem solving from different perspectives – 'teachers don't spoon feed us' and 'we're taught how to learn from our mistakes', we were informed. School is pioneering in its approach and is working towards Thinking Schools International status.

Even the youngest in the school evangelise the benefits of eg looking at problem solving from different perspectives – 'teachers don't spoon feed us'

University application process universally praised by parents and girls. Dedicated full time careers and UCAS advisor delivers 'loads of one-to-one advice,' say parents, plus programme to provide every opportunity for girls to build CV. Teachers described by all as 'really supportive', offering extra classes in preparation for eg medical exams. Visiting advisors are frequent fixtures, eg mock university interviews with admissions staff from Imperial College or staff at nearby Merchant Taylors' and endless internship opportunities both through school portal and GDST – one sixth former we lunched with was spending her summer interning at Nomura thanks to the latter, with another looking forward to her work experience in Beijing via the same route.

Games, options, the arts: Doesn't boast the most gleaming array of facilities we've ever seen and the field is tiny, but for what is essentially a London school, it's as well equipped as it needs to be. Stand out facility is the 25m pool – with everyone swimming all year round and weekly lessons for years 7 to 9. Sports hall has a new climbing wall used both

Academic superstars can coexist happily alongside their more pedestrian peers, with neither group feeling undue pressure

in PE lessons and by clubs. Gym also attractive and well equipped, apparently well used at lunch times by older girls. PE and games compulsory to year 11. Tons of extracurricular sports on offer to suit all tastes – hockey, karate, basketball, you name it. Try as we might, we couldn't get the girls we met to extol the virtues of school's sporting prowess and, with just three compulsory games sessions per fortnight on offer, we wondered whether school was perhaps not the most obvious choice for super sporty types. Parents reassured us, however, that cohort includes a number of outstanding gymnasts, swimmers and even a British team triathlete – we stand corrected, but worth investigating further if your daughter is sports mad. The overall message for sport was: 'it's about right'.

Performing arts centre looks newer than it is and includes an excellent drama studio, recital hall with a sprung floor plus well kitted out music tech room and a plethora of instruments from steel drums up. Plenty of opportunities for budding thespians to throw themselves into productions, most recently Narnia for the lower school, and although there's no space for such performances to take place in a grand theatre, the assembly hall does the job. Parents describe music as 'absolutely fantastic' – for all tastes and levels – from a 50 strong orchestra that plays 'everything' from classical to pop, to jazz bands and chamber choir. There's hours of fun to be had leafing through the booklet detailing all the extracurricular activities on offer with something for everyone – from the active to the cerebral.

Background and atmosphere: Founded in 1878 in Endsleigh Gardens, Bloomsbury, with around 25 boarders and a handful of day girls. Headmistress Miss Buchan-Smith, concerned about the unsavoury influence of the Euston area on her girls, moved the school to its current site in Northwood in 1893. The current front building – red-brick late arts and crafts with leaded lights – was opened for 20 boarders and just two day girls. The Briary, next door, accommodated little boys, and although they are long gone, school pays tribute to those who went on to fight and fall in the two great wars with an annual wreath laying at Ypres.

Joined Girls' Day School Trust (GDST) in 2013 as a precursor to joining with Heathfield School (75 per cent of their girls made the move to Northwood), already a member of the Trust, the following

September. Head reports that the governors thought 'long and hard' before taking up the rare offer of membership and all are delighted that belonging has not changed the culture of the school at all, 'merely provided a plethora of opportunities that a standalone school doesn't have'. Northwood girls now benefit from participation in GDST music and sport competitions, eligibility for travel scholarships, participation in conferences on eg Oxbridge application, as well as access to an alumni network numbering some 75,000 members, bringing a healthy pool of work experience and internships from which to fish. Staff also benefit from additional training and development opportunities, which bears obvious fruit in the classroom.

Most striking to visitors is the calm – almost serene – atmosphere that pervades the school. Smiling faces are everywhere to be seen and parents and girls report nothing but kindly and supportive behaviour between girls

Beyond the main building and with notable exceptions (the quaint William Morris-esque, parquet floored reception area and quirky, characterful library) the site wouldn't win any beauty contests and space is at a premium, but the combination of disparate buildings somehow hang together nicely in their urban setting to create a cosy atmosphere – and all aspects are highly functional. The homely sixth form common room buzzes with chatter. Most striking to visitors is the calm – almost serene – atmosphere that pervades the school. Smiling faces are everywhere to be seen and parents and girls report nothing but kindly and supportive behaviour between girls.

Pastoral care, well-being and discipline: Minor transgressions only in the main and these, mainly tiny bumps in the road to adolescence, reportedly dealt with 'brilliantly and sensitively' according to parents who were full of praise for the pastoral side of Northwood life. Reports of girls experiencing 'the grass is always greener' effect and returning within weeks of departure, particularly for other sixth forms. 'There's just something about Northwood,' said one mother: 'everybody knows everyone'. 'Incredibly strong' house system plays into this, with fiercely fought competitions ('the life blood of the school', according to one pupil) in anything and everything, the highlight being the house music competition in which every girl participates. Bullying is a 'no go zone', say pupils. Older girls pick up concerns of their younger peers and head reports 'very few' eating disorders or instances of self harm – highly commendable in an academic girls' school – 'we don't value aggressiveness'. What about lost sheep? 'We grab hold of concerns early and work in partnership with parents.' Indeed, parents appreciate this approach and seize opportunities to attend school for talks on subjects such as social media and cyber bullying.

Pupils and parents: Majority from British Asian backgrounds although all cultures and religions represented (there's a multi-faith prayer room for free use by girls as and when) and a more sensible and earnest cohort you'd be hard pushed to find. No reports of cliques, with the majority of non-Asian parents relishing the opportunity for their daughters to 'stay younger a little bit longer' due to the positive influence of other cultures. Wide reaching coach routes transport girls from Ealing, Edgware, Kenton, Gerrards Cross and Radlett. Proximity to Northwood station on the Metropolitan line gives easy access from both directions.

Entrance: Girls joining senior school from other prep or junior schools take the London 11+ Consortium cognitive ability test, with great emphasis on the interview. Another 20 or so join for A levels, with places conditional on GCSE results plus online test and interview. Occasional places in other year groups so worth a call if you're moving into the area.

Exit: Almost all stay on for A levels with vast majority moving on to Russell Group or new universities. Just one to Oxbridge in 2018 (English and French); this explained by school's demographic with hard working, dual income families often not wanting daughters to move away for uni – hence many take places up at London colleges or others within commutable distance. Generally several medics.

Money matters: A few means-tested bursaries – up to full fees for particularly deserving cases. Scholarships for academics, art, music and sport.

Remarks: If neighbouring options are too academic, too large or too aggressive, Northwood is (in the words of Goldilocks) just right. Unfettered access to a world of opportunities in a supportive and purposeful culture await. In the words of one parent: 'girls come out happy, healthy and rounded'. What more could you want?

Northwood College Junior School for Girls

Maxwell Road, Northwood HA6 2YE

01923 825446 | admissions@nwc.gdst.net | northwoodcollege.co.uk

Independent	Pupils: 400
Ages: 3–11	Fees: £11,280 – £14,700 pa

Linked school: Northwood College for Girls, 515

Acting head: Deputy Julie Maloney is holding the reins until a new head joins in January 2019.

Entrance: Oversubscribed for entry at 3+ and 4+ with around three applicants for every place. Gently selective with nursery and reception places offered after observation in play. Head meets all parents: 'we're looking for children who are ready for school.' Up to 10 new places at 7+, when applicants are assessed in maths, English and reasoning and by interview.

Exit: Almost all to senior school at 11+ with a small handful taking up state grammar places most years.

Remarks: Three purpose built buildings on same site and a handy hop, skip and jump from senior school – handy when girls reach year 6 and start to take a few lessons with their soon-to-be secondary teachers. Delightful Bluebelle House is home to early years girls – designed with a wonderful playground, outdoor explorer area (minibeast heaven), masses of IT and spacious, airy and inspiring classrooms where girls learn Spanish via action songs, yoga and ballet from age 3. Three reception classes of up to 20 girls also enjoy this space with life skills such as resilience already high on the educational agenda. Lessons we observed were engaging and interactive and girls highly articulate. Years 1 and 2 in Vincent House, with junior school housing years 3 to 6 – both immaculate, modern houses, with every available space proudly adorned with colourful art and meticulous handwritten work. Benefits from sharing facilities including swimming pool, sports hall and science block with senior school.

Not a negative word to be heard from parents – 'they've really brought our daughter out of herself – we love the inclusive atmosphere', raved one and indeed girls are nurtured rather than pushed and, happily, few are denied the right to move into the senior school. Majority from British Asian backgrounds although all cultures and religions represented (there's a multi-faith prayer room for

free use by girls as and when) and a more sensible and earnest cohort you'd be hard pushed to find. Thinking skills – pioneered by the whole school from nursery through to year 13 – taken very seriously by all with pupils able to explain the purpose of De Bono thinking hats with enthusiasm and clarity. All girls screened for SEN in year 4 and supported in small groups either within or outside the classroom. Around 30 girls receive EAL help.

Not a negative word to be heard from parents – 'they've really brought our daughter out of herself – we love the inclusive atmosphere'; girls are nurtured rather than pushed

Despite parents admitting that 'the academic is the most important thing,' school works hard to ensure balance with a dazzling array of extra-curricular clubs which take place either at lunch time or after school. Something for everyone, with all major sports represented, ballet, martial arts, masses of opportunities for musicians to do their thing and everything else from outdoor explorers and gardening to newspaper club. 'Really extraordinary' major stage production each year – recently The Wizard of Oz – with the whole of year 6 participating and many behind the scenes roles up for grabs for lower year groups. Super catering, with lunches (included in fees) freshly prepared on site and all girls from reception up eating together in dining room. Hot suppers also available (charged as extra) up to 6.00pm and there's a breakfast club from 7.45am – great for working parents.

We spoke to parents who had wanted their girls to have the option of moving to other secondaries at 11+ and won places at – in some cases – arguably more high flying schools. Invariably, none wanted to leave, thanks in no small part to the clever balance of nurture and academic rigour they enjoyed at Northwood. Definitely one for the list if you want an all-through, rounded education – not to mention avoiding the 11+ frenzy...

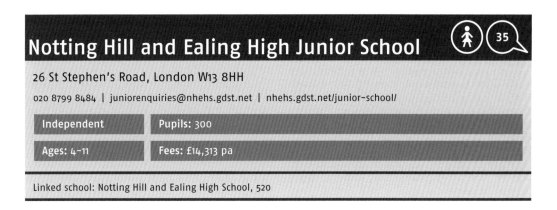

Notting Hill and Ealing High Junior School

26 St Stephen's Road, London W13 8HH

020 8799 8484 | juniorenquiries@nhehs.gdst.net | nhehs.gdst.net/junior-school/

Independent	Pupils: 300
Ages: 4–11	Fees: £14,313 pa

Linked school: Notting Hill and Ealing High School, 520

Head: Since 2013, Silvana Silva BEd (50s). She arrived at the school as a year 4 class teacher in 1989 and has stayed ever since. Deputy head for 11 years before taking the top job. A north Londoner by background, she attended St Michael's Catholic Grammar School in North Finchley and did her degree at Roehampton University. She always wanted to teach and previously taught at primary schools in west London. 'But as soon as I walked in here in 1989 I thought, this is for me,' she says. 'Everything has always been new and exciting.'

A positive, energetic and sympathetic head, she is very proud that the school was named as the Sunday Times independent prep school of the year in 2018. Much liked by pupils and parents. 'We offer academic excellence in a happy and relaxed environment,' she says. 'The girls have to be happy and they are our number one priority. Pastoral care is paramount for us.'

She still teaches both reception classes once a week and says it's the best part of her job. 'It's really important to get to know all the girls and their personalities,' she says. 'They are full of life and joy and love telling me about their day.

Married (her husband works for John Lewis), with one son who is doing his PhD at UCL. She's a great believer in 'healthy mind, healthy body' and in her spare time enjoys going to the gym, theatre and spending time with her family.

Entrance: The two main entry points are 4+ and 7+. At 4+, 100 applicants try for 40 places – two reception classes of 20 each. The girls are observed in groups of three or four doing 'nursery style activities' (playing, interacting and talking to junior school teachers). No formal reading or writing required. At 7+, 30 to 40 apply for an additional eight year 3 places. Girls are tested in maths, writing and verbal reasoning. Girls who do well in the test are invited back for a short, informal interview and a tour. The school is full but places occasionally come up in other years (mainly due to families relocating).

Exit: Virtually all progress to the senior school at the end of year 6. Confirmed, unconditional offers of places for the senior school are made in the spring term of year 5. The juniors still take the senior school entrance test with outside applicants though – so they can be considered for scholarships on an even footing. A few leave at 11 for other senior schools (such at St Paul's Girls', Godolphin & Latymer and Lady Eleanor Holles) but the assumption is that once they join the junior school they're here for the duration.

Remarks: The national curriculum is watched but certainly not slavishly followed. Girls do key stage 2 Sats – the head says teachers find them useful to track the girls' progress. 'It's all very low key,' she adds. 'There is a bit of preparation but no angst about them. It's just part and parcel of what we do.' Teachers focus on developing literacy and numeracy, with daily lessons in each subject. The school is rightfully proud of its integrated curriculum, introduced eight years ago. Designed 'to give meaning to humanities subjects', each year group from year 1 to year 6 is given a theme (anything from pirates to the First World War). When we visited year 6 pupils were studying the geography of the First World War battlefields and having philosophical discussions about what is worth fighting for.

Most subjects are taught by class teachers but science is led by a dynamic former research scientist from King's College London. She teaches girls from year 1 and enthuses them about the subject from the start – everything from snail races to learning how to purify water. 'We need to get girls passionate about science from a young age,' she says. Computing (lots of coding) and Mandarin are taught from year 1 onwards. French and German are offered as after-school clubs. Other clubs run at lunchtime and after school include computing, sewing, animation, art, touch typing and yoga.

Sensible levels of homework. Reception pupils get reading every evening, year 1s take spellings home and year 2s and up have homework – once a week in year 2, four nights a week in year 5 and every night in year 6 (but only for 30 minutes). Every so often homework is suspended and girls take part in an 'open homework' project – subjects range from hopes and dreams to heroines (choices included Mother Theresa, Rosa Parks and Malala Yousafzai; one girl nominated her granny). Girls have two PE lessons a week (gym, dance, netball, cricket), with weekly swimming from reception through to year 4.

The school is academically selective so while some have learning support for dyslexia and dyscalculia they must be able to cope with the pace of the curriculum. Support given one-to-one or in small groups. Strong links with the senior school. Girls from years 7 and 10 come and read to their junior counterparts, year 12s run a Minimus Club for year 4 girls and many pop in to say hello to their former teachers. Music, led by a former professional opera singer, is a tour de force. Girls take instrumental lessons from year 3 and there's an 80-piece orchestra. Plenty of opportunities to perform in concerts, bands and choirs too.

The junior school is located in a well-kept Victorian villa on a quiet residential road. It's on

She previously taught at primary schools in west London. 'But as soon as I walked in here I thought, this is for me,' she says

the same site as the senior school, with a green Astroturf, playground and south-facing garden at the back. Whole school assemblies are held twice a week in the junior hall but the junior girls also use the senior school's impressive hall and indoor swimming pool. The girls, in jaunty navy and red uniforms, walk across to the senior dining room for lunch. They all belong to one of four teams which compete for an annual team cup. Great emphasis placed on self-esteem, confidence and being happy at school and as girls progress through the school they take on responsibilities such as acting as 'playground pals' to younger pupils and elected reps on the school council.

Most pupils live relatively nearby. The majority have two working parents (lots of doctors, lawyers and media types) and the school runs a breakfast club from 7.30am and an after-school club till 6pm, both run by staff rather than an outside agency.

An academically excellent school that nurtures its pupils and helps them to develop into happy, confident girls. The head says that it's vital that the girls are happy – and they really are.

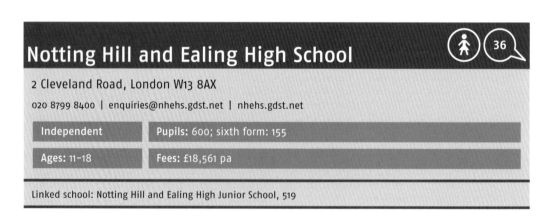

Notting Hill and Ealing High School 36

2 Cleveland Road, London W13 8AX

020 8799 8400 | enquiries@nhehs.gdst.net | nhehs.gdst.net

Independent	Pupils: 600; sixth form: 155
Ages: 11–18	Fees: £18,561 pa

Linked school: Notting Hill and Ealing High Junior School, 519

Head: Since January 2017, Matthew Shoults MA (40s). Educated at King's College School, Wimbledon, then read classics at Worcester College, Oxford. Spent two years on the civil service's graduate fast track scheme before deciding he wanted to be a teacher. After doing a PGCE at Cambridge he taught classics at King's, his old school, for four years. Moved to North London Collegiate School as head

of classics, becoming deputy head and then senior deputy. After 12 years there he was appointed to the top job at Notting Hill and Ealing High School.

The first male head in the school's 145-year history, he was struck from the start by its warmth and friendliness. During his first visit one girl told him: 'It's a school of conversations,' while another said: 'The teachers trust and believe in us.' 'Yes, it's academic,' he says, 'but it's a happy place to be. It's our job to nurture the girls – and nurture their ambitions. It's incredibly easy to progress here.' Parents are impressed by his energy and dynamism and like the fact that he's very visible around the school. 'He's bringing in new ideas and is really good for the school,' one told us. Another said that the girls respected him and found him 'down-to-earth and easy to talk to'. Head has launched a drive to get as many pupils as possible involved in public speaking. We attended morning assembly during our visit and after notices about the forthcoming inter-house maths challenge and an appeal for clothes and toiletries for refugees, a group of engaging sixth form girls led a presentation about how languages affect the way we think. The head encourages pupils to come up with new ideas – girls often put their heads round his door and say 'I've had an idea'. Recent suggestions, both implemented, saw the launch of a dissection society and an origami club.

Head sees all year 11s as they decide their A level choices and all year 13s before they leave. He teaches public speaking and debating to all year 7 pupils so he can get to know them, will teach Greek to sixth formers next year and already spends time helping girls with their university applications. He often describes people as 'a good egg' and was amused when sixth formers presented him with an egg box labelled 'a pack of good eggs'. Inside were six decorated eggs, one depicting the head. In his spare time he plays the violin, sings, does cryptic crosswords and 'spoils' his three godchildren. He's also a third of the way through climbing Scotland's 282 Munros.

Academic matters: Results are impressive – 92 per cent A*/A/9-7 at GCSE in 2018 and 65 per cent A*/A at A level. Most popular A level subjects tend to be maths, biology and chemistry but arts and sciences are equally represented. Girls can take virtually any combination of subjects (luckily the assistant timetabler used to be a railway timetabler) and even if only one or two girls want to do an A level subject the school will run it. Most take three or four subjects at A level (25 subjects to choose from, including history of art, economics, psychology and politics) and 10 or 11 at GCSE. EPQ is growing in popularity for sixth formers and year 12 students take a variety of enrichment courses, choosing from an eclectic list of topics, from medieval art to the psychology of happiness.

Languages are strong here. All study Mandarin in years 7 and 8, plus either French, German or Spanish. Most take two languages at GCSE. Excellent take-up of Mandarin at GCSE with two-thirds of grades A* in 2018 (18 entries in all). There's also a biennial trip to China. Latin is taught from year 8, with classical Greek offered from year 10.

Class sizes of around 24, with maths the only subject set (from year 8). 'We want to create a sense that they aren't competing against each other,' says the head. 'It's how they are doing themselves that's important.'

Two dedicated learning support staff offer extra help where needed. Parents say the academic side of the school is 'very solid' and praise the way it helps new year 7s transition to senior school life. 'They want to them to settle in their friendship groups and develop their confidence before the work ramps up,' said one mother.

Games, options, the arts: Sport is important (at the time of our visit the new director of sport had been shortlisted for the London's sports teacher of the year award). The site is compact but clever architects have managed to fit a lot into the space. New four-court sports hall is impressive, as are the Astroturfs and 25-metre indoor pool. Sixth formers can train as life guards. The new extension to the school has added a stunning rooftop dance studio and fitness gym, with views across the school. All pupils take part in sport, from mainstream sports like netball, hockey, tennis and athletics to activities like cross-country, trampolining, running, badminton, cricket, football, zumba, yoga and kickboxing. Many notable local and national successes, including winning the year 7 Middlesex cricket tournament and reaching the national finals in under-14 netball.

An enterprising sixth former was busy organising a fashion show at the school and had fixed for a national newspaper fashion editor and a representative from a well-known sports brand to attend

Music is a real strength of the school. A multitude of individual music lessons and plenty of opportunities to play in orchestras and ensembles and sing in choirs. Recent choral tours to Barcelona, Florence and Croatia. Less experienced musicians get the chance to build their confidence by performing in atrium concerts. Parents say drama is 'fantastic' (there's a studio space as well as the main hall). School play every year, with girls designing the sets, lighting and costumes as well as performing and directing. Art department is vibrant and exciting, boasting three purpose-built studios kitted out with everything from digital scanners to a printing press. Several girls a year head to do art foundation and architecture courses.

Vast range of extracurricular clubs, many of them student led. Work experience is compulsory in year 11 and most girls find their own placements. On the day of our visit an enterprising sixth former was busy organising a fashion show at the school and had fixed for a national newspaper fashion editor and a representative from a well-known sports brand to attend.

Background and atmosphere: The oldest school in the Girls' Day School Trust (GDST) portfolio, Notting Hill and Ealing High School was founded in Notting Hill in 1873 and moved to leafy Ealing in 1930. The site has been transformed in recent years – a dazzling reworking of the central core of the school retained the school's period façade and a sleek glass extension has been added at the rear, with a spacious library, ultra-modern assembly hall, music recital hall, recording studio and sports hall. The extension looks out over a tree-lined courtyard with lots of benches to sit on during the summer months. Parents like the school's size. 'It's like Goldilocks,' said one. 'Neither too hot nor too cold. Neither too big nor too small.'

Parents are impressed by his energy and dynamism and like the fact that he's very visible. 'He's bringing in new ideas and is really good for the school,' one told us

Sixth formers enthuse about their sixth form centre, a former children's home a five-minute walk away from the main site and equipped with six classrooms, common room, gym and café serving sandwiches, jacket potatoes, pasta, tea and coffee. Sixth form classes are small, girls don't have to wear uniform (no midriffs and no strappy tops) and they can go home in the afternoon if they don't have lessons. 'The sixth form girls like the fact that they get the support and outward-facing perspective but we aren't cocooning them,' says the head. Parents agree. One told us that her daughter had thrived in the sixth form. 'The environment is very nurturing but they are treated as adults too,' she said. Head of the sixth form reminds the girls of the importance of maintaining a healthy work-life balance – 'the vast majority are very sensible,' she says. Plenty of opportunities for leadership roles. Contenders for the role of head girl have to write a letter of application, make a speech and have an interview. All sixth formers are school reps and there's also a six-strong head girl team (including a sports captain).

Strong emphasis on helping others – girls of all ages raise money for chosen charities by running cake sales, nearly new sales, games and raffles. Strong links with the local community, including a Saturday morning Mandarin club for primary school children and a netball tournament for nearby primary schools run by year 10 girls.

Pastoral care, well-being and discipline: This is a school where pastoral care is prioritised as much as academic drive. When the head arrived he was struck by how 'joined-up' the pastoral care is. It's overseen by senior deputy head (pastoral) and staff work closely with parents. Heads of year meet form tutors every week to problem-solve and discuss any concerns. Girls can also talk to the school nurse and counsellor.

New year 7s are well supported via the big sister scheme (year 12s act as big sisters to them, offering help when they need it). Other activities include a picnic with year 8s and the chance to write a letter to their future selves, expressing their hopes and ambitions. Much to their delight, they receive it back in year 11.

All the girls we met were enthusiastic about being in an all-girls' school. 'It's far more relaxed without boys,' one told us. Parents say that issues and concerns are handled well – 'in a very thoughtful and individualised way'. In years 7 to 11 girls have to put their mobile phones in lockers when they arrive at school – 'if they are spotted with their phone we have a word with them,' says the head.

Pupils and parents: The pupils we met were enthusiastic, outgoing and full of charm. One parent told us that the girls were six months behind their central London counterparts when it came to social life and teenage parties– 'and we are very grateful for that,' she added. Girls predominantly come from Ealing, Chiswick, Hammersmith, Harrow, Notting Hill, Richmond and Kew. Travel links are good and 70 per cent travel in by public transport –tube, train and bus (the bus from Ealing Broadway stops right outside the school). They are a very grounded group of girls – 'in touch with reality,' says the head. Most parents work (lots of doctors, lawyers and media types).

Distinguished alumnae include historian Bettany Hughes, Labour MP Rupa Huq, stand-up comic Pippa Evans, London Grammar singer Hannah Reid and 2018 GDST alumna of the year Nirupa Murugaesu, the clinical lead for molecular oncology at Genomics England.

Entrance: Very oversubscribed but doesn't give out application numbers – 'because we don't want to put parents off'. Around 45 girls move up from the junior school each year, with another 50 coming from local primaries and preps. The school is a member of the London 11+ Consortium and entry now consists of a 75-minute cognitive ability test incorporating verbal, non-verbal and maths questions. All applicants to the senior school have a one-to-one interview. 'We are looking for girls with an inquiring nature,' says the head. 'We don't have a type. One of the fundamental aims of the school is for them to be themselves.'

Six or seven girls join the sixth form from other schools. Assessment is via a single paper consisting of a short essay on a subject of topical interest or news event, plus interviews with subject teachers and head of sixth form.

Exit: A handful leave after GCSEs, usually for co-ed independents and state schools. Some decide to head back within a few weeks and the school accommodates them if it can. Virtually all go straight to university (very few gap years), majority to Russell Group with five to Oxbridge in 2018. Recent exceptions include one girl who got a highly-prized BBC apprenticeship and another who opted to train as

a pilot. One or two a year head to US universities (head thinks numbers will grow).

Money matters: The GDST has been providing high-quality academic education at a reasonable cost for nearly 150 years and Notting Hill and Ealing High does exactly that. Academic scholarships worth up to 50 per cent of the fees and music scholarships worth 10 per cent of the fees are available for year 7s. For those entering the sixth form there are academic, art music, sport and drama scholarships worth five to 10 per cent of the fees. Means-tested bursaries available too (scholarships can be supplemented by these).

Remarks: A forward-looking school that provides a stimulating education in a friendly and nurturing environment. Academic achievements are excellent and these energetic, exuberant girls are definitely a force to be reckoned with.

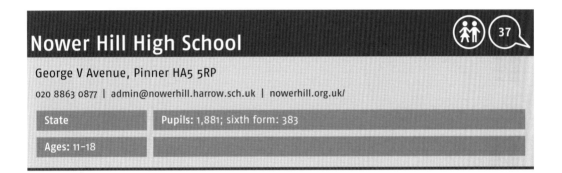

Nower Hill High School

George V Avenue, Pinner HA5 5RP

020 8863 0877 | admin@nowerhill.harrow.sch.uk | nowerhill.org.uk/

State	Pupils: 1,881; sixth form: 383
Ages: 11–18	

Head: Since 2012, Chris Livesey, BA from London in modern history. A Cheshire lad, who moved to London for his degree, continued his studies there (PGCE) and never went back: 'My first teaching job was at a comprehensive school in Wembley, and then I became deputy head at Nower High, where I stayed for the next 15 years before becoming head. I've basically had two long services in two schools.' Although he is loathe to admit that he must have been the natural choice to succeed the much respected former head teacher, we think few would've expected otherwise. One parent told us: 'Mr Livesey was always a well-respected deputy head and classics teacher and was always very visible.' Mr Livesey says that when he was offered the role of head teacher, he was 'extremely flattered to be entrusted with such a role at such a school' and wants to ensure that he gives the role his utmost level of commitment and hard work.

At 50+ years old, Mr Livesey manages to successfully combine a friendly and youthful demeanour with a straight up, very headmasterly, no-nonsense approach. One parent commented that 'children

really like him, but when he walks in the room there is complete silence.' He loved his own schooling and as a result remains passionate about education. 'I went to an independent school in Cheshire – school was fantastic.' This head doesn't strike us as someone who will ever take his job for granted; quite the contrary – he enthuses about his loyal and committed staff, 'a very strong team of senior leaders, teachers and support staff', the lovely pupils and the general vibe of the place: 'You only have to look at the school's history to see that since it first opened its doors in 1929, the school has only ever had seven head teachers.' Heads, it seems, are at Nower Hill for the long haul.

He insists on a clean and tidy school. One parent told us: 'Mr Livesey is forever picking up litter and he never asks anyone to do it for him.' And his presence has been noted by many: 'He is always on the school gates and walking around the school. He is transparent in a good way. He doesn't hide how he feels about where he wants the school to be.' Punctuality is very important to him, and he himself has something of a daily commute from

Twickenham Preparatory School

Richmond where he lives with his wife (an assistant head teacher in Richmond) and their three children.

Academic matters: This Ofsted outstanding school is well known in the area for its academic standards. One local parent told us: 'Nower Hill has always had a good reputation, now it has an excellent one.' Part of its success could be down to its class sizes of 25 pupils, spread across 12 forms in a year group, part of it could be down to the dedicated teachers 'who always have their lines of communication open to parents' to the point where one parent told us: 'I feel a bit sorry for the teachers. They work so hard during the day and then call or email us back straight away if we have a query.' Ofsted said: 'The leadership of teaching and learning is exceptional.' And the head added that part of the school's success is that 'we pride ourselves on working hard for all learners.'

One parent told us: 'I feel a bit sorry for the teachers. They work so hard during the day and then call or email us back straight away if we have a query'

In 2018, 75 per cent of students got 9-4 in both English and maths; 31 per cent 9-7 grades. At A level, 64 per cent of all grades were at A*-B, with 33 per cent at A or A*. 'For a not particularly competitive school, they still get the results,' one parent told us. Another said, 'The school does very well at stretching bright children, whilst at the same time providing a round education for everyone.'

The curriculum is wide and varied with 24 optional subjects offered at GCSE level (Mandarin offered as an extracurricular language), with more able students being offered the opportunity to learn ancient Greek and astronomy. An enthusiastic parent told us: 'The options in year 8 are fantastic. Students start their GCSE course in year 9 and they are given a chance to chop and change a bit for the first term and decide if it is the right course for them.'

Each student has been given their own tablet, which they can take home and use for homework. Quite extraordinary in a school of 1,900 pupils and clearly highlights the school's priorities in terms funding. One parent told us: 'It's things like this that make this school so progressive.' The head is quick to point out that this is an educational tool only and that students don't have access to Facebook or Twitter: 'Everything they need has been put on there for them.'

Parents have also welcomed an online app called Show my Homework where students, parents and carers can access homework details and retrieve and submit work online. Students also have their own personal portfolio where they can store all their electronic documents, allowing access to them in or out of school. It is part of the school's Managed Learning Environment (MLE) for which Nower Hill won the award for secondary schools.

Excellent facilities for students with disabilities, including ramps, improved corridor lighting, lifts, handrails on steps, widened doorways for wheelchair access and yellow lines to assist visually impaired students. Roughly 13 per cent of the school intake is registered with an SEN. For those students, a well-supported inclusion staff team is on hand to offer extra support, including a SENCo, qualified SEN teachers, Inclusion manager, behaviour manager, mentor and counsellor. There is also extra support for maths and English

Games, options, the arts: The school has a very long tradition of strength in the arts subjects, which was evident as we walked round. Astoundingly good self-portraits from GCSE students were on display as well as an interesting montage of student-designed film posters. Several of Nower Hill's art students have had their work displayed in local art galleries, national exhibitions and at the Mall Galleries. Many continue their art studies post A level, at well-respected art colleges. Photography also strong.

Drama is popular and taken up in fair abundance. Big scale biannual musicals, which have included The Lion King and Oliver! Watford drama winners recently. The dance department offers a wide range of extracurricular dance activities including contemporary dance, tap, ballet, Bollywood, street dance and modern. There are many performance opportunities available both in and out of school; school productions, a dance showcase, summer extravaganza and a performance at the Royal Albert Hall.

Musical students have a choice of a dozen ensemble music groups and orchestras to take part in, including a soul band, and school hosts concerts several times a year. Some 400 pupils have peripatetic music classes, and groups include everything from steel pan ensemble to African drumming to a full 51 piece school orchestra. Well-equipped recording studios. One pupil told us: 'This school really caters well in all departments and has something for everyone.'

Sports play a big part in the school and there is a wide range of activities. The faculty prides itself on 'giving very generously of its time'. Sports include netball, basketball, handball, rugby, trampolining and indoor athletics. All clubs are fully inclusive. School athletes compete at borough, county and national level with 'considerable success.' Sporting facilities include a 3G Astroturf pitch, two tiered grass playing fields, six tennis courts, six netball courts a multi-purpose sports hall, fitness suite and gymnasium.

A long tradition of strength in the arts. Astoundingly good self-portraits from GCSE students as well as an interesting montage of student-designed film posters

Aspiration is definitely a buzz word at Nower High, and an Aspire programme is run on Wednesday and Thursday lunchtimes for Y12 and Y13. This programme helps to develop 'interview, thinking and critical analysis skills, provides personal feedback and mentoring' to ensure students have the best possible chance at future employment. Training is also offered to become mentors for younger students and give older students the opportunity to run lower school science, sports and dance clubs as well as a variety of other leadership roles.

This school really puts a big 'C' in charity. It doesn't do things to tick boxes, or to excite an overzealous PTA. Pupils seem to be charitable to the core. When we were there, a dedicated area of the school hall had been given over to black bags, full of clothes and toys for Syrian refugees: 'We like to instill charitable values in children of a young age.' School fundraising events have included a leavers' ball, pizza and quiz event and charity sports fixtures against staff. There is also the opportunity for sixth formers to work voluntarily in an orphanage in Romania as well as with elderly people in the local community. Events are planned throughout the year to raise money for their chosen charity – St Marcellin's Children's Village in Zimbabwe.

Background and atmosphere: Formerly Headstone Council School, this red-brick building on Pinner Road first opened its doors in 1929. The school's purpose was to educate 292 5-14 year olds with an average class size of 50. The school soon expanded to meet the ever-growing number of children resident in rapidly expanding north Harrow and Pinner. Its steady expansion has withstood many a hitch including the Second World War, when many of its male teachers were called up for military service and the playing field was dug up for trenches and air raid shelters.

Redevelopment work continued throughout the 60s and 70s (when the school became Nower Hill) – continuing throughout the 90s, which saw

the start of a £2.75 million development programme, including a new 13 classroom block and the Gristwood Centre, housing music, dance and drama studios, a fitness suite and the sports hall. The school added a sixth form in 2006, which a few years later moved into its £4 million sixth form extension. The site was further enhanced in 2010 by the addition of a block of five science labs and a new English teaching block hosting 13 classrooms. This is one big site.

As a result, the site is a bit of a hotch-potch of buildings, none of them particularly pretty, but functional and purposeful and very much in keeping with large comprehensives. Plus, as every parents knows, schools are much more than bricks and mortar – and this school is so much more. The pupils who showed us around were extremely articulate, warm, kind and very proud of their school. Big mix culturally and harmonious atmosphere. Room after room was explained with equal enthusiasm (even the less aesthetically pleasing ones), and each montage on colourful walls was discussed in detail – especially those of past school trips. We were taken through a labyrinth of corridors and would've lost our bearings many a time if it weren't for our guides. There were a few nice touches we spotted on our tour, most notably the 'ancient' Greek columns outside the classics department (homage, possibly, to the head, who is partial to a bit of classics).

'I won't argue with a child about their hair. It's a very happy environment here'

Other things worth mentioning include the spacious library, well-equipped with books and computers, and six different outlets for food and snacks, including a cold canteen for grab-and-go pastas and salads and a hot canteen. However, one parent did say that the downside of such a large school is the difficulty in accommodating everyone: 'My son finds school dinners all a bit stressful and too much of an effort to have something hot. There are just too many other kids and often nowhere to sit. I think they should stagger it more.' Sixth formers have now been offered the incentive of a £1 coffee and cookie in the common room, instead of traipsing to the local café and wasting valuable time.

Pastoral care, well-being and discipline: Discipline is 'bang on', one parent told us: 'For a school with this many children, you really don't hear of many incidents like bullying etc, and if there are, they are dealt with quickly and appropriately.' By all

The pupils who showed us around were extremely articulate, warm, kind and very proud of their school. Big mix culturally

accounts Mr Livesey is a truly dedicated head, and he expects the same of his staff, where the well-being of his pupils are concerned. One parent told us: 'The teachers always walk out with the kids at the end of the day and often accompany them to the local shops. That way the shop keepers are always reassured that a grown up is with them.' Another said, 'You never ever see any Nower Hill pupils lighting up outside the school gates or nearby, like at other schools. The students here are very aware that they are representatives of the school and they wear their uniform proudly.'

Uniform is a very smart navy affair, with the odd splash of varying colours on the v-neck pullovers denoting the year group. All blazers have the school's crest with the motto 'service not self' emblazoned on it. Although strict on uniform, Mr Livesey does display a softer side, especially when questioned about the assortment of hair colour that passed us by (most noticeably green), on our tour of the school: 'I won't argue with a child about their hair. It's a very happy environment here and that's the main thing.'

In a school of this size, we wondered how feasible it is to oversee the well-being of all students and to prevent the more vulnerable ones from slipping through the cracks: 'We work very hard at keeping a large school, a small school', says the head. And indeed Nower Hill does seem to have a pretty robust infrastructure. There is a full-time attendance officer who works with parents around punctuality and is there to pick up on any possible issues. There are two co-ordinators for every year group and a well-staffed student support team. There are also two peer mentors for new students allocated to each class.

One parent told us: 'This school's motto should be above and beyond. They really do go the extra mile here. The lines of communication are always open if you need to speak to a teacher, and somebody always gets back to you pretty promptly.' Another told us how the school bent over backwards to help facilitate her daughter's studies after a long period absent due to ill health: 'Home tutoring was arranged for my daughter as soon as we needed it and the tutor was very impressed with the excellent support material provided to her from the school.'

Mr Livesey recently reintroduced a new house system to reflect the core values of the school. These six houses have been named after influential people who, together, inspire millions around the globe: Gandhi, King, Shabazz, Franklin, Bannister and Nightingale. The school sees the qualities of being well mannered, articulate, well behaved, hard working, smart and kind as part of the DNA, and reminders are displayed throughout the school. Ofsted said in the last report that: 'Student' behaviour is excellent..the school provides an orderly, welcoming environment entirely conducive to learning.'

The reintroduction of the house system has been welcomed by pupils. One told us, 'It's more fun and you become loyal to your house. It also promotes a healthy competition between the houses on things like sports days.'

As with any school, particularly of this size, disruptive pupils will always be an issue. However, Mr Livesey says that permanent exclusions are below the national average: 'We have very high expectations here. Any poor student behaviour is dealt with in a clear and consistent manner' through what the school calls its Ladder of Consequences. This includes an inclusion centre for students temporarily excluded from lessons, which is equipped with computers and other educational resources.

Pupils and parents: Pupils and parents pretty much reflect the general demographic of the local area of Pinner and north Harrow. Roughly 30 per cent white British, nearly half Asian and the rest a mixture of other ethnicities. Parents are largely professionals, pupils aspirational.

Entrance: Hugely oversubscribed. Approx 1,400 applications are submitted each year group for 324 places. Waiting list system is operated by the local authority. School catchment is roughly a mile, and you'll get in if you have a sibling or a looked after child. However, one unhappy parent told us: 'My only real gripe with the school is that the sibling policy stops at GCSE, so if you have a bigger age gap between your children, there is no guarantee at all that they will get in.'

Exit: Around 40 per cent leave after GCSEs, mostly to do vocational courses elsewhere. Nearly all sixth form students go on to university, with the rest choosing a gap year, an apprenticeship or employment. Quite a few medics and dentists each year; usually a couple to Oxbridge (one in 2018). Oxbridge admissions preparation with academic mentors who have themselves been to Oxford or Cambridge. Popular destinations also include elite art colleges and music conservatoires.

Remarks: If you live in the north Harrow area and are within catchment of this school, applying for it is a bit of a no-brainer.

Orley Farm School

South Hill Avenue, Harrow, Middlesex HA1 3NU

020 8869 7600 | office@orleyfarm.harrow.sch.uk | orleyfarm.harrow.sch.uk

Independent		Pupils: 496	
Ages: 4–13		Fees: £14,160 – £16,335 pa	

Headmaster: Since 2013, Tim Calvey (40s), formerly school's deputy head and art teacher, rocketed to headship following the sudden departure of his predecessor following an 'error of judgement' (worth googling, even just to learn what 'acrostic' means). Hailing from a teaching dynasty, grew up in Zimbabwe in the boarding house run by his father. Passionate about sport and art, got his teaching degree at Christ Church University before cutting his teeth at Northbourne Park School in Kent under an inspirational head 'who pushed all the boundaries,' then landing at Eagle House (Wellington College's prep) around the same time as Anthony Seldon took the helm at the senior school – spending a six year period there that 'shaped him.' In true Seldon style, impassioned by well-being and development – 'we have to find ways to release the pressure children are under.' A challenge indeed in this most competitive of postcodes.

Shades of Gareth Malone – sharp, quirky dress sense, warm charisma, palpable energy and a real human touch. Parents uniformly comment on how informal he is compared to other local prep heads. Happily donned Willy Wonka costume at behest of parent committee at recent Christmas Fair. Pupils describe him as 'effervescent' (well done that child's English teacher), 'enthusiastic' and 'funny' – the first head we have met known to wear Iron Man cufflinks. Rarely have we seen a head teacher so naturally connect with even his youngest charges, all of whom chat away to him merrily. If he ever fancies a change of direction, a career in broadcasting surely awaits. Feels 'huge duty of care' to bright children and warns destination obsessed parents that it's about the journey and that Orley Farm is 'not for them if they just want their child tutored – we don't want to be defined by either the name of the school or our grades.'

Lives on school grounds with wife Rachel, who teaches RS and science at the school, and his three children – all of whom have attended Orley Farm.

Entrance: Vast majority enter at 4+ from as many as 40 different nurseries with places oversubscribed by about three to one. Children are observed participating in a carousel of activities and head is clear: 'don't bother tutoring your 4 year old' – school is looking for 'sparky children' and doesn't expect them to read or write. Occasional places do crop up from time to time, mostly due to relocation, and around 20 places come up for year 7 when many girls, and a few boys, leave for 11+ schools. Short shrift given if potential parents are looking for prep merely as springboard to top schools. 'Have I put parents off with this attitude?' muses head. 'Probably.'

Exit: Huge breadth of destination schools with an impressive number to top academic schools (St Paul's, Westminster, Merchant Taylors' and Habs for boys and St Paul's, North London Collegiate, City of London and Godolphin & Latymer for girls), as well as Hampton, John Lyon, Aldenham, Northwood College and Notting Hill and Ealing Girls' School. A small handful each year to boarding schools.

Remarks: The only co-ed school in the area, Orley Farm occupies a Tardis-like plot fronted by a Victorian school building, tucked into a leafy residential area away from the less picturesque parts of Harrow proper. Having just finished an £11 million refurb programme, school boasts smart classrooms and facilities galore (barely a tatty corner in sight), plus not only the shiniest dining room for miles around but also a state of the art library designed to inspire the most reluctant of readers. Delightful grounds sprawl behind the main school building, providing space for all manner of activities – as well as the Orley Farm chickens (the box of freshly laid eggs we were given on departure, rather than the usual piles of self-promoting literature, could almost be a metaphor for how this school differs from others). Main playing fields amounting to some 40 acres are over the road, plus separate gym and sports hall, pool and Astroturf – how many London schools can claim such riches?

A holistic vibe in evidence at every turn. Recent introduction of the Creative Curriculum in pre-prep much welcomed by parents who feel it 'brings

Expeditions Week takes everyone from year 4 up all over the place from mountaineering in Wales to 'total immersion' in a French château

topics alive' for the school's youngest pupils, to the extent that they want to do more under their own steam when they get home. The Edge programme, which sees children participate in age-appropriate experiences from planning – then following unaccompanied – a route into central London on public transport to fixing a bicycle puncture or spending time with local elderly people, demonstrates that school is not just paying lipservice to developing EQ as well as IQ. You can't help feeling that an Orley Farm education is about so much more than just powering towards the next school. There is, however, a question mark over how unanimous parents are in supporting this approach – definite rumblings in evidence from those who would like school to fall into line with local academic hothouses and reports of parents demanding homework for their 5 and 6 year olds (then setting it themselves when not forthcoming). This is explicable by school's demographic, typified by its geography. Around 70 per cent of families are Asian, with the vast majority dual income professionals, 'incredibly committed to education,' according to head. Many Harrow School and some John Lyon staff in parent cohort. Pupils, thankfully, come over as carefree, likeable and down to earth – head 'can't stand arrogance.' Teachers reportedly 'go the extra mile' and pre-prep parents are delighted with recent appointments of young staff, whose ideas have been welcomed and implemented.

Curriculum broad, with majority of girls heading for 11+ and boys for 13+ exit. French and Latin in the languages department, with a taste of Greek at the top of the school. Gentle setting from summer term of year 2 and children are class taught for most subjects until year 5. Classes maxed at 21, often with smaller numbers in English and maths sets. Head says 'academic life is a given – we go a long way beyond what's expected.' Staff ratios are 'absurd,' he says, with a full time classroom assistant in every class up to year 4. Full-time SENCo plus some part-timers to assist those with additional needs. Around 30 children currently supported with anything ranging from organisational skills to mild dyslexia, with withdrawal avoided wherever possible. Open to taking children with greater needs, recently profound deafness, as long as they are able to successfully access curriculum.

DT and art in strong evidence, both with impressive studios. Head still teaches art – his lessons greeted with enthusiastic fist pumps from

pupils. Drama on curriculum to year 8; school has a new studio plus dynamic newish teacher who has breathed life into performances. Music, though, is the jewel in Orley Farm's crown, taught from the new music school, with choirs and ensembles galore ranging from the Fab Fives which sing 'funky' hits to the chamber choir which tackles three part harmonies with reported aplomb. Compulsory recorder for all in year 2 and over 90 per cent of all pupils learn a peripatetic instrument. Unsurprisingly, given facilities, sport high on agenda with 'strong' rugby and netball, a non-compulsory Saturday morning sports academy and A to E teams fielded whenever opposing schools are big enough to match their numbers. A few grumbles from parents that school could do more to develop those with less talent, but overall sports universally praised.

Four houses encourage 'healthy competition' amongst pupils and children are given positions of responsibility right from reception. We love the playground traffic light system used for solving disputes – no teachers involved, just worldly wise year 3 pupils to mediate spats. Each class has a form tutor as well as form teacher to monitor pastoral well-being. Psychodynamic counsellor on staff two days each week, with children able to self-refer for help with concerns related or totally unrelated to school (fears, phobias, stress). Extracurricular activities, known as 'hobbies', not as broad or varied as at some schools but solid, with all the usual suspects. Wonderful, annual Expeditions Week which takes everyone from year 4 up all over the place from mountaineering in Wales to 'total immersion' in a French château. Best of all, it's included in the fees.

Shades of Gareth Malone – sharp, quirky dress sense, warm charisma, palpable energy and a real human touch. Happily donned Willy Wonka costume at recent Christmas fair

Going places under fabulous head. If you're looking for a school to drive your child hard towards academic superstardom and a ticket to a top academic secondary, Orley Farm probably isn't for you. If, however, you want them to skip joyously into school every day, have time to play when they come home – and quite possibly land one of those coveted top school places on the grounds of their roundedness, likeability and passion for learning, get your name on the list and cross fingers and toes (tutoring won't work).

Radnor House School

Pope's Villa, Cross Deep, Twickenham TW1 4QG

020 8891 6264 | admissions@radnorhouse.org | radnor-twickenham.org

| Independent | Pupils: 420; sixth form: 81: 59 boys, 22 girls |
| Ages: 9-18 | Fees: £15,900 – £19,350 pa |

Head: Since January 2018, Darryl Wideman, previously head of Silcoates School in Yorkshire and with 25 years of experience in independent education, including nine years at Silcoates. He has an Oxford degree in ancient and modern history, and still teaches history to a range of age groups, including A level; he has also been deputy head at Ratcliffe College and taught at Millfield and Fettes.

Previous head Rosie Gill is now a non-executive director and works closely with the senior leadership team.

Academic matters: The school is taking its academic mission extremely seriously – but equally its commitment to the wider well-being of all its pupils and their families. Once you're in, they want you to stay and to work hard – and that, in practice, is what happens. The results tell a good story: 65 per cent of A level grades in 2018 were A*-B and 32 per cent at A*/A. At GCSE, 49 per cent of grades were 9-7, and at least as important was that the grades were earned from success across a broad spread of mainly traditional subjects, with many GCSE pupils taking two modern languages and Latin. The school doesn't want to be narrowly selective, but it emphatically wants pupils who may not believe themselves academically exceptional to achieve more highly than they (or their parents) might have believed possible.

'I can't praise the teaching too highly,' said parent. 'However clichéd it sounds, the teaching my children are receiving is directed towards them, and I really believe others feel the same.' Another added: 'We didn't want my son tutored within an inch of his life, and that's not necessary at Radnor. He's working hard, he's thoroughly stimulated. And the place feels personal.' The slight gender imbalance among pupils is ironing out nicely now, although boys still in the majority 60-40.

The school is emphatic that the effervescence and ambition of the pupils owes much to the calibre of the teaching staff. A lot of care goes into both recruitment and retention and the turnover is modest – 'you need a bit of change, but continuity is critical, especially if the quality is high'.

There are strong suggestions everywhere that this is a happy ship into whose vision staff subscribe wholeheartedly. Despite the nationwide moans of a paucity of teachers in maths and sciences, school has always had a strong field from which to make a selection. All appointments are qualified teachers.

'We didn't want my son tutored within an inch of his life, and that's not necessary at Radnor'

There are two SENDCos – one, dealing with children up to year 8, who advises the classroom teachers in strategies required to help pupils needing learning support. The other, working with older students, has a particular responsibility to ensure that such pupils are adequately prepared for public examinations, with consideration awarded in line with statutory allowances. The informal brief of both extends, of course, very much further – 'like any other teacher, they have to win hearts and minds'. The interests of the small number of children with mild learning support needs within the school are strongly championed by all constituencies.

Games, options, the arts: This is a school which likes its pupils to be active – but, equally, aims to get them to buy into this by friendly example. Football, rugby and cricket dominate boys' sport, and netball, hockey and rounders the girls'. But the school doesn't welcome gender stereotyping. Over 100 boys and girls are now rowing, and mixed football and mixed hockey are not merely popular but being taken very seriously. It's also part of the school credo that everybody represents the school in at least one sport once a year, come what may – an ambition made possible because there are always two teams for each major sport within a year group. There are no games fields on site, but the University of St Mary's, Twickenham, with all those lush playing fields, is only five minutes away by minibus. So nobody is going short of green spaces.

At the time of our visit, the school was busily preparing for its forthcoming production of Oliver! – to be performed at the St Mary's University theatre. It has good drama and music rehearsal spaces in house, each of which is much used for the biannual house music and drama concerts. The latter is a focal point in every Radnor House pupil's life, since the democratising ethos embraces the arts vigorously and ensures these events are truly school-wide. There are some hints that the impact of the arts (and of after-school clubs) doesn't hit home everywhere: 'There's still some way to go,' said one parent, 'before the great majority of pupils are really buying into what's on offer'.

Background and atmosphere: Radnor House is a very recent addition to the tough and competitive environment of senior independent schools. It was the brainchild of David Paton (a former head of sixth form at the Harrodian) who was head between 2011 when it opened and 2016. He retains the post of executive principal. In theory, it sounds a fraught arrangement; in practice, it seems to work excellently with Mr Paton spending a day a week here 'really to exchange news and share thinking'. There is also a heavy-duty advisory panel of governors including the former heads of Alleyns and Hampton.

There is an underlying commitment to transparency and accessibility. 'We see parents a great deal, because it's critical. We enjoy it, we value it, and we hope they do as well'

The school is housed in a handsome mid-19th century neo-Tudor fantasy, which was once the site of the home of the poet Alexander Pope – hence its name (Pope's Villa). There's a delicate and thoughtful balance which has been struck in its redevelopment: the reception areas (with a splendid glass atrium in reception) are of graceful proportions, and the back of the mansion overlooks the river. The combination of grass, water and sky reminds any visitor at a stroke that, whatever else, there is nothing humdrum here. There are lots of small staircases and moderate sized rooms, rather than great ballrooms, all piled high with IT, children's artwork and recent photographs of pupils in their various endeavours. The uniform is worn easily, comfortably – and the atmosphere is the opposite of starchy. Children (of all ages) meet adults' eyes and engage willingly and warmly, but there's no sense of their being ingratiating. A visit to the sixth form common room lunch break gave us a snapshot into something completely authentic

and reassuring: low-buzz comfortable chat, interspersed by bits of work and people plugged into their phones. There is a sense that the children know they are enjoying many advantages in life, but are busy, capable and unpretentious – and draw much inspiration from their teachers who clearly are cut from the same cloth.

The school is rightly proud that 'our community engagement goes a lot further than fundraising'. All projects wherever possible focus on 'personal engagement in the cause of social transformation' eg the annual Make a Difference Day in which every member of the school, staff and pupils, takes a full working day out to make some kind of civic contribution.

Pastoral care, well-being and discipline: Pastoral care is based around form groups – of 20 pupils – with a form tutor, and year groups of 60 under a year head. These are the proactive pastoral figures, and two members of the senior leadership team are there 'to guide, enthuse and, where necessary, to be reactive'. The house system has just been relaunched, mainly for sport and social purposes, but with sixth form pupils acting as heads of houses in an effort to lend kudos and foment useful initiatives. The deputy head (pastoral) fronts most of the bigger pastoral issues, but there is an underlying commitment to transparency and accessibility which the school believes embraces all the staff. 'We see parents a great deal, because it's critical. We enjoy it, we value it, and we hope they do as well.' There have been no recent exclusions – the usual challenges of children aged 9-18, especially those associated with IT, are ones the school recognises, but it finds that a gentle guide on the tiller is usually all that is required.

Pupils and parents: Half termly 'assessment' reports give all parents a terse overview of recent progress and levels of effort. In addition to these, there is a full written report for all years and two meetings a year between individual parents and teachers. Other meetings are arranged as and when the need arises, with all the staff, including the head, always being willing to find time to accommodate requests for face to face discussions.

Three school buses help draw in children from the school's impressively wide catchment – one goes to Chelsea, one to Ealing and the third to Wimbledon. Socially and ethnically, there is a real mix here and many parents are first-time consumers of independent schools. The pupils radiate enthusiasm rather than entitlement.

Entrance: The main point of entry for juniors is now year 5 (as the classes for years 3 and 4 have been phased out – a sign of the school's growing popularity). Children sit an English and a maths test and, if admitted, will be part of a cohort of 20 when they arrive. A further 40 places become available at the start of year 7, selection for which is decided via the 11 plus. There's also a sixth form intake: you need to put in an application in the autumn of year 11, and get ready to sit a range of interviews as well as taking the Yellis computer adaptive test. The underlying rationale is clear – its entry policy is sensible and humane. It becomes more obviously organised around academic testing the further up the school you go, but never to the exclusion of everything else. Siblings are prioritised, but only to the extent that they can fit in comfortably.

Exit: Brighton, Reading and Exeter currently popular sixth form destinations. No Oxbridge yet – 'but that's only a matter of time, and also only one of many ambitions we have for our wonderful pupils'. Some interest is being shown by pupils and parents in European and American universities – one off to the US to study liberal arts in 2018 – applications for which are being finessed by a dedicated member of staff. 'There is a trade-off, I suppose,' said one parent, 'between results and values. At Radnor House, I am confident they can achieve the first, and I'm certain they are achieving the second.'

Money matters: Lunch is charged separately, as are school trips, though a big effort is made to keep

The combination of grass, water and sky reminds any visitor at a stroke that, whatever else, there is nothing humdrum here

costs down. The fees aren't out of line with competitor schools, and the ethos of the school has the low-key quality which accompanies an underlying confidence. Some bursary help is available 'in exceptional circumstances' but this is part of the school's development has perhaps some way yet to go. Uniform is smart but not showy or expensive.

Remarks: Radnor House works hugely hard but has a sense of its underlying values and of the direction it wishes to follow – and these both mark it out as a credible and confident player in the independent school world. The atmosphere is calm as well as energetic, and the head and her colleagues communicate values which are humane and imaginative. It is now poised to become a school of first choice and thoroughly deserving of all the good fortune which comes its way.

Reach Academy Feltham

53-55 High Street, Feltham, Middlesex TW13 4AB

020 8893 1099 | admissions@reachacademy.org.uk | reachacademyfeltham.com

State	Pupils: 780; sixth form: 50
Ages: 4-19	

Headteacher: Since September 2018, Beck Owen, previously associate headteacher.

Executive headteacher is Ed Vainker MA (30s), previously principal since 2012. Following experiences as Teach First trainee in inner city schools and exposure to US Charter School movement, burning desire to set up school to right wrongs was born. His Eureka moment came in the US (he'd won an educational scholarship), when saw Waiting for Superman at cinema (got time wrong – was supposed to be Social Network but didn't want to waste babysitter) and stayed up all night, committing educational vision to paper. Serendipity was

the clincher: a mutual friend introduced him to Rebecca Cramer, school's co-founder and previously secondary head, now director of education.

The first in family to go to university (Bristol, geography) and a fellow Teach Firster, Rebecca shared Ed's sense of injustice over dismal prospects for bright but disadvantaged pupils who ended up with middling exam results, education and careers instead of the stellar opportunities they deserved.

The solution? A school where the partnership with parents wasn't just about education but everything from aspirations to parenting skills and diet. It needed to take the very young (makes Jesuits look like beginners) and stay small so teachers could get to know children, and their families, inside out. Families short on decent life chances were to be the prime beneficiaries. Feltham, only five miles from Hampton Court Palace but an awful lot grittier (government's latest deprivation index puts it in bottom third of areas for education) was the ideal location, particularly given authority's commitment to building new homes and schools for fast-growing population.

First pupils (reception and year 7) arrived in 2012 and a new primary and senior year has been added on each September since, making a full house in 2018.

Rebecca and Ed are idealistic but clear-sighted, offering practical help where needed (including carpeting bare floors in one family's flat) but never letting poverty become an excuse for low achievement. They're hugely impressive. Rebecca is praised for pastoral and psychological expertise while Ed's the systems and strategy man with a brilliant little black book stuffed with useful contacts and a virtuoso approach to getting what he wants from normally intractable public bodies ('pre-schmoozing' was mentioned).

Both have understanding partners and young children – 'was planning to have a school dog but got a baby instead,' says Rebecca, whose just crawling son was a cheery addition to the morning meet and greet squad on day of visit.

Rebecca and Ed are idealistic but clear-sighted, offering practical help (including carpeting bare floors in one family's flat) but never letting poverty become an excuse

Job could take over their lives but they work hard to ensure it doesn't and swear blind that a 5.30pm getaway is the norm, 'plus, of course, some email checking once the children are in bed,' says Rebecca. Personable and charming, though with the essential steely edge where necessary, they also have the ability to make others feel at ease. One parent, distraught when child launched into a tantrum at a get-to-know-you session, was instantly put at her ease by Rebecca. 'She came over and spoke to me like a human being and made me feel so relaxed.' Staff think they're pretty fab, too. 'Rebecca stays so calm, I've never seen her fazed or annoyed. She's always in control,' says one.

That said, children have a healthy respect for her. 'She's very much like "this is how it's going to be",' said one.

Now first stage one has been accomplished, it's on to phase two – a second school that will take

pupils even earlier – pre-conception, if they get their way – and 'hopefully' bring together NCT (currently nearest branches are in well-heeled Chiswick and Teddington), local GPs, midwives and just about everybody who can ensure that parents get proper support from the very beginning. It's due for completion 2019 (fast by most standards but boringly slow motion for Ed, who got this school up and running in just 10 months).

Ed and Rebecca now envisage training up a brace of successors who share their ideals but are happy to take on a going concern rather than a blank page while they work on further expansion. 'Would they be younger?' we asked. 'We are young,' say Ed and Rebecca, indignantly.

Academic matters: Social justice is the driver, goal transformational education ensuring that every able child gets top results. They've demanded, to some initial consternation, as big a proportion of families from disadvantaged backgrounds as possible.

Second impressive GCSE results in 2018 saw 31 per cent 9-7 grades, with 84 per cent getting 9-4 in both English and maths. School is already notching up the laurel wreaths, first all-through free school to garner an outstanding grade from inspectors and with good results (eg in year 1 phonics test) that put it way ahead of national averages. The acid test will come in 2021 when first year 11s home grown from reception sit GCSEs. The current year 4s are already working at same level as year 7 pupils – so it's looking good.

'We take an A at A level and work backwards,' says literature...'They expect great things for all of us,' agreed year 11 pupil. Only exceptions a couple of pupils who wouldn't cope with GCSEs, based here but taking vocational courses at other local colleges.

Crack team of teachers is key. Highly qualified and occasionally shoeless ('helps them feel grounded,' we were told), they're also known by their first names (means 'have power but don't feel bigger,' thought one pupil) and have no discernable 'off' button, replying to texts from early morning to late at night and over the hols.

'Seem to be there because they want to be there,' thought another. The few who don't self-select into new employment fairly quickly, but with 17 who've been here since the school first opened, most are clearly keepers.

Ark Schools group helps with training and all teachers, several former TAs among them, have a mentor and weekly observations. Though ethnically less diverse than pupils, it's not the whole story as a fair few also have first hand experience of achieving against the odds.

Curriculum is very much the school's own. Unsurprisingly, little quarter is given in lessons, from year 10s deep in semantic (and battle) fields as they analyse war poetry to year 2s dissecting Edgar Allen Poe's The Raven by way of a Hallowe'en treat.

There's role play to develop confidence for reception pupils and the involvement of senior school subject specialists (science, French) from year 3 onwards. Lesson length varies according to subject, little and often for languages but longer sessions (up to two hours for seniors) in literacy and numeracy, which dominate curriculum. Competence in both areas is a non-negotiable that's well understood by parents. 'If you want to go off and be a carpenter or something like that, there's no good learning that at school if your maths isn't brilliant,' said one.

Everyone is expected to take between eight and 10 GCSEs with art, music and MFL among the options – most bases covered though don't offer DT. Sixth formers (first entrants joined in September 2017) have choice of 18 A levels and two BTecs, plus electives (astronomy to photography – potential starter for extended essay project) and linked studies such as research techniques.

With pupils speaking 55 languages between them and English an additional language for 40 per cent, support network has to be robust – and it is, with before school catch up lessons and small group work for those needing a slightly slower pace.

Adjoining forest school may be more of a coppice but gets non-stop multi-purpose use – tents, mini-beast hotel and balancing wire slung between two trees

Don't shirk from SEN and school is impressively dyslexia friendly (white backgrounds routinely replaced with pastel shades – far easier to read), while new resources are being added (sensory room is on the way). Stress, however, that while school is small, class sizes aren't – it's 30 or so up to end of year 11 – so wouldn't be the right environment for child in need of extensive small group or one-to-one support.

That said, parents confirm that the school won't give up on pupils with additional needs without a fight. Under a handful so far have moved on to more specialist environments and it's brilliant with those it can support. Rebecca's prizewinning account of school life for bright, autistic boy resulted in trip to education conference in Bulgaria where his speech on need for greater understanding of SEN, he told us, had audience in tears.

Games, options, the arts: Sense of togetherness permeates everything, from play featuring

Both have understanding partners and young children – 'was planning to have a school dog but got a baby instead'

wisecracking teacher and pupil compere duo to school trips – six a year for primary pupils, with overnight stays from year 3, while all secondary pupils get a residential week in a university (Bath for year 7, York year 8 and Cambridge year 10) – 'a huge thing and a non-negotiable,' says Ed. Year 9s, meanwhile, work on Sports Leader UK and D of E qualifications (aim for silver in year 11). 'All part of making everyone part of the family,' said parent.

Smart thinking sees work experience happening in autumn half term to beat the post-GCSE rush. One year 11 boy encountered slebs on his – 'Dom Joly,' he breathed in star-struck tones, though not everyone's as happy. 'Rubbish,' said a girl, who had less fulfilling time with another firm.

Around 100 children learn a musical instrument in school (fair few enthusiastic beginners aiming for grade 4 in time for GCSEs) and even reception children, including the very shy, have acquired the confidence to perform in public within weeks of joining.

Art is also taking off, specialist teacher now installed, room uncommonly neat and restrained but filling up nicely with glittery stage sets ready to go for forthcoming production of Annie when we visited and some interesting individual work including year 9 pupils' rather beautiful Romero Britto-inspired designs.

Opening of second Reach Academy in 2019 or 2020, on a bigger site, should mean more outside space all round. In the meantime, sporting successes are coming (senior girls' football, cross-country and shot putt) while colossus of a sports hall also goes some way to compensate, as does its rooftop Astroturf (with views of glorious sunsets views over Feltham) – though one parent felt it could be used a bit more often.

SEN support extends to after-school clubs – yoga 'very good for those with dyspraxia,' says head of sport. They're popular with parents, with football, table tennis and trampolining all generally oversubscribed

Learning outside the classroom is a big feature, like so much here, plugging social as well as educational gap. Down on the farm that's a gated hop skip and jump from the playground, Nigel the farmer supplies and vets the livestock: beady-eyed chickens, hoping for seconds of mealworms (top favourites) have plenty of star quality but are comprehensively outshone by the two pigs. Pupils can volunteer to be young farmers and learn responsibility by working here after school.

Meat and eggs are sold to the parents who can also sample other edibles (spices, rhubarb and tomatoes and even a batch of home-made chutney), and there's also a virtuous circle, with pigs (sensibly not named) fed spare break time fruit (unlimited for all) though government diktats consign most other leftovers to landfill.

Adjoining forest school may be more of a coppice but gets non-stop multi-purpose use – tents, mini-beast hotel, and balancing wire slung between two trees. And though compact (you can definitely see the wood for the trees), it's an oasis to many of the parents who help out here. 'Like a day out – felt that wasn't in Feltham at all,' said one.

Background and atmosphere: No bureaucracy-heavy place, this. It feels fleet of foot – even on the 'phone. 'We'd rather deal with you ourselves,' says friendly receptionist, who offers to sort out the visit direct with the principal (none of this transferring your call to umpteen other extensions, all with a voicemail on the end).

School's small is beautiful ethos makes it a rarity not just in its home borough of Hounslow but just about anywhere in Greater London. It achieved star status early on, seemingly the must-see educational destination of choice for range of ambitious politicians. Year 11s we spoke to had previously been quizzed by David Cameron (school was final official engagement before his post-Brexit resignation). Others who've dropped in include Lord Adonis, Boris Johnston and Michael Gove (though we bet we were the only ones to be offered school pud – complete with bowl – as a goody bag present).

Area, though not picturesque, is brilliantly connected for trains, automobiles (and of course many, many planes) though some parents prefer to collect, on foot if necessary, rather than letting even secondary-age children walk back on their own.

Inside, however, the school, designed from scratch by founders, is a well-thought out and attractive oasis of calm, from the separate primary and secondary meet and greet areas and playgrounds to the move to unisex toilets ('the boys' smelled and the girls spent hours looking in the mirror,' says Rebecca).

Life centres round five phases, each with its assistant head, made up of one or more year groups in own area consisting of classrooms off a multi-purpose central space (nursery, in own single long room, the only exception). Unless location is key (science, music and art) it's the teachers who move. 'None of this 100 kids rushing through the corridors to get to a lesson,' said parent.

Plenty, as you'd expect, on the wish list. New library needs more books; embryonic music tech room more tech. Donations come from a range of sources – Teach First, for example, was persuaded to part with some old sofas – ideal for the new sixth form centre (first occupants in September 2017) which also boasts rooftop terrace and well-stocked fitness suite – but Ed and Rebecca are cautious about hitting the well-wishers' list too often. State education 'isn't really badly funded,' they reckon.

Pastoral care, well-being and discipline: There's a strong family feel here, starting at the gates (primary pupils enter to left, seniors to right), with handshake for all at start and end of the day 'without fail,' said parent. 'It feels lovely.' Inspirational quotes (JK Rowling, Ghandi, Martin Luther King) are juxtaposed with posters for Childline, and school is under no illusions as to some families' home life. For some, just getting children to school is an achievement, we were told by grounded family support worker. 'They deal with every angle of their upbringing,' said mother. 'Not just education but their social needs, too.' Practical support includes organising visits to the job centre, optician and food bank or – in one case – taking the children to feed the ducks at local pond to give parents a break.

Some pupils arrive so far behind their peers that may never achieve as much as they should, though progress can be dramatic – one primary school boy sitting quietly at the table to eat his lunch 'would have found it impossible when he first arrived,' we were told. Food really matters. For some children it's their first encounter not just with healthy diet but also with the social rituals of mealtimes. So there's food mindfulness in primary (distraction-free silence during first mouthfuls) to minimal choice menu, family service with older pupils serving younger ones, no packed lunches and home visits for serial non-eaters. Several new parents, initially nervous about fussy offspring, quickly reassured. One H2O refuser blossomed when was offered school's 'magic water for big boys.'

Crack team of teachers is key. Highly qualified and occasionally shoeless ('helps them feel grounded,' we were told), they're also known by their first names

Elsewhere, children are guided towards the right decision by impressively low key but authoritative staff. 'Don't need to shout and scream, just clap their hands and everyone stops,' said parent. Incentives include payslips for good work and behaviour – exchangeable for golden time (primary) and activities (senior pupils). 'You get a lot of messages coming home telling you to congratulate your child when they've done really well,' said parent. Nothing flabby about two-step sanctions, however. First time senior school trangressors talk through reasons for poor behaviour while serial (or serious) offenders sit on their own in lessons and at break for a day, decision to readmit to polite society decided by class vote and communicated by buddy.

Parents, too, shoulder their share of responsibility. If a phone goes off in a lesson, will be called in to remove offending item and confirm they understand why. Similarly, late arrivals get automatic 30 minute detention, 'bad traffic' excuse a non-starter. 'Would need to have affected every car in the whole area,' says Rebecca, implacably. Tough love it may be, but after the initial shock, every parent we spoke to understood why it was necessary and appreciated the active encouragement to join in school life. All have open invitation to have lunch or, if worried about child's progress, sit in on lesson. 'Very open – there's nothing to hide,' said one.

Pupils and parents: One of several rumours we heard was of places awarded to wealthy parents identifiable by posh cars at drop off and pick up time. We diligently scoured the Tesco and Aldi car parks opposite at 8.00am and can report a pronounced absence of luxury marques.

'Rebecca came to our house and did an amazing presentation,' said one parent. Those who took a leap of faith and got in early thank their lucky stars

Instead, there's a diverse community. Was 80 per cent ethnic minorities when first opened though there are now more pupils from lower income white families. Embryonic PTA, busily organising Christmas Fair when we visited, is doing best to create parent community – one mother, frozen out by the clique in previous, middle-class dominated primary, was full of praise.

Entrance: The school stresses – and stresses again – that its admissions procedure is completely transparent – if different to anyone else's. It doesn't stop suspicion creeping in, down to the long odds – over 1,000 families recently applied for the 120 reception and year 7 places (something that rivals even grammar school admissions) – that condemn majority to disappointment. Doesn't stop them trying (two parents turned up on day of visit to plead their case) – and second school can't come soon enough.

After looked after children come nursery pupils qualifying for early years pupil premium,

---

All have open invitation to have lunch or, if worried about child's progress, sit in on lesson. 'Very open – there's nothing to hide'

followed by exceptional medical and social needs, siblings, others qualifying for pupil premium, staff children and those living within admissions area (chosen by electronic ballot). Transition process is painstaking, particularly when it comes to identifying those with learning needs. 'We'll go in and make sure it's identified early,' says Rebecca.

Main feeder schools are Victoria Junior School and Oak Hill Academy, geographical area covering Feltham, Southville, Bedfont, Hanworth and Hounslow (though early adopters include those from slightly further afield).

At the start, school was canvassing for pupils – and how. 'Rebecca came to our house and did an amazing presentation,' said one parent. Those who took a leap of faith and got in early thank their lucky stars. Neighbours who didn't and are on the waiting list (which does move, but at glacial speeds), wish they'd done the same. In the meantime, the rumour mill is whizzing round at speed while school does its best to highlight transparency.

It's currently having to repeat the process for sixth formers as applications are slightly thin on the ground for early intakes – sheer newness means not yet a destination school for high achievers. We'd strongly recommend taking a look.

Exit: There's some relocation – including visa expiry. Some departures at end of year 11 (about half so far) as school sets the bar high for sixth form admissions – six 6s minimum, 7s required to study toughest subjects (eg maths, sciences, languages, history). Similar number of 9-4 grades will see you on to a BTec.

For those moving on, options range from The Heathland School in Hounslow to Springwest Academy and St Paul's Catholic School in Sunbury. One parent felt school should do more to help with search. Don't hold your breath or expect much in way of handholding – school expects parents to do their homework and research alternatives. 'We don't spoonfeed,' says Rebecca.

Money matters: Sixth form bursaries for everyone on free school meals. As and when hardship bursaries also available – no pupil will miss a school trip because of lack of money.

Remarks: 'It seems too good to be true,' said parent. 'We kept saying "what's the catch?" There is no catch.'

St Augustine's Priory

Hillcrest Road, Ealing, London W5 2JL

020 8997 2022 | office@sapriory.com | sapriory.com

| Independent | Pupils: 464; sixth form: 39 |
| Ages: 3–18 | Fees: £11,709 – £15,693 pa |

Head: Since 2012, Sarah Raffray BA (English and Latin, Manchester) MA (literature and modernity, Salford), 40s. With a career, seemingly, purpose-built for this post, Mrs Raffray is universally praised. She inherited a school with a venerable tradition but a recent, prolonged and very public upheaval accompanied by a mass exodus. It is a tribute to her energetic, frank and warm approach that the school is in such good heart and that it merits this, its first inclusion in The Guide. She knew what she was doing when she came here – 'I almost didn't apply but I had an "if not you, who?" moment and I absolutely believe in Catholic education, with a 21st century resonance. Unless you encourage people to sit still, go deeper and challenge things, everything becomes superficial.' School received an 'outstanding in all areas' diocesan inspection in 2016.

From St Mary's, Shaftesbury, where she'd been deputy head, Mrs Raffray had previously taught at St Mary's, Cambridge (head of sixth form) and St Bede's, Manchester. All good Roman Catholic schools and providing solid experience for taking on St Augustine's – less well-known than her earlier schools but, under her aegis, this is set to change – and not just in the locality. Not least among her achievements is the unity and community she plainly fosters – her parents tell us: 'she has recruited many really outstanding, teachers'; 'she is a figurehead with real presence'; 'a dedicated leader'; 'she walks the playground – it's good to see the boss of the shop at the door and she's not afraid to deal with difficult things..all her changes are good – she now needs to be even more ambitious'.

No fear of failing in that department. Lots of new initiatives and a wholesale upgrading of staff. Ten-year master-plan for capital development has commenced and will include a new hall, sports and drama facilities.

Head is relaxed, easy to talk to and very open. 'I can't bear the idea of a "safe" sixth form – we need to look after people but we need to be edgy too.. We're not afraid to say we got it wrong but we're learning all the time... ' One of the best appointments we have seen for years.

Academic matters: Small classes. A pervasive air of orderliness and atmosphere of quiet study. Pupils pay tribute to the outstanding teaching, especially of many newer appointees – 'they are real experts in their subjects,' enthuse parents. Range of subjects respectable but not huge – as you'd expect from a small school. IGCSEs now taken in all sciences, modern languages and English. Russian on offer, as well as Spanish and French. Ambition shown in the arrival of additional maths on the GCSE curriculum. Very good results in, especially, art, English and Latin GCSEs, biology and physics IGCSEs. In all, 66 per cent A*-A/9-7 grades in 2018. A level results suffer from too many post-GCSE leavers but that is changing. A very encouraging 40 per cent A*/A grades in total in 2018, with the retention of academic high-flyers in the current sixth seeing changes here. Far fewer leavers than previously but more still needing to be done. Girls would like thinking skills or critical thinking lessons. But the sixth form, newly relaunched, is ripe for expansion – with its new centre, enrichment programme and extended school day – and we are confident that, given another year or two and the school's reputation growing as it must, they will be turning girls away.

'Unless you encourage people to sit still, go deeper and challenge things, everything becomes superficial'

Good learning support from f/t SENCo plus f/t learning support/literacy teacher and much p/t help from subject staff and a dyscalculia expert. Parents of dyslexics appreciative of the support their daughters receive – 'my daughter outperformed all expectations and will now get a great crop of A levels – we never dreamed it'd be possible'. EAL also supported. School flexible over GCSE subjects when SEN hinders achievement – 'They let my daughter stop French – which she was never going to get. So sensible!' And all parents we spoke to praised the value added to their daughters' academic aspirations by the culture of the school.

Secured links with the French Embassy and Sorbonne in London, thereby officially becoming bilingual hub. Offers bespoke French intensive learning to a hand-picked few.

Some sense that the extra-bright could be stretched more but this, too, is on the way with a new Oxbridge group – open to all aspirants – from year 10 up. Also, blow-up pics of successful former pupils around the place, pour encourager.. Despite improving academics, this school is not striving to be another league-table topper and quite right too.

Games, options, the arts: With sports fields like nothing we have seen elsewhere in London, St Augustine's is uniquely privileged. And they're not just extensive but quite beautiful. Good new Astro used for team sports and athletics. Unsurprisingly, PE is a GCSE and A level subject. Much praise for new head of sport and team – 'a new energy,' said a parent. Hockey, netball and lacrosse on offer plus fitness and taekwondo. Matches played with enthusiasm. D of E is popular and girls rave about their trips eg skiing in Switzerland and Bulgaria, geography trips to eg Iceland and to Morocco where they helped build a girls' boarding school.

Surprises await. From the back of the building, the view over 13 acres of fields to the spread of the capital is astonishing. There are gardens, an apple orchard, a prayer garden, chicken runs

We were impressed, again, by the enthusiasm displayed in the art and photographic studios – much experimentation, colour and free expression in textiles, paint and modelling. Pupil art well-displayed in every corridor. Lots of musical activities too – choirs and ensembles and all backed, now, by tip-top equipment – IT etc – and super large music room. Carol concert held in nearby Ealing Abbey. School badly needs an all-purpose hall (and will, eventually, get one) but drama and music thrive notwithstanding and the chapel lends its own peculiar magic to events. Much success in eg Young Enterprise, Youth Speaks, Youth Games, maths challenges and various writing competitions and a sense of striving for achievable goals.

Background and atmosphere: The school was founded in 1634 by Mother Lettice Mary Tredway CRL (1595 –1677) a canoness regular and abbess who,

Junior school itself is lovely – lively, imaginative activities with some pleasing mess (we hate sanitised nurseries) and happy, occupied children

together with Miles Pinkney (Father Carré), founded a monastery for the English members of her Order in Paris. A pension for English ladies and a school were attached to the new monastery, of which Tredway was abbess till 1675, when illness compelled her to resign. The priory survived, along with the school attached to it, until the French Revolution, when the English canonesses were forced to flee. They returned home, where they were able to live out their life as a religious community. Eventually the community established itself as St Augustine's Priory in Ealing and the school has occupied its rather wonderful and surprising present site since 1915.

It's tucked into a corner off the North Circular as it rises to meet the A40, yards from the unlovely Hanger Lane Gyratory System – as the monster roundabout is grandiosely named. From the front, the school looks a hotch-potch of brick and pebbledash buildings of no particular distinction. However, surprises await. From the back of the building, the view over 13 acres of fields to the spread of the capital is astonishing. There are gardens, an apple orchard, a prayer garden, chicken runs, many mature and beautiful trees and the whole thing is an oasis. You don't hear the traffic, you just relax into this beautiful space. Many of the school rooms look over this – most notably, the exceptionally well-appointed sixth form common room and the art studio at the top of the building. The rear of the building also surprises – its monastic principles clear in the pastiche Norman windows, the row of windows on the floor above which would have been those of the nuns – now gone – and the simple cruciform architecture – more obvious when you walk the school itself.

'It feels like the countryside,' as a parent said. It also feels like a village community – lots of old girls and staff send their daughters here. Junior school occupies building at one end of the site – with its own meadow and nursery playground. Little demarcation between the junior and senior schools – seen as a plus by some while others feel there should be more of a 'step up' up at 11. Junior school itself is lovely – lively, imaginative activities with some pleasing mess (we hate sanitised nurseries) and happy, occupied children. Very orderly classrooms for older children and an air of productive purpose throughout.

We have seldom visited a school with so powerful a sense of commitment amongst its community. It's small – too small for a few – but the girls know each other and the strengthening of houses and inter-year activities are helping. Lovely features like the new outside theatre, the willow tunnels constructed by 'amazingly inventive groundsman' and a feeling that 'anyone who comes up with a good idea gets encouragement and, if need be, funding'. Lack of a proper school hall felt by everyone, but 10-year development plan now commencing should sort this as well as provide other much-needed facilities. All classrooms have names of saints or worthies – Thomas Aquinas houses science, St Cecilia music etc. Tuck shop and two refectories – modern, bright and with 'excellent' food. Whole school now bristles with new PCs.

Lovely features like the new outside theatre, the willow tunnels constructed by the 'amazingly inventive groundsman' and a feeling that 'anyone who comes up with a good idea gets encouragement and, if need be, funding'

Much of the interior is nondescript, though all is in good order – clean and spruce. But the chapel – even to heathens like your reviewer – is a source of pleasure. With balcony, vaulted roof, splendid marble columns and altar, and white walls, this Douai-inspired centre of the school life induces reflection and calm. Monday assemblies and three-weekly mass for each year held here. Little Muslim prayer room, but that this is a Roman Catholic school is inescapable. Life-sized statues of saints, crucifixes, pictures and pious posters and messages are everywhere, yet under half the school population is RC and not all those are practising. However, RC values underpin the school's teaching and the girls we spoke to were comfortable with the ethos, and felt the ethos of community and equality will stay with them when they leave. No-one felt oppressed by it.

Pastoral care, well-being and discipline: Very few problems. Some legacy of past difficulties persists but, as with everything here, a sense that Mrs Raffray and her team are on top of it and there is little left to do. 'We have changed our bullying policy. There are clear sanctions.' Impressive newish deputy has pastoral role among others. Universal praise for pastoral care and equipping the girls for the wider world: 'The school allows them to stay as children in an environment which wants them to grow up too early,' a parent told us. 'There are lots of leadership programmes and a growing sense of boldness and confidence.' 'Our daughters are very happy.' Big sister/little sister buddying between sixth form and year 7 newbies. Before and after-school care.

Pupils and parents: Roman Catholics (around 40 per cent of school's population) from Ealing and surrounds. Further 20 per cent are other Christians. Culturally and ethnically diverse, as you'd expect in this part of London – lots of Asians and mixed race families. Strong community holds all together. Middle class, professional families. Mostly from local primaries. School runs a minibus from Chiswick. No identikit pupil. Says head, 'The school has a tradition of accommodating girls who want to be different.' We met nothing but relaxed, articulate, smiley girls. Most famous old girl: actor and writer Phoebe Waller-Bridge.

Entrance: Ealing is well-served by good local state primaries – many of them RC. Nursery and reception places available but waiting lists now in years 3 and 4. Few places in years 5 and 6. At 11+, 60+ apply for c12 places via exam and interview. Places available for year 12. However, all this is set to change. This school is now a player and, notwithstanding the good local state provision, the school's site and, now, its academics and inclusive culture – along with the outstanding pastoral care and community feel – will drive custom. Get in quick.

Exit: Latterly a sizeable exit post-GCSE to state RC heavyweights, and local co-eds. That is set to change. All 18+s to higher education, mostly to good universities eg LSE, Warwick, Edinburgh, Newcastle and even Toronto, to read proper subjects. No Oxbridge in recent years but we met some impressive current candidates and would confidently predict success.

Money matters: Fees appreciably lower than those of local competitors. Worthwhile discounts for siblings. Academic/sports/music awards at 11+. Academic awards at 16+. All worth 10-20 per cent discount on fees. Bursaries for existing students in case of need.

Remarks: We came away with a bottle of their home-grown and pressed apple juice, and much more you couldn't bottle. This could be the school for which the cliché A Hidden Gem was invented, but we don't expect it to remain hidden for much longer under such inspirational leadership.

St Benedict's School

54 Eaton Rise, London W5 2ES

020 8862 2254 | enquiries@stbenedicts.org.uk | stbenedicts.org.uk

| Independent | Pupils: 1,076: 718 boys, 358 girls; sixth form: 218 |
| Ages: 3–18 | Fees: £12,990 – £16,845 pa |

Headmaster: Since 2016, Andrew Johnson (50) married to Dawn with two sons at university. Educated at the highly academic Skinners' School in Tunbridge Wells; on leaving he read modern languages at Bristol and then went straight into teaching. His degree landed him head of the subject at Winchester and then took him north, first to Birkdale School in Sheffield and then on to the top job at Stonyhurst, where he introduced the IB and embedded co-education.

His arrival here was announced as 'a real coup' by the governors and he is definitely on a mission to try and make the world sit up and notice this school. An easy, tidy man with a controlled sense of humour, who despite describing himself as 'not an office worker' obviously has impressive management skills. He has brought in an infusion of new blood at the head of the school, including a new deputy head, deputy head academic and bursar, and is confident that he can mesh the new with the old as far as staffing goes. Determined to get to know the pupils as well as the teachers, he tries to observe three lessons a week and cheer on as many of his vast array of rugby teams as possible.

Head of junior school: Since 2005, Rob Simmons BA MEd (40s), married with children and grandchildren. Schooled at St Benedict's; after a history degree and time abroad on voluntary service he returned to his alma mater to teach history at senior level, before winning the headship of the junior school. A trim, dapper dresser, he is not shy about his passion for aviation, planes neatly arranged on shelves and a favourite paperback, starring a Second World War aviation hero, tucked in amongst the history books. Hopefully, not just popular for the sugar content, he is starting 'Hot Chocolate (and marshmallows!) Friday' this term for one pupil from each class who has ticked all the right boxes during the week.

Academic matters: Nursery, rescued from its nissan hut island in the playground is now housed in the junior school, with an experienced head – 'I just love the little ones' – in charge. A full curriculum, including art, drama, music and computing alongside traditional subjects is taught from reception onwards and in keeping with AJ's new approach to academics higher up, they have recently introduced setting in maths and English from year 5. The new building has been designed with early years children in mind and there are cosy break-out spaces (including a ribbon bedecked 'rainbow' room) and a full-time SENCo who operates on both a group and one-to-one level.

In the senior school, AJ's conscious decision to raise the game academically – 'we want to give a greater sense of zip to academic life' – has already paid off with a much improved set of GCSE figures in 2018: 66 per cent 9-7 grades. AJ states that it will be a slower process, maybe up to five years, to make the same sort of progress at A level, but the results were still respectable in 2018 with 73 per cent graded at A*-B and 41 per cent at A*/A. He has instituted new practices such as monitoring the school's ranking against other independents rather than all schools, as well as frequent testing, so that 'we can be more straightforward about a pupil's ability'. He has also expanded the tutorial system so that all pupils from year 7 onwards have access to two form tutors.

Outings to the Lake District for the great outdoors and to Normandy to learn about baguettes and butter

After three years of studying a wide range of subjects, even including the option of Chinese in year 7, everybody aims at a minimum of nine GCSEs. Once in the sixth form most take three A levels with 40 per cent doing an EPQ in the lower sixth on subjects as diverse as phage therapy (how to crack treating viruses, to the rest of us) and the moral stance of Woodrow Wilson.

We asked various students whether they thought the school had particular academic strengths, but their tendency to give a wide variety

An impressive array of fitness machines and a full complement of professional staff to help would-be stars develop

of answers implied that they were confident about the teaching across the board. A source of pride to all was that one pupil beat entrants from nine other European countries to win the Youth Debating Competition in Budapest, an achievement proving that students feel confident to tackle projects well outside their comfort zone.

Some eight per cent of pupils receive SEN support from a full-time SENCo, operating alongside the new counsellor, whose brief is to listen to any problems that are brought to her by pupils or parents.

Games, options, the arts: Nursery and reception do PE including dance, but from the age of 7 serious sport begins. Girls start the autumn term with hockey, then netball in the spring, boys play rugby for two terms and both head to the cricket pitches for the summer term. Chosen by one parent partly because the senior school is 'sporty', rugby tops the bill with twice weekly fixtures, international tours and the chance to be part of a London Irish training scheme. Not to be left out, girls play tag rugby, but the emphasis is on netball and hockey and they have recently fielded teams who have successfully toured abroad. Everyone is encouraged, according to one parent, and there is a large indoor sports hall with an impressive array of fitness machines and a full complement of professional staff to help would-be stars develop. Fencing is very strong in the senior school. Add to this athletics, football, cross-country, rounders, swimming, badminton, basketball, volley ball and jiu-jitsu and you can see why the sporting side of the school often pops up when talking to parents.

Extracurricular offerings in the junior school range from the head's aviation club, which has proved so absorbing that one ex-member is now in the RAF, to the more grounded chess, gymnastics, ballet, sewing and drama. Staying on the ground, there are regular trips to museums and theatres and in years 5 and 6 residential outings to the Lake District for the great outdoors and to Normandy to learn about baguettes and butter. Older pupils are given over 60 options to widen their horizons, lots of D of E awards and charity work but also a massive music offering from rock groups to close-harmony singing. The cadet force signs up plenty of recruits and the less regimented can choose from arts, drama, dance, languages, science and extra sport.

Music is a strand that runs through the whole school from little ones singing in their nativity play past the juniors who all learn the violin in year 3 to the near professional spring and summer concerts, given in the abbey by senior pupils. There is a busy, buzzy art room at the top of the junior building full of enthusiastic children and imaginative mobiles, and in the senior school there is a new art, design and technology department. We were particularly impressed by a papier mâché tour de force, posing as a futuristic chair, and students showcase their work with two major art shows each year.

Drama is not timetabled in the junior school, although nativity and form plays are an annual event, but once in year 7 – 'we have a wealth of acting talent' – it starts to take regular billing. The middle school recently put on A Midsummer Night's Dream and 'Lord of the Flies' whilst the seniors staged West Side Story' and 'Amadeus.

Background and atmosphere: Nearly 400 years after the Reformation, the Benedictine monks of Downside decided it was time to expand from rural Somerset to suburban London. Initially known as Ealing Priory School, the school opened in 1902 with three boys and five pounds in the kitty, was given its current name in 1948 and has been fully co-educational since 2008.

The architectural chimera lying on the summit of a gentle slope above Ealing Broadway is composed of solid Edwardian villas, rather dreary brick buildings and a lot of tarmac sandwiched between unlikely golden doors and the 1900s abbey. Perhaps fortunately, the slightly weary creature is in the midst of a massive refurbishment.

A trim, dapper dresser, he is not shy about his passion for aviation, planes neatly arranged on shelves and a favourite paperback tucked in amongst the history books

They've already finished a building for the sixth form with art studios above, a small chapel featuring primary coloured windows, designed by a pupil, and an entirely revamped junior school in a modern Scandinavian style which ticks all the right eco boxes. Inside they've brightened up the reception area and the main school hall and there are plans in the pipeline to do up the more elderly classrooms. Parents' reactions are positive, with one saying that the school was 'a bit tatty', but now looks 'much fresher'. AJ would like to build a performing arts centre in the medium term and there is even talk of planting an avenue of trees once the builders have finally departed. A decidedly good idea as leafy, green trees would definitely improve the present overall monochrome effect.

Pastoral care, well-being and discipline: Rules are here to be obeyed and AJ is not shy of suspending pupils for a few days if they consistently break them or insist on remaining academically lazy, but he hopes that this can almost always be avoided by close monitoring of each pupil's progress both academically and socially.

In the junior school there are cheerful 'worry' boxes, and once in the senior school there are quiet rooms and the new chapel (complete with chaplain) as well as the counsellor who is always on site.

The recent conviction of a priest ex-middle school head for sexually assaulting pupils in the 1970s and 1980s, plus the departure in 2015 of the deputy head, following his arrest over indecent images (not involving any St Benedict's children), have resulted in extremely thorough measures to safeguard pupils. There is both internal and external monitoring of the internet and the last ISI inspection was passed with flying colours. Parents remark that the school is very hot on e-dangers and the modern pressures put on pupils via social media and selfies. In our opinion St Benedict's is aware of the mistakes of the past and has moved on.

The children who showed us round the lower school were smiley, charming and confident and all the older pupils were polite and articulate

Some 55 per cent of the pupils are Catholic, the remaining 45 per cent from other faiths including some seven per cent who have not signed up to any at all. The school is no longer marketed solely as a Catholic institution, but talking to students made us very aware that the Benedictine ethos is still incorporated throughout the curriculum. The visits to Lourdes, charity fundraising, weekly mass in the abbey and the voluntary service carried out by all members of the lower sixth, plus the attitude of pupils to staff and to one another, remind you that this is a school that takes faith and social behaviour seriously.

Pupils and parents: A large number of double income parents who work extremely hard in order to pay the below average fees charged here. In western London school terminology, St Benedict's is counted as middle of the road compared to some of its flashier rivals, but all parents that we talked to felt that it provided good value for money, very good pastoral care and that the new leadership team were pushing the academic standards to a higher level.

At the younger end the school the children are almost all very local but higher up the catchment area spreads significantly, and they now run regular transport from Hammersmith, Harrow and Richmond. The children who showed us round the lower school were smiley, charming and confident and all the older pupils were polite and articulate, if not appearing quite as sophisticated as some of their inner London contemporaries – not necessarily a bad thing.

Alumni include Julian Clary, Peter Ackroyd and the poet/songwriter Labi Siffre as well as a sprinkling of politicians (in particular Chris Patten) and rugby players.

Entrance: Entrance at 3 is non-selective; at 4 it is more formal, with children observed doing tasks in a classroom. For entry at 7 or above children are asked to do tests in maths, English and verbal reasoning as well as spending part of a day being assessed in a group and time in a class of their own age group.

At 11+ pupils from the junior school compete in the same exam as external candidates from local state primaries or preps, for the 120 places available. There are occasional spaces at 13+ and in the sixth form but the bar is on the rise with increasing numbers applying.

Exit: Some 70 per cent of juniors move up to the senior school, and around 85 per cent continue to the sixth form. Leavers head to universities from Aston and Bangor to Warwick and York. One off to Oxford in 2018 to study philosophy and theology, and one heading for St Andrews to study medicine.

Money matters: Academic, music and sports scholarships, worth up to 50 per cent of the fees, available at 11+ and sixth form for internal and external candidates. Bursaries available in the senior school are strictly means tested, but 'once a child is in, if a parent falls on hard times, we will do our best to help them'.

Remarks: The 'granular scrutiny' that the ambitious new headmaster is applying to all things academic and pastoral is already bearing fruit, and this school is definitely on an upward curve scholastically. If you then take into account all the new buildings and refurbishment programmes, this could soon become better known amongst the schools to the west of the city.

St Dominic's Sixth Form College

Mount Park Avenue, Harrow on the Hill HA1 3HX

020 8422 8084 | admissions@stdoms.ac.uk | stdoms.ac.uk

State	Pupils: 1,234	
Ages: 16–19		

Principal: Since 2013, Andrew Parkin (40s). Studied music at Durham and Cambridge and started his professional career in London at The St Marylebone Girls' School. Went on to be deputy head at Sion Manning Girls' School in Kensington and then St Augustine's High School in Westminster. 'For 18 years, I worked in fairly tough comprehensives, which probably explains why the hottest topics for me are teaching, learning, attainment, consistency and attendance and punctuality,' he says. 'But I love the way that here, we get to combine these with informalities such as addressing each other on first name terms, as well as a greater emphasis on independent learning – the result of which is fantastic preparation for university.'

Not someone to hide away in his office, he greets students on the gate, observes lessons, teaches general RE (and occasionally some music) and regularly chats to students and staff. 'I'm not really a number cruncher – I don't believe that is what headships are about.' Clearly passionate about his role ('I absolutely love it! I feel I've got the most perfect job, with happy students that work their very hard, and no discipline issues'), he is also a keen member of several committees in the wider sector. Among the key changes he's brought to the college are a strong emphasis on teaching and learning, more peer observations, a hands-on leadership team and embedding IT into learning. Students don't have a bad word to say about him. 'He seems to know everybody's name,' said one. 'He's so approachable and easy going.' Parents similarly keen: 'He is absolutely fabulous – a supportive leader who's not afraid to get his hands dirty, rather than being just a figurehead.'

Both interested and interesting, he is keen amateur musician and is chairman of the BBC Symphony Chorus.

Academic matters: Some 29 subjects available in more-or-less any combination. Maths, history, the three sciences, economics and psychology are the most popular A level subjects – with strongest results in maths, chemistry, biology, history and economics (in terms of attainment) and history,

classics, languages, music and art (in terms of value-added). In 2018, 32 per cent A*/A grades and 62 per cent A*-B grades at A level.

Option to change subjects in the first week or two if you really loathe geography or have just developed a passionate interest in Italian. Currently, students can take four subjects in year 12, dropping down to three in year 13, enabling them to keep options open. Offers level 3 BTec national and extended diplomas, ideally suited to those who don't like the sound of lots of final exams, which can be combined with one (extended course) or two (national course) A levels. 'BTecs are often undersold, but they afford our less academic students an opportunity to achieve highly and go onto the likes of York, Nottingham and London universities. The business studies one has validity and is taught well here,' claims the principal. College has also brought in a core maths programme, which enables students to keep up with maths without taking the full A level.

Not someone to hide away in his office, he greets students on the gate, observes lessons

Class sizes range from 2-25 and teaching is largely discussion-based. 'The teachers' subject knowledge is phenomenal – some have two degrees,' one told us. 'Teachers here are so inspirational and really passionate about what they teach,' said another, although be warned they are very hot on homework, being 'very strict on both completion and deadlines.' Professional development for teachers is a strength, with all having spent time in London schools. 'It's been great for them to see what life is like elsewhere – it's got them to reflect on their own practice and raise the bar,' explains the principal.

Good for those with physical disabilities – we met one wheelchair user, who couldn't praise the college highly enough. 'There's not one area I can't access,' she said. Students with hearing or visual impairments are equally impressed. Very few students with SEN, though. Support for them is 50 per cent classroom support, while the other half takes place in the Study Plus area, which other students access for anything from revision workshops to small project groups – all of which helps to prevent any stigma. 'Our son has Asperger's and the college has been brilliant – really going out of their way to help him on his terms and he got far better results than we thought he would,' one parent told us.

Offers the EPQ. 'They have a free choice of subject, but it makes sense to relate it to a subject they may do at university, and gives something to talk about at interview.' Large numbers of aspiring medics, so the college runs a programme of BMAT preparation and mock interviews. Excellent university and careers advice; has been awarded the Investors in Careers mark and has a designated HE and careers advisor. 'We're realistic and honest, and allow no poverty of aspiration.'

'With the sounds of nature and the London hum in the background, and the sheer talent of the students, it's all highly dramatic,' says the principal

Effort and achievement grades given every six weeks. 'Our monitoring is much more frequent than they have time to do in schools. All our staff are focused on the sixth form – not on settling in year 7s or helping year 9s choose GCSE subjects, or indeed behavioural issues.'

Games, options, the arts: State-of-the-art sports hall includes a multigym and hall for badminton, table tennis and five-a-side football, with its use juggled between A level PE students and general recreation. Sport is not compulsory, but the hall 'has increased motivation and attendance. We've been pleasantly surprised that participation rates have been very high.' Indeed, the principal encourages all students to utilise the multigym, which is open from 7.30am-5.30pm. Outdoor space includes a five-a-side football/netball court and a football field set among beautiful woodland. There's at least one team for each of football, rugby, tennis, basketball, table tennis and netball – 'Football trials are particularly popular, with around 100 students applying for just 11 places,' one student told us. They do well in local leagues, and some competitions further afield, particularly for football and badminton. There's a cycling club and golf club, plus opportunities for cheerleading and street dance for those less competitively inclined.

Music is part of everyday life – we heard the practising for the annual bands' performances when we visited. Decent numbers (around 25) do A level, while seven peripatetic teachers cover individual teaching of instruments including piano, flute, strings, guitar and drums. Choir and orchestra both popular and good, with termly concerts providing opportunities to perform. Department comprises of teaching space, recording studio and rehearsal rooms, and there's a newly installed electric organ in the chapel, that is used by keyboard players. 'I've been known to pop in to play it for half-an-hour myself,' admits the principal.

Top floor art studios could be bigger and better, but they do the job and are reassuringly cluttered with colourful resources and some very talented work. Three teachers cover art, art history and DT, and the sophisticated artwork and fashion creations are exhibited in the chapel annually, with several students each year going on to art and design courses. Drama studio is ok, but any lack of cutting edge practice areas doesn't put off keen thespians, who put on an annual musical production, plus various productions throughout the year. Great excitement about the devised pieces being showcased annually in the so-called 'shack' – a covered outside space for which the college hires in tiered seating. 'With the sounds of nature and the London hum in the background, and the sheer talent of the students, it's all highly dramatic,' says the principal, recalling that one performance required a pig's head having to be ordered from the butcher, then kept under health and safety conditions.

Volunteering and fundraising are important parts of the ethos. 'Charity efforts spring up out of nowhere.' Students do sponsored walks and sleep outs, work in soup kitchens, volunteer on a Catholic farm, join a pilgrimage to Lourdes. 'There's a philosophy of respecting other people and helping the wider community.'

Long list of day trips and residentials. 'London is used to the max – theatres, museums, concerts, Houses of Parliament and so on.' Among the regular overseas trips are Great Wall of China (general trip, open to all), Washington DC (history and politics students) – and there's an annual exchange with a school in New Jersey. Other recent trips have included music trip to New York, art trip to Rome, general trip to Venice and classics trip to Athens. Extracurricular activities not obligatory, but widely taken up – including everything from flower arranging to sports. Guest speakers regularly invited in – including The Spectator's editor Fraser Nelson, Sir Bernard Hogan Howe, Mark Damazer and Phillip Coggan.

Background and atmosphere: Opened in 1978 in what had been St Dominic's Independent Grammar School for Girls, run by Dominican nuns. Sits on a hill above a leafy, gated estate of substantial houses with large gardens that could have strayed from the Chilterns, and amazing views across London – as far as the City and Canary Wharf on a clear day. By the entrance to the 28-acre site is the chapel, a peaceful and atmospheric building with lovely stained glass, 'the heart of the college'. Assemblies (each year group gets four a year, which are supplemented by the principal's Sunday night emails on a theme for the week, such as 'What is truth?') and introductory talks take place here, as well as morning masses, and Muslim students use a side room for prayer. Four large blocks make up the key teaching areas – Hume (humanities), Catherine (maths, English, languages), Aquinas (sciences) and Siena (sports hall and psychology).

The most recently developed facility is the remodelled library – among the nicest we've seen, in which the £1m investment paid for a bright, airy space, with multicoloured seats and two glass-dominated mezzanine areas, with masses of study space and computers. 'It's well staffed and equipped – we love it,' one student told us. Indeed, it's generally packed until closing time at 4.30pm.

No common room ('We don't need one – we're not a school,' says principal), with students gathering instead in the spacious canteen, library and the Shack, where an all-day coffee kiosk augments the canteen offerings.

Faith is a major part of the deal here, with the principal big on the Dominican tradition – with links with its sisters and brothers all around the country. Mass is held every week, tutor groups take it in turns to choose readings, everyone studies RE. 'We want our students to develop on an academic, personal and spiritual level. We want them to critically examine their faith, to mix with people from other faiths and hear why it is important to them. It makes a tremendous difference to what we can offer and how they develop in later life,' says principal.

About 60 per cent of the staff is Catholic, but all buy into the ethos. Prayers are said each morning and each tutor period. 'It is a moment for thinking outside oneself – a lovely sharing moment.' Very good relationships amongst staff and between staff and pupils and overall, there's a real buzz around campus – the atmosphere is relaxed, informal, yet hardworking.

Pastoral care, well-being and discipline: Any student problems tend to be ironed out by teachers or the college counsellor, the latter whose hourly slots over two days a week are always packed out. 'If I could afford it, I'd have her here five days,' say the principal. One parent whose family had suffered trauma were particularly impressed by the pastoral offering. 'They could not have done more for my son.' Mental health issues, particularly anxiety, on the up, reports the college – but that's no different to what any other head tells us. In the main, things tick over pretty smoothly here – and students were aghast when we asked them if there was any bullying. 'Unlike a lot of sixth form colleges, where you get cliques, this one has a really warm and friendly atmosphere,' said one. Strong student voice – changing everything from more loo rolls in the toilets and better air-con to helping organise events like the annual talent show and cultural day.

'I insist every young person has someone to represent them because when they get to 16, many parents take a back seat, and that's not what we want here'

Electronic registration for every lesson means that everyone is accounted for: the pastoral team phones parent and student if the student is not in by 10am. If lateness becomes a regular occurrence, homework is late, a student shows lack of effort, or takes unauthorized absence, then they're put on warning. If they still don't pull their socks up, they are asked to attend supervised learning and teaching (detention basically – although they won't call it that). 'It's an opportunity for students who haven't worked hard enough that week to do so,' says the principal, although not many students wind up actually having to attend one. If there's still no improvement, parents are called in – again, it's very few students overall. Zero tolerance for drugs or violence, but no problems with either for many years – in fact, no temporary exclusions whatsoever in current principal's reign.

Pupils and parents: About 40 per cent Catholic, most of the rest Hindu or Muslim. Homogeneous in that all take their religious faith seriously, with the exception of one or two atheists (but no zealous ones, unsurprisingly). 'All students are serious about academic life – you need to be motivated and have a certain level of intelligence to get on here,' one student told us – indeed, the college offers virtually no vocational courses. And as there is a high level of competition for places, those who get in feel a great sense of gratitude. 'I feel really lucky to be here,' is something of a mantra.

White British is certainly not the majority here. 'Harrow is one of the most diverse boroughs in the area, and we are reflective of that,' says principal. Good mix in terms of class too – with many students the first in their families to aspire to university. Parents are nearly all highly supportive, with 97 per cent attendance at the annual parents' evening – doubtless helped by the fact that parents can drop in anytime between 9am-7.30pm and the principal stipulates that they do so. 'I insist every young person has someone to represent them because it's my experience that when young men and women get to 16, many parents take a back seat, and that's not what we want here.'

Entrance: About 40 per cent from its two partner schools, Salvatorian College and Sacred Heart Language College – the rest from over 100 other feeder schools, stretching as far as 1.5 hours travel away. 'I know someone who comes in from Kent,' one student told us, while one from Enfield told us it takes her 'an hour-and-10-minutes travelling one way – and that's on a good day.' 'Most of our students live in Harrow, but if you looked at a heat map of London, we'd have dots representing students' homes all over it, and I think that's great,' says the principal. 'At 16, people are old enough to make decisions and if they recognise excellence and are prepared to make an effort to get out of bed for it, then I'm all for it.'

Students from the main two feeder schools are guaranteed a place, providing they get at least five 9-4 GCSE grades including English language. All other applicants must get at least seven 9-4s and meet the individual subject requirements. These range from a 4 in English for religious studies to an 7 in maths for further maths. Priority to Catholics, then other practising Christians, then other faiths and no faith. Applicants must acknowledge their commitment to the religious values of the school in writing. Conditional offers are made in March and are based on academic references, including predicted grades. Any remaining places offered based on subjects with spaces and highest GCSE average score. Some spaces also become available after the first year. 'Many parents round here work abroad, so there's quite a lot of movement in the area,' explains the principal.

Exit: Around 90 per cent to higher education. London universities are very popular, as are Nottingham, Southampton and Warwick. Law and medical/biomedical subjects tend to top the tables. Fewer Oxbridge applicants than one might expect given the calibre of students (eight places in 2018), largely because so many are prospective medics (15 in 2018).

Money matters: Free if you're under 19. Excellent and enlightened system of bursaries for students and staff to fund specific projects and trips.

Remarks: Greatly sought-after college in pleasant leafy location with high academic standards and a strong Catholic ethos of care for each other. 'A lovely place to work and study,' say staff and students.

St Helen's School

Eastbury Road, Northwood HA6 3AS

01923 843210 | admissions@sthelens.london | sthelens.london

| Independent | Pupils: 1,162; sixth form: 146 |
| Ages: 3–18 | Fees: £13,841 – £17,448 pa |

Headmistress: Since 2011, Dr Mary Short BA PGCE PhD (50s) – did her PhD, in the politics of budget-setting in the 1920s, at Cambridge. Has taught undergraduates at Cambridge and pupils at independent schools including St Paul's Girls, City of London School and Haberdashers' Aske's Girls (deputy head). At St Helen's, she has upped the academic performance, partly by making the school more selective, but also by curriculum reviews, consistency of aims, better monitoring of performance, peer review of teachers, that sort of thing.

But a league table obsessive she is not and parents say she's made her changes through evolution, not revolution. 'I think my main contribution so far is making sure St Helen's understands what it is,' she says. 'In the past, the school knew what it wasn't, but wasn't sure what it did stand for. I'd say we're now firmly on the map as having academic ambition, but with very strong co-curricular.'

Our first impressions were of someone over-protective of her school and her girls; she later showed herself to be cordial, unpretentious and an impressive strategist. Parents describe her as 'businesslike.' 'She always makes time for you and is good at keeping parents informed, including through her blog which isn't some Ra Ra Ra newsletter, but a "here's what we're doing well and here's what we are trying to improve",' said one. But although she told us she has a very visible presence throughout the school, some juniors told us 'we don't see her very often.'

She has teaching in her blood and is married to a fellow teacher, with whom she lives in north London. Apart from history, likes walking, gardening and travel. Retiring in July 2019.

Academic matters: Not the top of the highly competitive north London academic tree, but no slouch. No visitor to the school is likely to leave without hearing the word 'ambitious' repeatedly. 'They want you to aim high, but there's not masses of pressure,' one girl told us. Think carrots not sticks, stretch not push, although gets crisper as they get older of course. 'We want independent thinkers and I always say it's the quality of the questions you ask in class that matter more than anything,' says head, although one parent told us 'you get the impression that it's the compliant, hard-working girls they really want.'

So vast are playing fields and floodlit courts extending in all directions that you realise most of this end of Northwood is St Helen's

In 2018, 52 per cent A*/A at A level, 79 per cent 9-7 at GCSE. Most girls take nine or 10 GCSEs, including a language, at least one humanity and a practical subject such as drama or DT. Reasonably even spread of success across subjects at GCSE, including maths and sciences. In sixth form, most take three A levels plus either an AS or EPQ. Popular subjects at this level are the sciences, maths, economics and history, with maths results particularly strong. Physics as ever with girls the slightly weaker relation, but school working hard on this and take-up is growing – the Heath Robinson Club is popular and interest in engineering is strong. Students are able to complement their A level programme with the St Helen's Portfolio, which comprises additional qualifications such as the European Computer Driving Licence; continue with languages they have studied to GCSE or acquire additional languages or study further mathematics; also recognises CCF, D of E, other clubs and societies. Girls rave about the Wednesday lecture series and university preparation courses.

French from year 1; then in year 7, girls choose two out of four languages – French, German, Spanish and Mandarin, as well as learning Latin; at GCSE, Italian and Japanese are additional options. No setting in prep, except two 'broad bands in maths from year 4.' In seniors, setting from year 7 in maths and at GCSE stage for sciences. But more 'differentiation in learning needs' and 'child initiated learning' than previously, says school. Lots of male teachers, lots of teachers who have had other professional lives before or even during teaching and a growing number of teachers who teach across both juniors and seniors, although fewer subject specialists teaching in prep than we expected. 'I encourage the teachers to use their own personal styles so the girls respond to their different personalities,' says head; inevitably pupils like some more than others. Parents praise the 'inspired teaching' in prep – plenty of competitions, incentives and outdoor learning. Homework starts in nursery with practising a sound a week, building up incrementally to around 40 minutes a day by year 6 and 60 minutes plus for seniors.

Thoroughly sympathetic to SEN, from the headmistress down. All pupils are screened annually from year 3 to year 11 to help spot any potential educational difficulties. Individual needs department with three staff provides support to pupils from age 7 both inside and outside the classroom. School can and does support autistic spectrum difficulties, mild dyslexia and dyspraxia, mild speech difficulties and children with hearing impairments. Support, but not separate teaching, for those who have English as an additional language. Some 350+ children currently identified as gifted and talented and supported with 'differentiated work schemes and activities.' 'I've got nothing but praise for SEN provision; we haven't had to push the school at any point,' one parent told us.

Games, options, the arts: Don't be fooled by St Helen's sedate hedges, modest perimeter walls and close proximity to Northwood town centre. So vast are playing fields, floodlit courts and pitches extending in all directions that you soon realise that most of this end of Northwood is St Helen's. Superb sports complex, including large indoor pool; new all-weather pitch. Lacrosse, netball, football, tennis, athletics, badminton, rounders, rugby and cricket all popular and many other games and activities available including pilates, aerobics, climbing and trampolining. County level for lacrosse, badminton and netball and national representation by individuals at swimming, gym, cycling, tennis and rugby. Supports those who excel (and need time off for national teams), but some parents feel girls at the less sporty end miss out: 'It's not sport for all here, with an elitist attitude to teams, and my daughter has no interest in fitness or sports now as a result.' All do ballet, PE, music and speech and drama as part of the prep school curriculum.

Art, DT and drama housed in the June Leader building, named after school's outstanding, and aptly named, head of 20 years (1966-1986). Art, having gone through a bit of a wobble, is now on the up with girls knuckling down to theory and individual skills when we visited. 'Art has a more academic feel now – no longer just a place to hang out,' says head. DT bubbling and well taught if not as jazzily equipped as some (though there is CAD and two 3D printers). Dance and drama (some joint with Merchant Taylors') much enjoyed, especially in the context of the annual House Arts festival – and again, there's popular take-up academically, with drama run as both a GCSE and A level. Plenty of performances, with recent examples including the prep school production of Matilda ('which made me weep,' says head), a musical written by the English teacher and performed by the middle school, and Kiss Me Kate! by the upper school. The Centre (multi-purpose space converted from old gym) also used for the performing arts and sport.

'Music has been great for years, but still gets even better year on year,' a parent told us, with numerous orchestras, choirs (the main one tours annually) and bands, again with much teaming up with Merchant Taylor's. 'Our jazz band played at their summer jazz night – it was wonderful,' says head. Around 250 girls do individual music lessons with peripatetic teachers. Plenty of varied opportunities for performing in school – new music centre – and the wider community, including regular concerts at St John's, Smith Square, London.

Collaboration with Merchant Taylors' also in CCF. D of E and Young Enterprise popular too. Visits from profs, writers and theatre companies. Co-curricular is bursting from every nook and cranny of the school, much of it student-led ('I've started up a foreign fiction book club for students and staff,' one girl told us), with hundreds of things for pupils to try and, when they latch on to one, the school will find ways of allowing it to be taken further. Particular successes in debating, maths and physics Olympiads, technology competitions. Lots of trips – Galapagos, Venice, Lake Tahoe, Ypres, Berlin, British Museum, galleries.

Background and atmosphere: Founded at the end of the 19th century with a vision of education for the whole child, which it still holds dear. A spacious school, trim and imaginative grounds. Dark green uniform up to 16; freedom in the sixth (including jeans). Plenty of recently completed developments eg Little Gables playground for pre-prep; junior school building with solar panels and green roof bringing all of key stage 2 into an exceptionally colourful, spacious and imaginative space; new

Co-curricular is bursting from every nook and cranny of the school, much of it student-led ('I've started up a foreign fiction book club for students and staff,' one girl told us) with hundreds of things to try

reception with glass corridor; new computer science labs; swish new dining room with fabulous food. Longworthe, one of the former boarding houses, is now used for before and after-school care in which pupils with busy parents can spend a long day – breakfast and tea included and quiet places for prep and recreation. 'The school provides very long hours of childcare for those who want it – you see girls as young as 3 left from early in the morning until quite late in the afternoon,' said one parent. Nicely decorated new sixth form block (much studiousness observed). Hard to think of any facilities the pupils could want for.

A culturally diverse school, with strong Indian, Tamil and Jewish (a strong JSoc and well-established links with the local synagogue) contingents, and reassuring lack of cliques. Notable absence of the unhealthily thin.

We were repeatedly assured the prep is an integral part of the whole and although they share many of the facilities of the senior school (sports, dining room, music), several girls and parents told us 'they feel like three very separate schools – it's a shame there aren't more links.' The nursery, Little Gables, and key stage 1, Gables, are in converted houses on site, each with own playground, while key stage 2s are in the stunning new purpose-built building, already noted. Happy atmosphere, bright uniform, civilised loos and teachers who call their charges 'ladies' while managing not to make the girls too precious. It is natural for girls here to stay the course – now from 3 to 18 – and continue to feel that it's all in the family. Oodles of gushing about it all from the girls. 'I would lay down my life for St Helens,' said one girl, who didn't appear to be joking.

Pastoral care, well-being and discipline: 'Even by the first parents' evening, I felt they 100 per cent knew my daughter – right down to the things that make her tick or anxious,' one parent told us. Indeed, pastoral care here starts with individual teachers, who are expected to notice and to care how the girls are, and to react supportively and promptly to any sign of trouble. As a result, while teachers talk of all the usual friendship problems, the girls shrug them off and prefects do not see dealing with social ills as a significant part of their remit. Relationships within houses, year groups and tutor groups all seem close, giving girls a variety of communities to turn to. Healthy awareness of issues such as self-harm and eating disorders and a part-time counsellor and clinical psychologist visit each week. 'My daughter gets very stressed about exams and they've been spot on in dealing with it – the pastoral lead at the school goes well beyond the call of duty,' said one parent.

Staff/student relationships palpably amiable. 'If I bumped into a teacher here and now, I'd probably wind up chatting to them for about five minutes – they're all so lovely,' said one sixth former. 'There are no doors closed here,' insisted another.

High expectations and clear boundaries, but it doesn't feel overly strict. 'These girls are conservative and from aspirational families in strong communities – we have very few behavioural problems,' says head. Warnings for forgetting PE kit, handing in homework late etc, but most girls go through their entire school life without a detention. Inner London problems kept at bay. Certainly no drugs incidents, or indeed temporary exclusions, in living memory. The occasional foolish misdemeanour is dealt with individually but 'sanely. It's never public, it's not about humiliation – ever.' You're allowed to slip here.

Pupils and parents: Northwood is affluent, with lots of large detached houses. But girls come from much wider area – good coach service covers Beaconsfield, Elstree, Barnet, Amersham, Ealing, Hemel Hempstead and points between. Others get the train and some – thanks to better car parking – are dropped off. The circle on the map gets smaller for juniors, though, and smaller still for nursery 'where girls are very local.'

'They want you to aim high, but there's not masses of pressure,' one girl told us. Think carrots not sticks, stretch not push, although gets crisper as they get older, of course

Resilient, personable and chatty girls. But while other heads encourage us to talk to their pupils without staff within earshot, visitor protocol here meant that junior girls came with an entourage of sixth formers and teaching staff (which inevitably meant no girl said she'd 'change a single thing'); the rules are the same for parents coming for individual visits during the school day, so visit on a working open morning if you want the low-down from the girls themselves.

Parents sociable, with thriving PTA. Old girls' network huge and devoted. St Helen's inspires great loyalty. Alumnae include Patricia Hodge, a great supporter, Vanessa Lawrence (United Nations), Lady Lowry, Luisa Baldini, Penny Marshall, Paula Nickolds (CEO John Lewis) and Maria Djurkovic.

Entrance: First point of entry is at 3 or 4 by observation and interview. At 7 by tests in English and maths and interview. School part of London 11+ Consortium which shares tests at 11- now a single cognitive ability test, plus interview; around 460 apply (around half each from state and independent sector) for approximately 100 places (sometimes more places are available due to bulge years) – not too terrifying as lots apply elsewhere too but school is increasingly candidates' first choice. Junior school girls have to sit the exam too, and up to 10 or so don't make the transition, either because they because they aren't academic enough ('in which case, we'd have conversations well before year 6,' says head) or they choose a competitor school. Just under half of the senior school places are filled by junior school girls. Occasional places available throughout the school. Interview and reference from current school as important as scores.

'Aim is to explore potential and to ensure that girls will be able to take full advantage of the curriculum and wider opportunities the school has to offer,' says the school. As ever true but never spelt out, parents should remember that they are on show too.

Between five and 10 join at sixth form. You need 7+ GCSEs at 6+ including good grades in the subjects relevant to the A level choices – 7s in sciences and maths; sometimes lower in humanities.

Exit: Much praise for the smooth transition from nursery to the juniors and from juniors to seniors. Around 15-20 per cent leave post-GCSE, most to co-ed or local state schools. All sixth formers to higher education. Three-quarters to Russell Group universities (London, Bath, Leeds, Warwick, Birmingham are popular). About a third science-related: strong bias to medical, biological and engineering courses, with a high proportion of dentistry and medical offers. Handful to Oxbridge annually (four in 2018); some parents feel the head makes too much of this ('It's always being mentioned'). Futures department, just off the sixth form study area, considered by the girls to be top notch.

Money matters: Currently supporting around 60 girls on means-tested bursaries (around 20 of those are on 100 per cent bursaries). These bursaries awarded annually either to girls whose parents could not otherwise meet fees or to girls whose families are experiencing temporary difficulties. Range of scholarships also available.

Remarks: By no means soaring the top of the league tables, but plenty of ambition for its pupils, academically and otherwise, with a strong underlying ethos of opportunity, progression and support.

Girls are so devoted to, and sentimental about, the school that you wonder if they're all sent on a PR course upon joining. All in all, an inspired educational offering with superb and spacious facilities and where there's pace but without the relentless pressure of some of its key competitors.

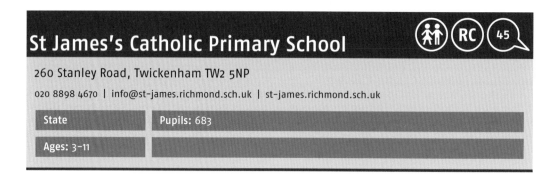

St James's Catholic Primary School

260 Stanley Road, Twickenham TW2 5NP

020 8898 4670 | info@st-james.richmond.sch.uk | st-james.richmond.sch.uk

State	Pupils: 683
Ages: 3–11	

Headteacher: Since September 2016, Louise Yarnell (30s) married to a teacher (not at St James's), with two small daughters (also not at St James's). LY told us, slightly ruefully, that there was no room at the inn due to the school not operating a 'children of teachers' policy. She arrived here from St Norbert's in Lincolnshire, which she had speedily transformed into an Ofsted outstanding school but then had to wait six years for a visit from the awarding powers. Her accent immediately gives away her origins from a part of the UK across the water, but she is now happily ensconced back in her husband's territory on the edge of west London, where she also went to college.

A bit cagey and slightly wary of us at first, she is clearly not only on top of the job but also proud of her school, so much so that she handed us a pre-written review, which was a very kind thought but we do like to write it ourselves. She invariably calls the children 'sweetheart' and some children definitely respond, one not-so-small girl flinging her arms round her as we walked round. There were mixed comments about her visibility around the school, but one parent remarked, 'she's very visible if you're late at the gate', and she came in for praise for her communication skills: 'The talk she gave at the carol service was a wonderful way to end the term'.

Entrance: At 3, 52 places in the nursery, almost 100 per cent moving up to reception. Parents say that they would be 'mad not to' and the remainder of the three form entry is filled from the four local Catholic parishes (priority is given to practising Catholics). The school is heavily oversubscribed and although the local birth rate is falling there

are still too many children for the available chairs. The only hope of a spot further up the school is if the removal vans are ordered and parents have to, reluctantly, move their child to another school.

Exit: Parents who want their children to continue being educated in a Catholic environment tend to opt for St Richard Reynolds Catholic High School in Twickenham. Up to a quarter of the children move on to independent senior schools, such as Hampton and Tiffin, but almost always in the same segment of outer London. Apparently, the school tends not to make direct recommendations on the next step with parents mainly doing the research themselves.

Remarks: With a site tucked down a cul-de-sac next to a golf club and opposite a tidy housing estate, an outsider would need to see the school hoarding to be sure they had arrived in the right place. Past the gates and in through the door is a smallish reception space furnished with 'outstanding' Ofsted citations and a plaster Madonna, her mantle toning happily with the emerald sofa cushions beside her. Immediately, you realise that this is a school not shy about proclaiming the importance of its faith and the attendant ethos.

Off the hall is the nursery where small people were stuffing woollen balls – masquerading as buns – into a play oven or experimenting with manoeuvring a motley selection of chickens and black labradors over a grassy hillock on a computer screen. Outside, others were exploring the current topic of the Arctic by enthusiastically shovelling fake snow over miniature walruses and seals but ignoring the polar bear lying on his plastic back.

Specialist French teacher. The approach is so successful that one parent told us she was 'blown away' that her 9 year old already spoke better French than her father

Past a screen featuring the four parish saints, together with their priests, the main school lies through double doors, surmounted by a plaque announcing that the block was opened by the Princess Royal. A long corridor, classroom doors interspersed with coat pegs and panels filled by pupils' work, provides the main artery and contains the lower years, with a floor above providing a home for the older children. There is an IT room, separate spaces where individual teaching can take place and an inviting library, complete with a librarian and a Narnia cupboard marked Book Shop. No secret world but plenty of books, provided by parents, which children can buy in instalments, but unlike the real world they can't take them home until they're fully paid up.

On the way to the playground outside is the George Tancred Centre for children with moderate autism, staffed by a team of six. It was nearly empty on our visit, proving the head's assertion that 'they are extremely successful at integrating them into the mainstream' to be correct. This was backed up by a parent saying that her son considered a child from the GTC as part of his class, even though she only came to some of the lessons. The teachers and assistants are all qualified and one small boy was certainly proud of his baking skills and made a good stab at pronouncing focaccia.

In contrast to the unremarkable façade, the back of the school is a glorious surprise with acres of grassy pitches and a newish PE building. Excellent use is made of this green paradise or muddy field (depending on the season), with children having at least two hours of games a week plus after-school clubs. They are borough champions in several sports ranging from swimming to tag rugby and even scooped a bronze medal in athletics at the London Youth Games, pretty good for a school where a class teacher is in charge of PE. In tune with their beliefs, there is even a contemplative spot furnished with benches and a gigantic pair of hands in prayer, sculpted by a parent.

Sats are consistently outstanding with French mentioned by all parents as brilliantly taught, partly due to the specialist French teacher who catches them very young. The approach is so successful that one parent told us she was 'blown away' that her 9 year old already spoke better French than her father, who was apparently somewhat

put out. In addition, to help the child with a linguistic bent, the school runs after-hours clubs in Latin, Polish and Mandarin. The work ethic is very strong, encouraged not only at school but also by a sizeable chunk of homework every evening and it is definitely a source of pride if your house wins the annual cup with points handed out for homework, manners and attendance as well as academic success.

Music is major here and LY's first appointment, a hugely enthusiastic and friendly music mistress, proudly showed us her shelf of brand new, yellow ukuleles. Parents affirm that she is 'fantastic' and has made music great fun: 'it's more mainstream now'. The weekly music lessons can be topped up by extracurricular music technology clubs, recorder groups and private music lessons and there are several choirs.

As you might expect from a Catholic institution, 'manners maketh man' in this school and the children leaped to hold open doors and answer questions politely. LY says that she cannot remember having a child sent to her for 'making a wrong choice' in her time in charge, and she has never had to face the unpleasant task of calling in a parent over their child's behaviour. We felt that we would also have minded out Ps and Qs when she hove into sight and that her plan to introduce a 'habit of mind passport' for the exceptionally well-behaved might be a bit daunting for some.

Head even persuaded one exciting father, who works for Virgin Galactic, to come and give a careers talk on building spaceships to an open-mouthed, goggle-eyed audience

The cerebral side is also encouraged by the accreditation of the school as a Thinking School in 2016. This strategy, based on Edward de Bono's Thinking Hats, puts controlled thinking at the core of the curriculum from day one. In practical terms this means more theme-based teaching with a new topic each half of the term, a change that children approve of, saying that it 'makes school more exciting'.

Large numbers of parents lend a hand, although the increase in numbers of working mothers means that there are fewer these days to help the mainly young (about two-thirds of the staff) teachers. There was zero evidence of this change causing a problem and the school gave the impression of running like clockwork, obviously partially due to the capable hands of the head. A larger staff turnover than one might expect but LY explains this by pointing out the cost of local housing, a serious problem for anyone on a state school wage.

The increase in working parents has led the school to organise a Breakfast Club and a Stay and Play scheme, which allow supervision from 7.30am to 5.30pm when necessary. Some of the only negative comments were around school meals: most of the children bring in packed lunches and there was not much enthusiasm for the food, particularly if you were not a meat eater.

The fairly affluent, middle class parents (miniscule percentage on free school meals) muck in by raising money (about £30k annually), used to buy anything from pianos to iPads, or by contributing worldly knowledge to help with assemblies. LY even persuaded one exciting father, who works for Virgin Galactic, to come and give a careers talk on building spaceships to an open-mouthed, goggle-eyed audience. Again as you would expect, charity fundraising is taken seriously with a different charity each week in advent and lent and pupils are in the thick of it.

A successful, orderly school believing firmly in putting children on the right path, not only in terms of academic achievement but also in their knowledge of themselves and their attitude to others, but might not suit those with a rebellious streak.

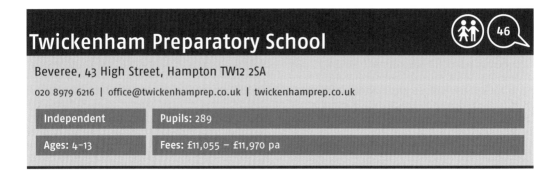

Twickenham Preparatory School

Beveree, 43 High Street, Hampton TW12 2SA

020 8979 6216 | office@twickenhamprep.co.uk | twickenhamprep.co.uk

Independent	Pupils: 289
Ages: 4–13	Fees: £11,055 – £11,970 pa

Headmaster: Since 2005, David Malam BA Southampton (history), PGCE King Alfred's College, Winchester (50s). Clever, very comfortable in his own skin and refreshingly candid. Like every other London prep head offering both the 11+ and 13+, he's reviewing the situation, though says there's no danger of losing common entrance, as long as leading senior schools (notably Hampton) retain 13+ entry. With odds slightly better at 13+ than at 11+ and those extra two prep years to enjoy – far better than being bottom of the heap in a senior school – what's not to like, he says.

Dreamed of pro career in either football or chess, taking both to a high level before studying history. Previous experience of running youth club at local church made teacher training a natural step. Initially worked in schools on the south coast, followed by a year in a Christian school in Cyprus. Started here in 1995 as history and games teacher, before becoming senior teacher and then deputy head in 1997.

Describes the job with welcome absence of corporate waffle. Though cites an impressive list of improvements, from mini amphitheatre to revamped grounds (including new sports surface) it's all outweighed by getting the staffing right. Teachers must 'genuinely enjoy working with children and see teaching as a vocation, not a day job,' (they all run a club). Approach was clearly paying off, judging by feedback from parents and pupils.

'[They] go the extra mile,' said one, praising willingness to take children to events at weekends nationwide 'and often abroad, too.'

Delights in pupil success (wears a tie in the school purple on Fridays for celebration assembly), particularly in areas that are close to his heart. Thinking skills and chess head the list (one pupil recently won gold for Britain in the Mind Lab Olympics).

Though he has done his time here (four children successfully and happily through the school and one still here), he still has a few years to go and so far, at least, appetite for the role remains undiminished.

Entrance: Non selective at 4+. Otherwise, it's occasional places only from reception onwards after assessments in English, maths and reasoning. If spaces permit, will take on a handful in year 6 to prepare for common entrance.

First dibs to staff children and siblings, followed by those deemed to be likely to benefit most from education here. Families who have registered are asked to sign acceptance form 18 months before start date. Deposit secures place – non-refundable if not taken up, deducted (with no interest) from final term's fees if it is.

Some pupils arrive at the school with undiagnosed needs, supported with, says head, 'best SEN in the area,' who gets rave reviews from parents. Parents, however, praise school's ability to identify barriers impeding progress – will work with speech and language therapists and implement social communication programmes. 'Provision for children with dyslexia is outstanding,' said one.

Focus, however, is on pupils who will do well academically. But while it's not the right place for those who might struggle to access the curriculum, head stresses that will talk to parents in year 5 or thereabouts about common entrance, if a pupil wants to stay, 'we would do our very best to keep them.'

Exit: Discussions about senior schools start in years 4 and 5. In 2018, three scholarships were taken up to St George's College Weybridge, Hampton School and Notre Dame. Most popular destinations were Hampton School (six pupils), Sir William Perkins School and Notre Dame (three pupils each). LEH, Surbiton High, SWPS, St Catherine's (Twickenham) and Notre Dame feature among the girls-only destinations. Recent most popular co-ed was St George's College. Others to Kingston Grammar and Radnor House.

Remarks: So good that last full ISI inspection dates from 2012 (there was also a regulatory compliance one in 2017). According to parents, however, all that was good then (just about everything) remains so. The only area with small question mark – IT – being sorted with help from ever generous Parents' Committee.

Name is misleading – was in Twickenham but moved to Hampton in the early 1990s after outgrowing original site. Not that this will need much explaining to the mostly very local punters, many from Hampton and Teddington, elsewhere Richmond and Twickenham plus a few from Sunbury, Molesey, Walton and Thames Ditton.

Many maintained sector escapees who find the school reassuringly normal. 'You don't forget where you've come from,' said one. School's home is a pretty listed building with modern, friendly additions including recent art and music block, complete with clock (also courtesy of parents) and railings, both in vibrant purple which also features in tasteful stripes down tracksuits, sensible exercise in restraint that stops assembly resembling a storm at a lavender farm.

Pre-prep has a semi secret location at the back of the attractive multi-purpose hall (eye-catching wavy roof, sprung floor, variable acoustics – older pupils would need keener hearing than ours to pick up more than the occasional word during otherwise delightfully inclusive whole-school assembly). Open the door and the light, airy kingdom of the 4 to 7-year-olds is revealed. 'It's about being loved, nurtured, feeling secure and taking risks,' says pre-prep head Mrs Barnes, an English specialist who has been at the school for 15 plus years and exudes warmth.

Freeflow rules outside with communal areas for all, while reception, year 1 and year 2 each have side-by-side plant-filled little gardens, with a secret leafy nature trail at the back, venue for (low) risk activities like building dens. Details-driven head of maintenance has even fitted nest boxes round the pre-prep building (RSPCA occasionally called in to rescue stranded fledglings) and prefers real grass over chilly perfection of artificial version (hurrah!), which is confined solely to reception garden after nature proved unable to compete with over-enthusiastic scootering.

Lessons are lively, from year 2, cutting out pyramids, sticking pinwheels in the top and then testing them courtesy of teacher's hairdryer, to popular prep history teacher who performs own songs. Jokes are terrible, say pupils, but it means the dates stick.

> 'It's about being loved, nurtured, feeling secure and taking risks,' says pre-prep head Mrs Barnes, an English specialist who has been at the school for 15 years

If displays were little restrained in places (art room was a bit too neat and tidy for our liking though '20 minutes ago, it would have been at a peak of messiness,' tour guide assures us), opinions aren't. Pupils have minds of their own and views they're keen to air, given half a chance, from reception upwards. ('We always put a chatty child by the door to talk to visitors,' says Mrs Barnes).

Ask one child what their favourite subject was and you won't be allowed to leave until everyone else in the class has told you theirs, too. 'Mine is ICT, because it stands for Ice Cream Tasting,' we were told by one impish year 4 pupil.

Inevitable and considerable planning goes on behind the scenes. Pre-prep subject coordinators (specialists for music, sport, ICT) work with prep team on curriculum development to ensure seamless transition. Even the library is sensibly organised, with fiction and factual books in different rooms, work and play carefully separated. There's do-able homework which increases in upper years but so gradually you 'don't really notice,' thought pupil.

School's not very secret weapon throughout is emphasis on mind games (think fun rather than interrogation) with focus on problem solving, timetabled through the school and taught by specialists.

Reception pupils might work out where to site farm animals (where do you put the pigs if they don't like talking to the sheep?); older pupils have more overt problem solving and strategy. Don't do things by halves – there's even a week-long mind festival (think cerebral sports day – synapse and spoon race?).

Does wonders for exam technique – 'Helps your brain,' confirmed year 3 pupil –and boosts resilience. Just as well given the inevitable cloud on the horizon, those horribly stressful 11+ and 13+ entrance exams.

Generally, they're managed with kindness and sensitivity by the school and with grace and good humour by pupils. We did pick up a few worries at the top end of the school. 'How are you feeling about your exams?' we asked one senior boy. 'Fine... and that's the biggest lie I've ever told.'

But that's down to the system, not the school. Parents and pupils stressed (and re-stressed) the quality of staff. 'Kind and nice,' said a pupil (and umpteen mums and dads, often adding 'nurturing' by way of ringing the changes). While there is pressure to do well, it often comes from within. 'I wanted to repay my parents for the investment they've made in me,' said a scholarship winner, and clearly meant it.

Ask one child what their favourite subject is and you won't be allowed to leave until everyone else has told you theirs. 'Mine is ICT, because it stands for Ice Cream Tasting'

Emphasis throughout is on knowing pupils inside out (can verge on over-cossetting for the occasional senior pupil) with teaching and support tailored accordingly. Setting (maths the biggy, though also small groups for English and French) is broad brushstroke rather than fiddly to avoid anyone feeling either singled out or sidelined.

Small details matter – one teacher writes end of week 'good news' note for each pupil – while rewards are all about doing better: credits and escalating precious metal merit certificates to year 6; recent switch to £5 Amazon vouchers for top years. 'Bet the teachers have never seen such good behaviour...' said year 6 girl of older boys. Demerits (for repeated transgressions – eg.not handing in homework) are tactically used: 'Year 6s letting off steam after pre-tests is time to monitor everyone carefully,' says member of staff. Can, but usually don't, result in 'sensible' detentions used, for example, to catch up with work.

School's not very secret weapon throughout is emphasis on mind games (think fun rather than interrogation)

Sense of being looked after is palpable. One of our guides may have done 40 or so tours but insists that the 41st (ours) is a treat (and we got bonus points for asking some different questions). Even the fish in two tanks by the entrance – tiddlers when they arrived, now approaching catch of the day size – seemed to exude contentment.

Rivalry does exist but is sensibly channelled. Would-be prep prefects nominate themselves, run hustings and incentivise the plebiscite with speeches and the odd song (sweets are banned). 'Odd maverick does get elected – and often surprisingly good,' says school. Otherwise, there's competition between the four houses, named for local notables. Each gets an assertive website write up, headed by surprising claim that David Garrick 'would be proud of some of our theatrical renditions of Boom–Chig–a–Boom in house assemblies.'

Presumably he'd also be impressed by the productions, mainly combining two year groups, younger as choir, older taking the main acting and singing parts, year 7 solo effort featuring cameo parts for staff. Sport has been seen as less of a focus, reinforced by trophy cabinet. 'Three-quarters ... are for chess,' pointed out tour guide. Perceptions are outdated, says Mr Malam, who reckons that sport is now on a par with other local schools and points to victories (winners of three football tournament in one term) as well as investment in good coaches and upping of fixtures.

Bar the normal anomaly of girls' vs boys' sports (several girls we spoke to wouldn't mind a crack at football and cricket, though we couldn't find any boys feeling the love for netball...) there's masses of choice. Curriculum also supplemented by numerous after-school clubs (one athletics/chess enthusiast – clearly a born multi-tasker – solves timetable clash by sprinting between the two) and extensive charity work (pupils involved in selecting deserving causes), with long term support for Street Child African and school in Malawi.

Mind games almost essential to winkle out wish list items from these happy parents. For girls entering the school at out of the ordinary times, it can be hard to break into well-established friendship groups. 'Not the same for boys – they have football,' said one, gloomily – perhaps another argument for shoehorning a girls' team on to the list?

Bar a few mild gripes about slightly variable lunches (hunger damped down by break time snacks, 'some the size of a three-course meal,' said a pupil) we'd rate this a must visit prep, which manages anxieties and aspirations of pupils (and parents) with aplomb and warmth.

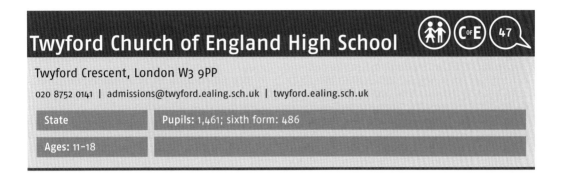

Twyford Church of England High School

Twyford Crescent, London W3 9PP

020 8752 0141 | admissions@twyford.ealing.sch.uk | twyford.ealing.sch.uk

State	Pupils: 1,461; sixth form: 486
Ages: 11-18	

Executive head teacher: Since 2002, Dame Alice Hudson MA (Oxon). Educated at Slough Girls' High and Leighton Park, where she was the first ever head girl. Read English at St Hilda's Oxford. Taught at Central Foundation Boys' in Islington and Maria Fidelis, Camden. Deputy head at Brentside High School, Ealing before joining Twyford in 2000, where she was deputy and acting head before being appointed head. Made a Dame in 2017 for services to education but, with typical modesty, at the time said she was 'taking one for the team.' Married with four children, most of whom have been educated here. Committed Christian. Loves cooking and a keen cyclist. Dynamic and inspirational. A force of nature.

Associate headteacher since 2013 is Karen Barrie, previously deputy head. Degree in maths from Manchester and still teaches one lesson a week. Softly spoken with a gentle sense of humour. Lives and breathes the school, admitting that 'Twyford has been my children.' Described by Dame Alice as 'the most brilliant headteacher the school has ever had.'

Together they make a watertight team. Highly visible at school events. One mother noted, 'They are greatly respected but are approachable, chatty and open.'

Academic matters: Superb results. In 2018, at A level, 44 per cent of entries were A*/A, 74 per cent A*-B. At GCSE, 85 per cent of pupils got 9-4 in both maths and English and 45 per cent of grades were 9-7. Unsurprisingly for a faith school, all pupils take GCSE religious education one year early, with knock-out results. Most pupils take nine GCSEs in total, with a the most able managing 10. 'We are a high functioning academic school,' explains Dame Alice, and few would argue with her. Yet, aside from the stellar results, she also wants pupils to learn to love their subjects. It's not just about league tables.

A specialist language college. In key stage 3, half of the year group takes two languages and

Latin is a core subject. Most pupils take either French, German or Spanish at GCSE, with a small proportion taking two. A minority takes Latin as an additional subject. French and Latin teachers train primary teachers in the borough in their subjects. Twyford is keen to share its expertise. Starry maths and science departments too. At GCSE, Twyford is in the top fifth percentile for progress in maths and science. Massive numbers take these at A level, some 30 of whom manage further maths too.

'The school expects the children to do well and never lets up on pushing them to be the best they can'

Strong sixth form, which has doubled in size from 250 to nearly 500. Twyford Additional Programme caters for around 50 high fliers each year who are likely to make Oxbridge or other top-notch universities, as well as those aiming to study dentistry, medicine or veterinary science. It 'aims to combine the extra skills and extended learning of the International Baccalaureate with the academic rigour and specialisation of A levels'. Focus is on developing thinking skills, presentation and honing interview techniques. Wide assortment of outside speakers wheeled in. Nearly all get A*/A for EPQ. Diverse range of essay subjects chosen including 'How far can humans travel in space?' and 'Was the English Civil War a '"War of Religion"?' One parent we spoke to said, 'The school expects the children to do well and never lets up on pushing them to be the best they can. There is a very, very high level of expectation and sometimes it can feel like a bit too much pressure. But it ultimately gets the results.' Another parent agreed: 'There is no escaping the fact that if you go to Twyford, you'll work hard.' No laziness tolerated, though setting from first years ensures not everyone has to proceed at a high-octane pace. Reports of huge piles of homework from year 8 onwards.

Less than five per cent of pupils in years 7-11 have an EHC plan, with a further four per cent on wider SEN register. The Alternative Resource Centre (known as ARC) has a specialism in supporting those on the autistic spectrum. A wonderfully quiet haven, especially compared to the deafening Uxbridge Road outside. Attachment disorder, anxiety and ADHD as well as dyslexia, dyscalculia and dyspraxia catered for. Those on the 'nurture programme' participate in about 85 per cent of mainstream lessons, but come to ARC for support in maths and English, on an individual and small group basis. They skip some language and humanity lessons, as well as singing, to attend these sessions. Support offered includes Lego therapy, homework and lunchtime clubs. A tranquil place for the vulnerable.

Pupils assessed four times a year, so school keeps a beady eye on performance. For those slipping through the net, swift action is taken to identify the cause of the decline. 'We quickly identify whether it is lack of effort, lack of support from home or poor behaviour,' we are told. Depending upon the cause, sessions are arranged with the school counsellor or behaviour consultant, parents are contacted, or pupils are pointed in the direction of booster groups or study clubs. All hands on deck to get the faltering up and running again. No-one is left to fall by the wayside.

There is no chance of school resting on its laurels with Dame Alice in charge. She is constantly looking at what could be done better. 'We are deeply aspirational'

Despite its academic successes, there is no chance of school resting on its laurels with Dame Alice in charge. She is constantly looking at what could be done better. 'We are deeply aspirational but averse to complacency. We are a self-evaluative organisation,' she tells us.

Strong core of committed teaching staff, with 85 per cent remaining static each year. When teachers do bolt, it is usually for positive reasons such as promotion elsewhere. Teacher recruitment can be challenging in some subjects, but head remains upbeat: 'We are perpetually appointing very good graduates.' Though some opt for in-house teacher training, others come armed with a PGCE. Plenty of non-Christian teachers but they must be 'in sympathy' with the Christian ethos of the school and be

happy to participate in institutional worship. New teachers are nurtured here. As Ms Barrie explains, 'Our training and support for staff has to be as tight as it is for the students.'

Games, options, the arts: Certainly, no lack of extra-curricular opportunities and head believes that 'the students have a richness of educational experience here'.

Twyford is a specialist music college, and parents consider the music department to be extraordinary. Currently over 20 ensembles, which have performed everywhere from BBC Songs of Praise (where the gospel choir was recent finalist in Choir of the Year) to St Paul's Cathedral. High spec music rooms, including recording studios, and professional-quality performance centre. Everything on offer including a traditional orchestra, laptop orchestra, brass collective and guitar and ukulele band. Pupils encouraged to perform internally and externally at every opportunity. 'The students don't just perform for themselves, they perform for others,' explains head. Fiercely-contested music competitions. Mammoth team of instrumental peripatetic teachers give lessons to more than 350 pupils each week. Drama department also firing on all cylinders. Whole-school musical productions (eg Grease, The King and I and Hairspray) staged at the end of the summer term. Lower school also puts on a Christmas show. Huge art department too, offering textiles, photography, computer-aided design, animation, print-making and clay.

Vast sports centre. Sports include rounders, netball, gymnastics, athletics, dance, football, cricket and hockey. Close links with professional coaches from QPR and WASPS, to develop most talented footballers and rugby players. Takes part in multiple local leagues and tournaments. An array of trophies stretching back to the 1980s reflects its sporting prowess. Twyford also competes regularly at county level cup fixtures for football, rugby and athletics. Girls' netball particularly starry, though one parent we spoke to claimed that 'sport for girls is not perfect. It is quite old-fashioned and what's offered to them isn't great. No girls' cricket or football or hockey.' For those less keen on kicking, throwing and hitting balls around, fencing, taekwondo and parkour await. Ominously-named The Cage is a fenced-off area for ball sports in the centre of the school. Though it resembles a prison compound, it is well-used and ideal for teenagers with surplus energy at break-time.

Plenty of chances for pupils to escape Acton. Trips punctuate the timetable. Language trips throughout Europe; cultural trips to Paris, Prague and Venice and sixth form historians visit St Petersburg. Active souls can ski or walk in the Alps. Closer to home, there are regular theatre and gallery trips. Parents pay for excursions, but a trip fund can be dipped into by those in need.

'We're big in the sixth form on what the students do outside of lessons.' Loafing around all summer would be heavily frowned upon

On top of their clutch of good grades, pupils are expected to add ballast to their CVs with work experience. Placements arranged everywhere from local primary schools and solicitors' offices to hospitals and local garages and even the Ritz kitchens. Some attend courses in hairdressing, childcare and carpentry, and others attend summer schools and workshops. Charity work also encouraged. 'We're big in the sixth form on what the students do outside of lessons,' explains Ms Barrie. Loafing around all summer would be heavily frowned upon.

Background and atmosphere: Twyford is part of a multi academy trust, along with William Perkin, the new Ada Lovelace and Ealing Fields, all in the same borough. 'We are stronger as a family than we were on our own. It has given us a competitive edge,' states Dame Alice. Much is shared between the schools in terms of front and back of house support, ranging from pastoral care, assessment and curriculum resources to finance and HR systems. Works brilliantly in terms of curriculum, as good lesson plans are shared on the intranet – particularly useful if one school has a weaker department. Not restrictive, however, and schools still have freedom to make own syllabus choices for themselves.

Twyford became a church school in 1981. School motto comes from St John's gospel, chapter 10 verse 10: 'I have come that you might have life, and have it to the full'. Pupils here are expected to live life to the full. This 10:10 ethos is shared by all the schools. Mostly Christian pupils, but all faiths represented. Two communions per year for each year group and the assembly we attended on epiphany was unequivocally religious. 'You need to know what you're getting into,' stated one parent.

The Elms, a grand Georgian building that houses reception, stands majestically at the heart of the school. Lawn in front is used by pupils to relax at break and lunch time. Jolly campus-style café serves hot food, with a canopy for those wanting a more Mediterranean experience. According to one mother, 'the real lack of variety on offer' at the café means her son is not alone in grabbing a meal deal at Tesco's instead.

Pastoral care, well-being and discipline: Pastoral support considered to be outstanding. Before each new cohort arrives, head of year 7 liaises with primary schools to ensure a smooth transition. Once here, year 7s have their own section of the school, as coming from a small primary to a whacking secondary presents its own challenges. Some older pupils are trained to become peer supporters to help with teething problems. One parent we spoke to commented that 'the nurturing side is strong and when my eldest had some wobbles in year 7 and in year 10, they couldn't have done more to support him. The school responds quickly to any problems and I have never felt fobbed off.' Chaplain comes in two days a week, one full-time counsellor. Seven tutor groups per year. Seven houses, named after cathedrals and abbeys: Truro, Wells, York, Fountains, Ripon, Durham and Canterbury. One mother we spoke to said that 'the school takes a lot of effort to make sure each child is prepared for the next stage in their education. In year 10, we had a one-to-one session with the head teacher to discuss our plans for A levels and university. They did this for every child in the year.'

Discipline has been tightened on Dame Alice's watch. You could hear a pin drop in assembly – not a single pupil was distracted or fidgety. Every pupil filed in past her, and each one was greeted warmly and reminded to stand up straight. Rules are strictly adhered to. Ms Barrie explains, 'We celebrate first. We reward positive behaviour and are not just punitive, but they need to understand the structure and rules.' Pupils left in no doubt about what is and is not acceptable, and one hapless boy who walked into assembly late when we visited was swiftly dispatched, with a late detention. Possession or supplying drugs, possession of an offensive weapon (including penknives), assaulting a member of staff or persistently disruptive behaviour lead to permanent exclusions. Pretty rare, though, and only a few each year are sent packing. Controversially, smartphones are banned, but 'dumb' phones (that only allow texts and calls) are allowed. Offending phones are confiscated until the end of term. 'The students know we might have to do a stop and search of their bags, if we have a good reason. If they are found with a smartphone, they know we'll confiscate it.' School not taken in by plaintive pleas of 'It's my Mum's phone and she must have dropped it in my bag by mistake this morning.' As one mother summed it up, 'The discipline if not for the faint-hearted. Zero tolerance for even minor things. You get a negative point for not having a rubber or talking in the corridor. But if you look behind the strictness you see a very kind heart, and senior management genuinely care about the children.' School runs efficiently but manages to retain the personal touch. Everyone knows where they are supposed to be at a given time and pupils scurry purposefully around the school towards their next destination. They do let off steam at certain points of the day, and break time can be pretty vibrant, but a sense of regimented order prevails most of the time.

Pupils and parents: Most hail from the Ealing area with large numbers from Brent, Harrow and Hillingdon and a few from Hounslow and Hammersmith & Fulham. Majority of parents are highly supportive and practically 100 per cent attendance rate at parents' meetings.

Around eight per cent of pupils in years 7-11 are eligible for free school meals. Just over half of the pupils are white, 31 per cent are black or mixed race. Christianity is the unifying factor. Fair amount of Polish spoken at home, as well as various other European languages and some Arabic. Not as multilingual in make-up as neighbouring schools.

Entrance: Oversubscribed. Some 190 places in year 7, with 150 foundation (Christian) places, 21 designated as world faith places and 19 music places. Details regarding length and frequency of attendance at church are pored over with a fine-tooth comb. As one mother reflected, 'Getting a place at Twyford is the hard bit. It's a full five years of nearly weekly attendance at church'. The music scholars' places have opened things up a bit. These places are offered to those with potential, as much as to those who have had money lavished on violin lessons from an early age.

A further 130-150 new pupils (out of 650 applicants) join the sixth form each year from elsewhere. Over 500 are interviewed, so a gargantuan exercise for the school. All applicants must 'be supportive of the aims, attitudes and values, expectations and commitment of this Church of England academy'. Minimum entry requirement is eight passes at GCSE at grade 5 or better, including maths and English. Each A level course has individual entry requirements, but generally a grade 6 or 7 in related GCSE courses is expected.

Exit: Around 65 per cent stay on into the sixth form. Those leaving post-GCSE tend to opt for local colleges offering more practical BTec courses.

Roughly 90 per cent of the sixth form heads for university, with about half to Russell Group. Birmingham, Manchester, King's, Leeds, UCL, Bristol, Kent and Sussex all currently popular, with the occasional one going overseas. Thirteen off to Oxbridge, and 12 to study medicine in 2018. Science courses most popular, followed by liberal arts, maths-related and creative arts. Ten or so take art foundation courses. Only one per cent takes on apprenticeships, in areas such as accountancy and journalism.

Money matters: Bursaries available in sixth form for students from low income families.

Remarks: A heady mixture of energetic leadership, strict discipline and high expectations. Ideal for your driven child who is keen to throw themselves into what is on offer. Not the place for the rebellious or unmotivated. Parents are full of praise and they consider their offspring to be lucky. As one mother put it, 'Twyford pupils are inspired, challenged and happy. It sets them up for life'.

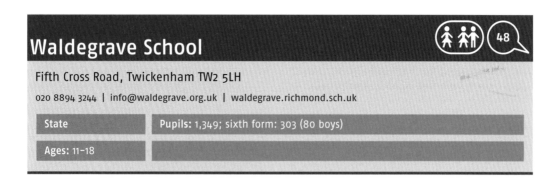

Waldegrave School

Fifth Cross Road, Twickenham TW2 5LH

020 8894 3244 | info@waldegrave.org.uk | waldegrave.richmond.sch.uk

State	Pupils: 1,349; sixth form: 303 (80 boys)
Ages: 11–18	

Headteacher: From January 2019, Elizabeth Tongue, currently senior deputy head at Tolworth Girls' School.

Head since 2006, Philippa Nunn, BSc from UCL in zoology, MA in educational management from Greenwich, PGCE and NPQH (50s). Appointed a National Leader of Education in 2011. Married with two daughters at local state schools. Was previously head of the Holt School in Berkshire, an all-girls 11-18 comprehensive. Started teaching science in 1987. Currently teaches ICT.

A calm, glamorous presence. Parents are all big fans. 'She's fantastic. She's a real person. Very approachable. As a mother of two girls she really understands.' Some staff have been teaching here for more than 25 years, which 'adds strength to the ethos of the school'. Introduced a house system to promote a greater sense of loyalty and belonging and to enhance student leadership opportunities.

A keen sports enthusiast, she plays hockey at Teddington, tennis and real tennis are passions. She's also training to become an Ofsted inspector.

Moving on in January 2019.

Academic matters: Consistently achieves good results in English, maths and science GCSEs. French, history, art, drama, RE always good too. The success rate in 9-4 grades is well above the regional and national average; 44 per cent of grades were 9-7 in 2018. Top of the Sunday Times Parent Power list for 11 to 16 schools for four years; now has a co-ed sixth form with 78 per cent A*-B, 43 per cent A*/A grades in 2018 A levels.

Parents are all big fans. 'She's fantastic. She's a real person. Very approachable. As a mother of two girls she really understands'

Quality of teaching is excellent. 'They're all so dedicated. I can't fault them,' said one parent. Achievements are recognised at assemblies throughout the year and at Celebration Afternoons at the end of the year. High academic standards are expected and some parents say that there is pressure on the students to get good grades. 'My daughter had to do French GSCE when she didn't want to do it as the teachers knew she would get a good grade.' But provision is made within the curriculum for all abilities, and modest acts such as helpfulness to the school or to others are duly acknowledged and rewarded.

Lessons are given in broad ability tutor groups initially, but setting for maths, science and languages occurs early on in the first years. In subsequent years, setting in other subjects if appropriate. All are entered for 6-10 GCSEs; some do up to 13 after discussion with parents and staff. Short course subjects such as ICT and PE well subscribed with good results.

Appointed as one of the first 100 Teaching Schools, and is also a National College for School Leaders National Support School. Designated area in an independent learning centre for gifted and talented girls and those with other special needs. Provides 'enhanced specialist teaching provision' for six girls with speech and languages difficulties/autism. With an incredible cultural diversity (43 different languages), EAL support is strong, even offering a lunchtime club for all age groups. On the subject of lunchtime, a great deal is compressed into a very short 35 minute break: careers advice, ICT, rehearsals for choirs and bands, puzzle club, homework clubs. Similarly, lots of before and after-school activities. A breakfast club at 8.00am every morning with badminton on offer at the same time for the more energetic. After school up until 4.00pm – choice is much more varied with a high take-up rate.

Games, options, the arts: Good range of sports offered – rounders, tennis, volleyball, athletics, rugby (with the Harlequins). Classes in the fitness suite, cricket, rowing (linked in with Walbrook Rowing Club) and table-tennis. Hidden from view from the road is a huge outdoor green area with tennis courts and marked-out running track. New sixth form block features four court sports hall.

School regularly wins regional netball leagues and was recently the Middlesex hockey champion. Also borough winners at netball and rounders. Running club is popular with 40 girls doing a 5k run twice a week with four teachers before school. (The head attempts to join them once every half term.) Head positively oozes enthusiasm, listing her school's sporting achievements. Another of her aims is to improve participation in sport. Gymnastics is strong – both a multi and traditional gym on site. A dance studio was funded through the National Lottery.

Extra opportunities include bridge, drama (big production every alternate year and an annual joint production with Hampton Boys' School), study skills, chess, art, music theory, ICT, choirs, rock bands and full orchestra. Art and music are both strengths. Year 7s all learn the recorder and in year 8 they get the chance to play the ukulele. When we visited we were blown away by the bird sculptures made in art lessons, inspired by their sister school in Madogo, Kenya.

After-school clubs include extra languages, eg Mandarin GCSE and there's even an astronomy club which parents can also attend. These cost extra but the pupil premium funds places for those who qualify.

Background and atmosphere: Original 1930s building has been added to over the years. Science labs are housed in newish block and brand new sixth form building opened in 2014, housing new sports hall and dining room. Outside play area transformed with money from the PTA with an outdoor theatre and landscaped surroundings. Food freshly cooked on site, and a biometric system for payment. Some girls take sandwiches. 'I don't want them having a slice of pizza and a muffin every day,' explained one parent. The girls themselves give this school a buzzy atmosphere. A former pupil remarked that 'all girls is a positive rather than a negative.'

Pastoral care, well-being and discipline: No real behavioural problems. First years are invited to spend a day in the school to find their way about and practise their journey to and fro – puts a stop to later excuses about buses being late. They also start the term a bit earlier before the older ones arrive. Prefects help out with the younger ones, organise charity events, welcome visitors and play an important leadership role in the school. Each tutor group elects a representative to attend the school council, which in turn represents the school at the Richmond School Student Council. All good training ground for debating and public speaking.

A local parent declares it a school where 'decent folk will be prepared to break all sorts of rules to get their daughters in.' Co-ed sixth form is making it even more desirable

School is honest about bullying and admits that, like the poor, it is always with us. However, stringent efforts made to put an end to it. Girls, staff and parents exhorted to report any incident straight away and assured that something will be done.

Pupils and parents: Although the school has no religious affiliation, the majority of the pupils are Christian. More than 25 per cent are from an ethnic minority. All come from the surrounding borough of Richmond, which is known nationally for its high level of professional parents. A local parent declares it to be the sort of school where 'decent folk will be prepared to break all sorts of rules to get their daughters in.' Co-ed sixth form is making this school even more desirable.

Entrance: Fully comprehensive intake. It is the only all girls' state school in Richmond so is always oversubscribed. Much to the head's relief, all admissions are dealt with by the local authority. Despite clear and rigid guidelines about admissions policies there are always appeals. Priority to those with special needs and those in public care or who are deemed by the LA to have a particular need, to siblings, daughters of staff and those living in priority areas. Most girls will have attended local primary schools in the borough. Six places are available in total in the school for those with speech and language difficulties or those on the autistic spectrum – invariably very oversubscribed.

Forty out of the 280 places in the sixth form are for boys but majority of girls' places will be taken by Waldegrave students. Five 9-4 GCSE grades needed for entry, with 6s in the subjects to be studied at A level.

Exit: In the past students have gone to Richmond Sixth Form College, Esher College, Strodes College or to sixth forms of independent schools. This has changed as the oversubscribed co-ed sixth form enables around 50 per cent of girls to remain at the school to study for A levels. Seven to Oxbridge in 2018; around half to Russell Group with one medic, one vet and one off to the US.

Remarks: A really buzzy school. 'It felt more dynamic than the other schools we visited,' said one parent. This school has so much going on that you're a lucky girl if you manage to get a place here. Now with the new sixth form you're even luckier.

North

Barnet
Enfield
Haringey

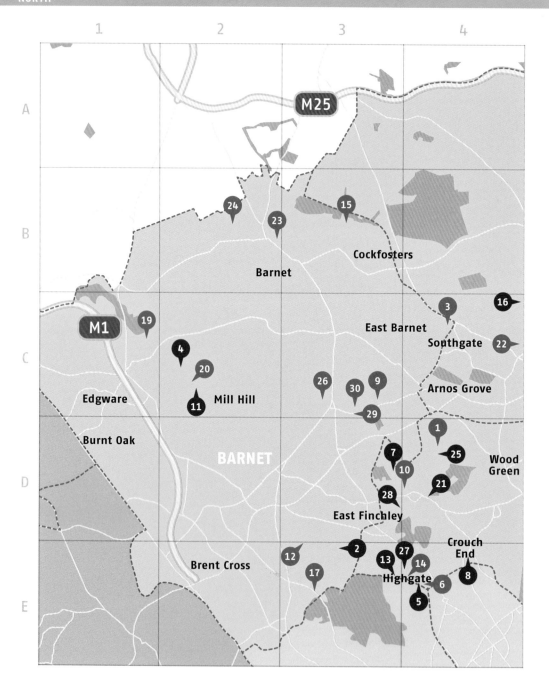

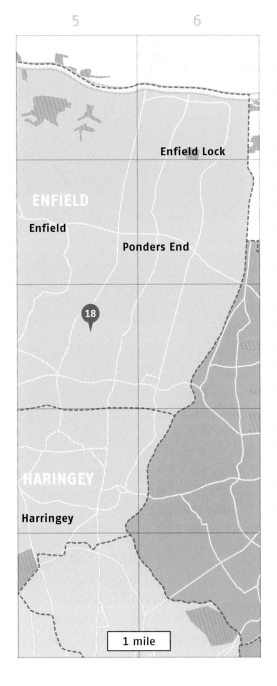

North London and its state schools

Barnet

Barnet, which stretches from Hampstead Heath to Hertfordshire, is mostly leafy and suburban. It includes Hampstead Garden suburb found in the early 20th century by Henrietta Barnet, whose eponymous grammar school in Central Square is one of the most sought-after in the country. The idea of the Suburb was to have houses for a range of incomes and gardens for every single person. So houses range from tiny to palatial, some Georgian but many Tudorbethan with flowers and tree-lined streets. Its greenery and ease into town has attracted many celebrities including Jonathan Ross to set up home. Barnet also includes Brent Cross shopping centre, the beginning of the M1, the suburbs that line the A5 as it cuts north to Edgware, and the open heathland of Hadley Common, with its duckponds and rural views. It is served by both branches of the Northern line.

Often talked about as having some of the best schools in London, Barnet is home to some of the highest achieving grammar schools – the aforementioned Henrietta Barnet School grammar school for girls qv, plus Queen Elizabeth School qv (boys), which regularly attract more than 10 applicants per place. The other popular grammar school in the neighbourhood is St Michael's Catholic Grammar qv (which is currently undergoing a major refurb expected to take just under two years to complete). Mill Hill County High qv awards a quarter of its places on aptitude (up to 24 technology, 24 music and 12 dance). Non-selective, but highly sought-after Ashmole qv, Compton, Wren Academy qv (50 per cent church places), ever popular Woodhouse sixth form college qv and Finchley Catholic High also do well. The newish Archer Academy is attracting increasing number of applicants including some of the bulge who previously went to Fortismere qv in Haringey. Hasmonean High is for orthodox Jewish children (boys' and girls' sections on different sites) and JCoSS qv is a cross-communal Jewish school.

Ark Pioneer Academy is a secondary school being developed on the former Underhill Stadium site, former home of Barnet FC. The school will be non-denominational and non-selective, serving the local community. The school plans to open with 180 places for year 7 pupils in September 2019.

Lots of faith primaries here too, including Monken Hadley C of E, St Mary's C of E, St Theresa's and Sacred Heart Catholic schools. Wren Academy has opened a primary school on the same site as has Ashmole Academy. There are several primary schools for orthodox Jewish families, including the Independent Jewish Day school and Menorah Primary. Popular secular primaries include Brookland, Garden Suburb, and Moss Hall infant and junior schools, Foulds, Monkfrith, Martin and Northside.

Enfield

Enfield is the northernmost edge of London, with the M25 dividing it from Hertfordshire and Epping Forest to the east. It has over 100km of rivers and waterways, copious parks such as the amazingly varied Trent Park, and numerous golf clubs. It also houses the Chickenshed theatre, home to the largest youth theatre in Europe, and Crews Hill, which is one of the largest specialist garden centres in the UK.

The town of Enfield sits where the suburbs give way to Hertfordshire countryside. Lee Valley Regional Park Authority runs open spaces and sports venues along the 26 mile long, 10,000 acre park. The park was created by a unique Act of Parliament as a 'green lung' for London. Southgate has mostly 30s houses built after the arrival of the Tube (Piccadilly line) and the opening of the North Circular road in the same year. Cockfosters tends to be a favourite of North London footballers and pop stars attracted by the large new houses with electric gates and security fences.

The borough's best known school is Latymer qv, a co-ed grammar school, which attracts over 2,000 applicants for 186 year 7 places. It will generally only make offers to those in 'inner' area postcodes which include parts of Waltham Forest, Haringey, Hackney and Islington as well as Enfield. Good non-selective secondaries in the borough include Highlands (which people are now moving home for) and Southgate.

Much excitement abounds for Wren Enfield, or 'Wrenfield' as it will be known – which had planned to open its doors to 180 year 7 students in September 2019, but has now been delayed. The school which will open on the Chase Farm Hospital site in the north west of Enfield, will be the sister school to the already hugely successful Wren in Finchley and hopes to create another 'close and inclusive community with a strong Christian ethos.'

Walker primary in Southgate is top of many local parents' primary school lists, as are Chase Side, Monkfrith, Eversley and Firs Farm. St George's RC, St Paul's C of E and Our Lady of Lourdes are among the most popular faith schools.

Haringey

Hilly Haringey is bordered by Highgate Golf Club in the west and Lea Valley in the east. Its westerly wards include some of the most prosperous – Crouch End, Muswell Hill and Highgate – and its easterly wards some of the most deprived. Highgate village is quietly residential with a definitely country atmosphere, Highgate and Hampstead golf courses nearby and independent Highgate School qv occupying much of the local land and property. Many young families move to the family-friendly areas of Muswell Hill and Crouch End to take advantage of the Victorian and Edwardian houses, the arty vibe, the busy shopping streets and breathtaking views over the city (best seen from Alexandra

Palace, which is undergoing a multi-million pound revamp). A branch of the Northern line threads the western edge, but otherwise there are no tubes in the area, though two overground train routes make their way en route to Hertfordshire and there are good bus services. House prices have had a meteoric rise in Haringey, arguably one of the sharpest inclines of any borough in London. This is largely down to its fantastic state schools.

Fortismere qv, at the top of the liberal, intellectual and media-centric Muswell Hill, has long been the comprehensive of choice for those fortunate enough to live close enough, but Alexandra Park School (APS) is vying for the crown and recently achieved much media hype after scoring better in international rankings than top performers like Singapore. Highgate Woods is increasing in popularity, so too is Heartlands High in Wood Green (near Alexandra Palace overground). It now takes much of the cohort who traditionally went to APS.

The much anticipated London Academy of Excellence Tottenham is a new, academically selective 16-19 free school which opened as part of the redevelopment of White Hart Lane in September 2017. The school is based on the 'phenomenally successful' model of its sister school LAE Stratford – named by the Sunday Times as the State Sixth Form of the Year for 2015-16.

The more westerly areas in particular abound with excellent primary schools: Rhodes Avenue qv, Coldfall qv, Muswell Hill qv, Tetherdown qv, Coleridge qv, St Michael's C of E qv and St James C of E. Several have expanded in recent years to cope with huge demand, but catchments are often rather less than half a mile.

Highgate Junior School

Alexandra Park School

Bidwell Gardens, London N11 2AZ

020 8826 4880 | office@alexandrapark.school | alexandrapark.school/

State	Pupils: 1,560; sixth form: 471
Ages: 11–18	

Headteacher: Since 2008, Michael McKenzie MSC PGCE (late 40s) – educated at a comprehensive in Birmingham, he read chemistry at Nottingham, followed by his teacher training at the Institute of Education. Head of year at William Ellis School in Camden which he cites as one of his 'most enjoyable times in education', then head of sixth form at LaSWAP and a brief stint at Parliament Hill School. Subsequently, deputy and associate head at Beal High School in Redbridge. Familiar and comfortable with Alexandra Park School's ethos before he applied, as the founding head had been his teaching mentor.

His reputation had preceded him and phrases such as 'the consummate PR man', 'fantastic salesman', 'smooth' were not an exaggeration. This head could sell sand to the Sahara – and it doesn't take Einstein to suss out how this once mediocre comprehensive has now become top of the league of schools in Haringey. The head says: 'If I am called a salesman, it's only because my commitment to the product – in this case education – is unequivocal.'

We finally meet (after trying to pin this head down for a while) and are greeted as if we were royalty – beaming smile, firm handshake and the exuberance of somebody who clearly delights in their job. Friendly and chatty – one could almost forget the purpose of our visit and drift into a non-relevant conversation. But be not fooled – this head is very much on the ball, and relishes the school's many achievements and outstanding students. He constantly finds his students 'very entertaining', and delights in meeting different kids every year. 'I have a student now. who is possibly one of the brightest I have ever come across. I am so excited to see how it pans out for that person..I am constantly motivated by bright pupils and those who want to challenge.'

He is a state school head through and through and says he could never be beguiled by the private sector. 'London has a very interesting education system. One of the strengths of this school is the mix. We still have pupils from as far afield as Tottenham from when school's catchment used to exceed five miles.' However, he is realistic that this diversity has changed over time, as the school's popularity has reduced the catchment to 0.7 miles

– which by virtue of its location (pricey Muswell Hill), will invariably make it more socially homogeneous. 'I can't control that element, but it will be a long time before that happens. There is still a good mix at APS, which keeps the school a little bit sane.'

Described by parents as being 'very much on the ball'; we imagine this head doesn't allow himself much downtime. Married, no children.

Academic matters: The proud recipient of a World Class Schools award, which means that APS belongs to a pretty exclusive club of only 19 schools nationwide. The award is given to schools who 'equip students with knowledge, skills and confidence to thrive in a challenging international environment where those who succeed take risks and continually pursue improvement.' APS's motto is 'success for all' and the school pulls off the very tricky achievement of being a successful London comprehensive welcoming the full range of abilities and social spectrum. 'Unlike other schools round here, it doesn't pick and choose. It's very inclusive,' said one parent.

> *This head could sell sand to the Sahara – and it doesn't take Einstein to suss out how this once mediocre comprehensive has now become top of the league of schools in Haringey*

The intake may be all-encompassing but the academic values remain traditional. 'We don't play any games with the curriculum,' says the head, and the school is notably strong on core subjects. 2018 results at GCSE: 84 per cent got 9-4 in both English and maths, with 40 per cent of grades 9-7. Most pupils take 10, including all three sciences. Spanish, French and Mandarin standard languages with Turkish also an exam option for GCSE and A level. Classics also a popular option with more than 120 pupils studying this at GCSE and A level.

Has specialist status as a science and maths school and an international school. More than 200 students last year had the opportunity of studying in partner schools in France, Spain, South Africa and China. Mandarin on the curriculum here and is more than token – students can spend time on an immersion course in Beijing, with 57 studying the language pre-GCSE, a dozen or so in the sixth form, and APS is one of a select group of schools in the Mandarin Excellence Programmae.

Some setting from year 7, depending on the department head – so maths and science are setted, English is not. When students first arrive, they are split into 'Alex' and 'Park' – one lot doing Spanish, the other French. This has been the subject of much heated debate as students are no longer offered the choice. One disgruntled parent told us: 'My family live in Spain, so I was very keen for my daughter to learn Spanish, but she was put into French and there is no room for movement.' Latin and classical civilisation popular. Arts and media studies – unsurprisingly in this heartland of the media classes – are notably good so, to counterbalance the trend, has opted for a specialism in science and maths, with a dramatic upswing in results. Good vocational curriculum, with BTecs in sport, business, art, salon services and catering, some taught at the College of North East London. 'It means children who might have been less engaged have something positive and interesting to do, and those taking academic exams have the space to focus,' said one parent.

Popular sixth form – in 2018, a creditable 33 per cent A*/A grades and 65 per cent A*-B grades at A level; 32 subjects on offer – strongest include English, French, physics and 'a really happening' history department.

The large bulk of students who fall in the middle are as well monitored as those at the extreme ends

Strong gifted and talented programme – pupils take early exams in maths, statistics, astronomy and classics. Astronomy has become so popular that the subject caused much controversy last year as the school didn't anticipate how many students would want to do the course, and spaces were limited. One parent told us: 'When we heard that astronomy was being offered as a GCSE, we jumped at the chance – we're middle class after all, of course we'd want our kids to do an extra GCSE!' However, there were many disappointed students who didn't get onto the course at first, 'but credit to the school, they listened to parents and extended the provision', putting an additional astronomy class to cater for all 60 students.

Also notable SEN support under dynamic head of special needs, with additional support in year 7 for those who've not yet achieved the requisite level in maths and English. This school seems to succeed where other large comprehensives fail, in that the large bulk of students who fall in the middle are as well monitored as those at the extreme ends. One parent told us: 'My daughter was very middling in her primary school and didn't have much confidence in her abilities. However, she has really thrived at APS, and whenever I go to parent evenings, one would think my daughter was top in everything.' Another parent told us: 'My son was really floundering before he came here, but he has really blossomed. The teachers get him.'

A National Teaching School, indicating the importance the school places on appointing the best practitioners and ensuring they receive the latest training. The teachers have been particularly praised as being a young and enthusiastic cohort with infectious enthusiasm – although, as with all schools, 'you do get the odd one who makes you think, why are they still here – are they unsackable?' Such is their dedication to the job, that the school is open on Saturdays and Sundays for several weeks before exams, for students who feel they need an extra bit of support: 'This is all off the back of the teachers, and not because I ask them', Mr McKenzie assures us.

Games, options, the arts: Busy, busy, busy. Specialist music and drama with a media suite and dance on offer. The school has a vibrant and very well-resourced music department with large numbers of students choosing to study music at key stage 4 and 5 and also a range of vocational courses including music technology. Extensive extracurricular programme including three choirs, orchestra and jazz band and the department organises an annual concert tour to Europe. More than 250 students take music lessons; 25 peripatetic teachers. Every student is expected to study music and drama each week. Large scale productions of Oliver! and Grease have included around 60 pupils running the entire event, from on stage to backstage to front of house. The school also has an annual Shakespeare performance.

Art also popular, 'one of the reasons my daughter chose this school.' Lucky pupils can draw inspiration in the stunningly bright art studio overlooking the golf course, which the head says he's been trying to claim for years as his office, 'but the art team won't let me.' (We were particularly struck by a fantastic portrait of Barak Obama drawn by a GCSE student.) Energetic visual arts with A levels in photography, art and product design, plus a creative and media diploma for those wishing to work on large-scale projects. Also a wonderful facility for textiles and those wishing to do fashion design.

The pupils we met were a lovely blend of savvy, street smart and witty ('the only thing that's missing at the school is a statue of me')

Though relatively limited on-site space for sport, games spill over into adjoining Dunsford Park and plenty of variety to suit all tastes. Basketball, football (West Ham's wonder youngster, Reece Oxford, is a recent ex-student), netball, rugby and cricket are main sports, but judo, aerobics, trampolining, tennis, badminton, wrestling and rugby also part of the offering. Online student newspaper. Eclectic range of after-school clubs includes astronomy, knitting, fashion, pursuit cycling and cheerleading.

Trips a big feature, with more than 120 throughout the year including student exchanges to China (for those studying Mandarin), geography in Iceland, French in the south of France, art in Madrid, politics in Washington and design in New York. Good careers advice with visits to universities and higher educational conferences.

Background and atmosphere: Local parents lobbied the local authority to create a new school in the area and APS was eventually founded in 1999 on the site of a former FE college. A relatively constricted site of five acres which feels more spacious due to the surrounding greenery of Muswell Hill golf course and Durnsford Park. The original mix of pleasant brick buildings, some from the 1950s, some from the 1980s, have been joined by a sleek modern extension (winner of a 2006 Civic Trust Award) and the sixth form centre. Extensive recent work has created a new humanities block, additional science labs, ICT suites and a media department.

Although visually impressive outdoor space was always a challenge, through clever remodelling of outdoor areas, the purchase of adjacent land and the use of the adjoining Durnsford Park, students now have a range of areas to eat lunch, play or just 'hang out'. This is particularly true for sixth form students who, although taught in the main school, now enjoy a separate social and study space and their own cafeteria. Mr McKenzie says: 'Now pupils don't wistfully look out onto all that beautiful green belt – they can actually benefit from it.'

Parents unanimous on the remarkably welcoming atmosphere: 'Everyone from the lady on the gate who checks uniform to the school receptionist makes you feel at home'. Even the police officer seeing kids onto after-school buses does it with a smile. Parents also enthuse about the school's multiculturalism and inclusiveness ('They really

try to be for everybody') and genuine concern ('It's far more nurturing than some of the other local comprehensives'). But concern is not cosseting. Mr McKenzie is also a very visible presence and is on the gate most days: 'He is very chatty to us parents – sometimes a bit too chatty and I worry that my daughter and her friends will think I'm terribly uncool hanging out with the head.'

Pastoral care, well-being and discipline: Traditional values apply. 'Kids need firm boundaries and it's important for the school to set them,' says the head. 'We expect them to be at school, on time, in uniform, ready to work.' Smart red and black kit is strictly enforced. 'There used to be a gang who wore their uniform in a special way and that's now all ended,' said one parent approvingly. Mr McKenzie also tries to clamp down on big clusters of students hanging around outside the local café at lunchtime, occupying the pavements. Not the school's best PR (although we have to say there are very few other places for them to go).

Behaviour in general is 'excellent' and school aims to keep it that way by instilling a sense of responsibility. 'We're training pupils to choose to do the right thing.' Misdemeanors are promptly and firmly dealt with – 'When my son got into a fight, there was absolutely no messing. They threw the rulebook at him'. Whilst Mr McKenzie considers himself to be fair, he is not one to pussyfoot around; 'This is definitely not a non-excluding school. If a child is making it difficult for other children to learn and we have exhausted all other options – we will exclude.'

'Other options' could include a trip to The Bridge, a prospect so mortifying that the mere mention is enough to make even the tardiest of students get their act together. One parent told us: 'My son is a bright child and generally well behaved, but has the potential to be swayed by peers. He was sent to The Bridge fairly early on, to deliver a message to a teacher. A stroke of genius'. According to that parent, the experience was enough to ensure that her son was 'never late or naughty in class again'. After further questions, it pans out that The Bridge is a fully staffed, self-contained base providing a wide range of interventions to those 'who present challenges in class.' One parent said: 'I imagine that children with a nervous disposition would probably be terrified.'

Drugs not a notable issue. 'It's bizarre,' says the head; 'at a previous school we had an incident every week. Here perhaps they're more savvy, more mature and are listening to our advice.' Weapons, too, had been conspicuously absent until just one recent incident in school – but the offender was promptly excluded.

Year 7 has its own 'transition manager', and one parent we spoke to, whose child had joined from neighbouring Rhodes Avenue, told us that 'there were a few opportunities during the summer term for new students to spend a day at APS and be taken around to orientate themselves.' Pupils remain in the same tutor groups for five years with a director of studies for each year. They're also supported by learning mentors and counsellors.

About 56 pupils with statements of special needs/EHC plans have mainly cognitive rather than behavioural difficulties and the school copes well with autism, Asperger's and Down's. One parent told us: 'I shopped around many schools before I chose APS for my son because of his very particular needs. I have to say, they have been amazing for him. If he was upset they would know about it. And nobody laughs at you here for being different.' The pupils we met were a lovely blend of savvy, street smart and witty ('the only thing that's missing at the school is a statue of me') – whilst polite and thoughtful. They shared one common notion – that they were all really happy to be there and felt listened to and looked after.

Communication between parents and school clearly a strong point – 'All my emails, however trivial, get answered promptly'. And various methods of positive re-enforcement are used: 'We often get phone calls home or postcards telling us how well our daughter is doing.' They also have a commendation system of silver, bronze and gold: 'Their rewards system is brilliant. It makes the pupils want to do well. '

Pupils and parents: Wide social spread, from the comfortable middle-class suburbs near the gates to some of the most deprived kids in the country – 'a high proportion on the cusp of social needs'. Middle classes tend to dominate the PTA, which runs endless jumble sales and bazaars and is strongly involved in the day-to-day running of the school, but the kids themselves mix well. Very supportive parents – 'Parents helped set it up and want to make it work'.

Entrance: Around 1,600 applications for 232 places. Usual priority to looked-after children, those with statements of special needs and siblings, then distance from the gates, which is now just under half a mile. The largest percentage (approx 20 per cent) from adjoining high-achieving primary Rhodes Avenue, as well as from Bounds Green, Our Lady of Muswell, Bowes, Coldfall, Coleridge, Hollickwood and Muswell Hill and another 30 or so local primaries.

Majority of existing pupils continue into sixth form of 340, with 70 or so joining from other local schools. External applicants for A levels should have at least five GCSEs at 9-4, with 6s in A level subject choice. (The head has been known to invite pre-A level students to his office, to lay out the pros of staying on at APS, if he gets a whiff that they may abandon ship for another local sixth form.)

Exit: Some 10-20 per cent leave after GCSEs. Around 60 per cent to Russell Group universities, including regular places at Oxbridge (five in 2018, and two medics). 'What is heartening is in the last three years these Oxbridge students have read a range of courses including English literature, law, history, maths, modern languages, music and natural sciences.' Other popular destinations include LSE, UCL, Manchester, Bristol, Bath, Nottingham, Warwick, Central St Martins, Queen Mary's and Newcastle.

Money matters: Training school and academy trust status bring in extra funding.

Remarks: A notably welcoming place for children (and adults) from across the borough. Not an academic pressure cooker but a school with high standards for all.

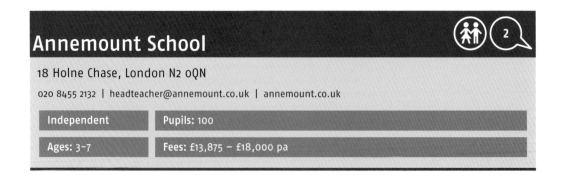

Annemount School

18 Holne Chase, London N2 0QN

020 8455 2132 | headteacher@annemount.co.uk | annemount.co.uk

| Independent | Pupils: 100 |
| Ages: 3-7 | Fees: £13,875 – £18,000 pa |

Head teacher: Since 1993, Geraldine Maidment BA MontDip. Educated at Northwood College, St Mary's Grammar School, and South Hampstead High School, Mrs Maidment followed a degree in German and art history from University College, London, with a stint at Sotheby's. Here, she realised she preferred people to objects. 'I'd taught children as a teenager, and loved the interaction. I realised that it was a vocation.' Started her career at Bassett House, then, when her own two daughters were tiny, launched Hilltop Nursery in a local church hall. In 1993, she bought Annemount, winning out against considerable competition. ('Mine wasn't the highest offer, but they felt I would continue the style of the school.') A two-year stint in the US with her late husband, an academic at the Open University, allowed her to take a masters in early childhood education at Denver University. An active member of the Independent Schools Association, she has been invited to speak on child and school-related issues on the radio, and continues to act as a consultant for families whose children have moved on to further stages of education. A talented linguist (she speaks five languages), she's also a very 'outdoorsy person', who enjoys music, the theatre and cooking. Parents undoubtedly respect and trust her. 'She cares deeply about the children and wants their happiness above all.'

Entrance: Not a school to encourage a call from the delivery room ('Having a baby is a time of great transition and your viewpoint may change'), but still sensible to sign up early. The school tries to keep families together, but admissions are on the basis of observation, with each child invited to a play session to ensure they're 'suited to the programme we offer and would enjoy it.' Most enter nursery at rising 3 or reception, but children considered at any point if the school feels 'they would thrive within the school community and peer group'.

Exit: Most sit 7+, though a few leave before ('There's no pressure about moving if that's part of the family's plans,' said one mother). At 7, to a broad sweep of north and central London schools. Popular co-ed options include Highgate, Belmont, Devonshire House and Northbridge House, with girls off to Channing, City of London, South Hampstead, Haberdashers' Aske's, boys to Haberdashers', UCS, Lyndhurst, St Paul's Juniors and St Anthony's. Head's office lined with individual files on each child and 'evidence-based' discussions about future schools start in year 1. 'We have a preliminary conversation to help parents draw up a shortlist,' says the head. Six months later this is revisited. 'Sometimes it's easy to fall in love with a school and lose sight of what is best for the child. We want children to be happy and shine, grow and mature into positive learners with good life skills.' Most parents respect the head's counsel: 'We knew she'd done this a million times before, so we completely trusted her.' Children are well prepared in a fun, relaxed way, with 7+ camps (in half terms and holidays) and 7+ clubs, and head has close links with the full range of schools, ensuring transition is as

smooth as possible. Not the place for those who expect hothousing.

Remarks: The school follows the national curriculum, and numeracy and literacy (with one-to-one reading daily) are taught to the highest standards ('excellent,' say the inspectors) by an ample supply of well-qualified, empathetic staff. Parents particularly praise how well staff understand their pupils. 'They really get to know them academically, socially and emotionally,' said one. Another commented, 'When I go to parents' evening, I always feel teachers are describing my children, and what pleases me as much is that my children are happy and confident enough at school to behave in the same way as they do at home.'

The school has had only two heads (the first remained in situ until she died aged 93) and has something of the feel of a secret passed on from generation to generation

Teaching equally successful at challenging the most able and supporting the struggling (though, perhaps, more of the former than the latter). The school has received an award from the National Association for Able Children in Education, and addresses ability largely through 'differentiation'. 'We look at who will benefit from being stretched and give them the opportunities to showcase their strengths. A singer or string player may be given performance opportunities, an able writer encouraged to enter competitions or discuss what they've been doing.' The school, however, does not label or segregate. 'We're not trying to single out children as a special and different. We want everyone to feel a valued member of the community.' Those with difficulties are given equally seamless support, with a specialist learning support teacher, closely monitored assessment and a well-planned timetable of booster sessions worked out with teachers and, where necessary, external experts. Homework – 'manageable and achievable' – encourages independence, and parents are expected to play their part, giving children real money when shopping, measuring with them in the kitchen.

Mrs Maidment's mantra is breadth, breadth, breadth, and this is undoubtedly one of the school's strengths. So, plenty of specialist teaching, with French taught by a native speaker (in situ for 20 years), chess by a coach who supports the British junior team. Budding athletes and dancers are also aided by professional experts. Music is central, and singing given emphasis both in lessons and clubs (choir). Highly popular violin programme, with instruments passed down via the PTA. 'They like carrying the case; they think everyone plays,' says the head, who believes that learning enhances study skills and develops the academic.

Hugely popular clubs (athletics, cookery, adventure, football, science and art) from reception. 'For such a small school, the extracurricular is amazing,' said one mother, whose children participate most days. No breakfast or after-school club, however: 'It's a school, not day care,' says the head firmly. 'Umpteen school trips', too, near and far, ranging from a summer walk around the school's leafy surroundings to Verulamium (St Albans), which inspire activities such as learning Roman numerals.

Kids clearly love the range of what's on offer. Asked about their favourite subject, all hands were raised and all activities included, from swimming and football to maths, science, and English. 'There are a lot of interesting things to do here,' stated one 6 year old earnestly.

Founded in 1936 as a gift to their former governess by some generous parents, the school has had only two heads (the first remained in situ till she died at the age of 93), and has something of the feel of a secret passed on from generation to generation. Housed in a low-rise private home, it has all the benefits of intimacy and scale suited to the very young and makes the most of this domestic mood (with birthday teas, for example, in the head's study.) Located in leafy Hampstead Garden Suburb – 'marvellous to park and safe to walk around' – it has a large and beautifully maintained garden studded with rose bushes and apple trees. This, thoughtfully subdivided into a sensory garden, a vegetable plot (where pupils harvest their own potatoes) and a woodland garden (where children can pile up logs), acts as the school playground.

More vigorous games like football – the school has its own team and strip – are played off site, while gym and swimming take place at Hendon Sports Centre. No dining hall and everyone brings their own lunch boxes.

Pastoral care is as critical as English and maths. 'We make every child feel safe and loved,' says the head, who sees developing independence as a key part of her brief. 'I want pupils to greet and be greeted with a handshake, speak in full sentences, express gratitude through letter writing, and manage their belongings from an early stage.' Parents encouraged to support these goals and most are impressed by the results. 'Even my 4 year old knows there's show-and-tell and will remember to bring something.'

All pupils given responsibility, with a school council from reception debating such issues as how to improve the library and which charities to support. 'Travel ambassadors' encourage safe walking and 'rangers' ensure everything in the garden is 'ticketty boo'. All year 2s given a go as head boy and girl. Disciplinary problems are rare. 'I've never heard of any,' said one parent.

Families generally live within a four-mile radius of the school, spilling out from Hampstead Garden Suburb into West Hampstead, Highgate and Alexandra Park. Parents, from all round the world, are mainly professionals, with the rest in media, business and sport. Most choose Annemount because they share its values ('We agree with Mrs Maidment that children should play outdoors, have time to be bored, just be children,' said one parent), and virtually all delighted with the outcome. 'We feel our children have been nurtured and encouraged and are incredibly happy,' said mother. 'The real benefit is that they started off by loving school,' commented another. 'I give it five gold stars.'

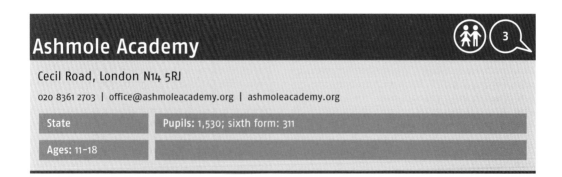

Ashmole Academy

Cecil Road, London N14 5RJ

020 8361 2703 | office@ashmoleacademy.org | ashmoleacademy.org

| State | Pupils: 1,530; sixth form: 311 |
| Ages: 11–18 | |

Head teacher: Since 1997, Derrick Brown MA MBA DipEd – degree subjects psychology and business. Formerly a scientist, but changed career when he realised it wasn't all about 'filling pretty liquids

into tubes. It was actually quite isolating and I'm a people person.' He was advised at the time to become either a teacher or a prison governor. He opted for the former. Prior to headship at Ashmole, he was vice principal at Leigh City Technology College in Dartford and then senior deputy at Cranford School – both schools much the same size and diversity of Ashmole and in comparable outer London suburbs.

Formerly a scientist, but changed career when he realised it wasn't all about 'filling tubes with pretty liquids. It was actually quite isolating and I'm a people person'

Early 60s, but 'nowhere near retiring.. I wouldn't know what to do with myself'. Quietly spoken, serious and tirelessly focused on getting things done, an outstandingly successful head. His drive and determination stem from his own 'not great' secondary school education which prompted him to challenge the state school system – in this case to turn a bog standard local comp into one with all the academic benefits of a private school education, without the fees. As he says: 'Why should only a privileged few have these opportunities? I want to make it available to all kids.'

Mr Brown vowed when he started at Ashmole to make an immediate impact on results: 'It was a fairly averagely performing school with not very high aspirations.' He took a hard look at the areas that were lacking and the following year results were already up by 10 per cent. 'I created partnerships with parents, worked on the discipline and talent scouted good teachers.' His 'football manager's mentality' of never being satisfied, and always finding something to improve on, has awarded Ashmole the title of 'super state school' according to the Evening Standard.

One gets the feeling that this head has little time or inclination for hobbies. With two grown up children of his own, any extracurricular activities he may pursue are of the more 'unusual' kind – which currently, he says, is revamping an old wreck he bought (we're presuming he means property). Although there's no resting on laurels for this head, he has already consolidated Ashmole's reputation as a provider of comprehensive education at its best.

Academic matters: This school hasn't been awarded the title of 'super state' for no reason. As the head says: 'Every subject excels here, no subject is weak.' Ofsted outstanding – it has managed to sustain many years of exceptionally high results. Strong value added. Entirely non-selective, so the results are impressive. Way ahead of the other non-selective schools in the area. 'There are no tricks here

– all the students come from the local community.' Anyone can do well here, we were told – boys, girls, the less motivated, 'everyone exceeds their personal best.' Classes are setted in main subjects – 'mixed ability doesn't work except in certain areas', says the head.

In 2018, 87 per cent got grades 9-4 in both English and maths, 41 per cent 9-7 grades. A levels 30 per cent A*/A and 62 per cent A*-B grades. French is popular and there's a very strong exchange link with the twinned town of Le Raincy, a suburb just outside Paris. Spanish and German are also offered at GCSE and A level, but less popular.

Students are closely monitored and undergo assessments after every half term. The head says: 'If we see underperformance, we can intervene and work with the child individually to make them improve.' However, one parent we spoke to disagreed. 'Ashmole is a great school if you are the academic, studious type. However if, like my daughter, you don't fit the mould, you're going to have more of a struggle there.' Teachers are also closely monitored and parents feel that there is quite a high turnover, although the school says it is similar to most London schools. But if this is the case, it is not an unhealthy state of affairs anyway, according to the head. He says: 'A stable school with no turnover can be a recipe for complacency and disaster.'

A third of the school has English as an additional language – support in place to make sure they progress, either through extra help or (mostly) in-class intervention. Around a seventh have some kind of SEN – about one or two per cent with EHC plans. Learning support is located within its own area, providing adequate space that caters for all needs. The weakest 30 or so students drop languages after year 8, taking BTec business instead, although this varies every year. These students have extra help with the basics.

We also noticed a lot of reading going on – in the canteen and elsewhere. The head told us that he insists every student carries a book of their choice around

Able, gifted and talented pupils – those who have all round ability across the core subjects of English, maths and science (around one in four students at Ashmole) – have their own programme designed for them. This bespoke Ashmolean programme involves a variety of activities which 'encourage aspiration,' whether this be by visiting higher education institutes or learning through Firefly, the school's virtual learning environment.

However, one unhappy parent called it an 'exclusive' club and a very 'rigid' system; 'most students who are on the programme come on it straight from primary school and there seems to be little movement.' She also said that much is made of the G&T students and the privileges offered to them, which makes the other students feel less worthy. Another parent disagreed, saying that her child has been 'on and off the programme many times according to her grades.'

Games, options, the arts: The opportunities are plentiful and the facilities wonderful. Huge floodlit Astroturf court, playing field, sports hall and separate studio for dance, aerobics and net sports, but no pool. Outdoor table tennis on offer, which proves to be a very popular lunchtime activity. Outstandingly successful in both boys' and girls' football; the boys' football team recently won the Barnet Cup and the girls' team reached the semifinal of the Middlesex Cup. Rugby also a biggie and the year 8 rugby team won the Barnet Saracens tournament recently. One parent told us: 'Even if your child is not the academic type, the sports on offer can give them the opportunity to shine.'

Much acclaimed music department. Amy Winehouse spent a few years here (although head, who was here at the same time, says: 'Amy left us quite early on to join the BRIT school'). Having a music specialism, they are able to employ the very latest technology. Music scholarships on offer to help those with talent develop their skills, and an increasing number of pupils take individual music lessons. A full range of extracurricular music programmes also on offer, including an orchestra, jazz band, chamber string group, junior string group, brass band, senior wind ensemble, Latin rock band, two choirs and show band for the annual school musical.

The result is a bright and spacious, well-mapped-out building, 'which is easy to navigate,' one parent told us. All subjects in their own sections and immaculately labelled

Drama popular – big, well-equipped studio and major musical production each year. Standards are high – recent 'fantastic' production of Hairspray. Impressive art studios and some astounding individual pieces of art. The school has its own radio station and two recording studios. Plenty of lunchtime and after-school clubs, including film club, debating societies, Mad for Books club, philosophy, homework clubs and numerous language clubs. Enrichment groups offer a choice of cultural, entrepreneurial and environmental activities. 'The options here are great,' a sixth former told us. 'We're bombarded with courses and clubs which enrich us as people.' He was not wrong.

Background and atmosphere: This is a different school, quite literally, from the Ashmole of yesteryear. It had survived in pretty dire conditions for years but, on his arrival in 1997, the head organised the sale of six acres of school land and began a visionary building programme with the proceeds. The design of the new buildings was the result of collaboration between the school, a very proactive parent committee and the architect. Rehoming happened in 2004 at a cost of £14m. The result is a bright and spacious, well-mapped-out building, 'which is easy to navigate,' one parent told us. All subjects grouped into their own sections and everything immaculately labelled. No chance of getting lost here. The only confusing things are the different coloured named staircases, like the 'orange staircase,' which in fact is blue. The head told us: 'When we designed the building we wanted to colour group it into sections so, for example, people could meet at the orange staircase, but this wasn't DDA compliant for partially sighted people, so everything has to be kept white and blue.' Lifts are also available for students with disabilities.

Large, wide corridors with beautiful wall displays, seriously impressive artwork and a convivial atmosphere. As we progressed from section to section we witnessed quiet classrooms (with the odd exception), with an atmosphere that encourages work and discourages messing around. 'We have a policy at this school that lessons should be silent, unless they require a discussion. It helps to keep the class focused.' We also noticed a lot of reading going on – by individuals in the canteen and elsewhere. The head told us that he insists every student carries a book of their choice around with them. 'There is no such thing as doing nothing,' he said. 'One can always read.'

Set in 28 acres of land in quiet, residential Southgate, the outside of the school is none too shabby either, especially for a London comprehensive. Plenty of outdoor space. Remarkably free of litter and immaculately kept lawns, outdoor classroom and environmental area, fully equipped with wooden table and benches. So much excess land that Ashmole primary school opened on the premises in September 2016. 'There is such a lack of primary schools in the area, it makes sense,' says the head. We say: Start booking your kids in now.

The new sixth form block, kitted out with its own Starbucks, was opened in 2014. This was many years in the waiting, needed £1.3 million (raised through fundraising events and tightening of the old school purse strings), two contractors and various other obstacles. One student told us: 'It's so exciting, I'm just upset I'll only have one year to enjoy it.'

Pastoral care, well-being and discipline: Big on discipline. 'Not for the free spirit,' one mother told us. Strict adherence to their uniform code expected – no exceptions or students will be asked to go home and change. Lo and behold: if pupils are caught outside the school premises with a shirt hanging out, they will be seriously reprimanded, sometimes even face a detention. Mobiles, too, are strictly forbidden, except for the sixth form – confiscated immediately if found and, to add to the humiliation, parents have to go in to school and pick them up. While this has been a bone of contention with many of the parents, who like to get hold of their kids after school hours, others feel it is a good thing. 'If nothing else because there have been some phone thefts in the area, but muggers know not to bother with Ashmole kids as they never have phones on them,' one parent told us.

The opportunities are plentiful and the facilities wonderful. Outdoor table tennis a popular lunch time activity. Outstandingly successful in boys' and girls' football

Zero tolerance of drugs, weapons and violence – on or off the premises. Much has been done to combat bullying, which has clearly been a problem at Ashmole in former years (as in many comprehensives of this size). CCTV cameras operate along main corridors 'to monitor any deviant behaviour that may occur' and when the new building was designed head specifically requested wide, open spaces free of 'little cul-de-sacs' where vulnerable students could be cornered. As Orwellian as this may sound, bullying is now virtually non-existent and parents are very grateful.

Disruptive or abusive pupils are sent to the individual learning room, where they are under supervision, have no contact with their friends and hate it. Two or three days there usually does the trick, but head will exclude for serious offences – roughly five permanent exclusions a year. 'We just can't let a disruptive child continue,' he says. 'They are given community service and various other deterrents, but if they are hell bent on being disruptive, they're out.' The result of this is a school in which pupils feel secure and comfortable and everyone knows the score.

Each key stage has its own learning mentors and key stage managers whom pupils know they can go to if they feel the need. Parents aren't so convinced. One parent we spoke to said: 'It's not always made clear who we should be speaking to, or emailing. I have left messages on several occasions and no one has responded. I think the communication between parents and year heads could be improved.' However, for the most part, parents and students we spoke to seemed extremely happy with the school. One sixth former told us: 'I've loved every minute of this school. The sixth form is like a big family, even for external students.'

A large amount of interaction between the year groups, encouraged by the cultural and charitable activities. Pupils feel they have friends in all years. Charity work plays a vital part in the general ethos of the school and every year students and staff raise thousands of pounds for a variety of good causes. Overall, the school has a general sense of self-discipline and a fostering of civilised behaviour.

Pupils and parents: Vast ethnic mix, as you'd expect from the Southgate area, though more Cypriots – Greek and Turkish – than anything else. Main religion is Christianity of all sorts, the second is Islam. Mostly working parents, but a supportive and hard working PTA makes big contribution to the school's development. Pupils are cheery, ambitious, focused and involved. Notable former students include: Amy Winehouse, former S Club 7 member Rachel Stevens, musician Stephen Sidwell, goalie Mark Bunn, Oscar winning producer Mark King, The Feeling lead vocalist Daniel Sells and Channel 5 tsar Sham Sandhu.

Entrance: More than 1,100 apply for the 232 places – of which siblings will take around 80. You'll get in if you have a sibling there, are a looked-after child or live very close – otherwise no chance. 'I wish I had bought on Cecil Road years ago. Houses must be worth a fortune now', one parent sighed. Up to 20 music aptitude places; these pupils, along with others who show talent, are placed on the music scholarship programme.

Exit: Up to 60 per cent leave after GCSEs, mostly for vocational courses elsewhere. The rest need to get 6s in the subjects they wish to study for A levels to stay on in the sixth form; fall-out of about 13 per cent after year 12. Around a third to a half of sixth formers to top universities; generally a few to Oxbridge (two in 2018, and four medics); others to places like Durham, Warwick, London universities, Nottingham, Leeds. Science, law and humanities are all popular.

Remarks: Slick, sensible and effective. Check out the housing market.

Belmont Mill Hill Preparatory School

The Ridgeway, Mill Hill Village, London NW7 4ED

020 8906 7270 | imanfredi@belmontschool.com | millhill.org.uk/belmont/

Independent	Pupils: 522
Ages: 7–13	Fees: £18,099 pa

Linked schools: Grimsdell Mill Hill Pre-Preparatory School, 595; Mill Hill School, 619

Head: Since 2015, Leon Roberts MA PGCE. Taught for four years in the state sector, moved to Keble Prep as head of history for the next four years then became deputy head (academic) of Belmont in 2004 before being promoted to senior deputy head (pastoral) in 2010 and finally taking on the headmaster's role. Married with three young daughters, including twins, he enjoys cricket (playing and coaching, both boys and girls), walking and watching Nordic Noir drama.

Down-to-earth, hands on and with the same energetic style as the outgoing head, he approaches the job with the same consultative and open style – he's building on a school which is in great shape (which he's been involved in creating) and adding his own mark.

Entrance: Automatic entry from pre-prep (Grimsdell) to prep (except in some very rare cases). This accounts for two-thirds of the school's intake. For external candidates, there are two main points of entry into the school – 7+ (year 3) and 11+ (year 7). Occasionally there are places available in other years – these are called 'chance vacancies'. Heavily oversubscribed from external candidates, so each expected to take reading, creative writing and maths tests together with a reference from their previous school

Exit: Some 95 per cent of Belmont students continue on to Mill Hill School, although all have to sit the entrance exam (for setting purposes; it is not a qualifying exam for entry). 'Children for whom Mill Hill is not the right school will leave at the end of year 6; once in year 7, the children have a place at Mill Hill at 13+ conditional on continuing good work ethic and good behaviour.' One parent felt that the fact that Belmont goes up to 13 is a massive advantage. 'At 13 they are desperate to make the next jump and are confident to do it. They are not little 11 and 12 year olds floundering around.' Occasional transfers to boarding schools eg Harrow, Tonbridge and Stowe.

Remarks: Established in 1912 following the success of its senior school Mill Hill, Belmont Prep School opened its gates with one student – Harold Pearse Soundy. By the summer term 1913, it had 12 pupils. Originally a boarding prep for boys, it has been a day school since the 80s and co-ed since 1995.

Situated on the relatively quiet part of Mill Hill's Ridgeway, the school is in an enviable location – set back from the road and flanked by large houses, beautiful greenery and a stone's throw away from the small but popular Belmont Farm. Hard to believe that a 25 minute train ride will take you to the centre of London. Harder still after meandering through some 35 acres of parkland to the rear of the school – taking in the panoramic views of the Totteridge Valley. Undoubtedly the school's selling point, the grounds and its facilities are impressive for a London-based prep school.

'Belmont was always a nurturing school, but the goalposts seem to be constantly changing and you feel like you are kept on your toes the whole time'

For a sporty child, this must be nirvana. The grounds host seven rugby pitches, 10 football pitches (of various sizes to accommodate different age groups), three cricket pitches, five cricket nets, five rounders pitches, two Astro mini hockey pitches, six Astro tennis courts, six netball courts, a fully equipped gymnasium and a small dance hall. Finally, a 1,500 metre woodland cross-country course known as The Oti (in memory of a former student who died of sickle cell anaemia). Pupils also have the use of the new 25 metre indoor swimming pool at Mill Hill School for swimming lessons and clubs. As one parent told us, 'Forget this school if your child has absolutely no interest in sport;

Set back from the road and flanked by large houses, beautiful greenery and a stone's throw away from the popular Belmont Farm

they'll be unhappy', commenting that it is the most disciplined department in the school.

Outdoor facilities also include a large wooden adventure playground, a variety of large established games including a giant chessboard, for children to use during break and lunchtime, and a gardening area where pupils tend seasonal plants and flowers. We spotted a little recycling area and then learned that Belmont has been awarded the much coveted Eco-Schools Green Flag Award.

After the spectacular exterior, the interior of the school comes somewhat as an anticlimax. The original 18th century house acts as the main entrance to the school and houses the function rooms, main reception area, staff rooms and the head's office. Whilst this has been tastefully refurbished (with the original beautiful winding staircase acting as the centrepiece), several of the classrooms on the upper level seemed on the cramped side and lacking in imagination. The science labs (in the Cloister Block) and the gymnasium particularly struck us as archaic and in need of a refurb.

That said, the Jubilee Hall, which accommodates most of the lower school classrooms, the dining/assembly hall and the head of lower school's office, is modern and airy. The school has a genial vibe, perhaps because it is not as formal as some of the other independent schools we have visited. Colourful and interesting displays of student work adorn the corridors, and the pupils we witnessed, whilst not particularly noisy, were 'spirited'.

Belmont pupils 'speak with confidence, whether in a classroom discussion, reading in an assembly or conversing with adults,' said their most recent ISI inspection. This was particularly evident on our tour when we met with school's council members – a bunch of 8+ year old boys and girls who were bright, articulate and bounced off each other like the future spokespeople they may one day become. They were confident, polite and hard pushed to find anything negative to say about the school. One bemoaned the fact that lunch should be better organised, whilst another commented incredulously that 'we've been to play other schools that don't even have their own cricket grounds' – which made him feel very lucky.

A Belmont child is a busy one. School opens at 7.30am for optional breakfast, and from there on in, a cascade of activities barely allows for an oxygen intake. Fifty clubs are on offer during lunchtime and after school, so if elastic or kicking a ball ain't your thing – why not try ancient Greek? Or perhaps origami, Dead Poets Society (we presume without Robin Williams), jazz band, Belle Plates or Bollywood dance, to name but a few. Popular after-school activities include chamber choir and horse riding. Fabulous trips (including a history trip to Venice) are offered from year 6 and above.

Clearly time is set aside for the curricular stuff, as results are well above national expectations. This, we are told, is achieved through 'excellent teaching' (ISI 2012), a broad curriculum that includes French from year 3 and Latin from year 6 and smallish class sizes. Teachers have annual performance reviews and their planning is monitored termly. No sluggards allowed here. A couple of parents we spoke to said that academia across the foundation has definitely been stepped up a notch over the past few years. One parent told us: 'Belmont was always more of a nurturing school, but the goalposts seem to be constantly changing and you feel like you are kept on your toes the whole time.' In school's view, 'High academic performance is our number one target.'

Fifty clubs are on offer during lunchtime and after school, so if elastic or kicking a ball ain't your thing – why not try ancient Greek? Or perhaps origami

Sats abolished in favour of continuous assessments from year 3. No longer follows the common entrance curriculum because nearly everyone goes through to the senior school. Instead, teaches 'a Mill Hill curriculum which gives the same rigour as the CE curriculum but tailored to enable our pupils to delve deeper into subject topics, with greater emphasis on problem solving and reasoning.' Places at Mill Hill are not unconditional, but any early problems, academically or behaviourally, are usually flagged up whilst the child is at Grimsdell (the pre-prep), so there are 'rarely any surprises.' School says that because Belmont is part of a foundation of three schools, it is important to look at the bigger picture. 'If we didn't feel a child could cope, we wouldn't allow them to progress to year 7.' These cases are few and far between, however.

The school has a small learning support department and is happy to accommodate children with mild cases of dyslexia and dyspraxia. Anything more severe, and 'we're not the school for them.' Small groups of gifted and talented children are arranged across the years, and most are prepared for the 11+ and 13+ scholarship awards.

Belmont is a Christian foundation based upon the principles of 'religious freedom'. Chapel services are obligatory, because if you start pulling pupils out, 'you lose the ability to say we can work together'. However, the school's pupils represent a wide range of faiths and cultures, so chapel services and assemblies are inter-denominational.

During our tour, we noticed the school undergoing building works – six new classrooms, two science labs and an impressive hall. Shortly after our visit, we discovered that Belmont, along with the other two schools in the Mill Hill foundation, was merging with the Mount School for girls (hmmm). The merger came as a great shock for parents who were informed by email, with no prior warning. School insisted that it was not planning a permanent expansion; pupil numbers have increased by some 55 or so, and boy:girl ratio is now more even. The Mount building now houses The Mount, Mill Hill International school.

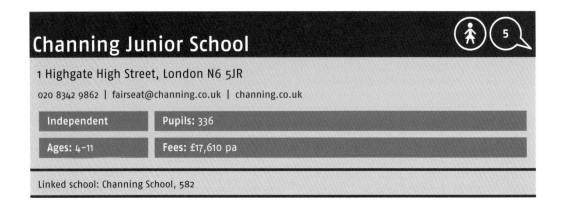

Channning Junior School

1 Highgate High Street, London N6 5JR

020 8342 9862 | fairseat@channing.co.uk | channing.co.uk

| Independent | Pupils: 336 |
| Ages: 4–11 | Fees: £17,610 pa |

Linked school: Channing School, 582

Head: Since September 2018, Dina Hamalis, previously academic director of Sarum Hall. Degree in education, specialising in English and history; spent five years at St Albans High Prep, moving to Highgate School (curriculum coordinator) then UCS pre-prep (SENCo, G&T and EAL coordinator) before joining Sarum Hall in 2011. She is an ISI inspector.

Entrance: Main entry at 4+. About 200 assessed (ie observed performing a range of 'nursery tasks') for 48 places (two classes of 24) in January before entry, then whittled down in a second round. 'We're looking for bright girls, who are interested, engaged and willing to have a go.' The school's increasing popularity means they're now first choice for most applicants. No 7+ entry; a smattering of vacancies higher up. Most families, however, are here for the duration.

Exit: The mode' is 'all-through', and the focus is to prepare girls well for the next stage, not for admissions elsewhere. ('We don't provide extra tutoring or practice papers'.) The assumption is that all girls will proceed to the senior school without further entrance testing. ('Not having to do the 11+ is a real advantage,' said one mother. 'It enables you to have a longer term view of education, which is very appealing.') In most years, a small handful leave for other schools. Some to board, some to the state (including highly competitive selective schools, like Henrietta Barnett and St Michael's Catholic Grammar), one or two to other leading independents. Children who would really struggle at the senior school are also gently guided elsewhere. 'It isn't a question of having a bar that has to be met. We want girls to thrive. Some children find the academic pace a challenge and flourish nonetheless, but if a girl's self-confidence starts to dip, we help the family find the best alternative.'

Remarks: Set opposite its senior school, behind high walls and tall gates in Highgate's traffic-packed high street, the school's rather forbidding exterior belies the pleasures within. Located in what was once Fairseat, the fine Victorian mansion of the Waterlow family, the junior school moved into its current accommodation in 1926, retaining a generous slice of the original gardens (the remainder was donated to the community to become adjoining Waterlow Park). The expansive house (with far-reaching views) now contains large, light classrooms, a performing arts studio, music rooms, a practical room for science, and plenty of elbow room for all. The gardens, with their mature trees, also house an adventure playground while three new outdoor learning areas (mud kitchen, classroom and a pavilion) are used by every class. All in all, 'it gives them a freedom rarely found in London. They can go into the bushes and make dens and still feel totally safe.'

A fundamental aspect of the school's approach is its personalised attitude to the academic; all are taught to a high standard, but not all are taught in the same way. ('One of my daughters needs – and gets – much more support than the other,' said a parent.) Bright and breezy teaching moves at a brisk, imaginative pace. (We watched girls create a 'storm' using a variety of sounds, for example, for a lesson on weather.) Specialists in ICT, modern languages. Art, DT, PE, drama and music throughout. Innovative new Spanish language programme engages all pupils in 'Spanish language and culture'. French also added in year 3.

IT firmly embedded from the off, with a dedicated IT room lined with Apple Macs, and iPads used as 'learning tools'. 'Somehow they see them as something completely different from the tablets at home. Here they're used as dictionaries, for creativity and for research.'

Reasonably heavy homework load. ('My daughter couldn't manage more,' said the mother of a girl in year 5), but it's cool to work hard and parents, pupils and students all have high aspirations. 'The school manages a good balance between stretching them academically, while still nurturing them and treating them as individuals,' said one parent. 'I feel my daughter's pushed about the right amount,' said another.

Designated additional learning coordinator works with classroom teachers to put together appropriate learning plans. Children are sometimes withdrawn from lessons to work in a quieter space, but always follow the same work as their classmates. Gifted and talented also given additional stretch.

'My daughter used to be very shy,' said a parent, 'but performing in everything from music assemblies to poetry readings has made her much more self-assured'

Attractive, well-used library with dedicated librarian, encouraging even the youngest to borrow, express opinions, and carry out research.

Music undoubtedly a strength, with enthusiastic head of music working closely with her equally energetic colleague in the senior school. Regular music lessons, plus plenty of opportunities to perform in music assemblies, orchestra, brass and wind bands, string quartet and choir. Wide range of individual music lessons, with vast majority taking classes in anything from saxophone to harp. (The school currently has four harpists.) Does its best to ensure girls find an instrument that 'fits their character' and lets parents borrow rather than buy in the early stages. Three girls recently invited to join the National Children's Orchestra, and usually several music awards to senior school. Art, with its own designated room, also vibrant.

The gardens also house an adventure playground and three outdoor learning areas. All in all, 'it gives them a freedom rarely found in London. They can go into the bushes and make dens and still feel totally safe'

Large sports hall on site (recently vacated by senior school, which now has its own), plus well-used netball and tennis courts. Swimming takes place elsewhere, and the school has its own playing field a brisk walk away, used for sports days and rounders matches. Pupils have competed at regional and national level in tennis, swimming and cross-country.

Has significantly boosted the extracurricular offering introducing in- and after-school clubs ranging from judo and gymnastics to fencing, ballet and chess (with one Grand-Master-in-the-making competing in the U11 World Chess Champions). Busy schedule of visits (eg Neasden Temple, Sky Studios, engineering workshop) and residential trips for older pupils.

Girls are well behaved – leaping to their feet to chorus 'Good Afternoon' – but building confidence is as critical as good manners. 'My daughter used to be very shy,' said a parent, 'but performing in everything from music assemblies to poetry readings has made her much more self-assured.' The atmosphere is friendly and bustling, girls engaged and enthusiastic. 'My daughter loves the school,' said one mother. 'If we ever discuss moving, she says she doesn't want to leave. She has a wide variety of friends – the school's not cliquey at all.'

Channing used to be very much a local school, but the increased intake and improved academic reputation mean that, while there are still plenty of locals (some whose families have attended the school for generations), the pool now spreads out five miles, with plenty arriving from Islington and beyond. Families are also more international than before, though still largely made up of a solid core of affluent professionals. Active parents' association arranges regular events and last year also helped raise £17,000 or so for charity.

Channing School

Highgate, London N6 5HF

020 8340 2328 | admissions@channing.co.uk | channing.co.uk

Independent	Pupils: 597; sixth form: 130
Ages: 11–18	Fees: £19,410 pa

Linked school: Channing Junior School, 580

Headmistress: Since 2005, Mrs Barbara Elliott, MA PGCE (60s). Mrs Elliott attended a girls' grammar school in Lancashire, then read French and Spanish at New Hall, Cambridge. Taught in both the independent and state sectors before arriving at Channing. Much liked by pupils and parents. Gets to know pupils well at the outset by inviting year 7s in for a chat. With experience of all-boys, all-girls and mixed schools, she remains a firm advocate of girls-only education. 'I've seen girls in co-educational schools sitting silently for years. Girls here are not without an interesting social life, but here they have the freedom to be themselves and try new things.' Like her pupils, there's nothing of the wallflower about Mrs Elliott, whose fashionable glasses and stripy tights signal her buoyant and breezy personality. Pomp and distance play no part in her regime (for example, she happily sat crossed legged for morning assembly in a charity swap with a junior pupil), and she runs the school with a light touch.With four adult sons, all now successfully established, she's an enthusiastic grandmother and dog-lover.

Academic matters: Channing is an academic school, but not one where academic achievement overrides all else. The intake here is slightly broader than at some of the local competition, and not every pupil will be cut out for straight A*/9s. ('Here, if a girl is outstanding at art, but not at maths, it's not the end of the world,' says the head. 'Some are exceptionally bright; others exceptional at something, but, naturally, not everything.') Every girl, however, should get the best she's capable of, and often significantly more than might be expected. ('Some achieve more than you'd have ever have thought possible.') At GCSE, most garner a pleasing string of 9-7s (84 per cent in 2018); at A levels, the dominant alphabet is again A*-A (62 per cent).

The sixth form is not huge – about 65 in each year – and nor is the subject range (19 on offer); the core is serious stuff and the conventional arts/science divide is roughly in balance, with biology and economics attracting similar numbers to history

and English (though few physicists). Maths tops the popularity stakes; biology and politics take away the highest grades. Good spread of languages, with Spanish, French, German and Latin all on offer at GCSE and A level, plus Greek as a twilight GCSE subject. Adelante programme from reception upwards aims to produce girls fluent in Spanish and with a love of Hispanic culture.

The school prides itself on the quality of its teaching. ('Our teachers are experts in pedagogy,' says the head.) The Independent Schools inspectors found teaching 'excellent', and also waxed lyrical about the 'exceptional' quality of 'pupils' learning and achievement'. No doubt at all that value is added here – in every direction. Good take up, for example, of the research-directed Extended Project Qualification (EPQ). Technology, too, thoroughly embedded, with all girls issued with a school iPad 'to support research, investigation, creativity and communication'.

Her fashionable glasses and stripy tights signal her buoyant and breezy personality

Special needs addressed by a qualified SENCo, called on to assist a range of difficulties, from profoundly deaf pupils to 30-or-so girls with mild visual impairment, dyslexia, or processing issues. 'We carry out appropriate assessment, but it's as much about helping teachers to adapt their teaching to meet individual needs.'

Games, options, the arts: Art and music both unusually strong. Art ('absolutely amazing,' said one pupil) is housed in roof-top studios with stunning views across London. Strong emphasis on drawing as the basis of it all, but art rooms are lined with Macs and scented by oil paint. Plenty achieve external glory, with recent prize winners in Young Art at the Royal College of Art. Student work also displayed (and sold!) at a north London gallery. Music, always strong, has undoubtedly been enhanced by the completion of the new music school, which has added 10 practice rooms, a technology room and a sound-proofed percussion studio. Record numbers now take external exams, including the first set of musical theatre awards (with 23 distinctions). Plenty of opportunity to perform in-house – annual and lunchtime concerts, plus informal recitals – and in formats that range from string quartets and guitar ensembles to a jazz band and contemporary music group. Recent finalists, too, in Voice Festival UK. Biannual international tours to eg Lisbon, Madrid, Vienna, Boston and Venice.

There's no prize-giving, and the most valued award is a Conabor Badge, bestowed on 'girls of good character' (or, as one recipient phrased it, 'for being good')

Limited running around space on site, so probably not a first-choice for those who live for goals and glory. Though 'we have county level sportswomen, and local netball clubs train here most evenings,' says the head. But if go-fight-win is not top of the agenda, keeping fit and healthy definitely is. PE compulsory throughout and newly refurbished multi-use games area plus sports hall make this a pleasure, with vastly improved opportunities for volleyball, badminton, cricket and dance, plus recent successes in cricket, tennis and football.

West End quality performing arts building recently completed and LAMDA classes very popular. Staggering range of school trips and activities, from history in Berlin and classics in Greece to a music tour to Madrid and regular theatre outings to the West End. Clubs follow prevailing interests and currently include feminist society, robotics, chemistry, classics, life drawing and creative writing.

Background and atmosphere: School housed in four tall and graceful Georgian buildings on Highgate Hill overlooking one of London's most beautiful and under-visited parks. Backing these, head has done a serious job of rearrangement, making the most of a relatively small site with the addition of a new complex (containing the music school, the gym and a sixth form centre). 'If you're investing in your daughter's education you expect 21st century facilities,' she says.

Established in 1885 by a Unitarian minister and two members of his congregation to educate the daughters of Unitarian ministers, the school's clientele has broadened, but it retains the founders' values of liberalism, democracy and religious tolerance. There's no prize-giving, for example, and the most valued award is a Conabor Badge, bestowed on 'girls of good character' (or, as one recipient phrased it, 'for being good'). 'Girls really aspire to be awarded this badge,' says the head. 'It's what most embodies the spirit of the school.'

Pupils are active and engaged, participating enthusiastically in both academic and extracurricular activities (15, for example, gained D of E gold recently, impressive numbers even for a much larger school). 'I've never worked in a school where the focus on advancement and learning is so great,' says the head. 'They all have a common purpose. They're very ambitious and focussed.'

Pastoral care, well-being and discipline: This is a calm and orderly place, but it has little to do with a system of tight rules and stern warnings. 'I'm not quite sure how the detention system works,' admits the head, who oversees 'a record of serious discipline' going back 13 years which takes up just two pages.

Strong emphasis on student leadership, with two officers in every form – 'they hunt in packs' – including two head girls. Older girls also apply to become 'school officers' with designated areas of responsibility. 'A lot of girls aspire to the leadership team,' says the head. 'They have real influence.' As well as 'advising constructively', year 12s set up and run clubs and have recently sat on a panel interviewing a teacher for a job. 'I hadn't done this before,' says the head, 'but they were so clear in their thinking, so mature and perceptive.' The code of behaviour is also co-written by the girls. 'We live together in this community.'

Head's priorities are 'integrity, independence, scholarship and altruism' – old fashioned virtues, adapted to a more complex modern setting. She acknowledges that the pressures on her students are greater than ever before – 'Not all girls sail through life without hitting stormy waters' – and the school works with parents all the way, helping minimise screen time and maximise mental and physical health. 'They believe in happy girls, rather than ones who are pushed,' said one mother.

Girls generally get on with minimal bullying and cliques. 'You know everyone here, you feel very comfortable and there is a real sense of joining together.' 'It's a very safe place,' said one parent. 'If your child is slightly quirky, you know they will still be fine.' However, we have had reports of recent less-than-sympathetic responses to teenage anxieties. Head appointed a counsellor on the advice of the sixth form.

Pupils and parents: Essentially a local school, so no fleets of coaches to far-flung locations. Most pupils walk or come by public transport, from a broad sweep round the gates. 'Mainly north and west, though we do get a few from east London.' Parents are cosmopolitan (South African, European, North American, Asian), highly educated ('At careers fairs, if you shout, "Is there a doctor in the house?", there's a rush') and value education ('expectations are very high'). They're also 'tremendously supportive'. Pupils, quite often the daughters of old girls, are confident and motivated, thriving in this relatively small school.

Entrance: At 11, 300-400 sit the London 11+ Consortium exams for around 56 places, joining the 40 or so coming up from the junior school to form four forms of 24. ('Junior school pupils don't have to sit 11 plus – it's a dream ticket,' says the head.) Will in future consist of a cognitive ability test (rather than maths and English exams) with great emphasis on the interview. For sixth form entry, applicants are interviewed and expected to achieve nine or 10 9-7 grades at GCSEs, with a minimum of 7 in the subjects they intend to study. 'I can sometimes bend the rules for existing students as we know they have firm foundations,' says the head, 'but we'd turn away someone from outside who didn't have the grades.'

Exit: A few leave at 16 – to board, to co-ed, to local state schools. The rest depart two years later for serious subjects at predominantly Russell Group universities. Two to Oxbridge in 2018, then UCL, Nottingham, Leeds, Exeter, Bristol. About half go on to science-related degrees (with a good smattering of medics and vets). The head takes a personal interest in all applicants, interviewing each girl.

Money matters: Not a hugely rich school, but still does its bit, with five per cent of annual income devoted to bursaries, 'supporting families who hit hard times'. Academic scholarships at 11 worth 10 per cent off the fees, but music scholarships (grade 5 with merit minimum required) are particularly good, with up to 50 per cent discounts. In the sixth form, art, music and academic scholarships (of up to 50 per cent off tuition fees) on offer to existing students ('We want to recognise their talent and potential, not find them sloping off elsewhere') as well as external ones. Bursaries also available at this point.

Remarks: A cosy, vibrant, local school in a very attractive setting, with high academic standards, up-to-date facilities and happy, motivated girls.

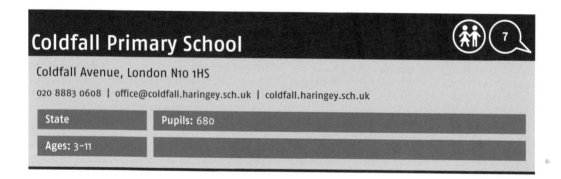

Coldfall Primary School

Coldfall Avenue, London N10 1HS

020 8883 0608 | office@coldfall.haringey.sch.uk | coldfall.haringey.sch.uk

State	Pupils: 680
Ages: 3-11	

Head teacher: Since 1996, Evelyn Davies (50s). Ms Davies is one of life's 'superheads', a woman who has taken a 'bog-standard' primary and transformed it into a star act with an 'outstanding' Ofsted, three-form entry and very happy parents. Most find her open-minded and approachable. 'I had an idea', commented one, 'and she immediately said "let's have a chat about it".' Hard working and well-organised, she gets things done. 'She's not ticking boxes, she really gets involved in the nitty gritty'. An active opponent of testing, testing, testing, she's even been to parliament to protest, winning the admiration of her local MP ('if I were the minister for education I would grab Evelyn Davies and put her as a key adviser. That way our children would be well educated in every sense of the word').

Entrance: Places given out using the standard local authority formula: children in local authority care, followed by special educational needs, siblings and distance from the gates. Recent expansion means a bit of leeway for those living a few streets away. Admission to full time nursery via the school.

Exit: A primary whose catchment fortunately straddles the borough's two highest flying comprehensives. The largest chunk of year 6 proceed to Fortismere, just next door. Sizeable (and growing) slice to Alexandra Park, down the road. Enviable success rate too, in grammar school entrance, then in dribbles to a wide range of local and distant establishments.

Many arrive at weekends to help with the gardening, and the thriving PTA organises summer and winter fairs, weekly coffee mornings

Remarks: This meticulously run school has everything going for it. Teaching here is enthusiastic and thorough, with staff constantly looking to improve performance. Academic standards are high and virtually every child reaches the government targets, many far exceeding them. Though the school has an 'unusually high' number of children with special needs, both those who struggle and those who excel are provided with plenty of booster classes. Not all parents, however, feel difficulties are necessarily dealt with sympathetically. 'Our son has considerable problems', said one, 'and we found the attitude very inflexible'. Behaviour is good and positive performance (particularly regular attendance) rewarded (classes compete enthusiastically for attendance teddies).

Facilities here can only be described as exceptional for a London primary. The original, large, low-lying Victorian schoolhouse, once a secondary school, has now been joined by a sleek, modern addition, providing extra classrooms and a new gym. Expansive grounds boast country-like playing fields, as well as two large and notably well-equipped playgrounds kitted out with basketball and netball nets, table-tennis tables and sheltered cabins. Pupils also benefit from the school's own allotments and nature trail, as well as access to nearby Coldfall Woods.

Sport played enthusiastically and successfully. Two hours of PE weekly overseen by a qualified sports coach and training approached with professional efficiency (gymnasts, for example, use flip cameras to study performance). Both boys and girls triumph in borough-wide competitions, boys winning recent golf and football championships, girls excelling in football and netball. Pupils also qualified for the London Youth Games.

Plenty of enrichment, in lessons and out, including chess (with championship-winning chess teams), French (taught by a native speaker), computer programming and cooking all part of the regular mix. Excellent range of clubs (including geology) and activities. Successful school choir has made appearances at the O2 and Barbican and one enthusiastic parent recently organised an entire week of dance with over 60 workshops and professionals imported from the West End. 'Things don't just happen here', said one mother. 'Everything is well planned and thought through'. Regular trips beyond the school gates include at least one visit to a museum, gallery and musical event for every pupil.

In the main (though not exclusively), parents are comfortably off Muswell Hill locals, so there's a good sprinkling of designer trainers in the playground, but this is low-key prosperity. Almost a third of pupils speak a language other than English at home. Both mothers and fathers (plenty of the latter at pick-up time) involved in making the school a success. 'All parents', said one enthusiast, 'are given an opportunity to contribute, not just non-working mums'. Many arrive at weekends to help with the gardening, and the thriving PTA organises summer and winter fairs, weekly coffee mornings, a Valentine disco, quiz night, fashion show and organic vegetable scheme. Sizeable sums are raised for playground, computer and PE equipment. 'There's a real feeling that everyone matters', said one mother. 'The kids are really blessed'.

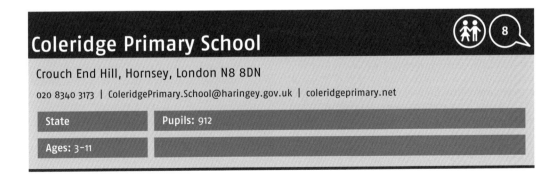

Coleridge Primary School

Crouch End Hill, Hornsey, London N8 8DN

020 8340 3173 | ColeridgePrimary.School@haringey.gov.uk | coleridgeprimary.net

State	Pupils: 912
Ages: 3–11	

Head: Since 2014, Leon Cheouke BA PGCE (40s). After a first degree in community studies at Manchester and a PGCE at Goldsmiths University of London, Mr Cheouke arrived at Coleridge in 2000 and, apart from a year teaching in New Zealand, has been there ever since, working formerly as deputy to his long-serving and popular predecessor. Continuity and growth have his model. 'He said he wasn't going to change much and he hasn't,' said one parent. 'He's kept the best bits, really listened to what parents want and cares about all the children rather than statistics.' Keen on politics, Dr Who and vinyl.

Entrance: Coleridge is a very large school (120 each year enter four reception classes), but, sadly for aspiring parents, Crouch End is an ever-popular destination for family existence, and siblings tend to elbow newbies out of the way. Mumsnet types moan, too, about affluent applicants guying the system by renting nearby. The only advice is live as near as you can (ideally, within quarter of a mile).

Exit: The majority to a strong set of local comprehensives (Highgate Woods, Alexandra Park School, Fortismere), plus a handful to state selectives (Laytmer), independents and home schooling.

Remarks: Coleridge is a super primary – in both senses of the word (with 960 pupils, it's the size of many secondaries). Long one of the neighbourhood's most sought-after schools, in 2007 it expanded onto two sites, doubling the number of slots available. New arrivals now start in the original 1960s low-rise, before moving across the road to the bright, old-meets-modern addition in year 2. Parents originally worried the expansion might damage the close-knit feel, but agree the mood has been maintained. 'Because the school is on two sites, you feel you're dropping off somewhere quite small,' said one. Many feel, too, the scale equips pupils well for life afterwards.

Teaching an undoubted strength (maths, considered by Ofsted 'impressive'), with staff praised as 'bright, funny and incredibly enthusiastic'. 'The teachers are well tuned in with the children; they listen to them and treat them as individuals,' said one mother. Results excellent, with large numbers of year 6 pupils reaching well above standards expected for their age (some, it has been whispered, with the aid of tutoring). 'Standards are high, but they still make it fun,' said one mother. 'They're very aware of not putting too much pressure on the children.' Careful monitoring and target setting ensure the approach to each child is tweaked for maximum benefit. Progress equally successful for those with special educational needs or struggling on the foothills of English, who all make 'outstanding progress'.

Everything done to make the day exciting and interesting. Philosophy taught weekly to enhance critical thinking and pupils regularly involved in lively political debate (the environment, housing, teachers' salaries), while the school's de-luxe scale allows for a raft of specialists (two for art, one each for music, PE and Spanish). Homework (classified as 'home learning' and operating on a long-term

timetable) is intended to develop research skills rather than become a domestic battleground. Two spacious libraries, with a dedicated librarian, are open to children in break and lunch.

Parents love the approach. 'They do a lot of art and don't concentrate all the time on maths, English and science,' commented one. 'I moved here because I liked the creativity'

The school holds the Arts Council's prestigious Artsmark Gold status for encouraging pupils to become involved with the arts, and the arts are, undoubtedly, a major strength. ('We've found that it's within the arts that children who may find the more academic areas of school life challenging are able to develop their "voice",' says the head). Art taught in a light, purpose-built studio and exhibitions held regularly, in school and out. Music excellent, with weekly singing assemblies and lively participation in choirs and competitions (Coleridge Royal Albert Hall choir, Crouch End Festival Choir, Sing Up competition). Dance and drama, too, made much of, with an annual whole-school play, dance classes (again with tailor-made space and links to The Royal Ballet), drama classes (with ties to the National Theatre) and numerous arts-related clubs held in lunch hours and before and after school. Parents love the approach. 'They do a lot of art and don't concentrate all the time on maths, English and science,' commented one. 'I moved here because I liked the creativity.'

Sports and games considered fundamental for healthy living and esprit de corps, as well as 'an integral part of the equal-opportunities practice' (so girls encouraged to play football, boys to dance). Gymnastics and games taught throughout, with older pupils learning netball, Kwik Cricket, athletics, tag rugby, tennis and football, some taught by specialist coaches. Swimming lessons at local pool. Frequent fixtures against other local primaries and sports day is a proper affair, with no dilly-dallying about all fair in love and sport, and school records recording 'x is the fastest at'.. ('The teachers decided to do this to challenge the children,' comments the head.) Outdoor education also delivered through regular attendance at forest school in nearby woods, where, as well as practical skills like putting up shelters, pupils develop teamwork and communication.

Huge range of after-school clubs (capoeira, meditation, fencing, drumming, photography, squash, art academy, tennis, school newspaper) and visiting talks (Highgate Woods feminist group – all former

Annemount School

pupils – on gender equality, a Google employee to launch a technology competition). Also, privately-run breakfast and after-school clubs.

Crouch End is cool and media savvy – the school's Glastonbury-themed fête gives you a clue, as does a recent outing to The Guardian newspaper (where else?) – and while pupils come from the usual metropolitan multi-stranded ethnic range, the less advantaged are not unduly well represented. (Those in receipt of the pupil premium is 'below average', states Ofsted, a relative rarity in London.) 'Now that the school is bigger, there are more people from the flats and estates, and it's bit more ethnically diverse,' commented one parent. Children, however, tend to have names like Esme, Flora and Felix, Planet Organic features in after-school snacks, and prominent on the noticeboard is an ad announcing 'half cello for sale'. Parents, on the whole, comfortably off (£13,000, for example,

raised at the summer fair), but also reasonably relaxed and school is warm and friendly, with parental involvement a major part of the ethos - 'I love the community feel,' said one. Though some comments, too, about a small number of the 'vocal and opinionated' who the school attempts to keep at polite arms' length. Pastoral care an undoubted strength (with professional, confidential counselling offered on a one-to-one basis). 'Moving towards' a house structure. No uniform.

Pupils of all ages are confident and articulate (with year 6 recent victors in the Winston Churchill Public Speaking competition, beating off considerable prep school opposition) – and happy. 'My son has really thrived here. He was quite shy before he went but he has made a lot of progress socially and really loves school.'

Now, as always, the It school in the neighbourhood.

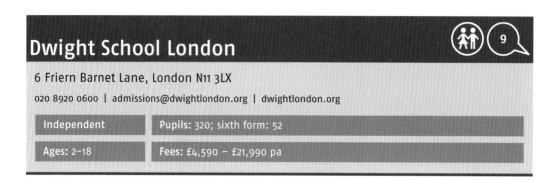

Dwight School London

6 Friern Barnet Lane, London N11 3LX

020 8920 0600 | admissions@dwightlondon.org | dwightlondon.org

Independent	Pupils: 320; sixth form: 52
Ages: 2–18	Fees: £4,590 – £21,990 pa

Head of School: Since January 2016, Alison Cobbin BA Dip Ed MBA (50s). Brought up in Australia and qualified as an English and history teacher at Macquarie University in Sydney. Moved to London in 1995 with her husband and then three young daughters; after a career break, joined Dwight (then Woodside Park School) as, variously, English, games and theory of knowledge teacher, IB coordinator and upper school principal. Moved to a SE London independent school as pastoral deputy head before returning to Dwight as head of school: 'I came back because I had made a shortlist of all the things I wanted from a school, and when this job came up it ticked all the boxes.'

The boxes it ticked were: co-ed, not too big, International, non-selective, and most importantly did the IB. Alison says once you've been to a school which upholds the values of the IB, it's very hard to go back: 'The IB is built on such a different philosophy – its broad base is so different. It's more collaborative than the English education system and does more than just work towards getting into the best university.' To which Andy Atkinson (upper school principal) adds: 'The IB is not subject

to government changes and grade inflation – you know that if a person achieved 40 out of a maximum 45 several years ago, that would still hold true many years later with the exception of the odd curriculum change.' We were sold.

The new leadership team of the upper school – Alison Cobbin and Andy Atkinson – have been called an exceptional team and inspiring to staff and pupils. One parent told us: 'Andy is a very strong character and has a real vision of what he wants to achieve. The profile of the school has definitely improved since they both came on board, as have the results.' Andy's international credentials are impressive. He was previously director of the two International Schools of London, and has taught extensively abroad. However, he says: 'There are not many IB schools like Dwight. It's a unique school in north London. Some of the kids are a little bit different, a little bit eccentric, and some are happy for the first time about coming to school.'

However, this is very much a leadership team of three. Lower school principal Matt Parkin BEd DipEd NPQH has been at the school since 2007. He has taught in the UK, USA and Indonesia and one could say has had a pretty colourful background in education. Following a seven year stint working in the state education sector in Devon, Matt was part of a start-up school in Houston, Texas. In the five years he was there he increased the school from 50-strong to 400. He was then offered a post to teach at 'one of the best schools in Asia' in Jakarta, Indonesia, which had an outdoor swimming pool, a theatre and a multi-media centre. As much of a draw as that was, Matt yearned for a school with an international outlook back home. 'There are not many of them around, and a job came up at Dwight, so I took it.'

Academic matters: Runs the IB programme at all levels. Year groups in lower school divided into two parallel classes with a maximum of 20 in each. Lots of child-inspired batiks, pottery and art help create a vibrant atmosphere. IB learner profile is displayed everywhere. IB primary years programme (IBPYP) well linked with the national curriculum, which keeps inspectorates happy and ensures children are well grounded with an international mindset. All lessons in each half of term based around one aspect of the curriculum. Specialist teachers for music, art, PE, French and EAL. Homework important and can be done at after-school club.

In 2018, average IB point score 30 (out of possible 45). One or two students each year opt to take a Dwight High School Diploma, earning IB course certificates rather than the full IB diploma. Average class size in upper school not normally more than 15, although we spoke to one pupil who had just three others in her geography class. 'It's great! Almost like one-to-one tuition.' Good results for IB middle years programme exams with several top students getting more than 60 points out of 70. One parent said the only downside of the IB from her point of view is that 'if you are weak in a certain area – such as maths or languages – you can't drop it, as you need to take one subject from each of the six subject groups.' However, there are choices within these.

Dwight also offers Pamoja Online courses which enable Dwight IB diploma students to take a wider range of courses while experiencing the kind of online learning that is increasingly common at university level. School says: 'These courses are fantastic. They are based in Oxford and provide a quality programme which is strictly monitored. There are over 50 different nationalities at Dwight and it's not always feasible to accommodate everyone, so these courses are a great online alternative. It is the equivalent of an IB course online.'

French is introduced in lower school, Spanish and Mandarin added as an option in upper school. Other languages considered on request at additional cost. (One Portuguese teacher does a lesson via Skype.) RE is not an IB subject, but world religion is. Photos throughout the school buildings depict many school trips, dramatic and music performances and community service activities, suggesting that a lot of learning is regularly extended out and about. After-school homework club for those who want extra help.

He has had a pretty colourful educational background. Part of a start-up school in Texas, he was then offered a post at 'one of the best schools in Asia'

Through the QUEST programme (at extra cost) the school can accommodate a range of learning needs, with the support of specialist teachers. EAL (also at extra cost) regarded as essential for children who lack English proficiency – two to five lessons a week, one to one or in a small group depending on needs. A mother tongue programme is available for Japanese pupils – the second largest group in the school (about 10 per cent) and some other languages (no extra charge is made if four or more students are in the same group and level). IB diploma students must be completely fluent in English.

A dedicated SENCo for the roughly 14 per cent on the SEN register: 'Because of the nature of this school, we're not equipped to deal with many pupils with very diverse needs.' But parents do say that what they like about Dwight is that it suits a great variety of children. 'I wanted a school where all of my children would be well served'.

Teachers are international and IB-experienced. Over 60 per cent come from overseas: 'London is a bit of a destination for teachers. For those not from abroad, they look at their IB training as a fantastic experience.' Parents speak enthusiastically about the teaching staff and their willingness to help and respond quickly to any parent concerns. One pupil told us: 'The teachers here are great – you can talk them about anything, even after school.'

Games, options, the arts: Games obligatory once a week for each year group – the school has its own sports field 10 minutes away by minibus and uses other local sports facilities. They compete not only with local and national schools but also with international overseas schools. One pupil told us. 'I love the sports here, there are lots of options and the school is even planning a trip to Venice to play beach volleyball.' Parents say they like the variety of sports on offer – not only the traditional ones but a wider range: rugby, football, basketball, track and field, sailing, ice skating.

Lots of after-school clubs and extracurricular offerings. Strong music – about 15 per cent learn an individual instrument; there are rock, jazz and chamber groups. The choir has sung at London's 02 in Young Voices, and for some lucky pupils, the 'highlight of their life' was performing with the Dwight New York choir at Carnegie Hall. Other clubs include cartoon club, sewing club, origami and magical maths.

Some have their activity week in Normandy (practising the French that they have been learning since they were 3) and some go on exchange to the Dwight School in New York

For the last period on Tuesdays, the pupils do mixed age group activities including community service projects. This helps to develop relationships across the ages, reinforcing the 'Dwight family' concept.

Lots of outings to concerts, theatres and galleries as well as trips home and abroad. Year 6 students spend a week at the Dwight School in New York, some year groups in upper school have their activity week in Normandy (practising the French that they have been learning since they were 3) and some of them go on exchange to the Dwight School in New York. Older students are developing a community service project in Nepal. They raise funds and students and staff travel there to do volunteer work. The arts dept has been to Vietnam to study music and dance; they have also visited Hollywood, India and Cuba.

Model United Nations conference is also popular. This year saw the school representing Saudi Arabia.

Background and atmosphere: The school was originally founded in 1972 by Dr Stephen Spahn, chancellor of the Dwight School in New York. Previously known as Woodside Park and North London International School, the school changed its name in a rebranding exercise to Dwight London School, to heighten awareness of its association with the Dwight family of schools that now has campuses in Seoul and Shanghai, with Dubai opening imminently. 'Dwight family' is a term used by staff and families alike. Dwight London has an advisory board of local parents and others who lend expertise and guidance and serve as a supportive sounding board for the principal in the strategic planning of the school.

The school is on four sites in two locations. Lower school is in Woodside Avenue. Kindergarten

and reception based in their own little house, The Lodge, with its own garden for play. Part-time options are available and there's a wraparound care programme from 7.30am to 5pm for the lower school.

Years 2 to 5 in the main building here have good sized, light classrooms with washing lines displaying student work. Each child has own drawer for storage. Computers everywhere. Media resource centres, a small library collection; great gym, which doubles up as the dining hall. Healthy food served from the kitchens next to it (where meals for the kindergarten are also prepared). Photos of all the year 6 students displayed in the passage with their personal blogs. Good music room and lovely art room. Whilst we were there we saw some wonderful examples of art which had been selected for the Dwight Travelling Art Show – a yearly event where the top 20 chosen art pieces make their way around the different Dwight campuses of the world. Well-equipped library with Harry Potter translated into an assortment of languages.

A recent popular addition to the school is the Dwight radio station which is broadcast online: 'This is another way we feel pupils can demonstrate their learning, without it just being test test test.'

Year 6 has a separate eco-building with easy access to the specialist classrooms and playground; school has green flag eco-schools status. If we were being finickity, we would say that the interior could do with a bit of sprucing up – a new lick of paint. The red, white and blue colours of their motif (which is painted virtually everywhere), becomes a little bit wearing on the eye after a while.

Playground not huge but much use made of local park for cross-country runs and scientific experiments plus compulsory swimming once a week at a local pool. They also regularly use the school's own playing fields a short bus ride away.

The upper school is in the former Friern Barnet Boys' Grammar School and in nearby Jubilee Hall. The main building has recently been refurbished and is clean, bright and welcoming, making very good use of light throughout. The administrative offices and faculty room share the same corridors as the classrooms, which must strengthen the sense of community. Every wall is full of original and creative student art and photographs, and there are posters with quotes from Gandhi, Martin Luther King and Nelson Mandela, who we learned are the role models for the three upper school student houses.

The Jubilee Hall holds more classrooms, two science labs, the upper school library and a pleasant canteen open throughout. This looks out onto an outside playground where students engage in a bit of exercise during break or lunch, and a small world garden beyond with picnic tables and benches. The school admits that conditions are a

The impression from parents and from our visit is that there is relatively little sense of the 'expat bubble' in this international school

little crowded, and they are on the lookout for new property in the area.

In recent years the Dwight community has collaborated to help families have a 'soft landing' when they arrive in London. A handy Welcome to London guide written and updated annually by the parents is found on the website with tips for families living in north London. Lots of welcome and goodbye rituals for students coming and going. There are also a variety of ways that rising year 6 students are supported as they move to the upper school. It's all part of the school's intention to give everyone a Dwight Hug. One parent told us: 'We were given a really warm welcome when we arrived and were immediately put in touch with the Parents' Association. The parent network at Dwight is fantastic.'

The individualised approach we heard so much about from parents was evident during our visit. We were shown around the school by an extremely theatrical and colourful student (who we definitely thought should be on TV) – and many others we spoke to were equally as quirky, interesting and slightly eccentric, with amazing back stories. Another seemed to be a science whizz who showed us her extraordinary end of M5 personal project (a culmination of their IB middle years) – and had created a working Enigma machine with morse coding etc.

Pastoral care, well-being and discipline: The IB philosophy and emphasis on tolerance and global understanding is reinforced everywhere in the school with big signs bearing the IB ethos (inquirers, reflective risk-takers, etc). Kids are divided into houses – Pioneers, Artists and Visionaries – and are awarded 'sparkies' (which refer to the IB philosophy of igniting the sparks of genius).

Kids seem happy, and although there is a uniform there are various options, so they can choose how casual or dressy they want to look. Parents love the small size of the school. 'It's a massive advantage. Everyone is known, everyone can shine and blossom.' One parent we spoke to who has home schooled her child for a while said that Dwight is the first school her son has been happy at: 'This school has literally been our saviour. I love the IB ethos in tailoring the work to your child's needs – it's so much more of a progressive approach.' The school recently introduced a vertical tutoring system, which encourages pupils to get to know other pupils from different year groups

Parents assure us that they were not aware of any incidents of bullying. With students from so many different cultures, school says it 'comes down hard on any form of bullying.' Drugs 'not an issue' either: 'the pupils that come here from abroad are often fairly naive and not part of that London culture.'

There is an LGBT community and a 'safe room' offered to those, who, for whatever reason, need to hang out alone for a while. 'For some pupils, this is the first time they have been able to express who they really are. This is often not the case in their home country.'

Door to door minibus service offered which collects pupils from as far afield as St John's Wood etc.

Pupils and parents: Dwight has a larger British student body than most other international schools in London (some 30 per cent), which seems to make it easier for international families to integrate into the local community. The impression from parents and from our visit is that there is relatively little sense of the 'expat bubble' in this international school. Long term families who joined the school in earlier incarnations (pre-IB) say they have been very pleased with the introduction of the full suite of IB programmes, and the interesting international experiences and friendships that Dwight's growing expat community brings. While they do see the turnover of families as a factor, many of these friendships endure and lead to exciting trips during the holidays to visit old friends who have moved on.

Entrance: Parents describe the school as 'selectively inclusive'. In all of our conversations (with parents and staff), no one emphasised 'academic results'. Though most enter in September, since the school serves expats, there are students entering throughout the year, from abroad and from local state schools. Interview and report from previous school only real requisites, as is a commitment and understanding of the IB programme. Interviews sometimes done via Skype.

Exit: About 75 per cent of lower school pupils move on to the upper school; some leave after the IBMYP, moving abroad or to sixth form colleges. University counselling programme in year 12, but it seems parents often start earlier, commenting they'd like to see a bit more attention to this area. Sixth formers mainly to university, a lot London based (eg SOAS, UCL and King's) with others to eg Scotland (Dundee and Aberdeen), to California and Waseda, Japan in 2018.

Money matters: Tuition is marginally less than other international schools in London. Extras include school trips and activities such as Model United Nations and some after-school activities. Good range of means-tested scholarships for families with an income of up to £120,000 pa (more if you have two or more children). These are awarded not for pure academic ability but for 'demonstrating the characteristics of the IB learner profile'. Also offers bursaries of between 25-50 per cent for children of visiting academics and NGOs. These are all available to current as well as new families.

Remarks: Dwight is a school where the education of the 'whole child' and the learning journey genuinely appear to be as important as exam results. A brave but rewarding choice for London born children ('none of my friends had heard of Dwight before', said one parent) – those looking for something a bit different and outside of the English curriculum. And a safe bet for International students who want the benefit of the IB in a more localised setting. The school does all it can to provide each student with opportunities to pursue their individual interests, all within the IB context. 'It's a kind school.'

Fortismere School

South Wing, Tetherdown, London N10 1NE

020 8365 4400 | office@fortismere.org.uk | fortismere.haringey.sch.uk

State	Pupils: 1,771; sixth form: 427
Ages: 11–19	

Co-heads: Since February 2018, Zoe Judge, previously director of sixth form, and Jo Davey, previously deputy head, who had been interim co-heads since September 2017.

Zoe Judge joined Fortismere in 2002 as a pastoral leader and a member of the English department, having begun her teaching career at a high-performing school in Barking and Dagenham. She was initially a head of year and has over the years taught English, media and film. In 2006 she joined the school leadership team as the assistant head with responsibility for key stage 3. In 2010 she became director of sixth form.

Jo Davey joined Fortismere as a part-time consultant in 2013 while deputy head teacher at Blanche Nevile School. She had previously worked in Camden schools as a history and politics teacher and as a school improvement consultant with responsibility for vulnerable groups.

Academic matters: A large proportion of bright, motivated pupils and also a greater than average number of pupils with SEN, with a relatively small mid range. In 2018, 76 per cent A*-B grades at A level, 42 per cent A*/A; at GCSE 42 per cent A*-A/9-7.

Every subject previously set from year 7; this has been loosened, but school still sets early for maths and science, whilst English is taught in mixed ability classes. 'We trust the faculty heads on that, but they must show that it works.' Relatively low class size of 24. Everyone learns French or Spanish in year 7 and promising linguists are offered Mandarin in year 8 (now a Pre-U in the sixth form). They are encouraged to take two languages to GCSE; around 80 per cent of pupils take at least one. The top 60 per cent are encouraged to take triple science GCSE.

Teaching standards mostly very high with the odd exception, say parents. 'They expect of lot of the students – I think they push them very hard. They encourage and extend them, particularly with the personal projects in the sixth form.' Reporting system to parents 'has improved. They tell you what your child's target is, what level they're performing at now and whether that's okay. I've mostly found teachers very responsive when I've emailed them.'

The sixth form admissions criteria are 'closer to a grammar school', with at least five grade 6s at GCSE required for A level, and 7s for certain subjects eg maths. The small number of vocational options, with five grade 4s at GCSE as a boundary, include music technology, ICT, business, media and sports science. School also teaches classical heritage and global perspectives Pre-U courses.

Maths a very popular A level, alongside history (teaching dubbed 'exceptional' by parents) and English. Respectable numbers pursuing biology and chemistry, and – as one might expect in this liberal, intellectual area – philosophy, psychology, government and politics and sociology, though linguists disappointingly few.

'Amazing' preparation for Oxford, said a parent. 'It was all very low key, but there are several young Oxbridge graduates teaching at the school, and they ran workshops, put on seminars, did mock interviews, and put pupils in touch with other students who'd been through the process recently. It was all there, but it was up to the kids to push themselves that much further.'

With its large, segmented site and high pupil numbers, possibly not the most suitable school for children with learning difficulties, but many choose it nonetheless, 'and we do a very good job with them'. Those with EHC plans – and there are a relatively large proportion of these, mostly with autistic spectrum and behavioural issues – have their own teaching assistant. However, 'we try to keep away from TAs velcroed to children', and they are included in class work as far as possible, with small group sessions to help them develop independent learning skills. Linc team helps those experiencing learning difficulties – temporary or permanent. The secondary department of the Blanche Nevile School for deaf and hearing-impaired children occupies an impressive building on the site. Some of its pupils join in the mainstream school activities.

Games, options, the arts: Fabulous newish music block, with recording studios, composing and practice rooms, plus multi-use performance spaces, mirrors the importance of the subject here (though few take it to A level). Symphony orchestra, big band and several choirs; community choirs and orchestras include parents as well as children; hosts Saturday music school. 'We play a key role in the local community.' School doesn't envisage the abolition of music aptitude places having any effect on the quality of music-making in the school. 'We have always had a lot of hugely musical students – it comes with the parent body.'

'We're a very artsy school. It's our natural default setting.' 'Fantastic' production of Little Shop of Horrors included the actual plant from the West End show

Impressive displays of art and fabulous photography coursework around the school on our visit, plus bright papier mâché aliens and rats created by younger year groups. Photography a popular A level and one can see why. Drama also 'massive'. 'We're a very artsy school. It's our natural default setting.' 'Fantastic' production of Little Shop of Horrors included the actual plant from the West End show;

sixth formers regularly take productions to the Edinburgh fringe, and help with GCSE drama performances.

Pathway round the playing fields can resemble a storm in the North Sea in inclement weather

Sports stars used to hone their talents largely outside school, but sport has been bolstered by increased amounts of time in the upper years plus the introduction of Colleges, or houses, which run weekly inter-college competitions and encourage non A team players to get involved. However, parents report that it is possible for the less athletically inclined to avoid breaking into a sweat, and it is fair to say that reports of sports team triumphs do not feature largely in school newsletters. Sports hall, tennis/netball/basketball courts, acres of playing fields and 'very popular' table tennis tables.

Large range of trips includes 'brilliant and very well organised' week in Beijing for Mandarin speakers, exchange visits to France, Spain, Senegal and India ('though you do have to queue up at 7am with your cheque to get a place on the popular ones,' commented a parent), D of E, outdoor pursuits in the Brecon Beacons, ski trips, field trips and cultural visits. A steady stream of authors, scientists, politicians etc comes to give talks; librarian organises team of pupils to shadow Carnegie medal deliberations, reading and reviewing shortlisted books; teams enter debating competitions.

Background and atmosphere: Large site amidst leafy Muswell Hill Edwardiana has been the setting for a series of schools of all sorts, including private, state grammar and comprehensive. Fortismere was formed in 1983 by the amalgamation of Creighton and Alexandra Park Schools (another Alexandra Park School has since opened nearby). Site includes a hotch-potch of buildings from its various incarnations. North and South Wings linked by a quarter-mile pathway round the playing fields that can resemble a storm in the North Sea in inclement weather. Accommodation beginning to show its age, but bright and cheerful. A multitude of notice boards – with college news, photos of trips, information on clubs.

Very much a community comprehensive with a relaxed atmosphere (subject to 'behaviour for learning' sanctions), and pupils strolling around in jeans and tee shirts. 'Proudly non-uniform', though with a veto on revealing too much skin or underwear. 'It's part of the ethos for children to be able to express themselves,' said a parent.

Pastoral care, well-being and discipline: Good transition system, with year 6s spending three days at the school in the summer term getting to know the site and teachers. Operates vertical tutor system, with 18 pupils of different ages from the same college in each group replacing old form tutor system. All staff – including admin staff – are tutors, 'which enables us to have small groups, and also increases student respect for non-teaching staff'. Mixed reviews from parents and pupils, some enthusiastic whilst others feel that the system needs time to bed in and become a tradition, and that they would prefer to spend the time with their peers.

Student leadership team, which includes head boy and girl and their deputies, has a meeting with the head each Monday. 'It has already had a real impact. They really challenge us about why we do things, and it makes us think about structures.'

Previous head's introduction of zero tolerance for lateness and absenteeism shocked some families and delighted others, with one parent terming it 'draconian.' 'The behaviour here was good, but we thought it could be better. If you are disrupting the learning of others, that is not negotiable. Parents complain, but when we tell them their child is stopping other people learning, they find that hard to justify.' Refuses permission for holidays in term time: 'We get a lot of poorly relatives in far flung places towards the end of the Christmas and summer terms.' In response to pupils' requests for carrots as well as sticks, Positive Points system gives house points for helpfulness, participation, tidiness etc and is widely reported in the newsletters.

> 'It is a very political school. We have to remember that parents don't just read the Guardian – quite likely they write for it too'

Pupils mostly very happy and have good relationships with staff, but some parents feel that the pastoral system is variable. Some teachers 'do resolve your issues,' said a parent, citing the 'novel and interesting solutions' to stress suggested by her daughter's college head. However, 'I had a very unsympathetic reaction from the school to a family death. I found their policies very inflexible.' 'They didn't seem to be sensitive to the needs of my younger daughter,' said another parent, whose children had joined from a different education system. 'I really didn't feel she got the support she needed, and I felt that no-one had an overview of the situation. I also had no response to a very carefully worded email about a pastoral issue that had upset her.'

Permanent exclusions rare, and usually for persistent defiance or repeated breaking of behaviour policies. Will swap recalcitrant pupils with other local schools. 'We're good at managed moves – they can be very effective.' Will also use outside providers such as local boxing and football academies for those who clearly need a different approach. 'We prefer to try something different before moving to permanent exclusion.' A parent commented: 'There are some wild and woolly kids, but they don't tend to disrupt classes.'

Works in collaboration with the mental health charity, Place2Be, to provide therapeutic counselling for students as needed.

Pupils and parents: Largely affluent, liberal, middle class families – artists and musicians, writers and actors – plus quite a few looked-after children. 'It is a very political school. We have to remember that parents don't just read the Guardian – quite likely they write for it too.' These are mostly cool kids, relaxed and confident, proud to be at Haringey's most popular comprehensive. 'My daughters' friends are lovely,' said a parent. 'They meet up to study and all help each other.' Ex-pupils include singers Michael Kiwanuka and Jess Glynne.

Entrance: Takes 270 pupils into year 7. Those with an EHC plan naming the school – and there are many of these – will automatically get a place. Then priority to children in care, those with particular medical, social or emotional needs, and siblings, with the remainder by distance, usually less than half a mile.

Takes 110 or so outside students into the sixth form, from state and independent schools. Requires 5+ 9-4 GCSEs for vocational A levels and 5+ 9-6s for academic A levels, with higher grades for certain subjects eg maths, from internal and external students. Those who don't perform well in year 12 are liable to be directed elsewhere.

Exit: Small numbers (around 30 per cent) move on after GCSEs, generally for more vocational courses. Nearly all sixth form leavers to university: Sussex, Leeds, Manchester and Bristol the flavour of the moment; 16 to Oxbridge or medical courses in 2018. English, philosophy, psychology, maths, law, geography all popular.

Money matters: Very active parents' association, the FSA, which underwrote the refurbishment of the sixth form centre.

Remarks: A popular and high-achieving comprehensive that successfully includes those with difficulties as well as extending the most able. School's vision is to have 'an active mind, a finger on the pulse and a big heart.'

Grimsdell Mill Hill Pre-Preparatory School

Winterstoke House, Wills Grove, Mill Hill Village, London NW7 1QR

020 8959 6884 | kandrews@grimsdell.org.uk | millhill.org.uk/grimsdell

Independent	Pupils: 189
Ages: 3-7	Fees: £6,852 – £14,895 pa

Linked schools: Belmont Mill Hill Preparatory School, 578; Mill Hill School, 619

Head: Since 2014, Kate Simon (40s). A current Grimsdell parent, Mrs Simon is no stranger to headship. Between 2002 and 2008 she was head of the junior school of the Royal School, Hampstead (now incorporated into North Bridge Senior) and from 2008 was head of Girls' Upper School at Garden House School in Chelsea.

Entrance: Heavily oversubscribed, due in part to it being non-selective at age 3 or 4. 'I don't feel comfortable with failing children at that age', says the head. Most pupils come from within a five mile radius and there is a 'multi-cultural mix.'

Exit: The majority of pupils continue on to Belmont school. However, if the school feels that a child won't cope there, discussions about alternatives take place from year 1. 'We have to be realistic', the school says.

Remarks: Unfortunate name for a very pretty school. On a beautiful autumnal day, Grimsdell was the antithesis of 'grim'. Situated on Mill Hill's Ridgeway, but accessed via a small and very lovely private road, the school occupies the rather grand Winterstoke House. Originally a vicarage for the vicar of St Paul's and sold to Mill Hill School in October 1923, Winterstoke House was purchased to become a school boarding house to host some 42 boys.

The school became Grimsdell in 1995 – a newcomer compared to the other two schools in the Foundation. The reason for its formation was largely due to a Mrs Grimsdell, widow of an Old Millhillian, who bequeathed a large part of her late husband's estate to Mill Hill School. Following a request from the school governors, Mrs Grimsdell agreed that the benefaction be applied to create a 'much required' pre-preparatory school, and Grimsdell opened its gates. The school is situated adjacent to Mill Hill School but has its own grounds – not quite on the scale of the other two schools, but more than adequate for a pre-prep school.

This is a cute, cosy school. Nothing grand and pretentious, despite the impression given by its exterior. We were seated in a colourful and bright reception area with a large aquarium to gaze at while we waited to meet the head. Familiar sounds of over-excited kids emanated from one or two of the classrooms (and we were particularly struck by one over-zealous music teacher doing something very strange with her arms!)

With a school that states boldly 'There is no such thing as bad weather, just bad clothing,' you had better be sure your little darlings have an interest in outdoor pursuits

All classrooms were light, airy and well equipped – particularly the Sunshine Room, which even in its name suggests something warm and nurturing. This is where pupils who need it go for extra one-to-one learning support. Specialist on-site teachers in music, PE and French are on hand and 4 to 7-year-olds have weekly keyboard lessons with a music specialist. The swimming pool at Mill Hill School is a great addition to the PE curriculum. Pupils use the theatre at Mill Hill School for concerts and performances. Cursive handwriting is taught from the start and we were quite amazed with the standard of year 1 handwriting displayed on classroom walls.

As with Belmont and Mill Hill School, Grimsdell's selling point is undoubtedly its idyllic surroundings. Pupils not only have access to 120 acres of beautiful parkland at Mill Hill school with its sports pitches, swimming pool and woodland, but they have their own great adventure playground and science garden to enjoy. A firm believer in the great outdoors, Grimsdell has its own forest school. Each session has a theme and activities can range from mini-beast hunting to fire building and cooking outdoors. With a school that states boldly in its prospectus 'there is no such thing as bad weather, just bad clothing', you had better be sure your little darlings have a healthy interest in outdoor pursuits. Forget this school otherwise – indeed discount the other two schools in the Foundation while you are at it.

Parents appreciate the expertise of the large Foundation, and the lack of pressure to take exams for future schools. One parent told us, 'Grimsdell is a secure and nurturing stepping-stone, which is illustrated by my own excited and eager children.'

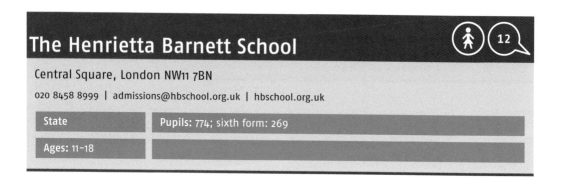

The Henrietta Barnett School

Central Square, London NW11 7BN

020 8458 8999 | admissions@hbschool.org.uk | hbschool.org.uk

State	Pupils: 774; sixth form: 269
Ages: 11–18	

Head: Since 2014, Del Cooke BSc MBA NPQH (50s), previously head of Sir William Perkins's School in Surrey. Maths graduate with MBA in educational management, her broad experience covers the comprehensive system, sixth form college, adult education and boarding at Cranleigh, where she was head of maths, housemistress and finally deputy head. Although relatively new, she is increasingly seen as the embodiment of HBS – smart, quick-witted, friendly and empathetic. 'The girls want to hang out with her. She is like them,' summed up one parent. We found her instantly likeable, not remotely intimidating and surprisingly low-key. Made no dramatic changes so far ('It's such a fantastic school, you'd have to be pretty pompous to come in and turn it upside down,' she says), but is known as a visible head, particularly interested in getting the girls' views on various aspects of the school, and is clearly keen to focus more heavily on celebrating individual achievements. No bad thing, point out some parents, who say the girls can be 'far too modest, and need reminding how amazing they are'. Has a passion for music, playing a number of instruments, including self-taught bassoon. Married with three sons.

Academic matters: Consistently top or very near the top of both the GCSE and A level league tables. In 2018, 95 per cent 9-7 at GCSE, 74 per cent A*/A at A level. Most do 11 GCSEs, three or four As. Results strong across all subjects at GCSE, with a bias towards maths and sciences at A level, which around three-quarters of pupils choose, although history and English also have a healthy representation. Languages prioritised, with French, German and Latin for all in year 7, plus Spanish for all in years 8 and 9. Plus an option of ancient Greek. No setting.

Myths about this school being an academic hothouse, where girls are worked like dogs, are prolific, and even the head was initially put off the job because she thought it would be so pressurised. 'I was resistant, assuming the girls would be working in a ridiculously intensive environment. But it's the girls who drive the pace of learning and if anything, the staff sometimes have to tell the girls to slow down!' says the head. Pupils and parents agree, with one saying her daughter had just been advised to 'take some time out of her revision schedule to do something more relaxing.' Girls are encouraged to be independent, albeit well-supported, learners from day one, with many setting up their own societies and visiting universities for extra lectures. During our visit, we saw one noticeboard with pages from HB Scientist, the sixth-form produced (and very professional looking) science magazine that is sold throughout the school, whilst plenty of posters around the school advertised forthcoming speakers that pupils have organised – Zadie Smith when we visited.

Competitive learning is frowned upon, making way for a supportive atmosphere and strong sense of co-operation, which everyone agrees is a huge aid to the girls excelling academically. Teachers could hardly be considered more dedicated, although many parents say more of them are needed. 'Every one of the teachers would be a good candidate for a head of department in a private school, earning 50-100 per cent more money, but they choose to stay here because of the quality of the school and the commitment of the girls, which makes them very, very special,' said one parent. Girls love the fact that many of the teachers have had (non-teaching) careers in their subjects, also praising the informal relationships they have with them and level of responsibility the girls are given. Homework is given if and when teachers feel it's required, rather than hours every evening for the sake of it.

Games, options, the arts: Historically sports not brilliant, although improved facilities – large multi-purpose Astroturf court for netball, hockey, football and volleyball – have helped, with the school increasingly winning at both a local and borough level and holding its own against some top private schools. Facilities also include a gym, a state-of-the-art fitness suite with a good range of exercise equipment and a variety of pitches available on the nearby Hampstead Heath extension. 'Sport is very much on the up,' insists the head and there's a long list of exercise alternatives, including zumba, fencing, tang soo do, yoga, fitness, indoor rowing, cricket, badminton and dance. Rugby and athletics are also increasingly popular. No swimming pool but occasional opportunities for swimmers to take part in school events.

Thriving music department, with a symphony orchestra that everyone agrees is a joy to listen to, especially at concerts in the nearby ambient St Jude's Church. There are other orchestras and plenty of choirs, along with all manner of bands, including swing and rock. All pupils study music in key stage 3 and many go on to GCSE. Plenty of private tuition in a wide range of instruments, including double bass, bassoon and French horn, and there is an organ scholarship. Great excitement about the music wing built in 2011. 'Previously, we were taught music in our classroom or temporary huts, so it's a major thing,' said one pupil, who showed us the well-stocked rehearsal room and studio, with several soundproofed practice rooms. The same wing is home to drama, another lively department with strong facilities, with recent performances including Hamlet (year 9s), a play about Henrietta Barnett (year 7s) and a school-wide Our Country's Good.

Recent trips included Iceland (geography) and Greece (classics). 'It was easily the best holiday I've ever been on, just unbelievably interesting and fun,' said one pupil

Mirroring this wing, on the other side of the main building, is the DT and art block. Downstairs, the spacious DT room is home to all kinds of interesting inventions, including a Batman-style wooden chair and scooter that changes colour when exposed to sunlight. Meanwhile, the upstairs art room is a fantastic space, with some seriously talented work on display across all media. The wrap-around balconies on both wings are both aesthetically pleasing and provide an outside space for students to work during the summer months.

Lots of extracurricular opportunities, including Mandarin, tobotics (year 8 team recently got through to world championships in USA), creative writing, philosophy society, LAMDA, and many pupil-led activities. For instance, sixth formers currently teach Japanese to younger ones, as well as running a current affairs club, with speakers (invited by pupils themselves) including Melissa Benn and Lucy Holmes.

'The school is the multicultural, meritocratic face of Britain,' said one parent, proudly

School trips, through each subject department, take every year group out once a year, with recent examples including Iceland (geography) and Greece (classics). 'It was easily the best holiday I've ever been on, just unbelievably interesting and fun,' said one pupil who went on the latter. French and German exchanges and Spanish trip to Seville. When we visited, 65 students were getting ready to head to the Rhineland for a music tour. Lots of day trips, particularly to theatres, museums and art galleries. Enrichment week, held in the summer, provides an entire week of outings. Own field study centre in Dorset, which every pupil visits for one week during her early years at the school.

Background and atmosphere: Founded in 1911 by formidable social reformer Dame Henrietta Barnett, the school is housed in architecturally stunning Lutyens designed buildings in upmarket Hampstead Garden Suburb. Not unlike the kind of buildings you'd find at Harvard of Stanford, it's also a beautifully landscaped campus. Facilities top-notch, particularly the colour-coded science labs and new swanky new wings for art, DT, music and drama, plus newly refurbished and extended library. Floors are polished parquet, classrooms are light and airy and corridors are tastefully decorated with everything from a recent photography competition to huge science-inspired pictures. Dining hall, where food is praised, and all-day café for year 10 upwards. Parts of the interiors could do with a lick of paint. But overall facilities feel spacious, with excitable students loving their environment, including after school, when something is going on pretty much every evening.

Pastoral care, well-being and discipline: 'No bells, no detention, no rules – it's so relaxed that if you came to school in your pyjamas no one would bat an eyelid,' wrote Tatler in its 2015 review, words that are now a source of great pride (not to mention humour) in the school 'simply because they are so true,' explained one pupil. Even a mention of the word 'discipline' will get you a blank look among pupils ('Why would you play up?' one said, genuinely bemused), whilst any occasional quirkiness that's perhaps inevitable among such an academic bunch is accepted as normal and certainly never teased. 'A few weeks ago, a whole class came out of art with painted-on moustaches and top hats from drama – it was so HBS,' laughed one girl. But this is no St Trinian's. Far from it, the girls' behaviour is impeccable and they always do their best, as well as being delightful and friendly. 'If a girl did step out of line, the teacher would just have a chat, adult-to-adult,' says the head, who believes it's the fact that the girls are treated like adults – with all the respect and trust that goes with that – that accounts for the lack of need for rules.

Bullying a non-issue, whilst part-time counsellors are on hand to deal with any problems. Currently a big push on reducing the stigma of mental health issues, with several noticeboards pointing to relevant resources. Strong student council, which is particularly strong in recruitment and raised funds for the new library, plus lunch council.

Pupils and parents: Girls are extremely bright and eager to learn, as well as both interesting and interested. Clear team spirit, where girls in different years bond naturally as well as through schemes like the student-led 'vertical families'. 'Of course, you get friendship groups, but absolutely no cliques,' said one pupil. 'It's a real community where everyone knows you and supports you,' said another. The school has always had a wide catchment area, based as it was on the vision of providing education to bright girls regardless of their means, although since the arrival of league tables, some pupils come in too far for the head's liking. ('I do question whether it's a good thing for some to travel really long distances.') Those in London mostly walk, cycle or get the bus or tube (Golders Green). There's also a parent-organised bus service to cater for those who can't easily get there by public transport.

Great ethnic mix – about a fifth Indian and a fifth white British, the rest from a variety of backgrounds. 'The school is the multicultural, meritocratic face of Britain,' said one parent, proudly. PTA provides refreshments at events, along with the odd quiz night, but not as active as some, particularly for socialising. 'It's inevitable, with families coming from such a wide area and diverse backgrounds,' said one parent, which

The spacious DT room is home to all kinds of inventions, including a Batman–style wooden chair and scooter that changes colour

probably also explains why after-school social life is not as vibrant as elsewhere.

Entrance: It doesn't get more selective than this, with 2800+ applying for 100 places. Some families move house once they have a place; others travel for long distances. Verbal and numerical reasoning tests in September, then the top 300 are invited back for English and maths tests in October. Pupils come from 50-60 primaries. Priority to looked after children and up to 20 on pupil premium who have been ranked in the top 300.

For sixth form, approximately 600 apply for a further 55-60 places, with six grade 7s at GCSE minimum requirement, including 7s in intended A level subjects. Girls already in the school are also expected to achieve this requirement, although in reality most far exceed it.

Exit: Around 10-13 per cent leave after GCSE, mostly to sixth form colleges. Twenty-four to Oxbridge in 2018. Lots of medics and dentists (36 medics, dentists and vets in 2018) and a good cross-section of all other subject areas Team of sixth form tutors provide UCAS advice, including raising expectations of what can be achieved. Alumni include Sarah Solemani (actress and television script writer), Ros Altmann (previously pensions minister), Baroness Evans of Bowes Park (leader of the House of Lords and Lord Privy Seal) and Debbie Wiseman (composer).

Money matters: Regular fundraising via PTA, pupil-led initiatives and a parental support scheme to which many parents regularly donate.

Remarks: One of the top academic state schools in the country, yet also one of the most liberal and nurturing; it's hard to exaggerate the emotional buy-in from pupils. 'The school becomes part of your DNA in a profound way,' said one. 'I don't know what happens when you get inside those four walls, but it is genuinely unique and stays with you for life.' Producing friendly, fun and delightful girls who come out with academic results that quite literally make the world their oyster, it's no wonder that top universities and employers love it too. 'My only sadness is that I can't see how it will ever be this good again,' said one pupil. A gentle and inspiring education for extremely bright girls, in a fabulous setting.

Highgate Junior School

3 Bishopswood Road, London N6 4PL

020 8340 9193 | jsoffice@highgateschool.org.uk | highgateschool.org.uk

| Independent | Pupils: 400 |
| Ages: 3–11 | Fees: £18,165 – £19,230 pa |

Linked school: Highgate School, 601

Principal of junior school: Since 2002, Mark James (50s), BA theology Nottingham University, followed by a PGCE in English from the London Institute and an MA from King's College London. Grew up in Somerset where he worked for a term at Wellington School: 'I had far too much fun running around with the kids and decided then that this was what I wanted to do.' He started his career in the state sector – Tiffin Grammar in Kingston – followed by a decade at Dulwich College, prior to becoming deputy head at King's Wimbledon School junior school: 'It was there I made the transition from senior school to juniors, after my wife suggested I give it a try. I loved it.' This is the head who had the task of transforming Highgate boys' 7-13 prep into a modern mixed junior 7-11 junior school: 'When the school took the decision to go co-ed with the ambition to be academic and selective it created a unique place in the market.'

Friendly, down to earth, all round nice guy – who certainly doesn't come across as being filled with a sense of his own importance, yet as principal of Highgate Junior School and head of admissions for the whole school, Mr James is THE guy to know for desperate parents vying for a place at the school. But he stands resolute and assures us that places at the school can only be obtained through a child's own merits and the Highgate assessment procedure: 'Parents can inevitably be disappointed if their child is not offered a place, especially if they already have a child in the school, but as I often say it has to be right for each child and the offer has to be justified based on the evidence we have'.

Popular with parents and pupils alike: 'firm but fair', 'approachable', open to ideas', 'knows all the pupils and parents', 'involved in everything.' He is an enthusiastic can-do character, with a boyish charm and sense of humour (as was evident from the large jellybean jar crammed to the brim in his office). Married to a teacher – they have two daughters both who have both gone through Highgate School. One parent told us: 'It helps that he's had kids who have gone all the way through the school, so he knows the score.'

Of his role at Highgate School, Mr James says: 'I feel very lucky that I like what I do – what's not to like?' We couldn't help feeling the same as we stepped out of his office into the splendour that is the newly built junior school.

Head of pre-prep since 2012, Diane Hecht DCE (50s). Previously deputy head of St Columba's Junior School in Kilmacolm, she came south as two of her grown-up children had settled in London and feels that she has found a wonderfully similar school in Highgate. 'The girls here wear exactly the same tartan skirts as at St Columba's – it was meant to be!' Warm, efficient and enthusiastic.

Entrance: Hugely oversubscribed – 350 try for the 36 places at 3+. Sane and lovely pre-prep head admits that assessing 2 year olds has to be on the arbitrary side, so do not be amazed if your astounding tot just doesn't astound on assessment day. Teachers observe them at play in groups, look for capacity to listen and follow instructions, general sociability – so don't make them learn their letters the night before.

This feeling of transparency was very much key to the design 'so that visitors can see great things going on rather than relying on pretty corridors of prepared displays'

At 7+ your child will be up against around 300 others battling it out for 50/60 places. Assessments at this stage consist of a reading test and an English and maths paper. Approx two-thirds of candidates will be invited back for a 'fun and interactive lesson' and a practical lesson which could be anything from art to music or science and, based on the outcome of that, will be invited for an interview: 'We are looking for an active and engaged child – a spark that sets them apart.' Other things count (where you live, parental statement etc), but not massively, it has to be said. No sibling policy, but 'every sibling is guaranteed an interview.' As far as school connections or being an Old Cholmeleian go, no preferential treatment we are told: 'oh no, that doesn't exist anymore.' Definitely have a plan B.

Exit: Nearly all go from the pre-prep to the juniors and nearly all go from there to the senior school. 'If your child has got into the school you're going to try your utmost to make sure they stay.' Plenty of warning given to those unlikely to thrive in the higher stages. Pupils generally only leave for financial reasons.

Remarks: There are schools (and we've been to many many private schools) – and then there's the £25m Highgate Junior School, so brand spanking new at the time of our visit, the imported fossilised stone was still setting. Tucked into Bishopswood Road – one of the many prestigious roads that line the route from Highgate to Hampstead – this two year undertaking (financed by the judicious sale of former boarding houses) was a project of deep consideration. The powers that be were very aware that whilst it was important for the school to have some sort of artistic mark to it, they didn't want the space to look like a museum, 'but one which would have appeal and comfort for our younger pupils.'

On entering the building one is immediately drawn to a breathtaking feature wall in the reception area, which was the work of a specially commissioned artist. Portland fossilised stone provided the backdrop with a design which gently curves its way to the upper level. Reptiles and amphibians of various kinds are sculpted into the walls and at various points throughout the school, to encourage children to explore and discover different surfaces and textures as part of their learning exploration. We were also told that this was based on the Fibonacci principle of combining maths with biological settings. (At this point we nodded sagely, had no idea what was being said and felt very inadequate.)

Light, space and fluidity are the core elements of the design. Entering the bright circular atrium, you can observe the goings on all around on both levels. This feeling of transparency was very much key to the design, 'so that visitors can see great things going on..rather than relying on pretty corridors of prepared displays.' The school offers bright and spacious classrooms, science laboratories, specialist rooms for art, DT, ICT, drama and music. Our favourite bit was the 360 retractable seat hall for assemblies and concerts etc. All classrooms, on the upper level or lower level, open onto a wonderful outdoor space. Balconies at the top – enclosed garden areas on the lower level with reading pods.

Lots of attractive work on show. Glorious herd of Elmer elephants made from plastic milk cartons and coloured paper

The outdoor space also includes a small amphitheatre, a literary garden and a wonderful adventure playground, all surrounded by the extensive Highgate playing fields. Simply idyllic.

However, as we know from experience, a beautiful building doth not a good school make, so this school had much to live up to. We were shown around by two lively and phenomenally bright pupils, one of whom will no doubt be the brains behind something quite wonderful in years to come. The only pupil we have met to date who was trying to explain the ergonomics of desk sizes in the class in relation to the seating. But he did this without any pretentiousness, or awareness of how quirky this might appear. As one parent told us, 'most Highgate kids are just regular kids, without an air of snootiness, or look at us – we're the rich kids. That's what makes it so special.' We had to agree: all the pupils we met were like any other – happy, spirited, at times noisy, curious and just very astute.

Hardly surprising when you consider what they have to do in order to get in at 7+ (if they don't come in via the pre-prep route). Once in, pupils can expect a challenging but fun time, 'the best' we are told. The day starts at 8.25am prompt and then it's full throttle into the learning day with the added injection of a smorgasbord of languages on offer. Unlike most other primary schools with 'only' French on the syllabus, Highgate Juniors can expect everything from French and German to Japanese, Gujarati and Russian, with the aim of instilling a love of languages, since they have no need to pass an entrance exam.

Teaching staff, who were praised by one parent as being 'beyond anything', struck us as being a particularly young and attractive bunch. A low turnover of staff and continuity throughout the school no doubt contributes to the school's success. Teachers are fairly heavily vetted and there is an open door policy for all classrooms, for regular observation: 'Each term we have roughly 30 observations, which are graded, and if they are not where we would hope they would be, we would need to do something to bring up their levels.' Fairly tough, some might say, but there are reputations to uphold.

Class sizes don't exceed 22, and are set from year 5 in maths. The school can cope with mild SEN, but because of its selective nature, numbers are quite small. Dedicated SENCo and part-time learning support person. School doesn't believe in much one-to-one; they adopt a more inclusive approach 'so that pupils don't miss out.'

Homework, we were told by both pupils and parents, was slightly on the heavy side. One parent told us: 'The workload can be a bit much at times, but my daughter doesn't struggle as she's used to it from pre-prep. I imagine if you come in at the 7+ stage, it might be more difficult.'

Academia aside, there is so much going on. 'Everyone has their chance to shine in the sun', says the head and sport is a biggie here. It would be difficult for it not to be with the phenomenal facilities on offer, both outdoors and at the Mallinson Sports Centre. Everyone gets the chance to play, we are told, and both juniors and seniors are known to do well in competitive sports.

Drama and music thrive. Many children take individual instrumental lessons and in addition to these, there is a school orchestra, and numerous ensembles. Drama is taught as a separate subject throughout the school, and there are termly drama productions within and across year groups. Active drama club.

Lots of extracurricular going on too. It's amazing that these young kids can cram it all in, but somehow they do. Robotics club, maths club, newspaper club, debating, Minecraft, Lego, creative literacy, chess and mosaic making are just a handful of what's on offer – not to mention the multitude of sports clubs (including water polo). Lunch time lectures are offered mainly by parents whose kids attend the school (and there is a veritable feast of who's who).

A very sociable school with 'a big heart', one parent told us. Tons of charitable events organised by the school's enthusiastic PTA. Indeed last year we were told they raised a staggering 50k for various charities, via the usual summer and Christmas fairs and school productions plus the less usual sales of teddy bears, friendship bracelets, umbrellas and pupil-designed cookbooks. Parents are in the main a prosperous bunch, but a couple of the parents we spoke to were not particularly high earners: they just decided to make their child's education a complete priority.

Pre-prep separately, delightfully (and permanently) housed. Starts at nursery – 18 morning or afternoon tots in lively spacious space both inside and out with smiley, lively teachers. Whole school theme of colour and light when we visited and lots of attractive work on show. Glorious herd of Elmer elephants made from plastic milk cartons and coloured paper. Lovely singing – the most in-tune bunch of rising 5s we've heard. An orderly, relaxed and friendly school. We saw much warm interaction between staff and small people and just wanted to stay and watch.

Highgate School

North Road, London N6 4AY

020 8347 3564 | admissions@highgateschool.org.uk | highgateschool.org.uk

Independent | **Pupils:** 1,400; sixth form: 317

Ages: 11–18 | **Fees:** £20,970 pa

Linked school: Highgate Junior School , 599

Head master: Since 2006, Adam Pettitt MA (40s). Oxford modern and medieval linguist. Taught French and German at Eton, Oundle and Abingdon and was second master at Norwich School, under Jim Hawkins, former head of Harrow – a formidable team. Has French wife and school-age children and is quite the most interesting, eloquent and thought-provoking head this veteran GSG reviewer has met in many a long school visit. Propelled by a sharply focused and incisively articulated moral and educational philosophy, Mr Pettitt is spare, brilliant and energetic. He must be an exacting – though supportive – man to work for. His pupils can only benefit from his firm commitment to outreach to schools and to those without their advantages, to placing an understanding of language at the heart of modern languages, and to educational values rather than exams and results. The results will follow where this approach leads. Parents are unstinting in their praise. The most inspiring head we've met in years.

Academic matters: Head has a refreshing disrespect for the bodies deserving of it: 'You choose the exam board on the basis that it will have the least distorting effect on the way you want to teach' – bingo! IGCSEs now in Englishes, sciences, langs and history and many subjects now opt for the Pre-U as an alternative to A levels. This can only enhance the nature and quality of learning. English and langs the first to head this way. Mr Pettitt the 'de facto head of MFL' at the time of our visit so langs getting the oxygen they needed and number of takers is sure to rise. Mandarin now through to sixth form; computer science a GCSE option. Maths much the most popular A level and, with further maths, has impressive results. Also strong are English, art, Latin, all sciences and RS. Tiny numbers take theatre studies, Greek, classics, music – school does not offer music tech nor other popular 'modern' subjects eg textiles, psychology and loses a few post-GCSE on that account. Number of subject options (24) felt by some to be a little limited, given the size of the sixth form, and some sixth formers would like more drama and art. However, good innovations include the 'knowledge curriculum' and 'critical method' courses. In 2018, 92 per cent A*-A/9-7 at GCSE and 75 per cent A*/A at A level/Pre-U. Lively, student-led conferences. Mr Pettitt takes all criticism on the chin and, given that over 70 per cent of the staff are his appointees, this – as everything else – is fast developing.

Several staff now working at local state schools as part of community partnership work – outreach is not a box ticking necessity here but an essential part of what it is to grow into a valuing and valuable person

Head's inclusive approach is just that: 'The quality of the way you learn is critical and every child's experience is equally important. Every day is important – I am most interested in the way each one of us teaches and learns.' IBAC – Independence through Buzz, Aspiration and Collaboration – the new acronym around the place. So this is not the school that was, nor the one people think they know. The fabric – see below – is radically changing and the character equally so. This is encapsulated in the sane and sensitively individualised approach to SEN. The Victorian main building is not good for those with mobility problems though school says 'we will try to make it work by moving our routines and schedules as far as we can.' Director of learning support covers all three schools and is a renowned expert in autism. The support for all conditions and syndromes as they emerge is individual, tailored,

supportive and 'concerned with management rather than labelling.' The very few with EAL needs are usually the very bright.

Games, options, the arts: Blessed with playing fields and space beyond the dreams of other London schools. If the educational philosophy and general zip in the place doesn't inspire you, the sporting facilities will. Girls' sport, some feel – school disputes – still catching up with boys'; football and netball still pre-eminent but plenty more on offer and played hard. Sports hall, pool, weights, Astroturfs, squash courts – it's all here. No country school could offer more.

Interior activities also privileged and currently being transformed by an enormous rolling building project that will add considerably to teaching space but also, it is hoped, to an eventual sixth form and arts campus. Drama and music thrive – many productions, concerts of all kinds and tours; art a little undemonstrative at the time of our visit but some lively colourful work around. Mills Centre provides studio and gallery space. Cultural life better displayed in the admirable school publications – professional-looking periodicals on history, politics, science, theatre and thought written and produced by pupils. Terrific range of clubs (they include vinyl and philosophy, beekeeping, LGBT soc and feminist society), trips, exchanges and tours – extracurricular is praised by many but not fully taken advantage of by all. 'I used to feel that some pupils' cultural references were limited to Arsenal: great though that club is, I want them to see and know so much more,' comments the head, happy to stress to parents that while these opportunities are on offer it is up to pupils to take them up.

Lots of charitable and outreach activities for both staff and pupils – several staff now working at local state schools as part of community partnership work. This very much part of the Pettitt ethos – outreach is not a box ticking necessity here but an essential part of what it is to grow into a valuing and valuable person.

Background and atmosphere: A school with an up and down history. Founded as the Free Grammar School of Sir Roger Cholmeley, Knight at Highgate, in 1565 – former pupils still known as Old Cholmeleians. Became Highgate School in the late 19th century – and no longer free. The chapel, undergoing terrific refurb at time of our visit, 'complete brick by brick restoration, new roof, stained glass windows repaired and cleaned, apse painting restored etc; lighting and heating to render God's work less chilly and gloomy,' in Mr Pettitt's inimitable phrases – and main buildings are 19th century. Some impressive bits – old gothic central hall with Norman arches, leaded lights, wrought iron balcony and cantilevered ceiling and splendid new Sir Martin Gilbert library in old assembly hall. A real library which, unlike so many schools' learning resource centres, actually has books in it, alongside all its rows of PCs, and an atmosphere to encourage concentration and study.

Playing fields and space beyond the dreams of other London schools. If the educational philosophy and general zip in the place don't inspire you, the sporting facilities will

By the 1960s, the school buildings (some considerably less felicitous), including boarding houses, were spread over the heart of Highgate Village – the premier north London suburb whose denizens refer to it as 'the village' and who are, understandably, rather smug about living there. Charter Building adds new subject rooms in a five-storey glass cube. All very high tech – interactive whiteboards and PCs everywhere. The whole site is now a mix of the new, light, glass-bound, airy and stylish, and the old, rather shabby, small passages and dark areas along which school operates a clever one-way system – but all likely to look a great deal smarter and more coherent in the next few years. Much tramping up and down the hill between the main buildings and the Mills Centre, playing fields etc, and each day sees orderly crocodiles with professional chaperones trailing along.

School suffered during the 70s and 80s and took time to recover its reputation. Girls joined the sixth form in 2004 and year 7 in 2006, and the whole school is now fully co-educational and fully rehabilitated. A Christian foundation and an inclusive one, with multi-faith assemblies and speakers from different religions on a weekly basis. House system – 12 houses – but no fanatical exclusive loyalty to these, rather a friendly rivalry in competitions etc and designed to encourage the mixing of year groups. 'It's a family school,' a parent told us. 'Not everyone is terrifically academic, though they really make the scholars work. They are very encouraging to everyone.'

Principal education sponsor of the London Academy of Excellence Tottenham, a new sixth form with Tottenham Hotspur as its business sponsor. This is the base for the Highgate Teaching Consultancy, offering specialist training in sixth form teaching which goes beyond exams.

Pastoral care, well-being and discipline: We saw only absorbed and concentrating classes with lively teaching. Discipline, as pupils gratefully pointed out, is not dependent on the whims of individual staff but 'whole school,' ie you know what is coming to you at every level should you transgress. Very little transgressing these days and we have seldom seen so few uniform infringements (has consulted on introducing gender neutral uniforms) – everyone is smart.

Small classes 'very well-monitored,' say parents. 'It's extremely well-run,' we were told. 'We are kept fully informed and have lots of email contact with staff,' another told us. 'The teaching staff are so enthusiastic and they really care about my children,' another enthused. Occasional loutishness clearly frowned on by majority of pupils, who are a civilised lot. 'We have sent all our children there – they're so different academically and in their characters – but all have been happy.'

Pupils and parents: From a wide area of north and more central London, though most live near, if not within walking distance. 'Not ruthlessly elitist,' as one parent put it but lots of City lawyers, accountants etc with clear idea of what they want from the school. Pupils are friendly, happy and articulate. Most seem proud to be at the school and keen not to jeopardise their futures. Notable OCs include Rt Hons Charles Clarke and Anthony Crosland, Michael Mansfield QC, Johnny Borrell of Razorlight, Ringo Starr's son Zak Starkey of Oasis and The Who, Orlando Weeks of The Maccabees and DJ Yoda, Phil Tufnell, Sir Clive Sinclair, Alex Comfort, Nigel Williams, Sir John Tavener, Barry Norman, Gerard Manley Hopkins and Sir John Betjeman. Doubtless, old girl Cholmeleians shortly to make their marks.

Entrance: Wildly oversubscribed at every stage – on a scale we see most commonly with the grammars. Six hundred apply at 11+ for the 90 places available when the junior school pupils have been accommodated. At 13+, only 6-8 places available; tests and interviews in autumn term of year 7. At 16+, some 120 for 30. At 11, around 60 per cent from state primaries and 40 per cent – mainly girls – from local preps. The tiny 13+ entry is mostly boys entering from the obvious preps – Arnold House, Devonshire House, The Hall, Keble etc.

Exit: Around a dozen, mostly boys, leave post GCSE to, mostly, Camden School for Girls, which has boys in the sixth. Around 90 per cent gain places at their first choice university – Bristol, UCL, Durham, Edinburgh and Leeds among most favoured; some now head to top US universities (six in 2018, plus two to Canada, two to Amsterdam and one to the Milan Institute of Fashion). Good numbers to Oxbridge each year – 32 places in 2018, plus six medics and two vets. Economics, English and languages are popular subject choices.

Money matters: Scholarships – music and academic – at all usual entry points and now purely honorary. 'Much kudos, but not just to the particularly brainy but to those who exemplify scholarship (persistence, creativity, setting own agenda, leading learning in the classroom, originality),' stresses head. Bursaries up to the value of 100 per cent fees available each year and most go to those who get all or most of that amount. School makes extensive efforts via primary school visits etc to reach those who need to know.

Remarks: A new school in all but site and name – co-ed, modern, delivering a first rate education to the lively minds and limbs lucky enough to get in.

JCoSS

Castlewood Road, New Barnet, Hertfordshire EN4 9GE

020 8344 2220 | admin@jcoss.barnet.sch.uk | jcoss.org

| State | Pupils: 1,250; sixth form: 297 |
| Ages: 11–18 | |

Headteacher: Since 2012, Patrick Moriarty MA Oxon MA (Ed) NPQH (early 50s.) Grew up in north London and attended Haberdashers' Aske's Boys School, before reading philosophy and theology at Oxford, then training as a teacher at King's College, London. Taught (RE and English) at Latymer in Edmonton, Bishop Stopford's School, Enfield, and Haberderdashers' Aske's School for Girls. Arrived at JCoSS in 2010 as deputy head. 'The opportunity of a new school was very exciting and I liked the fact that it was a faith school.' Despite his unlikely background ('I told them I wasn't Jewish and I was contemplating studying for the priesthood'), he started nine months before the school opened, helping 'finesse' the curriculum.

Breathtakingly energetic, genial and thoughtful, he has undoubtedly delivered on the promise of balancing an outstanding curriculum and outstanding pastoral care. Ofsted, pupils and parents agree on his manifold virtues. 'Exceptional,' say the school inspectors. 'The best head,' said a sixth former. 'He's done an amazing job,' agreed a parent. He's also recently received recognition at the Jewish Schools Award for his 'outstanding and inspirational leadership'. Married to a musician, his out-of-school hours involve heavy-duty family responsibilities (two stepchildren at degree stage and two primary age children). He's also curate of a church in Barnet. Perhaps unsurprisingly, little time left over to play the piano and organ.

Academic matters: High expectations of what would be achieved, and JCoSS's 2018 set of GCSE results certainly didn't disappoint, with 40 per cent 9-7 grades, immediately catapulting the school into the top 10 per cent nationally. At A level, 38 per cent of grades were A*-A (as good or better than many independents), and 67 per cent A*-B.

Largely academic curriculum with most students taking 11 or 12 GCSEs though 'set to reduce slightly in response to concerns about depth of learning and student well-being,' says school. Modern Hebrew compulsory in year 7 (alongside French). In year 8, students can opt out of Hebrew and consider Spanish or Latin. Twenty-eight subjects on offer at A level, including psychology, sociology and further maths. Good take up of religious studies, which achieves notably strong results, as do psychology, English and sociology. Six vocational courses, a mixture of BTecs and Cambridge Technicals in the sixth form (in health and social care, creative media, sport, IT and business). About 70 per cent of students do purely A levels, about 10 per cent purely vocational courses, others mix and match. 'Our aim is to break down the boundaries and get all our students successfully into university.' Energetic teachers, happy to go the extra mile, and teacher-pupil relations clearly strong. 'I feel my teachers are talented and charismatic,' said one student.

One of the distinguishing characteristics of JCoSS is the Jewish education. Students take six lessons a fortnight of Jewish education, five concentrating on Judaism, one on other faiths. 'The kids ask for it, and we feel part of being Jewish is loving your neighbour and understanding your neighbour's religion.' (At GCSE, the second faith studied is Islam.) Jewish education continues for all into the sixth form.

Provision for SEN commended by Ofsted as 'outstanding'. The school, after consultation with the local authority, decided to create a specialist autism unit, the PSRP, with seven places a year devoted to those on the autism spectrum who can access the national curriculum (regardless of faith). The aim is to integrate these students as far as possible into the mainstream. Some spend all their time with the rest; others about half. 'It's highly personalised,' says the head. 'It's a brilliant model because it allows the maximum flexibility and enables all students to recognise and celebrate difference.' One designated SEN teacher per year group in the PSRP, plus two or three learning support assistants, all with specialist training. Others with special needs (dyslexia, dyspraxia, etc) – about three or four a year – are also well catered for, with three SEN teachers and around 30 learning support assistants, given one-to-one support where necessary. 'Able and ambitious' programme enriches the core offering for those who excel in any area.

Games, options, the arts: Sport still relatively in its infancy and limited grounds mean it's unlikely to be a big priority in the immediate future. 'We need a wider range of sport,' said one student. Some all-weather pitches and a spacious well-equipped gym, plus a multi-gym. Some 150 external recent matches in netball, football and basketball, with pleasing results. Badminton and table tennis a particular strength (recent Barnet champions). Rugby offering improving with enthusiastic encouragement from the sixth form. Elite sports programmes (with Saracens rugby coaching, Brentford and Southend football trials). Broad range of after-school sports clubs include sports leadership, table tennis, trampolining and modern Israeli dance.

'Our aim is to break down the boundaries and get all our students successfully into university.' Energetic teachers, happy to go the extra mile

Large art department with enthusiastic participants. Keen musicians enjoy chamber choir, jazz band, orchestra, guitar surgery. Good range of community involvement and social action: Duke of Edinburgh, Amnesty International, primary school volunteering, Israel club.

Background and atmosphere: Traditionally, London has not had enough school places for Jewish families, and JCoSS was established to be a 'pluralist' Jewish secondary, where all who 'self-identified

as Jewish' would be welcome. 'Religiously, we were doing something different,' says the head. 'Here, whether you're Orthodox, Masorti, Reform or Secular, we believe that's a valid expression of tradition.'

Pupils feel the approach works well. 'At other Jewish schools, you might get the feeling that one person's opinion is not as good as another's, but that's not true here,' said one sixth former. 'There are Jews from lots of different backgrounds, but I've never seen an example of bullying on the basis of people's beliefs,' said another. 'We might disagree about Israel's stance for example, but we would debate it.' 'Religion is not pushed,' said a parent. 'It's discussed philosophically.'

The school is inclusive and ecumenical, with a strong stress on inter-faith activities, including visits to temples and cathedrals. Though 99 per cent of pupils are Jewish, last summer, for example, a Ramadan tent was erected in the grounds, where Christians, Jews and Muslims formed a circle of faith.

A long time in the making, the school finally opened on a leafy site in east Barnet in 2010, with 150 pupils and 15 teachers. In 2012, a sixth form was introduced and it is now full to capacity.

Spacious (£48m) modern building, with wide corridors, large, light classrooms (more added in 2017) and excellent facilities. Calm and order reign throughout. Kosher food for all, with cool café for use of sixth formers, staff and visitors. Tight security on the gates.

Students generally mature and focussed ('During my son's GCSE year everyone really settled down,' said a mother. 'I was amazed how motivated they all were.') The head boy and girl actively involved in bringing about change – getting everyone to donate blood, inviting in speakers from universities, etc. Also generous with praise for fellow students ('He's amazing at art', 'She did a wonderful job,' are constant refrains.)

Pupils clearly enjoy the school. 'There's never been a day when my son has not been happy to go,' said one mother. 'When I asked him if he wanted to consider somewhere else for sixth form, he said, "Absolutely not".'

Pastoral care, well-being and discipline: The development of each student as a 'Mensch' – a person of integrity and honour – is the backbone of the school, and moral worth very much emphasised and rewarded (one prize, for example, for kindness, is voted on by students, another awarded for 20 hours volunteering).

Growing house system, with head boy and girl, plus deputies. 'Students put themselves forward, and are interviewed; it's a proper process,' says the head. Discipline is relaxed but clearly defined ('Chilled,' said one parent, 'but not laissez faire.'). 'It's generally a very inclusive and friendly place, good natured and human,' says the head, who has overseen a few fixed-term exclusions, but only one permanent exclusion.

Pupils and parents: From the highly observant to the not observant at all, with a reasonable sprinkling of mixed marriages. A good chunk live fairly locally, but pupils come from as far afield as St Albans and Essex, Harrow and Hackney. Many arrive by school coach, where firm bonds are formed. Parents are predominantly university-educated Jewish middle class, but a reasonable number are aided by the pupil premium and free school meals. All tend, however, to be focussed on similar goals. 'The great majority of our students intend to go to university and get professional jobs in the future, and think and act in that way,' says the head.

Entrance: Around 720 apply for year 7 places here, with about 400 putting it as their first or second choice. The school is mixed ability, but priority goes to Jewish children (proved by attendance at synagogue or involvement with Jewish education plus volunteering in the Jewish community). To cater for demand, school increased places from 180 to 210 in 2017, with possible permanent expansion. Admissions process also changing, with less priority for feeder schools. 'We wanted to ensure there is room for children whatever primary school they have come from.' Order of acceptance is now: looked after children; siblings; 18 places on distance; staff

Has an unlikely background ('I told them I wasn't Jewish and I was contemplating studying for the priesthood')

children; then, by random ballot. The school does not expand the sixth form, merely fills the gaps. Minimum six 6s at GCSE for those considering A levels; five 4s for the vocational route. Jewish applicants are again given priority.

Exit: About 20 per cent leave after GCSEs. Some because they don't make the required grades, others to sixth form colleges or independent schools. At 18, virtually all to university, about half to Russell Group universities (Nottingham, Leeds, Manchester particularly popular), with seven to Oxbridge or medical school in 2018.

Money matters: Parents are asked for a voluntary contribution to help underwrite unfunded Jewish education.

Remarks: A school with a clear vision, which, in six busy years, has grown from a hopeful acorn to an oak of excellence. An inclusive place producing excellent results and happy, involved pupils.

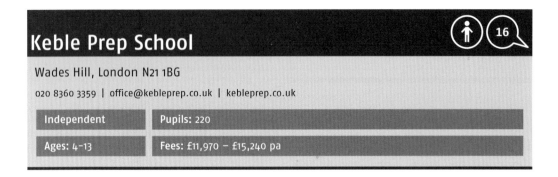

Keble Prep School

Wades Hill, London N21 1BG

020 8360 3359 | office@kebleprep.co.uk | kebleprep.co.uk

Independent	Pupils: 220
Ages: 4–13	Fees: £11,970 – £15,240 pa

Headmaster: Since September 2017, Mark Mitchell (40s) BSc from Leeds University, followed by a PGCE at Kingston University. He started his career as a science teacher at Ardingly College in Hayward Heath: 'I always wanted to teach, particularly science, so when I was offered a post teaching science at A level, I grabbed it.' However his main passion was teaching years 7 and 8, so he moved on to King's House School in Richmond followed by Feltonfleet school in Cobham. It was around this time he had his first child and, space being an issue, moved to Cheshire to the Terra Nova School where he was head of

science, followed by deputy head and finally head teacher. He was there for a total of 12 years. However, after separating from his wife, he moved back down south again to the job of head of Keble Prep. 'As soon as I came through the school gates it felt right.'

Tall, tanned and friendly, Mr Mitchell makes a good first impression. A northern lad from Yorkshire who was 'swayed' by the independent sector the first time he taught in a prep school: 'It was quite a big deal for me, I had no idea of the prep school world initially, having gone to a standard comprehensive in Hull, after but my first impressions of seeing the school and its grounds, there was no turning back.' On a more serious level he believes that there is much more freedom with the independent sector in terms of tweaking the curriculum and going outside the envelope a bit more, 'otherwise what's the point of calling it an independent school?' Plus, he says, 'children are children and they all come with their own issues whether they be in state or independent schools.

Parents so far have generally been positive about Mr Mitchell as new head teacher, and talk about how he has brought in fresh ideas to the school, which was slightly fraying around the edges. Recent changes have included a new maths programme, after-school activities for reception and year 1 and alterations to certain aspects of the curriculum. Plus he has done away with 'the random half days that were really difficult for working parents.' Some parents have said he is slightly less approachable than the previous head, 'but deals with issues straight away and effectively.' We get the impression that teachers are under more pressure than before with assessments every term.

Firm, too, on discipline: 'shaking hands, eye contact and opening doors will hopefully become ingrained.' But often, he says, the tightening up of standards comes from the boys themselves and is not led by him.

In any spare time, Mr Mitchell is a keen tennis player, cook and amateur baker – so much so that he has introduced a weekly cooking club for the boys run by a chef. He also enjoys reading and listening to music to unwind.

Entrance: Register a couple of years before entry at 4 but pressure on places is not intense. For some parents this school is an informed choice and they want a small Independent school – for others they have no choice as they live in a 'grey area' of schools in Palmers Green and couldn't get a place at a state primary school.

The school is non-selective, but before pupils start reception parents come for a meeting and their sons are observed doing jigsaws and playing games. 'The key thing is to ascertain that we will be a good fit for the child.' Probably not the school for a boy with a very specific or global needs, who is unlikely to be accepted. Some new entrants from the state sector at 11.

Exit: A small exodus at 11 to high-achieving local grammar schools and comprehensives, but school hopes to attract parents who understand the benefits of a school that runs to 13. 'We believe in 13+.' One parent did say, however, that her only criticism of Keble is that 'it needs to decide whether it's an 11+ or 13+ school, as many senior schools are changing their admissions policy.' However, she added that this was part of a 'bigger picture.'

At 13+, Mill Hill and St Albans are historically the two most popular choices, but horizons are expanding – 'we are sending boys to Highgate, Haberdashers, City, UCS, Westminster, Haileybury and St Columba's'. Wherever pupils go, the school does its utmost to ensure the best match between boy and school – 'we know the boys very well and recommend on personality'. A handful switch to the state sector – Ashmole, Finchley Catholic High and Highlands are popular choices, as are The Latymer and Dame Alice Owen.

Remarks: Driving to this lone prep school in an affluent suburban area of north London, (along roads such as Broad Walk, which make Bishops Avenue look like social housing) – we expected great things, so first impressions were slightly underwhelming, especially as we entered through the back for parking purposes. However, the minute we were ushered into the school, that feeling began to dissipate which was credit to the friendly staff who gave us coffee and plied us with delicious Fortnum and Mason biscuits.

Enthusiastic teaching and boy-friendly approach. 'We try to make it very hands on,' said one teacher. 'We make models and castles.' Parents praise staff highly

A small school, which hovers at around 200 boys in all, so class size is reflectively intimate, ranging from 12-15 in two parallel forms. In the early years the school follows the national curriculum, with add-ons such as French, which starts in year 3. The pace is accelerated and curriculum expanded as boys get older – 'we adapt it to the boys, easing into common entrance after 11'. Specialist teaching in music and PE in first two years, then further specialisation in art, ICT and French; by year 5, all subjects taught by specialists and switch to a senior school system where classes are split for English, maths, history, Latin etc.

Enthusiastic teaching and boy-friendly approach. 'We try to make it very hands on,' said one teacher. 'We make models and castles.' Parents praise staff highly. 'My son is motivated, interested and enthused. It's a great credit to the teachers,' said a mother. 'The teachers are incredibly encouraging,' said another. In the past, the school has been criticised for not necessarily stretching the brightest, but has spent time, effort and money rebalancing that equation. A director of studies now has a clear brief and the brightest are given differentiated teaching in class and one-to-one

Belmont Mill Hill Preparatory School

support out of it. Boys are setted in English and maths from year 5, with informal setting in science, French and humanities.

The philosophy, however, is very much 'each child is an individual' and the struggling are equally well guided, with the full range of SEN support which includes a full time dedicated SENCo and a team of three other assistants. Low percentage of SEN however, and whilst the school can deal fairly comfortably with dyslexia, dyspraxia, mild autism and Asperger's, they would advise a parent of a child with a more specific need to go through the state system as they just can't access the same level of support here. However, where possible, they will try and make reasonable adjustments. Parents say that the benefit of the small classes at Keble Prep is the individual attention their sons receive, and the safe and nurturing feel. As one parent told us: 'The teachers really know my child, and will flag up something immediately if there is an issue.'

This is a small site and facilities are relatively restricted but rebuild has brought more classroom space (although still fairly tight and a bit airless, which is something they are working on), a new science lab and an art room, allowing for relocation of the library, which had doubled as a music room. Limited space, too, for sports, although three new Astroturf courts have recently been put in, and a new playground area: 'The redevelopment of the reception playground splits the space into two areas to allow for free-flow indoor/outdoor play.'

Games, played twice a week, are taken seriously. Rugby, football, cricket and tennis are the main menu and a school minibus transports players to local and distant pitches. Rugby has put the school back on the prep school circuit, and more recently too has tennis – they recently won the first north London independent schools' tournament they have entered. Parents say that Mr Mitchell has really pushed sport at the school, and he says that he is trying to get a weekly fixture: 'I feel we punch above our weight with other schools but I would like to enter a few more national competitions.' Boys can also let off steam fairly regularly at nearby beautiful Grovelands Park, and the school is also looking into the option of a forest school.

Various lunch-time and after-school clubs on offer include puzzle club, movie club, cookery club and spy club as well as a common entrance drop-in club. Music has also been taken up several notches, with an assortment of orchestras, choirs and instruments on offer.

Has been going for 80 years and its aim now, as always, is to serve the local community, a community of small family businesses rather than City professionals. Many parents are first-time buyers. 'Our parents often want what they didn't have for themselves.' Many have Mediterranean roots (Turkish, Spanish, Greek, Italian, Cypriot) and a

firm belief in family, and the school reflects those values with a strong family atmosphere. Active parents' association that puts on summer and Christmas fairs, welcome evenings, curry nights, quiz nights etc. They have managed to fund a school minibus, some IT equipment and contribute to some of the playground revamp.

Very much a traditional prep, it retains distinctive black and yellow blazers, formal good manners and neatly brushed hair (long hair is definitely frowned upon). We did feel a tad sorry for the younger boys in reception who looked so stiff in their neatly knotted ties on the floor playing with plastic farm animals. We felt they had the rest of their lives to be City bankers. When we mentioned this to Mr Mitchell, he replied that this was something he had been planning to look into for the younger years, 'although I am aware that changing uniform is a major step so needs careful planning'.

Very much a traditional prep, it retains distinctive black and yellow blazers, formal good manners and neatly brushed hair (long hair is definitely frowned upon)

Pastoral care was more old school before Mr Mitchell became head, but he is very aware of concentrating not just on academia, but on producing grounded and well rounded individuals: 'We need to equip these boys with the right skill set for life and cultivate a culture that is supportive of them in sometimes dealing with failure.' For that reason he has introduced a new PSHE called Jigsaw which is built around mindfulness and reflection, which he hopes to instil into the boys. He has also put in worry boxes outside his office and around the school, where pupils can either jot down their concerns anonymously or ask to talk to someone about them.

A 'big brother, little brother' scheme matches older pupils with younger ones – evident and unaffected warmth stretching across the age divide. Pupil seem happy and well rounded, and as a final year pupil said: 'I love the school and I'm going to miss it when I leave'. Parents are equally positive. 'We chose it because it's very friendly and has a great identity that boys can relate to.' 'We love the school. It's a home from home. My son looks forward to going to school every day.' Keble is not a wealthy or notably well endowed place, but is undoubtedly a happy and safe haven, where all boys are treated with respect and respond in kind. A very secure place to start your school days.

King Alfred School

Manor Wood, 149 North End Road, London NW11 7HY

020 8457 5200 | admissions@kingalfred.org.uk | kingalfred.org.uk

| Independent | Pupils: 650; sixth form: 110 |
| Ages: 4–18 | Fees: £16,074 – £19,377 pa |

Head: Since 2015, Robert Lobatto MA Oxon PGCE (on the cusp of 50s), previously head of Barnhill Community High in Hayes. Married with two school age children. Educated at the Haberdashers' Aske's boys' school in Hertfordshire before reading history at Oxford, Mr Lobatto is firmly rooted in north London and its culture. Prior to coming here he spent 25 years in state secondary schools, head of history at East Barnet school, head of humanities at Highbury Fields, deputy head at Lister Community School in Plaistow and head (at only 40 years old) at Barnhill Community High School in Hayes. The one thing all his previous schools have in common is that they are 'big, urban and ethnically diverse', he says. At Barnhill 85 per cent of the school were from ethnic minority backgrounds, 60 per cent on free school meals.

His quiet and unassuming appearance belies a man of steel and purpose. While head at Barnhill he spent eight years setting up a multi academy trust, the Barnhill Partnership Trust, taking on and turning round a primary school in its wake. He brings a wealth of experience to his current role, and despite the stark difference in demographic, says that KAS is much more similar to his previous school than he anticipated. He left the state sector disillusioned with a diet of data and performance tables – the strap had been rubbing for too long on the same spot.

He finds the supportive parental body, the resources, the small class sizes and, above all, the genuinely child centred approach hugely refreshing. 'In the state sector we were making decisions for the school rather than for the children,' he observes. He enjoys being accountable to the governors (here known in Pullmanesque speak as Council rather than a governing board). His role here is less about admin, more about strategy. The strategy that he is particularly interested in developing is around learning – empowering the children to lead their own learning. While he believes in 'a rigorous academic education,' he says, 'real learning is about empowering the individual in the learning process.'

When challenged about what kind of child suits the liberal, relaxed ethos of the school, Robert muses, 'There genuinely is a place for everyone here as we are trying to bring out the best in each individual child. There is an alchemy about the place, they come out confident, well-balanced and articulate.' With the small numbers at King Alfred, you don't need 'heavy-handed behaviour management processes,' he suggests. He knows all the pupils, who he describes as 'delightful, easy to talk to and well behaved'. He still finds the time to teach history, which he enjoys and which gives him still greater insight into the pupils and the way the school operates. He relishes the strong ethos of working with the individual and says he is 'hugely experienced at dealing with complex behavioural issues'. There are certain goals to be achieved, however: moving forward the academics, particularly science, is one, working more with parents to help them support their children, as well as to provide inspiration to the school community, is another.

> 'There genuinely is a place for everyone here as we are trying to bring out the best in each. They come out confident, well-balanced and articulate'

A thoughtful man, Robert Lobatto clearly commands a great deal of respect. From groundsmen to junior school pupils, everyone we passed was keen to catch his eye and receive a nod or smile of recognition.

Head of lower school since January 2018, Karen Thomas, previously head of Kowloon Junior School in Hong Kong, and before that vice principal and PYP coordinator at Peak School there.

Academic matters: Focus here is not on exams and results, though there is a definite desire to see the pupils progress, excel and above all reach their potential. No tests, though the school keen to point out that the children's progress is monitored carefully. Barely any homework in lower school until year 5, although children take home reading books from reception onwards. 'When homework hits big time in year 10 the pupils have a massive shock', observed one parent. Lots of projects and creative building of volcanoes and the Great Wall of China, for example, between the age of 8 and 13. Pupils learn very much at their own pace and no one is told that they 'should' be at a certain point. 'This is fine if you are in it for the long term,' commented a parent, 'but if you decide to move your child you are likely to find s/he is way behind.' Another parent expressed it more positively: 'Bright and motivated children will do as well at King Alfred as anywhere else, but pupils who might have been crushed elsewhere do better. You must be prepared for the long haul and be patient as educational achievement is a longer process here than in other more pressurised environments.'

Relationships between pupils and teachers noticeably more personal than in most other London schools. This can lay the foundation for inspiring and motivational learning, and it is this individual approach that is at the heart of the ethos of the school and filters into every corner of school life, including the classroom.

At GCSE in 2018, 57 per cent of grades were 9-7. At A level over 30 per cent A*/A grades. However a much better indicator that the school is doing something right is its value added score. Progress between GCSE and A level is among the top 10 per cent in the country – there is a broad spectrum of ability here yet the progress pupils make is impressive.

Deservedly known to be a school for the creative arts more than for science, popular A levels here include art and design, history, politics and English. At GCSE high numbers do art and design and photography, and a good number choose performing arts and music studies, including a BTec group. More do French than Spanish, very few choose to do Latin, and food tech is now an option. Most of the 9-8 crop at GCSE is in English literature and history.

Additional support is available for students with mild specific learning difficulties – individually, in groups or in class. The progress of each student is monitored throughout their time at the school. Teachers build up a picture of pupils' learning profiles and identify those who might require specific intervention.

Games, options, the arts: If you want fierce competitive sport and silverware displayed in shiny glass cabinets, look elsewhere. Matches are often mixed – in age, gender (and competence). A successful match is one which everyone enjoys. Children of all ages are out kicking a ball on the field at the heart of the school, some are climbing trees, others working in the forge.

What makes Alfredians stand out is not the polish but the evident joy and collaboration they bring to their performances, and that all are encouraged to join in

Music has always been popular. Trendy boys play in bands (there is a popular after-school band club). Old school Alfredian teachers with long hair in ponytails inspire a number of pupils to perform in orchestras and ensembles. Large music tech room, complete with Macs, drums and cymbals, percussion keyboards and djembes. Plenty of space for drama, including a large theatre as well as a 'black box' studio. Years 7-9 performed Emil and the Detectives, years 10 and above in Chicago and Anything Goes. However considering the number of parents in the arts, particularly the performing arts, one parent commented that the school punches well below its weight. Another parent observed that the school does not dance to the obvious 'wow' factor. What makes Alfredians stand out is not the polish of their performance but the evident joy and collaboration they bring to their performances, and that all are encouraged to join in. While other schools at a choir competition may look impeccably groomed with perfect pitch, Alfredians will be seen in a colourful jumble, singing and clapping with gusto, supporting and encouraging each other, wreathed in grins. They are not a shambles, however – the lower school has won the Watford Music Festival first prize two years in a row, and the upper school reached the national school finals.

Industrious and inspirational art room – three rooms at the top of the building that overflows with ceramics, as well as charcoal drawings of leaves and plants.

In the senior school, years 7-11 required to make their choice of co-curricular activities from a wide range, from pottery to golf; sixth form options include screenwriting for films, emotional intelligence and Mandarin. Strong commitment to volunteering throughout, with pupils helping out at the local special school and raising significant sums for international causes (including building a school after the tsunami in Sri Lanka). Good careers advice (which kicks off in year 7) helps with GCSE and A level options and UCAS applications pre- and post-A level. As one might expect, green is high on the agenda – one of the first schools to introduce solar panels and recycling bins.

Everyone we spoke to talked glowingly of 'the village project' – a week in year 8 when all the pupils set up a camp in a corner of the grounds, plan their meals, cook them over a camp fire that they have built, plan the layout of their camp, and build where they will sleep. Adults take a background facilitating role so that the children can take control of their lives and manage the fundamentals they need to survive.

The Forge, managed by a female blacksmith, is another central feature of the curriculum that builds into the creative, hands-on craftsmanship that the school is so adept at instilling into its pupils. 'A wonderful outlet for those that are not so academic,' enthused one parent, who said how much the family enjoy building up a new iron poker selection around their fireplace. Children who have practical skills love being given a chance to shine at something so esoteric. The village project takes a mobile forge over to the camp to use during their week, an example of how King Alfred excels in integrating the curriculum and mixing up different opportunities that are offered here.

Background and atmosphere: Founded by parents in Hampstead in 1898, original aim was to provide an education based on what was best for the child and encourage learning for its own sake. Part of the progressive movement, KAS sees its kindred schools as Bedales in Hampshire and St Christopher in Letchworth. Moved to its current site, a leafy patch of north London opposite Golders Hill Park, in 1921, and has recently expanded, with a school building for the infants across the road from the main site at Ivy Wood, once the home of Anna Pavlova. The emphasis here is for little ones to be outdoors, doing craft, and tuning into nature. Attractive grounds with a mixture of periods and styles (new fitness studio, music and drama block, lovely arts and crafts dining hall) grouped around a central village-like common. Star attractions include a wooded amphitheatre, an arbour (Squirrel Hall), formed from the sheltering branches of two ancient chestnuts, and the farm, complete with chickens, rabbits, ducks and bees. This latter forms a key part of the outdoor education – not just a quaint accessory. Design technology here is of the old-fashioned carpentry kind, preserving creativity, and forms part of the hands-on creative ethos. Pupils start design from 4 years old.

The original ethos – liberal, progressive, egalitarian, child-centred – remains core to the school's values today. Parents and pupils agree that the needs of each child are foremost. 'They try to act holistically. They look at the individual and find out what makes them shine.' In many respects the school operates as a large extended family, without the rigid age divide found elsewhere. 'It's a really friendly school,' said one year 9. 'Older kids look

Children of all ages are out kicking a ball on the field at the heart of the school, some are climbing trees, others working in the forge

out for younger ones and you'll see sixth formers play with year 7s.' Most children seem to enjoy their time here. 'They skip into school every day,' said one long-time parent. 'Even after the holidays, they can't wait to get back.'

New Fives Court lower school building includes auditorium, cutting-edge art technology room with kiln and multi-purpose room for food science, rural studies and general science. ICT suite, learning support area and lower school library upstairs. Dotted around the site are climbing frames, sandpits and a gypsy caravan – all wood and natural materials.

Smiling groundsmen (always a good sign), colourful array of children, a refreshing indication of individuality. Discreet and rather beautifully delicate wrought iron gates secure the entrance to this charming oasis, off the busy North End Road. Blink and you'd miss it. Staff here are all very informal – streaming in and out of the staff room in all manner of clothes, except for suits and ties. Pupils also scruffy, and sometimes it's hard to tell the difference between staff and sixth formers.

A small school, with a total of 650 pupils from reception through to the upper sixth and fewer than 50 children in each year group, together with small class sizes – between 16 and 17 – makes for an intimate school community. This is enhanced by the village green atmosphere. School provides a genuine opportunity to develop personal relationships with both teachers and the wider school community.

Pastoral care, well-being and discipline: King Alfred will always give your child a chance. The school's detractors comment on a lack of boundaries and leniency in the face of transgression. 'Show us a London school that doesn't have its fair share of drugs and alcohol felons,' counter its supporters.

Robert Lobatto is regarded by many as introducing some much needed tightening – automatic expulsion for bringing drugs into school or using them in school. Otherwise the approach is more about discussion, reasoning with the offender and educating them as to why they have crossed a line. There are policies of internal exclusion (taking children out of lessons) and external exclusion (removing them temporarily from school) but, as with everything here, time is taken to explain, educate and be as fair as possible. 'We would always give kids many chances and do a lot of work to support and educate children about social media – drawing clear lines.'

This is above all a nurturing school. More carrot than stick. No hierarchies, very few rules but bullies will be suspended. However, probably not the place for a child who needs strong structures. Four counsellors and strong system of peer mentoring. No uniform but pupils tend to be unkempt rather than outrageous.

Pupils and parents: A fair smattering of A list celebrities, but 'which independent school in London doesn't have that' is the refrain. Plenty of parents who hated their school days seize the opportunity to give their children a chance to develop as individuals in a low pressure environment. Lots are Old Alfredians themselves who relish being part of this supportive community once more. Pupils, mainly from the wealthier suburbs of north London (Hampstead, Golders Green, Highgate, Muswell Hill), are confident and articulate and expect to be given equal weight as adults. Difficult to say what kind of child suits as often it can be counterintuitive. Blue stockings are given the chance to be bold, free spirits aren't squashed. One thing is certain, the parents need to be involved and supportive to make it work. More than in any other school the relationship is triangular, and all corners need to support to create success.

Entrance: Not selective at 4 but put your child's name down at birth. Date of registration decides visit order and over 200 apply for 40 places in reception. Always some places in year 7 though not normally more than 10. One hundred and twenty normally apply. 'We are looking for people who will get a lot out of King Alfred and give a lot to the school – those who are a good fit for our culture,' says Robert. Children don't just sit a few tests in maths and English but will spend a day at the school, will be asked to do group work, be interviewed in a group and will be assessed in the round. Do they have something about them? Are they sparky, confident, creative? At sixth form minimum of five 6s at GCSE – but school very flexible and inclusive, and will enable pupils to choose combinations that are individualised.

Exit: About 20-30 per cent leave after GCSEs, some to Camden School for Girls or other state sixth forms, others to UCS, Highgate or Francis Holland, for example. After A level, Bristol, Manchester and University of East Anglia popular choices. A few each year to do art foundation courses at eg Kingston or City and Guilds, and some to music colleges. Candidates choose to study a range of courses from business management (Sussex), industrial design (Brunel) and biomedical science (Kent) to English literature and film studies (UEA), history (Bristol), international relations (SOAS) and maths and philosophy (Leeds)

Money matters: Though not particularly well endowed, attempts to keep fees as stable as possible while keeping facilities up to date. No scholarships, a small number (about four) of means-tested bursaries in year 7 and sixth form.

Remarks: A wonderfully liberal education for the free spirits who balk at rigid structures and too much discipline, but KAS can also set free the souls of those children who have always been overly keen to conform. Not a school for parents obsessed with league table position, nor those who would prefer to delegate the education of their children completely. Success will depend on parents, child and school all rowing in the same direction.

The Latymer School

Haselbury Road, London N9 9TN

020 8807 4037 | office@latymer.co.uk | latymer.co.uk

State	Pupils: 1,369; sixth form: 439
Ages: 11–18	

Headteacher: Since 2015, Maureen Cobbett BA (modern languages) followed by a PGCE from Liverpool University. Originally from Birmingham, she started out as a languages teacher in French and German – both subjects to GCSE standard and French to A level standard: 'Teachers are often inspired by that one teacher they had at school. For me it was a memorable French teacher.' Prior to her post at Latymer, Ms Cobbett was head at All Saints Catholic School in Nottinghamshire and in that time took it from an underachieving school to the 'most successful comprehensive in Nottinghamshire.' However after seven years in the post, she decided it was time to do something completely different and the right time to pursue her ambition of working and living in London: 'I wasn't initially aware of the post of head teacher at Latymer; it was my sister who lived in London who made me aware of the school. She told me about the conversations she had heard on the train from lovely, well-mannered children'.

Before meeting this head, we didn't quite know what to expect. Yes, Ms Cobbett is fairly business-like by nature, very straighforward and definitely not concerned with winning us over – but during our meeting, we did witness a more affable and humorous side. Parents have clearly seen this side too. One told us: 'At this year's annual teachers' Christmas concert, she was there in the orchestra wearing a Christmas hat and playing the triangle.' And one pupil told us: 'She sometimes stops us in the corridor and tells us really bad jokes.' She is also popular with the teachers, we are told.

Since arriving at Latymer not all her changes have met with approval. Some parents were not happy by her immediate introduction of a stricter uniform policy. One parent told us: 'She definitely seems hung up on the uniform. It's fair enough if she wanted to change the jumper to a smarter one with a logo, but when she starts saying that girls have to wear tights, I don't think there needs to be that level of detail and it also gave the girls a little bit of choice'. However, a more satisfied parent said of her approach: 'I love what she's done with things like the school website. It's been updated and is much more professional now. Things just seem more organised'.

'The standard is amazing,' one parent told us, 'and what I really like is that the orchestras accept students of all abilities. It's not all about the top lot'

Whether or not she has divided opinion, one has to admire the daunting task of heading up one of London's most high achieving schools – not to mention in an uncertain financial climate. Ms Cobbett says: 'It's quite a depressing position to be in for most headteachers – they are facing funding being slashed and yet they are being asked to make standards rise. I don't see how the two go together.' That said, she remains passionate about

education born out of the values instilled in her when she was a child: 'I come from a low income Irish family, but my mum was very keen for us all to have a good education. All five siblings and myself went to grammar schools.' She adds: 'I love what I do. I never considered anything other than teaching and I love being around young people. It makes you feel young.'

Ms Cobbett has two grown up daughters. 'I waited until they were older and doing their own thing before I moved, so I didn't have to uproot them too.' Any free time she allows herself is often spent doing sports or going to the cinema and theatre.

Academic matters: Excellent GCSE results, making it the top performing school in Enfield borough and within the top six per cent in London, with 84 per cent 9-7 grades in 2018. Pupils must choose a MFL from French or German in Y7 and they can then choose between French, German, Russian or Latin in Y8, 'languages to get into Oxbridge with', one parent jokingly told us.

Students study 10 GCSEs and the vast majority take the EBacc subjects. Geography is very popular as are the sciences. At sixth form, maths is the most popular subject and the school offers 'nothing apart from an ashamedly academic programme', so no vocational subjects. (Sociology has recently been scrapped due to funding cuts.) The majority stay on at sixth form – if they achieve at least six grade 7s at GCSE – but another 50 join from other schools. A level exam results for 2018 were 63 per cent A*/A, and 88 per cent A*/B grades.

Parents agree that the school is 'very good academically' and it certainly makes plenty of effort to award academic achievement across all years. Year 13s are awarded prizes in specialist subjects too, such as mechanics, statistics and government & politics. Pupils who do not gain a subject prize have the opportunity to be awarded either a Latymer Lodge or school prize for gaining a high aggregate at A level. There are also open awards for special achievements in spoken English, creative work, instrumental performance, music composition and fieldwork, as well as prizes for service to the community, thus there is plenty of motivation to strive and to win here.

Where pupils have a special learning need, they will find help through the learning support department which also arranges mentoring for younger students from sixth formers. EAL students are supported well and achieve equally well at GCSE and A level. One parent told us: 'At Latymer, SEN could be children who are super bright but actually need additional support for areas in social interaction which they may lack.'

It is important that academic success is supported by 'a life outside school' and students are encouraged to take part in the wide variety of activities on offer. Languages are supported by school journeys and exchanges through links with Russia, France and Germany; there have also been exchange visits with the Mwambisi school in Tanzania; other trips include geographers going to Iceland, classicists to Italy, artists to Barcelona, skiers to the French Alps, music to Austria, Belgium, Germany, the Czech Republic and scientists to Honduras and South Africa.

Games, options, the arts: More than 17 different sporting activities offered, which may come as a surprise to some, who know Latymer as a predominantly academic institution. One parent said: 'The school does have very good sporting facilities and outside grounds, and, whilst they may not do as well as other schools, the opportunities are there.' New long jump and athletics facilities 'but could do with an all weather pitch', one pupil told us. The school encourages active lifestyles and rewards pupils' enthusiasm for sport with a number of awards that recognise outstanding achievement both in and outside school. These include rugby (played very competitively), hockey, football (for girls and boys), netball, cross-country, rounders, tennis and cricket. One pupil proudly told us: 'We have some of the top runners in the county.' Students in years 7 and 9 have the opportunity to spend a week at Ysgol Latymer, the school's outdoor sports centre in Snowdonia, for activities such as hill walking, orienteering, climbing, abseiling and canoeing.

Music is extremely strong. Wonderful facilities – we counted approx 10 practice rooms and a couple of well-equipped studios. A quarter of the pupils learn a musical instrument at standards ranging from beginners to beyond grade 8. There are five orchestras (including reed and brass), a concert band and several choirs. They perform at school concerts and many are invited elsewhere, such as the National Festival for Music. 'The standard is amazing,' one parent told us, 'and what I really like is that the orchestras accept students of all abilities. It's not all about the top lot.'

Latymer had art specialism and so the subject has a strong presence outside the department, with astounding work on display around the school. Experts visit to do talks and run special workshops in oil painting and sculpture, and the department runs visits to the London Institute, Tate Modern and Tate Britain as well as European trips. As a result, examiners have commented on the good grasp pupils have of contemporary artists. Drama is supported by trips out plus the big theatre productions that take place at the school each year; a main school production in November (recently Anything Goes), a junior production in July, and the house drama competition every other year. Recent house drama offerings – one by each of the six houses – based on The Diary of Adrian Mole. One of the pupils directing it told us with a groan: 'We have to do everything – cast it, direct it and cram it all in during lunch times and after school..but it is fun.'

Far from the dull, intellectual conformists we expected to meet, the students who showed us around were extremely well rounded individuals

If Latymerians have any spare moment to breathe after all of this they can enjoy a rich range of extracurricular activities that shape life at the school; over 60 different clubs and teams run before, during and after school, and at weekends. Lunchtime clubs are run by the students themselves ('a bit like freshers' week'), which include a debating society, an Afro-Caribbean society, LBGT society, gardening, chess and more. There is a Young Enterprise group, an economics society and clubs whose sole purpose is to raise funds for less fortunate people, particularly supportive of local charities such as the food bank in Edmonton.

Background and atmosphere: Tradition creates the atmosphere at Latymer. It was established in nearby Church Street in 1624 at the direction of Edward Latymer, a City merchant, who bequeathed certain property to trustees on condition that they were to clothe and educate 'eight poore boies of Edmonton'. His, and the 'generosity of the many others since', are remembered each year on the school's Foundation Day. Pupils are proud of this tradition and seem enthusiastic about the events that keep it alive. The school's motto – Qui Patitur Vincit (Who Endures Wins) – aptly sums up its spirit, and is the title of the annual talk. The school moved to its present location in 1910.

Once we found the school all was pretty quiet in the snug waiting area, except for an ill student who was dealt with sympathetically and sent to medical. This episode added a more human side to a school whose academic reputation has become somewhat legendary. It is the first choice school for many north London parents with an extremely clever child.

Far from the dull, intellectual conformists we expected to meet, the students who showed us around were extremely well rounded individuals – one of whom was quite possibly the biggest character we've met at any school we've visited. She was extremely entertaining, exceedingly bright and full of praise for Latymer and her six years there. The other student, also very pleasant, had just been offered a conditional place at Cambridge. They both felt very 'lucky' to have spent their secondary school years here: 'Yes, there is pressure, but nothing we can't deal with and there is a lot of support offered.'

Built on three acres of land and flanked by 12 acres of playing fields, which separate the school from the main A10 road, Latymer looks deceptively small from the front; one parent felt that planting a few more trees would help the aesthetics. Walking into the school is like walking back in time. It doesn't seem as if much would've changed since 1910, which arguably adds to its charm. We have become accustomed to sterile foyers in many other schools: the one at Latymer is a modest and cosy affair with oak panelled doors and simple but exquisite charcoal drawings adorning the walls, all hand drawn by students. The lady on reception remarked: 'It's not fair is it? Not only are these kids ridiculously bright, but look how they draw!' We had to agree.

Exquisite charcoal drawings adorned the walls. The lady on reception remarked: 'It's not fair is it? Not only are these kids ridiculously bright, but look how they draw!'

There are a number of outbuildings around the main one, added at various times over the school's life and capturing its spirit of progress: the Great Hall (1928), which seats over 1,000; the gymnasia and technical labs (1966); a performing arts centre (2000) and a sports/dining hall complex (2006). In 2010 the high-tech multi-purpose Seward Studio (performance space, auditorium, media studio, art gallery and drama theatre) was opened. The school also has a number of rooms dedicated to specialist teaching: 12 science laboratories, six fully-equipped technology rooms, and specialist ICT rooms with wireless networks. Also a very large, very well equipped library: 'I don't think there is anything I could need from a library that isn't here,' a student told us. Sixth formers now have a new modern common room equipped with a small café selling sandwiches and paninis etc (which is just as well, as the local eateries are pretty limited).

Pastoral care, well-being and discipline: The 186 pupils in each year are organised into six form groups, and each form group belongs to one of the six house groups. They remain in these groups throughout their school lives, meeting daily for registration and form periods, including, in the lower years, PSHE lessons delivered by the form tutor. Each year group also has a head of learning (first port of call for parents concerned about progress) who, along with the deputy head of learning, also acts as mentor. House culture is strong. Each has a senior pupil to lead, democratically elected. Senior pupils organise activities which are used to inject a sense of comradeship and teamwork across all year groups, and to make new year 7s feel fully inducted into life at Latymer. They do this via sports tournaments and various competitions such as cake-making, drama and music.

Pupils are expected to abide by the school rules and the home-school agreement they signed with their parents on joining the school, but the school views 'self discipline resulting from wanting to learn' as a more important deterrent to poor behaviour. One parent did say that students who go to Latymer are already self-motivated: 'I doubt there are many behavioural issues, but that said, clearly students are under immense pressure. However there is quite a lot of support offered to them and the school never gives up on its pupils.' Support comes by way of two counsellors who regularly visit the school, and pupils can refer themselves; a head of year and an assistant head of year who would be the first port of call for a troubled student; and a mentoring system, where students from years 12 and 13 are trained to mentor the younger students. The school has also recently introduced into the curriculum one lesson a week dedicated to 'pastoral time' – issues ranging from drugs to bullying etc.

One parent said that 'while the academic side is challenging, it is not to the exclusion of everything else.' Another said she has 'always felt comfortable emailing teachers direct if I have a concern or question.'

Pupils and parents: Anyone and everyone who is 'very clever', though the school wisely lists acceptable postcodes in its admission criteria (and suggests that no-one should apply from further than an hour's journey). Roughly 65 per cent of the school's cohort are from ethnic minorities. Alumnae include Dame Eileen Atkins, actor, Simone Butler, bass player with Primal Scream, and Syed Kamall, currently Conservative MEP.

Entrance: Only those 'deemed capable of achieving the highest grades at GCSE are considered' at this highly oversubscribed, selective school. Selection is by the NVR test as well as literacy and numeracy. A parents said 'it used to be harder to get into', but around 2,000 typically apply for the 186 places, so many are still disappointed. Priority is given to looked-after children and those who live in designated postcode areas in the boroughs of Hackney, Islington, Waltham Forest, Haringey and Enfield. Offers also made to around 20 per cent of students who live in these areas and show 'exceptional musical talent and achievement' akin to grade 5. A further 20 places are awarded to those on pupil premium.

Around 50 external students join the sixth form. Pre-requisites including living in designed postcode areas, getting at least six grade 7s at GCSE, including for proposed A level subjects, plus entrance tests for those applying to study maths and/or/sciences.

Exit: Around 95 per cent go on to university or other forms of higher education in music and art. The school does not 'push Oxford or Cambridge though plenty apply, and plenty get offers' (18 places in 2018); 19 medics, two dentists and three vets. UCL, Bristol, Nottingham and other Russell Group universities are also popular destinations; courses include aerospace engineering, medicine, law, Chinese, Russian and Egyptology.

Money matters: Funding cuts affect Latymer as all other state schools. Parents have been asked to make voluntary yearly contributions. The school says: 'The response from parents has been very positive and they have been very generous. They don't want the school to suffer'. The school has also been appealing to the LOSA (Latymer Old Students Association) for donations.

Remarks: A peek back in time shows that some well-known former pupils like Baroness Claire Tyler (Chair of CAFCASS and president of the National Children's Bureau), footballer Johnny Haynes and Sir Bruce Forsyth CBE all did well here. Pupils clearly still do. This is a zealously traditional school with pupils who show a healthy balance between hard work and play. Ofsted has a similar attitude and in its last report described the school as outstanding.

Mill Hill County High School

Worcester Crescent, London NW7 4LL

0844 477 2424 | admin@mhchs.org.uk | mhchs.org.uk

| State | Pupils: 1,740; sixth form: 452 |
| Ages: 11–19 | |

Headteacher: Since 2004, Geoffrey Thompson MA MBA (Ed) FCMI (50s). Formerly head of Duchess's Community High School in Alnwick, Northumberland. Educated at Campbell College, Belfast, then at St Catharine's College, Cambridge, where he read music. Started his teaching career at Langley Park School for Boys in Bromley, where he worked for 18 years, before moving to Norfolk as deputy head, then on to Northumberland. Though Mill Hill County has always been a school with high standards, his time in charge has improved it significantly. 'Having a vision and a blueprint is not my way,' he says. 'You have a set of principles and good judgement, you make decisions with other people and the place grows organically.'

A dapper soul, whose own tie is always immaculately knotted, he has a dry sense of humour and a delightfully precise command of the English language. Married to a teacher (who also works in the school), he has two daughters and a son. Out of hours, he enjoys reading, particularly modern history, travelling and music.

Academic matters: One of the country's highest performing comprehensives. With 60 per cent A*-B grades at A level in 2018, and 42 per cent 9-7 at GCSE, this is a school which believes in an academic focus – 68 per cent of pupils gained 9-5 in both English and maths. Apart from a handful of vocational qualifications in ICT and media, the curriculum is traditional, with a good range of modern languages (Spanish, French, German, Latin) and a quarter of pupils taking all three sciences at GCSE. In the sixth form – the largest in the borough – the 33 subjects on offer include sociology, psychology, economics and dance. Maths and science, however, are the most popular options (with 10 groups for maths).

Teaching strong throughout (with regular awards for science, geography and maths) and most subjects provide plenty of enrichment. In English, for example, there are Shakespeare and poetry workshops, in DT, direct links with industry. An undoubted strength of the school is the focused attention it offers for all. 'Every child is taught to their own individual abilities,' commented one parent. For those at the top of the spectrum, there are two members of staff to encourage A level students to aim for A*s and Russell Group universities, while those who struggle to make the 9-4 benchmark at GCSE are offered a one-year course in which to resit. At this juncture, too, the school participates in a Barnet-wide scheme which sandwiches vocational college training with English, maths and employment skills. Largest number of SEN pupils in Barnet with a department reflective of their very varied needs (including provision for blind children). A raft of teaching assistants provides in-class aid and specialist staff oversee classes and support students beyond. 'It's quite an operation,' says the head.

Games, options, the arts: The school prides itself on its extracurricular offering, but there's little doubt that music is the jewel in the crown. 'There are few local schools that can hold a candle to us,' says the head with legitimate pride. He himself rehearses all year 7s to appear in the Christmas concert and from time to time plays the piano at assembly or a duet alongside a visiting professional. Standards throughout are exceptionally high. Recently, for the fourth year in a row, the orchestra performed a joint concert with the Royal Philharmonic ('you have to be quite good for the RPO to come and play with you,' says the head). Meanwhile the school band featured alongside that of the Royal Air Force at the Watford Colosseum. Regular lunchtime concerts, major concerts twice a term, large-scale musical in the Easter term, plus an annual European tour for concert and jazz bands. A full range of other sounds, including gospel, African drum and steel drum. Boys participate as enthusiastically as girls – 'unheard of,' says the head – and one talented former pupil performs regularly at Ronnie Scott's.

In sport too, the school has become a 'force to be reckoned with,' particularly in boys' football and girls' netball. Basketball and rugby also on offer and table tennis played enthusiastically by all. Excellent facilities for sport include a range of pitches, three playgrounds, gym, sports hall and in summer, six-lane track and three tennis courts. Art thriving, with a weekly art club and life drawing workshop run by the Royal Academy for A level pupils. Numerous guest speakers and in-demand trips (languages to Barcelona and Normandy, politics to the US, annual ski trip) to inspire and raise aspirations. Good range of clubs run early morning and after school (which can be difficult for those who live at a distance), plus D of E, World Challenge and CCF (shared with nearby independent Mill Hill School).

Background and atmosphere: Originally opened in 1931 as Orange Hill Boys' Grammar School, which then combined with matching girls' grammar in the 1970s. Merged again with Moat Mount School in 1984 to create Mill Hill County High School. The school, fringed by a good expanse of playing fields and forest, now sits on a hilly site with panoramic London views. There, however, the picturesque ends, with well-used buildings crammed together in an intricate hotchpotch to accommodate more students than ever. 'It is overcrowded,' said one parent. 'They're the victims of their own success.' Older parts of the fabric include some fairly basic portakabins (which house dance and drama), but recent additions have provided modern labs, a sixth form centre, computer suites, seven new classrooms and an air-conditioned assembly hall.

Music is the jewel in the crown. Boys participate as enthusiastically as girls – 'unheard of,' says the head – and one talented former pupil performs regularly at Ronnie Scott's

The lack of elbow room doesn't seem to detract from the upbeat mood, with friendly and positive staff (on the day the Guide visited a member of the office team was ringing up a local primary school to ensure a forgotten jumper was returned to its owner) and parents praise the general sense of well-being. 'The school is very good at communicating,' said one. 'They keep us informed and I have the email addresses of all my child's teachers.' Another was grateful for the empathy shown at a difficult time. 'They were understanding and supportive when we had family problems.'

Not the easiest school to get to. No tube nearby, which contributes to the mood of semi-rural calm but can be difficult for those wanting to arrive early or stay late for clubs or games. Mill Hill became an academy in 2011, but still works closely with Barnet Council, particularly in its responsibilities for Oak Hill, a successful facility for 32 emotionally and behaviourally disturbed children, four and a half miles away.

Pastoral care, well-being and discipline: One of the first things parents tend to mention is the uniform policy. 'They're very strict on uniform,' said one. 'Everyone looks very smart.' The head sees uniform as a means of setting the expectation bar. 'We're very clear about what we say and insist that what we say is done. We aren't repressive, but you'd be unlikely to see anyone with their shirt tails not tucked in or their ties not tied.'

The head also spends one lesson a week making surprise visits to a range of classrooms. 'That way, you see what's happening. You chat to the children, look at their books. It's a co-operative relationship, but you could potentially see those same children in another context behaving badly.' The insistent focus on behaviour, attitude and good manners undoubtedly pays off. 'Most people who come across our students have positive things to say.'

Pupils and parents: About half the school's intake comes from the leafy and prosperous suburb of Mill Hill, with its high concentration of professionals and business families, but the intake is certainly not uniform. 'There are quite a lot of deprived children and the ethnic mix is huge,' says the head. It includes significant numbers of families who originate from the Indian sub-continent, Asia and Africa. Only a few, however, 'don't speak excellent English.'

Entrance: Mill Hill has entrance criteria guaranteed to drive north London parents into a neurotic frenzy, with 243 places at 11 sliced up into small print sub-sections. Lucky locals can benefit from one of the 90 guaranteed 'geography' places. But distance from the gates is frighteningly close (rather less than a mile). Siblings, too, are ensured a desk. After that children of members of the teaching staff (who have been working at the school for a minimum of two years). If there are 60 remaining places they are then awarded on aptitude and are split into: 24 for technology, 24 for music and 12 for dance. Technology is tested in two stages – a reasoning test in the summer term of year 5 whittles down about 1,500 to 240, the second round (in abstract reasoning and maths) held in September

cherry-picks the rest ('it's harder than getting into Oxford,' jokes the head). Music equally competitive, with up to 400 auditioning, in two sections: listening and performance. 'You can, however, play a snappy piece on the classroom xylophone and come out higher than a carefully coached grade 4 violinist.' Dance candidates are selected by audition.

The large (and heavily oversubscribed) sixth form admits a further 40 to 60 pupils out of 600 applicants, with minimum entry requirements of six grade 6s at GCSE, including English and maths. Those wishing to study science and maths need 7+s in their chosen subjects though, and most come garlanded with a string of 9-7s.

Exit: No one is ever asked to leave (except for disciplinary matters), but a fair few (27 per cent in 2018) move on after GCSE to local sixth form colleges, independent and grammar schools. Some 50 per cent Russell Group (one of highest representations of any comprehensive in the UK) with four to Oxbridge and four medics in 2018. Quite a number to drama and art-related degrees. A consistent trickle to the US.

Money matters: The transformation to academy status has released additional funds and these are now being used for building projects. Otherwise not rich, but not poor either.

Remarks: A cheerful, well-run school producing highly motivated, high achieving students. Exceptional music.

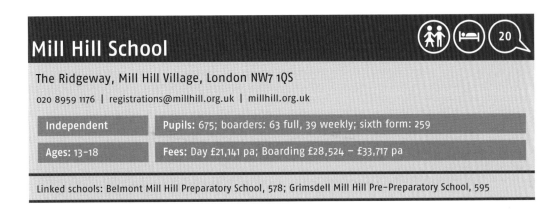

Mill Hill School

The Ridgeway, Mill Hill Village, London NW7 1QS

020 8959 1176 | registrations@millhill.org.uk | millhill.org.uk

| Independent | Pupils: 675; boarders: 63 full, 39 weekly; sixth form: 259 |
| Ages: 13–18 | Fees: Day £21,141 pa; Boarding £28,524 – £33,717 pa |

Linked schools: Belmont Mill Hill Preparatory School, 578; Grimsdell Mill Hill Pre-Preparatory School, 595

Acting head: Jane Sanchez, principal deputy head, is holding the reins after the resignation in August 2018 of previous head Frances King.

Founding head of The Mount, Mill Hill International School since 2014 is Sarah Bellotti BEd (50s). Mrs Bellotti is steeped in international education, having spent 20 years teaching English

in international schools in Rome and, latterly, nine years as the director of King's, Ely's International Study Centre. It has to be a dream job, this – a beautifully reimagined and refurbished school dedicated entirely to educating able children from overseas in English subjects via intensive language support to enable them to gain places at good

English boarding schools – and down the road from and sharing the facilities of the main school. And she fits the bill. Intense and intensely committed to the task: 'I passionately believe in the international community – we celebrate internationalism here' – she exudes focused excitement and a determination to realise the considerable potential here. She spent her first year 'going across the world' spreading the word and recruiting pupils. At the time of our visit, there were 66, including, interestingly, 10 day pupils who find in the flexible curriculum etc something to suit their individual circumstances. Her new school is perfectly placed and equipped to make a real impact on this market.

Academic matters: Pretty trad curriculum though some interesting novelties eg an IGCSE in further pure maths and A levels in computer science and psychology, not found everywhere. Popular A levels are English, business studies and maths – maths being the stand-out success story in terms of results here. Results, otherwise, are a spread. Not vast numbers of A*s and a range from A-C across the board (in 2018, 39 per cent A*/A grades). Popular GCSE options are geography, history, RS and French. Best results in all three sciences, art, Latin and statistics – latter popular and successful but replaced by further pure maths (see above) under exam reform. In 2018, 57 per cent A*-A/9-7 grades overall.

Lots of changes under the previous head's regime include an Innovation Hub – a room where techie things can be tried out. If the DT workshops and the work we saw there is anything to go by (eg stunning sliding work station) great things will emerge. Another innovation is three-weekly progress reports – 'Before, if you were really good or really bad everyone knew but no-one really noticed the in-betweeners. Now you are monitored and have targets. It is more pressure but it's helpful.' And, of course, to counter the pressure, they now have 'mindfulness' and drop-in, stress-reducing activities like colouring. It had to happen. There are masses of catch-up classes, clinics and individual support. It's all there for the taking – though some sense among parents that the extent of what's on offer isn't always made clear – 'If we'd realised, we wouldn't have had a tutor. It was there in school for us all along.'

Good trad Piper Library – impressively full shelves though some stock needs updating and the bookshelves unaccountably not labelled. Good stock of periodicals. F/t UCAS teacher can be found in sixth form centre – 'She's brilliant'.

Interestingly, 20 per cent of the school's population is on the SEN register and we were told over and again how supportive the school is of eg dyslexics. Previous head immediately enhanced the staffing and provision in general and the effects are obvious. 'Some of them are slow developers but

To counter the pressure, they now have 'mindfulness' and drop-in, stress-reducing activities like colouring. It had to happen

they can be absolutely the children we want and do well by.' Support is given by individual and small-group lessons which are timetabled not to cut across pupils' other periods, following and reinforcing aspects of the main curriculum and teaching study and organisational skills. Learning support assistants intervene in mainstream academic lessons to support particular pupils or groups. School mainly caters for pupils with mild to moderate specific learning difficulties but also accommodates some statemented pupils eg those with impaired hearing.

The majority at The Mount comes for the one-year IGSCE course, though you can stay for anything from one term to two years. No IB. Small classes with a maximum of 12 pupils. It takes children from 13-17. All teachers have EAL qualifications/experience. Flexible courses depending on the level of English you arrive with. Pre-A level programme. We met several students on our visits – clearly a happy, stimulated and cohesive group who were enjoying a first class education.

Games, options, the arts: Long and pioneering tradition in the arts. We remember coming for an arts festival some 30 years ago and the vitality we met then has only grown.

Famously sporty and, while having fun, sports are taken seriously here – girls' sports, seemingly, as much as boys'. 'We have fields and fields and fields,' pupils enthused. Partnership with Middlesex University provides high level support for elite athletes. Good to see extension activities with sports scholars – with specialist staff to help them build and challenge themselves. Remarkable number of representatives in local and country teams across a range of sports – netball, cross-country, cricket, golf and – new to us – bouldering. Lots of teams in eg rugby and hockey so not restricted to the real jocks. School magazine reports – written with an honesty rare in such publications – attest to the earnest approach and a capacity for self-appraisal we seldom see. However, some feeling among the pupils that there was, notwithstanding, a lack of ambition and acceptance of below par performances when a bit more get-go might tilt the balance.

'You don't have to be sporty,' said one parent; 'there's so much else to get involved in.' Exceptional music dept and no lack of ambition in its vast repertoire and the 230 concerts and services annually for which it provides the ensembles, choirs, soloists etc. 'The standard varies from professional to er, well.. but they are so inclusive – everyone feels they can have a go.' House music and house drama on alternate years involve – intensely – just about everyone, as does the music competition. Patrick Troughton Theatre (capacity 150+), a rigged stage in The Large ie main hall, and a spacious drama studio with seating for a small audience. We were impressed by the range of art media: 'They encourage you to try everything,' a non-artsy sixth former enthused. We loved the variety in what we saw – no production line stuff. Impressive range of activities on offer. 'There is masses to do,' and lists and lists of clubs, outings and trips bear witness to that.

The Mount could accommodate three times the present number – it is spacious, superlatively kitted out; no expense has been spared. While some facilities are shared with the main school, there is little lacking here – own DT studio, plenty of outside space. The only shared teacher is one of the PE dept. Excellent range of weekend activities, again, shared with the main school.

Boarding: Boarders make up a fifth of the school population and most are full boarders, based overseas. They come from around 15 countries from China to Spain. However, only a third of them need EAL support, which is given individually and in groups when needed. Small number of UK-based weekly boarders. Boarding is set to grow here and not just for overseas pupils. The market for weekly boarding in the London of busy working parents is buoyant and Mill Hill is beautifully placed to supply it. Vertically-aged houses; all but one are mixed. Good bonding activities for newbies. Enticing and varied list of compulsory weekend activities includes outings eg theatre and music trips, catch-up and revision classes, sports, clubs and interest groups – lots of choice. Day pupils come in for much of it. Boarding isn't state of the art – no en-suites here yet – but most are in two-bedders of reasonable sizes and all year 13 boarders in singles. Good games rooms.

When we visited The Mount there were, among its 66 pupils, 24 home languages spoken. School will not take more than 25 per cent from any one country. Boarding takes place in the main school and The Mount's boarders are fully integrated.

Background and atmosphere: Founded by nonconformist merchants and ministers in 1807 in the then village of Mill Hill, safely located away from 'dangers both physical and moral, awaiting youth while passing through the streets of a large, crowded and corrupt city'. It's not just safe but high – ought to be called Mill Hill-on-the-Hill – and looks over the northern suburbs much as a more famous, boys only, school on a neighbouring hill does, only

from a different angle. In many ways. A rare thing, a boarding school of this size – 120 acres – so close to the national hub and unique, now, in offering, as it does, coeducation from 3-18 with an inbuilt international school integral to its offering. In parkland with some glorious trees which still date from the planting of a former resident, the botanist Peter Collinson, the main building – colonnaded and with tall windows – makes a confident statement. Inside are some splendid rooms and many walls are lined with huge oil paintings of school worthies – again, this is a school which had, from its inception, no modest aims. Democracy rules here and even the grandest meeting room – The Crick – is open to bookings from pupils for meetings and discussions.

The main building – colonnaded and with tall windows – makes a confident statement. Inside are some splendid rooms and many walls are lined with huge oil paintings of school worthies

Countless additional buildings – many attractive, some functional – and dating from all eras. Walkways, staircases abound – 'You get used to stairs here'. We loved the rustic vernacular Winterstoke Library and were desperate to know what is housed in its little tower; we loved the McClure Music School (1912) redolent of an innocent age, and we loved the Favell Building (2007) – which houses humanities and the top floor of which is hung with huge flags from everywhere. Most recent addition: an Innovation Hub. An attractive chapel (1896) by Basil Champneys, architect of many notable scholastic buildings. The chapel – though obviously of Christian origins – is now very much an ecumenical hub, and actively celebrates all faiths and their key festivals. We visited over Harvest Festival but missed Rosh Hashanah, the week before, and heard about the preparations for Diwali on the week following. One of our guides explained about Ramadan and the difficulties of fasting. The chapel was decorated by self-portraits of the new year 9s who explain to the gathered classes why they depicted themselves as they had – an excellent way to start to get known and know others.

Away from the main corridor and atrium, some areas are pretty old-school Spartan and need painting or a general refurb. Others are mint and sparkling.

Strong and popular house system and here, unlike in many other schools, houses you belong to are actually physical houses – or, at least, parts of buildings. They are defined by a house colour scheme – you can't miss it in upper areas of the main building where the overhead light is retina-bendingly harsh. Parents praise the heads of houses: 'They deal with everything and they always phone you back'.

New sixth form centre is making staying on more attractive and the revamp is upping the profile and quality of what Mill Hill sixth form has to offer in general.

Outstanding food – we can't remember seeing – or scenting – better. The home-made cookies made us want to curl up and stay for the day.

School magazine reports – written with an honesty rare in such publications – attest to the earnest approach and a capacity for self-appraisal we seldom see

The Mount – formerly The Mount Girls' School – has been beautifully refurbished. It has lovely grounds, good-sized classrooms and a happy collaborative atmosphere. The pupils – from everywhere – mix well with each other and the boarders they share houses with in the main school.

Pastoral care, well-being and discipline: Universal praise for pastoral care – both when you need it and when you only need to know it's there eg on arrival in the sixth form. 'It was so welcoming!' 'It's not a school where people act up much,' we were told, 'and if you do hit trouble it doesn't define the rest of your time in the school. They try to help you and find out why.' Very rare chuck-outs, mainly for drugs and nothing recent. House structure is the bedrock of the overall care and support and much praise for house staff in general.

Pupils and parents: Boys vastly outnumber girls, especially in the sixth form. This is true in pretty much all co-eds but is markedly noticeable here, partly due to the number of local, first rate, girls' schools. However, again, the school is working on redressing this and, in any case, girls, evidently don't feel outnumbered and no-one complains that provision for them is second class. We did note an activity called 'programming for girls' and wondered.. Parents praise the inclusiveness – 'My three are all completely different and the school is brilliant for all of them'. Most day pupils live locally and are the, mostly, comfortably-off, ethnically mixed,

professional families you'd expect in this prosperous part of north west London. Active Parents' Association – clearly very popular.

Most Mount students based abroad but it could also be an option for recently relocated families, for local or other UK pupils whose education has, for any reason, been interrupted eg by sports prowess, filming, illness etc because of the flexibility and the intensive courses it offers.

Entrance: At 13+, 80 come up each year from linked prep Belmont, which means 70 places available for outsiders. However, places now offered in years 6 and 7 at Belmont – the prep school is expanding, particularly in hopes of attracting girls. Entry to the senior school from Belmont is not competitive so well worth investigating. Computer-based pre-testing in year 6 for external 13+ Mill Hill applicants in reading comprehension, verbal, non-verbal and numerical reasoning plus group activities and interview. Places also available via year 8 exams in maths, English, science, French and Latin (if learned) plus interview and report; 14+ places tested similarly.

At 16+, 22+ places available and candidates need at least two 7s and three 6s at GCSE.

Exit: Uncompromising chucking out post-GCSEs of those who didn't make the grade stopped by Previous head on arrival. At least two 7s and three 6s expected but there is flexibility – as there should be – for those who otherwise make a strong contribution to school life. We find this so heartening – not every school should be trying only to cater for the super-bright. Most of us aren't. Post-A level, one of the most impressively diverse list of leavers' destinations – in terms both of course and university – that we've seen. This suggests a real focus on developing the individual and not turning out an identikit product – we like this. Three off to Cambridge in 2018 (history, engineering and human, social and political science).

The list of notable Mill Hill alumni is equally multi-lateral: actors Jasper Britton, Patrick Troughton (Dr Who mk 2), Harry Melling (Dudley Dursley); Richard Dimbleby and Simon Jenkins; Francis Crick, Norman Hartnell, Bob Marshall-Andrews, Tanika Gupta and Dennis Thatcher.

Around 50 per cent from The Mount move to Mill Hill main school after, usually, a year. Some stay at The Mount for years 10 and 11. The rest to, mostly, other boarding schools better suited to their needs.

Money matters: More than 10 per cent of pupils receive some level of fee assistance and some few are on 100 per cent fee remission. Scholarships in academics, sports, arts all worth 10 per cent of fees – but bursaries available which can contribute, in a few cases, up to 100 per cent of the remainder. Three 100 per cent sixth form bursaries. Hardship fund may see you through short-term liquidity problems. 'Thorough' and regular means-testing, of course. Numerous smaller awards bring kudos and Mars Bar money. Some interesting one-offs eg The Grinton award – a senior school scholarship for a girl boarder who wants to study art and The Donald Hall award for someone who wants to take sixth form science.

Remarks: 'My school is a place where you can express yourself and do anything,' we were told. Spot on. Set to regain its pre-eminence in this part of the world, wider still and wider.

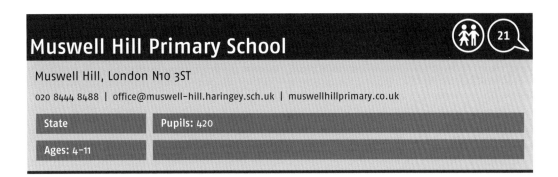

Muswell Hill Primary School

Muswell Hill, London N10 3ST

020 8444 8488 | office@muswell-hill.haringey.sch.uk | muswellhillprimary.co.uk

State	Pupils: 420
Ages: 4–11	

Head: Since September 2018, Mandi Howells, previously deputy head of Carlton Primary School, where she taught since 1996.

Entrance: One of the most heavily oversubscribed primaries in the borough (approaching 600 applicants for 60 places). Having a sibling already at the school or living nearby are the two quickest ways through the gates, but 'near' means very, less than a quarter of mile if you want a realistic chance.

Exit: The school sits midway between two of north London's best comprehensives, so why consider anywhere else is the general parental view. Most leavers proceed to Fortismere, a few to Alexandra Park. A trickle, 'for those who live in funny roads', to independents, plus a few to various sought-after nearby grammar schools.

Remarks: Its last full Ofsted (2006) deemed this an outstanding primary, and there's little evidence this view should change. Results in year 6 remain rock solid. Teachers are a happy mix of experience and enthusiasm; most are in their 30s, with a healthy sprinkling of men. 'We're very happy with the teachers,' said one parent. 'They're very approachable and supportive.' The new management structure (giving responsibility for a number of year groups to three assistant heads) means classroom time is always in the hands of a qualified teacher (and parents have 'a point of contact' for concerns, gripes, etc).

Children eased gently into school life with parents allowed to stay in the early days. Good support for the basics, too, with an informative 'phonics workshop' for those unfamiliar with the jargon. French from year 3 (but 'only a little'). Good ICT, with plenty of coding. Science skills developed beyond the curriculum with final year pupils introduced to secondary school methods with classes at Fortismere. Philosophy, reasoning and 'reflection' from reception. Regular homework, with daily reading, weekly maths and spelling, plus 'the odd project'. Comprehensive special needs strategy overseen by a SENCo, aided by learning support assistants in each class and out-of-school specialists when required.

The visual arts important here – 'There's a lot of focus on art,' said one parent. As well as the standard fare, there's an arts week, art award, and involvement with a 'working' artist. School orchestra and choir (both provided in after-school clubs).

An attractive, well-equipped playground for the youngest, good-sized courts and extensive running-around space (dotted with picnic tables) for their elders

Sport 'huge'. Netball, rugby, dance, cricket, gymnastics, basketball, athletics and hockey all on offer, with external specialists honing skills to a high standard and plenty in the way of inter-school competition ('The trophy cabinet's not big enough for the trophies we've received,' says the head). But, if winning is the aim, the attitude remains inclusive. 'Football Friday' fields eight teams and eight groups of supporters (plus appropriate team shirts) and regs require three girls from each team to be on the pitch at all times. Good range of well-organised after-school clubs, from cheerleading and chess, to cooking and capoeira. (Paid for) before- and after-school clubs extend the school day for working parents.

Formed by the merger of an infant and junior school in 2000, the school now occupies an army camp of 60s low-rise buildings. Located on the site of what was once Muswell Hill Railway Station, there's lavish outside space, with an attractive, well-equipped playground for the youngest, good-sized courts and extensive running-around space (dotted with picnic tables) for their elders, plus a delightful wooded area and wildlife garden.

'Joy, discovery and diversity' are the defining themes of schooldays here, and parents agree that this is 'a really nurturing' place. Reasonably relaxed in a north London way, so no uniform. ('It's quite liberal, but I like that,' said one mum). Generally 'millennial' in approach, so clothes recycling point on site and pupils encouraged to walk to school. Broad cross-section of ethnicity and income, but the prevailing mood solidly middle class. ('It would be lovely to go for ice cream; let's find a date.') Fundraising, too, tends to reflect the area, with a concert of Vivaldi's Four Seasons a recent moneyspinner.

Generally a friendly, upbeat place, with parents bonding in the active PTA, which raises funds through a multitude of events, from quiz evenings and cake sales to fairs and fireworks night. Also active gardening and nature groups involved in 'site development'. 'It's a very nice community and I've made some very good friends.'

Produces articulate, confident children, who enjoy their time at school. 'My son looks forward to school every day.'

Palmers Green High School

104 Hoppers Road, London N21 3LJ

020 8886 1135 | office@pghs.co.uk | pghs.co.uk

Independent	Pupils: 260
Ages: 3–16	Fees: £11,130 – £15,930 pa

Headmistress: Since January 2017, Wendy Kempster (50s) BSc PGCE. Originally from North Wales, Mrs Kempster studied maths at Reading University, where she went on to do her PGCE. Taught in Reading and Bristol, before moving north and taking time out when her children were young. Previously deputy head of Loughborough High, and assistant head and head of maths at Nottingham Girls' High. Attracted to PGHS because of the opportunity to know every girl: 'You can't do that in a school of 600 or 700.' Trained as an ISI inspector and an accredited advanced skills teacher, she's also been a school governor for over 15 years. Married to a fellow educator, she has three grown sons (all qualified or soon-to-be qualified as doctors). Enjoys singing, running, cycling, swimming, tennis – and mountains. 'I'm a country girl at heart, and every holiday I'm off to the mountains in the Lake District.' Down to earth and experienced, she appears to be keeping PGHS on a firm course and leading it to new heights.

Academic matters: The Sunday Times recently ranked Palmers Green in the top five small independent schools (though it has frequently hit the no 1 spot), and, its 2018 GCSE results bore out this accolade, with 79 per cent of I/GCSEs marked A*-A/9-7. Single class of about 25 in each year group ensures all girls get plenty of attention, and most make 'exceptional' progress at every stage from reception to GCSE. Parents particularly welcome specialist subject teaching (in art, DT, ICT, drama, PE and music) more-or-less from the get-go, with junior pupils sharing senior-school facilities.

Girls currently sit a mix of GCSEs and IGCSEs, depending on which exams the schools feels will best prepare them for A levels, and perform particularly well in maths, modern languages and all three sciences (where they are encouraged to reach high with lots of in-class and external enrichment, including visits from engineers and the RAF). Plenty of extra help, too, in a wide range of academic 'sugeries'.

French introduced in year 3, and year 5s enjoy a taster of Latin, German and Russian. French and Spanish on offer at IGCSE (with the option to take one or both).

Teaching, by well-qualified staff, strong throughout. 'Everything is very well managed,' said one mother. 'Pupils are happy and enjoy what they're doing in class. The teachers are nice, too, friendly and experienced.'

Learning difficulties tend to be mild, primarily dyslexia and a small number of autistic spectrum disorders. Support given in lessons ('Every member of staff has a teaching strategy to help girls,' says the head. 'We make sure the provision is not nebulous') with external specialists introduced as required. Extra classes before and after school and one-to-one tuition also available (sometimes at an extra charge). New push to stretch the able, gifted and talented.

Games, options, the arts: Not much in the way of outside space (a decent-sized yard, and an attractive early years playground) and limited numbers mean putting B and C teams together can be a challenge, so possibly not the best home for the super sporty. That said, as the head notes, 'The advantage of a small school is that everyone gets a chance to play in a team', and the school runs competitive teams in several sports, including netball and cross-country. All study gymnastics and dance on a half-term rota in the school hall, with outdoor games (netball, football, rounders, tennis and athletics) and swimming at grounds a short coach journey away. In addition, years 10 and 11 travel enjoy the facilities of a nearby leisure centre for trampolining, basketball, volleyball, aerobics, spinning and circuits. Wide range of sports clubs (netball, gym, fitness, yoga, rounders, tennis, football, athletics), too, and support given to those who wish to pursue a talent (such as ice skating) outside of school.

Artwork impressive, taught by a dynamic head of art, and girls pushed to achieve in everything from monoprinting to experimental work. About half take GCSE art, and many inspired to develop skills further in after-school art club. Recently refurbished and well-equipped music room. Timetabled instrumental lessons (clarinet, saxophone, flute, piano, singing, violin and viola, plus other options if requested). Girls given plenty of opportunity to perform in junior and senior school orchestras, four choirs, instrumental groups (recorder, violin, and woodwind) and a rock band club. A highlight of the calendar is the (highly competitive) annual house choral competition. Drama a popular GCSE option and junior school (including all year 6) star in annual play. DT has its own workshop with excellent facilities (3D printers, CAD etc), where girls in the junior school are taught in half-class groups, making everything from toy cars to fairground attractions.

Over 80 weekly clubs (before and after school and at lunch-time), including book club, debating (with inter-house competitions), ICT, literary society, film skool (sic), LAMDA exams and knitting. Most take D of E bronze. Lively range of visits (Science Museum, Downing Street, The Guardian), and visitors (Onatti Spanish Theatre, author talks, professional parental insight from parents who are dentists, doctors etc), plus residential trips (skiing in Italy, year 5 to Flatford Mill, year 7 bonding at PGL). 'The school provides a really rounded education,' said one parent. Well-stocked recently refurbished library offers an inviting place to read and study. Strong careers programme from the start of senior school. 'Because girls move on in the sixth form, we have to focus on this much earlier than other schools,' says the head, and all expected to undertake work experience in year 11.

'I'm a country girl at heart, and every holiday I'm off to the mountains.' Down to earth and experienced, she appears to be leading PGHS to new heights

Lunch, freshly cooked on site, is seasonal, farm-assured and free range, and includes a vegetarian option and sandwiches.

Background and atmosphere: Founded in 1905, by Miss Alice Hum, with just 12 pupils, by 1918 the school had expanded to 300 and moved to its present site. New classrooms and a dining hall added in the 60s and 90s, and the Elizabeth Smith Hall more recently to provide an additional venue for assemblies, workshops and exams. Despite its age, the school seems bright, modern and well kept, and the compact site makes it girl-friendly and intimate. Purpose-built PGHS nursery housed in its own building about a mile away.

The school's values are rooted in Miss Hum's Quaker beliefs – 'By Love Serve One Another' – and a recent survey of student opinion found an unusually harmonious and caring atmosphere. ('The girls comfort you with kindness and help you if you are stuck,' said one.) Girls, educated here for a long stretch, consider it a home away from home ('PGHS is like a second family to me,' said one year 6), and make regular return visits even after they've moved on. 'They love coming back,' says the head. 'They've been here longer than anywhere else and know they'll always be a Palmers Green girl.'

Today, the school is very much multi-faith (though traditional hymn books still in use, and carol service held annually in St John's Church, Palmers Green), but making a contribution remains important. PGHS shares adventures (such as the loan of Moon Rocks from NASA and study skills days) with local primaries.

PGHS is one of the last remaining girls'-only independent secondary schools in the area and head is a firm advocate of what single-sex can offer, giving girls the confidence to be themselves and achieve. ('When I was at school, they used to say, why do you want to do maths? That's not a girls' subject.')

Former pupils include Palmers Green legend, poet Stevie Smith, and actress Dame Flora Robson; more recently, telly stars Kathryn and Megan Prescott, award-winning poet Imani Shola, Lucy Collins, the first female naval submariner, and prima ballerina Marion Tait.

Pastoral care, well-being and discipline: The school's small scale means there's little danger of problems getting overlooked. 'We know everyone and there's no place to hide physically or emotionally,' says the head. 'Staff quickly spot if a girl who is normally happy is looking unhappy and pass on their comments straight away.' Teachers operate an open-door policy and pupils feel comfortable asking for help. ('I know I can trust any teacher with my problems, however small,' said one girl in the senior school.) House system creates bonds across the year groups ('Unlike bigger schools, you'll often find year 10s playing with year 7s, just as you would in a family,' says the head) and senior pupils mentor younger groups and take up roles of responsibility as head girl, house captains, prefects, etc. Junior pupils also take on roles of responsibility, while the culture of 'active citizenship' means girls are canvassed on decisions, such as the choice of caterers or the new school uniform (smart navy blazer and pink shirt for seniors, blue pinafores and summer boaters for juniors).

Strong careers programme from the start of senior school. 'Because girls move on in the sixth form, we have to focus on this much earlier than other schools'

Behaviour tends to the excellent. 'We have only very minor disciplinary problems,' says the head, 'and I haven't run a single detention since I arrived.' Mental health, on the other hand, high on her agenda. 'It has become a growing issue because of social media. We don't allow devices in school, which at least gives girls six or seven hours each day contact free.'

Parents comment favourably on the 'nurturing' environment and 'old-fashion values' (girls, for example, leap to their feet when visitors enter a classroom).

An unusually harmonious and caring atmosphere. ('The girls comfort you with kindness and help you if you are stuck,' said one)

Pupils and parents: Parents, from a broad mix of cultures and backgrounds, are not super rich; mostly hardworking professionals, who have similar aspirations for their daughters.

Entrance: Selective, but not quite as intimidatingly so as some other north London options. Many join in nursery, but further official entry points at 4, 7 and 11, plus occasional places elsewhere. Younger applicants are sifted on the basis of 'ability and aptitude'; at 11, tests in English, maths, and reasoning, followed by interviews for those who perform well. All current junior pupils sit 11+ alongside outsiders, but almost all proceed seamlessly to the senior school. 'Only very occasionally do we suggest to a parent that they consider another school,' says the head. Some preference given to siblings, but entry not automatic. 'We don't want a child to be out of their depth or unhappy.'

Exit: PGHS sees itself very much as an all-through nursery-16 school. 'We view it as a journey,' says the head, 'and we're very candid that, as a through school, we don't offer specific preparation for 11+.' Nonetheless, teaching and curriculum mean girls are very well prepared and some do move on at this stage, when parents are often looking for selective state options (Latymer, Dame Alice Owen's, Henrietta Barnett, etc). In year 11, girls carefully advised and guided in their choice of sixth form, when again, they tend to favour the state (Woodhouse College particularly fashionable at the moment among the usual spectrum), but independents (North London Collegiate, Highgate, Aldenham, City of London, St Alban's High School for Girls, Haileybury, Haberdashers' Girls) also well represented.

Money matters: Fees definitely on the good-value side. Scholarships at 11 to current pupils and incomers. Limited number of bursaries of up to 100 per cent, plus music awards (minimum grade 4 required), which fund lessons on one or two instruments.

Remarks: A small, friendly and nurturing school, providing a rounded education, with old fashioned values, and an excellent academic record that prepares girls extremely well to move on at sixth form.

Queen Elizabeth's Girls' School

High Street, Barnet, Hertfordshire EN5 5RR

020 8449 2984 | office@qegschool.org.uk | qegschool.org.uk

State	Pupils: 1,015; sixth form: 128
Ages: 11–18	

Headteacher: Since 2015, Violet Walker BSc (UCL), MA (Brunel), NPQH (50s). When Mrs Walker arrived as head at QE Girls, she must have felt she was returning home. Not only did she attend the school as a pupil in the 70s, she spent time here as part of her training as a maths teacher in the early 2000s. Before qualifying as a teacher, however, she had a pursued a number of other routes, qualifying and practising as both an accountant and a psychotherapist. Once launched in the profession, she rose rapidly, working as assistant head at Park High School, Harrow, and, most recently, as deputy head of Northolt High School for Girls (which she helped move on from special measures). Clearly seen as a 'safe pair of hands', her aim at QE Girls has been 'to marry the sense of tradition and what might be thought the old-fashioned values of my days with the very best of the latest in education.' This ambition has already been realised in a calm and competent fashion, and, since her arrival, the school's seen a rapid turn round of its academic fortunes. Both parents and pupils acknowledge her impact. 'The head seems a lot more in control,' said one mother. 'She really has her finger on the pulse,' commented another. A firm believer in what girls'-only education can offer, she acts as a coach for Women in Leadership, and her ambitions are 'for QE to be recognised as an outstanding school' and 'for girls to love school'.

Academic matters: In 2014, the school experienced a major shock when standards at this traditional high-flyer were called into question by Ofsted. Since then, a new head and a new Ofsted inspection have indicated the road to recovery is fully underway, with excellent recent results. At GCSE in 2018, 36 per cent of grades 9-7; at A level 25 per cent A*-A, 55 per cent A*-B. QE Girls is also now officially recognised as providing outstanding 'value added', with progress as well as achievement far above average. Teaching weaknesses (particularly of the most disadvantaged) have been resolved, with a raft of new appointments and energetic monitoring.

Girls enter year 7 from a wide range of local primaries and are quickly melded into a cohesive seven forms of 25-26. All study a largely academic curriculum, with most taking GCSEs in English, maths, science, at least one modern foreign language, history or geography plus an expressive art or technology subject. (They also study IT, RE, PE, PSHE.) Some career-oriented options, too, such as business studies and BTec in health and social care.

Teachers (including quite a few men) are enthusiastic, professional and popular. 'The teachers are really nice and you always feel comfortable going to ask for help' was a refrain heard repeatedly from girls across the age range.

Maths taught in sets from year 7 and maths and science (which came in for particularly criticism in 2014) are definitely on the up, with Ofsted praising the improvement for the middle ground. Not all parents, however, are entirely convinced by the transition arrangements. 'There has been a high turnover of maths teachers,' said one. 'My daughter finds that quite difficult as every teacher has a particular way of explaining things. Sometimes, she's just given worksheets and left to do them.' Science taught in a range of well-equipped labs, but no pressure to take all three (biology, physics, chemistry) to GCSE. 'You can go on to do medicine or science with double award,' said one teacher, 'so we generally only encourage those who really like science to do three.'

For many parents – and girls – the fact that it is single sex is also a definite plus. 'No annoying boys,' said one pupil succinctly

All start Spanish in year 7 and top-set linguists take up French in year 8 (with the option to continue with two languages to GCSE). Official praise for English, humanities and drama at GCSE, and DT gets the thumbs up from pupils – with girls enjoying the wide-ranging subject matter, which includes food ('I've just learnt how to cook a quiche,' said one enthusiast, 'and I'm going home to make another tonight'), metalwork, textiles and woodwork. Girls seem to flourish in what is often considered masculine terrain, and, according to a teacher who has taught in both single sex and co-ed schools, comfortably take on tasks they might have shied away from elsewhere.

Widening range of post-GCSE options (26), including business studies, DT, drama, media studies, music tech, further maths, psychology, philosophy, government and politics, photography and sociology. Also now offers a BTec in health and social care. The Extended Project Qualification (EPQ), which universities welcome for the way it fosters research skills, has also been widely embraced, with most of those taking it gaining A*-A. Sixth form class sizes are small (often under 10) and girls get close personal supervision from a 'pastoral mentor', a specialist in one of their chosen subjects. Good careers and university advice (including for Oxbridge and international options, though currently not many heading in these directions.)

Her aim has been 'to marry the sense of tradition and what might be thought the old-fashioned values of my days with the very best of the latest in education'

Well-resourced facilities for SEN with dedicated space and well-targeted support overseen by a SENCo and senior learning mentor. 'My daughter was struggling in English and I found the school very pro-active,' said one mother. 'They identified her problem and gave her extra help, which not only improved her work but boosted her confidence.'

Games, options, the arts: Extracurricular as well as curricular drama highly popular, with girls auditioning enthusiastically for speaking parts or stage management roles in the annual production (recently Peter Pan). Art and textiles demonstrate imagination and skill, and broad range of in-lunch and after-school clubs provide additional opportunities for sports fans (netball, boot camp, hockey, yoga, football), budding intellectuals (Reading the Classics, Scrabble) and creatives (LAMDA, jazz band, fashion show club and film club). ' I have decided to work in film,' announced one year 9, who'd recently launched her debut work. Excellent facilities for sport, with large on-site pool and gym, eight tennis courts and ample grounds for running around (or simply lounging). Teams and individuals compete at borough and county level, performing particularly well in athletics. Variety of choirs, orchestra

and bands (jazz, drumming, guitar, etc). Good range of trips and visits (PE to the Alps, English to Copenhagen, modern foreign languages to Spain) and all take part in an enrichment programme and work experience in year 12. Well-stocked library staffed by knowledgeable librarians. (Popular Accelerated Reader Scheme encourages reading more and reading more broadly.) Confidence also boosted by participation in the Jack Petchey's Speak Out Challenge.

Background and atmosphere: QE Girls traces its roots back to Elizabeth 1, when Robert Dudley, Earl of Leicester, requested a charter for 'the education, bringing up and instruction' of boys, and – at a future date – a school for girls. The boys' school was founded in 1573, the girls had to wait until 1888, when a small school of just 40 girls was eventually opened. Once a grammar school, the school went comprehensive in 1973.

One of the oldest girls' state schools in the country, it still enjoys the county council-funded building of 1909, but this has now been joined by a myriad of later additions (many erected in the 60s), plus general updating, replacing (after a fire), and extending to adapt to increasing numbers and new requirements. Very good facilities include an array of well-equipped science labs, technology rooms, drama studio, sixth form common room, spacious dining hall (with attractive views, outdoor snack bar and the latest thumbprint technology for cashless payment). The beautiful and extensive gardens are also a definite asset. Sixth formers have their own common room and silent study centre in the library.

Pastoral care, well-being and discipline: The school's stated goals are: to produce confident, independent, self-disciplined and considerate young women in an atmosphere that is calm, careful and purposeful, and they seem to be well on the way to delivering this outcome. In general, pupils are keen, articulate and poised. Though there will always be the odd disruptive force (and the odd exclusion), in general girls are well behaved and well mannered. 'I watch them going in and coming out,' said one parent. 'They always seem very well behaved, with teachers standing by to make sure they are.' Guidelines on behaviour are now firmer ('It's much stricter than it used to be,' commented one girl) but certainly not draconian. 'They let parents know if there's an issue, but they're not heavy handed about it.' Girls seem to enjoy the school very much and have excellent relationships with each other and teachers. For many parents – and girls – the fact that it is single sex is also a definite plus. 'No annoying boys, ' said one pupil succinctly.

Plenty of leadership roles in the sixth form (head girl, two deputies, designated senior prefects for student council, charity, sport, library, sustainability). Sixth formers also mentor younger girls, running clubs, supporting in lessons and acting as reading mentors, which provides a strong sense of cohesion across the school. The head is also a firm believer in preparing girls for the world of work, and as well as her own involvement with Women of the Future Ambassadors programme, ensures pupils have the opportunity to attend networking events with high-achieving women.

Pupils and parents: QE Girls sits in a leafy, primarily middle-class commuter suburb, and its intake is a fair reflection of its surroundings (though it also addresses the needs of a large nearby estate). This is north London, of course, so a rich ethnic mix, with school and parents celebrating diversity. 'For me, one of its main attractions is that there are people from all walks of life,' said one mother. Parents generally attentive and involved, with an energetic PTA organising a regular calendar of quiz nights, raffles, etc. Former pupils include Jane Duncan, president of the RIBA, singer Phildel, actress Stephanie Beacham and writer Anne Thwaite.

Entrance: A non-selective comprehensive, oversubscribed by about three to one at 11, when 180 girls are admitted using Barnet's 'community' criteria (looked-after children, then siblings, then distance from the gates). Very much a local school, many parents choose it because of its 'walkability', though transport links are also excellent with the tube just a minute away. Sixth-form admits a maximum of 25 new students depending on subject availability (and a GCSE point average of 5.5).

Exit: About half of those who enter at 11 proceed to the sixth form, often declaring how comfortable and happy they feel at the school. At that point, the rest tend to float off to co-ed comps and sixth-form colleges (Fortismere, Barnet College, etc). Virtually all those who remain gain entry to their first or second choice university. About a third to Russell Group, the rest to the full spectrum of higher education. (Popular destinations include: King's London, Brunel, Essex, Bristol, Leeds, University of Hertfordshire.)

> *Wide-ranging subject matter, which includes food ('I've just learnt how to cook a quiche,' said one enthusiast, 'and I'm going home to make another tonight')*

Encouragingly broad range of subject choice, too, from aerospace engineering, marine biology and mechanical engineering, to economics, law, graphic design and optometry. One medic and one vet in 2018. A few to high-level apprenticeships.

Money matters: Funds from the original endowment still benefit the school, providing financial aid for those who could not otherwise afford it to participate in activities and support for small capital projects (such as the 2016 Upper Courtyard redevelopment). PTA-raised funds (£10 a month is politely suggested) contribute to desirable extras like school minibuses, picnic areas in the grounds and ICT equipment.

Remarks: A relaxed, safe and friendly place, now with a firm hand on the tiller and rocketing results.

Queen Elizabeth's School, Barnet

Queen's Road, Barnet, Hertfordshire EN5 4DQ

020 8441 4646 | enquiries@qebarnet.co.uk | qebarnet.co.uk

State	Pupils: 1,235; sixth form: 310
Ages: 11–18	

Headmaster: Since 2011, Neil Enright MA (Oxon) MBA NPQH FRSA (40). Educated at St John's College, Oxford, and has worked here since 2002, rising to become head of department (humanities – a geographer), head of year, deputy head. MBA in 2010 from the University of London Institute of Education, which focused on aspects of leadership, management and systems of effective learning.

Gives a knuckle-crunching handshake and oozes authority, but is cordial, jovial and empathetic. Pupils admit they sit or stand up that bit straighter when he's around, 'but more because we want to impress him than assuming we'll be told off.' Tellingly, one of the first things he did was put a huge glass window between his (more company boardroom than headmasterly) office and the corridor, with pupils encouraged to drop in with any concerns. Although not a timetabled teacher ('the demands of my job don't allow it'), he takes geography lessons across all year groups when he can.

Converses easily with the boys, always eats in the dining hall at lunchtimes, attends every school event and has even been known to hang around at the bus stop after school to chat. Runs a very tight ship, with a well distributed leadership model. Areas of focus include driving innovation in the classroom and pastoral care.

Academic matters: Consistently top of the academic league tables, rivalling most schools, independent or state, in its exam results. Baseline assessment in year 7, then setting in all subjects (including sport), with half-termly tests thereafter. Testing very much part of the modus operandi. Many parents put off applying for fear of the stress (one parent told us she took her son out because 'the pressure was just too much'), but the school has heaps of motivational mechanisms in place, including personal tutors, who they see twice a day in groups, as well as having a one-to-one sessions every half term. Coaching and mentoring (including peer mentoring) also the norm. 'I arrived with good grades, but was a bit of a slacker, and the school soon sorted me out,' one pupil told us. Others talk about being 'carried along with the collective will to learn.' It also helps that hard grafting is admired, said another parent. 'In a lot of schools, you get teased for trying, but nobody's called a geek here. In fact, they somehow turn it around so that the boys look up to each other and respect others for trying hard in something, whether it's their subject or not.'

'I arrived with good grades, but was a bit of a slacker, and the school soon sorted me out,' one pupil told us

---

In 2018, 91 per cent 9-7 grades. Languages popular, with all pupils taking French, German and Latin from year 7 and continuing one modern language (at least) at GCSE, with Mandarin, Spanish and ancient Greek offered as extras. First school to become 100 per cent EBacc. A level choices are decided by tests in years 10 and 11 designed 'to tease out' aptitude. 'We don't rate GSCE results as a good

enough indicator,' explains head. Seventy per cent of boys do four A levels, most get four A*/A grades (83 per cent of grades were A*/A in 2018); only a handful don't take maths, two-thirds some science, many do a mix. No fluffy options whatsoever.

Arts facilities light and airy, with exceptional examples of mostly abstract work displayed throughout the school, including some choice pieces adoring the head's office

---

Strong teaching, with good gender balance, in every department. 'They go well beyond the syllabus and really care about you enjoying the subject and doing well,' said one pupil, with boys particularly enthusiastic about geography and history. 'Every lesson aims to push these boys up to their ceiling, which is made easier when there's such a narrow ability range,' says head. Boys say healthy competition pervades the classroom as much as the sports field, but there's plenty of group work, with many classes we visited organised with desks in clusters rather than in neat rows. Class sizes around 30, dropping to 15 at A level. Lots of homework (one and a half hours in year 7, one hour per subject per night at A level). Technology embedded in lessons, but not much use of tablets.

Enrichment throughout, with boys regularly taken off curriculum, and extra-long lunch breaks allowing for the myriad of clubs that also run before and after school (favourites include public speaking, karate and sports). Some clubs pupil-led, including an impressive politics one, with recent guest speakers including Vince Cable and Alistair Campbell. An expectation to do the Extended Project Qualification, with subjects ranging from photography to ancient history. Big push on symposia with high-performing girls' schools, including Henrietta Barnett, St Albans High School and North London Collegiate. 'Whilst there are huge benefits to boys learning in an all-male environment, boys also need to be able to work with young women,' says head.

Special needs at this school tends to be on the gifted-and-talented end of the spectrum, although school can accommodate mild autism, Asperger's and dyslexia and every department runs subject-specific clinics to support the struggling and challenge the most able. 'Because difference tends to be celebrated at this school, and the learning is so tailored anyway, our son's special needs have really been a non-issue in terms of his education,' said one parent.

The Henrietta Barnett School

Games, options, the arts: Rugby by far the strongest sport, with all participating in year 7. Fixtures list includes all major independent schools in the region. England under-16 head coach coaches the rugby squad and the school fields up to D teams on a regular basis. Rugby 7s has also been running since 1976, with school playing against 64 others, including Eton. Swimming, Eton fives, tennis, badminton, basketball, cross-country and fencing also popular. Plenty of county and national representation in bridge, chess and water polo. Eight-lane swimming pool, all-weather tennis courts, multi-gym and plenty of neatly trimmed green fields for team sports. But it's no big deal not to have sporting prowess in the obvious options, say students. 'I didn't like any of them, but have found I really do like tennis and swimming,' said one old boy.

Music department boasts three full-time music teachers, 17 peripatetic teachers and a music suite where boys can study A level music technology with all the latest recording equipment. Particularly strong orchestra and choir, both of which are open to all, plus chamber choir and ensembles, including Indian music, which boys run themselves.

Notable visual arts facilities, all open-plan, light and airy, with exceptional examples of mostly abstract work displayed throughout the school, including some choice pieces adoring the head's smart office. DT boasts all the latest equipment, with one pupil designing and making his own drone when we visited. Generally an academic attitude towards art, with many pupils interested in pursuing architecture.

Strong teaching, with good gender balance, in every department. 'They go well beyond the syllabus and really care about you enjoying the subject and doing well'

Whole school drama performances take place in Shirley Hall, which has a decent sized stage and 400 drop-down seats (otherwise flat against wall when the hall is used for low-impact sports). New spacious food technology facility.

Name a country and there's probably been a trip there. Recent rugby tour to Sri Lanka, geography trips to Iceland, Switzerland and Sicily, music tours all over Europe, plus well-established language exchanges to Germany and France and set trips to battlefields, among others. Head keen that it's not always the same boys benefiting, either due to cost or ability.

Background and atmosphere: Plenty of visual reminders around the school that it was founded in 1573 by Robert, Earl of Leicester, with a charter from Elizabeth I. Rebuilt in 1932 by Hertfordshire County Council in a noble civic style with terrazzo flooring, parquet and panelling, all kept in spotless condition. Still well-endowed with land held in perpetuity and its own Foundation Trustees, QE went comprehensive in the '60s, reverted to grant-maintained status in 1989 and became a grammar school once more in 1994.

Atmosphere is ordered, focused and positive and even at break times, there's no casual loitering. At lunchtime, for example, boys wolf down their lunch so they can fit in football or other activities before attending a lunchtime club. Meanwhile, in class, boys are absorbed and single-minded. You'll find no low-level disruption here.

Leadership responsibilities from year 11, when own suits are allowed. Ninety prefects voted for by staff and students, monitor lunch (fresh food produced daily), playgrounds and classrooms. School captain and house captains appointed from on high. Student voice heard through pupil conferences. Boys also involved in appointing new staff by attending a class, then giving feedback.

A 15-year estate strategy means there are always plans in place around buildings. Among the newest additions is a spacious new library, with 100 computer terminals and 15,000 books when we visited. 'When other school librarians tell me they struggle attracting pupils in their library, I'm amazed,' the librarian told us. 'Ours is so popular that we practically have to fend them off at lunchtimes.'

Café 1573 provides a Starbucks-like environment for sixth formers, whilst other years frequent the dining hall, a modern space also with its own branding and colour scheme. School even has its own (cashless) shop, selling everything from uniforms (much lower cost than in shops) to pens, with all profits ploughed back into the school.

'Pupil progression' (broader and less vocational than careers advice) embedded throughout, whilst loyal old boys come back to chat to sixth formers about university and subject choice. Some act as Oxbridge buddies for the next generation. Big programme of volunteering, with all sixth formers expected to do 40 hours over the school year (although most do much more), including working in libraries, charity shops, hospices, charity shops and even supporting the local MP's surgery.

Pastoral care, well-being and discipline: Pastoral care mainly from form teachers, and a real strength of the school's provision. Motivation comes from a plethora of rewards and praise, including house points, certificates, merit stickers (for younger boys), congratulatory emails and postcards sent home to parents, showcasing of achievements on the website and 'good notes' in the diary which must be signed off by parents (there are 'bad notes' too for offences such as persistent failure to meet deadlines, but these are far less frequent). Plenty of silverware prominently displayed to remind pupils of the school's achievements.

'When other school librarians tell me they struggle attracting pupils into their library, I'm amazed'

No real misbehaviour to speak of – pupils have good manners, wear their uniform well, and do their work when asked. Head puts it down to clear expectations, a strong sense of discipline that feels natural rather than forced, and rewards. 'Not the kind of school for boys who don't like taking orders or challenging the system,' said one parent. Indeed, there are fixed-term exclusions for persistent 'failure to carry out school protocols' or misbehaving in lessons and head says he would expel a boy on the spot for offences including violence aimed at staff, consciously creating racial disharmony or bringing drugs into school, although no boy has been expelled in his time. 'We make absolutely no exceptions and that message is very clear,' he says.

Pupils and parents: Contrary to popular opinion, this school is not full of middle-class families. Ofsted noted it's the national average in terms of deprivation, with quite a few boys in receipt of pupil premium. 'We take great pride in the fact that the school is a complete meritocracy,' says head. 'There is absolutely no other means of gaining admission than doing well in the test for maths and English.' Over 80 per cent of boys come from ethnic minorities, predominantly Asian. Around half speak English as a second language, although they're advanced bilingual learners and generally only need help with areas like idiom and inference, which the school happily provides. Many of the boys who make it to Oxbridge are the first generation in their family to go to university, and in recent years one was a refugee from Rwanda. Majority travel from London borough of Barnet, although there are boys from all over north west London and the surrounding home counties, who are served by good public transport links and a nine-strong coach system facilitated by the school. Pupils are quietly confident, grounded, polite and exude intelligence.

Parents are considered as key partners of the school, regularly communicated with via pupils' diaries, live reporting on the website and emails. 'I've never experienced a parents' association like it,' adds head of Friends of Queen Elizabeth, with parents doing everything from providing work experience and mock interviews to giving lectures, supporting concerts and fundraising. 'The annual Founders' Day Fete raises up to £25,000 and has parents taking the day off work the Friday before to help prepare,' says head, although a couple of parents told us it's 'unfortunately the same old faces that tend to help.'

Entrance: More than 2,300 boys apply for 180 places. Tests in September (register between May and mid-July), which although tough are made as comfortable as possible, with year 9s present to put applicants at ease, 'including playing hangman'. Boys told whether or not they have met the 'standard required' before they have to make their choice of schools, so they have nothing to lose by taking the test. NB Meeting the 'standard required' does not guarantee a place. Pupils come from around 90 primary schools, but the ability range is narrow, with most in the top 10 per cent nationally. Occasional vacancies between years 7 and 10, offered to those on the waiting list. No sixth form entry for external candidates. 'I see this as a seven-year education,' says head, who adds that he's seen too many schools that take external sixth formers essentially run as two separate schools. Automatic transfer to sixth form for nearly all students, although pupils have to be recommended for individual subjects.

Exit: Up to 15 per cent of boys leave after GCSE. Reasons include not making the grade; preferring a mixed sixth form; hankering after a more relaxed environment; looking for subjects the school doesn't teach, such as law and psychology; or winning scholarships to independent schools (although that's rare – most families pick this school over the private sector). Almost all who stay go on to top Russell Group universities, notably Nottingham, Imperial, UCL and Warwick. In 2018, 28 to Oxbridge, and 19 off to study medicine, plus one veterinary medicine. Typical subjects include economics, law, engineering and medicine. First-rate UCAS guidance provided to all boys.

Money matters: You wouldn't know it, walking around the school, but there's minimal state aid, with head saying he gets less money than many local comps. Gaps are filled with a voluntary £60 a month contribution from parents, funds from the Foundation and donations from parents, old boys and friends.

Remarks: A remarkable school that offers the top 10 per cent of learners from a diversity of backgrounds an exceptional and rounded education that even private schools struggle to compete with. Not for boys who may want to challenge the status quo, nor for the non-competitive. But for those who thrive in a highly ordered, hard grafting environment with an underlying sense of competition across all subjects, this is a great school that consistently turns out responsible young men with unbounded opportunities to succeed at university and their chosen careers beyond.

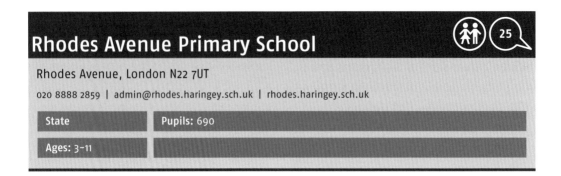

Rhodes Avenue Primary School

Rhodes Avenue, London N22 7UT

020 8888 2859 | admin@rhodes.haringey.sch.uk | rhodes.haringey.sch.uk

State	Pupils: 690
Ages: 3–11	

Headteacher: Since 2015 Mr Adrian Hall BEd (30s). After gaining his degree in primary education from Leeds University, he worked as a reception teacher at Castleton Primary School, then moved up the ranks to his first headship at Churchfield Primary School in Enfield, a post he had for eight years. During this time – in which he worked in a wide range of schools, some in deprived areas – he earned himself an NLE (National Leader in Education) in recognition of his work in supporting not only pupils but also teachers and leaders.

Instantly likeable, he is warm and laid back – a high-fives-in-the-corridor kind of head who wants children to feel comfortable in his presence. 'He's the best head teacher in the world,' one child told us, with others describing him as 'kind,' 'funny' and 'really nice.' 'They hero worship him – and he's a brilliant teacher,' said one parent – indeed he teaches year 4s once a week. But make no mistake – he is also highly efficient and savvy about all things educational, and the policies he's brought in around discipline and punctuality have been unanimously welcomed. 'He improved an already brilliant school – that's no mean feat,' one parent told us.

Parents and pupils alike welcome the fact that he greets them at the school gates every morning. 'Within a week of arriving, he knew every child's name and he always chats to us. What's more, if you put forward an idea, he's on the case. He's an incredible man,' said one parent. Another told us, 'This isn't a school where you don't go to the head because he's the last port of call – he and the teachers are seen as interchangeable. Even if he's not having a good day, he'll find time for you.'

When Mr Hall is not at school, he calls himself a 'water baby at heart' and loves swimming and rafting. He also tries to spend as much time with his family as possible and explore London and the world: 'My son is fearless so we spend many a weekend at theme parks.'

Entrance: Admission by means of the local authority criteria – which means that, in order of priority, it's looked after children and SEN, then siblings and after that, living as near as possible. With four applications for every place, this generally means within a quarter of a mile. Local estate agents are big fans – the success of the school, and its neighbouring comprehensive, has had a significant impact on local property prices.

Exit: The school backs directly on to Alexandra Park, one of the borough's best secondaries, and over half of pupils proceed there. Others to Fortismere and Latymer, with the remainder attending a wide range of schools including JFS, the Compton School, Greek School of London, Channing and Dame Alice Owen's.

Remarks: Undoubtedly helped by the fact that most families live within feet of the gates, this is a school with a true community feel – a vibe that parents say it has managed to retain despite moving to three-form entry of 90. What strikes you as you enter the contemporary buildings (set amongst immaculately kept grounds) is the atmosphere of both fun and of purposefulness – a combination that many primary schools aim for and fail, often spectacularly. If ever there was an argument that schools benefit from great architects, this is it – the interiors meld the original 1930s building with the more recent extensions to create bright, light and modern learning spaces that are a joy to spend time in. The wide, carpeted corridors of the main split-level building are so much more than mere walkways, with private music lessons, art exhibitions etc going on throughout. The classrooms are big and airy, with huge windows – and the spongy-carpeted library is somewhere that several children told us was their 'favourite place.' The art studio is well stocked; ICT suite is up-to-date; and there are two school halls – one purely for PE, while the other is also used for assemblies, lunch and performances. Nursery (now full time) and reception are housed in a single story building that also boasts nice, bright classrooms.

Outside, there are separate soft-ground playgrounds for nursery and reception; years 1-3; and years 4-6 – each well-equipped for the age group in question (younger ones get masses of toys under a large shelter; middle school gets a great climbing frame; older ones get the likes of table football and even a bandstand). And the chickens – a relatively recent addition, which has a nod to the school site's origins as a farm, and which is extremely popular with the children. 'We are lucky,' one of them told us – neatly summing up the pupils' sense of good fortune. They wanted to show off every single nook and cranny to us, revealing what is a clearly a huge sense of ownership and pride in their place of learning.

Teaching staff – who are made up of a good mix of thoroughly experienced and young and enthusiastic teachers – are themselves fun. In every classroom we visited – and in the staffroom too – there was a feeling of merriment, creativity, learning through doing and of getting things done with a smile and a light touch. And it clearly works. The school has for some years consistently dominated the local authority league tables, with reading progress in the top 20 per cent of schools in the country, and writing and maths in the top five per cent. Ofsted can barely think of a word of criticism. Sats results are outstanding, with the majority reaching the highest levels. Though the pupils tend to be of above average ability on entry, everyone we spoke to agrees the school goes above and beyond.

In every classroom – and in the staffroom – there was a feeling of merriment, creativity, learning through doing and getting things done with a smile and a light touch

Children are taught mainly by class teachers, with specialist teachers enhancing areas such as French, art and PE. Parents praise the themed approach to learning – with each year group studying a single topic every half term, with a cross-curricular approach thereon eg year 5's theme was Pole to Pole, when we visited – the history aspect speaks for itself, while in geography they learned about global warming and in English, they explored Shackleton's poems etc. 'You really get to see these themes come to life in the class assemblies,' said one parent – of which each year group or class does one a year.

Academic progress is charted minutely and parents kept well informed, with three parents' evenings and three reports a year. Strong support, too, for the struggling. 'My son has a special literacy person and she's fantastic,' said one parent. French taught from year 2 and 'parlez-vous' is supplemented with fun activities like a French breakfast, croissants included. Setting in years 5 and 6 for maths and English.

Homework is an ongoing debate among parents, with a 50/50 split between those who think there's enough and those who believe there should be more. As with the classroom teaching, there's an emphasis on making it enjoyable and it will often include a visit to somewhere in London, which the child then talks about in class. 'We try to merge home and school life as much as possible as home can be a real place of learning too,' says the head.

An 'inclusion leader' leads SEND, with a separate SEND lead in the early years centre – both cater for not only mild and moderate, but more severe, including pre-verbal and wheelchair using children. Their creative, child-focused support both in and outside the classroom has earned the school an Inclusion Quality Mark. 'My son has a specialist care team because of his needs and they were very impressed by how far the school was prepared to go to ensure he reached his full potential. It's just incredible,' a parent told us, while another said, 'Unlike other schools, they start with the child and adapt the school to them – rather than telling you how you have to fit in.'

Sport, music, art and drama are as high up the agenda as the three Rs and although, in the past, some parents felt that the obvious winners were celebrated to the detriment of the less brilliant, things are changing, with a push on inclusivity. 'We want every child to be able to compete, so we've introduced a squad system for football, for example, whereby 30 children get to compete, instead of the six children in the top team in the old system,' says the head. 'It's working – sport here is much more about participation than it used to be,' a parent told us. Not that the school intends to take a soft-touch approach to sport – indeed, it tends to sweep the board in local competitions, with shelf after shelf of silverware on display in reception. Minimum of two hours of PE a week, which includes netball, gymnastics, athletics and rugby at the core – as well as less obvious options including basketball, boating, golf and handball. Onsite facilities include the two sports halls and outside cage for netball and football, and they use public parkland just behind the school – visible from the head's office – for field sports. There are good links with the local tennis club, and year 4s upwards go swimming at a local public pool.

Drama regularly seeps into English lessons, and there are two extracurricular acting clubs, plus a whole-school Christmas production and class assemblies. Art is popular – with the specialist teacher teaching the likes of sculpting and printing, alongside more traditional art, the results of which are on display during the annual summer exhibition. 'We had to make a fish out of a trash can recently – I thought it would be rubbish, but it was amazing,' one child told us.

Music permeates the culture here, with many of the private music lessons by peripatetic teachers taking place in the corridors ('The real reason we do it is because we're short on private study areas – but the upside of this problem is that it's lovely to walk past the children learning anything from the cello to piano,' says the head). There's an orchestra, chamber choir, school choir and boy band – all of which publically perform – and children sing at the local tube station to raise money for charity at Christmas. Some year groups learn instruments as a whole, with past examples including cello, clarinet, recorder, drums and violin.

Extracurricular clubs include sports (ranging from cross-country to cricket), recorder, Spanish, French, street dance, coding, meditation, sewing, chess, pottery and drama. Lots of competitions entered and usually won, whether that's for the school's abundant and much-loved vegetable garden or for pupils' Christmas card designs. Breakfast club from 7.50am and after-school play centre on site 3.30-6pm, plus holiday clubs. Loads of trips and workshops, all related to the current topic, as well as two activity-based residentials – year 5 to Wales for a weekend and year 6 to Lincolnshire for a week.

Instantly likeable, he is warm and laid back – a high-fives-in-the-corridor kind of head who wants children to feel comfortable in his presence

This is a nurturing school, say parents, with a strong pastoral system, thanks to these key ingredients: class teachers that get to know the children well; deputy head is the lead in this area; school counsellor available one day a week; art therapy sessions available from the specialist art teacher; an open environment, in which children feel able to talk and communicate and feel they can see the head at any time; and a parent gym (in which parents can get support and guidance on issues like bedtime routines and healthy eating). Many parents, as well as the head, also believe that the no-uniform policy is relevant – 'It helps children feel comfortable and that they can really be

themselves,' he says – and although not all parents support it, many come round. One parent said, 'At first I thought, "What will they wear each day?" and where will the sense of identity be around the school? But it's so nice walking in with all those bright colours and you can see it just sets them free. And believe me, there's no shortage of identity in this school. I'm all for it now.'

'We are lucky,' one told us. They wanted to show off every single nook and cranny to us, revealing a huge sense of ownership and pride in their place of learning

Plenty of praise is the recipe for good behaviour – with stickers going a particularly long way. 'By and large, the children's behaviour is immaculate,' says the head – with children saying hello, holding doors open and arriving in the classroom ready to learn. Children who don't follow the 'golden rules' are given 'refection' and if that doesn't work, parents are called in. 'And if children are racist, fight or bully, then we would go straight to the parents,' says the head. But bullying is rare and there is less than a handful of temporary exclusions, if any, each year – which the head puts down to their focus on inclusion and accepting difference.

Parents increasingly prosperous and professional, although around six per cent of pupils are on free school meals. The parents are a sociable bunch – and very supportive too. Indeed, the PTA is buzzing, with recent purchases from its hectic cycle of events (including fairs, raffles, sales, fireworks etc) including more computers for the computer suite and redevelopment of the key stage 1 playground. Those with interesting jobs – astronauts or newspaper editors – come in to share their expertise. Around half of the children are white British, while the remaining predominant ethic groups are other white backgrounds and Asian.

There's a big student voice here, with the student council having voted to bring in vegetable growing areas, among other things. In fact, the school is big on the outdoors generally, with all teachers trained in forest school. Mixed views on the food. 'It's horrible,' more than one child told us, while a parent said, 'It's a shame as food used to be one of their shining glories.' The head acknowledges 'it's mass cooked,' but adds that 'there are 12 different choices in the salad bar – all selected with the help of the school council.'

This is a friendly, upbeat local school where pupils have fun, get excited about learning and have lots of opportunities around responsibility

– whether in school council, sports leaders and ambassadors, librarians, lunch teams, animal welfare etc. 'Pretty much every day, I thank my lucky stars that my kids go to this school. You can't ask for more than that.'

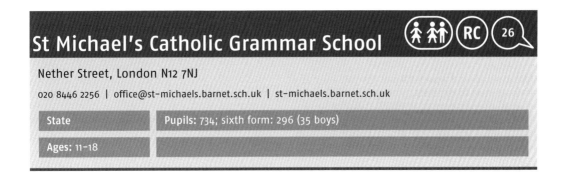

St Michael's Catholic Grammar School

Nether Street, London N12 7NJ

020 8446 2256 | office@st-michaels.barnet.sch.uk | st-michaels.barnet.sch.uk

State	Pupils: 734; sixth form: 296 (35 boys)
Ages: 11–18	

Headmaster: Since September 2017, Michael Stimpson BSc MSc MA MA PGCE NPQH (40s), previously head of St Bernard's Catholic Grammar in Berkshire. Degree in natural science and teaching certificate from Durham; went straight into teaching physics and much later completed his masters in astrophysics part-time through Queen Mary, University of London. He also holds two masters degrees in educational management (one in Catholic school leadership). Has spent most of his time in selective and Catholic schools, including a spell as head of sixth form at St Michael's. Keen on the role of extracurricular education – and of the Duke of Edinburgh's Award in particular, for which he has given up many weekends. He is married with three children and enjoys literature; walks in the wild bits of Britain and listening to the music of Westminster Cathedral Choir. He is a fellow of the Royal Astronomical Society.

Academic matters: St Michael's has won numerous awards (including Sunday Times State Secondary School of the Year) for providing an outstanding education and is now one of the country's leading secondary schools, always sitting within the top 20 grammar schools (often in the top 10) nationally at A level, usually in the top five at GCSE. 2018 saw 91 per cent A*-B grades at A level and 62 per cent A*/As. At GCSE, 81 per cent 9-7. Teaching is undoubtedly a strength ('There are very clever teachers who provide very good teaching,' said one parent) and the school works hard to maximize both pupils' and parents' aspirations. 'We give a great deal of time to thinking about it,' says the head.

All the girls accepted here are bright, but St Michael's still offers significant added value, with a packed, fast-paced curriculum ('You need to enjoy academic work and want to find out about things'). Almost all take 11 GCSEs, including a large compulsory core, which includes English, maths, history and/or geography, RS, a science (about a third take all three) and a modern foreign language (large numbers take two). Language offering particularly vibrant, with French, German, Spanish, Latin and Italian all on the timetable, and Japanese and Mandarin offered outside it. Italian and Spanish particularly popular A levels (as well as psychology, RS and maths). Sixth form has its own building ('St Michael's is really two schools, with two distinct regimes, a girls'-only school in years 7-11, and a co-ed sixth form college'). Only small numbers with special needs, but strugglers are provided with generous support. Homework is pushed hard. 'If you're ill you have to catch up on what you've missed,' said one mother.

Enjoys walks in the wild bits of Britain and listening to the music of Westminster Cathedral choir

Games, options, the arts: No playing fields and only a handful of courts, so team games not a forte (no hockey, for example), but a spacious new-ish sports hall (the largest school gym in Barnet) is used to the full to deliver high standard athletics, netball, volleyball, gymnastics, table tennis and badminton. Professional basketball and netball coaches bring out the best in nascent stars and the school is successful at local and regional level in a number of sports. The top performing school in the borough's inter-sports competitions for girls.

Academic music is excellent, with dedicated practice rooms and a recording suite, though the school is pushing for higher standards of extracurricular involvement. 'Lots of girls participate in choir and orchestra, but I would like us to have greater opportunities for high quality performance.' Large, well-equipped art and DT studio (offering material technology, food technology and graphics) with plenty of enthusiastic participants.

Good range of clubs (mainly in the lunch hour rather than after school as many pupils live far away) and trips (including skiing, modern languages and faith-centred activities, such as retreats and a visit to Lourdes).

Background and atmosphere: Founded by the Congregation of the Sisters of the Poor Child Jesus in 1908 as a prep school in the grounds of its convent. In 1958, a girls' grammar school was launched to share the site, and eventually the prep school was closed to allow the grammar school to expand.

Still quite a compact school housed in a motley collection of periods and styles. The Grange, which now accommodates the sixth form, was once a 19th century private house, and has the elegant proportions reflective of this history. The main school was built in the 1950s and comes with large windows and bright views. Modernisation is a constant theme (and drain on finances), but recent additions include an air-conditioned multi-media suite and sixth form study centre. Classrooms remain a mix of old and new, but all are equipped with interactive whiteboards. Attractive gardens, once the convent orchard, are graced by a monkey puzzle tree, large redwood and shrine to the Virgin Mary.

Attractive chapel with superior stained glass windows by Patrick Reyntiens, a master craftsman whose work also features in Liverpool and Coventry cathedrals

The school, which is voluntary aided, is conducted by its governing body as part of the Catholic church and the Catholic ethos remains fundamental. Prayers are said daily and every pupil attends a weekly religious assembly, as well as mass on feast days. But this is contemporary Catholicism. 'They go to mass, but they don't expect them to be cleaning the vestry floors,' said one parent. Attractive chapel with superior stained glass windows by Patrick Reyntiens, a master craftsman whose work also features in Liverpool and Coventry cathedrals. Girls put their faith into practice with charity work, helping in the community and giving food to homeless. Generally, the atmosphere is kind, warm and supportive. 'Academically, they push them to their limits, but they do look after them,' said one parent.'There's a very nice feeling to the school.' 'No one gets lost,' said another. 'It feels very safe.'

The school is currently undergoing a major refurb, which is expected to take just under two years to complete. Part of the main building (a four-storey teaching block housing the library, computer rooms, art, and some rooms for science, history and geography) will be replaced over 2018/19. During the building work, lessons will be moved to 'high-quality temporary accommodation' on-site and by January 2020 the new building should be completed and ready for use. This venture will 'replace a tired 1950s building with a new, more spacious and modern building.'

'We try to create a relaxed and happy atmosphere, but we expect high standards of behaviour'

Pastoral care, well-being and discipline: The primary aim here is the formation of responsible and committed Catholic citizens. 'We try to create a relaxed and happy atmosphere, but we expect high standards of behaviour, self-discipline and responsibility.' Those from bohemian families are advised to think carefully about their choice. Even those who aren't acknowledge that the regime is firm. 'There is very strong discipline, which can irritate the girls,' said a parent. 'They will stamp on anything – possibly too hard.'

The pre-GCSE years have a slightly old-fashioned air. 'There's no talk of drugs,' said one mother. 'They do go to parties, but there's no big modern teenage culture.' Girls leap to attention if the head is spotted in the corridor and pupil pressure as much as teacher pressure patrols the classroom. 'My daughter said to me in astonishment, "a new girl in the school keeps answering the teacher back. Nobody will be friends with her. We like our teachers. They're on our side; we're on theirs".'

In the pre-GCSE years, uniform strictly enforced, with purple skirts at the knee or close to it, no jewellery or make-up. In the sixth form, mufti is permitted and the dress code becomes 'decency'.

Pupils remain accountable for what happens outside the gates if in uniform. Few problems, however. 'Most people who come here are impressed by the behaviour and friendliness of the pupils.'

Pupils and parents: Cradle Catholics from all over London and the world, with increasing numbers of Eastern Europeans, particularly Poles. Not as skewed to the professional middle classes as some other grammar schools, with more new immigrants (33 per cent do not speak English as their first language at home).

Entrance: Not perhaps as tricky to get into academically as some of the other North London grammar schools (some 390 apply for 96 places), simply because of its single-sex faith criteria. That said, the Catholic hurdle is not for slackers. Applicants at 11 plus must provide proof of first holy communion and at least one parent must also be a Catholic with a written reference from their parish priest stating they attend mass on Sunday with the applicant. There is no catchment ('you can come from Sheffield if you want') but only girls who meet the religious criteria are allowed to sit the admissions tests (in verbal and non-verbal reasoning, English and maths). Sixth form applicants are not required to be Catholic (about 20 per cent come from other faiths) but 'must subscribe to the Catholic ethos'. At this stage, there are a further 60 places (open to boys and girls with at least six GCSE passes at 9-7, with at least a 7 in the subjects they wish to study and no lower than a 6 in English and maths). Boys in this relatively large sixth form remain in the minority, with about 20 a year. 'The boys have to be quite brave,' said one parent.

Exit: Roughly 20 per cent of girls leave post-GCSE, to nearby sixth form colleges, like Woodhouse, or larger co-ed selective schools. Most sixth formers go on to the older universities. In 2018, 12 to Oxbridge (including one vet to Cambridge), plus another vet and two medics. Nottingham, Warwick and Birmingham popular.

Money matters: St Michael's is a voluntary-aided school and parents are expected to contribute towards the cost of the buildings and facilities. 'The school would fall down otherwise.' An annual contribution of £275 a year is asked for and 90 per cent of parents contribute something. 'We don't go chasing the other 10 per cent.'

Remarks: A happy school, with firm discipline, high expectations and outstanding results.

St Michael's CofE Primary School

North Road, London N6 4BG

020 8340 7441 | admin@stmichaelsn6.com | stmichaelsn6.com

State	Pupils: 450
Ages: 3–11	

Head teacher: Since 2013, Geraldine Gallagher (40s), BEd Liverpool University. Was NQT in a 'semi-rural' primary school with a mixed catchment, then went inner city to work in a primary school in Hackney, an experience she called 'very good although challenging at times.' She left after a year to teach at St John Evangelist School in Islington where she worked her way up to becoming deputy head. Sixteen years later she was ready to embrace the demands of becoming a head and saw the post advertised for St Michael's CofE: 'I grew up in Islington so had heard of the school and it had always had a pretty good reputation, so decided to go for it.'

Focused, 'I've wanted to be a teacher since I was 14', grounded, and knows the score. Ms Gallagher was only too aware that this was not an easy school to take on, with its prominent milieu of extremely hands-on parents (a positive in many ways but could arguably marginalise the power of a new head). She says: 'In the main the parents here are very supportive, but like most people if things go out of kilter, they will let you know.' However, judging by the feedback we've had, she need not worry. One parent told us that Ms Gallagher has already turned things around for the better in so many ways since starting: 'Parents now know where they stand with her and with the school as she has clear rules and guidelines.' Another said: 'She is a fantastic head. Before she came there was a lot of discontent and the school was in quite a bit of turmoil. The school was operating on the ethos of an old head and it became a situation of us and them between parents and teachers. Ms Gallagher has brought consistency to the school and moved it forward.'

With three of her own children at the school, this head undoubtedly has a vested interest in its success, both academically and pastorally. As one parent pointed out, 'The ethos here is very much that you get out what you put in.' Married for 14 years, any extracurricular time that Ms Gallagher has is spent with her family on days out and the odd swim or two.

Entrance: Heavily oversubscribed at nursery and reception. Around 70 apply for 52 nursery places and 100 for the 60 reception places, which are allocated on a points system, 14 points being the maximum. (Four points for church attendance at St Michael's Church, three for living in N6. Thereafter, local Christians, siblings, other faiths.) Christianity very much part of the ethos. Open days every term and, if a vacancy is available, parents are welcome to look round. Places do arise, particularly in the higher years when some pupils leave for the private sector.

Exit: On the border of three boroughs – Haringey, Islington and Camden – St Michael's sends its leavers to as many as 30 secondary schools. About half to independent schools (many with scholarships), particularly Highgate, with which the school has a close association, and City of London, but also Channing, UCS, Westminster, North London Collegiate, Haberdashers' Aske's and South Hampstead, plus top grammars Henrietta Barnett, Latymer, St Michael's Catholic Girls and Queen Elizabeth School. A considerable chunk each year to Fortismere School, the popular local comprehensive in Muswell Hill.

Remarks: One of north London's most sought-after primary schools, St Michael's has high academic standards and a high proportion of pupils who reach well beyond the government's expectations at 7 and 11. This partly reflects the intake (largely middle class Highgate), but is also due to strong teaching – recently boosted by an overhaul of the teaching structure. 'Much more academic,' one parent told us; another said, 'The school is now back on track and on its way to becoming very successful again.'

The pupils were an astute, friendly bunch. We got treated to a spectacular card trick by one who said he loved the school because the teachers 'let me do magic'

The shift in the teaching structure came about following a period of upheaval at the time when Ms Gallagher was appointed head over two years ago. She says, 'I don't believe in old style leadership and pointing the finger. I knew the school had been though a difficult time, but I believe in working together to achieve the best teaching model.' This included bringing in several new members of staff and making some of the existing ones non-teaching heads of phases, which freed them up to

---

Troy, the 'legendary' school manager, ran into each classroom shouting that a spaceship had landed, amidst noises and lights

oversee the efficient running of the year groups. While some parents were initially resistant, others feel their children are really reaping the rewards. One told us: 'There is a huge difference in what my son gets for homework to what my older daughter got at that age. It was a bit haphazard before, now it's more structured – not hothousing, just wanting each child to reach their potential.'

This is a school that doesn't rest on its laurels – which it probably could do quite comfortably by virtue of its catchment. A dedicated teacher/parent partnership ensures that even the least engaged child will derive something because of the constantly stimulating and original methods of teaching. Pupils still enthuse a year later about how 'a spaceship landed in their grounds', which they were allowed to explore – after which they were encouraged to write a story about the experience. This was courtesy of some very innovative parents, who together with the English leader spent hours creating the spaceship, and Troy, the 'legendary' school manager, who ran into each classroom shouting that a spaceship had landed, amidst loud noises and flashing lights.

This year saw a campervan book bus parked in the grounds to encourage pupils to go in and read during break times (a cool spin on the old mobile library). Other stimulating learning tools include a charming open reading shed in the grounds funded by parents, a play pod with an assortment of recycled goods to encourage imaginative play and an allotment run by parent volunteers. We also loved the idea of a 'kindness wall', which we spotted in a couple of the classrooms, and which, we are told by one pupil, 'encourages us to write nice things about each other.' The pupils we chatted to were an astute bunch, happy and friendly. We even got treated to one spectacular card trick by a pupil who said he loved the school because the teachers 'let me do magic.' Another pupil told us that as a Muslim he liked how a Christian school 'embraces other cultures.'

Parents are an unusually energetic bunch – the school's Parents' Association (SMSA) is possibly the most committed we have come across. Last year alone they raised an astonishing £61,000, through events such as a bonfire night, battle of the bands, fun run and, the pièce de résistance, the annual parents' pantomime. This, we are told, can rival anything seen in the West End and is the highlight of the school calendar. One parent told us: 'What makes this school so special is the dedication of parents. Because we are a church school with no extra funding we can only get the extras we want if we raise the money ourselves. It does create a lovely community atmosphere, but forget it if you want a school where you can just drop your kids off and not get involved.' For a recent production of Dick Whittington, it was not unusual to see parents rehearsing or building sets until midnight, on top of the jobs they do during the day. Luckily for the school, parents include actors, musicians and set designers.

Excellent drama, with two or three plays annually, plus a nativity play and annual summer concert. A good range of sport – gymnastics, football, tag rugby, tennis, cricket, netball and basketball – taught in lesson time. Swimming, taught in years 5 and 6, is particularly strong.

Fantastic and varied extracurricular programme provides a wonderful resource for working parents. Breakfast clubs start as early as 7.45am and for the particularly energetic early bird fencing and gymnastics are offered. The quieter soul can indulge in a bit of Latin or creative writing, and an early morning maths club is also offered for 'invited pupils.' After-school activities include football, netball, dance, drama (led by the school's celebrated drama teacher, Bob Williams CBE), orchestra, French, chess and fortnightly film club (pupils have won several awards for film reviewing as part of the National Film Club).

Charity a big part of the school's ethos. On the day we visited parents were arriving with hampers to distribute to the local community and a busload of senior citizens arrived for their annual Christmas party. At this much anticipated event, year 6s dress up as waiters and waitresses to serve food and give out individually handmade cards and wrapped presents.

Good SEN department. Specific programmes designed for pupils who are classified as SEN or statemented (roughly 16 per cent), and access to regular sessions with art, occupational, and speech and language therapists. Each classroom has an adjoining intervention room for those who need extra help with maths, English etc.

The school is a couple of hundred yards down from pretty Highgate village – barely visible from the road, but as you approach the main gates the beauty of this building and its grounds can be appreciated. Founded in the mid-19th century as a school to train young locals to go into service, by 1852 it was on its current three-and-a-half acre site with the intention of not only providing an academic education, but also cultivating the spacious grounds as a farm. The green fields and listed Victorian buildings have since been joined by a block built in the 1970s, two large, well-equipped playgrounds and a large, new all-weather court. Both building and grounds are extensive and it is easy to lose one's bearings. The only gripe we heard from parents was about improving the concrete play area. One parent told us: 'I appreciate it is all about funding, and it's definitely better than it was previously, when it looked like a camp site, but there has been just talk for a long time.'

Tetherdown Primary School

Grand Avenue, London N10 3BP

020 8883 3412 | admin@tetherdownschool.org | tetherdownschool.org

State	Pupils: 417
Ages: 4–11	

Headteacher: Since 2013, Tony Woodward BEd music (late 40s). Started off teaching on his home turf of Solihull, West Midlands, at a 'challenging' primary school where he became music and art co-ordinator. He came to London in 1997 to work as head of juniors at Rushy Meadow Primary School in Sutton, where he stayed for the next four years. Following this he became deputy head at nearby Robin Hood Junior School, and then moved on to become head teacher of another local school, Warren Mead Junior – prior to his headship at Tetherdown. His work in Surrey also saw him as a local leader in education, supporting leaders of struggling local schools and as an additional Ofsted inspector.

Primary schools are where this head has always wanted to be: 'It means I get to work with a whole range of ages from 4 to 11 year olds.' His parents were both road safety officers who went into schools to teach, so being around this as a young boy gave this head a taste of how teaching can really make a difference to children. Indeed, in the last few years since Mr Woodward took over the daunting mantle of one of north London's leading state primary schools, he has already set about trying to make a difference to the school by introducing a lot more sport into the curriculum. One parent told us: 'Before Mr Woodward became head, the school was solely about academia and there was not much time factored in for anything else. '

Mr Woodward has since appointed a PE co-ordinator and a PE coach, and has set up a wide variety of sports clubs, both curricular and extracurricular, including football, netball, hockey, gymnastics and swimming. The school even won Haringey Sporting School of The Year recently and has won several trophies for football, tag rugby and cross-country. He is himself a keen sporting man (which is perhaps why it is so important for him) – trampolining was his specialty, and he came second in the European Championships at the height of his competitive career.

One parent praised the new rigour which Mr Woodward has imposed in his tenure at the school: 'There seems to be a lot more organisation around the admin side of the school and with regards to homework – which was getting a bit haphazard before he came on board.' Another said: 'Mr Woodward has a positive manner and a clear vision of how he wants things to be.'

Engaged parents who devote the same attention to reading rotas and library duty as they give to successful careers

This is a head whom we suspect quietly worms away behind the scenes rather than being a front of house guy. That's not to say his presence is not noted around the school (some say quite visible), but he doesn't come across as a massive PR man. He does the job he was employed to do, but don't expect a big sales pitch, or well rehearsed spiel. He likes to unwind by playing the piano and cooking.

Entrance: The school admits 60 pupils in reception, but there's still fierce competition to get in. In the past it was only siblings and those living feet from the gates who stood a chance, now at least an address in the same street might reasonably be expected to do the trick. (Needless to say property prices nearby have their own exotic micro-climate.) One family (we were told) was even in the process of building their own house virtually opposite the school to ensure entrance. Parents can view the school in the autumn term prior to entry, kids visit in the summer term before they start.

Exit: Lucky pupils whose parents bought wisely in the area are also pretty much guaranteed a smooth transition to one of the capital's best comprehensives. Smug parents, who've sorted it all by the age of 4, tend to assume their children will proceed to Fortismere, and the vast majority do go on here. The rest to North London grammar schools such as The Latymer or leading independents – including a fair chunk to Mill Hill School and Highgate and a few to Channing. ('This is Muswell Hill,' said one mother; 'parents tutor without hesitation.')

Remarks: Despite a recent Ofsted demotion from 'outstanding' to 'good', Tetherdown remains one of London's top performing primary schools. This is a school which regularly sits near the top of the local authority league tables and, even in an average year, over 50 per cent of pupils reach level 5 in English and maths. 'Teaching is consistently good, with some that is outstanding,' says Ofsted. Parents would agree, but there has been a high turnover of staff in recent years, which has been noticed and commented on by pupils. One told us: 'There were so many teachers and teaching assistants that came and went in year 4 – none of them seemed to last more than a few weeks, I'm not sure why'. However, the head is keen to point out that that was an exceptional year and not the norm (and the shortage was mainly down to maternity leave). 'There was a period of instability, but we are back on track and currently have a very stable staff team.'

One reason for its demotion by Ofsted was because 'a few high-attaining pupils are not always sufficiently challenged'. One parent told us: 'Tetherdown is a great local school if your child can just get on and do the work and doesn't need extra intervention in any way. However, if your child is particularly able or, conversely, has any special needs, it doesn't cater well for that.' However, another parent strongly disagreed: 'My child does require extra help and the school does have good SEN provisions – his needs were picked up on early on. But I would say that you do really do have to push for everything and communication is not as good as it could be.' Communication is something the school has been working on a great deal: 'We have an open door policy – parents are invited to feed in as well as receive feedback.'

With meticulous monitoring, more than a dollop of regular homework (one and half hours weekly up to year 3, then a whole lot more), and dedicated parents willing to supervise nightly reading from reception to year 6, you get some idea of how good results happen. The school follows the national curriculum but adds its own flourishes,

> *A good emphasis on making learning fun – whether tricky Tudor recipes or studying maths with the help of a visiting Maths Clown*

with a good emphasis on making learning fun – whether this be tricky Tudor recipes, studying maths with the help of a visiting Maths Clown or sharpening up those multiplication tables in Beat the Parents at Mental Maths. 'The children have a lovely education,' said one parent. Pupils are rewarded by pyjama days and a system of rewards. Pupils are grouped, extended and supported according to ability. Recent requirement for the inclusion of modern language teaching is provided by French lessons from year 2, and the school is looking into the possibility of Mandarin.

Plenty of stretching and thinking in all directions, whether in an opera workshop or an after-school street dance club. Plenty of creative parents, too, who come in to share their expertise. All children learn to play the ocarina (Peruvian recorder) and individual instrumental tuition, subsidised by the local authority, is provided during the working day. Sport, which was previously the weakest link, is now more expansive and better equipped. In year 6, all children learn swimming and travel outside the school for specialist coaching. Breakfast club and plenty of lunchtime and after-school activities eg choir, drama, gymnastics and spy club. Regular school trips include an annual outing to the seaside for years 2 and 5, as well as visits to the British and Science Museums and trips to the local mosque.

Virtually all parents and pupils live within a few surrounding streets and the school has always offered an exceptionally tight-knit community. Expansion has marginally diluted the atmosphere, but has brought advantages. 'It used to be very much like a village school, where everyone knew each other and older pupils looked out for the younger ones,' said one mother with children at both ends of the spectrum. 'That was comforting, but sometimes your child didn't have a particularly wide choice of friends. Now there's plenty of scope.' Indeed, the school prides itself on having a 'wide mix of cultures, religions, backgrounds and languages.'

All classes are supported by exciting innovations in technology and children learn to communicate learning through a variety of platforms, including multi-media presentations, pupil-led video articles, iPad technology and even create their own apps.

The school has no uniform and rules are kept to a minimum. 'We have just three rules. Respect yourself, respect others and respect your environment. If you respect yourself you are going to work hard to become the best you can.' Parents admire the way these principles are implemented. Those demonstrating behavioural challenges are given the same support as those with academic problems – with intervention and targets. Children are encouraged to get involved: with the school council; with each other's welfare (by becoming play leaders and buddies); and with the broader community (for example, running a soup kitchen at harvest time). They are also lavished with praise. Regular Achievements Assemblies recognise work, effort and attitude. Anti-bullying is promoted throughout the school (as was evident by a large wall montage entirely devoted to bullying), because bullying has been an issue in the past. 'We take bullying very seriously, like any school, but we make children very aware about bullying, we liaise closely with the parents and we always use circle time and assemblies to make children aware.'

Tetherdown is located in North London's prosperous, professional Muswell Hill and the parent body is a mirror of the locality, with plenty of engaged parents who devote the same attention to reading rotas and library duty as they give to successful careers. However, one parent said that the school could do more to maximise the use of parents: 'There are many parents like me who are at home now, and have a variety of skills and could help more, but the school is not as proactive as it could be at utilising us more.' School maintains that parents are welcome 'to volunteer their time to share their expertise, support admin tasks and promote the school's high expectations', although they have found that parents are most often taking the opportunity to return to work.

> *He is a keen sporting man – trampolining was his specialty, and he came second in the European Championships at the height of his competitive career*

Very active Parent School Association (PSA), which raised £25,000 last year and used the money to underwrite school trips, build a new woodland play area in the junior playground and contribute towards reading books and general resources. The head is very supportive of the PSA, which has been welcomed by parents. He says: 'Finance for the school is always one of our biggest challenges. This school is one of the lowest funded schools in Haringey because it is perceived as being in a wealthy area. What money we have, we invest in staff.'

Parents at the school are highly ambitious for their kids and for the school, 'some wanting a private school education from a state school.' One disgruntled parent told us: 'This used to be the school of choice in the area, but now according to our local newspaper, is the one you go for if you can't get into Coldfall, Muswell Hill or Rhodes Avenue.' We remain confident that it will resume that status again.

Woodhouse College

Woodhouse Road, London N12 9EY

020 8445 1210 | enquiries@woodhouse.ac.uk | woodhouse.ac.uk

State	Pupils: 1,364
Ages: 16–19	

Principal: Since 2013, John Rubinstein BSc (50s) – read maths at Sheffield University where he achieved a first class degree. It was during his PhD that he decided teaching was his vocation: 'Part of my duties as a postgrad was to teach undergraduates, which I really enjoyed, and I realised then that this was what I wanted to do.' His first teaching job was at a comprehensive in Manchester – prior to getting his first post in London. His third teaching job was at Woodhouse College in 1994 as a maths teacher. He stayed there for the next 10 years, only leaving when he was offered the post of deputy head at a school in Haringey. He came back to Woodhouse in 2008 as deputy head, and was promoted to principal five years later.

Originally from Yorkshire, this softly spoken head seems totally devoid of any of the salesman techniques often displayed by other heads. That's not to say he's not enthusiastic about the school or his pupils – he is clearly extremely proud of both – but no doubt he feels, as we do, that Woodhouse pretty much sells itself. Students and parents alike describe him as 'very approachable' and one student told us: 'Mr Rubinstein is always wandering around the learning zones and often spends ages with pupils helping them out. You can email him anytime and he always gets back to you.' Even after nearly 30 years in the teaching profession, maths is still his passion and he still teaches four maths lessons a week which equates to a full A level week: 'It keeps me in touch with students, with the experience of colleagues, but most of all because I love it.' He even taught his own daughter, who is an ex-Woodhouse student: 'I warned her that it might be slightly strange, but it worked out fine in the end.'

His wife is also a teacher and they have three children – two of whom attended Woodhouse and are now at university. Mr Rubinstein has many other strings to his bow – formerly an Ofsted Inspector for 15 years: 'I gave up a year ago as the workload was getting too much and I was fed up of staying in hotel rooms'; he also enjoys running and has taken part in many half marathons and 10k runs. 'I have done the Crouch End 10k run for 13 years in a row and now train some of my students.' Recently nominated the school caretaker for a CBE for 20 years of service to the school: 'He is the glue that keeps this community together.'

Academic matters: Woodhouse is one of the country's leading sixth form colleges, always in the top five nationally, usually in the top three. This is essentially an academic place, whose main focus is on A levels. In 2018, 35 per of grades were A*/A and 70 per cent A*-B.

Undoubtedly a key part of the success is enthusiastic, experienced and focused teaching. One parent told us: 'I can't say enough about the teaching at Woodhouse and how they inspire students. My son had no real intellectual curiosity before going there. Now all he wants to do is discuss the Russian revolution.' Another said, 'The teachers really seem to know our children individually and their particular traits.' The consensus seems to be that 'they're excellent at monitoring and keep their finger on the pulse.' Mr Rubinstein says that close monitoring of students is vital as some students choose the wrong subjects, and they are under so much more pressure than they used to be. 'If a student is underachieving, there will be a case conference and a discussion of perhaps reducing the amount of subjects they take. They will also be offered extra supervised study.'

Results are certainly not achieved by hothousing or editing. The principal welcomes the introduction of the new A level system, which returns to the old two year study programme with no exams until the end of the second year. He says that although results will change, 'we won't just be teaching towards an end of year exam. Pupils will be able to explore their subjects more deeply.'

Prides itself on providing 'a broad and civilising education' and all are expected to take part in 'enrichment'. Most relish the opportunities to develop new skills in everything from drawing to street dance

A wide range of options on offer, with 27 subjects in almost any combination. Maths is the most popular A level choice (with 45 per cent taking it) and results are notably strong. One of London's largest providers of A level science, with many going on to science-related degrees. Four languages, including Italian, and an abundance of 'ologies', from sociology to music technology and the extended project also available. The EPQ is taken by over 100 students each year and yields high grades. One parent said that 'the fantastic selection of A levels, including classical civilization, really excited my daughter when she was looking at sixth forms, and this is what swung it for her.'

Though the majority at Woodhouse tend to favour professional courses at university, social science and arts-based studies are strong, with thriving theatre studies, economics, English literature and geography. 'Independent learning' is high on the agenda. 'We want students to prepare for lessons, so they can understand and interpret the information, using the teacher and their fellow students as a resource,' says the principal. Motivated students respond well to this approach. 'Teachers assume if you're interested in your subjects, you will want to read around them,' said one. 'They don't force you to work, but they'll give you the resources and make themselves available to you,' said another.

An enormous amount of help is offered to pupils with their UCAS forms, and extra workshops and weekly presentations are laid on nearer the deadline. A teacher is on hand every Tuesday after school to offer any extra help for university applications, and Mr Rubinstein is also very involved in the process and runs mock Oxbridge interviews.

All students have access to two learning mentors – one for humanities, the other science and maths – to sort out any day-to-day tangles. One full-time SENCo, plus one part-time specialist providing individual support for those with dyslexia and dyspraxia and a learning mentor to help with study skills. The buildings are 99 per cent adapted for those with physical disabilities.

Games, options, the arts: Woodhouse prides itself on providing 'a broad and civilising education' and all are expected to take part in at least two six-week courses of 'enrichment', the majority of which take place on Wednesdays afternoons, when there are no lessons. Most relish the opportunities to develop new skills in everything from observational drawing to street dance. Duke of Edinburgh and Amnesty International also on offer.

Art is strong and some of the pieces we saw on our tour were simply outstanding – something we honestly weren't expecting: 'Traditionally the more academic subjects are most popular here, and although art and drama are taken by smaller numbers, they are very successful. Several of our graduates go on to art colleges.'

Dance is also a strong curricular subject here and the college has two lovely, bright, mirrored dance studios. Sports facilities, too, are good, with a new sports hall and new floodlit 3G football pitch. Official team sports include football (girls' and boys'), netball and basketball, but individualists can also enjoy cross-country, squash, trampolining and kickboxing. 'If there isn't a club that you'd like to do,' said one student, 'the sports department are happy to try and set something up.'

Music, which was previously a 'neglected' subject, now has its own dedicated separate building outside, with a well-equipped practice room and a music studio, which works in conjunction with other Barnet schools, and offers lessons from peripatetic teachers.

Original stately Victorian façade (deriving from its former incarnation as the home of ornamental plasterer Thomas Collins)

Woodhouse students like to get involved and there's an active college council, which has recently helped introduce a daily loan system for netbooks. Plenty of outside speakers and activities including art trips, foreign exchanges, a ski trip and the opportunity to undertake voluntary work abroad. Debating has traditionally been strong at Woodhouse and the college takes part in the Model United Nations competition, which hosts around 40 different debates a year in various institutions, including Woodhouse.

Background and atmosphere: Located in a pleasant leafy suburb, Woodhouse began its educational life as Woodhouse Grammar School in 1925, but became one of the capital's rare sixth form colleges in the 1980s. Today all pupils are aged between 16 and 19 and all are studying A levels. With some 700 new pupils a year, the college is significantly larger than a traditional school sixth form, but smaller than a FE college.

'Independent learning' is high on the agenda. 'We want students to prepare for lessons, so they can understand and interpret the information'

The original stately Victorian façade (deriving from its former incarnation as the home of ornamental plasterer Thomas Collins) has now been joined by a motley timeline of newer buildings, leaving it today with well-equipped facilities. The bright, open plan Learning Zone is one of the most recent innovations, offering space to work in solitary silence as well as in small groups, and supervised open-access IT. In 2014 the college managed to raise two million pounds for a two-story, purpose built mathematics facility. 'Quite a lot of students here can't work in silence at home and don't have the facility to do the "hard hours",' says the principal. 'We wanted to create learners who can work on their own.'

To this former Woodhouse student, the college internally is barely recognisable as the Woodhouse of yesteryear. However, what still remains is the strong sense of individuality that Woodhouse was always renowned for – and is still clearly evident in the students we witnessed strolling around the grounds. All creeds, colours, dress codes, hair colour, piercings welcome (well, maybe piercings not 'welcome', but they're there). One student told us: 'I never feel we are judged on anything here. We know grades matter, but that's really it.' Another student told us: 'I've never been as happy as I am coming here. I used to loathe going to school, but now I'm worried about my time at Woodhouse going too quickly.'

The students we met were indeed a happy and likeable bunch. They all felt extremely independent and loved the free rein the college allows them. However, one student grumbled that she tends to go out for lunch in North Finchley High Road (a five minute walk), as the canteen is too small and can't often accommodate everyone – a sentiment echoed by a parent, who suggested that perhaps the lunch hour should be extended.

Values here are traditional. 'We believe in honesty, hard work, mutual respect and taking responsibility for your own learning.' The

atmosphere is generally enthusiastic, as much for work as for play. 'Here it's cool to work, cool to be involved,' said one student. 'The atmosphere is incredible,' said another. 'There's a massive sense of community. There are always things happening.'

Pastoral care, well-being and discipline: Not every 16-year-old is ideally suited to the self-motivation required by an academic sixth form college, but here high expectations are supported by a well-thought-out tutorial system and plenty of individual guidance. Every student has their own tutor, 'My son sees a guy two or three times a week, whom he likes and respects,' said one mother. 'When he was having trouble at home, they really kept an eye on him.'

The principal is all too aware that students these days are under a lot more pressure than previously, 'and as a result are a lot more fragile and there is more self-harming.' For this reason, they invest time in what they offer pastorally, including a pastoral manager and a counselling service. One student told us: 'The pastoral care here is excellent. There's pretty much someone you can talk to 24/7, if you needed to.' Another said, they accommodate for everyone and there is even an LBGT community.'

The college sees itself as a bridge between school and university, and new students are eased into this more adult world with an induction day in the summer before they start. The enrichment programme helps aid new friendships beyond the classroom. 'Everyone makes friends ridiculously fast because there are so many people in the same position,' said one boy. However, one parent did say that her child found the transition from school to college 'socially quite daunting if you don't know anyone, as pupils are always rushing off to their different classes or study period – it's unlike school where you get to know your peers over time.'

The enrichment programme helps new friendships beyond the classroom. 'Everyone makes friends ridiculously fast because there are so many in the same position'

Boundaries are firm and there's zero tolerance on punctuality. 'It's an issue they have to grasp,' says the head. 'If they're not making the effort, why should other students suffer?' However, unlike most sixth forms, there is no morning registration, instead pupils go straight to their class and their ID registers them when they swipe it at the entrance turnstiles. One pupil told us: 'I much prefer it this way. It means we can go straight to our lessons and not waste time.'

Parents agree that discipline is firm but reasonable. 'They run quite a tight ship, but it makes them responsible,' said one father

In lessons, students are attentive. 'If a teacher leaves the room, people get on with their work,' said one boy. We witnessed some of the most attentive and eager students we've come across, who were happy to talk with enthusiasm about what they were learning. There is definitely a strong work ethic that exists here. 'Issues found elsewhere are not even on the radar here,' notes the principal gratefully. Standard formula of oral and written warnings, with a code of conduct signed by all parents and pupils, but exclusion is a rarity. 'We have pupils from quite challenged backgrounds, but I have thrown out just one student,' says the principal. Parents agree that discipline is firm but reasonable. 'They run quite a tight ship, but it makes them responsible,' said one father. 'When my son's attendance was only 90 per cent, he had to see the senior tutor every week. As his attendance improved, he went less frequently.'

Pupils and parents: An eclectic mix – 'some nerdy kids, some cool kids, all sorts, colours and creeds.' The core is probably typical of the reasonably prosperous 'squeezed middle' of north London, but with a far higher ethnic intake than you'd assume from the location, and a far higher proportion of those who require some type of financial support.

Parents tend to be involved and supportive, students upbeat, mature, outgoing and energetic. They clearly enjoy the school – more than half volunteered on the annual open day held on a Saturday. 'They want to do well and they want to enjoy themselves,' says the principal. 'They're trying to get the balance right of working hard and having a good social life.' A parent agreed: 'My son is so happy. He really appreciates the fact that people are there because they want to learn, not because their parents are pushing them. Most students here are trying to better themselves and work really, really hard.' Past students include journalist Johann Hari, comedian Michael McIntyre and actress Naomie Harris.

Entrance: Priority is given to applicants from one local secondary school, Friern Barnet (although that accounts for roughly 20 places and they still have the same entry requirements). After that, it's predicted grades and/or interview. Competition is ferocious (about 4,500 apply for 700 places), particularly for in-demand subjects. 'We can afford to be choosy,' says the principal, 'but we're looking for a range.' All applicants with minimum predicted grade requirements (evaluated on a points system, with specific grades for individual subjects) are given a 20-30 minute interview (with optional parental accompaniment) in the February/March prior to entry. 'We're looking for maturity,' said one teacher. 'We want them to demonstrate that they are committed to A levels and really want to work, but we also want people who will get involved on a wider basis.' The interview is frequently of as much benefit to the student as to the college. 'We often spend it giving careers advice,' says the principal.

Travel time is also taken into consideration. Students come from as far afield as Highbury, but the school 'generally considers an hour and a quarter by bus the maximum desirable distance.' Applications available from the time of the open day in November until the closing deadline in January. All candidates require a confidential report from their current school and must be between 16 and 18 when starting at the college. The college operates a waiting list for the reshuffle that often takes place after results day in August.

We witnessed some of the most attentive and eager students we've come across, happy to talk with enthusiasm about what they were learning. A strong work ethic exists

Exit: Over 95 per cent to university – slightly over 50 per cent to Russell Group universities, with the most popular destinations being London universities, Warwick, Kent, Manchester and Sussex. Most popular subject choices are economics, law, engineering, business and psychology. Fifteen to Oxbridge and an incredible 29 off to study medicine in 2018. Good advice about careers and courses, including a full time careers co-ordinator.

Money matters: Parents are asked for £100 contribution for the two-year stint, enabling the college to keep up to date with books and underwrite the enrichment programme and facilities (those who can't afford it, don't pay). A £50 refundable deposit also required for text books. The college has attempted to replace some money lost through EMA cuts with bursaries.

Remarks: An upbeat environment, with strong teaching and results. A firm stepping stone between school and university.

Wren Academy

👥 (C°E) 30

Hilton Avenue, London N12 9HB

020 8492 6000 | firstcontact@wrenacademy.org | wrenacademy.org

State	Pupils: 1,288; sixth form: 254
Ages: 4–18	

Principal: Since 2015, Gavin Smith (40s). He has a geography degree from University College London and a PGCE from the Institute of Education. He joined Wren Academy in 2008, having worked in various London secondary schools, and was part of the founding team responsible for the curriculum, assessment and enrichment programme. He is married with two young children.

Headteacher of the primary phase is Louisa Taylor.

Academic matters: This is a comprehensive, but the nature of the students in this leafy area means it is primarily an academic one. The biggest initial challenge was achieving a truly comprehensive intake: the previous school on the site had a very poor reputation and Barnet has a variety of popular state schools, including three grammars. However, within a short space of time Ofsted stated that 'the teaching at Wren is stunning', and this is not something you read very often. 'As well as maximising achievement – because children need that currency to move on – we teach learning skills and aptitudes. Children need the capacity to think for themselves. They are encouraged to seek out their own answers, to be flexible and take risks.' In 2018 at GCSE, 43 per cent 9-7 grades. Sixth formers achieved 53 per cent A*-B, 30 per cent A*/A in their A level exams.

Parents are enthusiastic. 'The teachers are very wisely chosen.' 'They're great at finding and encouraging talents.' 'They really encourage them to aim high.' Newsletters all include brainteasers for parents and pupils to solve, and articles on ways of building learning power.

English, maths and science are taught in single sex classes. 'This gives us opportunities to stretch children in gender-specific ways. For example, in English boys can look at their powers of reflectiveness and empathy, whilst in girls' maths classes we can encourage them to take risks and concentrate on answering quickly. It helps to broaden their skill sets, and they enjoy it.' Research suggests that girls taught in single sex groups are more likely to continue with maths and science, and a good percentage of girls choose single science GCSEs.

The school sets for English, maths, science and foreign languages from part of the way through year 7. 'We like to get data of our own rather than relying on Sats results.' Everyone studies a language (generally French, though some take Japanese or Spanish) and most are expected to take it to GCSE. Regular language days involve a range of linguistic activities. GCSE courses start in year 9.

The specialism of design and the built environment enhances rather than dominates the curriculum, says the school. 'It influences our culture and our ways of thinking about tasks. We have a high emphasis on creativity, and each task has a creative phase, a planning phase and an evaluation phase. But we also have the opportunity to plan projects in architecture and civil engineering.'

'The teachers don't tolerate any bad behaviour,' say parents. 'It is a lovely, safe environment for learning'; and indeed the school had a supremely ordered feel

Those who need extra help are identified at the beginning of year 7 and follow a six week key skills programme to help bring them up to speed. There are also after-school support groups that help with spelling and comprehension. Although some get one-to-one help from teaching assistants, 'the aim is for everyone to be unsupported in lessons eventually. We do what helps them to access the curriculum in the appropriate lesson.'

Games, options, the arts: The school week includes three extended days, with compulsory enrichment activities from 3-4pm. These range from samba band, Latin and knitting to debating. Staff and students learn together and either can win Excellent Learner of the Week awards.

Houses – named for Wren churches – give the main opportunities for sporting rivalry, but football, netball, basketball, badminton and athletics teams also take part in borough and regional competitions with increasing success. There's a sports hall, netball courts and a football pitch. Opponents have commented on Wren teams' good sportsmanship. Pupils can take sports GCSE or BTec, and enrichment options include rugby, trampolining and table tennis.

Art, design and technology very strong and creative – as one would expect in a school with a design specialism. Projects include designing sculptures of dream ice cream sundaes, creating a piece of artwork inspired by the River Thames and designing an Olympic stadium.

'In English boys can look at their powers of reflectiveness and empathy, whilst in girls' maths classes we can encourage them to take risks'

Music is keen – there's an orchestra, samba band, gospel choir, Indian drumming club – and increasing in quality as musicians move up the school and hone their skills. Drama also finding its feet; eagerly awaited annual school musical – eg Bugsy Malone and Hairspray. Wren's Got Talent showcases singers, magicians and musicians.

Background and atmosphere: Named for Sir Christopher Wren, designer of St Paul's Cathedral, which reflects its C of E status and specialism in design and the built environment. Opened in 2008 on the site of a failed school next door to Woodhouse College. Partly refurbished but mostly newly built, it has an open plan feel, with roof lights and large north windows, grey carpets and aluminium cladding. Steps leading down from the entrance hall to the library, 'the heart of the school', are lined by ledges where children can sit and chat, under treble-height rooflights, giving an amphitheatre-like atmosphere. There is a feeling of space and airiness throughout. Corridor walls are decorated with graphics of the footprint of St Paul's Cathedral, and with murals quoting inspiring biblical texts eg 'Be willing and available to provide support and guidance to others'.

The school is sponsored by the London Diocesan Board for Schools, hence its Christian character, and by Berkhamsted School, which provides some of the governors. The schools work together on areas such as curriculum development, Wren students go over to Berkhamsted for activities, including a year 7 residential retreat, and Berkhamsted sixth formers visited Wren to give their views on appointing a

new head of sixth form. 'It's a partnership, and we hope that both schools will get an equal amount from it.'

Primary school on the same site adjacent to the existing school opened in 2015; it is growing one year at a time and will in 2022 become a complete all-through school.

Pastoral care, well-being and discipline: 'The teachers don't tolerate any bad behaviour,' say parents. 'It is a lovely, safe environment for learning'; and indeed the school had a supremely ordered feel during our visit. Three different breaks and lunchtimes help. So does the design of the building: staff and pupils share unisex toilets, and there is no staff room, so everyone socialises in the restaurant. 'It's a philosophy that when staff and students share the same space there is passive supervision, and students feel secure. They're encouraged to sit in here and chat – it's part of the curriculum.' 'Focus days' concentrate on matters ranging from sexual health to university choices.

Much emphasis on good manners and courtesy. Common sanctions include litter duty and community service. There's a Reflection Room for 'those who would benefit from time on their own'. Pupils have a high degree of autonomy, with plenty of opportunities to get involved in the way the school is run, from becoming prefects to interviewing potential teachers to taking part in curriculum reviews. 'In return, they generally play their part. There's a high level of buy-in.'

The chaplain, who plays a counsellor-like role, is generally considered a good egg. The only parental criticism is that some feel the school doesn't take their views on board. 'When you start a new school you have to put in place structures that will work. We opened with a very clear idea of what we wanted. We've always listened and explained to parents, but we haven't always amended our ways as a result.'

Pupils and parents: A diverse range, about 25 per cent white British, and characteristic of this leafy outer-London suburb; mostly 'ambitious people who want to do well'. Pupils have taken GCSEs in 13 different home languages. Active PTA which organises quiz nights and festivals, organises second hand uniform sales and has raised funds for the gazebo, which offers a shady outdoor place to socialise.

Entrance: Takes 60 into reception, and 184 into year 7. Priority to looked after children, medical/social need, siblings and children of staff. Half of remaining places community (by distance), half foundation (church-goers). Internal and external sixth form applicants need at least five grade 6s at GCSE including maths, English and the subjects they want to study at A level; prospective maths, further maths, science and French students need 7+ grades in these subjects. At least 25 external sixth form places.

Exit: Some 50 per cent leave post-GCSE. Courses include biomedicine, engineering, architecture, law and economics; universities include Exeter, Manchester, Sheffield and Queen Mary. Four to Oxbridge and one medic in 2018.

Remarks: This young school has already established a reputation for high teaching standards, courteous students and excellent enrichment activities. Likely to go from strength to strength.

East

Barking & Dagenham
Havering
Newham
Redbridge
Tower Hamlets
Waltham Forest

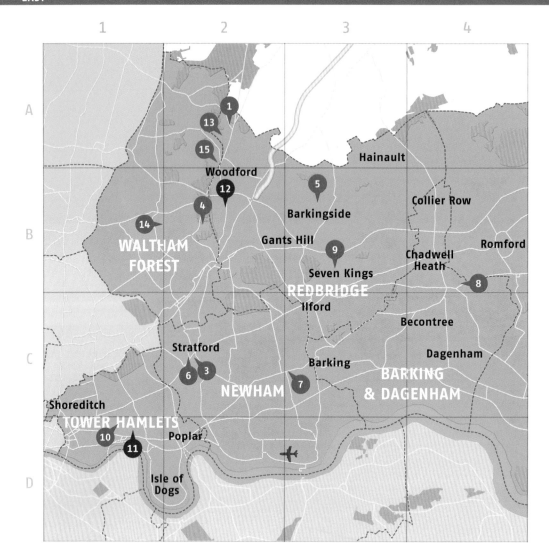

EAST

East London and its state schools

Barking & Dagenham

Barking and Dagenham, with the Thames as its southern boundary, stretches north to encompass the green belt area of Chadwell Heath. Barking was once a fishing port, with the country's largest fishing fleet until the mid-19th century. Dagenham was largely an agrarian village until the 1920s and the construction of the Becontree estate, the largest public housing estate in the world. Once, companies such as the Ford Motor Company provided settled blue collar employment (and the setting for Made in Dagenham, a dramatisation of the ground-breaking 1968 strike where female workers campaigned for equal pay). Now, most of the employment is in low-paid service industries. The borough has the cheapest housing in London and has become a magnet for first time buyers.

Robert Clack qv is a top secondary: this once-failing school was captained to success by the now-retired Sir Paul Grant, who took the helm in the late 90s, and is now massively oversubscribed. The Sydney Russell School – becoming an all-through school - is rated outstanding; Barking Abbey, Jo Richardson and All Saints Catholic School are all popular.

William Ford Junior School – linked with Village Infants on the same site – was founded in 1841, when Dagenham was a village surrounded by fields. Manor Infants/Manor Longbridge are also rated outstanding, as is Warren Junior School. Most Barking and Dagenham primary schools are large, with only a couple of faith schools having one form entry, and many with four or more forms in a year group.

Havering

Havering is the most easterly of the London boroughs. Its main town is Romford, a major metropolitan area, but it also includes large areas of green belt land. Romford, whose house prices are expected to rise in anticipation of Crossrail, claims to have one the largest and longest established markets in the country, established in the 13th century. Hornchurch and Upminster are quiet commuter towns with many 20s and 30s houses and easy access to the City by train and tube. Rainham Marshes nature reserve on the banks of the Thames, closed to the public for over 100 years and used as a military firing range, is now run by the RSPB and is a haven for birds and other wildlife.

Church-goers are privileged in the search for good secondary schools. Coopers Company and Coburn school qv in Upminster is one of the most popular secondaries and has a 'religious character': it will only consider regular worshippers from any of the major faiths. Admissions arrangements are convoluted: it gives preference to children of staff and former students; a certain percentage of places to those living in specific areas; 10 sport and nine music places. Other high performing secondary schools are both Catholic and both in Upminster: Sacred Heart of Mary girls' school and The Campion boys' school. Both give preference to practising Catholic families living in specific local parishes.

Ardleigh Green Junior and Scott's Primary, both in Hornchurch, are rated outstanding, as is Engayne primary in Upminster. Several Catholic primaries do well: St Peter's in Romford, St Joseph's in Upminster and La Salette in Rainham.

Newham

Newham – home of most of the Olympic Park, including the fabulous Zaha Hadid-designed Aquatic Centre – is also one of the most deprived boroughs in the country. It does however have rapidly improving public transport, including Stratford Station, Docklands Light Railway and – in future – several Crossrail stations. Plus London City Airport. Stratford is undergoing huge change, with over 10,000 new homes being built around the renamed Queen Elizabeth Olympic Park over the next 20 years. And of course it has the huge Westfield shopping centre – a magnet for most visitors, and a world away from the traditional East End high street.

Plashet School in East Ham is very well thought of, as are St Bonaventure RC school for boys and St Angela's Ursuline Convent school for girls (these two have a joint sixth form). Newham Collegiate Sixth Form Centre qv, which opened in 2014, has rapidly achieved excellent results. The newish selective sixth college, the London Academy of Excellence qv, is in Stratford; it was the brainchild of the heads of the local Kingsford Community School and independent Brighton College, one of its backers. Both of these achieve Oxbridge successes that leave some independent schools floundering. School 21, set up in 2012 by Peter Hyman – once adviser to Tony Blair – is developing into an extremely popular all-through school for 4-18 year olds.

Elmhurst Primary ranks highly, as do Vicarage, Central Park, St Stephen's Primary, St Edward's Catholic Primary and Upton Cross (which has expanded to five form entry on a new site and now has some 1,200 pupils). Tollgate in Plaistow is also rated outstanding, as is St Luke's C of E in Canning Town.

Redbridge

Redbridge is one of the greenest boroughs, with plentiful parks and open spaces, and the wooded expanses of Epping Forest just to its north. The M11 extension – built after years of protest, including an occupied treehouse in a 250 year old chestnut tree - pushes its way south to join the North Circular Road, and the Central line loops round and back again. Ilford, on the main train line to Liverpool Street, developed as a commuter town. South Woodford and Woodford Green have extensive inter-war mock Tudor developments, Wanstead Victorian and Edwardian terraces. Young professionals swap flats in Hoxton and Shoreditch for houses here with gardens and nearby green space.

Woodford County High for girls qv and Ilford County High for boys qv are the local selective grammar schools, with results to match (priority to high achievers who live within the school catchment areas). But there is also a high proportion of non-selective schools rated as outstanding, including Seven Kings School qv, Loxford School, Valentines High, Beal High, Oaks Park High, Chadwell Heath Academy and Trinity Catholic High. Understandably, a large proportion of pupils go on to university.

The primary schools are good too. Christchurch Primary, a secular school in spite of its name, is one of the largest in the country with five forms in each year group. St Bede's RC primary and Our Lady of Lourdes RC primary are high-achieving, as are Redbridge, Nightingale, Churchfields and Gearies.

Tower Hamlets

Tower Hamlets, one of the oldest parts of London (tribal, pre-Roman, silted and swampy at the time), was in more recent times home to most of London's Cockney dock workers. Wapping and the areas along that length of the river were lined with docks and warehouses for the thousands of ships and workers in London's port, characterised as well by Dickensian levels of poverty and crime. Those same docks, winding streets and riverside warehouses now contain very high end flats, served by the best butcher in east London and lively cafés and trendy restaurants (one, for example, in a converted power hydraulic station), but some areas still have high levels of poverty.

This is a vibrantly multi-ethnic borough – successive waves of immigrants, including Huguenot refugees, Irish weavers, Askanazi Jews and most recently Bangladeshis have congregated here. As well as the largest city farm in the country – the 32 acre Mudchute Park and Farm in the middle of the Isle of Dogs – it has the oldest surviving music hall in the world, Wilton's.

In the 90s it had some of the worst performing schools in the country; now it has some of the best. It reduced absences, set ambitious targets and used its extra funding as a deprived area to attract some high quality teaching staff and heads.

Sir John Cass's Foundation and Redcoat School qv is one of the most popular secondary schools. Although a C of E school, only a small minority of places are for committed Christians, and the vast majority of pupils, mirroring the ethnic make-up of the area, are Bangladeshi. In 2014 it was caught up in the controversy about Islamic extremism in schools, and downgraded by Ofsted from outstanding to inadequate, primarily over segregation of boys and girls and some sixth form Facebook activity. However, an inspection in October 2015 returned it to its former outstanding status. Mulberry School for Girls, with a similar demographic, is also rated as outstanding, as are Morpeth School and Swanlea School. St Paul's Way Trust, undersubscribed and rated as 'satisfactory' a few years ago, is now, in a new building with greatly improved reports, another of the most sought-after schools in the borough. A recent arrival is ELAM qv, East London Arts and Music, a sixth form music, games design, film and TV academy that has now moved into its own new building at Bromley-by-Bow.

Amongst many popular primary schools are Sir William Burrough qv with its international primary curriculum, Old Palace, Bygrove, Bonner, Old Ford and Clara Grant – interesting that many of the top-performing primaries in this area are secular. A controversial free school, Canary Wharf College (a primary in spite of its name) has hit the news for having only two per cent of pupils on free school meals in an area where most schools have 50 per cent, and limiting class sizes to 20. A second College opened in September 2014, again with 50 per cent of places for Christian church goers, and a senior school opened in 2016.

Waltham Forest

Waltham Forest is a borough of contrasts: the area south of the North Circular Road is mostly built-up and urban, with the socially and ethnically mixed population characteristic of inner cities – it includes one of the highest ethnic minority populations in Europe. The reservoirs along the western boundary are being transformed into an urban wetland nature reserve; the northern boundary blends into the edges of Epping Forest, and the area north of the North Circular is rather more suburban and leafy. At the end of the Victoria line, it is increasingly on the radar of those trying to keep ahead of the rising tide of house prices – and Walthamstow features not only the William Morris gallery but God's Own Junkyard, with its neon light creations. Walthamstow Village, the ancient heart of the town, is the site of a 12th-century church, 400-year-old almshouses and roads of highly desirable terraced houses.

Walthamstow School for Girls qv, which goes up to 16, is a flagship secondary; Highams Park is also popular. Leyton Sixth Form College has been judged the best college in London for sport.

St Mary's Catholic Primary in Chingford in the leafy northern part is highly rated, as are Henry Maynard, the massive Hillyfield Primary Academy (with seven classes in a year group and over 1,000 children on two sites), Greenleaf, Coppermill, Handsworth and Dawlish Road.

Ilford County High School

Bancroft's School

611–627 High Road, Woodford Green, Essex IG8 oRF

020 8505 4821 | stephanie.wallis@bancrofts.org | bancrofts.org

Independent	Pupils: 1,142; sixth form: 245
Ages: 7-18	Fees: £14,751 – £18,123 pa

Head: Since 2016, Simon Marshall (early 50s). Formerly headmaster of the English College in Prague and, before that, deputy head academic at UCS Hampstead and, in an earlier incarnation, head of English at KCS Wimbledon. A very calm and incisive communicator who has the underlying confidence to deal in nuance. He believes he has taken over a school which is already performing at a very high level, and his attention seems divided equally between maintaining all that is good, and trying to help all constituencies within the school think of themselves and their ambitions perhaps a little more laterally. No academic slouch himself, having read classics at Cambridge, where he was also a choral exhibitioner and did a PGCE. Thence to Oxford, where he took a degree in English literature and then a MPhil in 18th century studies. A keen mountaineer and runner, he enjoys gardening, music and theatre. Married to Eleanor.

One parent, steeped in the ancien régime, described him as 'a great listener, sensitive to tradition, but definitely working in his ideas. He's greatly liked, and the way he is celebrating arts and humanities is just what Bancroft's needs.'

Head of prep since 2012 Joe Layburn MA, previously acting head. MA in German literature from University College London, followed by a 15-year career as an investigative journalist and TV reporter, primarily for Channel 4. Retrained as a teacher and joined Bancroft's Prep in 2004. A steady pair of hands, popular with staff, children and parents. Author of a trilogy of children's books. Married with three children; two were educated at Bancroft's from prep onwards and one at a special needs school. Keen on running, cycling and West Ham United.

Academic matters: Notable results across the board (in 2018, 69 per cent A*/A grades at A level). Many go on to study medicine or engineering at top universities. The head is emphatic about the hard work and deep commitment of staff, but places a big emphasis too on the work ethic of pupils. Maths and physics are stellar, and all the sciences excellent. Arts, languages and humanities results are,

by any standard, very good. This slight asymmetry has less to do with teaching, about which all parties wax lyrical, than with the nature of the constituency: many families here are first generation users of independent schools, and there is an emphasis on traditional 'respectable' professions. One gets the sense the head may be keen gently to nudge pupils into believing there are more destinies for themselves than they might sometimes imagine. 'Bancroft's boys and girls have such heart and power,' he says, 'such creativity and imagination'.

The GCSE hit rate in 2018 was a whopping 85 per cent at 9-7. No obviously weak links but maths and science again at the heart of success. Perhaps rather fewer taking the more obviously creative subjects – art and music, for instance, or DT. Drama is now in the curriculum, but getting real momentum behind these is less about facilities (which are good) than about winning over sceptics. It all takes time. Modern languages have been the beneficiaries of this patient dedication. German, French and Spanish are all on offer from year 8; Russian becomes available in year 9 and Mandarin in the sixth form. A particular, enlightened feature is that subjects can be chosen not, as elsewhere, from 'blocks' but from the whole curriculum. Given that Bancroft's is not a rich school, and that staff are required to teach an average 31 periods per week, this flexibility is all the more impressive.

Head is emphatic about hard work and commitment of staff, as well as the work ethic of pupils

A terrific learning environment. The library, revamped with a stylish mezzanine floor beautifully integrated into the whole, is a proper scholarly resource – a place where pupils actually sit quietly and read. Given that library is all too often a euphemism for 'IT suite' these days, this delving among books redounds greatly to the credit of both staff and pupils. The latter evidently appreciate the librarians– 'they are fantastic – they get in anything you need'. The sixth form has a quiet study area and the Great Hall is used, amongst much else, for societies, debates and visiting speakers. IT everywhere – lots of rooms with new PCs, including a tiptop language lab.

Prep classrooms busy, not over-orderly and relaxed – we wanted to look at the displays, all of which seemed interesting and not as predictable as they so often are. We also approved some of the interesting work in progress, especially the lesson on moulds – 'We had to throw them away as they were beginning to smell,' was a rueful observation. Year 6 has critical thinking lessons – 'to expand our minds, to think out of the box, to widen our imagination,' we were told, earnestly. We were impressed by the sensible 'traffic light' system whereby pupils assess their grasp of what they have learnt and where they need help.

One parent, steeped in the ancien régime, described him as 'a great listener, sensitive to tradition, but definitely working in his ideas. He's greatly liked'

Learning support department screens all at 7+ and 11+. School has a dedicated SENCo and there are two part-timers in assistance. All new staff get some training in spotting those with learning difficulties but the head is mindful that all staff need encouragement to stay alert to those with learning difficulties: these will mostly be mild dyslexics and all will be given some kind of individual support – the precise nature of which depends on need, but may well involve one-to-one time. Lower sixth get help to 'develop individual learning skills'. 'They are wonderfully flexible over special needs,' said a parent.

Games, options, the arts: Sports are 'big' and well-resourced. Large playing fields on site plus vast sports hall with 25m pool. Five minutes' drive away is school's own West Grove with pitches, courts, tracks etc. Strong in all major sports – hockey, rugby, netball, cricket and tennis. Achievement to match – triumphs in netball, rugby and cricket as well as tours in these and hockey to, eg, Canada, Singapore/Malaysia, South Africa and Barbados. Historic complaints that sport is too elitist have become less strident but not disappeared: 'It's too often the same brilliant sportsmen getting the limelight,' said one parent. The school has taken these seriously and evolved B and C teams, along with soccer. There are practical constraints, not

least finding the necessary facilities and fixtures with other schools. 'I know they're working on this,' said one parent, 'and not before time. It's our one grouse about the school.'

There is a serious wish on the part of the head that sport should reflect the values the school is trying to impart. 'We're properly proud of all the sporting success,' he says, 'but we want to create ways in which the best kind of team experience is genuinely attainable to all who seek it. Sport should offer all our pupils a medium through which they can cultivate the kinds of strength and conditioning which will sustain them throughout their lives.'

CCF is huge, very popular and enthusiastically pursued by those who surprise themselves by how much they get out of it, girls as well as boys – 'It's taught me how to get on with people I'd never mix with normally'; 'It's good that the sixth form help with it – you can have a bit of a laugh with them'. Thriving D of E. Over 200 pupils are involved in it with 30 taking gold – 'doing my gold was the hardest thing I've ever done,' said one girl, 'and the best'. Also a Sea Scout group with cubs and scouts.

Equally, steadily increased provision for arts across the school. Music and drama enthusiastic and popular – annual concert in Drapers' Hall the big annual event, with bands, solo performances and musical mix the main features. HM particularly enthused (moved, really) by the recent TAAL production – a pan-Asian body run by the Hindu, Muslim, Bhuddist and Sikh Society, but involving pupils of all ethnic groups – which embraced dance and music of all kinds. 'It was an explosion of energy and creativity,' he says, 'and it tells a big story'. Vast range of instruments studied, with eight classical concerts each year. Jazz, rock and other genres all celebrated in addition to the main and chamber orchestras. A suite of Apple Macs to support composition. Two big drama spaces – the Great Hall and a fine performing arts centre. A recent triumphant production of Les Misérables but also Amadeus and Sweeney Todd. All year 7s and 8s do drama as part of the curriculum, and there is house drama production as well. Productions at Edinburgh Fringe Festival.

Art, electronics and DT departments are buzzy spaces. Art is well-displayed and the studios are wonderful oases of light and space, as well as excellently equipped. Excellent outcomes for the seriously committed – one recent leaver having secured a spot at Central St Martins. Pupils are given considerable latitude to be creative in design. After a period of staff turnover, DT is becoming more embedded and there are hopes that it will soon be on offer for A level. Like so many schools, the cultural leap to move away from the old woodwork/metalwork shop mentality hasn't happened overnight, but the head sees an emerging synergy not merely between art, DT and electronics but extending to physics and the sciences, with big potential growth in product design.

Background and atmosphere: Founded in 1737 by the Drapers' Company on behalf of Francis Bancroft as a school for poor boys; moved to Woodford from Mile End in 1889 into the present large and imposing red-brick Victorian gothic revival building – clearly designed to impress, with serious scholarly credentials by architect, Sir Arthur Blomfield, also responsible for Selwyn College, Cambridge. This is one of his more benign and attractive buildings, with towers, crenellations and oriel windows, a splendid central quad and admirably generous corridors which, though originally intended for 200 boys, still feel spacious for today's quadrupled numbers. Twisty, brick staircases and leaded lights which grab eager 10 year olds immediately – 'I chose it because it was like Hogwarts'.

Large Great Hall – typical of date and type. Excellent Courtyard Building with colonnaded atrium and sitting area, dining room (all seniors eat together, although the sixth form can exercise the option to eat in their common room). The food gets good press, too, in contrast to the dismal recollections of one old boy now a parent ('I'm pretty jealous, actually'). Some 1960s add-ons but much better later additions (such as enormous multi-purpose sports hall) and adjoining buildings, eg vast head's house now used for admin and offices too, with head's garden open to everyone for quiet time and 'well-respected'. Nice new physics labs and modern language rooms and DT suite.

This is one of his more benign and attractive buildings, with towers, crenellations and oriel windows

Integral chapel one of the best bits (complete with much-loved chaplain who is, says a parent, 'just extraordinary – you should hear what my children say about him. They leave chapel filled with fresh understanding about the need for mutual respect.') Each year group comes once weekly for an ecumenical service. Brass plaques to former heads and a vast stained glass east window set the tone for the services, which are inclusive in all ways, given the mix of pupils. Chapel also used for arts events – words and music etc, a classy extracurricular feature here.

Prep is in two conjoined, inviting-looking, modern red-brick buildings at the lower right hand side of the main school playing fields – two-storeyed and with big windows. Newish science, drama, music and DT rooms, a good-sized hall

with flexible seating – lots of IT and new laptops. The library, recently refurbished, is well-stocked and a good mix of fact and fiction. Outside space good and super all-weather surface for littlies with monster chess set and apparatus – not surprisingly, 'Everyone loves coming out here'.

Parental tributes to general efficiency of school and its communications. Sense of order, purposeful activity and common sense all-pervasive.

Pastoral care, well-being and discipline: Unstinting and uniform praise for pastoral care is very rare, and yet this is what our enquiries to a range of parents and pupils revealed. Tributes to the teaching staff, overall friendliness, care and attention given to individuals pour from everyone and are a delight to hear: 'My teacher is amazing – he's given me extra lessons every week'; 'They'll help with anyone – not just the Oxbridge candidates'; 'The teacher gave my daughter as much time as she needed when she was struggling'.

Staff respond especially to the wholehearted and aspirational nature of their pupils, who are so laudably devoid of a sense of entitlement. The system which facilitates such praise is based around form tutors – usually of between 13 and 17 pupils. There are also houses for competitive purposes. With 200 plus pupils in each, the heads of house and their deputies have a formidable challenge in knowing their charges.

The teachers seem also to believe pupils are overwhelmingly biddable and friendly. 'Of course,' says the head, 'teenagers can make mistakes'. Like every other school, helping youngsters to make sensible use of IT is a preoccupation for teachers and parents, but as HM says, 'adults don't always find it easy either.' He is trying to encourage a pastoral style which can be more generally proactive and – it follows on – pupils find it easy and unthreatening to volunteer fears and anxieties.

Pupils and parents: From as far away as Potter's Bar, Winchmore Hill and Cheshunt, though most from between 10 and 20 minutes' drive away. Transport from local tube station to encourage pupils to look out of town towards green space for schooling. Vast ethnic and social intake – 'very well-handled by school,' say parents. Most parents first-time buyers who 'work very hard to pay fees'.

OB notables include Dennis Quilley, Sir Frederick Warner, Sir Neil McFarlane, Hari Kunzru, Adam Foulds, Yolanda Browne, Andrew Saul, Anita Anand, Lord Pannick QC, Samantha Spiro and Mike Lynch.

Entrance: At 7+ into the prep – oversubscribed by about three to one. Testing in English – reading and writing – and maths takes place on beanbags. Children seen (and offered doughnuts) in small groups with head and deputy – it's 'as informal and low key as possible'.

Some 60 pupils come up from the prep school to the senior school at 11. Around 500 apply for 65 additional places. 'It's nice to be wanted,' says the head, 'but we want to stay well away from complacency'. There are entrance tests in maths and English plus interviews – 'we need to fashion something more imaginative.' he says. 'We're working on it.' In practice around a third of those whose first choice is Bancroft's will get in. Umpteen feeders, though several from St Aubyn's, Loyola and Woodford Green Prep. Around a half from state primaries.

Candidates for the sixth form sit the school's own entrance exam in two proposed A level subjects, need six 7s at GCSE plus the usual references. Around 20 places at this level – very few (around 10 per cent) leave.

Exit: Around 90 per cent of the prep moves to the senior school. Around 10 per cent leaves after GCSEs. Twelve Oxbridge places in 2018; 17 medics, dentists and vets. Popular current destinations are Birmingham, Exeter and Nottingham. Others off to Amsterdam, Maryland, Milan and Toronto.

Money matters: Bancroft's has always sought to keep its fees low. There's been a hike recently which has led to some mutterings, but the HM says ruefully, 'It's always a dilemma. We don't want to change our identity, but we must be able to plan for the long term.' He feels some of the building projects of earlier times could have been better conceived had there been less of the short-termism

Much-loved chaplain who is, says a parent, 'just extraordinary – you should hear what my children say about him'

which customarily happens when budgets are too tight.

Fifteen Drapers' scholarships offered annually at 11+ worth a quarter to a half of fees. No means-testing – based solely on performance at entrance exams. Also music scholarships worth half or quarter fees plus free tuition in one instrument. Several Francis Bancroft scholarship awards – means-tested but with a generous financial threshold, worth up to full fees, based on a sliding scale dependent on family income. Bancroft's Foundation set up in 2012 to mark 275th anniversary has already raised significant amounts to increase means-tested provision – enough to fund six Foundation scholars.

Remarks: An outstanding school – bright children, dedicated staff, and one of the most remarkable heads we've met. Given all its strengths, it deserves to be much more widely celebrated, although a deep part of its charm (and virtue) is that boastfulness and self-advertisement is off-limits. 'We can never repay what this school has done for our children,' said one parent. We wanted to shout it out from the rafters – this place is superb.

The Coopers' Company and Coborn School

St Mary's Lane, Upminster, Essex RM14 3HS

01708 250500 | info@cooperscoborn.org.uk | cooperscoborn.org.uk

State	Pupils: 1,386; sixth form: 450
Ages: 11–18	

Headteacher: Since 2013, Dr David Parry PhD MA MBA NPQH. Previously deputy head of the school since 2005, including a stint as acting headteacher. Did his teacher training at the Royal Central School of Speech and Drama (where alumni include Rupert Everett and French and Saunders); his BA in English and education, along with his masters in leadership and management, at Open University; and his PhD and more recently MBA at the UCL

Institute of Education. When we visited, he was studying for a GCSE in physics with year 11s. 'It's part of our growth mindset culture – all staff take on board a challenge to show the students anything is possible,' he explains, providing other examples of staff learning to play the saxophone, to sing, to learn a new language or to walk the three peaks. Staff told us this aspirational culture was always implicit, but Dr Parry has made it explicit. Also known for bringing in clearer systems, along with zero tolerance around behaviour. 'Students' behaviour was always good; now it's even better,' one staff member told us.

Prior to this school, he was deputy head at Caterham High School. 'And before that, I suppose you could say I was professionally promiscuous,' he laughs, pointing out that he worked across both the independent sector (where he taught Alan Sugar's children) right through to challenging state schools in London.

One of the most hands-on heads we've come across, he greets pupils every morning at the gate ('The subtext is checking on uniform, but it is genuinely nice to welcome them every morning,' he smiles) and says goodbye to them every afternoon. He is available outside for every morning break time, has a genuine open-door policy, eats in the dining room every day, gets involved in extracurricular activities and school trips, helps with UCAS applications and teaches English. 'As a head teacher, I don't know how you cannot teach,' he says. 'All of us are shop floor operatives in this school, no matter what our role. We don't want to run a school where leaders are remote.'

Parents see him as 'old school, but always open to new ideas,' ('the perfect balance,' said one) and pupils say he's the kind of head that 'instantly demands respect', but is 'very approachable.' We found him a solid, authoritative type, but extremely friendly, open-minded and forward-thinking.

Academic matters: There's an assumption that students will do well here ('It's built into their DNA that they will want to succeed,' says head) and they do, with the school consistently achieving near top GCSE results nationally, with 95 per cent getting 9-4 in both English and maths, 39 per cent 9-7 grades in 2018. They are especially strong in English language, English lit, mathematics and art and design, but pupils also do exceptionally well in RS, DT, textiles technology and music. The most popular GCSE choices are history, German, geography and sport/PE, and fair numbers also choose Spanish and French.

At sixth form, pupils are offered a wide curriculum of traditional subjects but are also introduced to new courses – media studies, psychology and politics. Popular choices are the sciences, especially biology ('We buck the national trend when it comes to STEM subjects a A level,' says head), business studies, history, maths and psychology. In 2018, 33 per cent A*/A grades, 67 per cent A*-B.

Spanish, French, German or Mandarin from year 7 (parents get to state a preference when they apply to the school), with a second language introduced in year 8, at which point Mandarin and German are also available. 'Modern languages are big strength of the school,' said one parent,

reflecting the views of others. Pupils are setted for maths in year 7 and there's an element of setting in languages and sciences at GSCE. Homework considered an essential part of shaping pupils' academic experience, particularly in relation to independent learning and thinking skills.

Teachers renowned for going the extra mile both inside the classroom and out. 'No teacher gets an interview until they've taught a lesson which we find to be good or outstanding,' says the head, who adds that for every applicant teacher, he asks himself two questions: 'Would I want to be taught by them? Would I want my daughter to be taught by them?' If either answer is no, they don't get in, he says. A fair amount of emailing goes on after hours, for which both students and parents are very grateful.

For every applicant teacher, he asks himself: 'Would I want to be taught by them? Would I want my daughter to be taught by them?' If either answer is no they don't get in

Despite high results, the school is always working on improving grades and has introduced Go 4 Schools, an online tracking programme, enabling parents and teachers to login at any time to monitor how the student is doing, with both individual grades and overall grades, target grades and how they can improve, enabling all three parties to monitor progress and make any necessary interventions to keep grades on track. 'It really helps cement the three way partnership between students, parents and teachers,' says head and parents agree. 'We have a good idea of both where our children are relative to where they need to be,' said one parent. The bottom 15 students in the year are provided with extra measures, as are the 15 at the top. SEN has a strong team of six staff members, mainly providing classroom-based help for children with issues ranging from dyslexia to autism, although less than one per cent of these have been statemented. 'For major SEN issues, other schools in the borough are better equipped,' admits head.

Although the school is very academic, we found it to be the antithesis of an exam factory, offering a broad and liberal education, with a major emphasis on extracurricular activities that all students are expected to get involved in. 'If you're the kind of person that just wants to go to school from 9am-3pm then go home and forget about school, this probably isn't the place for you,' one student told us. Whilst PE accounts for the majority of the 142 clubs on offer, other subjects include music, drama, IT and all the academic subjects right through to beekeeping, chicken keeping and robot building. Many of the school teams enter national competitions – 94 of them the year we visited, reaching national finals in 33 of them and world finals in two. The debating team reached the finals at Oxford University.

Games, options, the arts: This is the number one co-ed state school for sport, if you take as the criteria the number of national level finals reached across all sports. Also regularly enters for international events, with the triathlon team having reached the world finals, coming second mixed team, the year we visited. Students took part in the opening ceremony of the 2012 Olympics and were also involved in the handover of the Olympic Flame for the Rio Olympics. Regular competitions against leading independent schools, especially in athletics, cross-country, badminton and swimming. Not surprisingly, the students we spoke to were deeply proud of the school's exceptional achievements and aptitude.

The rich curriculum ranges from circuit gym training to trampolining, cricket and netball to indoor rowing and PE remains compulsory throughout the school years, even at sixth form. Facilities, including a swimming pool, are impressive and sports trips are notable, including rugby tours to New Zealand and Australia, athletics training in Lanzarote and tennis training in Florida. 'The attention to detail in the coaching is second to none,' said one parent. 'Nobody is left out, with everyone given a chance to thrive,' said another.

Well-equipped art studios, with a studio offering individual cubicles for pupils who need a designated area in which to work. An 'open house' policy approach encourages independent work and, along with the clearly outstanding levels of work on display, creates a wonderful 'art school' atmosphere. Pupils consistently have work displayed in exhibitions around the country.

Drama standards are high, with two roomy practice areas, including a state-of-the-art renovated theatre, with retracted seating. Plenty of performances throughout the year, including one main annual performance – Singing in the Rain the year we visited.

Music also strong, with five school orchestras (including an all ability one), two choirs and regular ensembles and concerts. Expect brass band more than rock music 'as we like to keep things traditional,' says head. Around 180 students are taught instrumental lessons in school, with 54 music exams in school alone – with many more students learning and being tested outside school. Students take part in music festivals and competitions, as well as playing at significant events, such as the Lord Mayor's Banquet, and at a more local level within school, for example during assemblies.

Amid 25 acres of greenery, and home to a pond visited by ducks and geese, the school feels spacious, neat and tidy and well cared for

'There's no shortage of volunteers and the inclusive and supportive ethos of the school means you never get students saying, "I don't think I'm good enough to play in front of my friends",' says head. Overseas trips, such as an eight-day Italy music tour to Lake Garda.

Huge range of extracurricular choice, with clubs before and after school and at lunch time, covering almost every conceivable area, from chess to fishing. Several clubs have been instigated and are run by pupils. 'The amount of opportunities is amazing – everyone tries something they never thought they would,' said one student. School trips are also big here, with around 40 domestic and 23 international ones every year. Besides the sport-based ones, there are language trips (year 8) and exchange trips (year 10) to support Spanish, German, Mandarin and French and other trips to explore interesting places such as Namibia and Botswana.

Background and atmosphere: A rich history dating back to 1536 when it was first established as a free school for boys. Its name came in 1552 when the Coopers' Company was asked to take over the running of the school. It was then located in Stepney, Tower Hamlets. In 1891, it joined foundations with the Coborn school for boys and girls and remained at sites at Mile End and Bow until it moved to Upminster in 1971. 'Our first students would have seen Shakespeare's plays,' points out the head, who sees their long history as central to the school's culture.

Now situated a good distance from the main road amid 25 acres of greenery, and home to a pond visited by ducks and geese, the school feels spacious, exceptionally neat and tidy and well cared for. And although some of the main school buildings from the 70s are looking tired, modernisation and development have seen new buildings regularly erected since the 80s, the latest being a sixth form block. Other smaller but notable modern developments include a solar panel roof, i-desks (with computers that pop up) and a state-of-the-art laser cutter. 'This school really listens to the students when it comes to the need for new facilities or equipment, so we never feel left behind,' said one student.

The school motto, Love as Brethren, appears quite literally in shining lights as you walk in the school and you won't find a student who doesn't believe it's central to school life here, with many using the hashtag

LasB when they sign off emails or post on social media. 'There's a real spirit of philanthropy and generosity of spirit here,' one student told us, and we too found the atmosphere to be happy and thoughtful, with students displaying a healthy level of boisterousness during break times, but heads down during class. Religion not in your face, but Christian values embedded into everyday life.

Pastoral care, well-being and discipline: Students describe the school as being a 'protective cloak' and 'like a family,' with the young people looking out for each other and staff on hand to help with any issues students may have. The school also buys into a student counselling service and clearly takes mental health issues seriously. 'Mental health is the single biggest issue facing today's young people,' says head. A house system, which consists of four houses, helps create vertical links, as well as the horizontal year groupings. Peer to peer mentoring, and around 150 sixth formers work with younger pupils.

Plenty of leadership opportunities, with a democratic process selecting school captains from year 12 pupils, who must apply for this prestigious position. The one boy and one girl selected hold office throughout their final year. School council plays a key role in the decision-making processes – including the appointment of senior staff. Pupils are given a sense of importance and are consulted on important developments. Reward system is fully utilised, including housepoints, certificates, postcards and phone calls home, letters from head and spotlight in assembly.

Bad behaviour here is simply 'uncool,' students told us. One pointed out that the rules are so well embedded into school life that nobody thinks the school is that strict

There isn't much room for making mistakes here, however, with zero tolerance of bad behaviour and very high expectations of conduct. These expectations, and the punishments for failing to adhere to them, are all outlined in both a contract that students have to sign before coming to the school, and a visually friendly charter. Staff are trained in them too, so that there is complete consistency, and parents are also expected to be on board. 'If students don't meet the standards, they can expect serious sanctions,' says the head. 'I'm quite happy to run Saturday detentions, for example, and I would

exclude.' Indeed, he had permanently excluded a student the week before our visit for intimidating behaviour towards a staff member, although permanent exclusions are rare. Talking when teaching, or not focusing in class, are considered as bad as writing on school walls. 'I explain to students that there are two types of vandalism here – damaging something and damaging the education of others – and I tolerate neither,' says head, with other rules including no mobile phones (except in sixth form), eating only in allocated areas and very strict uniform rules, with not a silly haircut or rolled up skirt in sight. But whilst it might all sound draconian, we found unanimous agreement from parents and students that the rules and consequences are fair and ultimately prepare young people for the world of work. Bad behaviour here is simply 'uncool,' students told us, with one pointing out that the rules are so well embedded into school life that in reality, nobody really thinks of the school as that strict. 'There's a strong sense of students not wanting to let down the school or betray its past,' adds the head. Bullying rare because, according to students; 'mocking just isn't what we do here.'

Pupils and parents: Most students from aspirational families. Around 80 per cent white middle class, the rest of a mixture of ethnic minorities. Although it's a Christian school, there's an eclectic mix from all recognised world religions. Many parents are supportive of the school and help out at school events, with an active PA of about 30 members – good for a secondary state school. They arrange various fundraising events including a monthly sale of supermarket vouchers to parents and staff and they had just raised enough funds for a new minibus when we visited. We found pupils to be articulate, grounded, respectful and polite – traits for which they are known throughout the local community. They are very proud of their school, as well as extremely appreciative of having a place there. Everyone is welcoming – greeting visitors with smiles and hellos, saying thank you, holding doors open and even singing to themselves as they pass by.

Entrance: Unusually large number of feeder schools (around 100). Admissions rules and catchment area complicated due to the school's historic links to east London and wish to preserve the principles of the Coopers' Company and Coborn Educational Foundation.

Over 1,000 applications for just 180 places and a fair number go to appeal. Ten sport and nine music places, which hundreds apply for. All other applicants must be actively connected to one of the main world faiths. Some places for children of staff and former students; others by promixity; others to those who live in specific areas including Havering, Brentwood and Billericay.

Most stay on to the sixth form after GCSE. Around 50 places for students from outside but, again, massively popular with over 700 applications. Applicants need at least eight 9-4 grades to be considered for a place, to be sympathetic to the school's Christian character and be willing to uphold its 'Love as Brethren' ethos by giving time to serve the school. Oversubscription criteria prioritise looked after children, highest predicted grades and then availability in specific sets. 'Our sixth form is equivalent to a grammar school, in terms of offering traditional subject choices and the fact that we take the cream of the crop,' says the head.

Exit: Around half leaves after GCSE for one of three reasons: to study a vocational course at college, to study different subject choices at other local schools or (a few) to take up an apprenticeship. Almost none leave to go into low-paid work. Around three-quarters of sixth formers to university, which is high for the area, of which a third go to Russell Group universities. Particularly popular are Warwick, Bristol, Durham, Birmingham, Bath, Exeter, Loughborough and Imperial. Four to Oxbridge in 2018.

School provides a range of opportunities to prepare for post school, including careers advice from year 9, conferences, workshops, competitions and special events at universities such as Nottingham and Cambridge. Many go on to study pure science subjects or vocational courses such as medicine, veterinary science and dentistry. Other popular subjects include psychology, economics, architecture, art history, journalism, politics and theatre design.

Money matters: The school allocates £10k to assist pupils that need help and also provides music and sports grants of up to £500 through a bursary system from The Coopers' Company and Coborn Educational Foundation.

Remarks: World class in the true sense of the word, this school is a dynamic, exciting place to learn, preparing students for successful lives. Dazzling reputation in the local community and largely responsible for increased house prices in the Upminster area. 'If you're not one of these things – academic, sporty or musical – it's probably not the school for you,' pointed out one parent, whilst students say you need to be willing to put in more time than regular school hours and more commitment than the bare minimum. 'There's no room for just plodding along here,' explained one. But for those that fit the mould, it's outstanding.

East London Arts & Music

London E3 3TA

0207 515 2159 | info@elam.co.uk | elam.co.uk/

| State | Pupils: 300 |
| Ages: 16–19 | |

Principal: Since the school opened in 2014, Charlie Kennard BA MA QTS (30s). Educated at Latymer Upper, read economics at Edinburgh, then went straight onto the Teach First programme. Taught for two years at Stuart Bathurst Catholic Secondary School in Wednesbury near Birmingham, working with some of the most economically disadvantaged children in the country; then joined the Teach First management team and subsequently became director of its sister organisation Teach for Malaysia. In 2012, happened to have a conversation with his brother Will, the platinum-selling musician of Chase & Status fame, decrying the lack of opportunities in the music business for young people from low-income families. ELAM opened two years later. No grass growing beneath Charlie's feet.

Youthful, fresh-faced, a child of the modern age and totally at ease with it, Charlie (all first names here) is also a man who genuinely believes in his students and works tirelessly to bring them on. A recent study found that 60 per cent of music chart acts had been educated at a private school compared with one per cent at the same point 20 years previously. He regards this as unfair and a waste of talent. 'Growing up, my brother and I were around professionals, whereas 60 per cent of the kids I was teaching in Walsall had neither parent working. Some of them were more talented musically than my brother – I've said this to him, and to his credit he didn't punch me in the face – but for them, succeeding in the creative industries was like a trip to the moon.' His mission is, quite simply, to put this right. 'We were impressed with the principal – his dedication and vision and ability to recruit great staff,' wrote a mother.

A popular and very active presence around the school – 'My boss is the students' – but also a calm, quiet individual who wears his commitment lightly and without the least zealotry. This is all the more remarkable given what he's achieved in such a short time: taking on the headship of this exceptional school at the age of 27, overseeing the construction of its state of the art premises on the site of a derelict warehouse, and leading it to its present success – it was rated outstanding in all areas by Ofsted in 2017. Sitting in his minimalist office, touched by his concern over our odd-looking cup of coffee from the school canteen and chatting comfortably, it took us a little time to realise we were in the presence of greatness. But we were.

Married to Victoria, a lawyer, with a baby daughter.

Academic matters: ELAM's ethos is straightforward: to enable young people to succeed in the creative industries through offering the right skills training plus access to high quality professional opportunities. 'There's often no straightforward route into the creative industries,' observes Charlie, 'so we're trying to create a clearer pathway, especially for those who can't afford to work unpaid until they get their foot in the door. It's vital not just to help students get their qualifications, but to get them started on the next step.'

The school originally offered music only, but now ELAM students can opt for one of three pathways: music, games design, or film and television production. Music trainees study for the BTec level 3 extended diploma in music. Games and film students study for the University of Arts London level 3 extended diploma in creative media production & technology. Both are equivalent to three A levels in UCAS tariff points and teaching time.

Having the different specialisms housed within the same school 'creates a great dynamism, and the trainees collaborate with each other.'

Everything taught here is underpinned by industry demand. 'The UK's creative sector is growing at a humungous rate. Music punches well above its weight in this country. Film and TV are going through the roof, not least because a high number of American productions are made here to take advantage of generous tax breaks. And there's a huge, huge industry demand for gaming skills.' From the outset, the school's approach has been to work with industry to define the curriculum. Universal Music UK was a founding partner and still offers 'unbelievably fantastic' support. Other partners include Decca, Lovebox, Virgin EMI, Abbey Road Studios, Lovebox, Polydor, Machinima Sboc – and more.

Trainees are worked hard from the off, and quickly come to relish the challenge of rising to professional level standards and deadlines. 'Before I came to ELAM I knew nothing about making games,' mused a year 12 student as he showed us an impressive virtual environment he'd created set in a submarine, 'but it's hands on here, you're thrown in at the deep end, it's about constant improvement. Coming here is one of the best things that's happened to me. It's amazing.' Teaching universally praised – 'They're brilliant professionals, they don't have to be teachers!' – but students were adamant that there was nothing relaxed about it. Meeting deadlines was hectic and often stressful, we were told, but they liked the professionalism of it. 'It's like you're an intern for a job.' 'They'll tell you if your work is rubbish. They're blunt with you and honest, and I think that's the best thing.' 'The learning here is quick, they don't mess around.'

Popular and very active presence around the school – 'My boss is the students' – but also a calm, quiet individual who wears his commitment lightly

Understandably, perhaps, some parents need to be convinced that the school is right for their child, particularly those whose offspring are academically successful and could have joined a more conventional sixth form; but once their child is here they appear to be very much won over. A parent of a student on the music pathway told us, 'The school does everything it can to provide the very best tuition, not just in music but in every discipline involved in the professional music industry. Above all, it teaches the importance of collaboration and the necessity of taking a collaborative approach. ELAM could not provide a better grounding for somebody looking to make music a career – whether as a performer or in other aspects of the industry.'

Maths and English are compulsory here, and an intrinsic part of the school's mission to enable young people to be industry ready. 'They have to be able to express themselves clearly and be comfortable with handling data – these days, the taste makers are the ones who can analyse trends'. Students who didn't achieve at least a 4 at GCSE must retake. School has a 100 per cent success rate for English resits; maths currently at 60 per cent. Those who have already passed these GCSEs when they arrive can opt to do either A level maths and/or English, or a level 3 qualification in quantitative reasoning plus the EPQ – both are equivalent to an

AS. Principal is unapologetic about these aspects of the provision, but readily concedes that not all trainees have full enthusiasm for them, and some of the young people admitted as much. 'I had to resit my maths, and the work for English is killing me, I'm not gonna lie,' sighed one, 'but I enjoy that I get to do the music I want to do, and get to meet industry people.' And personal reluctance notwithstanding, all the trainees agreed that the school was right to insist on it. 'The stuff they teach us, whether you like it or not, it's relevant,' said one. 'A level maths is very applicable to game design,' said another, who came to ELAM with a full crop of top grades at GCSE. 'I have these small moments when I'm using the maths I'm learning in my gaming and it's really exciting.'

Designated SEND team offers one-to-one, group and in-class support to the small number of students – around five per cent – who need it.

Games, options, the arts: Every student is given a mentor from their chosen industry, and additionally all trainees do two weeks' work experience every year with some pretty awesome companies. Universal Music alone offers around 40 placements, and the list of others reads like a Who's Who of hip commercial creativity: Spotify, Apple, YouTube, etc. 'For our least able kids those two weeks are transformative,' says Charlie, and everyone we spoke to raved about this part of the provision. 'I got to go to Red Bull Music for my work experience!' cried a young singer. Trainees soon find the confidence to set up their own projects, and these seemed to be happening everywhere we looked. We came across five personable young men who proudly gave us their business cards for the music production company they'd set up and did a good pitch to us there and then. We checked out their website afterwards – alive and banging.

School is equipped with industry standard facilities including an amazing 440-seat theatre and any number of live music rooms, recording studios and computer suites. Wherever we went, trainees were getting together to rehearse songs, practise riffs, do a spot of sequencing, or just strum a guitar and unwind. 'Everyone's basically learning from each other in this school – it's musically multicultural,' said a talented young pianist who broke off from his drumkit practice to chat to us. Everyone on the music pathway has one-to-one tuition in at least one instrument, and music theory is also taught.

Extracurricular activities not confined to the set pathways: Love Of Literature week had many trainees producing poems and plays. Sports provision, however, is meagre and when we asked the trainees about it we were met with perplexed silence. 'There's a football match on the 10th,' one lad finally volunteered, sending everyone else into

Maths and English are compulsory here, and an intrinsic part of the school's mission to enable young people to be industry ready

fits of giggles. 'We're terrible at all that,' admitted the principal. Trainees are educated in health and fitness issues, and yoga and dance teachers apparently come in from time to time, but no details about this were forthcoming. Given the amount of time the gaming trainees in particular spend in front of a screen, we were surprised at this deficiency.

Lots of music and media trips to large games and film expositions, workshops at places like the Royal Albert Hall. The school often gets invited to special events such as the Mercury Prize and the BAFTA Games Awards.

Background and atmosphere: Situated hard by the thunderingly noisy A12 and accessed from half-boarded up Bromley-by-Bow tube via a grim-looking subway, ELAM's surroundings can't be called pretty. But that, after all, is the point: the school was founded to help young people from low income backgrounds, particularly EastEnders, and the building itself stands tall and proud, clearly signed for all to see.

Once inside, ELAM gives out an aura of calm professionalism that is very engaging. Indeed, it doesn't feel like a school at all, but like a rather glitzy recording company with a more than usually young workforce. A small but pleasing display of pop art adorns the spacious entrance hall, trainees in casual clothes with headphones and creative hair styles move about with assurance and purpose, banter and music drifts down from above. All very civilised. No sixth form common room: staff and trainees alike meet in the canteen, so that staff can be seen having working conversations. 'You can't just tell someone what is not professional, you have to model it yourself,' insists principal, who wants ELAM to feel like a creative company rather than a school. Walls very bare at present, but high quality framed student art work is planned. Meanwhile, 'corrugated card round the edge of a noticeboard is not our vision'.

ELAM was supposed to be a two week summer project to 'enhance and inspire' creative youngsters in the area, but very quickly took on a powerful momentum of its own. Sir Nick Williams, former principal of the BRIT School and David Joseph, the CEO of Universal Music, urged that more was needed, for the sake of both students and the industry. 'The environmental factors of demand

and supply said that we needed to create a school,' recalled Charlie, 'My brother and I almost wanted it not to take off so that we could go back to our lives, but it couldn't be stopped.' The school began life up the road in Stratford as the guest of School 21, housed in their sixth form block and admitting 75 students. In April 2017 it moved to its present quarters and September 2018 saw it at its full capacity of 300, highly regarded by the community, the industry and the DfE, and '10 times oversubscribed'. By any standards, an astonishing success story.

Pastoral care, well-being and discipline: 'We've been super-tight with discipline,' commented Charlie, and the behaviour we saw was exuberant but controlled and respectful. Many of ELAM's year 12 trainees are technically year 13s because of having dropped out of their first year of sixth form elsewhere; but once here, a lot of the students' previous issues seem to dissolve of their own accord. As one trainee put it, 'In secondary school, they tell you what to do. Here, you have a creative imagination and they support it.' Another confirmed, 'I hated secondary school, hated everything about it, but I want to be here. As soon as you walk in, everyone's welcoming, friendly, passionate about what they do. You get to meet other people who like what you like, so we get to build and grow together.' Teachers are, say parents, 'accessible and approachable.'

ELAM was supposed to be a two week summer project to 'enhance and inspire' creative youngsters in the area, but very quickly took on a powerful momentum of its own

The school strives to instil professional values at all times, so punctuality and meeting homework deadlines are taught in that context, and are, according to parents, extremely effective. Likewise, dress code is relaxed but school is strict on anything too revealing, because it gives the wrong impression for work. Attendance is strictly monitored and any concerns are flagged up quickly. 'It is made clear to the trainees that opportunities such as good work placements have to be earned,' observed a parent, who rated the pastoral care as excellent. The catering looked mediocre when we visited, but the principal was already on it, with a new caterer appointed, and the school is looking into how this could also provide training opportunities for the students.

Perhaps the best endorsement for the school's approach comes from the trainees themselves, who take their role as creatives extremely seriously and are overjoyed to have landed at a school that does the same. 'If you're not serious, don't bother coming here,' was a comment from one year 12 lad that had everyone vigorously nodding. 'Never mind wasting your own time, you're gonna waste other people's time.' 'If you don't have passion, integrity and drive, you might as well not come here,' confirmed another trainee. The result is an atmosphere that is genuinely inspiring, according to parents. 'It is striking how students help each other and cheer on their peers at school concerts.'

Pupils and parents: A very heterogeneous cohort – some privately educated with a raft of top-grade GCSEs, some from the poorest council estates in Stratford with nothing, and 'everything in between'. Currently around 30 per cent of students on free school meals, but school is well aware of the increasing number of middle class families turning up at open evenings as the word spreads and will be 'aggressively recruiting from local comprehensives' to ensure diversity and balance.

Intake is from 22 London boroughs and beyond. A small number come from as far as eg Norwich, Wales and Newcastle. School is not registered as a boarding provider and therefore can't help with accommodation for the latter, but will put them in touch with other trainees who have done the same and who can recommend host families.

Entrance: Online application in which students' creativity and motivation is assessed. If the school is satisfied about these, applicants are invited to an assessment day. This includes a one-to-one interview and a problem-solving group activity with people they've never met before – the school here is looking for 'collaboration, integrity, communication.' Those applying to the music pathway must also do a performance. Once the day is finished, applicants are scored out of five, and only when it's identified the high scorers does the school look at their academic record and references.

Exit: Around 50 per cent to university or conservatoire: destinations have included Manchester, Newcastle, Goldsmith's, University of East London, Liverpool Institute of Performing Arts, BIMM, Leeds College of Music, the Academy of Contemporary Music. Most students on music or music-related courses. The remainder to a variety of apprenticeships or employment with companies such as BBC Radio 1 and 1xtra, Odd Child Music, PMR Records, Sony, Warner, Univeral Music, Apple and Spotify.

The school supports former trainees by allowing them access to ELAM rehearsal studios after they've left and by appointing some as ELAM 'ambassadors'. It also actively uses social media to promote the work of both current and former trainees. 'Our son feels that ELAM has provided him with an invaluable stepping stone towards his goal of being a professional performer,' wrote a grateful parent.

Occasionally students have dropped out owing to a misconception of what ELAM is about and the hard work and commitment that will be expected of them – we gathered that this had particularly applied to the Gaming pathway, perhaps unsurprisingly. School is therefore currently strengthening its initial assessment and induction process to ensure that all trainees thoroughly understand what's involved in 'turning the thing you like doing into the thing you do for work every day'.

Remarks: Hugely impressive, outward-looking, professional yet caring, and totally unique, this school really took our breath away. A godsend to any aspiring young creative lucky enough to come here, not least those who couldn't imagine how they would have fared anywhere else. Well on the way to becoming one of London education's hottest tickets. Apply early.

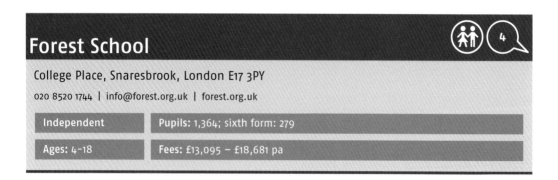

Forest School

College Place, Snaresbrook, London E17 3PY

020 8520 1744 | info@forest.org.uk | forest.org.uk

Independent	Pupils: 1,364; sixth form: 279
Ages: 4–18	Fees: £13,095 – £18,681 pa

Warden: Since 2016, Marcus Cliff Hodges (50s). An imposing man – looks tough and dynamic – but thoughtful and likeable, and very easy to meet. A career schoolmaster in the very best sense of the word: English degree from Cardiff, plus a masters from the Institute of Education; then teaching posts in Gstaad (for a year), followed by Bedford and Latymer Upper, where he became assistant head. Moved in 2005 to be head of the boys' senior school at Forest and in June 2016 was made acting warden before officially taking the top spot in December. No sense at all of being overawed by the job – 'it's actually a very liberating experience' – he is evidently devoted to a school he knows and understands intimately. A keen fisherman and mountaineer, he communicates calm dependability. Married with a 15 year old son (a pupil). 'Steeped in the place and a great appointment,' said one parent, adding, 'he's quite formal and old-fashioned in some ways. No bad thing.'

Head of prep school: Since September 2017 is James Sanderson (50). Friendly, direct, focused. Previously the deputy head of co-curricular at the senior school, and with 17 years at Forest already under his belt. Australian, a professional opera singer by background, he keeps a scholarly interest in early 18th century Italian vocal music. In addition to having been Forest's director of music at one stage, he has also taught languages and maths. Given his prominence within the school's hierarchy, and the close links between the prep and senior schools – 'we respect each other's autonomy and drive towards coherence' – hopes of a smooth transition are high. Keen on developing creative links between classroom learning and extracurricular life for children between the ages of 7 and 11, and muses of building up numbers at the pre-prep stage. 'We hate disappointing good applicants,' he says, 'but any expansion needs a huge amount of careful forethought.'

Academic matters: A highly efficient and effective feel to the teaching, and all backed up by excellent results. In 2018, at A level, 50 per cent of grades were A* or A, with 70 per cent A*/A for EPQs. At GCSE, 77 per cent of all grades were A*-A/9-7. Maths, science, English and history appear particularly strong. Less obvious drive to continue with modern languages, where the A level take-up is slight, but there is no glaring gender divide in subject take-up, nor in achievement. Masses of (trained) support for those with organisational difficulties and specific learning difficulties. The overall sense is of very capable and determined teachers and pupils – and of a school packed to the gunnels with bright pupils, and a few very high flyers. 'It's a high-achieving school,' said one parent, 'but not a hothouse. That's suited us. I really hope that it stays that way.'

At the most recent ISI report (true, back in 2011), teaching was judged 'excellent' and there is no sign of anything less than ongoing commitment. 'My teachers really mind,' said one girl, 'and it makes such a difference to the way we all work'. The warden agrees: 'There is masses of good practice,' he says, 'but the real challenge is to make teaching and learning tailored around each individual pupil. Not to pander to them, but to empower them'. Forest has made a big play of 'learning characteristics' – independence and flexibility are two of them. These are taken extremely seriously (not least by him) and are used as a constant reference point, particularly to help teachers reflect on the progress of those under their care.

Professional but pragmatic attitudes to special educational needs: basic screening tests are given to all pupils on entry and parents are at once told if extra support is needed. There is a learning support department with four qualified staff. The drive is to give support, whether that means specialist lessons to pupils or advising subject teachers how they can best help. There are pupils with EHC plans, but about 80 presently have IEPs.

Warhammer and chess clubs, well-known destinations for some who are less than extrovert or athletic, enjoy prominence, as do those for Manfood and cake decoration

The great singularity of Forest is its diamond structure. Between the ages of 4 and 7, the school is fully co-educational. Between 7 and the end of GCSEs, classes are single-sex. Eating, recreation, sport and most other activities all take place together – it's just that boys and girls learn separately. At sixth form, they revert to co-education. 'We haven't retained it as an historical curiosity,' says the warden. 'We believe in it. We think it's best.' And since Forest is a one-site school, he has good reason to claim the school is properly co-educational.

Games, options, the arts: Sitting, as it does, on 50 green acres on the edge of Epping Forest, the school has great opportunities to allow its pupils to immerse themselves in sport. The facilities are astonishing – with a sports centre on site and an Olympic swimming pool. Football, in the warden's words, 'is deep in the DNA of the school', but he is also convinced that the range of choice is sufficiently embedded that no one sport enjoys a monopoly of prestige. 'Having sufficient alternatives is critical if people aren't going to feel excluded,' he insists. The under 15 footballers have recently been in the ISFA final, and hockey is making a strong comeback, with three U15 players (two girls and one boy) in the England squad for the age group. Girls' football is also booming and the

school tries to cater to all tastes and talents, using the Olympic velodrome, West Essex golf club, local rowing clubs – the list is endless. All pupils have to do four games or activity periods per week, right up to their last year. 'It's simple,' said one pupil, 'they want us to have something to think about as well as our work. Otherwise, you can end up fretting.'

Very strong dance (musical theatre, street, ballet and tap) welds into performance. There's an annual multicultural music and dance spectacular – the so-called FUSION. With 14 houses each doing an annual production in the annual house drama competition, and with at least three big school productions every year, the school theatre is well used. The Michaelmas Play draws its cast from the whole school community. Recent productions include Oh What A Lovely War!, Nicholas Nickleby, Kes and Dick Barton – Special Agent! Paapa Essiedu, the Ghanian-born actor who played Hamlet in 2015 at Stratford, is an old pupil – and did theatre studies A level while here. A new head of DT has recently been appointed, and there are already clear indications of the booming significance art, design and technology play in the life of the school. For the past five years at least one pupil per year has won a place at a musical conservatoire.

Background and atmosphere: Began life as a proprietary grammar school in 1834; Forest's founders included the Spode industrialist William Copeland and the governor of the Bank of England, William Cotton. It grew sufficiently rapidly to have sacrificed some 100 old boys in the Great War, but the big growth came in the last century, with girls being admitted in 1981.

Notwithstanding the large number of pupils, the campus feels lively rather than crowded – more like a well-ordered village rather than an institution. The pupils exude purpose – modern, dynamic youngsters with an eye on what's happening next – but their manners lack that brittleness of some metropolitan children which can set teeth on edge. The way in which they wear their uniforms, and interact with their teachers and each other, corroborate the nice things they have to say about their school. In the words of a parent: 'All types of pupils and all kinds of achievement are celebrated. The teachers set the example and the older pupils take their lead from them and it seeps all the way down the school.'

The school communicates a palpable ethos of teamwork and service. The Duke of Edinburgh Award and CCF both recruit pupils in their hundreds. The school's contingent is linked to the Royal Green Jackets – which augurs a commendable degree of toughness. Civic engagement is highly prized: there is a close link to Haven House, a local children's hospice which costs £7,000 per day to function, and the school has sought to raise £7,000 per term on its behalf. 'We're not going to solve its funding,' says the warden, 'but our ongoing involvement is about more than money.' New initiatives are constantly springing up, most recently with pupils helping run a youth club in Chelmsford for young people with mental health issues.

There are also agreeable indications, in the vast selection of lunchtime and after-school clubs, that Forest embraces irony as well as all that is wholesome. Warhammer and chess clubs, well-known destinations for some who are less than extrovert or athletic, enjoy prominence, as do those for Manfood and cake decoration. Alongside the medicine, engineering and law societies, those of a less squeamish disposition may enjoy time spent at the dissection society.

Pastoral care, well-being and discipline: Discipline is low key, but the school does not shy away from addressing occasional poor behaviour. 'We have most of the usual teenage issues to confront,' says the warden, but he is also clear that sometimes the hardest situations have only a peripheral relationship to discipline. 'I believe the safeguarding here is outstanding,' he says, 'and that the whole ethos of pastoral care here is embraced by the staff.'

Sitting in 50 green acres on the edge of Epping Forest, the school provides great opportunities for pupils to immerse themselves in sport. The facilities are astonishing

Forest is, depending on how you look at it, two schools (or even three), albeit on one campus and sharing the same ethos and genus: there's the prep – which also contains a pre-prep and admits children from the age of 4; and the senior school, which children enter in year 7 and stay, in the usual way, until year 13. The latter is divided into a lower school for children of years 7 and 8, a middle school between years 9 and 11, and the sixth form. Each has its own head of section who oversees pupils' progress. In addition, there are housemistresses and housemasters with oversight on the pastoral care of individual pupils, supported by pupils' own tutors.

Houses exercise a big hold on pupil identity as well as holding considerable importance in terms of school competitions (note – these are about very much more than sport, and include art, dance, drama and MasterChef). There's also a chaplain (and a very beautiful school chapel) and year group services each week which all pupils are required to attend. It's has a very Church of England feel,

---

'We want clarity and confidence,' says the warden. 'This way parents become clued-up rapidly about what we see as important'

but the choice of hymns is reputedly calculated to avoid offending the susceptibilities of those of other faiths. 'I'd actually prefer it to be completely secular,' said a parent, admitting that was 'a minority view'.

Pupils and parents: Eight buses carry some 240 pupils to and from school every day from places as far afield as Epping, Docklands and Highbury, although many pupils make their own way to school using the excellent public transport links. Much thought and hard work also goes into liaison with parents. In addition to termly written reports and an annual parents' evening for each year group to discuss their children's progress with teachers, there is an additional yearly information evening for parents. These are packed into September. 'We want clarity and confidence,' says the warden. 'This way parents become clued-up rapidly about what we see as important over the next 12 months, and it gives them confidence and a good reason to work with us.' Lots of other events as well – the parental conference programme includes events on revision, drug awareness, IT and so forth. Links seem friendly but businesslike. There is no sense that this is a school which would ever allow an 'in-crowd' of parents to emerge – and is all the better for it.

Distinguished alumni abound: H Tubb and WJ Cutbill were founding members of the Football Association; Nasser Hussain and James Foster became England cricketers; Paralympic equestrian competitor Liz Stone won gold at Atlanta in 1996. Surgeon commander EL Atkinson was the man who located Scott's final camp on the ill-fated polar expedition. Leading the way in the arts and engineering are Ruth Buscombe and Chantelle Sampat at Sauber F1 and Toro Rosso respectively, whilst Ella Purnell and Nicola Walker are enjoying successful stage, TV and film careers. Less generally famous perhaps is squadron leader Geoffrey Wellum DFC, a renowned Battle of Britain spitfire pilot. He has credited Forest with giving him the spiritual support, courtesy of his time in chapel, to fight another day in the clouds.

Entrance: Oversubscribed, of course, like so many schools in Greater London. Selection for the pre-prep takes the form of a morning of low-key activities for which parents are asked – perhaps more in hope than expectation? – not to coach their children. At this stage there are about 150 applicants for 32 places (16 boys and 16 girls). There are further entry points at 7+, at 11+ (the start of the senior school, at which point some 120 pupils will be selected from at least 750 applicants) and 16+, where the school might well take in another 20 or 30 pupils, depending on availability.

Exit: Almost all the prep school pupils move into the senior school, unless families are relocating, and the same is true of the GCSE cohort. A few leave at this point (a quarter in 2017), sometimes because families are moving, and there will be a tiny contingent who decide it's not for them or who don't cut the mustard academically and get the necessary grades for sixth form. This is a high-octane environment: two pupils were awarded Cambridge places

in 2018 and almost all leavers go on to Russell Group universities. Four off to medical school in 2018, but the broad base of subjects studied at university testifies to the school's academic range and depth. One off to study Royal Northern College of Music and one to study liberal arts at UC Berkeley.

Money matters: There is a range of scholarships and exhibitions, for both academic and musical prowess, as well as bursarial assistance, depending on means.

Remarks: A powerhouse with a heart. The school has an immensely purposeful feel to it – no doubt influenced by the warden, but also by skilled and serious-minded teachers and parents.

Ilford County High School

Fremantle Road, Ilford, Essex IG6 2JB

020 8551 6496 | enquiries@ichs.org.uk | ichs.org.uk

State	Pupils: 1,016; sixth form: 298
Ages: 11–18	

Headteacher: Since 2015, Rebecca Drysdale BSc (40s), who joined the school in 2012 as deputy and then acting headteacher. It was whilst she was doing her degree in geography at Coventry Polytechnic (now Coventry University) that she first caught the teaching bug. 'I had spent a year doing the Marks & Spencer's management training course and immediately took to the personnel side of things. This, coupled with the fact that I loved working with young people, made me realise teaching would be a great career,' she explains. Did her PGCE at Reading, then worked her way up the ranks across two comprehensives and a secondary modern (Chalfont Community College, Bucks; Copleston High School, Ipswich; Charles Darwin School, Biggin Hill), followed by a 10-year stint as assistant headteacher at Edmonton County School.

'I can be scary when I need to be,' she says (and pupils concur), but so long as everyone toes the line, she has a jolly and genial demeanour, as well as being both earnest and refreshingly unassuming – the type you feel would roll her sleeves up and get stuck in whenever needed. Staff describe her as a 'true listener,' taking on board everyone's point of views, which means that when she does make changes, everyone tends to move forward

together. Teaches a little, 'but not as much as I'd like,' although she regularly does lunch and break duty, and students we talked to were clearly impressed at how often she chats to them in the corridors.

Sees her role as 'helping what was already a very good school to evolve,' although her attitude should not be mistaken for a lack of vision. 'I want this school to be the best grammar in the area,' she told us. 'I'd like to see people buying houses to try and get their sons into this school. I want people to move to Redbridge to come here.' Among the big changes she's made are overhauling the pastoral care system and increasing the emphasis on individual support for each child.

Academic matters: In 2018, 66 per cent 9-7 grades at GCSE, with strongest results shown in the sciences and mathematics. Everyone learns French and Spanish in years 7 and 8 takes takes one language at GCSE, though few take two or continue languages to A level. No setting before GCSE and only then in maths, science and English. Besides maths and sciences, other popular GCSE subjects include geography, history and English, and every child has to take at least one creative GCSE in the likes of PE (particularly popular), art, music and technology. 'We call it EBacc Plus,' says the head, who believes it enhances UCAS forms no end.

At A level, popular subjects include the sciences, economics, mathematics, history and government and politics. Most stick to academic rather than creative subjects, although sixth form enrichment ensures all students continue learning the arts. In 2018, 32 per cent A*/A grades. Subject-based reviews help to monitor each subject and data tracking to monitor pupil progress helps spot and tackle underperformance; not that there is much of that here, according to parents. Maximum class sizes, at 30 (and 26 in the sixth form), are at the higher end. The school funding crisis means that it can't run subjects with few takers eg languages last year.

Teacher profile on the older side, reflecting the low staff turnover and long-term experience. All teach their degree subject and many are examiners. Where possible, teaching is practical. Expect plenty of pongs wandering through the science block, for example, where one class was dissecting fish and another had their Bunsen burners all going when we visited. Meanwhile, a history lesson on WWII involved a mock trial for Hitler. In fact, all classrooms we visited were lively, with bright, perceptive students clearly hungry for detail and knowledge. Disappointing to walk past two classrooms with teachers shouting at their class, but maybe that's the price you pay for encouraging such energetic debate. School works on a two-week timetable.

Two-thirds of pupils with EAL requirements plus 30 or so who need SEN support. When we visited, there were students with cerebral palsy, hearing difficulties (including one who was profoundly deaf and also has vision impairment), plus all the usual – dyslexia to autistic spectrum. Can and does cater for wheelchair users, although there are some struggles with the old building – this will be made easier when the new ones are up. 'If students are bright enough to study here, we'll find a way,' says head, who says individual support takes place both in and outside the classroom.

But parental views are mixed on the quality of SEN support. 'My son has a physical disability and we were initially told by people in the area that this might not be the best school for him, but they've been amazing at meeting his needs, whilst still academically challenging him,' said one enthusiastic parent. 'I've been particularly pleased at how they've built up his confidence. SEN support here is very nurturing and they regularly suggest things I've never even thought of.' But others reported that the school's SEND knowledge was lacking, and their child was not well supported. We'd recommend a thorough quiz of the SENCo in regards

So long as everyone toes the line, she has a jolly and genial demeanour, as well as being both earnest and unassuming

to your child's condition, and requesting a detailed outline of the support that will be given to him.

The creative curriculum is big here, with students taken off timetable for six per cent of the time in year 7 and four per cent of the time in year 8. Mainly involves students working in small groups to build habits of mind that will stand them in good stead beyond school – leading a team, being a team player, debating, time management, structuring a piece of work etc. We saw it in action during our visit, with year 10s having created a morning of educational activities for year 7s on World Book Day. 'These students devised the plan, worked out the detail, came to me to pitch it, then carried it through,' says the head, who is loathe to call them 'soft skills' for fear of depreciating their value. Other examples include students pretending their plane has crashed on a desert island (they work out how they will survive), commemorating National Holocaust Day and committing to learning a new skill (usually off the list of activities from the Duke of Edinburgh award which, by the way, is an option from year 9 upwards). A particular favourite for students is the project that involves them researching an area of London, then taking a fellow student on a guided tour. The preparation is impressive, with students writing to the likes of Downing Street to request going through the magic gates. By the end, students have learned skills including independent research, preparing engaging speeches, navigating a map and using the tube.

Games, options, the arts: Cricket and football are by far the strongest sports here. 'Cricket is the most popular and we're good at it; football is also popular, but we're not always quite so good at it,' smiled one pupil. Swimming and rugby also well-liked, whilst other options include basketball, badminton, table tennis, rowing, sailing and rock climbing. Boys here have a competitive streak and sport provides a good outlet, but that's not to say it's all about the best people, with several boys reassuring us that sport is inclusive, including sports day, 'which is very much for everyone', and sports relief, 'in which each house completes a triathlon – meaning you can do just one bit of it if you want'. Duke of Edinburgh caters for those who prefer walking and expeditions to actual sports. 'The focus here is on fitness for life, not just elite players,' sums up the head.

On-site facilities include an artificial cricket strip, two football pitches and a 400m running track. The impressive sports hall (where we saw enthusiastic boys thrashing each other at table tennis) houses a heated swimming pool. There are also four badminton courts, a full size basketball court, with two small courts and provision for volleyball, five-a-side football, and tennis. Upstairs there is a fitness/weights room, an aerobics area and a viewing gallery (which doubles up as a drama studio) and a 'theory room for people taking GCSE or A level' – currently about 50 at GCSE and 10 at A level.

Oracy is new to the year 7 and 8 English/MFL curriculum and some work for LAMDA exams, but beyond that there's only student-led drama clubs – not great for aspiring thespians. Even whole school productions are rare, although you do get some smaller productions and boys enjoy the annual Speakout Challenge. Art is a different matter, with rich, bold and inspiring work on display – including drawings, paintings and sculpting. We also saw students working on some particularly impressive photography. 'Art is core to cross-curricular work here,' one pupil told us. DT also dynamic, with spirited pupils working hard.

'A lot of our international work involves video conferencing,' explains the head, with examples including a shared wildlife project with a school in Ghana

Provision for music is also good. 'This is my absolute favourite department. There are so many chances to learn and perform and there's plenty of sophisticated equipment,' one pupil enthused as he walked us through it. All students study music in years 7, 8 and 9. Over 100 children also have extra-curricular music lessons and some exceptional talent can be found here. Some lessons take place at the Redbridge Music School. Pupils have plenty of opportunity to develop their talents on piano, violin, cello, double bass, saxophone, drum, voice and more through orchestra, jazz ensemble, choirs and various bands. There are concerts and performances in London and abroad. But few pupils take art or music A level.

Extracurricular provision is largely sports-based and there's plenty of subject intervention to enable students to further and deepen knowledge in specific topics. Beyond that, there's a rich variety of clubs, groups and ensembles covering everything from astronomy to chess and gaming to debating club.

Day visits to all the usual galleries and museums (particularly for art) and fieldwork visits to the likes of Dover Castle, Epping Forest and the battlefields. Relatively thin on the ground when it comes to residential trips, however, with the exception of exchange trips (mainly to Spain, Germany and France), and sports trips have included Spain, USA and Caribbean in the past. 'We prefer to do lots of little things that help embed learning, rather than saving it all up for one big trip,' explains the head, who points out that there's no shortage of international focus. Indeed, the school has strong partnerships with schools and colleges in Germany, Spain, Switzerland, Denmark and Iceland and has British Council International School status. 'A lot of our international work involves video conferencing,' explains the head, who claims this makes the global emphasis of the school both more accessible and frequent, with examples including peer assessment with a school in Indonesia and a shared wildlife project with a school in Ghana.

Opportunities to volunteer are frequent, including sixth formers going into local primary schools to teach maths and modern foreign languages to small groups. 'I couldn't wait to do this because I remember how much it meant to me when an Ilford County High boy came and taught me in primary school,' said one pupil. A faith ambassadors scheme involves boys giving talks on what faith means to them (or not – one did a talk on atheism) and there's fundraising projects for local and national charities too.

Background and atmosphere: Founded in 1901 as Park High Grade School, the school was originally co-ed and located in Balfour Road. In 1929, the boys' school split, then moved to its present location in Fremantle Road in 1935. Although smack in the middle of a built-up residential area, the school has a secluded feel. And whilst the building itself is traditional (think sweeping oak stairwells, large wooden boards with lists of past notables and trophy display cabinets), the fabric of the school is undergoing dramatic change. Newly opened is a science block with 10 labs and six demonstration classrooms, a sixth-form centre, DT suite and more computer areas. 'We're bringing the school into the 21st century, with a purpose-built, modern learning environment that reflects our emphasis on learning through doing, but whilst still retaining the beauty of the original buildings,' says the head.

The school layout resembles a figure of eight, with two storeys of classrooms organised around the two adjacent squares, with green areas in the middle that pupils can use at break times. The layout makes it easy for new pupils to find their way around, although we wondered how students here cope with the jump from extremely overheated classrooms to really cold ones. At the front of the school is the hall where assemblies and concerts take place – a decent size with that familiar old-school, musty smell. A new learning resource centre and library is airy, bright and welcoming, and hosts regular live and video conference talks by visiting authors; other visiting speakers; and a reading ambassadors scheme where older boys support younger ones. 'I love it here – this is my favourite part of the school,' one pupil told us.

The atmosphere here is bustling, lively and purposeful. We'd like to have seen the school corridors livened up with more displays of student work, but where they do exist, they are imaginative and intelligent.

Pastoral care, well-being and discipline: 'You don't learn until you get stuck,' says the head and it's an ethos that pupils here really do seem to get, making for a supportive environment, which balances the healthy competition between the boys. Where possible, form tutors – who are generally responsible for pupil welfare and progress – stay with their class all the way up the school. Meanwhile, the vertical house system means all boys have a head of house looking out for them too. The system provides opportunity for the boys to develop stronger skills in leadership, mentorship and responsibility, plus opportunities to develop relationships across year groups, right to sixth form. A visiting counsellor is available; the school regularly accesses Redbridge services for young people; and there are all the usual talks on sex, drugs and rock 'n' roll through to forced marriages and knife crime. 'One charity came in to do a drama workshop on domestic violence and that was particularly powerful,' says the head.

Year 7s receive peer mentoring from trained older pupils in year 9, 10 and sixth form. 'They're a bit of a role model for the younger ones to look up to,' one pupil told us. For one pupil, who joined at sixth form, this was 'one of the things I liked when I came, people always willing to help'. He told us that bullying, or rather the lack of it, was another nice surprise for him, as at his previous school 'fights were a common occurrence. It was a radical change for me – since I've been here I haven't seen one'. The head certainly seems to have a healthy attitude towards bullying. Whilst not making any arrogant claims that deny its existence, she outlined a strict anti-bullying policy and clearly treats it robustly and quickly. 'My child was bullied, but when I contacted the teacher, he had it sorted out within two days and he took me through all the measures he'd taken,' said one parent.

Boys are generally well-behaved here – reports describe the behaviour as 'outstanding' – which is no doubt helped by the clear warning system and strict rules, for example on uniform. 'But boys will be boys and they are naughty sometimes,' acknowledges the head. Indeed, there was an incident the

Staff try to ensure parents understand what the career they have in mind for their son entails

day we visited. No permanent exclusions, although there had been 14 temporary ones half way through the academic year when we visited, mostly for fighting, saying mean things and bringing in banned substances. 'You are dealing with children and they make mistakes. The most important thing is to make sure they learn from them,' says the head.

Pupils and parents: Pupils come from a wide mix of ethnic backgrounds, with Asian (Indian, Pakistani and Tamil) the dominant group, then white British, white Eastern European and black Caribbean. They all come from the borough of Redbridge and some surrounding areas. 'The local authority drew up the smallest circle they could to fully encompass Redbridge, which means you get a little bit of neighbouring boroughs in there too, most notably Waltham Forest and Essex,' explains the headteacher, who describes the school as one of the few grammars left that are true community schools. 'We want it to stay that way,' she says firmly.

Pupils range from bubbly, stumbling and oblivious year 7s making their way between lessons, to the year 11s who are articulate, mature, friendly and inquisitive. In fact, the older pupils who showed us round asked us almost as many questions as we asked them – both rare and refreshing.

There's no PA here, to the disappointment of some parents, but parents generally have good involvement in the school, with almost 100 per cent attendance at parents' evenings and relevant meetings – and parents say that communication is good. The school does have some anxiety about boys whose parents 'have unrealistic aspirations for them' – the 'You will be a doctor!' brigade. But staff try to ensure parents understand exactly what the career they have in mind for their son entails, and to hit home that there are other jobs out there. 'If a boy's real interest and passion is for humanities and not science, fine, as that it is where he will get real satisfaction and achievement.' Work is also done from early on to emphasise that it's about the education, not just the grades. 'The qualifications will get you to the doorway, but you need more than that to walk through it – character, resilience and so on,' says the head.

Notable former pupils include Raymond Baxter, TV personality (Tomorrow's World), Sir Trevor Brooking, footballer, and David Miller, deputy chief inspector of Air Accidents. Lots of presentation evenings hosted by alumni, including some of these big names.

Entrance: More than 850 boys in the borough of Redbridge and nearby compete for the 180 places available each year by sitting the 11+ examination. The test, which has recently changed to CEM (aimed to unearth the brightest children, not the most tutored), is administered by the borough. School manages its own admissions to the sixth form, with places offered only to boys with 9-6 in their chosen subjects, plus at least eight 6s across the best of their GSCE results. 'It sounds counter-intuitive, but the idea is to get breadth as well as depth,' explains the headteacher. All sixth form entrants also require grade 4 or over in English and maths. Parents of pupils who get into this school say their sense of relief is huge, which is unsurprising given that it is the only boys' grammar in the borough.

Exit: Almost all (some 80-90 per cent) stay on to sixth form. Medicine and engineering are the most popular subjects chosen at university, although others include economics, architecture, dentistry, law and physics. Majority choose to study in London at eg King's College and UCL, whilst others go to Russell Group universities across the UK. 'If they're brave enough to go outside London, they're brave enough to pick far and wide,' says the head. One off to medical school in 2018 (in Bulgaria); generally several optometrists, pharmacists and biomedics.

Remarks: This is a school that delivers a very high standard of academic teaching and much more besides, producing young men who seem genuinely well prepared for the wider world. It's not for the faint-hearted, with firm rules and high expectations, but there's a strong support system to back it all up, with a caring head and exceptionally experienced teaching staff. We found boys well-adjusted, happy and hungry to learn.

London Academy of Excellence

Broadway House, 322 High Street, Stratford, London E15 1AJ

020 3301 1480 | office@excellencelondon.ac.uk | lae.ac.uk

State	Pupils: 460
Ages: 16–18	

Head Master: Since September 2017, Scott Baker MA PGCE QTS. After reading history at Cambridge, he began his teaching career at Robert Clack School in Dagenham in 1999. Has held senior leadership positions in state schools including Sandringham School in St Albans and The Henrietta Barnett School in north west London. He is the school's third head since it was founded in 2012.

Academic matters: Only 'facilitating subjects' offered (what some might regard as 'proper subjects' or 'subjects favoured by the top universities.') These 13 include psychology, philosophy and theology, politics, economics, further maths, French and Spanish. Maths and sciences are most popular at the moment. Very gradual increase in numbers taking modern languages. Students can also choose the Extended Project Qualification (EPQ). Additional languages offered outside the timetable include Mandarin, Italian, Bengali, Arabic, Urdu and Japanese. Opportunity to do an MPQ (mini project) in the first half of the first term, which is often developed into an EPQ. Exciting a thirst for learning and for academic endeavour is key here.

The scholars' programme contributes to this incentive and prestige. Those who achieve high grades in exams may be awarded Governors' scholarships or Merit scholarships – the prize being financial support for resources as well as more trips to Oxford and Cambridge.

Maths and science setted according to ability – other subjects grouped but not according to ability (there isn't a wide range of ability in other subjects, says school). Results are good – but some mutter that, considering the selective intake, they should be higher. However the first few cohorts were not especially selective, counters school (minimum five grade 6s at GCSE – now the minimum is five 7s) and they added a lot of value to relatively mixed ability groups. Year 12s must get at least three Cs in end of year exams to move up to year 13. In 2018, 61 per cent A*/A, 90 per cent A*-B at A level; ranked in top one per cent for value added by DfE.

For those students who need learning support (and there are around 40 on the schools' register with dyslexia, dyspraxia or ASD), the school says it takes a proactive approach to identifying any special needs. Not just those diagnosed with a

Sir John Cass Redcoat School

particular SEND will be given support. One of the assistant heads is the SENCo and learning coaches provide day-to-day support. School affirms that results for those with SEN match those without.

School day is long – the library opens at 7.45am, lessons start at 8.30am. At the end of the school day optional clinics take place where students can get further support. Teaching provision is effectively an 8am-6pm each day. Small tutorial-style groups and teachers who love their subjects make for lively, engaging lessons. Genuine participation and discussion rather than a more didactic approach. Parents wonder at the levels of support given to their children by the teachers: from Saturday classes and after-school clinics, to making themselves available by email until 11pm as well as during the holidays.

School regards itself as the 'academic pathway to top universities for students in Newham'. Three specialist 'pathways' are specified under the curriculum – law, medicine and Oxbridge – but there is bespoke preparation for a career in any field. High numbers (between 40 and 50) choose medicine. School says part of the secret of their success is the high quality of teaching – teachers are largely specialists in their field (the biology teacher is a former doctor) – with excellent subject knowledge and a passion for their subject. They are able to conduct university-style lessons with lots of interaction – students here are taught to think, no doubt balm to admissions tutors' ears.

Games, options, the arts: Thursday afternoons are dedicated to clubs and societies. These range from the medical society to the Bollywood Dance society. There are 31 in total to choose from (but if a student decides there is a demand for a particular society, the school will facilitate the running of it). Currently python programming, the newspaper society (merged with the feminist society) and history of art are just a few that are student-led. Debating and Model United Nations are popular, as is chess. A number of competitions organised against other schools. One boy told us proudly of how he set up the LGBT society and raised over £400 from bake sales and non-uniform days. We observed students building a robot in the STEM society, and participating in a refreshingly polite and intelligent discussion about Brexit. Our politicians could learn a lot from these students' ability to respect the viewpoint of others and listen attentively.

A number of physical activities take place on Tuesday afternoons – with a huge choice of 21 different sports from girls' and boys' football, rowing, sailing and pilates to basketball, climbing, canoeing, boxercise, volleyball, yoga and zumba. Games take place at a number of different venues including the Olympic Park, Redbridge Sports Centre, University of East London and Lee Valley. Athletics in the summer can get very competitive in the run up to sports day when all six houses compete against each other. Students we spoke to became hugely animated about their house's performance in the javelin.

School says part of the secret of their success is the high quality of teaching – teachers are largely specialists in their field (the biology teacher is a former doctor)

Drama and music a bit thinner on the ground. Apart from a guitar society there seemed to be little provision in the way of groups, orchestras or a variety of musical instruments. However music performances do take place during assemblies and there is a music room with a speaker system, microphone and guitars. Students get the chance to sing. There is a drama and improvisation society and a show takes place each term, which gives the students a chance to perform, whether it be a poetry recital, a band or dance performance. A play is produced in the summer after exams. Recently performed Macbeth directed by a teacher from Eton. The singers perform at a number of events, most notably at a reception at Lancaster House in front of the prime minister. One student we spoke to had high hopes of becoming an actor after completing his medicine degree. What provision we saw for drama was fairly sparse; however, since our visit school tells us that a student from the Central School of Speech and Drama now spends one day per week at the school, so that sixth formers have regular access to drama.

Plenty of school trips. The students we met were buzzing from one recent trip to see Dr Faustus and another to listen to Naomi Campbell at the China Exchange. A thorough outreach programme includes LAE students mentoring other students at local schools and voluntary work with local charities.

Parents thrilled with the opportunities their offspring have here. Opportunity is often their prime reason for choosing LAE, and is unparalleled here compared with other schools in the borough, they say.

Background and atmosphere: Founded in 2012, LAE was the brainchild of Richard Cairns, head of Brighton College, and Joan Deslandes, head of Kingsford Community School in Newham. They met on a bus in Beijing and found they shared a passion for the teaching of Mandarin (they both introduced compulsory teaching of Mandarin in their schools) as well as rigorous academic learning and a desire for social justice. Joan Deslandes needed somewhere to send her high fliers (Kingsford is an 11-16 school). Brighton College took two sixth formers each year from Kingsford, on full scholarships. These scholarships were funded by HSBC, which still continues to support the LAE today. However Joan Deslandes had another 40 high attainers at Kingsford, whose academic thirst still wasn't being met. With the inspirational energy of these two first class educators, the early seeds of the LAE were sown. Most agree that Richard Cairns was a driving force in gaining a groundswell of support from the independent sector, one of the innovative features of LAE.

The first sixth form only free school, it has the benefit of strong links with the independent sector. Six 'partner schools' – Brighton College, Eton College, UCS, Highgate, Forest School and Caterham – share resources, knowledge, experience and contacts. In addition strong links are being forged with Francis Holland and Putney High schools. The students are grouped into houses named after the partner schools. Some provide teaching support, and students from LAE are invited to seminars and talks at the partner school; others provide strategic advice, interview practice and contacts for university applications; others provide sporting facilities. Students in, say, Brighton house, will meet their 'sixth form buddies' at Brighton College, and will host a return visit from Brighton students.

Majority of parents haven't been to university themselves and, while very supportive of the aspirations of their children and the school, some confess to feeling daunted

School is housed in an unprepossessing 1980s former council office block on Stratford High Street. Functional and businesslike, but the edge is taken off by bright colours and idiosyncratic names (the large dining/study/common room area is called the agora – in Greek script), and walls throughout the building are adorned with wonderful large portraits of 'independent thinkers', from Coco Chanel and Elizabeth David to Srinivasa Ramanujan and Reverend William Buckland, saying profound things. All rooms are bright, light and airy, with tasteful wooden floors and pictures. Nothing here feels run down. All shiny, bright and fit for purpose. Many play chess in the agora during down time; 'we can't stop them playing chess,' remarked a teacher. Large comfy colourful sofas adorn parts of the space, with tasteful beechwood floors and tables and canteen for staff and students to eat together. School

They met on a bus in Beijing and found they shared a passion for the teaching of Mandarin as well as rigorous academic learning

currently in negotiations with the Department for Education to see if they can expand into the next door building, but wouldn't want to get too big 'and become a sixth form college'; the aim is 'to retain an independent school style of education.'

Pastoral care, well-being and discipline: Core values here are respect – and kindness; any breach of these and there's trouble. Students are driven academically so discipline tends to be good. They concentrate on the everyday stuff – uniform, lanyards (zero tolerance on these not being worn), punctuality, not handing in homework. Lines of communication with parents fluid – they too will know when their child has been late or failed to hand in work on time. School did have to exclude four students recently for inappropriate cyber activity – every head's current nightmare. All four were found places at other sixth form colleges. School is, and has to be, vigilant on cyber behaviour. This incident was picked up quickly, dealt with quickly and no shock waves ensued.

Students are grouped into six houses, with about 70 students in each house (from both year 12 and year 13). A head of house along with a team of five tutors in each house is in charge of these students' pastoral welfare. Each student's tutor is also responsible for their UCAS reference, PSHE and monitoring their academic progress. The tutor is the first port of call for parents. A tutor writes a report at the end of each term on the progress of the student, and parents also can meet the tutor and other teachers once a term.

We saw a mindfulness yoga session in full swing in the library. Plenty of opportunity to reflect and calm the mind, though in this instance it only seemed to be girls who were seizing this opportunity.

Pupils and parents: Unusually high proportion of first and second generation immigrant families – particularly Asian and black. Fiercely aspirational parents have a positive influence on the ambition of their children. School, painfully conscious of the very low representation of the white working class, has appointed a head of 'widening participation' to try to address this. Teachers remark on the curiosity of the students – they are kept on their toes, they say, by the students' complex questions.

Students are dressed smartly but, apart from the boys' blue and gold ties, not uniformly.

The students we met, a mixture of year 12 and year 13, were the kind of people you would want to represent your country – model citizens. Thoughtful, articulate, mature, polite and with an ease and confidence that belied the backgrounds of many of them. Their confidence apparently comes on hugely as they progress through the school. One parent observed how much responsibility her son is given, which contributes to his mature behaviour. There is much competition for the prestigious roles of house captain (there are only six) and prefect, again fostering a positive and responsible attitude.

Majority of parents haven't been to university themselves and, while very supportive of the aspirations of their children and the school, some are brave enough to confess to feeling daunted as to how to fund tertiary education. Although, they say, school is very good at explaining the route to university and assisting with strategy and tactics, very little information or explanation is given to parents as to how to cope with the financing of it. 'I think they are scared of putting anyone off,' suggested one parent.

Entrance: Minimum of five 7s at GCSE with at least 6s in maths and English. School gets about 3,000 applicants and will interview about 1,500 for 240 places – according to their predicted grades. Fifty per cent of places are given to students from Newham, other 50 per cent could come from anywhere. Some priority to those on free school meals.

Exit: Impressive – both in terms of the institution and the subject. Just under 60 per cent to Russell Group universities, a good number to STEM subjects, those who go to non-Russell Group universities mostly go to City, Greenwich, SOAS, Westminster or Bath. Most popular subjects are English and economics, closely followed by maths, biomedical sciences, history and politics and physics. Impressive 15 to Oxbridge in 2018 – a higher percentage than many top independent schools. However re-entry into year 13 is dependent on year 12s securing at least three C grades at their end of year exams.

About 15 each year take a gap year and come back during that year for advice and interview practice.

Money matters: School is lucky enough to continue to have the benefit of the HSBC funding that was a legacy of the Brighton scholars' funding. This is not a luxury, says school, but vital in a climate of continuing government cuts, 'and we ask a lot of our teachers. The HSBC support enables LAE to provide the complete education package which is experienced by the pupils of its independent school partners.'

The Hardship Fund, set up by the Worshipful Company of Innholders, provides financial support for trips and resources to those most in need, and the diligent few who are awarded scholarships also get financial help with resources and trips.

Remarks: London Academy of Excellence is – at the moment – is doing exactly what it set out to do. It provides a rigorous academic education to bright, aspirational students who are keen to seize the many opportunities that are on offer. Students here develop an easy confidence accompanied by a sense that they can do anything they set their sights on. An inspirational institution for anyone hard working and lucky enough to get a taste of it.

Newham Collegiate Sixth Form Centre

326 Barking Road, London E6 2BB

020 3373 5000 | enquiries@ncs6.org | thencs.co.uk/

State	Pupils: 503
Ages: 16–18	

Principal: Since 2014, when the school opened, Mouhssin Ismail (late 30s), former City banking and finance lawyer at Norton Rose Fulbright and one-time Essex cricketer. Nobody can have any reason to question Mr Ismail's deep seriousness and intensity of purpose. Very much admired and liked by all constituencies – 'there are many explanations for the school's success,' said one parent, 'but Mr Ismail is at the heart of each of them'.

Previously assistant headteacher at Seven Kings High School, with a reputation as an outstanding economics teacher (as he still is), Mr Ismail is conscious that much of his own story has resonance for his pupils: 'I am a local boy, from an ethnic minority. My parents were devoted to my interests, but they had little formal education. But they provided me with example, and they taught me the value of hard work.' He is married with a boy and girl – parenting and cricket-coaching with his young family soaks up most of his spare time.

He clearly relishes the job, but in a thoughtful and believable way. 'We've started on a journey and, yes, it's exciting. But it's still early days.' His key ambitions for the school are academic: 'We'd like 75 per cent A* and A grades, 35 places at Oxbridge annually – because, without this kind of success, too many of our kids just won't have the choices and chances'. But he is also clear that the school has an equal duty to try to make sense of the elite universities and workplaces to which he wants his pupils to aspire. 'So building up cultural and social capital to support them in their ambitions is as important and, believe me, we take it seriously'.

Academic matters: This is a selective school, but virtually all of the pupils have been at non-selective state secondaries before they arrive, and the results are staggeringly good. In 2018, their third ever A level cohort scored 90 per cent A*-B, trumping many of the local grammar and independent schools.

How do they do it? Selection plays a large part and so does academic intensity. The whole infrastructure is unapologetically geared towards high achievement

Unlike so many schools, state and independent, NCS is taking no shortcuts to get this kind of success. The A level curriculum in the core is pretty much confined to facilitating subjects recommended by leading universities: maths, further maths, English literature, economics, geography, history, psychology, religious studies, government & politics, chemistry, physics and biology are all offered. The glaring omission is the absence of foreign languages, ancient or modern. 'There just isn't the demand,' says the head, 'and we can't make it financially viable'.

Prejudice might suggest that this is a maths and science factory, but that isn't the case: 'our humanities results are also outstanding,' head explains, 'especially history and English'. In a school of some 500 pupils, overwhelmingly from ethnic minority backgrounds, this challenges many complacent assumptions. The staff (39 of them, two-thirds

Oxbridge-educated themselves) are teaching right to the top end, and clearly to great effect.

How do they do it, one asks? Selection clearly plays a large part in this, and so too does academic intensity. Classes start at 8.30am five days a week, and the whole infrastructure – iPads for all, study periods instead of free periods – is unapologetically geared towards high achievement. Almost uniquely in our experience, private study periods live up to their name – the sense is that serious study is being undertaken in silence by everyone there. There's also homework, of course but, as one girl suggested, 'It's sensible homework – it ties in what we've been doing, or what we're about to do – and it's about making us think.' One parent acknowledged that there was a lot of work, but added, 'I think it's up to parents ultimately, not schools, to try to ensure our children don't get overwhelmed. If we need to restore the balance, we should do that. The school is already playing its part.'

Another assumption might be that this makes for an examination sweatshop. That would be grossly to underplay the much richer vision of education which underpins the place. Classes end at 3pm, and the extra time this frees up allows for a massive enrichment programme, drawing off the school's super-curriculum. There are visiting lecturers (Ed Milliband, Lord Mervyn King and Professor Lord Robert Winston among many others) and pupils team up with PhD students at UCL with whom the school is partnered. There are also myriad networks with business and industry, and a range of non-examined cultural and academic courses – living testimony to the extent to which the school is embracing a tradition of liberal humanism. 'Our pupils, for all kinds of reasons, can quickly feel strangers anywhere outside London,' the head acknowledges. 'To prepare them for university and beyond, they need a great deal more than A levels'.

Special needs are acknowledged to the extent that those pupils who have been diagnosed as qualifying for extra time in exams may receive it, but there is no in-house specialist to supplement teaching. 'Very few pupils are involved,' explains the head, 'and our staff are always happy to put in any extra effort required.'

Games, options, the arts: The school encourages sport, but there is no specific provision for it within the timetable. The East Ham Leisure Centre is literally next door, and the fact that Friday school finishes at 2pm is an inducement for some students to go next door for a workout. The school also supports students taking Duke of Edinburgh Award, and there are music and drama societies. It has had huge success in debating, with one pupil recognised for being the first state school student to be judged Best Individual Speaker in the Eton Debating Competition.

'There are many explanations for the school's success,' said one parent, 'but Mr Ismail is at the heart of each of them'

But there just aren't the resources – human, material and, above all, time – to enable its pupils to experience drama, music and sport in the ways available to those from top independent schools. On the other hand, the school is committed to facilitating these experiences – through links with partner schools, and local initiatives. In the same spirit, it supports volunteering and outreach programmes.

The school is acutely aware that it needs to help its students to confront and understand much of the world in a way which is often taken for granted by independent school pupils. 'Being in London makes that a whole lot more possible,' says the head. Trips to theatres and museums, galleries and other landmarks, easily otherwise overlooked, are an integral part of every student's experience.

The school has facilitated an all-expenses paid work placement in Abu Dhabi with leading international law firm White & Case LLP and overseas visits to Kyoto, Japan to engage in science workshops with eminent Japanese scientists as well annual trips to Washington and New York, where students have visited the White House, Pentagon, UN headquarters and Columbia University. There is a real sense that the school is replicating many of the outstanding features of a private school education, providing its students with opportunities that would not necessarily be available in a normal state school.

Background and atmosphere: Having started life in 2014, working in partnership with Newham Council, NCS is – and feels – like a local school. Of course, it's made distinct by being selective, and also by occupying a splendid grade11* listed building in East Ham. At the start of 2018, it became one of the flagship schools of the City of London Academies Trust – assuring it, amongst much else, of access to a centre of wealth and influence.

The atmosphere which results is also distinct: it's utterly metropolitan, for one thing – no rolling acres here and only yards away from the bustle of east London – and multiracial and multi-ethnic.

When we visited the students were calm, friendly and articulate – very focused in class, but never robotic. There was lots of relaxed interchange between teachers and students, and plenty of smiles but, underneath it all, it was impossible not to recognise the deep ambition of everyone there. There's a school uniform, enforced strictly, with

students looking immaculate and professional at all times, worn not so much with pride (that may well be true) but with the same sort of calm pragmatism which characterised the whole place. They are busy young men and women and, in pursuit of their ambition: striking an attitude about uniform, or indeed about many of the things which exercise some more peach-fed youngsters, would seem rather frivolous here.

Pastoral care, well-being and discipline: Given that competition for places at NCS is intense, with approximately 3,000 applications being received for 300 places (driven by pupils as much as by parents), and that it is a day school, discipline is hardly an issue. 'Our parents value education highly,' says the head, 'and that's a cast of mind which they communicate to their children. The school benefits from that greatly. Of course, just like any group of 16-18 year olds, issues surface, but bad behaviour isn't one of them.' Managing work pressure, social media and the claims of competing friends may each occasionally call for help. So may no longer being at the top of the class – as so many were in their old schools.

If NCS continues to deliver, it could prove to be the standard bearer for a new generation of schools

Pupils see their tutors three times each week for 20 minutes – 'long enough for the basis of good relationships to be built up'. The head insists he and all his colleagues operate an open-door policy and pupils are insistent that this really happens. 'If I need help,' said one boy, 'I know that any of my teachers will be there to help at once.' Unlike many other schools, pupils are free to email teachers on work-related questions. 'It makes all the difference,' said one girl, 'and they reply so quickly.' A particular innovation are the weekly Ignite sessions – an hour each week – based around the ambition of nurturing good 'habits of mind' and dispositions.

The values which abound feel humane and collegial. 'When one of my friends got into Cambridge,' said one girl, 'the whole school was happy.'

Pupils and parents: NCS styles itself as a local school. Most pupils come from modest backgrounds – very often they are the sons and daughters of first generation Asians in Britain, who are ambitious for their children to have opportunities not open to them. They have the dynamism of achievers, and also the tolerance one associates with those living in a global city. As one girl put it: 'We're not usually rich, but we're not all deprived either. My parents went to university, which is a bit unusual, but not very.' One parent suggested that the creed of mutual respect and tolerance is a shock to a small minority of pupils, especially those whose earlier education hasn't prepared them for it. 'I believe this is happening,' he said, 'but it takes time'. Head insists he finds the parents 'invested in the school in ways which are helpful, and a pleasure to work with.'

Entrance: Entry comes mainly from the nine 'partner' schools in Newham – most are 11-16 academies. There are a small number of students from Tower Hamlets, Tottenham and Waltham Forest, and few may have to commute for up to an hour. 'We're quite determined that this will remain a school that serves Newham and students from east London, not least because of the work demands we make,' head insists. Despite applications from some independent school pupils, the trickle of middle class intake will not become a torrent. Selection criteria is rigorously academic – you have to get a 56 points from your top eight GCSEs (including English and maths) and then score between 7 and 9 in subjects being studied at A level (or 6 in some related subjects).

One parent admitted she'd been 'sceptical' about the school when her daughter first applied. 'But as soon as she arrived, my doubts started to fade. The teachers are so engaged. They really want to understand each pupil, and take a great interest in parents as well. Very different from what I was used to.'

Exit: The statistics make the scope of this school's ambitions perfectly clear. Ninety-five per cent of 2018 leavers went to Russell Group universities. Ten students went off to Oxford and Cambridge, and 20 to become medics/dentists. Three got offers to join KPMG or PwC. These are stats which will leave many independent school heads and parents slavering.

A lot of time and care is expended on helping prepare pupils to make UCAS applications, to excel at interview and – in every way – to outperform the expectations that might otherwise be made of them on the basis of their postcodes.

The sting in the tail is that pupils have to perform at all points in order to be invited to continue into the upper sixth.

Remarks: If NCS continues to deliver in the way in which it has begun, it will be the standard bearer for a whole new generation of schools. There are two irreducibles here: the enthusiasm and hard work of the pupils, and the way they are storming every educational citadel that confronts them. Of course, there is a concentration of talent – both of teachers and students – but that's just the start. The secret seems to owe much to unapologetically high expectations and a huge investment of time and care. That and bright children, no doubt.

The absence of rolling acres will put off some middle-class punters, of course, but they are hardly the target audience. It's a humane and imaginative society, as well as an academic powerhouse: a combination which should make a great many fee-paying schools sit up and take notice. For us, this is the real deal.

Robert Clack School

Gosfield Road, Dagenham, Essex RM8 1JU

020 8270 4200 | office@robertclack.co.uk | robertclack.co.uk

State	Pupils: 2,070; sixth form: 456
Ages: 11–18	

Headteacher: Since 2018, Russell Taylor BSc, previously senior deputy head. He grew up in Dagenham, is a former pupil here, gained a first class degree in economics at Queen Mary and trained as a teacher at the Institute of Education. He joined Robert Clack, his fourth teaching post, in 2002.

Academic matters: Some 40 per cent of pupils have SEN and over 50 per cent have free school meals, but results have improved steadily: in 2018, 43 per cent of pupils got 9-5 in both maths and English GCSE. At A level, 82 per cent A*-C and 22 per cent A*/A grades. These results are way above the national standard for a school with such a big cohort, one of the biggest in the country and expanding.

Specialist school in science, maths, computing and modern languages – no mean feat in such a strongly working-class school. Everyone takes

French and Spanish from years 7 to 9 and approximately 70 per cent take a GSCE in one of those. 'Our aim is to push that to 100 per cent,' says school, although French and Spanish A level take up is disappointing. Everyone takes double science, and 35 per cent take triple science, with others opting for the vocational applied science option – all with a healthy gender split. Other vocational options include health and social care, business studies, catering, beauty and ICT. Indeed, while many schools are cutting back their vocational provision due to their worry about league tables, this school ensures the vocational routes remain strong.

The ability range is massive, from those aiming at A*s to those who joined the school with a reading age of 5 or 6. Setting for every subject in years 7 to 9, then in core subjects of English, maths and science until GSCE options, where there is no setting at all. Lots of auditing of progress means significant numbers move right up through the sets, however. Parents and pupils feel homework levels are fair – enough to complement their studies, but not so much that it causes battles at home.

Learning support and mentor rooms where children can come to catch up on literacy and numeracy – perhaps because they've been off sick or they're upset because of family problems and can't cope amongst their peers. Meanwhile, SEN – which includes the whole gamut from mild dyslexia and ADHD to pupils with Asperger's, dwarfism, hearing and sight problems and cerebral palsy – all get plenty of classroom-based help if and when required, as do the gifted and talented. 'I've got cystic fibrosis and whenever I've had to miss school, the teachers help me catch up, without making me look singled out, and I get lots of passes to help me get the things I need whilst I'm in school,' one pupil told us. 'My son, who has Asperger's, had to leave his last school after just three months because it didn't work for him, whereas here their laid-back, but tailored, assistance in the classroom has enabled him to do really well,' said another. One parent of a student who had to take several weeks off due to Crohn's disease said home tuition had been set up, plus the head of year visited them both in hospital and at home. 'It's a big school, with a lot of special needs, but nobody gets missed and the focus on kids each achieving their full potential regardless of any barriers is phenomenal,' she said.

The sixth form is part of the North East Consortium with two other local schools, offering more than 40 courses at different levels. Over 800 sixth formers in the consortium, including some 550 at Robert Clack, many of whom are the first in their families to stay in education post-16. No minimum entry requirements, as courses range from a certificate in motor vehicle servicing to further maths, though students who want to take A levels must have at least five grade 4s at GCSE. 'Despite the ever-increasing risk from Ofsted, we don't set the benchmark too high because we want to give these children a chance.' Maths and sciences are the most popular A level courses, followed closely by English, history, economics and media studies. Courses in business, IT and sport popular, as is beauty therapy, taught in an on-site beauty salon – 'we give everyone the opportunity to be successful here'.

'My son had to leave his last school after just three months, whereas here their laid-back, but tailored, assistance in the classroom has enabled him to do really well'

Alongside a strict disciplinary procedure ('expectations of high standards are well-established and non-negotiable,' explains school), high quality teaching is seen as key to the school's success. 'Every child feels there is a pathway for them, with teaching that enables this pathway,' said one parent. The 'Robert Clack good lesson' template – which involves explaining to pupils the objective, interactive content and process of every lesson – is also much admired. 'The established and consistent approach means young teachers can come in and say, "I know for a fact this is what you're used to," and get on with teaching high quality lessons rather than trying to reinvent the wheel.' Teachers – whose ethnicity almost exactly represents that of the pupils – are seen as inspirational and often going well beyond the call of duty. 'They show enormous respect for the students – it's not just expected the other way round and these kids really value that,' one parent told us.

However, whilst the school was, until recently, one of 12 outstanding secondary schools fêted by Ofsted for excelling against the odds, it is currently feeling bruised by being taken down a peg to 'good' in 2013. The only category that has, according to Ofsted, dropped in standards, is the teaching – with the overall assessment remaining one most schools would kill for.

Games, options, the arts: It's sport, according to the previous head, that is largely responsible for turning this school around. 'It was the quickest, most visible way to espouse excellence. Sport develops things like pride, self-discipline, teamwork, confidence and empathy, all of which then feed through into other areas of school life. I really don't think we could have done what we have without sport.'

Today, it's considered no less important, with the school frequently borough champion at rugby, netball, football, athletics and cross-country. Boys and girls have competed at county and national levels at rugby and netball, and the school recently finished fifth in the country at athletics. A rugby academy attracts talented players to the sixth form. Pupils have competed nationally at sports ranging from netball to skiing and their team shirts are displayed proudly alongside photos and trophies. 'My son hated rugby when he arrived and now he adores it,' one parent told us.

A swanky leisure centre includes a sports hall and fitness suite, open to the local community outside school hours, and there's a new sports hall on the lower school site. There are also tennis and netball courts and a large playing field which includes a recent £5m all-weather, state-of-the-art surfaced pitch. Numerous sports clubs before, during and after school, as well as on Saturday mornings, range from hockey to dance to girls' boxing.

Boys', girls' and mixed school choirs go from strength to strength, including entering national song competitions, hosting musical exhibitions and helping local primary schools with singing. Ex-pupil Sandy Shaw gets stuck in enthusing pupils when she can, including attending concerts where she has been known to throw out a tune or two herself. Impressive school orchestra, with one student a member of the London Symphony Orchestra, plus a jazz group. Instrumental lessons are free and there are regular whole school performances combining music and drama, as well as regular visits to the West End.

Plenty of artwork displayed around the school, with light, airy and spacious facilities for both this and DT, both of which have reasonable take-up at GCSE. 'Take away art and you might as well take away some of our students' ability to breathe,' say staff, citing research showing that art can act as window into the soul among some children.

School trips include a French exchange, sixth form politics and history visits to Washington and New York and sports trips to Canada, Barbados, Germany and South Africa. Cultural visits to Italy and Spain; expedition visits to Egypt and Latin America. Residentials to Isle of Wight and day trips to France, among others. Staff insistent that these trips are critical to children's development and the school (and students) raise funds to ensure nobody misses out.

Background and atmosphere: This is a mammoth – and expanding – split-site school, named after local legend Robert Clack, who was mayor from 1940 to 1942 and a champion for social justice. 'The values by which Alderman Clack lived his life are the values that permeate the daily ethos of the school, the values of mutual respect, compassion, discipline, high expectations and aspirations, and hard work.' The lower school site, which houses

Pupils have competed nationally at sports ranging from netball to skiing and their team shirts are displayed proudly alongside trophies

years 7 and 8 and most of year 9 (as well as some sixth form classes), opened in 1935, the upper school buildings, half a mile away, in 1953.

It is one of the most deprived areas in the country, with the tower blocks of the Becontree Estate – one of the largest in England – casting a shadow over the playground. Yet this is one of the most ordered, neatest schools we've come across – no litter in sight and, as one teacher put it, 'an oasis of calm in the midst of the chaos outside.' Despite the vast number of pupils, there are only a few 'pinch points' that lack space, the dining hall among them. The shabby prefabs put up 'temporarily' in the '40s have been replaced by newer (still prefab, but higher quality) buildings which provided the lower school with 18 new classrooms, and there's a good science block and media block with facilities for drama, music and media studies, as well as the spotless beauty salon. No shortage of computers and whiteboards and lots of students' work displayed neatly throughout the corridors. No lockers, though, which bothers some parents. 'I worry for my son's back, having to carry everything around with him all the time – he's only little,' said one.

Pupils also impeccably neat in blazers and ties (not a rolled up skirt or shirt hanging out here), orderly in corridors (although several students moaned about the one-way system) and attentive in lessons. Students we met wore plenty of badges, reflecting the school's emphasis on providing leadership responsibilities. Racism issues minimal, with students mixing in genuinely diverse groups outside classes. 'When the school changed, the head dealt with all issues of racism personally, and now the school's values of tolerance and respect for others are just normal,' one parent told us. School recently introduced its own hijab as part of the school uniform, after consulting for a year with all the Muslim female students in the school and their families. Active school council made up of 300 pupils (again more or less reflecting diversity of the school).

A breakfast and homework club – along with masses of extracurricular clubs in everything from cheerleading to astronomy and sports to debating – mean students often arrive as early as 7am and don't leave until gone 6pm. 'They don't just come home and hang around on the streets because they feel really supported to pursue their interests,' said one parent. 'The clubs have taken my kids to another level,' said another. Even the library – where the homework club takes place daily – is very popular. 'It's a safe, quiet and friendly place that you can get on with your homework,' said one student. Even outside the school, there's little trouble, with Robert Clack kids known locally for being respectful and well-behaved – a far cry from days of old.

A third site, for years 7-11, opens in 2020.

Pastoral care, well-being and discipline: 'We must not underestimate the importance of being happy, especially at school.' Every positive action gets a reward and every negative action is followed with a consequence – and every student knows it. Praise includes colours for sport, music and performing arts; lots of merit awards during assemblies; notes home to parents; words of praise from head, among others. Meanwhile, the strict disciplinary procedure ('expectations of high standards are well-established and non-negotiable') means detentions for low level offenses such as chewing gum, forgetting homework etc. Two such boys stood in one corridor when we visited, looking suitably sheepish. Pupil referral unit handles more serious transgressions, such as disrupting lessons, starting a fight or playing truant, with the ultimate sanction sending them home. It's all about nipping problems in the bud, along with consistent and clear boundaries, say staff – and it works, with no permanent exclusions for over 10 years and pupils agreeing rules are generally fair.

Pastoral care – mainly from form teachers and school counsellor – admired by parents, who say children feel very safe here. Bullying a non-issue, which pupils put down to CCTV throughout the school and an ethos among students of looking after each other. 'I spilled my drink in the dining hall the other day and an older boy came rushing over asking if I was OK,' one pupil told us. 'My teenage son isn't the easiest to deal with and has had quite a lot of problems, but staff have put in so much time to steer him on the right path,' one parent told us. 'It's amazing how they've worked with him.'

Pupils and parents: Largely from the surrounding estates, though proximity to the school puts a premium on the prices of the few houses for sale in the area. Huge (and increasing) numbers of single parent families, as well as those with several generations of unemployment. This is an area with some severe poverty issues and one of the fastest changing demographics in the country. The school largely reflects this demographic, with around 45 per cent white working-class; 35 per cent Afro-Caribbean; 15 per cent Asian (mainly Bangladeshi); and the rest mixed race. Pupils are polite, resilient, articulate and hard-working. And although they are typically from underachieving backgrounds, the school says

most parents work in partnership with the school. School employs a parental adviser who visits families under stress and helps with housing, clothing and food allowances.

Entrance: Some 2,000 applications for the 360 places in year 7. Looked-after children get priority, as do those with special educational needs, then by distance from the upper school site – generally within just one kilometre. Large numbers from other schools join the sixth form.

Ex–pupil Sandy Shaw gets stuck in enthusing pupils when she can, including attending concerts, where she has been known to throw out a tune or two herself

The new site that opens in 2020 will enable a further expansion of places.

Exit: About 60 per cent of pupils move up to the sixth form, up from around 20 per cent 10 years ago. Around half of those go on to university. Usually a couple to Oxbridge (two in 2018, one to study medicine, plus seven other medics). A handful to UCL, Queen Mary's and Royal Holloway respectively, with other high profile Russell Group universities also featuring regularly among destinations. Some 70 per cent study maths and sciences, with the remaining 30 per cent covering virtually every subject going. The remaining half of sixth formers go straight into work (many on apprenticeships), with significant numbers moving into the City. Plenty of careers advice and help with UCAS applications, and the school has high value partnerships with the likes of the The Worshipful Company of Chartered Surveyors, The Prince's Teaching Institute, Teach First and Business in the Community, all of which provide pupils with work experience or routes into careers, as well as promoting the work of the school.

School is working hard to build up alumni, with 2,000 ex-pupils so far involved in helping with interviews and work experience, as well as providing access to their networks.

Remarks: An exceptional comprehensive in one of the most deprived areas of the country. All roads here lead back to the ethos of the school, which is all about being inclusive, mutually respectful and aiming high. The school is a source of huge pride for staff, parents and pupils, where every single young person is both encouraged and supported to reach their full potential.

Seven Kings School

Ley Street, Ilford, Essex IG2 7BT

020 8554 8935 | contact@sevenkings.school | sevenkings.school/

State	Pupils: 1,783 (including 360 in the primary school); sixth form: 523
Ages: 4–18	

Head: Since September 2017, Jane Waters, previously head of secondary. She joined the school in 2007.

Head of primary school: Since its opening in 2015, Kate Beaumont.

Academic matters: If achieving top grades is your priority for your kids, then you have very little to fret about at Seven Kings. Despite its 'very average' intake, Seven Kings seems to sail effortlessly to the top of the league tables. Eighty-two per cent of GCSE candidates in 2018 achieved 9-4 in both English and maths; 37 per cent of grades were 9-7. The hugely oversubscribed sixth form produced respectable results – 47 per cent A*/B grades and 18 per cent A*/A.

This is a school that starts with outcomes required, then finds the best means to achieving them. 'This is no exam factory, but we do know the syllabus and the exam requirements, and we also know the kind of teaching that works.' Pupils concur that the teaching is both vibrant and innovative, with faces in classrooms looking hungry to learn when we visited. 'Teachers here bring subjects alive,' one pupil told us. 'There's constant encouragement to probe the teachers because they want everyone to grasp the subject really well,' said another, who added that even if you email a teacher at 8pm, you often get a reply. High expectations for teachers, who are expected to enthuse children at every opportunity (they must engage with at least six students when on 20 minute break duty, for instance). 'Someone once said, "You just do what it says on the tin when it comes to teaching," and it's one of the best complements we've had.'

Monitoring, tracking and a 'can-do' culture also contribute to academic success. 'You won't find a pupil we haven't spoken to in the past three weeks about their learning'; every student receives two formal one-to-one interviews about their academic progress per year, in addition to many more informal ones. Pupils praise the marking system that means they've given comments, rather than grades. 'Understanding what you've done well and what you can do to improve is more helpful than just a mark,' explained one. Also popular is the 'passport' that all kids in KS3 get. 'The children get visas to add in for good work, eventually being made a "scholar"'; school encourages a strong triangular relationship between students, teachers and parents to ensure that everyone is on board with learning outcomes in a well-communicated way.

English, maths and science by far the strongest subjects, with learning for science very practical (one of the labs is university-level), meaning that bangs and smells are part of the fabric of school life, with around 50 experiments going on a day. 'Students rave about science here'; school is a recognised centre of excellence in this subject, with some staff sitting on the boards of top science organisations.

Three languages on offer – French, Spanish and Mandarin – with well over two-thirds of the students studying at least one language at GCSE. Setting only in maths 'because all the evidence shows that setting doesn't work and puts a ceiling on young people's achievement,' says the head of secondary school. 'Research on boys in second sets, for example, shows that they are much more likely to move to the third set than the first set.' Plenty of academic after-school clubs, as well as after-hours opportunities providing support with homework and coursework. Plus other clubs for sport, arts, dance, radio, Amnesty International, Model UN, chess, model airplanes, astronomy, film and more.

Eighty per cent stay onto sixth form, where students get to choose from 22 A levels, of which science and maths are the most popular. One pupil, who moved from another school into the sixth form, told us, 'Teachers here give you a step-by-step guide to research, writing essays and getting through exams, whereas at my previous school, you're just expected to get on with it yourself.'

Seven Kings has a national reputation as a centre of excellence for disabled children. There is a specially adapted entrance and well-equipped medical centre, plus the classrooms are accessible by wheelchair. 'We are unbelievably inclusive, which brings such a richness to the school.' In addition, there's a well-staffed highly-skilled SEN department (23 per cent SEN when we visited, with 54 with EHC plans), providing exemplary provision. 'If we can get it right with vulnerable children, we can get it right with all of them'; they cater for the usual range of special educational needs.

Games, options, the arts: Two hours a week of PE, with very few complaints from pupils. Football, cricket, netball, rugby, long-distance running and athletics all core to the curriculum, with notable successes in cricket, football and long-distance running. Judo and fencing recently added to the growing list of sports. Facilities include an Astroturf pitch, front field, sports hall and gym, along with table tennis tables dotted throughout the outside areas.

Music highly valued, with spacious and well-equipped practice areas. Years 7 and 8 are on a scheme whereby the whole class learns a particular instrument together, with past examples including recorder, clarinet and trumpet. There's a school orchestra, jazz band, ensembles (including strings), as well as student led bands. Staff are employed to teach guitar and drums, as well as 35 lessons a week with peripatetic music teachers.

Science very practical (one of the labs is university-level), meaning that bangs and smells are part of the fabric of school life, with around 50 experiments going on a day. 'Students rave about science here'

Plenty on offer for aspiring performers, including an extra period for drama in year 7 and 8 and all students in year 8 expected to take part in story telling to parents. 'We think it's is a great way of developing confidence and oral skills.' KS4s put on an annual community play, focusing on issues relevant to them, with examples including the riots and refugees. Meanwhile KS3s perform monologues, as well as group productions. West End theatre groups regularly invited into school to do workshops, with students also being invited on trips to theatre performances, and there are whole school performances annually too.

School day trips to museums and galleries, as well as residentials to the likes of Berlin (history), Barcelona (art and culture), Vesuvius (geography) and Japan (science).

Background and atmosphere: The school started life as girls' grammar in the 1930s, and some remaining original features give a feel of the inter-war years, with an expansive spread of low rise brick buildings and a Betjemanesque assembly hall ideal for listening to the clock ticking away the exam minutes. Modern additions include the lecture theatre, glass entrance hall and shiny new science labs. Stand-out facilities include the spacious and well-used library; the DT facilities with impressive window displays of students' work; the well-resourced sixth form private study areas; and the sixth form common room, a great space with youthful wall art. Lots of colourful displays of students' work throughout the school, including huge canvases of artistic portraits. Inside the tall-windowed classrooms, the focus is on learning.

This is a place where the school motto is more than some inaccessible Latin phrase that nobody can pronounce. '"Friendship, excellence, opportunity" are what we're all about on every level,' says the school, with pupils and parents agreeing wholeheartedly. Mutual respect is also more than a hollow phrase, with students allowed in their classroom at all times, including break ('it's their school, so their classroom') and students overwhelmingly report that they feel valued by teachers. 'The head thanked the parents for giving them such great students at a recent event – and that pretty much sums up the attitude towards the kids here,' one parent told us.

You'll find no shortage of leadership opportunities and student voice, with a vast array of headship roles for students, as well as plenty of pupil involvement in everything from designing the new primary school and its uniform to observing and feeding back on lessons and providing ideas to improve learning. You'll even find students on the school gate to monitor lateness 'because there's nothing like having to explain to your peers why you're not on time,' says the head of secondary. Peer mentoring also popular. We found the older students confident and articulate, although the school says a lot of work goes into achieving that. 'Many come in quite passive and quiet, but our mantra is that a quiet student isn't a good learner,' says the deputy head. Innovative courses and workshops help, including a day of circus skills in year 7 (which takes pupils out of their comfort zone and reminds them that if you put your mind to it, you can often do things you never thought you could) and a teambuilding day in year 12. Staff get similar treatment. 'For example, we got new staff to do The Big Paint, which reminds them about how it feels doing something new – like the kids have to every day – and helps develop empathy,' explains the head of secondary.

Pastoral care, well-being and discipline: Seven Kings serves a neighbourhood that has social problems and deprivation typical of many parts of urban

London. But despite its relatively stark surrounding streets – and the fact that many students come from difficult backgrounds – the school itself is an oasis of purposeful calm. Discipline is assumed, corridors are quiet, classes orderly. That's not to say there's no bad behaviour. 'We have 1,500 hormonal kids. Of course we have discipline problems.' Most are nipped in the bud, though, thanks to clear expectations and sanctions (mostly detentions), with exclusions kept to a minimum. 'What helps the most is that we can get it right with each child because we know them on an individual basis,' says the head of secondary school. 'For example, this week, a boy was misbehaving and when we looked into the cause, it turned out he didn't feel he was achieving success in class. Once we dealt with that, the problem stopped,' she says. The point is, she continues, that children often don't have the skills to navigate their way through what is a very complex world to grow up in 'and we never forget that when we're dealing with these young people.'

No wonder pastoral care and well-being are high on the agenda of every member of staff at this school, with particular attention from form tutors, year leaders, staff mentors and the full-time student counsellor. The school also buys in counselling support from outside agency Here and Now as and when required, as well as offering yoga and meditation sessions and occasional 'drop down days,' when the timetable is collapsed to focus on issues such as how to revise and stress management. 'In year 10, my daughter suffered from clinical depression. Her grades dropped and she didn't want to be in school. But the school pulled out all the stops to help her and she's now thriving at LSE,' one parent told us.

This is a school that starts with outcomes required, then finds the best means to achieving them. 'This is no exam factory, but we do know the syllabus and the exam requirements, and we also know the kind of teaching that works'

Bullying happens, but is rare. 'I experienced it in year 7,' one student told us, 'but the teachers took it really seriously and managed to stop it.' Pupils value diversity here – ethnically and in terms of disability, among other things – which students say helps in promoting a culture that values difference. No-one from years 7-11 let offsite at breaks or lunchtimes. Lots of talks around drugs, drinking and smoking, sex, eating disorders and cyberbullying.

Pupils and parents: This is a neighbourhood comprehensive, with students mainly living within a one-mile radius (some years, it's just half a mile) and coming from around 40 feeder schools (although most come from just four of these). More than three-quarters come from Indian, Pakistani or Bangladeshi backgrounds and 19 per cent are on free school meals. In the main, parents are very involved in their children's education – something that is very much encouraged, with curriculum evenings, a 'test the temperature' evening (parents' evening early in the term), as well as breakfasts with the senior leadership team. Parents even get the opportunity to be taught a lesson to see how it feels, followed by help from staff in how best to support their child's learning ('for example, we encourage parents to say, "Tell me something about your day" rather than just "How was your day?" which is a closed question,' explains the head of secondary school). 'By the Christmas holidays in year 7, parents really know what we're all about.' Parents aren't, however, a cake-baking, raffle-holding crowd and, to the disappointment of some parents we spoke to, there is no PTA. The kids themselves work hard and, and on the whole, behave well. 'They are bright and ambitious and absolutely gorgeous.'

Entrance: Over 2,000 local candidates apply for the 180 year 7 places, with a waiting list well into the hundreds. As it's completely non-selective, children in the looked after system/those with a statement/ EHC plan are prioritised (following the admissions code), followed by siblings, after which it's down to distance. Around 80 per cent go through to the sixth form, with around 2,000 applying for the remaining 140 places. Successful applicants need six 4s or above at GCSE, with 6s in their chosen A level subjects (7 for science and maths).

The Seven Kings Primary School opened in 2015 with 120 reception children. The impressive looking new-build forms part of the new all-through school which will grow by 120 places a year.

Exit: Out of 180 students, some 50 per cent go on to sixth form. The rest leave after GCSEs, mostly to do vocational qualifications, other courses, apprenticeships or go straight into jobs. Of those who leave after sixth form, 95 per cent go to university – about a third of those to Russell Group, including York, Birmingham, Leeds, Nottingham, Bristol, Bath, Cardiff. LSE, Imperial and Kings. Around half choose science degrees, with three medical students in 2018, plus one off to Oxbridge. The rest go to other good universities ('Some choose not to go to a Russell Group') or destinations such as internships in the City. The remaining five per cent who don't go to university either take a gap year or go into apprenticeships (one had just gone into Louis Vuitton when we visited), art college or straight into the jobs including in the City.

No shortage of help with UCAS applications, and careers advice is embedded into the curriculum from year 7, with lots of work experience and enrichment. 'Opportunities that look good on your CV or university application aren't just encouraged – they are really promoted,' said one student

Remarks: This is a school with high aspirations, and the academic rigour can be tough because of the pursuit of excellence. But the results prove it's achievable, with a wide range of strategies ensuring that every student is pushed to reach their full potential. But there's fun to be had here too, with students clearly enjoying school life. Particularly notable is how respected they feel by the teaching staff, which clearly contributes to the good behavioural record. Parents who send their offspring here can be confident they will reach or exceed expectations, as well as coming out well-rounded and ready for university and/or a decent career.

Sir John Cass Redcoat School

Stepney Way, London E1 0RH

020 7790 6712 | info@sjcr.net | sjcr.net

State	Pupils: 1,440; sixth form: 435
Ages: 11–19	

Headteacher: Since 2016, Paul Woods BA PGCE (40s). Originally from Enniskillen in Northern Ireland, he studied French and politics at Kingston University and did his teacher training at the University of North London. Previously head of Bishop Stopford's C of E School in Enfield. Lives in North London, where he began his career as a French and Spanish teacher, moving up the ranks to deputy head, after which he moved to Barking 'because I wanted to work in a more challenging location.' Later moved into his first headship at Bishop Stopford where, in his first week, the school was told by Ofsted that it 'required improvement' and he set to work getting it up to a 'good' status two years (to the day) later.

Students say his office door is always open 'except for meetings,' which encourages an informal drop-in approach. 'And he's nearly always in the corridors at class changeover and break times, when any one of us can chat to him – and we really do,' said one. With his easy, gregarious, one-of-us manner, it's easy to believe. 'This is a social institution, so what would be the point in sitting in an ivory tower or diarising everything?' he asks, adding that most things students talk to him about take all of 30 seconds. 'Then the issue is off their mind and they can get on with their studies.' Parents, in the main, have little to do with him. 'There's always someone to help you as a parent at the school – it's just not usually the head,' commented one, although there are obvious exceptions.

Teaches French (to year 10 the year we visited), while back in his office he is clearly a man with a plan, listing a lot of exciting proposals for the school from ensuring closer links between the different levels of leadership to a greater focus on the whole child – all with an infectious enthusiasm. 'One of my plans is a cultural entitlement programme because I want to be able to say to every single student, "You can expect this number of theatre trips, this number of day trips and this number of clubs to join".'

Academic matters: Consistently near the top of the value-added tables and has three times been ranked the most improved school in the country. Most students come in with lower than average achievement, but in 2018, 69 per cent got 9-4 for both English and maths at GCSE with 25 per cent A*-A/9-7 grades – good results in English, maths and science. Students come from over 50 primaries (most feeling like the cat that got the cream when they get a place), but many have difficult home lives. 'Our first focus is on behaviour, on creating a climate for learning. Then we engage them with exciting teaching.'

Indeed, Ofsted's latest report (outstanding), in November 2015, talks of 'high quality and energetic teaching' – something the students also rave about. 'You're never bored and teachers give their all to make sure you both keep up and that you're kept enthused – they have very high aspirations for us,' said one. Monitoring of student progress is meticulous, with school targeting those who need extra help in a range of ways, from one-to-one help to subject clinics for small groups. 'I'm a big fan of their marking system too – there's always such detailed feedback,' one parent told us.

Setting for maths, English, science and RE from year 7, but with plenty of scope to move up or down according to individual needs. As a specialist language college, it is perhaps surprising that students only study one language for the first three years (it used to be two) from a choice of French, Spanish and Bengali, continuing at least one to GCSE. That said, many take more, with a wide choice of languages in twilight classes (for parents as well as pupils) including in Arabic, Japanese, Korean, Mandarin, Italian and Turkish – and many pupils take a GCSE in their own native language in KS4. Many go on French or Spanish exchanges and there are many international links and partnerships which have involved students visiting Poland, Italy and the Czech Republic.

There are vocational as well as academic courses at KS4, for example in food tech and business studies. In fact, there's an impressive emphasis on business and enterprise here, including strong links with Canary Wharf and City firms, with some offering work placements, scholarships to cover university fees and jobs after graduation to talented students. Sixth form business studies students can have mentoring from business partners, visits and seminars, lectures and summer internships.

'He's nearly always in the corridors at break times, when any one of us can chat to him – and we really do.' With his gregarious, one-of-us manner, it's easy to believe

The large sixth form, with some 500 pupils, has its own centre, including a library, IT suite, common rooms and a popular café. But students say this can be a double-edged sword ('Great for sixth formers to essentially get their own school, but we rarely see them,' explained one student), so is something the head is addressing. A level subjects offered alongside a variety of vocational courses and GCSE retakes – with most popular and successful subjects including maths, science and English, with wide take-up for psychology, RE and sociology too. In 2018, 17 per cent A*/A, 50 per cent A*/A. Many students come in from elsewhere to join those moving up, and quite a few have relatively low qualifications. Some start with intermediate level courses then move up to higher levels en route to university.

We were impressed how drama is used to address certain pastoral themes that come up in school

Around 10 per cent of pupils have SEN and the school has a large learning support team dedicated to supporting them. Learning mentors and assistants work through teachers and directly with pupils, helping to track their progress and ensure they know what they need to do to improve – and there are regular extension and catch-up classes. 'They're really good on SEN – I couldn't fault it,' one parent told us. Gifted and talented students are also identified for extra support.

Teachers seem to be as keen to work here as young people are to study here, with large numbers of applications for most teaching posts. 'We are high profile and attract high quality applicants,' explains head, pointing out that he just recruited a new physics teacher, with a first class degree. 'It's unheard of in London,' he says, as if still incredulous at his find, adding that many past students come back to teach – 'something we're extremely proud of.'

Games, options, the arts: Among the most successful schools in Tower Hamlets when it comes to competitive sports – 'a tremendous achievement when you look at the limitations of the site,' says head – and we agree. Indeed, outside sports facilities consist of a less than a handful of courts that double up as the playground – and although there's an indoor swimming pool (everyone learns to swim by the end of their first term), it's pretty shoddy, as is the indoor fitness suite currently housed in a portacabin. Decent sports hall, however, while the likes of running and football take place at offsite at nearby Spider Park (which has tracks and Astroturf) and annual sports day is at Mile End Stadium. Table tennis, boxing and fencing are also on the agenda. 'They try to get you enthused about some kind of exercise, although it doesn't work for everyone,' one student told us, and parents agree.

Visual arts no great shakes, but drama is hugely popular (including at A level – a joy to see), with a particularly dedicated and popular head of department, who ensures GCSE students get access to at least four operas and/or musicals, which they use to reflect on their own work. Actors regularly perform at The Half Moon Theatre – and we were impressed how drama is used to address certain pastoral themes that come up in school, with students writing and performing plays on these subjects.

Lively (and noticeably experimental, when we visited) music department, with over 100 students in every year group having individual music lessons. The steel band has played at the Albert Hall, the Mansion House and for the Lord Mayor's Show, and have won various awards. There's also a gospel choir, orchestra and various string ensembles.

Clubs are mainly focused on sports, but there's also Equality Group ('which deals with everything from homophobia to sexism' – Ian McKellen having recently been invited to the school to talk on LGBT issues when we visited), Amnesty International, Whitechapel Mission, plus charity club, debating club and Christian and Muslim unions, among others. Student-led clubs are disappointingly thin on the ground, but head plans to address this. Residentials have historically not taken place during term-time, but again this is set to change – with access to The Hampshire Cass Mountain Centre in Wales making whole year group residentials a possibility.

Background and atmosphere: Formed in 1964 by the governing body of Red Coat School (established in 1714 for boys born within Mile End Old Town) and the governors of the Sir John Cass Foundation (a charity set up in 1710 by Sir John Cass for poor children in the East End of London). The school is owned by the Foundation, one of London's oldest educational charities, and Founder's Day in St Botolph-without-Aldgate church is one of the highlights of the school year. Its present site dates from 1965 and has been refurbished over the years since to include up-to-date science labs and learning centres stocked with computers – as well as an attractive glass-fronted main building. Classrooms vary in both age and size and while most are light and airy, some were exceptionally hot on the summer's day we visited (to be fair, school is trying to secure aircon – 'it's all a matter of funding'). Although it's in the middle of the East End, the school boasts a deceptively rural-seeming setting with a city farm opposite, a park next door and the school church and its tranquil graveyard beyond.

The library is open before and after school and on Saturday mornings, with learning mentors around to help. 'Many students have no computer at home, nor quiet space in which to do homework.' The great hall with stage and balcony doubles as a lecture theatre and can accommodate large (although sadly not quite the whole school) assemblies. 'These are important for setting the behaviour tone for the school.' Uniform is traditional, including a blazer, and while sixth formers wear their own clothes, they are expected to dress smartly. Although this is a C of E school, around 90 per cent of students are Muslims and two multi-faith rooms (one male; one female) cater for both. Cashless cafeteria serves hot food, while cold food is served from a hatch on the playground; sixth formers have their own indoor café. 'Food is good here, although we're pleased the head is on the case about getting more variety,' one student told us.

An orderly atmosphere pervades, with a high level of attentiveness during lessons. But kids will be kids and, refreshingly, that's allowed too – apparent in the corridors between lessons, albeit with classical background music and a strict one-way system (and certain routes for certain year groups) encouraging an overall sense of calm.

Pastoral care, well-being and discipline: The emphasis on security is palpable, with tall black, alarmed fences surrounding the school and quite a rigmarole to go through when arriving as a visitor at reception, along with CCTV cameras throughout the school and staff checking on destinations of those wandering the corridors between lessons – all of which, say staff and students, discourage vandalism and help students feel protected. Equally noticeable (many visitors comment on it) is the mutual respect. 'First of all we make them feel secure and safe, then we start to cultivate respect for all,' explains head, who describes the school as 'strict but not punitive.' Students concur, saying many of them go through school without a detention (most are given for lateness or failure to hand in homework). Students praise the fact that they (and their parents) are each assigned a named adult, whom they can approach about any personal problems – 'and heads of year are very approachable too.' There's also one full-time qualified counsellor.

'The children are happy here,' concluded one parent. 'They know what's expected of them and they get down to work.' A lively school council makes regular suggestions

Head insists that 'the high standards and quality of teaching, along with the consistent approach by staff' are relevant pastorally too. 'It means everyone is focused on why they're here and is the reason I believe we have to do very little firefighting pastorally.' 'The children are happy here,' concludes one parent. 'They know what's expected of them and they get down to work.' A lively school council makes regular suggestions for change – all the usual issues, including getting more playground equipment.

By all accounts, very little racial tension and very few exclusions – with only one temporary (and no permanent) exclusions in the last three years. Drugs very rarely a problem; carrying weapons even less so – both prolific problems in the local area. 'We do very occasionally have some challenging behaviour, but it does not threaten the learning environment. We try hard not to exclude if we can possibly avoid it.'

Pupils and parents: About two-thirds of the students are Bangladeshi, the rest from a variety of ethnic minorities, including many Somali refugees. Around 70 per cent receive free school meals. Although there's no formal parents' association, parents are mostly very supportive of the school and its high expectations for their children. Good communications between school and parents – 'I've always had quick responses from them,' said one. Students form strong peer groups. 'There's a very strong ethos of care for one another,' said a parent.

Entrance: Some 1,200 applicants for 208 places. Everyone is placed in one of four ability bands, assessed by the standard Tower Hamlets numeracy and literacy tests in year 5, with equal numbers of places offered from each band. This is a C of E school, so it does allocate a minority of places to committed Christians, with 40 places going to worshippers in a recognised Christian church, with looked-after children, social and medical needs, living in one of the listed parishes and then siblings in order of priority. The other 152 places have a similar priority order, but 20 are offered to first-born children. Families in the area tend to be large and siblings would otherwise monopolise the intake. Distance from the school is the tie-break. Sixteen places (four per band) are also allocated to those who score highest in the school's language aptitude test.

The sixth form is also highly oversubscribed, with over 1,000 applicants for 300 outside places. Most A level courses require five or more 9-4 grades at GCSE including English and maths, with some higher stipulations eg grade 8 in maths for maths or further maths A level (whereas with other subjects, including English, they'll consider a grade 6). But those with lesser qualifications can take lower level courses, and the majority of pupils from year 11 go through to the sixth form.

Exit: Up to half of students leave after GCSEs – usually to another sixth form or straight into a job. A quarter leave after year 12. And of those who go through to year 13, almost all go on to university, while others go into apprenticeships, voluntary work or employment. Of those who go down the university route, around 40 per cent go to Russell Group universities, the vast majority (for social and cultural reasons) choosing London universities, with Kings, UCL, Imperial and Queen Mary proving particularly popular. Has had several successful Oxbridge candidates (one to Cambridge in 2018, plus two medics). While there's quite a range of courses studied, these do tend to be heavily dominated by sciences and maths.

Remarks: A beacon of excellence in one of the most deprived areas of the capital (and indeed the country), which takes in students with low levels of attainment and sends most of them off to university where they get laudable results. If your child is prepared to behave well and knuckle down to work, the expert teaching and high aspirations here will almost certainly see their grades go from strength to strength (and that goes for those who enter from one of the higher bands too).

Sir William Burrough Primary School

11

Salmon Lane, London E14 7PQ

020 7987 2147 | admin@sirwilliamburrough.towerhamlets.sch.uk | sirwilliamburrough.net

State	Pupils: 379
Ages: 3–11	

Headteacher: Since 1995 Avril Newman (60s) BEd, first class honours from Goldsmith's, who has spent her whole teaching career in Tower Hamlets. She is a national leader of education, a JP and has been honoured with a Freedom of the City award. A lover of theatre, books and travel, she is married with two grown-up children. Mrs Newman cited her greatest achievement as the integration of rigorous attention to academic standards with high emotional intelligence; qualities she noted 'don't always go together' but, in this case, are evidently modelled from the top. A warm, positive and articulate woman whose delicate stature belies a strong and dynamic force. She believes that every child should aspire to the highest possible standards in reading, writing and maths regardless of social or cultural background; the testimony of which lies in the reputation and success of the school and the low turnover of staff. One parent remarked: 'She is amazing, she really listens', and another described her as 'very accessible' and 'very good at dealing with a problem'.

She has an open door policy, literally (during our visit the lively community toddler group was in full swing just outside her office), and encourages parents to come in and talk face to face with her about any problem. Communication between the school and parents includes monthly Cup of Tea Mornings, described alternately by one parent as 'Avril meetings', providing a forum where parents make suggestions as to how things can be improved.

Back in 2011 Sir William Burrough was one of the first primaries to become a converter academy in Tower Hamlets which, at the time, was politically controversial. Now, she observes: 'We are waiting for the future to catch up with us.' Whilst there was mention, sensibly, of succession planning, Mrs Newman added that she has 'no plans to leave soon'. When the time does come for her to retire, she is confident that the strong deputy and leadership team will ensure there is a smooth transition and stability will be maintained.

Entrance: A highly oversubscribed school in a highly populated area means that the appetite for places is fierce: most recently 180 applications for the 45 places on offer in reception. Customary priority is given to looked-after children, siblings then proximity – and last year you needed to live very close indeed (within 260m). The recent changes to the welfare system have resulted in some local families moving away so places in the later years do crop up.

Exit: Mostly a spread of local secondary schools with the occasional child attending an out of borough independent or grammar.

Remarks: In a densely urban area with the entrance tucked up a dreary back street, there is something quite magical about stepping through the gate into the friendly and colourful atmosphere that immediately greets you. For a Victorian building spanning three floors, it is surprisingly light and airy with windows open and homely curtains billowing against a soft breeze. Children's artwork adorns all surfaces, proudly including some deft pencil drawings depicting, as one articulate boy observed, 'sociality in the city', as well as a net suspended from a classroom ceiling decorated with sumptuous rainforest paintings; a project complimented by a trip to Kew Gardens, one of many trips to take full advantage of the city's resources.

The classrooms are roomy and colourful, all with interactive whiteboards, and the library has a calm, attractive ambience. Unusually for a state primary, there is a dedicated and fully-equipped computer room backed up by widespread use of iPads. The recently refurbished reception classrooms are calm and comfortable with integrated toilets and a separate outdoor play space. The indoor gyms are a bit on the small side but there are two of them, and for physical activity they are more than made up for by the fine outdoor provision. A series of outdoor spaces surrounds the school building, including a dedicated 'dance space' where children can dance to music outdoors during lunchtime; two multi-sport pitches; a netted cricket area; and a vast array of play equipment including a trampoline. When we visited, during playtime all children were busy climbing, skipping, playing table football or foraging in the wooded area making 'camps'. An advantage of reigning for 20 years, Mrs Newman has overseen the planting and maturing of the lush trees that encircle the playground, adding an abundance of green to this urban oasis.

When we visited during playtime children were busy climbing, skipping, playing table football or in the wooded area making 'camps'. Lush trees encircle the playground

Sats-wise, over the last three years 95 per cent of pupils achieved level 4 or above in the three Rs, well above the national average, and most recently 29 per cent reached level 5 or above. A National Support School, SWB is amongst the 200 top performing primary schools and in the top eight per cent for the progress of all children, regardless of background, the hard data testimony to the school's academic approach. All children, apart from those with particular special needs, have learnt to read and write (in cursive!) by the end of reception, when they partake in a graduation ceremony complete with mortar boards and gowns. Once the basics are established, the Accelerated Reader and Accelerated Maths schemes kick in: online, personalised programmes which motivate through quizzes, prizes and international competitions. Families are able to win what amounts to a small library between them once they have read a million words: 'our way of ensuring children have books at home'. Other incentives include a maths Olympics, where children win rosettes for knowing their times tables, and a spelling bee.

All this takes place in the mornings, with the afternoons dedicated to the creative, experiential learning of the International Primary Curriculum (IPC). Sir William Burrough was one of the first primary schools in the country to introduce the IPC, which adopts a global perspective alongside a thematic, topic-based approach to learning. In a project on the Romans, children traced each other's bodies to create a life-size collage and went on to act out The Battle of Marathon. The children make their own movies and animations using iPads and, if the plot demands it, a green screen.

An energetic and effective use of partnerships brings in professional coaching in fencing, judo, rugby, hockey and handball alongside reading, number and chess partners from City firms. A recently established link with the Worshipful Company of Musicians complements the already lively musical culture in the school, including a 60-strong choir and a ukulele ensemble. They even have a choreographer-in-residence who ensures that every child in the school gets moving, appreciated particularly by one parent who felt that 'dance is fantastic' at the school. After-school clubs include film and animation, Spanish, sailing and debating. Years 3 to 5 build up their independence on residential trips offering challenge and outdoor adventure. Year 5s and 6s get to learn Latin. There is a breakfast club from 8.30am and a teatime club that runs until 4.30pm, facilities that were much appreciated by many of the working parents we met.

The school's You Can Do It programme 'keeps levels of confidence and resilience high, and is deeply woven into relationships of respect, tolerance, kindness and courtesy'. We saw this in action as children held open doors, enquired about the welfare of others and remarked that 'we all comfort each other'. There is an emphasis on continual practice and one pupil commented that 'if you are unsure, there is always a teacher next to you'. A caring infrastructure is evident from the youngest to the oldest: there is a room dedicated to part-time and summer-born reception children and year 6s were helped to feel calm before their Sats through afternoon yoga sessions. There is also a system of

In a project on the Romans, children traced each other's bodies to create a life-size collage and went on to act out The Battle of Marathon

peer support via year 6 school monitors, who look out for the younger children, and year 4s who help the reception classes learn to read.

All SEN support is offered in the classroom by teachers and TAs 'in the moment of learning' rather than in separate sessions or groups. This is a genuinely inclusive school with an expansive cultural mix. A small majority of pupils are from Bangladeshi heritage, others are of Somalian, Eastern European, Chinese and white British backgrounds. Some 75 per cent of pupils speak English as an additional language, though most are London-born and speak English when they arrive: the school's mastery of words proclaimed by repeatedly finishing as runners up in the English Speaking Union's Pan London Debating Tournament. Parents describe it as 'like a family', 'creative, friendly, inclusive' and one pupil commented 'they accept everybody who comes here'. When faced with the question of what the school might be able to do better, the pupils understandably struggled: 'I would change the sausages into hot dogs' and 'get a bigger trampoline' were about it.

Over her 20+ years as headteacher, Avril Newman has been inspired by the words of John Tomsett: 'A truly great school grows like an oak tree over many years'. Under the talented and passionate guidance of its head, Sir William Burrough has matured well like the trees in the playground. A happy, inclusive and high-achieving urban primary.

Snaresbrook Preparatory School

75 Woodford Road, South Woodford, London E18 2EA

020 8989 2394 | office@snaresbrookprep.org | snaresbrookprep.org

Independent	Pupils: 164
Ages: 3–11	Fees: £8,922 – £11,934 pa

Head: Since September 2018, Ralph Dalton BEd, previously senior deputy head pastoral at Woodford Green Prep.

Entrance: Most come in at nursery and go though to year 6. There is a low-key family interview with the head. Places higher up subject to a family interview and in-class assessment. Pupils come from various nurseries in the local area, from Canary Wharf and Stratford out to Epping, Woodford Green, Romford and Loughton, and beyond.

Exit: Bancroft's, Chigwell and Forest most popular local destinations, alongside City of London schools and St Edmund's Ware. Others to local grammar schools Woodford County High and Ilford County High.

Remarks: Small size and family atmosphere mean pupils settle in quickly. 'You don't have to be scared to talk to a year 6 because everyone knows each other,' a pupil said. One parent said that during her son's first year at the school he has 'waved to and greeted any older pupil we met in the street. And the bigger kids have invariably waved back.'

The main school is set in a 1930s Victorian house and was managed by the same family for 50 years. Its small, quaint classrooms are close together and the corridors are dainty, but it is an intimate rather than cramped feel. The nursery and reception are housed in a separate, purpose-built building overlooking a small playground, with the hall and a multi-purpose library room on the other side of the playground. Beyond that is a covered sensory garden, designed and constructed by an architect governor. The children grow plants here, and experiment with different climates and seasons. There is a huge blackboard where they chalk to their heart's content and above it a huge, colourful mural painted by year 6s.

The governors are very much involved in everyday school life, often to be seen popping in and out. They helped to extend the hall to create more storage space, they have helped decorate the staff room and to build the new canopied decking area outside the nursery so pupils can enjoy year round outdoor play free of leaves and rain. 'They are very sensitive to the needs of the staff and children.'

Single form entry, with class sizes of roughly 24 in the infants and 18 in the juniors, and plenty of classroom assistants. 'It is mixed ability here. What is exciting is seeing children who didn't come in as high fliers leave having made massive progress.' Most extra support for those with learning difficulties is provided in class, with a part-time specialist available as required.

French from nursery, optional German and Spanish, year 6s learn Latin and also embark on self-directed projects. Lots of investment in IT. We saw year 5s listening to a live commentary on an Arsenal v Southampton match and learning how to extract key information from a database to write up their news reports.

The school adventure service challenge is 'like a mini Duke of Edinburgh... we do camping, rowing, bird watching, cooking and it's lots of fun,' say pupils. Years 4 and 5 were excited about the annual trip to France where they visit a chocolate factory in Boulogne (they like this better than the snail farm). Whilst in France they spend time with penfriends and complete a shopping task in French, although some confess they have found ways around this: 'Luckily the lady that was serving us knew English'. Year 5 has a history trip to York and year 6 an end of year trip to Shropshire.

Years 4 and 5 were excited about the annual trip to France where they visit a chocolate factory (they like this better than the snail farm)

Before and after-school clubs include the usual range of sports plus country and maypole dancing, scooter club, creative writing, art club and knitting. Popular sports are football and netball, and considering how small the school is, they do well: 'Once we played in a tournament and there were two Snaresbrook teams in the football play-off and they ended up playing each other,' a pupil said with pride. There are no fields here so pupils take a minibus to Redbridge Sports Centre and Ashton playing fields.

One parent commented: 'I feel the school works hard to optimise the use of space available.' At breaktimes a daily games timetable saves the tiny playground from being dominated by football (football still an option at lunchtime when playtimes are staggered) and the children can try out a different game each day. 'Our new games teacher came up with the idea,' said a pupil. It was inspired by Olympics sports such as handball, dodgeball and basketball. Most of the children take part and girls and boys play together. Other activities are on offer, too – they can read, do art, play table tennis.

When we visited, years 1 and 2 were in the hall preparing for a dress rehearsal of Rise and Shine. 'All have a part to play in the production,' said their teacher. The school tries to offer a taste of a wide range of drama and music, and each class gets a chance to perform. 'Lots of parents come to see the productions whether they have children in that year group or not.' Around 20 per cent of children learn to play the recorder, violin or flute.

House system gives everyone a chance to shine in different areas. 'Browns usually win on sports day, blues dominate swimming, yellows are good at choir singing and pancake races,' a pupil told us, 'so we each have our fair share of glory'. The many charitable and fundraising activities include readathons, movie nights to raise funds for Redbridge Night Shelter, sports events for the NSPCC and Great Ormond Street and harvest collections for the British Red Cross. Year 4 girls created a magazine, 'packed with quizzes, gossip and pictures. They made £61 by selling it to everyone'.

Pupils help inside school too. A year 6 pupil said of the nursery: 'We come in our free time and help the children and teachers with projects. It's also fun for us as this was our room when we were in the nursery.' It invokes a sense of service: 'This morning I was holding the door for a parent and I heard one of the year 4s say, "Dad, when I'm in year 6 I will be able to hold the door, I will say good morning to everyone".'

Support is good, say parents, with teachers always willing to discuss and address problems. Plenty of incentives and rewards for doing well, including Good Marks assemblies and commendation awards. The merit board includes an award to teachers for 'making a good start on the return after holidays'.

A new system of online live reports, with up-to-date comments from teachers that parents can access at any time, has replaced yearly written reports. The plan is to produce a detailed picture of how each child learns and how they are progressing.

Very active parents' association – '40 donations for the bake sale the other day', said a member – with an impressive participation rate considering that many, if not most, families have two working parents. Hotly-contested annual pancake race involves children, staff and parents.

Trinity Catholic High School

Mornington Road, Woodford Green, Essex IG8 0TP

020 8504 3419 | admin.trinitylower@redbridge.gov.uk | fc.tchs.uk.net

| State | Pupils: 1,627; sixth form: 417 |
| Ages: 11–18 | |

Headteacher: Since 1981, Dr Paul Doherty OBE BA DPhil (Oxon) FRSA (70s). Middlesbrough born and bred, he originally studied for the priesthood at Ushaw College in Durham. After gaining a history degree at Liverpool University, he won a state scholarship to Exeter College, Oxford, where he met his wife with whom he had seven children. Having decided the academic world was not for him either, he became a secondary school teacher, working in Ascot, Newark and Crawley before being appointed as headmaster to Trinity.

'An inspiration' is the phrase you'll hear more than any other about this larger-than-life character and despite him being in his 70s, pupils, parents and staff alike seem terrified at the mere thought of him leaving. We found him solid and commanding, yet friendly and open-minded – a winning combo that helped lead him to getting an OBE in 2012 for services to education and that helped lead the school to gaining five consecutive outstanding reviews from Ofsted. Doesn't teach, but very much part of the furniture across both school sites, where he eats with pupils in the dining room, holds regular question-and-answer sessions and invites every child to see him on their birthday, presenting them with a card, sweets and £1 coin. 'He's always reminding us that we should treat every child here as our own,' one staff member told us. 'Perhaps not the most politically correct of heads, but I rather like that,' commented a parent, while others also praise the 'strong management team' he has around him.

Also a novelist and writer of non-fiction, with over 100 books to his name, some translated into 20 languages. Has written under various pseudonyms including CL Grace, Paul Harding, Michael Clynes, Ann Dukhas and Anna Apostolou – although he now writes only under his real name. His seven grown-up children were all educated at Trinity.

Academic matters: Setting in maths from year 7, but in no other subject. 'Mixed ability classes work,' insists the head – and they have the results to prove it, with 89 per cent of GCSE candidates getting 9-4 in both English and maths in 2018, and 34 per cent of grades at 9-7. Strong results across the board, particularly in the core subjects of English, maths and sciences, with pupils also doing exceptionally well in art, computer science, child development, English literature, dance, drama and food tech. Popular GCSE choices include history, computer science, languages and triple science.

At sixth form, 28 A levels are offered – mainly traditional subjects 'due to Russell Group demands'

– although media studies, psychology and sociology also available, all with decent take-up. In 2018, 47 per cent A*-B and 21 cent A*/A grades, with strongest results in chemistry, French, Spanish, English language and literature.

Spanish and French from year 7, with Latin available in years 7 and 8 as a 'twilight course'. They don't hold back on homework which, perhaps inevitably, isn't to everyone's liking. 'I think they should give less in years 7 and 8 so that the children have more time to develop outside interests,' said one parent, while another commented, 'My child had to drop an A level due to the workload he was expected to get through at home.' Tracking of students is meticulously detailed and well communicated to both pupils and parents, and the school's monitoring and evaluation of this system is widely chronicled (including by Ofsted) as being second-to-none. 'We all know exactly where we should be in every subject – it's incredibly thorough,' one student told us. Meanwhile, a teacher said, 'It's very fluid so that we can raise standards where we need to and likewise, add in interventions where students aren't reaching their targets' – the likes of which include subject clinics and Saturday school.

The school's approach to SEN (110 on SEN register, including 30 EHC plans when we visited) is no less painstaking, with one parent praising the 'systematic approach to ensuring children get help both inside and outside the classroom – I couldn't fault it.' Adapting the curriculum is not uncommon – for example, so that a student can take six GCSEs instead of the more usual nine, with a bespoke curriculum and booster classes where needed. 'They've supported my daughter thoroughly without ever making a big deal of her special needs, and it's all coupled with clear expectations that she has to work as hard as she can. It's a great philosophy and has worked wonders for her.'

'It's very fluid so that we can raise standards where we need to and add in interventions where students aren't reaching their targets' – the likes of which include subject clinics

In short, a highly academic school – but an exam factory this is not, with several parents reporting that their multiple offspring's different academic levels were all catered for. 'One of my child found studying a breeze; the other really didn't, and the school managed both perfectly, finding their full potential but never making them feel over-pressured,' said one.

Games, options, the arts: All the usual suspects are on offer, including hockey, netball, football and rugby, and frequently wins competitions. Less traditional options include cycling (the school has bought in bikes), sailing (at Fairlop sailing lake), badminton and dance (to GCSE), and some parents told us the school was good at 'encouraging fitness – essential in the current climate.' Only a sports hall on site, however, with other facilities a 10 minute coach ride away; parents we spoke to either told us their children weren't interested in sport (telling in itself?) or that their very sporty child had been 'disappointed'.

'They've supported my daughter thoroughly without ever making a big deal of her special needs'

The art suite – which includes three art studios, plus a smaller workroom – produces some striking artwork, which is displayed throughout the school. Visits to galleries often involve mixed year groups 'so they can learn from each other' and visiting artists are regularly invited to work in the workroom, with students observing them in small groups. This approach is extended to pupils too, with younger ones frequently invited to watch and critique older ones producing their masterpieces. Meanwhile, teachers are encouraged to inspire students through their particular area of specialism.

The focus on drama tends to be more academic than extracurricular, with no all-school productions. But there's plenty to shout about when it comes to value added, with very successful results at GCSE, although this attracts relatively small numbers, usually around 20 a year.

Parents itching to watch their little cherubs perform have more joy when it comes to music, however, with the Christmas carol concert and rock and pop concerts among the popular annual events. There are also plenty of one-off performances from the various school orchestras, choirs, ensembles and school bands – plus regular music festivals and competitions. Around 60 students from every year group from years 7 to 9 are taught instrumental lessons by a peripatetic teacher (some in groups), with numbers starting to trail off after that. The annual music tour, which involves a different European destination each year, is well attended. 'Trinity really feels like a musical school – you often see pupils performing, sometimes as a background at lunchtimes while you eat,' one pupil told us.

There's a comprehensive extracurricular timetable, resulting in many pupils staying on until 5pm at least a couple of times a week. Clubs focus on sport, music, IT and all the academic subjects right through to war gaming and chess (popular with the quieter pupils). This is a lead school in outdoor education, with a greater take-up of D of E (bronze, silver and gold) within the school than across the rest of Redbridge as a whole. At least one or two school trips every week to theatres, museums etc and some residentials too, including a recent ski trip to Austria, film and media studies visit to LA and regular teambuilding trips to Wales.

Background and atmosphere: The school is split between two sites, with the upper site (main site) on Mornington Road and the lower site on Sydney Road, a five to 10 minute walk away. The lower site (originally the local secondary modern school, St Paul's) is home to years 7, 8 and 9, while the upper site (originally Holy Family Convent School, the local girls' grammar – which merged with St Paul's in 1976) is home to year 10 upwards. 'It makes starting at this vast school much less daunting for year 7s,' one parent told us – pupils concur. That said, due to specialist facilities being split across the two sites (music is based in lower school, while most science labs are mainly in the upper school, for example), all pupils access both sites, with older ones often walking between them two or three times a day. 'We used to move the teachers around, but now we move the pupils – much better for fitness.'

The upper site is made up of nine buildings, dating between 150 and two years old: Trinity House, Keswick House, Rackham House, Monteluce House, Pelham House, Grainger House, St Joseph's House, Vincent House and Becket House – each home to a different subject area ranging from humanities to food tech. Meanwhile, the lower site is made up of a single 1960s building, with a remote science laboratory in the playground called the Padua Centre (named after St Anthony of Padua). 'This is where the snakes and geckos are kept – you can borrow these over the holidays,' a pupil told us excitedly.

Remote science laboratory in the playground. 'This is where the snakes and geckos are kept – you can borrow these over the holidays,' a pupil told us excitedly

Inside, much of the school looks tired and in need of a lick of paint, and everyone agrees they are limited by space – there's no dedicated canteen, for instance, and the library doesn't look anywhere near big enough for 1,750 pupils. 'The school was designed for six form entry – we're now eight form

entry.' We felt it in the lower site during wet play, with every single pupil crammed in the corridors and main hall. That said, the facilities are good and some areas, such as common rooms, are surprisingly roomy, albeit unimaginatively designed with a sea of conference-style blue chairs and magnolia paint.

The annual music tour, which involves a different European destination each year, is well attended. 'Trinity really feels like a musical school – you often see pupils performing'

You will be in no doubt that your child is a Catholic school, with daily mass at 8.30am and prayers in the morning, at midday, at 3pm and before all meals. There's a chapel on both sites, plus a chaplain who puts a Catholic slant on any counsel provided to the pupils, while pictures of the pope adorn several noticeboards. But that doesn't mean pupils are spoon-fed religion – in fact, they are actively encouraged to question their faith. 'Some students wind up atheist and that's not seen as a problem – all views are welcomed,' one pupil told us. Overall, there's a culture of learning – when we visited, all classroom doors were firmly closed, all desks faced forward and all pupils looked engaged. Once the bell goes, though, there's all the noise and excitement you'd expect when hundreds of tweens and teens are able to let their hair down, if only for a few minutes between lessons.

Pastoral care, well-being and discipline: 'Firm but fair' is how most pupils and parents describe discipline here and it clearly does the job – pupils are well behaved and there have been no temporary or permanent exclusions for at least three years. 'All the students know the rules and that there are clear consequences if you break them,' explained a parent – notably detention (lunchtime or after school), community service (litter picking etc) or Saturday school, albeit with a warning system first. The most heinous crime, it seems, is distracting others in lessons, although pupils told us the school is also particularly hot on uniform and giving in homework on time. 'We have zero tolerance for lessons being interrupted – teachers are here to teach and pupils are here to learn,' the school told us – and a daily logbook is sent round to all classes so that teachers can record any misbehaviour, even if it's only a warning. 'It means teachers know they

Snaresbrook Preparatory School

are well supported and students know the teachers talk to each other.'

Pastorally sound. 'Teachers are approachable, with most regularly reminding us that they are available if you are struggling either emotionally or practically,' said one pupil. In addition, each year group has a head and assistant head, who – together with the school chaplain – encourage any pupils to come and see them if they want to. There's also a big prevention strategy to help stop issues ranging from bullying to radicalisation becoming a problem in the first place. Plus, there's plenty of leadership and peer mentoring type opportunities, including a prefect system and Guardian Angels (whereby sixth formers look out for younger ones).

Excellent communications between school and parents all helps, say parents. 'There has never been a time when I haven't known what's going on with my child – they tell you when they're doing really well, when they're struggling and when they really play up,' one parent told us. 'When things go wrong, they get you involved quickly so they can resolve it and move on,' said another.

Once the bell goes, though, there's all the noise and excitement you'd expect when hundreds of tweens and teens are able to let their hair down, if only for a few minutes

Pupils and parents: A great diversity of backgrounds and ethnicity, with 47 per cent minority ethnic (predominantly Black Caribbean), with the common denominator being – surprise, surprise – Catholicism (93 per cent). Although there's no PA, parents feel involved and there's almost full attendance at parents' evenings and a good turnout at events such as cheese and wine evening. We found pupils to be chatty, grounded, community minded and well-mannered, with a real pride for their school. Alumni include Tamzin Outwaite (EastEnders actress), Kele Okereke (musician), Matt Ward (record producer/songwriter), Gary Lucy (actor), Christine Ohuruogu MBE (Olympic, world and commonwealth athletics champion), Catherine Dalton, Dan Lawrence and Nicholas Browne (cricketers).

Entrance: The four main feeder primary schools are St Antony's Woodford, St Mary's Chingford, St John Fisher Loughton and Our Lady of Lourdes Wanstead – although pupils come from around 50 in total. Looked after children get priority, then it comes down to Catholicity and distance of Catholic primary school. Over 1,000 applications for the 240

Doesn't teach, but very much part of the furniture across both sites, where he eats with pupils in the dining room, holds regular question-and-answer sessions and invites children to see him on their birthday

places and many go to appeal, with long waiting lists further up the school.

Over three-quarters stay on to the sixth form after GCSE, for which the entrance criteria is 9-6s at GCSE for the subject they want to study. Around 50 more join from outside (depending on numbers staying on), although that figure has dipped recently as some local schools have introduced sixth forms. 'It's a shame as we could accommodate more than 50,' says school. Unlike the rest of the school, sixth formers don't have to be Catholic, but they must be willing to uphold the school's religious ethos.

Exit: Nearly a quarter leaves after GCSE – usually to study a vocational course at college or different subject choices at other local schools. A few do apprenticeships. Around 80 per cent of sixth formers to university, of whom approximately 45 per cent go to Russell Group universities. No particularly dominant universities or subjects – 'there's such a range, from law to technical theatre and they head off all over the country.' Around five medics a year. Three Oxbridge places in 2018. Pupils praise the university and careers advice service – 'There's nothing they can't help you with.'

Money matters: Parents are generous in their financial support, with a Gift Aid scheme in place for those who donate either via standing order or one off donation. Trinity holds funds to support those in need and parents/guardians are encouraged to contact the head if financial support is required. Strong links with local community groups also ensure that families are well supported.

Remarks: A strict, disciplined Catholic school with a strong pastoral system to ensure young people stay on the straight and narrow. This, together with the excellent teaching and monitoring, makes this a place where young people of all abilities thrive academically. Standards haven't slipped here in decades and it doesn't look like they're about to start any time soon.

Walthamstow School for Girls

Church Hill, Walthamstow, London E17 9RZ

020 8509 9446 | info@wsfg.waltham.sch.uk | wsfg.waltham.sch.uk

State	Pupils: 900
Ages: 11–16	

Head: Since 2012, Meryl Davies BA (50s), who we found to be easy-going, enthusiastic and energised. Prepared to go against the grain if it's in the best interests of the school – which staff, parents and students unanimously admire – it feels like there's really nothing this determined head couldn't handle. Having studied French and linguistics at Sheffield University, she stayed on to do her PGCE. 'I loved my own schooling in North Wales, so teaching was a long-time ambition,' she says. Immediately attracted to some of the more radical teaching techniques of the 1980s and the more gritty comprehensives of inner London, she found the reality was quite an eye-opener as a young whippersnapper, but one she nonetheless embraced, with one of her earlier jobs working on a London barge with school refusers to get them back into mainstream schooling. 'Working at the raw edge of education is an experience I think all teachers should have – you get to really understand what makes young people tick,' she says.

After moving on to Graveney School, Tooting, she moved up the ranks to assistant head, then took up a deputy headship in Elliott School, Putney, one of the biggest London comps at the time (where she was seconded briefly to take on a headship of a school on special measures). She then moved to Cator Park School for Girls, Bromley, before coming to Walthamstow in 2012. Disappointingly, results dropped a whopping 14 per cent after just a few months of her joining, but it's widely acknowledged this was largely down to an earlier decision to get all year 11s to do a pilot course of double maths. With fine grading among the tactics she's since introduced, results are not only back on track, but the best the school has ever had. Seen by staff as an enabling, empowering leader, she regularly encourages others to front meetings. She teaches French to the lower school, runs a Monday surgery for parents and answers emails at weekends, seeing her job as 24/7.

'Teaching has been my vocation and London schools have been my life and passion,' she says. 'It sounds trite, but if you think about how many lives we have an impact on, I think working in education is an amazing opportunity and responsibility.' Lives in South London with her partner and has three grown-up children.

Academic matters: Excellent results across the board, with the school consistently among the top performing non-selective schools in the country. 'There are no specialist subjects at this school – we aim to do well in everything,' explains head, although the school has a specialist status in maths and computing, which has done no harm to results in these areas. In 2018, 77 per cent of students gained five or more GCSEs (including maths and English) at 9-4 and 28 per cent were 9-7 grades – some of the best results the school has ever had, which the head attributes to a combination of high expectations, inspirational teaching, regular monitoring and target setting and a broad approach to learning experiences.

> *'There are no specialist subjects at this school – we aim to do well in everything,' explains head*

No setting, except in maths from year 7. 'Historically, the school has never done it,' says head, 'and this works for us.' French or Spanish from year 7, with a taster in Urdu, and Latin also available at GCSE. At the end of year 8, students take part in the Languages Festival, a celebration of all languages spoken or studied in the school and the girls perform in a foreign language in front of their year. Latin offered as an additional language at GSCE.

Targeting and monitoring are huge, with personalisation of study plans meticulous in detail – one of the key reasons no student seems to get left behind. 'It's forensic,' smiles the head, who can talk at length at how girls are identified for different types and levels of help, depending on their individual needs and the way they learn. Peer mentoring is also a focus, with older pupils trained to work regularly with younger ones around student support.

A tour of the classrooms revealed engaged students contributing animatedly and with much smiling. Students we spoke to agree this is the norm, with plenty of references to 'engaging,' 'interactive' lessons that 'are never dull.' 'Teachers want to see that everyone is on board and thriving in their subject,' said one student. The head points to the growing focus on sharing good techniques around teaching and learning, which she hopes will improve consistency of teaching methods across the school (something they've been criticised for in the past). Low staff turnover, with one parent commenting, 'Lots of teachers have been here a very long time and it means they have strong attachments to the school.'

'We all have a great sense of pride when our artwork is displayed – there's a feeling of "I did that and my school appreciates it",' one student said

Phrases like 'That's not good enough' are not part of school life here, where the emphasis is on enabling and encouraging effort in much more positive ways. 'You won't hear it said to the students or staff,' says the head firmly. 'We pride ourselves on having a healthy atmosphere where we make people feel confident, not self-doubting.' The school motto, 'Neglect not the gift that is in thee,' resonates here, according to staff and students, who add that school is, in the main, fun.

Whilst the school doesn't claim to stand out in terms of SEN, around a quarter (nearly 24 per cent) require SEN support (almost double the national average for schools) and a similar figure (27 per cent) speak English as a second language. No wonder the language and learning department has a 16-strong team (some of whom are teaching staff), catering for the usual remit – everything from mild dyslexia to mobility problems (there's good wheelchair access here). Most support is classroom based and there's a plenty of focus on looking ahead so that gaps are prevented from widening where they needn't. 'I've been massively impressed by how much effort the department puts into my daughter's needs and how well they communicate with us about it,' one parent told us. 'The school is incredibly personalised and inclusive.'

Games, options, the arts: 'Sport is a large feature of this school,' states the head and there's certainly no shortage of options – cricket, basketball, tag rugby, football, rock climbing, netball, trampolining, dance, self-defence and more – which are mainly offered on site, either in the sports hall or so-called MUGA (multi-use games area), which consists of a large, hard-surfaced area of courts. Sadly, no school field, although there is some outside green space, including a landscaped woodland area, which is sometimes used for PE. Meanwhile, the local YMCA, which is in easy walking distance, is used for swimming and fitness classes. The school regularly competes against other schools, and there is some representation at regional level and occasionally national, with one former student having made the Olympic squad for volleyball, and another for athletics. School is also involved in the NEC Wheelchair Tennis Masters. 'Some other schools around here don't seem to value sport, but this one really gets that link between physical exercise and learning well in the classroom,' one parent told us.

Impressive art facilities, consisting of two main studios, which are spacious, bright and airy, with students' creations in everything from ceramics to textiles and graphics to portrait work exhibited throughout the school. A particularly attractive year 8 Grayson Perry vase project, displayed in glass cabinets in one major corridor, couldn't help but catch our eye. 'We all have a great sense of pride when our artwork is displayed – there's a feeling of "I did that and my school appreciates it",' one student said. Lots of cross-curricular projects, such as maths through art, plus plenty of visits to galleries and exhibitions. The school runs an annual exhibition of self-portraits by year 7s, which appears as part of the Walthamstow Arts Trail, attended by celebs and general public, and which raises money for their link school in Pakistan.

Drama very popular and seen as a key part of increasing the girls' confidence and ability to speak out, with lots of performances by individual year groups and whole-school performances every other year, such as The Wizard of Oz. Strong links with the Unicorn Theatre in London Bridge. School also involved with Shakespeare Schools Festival.

'Some other schools around here don't seem to value sport, but this one really gets that link between physical exercise and learning well in the classroom,' one parent told us

The biggest things to come out of the music department here (which has two music classrooms and a decent number of practice rooms) are the highly acclaimed steel pan bands, which regularly perform in public spaces, including the Royal Albert Hall. It's been a tradition at the school for decades, with a steel band ensemble in every year

> *Some attractive break-out areas, including one with brightly coloured orange and black sofas, known by the girls as the Easyjet Lounge*

group, which rehearses every morning. There's a whole school orchestra, although it's not huge, plus school choir and various ensembles and bands, some of which are student led. Four peripatetic teachers come in to teach instrumental lessons. The annual Modern Languages Festival involves each class in year 8 learning a song in the language they study and performing with their class in front of the entire year group. Dance is also valued, and seen as key to team-building.

Food tech is innovative, with plenty of competitions and links with outside organisations – ranging from an annual project with foodbanks, in which students learn to make dishes with very limited resources, right through to trips to fine dining restaurants in top hotels.

Extensive enrichment, including trips (eg black history month trips), workshops (eg in STEM, and also for young lawyers and for young doctors), events (eg Girls Can Crafting and Coding Event), entry to competitions (eg WSFG Cycle Planning Awards, Jack Petchey Speak Out Challenge) and links with other schools (eg primary schools are invited to the school for science days). The girls even run their own bank, through a longstanding link with MyBnk.

Extracurricular clubs include multimedia, origami, languages, sport, gardening, engineering and debating. 'Whilst these clubs are not compulsory, they are actively encouraged,' says the head. We attended a meeting of the International Club, where a group of students were busy planning all kinds of exciting initiatives, particularly schools they have strong links with overseas – including the Goodwill Secondary School in Roseau and Dominica and Ambore Read Foundation School, Ambore, Pakistan. Plenty of fundraising for the school in Ambore (over £15k to date), while teachers have travelled there to officially open the school and deliver lessons. 'These international links are frequently the subject of school assemblies and we are currently exchanging messages with students in Dominica via our Google Community,' says the head. School also has live penpal links with schools in France and Spain and holds the British Council International School Award (for outstanding development of the international dimension in the curriculum).

Background and atmosphere: Main building – with the classic grade 2, red-brick grammar school look – was built in 1911, although the school itself dates back to 1890, when it was opened as a private school in West Avenue, which later moved to nearby Church Hill House. In 1911, the school was taken over by Essex County Council and in 1913 moved to its present site on land originally part of the Vicars Glebe. The school has since been enlarged in 1918, 1928, 1962, 1974 and 2010 and the resulting combination of new and old builds works seamlessly, with no need to even leave one building to enter the next. After a period in the late 20th century as a grammar school, then as a senior high school for 14-18 year-olds, in 1986 the school once again became a school for girls aged 11-16.

In the old part of the school, expect oodles of original features, from the parquet flooring and wall tiles to traditional radiators, with the oak panelled school hall forming the centrepiece, whose walls bear the names and achievements of past students. At the other end of the spectrum is the 2010 building, which includes the new Norris Hall, providing an impressive theatre-style auditorium. Spacious classrooms and labs boast masses of natural light, and there are some attractive break-out areas, including one with brightly coloured orange and black sofas, known by the girls as the Easyjet Lounge. A vast dining hall has mixed reviews of the food from students and the library is a good size. Everywhere – and we mean everywhere – is scrupulously clean and tidy.

> *Highly acclaimed steel pan bands, which regularly perform in public spaces, including the Royal Albert Hall. It's been a tradition at the school for decades*

Outside, the stand-out feature is the Greek Theatre, built in the 1920s and which has a circular arena with steps up to a stage on one side and pillared portico on the other. There's a reasonably sized green space surrounding the theatre, plus a rooftop area (to the 2010 building), accessible from ground level, with plenty of chairs and tables. Students also use the MUGA area at break times. Overall, there's a rural, village feel here, even though they're only five minutes from the Victoria line – with enthusiastic students clearly enjoying their environment and plenty of reassuring signs that they're genuinely having fun. The only rude interruption to all this is the hideous end-of-lesson 'bell' that sounds more like some kind of nuclear alert.

The school day runs from 8.45am-3.30pm, although breakfast club students arrive from 7.30am and extracurricular activities run after school daily, with girls also given the opportunity to stay on to do work after school if, for example, they struggle with finding the space and quiet to do so at home.

Pastoral care, well-being and discipline: Pastoral care primarily comes from form tutors, with students describing teachers as 'approachable' and 'caring', and girls clearly feeling safe and nurtured. Peer support is also strong, with some formal mechanisms in place, although for the most part, it's natural, with students instinctively looking out for one another, especially lower down the school. A part-time counsellor is accessible via referral from teachers and learning mentors, and there's plenty of emphasis on exploring issues that others school shy away from – from female genital mutilation to forced marriages. The school is Stonewall approved and there's no shortage of multicultural events and projects to ensure everyone's background feels valued. Big on fundraising, especially for linked schools in other countries. Transition for year 7s is notable, with the school running a highly successful summer school to get a head-start on team-building, and the school has recently introduced a mindfulness course for year 11s.

Strong student council (which, like most, seems to focus on food and toilets) and plenty of leadership opportunities, including interviewing staff, which reflect the emphasis on trust being given to the girls. 'Teachers are strict when they need to be, but for the most part, there's a strong reliance on self-discipline here,' says the head. Indeed, although there are school rules, you're more likely to hear talk of rights and responsibilities, with girls very much feeling a sense of ownership in this school.

The school is Stonewall approved and there's no shortage of multicultural events and projects to ensure everyone's background feels valued

Bullying occasionally occurs as it does in any school, says the head, although there are plenty of anti-bullying policies and the fact that this is a 'telling' school means students are quick to speak out not just about themselves, but any friends in trouble. 'Our staff are trained to notice signs,' adds the head, 'and when it happens, we involve parents quickly.' No permanent exclusions as long as

Parents equally, if not more, aspirational, expecting a lot from their girls, with almost 100 per cent attendance at parents' evenings

anyone can remember, with fixed term exclusions well below the national average, usually given out for very rare instances of aggressive behaviour.

Pupils and parents: Multi-ethnic population, with students from over 50 countries – a great source of pride for the school, which celebrates this rich diversity in everything from assemblies to individual projects. Majority of students from Pakistani origin, followed by white (not just British), then black Caribbean and black African, with the fourth largest group being Indian. 'Mind you, this changes all the time,' points out the head. Girls seem confident, articulate, aspirational and optimistic. 'I could take any of my daughter's friends and they'd have a very clear idea of where they want to be in two or three years' time,' said a parent of a year 10 student.

Parents equally, if not more, aspirational, expecting a lot from their girls, with almost 100 per cent attendance at parents' evenings, consultations about subject options etc. Parents are also regularly invited to take part in questionnaires and parent forums and they are consulted about policy. No PTA, however, which is a disappointment to some parents.

Former pupils include Baroness Scotland, Jacqui Harper (BBC news) and Jeanette Kwakye (Olympic sprinter).

Entrance: Heavily oversubscribed, with some 700 applying for 180 year 7 places. Non-selective, the school follows the borough's entrance criteria, which favours girls in the looked after system/those with an EHC plan, followed by siblings, then it's down to distance. Those who get in mainly live less than a one mile radius. Occasional places further up the school when families move out of the area.

Exit: Vast majority of girls go on to sixth form college or local school sixth forms. 'They clammer to have our girls,' says head. The two main local colleges are Sir George Monoux Sixth Form College and Leyton Sixth Form college, whilst schools include Highams Park, Heathcote, City and Islington, Latymer, City of Westminster and Forest School. Most go on to study for A levels, with a heavy emphasis on sciences, whilst a few do BTecs. 'They are career savvy and know exactly what they want to study and why,' says head. Those after more specialist courses are prepared to travel, with some commuting up to a couple of hours every day.

Remarks: This is a relaxed and happy school, yet it's purposeful, vibrant and aspirational. The strong academic atmosphere, which is backed up by a great pastoral system, means there's no reason any girl should get left behind. We were particularly encouraged by the extent to which girls are encouraged to express themselves and to challenge stereotypes and indeed the status quo where appropriate. A true community school that believes passionately in the research that a single-sex environment empowers girls to realise their potential, this is a place that proves with the right teaching and school culture, anyone can thrive.

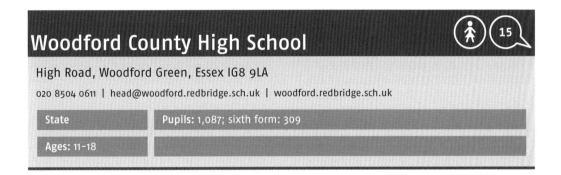

Woodford County High School

High Road, Woodford Green, Essex IG8 9LA

020 8504 0611 | head@woodford.redbridge.sch.uk | woodford.redbridge.sch.uk

State	Pupils: 1,087; sixth form: 309
Ages: 11–18	

Headteacher: Since 2010, Jo Pomeroy (early 50s), MA in English language and literature (St Andrews), BEd (Open), NPQH. Spent two years in a comprehensive in rural Scotland before going to work in France at a mixed grammar school for three years. It was at this high achieving international school that she became aware of 'what can be achieved', 'what is possible' and 'what bright students are capable of if they are given enough challenge,' she says. So the aim here 'is for students always to be working just beyond what they are comfortable with'. Back in the UK she spent another three years working in a comprehensive school with strong bias towards European languages and at that point 'got interested in management, in getting into position where you could make a bigger change'. Sure enough, at her next appointment at a girls' grammar in Surrey, where she spent 16 years, she eventually became deputy head. 'There is enormous satisfaction in seeing incrementally what can be achieved in one place,' she says. Academic life at Woodford is very much influenced by this passion for great leadership as well as head's English teaching background. 'What excites me the most is working from what you may be able to stimulate in your own life and career and then being able to share that with students so that they can enjoy challenges themselves.'

Academic matters: Best results in Redbridge. These are bright girls taught by committed teachers, a third of whom have been here for over 10 years. As a selective school (there are only some four students with SEN), it has maintained an outstanding record of achievement, with 81 per cent 9-7 grades at GCSE in 2018. And these stats despite most students – in fact well over half of the school population – speaking English as a second language. 'The joy of being in a school like this is that it is self-propagating: when students come in and they see other students valuing learning and success, and working hard on collaborative projects, it really affects everything else they do.'

This school models leadership extremely well. It has an impressive mentoring structure in place where older pupils mentor younger ones. There are literacy mentors who provide targeted additional support for year 7s where needed, and this 'sustained focus on academic literacy across the curriculum has been highly successful'. Head says, 'I have an interest in a great many subjects and I think the joy of English being my subject is that it takes you into everything, history, philosophy, art and music, and it is wonderful being able to inves-

> *The girls lack nothing in terms of modern resources, thanks to a very active PFTA and generous sponsorship of STEM resources from the Wolfson Foundation*

tigate and enjoy literature and other languages as well.' These pupils have the opportunity to be mentored in other subjects as well, by sixth formers who relish the opportunity to 'give something back', though 'teachers still keep a close eye...'

In some classrooms desks are arranged to encourage interaction between students, not only with teachers. In the English department, year 7s are introduced to Shakespeare texts usually reserved for later years and invited to write an essay on what they have learnt. They also have lots of opportunity to visit theatres. Pupils take two languages from year 7 (French and either German or Latin). English, languages and science are all strong here and nearly everyone takes triple science GCSE. Lots of information and support provided to both students and parents on choosing options. GCSE computing now offered and in KS3 an integrated DT, electronics and programming course.

In the sixth form, where roughly a quarter of students come from other schools, girls either take four A levels, three plus the EPQ or three plus AS maths over two years. Woodford maintains good A level results with 79 per cent A*/B grades, 16 per cent A* in 2018, with students off to Oxford and Cambridge and many on to medical careers. Academic mentoring and university preparation at sixth form, and guidance to final transition here is second to none, or in one parent's words, 'really very strong'.

'What excites me the most is working from what you may be able to stimulate in your own life and career and then being able to share that with students'

Games, options, the arts: Head's commitment to leading a school that offers plenty of opportunity to be stretched is evident across the whole curriculum. Reasonable range of games on offer – badminton, athletics, netball, rounders, gymnastics and dance – and girls can pursue their interest in multicultural dance options such as Bhangra, African and street dance. Games either take place outside on the field and tennis courts or indoors in the newly built Lottery funded sports hall, which looks gorgeously fresh next to the main school building, already well over 100 years old when it opened as a school in 1919. Outdoor Greek theatre recently restored. The girls do well at games; they recently reached the UK badminton national finals, and they seem willing to try their best at everything, keen or not: 'Sport, I'm not good at, but it's a popular subject.'

Pupils speak highly of the sports leadership qualification offered in years 10 and 11: 'It gives you skills in being responsible, listening skills and classroom theory. We learn to create lesson plans.'

'We have house competitions,' head says, 'and sometimes there can be more drama offstage than on stage'

Another said it 'opens us up to new areas; we realise there is more to our skill set and that motivates and opens us up to aim higher'. D of E also offered.

School does well at art and has had pupils featured in a Saatchi exhibition. Major drama event each term as well as an annual musical (recently Anything Goes!) plus a summer production run by teachers and a spring production organised by students. A beautiful patchwork tapestry displayed under glass in the technology department harks back to the days when the school offered textiles. These days the girls focus their design skills in technology, where they recently emerged winners of the National Technology Design Prize, of the Talent 2030 Engineering Prize (sixth form) and of the Faraday Challenge (year 8).

Instrumental and vocal lessons at all levels on offer, though most who learn do so out of school. Many are involved in one of a large number of ensembles and clubs: guitar, singing, Carnatic music. There is a large junior choir and band, a folk group, a brass project (all year 8 pupils learn a brass instrument), woodwind ensemble, and a staff choir too. Girls also participate in the biennial Redbridge Choral Festival at the Royal Albert Hall.

Lots of trips to support lessons and extracurricular activities, including expeditions to eg Ghana, Morocco, Indonesia, China, Cambodia and most recently Nepal. Annual geography trip to Iceland.

Sixth form enrichment programme includes dance, cookery, computing, BSL sign language, art, sports and an extended period of voluntary service. Older students preside over all manner of different extracurricular opportunities, such as talks, clubs and charity events, and there is a society for everything – even to discuss current affairs. 'We have house competitions,' head says, 'and sometimes there can be more drama offstage than on stage.' But because there is no adult intervention the girls learn to work together and develop great teamwork skills – 'a real success and selling point of the school.' All comes good in the end, as evidenced by the year 11-led assembly held on the morning of our visit. In their well-structured presentation the girls demonstrated what they had learnt about self, learning and approaching life, showing extraordinary wisdom and the ability to work together. Head says, 'They listen to each other very well, and coming up the school younger students see this and that sets their aspirations.'

Background and atmosphere: Main building dates from 1768 when it was built as the country manor home of the Highams; school opened here in 1919, and its venerable features lend an atmosphere of tradition – from the beautiful open air Greek theatre that stands in the grounds near to the tennis courts, to the hymnals still used in assemblies – 'I'm not a Christian but I enjoy it', a pupil remarked.

With its small classrooms, narrow stairwells and corridors, the school has an intimate feel. Massive development the Centenary Centre opened September 2017 with new science labs, computer facilities, classrooms and outdoor learning areas. Refurbished rooms in the main building provide new food and nutrition rooms and an Innovation Lab. The girls lack nothing in terms of modern resources, thanks to a very active PFTA and generous sponsorship of STEM resources from the Wolfson Foundation.

Pastoral care, well-being and discipline: Pupils receive support from their form tutors and also have prefects to help school life run smoothly. 'Teachers are approachable, and there are some small classes so you get to know everyone.' When issues of bullying come up, 'once staff are aware of it the response is immediate and caring'.

Lots of careful thought has gone into ensuring peer support is strong. 'Our greatest glory is not in never failing but in rising up every time we fail,' says a poster on the PSHCE board in the corridor. The board provides information about the peer support service run by older pupils. 'So important,' said a pupil; 'petty things getting out of hand is rare.' Pupils say they 'can't imagine peer support not being there. It's natural.' Also, 'Form prefects develop close relationships so you stay in contact even after leaving, like on Facebook.' House groups are active and help mobilise the girls to get involved in drama performances and fundraising events for the chosen recipient of charity week. Events like the five-penny race are popular and encourage heated competition, raising as much £2,000 in one hour.

Lottery funded sports hall looks gorgeously fresh next to the main school building, already well over 100 years old when it opened as a school in 1919

Career support is good. There is a university success board to inspire the girls and year 11s have a review day including one-to-one meetings with teachers. Former students of the school are generous with their time, providing inspirational role models for current students throughout the year at careers events and prize givings. Year 12s spend two hours per week in voluntary service, often working with children or the elderly or the disabled. 'It's a steep learning curve and you find yourself going back for several months.'

Its venerable features lend an atmosphere of tradition – from the beautiful open air Greek theatre near to the tennis courts to the hymnals still used in assemblies

Pupils and parents: Multi-ethnic population: over 40 languages spoken here and there is a significant Tamil and Indian population. One parent said, 'My daughter benefits from being with children from many different ethnic backgrounds'. Parents support the PFTA as an opportunity to solve many of the school's cash problems (£25,000 raised for an Innovation Lab in 2017; has previously funded a digital language lab, a minibus and external lighting).

Girls seem confident, resilient and creative. Former pupils here include Lucy Kirkwood, playwright (RSC, National Theatre), Sarah Winman, best-selling novelist (When God was a Rabbit) and Peggy Reynolds, Radio 4 broadcaster in the arts.

Entrance: Massively oversubscribed for year 7 places and has recently expanded from four forms of entry to six (180 girls). CEM entrance tests are used for the borough's only two grammar schools (the other being the brother school, Ilford County for Boys). Up to 10 per cent of places given to girls eligible for pupil premium who score above the pass mark. It is one of just three all-girls schools in the area (the other two are independent and Catholic). Common catchment area with boys' grammar school. Head says the girls are tested on 'wit rather than what's been studied in the classroom'. Nearly all girls stay on to the sixth form, joined by 30 or so from other schools.

Exit: A few (around 10 per cent) leave post-GCSE but nearly all that stay go on to university. Subject choices are academic but varied: physics, law, medicine, languages (most likely French), mathematics, geography, English or economics. A few go on to study business or architecture. Some success in applications to top universities and competitive courses with 10 Oxbridge places in 2018. Other destinations include UCL, Queen Mary's, Kent, King's College London, Birmingham, Nottingham.

Remarks: With the great pastoral and peer support in place and strong academic atmosphere there is no reason why a pupil should not do well here. The message from pupils to any year 6s considering the school is: 'If you love academic study, close relationships with teachers, clubs and societies, and you want to get involved, this is the place for you.'

Schools for special educational needs

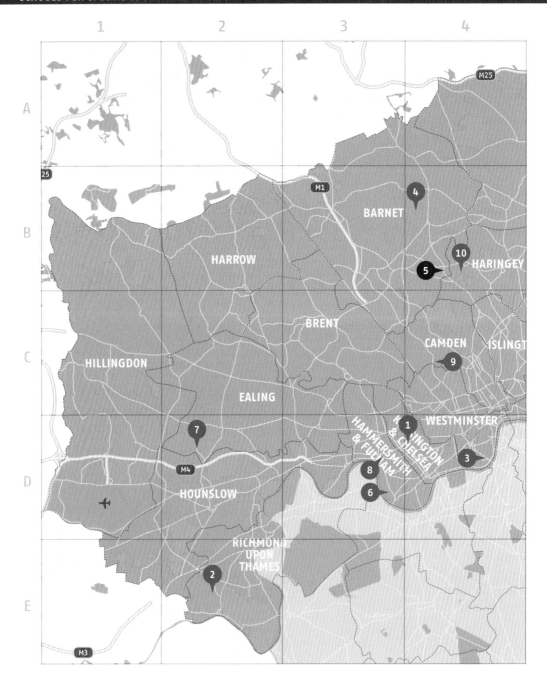

SCHOOLS FOR SPECIAL EDUCATIONAL NEEDS

Schooling for children with special needs

The scramble for London places has an extra layer of complexity when your child has additional needs. It's not just the decision between state and independent, but also between mainstream and specialist. And the financial considerations are greater – learning support is usually charged as an extra in mainstream independents, and specialist school places are expensive, meaning you may have to fight for state funding. And while state mainstream schools will all talk the talk about inclusive education, finding those that truly do well by special needs children is another matter.

How do I know whether my child has special needs?

If your child has a difficulty that makes learning harder for them than most children of the same age, then they may have a special need. Sometimes the difficulties are apparent from early childhood, but other conditions such as mild autism spectrum disorders, auditory processing difficulties or dyslexia may not become clear until well into their schooling. And other factors outside of any disability can affect a child's ability to learn, and can be counted as a special educational need – such as mental health disorders, or the after-effects of early trauma in adopted children.

Signs of an undiagnosed special need include:
- poor school performance which does not tally with the child's general ability
- frequent reports of misbehaviour or failing to pay attention in class
- a dislike of going to school, or onsets of headaches/tummy aches when it is time to go to school
- refusal to put pen to paper, even though articulate
- regular clashes over homework

- poor handwriting, presentation and pencil grip
- difficulties in understanding the nuance in language, social expectations, or making friends
- clumsiness or lack of spatial awareness
- and feelings of frustration or anxiety which may manifest as angry outbursts.

A common problem

If your child needs extra help at school they will be far from alone. Between 15 and 20 per cent of all children have some form of additional need. Around three per cent have more significant needs, and this is the group that qualifies for an Education, Health and Care plan (EHCP), which can provide the funding for a special school place or additional help within a mainstream school, and priority in school admissions. Those who do not qualify for an EHCP receive support from the school's own resources under a system known as SEN Support, and they are subject to the same admissions criteria as other children.

Where do I go for help?

For a young child, your GP or health visitor can advise on specialist assessments, for example from a speech therapist where there are possible issues with speech and language, or an occupational therapist for concerns over co-ordination. Waiting times to see NHS therapists are lengthy, and if you can possibly afford it, it will be worth organising one privately.

For a school age child, your first port of call should be the class teacher or the school's special educational needs co-ordinator (SENCo). Outline your concerns, and ask what they can do to help. If they dismiss your concerns, start to keep a record of instances which demonstrate your child is struggling – things your child tells you about their school day, occasions when the child has been upset and reluctant to go to school, any times the class teacher calls you in to report some problem that day. Then demand a meeting with the headteacher, and present your documentary evidence. We hear of too many occasions when parents are fobbed off – stick to your guns if you suspect things are not right.

Schools may then suggest organising an educational psychologist's (EP) report which will be able to identify any difficulties. However with current cutbacks and the shortage of EPs, we hear that schools are becoming increasingly reluctant to pay for these, while the wait to see a local authority EP can now be up to two years. Again, if you can possibly pay, it's worth commissioning one privately (our SEN team can provide details of ones in your area).

State or independent?

You have a right to name any state school for your child with an EHCP (although for a selective school, they would still need to pass the entrance exam) in conjunction with your local authority. The LA is likely to be less receptive to naming one outside your own borough, as this is more costly for them. All schools are required by law to make any necessary adjustments, or to supply extra provision, that your child may need. The only grounds on which they can refuse a place to your child is where this would interfere with the efficient education of other children, or would not be an efficient use of resources. The schools' application of this premise varies hugely, from those who just toe the legal line, to those where the head truly embraces the idea of inclusive education, and is supported by a well-qualified and enthusiastic SENCo. Winkling out these gems is no easy task, and schools that aren't welcoming will use subtle ploys such as having no

SENCo available at an open day, or generally making you feel so unwelcome that you won't bother applying.

Independent schools have more freedom to select pupils. If they don't want to accept your child there is little you can do – even if you have grounds to challenge this decision under equality law, you are likely to be disinclined to do so when a school has taken this attitude. A few are genuinely welcoming to children with special needs, but they tend to have a quota on how many they admit in order not to overwhelm the special needs staff, and any such London places are usually snapped up at reception entry. Others will look at each child on merit, but the reality is there is little chance of a place for anything beyond mild needs.

It is possible, but rarely achieved, to get state funding for an independent school. Parents have successfully argued for this on grounds of school size/class size/peer group.

Mainstream or special school?

Most parents start with an inbuilt reluctance to contemplate a special school; but equally they can feel a huge sense of relief when their child has been placed in a specialist setting.

The right option for your child will depend very much on their individual circumstances. The biggest misconception is that a special school will somehow quash any potential – in fact a child who has floundered in mainstream can suddenly make huge leaps when the teaching is properly tailored to their needs, or when their self-esteem is restored. And behavioural problems can disappear overnight when children find themselves in a setting which understands their frustration and has the means to break through. It is possible to take a full range of GCSEs in a special school; they should enable a pupil to work to the best of their ability.

Any additional therapies needed will be more readily

available in a specialist school, and it can make all the difference that staff at these schools have specifically opted for special needs teaching. The downside is that these places are more costly, so you need to ready yourself for a fight, and may need to take the LA to Tribunal.

Conversely, some children with milder or transient needs will be better within a mainstream school. But the quality of support available can be extremely variable, so it is important to do your homework about exactly what provision there will be, and how inclusive. At primary school in particular, inclusion can mean the child spends their days working separately in the corner with a teaching assistant. Therapy provision will be delivered by external agencies, can be patchy, and will be an add-on, instead of infused through every part of the day as in a specialist school.

Be sure to have an individual meeting with the head and SENCo – are these people you will be able to deal with readily if there is an issue? Are they enthusiastic about the idea of taking your child, do they have knowledge and experience of their condition? Look for evidence of understanding across all teaching and support staff, rather than an attitude that this is a matter for the learning support department. And beware the well-meaning but inexperienced – it can become wearing when you have to keep close tabs on everything.

Can we help?

The Good Schools Guide website has informative features covering the various types of special needs, your legal rights, how to get an EHCP, family issues plus reviews of special schools across the country. See www.goodschoolsguide.co.uk/advice-service/special-educational-needs-service for individual help.

Abingdon House School

Broadley Terrace, London NW1 6LG

0203 750 5526 | ahs@abingdonhouseschool.co.uk | abingdonhouseschool.co.uk

Independent	Pupils: 70
Ages: 5–17	Fees: £31,050 pa

Headteacher: Since January 2018, Tanya Moran, following the sudden departure of Mr Roy English. She joined from The Independent School, which has closed following its purchase by Abingdon's owner, The Cavendish Group. A maths and science teacher, she has also taken pastoral and well-being roles in postings including head of year and deputy head at The Harrodian.

Academic matters: Classes are named after endangered species such as rockhoppers, sea turtles and panthers and are kept small (max eight in younger years and 12 in older years). Age groups are mixed and the emphasis is on flexibility across classes to meet a child's changing needs. As one mum put it: 'They group them according to emotional ability and how they fit in.' Smaller groups and pairs are formed for maths and literacy as well as therapy sessions.

The national curriculum is adapted to a thematic approach so that children who attend nurture groups or extra therapy sessions don't miss out on vital stages. We witnessed a group of the youngest children unaware it was a numeracy lesson, as they sang and jumped to 20. Elsewhere, sensory supports were used, some children with adapted chairs while others had a screen to minimise distractions. Laptops and iPads are available for each child as well as a designated ICT room with a cluster of desktops. A giant model of a dissected frog leaps at you in the modest science lab, which doubles as the library. Another classroom houses a venerable pet turtle.

Games, options, the arts: Sports specialist teacher oversees taekwondo, yoga and games and the children get to visit a neighbouring playground and swim at a local leisure centre. Basketball, cricket and football are played on a nearby all-weather pitch, although one parent remarked: 'I don't think games once a week is enough – they are a bit fair weather.' School strenuously denies it.

Nonetheless, what the school lacks in hearty outdoor facilities, it makes up for in culture. On the top floor, music, DT, art and drama are synthesised in a whitewashed garret known affectionately as 'creative central.' An inspiring music teacher was showing how to make rhythmic patterns from homespun instruments, conjuring a tiny steel band from catering-size food cans from the kitchen. DT students construct their own cajon (Latin American drum) from scratch. Rainbow rugs on the floor and table football make this a cool place to hang out at break. The children are encouraged to try out the instruments on show: ukulele, guitar, keyboard, trumpet, as well as lots of percussion. The first term's one-to-one tuition is free, then the child can opt to take up the instrument as an extra and many have progressed with great success (music exams to grades 4 and 5). Others had formed a funky five piece band to entertain the parents at the termly school show.

A giant model of a dissected frog leaps at you in the modest science lab, which doubles as the library

Round the school the children's artworks testify to the popularity of the subject. A magnificent big game trophy sculpted in paper sits outside the art room, still life drawings and textiles adorn the walls; toy theatre shows make the most of the limited space in-house, while the end of term concert takes over the neighbouring church hall. The school won the Independent Schools Association 3D figures category with some witty papier mâché Olympians. A visit from the ASD artist, David Downes, provided an inspiring role model for these children.

Background and atmosphere: Established in 2004 and originally occupying two terraced houses in Kensington, Abingdon House moved to Lisson Grove in 2010 – to the site of a former theatre school (Amy Winehouse's graffiti still exists behind a wall on the upper floor). Hidden behind Marylebone station, the traditional Victorian schoolhouse stands sandwiched between church buildings and a Turkish hammam. It is a densely urban area, buses and Boris bikes mixing with office workers and their sandwich bags. Nevertheless, the buildings are beautifully maintained, making the most of the original structure to create a clean and practical space. Fun touches include blue and yellow handrails, to avoid collision on the stairs.

An economy-sized dining room delivers 'fabulous food' according to one mum, and is presided over by a popular caterer with a can-do attitude to fussy children and parents. There is a compact hall which morphs into an indoor play area with colourful wall-mounted climbing frame. Alternatively, children can choose one of the play courts at street level to bounce on a trampoline or play with giant Lego and outdoor games. There is no disguising the compromised outdoor space, but these are city children and one parent assured me they get to experience the best that the metropolis can offer by stepping out in their high-vis vests to Regent's Park and London Zoo. Westminster is cultivating a local wildlife park, which offers pond-dipping and vegetable-growing opportunities, but as one parent put it, 'if you have a boy who needs to play rugby, it's not necessarily for him'.

Local wildlife park offers pond-dipping and vegetable-growing opportunities, but as one parent put it, 'if you have a boy who needs to play rugby, it's not necessarily for him'

The children arrive each day by private transport or school bus from up to 10 miles away, in neat royal blue blazer with gold trim and sporting a traditional school cap. Boys outnumber girls six to one. Early starters eat at a breakfast club and there's homework club after school for children who find it difficult to get down to it at home. One mum happily paid the extra cost for her daughter – 'homework club works beautifully for her, she doesn't want to do it with me.' It includes 10 minutes reading a day, and is supplemented by spelling and other subjects as the children get older. Art club, sports, Lego, computer and swimming club are also popular, dance club ranges from flamenco to street dance and many of the activities come free of charge.

Being in the heart of the city gives the teachers plenty of choice when it comes to day trips: Kensington museums, Imperial War Museum, London Aquarium and Kew Gardens. One mum was disappointed that there were no residential school trips – 'I think they could because they have a great staff ratio there.'

Pastoral care, well-being and discipline: Discipline does not appear to be a problem. 'They are a good group of kids, it has a very nice vibe to it,' remarked one mum; behaviour is managed consistently by staff. A rainmaker is used in class rather than a raised voice, which might stress an anxious child. There is a traffic light system to give warnings. Stickers and a merit chart contribute towards 'golden time,' which comes in the form of a fun activity or outing to the park. Parents confirmed it worked – 'the school stops any bullying developing...it's a very big preoccupation for SEN parents.'

Therapy and staffing: Teachers are supported in class by therapists (speech and language; music; play) as well as frequent input from physio and OT. The school's enlightened understanding of the importance of speech and language support in building a child's confidence is palpable; parents can opt for extra one-to-one after school too. Physio and OT (known as 'Cosmo') is invisibly woven into lessons two or three times a week, perhaps as beanbags or climbing the apparatus. Lessons are peppered with sensory breaks, disguised as fun. Parents praised the inclusion of the learning support, not only for saving them the trouble and expense of outside tutors, but for genuine inclusiveness, 'she didn't feel excluded or singled out'.

Pupils and parents: Children have a range of difficulties including ASD, Asperger's, dyspraxia, dyslexia, ADD, speech and language or social communication problems. Many arrive with poor self-esteem and social anxiety from mainstream schools.

Parents contact their child's teacher through the home/school book and are confident that they are being kept informed – 'communication is kept open,' we were assured, by email and phone.

Entrance: Children are taken after a two-day multi disciplinary assessment with teachers and therapists, which includes a try-out within the classroom. 'Paperwork isn't everything. We take our admissions on the individual, not on any particular difficulty.' As a consequence the classes are both mixed ability and mixed socially. Many children are privately funded, some by their LA; from both north and south of the river; 25 per cent from overseas. The school supports parents with tribunal applications.

Exit: 'We don't see ourselves as a through school. The majority we plan to get back to other schools.' Staff estimate a school career at Abingdon House for most children of between one and three years. Some go on to nurturing independents like The Moat, Portland Place, Wetherby and St Augustine's Priory while others go to mainstream state secondaries.

One of the parents voiced their worries about leaving – 'most parents are sweating on the top line about where their kids go to when they leave,' she said. She mentioned there was some help with transition to further schools but felt more could be done to build formal bridges to other schools.

Money matters: Places can be self-funded or paid for by the local authority.

Remarks: For a London child with specific learning difficulties, this is a thoughtful and nurturing find. Self-esteem thrives with the seamless inclusion of therapies within the curriculum and generous ratio of expert staff. Shame about the lack of playground space, but nevertheless, the charming, Victorian setting is brought to life by chattering youngsters, particularly in the vibrant art and music studio – a specialist oasis in the heart of the city.

Clarendon School

Clarendon Secondary Centre, Egerton Road, Twickenham, TW2 7SL

020 3146 1441 | info@clarendon.richmond.sch.uk | clarendon.richmond.sch.uk/about/

State	Pupils: 100
Ages: 4–16	

Headteacher: Since 2006, John Kipps BSc PCGE NPQH (early 50s). A local man, he grew up in Hounslow and was educated at Latymer Upper before studying for a degree in geography and biological sciences at Exeter University. He started his teaching career at St Mary's and St Peter's C of E Primary school in Teddington where he coordinated, at various times during his four years there, the music, art, science and technology curriculum. In his fourth year his class did an inclusion project with a group from Clarendon and, he says, he knew from that moment that this was the school he wanted to work in. He has been here ever since and his wholehearted commitment to the place seeps from every pore.

He has taught at the school for more than 23 years, starting as a teacher and, before becoming head, working as deputy head for nine years. He has two grown up daughters. Deeply professional, Mr Kipps evidently loves the job and this is reciprocated. As we walk round the school he is greeted by warm smiling faces, of both staff and pupils, and he is as proud of their achievements and progress as a parent would be. Parents describe him as having 'a lovely calm influence. He's not around a lot but he's always in the background.'

He has seen the school go from strength to strength during his headship. It has taken on management of two external centres – The Gateway Centre (a 20 place unit for pupils aged 11-16 with a diagnosis of autism) and the Newhouse Centre (a 23 place unit for secondary aged pupils with social, emotional and mental health difficulties). He also manages a large team of peripatetic learning support assistants who work alongside pupils with physical and sensory needs in mainstream schools.

Summer 2018 saw the school dividing into secondary and primary sections, both at new sites: the secondary school to the newly developed Richmond College site, and the junior school to Buckingham Road, Hampton.

A wealth of equipment to tickle the senses from a bubble tube to a ball pool rich with changing colours

Mr Kipps is a man who sees the big picture as well as the fine detail. Expert at finding creative ways of tapping into resources, he says the 'school is well resourced, though finances are complex'. Grandiose schemes don't substitute individual attention and care for each pupil. A genuine man who doesn't need frills; your child would be lucky to find themselves under his care and leadership.

Academic matters: A school originally for pupils with moderate learning difficulties, the needs of its pupils have become much more complex in the last five years. A number of diagnoses from the autistic spectrum (some high functioning, some low functioning) to ADHD and sensory difficulties. Most pupils are verbal, some have difficulties with socialising, whilst a very few can occasionally exhibit some challenging behaviours as a result of their diagnoses.

Small class groups with between 10 and 12 pupils taught by a teacher and one, sometimes two teaching assistants. Two specialist classes in the secondary part of the school in groups of six with three adults: one for children with complex autism but relatively high functioning who need the support of a small group; the other composed of children with severe learning difficulties but whose social skills are relatively well developed.

All pupils do art GCSE, a few do maths and some choose to do PE. Year 9 pupils go to Hampton Academy to do their PE GCSE course. Entry level certificates offered in 12 different subjects – these courses start in year 10 (GCSE courses start in year 9). Impressive design technology facilities and pupils can take a qualification in DT. A food technology room is well equipped and well used and cooking one of the most popular clubs. Important skills – how to use a dishwasher, iron etc – are honed here. Lots of practical courses including site management, catering and child care.

A food technology room is well equipped and well used and cooking is one of the most popular clubs. Important skills – how to use a dishwasher, iron etc – are honed here. Pupils take practical courses

---

Secondary school classes are chronologically grouped (between years 7 and 11). Each classroom has a private work station for each child on the autism spectrum at the back of the room and then a circle of desks close to the teacher at the front. Each work station has a visual timetable and each child has an in tray and out tray to assist with organisation. In every class group each child may be doing something different – lessons here are bespoke. The same class teacher takes the majority of lessons – even for 16 year olds – as continuity is most important. Specialist teaching for some subjects, however, eg science. A manager for additional needs (no SENCo here) manages and oversees provision of extra support.

Parents praise the effective way the school prepares the children for transition. Year 11 spends one day each week at Richmond College with a member of staff to get used to and prepare for the post-16 transition.

Games, options, the arts: Music and the performing arts are a big part of the day and an important part of the curriculum, avers Mr Kipps. Free tuition is offered on keyboard, guitar, drumming (especially popular) and violin. In years 8 to 10, 25 children go away for a week to Leiston Abbey in Suffolk to put on a play – the rest of the pupils do an activity week. One option is sport focused, the other cultural. A big annual production takes place in the gym. Juniors do a Christmas production – 'a nativity or something more wacky,' we're told.

There is a wide variety of physical activity offered, from swimming and bowling to cross-country, sprinting and football, wheelchair rugby, basketball and javelin. Juniors go horse riding every week to Bushy Park. All pupils swim in the nearby Hampton Open Air or Lady Eleanor Holles pools. The school gym is well used throughout the day and there is a climbing wall on site where year 11 can practise before their outdoor pursuits trip. Yoga is popular – particularly among the younger pupils, who practise early in the morning.

An innovative activity is cycle maintenance. In a corner of the school there is an enormous stash of bicycles that have been picked up by the police (they give the school about a 100 bikes a term). A cycle maintenance tutor helps students to restore the bikes to their former glory and many are then sold at Kingston market. Pupils come in from other schools to help work on the bikes and there are lots of cycling activities.

After school clubs include musical theatre, tag rugby, wheelchair basketball and nails and beauty.

Background and atmosphere: By the start of the autumn term 2018 all pupils should have left the unprepossessing old 60s building for their shiny new campuses.

The school recognises that it's not just the pupils who need support, and families can seek the help of family support workers by simply booking an appointment.

Staff here are long serving – one teacher has been here since the 1970s, putting Mr Kipps's 23 years in the shade. However, they are by no means stuck in their ways. Head describes his staff as 'very positive and open to change'. He is also blessed with an excellent governing body that is not only hardworking, high powered and diverse but also hugely supportive as well as challenging. Unafraid of Ofsted, Mr Kipps welcomes their recommendations. Parents are effusive about the quality of the staff here. 'Their commitment and dedication are unsurpassed,' said one experienced mother. 'It is like a giant family,' said another. 'Everyone down to the caretaker is involved.'

Pastoral care, well-being and discipline: Emphasis here is very much on rewards and incentives rather than sanctions and punishments. There is a house point system and pupils are awarded bonus points at the end of each day for following the rules in every lesson. Each point is worth one penny – 400 points amounting to £4.00. Pupils are allowed to spend their points in a shop and the house that gets the most points at the end of term has a day out – eg ice skating and pizza; the pupils can choose. Detentions after school can happen – but are 'highly unusual – not least because it doesn't work for some parents, and I haven't had to give any this term,' says Mr Kipps. Unwanted behaviour is logged onto a monitoring system and referred to the head, who then looks into why this is happening. 'It's the root cause that we need to tackle,' he says.

In a corner we saw an enormous stash of bicycles that have been picked up by the police (apparently they donate about 100 bikes a term to the school)

Mr Kipps reports on the 'incredible academic progress' that has resulted from family therapy sessions that are provided one day a week for a small group of parents and their children.

All the staff here are Team-Teach trained: a nationally recognised programme that trains teachers to de-escalate situations. Children are handled in a dignified way and with respect, and as a result the behaviour here is well managed. 'It's highly unusual to raise one's voice to a child,' affirms Mr Kipps.

Therapy and staffing: A dedicated team of teaching assistants – with a mix of profiles: some are career TAs who bring a wealth of experience, others are graduates who are thinking about a career in teaching but nonetheless, says Mr Kipps, 'are very hands on'. Speech and communication is given strong emphasis here. Three speech and language therapists work on site and while occasionally a pupil is taken out of class, much of it is delivered as part of the teaching. Art therapy and counselling also available on site. Occupational therapy and physiotherapy takes place on site for individuals and small groups. As well as individual programmes delivered by professional therapists, some TAs are trained to offer ongoing therapy support for other pupils. Speech and language and occupational therapies are a commissioned NHS service (with the inevitable rationing that brings) whilst art therapy, music therapy, psychotherapeutic counselling, educational psychology and family therapy are bought in.

A magical 'sensory room' is lovingly maintained to support pupils with sensory impairment. Inside this Aladdin's den is a wealth of equipment to tickle the senses from a bubble tube and infinity panel to a ball pool rich with changing colours, moving images and music. Up to three children at a time can benefit from timetabled sessions in here.

Pupils and parents: Forty-five per cent of pupils are on pupil premium. Forty-four per cent from ethnic minorities. Richmond is perceived to be one of the more affluent London boroughs but pockets of it are very deprived, and Clarendon is more a reflection of these areas than the Richmond of Zac Goldsmith. The catchment is very wide – many pupils come from some distance outside the borough. The number of professional parents is low and the PTA struggles to build a network of volunteers – fundraising in this area can be a battle. 'While parents are wary about getting involved, once they do, they commit wholeheartedly,' observed one parent.

A healthy ratio of 60 boys to 40 girls (more of a balance than a lot of schools of its profile). Twenty-eight per cent of pupils have been diagnosed with autism, about 10 per cent with Down's syndrome. What strikes you most about the children here, however, is their confidence. They will chat to you as you pass, tell you what they have been up to. A positive attitude permeates the place. We were also told by a number of parents how supportive the pupils are of each other. A particularly touching story was of a talent show put on by the PTA. The children performing lost their nerve and froze – the audience of children rose to their feet to clap and cheer them on – the staff held back and allowed the children to help

Entrance: A reception to year 11 school, newly on two different sites. You will need an EHC plan to apply. Once paperwork is received from the local authority, the school will visit the family and a decision is made within three weeks. Year 3 and infant class entrants tend to have complex needs. At year 7 several join who have coped through primary school but can't manage mainstream from 11. There is also an influx of pupils into years 8 and 9. School was 'over full', but will have room for expansion on its new sites.

Exit: Virtually all pupils go on to Richmond College for the sixth form. The rest, with more complex needs, tend to go to special schools with sixth forms or colleges closer to home. All pupils go on to further schooling or college.

Remarks: An inspirational school. The dedication of the staff and the management team, including the governing body, make for a genuinely nurturing environment which is well-equipped to handle the not insignificant challenges it faces on a daily basis. The students' support of each other is striking, as is the 'can do' attitude of the staff – whether it be cycle repairs and entrepreneurship, or taking the children off for a week to put on a play. You can feel confident that your child will not only be well looked after but also become empowered to reach his or her potential.

Fairley House School

30 Causton Street, London SW1P 4AU

020 7976 5456 | office@fairleyhouse.org.uk | fairleyhouse.org.uk

Independent	Pupils: 212: 143 boys, 69 girls
Ages: 5–16	Fees: £31,827 pa

Headmaster: Since 2013, Mr Michael Taylor BA PGCE FRGS (40s). A geographer, he came here from four years as deputy head at More House near Farnham, another good specialist school. He clearly gets on well with both parents and children. Parents say 'boyish', 'deals with problems well', 'has a laugh with the pupils but keeps their respect', 'hands shaken, greeted by name, knows if they have been away'.

Previous principal, Jackie Murray, is now school's principal educational psychologist. Still a force in the land.

Academic matters: Most pupils have a diagnosis of specific learning difficulties, usually dyslexia and/or dyspraxia and the related conditions ADD, ADHD and Asperger's. Also able to accommodate some pupils who have non-conventional learning styles and find mainstream schools inaccessible.

Regularly inspected and accredited by CReSTeD, the register for specialist schools with provision for dyslexia and SpLDs. Pupils are split into a junior department – 5 to 9 years – and a senior department – 10 to 16 years, class size usually 8-12 pupils. The main emphasis being on numeracy and literacy, everyone is put into a small group to match their ability and skills for maths and English and rejoins their class for other subjects. Children are taught to understand their own learning styles and shown strategies to overcome barriers to learning to achieve their targets. The aim is to return children to mainstream schools as soon as they are able, which school has great success in doing. Test results such as Sats are very respectable, especially from children who can have quite pronounced difficulties.

Every child has an IEP which is regularly reviewed by the trans-disciplinary team to monitor progress and ensure that individual needs are being catered for. Mornings start with exercises; depending on the individual, this could be physical, orthoptic or attention focused. All the classrooms, including the science lab, are buzzing with activities, visual reminders and clues, anything that is memorable: models made by the children, word banks for a current history topic or colour-coded parts of speech.

> *All the classrooms, including the science lab, are buzzing with activities, visual reminders and clues, anything that is memorable*

Every teacher has specialist qualifications which ensure that all classes are fully accessible and multisensory. 'Having teachers who are nice to you and understand has changed my life,' said a 10-year-old. The learning support is an integral part of the whole school approach to teaching. The transdisciplinary approach is used across the curriculum, helpfully allowing therapy delivery to be linked to specific subjects and development. Homework is colour-coded to help with organisation, and deadlines must be met to prepare the children for returning to mainstream school. Help and advice is on hand for those who get stuck.

Parents thrilled to have found the place. A typical story: 'His previous school [a well-known London prep] had given up on him: "He will never learn his times tables". He had shut down completely. On his first day here he learned his nine times table. He has made huge progress, so much more confident, maths is no longer an issue.' Or: 'It was like letting a different child into my house. Cool and collected where he had been crying and angry.'

Games, options, the arts: Wonderfully imaginative art displays line the corridors and even the ceilings are decorated in many areas of the building. Pupils make their own ceramic tiles depicting various scenes from history and also design and execute murals. The most recent addition is the newly-built art studio and kiln room. The children enjoy a great variety of artistic activities including textiles, fashion, design and technology, sewing and puppet-making.

Homework is colour coded to help with the organisation, and deadlines must be met to prepare the children for returning to mainstream school. Help and advice is on hand for those who get stuck

A range of sports – all the traditional ones, alongside canoeing, fencing and yoga. Although doesn't have its own playing fields, they make good use of local facilities at Battersea Park and the Queen Mother sports centre. Music and drama are taught as separate subjects and integrated into other curriculum areas to help children develop good communication skills. Everyone is encouraged to learn a musical instrument and the school runs its own acting awards and music medals scheme. Parents pack into the termly dramatic and musical productions.

Extracurricular activities include museum and theatre trips along with a wide choice of lunchtime and after-school clubs. Club options change regularly depending on the clientele and demand.

Background and atmosphere: Founded in 1975 by a speech therapist, Daphne Hamilton Fairley, as a charitable trust in memory of her oncologist husband, killed by an IRA bomb. The upper school site, originally a church, has been cleverly converted into a four-storey building. The junior school pupils are housed in a Victorian infants' school in the shadows of Lambeth Palace, backing on to Archbishop's Park, complete with sports facilities and an adventure playground for the children's use. Both buildings are well decorated, with a lot of space dedicated to the children's achievements, visual timetables and fantastic works of art. The atmosphere is purposeful, peaceful and well organised, encouraging pupils to be themselves. Lots of smiling and cheerful faces – nobody should feel the odd one out here.

Pastoral care, well-being and discipline: Structured mentoring system involving 18 members of staff to whom children can refer themselves. Aim is to work in a strong partnership with parents to help ensure things do not go wrong for pupils due to simple misunderstandings. Seems to be working, as parents feel pastoral care has improved over the last few years. 'Not too strict. Jokey,' said a parent, but at the end of the day kids waiting for the bus are orderly, and board quietly.

Therapy and staffing: Depending on the individual needs of the pupil, speech therapy and occupational therapy are incorporated into classroom learning, art, drama and sports. Younger children will be making 'ch' out of chocolate buttons whilst older ones are baking round pies to help understand and remember the mathematical sign pi. Children are taught to touch-type once they have achieved a reading age of approximately eight years. In-house speech and occupational therapists run their own sensory integration programmes and motor coordination classes. The therapy staff organising the motor coordination classes have been specially trained in America and continue to attend training in the USA to keep up to date.

Pupils and parents: Scattered all over London, and a few from the edges of the home counties – requires an effort to get to know other families. Everybody and anybody affected by neuro-diversity. By all accounts, lots of very supportive and enthusiastic parents who are keen to get involved with school activities. Most recently the parent group has fundraised to update and restock the school library. Weekly newsletters, back-up information on the website and parents can use a communication book or email teachers. Comprehensive, well-designed website, but not 'reader friendly' as yet.

Entrance: Children are invited to spend two days here, where they will have a transdisciplinary all-round assessment to ensure that the school will be able to meet their needs. After the assessment, parents are provided with reports from an educational psychologist, speech therapist and occupational therapist and then invited for a conference to discuss how the school can help and support their child. Assessments cost £290–£890. In the event of the school not being able to offer a place they will suggest other options to parents.

Exit: The average stay for pupils at Fairley House is approximately two/three years. Depending on when a child arrives at the school, there is a tendency for the Fairley programme to end at odd ages (from an entrance point of view) like 12 or 14, which some potential next schools get stuffy about. Some parents clearly feel that the school could be more helpful in the search for where to go to next. Top destinations are Bedales (senior and junior), DLD College, Hall School (Wimbledon), Kingham Hill, Millfield (senior and junior), Milton Abbey, Portland Place, Bedes (senior and junior), St Christopher and Windlesham House – but there are a wide range of others who welcome Fairley pupils.

Money matters: A few bursaries are available for trainee teachers. As yet, unable to offer bursaries to

pupils, but will assist parents with tribunals and the EHCP procedure. Approximately 26 per cent of pupils have an EHCP/ statement of special educational needs and are funded by their local authorities.

Remarks: Certainly good value for money, but the fees are terrifying and beyond the reach of many without local authority funding. A remarkable school for its holistic, multi-sensory and transdisciplinary approach. A beacon for children with learning and processing differences and parents who have been tearing their hair out trying to cope in other situations.

The Holmewood School London

88 Woodside Park Road, London N12 8SH

020 8920 0660 | enquiries@thsl.org.uk | thsl.org.uk

Independent	Pupils: 45: 43 boys, 2 girls; sixth form: 9: 8 boys, 1 girl
Ages: 7–19	Fees: £63,000 pa

Head: Since April 2016, Lisa Camilleri BA QTS PGDip autism PGCert educational leadership, former deputy principal of NAS Radlett Lodge School, full of bright ideas and bringing wide experience. Keen on building community links and establishing an outreach and inclusion programme including training for autism teaching leaders.

Academic matters: Range of pupils is quite wide academically as you would expect in a school for high functioning autism, Asperger's, SLCN, SpLD and 50 per cent with ADHD. Some pupils deemed unteachable before coming here and many have had multiple school failures.

Pupils work towards five GCSEs but approximately 20-30 per cent take pre-GCSE entry level certificates in English and maths instead if academic levels or anxieties preclude GCSEs. Individualised approaches help each pupil to achieve to their best level. Those taking GCSEs do so in subjects where they feel most confident. Current choices are from English, maths, ICT, science, art and design, drama and languages where relevant and suitable. Sensibly, teaching is across ability not age levels. Some very bright ones go on to A levels. In a typical sixth form, one will be doing two AS levels, one doing one AS level, and others resitting GCSEs to improve grades in maths or English. Others follow functional life skills and social skills programmes. Some are based at Holmewood (THSL)

where they study functional literacy and numeracy, and access college with a TA (popular choices are a BTec in gaming and a BTec in childcare).

The school focuses on being positive about what students can do and one sixth former did work experience with Sega. Really small class sizes of three to six pupils plus subject teacher and two TAs. Average staff to pupil is one-to-two. Certain pupils have one-to-one or two-to-one.

Standard lessons in the morning are double at 90 minutes with breaks as needed. Most often they are movement breaks: run, jump, or do something OT based. Pupils are calmer, quieter and more focused as a result. Much work goes into encouraging self-regulation. Different systems in place for each pupil to identify that they need to take a break or to respond positively to a suggestion that they might need a break.

An almost paperless school. Pupils work on Google Chromebooks and with Google Classroom. Suggestions from parent partnership led to homework being done online, and marked online. Parents can log in and see what is going on. Real understanding that THSL pupils often need to separate home and school, and homework leads to anxiety and meltdowns. There is an after-school homework club.

Games, options, the arts: School hall is used for indoor sports like dance and yoga and a recent visit from a golf pro. Most school sport takes place off site and is generally individual sports like badminton, kayaking, ice skating, horse riding and golf, using local parks and leisure centres.

Most school sport takes place off site and is generally individual activities like badminton, ice skating, horse riding and golf, using local parks and leisure centres

THSL has a qualified forest school teacher on staff who develops skills such as how to light a fire with flints, cook sausages outside etc. Regular trips to a forest school on a farm near Mill Hill are highly sought after. Secondary pupils and sixth formers go on school journey week in the Isle of Wight to develop their life skills and independence, and have a chance to live away from home. Pupils are minutely prepared for the trip and know exactly what is going to happen and when. They go in small groups with high staff ratios, and staff do all the activities with them. A recent trip included surfing, tree climbing and cycling.

After-school activities are not possible due to diverse age range, local authority transport and general logistics, but once a week they have the choices of art, football, music and coding club. All the parents we spoke to wished there was more after-school life for their children.

Background and atmosphere: Tucked away in Woodside Park, first impressions are of a cramped and down-at-heel building. Don't be put off. The administration team sit cheek by jowl but are friendly and knowledgeable. The atmosphere is calm and friendly and you hear a lot of laughter from staff and students alike. Both the junior and senior parts of the school share break times in the relatively small but safely fenced playground and you can see staff members getting stuck in playing alongside the children and modelling social skills and interaction. Parents feel that this works and 'the kids all get on really well'. Five minute warning before the end of break understands the need for predictability and consistency and anxiety around transitions.

We were struck by some original approaches. We particularly liked the 'conversation menus' which pupils pick up at lunchtime along with their cooked lunch, in order to provide a framework for chat and social interaction with peers and staff. As a result we didn't see any of the usual problems of unstructured time. The food looked and smelled good and not a whiff of overcooked cabbage anywhere.

Now owned by the Cavendish Group, and has an additional site at the Sternberg Centre on East End Road in Finchley. The sixth form is currently based there, and a rise in numbers is expected.

School runs for 35 weeks a year with one holiday week of daily forest school where they build dens, make fires and have outdoor adventures. For parents the long holidays can be incredibly hard.

Pastoral care, well-being and discipline: Strong emphasis on self-esteem and well-being. Behaviour management based on commitment to consistency, training, having clear policy and guidelines. Collaborative approach with pupils to help them to understand and communicate how they are feeling. Behaviour management plans regularly updated, and focus on working out what is really happening for a child who might be kicking off. Acceptance that conventional consequences rarely work for ASD children but their peers need to see a consequence. Discipline involves anger management programmes, and talking to on-site psychotherapist. Other flexible options including contracts, mediation and scales of justice approach, said to be very effective.

Therapy and staffing: Therapy is timetabled but speech and language therapy is integral and aims to be functional and practical and includes a girls' group and Lego therapy. Therapies are a key part of the school's approach, seen as fundamental tools to access learning and teach students the experience of being calm (many do calming yoga). It's a committed approach and it seems to work. Experienced therapy team all on site includes one full-time SLT, part-time SLT, full-time OT/sensory integration specialist plus assistant, and a child and adolescent psychotherapist on site four days a week. There's also a part-time drama therapist, music therapist and reflexologist.

You can see staff members getting stuck in, playing alongside the children and modelling skills and interaction

Fifty per cent of pupils have ADHD as well as ASD. Interestingly, only a few are medicated, as the school environment and therapies seem to work for them.

Full staff training weekly, and induction training for new staff takes a whole term and includes instruction from all the specialists on site. Most TAs have level 3 NVQ in teaching assistance, and they all attend every staff meeting.

Pupils and parents: For pupils aged 7-19 with high functioning autism, Asperger's Syndrome, language, communication and social pragmatic difficulties and those associated with ADHD and specific learning difficulties. Many with co-morbid diagnoses: ADHD (50 per cent), challenging behaviours (40 per cent), anxiety and ODD. Many with a late diagnosis of autism and/or history of multiple school failures. Pupils come from 13 different local authorities, as far south as Southwark and as far west as Heathrow. Some 25 per cent are picked up by parents, many have LA transport and seven pupils can now travel to school independently after six months' travel training from THSL.

Active parent partnership group works together to solve homework issues and to get other parents involved. Run a bit like a governing body. Parents report 'everyone has their say' and there is a supportive focus on helping parents to engage better with their children.

Entrance: Via local authorities and direct parent referrals. We found Anna in admissions knowledgeable and approachable. Many have 'failed' at other schools. Taster sessions for potential pupils which can last one day, one week, even half a term. Assessment based around whether THSL can meet needs, whether child fits current profile of the class etc. The real question is whether the whole THSL experience would be right for the child. School has supported parents through tribunals, and developed positive relationships with LAs. THSL understands and is clearly not afraid of the behaviours that come with often co-morbid diagnoses including anxiety, oppositional defiant disorder, ADHD and challenging behaviour. The real issue is space. 'There are only so many safe spaces when someone is kicking off'.

Exit: Majority of 19-year-old leavers continue into some form of further education. Recent leavers went to LaSWAP sixth form in Camden, Coulson College – to do A Level maths and BTec in engineering – and to a residential college in Somerset. Careers fair every year and THSL actively cultivates local employers to provide work experience for older pupils. Careers notices and ideas well displayed in school hall and impressive expectations to prepare all pupils for employment.

Money matters: Fee includes all therapies but cost for any one-to-one is extra. International students often self-fund, as do a few other UK students, but about 95 per cent of the pupils receive LA funding.

Remarks: THSL is best suited for pupils with average to above average academic ability, although it will consider those working just below average where they can aim to close that gap. Pupils need to be verbal, but high anxieties, low self-esteem and multiple diagnoses are par for the course.

We like the fact that this school is definitely not fazed by challenging behaviour – the only thing that stands in their way is the limitations on managing it owing to space in the current building.

We saw a judicious balance of tough love combined with a deep understanding of pupils' vulnerabilities, and a determination to enable its pupils, however complex their presentation. A clear level of understanding of their pupils who may have 'the body of a 15 year old and the social and emotional functioning level of a 5 year old'. Parents feel 'supported for the first time in years' and confident that the school will 'never give up on them'.

Limespring School

Park House, 16 High Road, East Finchley, London N2 9PJ

020 8444 1387 | info@limespringschool.co.uk | limespringschool.co.uk/

Independent	Pupils: 18 full time, 10 part time
Ages: 7–11	Fees: £21,600 pa

Head: Since 2012, Denise Drinkwater MSc OCR Cert SPLD, married with three grown up sons. She started the school with just a handful of pupils and works with passion and zeal, inspiring pupils and staff. Originally a maths lecturer at North London University after a degree at UCL, she stopped working full time in order to look after her three sons. She started teaching one-on-one in various schools ending up with some 30 individual pupils. She also gave training sessions as a consultant special needs teacher and realised that rather than race around teaching and training, she should open a school and run both training courses and teaching from there. She has no teaching qualification but is taking an MA in inclusive and special education to consolidate her understanding further. Her enthusiasm and drive keep the school moving forward, with everyone mucking in and helping. She still teaches, showing good practice and staying in touch with the pupils and especially helping with the maths teaching. Pupils are not 'coddled,' according to one parent who said that she 'tells it as it is' and is 'honest with a straightforward approach'.

Entrance: No deadlines for entry: pupils come after struggling at primary or on diagnosis of specific learning difficulty. Some from Fairley House, having found the distance too difficult or exhausting, some are sent for a few hours a week by local primaries who can't support them properly and pay using their pupil premium. An interview and assessment by the head will result in quick decision – a joy for parents who are used to being put off. One parent said that her child was assessed so well that it felt 'like the school knew him inside out and completely understood his struggles'. Her child said, 'They understand me there'. The school takes children of average ability with dyslexia and often they may have secondary difficulties, but the school does not take children with ADHD or speech and language difficulties or complex needs.

Only four classes with a maximum of eight children in a class, good mix of boys and girls. Not a cheap option but very few extras and almost individual lessons. Some bursaries and scholarships available.

Exit: Most stay until the end of year 6 when the aim is to move all children into mainstream schools – Aldenham School, Millfield School, Immanuel College, Heathside as well as local state secondary schools or specialist schools – Fairley House, The Moat. Some pupils only come for a year or two and some pupils, whose schools have no special needs teaching that suits, only attend for a few hours a week and get more therapeutic and focused learning with special needs teachers.

Remarks: Rare for north London, this very small school provides focused and individualised learning for pupils with dyslexia or dyspraxia, or other learning difficulties such as mild autism spectrum disorder or dyscalculia (diagnosed or not). Four classes in a modern purpose-built block for full-time pupils and several smaller rooms for part-time pupils, some who come in for just an hour a day.

School starts with 'shake up and wake up', some exercises as a way of preparing them for learning and setting a routine. Morning classes spent on literacy, maths and touch typing, with afternoons for topic work – history, geography, science and enrichment activities.

Lunch, prepared in the nursery school kitchens adjacent, is eaten as quickly as possible all together, with teachers taking turns to clear up, so that pupils can get out to the local park for playtime.

Aim is to give enough individual learning as possible to bring up reading and writing skills to an age-appropriate level. Pupils arrive with bruised confidence and a feeling of failure, so finding alternative ways of teaching so they can learn to read and write fluently is a priority. They also learn touch typing as part of timetabled lessons (there are eight computers in IT room) to allow for freer and faster expression of ideas. The school follows an adapted national curriculum with plenty of time on spelling techniques, organising their own learning and planning before writing. Overlearning, multisensory learning and fun enables children to work out what way of learning works best for them and to help with the primary goal of getting them ready for mainstream secondary school.

Parents appreciate 'the attention to the individual', 'that nothing is too much trouble for teachers' and 'the high teacher to pupil ratio'. Some liked the fact that their children are not burdened with homework and reading logs

For the pupils with dyspraxia, plenty of visual perception skills – puzzles, threading, use of counters, odd one out games. Little need for separate therapy sessions when this kind of work is incorporated in class lessons. A maximum of eight pupils in a class means plenty of opportunities for individual support and carefully planned lessons. Parents appreciate 'the attention to the individual', 'that nothing is too much trouble for teachers' and 'the high teacher to pupil ratio'. Some liked the fact that their children are not burdened with homework and reading logs, so it wouldn't suit parents who are very focused on academic results, and indeed one parent felt that there was 'too much enrichment activity and more studying is needed'.

Art a definite strength in the school thanks to an inspirational (and qualified) art teacher – wonderful examples of collaborative and individual art in a wide range of media – papier mâché, clay, collage, watercolours and sculpture to name a few we saw. Cross-curricular learning used in art as in all subjects – biology and art, exploring the senses, body parts, colour wheel, historical costume etc. Music taught within class teaching, concentrating on how music makes you feel, mindfulness and reactions to music rather than formal teaching. Opportunities to play during assemblies for those who learn instruments outside school. Sports in the local recreation ground at break time, and in school there is yoga, san juro martial arts and dance (hip hop), all resulting in a big end of year performance.

Trips to plays and musicals are popular with parents and children alike, who see it as 'connecting learning with something they can see for themselves'

Parents said the school was 'active in terms of breaks and outside activities with plenty of educational trips'. Drama weekly – partly as therapy, partly as a chance for children to learn about expressing and reading moods as well as preparing to speak in public. Trips to theatre for plays and musicals popular with parents and children alike who see it as 'connecting learning with something they can see for themselves'. Four trips a term outside school as part of enrichment with the resulting usual split of opinion between those parents who like the breadth of learning and enrichment activities and those who would like more time spent on

academic learning. Pupils, needless to say, love the outings.

Breakfast club and homework clubs cater for parents who work or travel from afar. The atmosphere is intimate, with each child knowing every other and staff all working together, giving a hand with washing up and making costumes and supporting every child or weepy parent as well as preparing lessons, sharing ideas and creating individualised learning programmes for pupils. Parents appreciate the fact that open door isn't just a policy but a reality, and they all reported they could go straight to any teacher or the head with requests, concerns or complaints. Pastoral care by Julie, who is 'like a mum in school who keeps an eye out for a worried face or uncharacteristic behaviour – both parents and pupils!' Children are supportive and 'we are all kind to each other'. This was confirmed by parents who said that a birthday party involves inviting the entire school as they are all friends.

Despite the fact that there are no qualified teachers apart from the part-time art teacher and the head of learning, parents praised teachers highly for giving pupils the 'confidence to believe in themselves and to put their hand up to ask for help rather than hiding at the back of the classroom'.

Parents reported unanimously that their children found it 'transformational' and were 'very happy' with more confidence and self-esteem. A wonderful haven for north London pupils with learning difficulties.

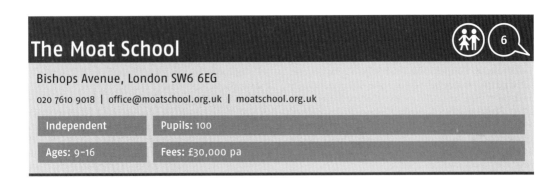

The Moat School

Bishops Avenue, London SW6 6EG

020 7610 9018 | office@moatschool.org.uk | moatschool.org.uk

Independent	Pupils: 100
Ages: 9–16	Fees: £30,000 pa

Headteacher: Since 2013, Clare King. The school has truly been a life's work for her – she joined as a newly qualified teacher, became head of IT then director of studies, and took an MBA on her way up to head.

She has a deep connection with dyslexic children, having witnessed the difficulties her brother with the condition encountered. There was a youthful nannying spell in the US looking after a boy with cerebral palsy, and a stint with Camp America working with children with MLD. Returning to the

UK, a quick turn in recruitment to pay off her debts was enough to demonstrate that corporate life was not for her.

She sweeps through corridors, Mary Poppins-esque, trilling out 'Hi darlings', and receiving hugs and high fives in return. She has that buoyant energy that would persuade you out on a long walk in a rainstorm when you had a log fire and box of chocolates in front of you. 'She is so bright, cheerful and positive that my daughter finds her easy to talk to and very supportive. I think she is a great role model for girls,' one parent said. 'Miss King's enthusiasm and zest for life is wonderful and the school is so warm and welcoming as a result,' said another.

A GSG tour will always see a head demonstrating how they know each child individually – trust us guys, we know when it is faked, and this one is the real deal. Honesty is a key part of her approach. 'I like everything to be transparent. I want to know what is going on at home, and for parents to know what is going on at school,' she says. It's not the first time we've heard this, but this time we saw the evidence. King talked to us frankly about her personal life, and the challenges of the job – the sign of a person who lives life out in the open.

Loves a bit of a sing, and confessed to us that she will 'always wangle a cameo in school plays'

'Clare is very frank about everything; that's how I like it. It's really refreshing to feel like nothing is being hidden,' a parent told us.

She readily admits that it's easy to get the work-life balance out of kilter in this role. Her remedy, a partner in finance who bans shop talk at home. And a family place in Cornwall with no road access, no phone signal or internet, where she takes surfing breaks.

One parent described her as 'a participatory and hands-on sort of head, even subbing a role as Alice in Wonderland in the school play with an hours' notice when a student couldn't do it'. He perhaps didn't realise she was only too delighted. Loves a bit of a sing, and confessed to us that she will 'always wangle a cameo in school plays'.

Academic matters: 'We're an academic school, the children are expected to do GCSEs, and to go on to a sixth form,' King says. The core curriculum involves sitting six GCSEs, and potential students need to be able to manage that. Most do the dual award in science, but those with a particular aptitude for science can do all three. All students take English language, while candidates with stronger literacy can take English literature as well. There is an option to take entry levels in English and maths for those that cannot manage a GCSE, and there's also a BTec course in Jamie Oliver home cooking.

Dyslexia is the school's specialism, but it's rare for a child to have the single diagnosis – there is often dyspraxia and dyscalculia too, and about 20 per cent of the pupils have high functioning autism (it's a ratio which King will not exceed, which can mean some disappointed parents).

It has two form entry, but pupils are split into three groups by ability for English, maths and science. Class sizes are a maximum of 10 (five for practical lessons such as DT and food tech), with a 1:5 staff ratio. Lessons are one hour, with movement breaks and brain gym built in. There are all manner of fiddles on the desks. Some children are in trackpants and sweatshirts rather than school uniform – a simple solution to avoid dyspraxic tangles on PE days: they just come in wearing their PE kit.

On an end of term visit, we saw reams of lively quizzing going on as pupils reviewed what they had learned over the term. Year 11s were revising waves and the universe – 'Miss, I'm winning,' a boy told the head triumphantly.

We saw several examples of this buoyed up self-esteem. 'Miss, my story is amazing,' said a boy in a year 8 literacy class. Not something you might expect to hear in a class of dyslexics – nor, 'Can Michael Rosen come to our school?' from another pupil.

Teaching is excellent, parents said. 'A quiet supportive learning environment, where staff chunk and present lessons suited to each pupil meaning many exceed expectations,' was one description. A poor teacher was swiftly removed, as a parent told us, 'One teacher I was concerned about was quickly gone, it was clear it wasn't a good match and was dealt with.'

Homework quantities and targets 'are sensibly arranged so as not to be overwhelming or dismaying to children and also parents', and often with a practical bent, as a parent described: 'For food tech [my daughter] needed to write out the steps to doing the washing up. This was inspired, as she certainly learns from both visual as well as practical. We did the washing up together and then she was able to write the steps involved.'

We saw reams of lively quizzing going on. Year 11s were revising waves and the universe – 'Miss, I'm winning,' a boy told the head triumphantly

All pupils have timetabled 'skills for learning' groups which incorporate therapy and work on individual targets. They are taught for this in mixed year groups, according to their main need. 'It helps us with talking and reading', and to 'get better at stuff', pupils told us.

'The Moat seems good at making a lesson achieve several targets at once: for example, a "social" session was framed as a touch-typing lesson which offered the opportunity to engage with texts about social encounters, and provide the basis for group discussion,' said a parent.

Games, options, the arts: It's idyllically set for a London school, bounded by the greenery of Fulham's Bishop's Park, but outdoor sports facilities are limited and of the public variety. 'Parents with very sporting/athletic children should bear this in mind,' warned one. But they use the public tennis courts opposite the school, play football in the park, and go out to a climbing wall and to row on the river. There are school skiing trips too.

There's plenty to engage the creative child. We heard some very good reports on the art teaching which has resulted in children winning national awards. 'He loves photography and was allowed to bring home a very expensive camera to take pictures over the weekend. This support is wonderful for my son and makes him feel valued,' reported a parent.

Performing arts are embraced with gusto. The school panto was 'a triumph,' we heard, and they regularly roll out the greasepaint – Hamlet, Julius Caesar, The Lion, the Witch and The Wardrobe among their recent productions, as well as their own version of a classic – Charlotte and the Chocolate Factory. A couple of pupils have their sights set on The BRIT School (performing arts), but everyone gets involved in tickets, lighting and so on.

There's peripatetic singing, drums, guitar; bronze and silver D of E. 'We're a small school but we try to give as many opportunities as we can,' King says. There are even out of school activities in the school holidays organised by teachers, such as cooking and cycling.

After-school clubs have been ditched as unworkable with pupils arriving from 21 different boroughs, often with a long journey and a rigid taxi time. Instead the last lesson of the day is known as enrichment, and there's a choice of creative, sporting, and community activities, all underpinned with social communication work.

Background and atmosphere: It's palpably cheerful inside. The potion, as a parent described it, 'is an acceptance of others, celebration of your talents (which they will find), joyful eccentricity and a low anxiety environment. Resulting in happy, achieving children.'

Parents are impassioned about the school, and are surely the most contented bunch we've yet met on our reviewing travels. One even described it as 'an educational paradise in Fulham'. But there has been a landing on their paradise beach in the form of the school's acquisition in late 2017 by the Cavendish Group. It has closed down and transferred in pupils from another of its schools, The Independent School, as well as transferring across a group of senior pupils from another, Abingdon

She sweeps through corridors, Mary Poppins-esque, trilling out 'Hi darlings', and receiving hugs and high fives in return

House. It has meant a sudden growth in the school's population, as well as new joiners with differing needs to The Moat's usual remit – which is inevitably causing parental anxiety. It also means the upper years are now choc-a-block.

Parental views on the changes are mixed – some are hopeful it will mean additional resources and greater security for the school, others are concerned by the immediate impacts – 'a negative one for many children. In two areas – teaching/ disruption – and social/anxiety. Children with more challenging issues and a very different profile have arrived. The school and new children need time to adjust, but it has been painful at a deeper level than expected,' we were told.

Pastoral care, well-being and discipline: There has been a key recruitment in the form of Arly, the 'wonderful' school therapy dog. He joins two human counsellors – we saw one at work in a lamplit room, a boy with his hands in a sandpit working through his problems.

We heard tale upon tale of children miserable in mainstream brought back to life here. 'When she started in year 7 [my daughter] could barely read or write and had rock bottom confidence. The Moat taught her to believe in herself and she now reads and writes to a level which is beyond my initial hopes for her. They provide wonderful personal development and support,' said one. The slight downside, she added, is that it shelters you from everyday life, and leaving this environment fills both parent and child with fear.

Parents said the school also supports them to manage issues in the home with their child. 'They never give me, as her parent, a difficult time. We work together for my child's benefit. I feel very much part of their team,' one said.

There's a great air of letting children be, and no sticking to rigid school rules which don't really matter. 'My son has long hair to the middle of his back. He asked Miss King if his hair would be a problem as he likes to have it different colours but he ties it back. Miss King's reply was "You may have your hair whatever colour you like just as long as you wear full uniform from the neck down." So he has worn full uniform with blue, blonde and purple hair.'

There are children wearing headphones because the noise bothers them, or because they are allowed to listen to music at times. Another goes shoeless when he wants to. 'In his previous school he would just take his shoes off and get very distressed as teachers would be trying to get them back on, as he couldn't tell them he needed them off,' his parent said.

Bad behaviour is dealt with in the 'responsible thinking classroom' (RTC) – through a combination of discipline and support. If a behavioural matter is not quickly resolved in the classroom, the teacher will send them to the RTC. They might only be there for 10 minutes, longer if need be. But it allows the lesson to continue, and the pupil to feel listened to.

No phones are allowed throughout school day, and they have screen-free Wednesday, when laptops are banned from morning and afternoon breaks to encourage conversation.

Therapy and staffing: There are three in-house speech therapists, one OT (a second is being recruited – much needed, say parents), and two school counsellors. The TAs are all graduates, and they are required to take a SpLD level 3 qualification in their first year, and several are also going through teacher training. There is one TA to a class to enable the 1:5 ratio, but there is no one-to-one; children must be able to operate independently. Teachers are required to do a masters in SpLD within two years of joining.

The occupational therapist has worked wonders on her child's independent skills, one mother told us. 'She can tie her own shoe laces, is learning to tell the time, getting herself dressed in the morning, buttering her bread and wanting to be more involved at home with setting the table etc. We really like the fact the school promotes the children developing their life skills.'

Pupils and parents: There's a broad socio-economic mix, from children living in deprivation to around one-third whose parents can pay the not inconsiderable fees. The latter group contributes to a better than average crop of work experience opportunities for the year 10s – the Houses of Parliament, and restauranteur Ottolenghi among them.

The Parents' Association is healthy, and there's warm support offered to battle weary new parents, as well as long termers, we're told. 'Parents are incredibly supportive of each other. There is a real sense amongst staff and parents of wanting the school to work for everyone. At the prize giving earlier this year, there was an atmosphere of pride for every young person who had achieved,' one said.

If you are seeking a place for a daughter, the girl ratio is particularly notable for a specialist school – across the school they make up one-third of pupils, in itself unusually high, but in year 7, there are even numbers of boys and girls.

Relations between parents and teachers are good. 'I feel that I am listened to and the views of my son are listened to. I don't feel that I am fighting for answers from the school when I ask questions. I feel valued as a parent, and know that nothing would be too much trouble to help myself or my son,' said a parent.

They are promised an email turnaround in 24 hours, and parents confirm they get this. They have direct email contacts for their child's form teacher, pastoral contact and support for learning contact. They are updated at least weekly, and one said 'We feel really engaged because they are so proactive and we get regular feedback'. Everyone has an annual review, regardless of whether or not they have an EHCP.

'He loves photography and was allowed to bring home a very expensive camera to take pictures over the weekend. This support is wonderful'

Because pupils come from far and wide, it can make managing friendships more difficult. 'It is important to ensure your child has interests and opportunities to develop friendships in their local area and that you are happy to put in the effort and time to support developing school friendships,' cautioned a parent.

Entrance: The biggest entry point is at year 7 'when preps are weeding out'. New year 5 and 6 classes were opened in 2016, taught as a joint class, currently with only five children in it, so it would be canny to grab a place ahead of secondary transfer rather than waiting for all the competition at year 7. Head hopes to eventually take year 4 pupils as well; another wish is to move to three form entry for the bursting years 7, 8 and 9.

Get the ball rolling by sending in paperwork (EHCP, school reports, etc). If your child looks a good fit on paper, they will have a two day trial where they will join a class and meet therapy teams, and the SENCo. 'I get feedback from every member of staff, on how they interacted at breaktime, in class, how they get on socially. I won't take them if we can't meet need, or the dynamics of the class mean it's not going to work,' says head. Red lines? 'An absolute no to behavioural problems'. Other situations which might result in disappointment are where a child requires more therapy than the school can provide, or has high levels of anxiety resulting from a mental health condition (but it has taken school refusers where it has taken a term to get them into school).

Exit: It's a sore point with parents that the school ends at 16. Transition evenings for years 10 and 11 help parents to find follow on places, with pupils typically heading for Canbury, DLD College, St Charles Catholic Sixth Form College, Bredon or local FE colleges.

Money matters: Some 70 per cent of pupils are local authority funded, but there's a good core of self-funders. The school is able to provide Tier 4 and 2 sponsorship for non-UK nationals. Therapy is included in a flat fee price.

Remarks: Sits like a pot of gold at the end of the weary path trodden by parents of a child with special needs. But like the pot at the end of the rainbow,

it might prove elusive. Currently crammed to the rafters, so unless it finds a way to expand, you'll have a job finding a place.

Immensely popular and likeable head who has got the blueprint for the school bang on by being clear and unwavering about the intake. So we have to be concerned about how it is changing under Cavendish ownership; early days, we'll be keeping a beady eye.

And King is like the pin holding this rare butterfly to the board. She's still a young woman, so what happens when she must eventually move on? But as a good leader she has built a strong team around her who, parents say, appear to have the ability to take the school forward if she moves.

The National Autistic Society Sybil Elgar School

Havelock Road, Southall UB2 4NY

020 8813 9168 | sybil.elgar@nas.org.uk | autism.org.uk/sybilelgar

Independent	Pupils: 72; sixth form: 32
Ages: 4–22	Fees: All funded by LA

Principal: Since 1994, Ms Chloe Phillips MSEN DipEd DipManagement. Previous experience includes teaching primary-aged pupils, some of whom were emotionally vulnerable. Clearly relishes her position: 'I love being head teacher here. I feel so privileged. There is always a project on the go.' She has a great sense of vision for her school, constantly seeking better provision for these pupils. Passionate about all things to do with autism: 'We are all on a journey. We feel we learn more from the students, than they do from us. We still have another journey to do, though, which is supporting adults with autism.' Though not always highly visible to parents, an inspirational head, well supported by her dedicated staff.

Likes to make the most of the capital. 'I enjoy London. I also like hill walking and the fresh air but mostly London and all that it offers ... the theatre, the Opera House and good food,' she says with relish. Bubbly and animated, with a ready laugh, though apparently a hard taskmaster too.

Academic matters: Sybil Elgar is a special school for pupils with autistic spectrum disorders. They all have profound learning, social and communication

difficulties, and some 60 per cent have no language skills at all. Others can make sounds but struggle to make whole words. School strives to teach its pupils self-confidence, empowerment and self-esteem as well as the importance of valuing others. Roughly 90 per cent boys.

Based on three separate sites throughout west London, the school is owned and managed by the National Autistic Society. Early years, primary and secondary are catered for in a low-rise building in a part of Southall that can best be described as being 'under development'. Separate further education unit (16 to 22 years) in Acton. A residential house in Ealing offers flexi-boarding for up to 17 students from Monday to Friday, as well as occasional weekends and parts of school holidays. Minibuses zip back and forth between the three sites.

All students have EHC plans and each has a personalised curriculum and individual timetable. School teaches subjects in a practical way, playing to students' strengths. The national curriculum is followed but underpinned by SPELL (Structure, Positive approaches and expectations, Empathy, Low arousal and Links) which has been developed by the NAS. Focus is on creating a highly structured, low stress and predictable environment with clear expectations.

The primary timetable allows for plenty of child-initiated activities each day, often beginning with an exploration of the sensory box. This is followed by maths or phonics. Then arts and PE dominate the afternoon, before more child-initiated activities at the end of the day. The secondary timetable includes heaps of art, DT, music and computer skills too, alongside academic subjects.

'Pupils feel quite grown up as they see the other students walking about the place. They also have shops and a café nearby, so it's real life learning'

At 16, pupils move over to the Woodlands unit. This bright block is located on the site of Acton Community College; currently 40 sixth formers. 'Pupils feel quite grown up as they see the other students walking about the place. They also have shops and a café nearby, so it's real life learning,' says head. These older pupils choose whether to focus on art, dance, catering or drama. Wonderful cookery department where the pupils learn to make simple meals such as pasta, scrambled eggs and pancakes. Lingering aromas on the day we visited suggest they are proficient chefs. 'We must let the students feel good about themselves. We promote empowerment and choice. Everything we do is a blueprint for the future,' says head.

Older pupils are often out and about in the afternoon: either swimming, visiting the library, or going to the park. Others hone their entrepreneurial skills in the local market where they run a stall, which involves organising the rental, researching the market and deciding what to sell. When we visited they had just completed making pottery Valentine's Day hearts which were due to be sold the following week. Plenty of opportunities for work: with high street businesses such as McDonald's and Oxfam, or as rangers in Acton Park. Pupils are certainly not kept locked away, and 'school is proactive in looking to extend links with the community'. Head very aware of importance of equipping them with skills for life beyond the school gates. They learn how to handle office environments, cafes and shops.

At the Southall site, class sizes no bigger than eight, with primary ones much smaller, often just a couple of children. Minimum staff to student ratio 2:5, but sometimes one-to-one. Warm, trusting and respectful relationships between staff and pupils.

Two parallel classes per year group which take into account peer relationships as well as ability.

Regular assessment of pupils using Performance (P) or Milestones (M) levels means that the school has a good grasp of each student's current attainment. Some pupils work at level 1 of the national curriculum but level 2 is pretty rare. The TEACCH (Treatment and Education of Autistic and related Communication Handicapped children) approach is used to structure learning activities, with visual prompts given to pupils when possible to reinforce the spoken word. KS4 pupils work towards ASDAN accreditations and OCR qualifications. In the sixth form, every pupil gains social and vocational skills and qualifications. 'We operate in a similar way to all other schools, with clear objectives and target setting. We assess and review their progress. Every single child here can learn and move forwards.' Pupils also self-assess, with thumbs up or thumbs down if not through language.

The post-19 provision was newly added in 2018. Also based at the Woodlands building, they follow a curriculum of English and maths, work skills and employability, life skills, and arts, sports and enrichment activities.

Games, options, the arts: Very successful creative and expressive arts curriculum that includes plenty of art, music, drama and dance. 'My son has been given every opportunity to learn how to choreograph, for example,' commented one happy parent. Range of opportunities to perform, from music and movement displays to playing drums in the school band. Clubs during the school day include strategy games and dance while formal PE sessions include aerobics, Pilates, and zumba. School has exclusive use of adjoining sports grounds, including a football pitch, throughout term time, and a lively sports day is held there each summer.

'My son has been to more West End shows than I have. They always manage to get amazing seats too!' remarked one delighted parent

Head enjoys getting all the pupils out into the wider world. Activity weeks in the summer holidays. Plenty of opportunities to visit local shopping centres and restaurants, attend youth clubs, discover local museums and theatres and use public transport. Excursions to local theme parks, animal parks and Chelsea football ground have also proved popular in the past. 'My son has been to more West End shows than I have. They always manage to get amazing seats too!' remarked one delighted parent.

A recent trip to Poland to take part in the arts festival there was a huge success; there have also been high-profile visits to St James's Palace and 10 Downing Street.

Boarding: Residential care is located four miles from school in quiet Corfton Road. Currently eight pupils here, each with their own bedroom and access to a spacious kitchen, sitting room and garden. They are given responsibility for making their own bed, putting their clothes in the washing machine, clearing tables and cooking their own meals. Some pupils come here occasionally for short breaks, often overnight or for the weekend, in order to sample living away from home, to gain extra independence and to give their families a rest. 'It's wonderfully flexible,' said one grateful parent.

Background and atmosphere: Set up in 1965 by Sybil Elgar, a pioneer in the field of autism and the UK's first autism-specific teacher. She opened this school – allegedly the world's first for children with autism – with just eight pupils. Given that Sybil Elgar was born in 1914, the current head roars with laughter when people confuse her with the founder.

Head enthuses, 'I couldn't want for a better set of parents. Their commitment is extraordinary, especially as many are juggling other mainstream siblings'

School moved to its Southall site in 1994. Much more attractive inside than out, with a huge atrium filled with attractive displays. Surrounded by fantastic playgrounds with autism-friendly equipment and a quiet courtyard for those who need time to themselves. Playgrounds are divided into four areas: two with climbing and play equipment; two with athletics tracks, basketball courts and football pitches. Coloured paths around the playground help pupils to negotiate their way around: red waiting area, green play area and blue is where children can move freely. Whole school is exceptionally well-equipped, including an art studio, ICT suite, multi-sensory room, food technology teaching kitchen, science labs, music therapy room, gym and yoga spaces and a speech and language room on site. A café serving nutritious snacks is run by older pupils to help with social and money skills.

Sixth form block has wonderful hi-tech room complete with an audio-visual system that involves the pupils interacting with different coloured light beams. It encourages sensory exploration, helps

with communication and is just great fun. Pupils look forward to their time in here.

Recent Ofsted inspection awarded school an outstanding rating.

Pastoral care, well-being and discipline: Pupils are taught early on what is appropriate behaviour and what is not. They learn that you only kiss your family and that hand-shaking is a more appropriate way to greet others. Head explains the importance of being able to protect themselves. 'They need to be able to say "No, I don't like that," either through language, signs or symbols.' School works to empower the pupils at every stage.

On-site psychologist analyses what has triggered behavioural problems and works out what can be done in future to lessen outbursts. According to one parent, 'She's wonderful. So calm. Always looks like she has just stepped out of a yoga class! She even accompanies me to medical appointments with my child.'

Therapy and staffing: All staff are trained in autism, including bus drivers. A range of on-site support includes an educational psychologist, behaviour co-coordinators and speech and language therapists as well as occupational therapists. These therapists look after pupils holistically.

Pupils and parents: 'We are a diverse, multicultural school,' says head. Most come from families where English is not the first language, with much Farsi and Urdu spoken at home. Pupils travel in from all directions, 'up to one hour 15 minutes but no more'. School serves 15 authorities all over London.

Good communication between home and school, through phone calls (daily if necessary) and messages in the diary. An open door policy with parents. Head of care offers practical advice to parents, such as how to support siblings. Workshops deal with a variety of issues from transition and sensory issues to care plans and behaviour management. School does home visits to prepare the child's programme, explain how parents can best support the child at home and to help with entitlements to benefits. 'We tell parents we are here to work together and to make their lives easier.' Head feels keeping parents involved and on side is vital, as they know their child better than anyone else. Parents feel well informed, including through formal termly parent meetings. One of the highlights of the school year is the summer social and graduation ceremony, to which parents and old pupils are invited. Head enthuses, 'I couldn't want for a better set of parents. Their commitment is extraordinary, especially as many are juggling other mainstream siblings'. Parents are genuinely grateful to have their children here: 'This place has given my son a life. He has always been encouraged, without criticism or impatience. He has made friends here too, from the moment he arrived.'

Entrance: Pupils are only accepted if they have a diagnosis of autism. Step-by-step admissions procedure is designed to cause as little stress as possible for the child. Parents must contact their local authority and then make a joint application to the school. The pupil is then observed at home or in their current school. Following an interview and on-site assessment, the school decides whether the pupil can be supported fully, whether their needs can be met at Sybil Elgar and checks for peer compatibility. Referral system is thorough 'as we don't want to set anyone up for failure.'

Originally just a secondary school, but primary age children are now coming here in dribs and drabs and school intends to enlarge this part of the school. Pupils accepted all year round. 'Some pupils start in mainstream schools and it often doesn't work out, once their autism becomes more obvious, so then they come to us'. Others are school refusers who have been out of school for a considerable amount of time. Some start at the school as late as 17 or 18. School is prepared to take pupils as and when it seems right, irrespective of age. Rare for pupils to go back to mainstream school once they are here, as they all have such complex needs. One satisfied parent felt 'this school has been just

perfect for my son. As far as I know, no one has ever been excluded, though the pupils' behaviour can be quite challenging, as you'd expect.'

Exit: Transition team helps pupils and parents with options for leavers. Some are able to hold down jobs once they leave, others go to a range of special needs colleges, to supported living or to residential places. A pupil who has just completed his university degree recently visited, making head justifiably proud. Each pupil leaves with their own Transitions Passport, which details their skills, interests and aspirations. School certainly does all it can to smooth the path on to the next stage of their lives.

Money matters: Local authorities fund places, including transport to and from school, with a chaperone if needed. Parental fundraising for extras such as playground equipment. Businesses also donate materials including Lego pieces and iPads.

Remarks: A wonderfully calm, supportive and outward-looking school, led by a motivated head. All pupils are able to make progress and build self-confidence. The head has certainly achieved her aim of making sure that 'autism is not a barrier to learning.' For these autistic pupils with their complex needs, there cannot be many better places to be.

Parayhouse School

Colet Gardens, Hammersmith, London W14 9DH

020 8741 1400 | a.sullivan@parayhouse.com | parayhouse.com

| Independent | Pupils: 46 |
| Ages: 7–16 | Fees: Most funded by LA |

Head: Since 2018, Mrs Eileen O'Shea. Has had a finger in many pies which contribute to the various roles demanded of a modern head – her career includes stints in an architectural practice, advertising, and as an NHS project manager.

Began her teaching career in an inner city mainstream, but was drawn to the pupils at the margins. She has held posts as an advisory teacher for Westminster Induction Service, working with refugees and asylum seekers, and in pupil referral units – as acting head at Ashley College in Brent, and as deputy head at Brent Health Needs Education Service – working with a cohort with a range of complex special needs, mental and

physical health needs, and social, emotional and behavioural difficulties.

She is a certified yoga teacher, with a particular interest in yoga and relaxation techniques for therapeutic purposes. Home is in north-west London with her husband and four children.

Academic matters: A non-maintained special school that caters for pupils with moderate to severe learning difficulties. All pupils have speech, language and communication needs identified as a significant part of their EHC plans. Can support children with diabetes, epilepsy, asthma, visual and hearing impairment, Asperger's, Fragile X and Prader-Willi syndrome. Specialism in Down's syndrome, and more than 30 per cent of pupils here have it, but rarely as their sole difficulty. 'Nobody here has just one issue going on,' explains head. Unable to meet social and emotional behavioural difficulties or autism as the sole difficulty.

'It's important that we're seen as a school and not as a unit or an offshoot. We do everything that is done in a mainstream school, including parents' evenings, sport, uniform and so on,' states head. Specialised and individualised curriculum tailored to the differing needs of every pupil. As one parent commented, 'All special schools pay lip service to this, but Parayhouse really delivers.' Support offered on one-to-one and small group basis throughout. Speech and language at the heart of everything. Three possible pathways: a life-skills based curriculum working in small steps within the P scales; an adapted national curriculum, generally key stage 1, focusing on English, maths and PE; the more able follow a key stage 2-3 national curriculum in English, maths, science, PE, art, food studies and history, up to level 1 in maths GCSE. AQA awards also offered.

Five classes: Pluto, Saturn, Neptune, Jupiter and Mars. Groupings by age, ability and language skills. Can be as much as five-year age span within a class. Three forms cover primary type timetables, including earlier lunch and more breaks within lessons, and the other two classes cover a more demanding secondary timetable. First three lessons provide a 'solid start to the day', usually English and maths. Head explains that morning break is called fitness because 'we keep them on the move.' Afternoon break is more relaxed, because 'otherwise we are on their backs the whole time. If they just want to flap a leaf in the corner then that's fine.'

In the afternoon, foundation subjects feature heavily including sport, drama and life skills. Food studies for older pupils takes place in the swish kitchen next door in the Inclusive Learning block. 'Very functional, such as making drinks, snacks and hot meals. Baking fairy cakes is fun but it's not going to be part of their everyday life beyond,' states head. Pupils also learn social and practical life skills such as how to do laundry, attend to personal hygiene, take public transport, read menus and ensure personal safety. In-house course offered on sex education. ICT is taught throughout the school with an emphasis on real life application. Online safety is the priority.

On arrival, baseline attainment is assessed in areas such as speech and listening, reading and writing. School has developed its own bespoke curriculum and assessment system. Rigorous tracking of pupils' performance, so quickly identified if someone is not progressing as expected. High expectations of pupils and the parents we spoke to believe their children are pushed to achieve. 'It's not just day care here,' explained one mother. Termly

targets set for each pupil, which are regularly reviewed. Another parent we spoke to commented, 'At Parayhouse, they try to delve into your child and what will unlock your child's learning'.

Games, options, the arts: Annual residential trips for all pupils in the summer term. Mostly funded by fees but parents asked for contribution too. Some happily stump up large amounts but equally many cannot give a penny. Years 3-8 spend three nights away and older ones stay for a week and experience self-catering. On-site activities offered. Occasionally a pupil might give it a miss but head explains residential trips are 'not an optional extra, they are very much a case of putting into practice what has been learnt in the lifestyle curriculum'.

Annual sailing day for the whole school, including a barbecue lunch, is one of the highlights of the year. Head confesses, 'The first time I went, I nearly had a heart attack.' The pupils love every minute, especially when they end up splashing away in the water. Parents come too but stay on dry land.

'It's important that we're seen as a school and not as a unit or an offshoot. We do everything that is done in a mainstream school, parents' evenings, sport and so on'

Pupils take part in sport within the community including panathlon challenge (football and athletics), West London Swimming Gala and Special School Athletics. Yoga is very popular, especially for those with cerebral palsy or anxiety who need 'a tool to dial themselves down.' Sports day celebrated by all.

Art, drama and music all taken seriously because 'we are always on the look-out for ways for these children with speech and language difficulties to express themselves non-verbally'. Art teacher in school two days a week. More able can take entry level art and some creative masterpieces exhibited all over the art room. School boasts an Artsmark award. 'Drama is massive,' says head. When we visited, the pupils were madly rehearsing Romeo and Juliet for the Shakespeare Schools Festival. Staff and parents watch the performance at a professional theatre and pupils relish being in the limelight. Whole-school production at Christmas, when music comes into its own, with all songs in sign language. Everyone joins in and has an absolute ball.

Tiny number of clubs offered. A girls' group takes place one lunchtime, where they enjoy 'female grooming' such a nail painting, applying face creams

They have fun, at the school birthday party, where stalls are festooned with bunting, or dancing energetically at the Christmas disco

and hair styling; they also play music and learn to make polite conversation. Helps with bonding of girls across the year groups, as they are in a minority. Thursday club offered after school at an external location and revolves around cooking, arts and crafts, gym, pool, table tennis and playing with train sets. Transport there arranged by school but parents pick up. 'We would like to do more after school but shared transport makes this difficult. It is a big sadness to me that the Thursday club is still exclusive,' states head. One parent we spoke to felt the school should offer more clubs, though another disagreed, saying that most children were too dog-tired by the end of the school to take on any more activities.

Background and atmosphere: Since 2016, housed in an unglamorous 1970s red brick building off the noisy Talgarth Road. Occupies the ground floor of Hammersmith College, bang next door to their Inclusive Learning division which offers provision to 16-25 year olds with special needs. Not the most beautiful school we have visited, with some gloomy windowless rooms, and the much-used hall could do with a lick of paint, but classrooms are bright and spacious. Though security is of pupils is vital, the high fences, with multiple doors and gates to negotiate feel intimidating. A new build is proposed – watch this space.

Family atmosphere at the school, with a remarkable sense of calm. Maximum 48 pupils. Head tries to start with smaller numbers in the autumn term to give new pupils enough support and attention and then builds up numbers as the year progresses.

School is good at celebrating achievement in the weekly assembly, whether for good behaviour, academic success or effort. All pupils receive a record of achievement on leaving. Pupils and their families have fun, too, either outside at the school birthday party, where stalls are festooned with bunting, or dancing energetically at the Christmas disco. Staff love getting to know siblings on these occasions and parents agree the whole family is welcomed in by the school.

Pastoral care, well-being and discipline: Pupils feel safe and secure, both emotionally and physically. Many arrive in a fragile state with low self-esteem but are nurtured and succeed here. Head tells us that 'most of the children would happily talk to any member of staff if they had a problem'. She

has an open-door policy and staff and children are constantly buzzing in and out of her room.

One parent commented that her child has proper friends for the first time here. The school is good at telling parents about blossoming friendships within the classroom and encourages play dates. 'Parayhouse cares for the whole child, including once the school day has finished. The staff really like the kids and genuinely want them to be happy,' said one parent.

Breakfast is provided, and enthusiastically devoured by those who have trekked miles across London to get here. Usually toast and cereal though pupils were going through a porridge phase when we visited. They munch in their classrooms and are expected to wash up afterwards, just as they would at home. No wraparound care offered. Head admits that summer holidays are long and that parents and pupils alike could benefit from extra provision.

Therapy and staffing: Staff is made up of teachers, occupational therapists, an art therapist and five speech, language and communication therapists as well as learning support assistants. OTs help with personal activities needed for daily living including using cutlery and fastening clothing. SLCTs focus on reading, vocabulary and narrative skills. Art therapy occurs on an individual basis. High staff to pupil ratio. First three classes boast a teacher, three learning support assistants and speech therapist in the morning, with two learning support assistants in the afternoon. Top two classes have their own teacher as well as two assistants and share a speech therapist.

Family support manager is rated highly by head and parents: 'She even does visits in the evenings, at weekends or in the holidays'. She carries out home sessions before the child starts at the school. Also smooths the transition to the next stage of schooling, helping with interviews and arranging work experience placements for the oldest pupils at Foxes hotel in Minehead. Head explains, 'We try to give parents the support that they need while also helping their children become independent. That is our goal'.

Long-serving staff. More than 60 per cent have been here for more than three years. 'There are certainly some old timers!' mentioned one parent. 'They know what they're doing,' said another. 'The teachers are firm, fair and fun.' Head is realistic about staff leaving: 'As a small school we do expect shift. There is a limit to what we can offer here. We are a stepping stone and take a pride in that. We cannot offer head of department to everyone, so cannot lure them to stay that way.' Lots of young male teachers, from different ethnic backgrounds, who act as positive role models to the boys.

Pupils and parents: Wide range of social and economic backgrounds represented here. Forty-two per cent on free school meals but some are from affluent middle-class homes. Broad ethnic mix, and 45 per cent have EAL. Largest single group is white British but sizeable contingents from Somalia and the Caribbean, as well as refugees from war-torn parts of the globe.

Pupils come from more than 12 local education authorities, right across the capital. Pupils trek in from as far afield as the Isle of Dogs, Brent and Richmond. Most pupils are ferried here by local authority transport, with a tiny number brought by parents. Sharing daily transport means that friendships develop across the age range, though the downside is the dearth of parents at the school gates.

Good relationships between staff and parents. Weekly newsletter keeps families well-informed. Open evenings and parents' meetings twice a year and the parents we spoke to felt they were kept fully in the loop. Friday assemblies open to all. Most parents are very supportive and come out in droves at school events. 'Our parents are fabulous,' says head. Most families actively want Parayhouse as their child's school, so tend to be onside from the start. Those that are less smitten initially are quickly won round.

Entrance: Pupils can enter the school at any stage provided there is a vacancy. Most come at the secondary transfer stage as 'many can just about hang on in a mainstream school through the primary years, with one-to-one support'. Some, usually those with most extreme difficulties, arrive at 7. Can be referred by parents, LA or education professionals. Parents tour the school and meet head, initially without their child in tow. This is followed by minimum two days of observation ('as opposed to assessment') of the pupil in their potential year group. This is flexible, so could just be an hour or two at a time. 'We need to unpack the needs of the child,' explains head. 'We must be certain that we can support them'. Medical and psychological reports required and every child has an Education, Health and Care Plan 'though we have never accepted a child just on paper'. Pupils turned away if school cannot provide sufficient support or if child does not require this level of care and would be better off placed elsewhere. Head admits it can be heart-breaking to turn down a child and some parents become distressed if school won't accept their child, 'but we have to be realistic'.

Exit: At 16, the school aims to return the pupils to their borough, as they begin to start their adult life. They move on to a range of further education opportunities. Some opt for non-vocational or academic courses, others prefer vocational training, while a minority might move on to residential provision. Recent leavers' destinations include Westminster Kingsway College, Oaklands, Paddock and Highshore. Last year, one pupil effortlessly headed next door to the Inclusive Learning department to continue his education.

Money matters: Not-for-profit organisation. Became a registered charity in 2000. Pupils' fees are usually agreed and funded by local authority. Some parents work for companies who pay the fees and occasionally an embassy foots the bill. All therapy is included.

Remarks: As one parent commented, 'There might be glitzier facilities elsewhere but I can't fault the school.' For the right child, this school is nothing short of a godsend.

Swiss Cottage School

80 Avenue Road, London NW8 6HX

020 7681 8080 | admin@swisscottage.camden.sch.uk | swisscottage.camden.sch.uk

State		Pupils: 236	
Ages: 2–19			

Principal: Since 2016, Vijita Patel (40s), previously deputy head since 2012; hails from the States, where she took her first degree initially in maths and sciences, though converted to primary education after meeting a child with autism at risk of exclusion. Her dissertation on legislation and barriers to schooling for children has been a constant interest and may explain her involvement in London Leadership Strategy and input in the DfE SEND policy, which has given her a chance to visit other schools and look at priorities and good practice. She did her teaching practice in Brent and then worked for nine years at Woodfield School, where she grew from class teacher to head of English and maths, eventually becoming assistant head. Having taken her NPQH, she came to Swiss Cottage School as deputy head and worked on staff training and professional learning.

Parents say that although she had large shoes to fill after last head, who was here for more than 20 years, the change has been smooth and they 'feel in good, safe hands'. She is a theoretician and administrator, and her original maths interest is standing her in good stead as the school works towards having better systems for monitoring progress in special needs schools. The fact that Swiss Cottage School is also a Teaching School and has a very active Development and Research Centre requires particularly scientific and organised thinking, and this diminutive, young-looking head clearly communicates well and has a vision that draws her senior management team tightly behind her. Presumably she delegates well as she also spends considerable time working with outside agencies and looking at wider educational policy changes. Parents call her 'exceptionally bright, an amazing head' and say she is 'dynamic and approachable and warm'. 'She is brilliant' and 'she really listens well'. She has one daughter and is married to another school head.

Academic matters: All pupils have EHC Plans, about half relating to autism spectrum disorder. A quarter have severe learning difficulties, with the rest having complex and multiple learning difficulties. Many children are pre-verbal and many have physical disabilities – profound and complex syndromes supported by in-house nurse and at least two teaching assistants per class, often more. For those with challenging behaviour there is positive behaviour therapy and risk assessment, not only to protect students but also to look for trends and work out solutions. Cerebral palsy, Angelman syndrome, Fragile X, autism spectrum disorder – this school has experience of all and more.

'There is actual learning here, they are learning to read and write,' said one parent

Classes are mixed in various ways – according to both physical and academic needs and social interaction as well as by age. This flexibility means that learning can be appropriate to the group, though each child has an individual learning programme. Small classrooms, each with outside space and an area for withdrawing children for some quiet or for individual therapies or learning – bright and full of displays of children's work. There are 186 staff (including 96 teaching assistants), which means the staff to pupil ratio is good (though no 2:1 assistant to pupil in evidence). We saw creativity in teaching strategies – history taught via experiences of people in another era: the smells, for example, or a home lit by candles. Goals and progress are set and recorded in the Evidence of Learning online record, which then sets next goals and timings to match child's progress.

Parents call her 'exceptionally bright, an amazing head' and say she is 'dynamic and approachable and warm'. 'She is brilliant' and 'she really listens well'

The younger children have their own playgrounds and lower school areas; pupils are given more space and freedom as they move up the school, with 16+ having their own roof terrace. Many 'pre-verbal' ('we think that most have the potential to speak and so prefer that term to non-verbal') and so language and communication is a large part of the learning here. Three separate curricula pathways according to ability of the child, with formative assessment fortnightly to 'celebrate successes'. Efforts made to 'assess without levels', finding a way to quantitatively assess qualitative improvements in pupils. By 16 and 18 years pupils take qualifications where appropriate in life and living skills, and maths and English at AQA entry level, and attain awards such as arts award, horticulture awards, languages, and even GCSE.

Parents were appreciative that pupils are encouraged to become independent and not reliant on a teaching assistant. 'There is actual learning here, they are learning to read and write,' said one parent. 'My child likes the activities and has friends and is very happy and wants to come to school each day – even in the holidays!' Older pupils (those who do not go on to colleges) are able to stay on and continue having therapeutic input, as well as learn and get work experience – either in school working on newsletters and pamphleting, helping in office duties or chores, or, where possible, on sheltered work placements. These older pupils also use the vocational room to learn cooking and hairdressing and life skills. There is a three room flat at the top of the school for respite for parents and to practice independent living skills. Parents appreciate emphasis on real life skills – 'shower class, shopping, dressing, chopping and cutting, how to use the toilet – these are skills that my daughter will need forever'.

The school works to an extraordinary degree with a range of related partners in a child's education – parents, therapists, social workers, who are encouraged to come to the school whenever possible. This linked up way of working for children's wider welfare is supported by a team of family support workers with an inclusion teacher, who can help in a myriad of ways – chasing benefit claims, respite care, helping with housing and medical appointments, ensuring the parents are supported so the child can flourish. 'This school gives more than necessary, it goes over and above its role as a school and makes things work for the whole family,' head says.

The communication is critical as parents often don't hear from their children what was learned at school, but parents said that they could look at the website and see the weekly newsletter, read the daily home/school diary, see the teachers at any time and attend progress meetings. Of particular interest is the new Evidence for Learning online app, which is accessible to parents and gives a running record including videos, pictures and notes of what their child has been doing, and progress both in their work and their personal development. This degree of team working is a rare and precious strength. 'My child can't say what she has done at school but I can read what teachers have said and so my child knows we are communicating. And every Sunday I write what we have done at the weekend so teachers can use this in school.'

Games, options, the arts: This is central London so little outdoor space, but what they have has been landscaped and is used effectively, if a little worn at the edges. Each classroom has its own outside space which, particularly in the lower school, is used as part of the classroom. There are swings and slides and bikes and we liked the road skills area for learning road safety. A running track winds round a well-used horticultural area and there's greenhouse for growing vegetables and plants. Plenty of small, safe areas for being outside. Training on an all-weather terrain for five-a-side football, basketball and athletics prepare pupils for Panathlon Challenge as well as building good health and confidence. The cricket club is popular and plays fixtures. The warm, clean swimming pool is used for timetabled therapeutic lessons. Three school buses for taking pupils to local Primrose Hill or elsewhere for outings.

Art a good feature in the school with mixed media and plenty of colour – displays abound, not only in classrooms but also in shared corridor and dining room areas. Plenty to stimulate and inspire. Dance and drama in dedicated studio with dressing up and face paint encouraged. Music room for lessons and instrument learning – piano, guitar and drums. Music teacher goes into classrooms; we saw the guitar being used as a marker for a transition to another activity. Music, drama and sports clubs at lunch time and at weekends and holidays. Pictures of the pupils on their school trips, not only in London but also to the countryside or seaside on residential stays for horse riding, rock climbing and sailing. No mollycoddling of these children, who are encouraged to be resilient and independent. Pupils higher up the school are developing attitude and confidence from interactions and responsibilities – 'I serve drinks and cakes to parents. I am good at welcoming and being friendly'.

Parents are thrilled with the after-school clubs that have started: 'they make it feel like the children have choices and outside interests'. There's yoga, ballet, sports, paid for by parents.

Background and atmosphere: The current building was completed in 2014 after a £25 million refurbishment under a PFI scheme. Wide corridors, airy practical classrooms with large windows, both to playground and to internal corridors so the (many) visitors can see activities in class. Fairly full and chaotic classrooms: 'children do create mess,' said one parent, so perhaps hard to keep these clean as a result? There are separate areas for lower, middle and upper school, allowing the pupils a sense of progression through the school. And there are well planned, if small, outdoor spaces. State of the art facilities and really practical and well thought out spaces for pupils' wheelchairs, eating, changing and moving around make this a pleasurable place to be and presumably for the pupils to learn in, and staff seem well catered for with spacious staff rooms and outside areas.

Residential stays for horse riding, rock climbing and sailing. No mollycoddling of these children, who are encouraged to be resilient and independent

Parents said it 'is a happy environment and my child is doing well here'. This school feels purposeful, effective and serious and the good practice is spread far as it is a Teaching School with initial teacher training courses for inclusive education, a National Support School (supporting other schools requiring improvement), and regularly runs conferences and training for practitioners as part of continuing professional development and learning. This is an inspiring and proactive hub for spreading the message of good, inclusive

The inclusion teacher can help in a myriad of ways – chasing benefit claims, respite care, helping with housing and medical appointments

special needs education. Teachers spoke of their school and their individual areas of responsibility with pride and high aspirations, and the learning doesn't stop when training is finished as there is a policy of peer coaching and 'reflective dialogue', which is ideal for a new trainee and allows staff to feel positive and supported. A busy, upbeat mood pervades – no room for slacking here by anyone.

Pastoral care, well-being and discipline: The school works to ensure that these vulnerable children are given the skills to keep safe – talking about relationships, use of social media and mobile phones, keeping safe online and how to watch for potential dangers and minimise and resolve risks. In these practical ways they educate the whole child in collaboration with parents and other caregivers. We spoke to pupils who knew how to introduce themselves and ask appropriate questions, they showed us the work experience they felt they were good at – real life skills in action. Sensory Stories for Children are used to promote mental well-being for pupils with learning disabilities, so it is not only the physical and educational needs that are met at this school. 'We built a social story for my daughter to help her understand about getting her periods.'

Therapy and staffing: Part of the school building houses a small NHS department for the therapists to work from – speech and language therapists, occupational therapists, dietitians and nutrition experts, psychotherapists, psychologists and medical staff. There are sensory rooms, soft play rooms and a warm hydrotherapy pool. NHS staff not only work with pupils, but also engage with parents so that the therapies can continue in school, in the classroom and at home. We saw a speech and language therapist who had managed to get funding to allow her to teach Makaton to a group of parents who were preparing to present Who's Going on A Bear Hunt to a class – this brought parents into school, making their child's education a real partnership, and was also chance to support parents and give them tools to use at home with their children. All way beyond the limitations of the therapies prescribed in the pupils' EHC plans. As well as excellent facilities and staffing, the school makes the most of technology – with pupils using iPads to speak if necessary – 'it gives my daughter a voice

as she presses the button and a voice expresses her choice' – and for increased interactivity.

Pupils and parents: Pupils virtually all from Camden and a mix of white British, Somali, Bangladeshi, and well over half the families with English as a second language, reflecting the cultural diversity of the borough. Camden places pupils here mostly from mainstream, but as places are scarce inevitably the school sees itself taking children with more extreme needs.

Parents can be part of the parent forum of 28 parents who meet together, as well as individually meeting the teachers. There is a family learning week each half term when parents can attend the class, observe the teaching and share good practice and good communication methods used at school, so they can be mirrored and practised at home. Family workshops take place each week and are a chance for parents to learn Makaton, English as a second language, gardening club, knitting – anything that will help include them despite the fact that often their children are brought into school by bus or taxi. We saw parents doing communication training, which was also used as a chance to get parents into school. 'Many parents do not speak English and women are often reluctant to attend without their husbands, but we use the chance to show what we have been doing in school so that it can carry on at home'. 'I was given training to use the iPad so my child can use the same communication method at home and at school'. 'It works as a big family and support system for me and other parents like me who might otherwise feel isolated with a special needs child'.

Entrance: Great demand for places and continuously oversubscribed (not surprising after six successive 'outstanding' Ofsted reports). Camden allocates places and pays fees. Admissions policy cites desire for pupils to be local with parental commitment and states it is a school for complex learning difficulties and disabilities. School believes that early intervention is ideal and so prefers early referrals, only taking children in the last two years of school in exceptional circumstances. This school is getting demand from more and more profoundly disabled children since the closing of nearby Jack Taylor School.

Exit: A few are able to leave at 16 to local colleges; those with profound learning difficulties stay on and work towards transitioning ideally to employment, with work skills and supported internships a major part of those last two or three years. Others stay on to 19 and then move to residential care.

Money matters: Active trustees and a Swiss Cottage School Charity that holds events and works with local businesses to raise funds for extras. The research centre and conferences are the real earners, raising money from training and expertise.

Remarks: Swiss Cottage School is a centre of excellence with fantastic resources, focus and interdisciplinary team work. The result of this success means that it is oversubscribed and pupils have increasingly complex needs. A child with moderate or profound learning difficulties will be really well looked after, given individual goals and taught here with new trainees and teachers using the latest methodologies in a safe, if well used, environment.

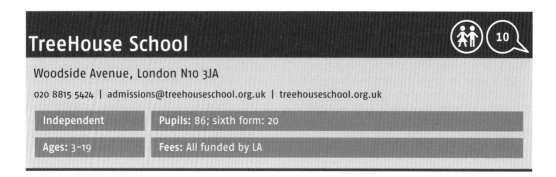

TreeHouse School

Woodside Avenue, London N10 3JA

020 8815 5424 | admissions@treehouseschool.org.uk | treehouseschool.org.uk

| Independent | Pupils: 86; sixth form: 20 |
| Ages: 3–19 | Fees: All funded by LA |

Headteacher: Since 2016, Kerry Sternstein, who joined TreeHouse School from Shaftesbury High where she had worked for 19 years, 18 years as deputy head and nearly two years as head of school. She set up 'a cutting edge' autism resource centre which taught pupils in five distinct areas according to the needs stated on their EHCP. This experience no doubt prepared her well for her headship at TreeHouse, where she is reinvigorating the curriculum and creating a similar emphasis on extending life experiences and opportunties.

Originally from Leeds, she moved south as a newlywed and started her teaching career as an English teacher, moving rapidly to become deputy head of English. Part-time jobs while her two children were young led her into special needs teaching, and after returning to full time she became a head of learning support.

As well as teaching, she continued to develop training courses for TAs and teachers and has also mentored and tutored teachers as part of their teacher training. This background in training others comes from a belief in the need to share good practice and her passion to motivate and inspire staff seems to be paying off at TreeHouse. She says it is important 'to share your enthusiasm with others, as this has a knock on effect to pupils'. A dynamic and energetic investor in people, she engages with both staff and pupils and works hard to engage parents, who say, 'she is experienced and confident and so there is more communication and information', with classrooms 'no longer out of bounds for parents'. She is seen around the school as well as directing curriculum changes and overseeing both academic and therapeutic practice from her bright and well-designed office, which is 'the go to place in school for any issue'. Emphasis on creating a strong school that has its own identity within the Ambitious about Autism charity has resulted, parents say, in 'greater transparency' and a 'tighter organisation'.

Academic matters: Small classes with pupils grouped in both age and ability levels – class sizes of around seven. Pupils sometimes arrive pre-verbal with about 65 per cent eventually able to use language to communicate. Some need up to two to one to support their behaviour needs initially. All pupils have significant learning difficulties, many are years behind their peers, and there is an emphasis on behaviour management and reducing barriers to learning rather than academics, however pupils make evidential progress. 'Not the school if you expect calm all the time; many pupils have challenging behaviour,' said one parent. Bright classrooms, with interactive whiteboards – we saw young pupils waiting patiently (a skill for some) to get onto the board, where they focused and worked to develop hand-eye coordination and fine motor skills. Every pupil has at least one-to-one support and individually planned goals.

Older students are involved in the school shop to enhance life skills and prepare for independence

The curriculum is based on academic as well as social and functional skills, whilst following the national curriculum as far as possible, which allows some pupils to gain entry level qualifications in maths and English. The curriculum up to 14 years is aimed at developing communication and independence and in, key stages 4 and 5, to preparing for adulthood. There may be more emphasis on behavioural issues than academic, parents saying 'sometimes we are concerned that not much is demanded of our child academically: we see him sitting on a sofa, looking out of the window and hiding behind poor language skills'. Another parent said, however, 'We have been in contact with teachers asking for homework as we would like our child to be stretched academically, and the teachers have responded promptly'.

There are daily lessons in English with language and communication seen as critical for accessing the curriculum and taking a place in society. Similarly, daily maths planned by specialist head of maths, with emphasis on using maths to develop logic, establish connections and patterns and life skills. This can then be used in practical ways to help with money, time and space, and older students are involved in the school shop to enhance life skills and prepare for independence. Early interventions take place if any pupils need extra input in their learning. TreeHouse has daily personal, social and health education (PSHE) lessons to work specifically on educating pupils to lead healthy lives, including relationships education, staying safe, understanding others and making responsible choices. ICT is inevitably hugely relevant for these pupils because they tend to gravitate to the safety of a screen for interaction, and so whilst they are at school, screens are used primarily to develop communication (for literacy, communicating with others, as well as using technology for art and creativity). No use of iPads while eating, for example: 'we want children to look around them rather than at a screen'. However, parents felt that 'technology could be used more creatively, especially since pupils may end up using ICT in work'.

By key stages 4 and 5, daily activities include meal preparation, enterprise and work-related experiences which 'use work as a context for learning', including horticulture, working in the school shop, office skills and learning about money and dealing with people. This emphasis on preparing for independence is furthered in the sixth form with pupils going on supported community placements wherever possible (charity shops, sports clubs, allotments, local church) with daily maths and English lessons being about functionality. Parents praised work on transition, including taking pupils on open days and taster days to workplaces and colleges. 'They are very enterprising in the way they support pupils for transition'. Vocational skills in areas such as catering, performing arts, sports, retail experience and horticulture. Pupils leave with foundation level qualifications and OCN at entry level for English and maths. Parents appreciate the way 'life skills are incorporated in the curriculum – self care, road safety, money, health'.

Games, options, the arts: A wall with sporting trophies is a new addition to the school as it develops its sporting presence and prowess. Pride of place was the trophy for coming third in recent Panathlon Challenge. Full-time head of PE as well as supporting teachers to ensure pupils get as much time moving as possible – football, bowling, horse riding, bouncy castle, swimming, fitness. They take part in in Sports Relief Day, Jack Petchey competitions and Duke of Edinburgh. Trips to local woods as part of 'healthy living' emphasis within PE curriculum. A yoga teacher is a popular presence, giving classes for all 4-14 year olds. Parents like the fact that pupils are regularly taken out and the school is not restricted by the need for safety precautions and labour-intensive support. 'My son has started to enjoy swimming and horse riding as well at school'.

Pupils are regularly taken out and not restricted by needing safety precautions and labour-intensive support. 'My son has started to enjoy swimming and horse riding'

They do art in school as well as outings in the school bus to exhibitions at the Tate and Royal Academy. Wide-ranging materials for sensory and therapeutic input – silk painting, mosaics, watercolours, acrylic paints, ceramics. There is an artist in residence whose remit is to engage with students and who is developing a 'pupil voice canvas' with huge bold paintings that can be seen round the school. An art therapist works to ensure art is used proactively to improve pupils' well-being.

Music lessons aid pupils' self-expression. Weekly music classes with specialist teacher for those up to 14 years and then weekly 'expressive arts' class which is wider and includes music composition and musical theatre. Some music making – drums, brass band. End of term performance gives pupils an audience for their musical skills.

Interesting pods within the school, one that functions as a shop and one that works as an office and provides a space for work experience for students, who laminate and photocopy and sell snacks.

As many enrichment activities as possible take place, inside and outside school. Cross-curricular day trips to a café, to a museum, to the park, to the leisure centre, and the opportunity for residential visits of increasing length as pupils develop confidence. Some clubs at lunchtime – board games, sports, art and music – to give pupils a voice and a choice of activity, as well as providing structured leisure time. They also have links with mainstream local schools, who visit and share time with TreeHouse pupils in 'reverse inclusion'.

Background and atmosphere: Originally set up by parents of children with autism to ensure a safe and pleasant learning environment, this school has some celebrity status within the autism world: it was one of the early specialist autism schools with its mission to 'make the ordinary possible for young people with autism'. Lots of emphasis on Applied Behaviour Analysis (ABA). However, the current head is working hard to make 'it feel more like a school'. A wonderful light, purpose-built space with the charity (Ambitious about Autism) and staff rooms on one floor, the lower school filling the ground floor and older pupils' classrooms above. Despite lockable doors separating areas and small breakout rooms, the school feels very open, thanks to large glass doors and huge windows. It is not a state school so has control over how it is run and which pupils to accept. Large grounds and good facilities, from the lunch room to the office pod. More use could be made of the extensive outdoor space, though a planted sensory garden is being developed, there is a cycle path route for road safety training and some equipment – trampolines and table tennis tables – for use in the playgrounds. The front area seems underused and parents felt 'there is not enough variation in outside activities to engage in'.

Pastoral care, well-being and discipline: There are six weekly review meetings to check individual goals and progress for new pupils, termly IEP reviews and the annual reviews of EHC plans. Tight reviews and communication between staff and parents help to keep pupil behaviour monitored and supported. Pupils do get agitated but 'we can deal with challenging behaviour based on distress or disruption' thanks to sufficient well-trained staff and good systems. Distressed pupils supported whilst other pupils kept separate and calm to avoid spread of anxiety. We saw pupils bouncing from space to space exploring while a support teacher alongside ensured safety. We also saw an overwhelmed pupil surrounded gently by support staff until ready to resume activities. Parents say, 'shouting and aggressive behaviour is managed very well, but that is part of what a substantial number of the pupils display'. Interventions kept to a minimum since pupils are constantly watched over. The consistent behaviour management systems seem to give pupils the security they need to become open to learning. 'I like school – everything, especially break time,' commented one pupil. When break

times can be very worrying in mainstream schools, that is indeed good news. Parents all said that they felt there were 'extremely good procedures in place for the challenging population and safety is paramount'. They felt that their children were kept very safe in a respectful and sensitive manner.

Therapy and staffing: The 144 staff keep the 86 pupils well supported. There are efforts to recruit more male staff and older staff as well as the good supply of young psychology students. This, together with concerted efforts at staff development and well-being (staff breakfasts, trusting staff more, encouraging them to leave school early on Fridays), is helping to improve staff retention – 'it is a challenging job and there is burnout'. Parents say that 'the school attracts the more extreme end of challenging behaviour, accepting pupils who have been rejected by other schools'. Seven behaviour analysts work with pupils to ensure their openness to learning. Gradual move towards Positive Behaviour Support (PBS), underpinned by Applied Behaviour Analysis (ABA) programmes.

There is an artist in residence whose remit is to engage with students and who is developing a 'pupil voice canvas' with huge, bold paintings round the school

Two full-time speech and language therapists and one full-time occupational therapist (all school based) have time with pupils both in individual spaces and within the class to ensure therapy is carried through. There are also art and yoga therapists. Communication systems include PECS and Makaton. No school nurse but qualified first aid trained staff look after pupils who have medical needs.

Pupils and parents: Pupils come from ridiculously far away – up to an hour and a quarter journey time each way, from all London boroughs – as there is so little provision elsewhere. As a result, it is often hard to get parents to be involved, so they are all called prior to the three annual parents' evenings to encourage good turnout, which seems to be working. The parents' evenings are also used as information sharing on topics such as reading, residential trips etc. Ethnically diverse pupil group, but predominance of boys (85 per cent). About a quarter of pupils on pupil premium. A family liaison officer helps support parents with matters such as transport and transition, and encourages family engagement.

Entrance: Transparent admission policy – all pupils have a diagnosis of autism or related communication disorder, and all have an EHCP. The school reviews reports to see if they would be able to meet needs, followed by detailed assessment at home or present school and an equally detailed assessment at TreeHouse. Then they need to agree LA funding. TreeHouse suits those with complex autism and learning difficulties. The school looks to see whether any current difficult behaviour is due to distress and would improve at TreeHouse, and whether the pupil could benefit from the teaching available. Careful matching of pupils to classes and current population to ensure good balance and integration in each class. A parent said, 'The admission process was extremely supportive and not at all stressful for us as parents, which was very different from what we experienced at some other schools. The admissions officers were clear and prompt, and a very courteous team of teachers and behaviour analysts did his assessment very quickly, while keeping me informed about progress.'

Exit: Most pupils go on to some post-school placement – some to the new Ambitious College run by the same charity that supports TreeHouse. Parents said, 'transition help was excellent, with discussions about placement and help with taster days at colleges'.

Money matters: Close link between Ambitious about Autism charity in the same building and the school. The charity supports the school as well as having a large team that raises funds and awareness about autism, and works to influence national policy. Aims to have TreeHouse as a centre of excellence for autism teaching as well as a centre to teach others. Twelve governors for three year terms include an ex-special school head, parent governors, community, LA and staff governors. No shortage of money for facilities and teaching – this is a well-resourced school.

Remarks: Relatively new, dynamic head is injecting the school with vigour and rigour. Staff are engaged and valued and as a result pupils are sure of support, and feel safe enough to be able to learn and develop in this exciting building. Pupils achieve more than parents could ever have imagined thanks to well-thought-through curriculum and individually set goals.

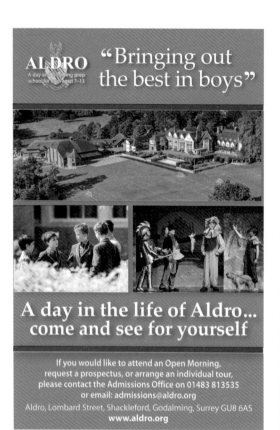

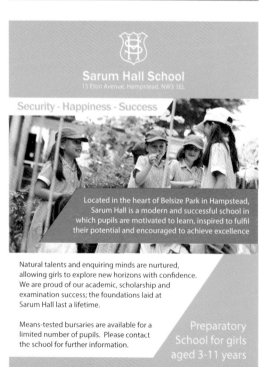

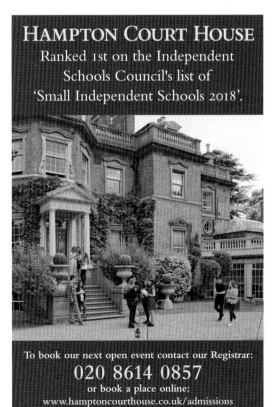

City slippers – boarding schools for Londoners

Boarding, like sheep herding, polytunnelling and plume scrumpling, is something many Londoners assume to be a predominantly rural activity. Whether this adds or detracts from its appeal is down to the individual but boarding, especially weekly boarding, is an increasingly popular option. It's no coincidence that boarding schools whose yield per hectare, if not quite a match for top cash crops, comes close, hit greatest density levels within easy reach of London's top postcodes – no more than a sonic boom's echo from Heathrow or Gatwick.

Some families who have never before considered the idea of boarding wonder whether the bracing two-hour trek across London to and from that excellent day school (and in the dark both ways during winter) really is as character forming as they'd hoped. For such families, boarding can seem life-enhancing, making it possible for their children to start early and stay late with food and friends provided – and without a punitive journey at the beginning and end of the day

Full boarding

Most famous of the lot are Eton, Harrow, Radley and Winchester. While other schools have not just rolled over in response to parental requests for part-time boarding but also offered to juggle a couple of hoops with their front paws, there are no such concessions here. When boys only full boarding for all has worked for centuries, you can't really blame them.

It's the same story for the girls at schools such as Downe House, Wycombe Abbey and Tudor Hall, which although they take a handful of day pupils are essentially full boarding in ethos. Parents who don't buy in to the idea of boarding the traditional way are gently – but firmly – advised to look elsewhere.

Weekly and flexi-boarding

Many schools make a virtue – and success – of combining education with what can feel like a large-scale bed and breakfast operation: some pupils day only, some there pretty much full time, others opting for in-school sleepovers because of parental commitments, exam revision, late night play rehearsals or early morning training

Girls-only establishments offering boarding and day places within or close to the M25 include Woldingham in Surrey, Marymount in Kingston-upon-Thames and St George's Ascot to the south and south west, while the Royal Masonic School for Girls and Queenswood fill a similar niche north of the river. Boy boarders, meanwhile, can opt for St Paul's School, Whitgift or Dulwich College, though day pupils predominate at both.

Those in search of a co-ed environment are, if not spoiled for choice close to London, far from being deprived, with Mill Hill School in north London and, farther afield, Aldenham and Haileybury in Herts, Sevenoaks in Kent and Epsom College and City of London Freemen's School in Surrey, among others.

Schools for skills

Then there are the specialists – such as the Purcell School (music) and Tring Park (performing arts) – where boarding helps the super talented to hone their skills in and out of hours, free from tube strike blues and similar aesthetic lows; the different (eg St Christopher in Letchworth, set up by the Theosophists); and the new (flushed with the success of its first boarding house, Whitgift School, in the non-plush territory of south Croydon, is already mulling over a second).

Even costs don't necessarily need to be sky high if you opt for a state boarding school such as Cranbook (selective), St

George's Harpenden (church-goers) or Gordon's (all-comers), where parents pay for accommodation while teaching comes courtesy of the ever-generous taxpayer.

For any dyed in the wool Londoners who come over all faint at the prospect of breathing air outside the congestion zone, no longer enhanced with flavoursome carcinogens, it's hard to beat boarding, literally, on your doorstep. Westminster School, with 185 or so boarders (including girls, admitted in the sixth form), is pretty much as close as you can get to total immersion in the beating heart of the city without squatting in Big Ben. 'You get that sense of community,' says a former Westminster parent. 'You have more time to get involved and people tend to stay late anyway.'

For some London parents, day places will always be the educational black, the only goal worth pursuing, with boarding the reserve choice when all other options have been exhausted. Others, relishing the out of hours opportunities, from extra tuition to drama, debate, music and sport, feel very differently. Costs permitting (and boarding is, undeniably, costly) it could well be worth taking a look at both.

For detailed information and reviews of the UK's best independent and state boarding schools, including those outside London, see Good Schools Guide Boarding Schools or visit our website (www.goodschoolsguide.co.uk).

Because no-one said you have to do it alone.

Our consultants know the best schools for every type of special need.

The Good Schools Guide Education Consultants

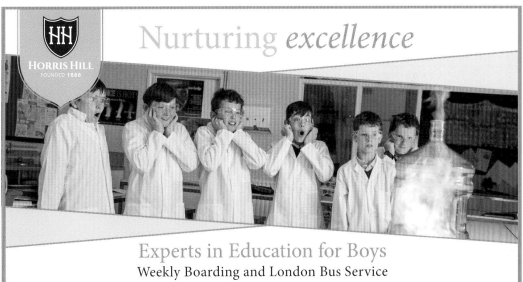

Tutors and tutoring – a Londoner's view

Tutoring is endemic in the UK these days, and nowhere more so than in the capital, where the top agencies have parents queuing up to pay £80+ an hour to buy their child an advantage. They'd have you believe that without a tutor your toddler will miss the academic boat, but keep your head – there's still plenty of time.

Two is too early

Seriously, there are folks out there offering to tutor children as young as 2, but don't be taken in. Spend the money at one of London's wonderful bookshops and read to your child instead. What pre-school-age children need is not tutoring and angst, but time and love from the grown-ups who care for them. If you're reading this article, you are by default an educated, thinking parent who wants the best for your child, so give her the treasures of your mind, your vocabulary, your tastes; they will far out-class anything a tutor can provide.

A clear reason

When do you need a tutor? Put simply, when there is a clear and specific reason for using one. Your child may need help with the 11+ or 13+ entry to an academically selective senior school, particularly from a state school. Or perhaps he's struggling with a particular GCSE/A level subject. Or she may be falling behind at school. Or he may have missed school through illness or some other crisis. Where there is a known goal to work towards, or a genuine problem to address, tutoring comes into its own.

For a shy child who's underperforming, a friendly tutor can be a godsend. Free from the distractions of the classroom and other pupils, he or she can sit quietly with your child and concentrate solely on whatever's confusing her, filling in gaps in her knowledge and building up her confidence. Grades start to improve, and the child becomes a happier learner, keener to put her hand up in class and more relaxed about going to school. For a teenager who's struggling with maths, demoralised by always coming last in his set and stressed about approaching exams, quality one-to-one teaching from someone with no preconceptions about him can make the difference between failure and success; between giving up and keeping on.

Or it could be that you're putting your child through the state system to begin with while you save up for the independent senior school you hope he'll attend. But an over-stretched primary school teacher, with 30 children to get ready for their Sats, will have no interest in helping Harry prepare for independent school entrance, and even mention of the local grammar school is unlikely to get a sympathetic response. After all, from her perspective, selective education isn't what school's about. No matter how bright your child is, he'll be up against other children who have been intensively coached so tutoring is pretty much essential unless you are confident about your ability to fill in gaps.

A real need

Perhaps you feel your child needs a tutor even though he's already at a good preparatory school. Well, maybe. Be very sure, though, that the need is real. You are already paying a fair whack for his education at a school whose job it is to prepare him to secondary school exams. Depending on where he is, a year's tutoring in the run-up to common entrance may make sense, if only because it'll bring you peace of mind. But to have your tutored 7-year-old win a place at a high-achieving prep, and then immediately start having him tutored some more just because everyone else is doing it, will only exhaust him and your bank account. Wave him off to St Brainiac's with a proud smile, and let the school do its work.

On the other hand, if you've just relocated to the UK from overseas, using a tutor is an excellent way to get your kids up to speed with the English system and help them to feel more assured and comfortable in lessons. This in turn will help them to make friends, and the whole settling-in process will be smoother. For a child in a new country, confidence is key.

Where to look

If you want a tutor for your child, how do you find one? The best way should be word of mouth, of course. However, tutoring is one of those things parents usually do in secret, either because they don't choose to tell it around that their child struggles at school, or because they've no wish to increase the opposition's chances in the race for places. Try asking a friend with an older child, who won't begrudge your using what they no longer need. If this doesn't bring results, don't worry. This is London, and you have plenty of options.

Tutor companies

The first of these is to approach a tutor company. We review many of the best of these on the Good Schools Guide website, and using them has a number of benefits. They'll be skilled at matching your child to the right person, and will give you redress if you're not happy. The work of looking will be taken off your hands, and, since the tutors usually come to you, the whole process becomes very straightforward. This is the most expensive way of employing a tutor, however. Almost all companies will charge you a registration fee, which can be anything from a few quid to a hair-raising £180, and the hourly rate for tuition will be high (be prepared for at least £45), because the company will take a cut before paying the teacher.

Some of the really big tutorial companies cover too wide a geographical area to interview all their tutors in person, but they will have interviewed them by phone, and checked their references and DBS record.

Online search

A cheaper option is finding a tutor online. There are a number of websites on which tutors can advertise, and whose contact details you buy, usually for around £20, after you've had an exchange of messages with your selected tutor to see if they're the right fit. Tuition rates vary from around £16 ph – probably an undergraduate trying to earn a bit of extra cash – to £45+ ph for an experienced and qualified teacher. The website companies run checks to ascertain whether the tutor advertising is who they claim to be, but otherwise it's down to you to judge people's suitability. Use your common sense. If a person's replies to your messages are semi-literate, don't engage them as an English tutor.

Do your homework

Whether you're paying top whack for Kensington's finest hand-picked Oxbridge scholars, or searching through the online jungle with only your five wits to guide you, there are some measures it's sensible to take. After all, this is your child. Self-employed individuals are unlikely to be DBS-checked, because the law prevents them from running a check on themselves, so ask to see references or to speak to previous clients. In fact, do this even if they are DBS-checked. Interview the tutor on the phone before fixing a first date, and don't feel pressured into accepting someone who doesn't sound right. Don't be afraid to sit in on the first lesson, and afterwards ask your child what she thought. If the tutor is travelling to you, check that they can get there easily. Don't believe them when they say they can get from Wood Green to Putney in half an hour; they absolutely can't. Lastly – and this wisdom comes from years of weary experience – insist on punctuality. A tutor who is routinely late will soon drive you up the wall.

In short, if you do your homework your child's tutoring experiences should be happy, productive and affordable. Good luck.

Because no-one ever said

'I want the second best
school for my child'

THE
GOOD
SCHOOLS
GUIDE

Call our consultants to find the
right school for your child.

The Good Schools Guide Education Consultants

0203 286 6824 | goodschoolsguide.co.uk/consultants | consultants@goodschoolsguide.co.uk

A word on child protection

If you are preparing to entrust your child to a school –
whether day or boarding – you will most likely assume that
your child will be safe and that all members of the school's
staff will take the greatest care to ensure that this is always
the case.

The chances are that your expectations will be fulfilled.
Unfortunately, in a sad minority of cases that is not what
happens.

We have all read news reports of bullying and abuse and
may have shuddered at the thought that those very people who
smilingly welcome our children into their care may be the last
people to whom we would entrust them, if we knew all.

A flood of historical allegations against schools, court
cases, mobile phones, flexi-boarding, more parental
involvement, the internet, sex education and heightened
awareness have together helped usher in some sunlight
and fresh air. Schools are now a less than perfect setting for
paedophiles and bullies. Child protection policies, found
on every school website, usefully make plain the possibility
of abuse at schools – something rarely contemplated a
generation ago.

Abuse can occur at any school, anywhere. Fame is no
protection, and nor is obscurity. Some kinds of school,
though, need to take particular care – and whether they
do should be obvious to you when you visit. International
schools have transient pupil populations, and teachers whose
histories may be overseas and hard to research. Specialist
music teaching necessarily involves a good deal of physical
contact with the teacher and the pupil alone in a closed
room. Religious schools can have a system of authority that
keeps abuse concealed. Boarding schools can become very
closed worlds. Special schools may have to deal with a large
range of communication and emotional difficulties.

What can you do?

Parents do well to warn their children – gently but seriously – of the dangers, however remote these may be, so they feel that it is easy to speak to you should they meet them. It is worth pointing out that abuse can come from anyone – including a teacher or an adult they know well, or from another child at the school.

Raise your own antennae at any school you may be considering. You can inquire about the steps taken to safeguard children in the same way you might ask about bullying or learning support. As always, much can be gleaned from the head's attitude when questions about child protection are asked. Is he or she ill at ease? Defensive? Or happy to engage, and proud of the steps their school has taken? Openness is what you're looking for.

How easy is it for a child, or a parent for that matter, to report an incident? Schools make this possible in a variety of ways; what matters is that passing on concerns is a routine thing (children and parents do it about lots of things all the time), and is welcomed by the school, and is low-stakes: the person registering the concern knows that they are not putting their relationships within the school at risk, let alone threatening someone's place in the school. That may seem an odd thing to say, but if you fear to report, say, careless management of a museum trip because it will harm an otherwise much-loved teacher, you probably choose to stay mum. Your concerns have to cross a high threshold before you communicate them, so you never pass on those troubling observations that may be the outward indication of serious problems. To be safe, schools need to hear the little voices, not just the shouting.

Do not think less of a school because a case of abuse has been brought to light there. Tabloid coverage can be the price the school has to pay for handling a case of abuse or bullying openly. It is inevitable that abuse will occur somewhere. What matters is how well the school deals with it, how well it performs in bringing the abuse to light and how open it is on the subject with current and future parents.

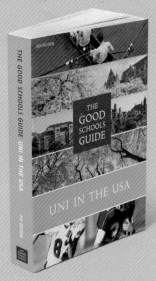

Further reading

The Good Schools Guide

Features independent and unbiased views of over 1,200 state and independent schools throughout Britain, written by parents for parents.

The Good Schools Guide Boarding Schools

Reviews 350+ boarding schools across Britain, independent and state, with advice on when to start boarding, applying from abroad, sex and drugs and homesickness, boarding for a child with SEN.

The Good Schools Guide online subscription

All the reviews plus details of every school in Britain, with exam data, catchment maps, university entrance information. Advice on choosing a school, SEN, tutors, talented children and much more.

Uni in the USA

Written by students who have been through the US system, features in-depth descriptions of 65 US universities, plus the inside track on getting in and preparing for life across the pond.

Uni in the USA and Beyond online subscription and ebook

Also includes unis in Europe and the East, from Alberta to Abu Dhabi, and advice from SATS to visas.

The Good Schools Guide International online subscription

The one-stop educational shop for expats, it reviews the best state and independent schools round the globe, plus insider knowledge on life overseas.

All available via www.goodschoolsguide.co.uk/shop-online

London North school index

School	Section	Page

List of advertisers

Advertisers

House ads

Notes

Notes

Notes